The Healing Power of Emotion

The Norton Series on Interpersonal Neurobiology
Allan N. Schore, PhD, Series Editor
Daniel J. Siegel, MD, Founding Editor

The field of mental health is in a tremendously exciting period of growth and conceptual reorganization. Independent findings from a variety of scientific endeavors are converging in an interdisciplinary view of the mind and mental well-being. An interpersonal neurobiology of human development enables us to understand that the structure and function of the mind and brain are shaped by experiences, especially those involving emotional relationships.

The Norton Series on Interpersonal Neurobiology will provide cutting-edge, multidisciplinary views that further our understanding of the complex neurobiology of the human mind. By drawing on a wide range of traditionally independent fields of research—such as neurobiology, genetics, memory, attachment, complex systems, anthropology, and evolutionary psychology—these texts will offer mental health professionals a review and synthesis of scientific findings often inaccessible to clinicians. These books aim to advance our understanding of human experience by finding the unity of knowledge, or consilience, that emerges with the translation of findings from numerous domains of study into a common language and conceptual framework. The series will integrate the best of modern science with the healing art of psychotherapy.

A Norton Professional Book

The Healing Power of Emotion

Affective Neuroscience, Development, and Clinical Practice

DIANA FOSHA
DANIEL J. SIEGEL
MARION SOLOMON
Editors

W. W. Norton & Company
New York • London

For information about special discounts for bulk purchases, please contact W. W. Norton Special Sales at specialsales@wwnorton.com or 800-233-4830

Manufacturing by R.R. Donnelley, Harrisonburg
Book design by Bytheway Publishing Services
Production manager: Leeann Graham

Library of Congress Cataloging-in-Publication Data

The healing power of emotion : affective neuroscience, development, & clinical practice / Diana Fosha, Daniel J. Siegel & Marion F. Solomon, editors. — 1st ed.
    p.   cm. — (The Norton series on interpersonal neurobiology)
"A Norton Professional Book."
Includes bibliographical references and index.
ISBN 978-0-393-70548-5 (hbk.)
1. Emotions.   2. Affective neuroscience.   3. Neuropsychology.   I. Fosha, Diana.   II. Siegel, Daniel J., 1957–   III. Solomon, Marion Fried.
   BF531.H373   2009
   152.4—dc22   2009026135

ISBN: 978-0-393-70548-5

W. W. Norton & Company, Inc., 500 Fifth Avenue, New York, N.Y. 10110
www.wwnorton.com
W. W. Norton & Company Ltd., Castle House, 75/76 Wells Street, London W1T 3QT

1   2   3   4   5   6   7   8   9   0

Contents

Introduction

Diana Fosha, Daniel J. Siegel, & Marion Solomon

HARDWIRED TO CONNECT with each other, we do so through emotions. Our brains, bodies, and minds are inseparable from the emotions that animate them. Emotions are at the nexus of thought and action, of self and other, of person and environment, of biology and culture. *Emotion* is a term that evokes many connotations, from the way we "feel" to the ways our lives are integrated across time. Specific emotions include love, joy, pain, fear, anger, gratitude, grief, care, closeness, awe, shame, excitement, agony, passion, and compassion. At one end of the continuum, we find extreme emotional states such as helplessness, terror, despair, and immobility; at the other, faith, enthusiasm, curiosity, tenderness, aesthetic wonder, ecstasy, wisdom, awe, vitality, and even transcendence.

We live in exciting times of shifting paradigms and emerging frontiers. The neuroscience revolution that has already changed our field has revealed the primacy of affect in the human condition. The Norton Series on Interpersonal Neurobiology, of which this book is a part, documents this revolution. This integrative, cross-disciplinary book at once reflects and expands that paradigm shift.

In parallel fashion, in the field of psychotherapy the locus of therapeutic action has begun to shift in emphasis from models favoring cognition—and, accordingly, top-down interventions—to models that assert the primacy of bodily rooted affect. Such experiential or "bottom-up" therapies consider insight to be the *result*, rather than the agent, of therapeutic change; they maintain that the deeper the *bottom* (in evolution, in the body, in the brain), the higher the *top*, and—not incidentally—the more effective and efficient the treatment. At one time marginalized, treatments that focus on emotion and the somatic manifestations of psychological processes are receiving fresh consideration. Moreover, increasing evidence about the plasticity of the brain throughout the lifespan is beginning to influence not only our techniques and effectiveness, but also to galvanize our therapeutic hopes and ambitions.

Just as emotionally traumatic events can tear apart the fabric of individual psyches and families, emotions can also act as powerful catalysts for healing. Like emotion, healing too is also gaining scientific respectability: We are starting to understand that healing is a process with its own characteristic phenomena and mechanisms, one that needs to be elucidated in its own right—and that emotions are at the core of it.

How do we regulate emotion in a healthy way? How do we foster environments conducive to its flourishing and reciprocity, the stuff of communication and resonance, of optimal health and effectiveness of action, of resilience, and of caring relationships? How do we do so without becoming flooded and overwhelmed? How can we use emotion to repair and heal, to grow and learn? How do we use emotion to mend ruptures caused by emotion? These questions, central to all clinical endeavors, are explored from a variety of perspectives in the chapters that follow.

This book provides the conceptual underpinnings for an *experiential clinical therapeutics* supported by neuroscience and developmental research. Although the contributors—neuroscientists, developmentalists, and clinicians—operate in different realms, all share certain assumptions about the primacy of emotion, the importance of engaged, empathic relatedness for the regulation and processing of emotion; and the value of experiential models of treatment that privilege bodily rooted experience. And while each author focuses on one part of the whole, we are all talking about the same elephant. Given the breathtaking variety of views on emotion, the resonant synchrony of the parts and the coherence of the whole is exhilarating. Just listen to physicist Richard Feynman:

> Which end is nearer to God, if I may use religious metaphor, beauty and hope, or the fundamental laws? I think that the right way of course, is to say that what *we have to look at is the whole structural interconnection of the thing;* and that all the sciences, and not just the sciences but all the efforts of intellectual kinds, are an endeavor to see the connections of the hierarchies, to connect beauty to history, to connect man's history to man's psychology, man's psychology to the working of the brain, the brain to the neural impulse, the neural impulse to the chemistry, and so forth, *up and down, both ways.* And today we cannot, and it is no use believing that we can, draw carefully a line all the way from one end of this thing to the other, because we have only

just begun to see that there is this relative hierarchy. And I do not think either end is nearer to God. (1965, p. 125, emphases added)

Below is a narrative of the trajectory by which we seek to deal with "the whole structural interconnection of the thing" we call emotion, not only "up and down, both ways," but also left and right, both ways. In the chapters of this book, *down* is deep into the brain (brainstem, limbic system) and body; the implicit *middle* is where life is lived—in development, in day-to-day life, in psychotherapy—and where emotions "do their thing," for better (health) or for worse (psychopathology). *Up* refers to the realms for which we strive when we speak of healing, well-being, and the pursuits and qualities of being under the aegis of our best and most flexible natures. Because, after all, "Human emotion is not just about sexual pleasures or fear of snakes. It is also about the horror of witnessing suffering and the satisfaction of seeing justice served; about our delight at [a] sensuous smile . . . or the thick beauty of words and ideas in Shakespeare's verse; about . . . any Mozart, any Schubert; and about the harmony that Einstein sought in the structure of an equation" (Damasio, 1999, pp. 35–36).

The first six chapters of this book provide the neuroscientific and developmental underpinnings for an emotion-based, bodily rooted experiential clinical approach. The next five are written by clinicians whose contributions to understanding emotion emerge from clinical work with individuals, couples, and families.

We begin with emotions as ancestral tools for living (Chapter 1), and then examine how, through bidirectional communication between brain and body, they are regulated by the autonomic nervous system. In Chapter 1, Jaak Panksepp describes the building blocks of the system, the seven *emotional primes*, as he calls them, the primary behavioral motivational systems that are at the core of what animates us: Seeking, Fear, Rage, Lust, Care, Panic (separation distress), and Play. Not learned, not secondary, "presyntactic," in no way dependent on experience or cognition, they are the constituents of our fundamental experience and adaptation. In the vitality of the emotions, Panksepp finds a corrective for social ills and sees vigorous play as essential to the well-being of our children. Before he is done connecting "up and down, both ways," he offers reflections on identity, the core self, and neuropsychiatric definitions of the soul.

From the subcortical regions of the central nervous system (CNS), where these vital biobehavioral systems that that we share with our fellow mammals originate, we move to the autonomic nervous system (ANS) and to the body: Evolutionarily speaking, we take both a step *down* (to reptiles) and a step *up* (to the specifically human) with Steven Porges's Polyvagal Theory of Emotion (Chapter 2). We step down—to the brainstem, to the visceral organs—to contact the legacy of our reptilian ancestors in the activation of the dorsal vagal complex under conditions of life threat; and we step up to the evolutionarily newest aspects of the parasympathetic nervous system, the ventral vagal complex, and the entrainment of the Social Engagement System under conditions of safety. Porges's work makes clear that how we engage with one another, how we are able to regulate emotion, even what emotional response (e.g., aggression or play) is evoked in us cannot be considered apart from differential *neuroception*, that is, the nervous system's perception of the situation. This hardwired assessment of safety or threat determines which aspect of the ANS (old parasympathetic, sympathetic, or new parasympathetic) comes online to mediate emotional experience.

Next we see how these elements come into play in development and operate throughout the lifespan. Whereas Panksepp and Porges focus on primal emotional systems and their regulation in brain and body, the developmentalists Colwyn Trevarthen and Ed Tronick show us the neurobiological richness and complexity of babies and their relationships with caregivers and companions. The primacy of the affect revolution and the bottom-up orientation of experiential therapies find their evidence in development, for they go hand-in-hand with the revolution that rescued infants from assumptions of passivity and blankness: Developmental research shows infants to us as fundamentally active beings endowed with supreme intelligence, with talent and gusto for meaningful interactions, which their brains and bodies are wired to undertake from—literally—the first day of life.

In Chapter 3 Trevarthen outlines how emotions operate in all spheres of human endeavor and serve many functions. He shows them as forces for the healthy intersubjectivity that is at the core of healing not just our individual selves but also our relationships and even our culture. Reaching *down* into neurophysiology and evolutionary history and *up* toward community and culture, emotion for Trevarthen allows individuals to participate in the music and dance of interrelatedness toward establishing sympathetic companionship and transmitting the value of human community throughout the lifespan, the upper reaches of the human endeavor. Tronick (Chapter 4) regards meaning-making as fundamental and us as meaning-seeking creatures from birth throughout the lifespan. He defines meaning as coherence and organization at any level of "the structural interconnection of the thing" (neurophysiological, cognitive, relational, or emotional) on the part of the individual or the dyad, or presumably the group. He connects down and up via the relational psychophysiology of emotional communication in dyads, be they infant–caregiver or patient–therapist. Dyadically coordinated and complementary states of the ANS yield expanded states of consciousness that we reach as a result of these coordinated interactions transacted through emotional communication; when they go well, resonance is amplified, and each member of the dyad is transformed.

Back in the CNS, we then go lateral to explore the contributions of right and left hemispheres in emotion regulation. Allan Schore (Chapter 5) focuses on the crucial role of the right hemisphere, especially the right orbitofrontal cortex, in the regulation of subcortically generated emotion and of its ANS arousal. Given the primacy of the right hemisphere in emotion and attachment regulation, Schore addresses the importance of regulating the sympathetic arousal of the "vehement emotions," Pierre Janet's (1889) term that captures the intense urgency of dysregulated emotions. When not supported by an attachment matrix (due to either trauma or neglect), the sympathetic arousal that characterizes these emotions overwhelms the individual's regulatory capacities and triggers the parasympathetic-mediated shutdown of dissociation as a survival mechanism. Schore discusses how recruiting attachment dynamics to the therapeutic situation to regulate emotion can gradually render dissociation vestigial and maximize the effectiveness of the individual's emotion regulatory capacities.

We continue our neurobiological journey by focusing on the integrative structures, both subcortical and cortical, where the mechanisms that optimal development and therapeutic change seek to recruit are in the foreground.

Integration is at the center of how Daniel Siegel construes emotion. In Chapter 6 he considers the powerful role of the prefrontal cortex in the transformative integration that he deems emotion to be. Siegel's discussion highlights how human relationships form and nurture the self-regulatory circuits that enable emotion to enrich, rather than enslave, our lives. The discussion takes us into the realm of mindfulness, a time-tested tool of experiential treatments for emotion regulation, and Siegel gives us a detailed description of the qualities of coherence (Connected, Open, Harmonious, Engaged, Receptive, Emergent, Noetic, Compassionate, and Empathic), complexity, and flow characteristic of optimal health and well-being—the very processes and qualities that experiential therapies aim to entrain and bring about.

Along the way from body and brainstem to limbic system to prefrontal cortex, we also encounter other phenomena and processes salient to a comprehensive understanding of emotion. These include phenomena of resonance and mirror neurons (Chapters 3, 4, 6); phenomena reflecting the contributions of the insula, anterior cingulate; and of the temporal and parietal cortices to vital body–emotion–environment integrations (Chapters 1, 2, 5, 6). We explore some preliminary neurobiological ideas about the wired-in, affective basis of the core self, which Panksepp hypothesized to be "concentrated in central midbrain regions such as the periaqueductal gray and ramifying through the core of the higher brainstem to medial cingulate/frontal regions," and possibly involved in the recognition processes by which emotional transformations are assimilated into the self (see Fosha below and Chapter 7).

At this point, our discussion takes us into the laboratory of the clinical situation, where the foregoing basic ideas about emotions, the brain, and the body in development and in relationship are applied in the service of healing. Detailed case presentations are an integral part of the clinical chapters that follow. Fosha's accelerated experiential dynamic psychotherapy (AEDP), Ogden's sensorimotor psychotherapy, Solomon's attachment- and neurobiology-informed work with couples, Johnson's emotion-focused therapy (EFT) with couples, and the attachment-focused family therapy of Daniel Hughes—all these therapies involve moment-to-moment tracking of somatically based and subjectively felt emotional experience in the context intersubjective and attachment-based relatedness, and all reflect the integration in action of the phenomena and processes elucidated by the neuroscientists and developmentalists.

Diana Fosha's work focuses on emotion-based transformation and the energy and vitality that the experiential processing of the vehement emotions yields to the individual (Chapter 7). Noting that the process of emotion-based healing is marked, moment to moment, by invariably positive somatic/affective markers, and that transformation is not only a desired outcome but also an experience and a process, she outlines the phases of the transformational process: from dysregulation (her *down*), to processing first emotions and then transformational experience, to the calm of core state (her *up*). She elucidates a new phenomenology of transformational experience, constituted of vitality affects, receptive affective experiences, healing affects, and core state.

Also working with adults, Pat Ogden elegantly shows us how the body is a powerful resource for the regulation of emotion. Central to this regulation is the capacity to transform compromised strategies for the regulation of ANS arousal through working within and at the edges of the window of affect tolerance. She takes the action intrinsic in emotion and sensation and explores the importance of action and movement for motivation and vibrancy, a theme also sounded by Trevarthen. She systematically shows us how to work with trauma-related and attachment-related tendencies, distinguishing emotions and sensations and defining overlap in bottom-up processes. Ogden's work illustrates the clinical uses of Porges' polyvagal theory of emotion and shows how the capacity for zestful, flexible play specifically, and expanded affect tolerance more generally, are a culmination of therapeutic success.

In Chapter 9 Marion Solomon reflects on the neurobiology of attachment in partnerships and shows us relational psychophysiology in action by forging a physiological linkage, whether between the members of the couple coming for therapy or the therapist–couple pair. Solomon carefully tracks both the level of arousal in each member of the couple and her own somatic experiences, while also encouraging a mindful attitude toward the emotions. Further, she demonstrates how recent findings on neuroplasticity can contribute not only to regulating the nervous systems of traumatized individuals but also to healing relationships. Regulating and reregulating emotion can change the brain, and by extension, our old toxic patterns of behavior, and, when conditions of safety obtain, can transform "intimate enemies" back into "intimate partners" once again.

In Chapter 10 Susan Johnson discusses the extravagant transformational power of emotions, which can be harnessed to repair attachment injuries. No longer the exclusive province of poets and mystics, the emotion of love, in Johnson's work, lands squarely in the science of attachment and emotion. Like Fosha, Johnson is interested in the phenomenology of emotions associated with the different phases of transformation. In working with couples, this involves the shift from the rigid secondary emotions that partners use to conduct their warfare (and protect themselves), to the excruciating primary emotions associated with loss or abandonment, to oxytocin-mediated "softenings" and the emergence of tenderness and empathy. These primary "soft" attachment emotions not only heal attachment wounds but further bond a couple and make life worth living.

Daniel Hughes's attachment-based family therapy completes our trajectory (Chapter 11). Noting that working with emotion in family therapy is different from individual therapy—that is, the object of the emotion is present—he focuses on fostering the constructive *communication* of emotion (rather than its expression). Hughes illuminates the profound regulation that intersubjective qualities can bring to emotional communication between family members. And indeed, empathy, playfulness, acceptance, and curiosity—the elements of his therapeutic stance—go a long way toward repairing the disruptions and healing the traumas of and between children and their parents. They also bring about magical "moments of absorption," moments of healing emotions in which new ways of being together are forged.

1

Brain Emotional Systems and Qualities of Mental Life

From Animal Models of Affect to Implications for Psychotherapeutics

Jaak Panksepp

BASIC EMOTIONS ARE fundamental powers of the human mind that are of utmost importance for both mental health and mental disorders. It is clear that all mammalian brains inherit a variety of emotional dispositions as ancestral tools for living. These systems, including ones for SEEKING, FEAR, RAGE, LUST, CARE, PANIC (separation distress), and PLAY, are of critical importance for generating primary-process affective states—basic psychological states such as urgent interest/desire, anxiety, anger, eroticism, nurturance, sadness, and joy.

These fundamental emotional powers of the mind, which are closely affiliated with a variety of bodily states and nonspecific brain arousal systems (e.g., norepinephrine and serotonin), concurrently generate distinct emotional action tendencies as well as raw feeling states that rapidly get linked to a variety of events in the world through classical conditioning and other basic learning mechanisms. When these ancient emotional forces of the human brain become tempestuous—dysregulated beyond our understanding—overwhelming psychological problems can emerge. In humans, emotional dysregulations are invariably accompanied by cognitive "stuff"—entangled in attributions, ruminations, and all sorts of hopes, plans, and worries. When cognitions become embroiled in primary-process emotionality, emotions and the affiliated cognitions can no longer be readily distinguished. Indeed, many psychologists envision them as part and parcel of the same psychological process. This is not a scientifically wise choice, since primary-process emotional affects are initially *unconditioned*, "objectless," neuroevolutionary, affect-laden response tendencies arising from very ancient lower regions of the brain, whereas practically all human cognitions are thoroughly *conditioned* by life experiences and language processes located within higher neocortical brain regions. Thus, cortical cognitions and subcortical emotional arousals do need to be distinguished if we want to understand how the brain eventually blends them into highly interactive mental wholes. From my perspective, social constructivism and basic emotion perspectives can coexist, and even thrive, within the complexities of brain, body, and world (Panksepp, 2007c).

Affective neuroscience has demonstrated that primary-process, *prepropositional emotional energies* have a mind of their own—an ancient form of phenomenal consciousness that preceded language and sophisticated human thoughts by hundreds of millions of years of evolutionary time. These are the mental "energies" I discuss in this chapter, and I envision how they might be addressed in psychotherapeutic practice in the service of better affect regulation.

An understanding of how *primary-process emotion* can either enrich or derail human lives is essential for scientific progress in all types of psychotherapy, as well as in the generation of a new basic neuroscience foundation for psychiatry and psychotherapy. A neurobiological understanding of the primary-process affective storms—perturbations of the *core self* (Northoff & Panksepp, 2008; Panksepp & Northoff, 2008)—is critically important not only for providing guidance in the development of new psychotherapeutic perspectives but also for new medicinal developments (Panksepp, 2006; Panksepp & Harro, 2004). Since I have summarized the basic neuroscience issues and affective neuroscience strategies many times (most recently, Panksepp, 2007c, 2008a), my primary goal here is to introduce some ideas that may take us toward new affective balance therapies—experiential therapies that may complement well-established cognitive–behavioral, interpersonal, and psychoanalytic therapeutic traditions.

Instinctual Antecedents of Primary-Process Psychological Entities

We are finally in an era where most thoughtful investigators agree with Freud's deep belief in the biological foundations of the psyche, but not necessarily Freud's psychoanalytic metapsychologies, with all their conceptual baggage, creatively constructed from limited, culture-bound clinical observations. At present, the most interesting discussions in psychiatry and psychotherapy are emerging from new interdisciplinary frontiers: (1) developmental social neuroscience (Schore, 2003a; Siegel, 1999; Stern, 2004), (2) an emerging neuropsychoanalysis (Solms & Turnbull, 2003), (3) a human and animal affective neuroscience (Panksepp, 1998a), and (4) new visionary perspectives on autonomic nervous system regulations that need to be coherently integrated with higher brain processes (see Porges, Chapter 2, this volume). These scholars are finally grappling not only with the affective nature of the human mind, but also with the deep emotional nature of the mammalian brain. It is now clear that affective values are built into the nervous system as birthrights, but not ethical and moral values, which are epigenetic emergents of developmental landscapes.

The correct view of basic emotions should eventually transform our conception of human nature, emotional disorders, our visions of core consciousness and affect regulation, the nature of object relations, and ways to achieve emotional homeostasis through therapeutic and lifestyle changes. This synthesis cannot be achieved without a correct foundational vision of how *primaryprocess affects and emotion* are organized in the brain, and how all of that relates to the massive cognitive plasticity of the mammalian brain (Doidge, 2007), especially the massive culture-induced plasticity of the human brain. Emotional and other affective systems lie at the core of such plasticities.

The only reason that cognitions have been so commonly envisioned to lead the way is because many practitioners of cognitive science, and hence most psychotherapeutics, have yet to assimilate the evidence about brain emotional systems from basic affective neuroscience principles. This bias is partly a residue of behaviorism, a very incomplete science that many have now rejected because of its narrow "externalist" prison-house mentality, which had just one precious gem to offer psychotherapy—behavior modification based on the rearrangement of reinforcement contingencies, in the context of no coherent vision, even a rejection of the affective interior of the mammalian mind. However, that externalist view continues to skew cognitive thinking in the field and to lead to continued conceptions of organisms as "passive" association-based, information-processing machines. What a deep neuroevolutionary psychology, based on a cross-species affective neuroscience, can now offer is a more realistic alternative—an "active" organism view wherein all mammals are endowed with rich neurobiological, internally experienced emotional processes. (For a thorough elaboration of such issues, see Northoff & Panksepp [2008] and Panksepp & Northoff [2008], a view that highlights how the active organismic concepts need to replace the passive "information-processing" views of behaviorism and cognitive science.) We can move in uniquely new directions through an understanding of primary-process emotions—namely, those brain–mind processes that constitute the neuroaffective complexities that lie under those behavioristic oversimplifications called "rewards," "reinforcements," and "punishments" (Panksepp, 2005b) and that guide the social constructions and clinical reconstructions of human minds.

Dan Siegel said it well in the foreword to Louis Cozolino's (2002) synthesis of clinical and neuroscientific approaches to the human mind: Clinicians, he said, immerse themselves "in the stories of individuals who come for help in feeling better. . . . Whatever the approach, lasting change in therapy occurs as a result of changes in the human mind . . . which involve changes in the functions of the brain. Exactly how the mind changes during the therapeutic process is the fundamental puzzle that the synthesis of neuroscience and psychotherapy seeks to solve" (p. XX). In my estimation, a most critically important scientific aspect of the puzzle of how the mind changes during the therapeutic process is how human brains generate *primary-process emotional feelings*. Here I explore how an understanding of such foundational issues may help us construct more effective affective balance therapies that include how embodied affects interact with cognitive processes and conditions of the body, and how personal growth and mental remolding can be achieved through psychological as well as somatic interventions.

Although psychotherapy has traditionally sought to deal more with the cognitive–emotional labyrinth of individual lives, a few revolutionaries have attempted to refocus the discussion toward affective issues (Fosha, 2000, 2001, and Chapter 7, this volume). I explore how such therapeutic models can be integrated with our emerging understanding of universal emotional principles of the mammalian brain. While psychotherapy must obviously continue to deal realistically with individual lived lives, we are finally entering an era where evidence-based affective views of the mammalian brain can provide an understanding of *cross-mammalian, universal, affective-emotional processes* that may provide a scientific foundation for new affective and body oriented therapies. Because we are beginning to comprehend the neurodynamics of primary-process emotion, we can also envision new variants of affective balance therapies (ABTs—see below).

Emotion as Inherited Ancestral Tools for Living

There is only space enough here to outline a few key issues arising from affective neuroscience (for more detailed coverage, see Panksepp, 1998a, 2005a).

My goal is to highlight how an understanding of primary-process emotions in the human brain–mind has (1) been illuminated through evolutionarily informed animal models of basic emotional systems, (2) provided a novel foundation for psychiatric and psychological science, and (3) can provide new ideas for the development of new biological and psychotherapeutic interventions. Key questions I address here include: How is raw affective experience created within the brain? How do the mental changes of these affective experiences relate to emotional disorders? What are the implications of this knowledge for achieving emotional homeostasis, greater feelings of well-being, and healthier outlooks on life?

The most effective current strategies for getting at the core nature of emotional feelings recognize that prepropositional affective processes can, at least early in development, exist in the brain independent of the enormous complexities of learning, as well as of associated cognitive processes with which they always interact later in real life. In their raw primary-process form, they are best studied in animal models where the detailed neuroscientific work can be done.

In contrast, the study of human beings is essential for characterizing the cognitive–affective aspects of mind that become imbalanced during the affective storms created by primary-process emotional imbalaces. By understanding the neurobiological nature of our cognitive apparatus, which is dynamically and developmentally constructed from life experiences, we are in a better position to understand how we might undo faulty programming, some of which has epigenetically become part of the maladaptive hardware of the brain. Here we envision "cognitions" to be those brain information-processing functions that are integrally linked to the sensory–perceptual portals of the mind, whereas raw "emotions and affects" reflect some of the most important within-brain organizing principles for understanding the powers of our ancestral mind. Whereas the cognitive aspects are linked more to the programming of each individual's development, raw emotions and affects represent our ancient, inherited tools for living.

A foundational understanding of basic emotional-affective feelings can be derived from a study of our animal emotional circuits, all of which are subcortically concentrated. Animal models have definitively demonstrated that all basic emotional operating systems are organized in deep prepropositional, precognitive subcortical regions. What this means is that the raw emotional tools for feeling and living are not created by lived experiences, although they may be shaped by them. When we are first born, we are cognitively "dumb." Emotions simply allow us to act and feel in certain distinct ways, without containing any intrinsic knowledge about how the present world is organized.

They are ancestral memories, successful solutions to living encoded in genetically dictated brain systems. How these raw emotional tools, provided by Mother Nature, link up to world events is of momentous importance for lived lives, sometimes proceeding smoothly and efficiently, promoting mental health, sometimes chaotically and inefficiently, promoting mental turmoil.

In other words, the raw emotional processes are, at birth, minimally connected up to busyness of world events. There are only a few evolutionarily derived "sign-stimuli" to set them off—such as pain, promoting fear, and the thwarting of SEEKING urges, promoting anger. They gradually get linked to cognitively detailed personal experiences. In other words, most of the "object relations" of emotional systems to world events have to be learned, and so there is a vast variety of emergent processes that can differ substantially among individuals in their personality development. For those who have had the fortune to be reared in supportive, mental-health-sustaining early environments, highly adaptive world relationships emerge. Among those whose "object relations" have emerged in the midst of various negative affects, there will be learned patterns that can disrupt the smooth flow of living for a lifetime. By reintegrating better object relationships in the context of ABTs, people can gradually become masters of their own affective-emotional dynamics, rather than being mastered by them.

Currently, psychotherapeutically relevant cognitive issues remain more slippery than our understanding of basic emotions. We can easily reach moments of therapeutic clarity in the midst of clinical sessions only to rapidly have all that progress slip away when clients, on their own between sessions, regress to their old cognitive–affective habits. This is because each of the primary-process emotions has enslaved large cognitive territories for its own self-serving purposes. The stranglehold that self-centered emotional systems can have on cognitive processes can be overwhelmingly robust. "Reconsolidation" of affective–cognitive memories needs to be a prime concern of therapy. As I consider toward the end of this chapter, it might also be possible to solidify therapeutic change if we learn to infuse therapeutic emotional–cognitive change more directly from affectively rich body dynamics into the process or restructuring of mind.

For long-term success, we must be able to bring affects and cognitions into a new harmony, using therapeutic strategies that deal forthrightly with the primary-process affective processes in the realm of affect regulation and affective–cognitive restructuring, rather than just the secondary and tertiary cognitive representations of these processes. Mental health ultimately means that an individual, through rich emotion-affirming encounters with living, has integrated his or her life in such a way that the emergent self-structures, deeply affective (Northoff & Panksepp, 2008; Panksepp, 1998b; Panksepp & Northoff, 2008), can steer a satisfying, cognitive course through future emotional jungles of lived lives.

Growing a Better Understanding of Human Affective Life Through Animal Models

Both human and animal brains are functionally structured entities, evolutionarily layered, where the foundational lower aspects of mind constrain the developmental trajectories of the higher cognitive aspects that vary considerably among different species and different developmental trajectories. Although all layers are interactive, with many neuronal and psychological interconnections between higher and lower brain regions, the basic principles of subcortical emotional organization are so strikingly similar in all mammals that credible translations can be made from brain research on those systems in animal models to principles of great importance for understanding the human mind. This does not mean that there will not be abundant differences in fine detail across species, but that general principles can be derived—that shared psychobehavioral dynamics and underlying neurochemical codes can be identified.

It is scientific fact, *and not just conjecture,* that a series of cross-mammalian emotional systems has been revealed through animal brain research. These emotional systems, concentrated heavily in the medial structures of the brain—from the midbrain periaqueductal gray, through the medial regions of the diencephalon (both hypothalamus and thalamus) to basal forebrain nuclei; ranging from the bed-nucleus of the stria terminalis, preoptic area, septum, and basal ganglia (e.g., the nucleus accumbens), up toward the amygdala, insula, and various medial frontal lobe structures (including the anterior cingulate cortex, orbitofrontal cortex, and medial prefrontal cortex)—all figure heavily in the genesis of a variety of emotional or clinical disorders (Panksepp, 2004b, 2006). The amygdala is *not* the center of our emotionality. All of the above structures are especially important for our diverse emotional-affective arousals.

How do we know that such core executive emotional networks for emotion do exist? We can activate a variety of instinctual emotional responses merely through electrical stimulation of the same subcortical brain regions in all mammals ever tested. Likewise, ethological animal models of emotions have long supported the existence of at least seven basic emotional systems. Such approaches confirm that all basic emotional systems are concentrated in homologous subcortical regions of the brain (Panksepp, 1998a, 2005a). Thus, there are three critically important lines of evidence:

• First, an ethological analysis of natural behavior patterns has demonstrated from time immemorial (including Darwin's [1872/1965] superb analysis and synthesis) that animals exhibit a series of emotional behavior patterns that are strikingly similar across mammalian species, including humans.

• Second, most of our functional knowledge about the underlying systems has been derived from studies using electrical brain stimulation (ESB) and chemical brain stimulation (CSB). A large variety of very similar emotional behavior patterns can be evoked by application of localized ESB and CSB within specific neural regions, which have been *intensively* studied only in nonhuman mammals. This does not mean that there are "centers" for emotions; rather there are specific places ("sweet" and "sour" spots in the brain) where the underlying widely ramifying networks can be aroused to provoke global, coherent, emotional state changes in all mammals, as well as birds and reptiles (although the data base is not as rich as for mammals).

• Third, these systems are neither informationally encapsulated "modules" or mere behavioral "output" systems (as some social constructivists continue to claim; Barrett, 2006). Rather, they are affectively tinged emotional integrative systems that interact with many higher and lower brain processes. Neither animals nor humans are neutral about such arousals. Animals either approach (and turn on) or avoid (or turn off) such central state shifts. These conclusions, with the needed psychological resolution, were confirmed in humans, mostly in the era of psychosurgery—affective shifts, closely related to the kinds of instinctual emotional arousals seen in animals, can be induced in humans (Heath, 1996; Panksepp, 1985). The fact that we now have a credible scientific way to understand how raw emotional affects are engendered in the brain has enormous implications not only for the development of new forms of psychotherapy but also for a new psychiatric systematics not yet institutionalized in documents such as the *Diagnostic and Statistical Manual of Mental Disorders* (Panksepp, 2004a, 2006).

Let us briefly consider the seven basic emotional systems that are solidly and consistently supported by a cross-species affective neuroscience. They are SEEKING, FEAR, RAGE, LUST, CARE, PANIC, and PLAYfulness. These emotional systems are labeled in capitals primarily to minimize mereological fallacies (i.e., part–whole confusions) but also to highlight that specific brain systems are being discussed. The capitalization is used to alert readers to the claim that these emotional primes may be *necessary* brain systems for those types of emotional behaviors and feelings, although by no means *sufficient* for the higher-order cognitive–emotional manifestations that may arise from these systems engaged in real-world activities. These systems make organisms "active agents" in the world: Animals that seek to engage and understand affectively relevant world events as opposed to simply being passive stimulus–response or information-processing behavioral robots (again, detailed coverage of these systems is available in Panksepp, 1998a, 2005a).

Let me focus on the Big 7 by starting with the SEEKING system, a most intriguing and highly generalized emotional system—one that all the other emotional systems may depend upon for their own appointed affairs. This system remains poorly recognized in most psychological theories, partly because it is involved in all motivational processes. It has been mislabeled as "the brain reward system" by behaviorists not interested in the nature of emotions. As we have repeatedly discussed, a brain reward system is a highly misleading concept (Ikemoto & Panksepp, 1999). Yes, mild arousal of the SEEKING system feels good in a special way, but this good feeling is not at all like a consummatory reward. It is the epicenter of the excitement of living, much of which consists of the *pursuit* of rewards. Perhaps the SEEKING system needs to be recruited for all highly effective educational and psychotherapeutic activities.

1. **The SEEKING/Desire System** (for most recent reviews, see Alcaro et al., 2007; Panksepp & Moskal, 2008). Where would we (or other animals) be if we did not have an active "explorer" inside the brain to find resources, to make new discoveries, and to serve as a foundation for practically all the libidinal aspirations of the human heart? The SEEKING system mediates appetitive desire—that is, the urge to find, to consume, and at times to hoard the fruits of the world. It is constituted of many chemical systems, but the one that provides major psychobehavioral "push" for the system, and hence best serves to highlight its anatomy, is the mesolimbic dopamine system that arises from the ventral tegmental area (VTA) and projects through the lateral hypothalamus to the ventral striatal nuclei, especially the nucleus accumbens, olfactory tubercle, and further up to medial cortical regions. This "appetitive motivational system" energizes the many engagements with the world as individuals seek goods from the environment as well as meaning from the everyday occurrences of life. We can now also recognize this system as a major foundational substrate for Spinoza's concept of *conatus*—a system that energizes our "intentions in actions."

Animals come to "desire" to self-activate—to self-stimulate—this system in addictive ways. Activation of the system is "rewarding." Practically all addictive drugs (especially the psychostimulants) and addictive behaviors (e.g., compulsive gambling, sex, listening to music) derive motivational push and craving from the dopaminergic part of this positively motivated SEEKING system. Although highly resolved cognitive information descends into this system, the dopamine neurons of the VTA pass on a simple message: to behave in appetitively aroused, goal-directed ways, increasingly directed toward environmental cues that predict rewards as well as safety in dangerous situations.

Recent work indicates that this system contributes substantially to sociosexual bonds and loving feelings, even to musical thrills. Rather than being "the reward" system, this is better conceptualized as a "well-being" system. The many interactions of the SEEKING system with higher brain regions highlight the degree to which basic emotive state-control systems can link up with cognitive systems that mediate secondary learning and tertiary thought processes, leading ultimately to awareness and thoughtful appraisals. It is best to recruit this system in every form of psychotherapy, for it is a generalized substrate for all the other emotional processes, from the establishment of libidinal social bonds to the seeking of safety in dangerous situations.

2. **The FEAR/Anxiety System** (for recent review, see Panksepp, 2004a). A basic FEAR system, remarkably similar across all mammals, provides a sentry function to alert organisms to all kinds of dangers that threaten the integrity of the body and of life itself. The core of this system interconnects central amygdalar regions via the ventral amygdalofugal pathways (VAFP) to anterior and medial hypothalamic regions, and then on to the periaqueductal gray (PAG).

All along the trajectory of this transhypothalamic system, freezing and flight responses can be elicited with localized ESB, accompanied by appropriate autonomic arousals. Activity in this system is the unconditioned response that mediates classical conditioning of fear, with frozen postures when arousal of the system is modest, and with intense flight when arousal is stronger. These functions diverge in the midbrain, with flight (a putative high dopamine state) being mediated by dorsal PAG structures while freezing (perhaps a low dopamine state) is elaborated more ventrally within the PAG. The associated affective state of trembling and uptight trepidation, especially when triggered by physical pain, readily becomes associated with many world events—with specific contexts coded in the hippocampus and with more discrete cues, like spiders and vipers, via the lateral amygdala (LeDoux, 1996). Humans stimulated in these same brain regions report being engulfed by an intense free-floating anxiety that appears to have no environmental cause.

This system generates pure trepidation, the "fear itself" that President Roosevelt emphasized when he rallied the country to fight World War II with the slogan "The only thing we have to fear is fear itself."

This system is especially important for promoting generalized anxiety disorders, neurotic disorders, and specific phobias. It is possible to produce symptoms of posttraumatic stress disorder (PTSD) simply by repeatedly stimulating this system, which leads to what Bob Adamec has called "limbic permeability," whereby minimal stimuli develop the capacity to trigger full-blown PTSD symptoms (Adamec & Young, 2000). There is a host of neuropeptide chemistries along this system that are potential targets for development of new antianxiety and antitrauma medications (Panksepp & Harro, 2004; Panksepp, et al., 2007), which currently include cholecystokin and substance P antagonists as well as cycloserine and corticosteroids that can modulate memory reconsolidations (Adamec & Young, 2000; De Quervain, 2008).

3. **The RAGE/Anger System** (for recent reviews, see Panksepp & Zellner, 2004; Siegel, 2005). To the best of our knowledge, this system is the primal source of angry feelings, closely paralleling the FEAR system but with nuanced differences. For instance, in the amygdala, corticomedial areas elaborate rage whereas basolateral areas mediate fear; similarly, the RAGE components descend to the medial hypothalamus via the stria terminalis, whereas the FEAR components descend via the VAFP. Activation of some of these sites has been found to provoke sudden anger attacks in humans (e.g., Sano, et al., 1970). Normally, anger is readily aroused by restraint and frustration, particularly when organisms do not get what they SEEK and want. This system is often intertwined with the FEAR system, with which it probably interacts in reciprocating ways during agonistic social encounters. As with all other basic emotional systems, higher cortical processes, especially in the frontal lobes, can provide inhibition, direction, and other forms of cognitive regulation over this impulsive urge, yielding internalized irritability, hatreds, and resentments.

Many emotional problems result from the inhibition of anger. Aggressive irritability is also highly dysregulated in trauma, both in terms of inappropriate aggression toward others as well as directed internally toward the self. For instance, when children are demeaned, ignored, sexually abused, or beaten, such domestic atrocities generate intense anger and irritability, often toward caretakers, but often also toward themselves. Obviously, traumatized children need to be rescued from their maladaptive environments before any therapeutic interventions can work. When the time is ripe, such children need to be gently reintroduced to a secure social base, with abundant laughter and the PLAYful joy of life (see below). Such positive affects may automatically help diminish the long-term emotional wounds inflicted by abuse.

Conversely, the experience and occasional expression of anger, in a regulated fashion, may be highly adaptive, leading to feelings of empowerment, assertion, and an overall sense of dominance. Affective therapies that permit the honest expression of angry impulses could help set the stage for learning better regulatory strategies.

4. **The LUST/Sexual Systems** (see Pfaff, 1999). There is a core sensualist system in everyone. Sexual urges have robust instinctual substrates. LUST networks, somewhat different in males and females, link up with SEEKING urges to provide gender-specific libidinal drive. Overall, the medial amygdala and preoptic area are especially important for male sexual urges, with an abundance of the neuropeptide vasopressin at the core of this system. In contrast, female sexuality is more strongly regulated by oxytocin circuits that find their origin in the basal forebrain and anterior hypothalamic regions, which project heavily into the medial hypothalamus for the consummatory phase of female sexual behavior, even though the appetitive phase is more likely to be facilitated by dopamine SEEKING urges. While humans can exercise extensive restraint over such urges because of the power of their higher cognitive mechanisms, most other animals follow no such cultural mandates. That means that erotic impulses are often especially thwarted in human societies, blocking the free flow of libidinal "energies."

In any event, gender-typical sexual systems are laid down, under specific gonadal hormonal influences, early in development, before babies are born, but these potentials are not fully activated until puberty, when gonadal hormones are secreted in abundance to arouse specific neuropeptide sex regulators that promote intense, but somewhat distinct, desires in males and females. Testosterone promotes vasopressin transmission, which may intensify male sexual assertiveness as well as jealousy (Panksepp, in press), whereas estrogen promotes oxytocin transmission in the brain and female-typical receptivity. Because of the way male and female bodies get organized during gestation, male-type desires can flower in female brains and female-type desires can thrive in male brains. These peptidergic circuits have been implicated in human sexuality and homosexuality, and they "light up" dramatically during human orgasms (Holstege, et al., 2003).

Of course, problems in libido are pervasive in psychiatric disorders, but instead of being a primary problem, they are often seen as subsidiary symptoms, except for distinct pathologies such as pedophilia. The need for specific libido-modulating pharmacological agents remains in great demand in this era of fine medications for erectile dysfunctions, with hardly any yet available for libido dysfunctions (e.g., abnormally low desire).

5. **The CARE/Nurturance System** (for a comprehensive neuroscience

summary, see Numan & Insel, 2003). Mammalian infants would not survive unless mothers were sincere and devoted "nest builders"; fathers typically have weaker CARE urges in their brains and hence have diminished motivation for caretaking behaviors. These systems are richly represented in anterior cingulate regions, downward to septal and nearby preoptic regions, then on to the VTA, where interactions with dopamine-based SEEKING mandates help add to the urgency of maternal intent. Maternal nurturant instincts, activated prior to birth by changing tides of hormones—increasing estrogen, prolactin and oxytocin along with diminishing progesterone—help prepare the mother for the arrival of the infant, sensitizing her brain to help assure that interaction with the newborn is a special delight. Oxytocin and prolactin are especially important in engendering the sustained touching required for nurturant care and milk sharing, as well as promoting confident and trusting can-do attitudes. Perhaps all these changes can be conceptualized as increased "confidence" (Panksepp, 2009).

As with all emotions, there is variability in the intensity and devotion of CARE energies arising from the overall emotional strength and resilience of the caretaker. The more devoted patterns of nurturance, such as abundant anal–genital licking in rats, facilitate psychobehavioral stress resistance and cognitive–emotional improvements in offspring (Szyf, McGowan, & Meaney, 2008). The neurochemistries of maternal care, especially heightened secretions of oxytocin, facilitate maternal moods that facilitate strong bonding with offspring—brain changes that are foundational for nurturant love.

The potential of agents such as intranasally applied oxytocin in ameliorating variants of depression, especially postpartum depression, and promoting prosocial moods deserves evaluation. Dysregulations in nurturant motivation may eventually be found to contribute to many emotional endophenotypes in some future, affective symptom-based biological psychiatry.

6. **The PANIC or GRIEF/DISTRESS System.** When young children get lost, they are thrown into a PANIC because they possess separation-distress circuitry, a major source of *psychic pain*. They cry out for care, and their feelings of sudden aloneness and distress reflect the ancestral neural codes of the separation-distress system from which adult sadness and grief are constructed. Indeed, there is a robust Sad Poet—nourishing existential attitudes—within most of us. The intrapsychic pain of social loss arises, in part, from brain systems that mediate separation-distress calls (crying). Brain chemistries that exacerbate feelings of distress (e.g., corticotropin releasing factor) and those that powerfully alleviate distress (e.g., brain opioids, oxytocin, prolactin) figure heavily in the genesis of social attachments and perhaps the regulation of depressive affect (Nelson & Panksepp, 1998; Watt & Panksepp, 2009). These

systems parallel the CARE system to a substantial extent, for mothers need automatic detection mechanisms for when care is most urgently needed. Again, the anterior cingulate, ventral septal, and dorsal preoptic areas, as well as the bed nucleus of the stria trerminalis, dorsomedial thalamus, and the PAG figure heavily in the generation of sadness, grief, and crying (Herman & Panksepp, 1981; Panksepp, et al., 1988).

It is hard to imagine how therapy could yield successful outcomes if there were no sense of warmth, attachment, and care between clinician and client. If therapists cannot assume an interpersonal stance in which they resonate with the psychic pain of the client, there can never be that sense of trust that is critically important for the healing touch—the foundation of the clinically very useful placebo effect—to take hold in the client's mind. There will always be a residue of suspicion of manipulation as opposed to the deep acceptance that opens the portals for change—for feelings of redemption and salvation, without narcissistic transference, that should lie at the core of every therapeutic interaction. The attitude of CARE—nurturant verbal guidance through the affective possibilities of life—is essential for the empathic stance that is essential for therapy.

CARE and PANIC/GRIEF/Separation distress are the Janus-faced twins of deep social attachments, and it will be interesting to see how their shared chemistries, especially oxytocin and endogenous opioids, can eventually be used therapeutically. These are the chemistries that are currently most likely to increase or decrease our capacity to create intersubjective spaces with others. Medicinal use of such social chemistries may one day allow clinicians to selectively enhance prosocial emotional feelings that may promote therapeutic progress. Many of us are waiting to see if supplementing therapeutic situations with nurturant activities can promote the release of endogenous opioids and oxytocin, but also whether supplementation with such hormones (e.g., intranasal oxytocin before a therapy session, perhaps in both therapists and client) could enhance therapeutic flow by allowing both to work more effectively in the present intersubjective moments.

Precipitous arousal of the separation-distress system may be one of the underlying causes for panic attacks (Panksepp, 1998a; Preter & Klein, 2008). Our understanding of the psychobiology of social attachments, which has largely arisen from work on these neurochemistries, is also being link up with some preliminary understanding of childhood disorders such as autism. Some children may be socially aloof partly because they are addicted to their own self-released opioids as opposed to those activated by significant others (Panksepp, Lensing, Leboyer, & Bouvard, 1991).

Although social-isolation-induced psychic pain is pervasive in many psychiatric disorders, the PANIC emotional system stands out as a major vector, heads and shoulders above others, in one psychiatric syndrome. That is depression and its many variants. Ultimately it is the pain of social loss, whether the loss of Mommy when one is young or social status when one is older, that opens the gateway to depression. The chronic sense of aloneness when social bonds have gone sour pervades many psychiatric syndromes, and it is the despair that follows the initial phase of acute protest that typically accompanies loss of social support or chronic stress, which sets in motion many symptoms of depression (Watt & Panksepp, 2009). Our understanding of the basic chemistries of the social brain has barely started to impact psychiatric practice. For instance, "safe opioids," such as the mixed mu-opioid receptor agonist/antagonist, deserve a more prominent role in psychiatric practice (Bodkin, et al., 1995). Such issues should come to the forefront when psychiatry begins to once again discuss the nature of brain emotional endophenotypes and the nature of basic affects (Panksepp, 2006).

Even though we currently have abundant research on fearful behaviors, there is attention given to the conditioning of anxiety-like behavior but little discussion of the underlying FEAR circuitry. Although there is some attempt to relate such data to psychiatric disorders, such as panic attacks (Busch & Milrod, 2004), it is often forgotten that in people with anxiety disorders, it is the internal feeling of tension and persistent negative affect that lies at the heart of their clinical problems. However, negative affect that accompanies panic comes in several forms, suggesting that at least two distinct types of underlying processes need to be considered in panic disorders. The panic attack itself is a precipitous disconnection from the comforts of the everyday world, where a "black hole" opens up under an individual and his or her whole sense of security is temporarily demolished, often in a time-limited ways as the emotional storm runs its course. Many simply see this as a sudden fear response; an alternative view is that this precipitous feeling of discomfort arises from sudden arousal of the PANIC/separation-distress system (Busch & Milrod, 2004). According to this nontraditional view, the FEAR system is largely involved in engendering the anticipatory anxiety that begins to fill the time between successive panic attacks. As people begin to feel anxious about being victims of unpredictable panic attacks, they become chronically anxious. Thus, while the feeling of panic may be due more to the PANIC/separation-distress system, the anticipatory anxiety is probably due more to the sustained arousal of the FEAR system (Panksepp, 2003; Preter & Klein, 2008).

If this view is correct, then animal models as well as the clinical therapeutic enterprise need to be clear about how these two anxiety states differ. Do they have different sources in the brain? How do they interact? What needs to be done about each type of dysregulation? With a better understanding, we might be able to educate clients on how to best manage the unusual triggers in their emotional systems. For instance, perhaps when a panic attack is about to start, slow, deep rhythmic breathing, along with the concurrent active expression of happy movement dynamics, could abort the forthcoming attack (see further discussion below, on possible ABTs). Then it might be a very different issue as to what we might do to minimize the sustained anticipatory anxiety that chronically darkens a person's life. Perhaps physical exercise along with meditative/mindfulness practices would help minimize such mood problems, allowing individuals to learn how to self-manage panic attacks. Of course, the role of different medications in the control of each should always be kept in mind (Preter & Klein, 2008) in case the psychotherapeutic maneuvers prove less effective than desired.

7. The **PLAY Systems**. There is a jester in all of us. Thank goodness, for it can make play out of work—including, potentially, psychotherapeutic work. These networks of the brain have been the most recent revelations of affective neuroscience. It is noteworthy that the neocortex is not needed for this emotional urge, just as it is not needed for any of the other primary-process emotions (Panksepp, Normasell, Cox, & Siviy, 1994). However, it is becoming clear that play has most remarkable effects on the cortex, programming it to become fully social, as long as the play energies are well used (Panksepp, 2008b). The core of the PLAY system is within medial zones of the thalamus (the parafascicular area, rich in opioids, is especially important; Siviy & Panksepp, 1987), as are ascending dopamine systems, which seem to be integrally important for the joy of laughter (Burgdorf, et al., 2007).

It is a blessing that the urge for social play—for joyous physical engagement with others—was also not left to chance by evolution, but is built into the instinctual action apparatus of the mammalian brain. Although PLAY circuitry has not been mapped with brain stimulation as completely as the other emotional primes, a laughter-type component is now well mapped in a rodent model (Burgdorf et al., 2007).

Playfulness is probably an experience-expectant process that brings young animals to the perimeter of their social knowledge, to psychic places where they must learn about what they can or cannot do to each other. Play allows animals to be woven into their social structures in effective but friendly ways. Young animals physically engage with each other in order to navigate social possibilities in assertive, joyous ways. Although many play actions consist of vigorous chasing, pouncing, and wrestling, these only highlight that young animals are exercising potentials for social dominance through positive social interchange. Young animals readily communicate how much they enjoy these activities, partly by play vocalizations (e.g., 50 kHz chirps in rats) that can also be induced by tickling them. We have recently challenged our colleagues to consider that joyous "laughter," so common in human play, also exists in other species (Burgdorf & Panksepp, 2006; Panksepp & Burgdorf, 2003; Panksepp, 2007b).

I would suggest that any therapist who can capture the therapeutic moment in mutually shared play episodes will have brought the client to the gateway of happy living. To the extent that the client can be held there, in both body and mind, the therapist will have offered one of the greatest emotional gifts that psychotherapy, especially child therapy, can ever provide. At the end of this paper I briefly return to this most joyous of brain emotional systems that is so richly expressed in body dynamics that are, perhaps, the foundation of dance. It should have a very special place in body therapies, from childhood to old age.

Higher-Order Emotions

There are, of course many other basic affects, from disgust to sweet delights, from hunger to thirst, but those are properly called sensory and homeostatic affects, not *emotional* ones. The emotional feelings are the ones that figure most prominently in the genesis of psychiatric disorders. There are also a host of socially constructed emotions, from guilt to jealousy to shame, that arise from the basic emotional system interacting with learning as well as higher cognitive and cultural processes (secondary and tertiary processes; for a discussion of jealousy, see Panksepp, in press). All are rooted in the emotional primes, but they take on their form from specific life experiences rather than any known evolutionary epistemology that exists in our genetically dictated brain networks.

Very briefly, the affective neuroscience view of affect generation in the brain is linked dynamically to the intrinsic instinctual action repertoires of brain emotional systems. This can be a two-way street. We can utilize our explicit, voluntarily activated expressions of emotional actions to modify our mood states, and the more dynamically we generate emotional actions, the more affective strength we can engender (Panksepp & Gordon, 2003). Might we be able to use these "energies," especially the positive emotions (SEEKING, LUST, CARE, and most certainly PLAYful dynamics), in conjunction with cognitive restructuring, to solidify therapeutic change? Might they be utilized to help reconsolidate aversive memories so that more adaptive, affectively gentle, remembrances replace stress-engendering ones?

The prevailing cognitive view of mind remains starkly incomplete without the affects. A common belief among cognitively oriented scholars, albeit not therapists who deal with troubled human lives, is that being scared (derived from the basic feeling of fear) is caused largely by the way people think. That is the more obvious part of cognitive–affective dynamics. The alternative they rarely consider, which every clinician must face, is that FEARful, RAGEful and PANICy feelings have a mind of their own, a raw affective consciousness, that interacts with, and can run roughshod over, cognitive awareness. The internal forces of anxiety can restructure the cognitive apparatus so that troubled people can no longer recruit the power of their universal SEEKING urges and the positive social affects, from loving CARE to joyous PLAYfulness, that open up the rich possibilities of a deeply inquisitive, satisfying, and LUSTy life. One reason eye movement desensitization and reprocessing (EMDR) therapy may work (Bisson, et al., 2007) is because it sets in motion a SEEKING-exploratory urge that can help restructure the way trauma has solidified in the brain. For instance, investigative eye movements and similar exploratory movements may allow therapeutic reconsolidations to be promoted because the SEEKING-exploratory system is well designed to lay down new memories, and because every aroused emotional state can exert commanding influences over cognitive restructurings. This is what future ABT approaches may seek to maximize.

The primary-process affects are internal signals indicating the various intrinsic zones of comfort and discomfort in living. These positive and negative affects indicate the presence of an array of *life supporting* and *life-detracting* environments. Through our affects we can learn more about such conditions of living by being connected to real-world events. The aim of therapy must be to restore a healthy appreciation for the mental and environmental conditions that promote well-being. I would anticipate that clients will often experience enormous relief to simply be educated about their emotional primes and to recognize how they can become masters over these primes rather than being mastered by them. The mere act of learning about them as ancient evolutionary tools for living can take an enormous burden off troubled minds. A better understanding of our ancient emotional energies may allow individuals to better deal with the upsetting feelings of the brain and to develop cognitive habits that help engender more positive feelings.

We must worry about the current status of biological psychiatry and the neuroscientific approaches to psychiatric disorders, wherein the varieties of affective experiences are all too often excluded from the active discussion of what is going on within the brain–mind during psychiatric problems. Indeed, an understanding of the emotional–instinctual action dynamics of the brain provides (1) a scientific way to understand how primary-process affective processes are generated in the brain (a topic extensively discussed elsewhere: Panksepp, 2005a, 2005b, 2008c), and (2) a way to envision how we might be able to recruit such bodily dynamics within experiential, affective, and body-oriented psychotherapies. For instance, one could envision inclusion of very basic emotional exercises, such as simulated "pure" laughter, within therapeutic interventions (Panksepp & Gordon, 2003). Such ABTs may provide an evidence-based way to modify emotional feelings directly, and to use such therapeutically facilitated affective attitudes as a foundation for restructuring the cognitive dynamics with which individuals can confront the world with more confidence and an overall better understandings of the universal principles that underlie emotional-affective state generation and regulation.

The Epistemology of Emotional Affects

Cognitions are not the only pathway to emotional affects. Emotional bodily dynamics are more intimately intertwined with the basic affects of the brain. The subcortical localization of the basic emotional system has been dramatically confirmed by that fact that investigators can surgically eliminate all neocortex at birth in various experimental animals, and they grow up to be seemingly normal creatures as far as their basic sets of emotional energies are concerned. They exhibit exploratory urges and seeking behaviors, fear, anger, lust, maternal care, and playfulness. The last is especially surprising (Panksepp et al., 1994), since physical play is such a dynamically flexible behavior. This kind of brain damage, inflicted to adults, certainly impairs all these kinds of behaviors more severely, probably because these urges are cognitively rerepresented in the brain, to the point where there seems to be no distinction between emotions and cognitions. The retention of basic affective tendencies is also evident in young humans missing higher regions of their brains (Shewmon, et al., 1999). What this research implies is that we can work more directly with emotional feelings through body dynamics than cognitive inputs.

Affective Balance Therapies

The emotional rudiments of the mind are thoroughly biological. The guiding principle is that raw affects arise from large-scale neural networks that generate instinctual emotional behaviors, rather than from higher self-related brain regions that mediate the cognitive awareness of our existence. Since these subcortical dynamics—large-scale analog network functions—are the wellsprings of emotional life, it may be useful for psychotherapists to more clearly envision the nature of these psychic energies to more effectively deal with them in therapeutic interactions. Each emotional system can be evaluated prior to and during therapy, as might be done with the Affective Neuroscience Personality Scales (Davis, et al., 2003).

Emotional feelings go hand in hand with emotional action dynamics and constitute distinct affective varieties of mental experience. The resulting affective dynamics have an identifiable bodily feel to them as primordial phenomenological-experiential states that we call "affective consciousness" (Panksepp, 2005b). Although these dynamics emerge from subcortical brain networks that we share with other animals, they could be recruited more effectively in psychotherapeutic environments, especially experiential–affective and body-oriented therapies, to help directly modulate how one emotionally experiences the world. As we learn to express such emotional dynamics creatively with our whole bodily apparatus, we can come to control and further explore our basic emotional feelings.

So, in a deep neurophenomenological sense, what are emotional feelings? To the best of our knowledge, emotional feelings arise from wide-scale neurodynamics that establish characteristic, mentally experienced "forces" that regulate and reflect certain types of action readiness within the nervous system. Let us briefly consider these dynamics. The distinct dynamics are evident in the pounding force of anger, the shivery feelings of fear, the caress of love, the urgent thrusting of sexuality, the painful pangs of grief, the exuberance of joy, and the persistent "nosy" poking about of organisms seeking resources. Practically the only way we can understand how mammalian brains generate raw emotional experience is by having workable (i.e., animal) neuroscience models where the necessary detailed work can be done.

It has long been known in psychological science that emotional feelings can be induced by simulating emotional actions. Often this response has been studied via facial actions, but even more dramatic effects can be achieved with whole-body dynamics (Panksepp & Gordon, 2003). How such voluntary control over affective states can be harnessed in psychotherapeutic situations remains to be studied systematically. It seems fairly straightforward to bring such affect-specific energies to bear on all varieties of experiential, affective, and body-oriented psychotherapies, what here I am calling the ABTs. These highly focused emotional exercises could contribute greatly to sensorimotor psychotherapeutic approaches (Ogden, Minton, & Pain, 2006), providing a ready opportunity to educate people about the primary-process aspects of their emotional lives.

To become a master of our emotional dynamics in this way should help pave the path toward emotional homeostasis in a variety of situations. Pursued on a daily basis, such emotional exercises may constitute a strengthening of our "emotional muscles" in ways that can counteract the effects of various past traumas and inoculate our emotional circuits against future adversities. A great deal of basic science, using appropriate methodologies (e.g., double-blind procedures) that combine cognitive–emotional interventions with existing body therapies (Ogden et al., 2006), needs to be done in this realm to evaluate the efficacy of various specific techniques. These techniques need to be studied not only in the context of interventions aimed at healing human suffering but also in terms of self-actualization for those with no urgent problems who wish to improve their humanness and mental healthiness.

Playful Affective and Body-Oriented Therapies

Play may be the most underutilized emotional force that could have remarkable benefits in psychotherapy, especially with children. There are, of course, many play therapies, but most of them are structured "fun" activities that have no resemblance to the bodily vigor, spontaneity, and creativeness of "real" physical PLAY. Indeed, there are good reasons to believe that one of the main functions of PLAY circuitry is to help construct social brains (Panksepp, 2007c, 2008b). The cortex, at birth, is largely a *tabula rasa* that needs to be socialized under the influence of basic tools such as physical PLAY, which Mother Nature provided for the epigenetic construction of the social brain. This construction may be best achieved by utilizing PLAY to shape the many plasticities of the brain in a way that creates fine-tuned social brains that work optimally in the environments in which young animals find themselves in their struggle to mature. Psychiatric distress can be conceptualized as overturned tables that need to be set right again, and there is unlikely to be any stronger emotional aid than that contained in the joyous potentials of PLAY.

If we do not build social structures that promote joyous childhood play in our own children, we may be promoting cultural attitudes that facilitate problems such as attention-deficit hyperactivity disorder (ADHD). Human children, just like rats that are not allowed safe places to exercise their urges for rough-and-tumble engagement, will develop heightened motivations to play. The likelihood of play-starved children becoming playfully impulsive within the classroom increases, as do diagnoses of children with ADHD, who, all too often, are destined to receive psychostimulants. Such drugs are among the most effective inhibitors of physical play urges. On the other hand, animal models already confirm that ADHD-type impulsivity can be reduced, in the long run, with extra rations of rough-and-tumble play throughout early development (Panksepp, et al., 2003).

Early play may be essential for the emergence of well-modulated social abilities. The use of abundant natural play in early childhood as a way to strengthen positive social affect circuits of the brain, and hence perhaps to not only provide substantial prophylaxis for ADHD but also depression, desperately needs to be investigated in large-scale sociocultural studies. Elsewhere I have proposed the development of concepts such a "play sanctuaries" for our 2- to 6-year-old preschoolers (Panksepp, 2007a, 2008b).

The same points can be made for adults. Playfulness is an underutilized "force" with which to reroute mature lives onto positive affective tracks. First, it is becoming clear that robust physical activity may be as good an antidepressant as any of the medicines that dampen emotionality (see Watt & Panksepp, 2009, for overview). Second, it seems likely that play urges in adults can be reenergized by various types of bodily activities—from dance to sports—much of it hopefully facilitated by artistic accompaniments, such as music and dance, that are partly designed around the rhythmic motor impulses of the body (Panksepp & Trevarthen, 2008). Marathon organizers, recognizing the power of such motor rhythm facilitators, are beginning to ban iPods so that music listeners will not have undue advantages over the silent plodders. Clearly, music and the other arts need to be incorporated into all therapies that are clearly concerned with the human spirit.

The flow of cognitive activities is considerably more dependent, during early life, on the lower emotional powers, when cognitive skills and ability for self-regulation remain poorly developed. It is also useful to remember that all basic emotional systems are plastic, getting sensitized (stronger) with use and desensitized (weaker) with lack of use. These two basic processes of sensitization and desensitization have many etiological implications for understanding how emotional distress can intensify and become chronic; they also may have therapeutic implications for the long-term regulation of distress as well as positive affect. For instance, depression is much more likely to occur in adults who have experienced chronic lack of support and insecurity during childhood. Children who have had a secure base internalize that security for a lifetime, a phenomenon now detailed in animals (Szyf et al., 2008). Can adult affective lives also be restructured? The massive plasticity of the brain (Doidge, 2007) suggests that this achievement is likely, albeit not to the extent as occurs during early development, when the neocortex still resembles a *tabula rasa* (Sur & Rubenstein, 2005).

On Treating Human Souls: Emotional Endophenotypes and Psychiatric Authenticity

Future development of ABPs can be facilitated by clearer, scientifically valid visions of how primary-process emotionality is organized within human brains, and how self-related information processing (Northoff et al., 2006; Panksepp & Northoff, 2009), within a cross-species core affective self (Northoff & Panksepp, 2008), helps program the rest of the cognitive apparatus. How do affective feelings, the neurosymbolic indicators of basic survival values, arise from neural activities? How are primary-process emotions of anger and fear, joy and sadness actually encoded within the brain? What does it mean when libidinal energies and core emotional values become imbalanced? What does it mean when excessive emotional energies permeate human souls? "Souls?" Indeed, we may need such concepts—which may be isomorphic with the affectively rich core self around which so much of our mentation revolves.

Although debatable, I suspect the biological "soul" or "core self" is a coherent and completely neurobiological process, barely studied, with its epicenter running deep in brain–mind evolution. In brief, convergent evidence suggest that we share relatively homologous ancient animalian core selves with many other creatures of the world. Because of this shared base, pet-assisted therapy can use the natural emotional vitalities of our fellow creatures to provide examples of how humans can live more joyously. We are all inheritors of core selves that are neurodynamically quite similar, to the best of our knowledge.

Such neurosymbolic representations of the organism are presumably laid out in primitive viscerosomatic coordinates concentrated in central midbrain regions, such as the PAG (Panksepp, 1998b). These body images ramify through the core of the higher brainstem to medial cingulate/frontal regions, and may be shifted into distinct emotional field dynamics (large-scale network activities that directly generate distinct types of behavioral–instinctive urgencies) by a variety of impinging neurodynamics arising from emotional command systems (Lewis, 2005). This core process for primal self-representation, which developmentally matures to permit self-related information processing, may be a source of psychic coherence that is developmentally linked to higher medial cortical rerepresentations of the more primitive core processes (Northoff et al., 2006; Northoff & Panksepp, 2008). However, with excessive and repeated emotional storms, this core of psychic stability may engender natural varieties of emotional disequilibrium.

If this vision is a reasonable approximation of core brain–mind dynamics, then the key scientific mystery of brain function that directly impacts psychotherapeutic practice and understanding becomes the neural nature of emotional feelings, especially cravings that have become manically extreme or diminished beyond levels that support normative living patterns. Such complex network dynamics are hard to see directly in cognitively regulated clients; they must be inferred by clients' willingness to reveal their core feelings. The "bread and butter" of experiential approaches is the use of techniques designed to get through the "defenses" and the "blocks against affect" of cognitively hyperregulated patients, so as to tap into somatically based emotional experience (Fosha, 2000). A therapist will see more clearly how these dynamics are interwoven with higher cognitive information processing. However, recent advances in basic cross-species affective neuroscience, supplemented now with modern functional human brain imaging, are making clearer visions of the core issues more approachable and comprehensible (e.g., Northoff et al., 2006; Northoff & Panksepp, 2008). This area could constitute a major neuroscience contribution to the therapeutic enterprise. Much of the core knowledge has so far come from basic animal studies; of course, the cognitive ramifications must be derived from new and more sensitive human work—a *psychoethology* that does not yet exist.

To develop a psychoethology devoted to understanding the neural nature of affective-emotional processes, the brain- and affect-free "functionalist" cognitive revolution that came to rule psychology and gradually germinated cognitive neuroscience with the discovery of brain-imaging technologies, needs to internalize important messages from animal affective neuroscience that currently remain ignored: (1) Essentially all instinctual expressions of basic emotions remain intact after neonatal decortication. (2) Various basic emotions can be aroused from subcortical brain regions, but only by activating specific neurochemical circuits. (3) The generation of primary-process affective mentality is a subcortical, not a cortical, function of the brain. Thus, for neuroscience to provide greater assistance to biological psychiatry and psychotherapeutics, investigators need to devote as much attention to the lower affective properties of animal brains as they do to the higher cognitive aspects of human minds.

An especially important skill for a therapist is to be able situate a client properly in affective space. Our own efforts in that direction have led us to construct a new personality scale, the Affective Neuroscience Personality Scale (ANPS), that offers a straightforward way to evaluate the status of clients on all of the emotional primes except LUST. "Spirituality" was added instead, since that is so important for getting people over the hump of addictive disorders as well as, more widely, for finding the path to a life well lived. The ANPS is freely available for clinical use and research (Davis et al., 2003; tests are downloadable in various languages from *www.anps.de*).

Since the dynamics of basic emotional systems control many affective qualities of mental life, psychotherapists need to evaluate not only where individuals lie on these emotional dimensions, as can currently be best estimated with the ANPS, but they also need to clearly envision the major emotional forces that may have become imbalanced in forms of emotional distress. Emotional endophenotypes may provide such guidance for clinicians and also for neuroscientists who wish to contribute to our emerging knowledge of raw emotional feelings (Panksepp, 2006). These affective ancestral voices of the genes arise from ancient, subcortical neurodynamics and proceed to profoundly effect (and affect) the whole cognitive apparatus. There is abundant room here not only for development of new medicines that directly target affective imbalances in specific emotional systems, but also to recruit the often latent psychological and affective resources of clients to personally counteract many of those sustained emotional storms that are currently conceptualized as psychiatric disorders.

Conclusion

As every cognitively oriented therapist knows, in adults cognitions can readily modify emotional responsivity in useful ways; to some extent that insight lies at the heart of many, if not most, psychotherapeutic approaches. But that is not really true of the bottom-up approaches featured in this book. In these approaches, insight is something that emerges as a result of therapeutic transformation; insight is not the primary agent of transformation, but rather a *consequence* of it. Emotional action guides perception. However, therapy is less effective if past insecurities have crystallized as a shifted sensitivity of an emotional system.

Therapists who know how to conceptualize the basic emotions as distinct control processes, and to respect the developmental power of such psychic energies, may be able to promote more lasting therapeutic change than those who seek to remain simply at the cognitive level. Therapists able to engage with clients deeply and empathically, gradually reflecting on the deeper and fluctuating emotional feelings of clients and drawing out and reframing the associated cognitions, are more likely to be helpful than individuals less skilled at working on primary-process emotional levels.

In sum, psychotherapists need to internalize a better understanding of the nature of the basic emotional energies in order to deal more effectively with those prominent factors in all psychopathological and productive psychotherapeutic equations. From the brain perspective, the nature of affect may be the most important issue not only in developing new animal models of psychiatric disorders, but in optimizing the way clinicians must conceptualize the foundational aspects of their clients' problems. One reason that furrow of scientific understanding has not been cultivated more vigorously is because the emotional feelings of animals have been marginalized by the same scientists best positioned to do substantive work on such critically important brain issues. Regrettably few behavioral neuroscientists have envisioned how their many objective scientific approaches could illuminate the fundamental nature of affective subjectivity (Panksepp, 2005a, 2005b).

As we continue to cultivate this furrow of understanding—the cross-species understanding of primary-process emotional systems—we may be in a much better position to facilitate restoration of affective homeostasis through not only new mind medicines but through our understanding of how old feelings can be integrated into new cognitive structures. Scientifically, an understanding of the "whole" psychic apparatus can only be achieved gradually through a thorough understanding of both the neuronal and psychological "parts"—at both affective and cognitive levels of mind–brain organization.

ACKNOWLEDGMENTS

I wish to thank Diana Fosha for valuable editorial advice. This work was partly supported by the Hope for Depression Research Foundation.

2

Reciprocal Influences Between Body and Brain in the Perception and Expression of Affect

A Polyvagal Perspective

Stephen W. Porges

EMOTIONS, AFFECT REGULATION, and interpersonal social behavior are psychological processes that describe basic human experiences in response to events, environmental challenges, and people. These processes shape our sense of self, contribute to our abilities to form relationships, and determine whether we feel safe in various contexts or with specific people. Although these processes can be objectively observed and subjectively described, they represent a complex interplay between our psychological experience and our physiological regulation.

These psychological–physiological interactions are dependent on the dynamic bidirectional communication between peripheral organs and the central nervous system connecting the brain with these organs. For example, the neural circuits, providing a bidirectional communication between the brain and heart, can trigger either a rapid increase in heart rate to support protective fight/flight behaviors, or a rapid decrease in heart rate to support social interactions. Peripheral physiological reactions can be initiated by the brain that detect features of danger in the environment, and alternatively, changes in our peripheral physiological state can feed back information to the brain and alter our perceptions of the world. Thus, affect and interpersonal social behavior

27

are more accurately described as biobehavioral than psychological processes, since our physiological state can profoundly influence the quality of these psychological processes, and our feelings can, in turn, determine dynamic changes in our physiology.

Our nervous system functions as a sentry by continuously evaluating risk in the environment. Through neural surveillance mechanisms (i.e., neuroception—see below), our brain identifies features of risk or safety. Many of the features of risk and safety are not learned, but rather are hardwired into our nervous system and reflect adaptive strategies associated with our phylogenetic history. For example, low-frequency sounds elicit in mammals a sense of danger associated with approaching predator. This reaction is shared with other vertebrates, including reptiles and amphibians. Due to our phylogenetic history, the rumble of low-frequency sounds shifts our attention from social interactions to potential dangers in the environment. In contrast, high-pitched screams from another mammal (not just our children, but also our dogs and cats) elicit a sense of urgent concern or empathy for another who may be feeling pain or injured. With humans high-frequency screams shift our attention to the specific individual who is screaming. Through exposure and associative learning, we can link these features with other events. *Specific features in the environment recruit physiological states differentially associated with feelings of safety, danger, or ultimate demise (i.e., life threat). Each of these states is characterized by a specific set of capacities for affect regulation, social engagement, and communication* (Porges, 2003).

Current research in affective neuroscience focuses on brain structures and neural circuits related to specific motivational and emotional processes (e.g., Panksepp, 1998a). These important discoveries emphasize cortical and subcortical structures in the emergence of the complex affective repertoire of humans and their contribution to social relationships (e.g., Schore, 1994, 2003a; Siegel, 2007). However, underlying these contributions are details of an important and often overlooked neurobiological substrate: the neural circuits mediating the reciprocal communication between body states and brainstem structures, which have an impact on the availability of these affective circuits. These underlying circuits not only promote feelings (e.g., Damasio, 1999), but also form a bidirectional circuit (e.g., Darwin, 1872/1965) that enables mental and psychological processes to influence body state, and to color and, at times, to distort our perception of the world. Thus, the study of affective processes, especially in their prosocial and healing roles, requires an understanding of the neural circuits both between higher brain structures and the brainstem and between the brainstem and the visceral organs (e.g., the heart) mediated through the autonomic nervous system. All affective or emotional states are dependent upon lower brain regulation of the visceral state and the important visceral, tactile, and nocioceptive cues that travel to the brain from the periphery. Moreover, there are distinct visceral regulatory states that foster different domains of behavior. These states do not preclude the important bidirectional information from higher brain structures.

This chapter emphasizes the neural regulation of observable facial movements and concurrent subjective visceral experiences that characterize the expressions, feelings, and perceptions of emotion and affective state. The chapter uses the Polyvagal Theory (Porges, 1995, 1997, 1998, 2001b, 2003, 2007) as an organizing principle to explain the role of the visceral state in the accessibility of prosocial emotions and restorative affective states. The Polyvagal Theory is an attempt to reorganize our conceptualization of the autonomic nervous system with a focus on the specific neural circuits involved in regulating visceral organs for specific adaptive functions related to affect, emotions, and social communication behaviors.

The Polyvagal Theory interprets social interactions and emotion as biobehavioral processes. Thus, the theory is particularly important for psychotherapists, who focus on the social interaction within the therapeutic setting and forego pharmacological interventions. By treating the social interaction as a biobehavioral process, it is possible to conceptualize a therapeutic treatment that relies not on pharmacological manipulations but, rather, on the profound positive impact of social interactions and interpersonal behaviors on the neural regulation of body state and behavior. By exploring these bidirectional biobehavioral processes, psychotherapeutic treatments may change the neural regulation of physiological state, which in turn will support further benefits from interpersonal interactions.

Emotion, Motion, and Visceral State: Features of Mental Health

Regardless of the operational, and often arbitrary, distinction between emotion and affect or between emotional expressions and feelings, the measurement of physiological states (e.g., autonomic, endocrine, and muscle activity) needs to be embraced in affective neuroscience, particularly if there is to be a functional dialogue with experiential clinicians. In most cases, *physiological state* has been conceptualized as a correlate or a consequence of higher brain structures (e.g., cortex) presumed to be driving emotion and affect. However, it would be naïve not to explore the connections and potential bidirectional influences between peripheral physiological states and the brain circuits related to affective processes.

Physiological state is an implicit component of the subjective experiences associated with specific psychological constructs such as anxiety, fear, panic, and pain. The convergence between physiological state and emotional experience is neurophysiologically determined, since the metabolic requirements necessary to modulate the muscles of the face and body require supporting changes in autonomic state. All emotional and affective states require specific physiological shifts to facilitate their expression and to reach their implicit goals (e.g., fight, flight, freeze, proximity).

Through the study of phylogenetic shifts in the vertebrate autonomic nervous system, it is possible to link the different expressive features of emotion in humans with the phylogenetic transitions in visceral regulation observed in vertebrates. Physiological monitoring provides an important portal to monitor these reactions, since some affective responses are often not observable in overt behavior. For example, the convergence between the neural mechanism mediating autonomic state and facial expressions phylogenetically occurs in the transition from reptiles to mammals (see Porges, 1995, 2007).

There is a rich history of research linking the neural regulation of face and viscera (e.g., heart) with brain circuits. Gellhorn (1964) elaborated on how proprioceptive discharges from facial muscles influence brain function and promote changes in visceral state, thus providing an example of the bidirectionality between peripheral and central structures as well as a neurophysiological basis for the assumed relation between facial expression and body feelings. Even earlier, Darwin (1872/1965) acknowledged the important and often neglected bidirectional relation between the brain and the heart in *The Expression of Emotions in Man and Animals*: "When the heart is affected it reacts on the brain; and the state of the brain again reacts through the pneumo-gastric [vagus] nerve on the heart; so that under any excitement there will be much mutual action and reaction between these, the two most important organs of the body" (p. 69).

Although Hess (1954) was awarded the Nobel prize in physiology or medicine in 1949 for his work emphasizing the importance of the central regulation of visceral state, journals in contemporary affective neuroscience (e.g., *Nature Neuroscience*) and biological psychiatry (e.g., *Biological Psychiatry, CNS*) express a disconnect between subjective affective experience and visceral state regulation. Contemporary affective neuroscience, with the aids of both imaging techniques and neurochemistry, has focused on brain structures contributing to various neural circuits involved in adaptive behaviors with apparent motivational objectives.

Panksepp (1998; see also Chapter 1, this volume) organizes affective experiences into seven neural-based motivational systems that include SEEKING, RAGE, FEAR, LUST, CARE, PANIC, and PLAY. However, missing from these functionally adaptive motivational circuits is the role that neural regulation of visceral state plays in potentiating or dampening these circuits. For example, if an individual is in a physiological state characterized by vagal withdrawal and high sympathetic excitation, body feelings of a fast pounding heartbeat are experienced, the threshold to react aggressively is low. In contrast, in a physiological state characterized by an engaged myelinated vagus, sympathetic and hypothalamic–pituitary–adrenal (HPA) axis reactivity are dampened, and that physiological state is experienced as "calm." Intrusive stimuli that previously would have triggered aggressive behaviors when the vagal activity is withdrawn will now result in a dampened reaction. Accompanying this change in physiological state are options to further dampen reactivity through social interactions.

Most proponents of affective neuroscience embrace a science of parallelism that links either observable emotional expressions or subjective experiences with a "neural" specificity that is concretized and assumed to be validated either by imaging studies that identify activation of brain areas or blockade studies that interfere with appropriate functioning of these circuits. Thus, to many affective neuroscientists, affect resides solely in the brain and does not require inputs or outputs linking the body to the brain. Missing from this research agenda and theoretical explanation is an appreciation of the necessary contributions of both the sensory inputs and the motor outputs from the central circuits. Focusing on the central circuits, without studying the sensory and motor contributions, is like studying the behavior of a thermostat independent of information regarding both ambient temperature and the capacity of the heating, ventilation, and air conditioning system.

Hess was aware that, although the components of a feedback circuit might be identified and studied independently, the functioning of independent parts did not explain how the system, as a whole, functioned dynamically during the moment-to-moment challenges of life. This limitation was, in part, dependent on the methodologies of the day that required pharmacological, surgical, or electrical manipulations to block or stimulate "global" branches of the autonomic nervous system that either shared a specific neurotransmitter (e.g., acetylcholine, epinephrine) or an easily identifiable nerve (e.g., vagus) that could be cut or stimulated.

Within the field of mental health, there is a similar acceptance of a disease model without a focus on the intervening feedback circuits that mediate the features of the disorder. Within psychiatry, anxiety and depression are defined by clinical features and not by a measurable physiological substrate. The prevalent strategies in mental health research that use neurophysiological variables (e.g., imaging, autonomic measures) are not directed at defining anxiety or depression, but use neurophysiological variables as correlates of a clinical diagnosis. The value of taking a different perspective can be illustrated with the construct of anxiety. If anxiety were viewed as dependent on a shift in autonomic state in which an individual's physiological state is dominated by the sympathetic nervous system, new clinical research strategies might emerge that focus on characterizing how states of anxiety and a vulnerability to being anxious would be potentiated or dampened by different autonomic states. Treatments would then be developed either to (1) dampen sympathetic tone or (2) enable the individual to move to environments or shift contexts that are less likely to trigger the increased reactivity associated with higher sympathetic excitation. Unfortunately, most researchers in psychiatry and psychology express little interest in the mapping autonomic regulation as a "vulnerability" dimension for various psychiatric disorders and behavioral problems, even though visceral features are often symptoms of the disorders they are treating.

Clinical disciplines rarely acknowledge the proximal functions of the visceral state. Likewise, clinicians seldom monitor the expression of vagal withdrawal or sympathetic excitation in their patients. Such a shift in autonomic state would be manifested in several physical and psychiatric symptoms, including flat affect, difficulties in auditory processing, hyperacusis (i.e., auditory hypersensitivities), tachycardia, and constipation. In addition, conventional models of mental disorders neglect the contribution of neurophysiological mechanisms in dynamic interaction with contextual cues in the environment. In contrast, these disciplines have embraced distal constructs related to the functions of receptors within the brain that lead almost reflexively to drug treatment, while generally failing to recognize the important role of visceral state and visceral afferent feedback on the global functioning of the brain. This strategy is far from parsimonious and does not take into account either the phylogeny of the mammalian nervous system or the intervening neurophysiological and biobehavioral systems along a continuum from genes to behavior. Rather these disciplines have assumed that clusters of observable behaviors or subjective experiences are linked parsimoniously and directly to neurochemical levels in specific brain circuits. Thus, they overlook the important potential of psychological and behavioral interventions (including changes in environment) that would be therapeutic by virtue of their direct influence on physiological state, without necessitating pharmacological treatments.

State Regulation and the Autonomic Nervous System:
A Historical Perspective

For over a century, researchers have measured autonomic variables (e.g., heart rate, palmar sweat gland activity) as indicators of emotional state related to perceived stress (e.g., fear, mental effort, workload, anxiety). Historically, arousal theories (e.g., Berlyne, 1960; Darrow, 1943; Gray, 1971) provided scientists who study brain–behavior relations with a model that assumed that activation of peripheral physiological measures regulated by the sympathetic branch of the autonomic nervous system were sensitive indicators of brain "arousal" or "activation." This view was based on a rudimentary understanding of the autonomic nervous system in which changes in easily measured peripheral organs (e.g., heart, sweat glands) were assumed to be accurate indicators of how the brain was processing emotional stimuli. Usually, emotional states were associated with fight flight behaviors and the sympathetic–adrenal system (e.g., increases in heart rate, sweat gland activity, and circulating catecholamines) as initially described by Cannon (1928a). Based on Selye (1936, 1956), emotional states were also associated with increased activity of the HPA axis (e.g., increases in cortisol). From a psychological level, arousal theories emphasized fight-flight behaviors and neglected or minimized the importance of both prosocial affective states that facilitated social interaction and also the defensive strategy of immobilization (e.g., fainting, death feigning).

An acceptance of a unitary arousal system is assumed in several research domains, including investigations of sleep, deception, sexual behavior, and anxiety. Moreover, this assumption has led to research on cortical "arousal" and the use of electroencephalography (EEG), single photon emission computerized tomography (SPECT), functional magnetic resonance imaging (fMRI), and other imaging technologies that accepted the arousal construct with little interest in the distinction between activation of neural pathways that were excitatory or inhibitory. This approach resulted in difficulties in establishing whether "activation" represents the turning on or the turning off of a specific neural structure. From a physiological level, arousal theories emphasize an assumed continuity between central cortical activation and peripheral arousal marked by increases in the activity of the sympathetic nervous system and the adrenal hormones. However, arousal theories have neglected both the importance of the parasympathetic branch of the autonomic nervous system and the bidirectional communication between brain structures and visceral organs.

The continuity between brain and peripheral arousal created a research environment that neglected several important factors, including (1) an under-standing of the brain structures that regulate autonomic function; (2) how these structures evolved from the most primitive vertebrates to mammals; (3) how the autonomic nervous system interacts with the immune system, the HPA axis, and the neuropeptides, oxytocin, and vasopressin; and (4) the co-evolution of stress and coping strategies with the increasing complexity of the autonomic nervous system. Missing from this dialogue is a discussion of the role of the parasympathetic nervous system and especially the vagus (the 10th cranial nerve) with its bidirectional portal between the brain and specific vis-ceral organs such as the heart.

The Polyvagal Theory: A Primer

The Polyvagal Theory emerged from the study of the evolution of the verte-brate autonomic nervous system. The theory assumes that many of our social behaviors and vulnerabilities to emotional disorders are "hardwired" into our nervous system. Based on this theory, it is possible to understand various as-pects of mental health and to develop treatment techniques that can help people communicate and relate better to others. The term "polyvagal" com-bines *poly*, meaning "many," and *vagal*, which refers to the important nerve called the "vagus." To understand the theory, we need to investigate features of the vagus nerve, a primary component of the autonomic nervous system. The vagus nerve exits the brainstem and has branches that regulate several organs, including the heart. The theory proposes that the two branches of the vagus are related to different behavioral strategies: One is related to social interactions in safe environments, and the other is related to adaptive re-sponses to life threat.

Historically, the autonomic nervous system has been broken into two op-posing components, one labeled *sympathetic* and the other *parasympathetic*. This organizational model was used to describe the function of the autonomic ner-vous system in the late 1800s and the early 1900s. In the 1920s this paired-antagonism model was formalized (Langley, 1921). This model characterized the function of the autonomic nervous system as a constant battle between the sympathetic nervous system associated with fight/flight behaviors and the parasympathetic nervous system associated with growth, health, and restora-tion. Because most organs of the body, such as the heart, lungs, and gut, have innervations from both sympathetic and parasympathetic components, the paired-antagonism model evolved into "balance theories." Balance theories at-tempted to link "tonic" imbalances to both physical and mental health. For example, a sympathetic dominance might be related to symptoms of anxiety, hyperactivity, or impulsivity, whereas a parasympathetic dominance might be related to symptoms of depression or lethargy. In addition to the tonic features of autonomic state, the paired-antagonism model also was assumed to explain the reactive features of the autonomic nervous system. This dependence on the construct of "autonomic balance" is still prevalent in textbooks, despite an intervening century in which neurophysiology documented a second vagal pathway involved in regulating autonomic function. Unfortunately, this new knowledge of the second vagal pathway has not permeated the teaching of physiology, which still is dominated by descriptions of the paired antagonism between the sympathetic and parasympathetic components of the autonomic nervous system.

The primary parasympathetic influence to peripheral organs is conveyed through the vagus, a cranial nerve that exits the brain and innervates the gastrointestinal tract, respiratory tract, heart, and abdominal viscera. The vagus can be conceptualized as a tube or conduit containing several sensory and motor fibers originating or terminating in different areas of the brainstem. For example, vagal motor pathways that regulate the lower gut originate in the dorsal nucleus of the vagus; the vagal pathways that regulate the heart and the lungs originate in the nucleus ambiguus; and the vagal pathways sending sensory information from the gut terminate in the nucleus of the solitary tract. Proximal and interactive with the nucleus ambiguus are the source nuclei that regulate the striated muscles of the face and head.

The Polyvagal Theory proposes that the autonomic nervous system reacts to real-world challenges in a predictable hierarchical manner that parallels, in reverse, the phylogenetic history of the autonomic nervous system in vertebrates. In other words, if we study the evolutionary path of how the autonomic nervous system unfolded in vertebrates (i.e., from ancient jawless fish to bony fish, amphibians, reptiles, and mammals), we learn not only that there is an increase in the growth and complexity of the cortex (the outer layer of the cerebrum), but also that there is a change in composition and function of the autonomic nervous system. In mammals, the autonomic nervous system functions as a hierarchical system that parallels phylogenetic states in reverse and not as the balance between sympathetic/parasympathetic systems.

The phylogenetic changes in the autonomic nervous system (including changes in neural pathways and brainstem areas regulating the peripheral organs) determine how the autonomic nervous system reacts to challenges. In humans and other mammals, the hierarchy is composed of three neural circuits, with the newer circuits having the capacity to override the older circuits. Under most challenges in our environment, we initially react with our newest system (i.e., myelinated vagus). If that circuit does not satisfy our biobehavioral quest for safety, an older circuit spontaneously reacts (i.e., sympathetic nervous system). Finally, if the former strategies are unsuccessful, as our last option, we reflexively trigger the oldest circuit (i.e., unmyelinated vagus). Functionally, in humans, the older vagal circuit is involved in adaptive reactions characterized by immobilization and decrease in metabolic resources, while the newer vagal circuit is involved in regulating calm states that promote both spontaneous social engagement and health, growth, and restoration. Along the phylogenetic hierarchy, between the two vagal circuits, is the sympathetic nervous that supports fight and flight behaviors.

The Polyvagal Theory: The Biobehavioral Quest for Safety, Survival, and a Painless Death

To survive, mammals must determine friend from foe and when an environment is safe, and they must be able to communicate to their social unit. These survival-related behaviors limit the extent to which a mammal can be physically approached, whether vocalizations will be understood, and whether coalitions can be established. Moreover, these behavioral strategies, which are used to navigate through the "stress of life," form the bedrock upon which social behaviors and higher cognitive processes can be developed and expressed. Thus, learning and other expansive mental processes must be structured, manipulated, and studied within the context of how the environment fosters or ameliorates stress-related physiological states.

The Polyvagal Theory proposes that the evolution of the mammalian autonomic nervous system provides the neurophysiological substrates for affective processes and stress responses. The theory proposes that physiological state limits the range of adaptive behaviors and psychological experiences. Thus, the evolution of the nervous system determines the range of emotional expression, quality of communication, and the ability to regulate body and behavioral state, including the expression and recovery of stress-related responses. Relevant to adaptive social and emotional behaviors, these phylogenetic principles illustrate the emergence of a brain–face–heart circuit and provide a basis for investigating the relation between several features of mental health and autonomic regulation.

Via evolutionary processes, the mammalian nervous system has emerged with specific features that react to challenges to visceral homeostasis. In general, the domains of homeostasis, which have been monitored, have focused on the visceral systems involved in cardiovascular, digestive, reproductive, and immune functions. For example, studies have evaluated how long it takes the heart rate to recover following a challenge to a prestress level. Adaptive coping requires minimizing the magnitude and duration of this deviation, whether the deviation is observed in rising heart rate, blood pressure, or cortisol levels or in disrupting digestion.

By investigating the phylogeny of the regulation of the vertebrate heart (e.g., Morris & Nilsson, 1994), three principles can be extracted. First, there is a phylogenetic shift in the regulation of the heart from endocrine communication, to unmyelinated nerves, and finally to myelinated nerves. Second, there is a development of opposing neural mechanisms of excitation and inhibition to provide rapid regulation of graded metabolic output. Third, with increased cortical development, the cortex exhibits greater control over the brainstem via direct (e.g., corticobulbar) and indirect (e.g., corticoreticular) neural pathways originating in the motor cortex and terminating in the source nuclei of the myelinated motor nerves emerging from the brainstem (e.g., specific neural pathways embedded within cranial nerves V, VII, IX, X, XI), controlling visceromotor structures (i.e., heart, bronchi, thymus) and somatomotor structures (muscles of the face and head), which results in a neural circuit that functions to facilitate social behavior and to maintain calm behavioral states.

These phylogenetic principles illustrate the emergence of a brain–face–heart circuit and provide a basis for investigating the relation between several features of mental health and autonomic regulation. In general, phylogenetic development results in increased neural control of the heart via the myelinated mammalian vagal system that is paralleled by an increase in the neural regulation of the facial muscles. This integrated system can "cue" others of safety and danger, while promoting transitory mobilization and the expression of sympathetic tone without requiring sympathetic or adrenal activation (i.e., raising heart rate by the removing the myelinated vagal inhibition from the heart). Functionally, this phylogenetic progression provides a system that can respond rapidly (i.e., via myelinated pathways) and selectively regulate the magnitude (i.e., via opposing inhibitory and excitatory circuits) and specificity of the features (e.g., via calming or excitation and linkage of autonomic reactivity with facial muscles) of the reaction. With this new vagal system, transitory incursions into the environment or withdrawals from a potential predator can be initiated without the severe biological cost of the metabolic excitation associated with sympathetic–adrenal activation. Paralleling this change in neural control of the heart is an enhanced neural control of the face, larynx, and pharynx, which enables complex facial gestures and vocalizations associated with social communication. This phylogenetic course results in greater central nervous system regulation of behavior, especially behaviors needed to engage and disengage rapidly with environmental challenges. These phylogenetic shifts, which promote a greater bidirectional communication between brain and viscera, provide opportunities for mental processes, including voluntary behavior, to impact on body state. Thus, a greater understanding of the circuit mediating these interactions might lead to functional models of intervention that would both calm the visceral state and promote more prosocial interactions. Consistent with this trend, new research and clinical programs are emerging. For example, the Cleveland Clinic has created the Bakken Heart–Brain Institute and has run annual Heart–Brain Institute Summits to bring together researchers, clinicians, and others to stimulate greater collaboration and understanding of the heart–brain link and to positively impact research, education, and patient care.

Three Phylogenetically Defined Autonomic Circuits Supporting Adaptive Behaviors

The Polyvagal Theory emphasizes and documents the neurophysiological and neuroanatomical distinction between the two branches of the vagus (i.e., 10th cranial nerve) and proposes that each vagal branch is associated with a different adaptive behavioral and physiological response strategy to stressful events. The theory describes three phylogenetic stages of the development of the mammalian autonomic nervous system. These stages reflect the emergence of three distinct subsystems, which are phylogenetically ordered and behaviorally linked to *social engagement, mobilization,* and *immobilization.* With increased neural complexity, due to phylogenetic development, the organism's behavioral and affective repertoire is enriched.

The Polyvagal Theory (Porges, 1995, 1997, 1998, 2001b, 2003, 2007) emphasizes the phylogenetic origins of brain structures that regulate social and defensive behaviors. For example, prosocial behaviors cue others that the environment is safe. Safe environments signal the individual to dispense with the hypervigilance required to detect danger and allows this precautionary strategy to be replaced with social interactions that further calm and lead to close proximity and physical contact. The prototypical prosocial behaviors in mammals are related to nursing, reproduction, interactive play, and being able to be calm in the presence of another. In contrast, defensive behaviors could be categorized into two domains: one related to mobilization, including fight and flight behaviors, and the other related to immobilization and death feigning that might be associated with dissociative psychological states. Within this dichotomy of defensive strategies, freezing behavior that requires increased muscle tension in the absence of movement, such as stalking or vigilance behaviors, is categorized in mobilization. In contrast, immobilization is associated with a decrease in muscle tension and often with fainting and other features of decreased metabolic activity. From a health perspective, the prosocial behaviors trigger neurophysiological circuits that not only support affect regulation and social interactions, but also promote health, growth, and restoration.

Relevant to adaptive social and emotional behaviors, the Polyvagal Theory makes the following assumptions:

1. Evolution has modified the structures of the autonomic nervous system.
2. The mammalian autonomic nervous system retains vestiges of phylogenetically older autonomic nervous systems.
3. Emotional regulation and social behavior are functional derivatives of structural changes in the autonomic nervous system in response to evolutionary processes.
4. In mammals, the autonomic nervous system response strategy to challenge follows a phylogenetic hierarchy, starting with the newest structures and, when all else fails, reverting to the most primitive structural system.
5. The phylogenetic stage of the autonomic nervous system determines the behavioral, physiological, and affective features of reactivity to people and objects in the environment.

The phylogenetic orientation focuses our interest on the parasympathetic neural structures and neurobehavioral systems that we share with, or have adapted from, our phylogenetic ancestry. First, there are three response systems proposed in the Polyvagal Theory: (1) cranial nerves to regulate the face and to mediate calm autonomic and behavioral states, (2) sympathetic–adrenal system to increase metabolic output, and (3) an inhibitory vagal system to decrease metabolic output and promote freezing and defecation. These three response strategies are the products of distinct neurophysiological systems. Second, these distinct neurophysiological systems represent a phylogenetically dependent hierarchy, with the use of cranial nerves to regulate facial expression emerging in mammals (well developed in primates); the sympathetic–adrenal system shared with other vertebrates, including reptiles; and the inhibitory vagal system shared with more primitive vertebrates, including amphibians, bony fish, and cartilaginous fish (see Porges, 1997, 1998). The three systems represent different phylogenetic stages of neural development. This phylogenetic development starts with a primitive behavioral inhibition system, progresses to a fight/flight system, and, in humans (and other primates), culminates in a complex facial, gestural, and vocalization system. Thus, from a phylogenetic perspective, the nervous system of vertebrates evolved to support a greater range of behaviors and physiological states, including states that we often associate with social engagement behaviors.

How the "Mammalian" Autonomic Nervous System Fosters Prosocial Behaviors via a Vagal Brake

The mammalian vagus (i.e., myelinated efferent pathways) functions as an active vagal "brake" (Porges, Doussard-Roosevelt, Portales, & Greenspan, 1996) in which rapid inhibition and disinhibition of vagal tone to the heart can support behavioral mobilization or self-soothing and calm in an individual. When the vagal tone to the pacemaker is high, the vagus acts as a restraint or brake limiting heart rate. When vagal tone to the pacemaker is low, there is little or no inhibition of the pacemaker. Due to vagal influences in the sinoatrial node (i.e., the heart's pacemaker), resting heart rate is substantially lower than the intrinsic rate of the pacemaker. Neurophysiologically, the vagal brake provides a mechanism to support the metabolic requirements for mobilization and communication behaviors; functionally, the vagal brake, by modulating the visceral state, enables the individual to rapidly engage and disengage with objects and individuals and to promote self-soothing behaviors and calm behavioral states. Thus, withdrawal of the vagal brake is associated with adaptive states of mobilization, and a reinstatement of the vagal brake with calm behavioral recovery. In mammals, the primary vagal inhibitory pathways occur through the myelinated vagus originating in the nucleus ambiguus.

By transitory down-regulation of the cardioinhibitory vagal tone to the heart (i.e., removing the vagal brake), the mammal is capable of rapid increases in cardiac output without activating the sympathetic–adrenal system. This mechanism enables the ability to rapidly shift states from calm engagement to precautionary states of vagal withdrawal, which rapidly increase cardiac output to support movements. But, unlike the sympathetic–adrenal strategy, which is slow to initiate and slower to dampen, reengaging the vagal brake instantaneously down-regulates cardiac output to produce a calm physiological state (Vanhoutte & Levy, 1979). By withdrawing the vagal brake, rather than stimulating the sympathetic–adrenal system, mammals have an opportunity to rapidly increase metabolic output for immediate, but limited, mobilization. If the duration and intensity of mobilization are increased, then the sympathetic nervous system is activated.

A withdrawal of the vagal brake facilitates the recruitment of other neural mechanisms (e.g., excitation of sympathetic, or the unmyelinated vagal, pathways) and neural chemical mechanisms (e.g., stimulation of the HPA axis) to regulate physiological state. Thus, consistent with the polyvagal theory, if the vagal brake is not functioning or will not serve the survival needs of the organism, then the phylogenetically "older" systems (e.g., the sympathetic–adrenal system or unmyelinated vagus originating in the dorsal motor nucleus of the vagus) will be recruited to regulate metabolic output to deal with environmental challenges. For example, if the vagal brake is not functioning, there is the potential for greater dependence on the sympathetic excitation of the cardiovascular system. This dependence on sympathetic excitation to regulate cardiac output may create health risks (e.g., hypertension) and lead to difficulties in modulating behavioral state (i.e., rage, panic, aggression). Consistent with assumptions of the Polyvagal Theory, the vagal brake contributes to the modulation of cardiac output by decreasing or increasing the inhibitory vagal control of the heart to influence rate and thereby adjust metabolic resources to support either mobilization or social engagement behaviors.

The Social Engagement System

As mammals evolved from more primitive vertebrates, a new circuit emerged to detect and to express signals of safety in the environment (e.g., to distinguish and to emit facial expressions and intonation of vocalizations) and to rapidly calm and turn off the defensive systems (i.e., via the myelinated vagus) to foster proximity and social behavior. This recent neural circuit can be conceptualized as a Social Engagement System. This system involves pathways traveling through several cranial nerves (i.e., V, VII, IX, X, and XI) that regulate the expression, detection, and subjective experiences of affect and emotion. Neuroanatomically, this system includes special visceral efferent pathways regulating the striated muscles of the face and head (i.e., special visceral efferent) and the myelinated vagal fibers regulating the heart and lungs (see Porges, 1998, 2001b, 2003).

The Social Engagement System is an integrated system with both a somatomotor component regulating the striated muscles of the face and a visceromotor component regulating the heart via a myelinated vagus. The system is capable of dampening activation of the sympathetic nervous system and the HPA axis. By calming the viscera and regulating facial muscles, this system enables and promotes positive social interactions in safe contexts.

The somatomotor component includes the neural structures involved in social and emotional behaviors. Special visceral efferent nerves innervate striated muscles, which regulate the structures derived during embryology from the ancient gill arches (Truex & Carpenter, 1969). The social engagement system has a control component in the cortex (i.e., upper motor neurons) that regulates brainstem nuclei (i.e., lower motor neurons) to control eyelid opening (e.g., looking), facial muscles (e.g., emotional expression), middle ear muscles (e.g., extracting human voice from background noise), muscles of mastication (e.g., ingestion), laryngeal and pharyngeal muscles (e.g., prosody of vocalizations), and head-turning muscles (e.g., social gesture and orientation). Collectively, these muscles function as neural gatekeepers detecting and expressing features of safety (e.g., prosody, facial expression, head gestures, eye gaze) that cue others of intention and control social engagement within the environment.

The phylogenic origin of the behaviors associated with the Social Engagement System is intertwined with the phylogeny of the autonomic nervous system. As the muscles of the face and head emerged as social engagement structures, a new component of the autonomic nervous system (i.e., a myelinated vagus) evolved that is regulated by the nucleus ambiguus, a medullary nucleus ventral to the dorsal motor nucleus of the vagus. This convergence of neural mechanisms produced an integrated Social Engagement System with synergistic behavioral and visceral components as well as interactions among ingestion, state regulation, and social engagement processes. As a cluster, difficulties in gaze, extraction of human voice, facial expression, head gesture, and prosody are common features of individuals with autism and other psychiatric disorders in which the Social Engagement System is compromised. And thus, we infer from the functioning of the face and the prosody of the voice, difficulties in both social engagement behaviors and physiological state regulation.

Interneuronal connections between the source nuclei (i.e., lower motor neurons) of special visceral efferent pathways and the source nucleus of the myelinated vagus provide an inhibitory pathway to slow heart rate and lower blood pressure—which, by actively reducing autonomic arousal, promote the calm states necessary to express social engagement behaviors and to support health, growth, and restoration. The brainstem source nuclei of this system are influenced by higher brain structures and by visceral afferents. Direct corticobulbar pathways reflect the influence of frontal areas of the cortex (i.e., upper motor neurons) on the medullary source nuclei of this system. Moreover, feedback through the afferent vagus (e.g., tractus solitarius) to medullary areas (e.g., nucleus of the solitary tract) influences both the source nuclei of this system and the forebrain areas that are assumed to be involved in several psychiatric disorders (e.g., Craig, 2005; Thayer & Lane, 2000). In addition, the anatomical structures involved in the Social Engagement System have neurophysiological interactions with the HPA axis, the social neuropeptides (e.g., oxytocin and vasopressin), and the immune system (for overview, see Carter, 1998; Porges 2001a).

Afferents from the target organs of the Social Engagement System, including the muscles of the face and head, provide potent afferent input to the source nuclei regulating both the visceral and somatic components of the Social Engagement System. Thus, activation of the behavioral component (e.g., listening, ingesting, looking) could trigger visceral changes that would support social engagement, whereas modulation of the visceral state, depending on whether there is an increase or decrease in the influence of the myelinated vagal efferents on the sino-atrial node (i.e., increasing or decreasing the influence of the vagal brake), would either promote or impede social engagement behaviors. For example, stimulation of visceral states that would promote mobilization (i.e., fight or flight behaviors) would impede the ability to express social engagement behaviors.

Relevant to psychiatric disorders are the specific deficits in both the somatomotor (e.g., poor gaze, low facial affect, lack of prosody, difficulties in mastication) and visceromotor (difficulties in autonomic regulation resulting in cardiopulmonary and digestive problems) components of the Social Engagement System. For example, clinicians and researchers have documented these deficits in individuals with autism. Thus deficits in the Social Engagement System would compromise spontaneous social behavior, social awareness, affect expressivity, prosody, and language development. In contrast, interventions that improve the neural regulation of the Social Engagement System, would hypothetically enhance spontaneous social behavior and state and affect regulation, reduce stereotypical behaviors, and improve vocal communication (i.e., enhancing both prosody in expressive speech and the ability to extract the human voice from background sounds). This is more than a plausible hypothesis. We have not only demonstrated relations between vagal regulation of the heart and social engagement behaviors, but have also demonstrated, in preliminary studies, (Porges, Bazhenova, Carlson, Apparies, & Sorokin, unpublished) that it is possible to improve social engagement behaviors in autistic individuals by engaging the neural regulation of the social engagement system (i.e., stimulating the neural regulation of the middle ear muscles with exaggerated prosodic acoustic stimulation). This research provides an empirical basis with which to understand the interpersonal social features, such as prosody and facial expressivity, that characterize individuals who effectively calm and soothe others.

Disorders of the Social Engagement System:
Maladaptive or Adaptive Behavioral Strategies?

Several psychiatric and behavioral disorders are characterized as difficulties in establishing and maintaining relationships. Diagnostic features often include those associated with difficulties both in expressing social behavior and in reading social cues (i.e., social awareness). These features are observed in a variety of psychiatric diagnoses, including autism, social anxiety disorder, posttraumatic stress disorder, and reactive attachment disorder. From a psychopathology orientation, these clinical disorders have different etiologies and features. However, from a polyvagal perspective, they share a core component. This core component is characterized by a depressed social engagement system with the consequences of poor affect regulation, poor affect recognition, and poor physiological state regulation. Although a compromised social engagement system results in "maladaptive" social behavior, do these asocial behavioral strategies have "adaptive" features? The phylogeny of the vertebrate autonomic nervous system serves as a guide to understand these adaptive features.

Through the lens of the Polyvagal Theory, the vertebrate autonomic nervous system follows three general stages of phylogenetic development. In the mammalian autonomic nervous system the structures and circuits representing each of the stages remain, but have been coopted for various adaptive functions. The neural circuit associated with each stage supports a different category of behavior, with the phylogenetically most recent innovation (i.e., the myelinated vagus) capable of supporting high levels of social engagement behavior. Since the neural regulation of the "new" mammalian myelinated vagus (i.e., the ventral vagus) is integrated into the Social Engagement System, when this system is compromised, the effects are both behavioral and autonomic. The resultant changes in autonomic state compromise spontaneous social engagement behaviors and minimize states of calmness while supporting a range of adaptive defensive behaviors. Specifically, the compromised social engagement system is associated, neurophysiologically, with a change in autonomic regulation characterized by a reduction in the influence of the myelinated vagus on the heart. This reduction results in difficulties in behavioral state regulation and a loss of neural regulation to the muscles of the face, mediating the flat affective expression often observed in several clinical disorders. The removal of the regulatory influence of the myelinated vagus on the heart potentiates (i.e., disinhibits) the expression of the two phylogenetically older neural systems (i.e., sympathetic nervous system, unmyelinated vagus). These two older neural systems foster mobilization behaviors of fight and flight via the sympathetic nervous system, or immobilization behaviors of death feigning, freezing, and behavioral shutdown via the unmyelinated vagus. Thus, withdrawal of the myelinated vagal circuit provides access to the more primitive adaptive defensive systems at a cost. If the removal is prolonged, there is an increased risk for both physical (e.g., cardiovascular disorders) and mental (e.g., anxiety disorders, depression) illness as the protective antistress and self-soothing features of the myelinated vagus and the associated prosocial features of the Social Engagement System are lost.

Neuroception: Contextual Cueing of Adaptive and Maladaptive Physiological States

To effectively switch from defensive to social engagement strategies, the mammalian nervous system needs to perform two important adaptive tasks: (1) to assess risk, and, if the environment is perceived as safe, (2) to inhibit the more primitive limbic structures that control fight, flight, or freeze behaviors. In other words, any intervention that has the potential for increasing an organism's experience of safety has the potential of recruiting the evolutionarily more advanced neural circuits that support the prosocial behaviors of the Social Engagement System.

The nervous system, through the processing of sensory information from the environment and from the viscera, continuously evaluates risk. Since the neural evaluation of risk does not require conscious awareness and may involve subcortical limbic structures (e.g., Morris et al., 1999), the term *neuroception* (Porges, 2003) was introduced to emphasize a neural process, distinct from perception, that is capable of distinguishing environmental (and visceral) features that are safe, dangerous, or life threatening. In safe environments the autonomic state is adaptively regulated to dampen sympathetic activation and to protect the oxygen-dependent central nervous system, and especially the cortex, from the metabolically conservative reactions of the dorsal vagal complex. However, how does the nervous system know when the environment is safe, dangerous, or life threatening, and what neural mechanisms evaluate this risk?

Neuroception might involve feature detectors involving the temporal cortex (see below), since the temporal cortex responds to familiar voices and faces and hand movements and can influence limbic reactivity. Thus, the neuroception of familiar individuals and individuals with appropriately prosodic voices and warm expressive faces translates into a social interaction promoting a sense of safety. In most individuals (i.e., those without a psychiatric disorder or neuropathology), the nervous system evaluates risk and matches neurophysiological state with the actual risk of the environment. When the environment is appraised as safe, the defensive limbic structures are inhibited, thus enabling social engagement and calm visceral states to emerge. In contrast, some individuals experience a mismatch wherein the nervous system appraises the environment as dangerous, even when it is safe. This mismatch results in physiological states that support fight, flight, or freeze behaviors, but not social engagement behaviors. According to the theory, social communication can be expressed efficiently through the Social Engagement System only when these defensive circuits are inhibited. Neuroception represents a neural process that enables humans to engage in social behaviors by distinguishing safe from dangerous contexts. Neuroception is proposed as a plausible mechanism mediating both the expression and the disruption of positive social behavior, emotion regulation, and visceral homeostasis.

New technologies, such as fMRI, have identified specific neural structures that are involved in detecting risk. The temporal lobe is of particular interest in expanding the construct of neuroception and in identifying neural mechanisms that, by detecting and evaluating risk, modulate the expression of adaptive defensive behaviors and autonomic states. Functional imaging techniques document the involvement of the temporal cortex, fusiform gyrus, and superior temporal sulcus in the evaluation of biological movement and intention including the detection of features (e.g., as movements, vocalizations, and faces) that contribute to an individual being perceived as safe or trustworthy (Adolphs, 2002; Winston et al., 2002). Slight changes in these stimuli can be appraised as posing threat or, alternatively, signally endearment. Connectivity between these areas of the temporal cortex and the amygdala suggests a top-down control mechanism in the processing of facial features that could inhibit activity of the structures involved in the expression of defensive strategies (Pessoa et al., 2002).

Neuroanatomical and neurophysiological research with animals provides additional information regarding the modulation and inhibition of defensive behaviors via well-defined connections among the amygdala, the periaqueductal gray (PAG), and the autonomic nervous system. The PAG is a heterogeneous midbrain structure that consists of gray matter surrounding the cerebral aqueduct that connects the third and fourth ventricles. Studies have identified areas of the PAG that are organized to regulate flight, fight, or freeze behaviors and the autonomic states that support these behaviors (Keay & Bandler, 2001). Stimulating rostrally within the lateral and dorsolateral PAG produces confrontational defensive behaviors (i.e., fight), whereas stimulating caudally within the lateral PAG and dorsolateral PAG produces escape behaviors (i.e., flight). Autonomic shifts (e.g., increases in heart rate and blood pressure) parallel these behaviors. In contrast, stimulation in the region of the PAG ventrolateral to the aqueduct (vlPAG) evokes a passive reaction of immobility, a drop in blood pressure, and a slowing of heart rate. Interestingly, excitation of the vlPAG evokes an opioid-mediated analgesia that might adaptively raise pain thresholds and promote the dissociative states that are frequently reported by trauma victims. In addition, there is evidence of a functional connection between the central nucleus of the amygdala and the vlPAG that both blunts the perception of pain (i.e., antinociception) and promotes immobilization (Leite-Panissi, Coimbra, & Menescal-de-Oliveira, 2003). Consistent with the polyvagal theory, the vlPAG communicates with the dorsal vagal complex (associated with immobilization in response to life threat), whereas the lateral PAG and the dorsolateral PAG communicate with the sympathetic nervous system (associated with mobilization behaviors of fight/flight in response to danger).

The detection of safety subdues the adaptive defensive systems dependent on limbic structures and enables the functioning of higher brain circuits related to frontal and temporal areas. This process may provide a plausible model through which a neural detection of risk (i.e., neuroception) would modulate behavioral and physiological states to support adaptive behaviors in response to safe, dangerous, or life-threatening environments. In the absence of threat, inhibitory projections from the fusiform gyrus and the superior temporal sulcus to the amygdala would be available to actively inhibit the limbic defense systems. This inhibition would provide an opportunity for social behavior to emerge. Thus, the appearance of a friend or mate would subdue the limbic activation with the biobehavioral consequences of allowing proximity, physical contact, and other social engagement behaviors. In contrast, during situations in which the appraisal of risk is high, the amygdala and various areas of the PAG are activated. The amygdala and PAG share connections only through the central nucleus of the amygdala (Rizvi et al., 1991).

Based on the relative risk of the environment, both social engagement and defense behaviors may be interpreted as either adaptive or maladaptive. For example, the inhibition of defense systems by the Social Engagement System would be adaptive and appropriate only in a safe environment. From a clinical perspective, it would be the inability to inhibit defense systems in safe environments (e.g., anxiety disorders, posttraumatic stress disorders [PTSD], reactive attachment disorder) or the inability to activate defense systems in risk environments (e.g., Williams syndrome, a genetic disorder with a behavioral repertoire characterized by engaging without detecting or respecting the emotional state of others) that might contribute to the defining features of psychopathology. Thus, an invalid neuroception of safety or danger might contribute to maladaptive physiological reactivity and the expression of the defensive behaviors associated with specific psychiatric disorders that include, in their diagnostic criteria, a social deficit (e.g., autism, social anxiety, Williams syndrome) or fear (e.g., various phobias, obsessive–compulsive disorder) (Leckman et al., 1997). However, in most individuals neuroception accurately reflects risk, and there is a consistency between the cognitive awareness of risk and the visceral response to risk.

The features of risk in the environment do not solely drive neuroception. Afferent feedback from the viscera functions as a major mediator of the accessibility of prosocial circuits associated with social engagement behaviors. For example, the Polyvagal Theory predicts that states of mobilization would compromise our ability to detect positive social cues. Functionally, visceral states color our perception of objects and others. Thus, the same features of a person engaging another may result in range of outcomes, depending on the physiological state of the target individual. If the person being engaged is in a state in which the social engagement system is easily accessible, the reciprocal prosocial interactions are likely to occur. However, if the individual is in a state of mobilization, the same engaging response might be responded to with the asocial features of withdrawal or aggression. In such a state, it might be very difficult to dampen the mobilization circuit and enable the Social Engagement System to come back online.

The insula may be involved in the mediation of neuroception, since it has been proposed as a brain structure involved in conveying the diffuse feedback from the viscera into cognitive awareness. Functional imaging experiments have demonstrated that the insula has an important role in the experience of pain and of several emotions, including anger, fear, disgust, happiness, and sadness. Critchley et al. (2004) propose that internal body states are represented in the insula and contribute to subjective feeling states, and they have demonstrated that activity in the insula correlates with interoceptive accuracy.

Modifying Old Neural Circuits for New Bodies: Co-opting the Immobilization Defense System

Immobilization as a defense system is phylogenetically old and is associated with reduced metabolic demands and increased pain threshold. In reptiles, which have a larger tolerance for reductions in oxygen, immobilization is a very effective defense strategy. In contrast, since mammals have a great need for oxygen, the inhibition of movement coupled with a shift in autonomic state to support the immobilization behavior (i.e., apnea and bradycardia) can be lethal (Hofer, 1970; Richter, 1957), such that death feigning can lead to death. In humans, fainting or dissociating in anticipation of death or painful injury reflects a less extreme form of this response.

However, several aspects of mammalian social behavior require immobilization, but do so in the absence of life threat. In these contexts, an immobilization without fear is required. Immobilization without fear is accomplished by coopting the structures that regulate immobilization in response to life threat to serve a broad range of social needs, including reproduction, nursing, and pair bonding. The area of the PAG that coordinates freezing behavior, as a part of the primitive immobilization defense system, has been modified in mammals to serve their intimate social needs. In addition, it has been reported that the vlPAG is rich in receptors for oxytocin, a neuropeptide associated with parturition, nursing, and the establishment of pair bonds (Carter, 1998; Insel & Young 2001).

Through the process of evolution, the immobilization circuit has been modified to enable prosocial behaviors associated with reproduction and nursing. This circuit enables humans to sleep safely with each other and babies to safely nurse on the breasts of their mothers. Overlapping with the area of the PAG that organizes immobility (i.e., vlPAG) are areas that, when stimulated, produce lordosis and kyphosis. The lordosis reflex is a hormone-dependent behavior displayed by female rodents and other mammalian species during mating. In most mammals lordosis involves the female immobilizing in a crouched posture with her hind end available to the male for copulation. Neural tracing studies have demonstrated that the vlPAG is part of the neural circuit involved in regulating lordosis (Daniels, Miselis, & Flanagan-Cato, 1999). Kyphosis is an upright arched back posture that is accompanied by inhibition of limb movements. Kyphosis is stimulated by nipple attachment and provides an opportunity for the dam to feed a large litter simultaneously. When dams initiate a nursing bout, their behavioral state shifts immediately from high activity to immobility (Stern, 1997). When the caudal portion of the vlPAG is lesioned, there are important consequences: (1) kyphotic nursing decreases, (2) litter weight gains decrease, and (3) the lesioned rats are more aggressive and more frequently attack strange males (Lonstein & Stern, 1998). Humans, similar to other mammals, have co-opted this ancient immobilization circuit to support nursing and reproductive behaviors.

Modifying Old Neural Circuits for New Bodies: Co-opting the Mobilization Defense System

Often the playful rough-and-tumble behaviors observed in mammals are interpreted as preliminary exercises to develop adaptive defensive and aggressive behaviors. However, play is also inherently motivating and provides a unique and positive experience (Panksepp, 1998a). Play, at least rough-and-tumble play, is characterized by mobilization. Thus, play shares with the defensive fight/flight behaviors a neurophysiological substrate that functionally increases metabolic output by increasing sympathetic excitation. Concurrent with the sympathetic excitation is a withdrawal of the myelinated vagal pathways that characterize the vagal brake. Just as the primitive mechanisms mediating immobilization in response to life threat can be coopted to support loving and nutrient processes, so can mobilization mechanisms be coopted to facilitate both defensive flightfight behaviors and the pleasurable play.

How is play distinguished from aggressive behavior? More importantly, are there neuroceptive processes that either dampen or potentiate aggressive retaliation? If we observe play, we can reliably observe cues that lead to either aggressive or calming behavior. Frequently, play leads to acts that are painful and potentially aggressive. For example, often a playmate is injured—an event that may occur with various mammalian species. When puppies play, they may bite too hard and elicit a painful cry in the playmate. When a human is playing with a dog, the dog might accidentally be hit in a vulnerable and tender place such as the nose. When humans play a sport such as basketball, an individual may be hit in the face with an elbow. How are these situations diffused? What processes enable anger to be contained and play to be resumed?

Access to the Social Engagement System can transform potential aggression to play. The Social Engagement System cues others that the intentionality of the behavior is benign. For example, a fight is likely to occur if the individual who accidentally hits another in the face while playing basketball walks away without diffusing the tension through a face-to-face expression of concern. Similarly, play will not continue if playing puppies do not make face-to-face engagements after an accidental, but hurtful, bite. Consistent with the importance of the social engagement system in the process of play, autism is associated with a lack of noninteractive (i.e., parallel) play. Thus, access to the Social Engagement System is critical in defining mobilization as play and not aggression. Team sports, which are prevalent in our culture, involve mobilization strategies that require face-to-face interactions to signal intentionality, and they all integrate features of the Social Engagement System with mobilization.

Jogging and other forms of exercise also result in a physiological state similar to team sports or rough-and-tumble play. However, unlike exercise, a "polyvagal definition" of play requires reciprocal interactions and a constant awareness of the actions of others. Play is different from fight/flight behaviors. Although fight/flight behaviors often require an awareness of others, they do not require reciprocal interactions and an ability to restrain mobilizations. Play recruits another circuit that enables aggressive and defensive behaviors to be contained. The rapid recruitment of the Social Engagement System results in an immediate face-to-face evaluation of whether there is intentionality in the event that provoked the painful response. Areas of the cortex, such as the superior temporal sulcus, provide a plausible location for this neuroceptive process. The superior temporal sulcus has been proposed to evaluate biological movement and intentionality. Thus, it is through this area of the brain that familiar voices, calming gestures, and appropriate facial expression can rapidly diffuse a possible physical conflict. Even dogs that whimper after being hit on the nose or bit on the leg while playing will rapidly make a face-to-face engagement and wait for a gesture that provides the reassurance that the event was not intentional.

How does the Social Engagement System calm us down and keep us from expressing inappropriate aggressive acts? First, there are inhibitory pathways from the temporal cortex that dampen the limbic reactivity associated with defensive behaviors. Second, as Gellhorn (see above) noted almost 50 years ago, facial muscle activity influences the brain structures that regulate visceral state. This effect is frequently observed in mammals of all ages, from very young infants who use sucking behaviors to calm, to older individuals who use conversation, listening, smiling, and ingesting to calm. Consistent with and in contrast to these strategies of defusing conflict, walking away or turning the head away from the conflict can trigger a violent reaction.

By investigating the unique physiological mechanisms involved in play, we uncover the unique properties of reciprocal interactions that may define play and distinguish it from exercise and other solitary behaviors. Play requires (1) turn taking in expressive motor movements and (2) reciprocal receptive inhibition of activity. These are also both observed in talking and listening, in throwing and catching, and in hiding and seeking. When there is mutual activity and contact, such as occurs in rough-and-tumble play, there are more opportunities for cues to be mistaken and aggressive behaviors to unfold. However, if face-to-face engagement occurs rapidly with the appropriate features of concern and empathy, then the physiological state that was driven by the physical contact is evaluated for intentionality and diffused with the appropriate cues exchanged between two Social Engagement Systems involved in the exchange. Although play may share some of the neural mechanisms involved in fight/flight behaviors, unlike solitary exercise, play requires dynamic neural regulation of state to ensure safe interactions. Thus, both sympathetic activation to increase metabolic output to support motor activity and the vagal brake to restrain mobilization and to support the function of the Social Engagement System are recruited to maintain a mutual playful activity.

Another adaptive process involves the coactivation of sympathetic excitatory and vagal inhibitory processes. This process is associated with sexual arousal, another vulnerable state that evolved to require face-to-face interactions when evaluating intentionality of physical contact to determine whether the behaviors are caring or hurtful.

Summary

The Polyvagal Theory is an attempt to reorganize our conceptualization of the autonomic nervous system with a focus on the neural circuits involved in regulating visceral organs for adaptive functions, including functions in the domains of affect, emotions, and goal-directed behaviors. The theory identifies specific variables that can be used to dynamically evaluate the changing neural regulation of adaptive circuits. Implicit in the theoretical model are four prominent features that impact directly on the development of testable hypotheses: (1) the role of specific brain structures and neural circuits in regulating the autonomic state; (2) the justification of developing methods that can distinguish and track the dynamic vagal output to target organs through the myelinated vagus, originating in the nucleus ambiguus, and the unmyelinated vagus, originating in the dorsal motor nucleus; (3) the role of visceral afferents and sensory feature detectors in relation to the switching that occurs among the neural circuits regulating the autonomic state; and (4) the relation between the regulation of visceral organs and the regulation of the striated muscles of the face and head involved in social engagement behaviors, including affect recognition and emotional expression.

The Polyvagal Theory suggests that affective or emotional states are dependent upon lower brain regulation of the visceral state and the important visceral, tactile, and nociceptive cues that travel between the brain and the periphery. Through the lens of the Polyvagal Theory, bodily states foster different domains of behavior. Specifically, the neural regulation of five physiological states has been described, and each state has been linked with a specific biologically based behavioral repertoire:

1. *Social engagement:* A state dependent on a well-defined social engagement system that promotes positive social interactions, reduces psychological distance, and promotes a sense of safety between people.
2. *Mobilization—fight/flight:* This state supports fight and flight behaviors and requires an increase in metabolic output.
3. *Play and foreplay:* A blend of the above. Play is a hybrid state requiring features both states of mobilization, "arousal," and social engagement.
4. *Immobilization—life threat:* This state is associated with life threat and is characterized by a reduction of metabolic output and shutdown behaviors. This primitive neural circuit works fine for reptiles but is potentially lethal in mammals.
5. *Immobilization without fear:* This state is associated with prosocial and positive states that require a reduction of movement without the massive reduction of metabolic resources. This circuit recruits pathways from the immobilization circuit and is used during nursing, childbirth, reproductive behaviors, and digestive and restorative processes.

Functionally, these five states color our perception of objects and others. Thus, the same features of a person engaging another may result in range of outcomes, if the target individual is in a different physiological state. If the person being engaged is in a state in which the social engagement system is easily accessible, the reciprocal prosocial interactions are likely to occur. If the individual is in a state of mobilization, the same engaging response might be responded to with the asocial features of withdrawal or aggression. This stimulus–organism–response model is reminiscent of Woodworth (1928), who postulated an S-O-R model, with an active organism intervening between stimulus and response. In the Woodworth model processes internal to the organism mediated the effects of stimuli on behavior. In the Polyvagal Theory, neuroception is an S-O-R model. Within this context, autonomic state is an intervening process that contributes to the transformation of the external physical stimulus to the complex internal cognitive–affective processes that determine the quality of the interpersonal interaction.

The five states described above provide a good fit with the underlying physiological states required to successfully express the seven neural-based systems described by Panksepp (1998a; see also Chapter 1, this volume). Moreover, the polyvagal perspective, with its emphasis on phylogenetic shifts in visceral regulation, provides a unique insight into the use of psychological constructs. For example, the Polyvagal Theory leads to three different visceral phenotypes for the emotion of fear. One type is characterized by mobilization strategies consistent with the features of fight/flight behaviors. A second type is characterized by immobilization (e.g., death feigning), a biobehavioral state that, due to metabolic depression, can potentially be lethal for a mammal. In humans this might be observed as fainting, defecating, and/or dissociating. A third type is more of an appraisal and involves a transitory depression of the Social Engagement System as a precautionary response to evaluate intentionality of behaviors. If behavior is detected as dangerous, then the sympathetic nervous system is activated to support the fight/flight mobilization behaviors. All three are "fear" responses, but they have different behavioral topographies and different underlying neurophysiological substrates. Thus, the understanding of affective experiences and the strategy of organizing these experiences into psychological constructs such as "emotions" may be informed by an understanding of the covariation between the specific phylogenetic shifts in the neural regulation of the viscera and the adaptive nature of these various affective states in phylogenetically older vertebrates

Concluding Comments

To optimize the strategies for studying the bridge between nervous system function and clinical disorders as well as affective experiences, affective neuroscience will need to incorporate methodologies and to test hypotheses based on our expanding knowledge of neurophysiology and the central structures involved in both appraisal of context (i.e., neuroception) and neural regulation of visceral state. These questions have motivated previous (e.g., Cannon, Darwin, James, Gellhorn, Hess) and contemporary (e.g., Critchley, 2005; Ekman, Levenson, Friesen, 1983; Thayer & Lane, 2000) researchers attempting to bridge the gap between visceral states and the subjective labels of affective experiences (i.e., emotions). To close this gap, new methodologies are necessary that are capable of evaluating dynamic changes in, and interactions among, various physiological variables (e.g., respiration, heart rate, blood pressure, vasomotor tone, motor activity) in a changing context. In response to these needs, the Polyvagal Theory was developed.

The Polyvagal Theory provides a perspective to demystify features of clinical disorders. The theory includes principles that organize previously assumed disparate symptoms observed in several psychiatric disorders (i.e., a compromise in the function of the Social Engagement System). Moreover, by explaining features of disorders from an adaptive perspective, interventions can be designed that trigger the neural circuits that will promote spontaneous social engagement behaviors and dampen the expression of defensive strategies that disrupt social interactions.

3

The Functions of Emotion in Infancy

The Regulation and Communication of Rhythm, Sympathy, and Meaning in Human Development

Colwyn Trevarthen

In healthy families, a baby forms a secure attachment with her parents as naturally as she breathes, eats, smiles and cries. This occurs easily because of her parents' attuned interactions with her. Her parents notice her physiological/affective states and they respond to her sensitively and fully. Beyond simply meeting her unique needs, however, her parents "dance" with her. Hundreds of times, day after day, they dance with her.

There are other families where the baby neither dances nor even hears the sound of any music. In these families she does not form such secure attachments. Rather, her task—her continuous ordeal—is to learn to live with parents who are little more than strangers. Babies who live with strangers do not live well or grow well.

—Hughes (2006, p. ix)

EMOTIONS HAVE HEALING power because they are *active regulators* of vitality in movement and the primary *mediators of social life*. From infancy, emotions protect and sustain the mobile embodied spirit and oppose stress. And they do so in relationships between persons who share purposes and interests intimately (Trevarthen, 2005a). By marking experiences with feelings, emotions allow us to retain a record of the benefits and risks of behaviors, and they give values to the intentions and goal objects of those behaviors (Freeman, 2000; Panksepp, 2005a). Most importantly, human emotions link persons in the life of family and community; they communicate the well-being, cooperation, and conflicts of our engaged lives (Smith, 1759/1984; Zlatev, et al., 2008).

The growing life of children is protected by powerful moral and aesthetic feelings that assist them to learn in companionship with adults, to gain from their larger experience, and to become actors with adults in a meaningful world, with its conventional likes and dislikes and demanding practical tasks (Bråten, 1998; Dissanayake, 2000; Donaldson, 1992; Reddy & Trevarthen, 2004; Trevarthen, 2002, 2005a&b). With the guidance of emotions that engage them with others and that estimate how they are appreciated, individual human beings find roles and personality in society, while mastering the historically accumulated knowledge and skills of a culture (Gratier & Trevarthen, 2008; Legerstee, 2005; Stern, 2000; Trevarthen, 1989, 1998, 2001a). Learning about persons and things plays an essential creative role, but there is a strong and willing foundation of motives and innate emotions that *animate and evaluate* learning. In a way, that is what I mean by *movement*: how we are animated by innate motives and emotions. Even infants experience *pride* in achievements, *shame* for failure, and *guilt* for wrongdoing. Pride and shame are *basic* self-and-other human feelings, essential to the work of relationships and the regulation of consciousness; they are not learned social techniques (Draghi-Lorenz, Reddy, & Costall, 2001; Reddy, 2005, 2008; Trevarthen, 2009; Trevarthen & Reddy, 2007). Each young person's place in the community is regulated by other basic feelings, such as *admiration* and *envy*, which cannot be reduced to sensations of pleasure and pain in a single self (Hart & Legerstee, in press).

In a psychology that places interpersonal experience at the heart of human understanding (Reddy, 2008), all the functions of emotion may be seen as acting their part in the intuitive, "self-teaching" life of an infant or toddler, and to be doing so before language gives articulation to any interpretations, beliefs, or explanations. Cognitions and "theories of mind"—though they may elaborate and guide emotions with experience—cannot, by themselves, either *form* emotions or *heal* them. Empathy, or *thinking about* the emotions of others, is not enough. What is required for emotional life with others to thrive is the genuine reciprocal *sympathy of impulses and feelings* and *intuitive companionship of purposes* achieved through the coordinated vitality of dynamic "relational emotions" with persons (Stern, 1993; Panksepp & Trevarthen, 2008). As is clear in the original Greek, *em-pathy* is a one-sided projection into (or taking in of) an emotion "about" an object by the self, whereas *sym-pathy* is a creative sharing of feelings, of whatever kind, "with" an other or others—seeking immediate mutual sensibility between friends or opponents (Smith, 1777/1982). The difference is that in sympathy, there is the motivation for cooperation and the social negotiation of a role (Reddy & Trevarthen, 2004), even between infants in groups (Bradley, 2008).

In this chapter I discuss findings about the emotions of infants that help explain how self–other motives and emotions guide intentions and cognitions in adults. I review facts about the formation of neural systems in the brain of the human embryo and fetus that, though homologous with systems in other species, shows unique adaptations for more elaborate, cooperative inter-individual efforts. The comparative account leads to a theory of the functions of specifically human emotions for (1) subjective regulation—informing the actions *of the Self* as an active embodied agent (*moving*) that has multiple purposes; (2) the intersubjective regulation of *being moved*—acting *with others* in intimate relationships and for the negotiation of a place or "identity" in a social world or community; and (3) the intergenerational translation of *meaning in culture*— the understanding of knowledge and skills.

A New Theory of the Infant Mind and A New Brain Science of Communication

Four decades ago a different descriptive method for conducting empirical research on the consciousness of infants led to a better appreciation of innate human talents and of positive feelings for intersubjective life and for the learning of meaning (Trevarthen, 1977). It also led to a new theory of basic motives that animate shared life, motives that previously had been relegated by reason to a defensive "unconscious" ruled by disturbing emotions. Medical and psychological science, focused as they have been on the elaborated rules of talk and rationality, had concluded that these talents were absent at the preverbal stage of life. The prevailing view was that a newborn infant is an organism with reflexes adapted to respond to maternal care for the body and its vital functions, aroused or soothed by stimuli, but lacking a coherent awareness of an active self and therefore incapable of a "mental' response to the intentions of an other. In that view, the "emotions" expressed by the baby were mere signals of physiological discomfort or need. For instance, smiles were regarded as automatic, mindless expressions of visceral stimuli. As Brazelton put it, "The old model of thinking of the newborn infant as helpless and ready to be shaped by his environment prevented us from seeing his power as a communicant in the early mother–father–infant interaction. To see the neonate as chaotic or insensitive provided us with the capacity to see ourselves as acting 'on' rather than 'with' him" (1979, p. 79).

The use of films of young infants and their mothers in secure and intimate communication to make detailed analyses of timing and expression enabled Daniel Stern and colleagues in New York (Stern, 1971, 1974; Jaffe et al. 1973; Stern et al., 1975; Beebe et al., 1979), and a group of us at Jerome Bruner's Centre for Cognitive Studies based at Harvard (Bruner, 1968; Richards, 1973; Ryan, 1974; Trevarthen, 1974, 1977, 1979), to show that infants are actually born with playful intentions and sensitivity to the rhythms and expressive modulations of a mother's talk and her visible expressions and touches. Later, Stern described the phenomenon that guided the patterns of movement infant and mother performed together as affect "attunement" (Stern et al., 1985; Stern, 1985/2000). Condon and Sander (1974) demonstrated that the interpersonal timing of mother–infant interactions had the fine-tuning found in film studies of conversational regulations between interacting adults.

As the development of the infant's behaviors was traced through the first year, it became clear that infants evoked "intuitive parenting"—that is, communication of dynamic mental states and the building of shared narratives of experience or "meanings" that have the rhythmic and melodic property of what Hanuš and Mechtild Papoušek called "musicality" (Papoušek & Papoušek, 1987; Papoušek, 1996). As Mary Catherine Bateson (1979) had concluded, clearly the infant's skills, with their stimulating effects on the mother's expressions, were adaptations not only for the learning of the symbols of language but also, as she put it, for other conventions of culture, including "ritual healing practices." She called the intimate engagements between a mother and her 9-week-old infant "protoconversations." Thus, the paths of discovery of the 1970s and 1980s led a number of us, independently, to accept *infants as persons, instinctively endowed with emotions, seeking companionship in knowledge and skills.*

Since the 1990s brain science, too, has developed observation methods that reveal activity in living brains while individuals are engaged in responding to one another's movements (Rizzolatti & Arbib, 1998; Decety & Chaminade, 2003). We now know that there are widespread events in both cortical and subcortical regions of the brain that are specific to emotions and intentions, and that these *animate* the acquisition of conceptual knowledge or motor skills (Schore, 1994; Panksepp, 1998a, 2005; Damasio, 1999; Gallese, 2005; Trevarthen, 2001b). It has been made abundantly clear that the dynamic and body-related features of the brain activity that are directing and evaluating movements being made by one individual are responded to by the brain activity of another person who feels them by immediate sympathy (Decety & Chaminade, 2003; Gallese, 2003; Gallese et al., 2004; Panksepp & Trevarthen, 2009).

Actions, even a newborn's, are intelligent and conscious (Trevarthen & Reddy, 2007; Trevarthen, 2009). The motives that coordinate their movements are the foundation of experience. The human brain is an organ evolved to formulate plans for moving, for evaluating the prospects of action emotionally, and for sharing their motives and feelings socially. The emotional expressions of one person and the sympathetic response to them excited in another individual are associated with increased activity in the same brain regions in both individuals, with the active systems including subcortical, limbic, and neocortical elements. Most remarkably, the regions of the cortex involved in both making and recognizing coordinated patterns of facial and vocal expressions, including those that will eventually produce and receive language, are already specialized for these functions in a 2-month-old infant (Tzourio-Mazoyer et al., 2002). Clearly, the human brain is both an intentional organ and an intersubjective one before it is a linguistic one, and emotions that regulate moving and being moved in intimate contact are its primary medium of communication.

Thus, developmental psychology and functional brain science come together, presenting new evidence that the infant brain is anatomically and functionally equipped with intentions and feelings. The infant brain also has within it the emotional foundations for learning and articulating symbolic conventions by identifying with the intentions and feelings other people express in their movements—the meanings of their actions (Kühl, 2007). A new psychology of infancy, of infant mental health, and of the foundations of human cooperative mental life and collaborative actions has been found (Trevarthen & Aitken, 2001).

The Psychobiology of Motives and Emotions in Infancy

To explain the competence of even newborn infants for sensitive interactions of two kinds—"body function regulating" and "psychological mind linking"—we need a psychobiological theory of emotional evaluations that are *actively generated* in the subcortical core of the brain, in neural systems, formed and functioning before birth, that underline motivation (Merker, 2006; Panksepp & Trevarthen, 2008). This theory needs to come first, before a theory of the *plasticity* of a massively impressionable cerebral cortex under the influence of imposed stimulation, rewards, and punishments. Neuropsychological researches, as well as studies of the neurochemical systems of emotion in animals, have proved that subhemispheric "environment expectant" systems activate and direct the conscious regulation of rhythmic skilled actions and the retention of episodic experiences in development (Panksepp & Trevarthen, 2009).

All adaptive actions—that is, the "movements of life"—operating at different time scales and through different periods of felt, imagined, and remembered experience, depend upon activity in innate neural networks that generate body-related space and time in motor actions, and that regulate them via sensitivity to the pace of events within and outside the body (Trevarthen, 1999, 2008b). The engagement of an infant's actions and experience with expressions of other persons is determined by a shared sense of "attunement" for measured rhythms of moving in the present (Stern et al., 1985; Stern, 1999, 2004), and a progressive, "narrative" sense of time (Malloch, 1999, Gratier & Trevarthen, 2008). In this sense of time, the flow of energy in action and of excitement in anticipation of experiences connects the few seconds of present activity with both an imagined future and a remembered past (Trevarthen, 1999). From infancy, human interactions exhibit the "pulse," "quality," and "narrative" dimensions of what Stephen Malloch (1999) has defined as "communicative musicality." A theory of the *biochronology of human movement* and the communal ritualization of actions interprets these panhuman regularities of intersubjective life in neurobiological terms (Malloch & Trevarthen, 2009; Osborne, 2009; Trevarthen, 2008a, 2008b).

When we are in the presence of others, even when they are at a distance and "public," we can sense their states of interest, motivation, and self-regulation from their postures (or attitudes) and gestures in relation to circumstances, from the speed and modulation of their movements, and, if they vocalize, from the rhythms, pitch, intensity, and quality of their voices. We do not need to hear what they say. We are alert to how and where their eyes look, to the changes in facial expression, to the subtle variations of hand movement, as well as to prosodic changes in their vocalizations and speech. Most especially, we are alert to how these behaviors respond to our own motives and feelings. In very intimate contact, we feel the gentleness of their touch, sense the tension of their body, and perceive their breathing and the faintest changes in vocal expression. We gain dynamic information of their motives and cognitive state from both the movements of their body to engage with or move in the world, and from the changes of their inner proprioceptive (body sensing) and visceral states, which are made evident in their expressions and gestures (Trevarthen, 2001b, Trevarthen et al., 2009, in press). In clinical work, information may be obtained from what people say they feel, believe, or think about, and who is important in their lives. But the clinician should also know that the more intuitive expressions of the body and its affective state are also significant and will be informative about his or her contact with the client in the present moment and throughout the course of therapy (Stern, 2004).

Charting the Uses of Human Emotion

Ethologists describe emotional signals of animals that mediate in essential transactions of hunting (between predator and prey as well as in coordinated group predations), of courtship, mating, and parental care—all to sustain the cooperative society of the species. Each species has a subtle "vocabulary" of emotional signals conveyed by body movements, and many show evidence of learning the "conventions" of expression that hold together a family or larger group in the pursuit of collaborative activities (Wallin, Merker, & Brown, 2000).

The Social Emotions

In human affairs we accept that all our contacts and relationships are colored by affections of one kind or another. We have changing moods of self-confident *happiness* or exhausting *sadness* and *anxiety*, and these are sensitively appreciated, with more or less consideration, by other people. The ways in which others respond to our emotions affect us, giving us feelings of *love* and *admiration* or *dislike*, or, in cooperative affairs, of *pride* in the achievements we offer for their approval, or *shame* if we perceive we have acted badly or failed to do what was expected of us. We also situate ourselves in relation to the behaviors *between* others, experiencing admiration or envy, or generous pleasure or jealousy for their achievements and actions together. Even infants and preverbal toddlers are sociable beings in this sense, equipped with feelings that reflect their sense of how they fit in with peers in groups (Selby & Bradley, 2003; Nadel & Muir, 2005; Bradley, 2008; Hart & Legerstee, 2009, in press). Moreover, each of us feels we are a person who owns a character that is most succinctly described in emotional terms, telling how we seem to *feel* about what we do and about life with others: We are *confident* or *timid* in social presentation, *quick* or *slow* in thought and action, *modest* or *opinionated* about our views, *considerate* or *impatient* with others, *creative* and *adventurous* or *methodical* and *controlled*, *likeable* or *disagreeable*. In all their aspects, human emotional behaviors appear to be adapted to express both how we regulate our intentions and experiences and how we live with others, in relationships and in society.

Emotional forces within and between us exist in the present moment, but they also powerfully influence both what we *imagine* or *anticipate* may happen in the future and what we *remember* of a past that may be as long as the story of our life. Most importantly, emotions give the individuals we meet and interact with roles on our "personal narrative history." All our histories gain social meaning by the conventions of the aesthetic and moral judgments that we invent for them, and our cultural creations serve to build a "habitation," so to speak, in which practical actions have conventional values that reflect the emotions we share. A child learns, by negotiation with companions, different social uses for the emotions with which he or she is born (Nadel & Muir, 2005; Gratier & Trevarthen, 2008).

Infants are born not only with proprioceptive regulation of the movements of a whole conscious subjectivity or self, in the present; they are also meaning-making subjects with playful intuitions that require imaginative companions who will validate those meanings, helping new ideas for moving grow in usefulness, intersubjectively. Infants have emotions that care about the sharing of humanly invented meanings, giving them the value of "human sense" (Donaldson, 1978). Joint attention to events pointed out in the world is not enough, and words are not necessary. The crucial element is an affectively loaded *mutual attention* and "altero-ceptive" regulation of actions made together—the sympathy of interests and emotional evaluations expressed in movement that make cooperative awareness and joint enterprise possible and memorable (Bråten & Trevarthen, 2007).

The Embodiment of Emotions as Active Principles, Not Mere Reactions

Emotions, defined by Stern (1993) as protectors of vitality in relation to goals for actions and in relationships, not just as categories of facial expression, evidently are epigenetic regulatory states or "agencies" that grow in the mind of an organism and that adapt in *creative* ways, or make fitting the motives of actions (Whitehead, 1929). They make the images and plans for doing things with movement safe and workable, so that they may best fit environmental contingencies. Other persons' sympathy enables the emotions expressed to become more than a self-expression—they acquire an intersubjective or moral value in the transactional space between self and other. The promotion of safe and workable contact with others must take account of their feelings, too, and must react to the contingencies that arise in communicative exchange of expressions and actions with them.

Key functions of emotion in attachments and the regulation of meaningful human life are as follows.

• *Integration and connection with the regulation of body functions.* Emotions have evolved to be both corrective and integrative for living, *inside* the body of an active, mobile agent or self. Emotional changes of intentions in the central nervous system (CNS) are coupled with, but not caused by, autonomic nervous system (ANS) mediated feelings of visceral and autonomic need that adjust and maintain vital state and energy resources of the body in all its organs (Trevarthen et al., 2006).

• *Attention, orientation, and focusing of perception to find external goals for moving.* At the same time, emotions "pay attention" to the world *outside* the self, aiming the foci of consciousness selectively—by locomotion and by "partially oriented" movements of limbs and special sense organs that pick up information in the several modalities—always aiming to find out what the self can perceive of what the environment may afford for future action.

• *Adaptive mapping in the brain of the body in "behavior space."* Emotions judge the different prospects of moving in one dynamic body-centred representation of space and time for behavior, an egocentric "behavior field." Emotions and emotional regulations are an intrinsic part of this adaptive mapping in the brain of the space in which a body behaves (Trevarthen, 1985).

• *Future orientation for action through time.* The adaptive function of any emotion in the perception of circumstances in the world, whether it is directing positive approach behavior or negative withdrawal, must be *prospective*—aimed to either protect the future life of the animal against possible stress, or to favor the acquisition of benefits from immediate or more distant objects and events. Human emotions depend greatly on imaginary events and circumstances, which bring great creative benefits that prepare for adventures in experience, but also the possibility for distortions in the sense of reality and its prospects, as in the delusions of schizophrenia. Anxiety from the past, real or imagined, can make the future unbearable. Emotions are the innate evaluative part of the perceptual space, weighing motives for future action in an imagined world. This world has other possible times and spaces—which multiplies the possibilities of egocentric experience.

• *Memories built with emotional ties to past actions.* An animal may profit from experience only if the state of affairs in the present is given appropriate or reasonably accurate emotional values that might be valid on other occasions. The emotions evoked by a situation or object are drawn from the emotions of past moments in which the same or similar situations or objects were encountered. There is a reliving of the actions with their feelings in perception; these feelings may qualify the uptake of information from the present. *Emotions associated with past experiences change the processes of motivation:* They can give rise to harmful phobias, addictions, and obsessions, or to aesthetic or moral evaluations that provide valuable guidance for experiencing satisfying actions in the present or to seek in the future. All creative activities are guided by emotions in this way.

• *Sympathy for intentions and feelings in others.* Even in primitive forms, animal emotions may be adapted for *social* regulatory powers, in the behavior space *between individuals, intersubjectively,* and these capacities are greatly elaborated in evolution (Wallin, Merker, & Brown, 2000). Social emotions of human beings, such as love, hate, pride, and shame, amplify or restrict the powers of individuals for profitable engagement with the environment by making their behaviors *cooperative* or *competitive.* Emotions between members of a couple or among members of a larger group determine how well their actions may be combined, and how well their separate experiences are shared and understood. This is true when the communication is entirely nonverbal, and remains true even when the messages communicated are intricately rational and codified in symbols. Indeed every invented symbol or agreed-upon communicative sign has both a *pragmatic reference* and an *emotional appeal.* In the creative movement of music, poetry, drama, and literature, even in philosophy, the emotional forces are strong, and they hold all elements of the story together in the composition of an affective narrative (Smith, 1777/1982; Lange, 1942; Fonagy, 2001; Kühl, 2007).

• *Development of shared understanding in a world of cultural meaning.* The communicative powers of emotion, active from birth in human beings, animate the formation of both life-supporting attachments for a long dependency on parental care in childhood, and the development, through lifetime *cultural learning,* of the accumulated consciousness of a historic community going back many centuries (Bruner, 1990; Feldman, 2002). Harmonious progress of society depends on aesthetic and moral emotions that give members a common set of values, which may or may not be articulated in beliefs or encoded in rules or laws.

Language itself depends on the emotional expressions alive in conversation. It has evolved and develops from a capacity to tell stories by *mimesis* (Donald, 2001), and every mimetic performance or narration is animated and carried forward by rhythmic transitions of emotional states—of expectancy or anticipation, of excitement as risks are encountered and overcome, of satisfaction in achievement, and of calm reflection after all is concluded. The poetic or creative processes reflect the "playful" emotions that make the narrative important, and the narrative is informative by virtue of how the facts it specifies fit in the "argument," or the "drama" of what the protagonists are doing (Turner, 1996; Bruner, 1990). These are the motivating "musical" principles that guide a toddler into meaning and language. It is likely that, in the evolution of human understanding, sharing of experience by a gestural and vocal "musi-language" preceded use of words in language to specify ideas with more precision (Wallin et al., 2000).

Emotions in the Total Design of the Brain

Emotions regulate practical functions of perception, cognition, and memory as well as the generation of coordinated and controlled movements. Correspondingly, the anatomy of emotion, established in the embryonic brain before any movements are executed, is both centrally or medially integrated and widespread in its influences (Panksepp, 1998; see also Chapter 1, this volume). The expression and reception of emotional signals engage all motor organs and all modalities of sense, and a specially adapted emotional motor system (Holstege et al., 1996) conveys enhanced evidence of psychological states and their changes between persons.

The areas of the human cerebral neocortex adapted to perceive live communication and to generate the intricate patterns of expressive movement, as in speaking, are the *most enlarged* in comparison with other species, and they are identifiable before birth. More space is allocated in the human cortex for activating *organs of dialogue*: for the eyes and their movements that signal direction of interest and focus of attention; for the hands and their use in modulated gesture as well as in skilled manipulation; for hearing of expressive sounds; and for articulations of the vocal tract, jaws, lips, and tongue to make the sounds that carry meaning with feeling.

In readiness for the exceptionally long postnatal development of the human cortex, new territories of the prefrontal, parietal, and temporal parts of the primate brain have also expanded in the evolution of humans. These have key importance in the social and cultural development of the child, and they gain unique asymmetry in the skills of intelligence they assimilate through education, most notably in the production and reception of language (Trevarthen & Aitken, 1994). Limbic parts of the cortex that integrate regulations of internal state with cognitive appreciation of objects in the outside world are also greatly elaborated in the human brain, and they continue to grow throughout life. They, too, are asymmetric and give different motives and learning potential to left and right hemispheres (Trevarthen, 1996) (Figure 3.1).

Throughout the vertebrates there is an asymmetry in the vital self-regulatory functions of the core neural systems that mediate between visceral and somatic needs. The left strand of neural systems is more dopaminergic and environmentally challenging or *ergotropic*; the right is more adrenergic and restorative and protective of bodily functions or *trophotropic* (Hess, 1954).

The right half of the child's brain has greater responsibility for *receiving*, for "apprehensive" affective regulation, whereas the left half is more *giving*, "asser-

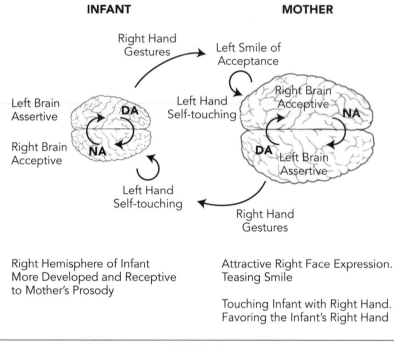

FIGURE 3.1
Asymmetries in functions of the cerebral hemispheres, and in communicative behaviours. The neurochemical activation and arousal systems are also asymmetric: DA = dopaminergic motor activation; NA = noradrenergic sensory arousal of attention.

tive," or proactive in expressing communicative intention toward the mother (Trevarthen, 1996). For the first 18 months, the right hemisphere of the infant brain is more advanced and growing faster than the left. This asymmetry is associated with the intense involvement of the infant in establishing attachments to the mother and a few other intimate givers of care and affection. In the second and third years, as the child develops more powers of communication and self-expression, more social independence, and begins to master the articulation of language, the left hemisphere shows a growth spurt. But even in the neonatal stage, there are asymmetries in the *reception* (more right hemisphere) and *production* (more left hemisphere) of communicative signals, including those for emotions. This deep complementarity of emotion systems supports the elaboration of human cerebral asymmetry for cognitive functions and the acquisition of cultural skills, including language.

The Neural Nets of Self-Control

The motivational and emotional basis for the special human sensory and motor capacities to make and receive expressions of communication and the
regulation of their affecting qualities and dynamics occur subcortically, centered on the periaqueductal gray (PAG), where all emotion-mediating neurochemical systems converge on a coherent self-representation of the organism
to constitute a primordial "core consciousness" (Damasio, 1999; Panksepp,
1998; Merker, 2005) that is sensitive to positive affective influences from other individuals, transforming them into rewarding neurochemistry (Panksepp,
2005).

Conscious control of movement in a complex, highly mobile human body
with many "degrees of freedom" (Bernstein, 1967) depends on a unique central
time sense and core control of effort in whole-body biomechanics—integrating a flexible trunk with head, arms, and legs, with "prospective control" (Lee,
2005). This rhythmic control, coherence, and regulation of energy are mediated by a widespread subcortical system of neural connection. An integrated
intrinsic motive formation (IMF) coordinates the parts of a mobile body and
is formed in subcortical and limbic systems of the embryo before the cerebral
cortex. The IMF functions throughout life to (1) direct the movements of the
sense organs and effectors to select goals and objects in the environment, (2)
evaluate their benefits or risks for the life of the whole self, and (3) express its
states and react to the movements of other selves while detecting their intentions and feelings (Trevarthen & Aitken, 1994; Panksepp & Trevarthen, 2008).
In part, this self-integrating neural system operates independently of the neocortex (Merker, 2005, 2006); when neocortical refinements of perception and
skill in movement and knowledge are being acquired and become active in
guiding behavior, they are integrated with the subcortical orientations and
emotional assessments. In short, emotions play a creative role in the regulation and development of an individual's cognitions and learning throughout
life.

The fetal brain is already built as "intentional" in this experience-seeking
sense, and the lifetime integrity of the self depends on this intentionality (Zoia
et al., 2007). The mind of a fetus, though lacking all experience of the world
and all rationality, has a clearly marked latent power to be both an intentional
agent and a person who must relate to other persons. From their first appearance, movements of the body exhibit an intrinsic motive pulse (IMP) that is
expressive—the rates of motor rhythms vary with the intensity of effort and
with the "confidence" or anticipated experiences associated with the intentions to perform actions (Trevarthen, 1999). The core integrative and regula-

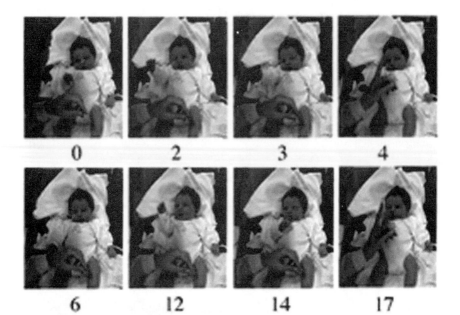

FIGURE 3.2

Manifestations in newborn infants of conscious interest in persons, seeking to engage with their expressions. Above: Photographs from video made by Dr. Emese Nagy, who studies neonatal imitation, of an infant less than 2 days old in a hospital in Hungary. The infant first watches its own hand (1 to 3), then attends as E. N. presents her index finger (4), the infant waits, then raises its hand and looks at it (12), then partly extends an index finger to imitate while looking intently at E. N. (14). E. N. is provoked to repeat her movement while the infant watches the finger intently (17). (The numbers mark seconds after the beginning at 0). Below: An infant 30 minutes old imitates tongue protrusion. Another, also 30 minutes after birth, follows a ball being moved playfully by a person. The infant tracks the animate movement with eyes, mouth, hands, and one foot (Photos by Kevan Bundell).

tory systems of the brain constitute the motivated self and define the functions of its consciousness and their emotional regulation and development (Panksepp, 2001; Merker, 2005, 2006).

Emotions as Visceral and Motor Regulators of the Self, Relationships, and Communities

The life-sustaining activities of the autonomic nervous system (ANS), which begin in the human embryo weeks before the cerebral cortex cells appear, take responsibility for maintaining the "internal environment"—regulating blood chemistry, circulation, respiration, digestion, and the immune system responses. These activities have also evolved to sustain the vitality of the social organism.

The parasympathetic nerves of the ANS in humans include special visceral efferents of the head—of cranial nerves 3, 7, 9, and 10, which, assisted by nerves 4, 5, 6, 11, and 12, not only regulate looking and seeing, blood circulation, breathing and respiration, eating, digestion, and excretion, but also express emotions that control social contacts and relations (Porges, 1997). All the muscles of human communication—of the eyes, face, mouth, vocal system, head, and neck—which are constantly active in conversation expressing emotions and thoughts, and which have disproportionately large representation in the sensory and motor "maps" of the neocortex, receive excitation from these cranial nerves (Aitken & Trevarthen, 1997; Trevarthen, 2001b). The activities of sympathetic and parasympathetic neurons are made evident for the benefit of social partners in specially adapted states of emotional expression (Panksepp, 1998; see also Porges, Chapter 2, this volume).

In a momentous evolutionary step, human hands, in addition to their extraordinary dexterity in manipulation, have become associated with the above organs of communication as supremely adaptable organs of gestural communication, capable of conveying sensitive interpersonal feelings by touch and rhythmic caresses, as well as of acquiring a language ability equal to that of speech (Trevarthen, 1986). Infants can imitate not only expressive forms of vocalizations and facial movements (e.g., tongue protrusion), but also isolated and apparently arbitrary gestures of the hands (e.g., index finger extension; see Figure 3.2), and they use them to establish an intersubjective engagement regulated by emotions (Kugiumutzakis, 1998; Nagy, 2008).

The movements of the infant's voice, face, and hands, are adapted for interpersonal transmission of impulses to know and do in dialogue, and all are potent vehicles for the communication of emotions and states of sympathetic motivation. The graphic hand movements of a young infant that, like the accompanying expressions of the face, show approach or withdrawal, pleasure, fear or anger, protection of the eyes or face, exploratory curiosity and surprise, are not learned. They are part of the innate emotional system for self-protection and for self–other communication.

Research on the subtle regulation of communication with infants has brought greater appreciation for the dynamic and expressive principles of nonverbal communication between human beings of all ages. The combined operation of visceral and somatic "mirror" reactions between mother and infant gives, in ways we do not fully understand, the infant means of expression and access to the other anticipatory "motor images" and "feelings" and permits direct motive-to-motive engagement with a companion as well as interest in a shared environment and what is being done in it. *Thus arises the psychological phenomenon of intersubjectivity, which couples human brains in joint affect and cognition, and mediates all cultural learning* (Trevarthen, 1998; Trevarthen & Aitken, 2001). A child must learn what other people know and do by intersubjective sympathy for their actions and their emotional qualities. How states of body and mind are shared has become an active new field of enquiry in phenomenological psychology and philosophy (Zlatev et al., 2008).

How Developmental Changes in Motives Determine Cultural Learning

Internally generated age-related changes in what infants prefer to do and in what interests them are evidently adapted to regulate adult attentions, as well as to regulate infants' own developing consciousness and experience (Trevarthen & Aitken, 2003). Some emotional expressions and reactions of infants are obviously related to eliciting maternal care and protection for the body. These can be called *emotions of attachment.* But other more complex innate emotions are adapted to promote sharing of actions and experiences, and for expressing evaluations of objects located and identified by the infant's intentions or desires—that is, by the infant's *mind.* These are *emotions of companionship* that control the cooperative quality of activities and interests in friendship with identified persons (Trevarthen, 2001a, 2005b). These emotions show regular age-related changes through infancy. They define cooperative interests in the shared world and enable the child to be educated in socially shared meanings, knowledge, and skills. They are the human emotions of cultural learning.

John Bowlby (1988) formulated attachment theory with support from ethological evidence of the effects of maternal deprivation in rhesus monkeys.

Early body contact plays a critical role in the development of appropriate social behavior, and disruption of early contact results in stress and later pathological behavior. Research on newborn rodents, cats, and primates shows that their rapidly developing brains depend on parental support. The quality of parental support determines how the brain will grow, and neglect or stress can damage the brain (Schore, 1994).

We are born more immature than other primates, with sensitivity to the emotions of persons who offer intimate attention with their whole body (Brazelton, 1979; Brazelton & Nugent, 1995). Adults in states of distress or suffering from illness or aging have a comparable need for affectionate and sensitive response.

Young infants respond with exquisite sensitivity to the touch, movement, smell, temperature, etc., of a mother. Newborns gain regulation from the rhythms of maternal breathing and heart beat, and fetuses are sensitive to maternal vocal patterns (Fifer & Moon, 1995). Infants' arousal and expressions of distress are immediately responsive to stimulation from breastfeeding. These interactions are not merely physiological. For example, the response to breast milk is facilitated if the newborn has sight of the mother's eyes. The newborn infant is ready to perceive and respond to the interest of her eyes and to respond to her oral expressions of emotion. The communicative precocity of human newborns indicates that emotional responses to caregivers must play a crucial role in early brain development (Schore, 1994). Indeed, the infant's endocrine status, neurochemistry, and brain growth respond to maternal stimulation, which cannot be fully substituted by artificial clinical procedures; this responsiveness can be demonstrated to a new mother and father so that they can provide sympathetic, loving attention that will help the baby's "social brain" grow (Panksepp, 2007).

Remarkable evidence that this precocious interpersonal sensitivity includes interest in *sharing new ideas* comes from research that shows us how, and for what purpose, newborns imitate (Nagy & Molnàr, 2004). If the procedures a researcher uses are not merely enacted to elicit responses, but are administered at intervals in *attentive and "respectful,"* ways, it becomes evident that a newborn baby is not only capable of *imitating* single arbitrary gestures, such as tongue protrusion, extension of an index finger or two fingers, or a firm closing of the eyes (see Figure 3.2). Given an opportunity by a waiting partner, the infant is interested in *eliciting or initiating* an imitation by repeating such a movement as a *provocation*, seeking a response. Moreover, these complementary actions are accompanied by different autonomic or emotional states of self-regulation. Synchronous with imitating, the newborn shows a heart acceleration, and when the infant makes a provocative movement attending to the other person to receive his or her response, the heart decelerates. This reciprocity of emotional regulation makes possible the intense cooperation in experience on which all human cultural enterprise depends (Trevarthen, 2005a).

Prefrontal "mirror neurons" have been taken as possible candidates for the mechanism that enables infants to imitate, to associate emotion with imitation of others' movements, and to develop language (Rizzolatti & Arbib, 1998; Gallese, 2005). However, given the relative immaturity of the frontal cortex in infants, it is more likely that unidentified *subcortical* components of a "mirror system" are involved in many imitations that neonates perform. The Mirroring of actions involves multimodal or transmodal sensory recognition of intentions in movements by many regions of the cortex; moreover there are many multimodal, affect-regulating neural populations in the brainstem. These are integrated within extensive systems that formulate motor images for action and expression (Damasio, 1999; Holstege et al., 1996; Panksepp, 1998). The distribution of activity in the brain of an infant a few weeks old when giving attention to a picture of a woman's face, indicates that the "sympathy system" of intersubjective communication (Decety & Chaminade, 2003) is well formed when the baby is born (Tzourio-Mazoyer et al., 2002).

A Map of Three Complementary Uses of Human Motives and Emotions, and Two Kinds of Ritual for Collective Action with Others

Ways of Acting with a Human Body and Steps to Share Meaning before Language

We can distinguish three ways in which the prospects of the mind are made effective in the service of life as a social being—three worlds in which the animal self or psyche seeks to move well—that is, to engage in action that is effective and has efficient prospective control (Trevarthen, 2001a; Trevarthen et al., 2006): (1) The *well-being of the body of the self* is sustained by the brain in cooperation with the hormonal systems that control distribution of vital resources and the economy of energy which, in turn, sustain the whole organism in health. (2) *Engagements of the self with the physical world* must be directed *subjectively*, by intentions that perceive objects and events and how their substances and other properties and processes can be used. (3) In *communication with an other*, or conscious subject, there is an additional need to be able to detect the probable reactions of that other, *intersubjectively*. Communication of emotions

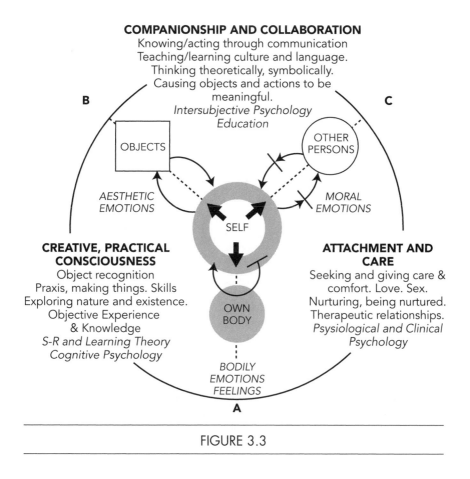

FIGURE 3.3

is required to negotiate any cooperation in purposes and experiences with an other (see Figure 3.3).

An infant is born with these three regulations, but the motives that integrate control of actions and experiences change greatly as the child's body and mind grow, transforming the ways in which the self functions in the body, with objects, and in the world of people. We can distinguish two paths available to the child that, if all goes well, lead to enthusiastic and practical life in society. These correspond to the two kinds of ritual by which communal life was celebrated and regulated in ancient Greece: the rites honoring the gods Apollo and Dionysos. Each gives the body and mind different tasks, and each has its own emotions. The reasoned Apollonian regulation of dealing with mastery of the physical world, practically, technically, and scientifically, differs from the Dionysian love and exuberance of the body in human company, which releases pleasurable energy of action and imagination as cultivated in the arts.

Enthusiasm, literally meaning a state of "having the gods within," motivates adventurous action of all kinds. Its purposes can be ordered *practically*, with studied reference to physical reality that sets limits to movement and offers ways by which projects can be carried out in a world that may be ordered by human-made structures and procedures or rituals. Or the enthusiasm for acting can be guided in more *self-aware and passionate ways* and by sympathetic respect for the wishes and feelings of others, and for the pleasures they gain from moving and sharing movement in creative artistic ways. All cultural rituals, practices, and creations can benefit from *both* of these ways of being "inspired by the gods," but the motivations of individuals differ. There is a tendency in ordered society for either science, technology, and commerce, on the one hand, or artistic creativity and the pursuit of beauty and pleasure of movement in spontaneous intimacy, on the other, to take precedence, thus distorting the social enterprise.

How Emotional Narratives Become the Discourse of Language

Early protoconversational engagements with infants, in the first 4 months, manifest the direct person-to-person emotional regulations of "primary intersubjectivity" (Trevarthen, 1979). Protoconversations are succeeded by rhythmically structured "musical" games—first, person–person games with communication itself in ways that manifest the playfulness so evident among young mammals (see Figure 3.4), and then "person–person–object games" objects that attract the interest of the infant who is beginning to explore with the aid of hands and mouth. At 9 months, a change occurs that initiates "secondary intersubjectivity" (Trevarthen & Hubley, 1978). Now the baby is becoming interested in sharing the ways companions use objects, and he or she makes practiced movements to engage with the world of things. The baby's willingness to cooperate in a task and to make "protolinguistic acts of meaning" (Halliday, 1975), transforms the ways in which parents speak to the infant. Questions and rhetorical comments are rapidly replaced by instructions, directives, and informative comments that the infant now attends to and tries to follow. This is the start of cultural information transfer between generations.

Research on communication with infants has clarified the innate and developing foundations of these playful behaviors, and, thus, of memory and meaning (Trevarthen & Aitken, 2001; Reddy, 2008). It has demonstrated how

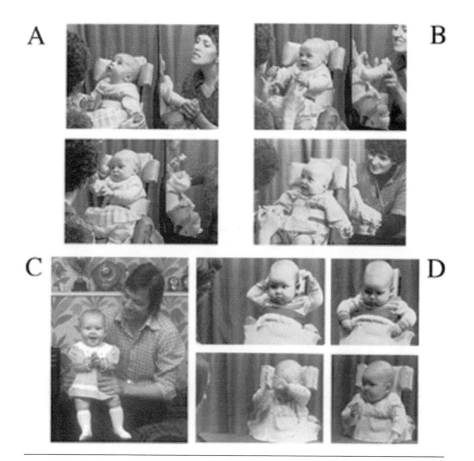

FIGURE 3.4

After 3 months, infants' bodies become stronger and their consciousness is more complex. A: A 4-month-old infant is curious about the room and concentrates her attention on an object presented by her mother. B: When her mother starts a rhythmic body game, the baby is both intensely interested and pleased. At 5 months she is attentive and participates in a "ritual" action game, "Round and round the garden," composed as a rhyming 4-line stanza with a lively iambic pulse. The infant has learned the song and vocalizes at the end in synchrony with the mother, matching her pitch. C: A 6-month-old sitting on her father's knee smiles with pride as she responds to her mother's request to show "Clappa-clappa-handies." D: The same 6-month-old shows her uneasiness and withdrawal in front of two strangers, a man and a woman, who attempt to communicate in friendly but unfamiliar ways. The infant appears to experience shame as well as distress.

actions in real time are shared between persons of all ages, enabling them to collaborate in intersubjective and collective acting, remembering, and recalling. The nature of cultural learning and historically contrived "communities of meaning" and their languages depends upon these vital engagements of minds and bodies (Donald, 2001).

The key factors in language development are intersubjective or communal, not one-head rational. A child comes to understand and use words naturally in intersubjective, two-head relationships with older talkative companions, then with same-age friends, sharing imaginative journeys and projects. The psychological motives that make a human body move with inventive grace are infectious. We sense one another's psychic states by a direct transfer: mind to body—body to mind. The rhythms and expressive alphabet of this communication, the music and dance of it, are brought to light by research on unconscious postures, gestures, intonations, and facial expressions of conversation (Fonagy, 2001), and especially from detailed analysis of how infants communicate, and how adults adjust their communication to meet young, unsophisticated minds (Reddy, 2008).

Observations made from home movies of infants under 1 year who, in the second or third year, were diagnosed as having autism spectrum disorder, indicate that the first or primary failing concerns these rhythms of attending and moving, and that this in turn causes problems with parental responses that can exacerbate the child's developmental difficulties, further weakening their intersubjectivity (Trevarthen & Daniel, 2004; St. Clair et al., 2007; Aitken, 2008).

Rhythms of the Embodied Self and of Cooperation: Synchrony and Sympathy

All animal actions take the form of rhythmic or pulsing measured sequences of movement—regulated through time and across a great range of times, from minimal perceptible intervals to days, seasons, and lifetimes (Osborne, 2008; Trevarthen, 2008a). Brains are networks of dynamic systems all obedient to rhythms that flow in unison (Buzsaki, 2006), orchestrating their effective actions to fulfill future-sensitive (motivated) desires and to be capable of recollecting past experiences of being. Without the coordinated regulation of spontaneous neural activity through time, there is no other way all these muscles of my body can work in collaborative efficiency—imaging and executing their forces in synchrony and succession in the present moment, with respect for *past* achievements and difficulties, and in realistic appraisal of *future* pros-pects—modifying inclinations and desires for the future that are founded on experiences past. It takes a coherent sense of time. Moreover, there would be no way for me to sympathize with another person's intentions and feelings if we could not share the rhythms of this self-synchrony to establish inter-synchrony (Condon & Ogston, 1966).

Cerebral representations of movement in time, anticipating reafferent stim-ulation, stimulation fed back from the moving body and its parts (preparations for which are established in the brain of a fetus), can explain the abilities of infants, even newborns, to produce rhythmic and melodic forms of movement that match the timing of adult movements, and to enter into a "dance" of syn-chronized, imitative, or complementary interactions with the adult (Beebe et al., 1985; Stern, 1971, 1999). These cerebral representations explain the sen-sitivity that young infants have to precisely controlled contingent stimulus effects of their own actions, the coordination they achieve between others' movements and their own, and the distress that is caused when a partner's movements (i.e., his or her actions and reactions) are noncontingent (Murray & Trevarthen, 1985; Nadel, et al., 1999).

The Communicative Artistry and Practical Technique of Human Emotions

Birds, whales, and gibbons have the motivation to communicate vocally by species-specific expressive displays shaped innately, or genetically. But they also learn the songs of their group, strengthening the community by keeping "traditions" alive in a transgenerational composition of songs (Brown, 2000; Payne, 2000; Merker, 2008). Sounds of the human voice have comparable functions and are also organized in narratives of aesthetic and moral feeling in the storytelling performances of song, the musicality of which can be imitated by instrumental music (Malloch & Trevarthen, 2008). "Tone of voice" (Fon-agy, 2001) and the "vitality affects" of voice and gesture (Stern, 1993, 1999) determine the interpersonal effect of utterances, even in communication me-diated by conventional signs or text of any kind (Brandt, 2008). Aesthetic or poetic principles influence the factual message, giving its story a "literary" coherence of motivation (Bruner, 1990; Turner, 1996; Fonagy, 2001; Kühl, 2007).

The dynamics of human emotion and their special adaptations for trans-mission of products of invention between individuals are richly displayed in the temporal or dramatic arts, especially song, music, and dance (Smith, 1777/1982). These cultivate the motivational base or inner subjective context that is alive in all rational thought and all culturally elaborated practices, techniques, and explanations. Human meanings and beliefs are made strong and given meaningful and memorable shape with the passionate support of musical, poetic, and prosodic forms of expression—that is, with "musical semantics" (Kühl, 2007). The social brains of children are nurtured by the musicality of communication with companions, adults, and peers.

How Primary Self–Other Regulation Leads to the Creation of Meaning

There are . . . two sides to the machinery involved in the development of nature. On the one side there is a given environment with organisms adapting themselves to it . . . The other side of the evolutionary machinery, the neglected side, is expressed by the word creativeness. The organisms can create their own environment. For this purpose the single organism is almost helpless. The adequate forces require societies of cooperating organisms. But with such cooperation and in proportion to the effort put forward, the environment has a plasticity which alters the whole ethical aspect of evolution.
—(Whitehead, 1929)

In a human community, individuals transform their relationship to the environment, their adaptation to its benefits and dangers, by the cooperative creation of a culture with its historically contrived rituals and beliefs, its techniques and arts, and its language. The foundations for this transmission of knowledge and skills across generations and hundreds and thousands of years, which gives humans a collective power over nature that Alfred North Whitehead claims changed "the whole ethical aspect of evolution," is established in the development of every human body and brain. Infants are born motivated for cultural learning (Trevarthen & Aitken, 2003). These changes are associated with transformations of the emotional powers and needs of the child to which parents must adapt by changes in their "intuitive parenting" (Papoušek & Papoušek, 1987).

How Infants' Emotions Grow with Responsive Parental Support

In the last 10 years, many findings have been made in support of the new concept of infants' "innate intersubjectivity" (Trevarthen, 1998; Trevarthen & Aitken, 2001), which is accepted as building a coconsciousness that enables the child to achieve mastery of cultural learning and that provides the essential foundations for understanding and using language (Bråten & Trevarthen, 2007).

Using the idea that infants have innate motives to guide their life with others, we have charted four periods in the first year of life, marked by age-related changes in the capacities of the baby to regulate actions and awareness—periods in which the foundations of experience and the relationships with parental care are established and transformed (Trevarthen & Aitken, 2001, 2003). Step by step, the expectations of the baby are guided by new motives to move in new worlds. These steps on the way to meaning in life with others are separated by short periods of rapid change, during which the motives of the child are transforming from within, apparently generated by transformations in the brain, some of which have been identified (Trevarthen & Aitken, 2003). These periods of change correspond to the "touch points" that Brazelton (1993) has noted give parents an opportunity to discover new ways of intimately sharing life with their infants, and to foster development.

The fate of each step in development depends on the capacity of "intuitive parenting" to respond to the infant's changing needs (Papoušek & Papoušek, 1987, 1997; Gomes-Pedro et al., 2002). If the mother of a baby is depressed and incapable of responding happily to the baby's appetite for lively care and communication, this can cause problems in development of the infant's self-confidence and understanding (Murray & Cooper, 1997; Robb, 1999; Marwick & Murray, 2008). Both the positive emotions in sensitive and mutually supportive communication and the negative emotions that disrupt communication in insecure or failing relationships can be related to their effects in the development of the child (see Figure 3.4). They also indicate various ways in which therapy can help when the individual is failing to cope, whether with self- or other-related difficulties.

As the infant becomes more active socially by 3 or 4 months, he or she can engage in playful encounters with siblings. It is particularly significant that by 6 months, the social emotions of *pride* and *shame* come online. The emotion of pride in performance of a learned ritual that is part of a favorite action, song, or game routinely shared with a parent is in contrast with manifestations of wariness, avoidance, and shame in an engagement with a stranger who not only looks and sounds unfamiliar, but who does not "know the game" (Trevarthen, 2002). This social sensitivity, regulated by the interpersonal "moral emotions" of *pride* and *shame*, becomes most evident just before a major transformation in the infant's interests and emotions, for example, the transition to secondary intersubjectivity at 9 months, each of which has effects on the behavior of an attentive parent. If a parent is "attuned" to the eagerness of the infant to act in demonstrative ways and to have these self-conscious performances noticed and responded to with signs of pleasure and attentive admiration, and if the parent's actions make him or her a part in the play, the child is manifestly happy and motivated to repeat the performance or, alternately, to create another diverting behavior (Reddy, 2008). Parents who respond with affection gently tease the infant and are quick to respond with humor to attempts of the infant to tease (Reddy & Trevarthen, 2004). Such behavior brings out the emotions of playfulness and focuses attention on rituals that may be learned as skills (Eckerdal & Merker, 2009).

A sad and detached mother is not a companion in playful invention of games. Furthermore, she may be insensitively stimulating or coercive, eliciting avoidance or protest (Gratier and Apter-Danon, 2008). *Infants are equipped with defensive emotions that repel unsympathetic communication.* These defensive emotions can further trouble the relationship and may be accompanied by stress that harms the infant's motivations and limits learning. Forms of therapy that aid a mother to provide more sympathetic and playful response to her infant—for example, video interaction guidance (VIG), which selectively identifies and reinforces moments of positive contact, can evoke the mother's pleasure in her infant and in the joy and pride that her child expresses (Schechter, 2004; Fukkink, 2008).

If the parents are available and in good humor, they find the infant a delightful, teasing playmate, and they share action games and nursery songs, which the infant quickly learns. Thus, many months before any awareness of the purposes of language or the ability to speak, a baby, if given the kind of affectionate support that comes naturally to happy parents, is becoming part of the musicality and ritual activities of a particular culture, enjoying appreciation by proud family members.

Testing the Time Sense and Emotional Quality of Engagement

Two kinds of perturbation or separation have been used to test the mutual emotional regulation of intersubjective contact between a mother and a young infant. This kind of research was necessary because there was, in the 1970s, strong theoretical denial that an infant just a month or 2 old could be capable of self-awareness, let alone awareness of an other, and capable of responsive, well-timed engagement motivated by purposes and emotions.

The first technique, implemented independently in the early 1970s by Ed Tronick et al. (1978) and Lynne Murray (Trevarthen, 1974, 1977; Trevarthen et al., 1981; Murray & Trevarthen, 1985), required a mother who was in the process of enjoying a protoconversation with a 2-month-old to stop being expressive and to hold her face immobile, with a neutral expression, in front of the baby for a minute. This "blank face" or "still face" procedure provoked an immediate response from the baby. First, the baby became attentive and sometimes made attempts by smiles, vocalizations, or gestures to appeal to or stimulate a response from the mother; then the baby became withdrawn, avoiding the mother's gaze, with signs of distress and confusion. The baby looked depressed. This finding agreed with those from studies showing that infants of mothers suffering from postpartum depression could appear withdrawn and depressed and express themselves with a depressed vocal musicality (Field et al., 1988; Field, 1992; Murray and Cooper, 1997). Subsequent observations of infants with mothers who manifested a bipolar psychosis further indicated that a baby confronted with insensitive and repetitive stimulating behaviors makes efforts to compensate by being watchful, hyperactive, and having a "false cheerfulness" (Gratier & Apter-Danon, 2009).

The second test, developed by Lynne Murray (Murray & Trevarthen, 1985) following experiments on mediation of communication with infants by television images by the Papoušeks (Papoušek & Papoušek , 1977), required that mother and 2-month-old should first engage in communication while in separate rooms by means of a two-way video–sound link, which proved not difficult for them to do (see Figure 3.5). Then a short segment of the mother's happy communication was replayed to the baby. In this scenario the baby showed expressions of surprise, confusion, withdrawal, and sadness, much as occurs for the still-face procedure. This response proved that the infant was immediately sensitive to the "contingency" or live and sympathetic timing of the mother's expressions. The communication had the right expressions in the right sequence but was out of synch with the infant's behavior. This experiment has been replicated (Nadel et al., 1999). Further, the complementary test has been conducted in which the baby's behavior in a live period of communication was replayed to the mother without warning (Murray & Trevarthen, 1986). The mother senses that "something is wrong," but does not know what it is, and might blame herself for her baby's apparent unresponsiveness. Human communication has to occur in real time, in all its creativity and unexpectedness, as in the improvisation of a jazz duet (Gratier & Trevarthen, 2008).

Conclusions: How the Roots of Emotional Communication May Be Restored

Detailed empirical research on the emotional behaviors of infants and young children in real-life situations where their motives are in active engagement with actions and expressions of others leads to an appreciation of the positive role of emotions in development and well-being in relationships (Donaldson,

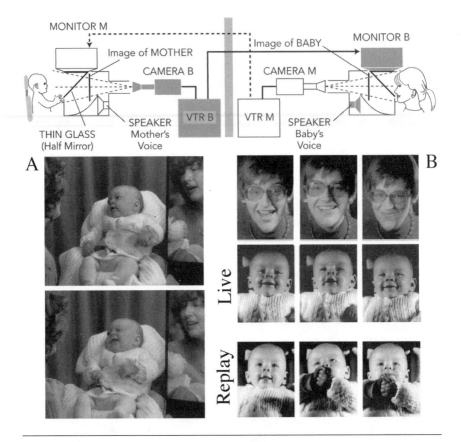

FIGURE 3.5

Complex expressions of social engagement in co-consciousness between young infants and their mothers. A: A 6-week-old girl looks intently while her mother (seen in the mirror) speaks, then smiles as her mother pauses. B: Pictures from an engagement between an 8-week-old infant and her mother mediated by Double Television in an experiment by Lynne Murray. In the "live" condition, mother and daughter enjoy a "protoconversation" in which the infant is both highly expressive of many happy emotions, and tightly coordinated in time with her mother's expressions and utterances. When the same 1 minute of the mother's behaviour is "replayed," the infant is immediately disturbed and becomes withdrawn and depressed. Infants are very sensitive to the contingency of a partner's behaviours with their own.

1992; Nadel & Muir, 2005; Reddy, 2008). Emotions are organic or "live" processes that are "creative," asserting their vibrant influence on emerging intentions, experiences, thoughts, expectations, and memories from birth and before. They should not, as A. N. Whitehead (1929) has said, be formulated as "products of logical discernment." Scientific experimentation on the nature of emotions has, however, been guided by rational *objective* and *causal* explanations of the ways animals and people react to stimuli. It has adopted a "third person" position, measuring behavioral events in individuals from the point of view of an outside observer. It has supported a belief of industrialized Western cultures that a child's negative or defensive emotions have to be "regulated" to keep them in balance and their pro-social feelings "developed" by a plan of training to inculcate culturally approved norms (Bierhoff, 2002). Support for a natural science of the whole range of relational emotions, one that follows a method of observation pioneered by Charles Darwin (1872), has come from neuroscience in recent decades (Panksepp, 1998, 2002, Chapter 2 this volume). Emotions are intrinsic principles that regulate adaptive life in the phenomenal world of movement—in relationships and communities, in commerce and politics, and especially in art.

The expressive/communicative activities and social customs that most directly represent the fluidity and creativity of human emotions are those of drama, music, and dance—naturally enjoyed ways of articulating and coordinating the limbs and self-regulatory organs of the body, coupling their tensions and impulses in rhythmic ways that seek to preserve energy and to channel it in most effective ways in obedience to an IMP. That communication between a mother and a young infant can be described accurately by a theory of "communicative musicality" is clear evidence of the source of human collaborative awareness in intimate creative expressions or a poetry (making) of stories. The notes, phrases, and evolving episodes of emotional narratives create and carry meaning, sustaining the rituals of culture (Gratier and Trevarthen, 2006; Malloch and Trevarthen, 2009).

The Message for Therapy and Education

Acting directly in response to the moral forces of relating evident in young children, taking note of the delight experienced in both directions, as from mother to infant and from infant to mother, has an importance that goes beyond what reason can explain or behavioral or cognitive training can achieve. Once a shared story is being written within the fun of its valued rituals, many meanings can be discovered and thought about with self-confidence and in confiding friendships. Rituals of teaching/learning and the "healing practices" to foster well-being in those who suffer from anger, fear, anxiety, and confusion depend not primarily on informational structures or "instruction" or on "training" of behaviors, but on sympathetic encouragement of the innate tendencies of all human beings—even the youngest or most debilitated—to share pleasures and to learn new meanings in nurturing company.

The therapist working with a person who has become confused by anxiety and fear and whose energy of enthusiasm has gone has a choice: try to make sense of the reasons and causes of the emotional loss, or try to seek, by sensitive provocation and positive belief, a form of appreciation that will evoke some signs of playfulness and hope for enjoyment in sharing the surprises of a human engagement in which there is no dislike or rivalry.

Infant research supports the use of nonverbal intersubjective therapies, such as music therapy, movement or dance therapy, drama therapy, pictorial art therapy, and body psychotherapy because these approaches accept that we are all equipped with a sensitivity for movement and qualities in movement, not only in our own bodies but in the bodies of others we touch, see, and hear. Moreover, "art therapies" have the benefit of accepting the assumption that we are story-making creatures, and that our own autobiography, and its main supportive characters, is the story that affects us most deeply.

Work with abused and emotionally disturbed children, or those with a constitutional disorder such as autism or Rett's disorder, demonstrates the need in therapy or special education for communication at an intimate emotional level (Malloch & Trevarthen, 2008), whatever procedures are put in place in the routines of experience or the layout of environmental affordances and contingencies by training programs. Training in how to regulate life for the self and with other persons has beneficial effects only if the communication—the process of sympathetic intersubjectivity by which it is implemented—is good.

From his own practice and from observing the benefits of skilled therapeutic work of others, Dan Hughes (2006) has identified the primary principles of engagement and reconstruction in his dyadic developmental psychotherapy, as follows. Here Katie is an abused child, now about 8 years old, Jackie is her principal adoptive parent, and Alison is the therapist. All these characters are fictional, based on Hughes's experience of many cases.

> The psychological treatment of Katie . . . involved providing her with a series of complex integrative affective and reflective experiences. The central features of her treatment involved intersubjective affective experiences of both attunement as well as shame reduction. . . . Within [an] atmosphere of trust, Allison and Jakie employed empathy and curiosity, always grounded on acceptance, to explore with Katie various experiences of shame from her

past and present life. Shame-reduction occurred by bringing the incident to Katie's awareness, actively communicating empathy for her distress, and then through co-creating the meaning of Katie's new affective and reflective states. This enabled her to integrate her fragmented self, increase her sense of self-worth, and enhance her ability to develop attachment security with Jackie. When Alison sensed and was responsive to Katie's affective states, she provided her with both primary and secondary intersubjective experiences. The experience was most therapeutic when it occurred in a manner that involved eye contact, facial expressiveness, rich and varied voice modifications, and a wide range of gestures and movements. Allison's voice moved easily from loud to soft, rapid to slow, with periodic long latencies in which she and Katie were wondering about a problem and its solution. Alison giggled and laughed, moved her face close and pulled away and demonstrated empathic sadness, fear or anger, closely attuned with Katie's affective state quite readily in her facial and vocal expressions. While exploring the immediate interaction as well as a recent or distant event, she sat close to Katie and frequently touched her. Such physical contact greatly facilitated the communication and shared affect. Physical contact was as effective as voice tone and facial gestures in co-regulating various emotional themes of joy, excitement, shame, anger, sadness and anxiety. (p. 279)

The same principles of enhanced intimacy and sustained attention to the other are important for helping children with autism or other developmental disorders. Furthermore, being in touch with the deepest sources of emotional expression is necessary to open communication with very senile people and in those with severe mental handicaps (Zeedyk, 2008).

Therapists seek to change the feelings that affect their patients' experiences so as to make them more confident, better able to adapt to life situations and relationships, and happier. To do so, they must find ways to engage with the motives that light up body and mind with emotions. Thus, they must move with the patient in the performance of real desired projects and tasks, not only tasks that exist as stories in talking. The rhythmic expressive foundation of emotional dynamics is the same for all spoken and unspoken "dances" of the mind. Emotions are how we dance together and doing so is at the heart of the human enterprise.

4

Multilevel Meaning Making and Dyadic Expansion of Consciousness Theory

The Emotional and the Polymorphic Polysemic Flow of Meaning

Ed Tronick

PSYCHOTHERAPY IS ABOUT changing the meaning people make about themselves in the world. Indeed meaning—private meaning—is a core concept in approaches as varied and contentious as psychoanalysis, psychodynamic, psychotherapy, cognitive–behavioral therapy (CBT), dialectical cognitive therapies, dyadic therapies, attachment and relational therapies, and even "alternative" body psychotherapies (Tronick, 2007; Harrison & Tronick, 2007; Ogden, Minton, & Pain, 2006; Modell, 1993). Nonetheless, I believe we have misconstrued the nature of meaning in deep ways that limit our understanding of how humans function, what meaning "is," and how individuals change their meanings. In essence we have tended to limit and categorize meaning into the domain of the explicit, mostly to the domains of language, symbols, and representations. We do this limiting in part because our cognitive processes tend toward chucking reality into categories, so it is hard for us humans to do it other ways. We also do it because our thinking is colonized by language, which in turn feeds back and further reifies the categorizations. Furthermore, the culture of science and its demand for the explicit also plays a role. Finally, we are very impressed with our ability to name things because it gives us a feeling that we know and control whatever it is we name. This thinking holds much truth about the meaning we make of ourselves in the world. But not the whole truth.

Meaning is Biopsychological

Meaning is biopsychological. It is made by polymorphic systems operating at multiple levels of the individual. These polymorphic systems create qualitatively different forms of meaning, what Freeman (2000) refers to as *actualizations of meaning*, which at best only messily fit together. Moreover, meaning is not one thing—one meaning. Meaning is a layered flow over time of the different meanings emerging from the multiple levels and processes that make meaning. Meaning is a laminated polysemic flow or bundle (A. Harrison, personal communication, 2008) that affects itself as it flows into the future. Yet, this flow of meanings has to be assembled by individuals into a coherent sense of themselves in the world, into what I will call a *state of consciousness*. No simple task.

Bruner (1990) has said that humans are meaning makers. They make meaning to gain a sense of their self in relation to their own self, and in relation to the world of things and other people. These meanings are held in the individual's state of consciousness. A state of consciousness is the in- or mostly out-of-awareness polysemic meanings made by the totality of an individual's biopsychological processes. Some meanings are known and symbolizable, some are unknown, implicit but with "work" can become known, and some may be unknowable. More on that later.

The meanings contained in a state of consciousness organize individuals' presence, way of being in the world. For example, it is the comfortable and inexplicable feeling one has in a loved childhood home or the unknown shearing discomfort in one's body, the feeling of a need to stretch and move, when in a house of an unknown trauma. Meanings are self-organized, regulated internally and private as well as dyadically organized, regulated with others, and shared. When self-organized meaning-making is successful, new meanings are made and become part of the individual's state of consciousness. When meanings are dyadically organized, a *dyadic* state of consciousness emerges between the individuals and contains new cocreated meanings, which in turn can be appropriated by each individual into his or her state of consciousness.

Successful self- or self-and-other creation of new meanings leads to an expansion of the complexity and coherence of the individual's state of consciousness. And successful creation of self and dyadic states of consciousness has experiential and functional consequences. So does unsuccessful meaning making. Successful meaning making carries with it a sense of expansion and positive affects; these feelings cascade and affect themselves, perhaps leading to a feeling of exuberance and aliveness, or an oceanic feeling of wellness. When successful meaning is made with another person, a feeling of connection and synchrony emerges, a mutual sense of being together in a special state. Failure to evoke meaning generates negative affects, fearfulness, anxiety, and a constriction and shrinking. These too feed on themselves, leading to radical qualitative changes in state. We see these shifts in our patients during those moments of new insight or when there is the catastrophe—a failure to make meaning (Modell, 1993)—and we must also recognize that we are participants in these processes.

What do I mean by saying that meanings are biopsychologically polymorphic? Meanings include anything from the linguistic, symbolic, abstract realms, which we easily think of as forms of meaning, to the bodily, physiological, behavioral, and emotional structures and processes, which we find more difficult to conceptualize as forms, acts, or actualizations of meaning. The difficulty arises because these polymorphs are made at every level of the organism, from the physiological to awareness, and also because we are forced to use language to discuss meanings that are inherently nonlinguistic and outside of explicit awareness. However, it is possible to comfortably integrate these ideas about meaning under a principle of singularity. The concepts of mind, body, and brain may be useful concepts or not, but they reflect the operation of the way our cognitive processes cut up the world. As such, they do not necessarily reflect or encompass the way the individual operates. Rather, there is a singularity, a concept related to how all subprocesses in a system not only purposively operate at the local level but also function in the context of the operation and goals of the whole system. All systems making up the whole individual—the totality of human biopsychological processes, including, but not limited to, what we call mind, brain, and behavior—operate to gain information about the world in order to act *in* and *on* the world in alignment with their intentions and goals as well as to create the individual's unique, singular purposes, intentions, meanings, and sense of self in the world.

One domain of meanings that we often find difficult to conceptualize as meaningful purposive elements of our state of consciousness is that of emotions. Freud spoke about primary and secondary processes, and though not fully clear about how they served as forms of meaning, he implied, and it has come to pass, that it is the secondary processes that are instantiated as meanings. Witness only that insight—an explicit, symbolized, linguistic form of meaning—was crowned the king of the change processes—whereas primary-process meanings constitute the domain of the unwashed peasant. Emotions were disorganizing, disrupting, disquieting, or even without organization. They were infantile, immature, and had to be grown out of, if one were to come to know the world and oneself.

Other perspectives are not so demeaning of emotions. Emotions have been seen as the intensifiers of meaning or catalysts of meaningful actions, a kind of unidimensional gain-amplifying process, in a manner similar to the way Philip Roth amplifies reality in his novels. Alternatively, they have been conceptualized as adding qualia (value) to experience, in an afterthought kind of way, via an appraisal process comparing the individual's goal to the outcome (Izard, 1977). Emotions are also almost always seen as existing in a small fundamental set in the individual, and though the core set may be elaborated into more complex blends, it does not show qualitative developmental changes (Ekman & Oster, 1979). Further, emotional processes are viewed as separate from cognitive processes, though in some views they are linked to bodily processes.

In these and other conceptualizations, I think we have misconceived, or at least missed, perhaps the most critical features of emotions. For me, *emotions have meaning.* Emotions are elements of meaning, being perhaps even the foremost and principal elements assembled in humans' state of consciousness. And though emotions are elements within the individual (the essentialist or individual psychology perspectives), I believe that they are both internally created in new emergent forms, as well as dyadically cocreated in new emergent forms with both externalized others and internalized objects. Thus, emotions are not fixed elements. They evolve over moments. Old ones change, new ones emerge, nuanced forms abound. They change and develop through emotion-organizing processes, and through the interaction of those process with other processes (e.g., cognitive processes). Further, when emotional meanings are self-created or cocreated in a state of consciousness, their creation has consequences for the formation of relationships, ongoing emotional experience, and the growth of the individual: how the individual thrusts him- or herself into the world (Freeman, 1994).

Infants and Meaning Making

My view of emotions developed out of my work with infants (Tronick, 2007). From Freud onward infants had been viewed as disorganized and/or only responsive to internal processes and/or without intention or contact with reality. Freud shared this view with William James, but notably, not with Charles Darwin or Melanie Klein. This view persisted well into the 1980s and still lingers today, with the related ideas that infants lack language and explicit memorial or cognitive processes. Piaget (1952) saw the infant differently. Though he was not particularly concerned with emotions, he was deeply concerned about meaning and adaptation. He saw the infant as making *sensorimotor* meaning of the world. Things in the world were what the infant could do to them. Objects as different as bottles, breasts, and rattles were the same to the infant because the infant sucked on them. The meaning of these objects was the action that could be performed on them—they were categorized as suckable. The meaning would change as the infant developed new motor capacities, such that rattles and keys were shakable, but not bottles or breasts. Later in development other processes would supersede motor processes and, eventually, in adulthood, there would be language, symbolization, and abstraction. However, given our adult symbolized, abstract, language- and narrative-based view of the world (e.g., this chapter), it takes a special effort for us to think that a thing is not a thing, but *is* the action done to it; the sense of the thing to the infant is, in Bruner's phrase, a literal *act of meaning*.

Emerging from this perspective was the notion that the infant was competent, but the competence was primarily in the perceptual and cognitive domains. As part of this effort, and based on Gibson's (1988) theory of affordances, I carried out a study of infants' reactions to impending collision with a virtual object (Ball & Tronick, 1971). The stimulus was an expanding dark optic array—a looming shadow. Infants as young as 11 weeks reacted to this display by putting their hands in front of their face and turning their head away—a defensive posture. As indicated by these actions, the shadow was something they *experienced* as threatening, and they ducked away from it. Though it may also have been novel or interesting, it had meaning about their relation to the event—it was dangerous to them. In saying this, I do not think that the infants had a sense of their own self or of the object *qua* object, and I am sure that they could not reflect on the event or their reaction. And though we don't truly know the infant's experience, nonetheless, they gave evidence of an organized state of consciousness in which the looming shadow had meaning, and critically this meaning was made without language or symbols. It is hard to move into the experience of an infant, but try thinking of other cryptic examples, such as individuals with apperceptive visual agnosia who move among objects and handle them in the visual world, but do not *see* them. Yet we know by their avoidance of objects and how they handle them that these individuals have a state of consciousness in which the "visual" world has meaning for them, but it is as radically different from the normal adult's state of consciousness as is the infant's state of consciousness. That is, both ways of knowing the world are beyond our ability to put into words.

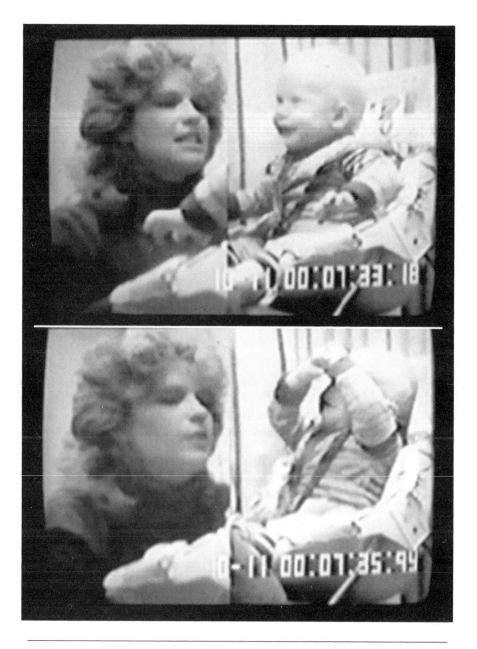

FIGURE 4.1
Infant's reaction to mother's anger indicates a state of consciousness.

In a related example, we have seen an infant react to an angry facial display by his mother as she attempts to get him to let go of her hair (Figure 4.1). The mother's angry facial expression and vocalization lasts less than half a second, but the infant detects them and immediately brings his hands up in front of his face, partially turns away in the chair, and looks at her from under his raised hands. Her angry face, perhaps the first he has ever seen, is not just interesting or novel. He apprehends it as a threat; something dangerous is about to occur and he organizes a defensive reaction to protect himself from what seems about to happen. And the mother almost immediately realizes it too. She changes what she is doing and using cajoling actions tries to overcome the rupture and to change his experience. At first he stays behind his hands but over the next 30–40 seconds begins to smile, and then smile and look at her.

The infant's defensive reaction to the angry face is an obvious state of consciousness, organizing the infant's way of being in the world, as is the change and shift in his state of consciousness as he begins to smile and look at her. However, as with sensorimotor meanings or apperceptive visual agnosia, we have to be cautious about what we think the infant *knows*. In this case, I don't think the infant knows what the danger may be, as might an older child, but the angry face makes him feel threatened by what is happening. He experiences (let's call it) threat, but we do not know what he might know, if anything, about what or where the threat is. Perhaps the infant's experience is analogous to a sense of doom people experience when no doom is obvious; it just is. And when the mother smiles, he smiles back, knowing that his world is again safe, but he does not know what makes for the feeling. It is important to note that the infant reacts as a whole system. Arms, posture, facial expression, gaze, and (we were measuring it) his physiology changed in reaction to the threat, and then continued to change as the disruption was repaired and the threat changed to safety and pleasure. The reactions were not only reactions of mind, body, and brain, but of many processes at multiple levels of meaning making, which were organized into coherent whole system reactions. Further, though we failed to talk to the mother about her reaction to her infant's reaction, we know, based on her actions, that she picked up on what was happening, changed what she was doing, and worked to change her and her infant's states of consciousness. In particular, we do not know if she was aware of the angry face she had made. Indeed, when we first saw the infant ducking, it took several viewing of the tapes for us to become aware of her angry face.

Emotions, much like the infant's sensorimotor actions on things, are one of the polymorphic meaning-making systems for the infant. Moreover, given the precocious sophistication of infants in responding to and expressing emotions, compared to their ability to act skillfully on the world, *emotions may be the foundational form of their sense making* (Tronick, 1980). Perhaps too mechanistically, infants can be thought of as emotion-meaning-making devices. They do not simply differentiate one emotion from another, or respond to the novelty of an emotion. Rather, emotional input has meaning. The meaning is inherent in the emotion processing and does not need to be translated by the infant into some other form. It does not have to be appraised or evaluated by other (e.g., cognitive) processes, though it likely becomes part of those processes. Perhaps an analogy is that the digestive system (emotion-meaning system) takes in nutrients (emotions) and makes them into useful energy and building blocks (meanings), and some things that are not nutritious (lip smack) cannot be digested (lack meaning, are sense*less*). As adults, we try to capture the world with language, which makes it difficult for us to even fathom what it would be like to have states of consciousness that were primarily emotional. Just think of the emotion of joy that is the glorious meaning of a grandchild coming at you with arms widespread, jumping into your arms.

It may help us to appreciate emotions as a form of meaning about our relation to world by considering the ways in which they are similar to, and different from, cognitions. The meaning adults make upon being alone in a dark, shadow-filled, unknown city is fear, anxiety, and creepiness. This meaning exists, side by side, with other forms of meaning conveyed in words and symbols by self, friends, and guides who say that the city is completely safe. Yet often adults remain stuck in the emotional meaning; it determines their sense of the world—danger. Things and people no longer are what we explicitly (cognitively) know them to be; now they are frightening, be they garbage cans or people. In fact, even when a person knows that the thing in the corner is a garbage can, it often still only means—only *is*—terror. The meaning is inherent in the person's scared state of consciousness.

The emotions do not carry meaning about episodic time, about digital yes/no categories, or boundaries, as do cognitions. Though they come in sequences, they do not have a narrative structure and they do not have a grammar. They also motivate the individual to action, whereas cognition can occur without action. Emotions also may motivate acts, though the target remains unspecified. Fear without knowing what is fear provoking can still lead to flight. Rage when one does not know what is provoking the rage is still rage. Paradoxically, it is almost as if emotions have no connection to the external world, though they move us into the world. In these ways, they are like Freud's view of primary process, and they share the timelessness of the unconscious, but they are not primary processes in the way Freud and James spoke of them.

Meaning as a Polysemic, Polymorphic Flow

Emotions are only one of many meaningful elements in a state of consciousness that are part of the hierarchically multileveled organization of individuals' way of being in the world. A state of consciousness is a dynamically changing biopsychological state integrating biological and psychological meaning, purposiveness, and intentions made at every level and site of operation in the organism, from physiology to awareness. As Freeman (2000) puts it, all organismic processes have purposes. The meanings from different sites at different levels emerge over different time spans (milliseconds to minutes or even longer), such that there is a temporally laminated flow of meanings about the same event, and these actualizations of meaning become part of the flow of meaning as it moves forward in time.

Let me give an overly concrete example (Dan Siegel, personal communication, March 2006) of different elements of meaning that I think makes it clear that the elements of meanings are different from one another and are not transmutable into the other. A father is walking through the brush in the desert with his son when he suddenly experiences a feeling of terror and pushes his son away from a bush just before a snake moves across their paths. What is the meaning of this event? Likely, the father detected a movement in his peripheral visual field that led to an automatic defensive reaction, at the level of spinal reflexes and early visual processes, of backing off. He jumps away without any awareness, plan, or intention, though there is a biological purposiveness to the action. There is no identified object, just the reaction. As the meaning-making sequence progresses, the amygdala is activated because of its role in evaluating visual input. The sympathetic nervous system is also activated. Attention gets focused on the environment for other dangerous elements.

These reactions and processes all occur before awareness of the event. But clearly there is a meaning to the event as actualized in the father's behavior, though the event is not yet identified as to what it is, and the meaning in the moment could be incorrect. The son is pulled away simultaneously. With the engagement of this circuitry, meaning takes an emotional form—fear, terror—but the meaning is not yet tied to a named target. Having moved away to a safer position, both father and son experience (outside of awareness) a parasympathetic response beginning to shut down the fear and arousal. Then there is an engagement of cortical cognitive and executive processes that evaluate the situation, detect a target, and further inhibit the fear reaction. Whereas the subcortical processes occur in milliseconds, these cortical processes take seconds or even longer as they unfold. There has been a polysemic cascade.

What I want to focus on is the importance of recognizing that there is not a single meaning, but rather a laminated flow of meanings that emerge over time from multilevel meaning making systems, what Harrison (personal communication, April 2008) calls a polysemic bundle or flow. The automatic reaction may have occurred, but had the target been a bird, the cascade of meanings would have unfolded differently. It seems to flow logically, but it also is the case empirically that the body and brain processes engaged are not equivalent as different meanings unfold. The automatic response engages reflexive spinal and perhaps other visual circuitry, circuitry that is completely different from the circuitry of the autonomic nervous system, or the circuitry of the amygdala fear system, or that of the cortical circuits. And though each form of meaning influences the others, each meaning is qualitatively different from that made by others. Think only of a "father" as having nothing more complex than the amygdala and the spinal jump-back reflex, a father that has only McLean's reptilian brain. The McLeanian father would have experienced one meaning totally reflexive and out of awareness, followed by an emotional meaning of terror. There might not be a target, no cognitive evaluation. We can also only wonder if this reptilian-brained father would have pulled his son out of harm's way.

These different meanings emerge over time and are incorporated into a state of consciousness over time. Thus the meaning made is hardly instantaneous. In this example, the target and location, time and context are certainly not in the reflexive meaning or in amygdalar meaning, but in the hippocampal and cortical meaning, and eventually may be incorporated into a narrative of the event (It was about noon, and we were walking along the path, when . . .”). But keep in mind that although the narrative meaning comes to colonize the experience, it is never equivalent to the flow of the meanings *experienced*. It comes after the experience of the other meanings and is incorporated into the flow of meaning forward in time.

One other point: These laminated events do not constitute a linear sequence of meaning making. Rather, they are part of the operation of the whole brain and body: The steps in the sequence are both the content (products) of the processes and the constituents of the meaning. Whole-brain processes contextualize the meaning. One reason the father is vigilant is because he knows they are in the desert. Had he been in his house, the reaction to a similar noise would have been different. Thus, meaning-making processes that are continuously operating in the background "prime" for certain other meaning-making processes. Another example, the reaction to protect the son, whether learned or innate, is also a priming of the father's meaning-making systems. Simply put, the father's state of consciousness *always* includes his son in his own sense of self and his reactions. It is his way of being. And the meanings made over time constitute the meanings that will continue to be made. Had the target been a bird, or had the father or son tripped, other meanings would have flowed and constituted the ongoing meaning-making process. Thus a state of consciousness integrates individuals' current sense of place in the world with the past sense of self and with the continuous temporal flow of meanings emerging in every moment. And it is always dynamically changing.

Messiness and the Creating of the New

It should be obvious that a critical characteristic of a multileveled temporally laminated flow of meaning making is that the process of regulating and creating meanings is inherently messy. By *messy* I mean that, within the individual, the multileveled processes constituting meaning operate on different time scales: one-tenth of a second for perceptual processes, reflexes, reaction times, brainstem, and parasympathetic responses, but larger time units for the integration of perceptual input and memorial processes, and the operation of mirror neuronal networks, and even full seconds for complex cortical processes. These different time scales make it difficult to coordinate them. Their coordination is further complicated by the continuous feedback effects that each of the actualizations of these systems has on itself and on other systems (e.g., the inhibition of cortical processes upon limbic activation). Also, the systems serve different purposes and sometimes cross-purposes. For instance, the parasympathetic system functions, in complicated ways, to down- or up-regulate the sympathetic system, which functions to down- or up-regulate arousal, and both affect the amygdala as it functions to generate emotional reactions. There is no reason to assume that they will all be fully coordinated.

In recent research on what we call *relational psychophysiology* we have looked at the interplay of the multilevel processes of meaning and meaning making and found a good deal of messiness among different systems (Ham, 2008). For example: Infants' emotional expressions, cardiac reactivity (heart rate, parasympathetic reactivity, Respiratory Sinus Arrhythmia), and sympathetic reactivity (skin conductance) were evaluated during the Face-to-Face Still-Face paradigm (FFSF). In a neat (i.e., not messy) system one might expect reciprocal relations among these different systems: high arousal levels with intense emotional expressions, low parasympathetic reactivity, and high heart rate. Certainly we found some of these relations, but more impressive was the messiness of the relations. As expected, infant angry protest was positively related to cardiac reactivity across the episodes of the still-face situation, and it was negatively related to parasympathetic reactivity, but only in the play episode and unexpectedly not in the still-face. Also, unexpectedly, there was no relation between angry protest and sympathetic reactivity in any of the episodes. Other relations among other behavioral and physiological measures were much the same kind of mix. Adding to the complexity (messiness) of the findings was what appeared to be striking individual differences in the behavioral and physiological relations among the infants. There are likely many reasons for the findings, but they are not of concern here. Only the messiness is of concern because it speaks to the complexity of the interplay among the meaningful elements making up a state of consciousness.

In the study we also wanted to evaluate the relations and coordination of these meaning-making systems between the infant and the mother, so we simultaneously coded maternal emotions and behavior, recording cardiac reactivity, parasympathetic reactivity, and sympathetic reactivity. As was found for the messiness of different meaning-making systems in infants, we found dyadic messiness among the meaning-making systems of the infants and mothers. When infants were protesting during the play episode, maternal parasympathetic reactivity was negatively related to protest, whereas during the reunion episode maternal parasympathetic reactivity was positively related, cardiac reactivity was negatively related, and sympathetic reactivity was positively related. Infant and maternal sympathetic reactivity and cardiac reactivity were unrelated over the still-face and reunion episodes but were positively related during the play episodes. In this case, in a sense, one system, the sympathetic reactivity, is saying "Get more activated and continue what we are doing together," whereas the other system, the parasympathetic, is saying "Slow down, we need to pause." A primary conclusion from these findings is that the different purposive systems of the infants and mothers were related to each other and affecting each other, but the coherence among the systems was at best imperfect: It was messy.

Both the messiness within the infant and mother[1] and in their dyadic relations should be expected for two reasons. First, these systems operate at different levels within individuals and operate on different time scales. Moreover, they have different purposes and contribute different meanings to the infants' and mothers' states of consciousness, respectively. The parasympathetic system is, in part, operating to regulate the activation of the sympathetic system, and both further regulate the emotion-generating activity of the amygdala. Or, to "debrain" this explanation, the purpose of one system is to dampen

---

1. The findings on the mothers need not be reported beyond noting that there was messiness of their meaning-making systems as well (see Ham & Tronick, 2009).

down the intensity of the individual's reactions, whereas another system is trying to increase that activation, and both are interacting with an emotional system that is generating qualitatively different emotional meanings over time. The totality of these different psychobiological purposes contributes to—that is, provides the elements and actualizations of—meaning in the infants' and the mothers' state of consciousness.

The second reason is of a different order of magnitude. Messiness is the wellspring of change and the stuff out of which new meanings emerge. Systems that are fixed, static, and tightly controlled do not change. They remain the same even if they are complicated. For example, spacecrafts have enormously complicated control systems, but they do not develop; nothing new emerges within them. They have a singular purpose; variability is limited, and if variability gets too great, the spacecraft simply fails. By contrast, self- and dyadically organized systems generate new meanings. Self-organized private meaning making, such as self-reflection or mentalization (Fonagy & Target, 1998), may lead to a new insight. So might engaging with another person. Either may generate a new state of consciousness.

Emotions are no exception. Individuals self-organize their emotions into a messy state of consciousness along with other polymorphic elements of meaning. As a consequence, the emotional meaning changes and, at times, new emotions emerge. For example, we don't see the emotion of shame in infants, but it does emerge later in development as emotional, cognitive, and cultural process become integrated into an emerging meaning. It may seem odd to think of emotions as changing, no less that they can be qualitatively different over time, because we tend to think of them as a fixed set of primary and secondary (blended) encapsulated entities that are universally shared (Ekman, 1980; Izard, 1977). In that kind of thinking, to the extent that emotions do change, the change is construed to be under maturational control; once they mature, they do not develop.

But I think emotions change. They become more nuanced and subtler, richer and textured. New ones emerge—guilt, intimate love. They also are changed and modified by other processes, such as bodily processes (pubescence) or cognitive processes (abstract thought). Dyadic processes change emotions and generate new ones, such as *relational emotions* (feeling in synch with another; Fosha, 2001). These dyadic processes may also be messier than self-organized emotional meanings because each individual brings his or her own meanings into a meaning-making exchange, enabling a possible cocreation of new emotional meaning between the two. Indeed, I think it is likely that certain emotions are not only cocreated by two individuals but also exist only in, and are specific to, their relationship (e.g., the bubble of a blip of

warming love that might come with a shared glance that is unique to one relationship).

Thus emotions are cocreated by an interplay of the active self-organized
emotional meanings in the individual and the actualized emotional meanings
of the other interactant as they mutually affect the self-organized emotional
meanings in each other. The mutual interplay is an ongoing, continuing process of exchange that leads to shared meanings states—dyadic states of consciousness—with meaningful and "agreed-upon" elements of emotional
meaning between the interactants. These dyadic meanings are appropriated to
the meanings in each interactant's state of consciousness. The possibility of
cocreating shared meanings—dyadic meanings—dampens the solipsistic view
of private meaning.

Emergent Consequences of States of Consciousness

For some, the creation of dyadic states of consciousness or intersubjective
states—states of shared meanings—is a sort of end state of interactive meaning-making processes (Trevarthen, 1985, 1998; Stern et al., 1998; Stern,
1977). But nothing could be further from the truth. The self-organized creation of new meanings in a state of consciousness, and especially the cocreation of a dyadic state of consciousness, has powerful consequences that
continue to unfold. What are some of them? First there is an objective consequence. When new meaning is created in a state of consciousness, it "objectively" fulfills the first principle of systems theory: A biological system must
gain resources to maintain and expand its complexity and coherence or else it
dissipates. Indeed, when a dyadic state of consciousness is formed, there is an
expansion of the complexity of each individual's state of consciousness as each
incorporates the new meanings in the dyadic state into his or her own state of
consciousness.

Beyond the objective, there are subjective experiential and developmental
consequences. The self- or cocreation of new meanings leads to an *emotional
experience* of expansion, wholeness, and growth, and it is marked by positive
affect. A critical experiential, as well as objective, consequence that comes out
of cocreating a dyadic state of consciousness is to feel connected, that is, to be
in relationship to the other person. In fact, I believe that the creation of new
meanings with another is the process leading to the formation and growth of
relationships. We create something new together and consequentially feel
connected to each other, rather than feeling connected because of some mysterious chemistry.

Meaning Making, Attachment, and Relationship Formation

Privileging the process of meaning making leads to a different take on how attachments are formed. When new meanings are cocreated, they generate a variety of emotions and qualities—intimacy, love, playfulness, excitement. This may sound like I am talking about the quality of attachment, but I am not. Attachment relationships have different qualities, and we have confused ourselves with the overly broad usage of attachment constructs. The different attachment classifications—the A, B, C, or D—are primarily about how individuals deal with safety, feelings of security, and the reduction of fear in the context of relationships. But these are not the only, indeed hardly, feelings and qualities in relationships. Years ago, Hinde (1979) emphasized that relationships have a variety of qualities and intensities, and that there are a whole bunch of ways of being together in relationships. Furthermore, relationships with one person become increasingly differentiated from relationships with other people who have other qualities and ways of being together in a relationship (Tronick, 2003). We simply don't do the same things with everyone; we have different ways of being with people that go beyond four, five, or even ten categorical forms. Relationships between children and their mothers, for example, are likely to be the most differentiated because mothers and children do so many things together and make so many new meanings together. Moreover, this process of differentiation continues throughout childhood and into adulthood, when security is hardly the issue. The relationship typically has a lifelong course, making it unlikely that it is fixed early in development. Furthermore, its differentiation, specificity, and changing qualities make it difficult to see how the mother–infant relationship could serve as a prototype for other relationships; it is too differentiated, too specific. Even were the mother–child relationship the model for other intimate relationship, new meanings and new ways of being together in those relationships would be cocreated and the relationship would become increasingly distinct from its initial starting point.

Importantly, security and other relational qualities noted by Hinde can and must be conceptually and empirically dissociated. To start, intimate relationships may or may not be secure. An abused child or adult may love the abuser but not feel secure with him or her. A child may be attached, feel secure with many people, but love only one of them. In the domain of psychopathology, to think that the infinite forms and variety of neuroses and psychopathology emerge from failure to feel secure in early relationships is foolishly constrictive. Aren't there individuals with personality disorders or depression who were in safe and secure relationships during their childhood? And, following

Hinde, could the quality of "normal" relationships, their enormous variety within and across individuals, be traced back to feelings of security. These and many other anomalies do not allow us to make attachment quality (A, B, C, D) equivalent to relationships.

Put another way, the processes of forming relationship and personality qualities and the processes of security making may overlap and normally do overlap, but they are not the same, and we need to begin to appreciate how they differ. A person can foster security and have a limited relationship, or have a highly differentiated relationship that does not provide a sufficient sense of security. For example, the unique being together of a child and his or her grandparents may not provide sufficient security for the child to stay overnight with them, but doesn't their relationship have a specialness that is not the same as the security or qualities of the relationship the child has with his or her parents? So what is it that grandparents or parents or anyone in a relationship does that leads to differentiated relationships?

Attachment theory emphasizes sensitive caretaking as the process underlying the development of relationships, but for me it does not seem adequate to account for the varieties of normal and abnormal, the uniqueness and the specialness of relationships. Sensitivity is a process of appropriately responding to the child's needs and intentions. A basic need of a child is to feel secure; at its base, sensitivity is a way of being with a child that reduces fears and anxieties. Thus, sensitivity may be adequate for generating the categorical qualities of relationships. But granting the security-enhancing function of sensitivity, it is still not adequate to the task of accounting for the qualities of relationships because it is one-sided and does not fully recognize the self-organized and active role of the infant in the relationship—that is, what *the infant* brings to relationship formation. Importantly, sensitivity is also not sufficiently rich, as conceptualized or studied, to generate anything new or as variegated as the qualities and varying intensities of relationships. Indeed in van Ijzendoorm's (1995) review of sensitive caretaking, as empirically studied, it does not even seem adequate to account for the development of the different categories of attachment: van IJzendoorm's sensitivity gap. Thus I think a more variegated and nuanced process is needed, and I think that the process of meaning making, of creating something together, is possibly that process.

Meanings come in infinite multileveled polysemic forms, all of which are aimed at increasing complexity or coherence. When meaning making is successful, new meanings are cocreated, new ways of being together are created, and these qualities are incorporated into the states of consciousness, the ways of being of the individual. Think of all the times when we talk about a person whom we love that we begin by saying "We used to do *blank* together." The *blanks* are infinite and different for each person and each relationship. And they lead to a variety and subtlety feelings in each individual and between them, and further differentiation of ways of being together.

By contrast, when meaning making fails to increase complexity, it is generally because the meaning-making processes have been saddled with the aim of maintaining current levels of complexity and staving off dissipation. The experiential consequences of not making new meanings within oneself or with others are damaging and invariably accompanied by negative affects (Tronick, 1989, 2003). Failure comes with a feeling of constriction and immobilization. There may even be a feeling of fear because new resources are not being appropriated and the individual's sense of organization becomes threatened. In the extreme, a feeling of annihilation may be experienced. "I don't know what's going on. I'm coming apart!" There can be a failure of the relationship, a constriction and limitation of ways of being together. These feelings lead to meaning-making processes of any sort that will maintain the individual's current level of complexity and coherence. And critically, the meanings made may be desperate and out of touch with reality or the self, yet they are infinite in variety and related to the unique way in which the individual self-organizes. These desperate meanings lead to problematic meaning making in dyadic relationships, particularly with those who are often the source of the senselessness. Such desperation can generate a variety of remarkable personality organizations and psychopathologies. Think of the chronically traumatized child who self-organizes dissociated states and a bizarre sense of self and others to maintain some semblance of coherence; or children of pathological or drug-dependent parents who cannot make sense of their ways of being with their parents, yet *must* make sense in some way in order to keep functioning; or the children of narcissistic parents, who in trying to make sense of how to be with the parent, have to give up their own feelings and intentions or else face a devastating emotional dismissal.

Implications for Therapy

This biopsychological multilevel view of meaning making has many implications for therapeutic processes. For me, therapy is a process of changing individuals' biopsychological state of consciousness, their sense of themselves in relation to the world. To start, one can ask what biopsychological domains does the therapist work in; that is, what level of meaning must be addressed to induce change in a patient's state of consciousness? In the Boston Process of Change Group (BPCG; Stern et al., 1998; Tronick, 1998), we argued that the change process could be found in the "something more," rather than in insight. The "something more" was the domain of the implicit. This argument was somewhat correct and somewhat incorrect for several reasons. Adults and children make meaning explicitly with the use of language. Words, insights, and cognitions in awareness are elements in an individual's state of consciousness. Working on changing a patient's explicit sense of his or her place in the world *can* produce change. Think of the varieties of cognitive therapies and insight-oriented therapies. Meaning-making processes also affect one another, so even if a problematic meaning were located outside the explicit domain of language or narrative (e.g., the memory of a trauma, an emotional state unlinked from an episodic memory), changing the narrative meaning—the explicit—will have "downward" causal effects on other levels of meaning. Of course, the inverse is true as well. Working on levels of meaning such as emotional meaning or bodily meanings can lead to changes in a patient's state of consciousness and have effects on his or her explicit sense of self. This perspective suggests that all levels of meaning affect all other levels of meaning—which is likely the case. But we can also ask if, at times, one or another domain should be privileged for therapeutic focus.

The answer is hardly simple and likely still unknown, but we can perhaps find some guidance in a multileveled biopsychological approach. With any patient, it would seem necessary to evaluate the level of what is problematic in his or her state of consciousness. Is it, as a cognitive therapist might argue, in the patient's automatic thoughts? Or is it, as a relational therapist might propose, a problem in the individual's way of being with others? Or is it an emotional issue? Trauma is often treated with talk therapy, yet van der Kolk (1994; van der Kolk, McFarlane, & Waisaeth, 1994) argues forcefully that the problem is "located" in bodily processes and that talk or relational therapy is not enough to induce change. He goes even further—and I think with some hyperbole—to say that the relationship is not important for trauma-healing bodily change processes.

Thinking of us in the multilevel meaning-making camp suggests that the therapy ought to be specifically (or at least, better) fitted to the level of the problem. Emotional issues may need to be addressed using an emotion-focused experiential therapeutic approach; traumatic issues that distort bodily (e.g., autonomic) functioning may be best changed using body-focused or somatic techniques; and distorted self-narratives that constrict other meaning-making systems may require work in the explicit domain of talk psychotherapy.

Of course, problems do not come in compartmentalized forms because, over time, initial causes affect other levels. Thus, what is most likely is not only that therapeutic work may need to take place in multiple domains, but the domains addressed initially may need to change over the course of the therapy. Initial work may focus on feelings of security and anxiety regulation, whereas later work may focus more on memorial processes and associations. Pat Ogden's approach with trauma patients focuses on bodily processes, though not exclusively, and it seems to me her focus changes as the patient changes (Ogden et al., 2006). The principle may be that, whatever domain is being worked on, the therapeutic input may need to be fitted to that level (Sander, 1977). In particular, it may be that the therapeutic input that fits what the level is "designed" to process is likely to be most effective in inducing change: Emotions may most effectively change emotions, bodily processes change bodily processes. But again, the "fittedness" cannot be exclusive of other inputs.

A related implication of the limitations of one domain of meaning making excluding other domains is that the therapist and patient may need to be in shared states of meaning making to be receptive to meanings made by the other and to cocreate new meanings. Limiting the variety of receptive states to only one or another state may preclude an exchange of meaning and lead to a feeling of not being heard by the patient and confusion for the therapist. For example, working in an explicit insight-oriented approach may be facilitated when the therapist and the patient are in focused cognitive states, whereas working on an emotional issue may be facilitated by the therapist being in a state that allows for emotional resonance. More generally, as suggested by the work of T. Ogden (1994) and Bion (1972), the range of states of the therapist and of the patient and therapist working together may need to be expanded.

There is an implication about a multilevel view of meaning that may be disquieting—it is for me: Not only may there be meanings that are out of awareness, but there may be meanings that are not possible to bring into awareness. Bollas (1987) writes about the *unthought known*, implying that the unknown can eventually be named, and that an emotion or event that is deeply hidden away can be brought into awareness. The second possibility here is more extreme: There may be meanings that are in our state of consciousness and affect our way of being in the world but that *cannot* be known. A meaning-making process such as an emotional process affected by early experiences that *shapes the form* emotions can take, is unknowable. Even if we were to extract an explicit account of how early experience distorts a plastic meaning-making system, the sculpting experience would remain unknowable. For example, early experiences of loss that bias the reactivity of the parasympathetic system, leaving one fearful and hypervigilant, are out of awareness. However, certain meanings being unknowable does not mean that meaning cannot be worked on, but they can be, in multiple ways. Bodily processes can be retuned with body-oriented therapies, and emotional regulation and experiencing can be shifted through emotional and relational experiences, and by the interplay of other forms of meaning.

There are reciprocal or parallel effects for therapists and how we think about therapy. One is the obvious: There are *"unknowables"* for the therapist. These unknowables affect how the therapist interacts with the patient and affect the therapist's countertransference. Therapists may have to do what they do without necessarily understanding why they do it, because the reasons, historical or dynamic or otherwise, for what they do might not be knowable. An implication is that therapeutic work might be going on for reasons that are not knowable, yet this unknowable work could be an essential part of the change process. I find this an especially disquieting idea.

What are the reasons for meaning being unknowable? Our use of language, in part, accounts for the unknowable. Language dominates the therapeutic experience in many ways. Narratives, for example, are post session accounts that cannot possibly capture the flow of a therapeutic session for several reasons. The narrative structure is imposed on the session without recognition that the session *did not have to unfold the way it did*. It could have gone differently. Narratives lose the reality of unpredictablity by trying to maintain a canonical form with a beginning, middle, and end. Moreover, the therapist, in narrating the session, has an investment in presenting the session as having worked, in terms of his or her effectiveness. Another form of colonization by language is the demand for the explicit: It robs emotions, and other forms of meaning, of their richness. One cannot assert that words such as *sadness, anger,* or *joy,* ascribed to a patient, can capture the flow of experience, no less its thickness and resonances. Less recognized as an issue but nevertheless important is the argument that because language is best at capturing the explicit, it privileges the reception of the explicit and loses, or at least downplays, the meanings made in other domains. Although we often say, "Of course, this account of the session is missing so much," we move on quickly and hardly attempt to take the missing meaning into account.

There are also deeper reasons why certain meanings are unknowable that are unrelated to language and the explicit, but to the multilevel process of meaning making. As I argue here, meaning is multileveled, such that much meaning is not exchanged in the explicit: Much of that exchange is already out of awareness, and, to make things worse, some of these meanings are not knowable. Yet, these forms of meaning have powerful effects on the patient's and therapist's states of consciousness and on their cocreation of meaning. The totality of the polymorphic and polysemic flow is part of the change process, because all the forms of meaning are part of the process of meaning making. Thus, we are unavoidably engaged in therapeutic processes, some of which are unknown, but perhaps knowable, and some of which may be unknowable. It seems that at least part of the change process is inherently cryptic because of the limitations of what we, as biopsychological beings, are able to know and bring into awareness.

Many questions and issues emerge if we accept this idea of cryptic processes and multilevel meanings of meaning making. One is, How is it that therapeutic processes, be they emotional, relational, dynamic, cognitive, or whichever, seem to demonstrate that their putative change mechanisms work when they are studied? One current answer is that the quality of the (*therapeutic*) relationship is the agent of change, whatever the particular therapy model. However, that doesn't tell us very much because the qualities of the relationship are not specified and seldom is any alternative evaluated against the relational hypothesis; it is a default explanation. Putting aside the often horrific quality of the research and its self-serving nature, the likelihood is that whatever process is hypothesized as the change process under investigation (e.g., insight, schema change), in the actual session, moment by moment and over sessions, the change process involves, intertwines, and co-occurs with other levels of meaning that do not enter into the theory's explicit self-accounting. A CBT researcher may claim that the change seen in a case is related to getting rid of automatic thoughts, but it is unlikely that that riddance has operated independently of other meaning-making processes, such as emotional exchanges and regulatory processes. The tyranny of theories is such that they leave out of consideration of other possible change processes. One simple way to put this—and we have known this for some time—is to say that the linkages between theories and actual practice are weak, loose, even nonexistent.

Beyond the Moment by Moment

What might be the change process and what does it look like in the moment by moment and over time? In the BPCG, we argued for the importance of looking at the "something more" of therapy, with the "something more" referring to implicit change processes of meaning. I think this idea is very powerful. However, we need to recognize that meaning making is multileveled and far richer than the dichotomy of the implicit and the explicit. Thus, I think we need to see is that the *what* that changes are states of consciousness that are assemblages of multiple levels of meaning and that change processes need to work at the totality of these levels. Fosha's (2000, 2001, 2002; see Chapter 7, this volume) accelerated experential dynamic psychotherapy (AEDP) model and Bion's (1972) work emphasize the need to work at many levels to generate coherence in self- and dyadically organized states of consciousness. But what does such work look like?

In the BPCG we used mother–infant research as a guide and mutual regulation model (Tronick, 2007) and dyadic states of consciousness to organize our thinking about the therapeutic process. We did this in part because infants lack the explicit and because their moment-by-moment exchanges have been carefully studied. However, when we turned to examine analytic therapeutic exchanges, we actually operated in the domain of the explicit. We took case reports and narratives and did text analyses, though we spoke as if we were *in* and *analyzing* the domain of the implicit. Furthermore, even if we had not been only in the domain of the explicit and were doing some work in the implicit (they do overlap some), we certainly were not in the multileveled domains of meaning that are simultaneously present in the analytic exchange, or any other therapeutic interchange, for that matter. The problem of being in the realm of the explicit and using language and narratives permeated much of our work, yet the problem seems to go unrecognized (Boston Process of Change Group, 2002). Thus, we claimed a theoretical evidence linkage, but at most it was an enticing metaphor. One possible way out of this dilemma is to measure other domains of meaning making, such as relational psychophysiology during therapeutic sessions (Ham & Tronick, 2009), and to actually look at what goes on in the moment during different therapies (Safran & Muran, 2003). The experientially oriented theories of Ogden et al. (2006), Fosha (2000), Johnson (2004), and Hughes (2007) use video to track the moment-by-moment process of exchange. This method certainly should prove to be enlightening, though we must be cautious and wonder about how much of the unknown the recording can capture or how much we will be able to actually see.

But there is also something that goes on beyond the moment and becomes a constraint on a way that meaning is made. It is how the past is formed and how it becomes a constraint on the present. Again borrowing from microanalytic analyses of mother–infant interactions, the BPCG focused on the moment by moment as if it were the only time unit of the change process. But there isn't only the present moment, and furthermore, other meanings constrain the present moment. From a dynamic systems theory perspective, there are changes that occur in real time that may be highly unstable, but with reiteration become increasingly stable. They become the constraints that operate on the range of real-time possibilities and on future directions. An analogy is to think of how drops of rain (moment by moment) come to shape a landscape; and with the shaping, the pathways in the landscape (constraints of the past) where the rain can flow become increasingly limited; however, at the same time and over time, these pathways continue to be shaped by the rain (Granic, 2006).

Therapy operates moment by moment, constrained by how the reiterated moments have shaped the landscape of states of consciousness, and by ongoing reciprocal effects of moments and constraints. Constructs such as "representations of interactions that have been generalized" (RIGS; Stern, 1977), model scenes (Lachmann & Beebe, 1999), transference, internal working models (Ainsworth, Blehar, Waters, & Wall, 1978), self–object–emotion configurations (Fosha, 2000), and such, when not seen as fixed or reified but as constraints that operate on the present, are extremely valuable. To emphasize a point, it is important to remember that they also continue to be changed by what is going on in the present (Lachmann & Beebe, 1999; Stern, 1977).

The work of Freeman (1994) provides guidance on how to use these ideas to deal with the relations between the present moment and past constraints. Freeman has shown that the electroencephalography (EEG) activation pattern for an odor in the olfactory cortex of the rabbit is different each time it is experienced. Second, different odors nonetheless produce activation patterns and responses that are differentiated from one another. Third, when a new odor is introduced, the organization of all the individual EEG patterns of the previously experienced odors and the overall olfactory cortical pattern are changed. The specific patterns and the overall patterns operate as constraints, yet they are constantly changing such that there are no fixed patterns or archetypes. Nonetheless, the response to an odor is veridical, that is, the rabbit finds the food or (usually) avoids the predator. Freeman's interpretation is that there is a dynamic array of olfactory activation patterns that reciprocally influence one another. This array of patterns is contextualized in a changing overall gestalt of the olfactory cortical space that allows for the recognition of different odors. Though not part of Freeman's account, an assemblage of activation patterns in response to a set of odors from a particular terrain could be thought as the rabbit's integrated knowledge of its place in the world; that is, as a state of consciousness reflecting the rabbit's meaning making.

I applied Freeman's thinking to relationships and what I called relational activation patterns (RAPS; see Tronick, 2003), and here I would like to apply it to one particular polymorphic form of meaning, namely, the emotions. Applying Freeman's model to emotions is easier than applying it to relationships because Freeman's work is based on the olfactory system, which has many meaningful emotional consequences (Panksepp, 1998a). Emotions, and what might be thought of as emotional activation patterns (EMAPs) in the brain, are activated by a variety of internal and external events. EMAPs are dynamically assembled in a functional emotional meaning-making multiloci and multilevel network (e.g., the autonomic nervous system, limbic system, cortical areas, mirror networks: Schore, 2001, 2003a, 2003b; Freeman, 2000) that creates emotional meanings. As with the assembling of many activation patterns of odors for a particular terrain, an EMAP is not a fixed form but one that changes in relation to other EMAPs, to its own reiteration, and to the overall gestalt of EMAPs in the emotion meaning-making network. That is, as Freeman would see it, in the process of making emotional meaning, much of the brain operates as a whole over time and reciprocally affecting itself.

This conceptualization of EMAPs is both dynamic and specific. Dynamically, each time infants experience a particular event, their EMAPs and their assemblage change in an analogous way to the change in the activation pattern of the reexperienced odor. As a consequence "all" of the infants' emotional meanings are changed. In addition, when an EMAP is reinvoked by an event, the change is not divorced from its past. Rather, it is influenced by the integrated assembling of the meaning of emotions of already existing EMAPs and their gestalt; that is, the raindrops of emotional meaning are influenced (and influence) by the emotional landscape on which they fall. Thus, EMAPs are subject to a host of changes that make each emotional experience dynamically singular (unique, but not fixed and forever static) and capable of influencing other emotional meanings and other levels of meaning in unique ways.

Infant Emotional Dynamics

A final implication of multilevel meaning for the study of emotion is that there are emotional psychodynamics in infants. At a straightforward level, there are multiple emotions and multiple other elements of meaning in states of consciousness that can have conflicting purposes and meanings at one point of time and over time. Angry emotions come in conflict with inhibitory regulatory processes. Furthermore, emotional meanings in the moment may not fit well with the Gestalt of the individual's emotional landscape. A depressed emotional landscape channels the pleasurable meaning of joy into a preworn landscape of withdrawal and sadness or neutral affect. These conflicting meanings make for the messiness of states of consciousness, and their resolution may generate something new, but the conflict may linger. But, again, the landscape is not fixed, and chronic exposure to joyfulness, with reiteration, is likely to shift and change the emotional landscape over time. Or as Main has shown, a "good" relationship can shift the insecurity of past traumatic relationships into a more secure domain (Main, 2000).

A more intriguing possibility is the presence of a dynamic conflict among meanings in infants. To avoid theoretical conflicts here, I would like to think of a dynamic conflict in a most general and typical psychodynamic manner. In the unconscious, there are thoughts or representations that are intolerable that have to be kept out of consciousness. Given that meaning is multileveled, any and all of these levels can contain meanings that clash with meanings at the same or other levels. The dynamic conflict to which I refer would be a conflict among polymorphs of meanings; the polymorphs might be subjected to some of the classical analytic mechanisms for keeping them out of consciousness (e.g., denial), or to powerful experiential mechanisms that are unique to each individual, or to mechanisms we do not yet understand. Consideration of the unknowable meanings and their effects on other forms of meanings makes this hypothesized dynamic conflict among polymorphs of meaning even more complicated and likely more powerful. The infant experiencing an approach–avoidance conflict freezes and cannot move in an organized direction, and experiences terror. One consequence of this hypothesis is the recognition that, even though infants do not have the usual array of explicit and representational processes that are thought to generate dynamic conflicts, they do have meanings that can come into conflict. Think of the love and hate Melanie Klein wrote about or the separation–individuation conflicts identified by Mahler (Mahler, Pine, & Bergman, 1975). One can only wonder what regulatory or "defense" mechanisms infants and young children truly possess for coping with their intolerable conflict.

I would hypothesize that these conflicts are formative and constitutive of psychological issues in infancy and childhood and, perhaps, affect the whole lifespan. How these conflicts are dealt with constitutes one of the fundamental processes that shapes the emotional landscape. Furthermore, I would hypothesize that parents are affected by these dynamic conflicts of their infants, and that infants are able to take on and participate in the dynamic conflicts of their parents. Such reciprocal effects during infancy are likely to have longlasting consequences because they become part of how the infant qua child and parent interact over time, so they are chronically reiterated, deeply cutting the "landscape."

Conclusion

Thinking about meanings and meaning making in a temporal and biopsychological multileveled way is distinctly different from the ways in which we typically think about meaning as symbolized, explicit, and categorical. By do-

ing so, I believe that we overcome some important issues, including the co-
nundrums over mind and body, mind and brain, and brain and body. Seeing
these myriad biopsychological processes that make up the whole individual
(the whole system and all its components) as meaning-making systems provides a unifying conceptualization that makes sense of the individual's place in
the world.

In particular, we can better understand the emotions as a system of meaning, along with cognition and other levels of meaning, without having to make
one or another preeminent. We can also focus on what kinds of meanings
each is able to constitute. At the same time, we do not get caught up by sequentially localized models of meaning making, but are able to work with the
apparently paradoxical interplay of localized functions and the gestalt of contexts. In a multileveled view, local functions are always contextualized by the
whole, and the whole is affected by the local. The same view helps explain the
moment-by-moment experience and the integration of moments into larger
units of meaning that, in turn, affect meaning making in the moment. Lastly,
it opens up a far broader way of understanding therapeutic processes and demands the inclusion of multileveled interventions with a full recognition of
the known and unknown meanings and processes that are at play.

5

Right-Brain Affect Regulation

An Essential Mechanism of Development, Trauma, Dissociation, and Psychotherapy

Allan N. Schore

THERE IS CURRENTLY AN increasing awareness, indeed a palpable sense, that a number of clinical disciplines are undergoing a significant transformation, a paradigm shift. A powerful engine for the increased energy and growth in the mental health field is our ongoing dialogue with neighboring disciplines, especially developmental science, biology, and neuroscience. This mutually enriching interdisciplinary communication is centered on a common interest in the primacy of affect in the human condition. Psychological studies on the critical role of emotional contact between humans are now being integrated with biological studies on the impact of these relational interactions on brain systems that regulate emotional bodily based survival functions.

By definition, a paradigm shift occurs simultaneously across a number of different fields, and it induces an increased dialogue between the clinical and applied sciences. This transdisciplinary shift is articulated by Richard Ryan in a recent editorial of the journal *Motivation and Emotion*:

> After three decades of the dominance of cognitive approaches, motivational and emotional processes have roared back into the limelight. . . . More practically, cognitive interventions that do not address motivation and emotion are increasingly proving to be short-lived in their efficacy, and limited in the problems to which they can be applied. (2007, p. 1)

Echoing this perspective, the neuroscientist Jaak Panksepp now boldly asserts:

The cognitive revolution, like radical neuro-behaviorism, intentionally sought to put emotions out of sight and out of mind. Now cognitive science must re-learn that ancient emotional systems have a power that is quite independent of neocortical cognitive processes. . . . These emotional substrates promote cognitive–object relations, optimally through rich emotional experiences. (2008c, p. 51)

And in the psychotherapy literature Karen Maroda sets forth this challenge:

From my experience there are more therapists who have painfully sat on their emotions, erroneously believing that they were doing the right thing. For these therapists, the prospect of using their emotional responses constructively for the patient is a potentially rewarding and mutually healthy experience . . . perhaps we can explore the therapeutic nature of affect, freeing both our patients and ourselves. (2005, p. 140)

In contrast to the prevailing privileged status of verbal, conscious cognition, I have suggested that emotional communications between therapist and patient lie at the psychobiological core of the therapeutic alliance, and that right-brain to right-brain emotional processes are essential to development, psychopathology, and psychotherapy (Schore, 1994). Indeed, recent clinical research reports that the more therapists facilitate the affective experience/ expression of patients in psychotherapy, the more patients exhibit positive changes; furthermore, therapist affect facilitation is a powerful predictor of treatment success (Diener et al., 2007).

In this chapter, after a brief introduction, I discuss the interpersonal neurobiology of the essential right-brain process of nonconscious affect regulation in development, in psychopathogenesis and trauma dissociation, and finally in the change process of psychotherapy.

Regulation Theory and the Primacy of Affective Structures and Functions

A central theme running throughout all my work is the exploration of the primacy of affective processes in various critical aspects of the human experience. Lane stresses the evolutionary functions of both implicit and explicit affects:

Primary emotional responses have been preserved through phylogenesis because they are adaptive. They provide an immediate assessment of the extent to which goals or needs are being met in interaction with the environment, and they reset the organism behaviorally, physiologically, cognitively, and experientially to adjust to these changing circumstances. (2008, p. 225)

The right brain implicit self represents the biological substrate of the human unconscious mind and is intimately involved in the processing of bodily based affective information associated with various motivational states (Schore, 1994, 2003a, 2003b). The survival functions of the right hemisphere, the locus of the emotional brain, are dominant in relational contexts at all stages of the lifespan, including the intimate context of psychotherapy.

Lichtenberg observes a central focus of the psychotherapeutic encounter:

To appreciate the patient's motivation, we need to . . . discern the emotional experience he or she seeks. At times, the goal sought will be self-evident to patient and [therapist]. At other times, the goal will lie *out of awareness* and will be difficult to ascertain. . . . The golden thread in assessing motivation lies in discovering the affect being sought in conjunction with the behavior being investigated. (2001, p. 440, emphasis added)

Relevant to the renewed interest in emotion in models of the change process in both development and psychotherapy, there is now a growing body of evidence which indicating that "in most people, the verbal, conscious and serial information processing takes place in the left hemisphere, while the unconscious, nonverbal and emotional information processing mainly takes place in the right hemisphere" (Larsen et al., 2003, p. 534). The right hemisphere is dominant for the recognition of emotions, the expression of spontaneous and intense emotions, and the nonverbal communication of emotions (see Schore, 2003a, 2003b for references). The central role of this hemisphere in survival functions is outlined by Schutz:

The right hemisphere operates a distributed network for rapid responding to danger and other urgent problems. It preferentially processes environmental challenge, stress and pain and manages self-protective responses such as avoidance and escape. . . . Emotionality is thus the right brain's "red phone," compelling the mind to handle urgent matters without delay. (2005, p. 15)

Furthermore, an important ongoing trend in interdisciplinary studies is a focus on not just emotion but *unconscious, implicit* emotion. At the beginning of the last century Freud speculated, "Unconscious ideas continue to exist after repression as actual structures in the system *Ucs*, whereas all that corresponds in that system to unconscious affects is a potential beginning which is prevented from developing" (1915/1957, p. 178). In my own work on unconscious affect, I have suggested that bodily based affects are the center of empathic communication, and that the regulation of *conscious and unconscious feelings* is placed in the center of the clinical stage (Schore, 1994, emphasis added). Maroda (2005) challenges therapists to ponder an essential clinical problem: "How do you relate empathically to an unexpressed emotion?" (p. 136). I argue here that unconscious affects can best be understood not as repressed but as dissociated affects. Later-forming repression is associated with left-hemispheric inhibition of affects generated by the right brain, whereas early-forming dissociation reflects a dysregulation of affects resulting from the dis-integration of the right brain itself.

Although this topic has been controversial, neuroscience now demonstrates a right hemispheric dominance in processing of *unconscious negative emotion* (Sato & Aoki, 2006). Other studies document a cortical response to *subjectively unconscious danger* (Carretie, 2005). For example, basic research on the neurobiology of survival mechanisms clearly shows that the emotion of fear "is not necessarily conscious; a fearful response may be evoked even when one is not fully aware of being 'afraid.' . . . As with emotion itself, the enhanced memory for emotional experiences may proceed at a relatively subconscious level, without clear awareness" (Price, 2005, p. 135).

Neurobiological studies also demonstrate that the right cortical hemisphere is centrally involved in "the processing of self-images, at least when self-images are not consciously perceived" (Theoret et al., 2004, p. 57). Deep psychotherapeutic changes alter not only conscious but unconscious self-image associated with nonconscious internal working models of attachment. Both unconscious negative emotions and unconscious self-images are important elements of the psychotherapy process, especially with the more severe self pathologies.

Thus, the essential roles of the right brain in the unconscious processing of emotional stimuli and in emotional communication are directly relevant to recent clinical models of an affective unconscious and a relational unconscious, whereby one unconscious mind communicates with another unconscious mind (Schore, 2003a). In a number of writings I have described in some detail the fundamental role of right-brain to right-brain communications across an intersubjective field embedded within the therapeutic alliance (Schore, 1994, 2002a, 2005b, 2007). This dialogue of ultrarapid bodily based affective communications in patient–therapist (and infant–mother) attachment transactions occurs beneath levels of conscious awareness in both members of the dyad.

Another area of common intense interdisciplinary interest is the self-regulation of emotion. Affect regulation is usually defined as the set of control processes by which we influence, consciously and voluntarily, our emotions, and how we experience and behaviorally express them. However, "Most of moment to moment psychological life occurs through nonconscious means. . . . Various nonconscious mental systems perform the lion's share of the self-regulating burden, beneficently keeping the individual grounded in his or her environment" (Bargh & Chartrand, 1999, p. 462). Greenberg now asserts, "The field has yet to pay adequate attention to implicit and relational processes of regulation" (2008, p. 414). Applying this principle to psychotherapy, Ryan notes, "Both researchers and practitioners have come to appreciate the limits of exclusively cognitive approaches for understanding the initiation and regulation of human behavior" (2007, p. 1).

Indeed, a large body of data suggests that unconscious affect regulation is more essential than conscious emotion regulation in human survival functions (Schore, 1994, 2003a, 2003b, 2007). There is agreement among both scientists and clinicians that this essential adaptive capacity evolves in early attachment experiences:

> The developmental achievement of a sense of self that is simultaneously fluid and robust depends on how well the capacity for affect regulation and affective competency has been achieved. . . . When these early patterns of interpersonal interaction are relatively successful, they create a stable foundation for relational affect regulation that is internalized as nonverbal and unconscious. Thus, further successful negotiation of interpersonal transactions at increasingly higher levels of self-development and interpersonal maturity is made possible. (Bromberg, 2006, p. 32)

Right-Brain Processes in Development: The Interpersonal Neurobiology of Secure Attachment

As summarized in a recent contribution on modern attachment theory (Schore & Schore, 2008), the essential task of the first year of human life is the creation of a secure attachment bond between the infant and his or her primary caregiver. Secure attachment depends upon the mother's sensitive psychobiological attunement to the infant's dynamically shifting internal states of arousal. Through visual–facial, auditory–prosodic, and tactile–gestural communication, caregiver and infant learn the rhythmic structure of the other and modify their behavior to fit that structure, thereby cocreating a specifically fitted interaction. Developmental researchers now describe this nonverbal intersubjective communication in a way that is congruent with the models of nonconscious communication discussed above.

> Preverbal communication . . . is the realm of non-consciously regulated intuitive behavior and implicit relational knowledge. Whether information is transferred or shared, which information gets across, and on which level it is "understood," does not necessarily depend on the sender's intention or conscious awareness. (Papoušek, 2007, p. 258)

During these bodily based affective communications the attuned mother synchronizes the spatiotemporal patterning of her exogenous sensory stimulation with the infant's spontaneous expressions of his or her endogenous organismic rhythms. Via this contingent responsivity, the mother appraises the nonverbal expressions of the infant's internal arousal and affective states, regulates them, and communicates them back to the infant. To accomplish this regulation, the mother must successfully modulate nonoptimal high *or* nonoptimal low levels of stimulation that would induce supraheightened or extremely low levels of arousal in the infant.

In play episodes of affective synchrony, the pair experience a condition of resonance, and in such, an amplification of vitality affects and a positive state occurs. In moments of interactive repair, the "good-enough" caregiver who has misattuned can regulate the infant's negative state by accurately reattuning in a timely manner. The regulatory processes of affective synchrony that create states of positive arousal and of interactive repair that modulates negative arousal are the fundamental building blocks of attachment and its associated emotions. Resilience in the face of stress and novelty is an ultimate indicator of attachment security (Schore, 2005a).

These adaptive capacities are central to the dual processes of self-regulation: *interactive regulation*—the ability to flexibly regulate psychobiological states of emotions with other humans in interconnected contexts; and *autoregulation*—which occurs apart from other humans in autonomous contexts. According to Pipp and Harmon, "It may be that . . . we are biologically connected to those with whom we have close relationships. . . . Homeostatic regulation between members of a dyad is a stable aspect of all intimate relationships throughout the lifespan" (1987, p. 651). The evolutionary mechanism of attachment—the interactive regulation of emotion—thus represents the regulation of biological synchronicity *between* and *within* organisms (Bradshaw & Schore, 2007).

In line with earlier proposals that emotional attachment experiences during early critical periods of development facilitate the experience-dependent maturation of emotion regulatory brain circuits (Schore, 1994), neuroscientists now assert:

> The mother functions as a regulator of the socio-emotional environment during early stages of postnatal development. . . . subtle emotional regulatory interactions, which obviously can transiently or permanently alter brain activity levels . . . may play a critical role during the establishment and maintenance of limbic system circuits. (Ziabreva et al., 2003, p. 5,334)

It is well established that the human central nervous system (CNS) limbic system extensively myelinates in the first year and a half and that the early-maturing right hemisphere—which is deeply connected into the limbic system—undergoes a growth spurt at this time (Gupta et al., 2005; Howard & Reggia, 2007; Moskal et al., 2006; Schore, 2003a; Sun et al., 2005).

The right hemisphere also has tight connections with the involuntary autonomic nervous system (ANS) that controls visceral organs, effectors in the skin, and the cardiovascular system, and is responsible for the generation of vitality affects. Via a right lateralized vagal circuit of emotion regulation, "the right hemisphere—including the right cortical and subcortical structures—would promote the efficient regulation of autonomic function via the source nuclei of the brain stem" (Porges, Doussard-Roosevelt, & Maiti, 1994, p. 175). Affect-regulating attachment experiences specifically impact cortical and limbic–autonomic circuits of the developing right cerebral hemisphere (Cozolino, 2002; Henry, 1993; Schore, 1994, 2005a; Siegel, 1999). For the rest of the lifespan, internal working models of the attachment relationship with the primary caregiver, stored in the right brain, encode strategies of affect regulation that nonconsciously guide the individual through interpersonal contexts.

Earlier speculations (Schore, 1994) are now supported by current studies which observe that right lateralized limbic areas responsible for the regulation of autonomic functions and higher cognitive processes are involved in the "formation of social bonds" and are "part of the circuitry supporting human social networks," and that the "the strong and consistent predominance for the right hemisphere emerges postnatally" (Allman et al., 2005, p. 367). In very recent work on mother–infant emotional communication Lenzi et al. (in press) offer data from a functional magnetic resonance imaging (MRI) study "supporting the theory that the right hemisphere is more involved than the left hemisphere in emotional processing and thus, mothering." Also confirming this model Minagawa-Kawai et al. (2009, p. 289) report a near-infrared spectroscopy study of infant–mother attachment at 12 months and conclude, "our results are in agreement with that of Schore (2000) who addressed the importance of the right hemisphere in the attachment system." Summarizing this data, Rotenberg asserts:

> The main functions of the right hemisphere . . . the ability to grasp the reality as a whole; the emotional attachment to the mother (Schore, 2003a); the regulation of withdrawal behavior in the appropriate conditions (Davidson et al., 1990); the integration of affect, behavior and autonomic activity (Schore, 2003a) are the basic functions of survival (Saugstad, 1998) and for this reason are the first to appear. (2004, p. 864)

The Interpersonal Neurobiology of Attachment Trauma

During the brain growth spurt (last trimester of pregnancy through second year), relational trauma-induced arousal dysregulation precludes the forementioned visual–facial, auditory–prosodic, and tactile–gestural attachment communications and alters the development of essential right brain functions. In contrast to an optimal attachment scenario, in a relational growth-inhibiting early environment, the primary caregiver induces traumatic states of enduring negative affect in the child. This caregiver is inaccessible and reacts to the infant's expressions of emotions and stress inappropriately and/or rejectingly, and therefore shows minimal or unpredictable participation in the various types of arousal-regulating processes. Instead of modulating stimulation, the caregiver induces extreme levels of arousal, very high in abuse and/or very low in neglect. And because the caregiver provides no interactive repair, the infant's intense negative affective states last for long periods of time. These deficits in maternal function outwardly reflect the mother's own internal stressful states of dysregulated arousal.

Psychophysiological studies of human maternal behavior directed toward infants clearly indicate that

> stress is an important factor that may affect social interactions, especially the mother–child interaction. Mothers during stressful life episodes were less sensitive, more irritable, critical and punitive. . . . Moreover, stressed mothers showed less warmth and flexibility in interactions with their children. . . . Overall, stress seems to be a factor that has the power to disrupt parenting practices seriously and results in a lower quality of the mother–child interaction. (Suter et al., 2007, p. 46)

These authors demonstrate that stress impacts the female's autonomic nervous system and specifically disrupts her right hemisphere.

On the other side of the mother–infant dyad, interdisciplinary evidence indicates that the infant's psychobiological reaction to traumatic stress is comprised of two separate response patterns: *hyperarousal* and *dissociation*. In the initial hyperarousal stage, the maternal haven of safety suddenly becomes a source of threat, triggering an alarm or startle reaction in the infant's right hemisphere, the locus of both the attachment system and the fear motivational system. This maternal stressor activates the infant's hypothalamic–pituitary–adrenal (HPA) stress axis, thereby eliciting a sudden increase of the energy-expending sympathetic component of the infant's ANS, resulting in significantly elevated heart rate, blood pressure, and respiration—the somatic expressions of a dysregulated hypermetabolic psychobiological state of fear/ terror.

A second, later-forming reaction to relational trauma is dissociation, in which the child disengages from stimuli in the external world—traumatized infants are observed to be staring off into space with a glazed look. This parasympathetic dominant state of conservation/withdrawal occurs in helpless and hopeless stressful situations in which the individual becomes inhibited and strives to avoid attention in order to become "unseen" (Schore, 1994, 2001). The dissociative metabolic shutdown state is a primary regulatory process, used throughout the lifespan, in which the stressed individual passively disengages in order to conserve energies, foster survival by the risky posture of feigning death, and allow restitution of depleted resources by immobility. In this passive hypometabolic state heart rate, blood pressure, and respiration are decreased, whereas pain-numbing and blunting endogenous opiates are elevated. It is this energy-conserving parasympathetic (vagal) mechanism that mediates the profound detachment of dissociation.

In fact, there are two parasympathetic vagal systems in the brainstem medulla. The ventral vagal complex rapidly regulates cardiac output to foster fluid engagement and disengagement with the social environment, and it exhibits rapid and transitory patterns associated with perceptive pain and unpleasantness—all aspects of a secure attachment bond of emotional communication. On the other hand, activity of the dorsal vagal complex is associated with intense emotional states and immobilization, and is responsible for the severe hypoarousal and pain blunting of dissociation (see Figure 5.1). The traumatized infant's sudden state switch from sympathetic hyperarousal into parasympathetic dissociation is described by Porges as "the sudden and rapid transition from an unsuccessful strategy of struggling requiring massive sympathetic activation to the metabolically conservative immobilized state mimicking death associated with the dorsal vagal complex" (1997, p. 75).

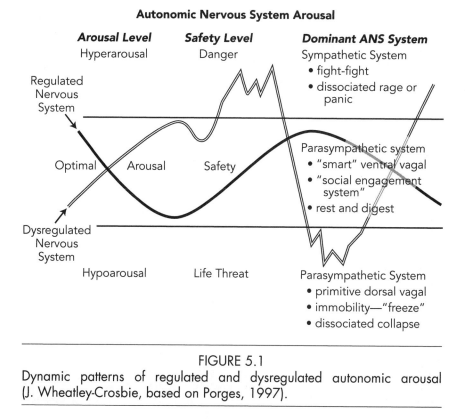

Autonomic Nervous System Arousal

Arousal Level	**Safety Level**	**Dominant ANS System**
Hyperarousal	Danger	Sympathetic System

FIGURE 5.1

Dynamic patterns of regulated and dysregulated autonomic arousal (J. Wheatley-Crosbie, based on Porges, 1997).

Porges (1997) describes the involuntary and often prolonged characteristic pattern of vagal outflow from the dorsal vagal nucleus. This long-lasting state of dorsal vagal parasympathetic activation accounts for the extensive duration of "void" states associated with pathological dissociative detachment (Allen, Console, & Lewis, 1999), and for what Bromberg (2006) calls dissociative "gaps" in subjective reality—"spaces" that surround self states and thereby disrupt coherence among highly affectively charged states. These gaps are also discussed in the developmental psychoanalytic literature. Winnicott (1958) notes that a particular failure of the maternal holding environment causes a discontinuity in the baby's need for "going-on-being," and Kestenberg (1985) refers to as "dead spots" in the infant's subjective experience, an operational definition of the restriction of consciousness of dissociation. At all points of the lifespan, dissociation is conceptualized as "a basic part of the psychobiology of the human trauma response: a protective activation of altered states of consciousness in reaction to overwhelming psychological trauma" (Loewenstein, 1996, p. 312).

Dissociation in infants has been studied with the still-face procedure, an experimental paradigm of traumatic neglect. In the still face, the infant is exposed to a severe relational stressor: The mother maintains eye contact with the infant, but she suddenly totally inhibits all vocalization and suspends all emotionally-expressive facial expressions and gestures. This intense relational stressor triggers an initial increase of interactive behavior and arousal in the infant. According to Tronick (2004), the infant's confusion and fearfulness at the break in connection is accompanied by the subjective response, "this is threatening." This stress response is then followed by bodily collapse, loss of postural control, withdrawal, gaze aversion, sad facial expression, and self-comforting behavior.

Most interestingly, this behavior is accompanied by a dissipation of the infant's state of consciousness and a diminishment of self-organizing abilities that reflect disorganization of many of the lower level psychobiological states, such as metabolic systems. Tronick (2004) suggests that infants who have a history of chronic breaks of connections exhibit an "extremely pathological state" of emotional apathy. He equates this state with Spitz's cases of hospitalism, Harlow's isolated monkeys, Bowlby's withdrawn children, and Romanian orphans who fail to grow and develop. Such infants ultimately adopt a communication style of "stay away, don't connect." This defensive stance is a very-early-forming, yet already chronic, pathological dissociation that is associated with loss of ventral vagal activation and dominance of dorsal vagal parasympathetic states.

In parallel to still-face studies, ongoing attachment research underscores a link between frightening maternal behavior, dissociation, and disorganized infant attachment (Schuengel, Bakersmans-Kranenburg, & van IJzendoorn, 1999). Hesse and Main (1999) point out that the disorganization and disorientation of type "D" attachment associated with abuse and neglect phenotypically resembles dissociative states. In recent work, Hesse and Main observe that when the mother enters a dissociative state, a fear alarm state is triggered in the infant. The caregiver's entrance into the dissociative state is expressed as "parent suddenly completely 'freezes' with eyes unmoving, half-lidded, despite nearby movement; parent addresses infant in an 'altered' tone with simultaneous voicing and devoicing" (2006, p. 320). In describing the mother as she submits to the freeze state, they note:

> Here the parent appears to have become completely unresponsive to, or even aware of, the external surround, including the physical and verbal be-

havior of their infant. . . . We observed one mother who remained seated in an immobilized and uncomfortable position with her hand in the air, blankly staring into space for 50 sec. (p. 321)

In an electroencephalograph (EEG) study of 5-month-old infants looking at a "blank face," Bazhenova, Stroganova, Doussard-Roosevelt et al. (2007) report increases in vagal activity "over the right posterior temporal scalp area and over anterior scalp areas. . . . This observation suggests greater right hemisphere involvement in face processing during blank face" (p. 73).

During these episodes of the intergenerational transmission of attachment trauma the infant is matching the rhythmic structures of the mother's dysregulated arousal states. This synchronization is registered in the firing patterns of the stress-sensitive corticolimbic regions of the right brain, dominant for survival and the human stress response (Schore, 1994; Wittling, 1995). Adamec, Blundell, and Burton (2003) report findings that "implicate neuroplasticity in right hemispheric limbic circuitry in mediating long-lasting changes in negative affect following brief but severe stress" (p. 1,264). Gadea et al. conclude that an intense experience "might interfere with right hemisphere processing, with eventual damage if some critical point is reached" (2005, p. 136). Recall that right cortical areas and their connections with right subcortical structures are in a critical period of growth during the early stages of human development. The massive ongoing psychobiological stress associated with dysregulated attachment trauma sets the stage for the characterological use of right-brain unconscious pathological dissociation over all subsequent periods of human development.

Right-Brain Processes in Psychopathogenesis: The Neurobiology of Pathological Dissociation

In the neuropsychoanalytic literature Watt contends: "If children grow up with dominant experiences of separation, distress, fear and rage, then they will go down a bad pathogenic developmental pathway, and it's not just a bad psychological pathway but a bad neurological pathway" (2003, p. 109). Neurobiological research on patients with a history of relational trauma also demonstrates continuity over the course of the lifespan in the expression of this primitive autoregulation defense. It is commonly accepted that early childhood abuse specifically alters limbic system maturation, producing neurobiological alterations that act as a biological substrate for a variety of psychiatric consequences, including affective instability, inefficient stress tolerance, memory impairment, psychosomatic disorders, and dissociative disturbances (Schore, 2001, 2002b).

In a transcranial magnetic stimulation study of adults Spitzer et al. report: "In dissociation-prone individuals, a trauma that is perceived and processed by the right hemisphere will lead to a 'disruption in the usually integrated functions of consciousness'" (2004, p. 168). And in fMRI research Lanius et al. (2005) show predominantly right-hemispheric activation in posttraumatic stress disorder (PTSD) patients while they are dissociating.

These and other studies are presently exploring the evolution of a developmentally impaired regulatory system over all stages of life. They provide evidence that orbitofrontal (ventromedial) cortical and limbic areas (anterior cingulate, insula, periacqueductal gray, amygdala) of particularly the right hemisphere are centrally involved in the deficits in mind and body associated with a pathological dissociative response (Schore, 2003a, 2003b, in press). This hemisphere, more so than the left, is densely interconnected reciprocally with emotion-processing limbic regions, as well as with subcortical areas that generate both the arousal and autonomic (sympathetic and parasympathetic) bodily based aspect of emotions (see Figure 5.2). Sympathetic nervous system activity is manifest in tight engagement with the external environment and high levels of energy mobilization and utilization, whereas the parasympathetic component drives disengagement from the external environment and utilizes low levels of internal energy (Recordati, 2003). These components of the ANS are uncoupled in traumatic states of pathological dissociation.

In line with the current shift from "cold cognition" to the primacy of bodily based "hot affects," clinical research on dissociation is focusing on "somatoform dissociation," an outcome of early-onset traumatization, expressed as a lack of integration of sensorimotor experiences, reactions, and functions of the individual and his or her self-representation (Nijenhuis, 2000). Thus, "dissociatively detached individuals are not only detached from the environment, but also from the self—their body, their own actions, and their sense of identity" (Allen et al., 1999, p. 165). This observation describes impaired functions of the right hemisphere, the locus of the "emotional" or "corporeal self." Crucian et al. describes "a dissociation between the emotional evaluation of an event and the physiological reaction to that event, with the process being dependent on intact right hemisphere function" (2000, p. 643).

I have offered interdisciplinary evidence indicating that the implicit self, the human unconscious mind, is located in the right brain (Schore, 1994, 2003b, 2005b). The lower subcortical levels of the right brain (the deep unconscious) contain all the major motivational systems (including attachment,

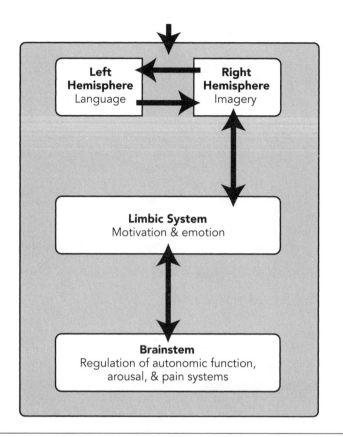

FIGURE 5.2

Vertical axis of right-brain cortical–subcortical limbic–autonomic circuits and subsequent connections into the left brain. Adapted from Kirmayer (2004).

fear, sexuality, aggression, disgust, etc.) and generate the somatic autonomic expressions and arousal intensities of all emotional states. When optimally functioning, higher orbito-frontal limbic levels of the right hemisphere generate a conscious emotional state that expresses the affective output of these motivational systems (Schore, 1994). This right lateralized hierarchical prefrontal system performs an essential adaptive motivational function: the relatively fluid switching of internal bodily based states in response to changes in the external environment that are nonconsciously appraised to be personally meaningful (Schore, 1994).

On the other hand, pathological dissociation, an enduring outcome of early relational trauma, is manifest in a maladaptive, highly defensive, rigid and closed system, one that responds to even low levels of intersubjective stress with parasympathetic dorsal vagal hypoarousal and heart rate deceleration. This fragile unconscious system is susceptible to mind–body metabolic collapse and thereby a loss of energy-dependent synaptic connectivity within the right brain, expressed in a sudden implosion of the implicit self and a rupture of self-continuity. This dis-integration of the right brain and collapse of the implicit self is signaled by the amplification of the parasympathetic affects of shame and disgust, and by the cognitions of hopelessness and helplessness. Because the right hemisphere mediates the communication and regulation of emotional states, the rupture of intersubjectivity is accompanied by an instant dissipation of safety and trust.

Dissociation thus reflects the inability of the vertical axis of the right brain cortical–subcortical implicit self system (see right side of Figure 5.2) to recognize and process external stimuli (exteroceptive information coming from the relational environment) and on a moment-to-moment basis integrate them with internal stimuli (interoceptive information from the body, somatic markers, the "felt experience"). This failure of integration of the higher right hemisphere with the lower right brain induces an instant collapse of both subjectivity and intersubjectivity. Stressful and painful emotional states associated with intensely high or low levels of arousal are not experienced in consciousness, but remain in implicit memory as dysregulated dissociated unconscious affects (Schore, in press).

This developmental model of relational trauma describes the psychoneurobiological mechanisms that underlie Janet's conceptualization of dissociation. As described by van der Kolk et al.:

> Janet proposed that when people experience *"vehement emotions,"* their minds may become incapable of matching their *frightening experiences* with existing cognitive schemes. As a result the memories of the experience cannot be integrated into personal awareness; instead, they are split off [dissociated] from consciousness and voluntary control. . . . extreme *emotional arousal* results in failure to *integrate* traumatic memories. . . . The memory traces of the trauma linger as unconscious "fixed ideas" that cannot be "liquidated." . . . They continue to intrude as terrifying perceptions, obsessional preoccupations, and *somatic reexperiences*. (1996, p. 52, emphasis added)

There is now agreement that "traumatic stress in childhood could lead to self-modulation of painful affect by directing attention away from internal emotional states" (Lane et al., 1997, p. 840). Given that the right hemisphere is dominant not only for regulating affects but also for attention (Raz, 2004), negative affect (Davidson & Cacioppo, 1992), and pain processing (Symonds et al., 2006), the right-brain strategy of dissociation represents the ultimate defense for blocking conscious awareness of emotional pain. If early trauma is experienced as "psychic catastrophe," the autoregulatory strategy of dissociation is expressed as "detachment from an unbearable situation," "a submission and resignation to the inevitability of overwhelming, even psychically deadening danger," and "a last resort defensive strategy" (Schore, in press).

Right Brain Processes in Psychotherapy: Unconscious Affect, Transference, and Primary Process

At the beginning of this chapter I suggested that the regulation of not only conscious but also unconscious affects is an essential mechanism of the psychotherapeutic change process. All forms of therapy currently view affect dysregulation as a fundamental condition of every psychiatric disorder (Taylor et al., 1997), including personality disorders (Sarkar & Adshead, 2006), and therefore share a common goal of improving the effectiveness of emotional self-regulatory processes (Beauregard, Levesque, & Bourgouin, 2001). In terms of regulation theory defense mechanisms are forms of emotional regulation strategies for avoiding, minimizing, or converting affects that are too difficult to tolerate. Treatment, especially of early-forming severe psychopathologies, must attend not only to conscious dysregulated affects but also to the early-forming survival defense that protects patients from consciously experiencing overwhelming painful negative affects—dissociation. This bottom-line defense thus represents the major counterforce to the emotional–motivational aspects of the change process in psychotherapy (Schore, 2007). This clinical principle is supported by research demonstrating that insecurely attached dissociative patients dissociate as a response to negative emotions arising in psychodynamic psychotherapy, leading to a less favorable treatment outcome (Spitzer et al., 2007).

Basic research suggests that "while the left hemisphere mediates most linguistic behaviors, the right hemisphere is important for broader aspects of communication" (van Lancker & Cummings, 1999, p. 95). Incorporating these data into the regulation theory model of the psychotherapeutic process, I have delineated the central role of implicit right-brain to right-brain nonverbal communications (facial expression, prosody, gesture) in unconscious transference–countertransference affective transactions—an essential treatment element of severe psychopathologies and a common mechanism of all forms of psychotherapy. Interdisciplinary data and updated clinical models lead me to conclude that the right hemisphere is dominant in treatment, and that psychotherapy is not the "talking cure" but the affect communicating and regulating cure (Schore, 2005b).

Clinical workers now describe transference as "an established pattern of relating and emotional responding that is cued by something in the present, but oftentimes calls up both an affective state and thoughts that may have more to do with past experience than present ones" (Maroda, 2005, p. 134). In a parallel formulation, neuroscience now documents that the right hemisphere is fundamentally involved in the unconscious processing of emotional stimuli (Mlot, 1998), and that

> the right hemisphere holds representations of the emotional states associated with events experienced by the individual. When that individual encounters a familiar scenario, representations of past emotional experiences are retrieved by the right hemisphere and are incorporated into the reasoning process. (Shuren & Grafman, 2002, p. 918)

Furthermore, "the right hemisphere operates in a more free-associative, primary process manner, typically observed in states such as dreaming or reverie" (Grabner, Fink, & Neubauer, 2007, p. 228). In line with current developmental and relational models I have argued that right-brain to right-brain communications represent interactions of the patient's unconscious primary-process system and the therapist's primary-process system (Schore, 1994), and that primary process cognition is the major communicative mechanism of the relational unconscious.

Enactments, Autonomic Arousal Dysregulation, and Dissociation

Primary process right-brain to right-brain nonverbal communications especially predominate in the stressful transference-countertransference contexts of clinical enactments. In a major contribution integrating clinical models and neurobiological data, Ginot (2007, p. 317) convincingly argues: "Increasingly, enactments are understood as powerful manifestations of the intersubjective process and as inevitable expressions of complex, though largely *unconscious self-states and relational patterns*" (emphasis added).

In line with earlier neuropsychoanalytic speculations (Schore, 1997) and in support of the central thesis of this chapter, Ginot observes:

> This focus on enactments as communicators of affective building blocks also reflects a growing realization that explicit content, verbal interpreta-

tions, and the mere act of uncovering memories are insufficient venues for curative shifts. . . . As intense manifestations of transference–countertransference entanglements, enactments seem to generate interpersonal as well as internal processes eventually capable of promoting integration and growth. (2007, p. 317–318)

She concludes that these "unconscious affective interactions" "bring to life and consequently alter implicit memories and attachment styles" (p. 318). Recall the hypothesis of Stern et al. (1998) that "implicit relational knowledge" stored in a nonverbal domain is at the core of therapeutic change.

In previous neuropsychoanalytic work, I offered interdisciplinary evidence deomonstrating that the right hemisphere is the locus of implicit memory (Schore, 1999). In discussing the right hemisphere as "the seat of implicit memory," Mancia notes: "The discovery of the implicit memory has extended the concept of the unconscious and supports the hypothesis that this is where the emotional and affective—sometimes traumatic—presymbolic and preverbal experiences of the primary mother–infant relations are stored" (2006, p. 83). Implicit memories of dysregulating ultra-high arousal experiences are stored and expressed in sympathetic dominant rapid extreme increases of autonomic arousal associated with heart rate acceleration. Conversely, implicit memories of dysregulating ultra-low arousal experiences are stored and expressed in dorsal vagal parasympathetic dominant rapid extreme decreases of arousal associated with rapid heart rate deceleration. The principle of the state-dependent recall of implicit memories thus applies to each of these two domains: Achieving a particular bodily state is necessary to access certain affects, behaviors, and cognitions.

It is often overlooked that affects reflect an individual's internal state and have an *hedonic (valenced)* dimension and *an arousal (intensity-energetic) dimension* (Schore, 1994). A body of studies now demonstrates that the right hemisphere is generally more important than the left in activating arousal systems (Heilman, 1997; Meadows & Kaplan, 1994), yet more capable of operating at reduced arousal levels (Casagrande et al., 2007). The right brain is superior in processing emotional arousal and in the automatic response to emotional stimuli (Gainotti et al., 1993), and it is dominantly affected by feedback of bodily stress-induced arousal (Critchley et al., 2004). As opposed to left-brain "anxious apprehension," expressed in cognitive anxiety, worry, verbal rumination, and muscle tension, right-brain "anxious arousal" is associated with panic states and somatic symptoms, including shortness of breath, pounding heart, dizziness, sweating, and feelings of choking. In this latter state the right side of the brain continuously monitors the external environment for threat and "exerts hierarchical control over the autonomic and somatic functions for re-sponding to threat" (Nitschke et al., 1999, p. 635).

In states of right-hemispheric hyperarousal that generate a massive density of intense sympathetic-dominant, energy-expending, high-arousal negative affect, arousal levels are so extremely elevated that they interfere with the in-dividual's capacity to adaptively engage with the social (object relational, in-tersubjective) environment. Bromberg (2006) links trauma, at any point in the lifespan, to autonomic hyperarousal, "a chaotic and terrifying flooding of af-fect that can threaten to overwhelm sanity and imperil psychological survival" (p. 33).

In contrast, states of right-hemispheric parasympathetic-dominant, energy-conserving hypoarousal generate a massive density of intense low-arousal negative affect. In these latter affective states arousal levels are so extremely reduced that they interfere with the individual's capacity to adaptively disen-gage from the social environment. Thus, early relational trauma, reactivated in transference–countertransference enactments, manifests in dysregulated autonomic hyperarousal associated with sympathetic-dominant affects (panic/terror, rage, and pain), as well as dysregulated autonomic hypoarousal and parasympathetic-dominant affects (shame, disgust, and hopeless despair).

In terms of Porges's (1997) polyvagal model (see Figure 5.3), the sympa-thetic hyperarousal zone processes states of danger (fight/flight), whereas the dorsal vagal hypoarousal system is dominant in states of life survival/threat (see Schore, in press). Recall that the early development of these two stress-responsive psychobiological domains is directly impacted by dysregulated (abuse and neglect) attachment experiences. These imprinted right-brain im-plicit memories of the hyperarousal and dissociative-hypoarousal responses to early relational trauma are reactivated in the transference–countertransfer-ence.

Clinical work in these dyadic enactments implies a profound commitment by both therapeutic participants and a deep emotional involvement on the therapist's part (Tutte, 2004). In these highly stressful contexts the therapist's affect tolerance is a critical factor in determining the range, types, and intensi-ties of emotions that are explored or disavowed in the transference–counter-transference relationship and the therapeutic alliance (Schore, 2003b).

A general principle of this work is that the sensitive empathic therapist al-lows the patient to reexperience dysregulating affects in *affectively tolerable doses in the context of a safe environment, so that overwhelming traumatic feelings can be regulated and integrated into the patient's emotional life.* In agreement with Ogden et al. (2005), Bromberg (2006) also points out that the therapeutic relationship must "feel safe but not perfectly safe. If it were even possible for the relationship to be

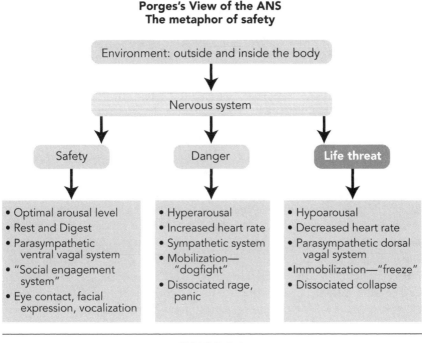

Porges's View of the ANS
The metaphor of safety

Environment: outside and inside the body

Nervous system

| Safety | Danger | Life threat |

- Optimal arousal level
- Rest and Digest
- Parasympathetic ventral vagal system
- "Social engagement system"
- Eye contact, facial expression, vocalization

- Hyperarousal
- Increased heart rate
- Sympathetic system
- Mobilization— "dogfight"
- Dissociated rage, panic

- Hypoarousal
- Decreased heart rate
- Parasympathetic dorsal vagal system
- Immobilization—"freeze"
- Dissociated collapse

FIGURE 5.3

Porges's polyvagal model of the autonomic nervous system. Adapted from Porges (2006).

perfectly safe, which it is not, there would be no potential for safe surprises" (p. 95). This affect-focused work occurs of at *the edges of the regulatory boundaries of affect tolerance* (Ogden, Chapter 8, this volume), or what Lyons-Ruth describes as the "fault lines" of self-experience where "interactive negotiations have failed, goals remain aborted, negative affects are unresolved, and conflict is experienced" (2005, p. 21).

The usual concept of "window of tolerance" used by Ogden, and Siegel, describes the range of optimal arousal to sustain secondary-process cognition (conscious, verbal, explicit) and striatal motor activities (voluntary action; controlled overt behavior). These cognitive and behavioral functions are dependent upon a moderate rather than high or low arousal range, represented by a classical inverted U. This window of optimal verbal processing and overt behavioral expression reflects moderate arousal levels that sustain left-hemispheric functions. Current cognitive–behavioral and insight-driven clinical models operate in this arousal range and focus on these left–hemispheric functions.

On the other hand, the right brain has a different range of arousal tolerance to sustain its unique nonconscious psychobiological functions and can operate at very high or very low arousal levels. Right-brain "windows of affect tolerance" thus refers to an optimal range of arousal for different affects and motivational states, which vary in arousal intensity. This affect tolerance is severely restricted in the emotional deadening defense of pathological dissociation. *An expansion of both negative and positive affect tolerance is a goal of the affectively focused psychotherapy described in this chapter.*

In such work, at some point the threatening dissociated affect must be activated, but in trace form, and regulated sufficiently so as not to trigger new avoidance. "The questions of how much and when to activate or to permit this activation, so as to repair the dissociation rather than reinforce it, must be addressed specifically for each patient" (Bucci, 2002, p. 787). According to Bromberg, "Clinically, the phenomenon of dissociation as a defense against self-destabilization . . . has its greatest relevance during enactments, a mode of clinical engagement that requires a [therapist's] closest attunement to the unacknowledged affective shifts in his own and the patient's self-states" (2006, p. 5). This self-destabilization of the emotional right brain in clinical enactments can take one of two forms: high-arousal explosive fragmentation versus low-arousal implosion of the implicit self.

Coconstruction of Intersubjective Fields

Visualize two planes of one window of affect tolerance in parallel to another: One represents the patient's window of affect tolerance, the other the therapist's. At the edges of the windows, the regulatory boundaries, the psychobiologically attuned empathic therapist, on a moment-to-moment basis, implicitly tracks and matches the patterns of rhythmic crescendos/decrescendos of the patient's regulated and dysregulated ANS with his or her own ANS crescendos/decrescendos. When the patterns of synchronized rhythms are in interpersonal resonance, this right-brain to right-brain specifically fitted interaction generates amplified energetic processes of arousal, and this interactive affect regulation, in turn, cocreates an intersubjective field.

The dynamic intersubjective field is described by Stern (2004) as "the domain of feelings, thoughts, and knowledge that two (or more) people share about the nature of their current relationship. . . . *This field can be reshaped. It can be entered or exited, enlarged or diminished, made clearer or less clear"* (p. 243, emphasis added). In my work on the interpersonal neurobiology of intersubjectivity, I have asserted that the right hemisphere is dominant for subjective emotional experiences, and that the interactive transfer of affect between the right brains of the members of therapeutic dyad is therefore best described as intersubjectivity (Schore, 1999). *An intersubjective field is more than just an interaction of two minds, but also of two bodies,* which, when in affective resonance, elicit an amplification and integration of both CNS and ANS arousal (see Chapter 3 of Schore 2003b on the communication of affects in an intersubjective field via projective identification).

At present there is an intense interest in how the body can be incorporated into psychotherapeutic treatment. The solution to this problem is to integrate into clinical models information about the ANS, "the physiological bottom of the mind" (Jackson, 1931). This system generates vitality affects and controls the cardiovascular system, effectors on the skin, and visceral organs. Stress-induced alterations in these dynamic psychobiological parameters mediate the therapist's somatic countertransference to the patient's nonverbal communications within a coconstructed intersubjective field. In previous writings on the psychophysiology of countertransference, I stated:

> Countertransferential processes are currently understood to be manifest in the capacity to recognize and utilize the sensory (visual, auditory, tactile, kinesthetic, and olfactory) and affective qualities of imagery which the patient generates in the psychotherapist (Suler, 1989). Similarly, Loewald (1986) points out that countertransference dynamics are appraised by the therapist's observations of his own visceral reactions to the patient's material. (Schore, 1994, p. 451)

Recall that the ANS contains dissociable sympathetic energy-expending and parasympathetic energy-conserving components. Extending this intraorganismic concept to the interpersonal domain, two dissociable intersubjective fields can be cocreated: (1) a sympathetic-dominant high-energy intersubjective field that processes state-dependent implicit memories of object relational and attachment transactions in high arousal states (see Table 5.1); and (2) a parasympathetic-dominant low-energy intersubjective field that processes state-dependent implicit memories of object relational and attachment transactions in low arousal states (see Table 5.2).

Note the contrast of somatic transference–countertransferences in the dual intersubjective fields. Also, the form of primary-process expressions in affect, cognition, and behavior differ in altered ultra-high- and low-arousal states of consciousness. Thus the high and low arousal states associated with, respectively, terror and shame will show qualitatively distinct patterns of primary-process nonverbal communication of "body movements (kinesics), posture, gesture, facial expression, voice inflection, and the sequence, rhythm, and pitch of the spoken words" (Dorpat, 2001, p. 451). Recall that sympathetic nervous system activity is manifest in tight engagement with the external environment and high levels of energy mobilization and utilization, whereas the parasympathetic component drives disengagement from the external environment and utilizes low levels of internal energy. This principle applies not only to overt interpersonal behavior but also to covert intersubjective engagement–disengagement with the social environment, the coupling and decoupling of minds–bodies and internal worlds. Models of the ANS indicate that although reciprocal activation usually occurs between the sympathetic and parasympathetic systems, these two systems are also able to uncouple and act unilaterally (Schore, 1994). Thus the sympathetic hyperarousal and parasympathetic hypoarousal zones represent two discrete intersubjective fields of psychobiological attunement, rupture, and interactive repair of what Bromberg (2006) terms "collisions of subjectivities."

It should be noted that just as emotion researchers have overemphasized sympathetic-dominant affects and motivations (fear, flight/fight), so have psychotherapists overly focused on the reduction of anxiety/fear or aggression/rage states. One outstanding example of this continuing bias is the devaluation of the critical role of dysregulated parasympathetic shame and disgust states in all clinical models. Similarly, psychodynamic models have highlighted the roles of rage and fear/terror in high-arousal enactments, and subsequent explosive fragmentation of the high-energy intersubjective field and the implicit self. As a result there has been an underemphasis on the low-energy parasympathetic-dominant intersubjective field. This is problematic, because

TABLE 5.1 High-Energy Charge Intersubjective Field

Hyperarousal = hypermetabolic CNS–ANS limbic–autonomic circuits = stressful, sympathetic-dominant, energy-expending psychobiological states

- High-energy explosive dyadic enactments; fragmenting of implicit self
- Sympathetic-dominant intersubjectivity; overengagement with social environment
- Somatic countertransference to communicated high-arousal affects expressed in heart rate acceleration; focus on exteroceptive sensory information
- Regulation/dysregulation of hyperaroused affective states (aggression/rage, panic/terror, sexual arousal, excitement/joy)

TABLE 5.2 Low Energy Charge Intersubjective Field

Hypoarousal = hypometabolic CNS–ANS circuits = stressful, parasympathetic-dominant, energy-conserving psychobiological states

- Low-energy implosive dyadic enactments; collapsing implicit self
- Parasympathetic-dominant intersubjectivity; dissociation/disengagement from social environment
- Somatic countertransference to communicated low-arousal affects expressed in heart rate deceleration; focus on interoceptive information
- Regulation/dysregulation of hyporaroused affective states (shame, disgust, abandonment, hopeless despair)

clinical work with parasympathetic dissociation—that is, detachment from an unbearable situation (Mollon, 1996)—is always associated with parasympathetic shame dynamics.

In my very first work, I proposed that the parasympathetic low-arousal state of shame, subjectively experienced as a "spiraling downward," represents a sudden shift from sympathetic hyperarousal into parasympathetic dorsal vagal hypoarousal (Schore, 1991). Recall that the collapse of the implicit self is subtle, signaled by amplification of the parasympathetic affects of shame and disgust, and by the cognitions of hopelessness and helplessness—common accompaniments of traumatic experiences. Working deep in the low-arousal intersubjective field, Bromberg (2006) observes that shame is present in those patients who "disappear" when what is being discussed touches upon unprocessed early trauma, and that shame is the most powerful affect a person is unable to modulate. He concludes:

> The task that is most important, and simultaneously most difficult for the [therapist], is to watch for signs of dissociated shame both in himself and in his patient—shame that is being evoked by the therapeutic process itself in ways that the [therapist] would just as soon not have to face. . . . The reason that seemingly repeated enactments are struggled with over and over again in the therapy is that the [therapist] is over and over pulled into the same enactment to the degree he is not attending to the arousal of shame. (p. 80)

Perhaps the most pointed observation is made by Nathanson:

> The entire system of psychotherapy, as we had been taught it, worked only if we overlooked the shame that we produced day in and day out in our therapeutic work. . . . It became clear that post-Freudian society had been

treated for almost everything *but* shame, and that the degree and severity of undiagnosed and untreated shame problems far exceeded anything we had ever imagined. (1996, p. 3)

Clinicians and researchers need to pay more attention to the energy-conserving parasympathetic-dominant intersubjective field of psychobiological attunement, rupture, and repair.

Interactive Affect Regulation as a Central Mechanism of the Change Process

Various authors have described the subtle psychological activities of the sensitive clinician who scaffolds the cocreation of an intersubjective field with the patient. Bromberg observes:

When [a therapist] gives up his attempts to "understand" his patient and allows himself to know his patient through the ongoing intersubjective field they are sharing at that moment, an act of recognition (not understanding) takes place in which words and thoughts come to symbolize experience instead of substitute for it. (2006, p. 11)

The dyadic nature of this deep affective exploration of the self was noted by Jung's (1946) suggestion that the clinician must go to the limit of his subjective possibilities, otherwise the patient will be unable to follow suit. According to Lichtenberg (2001), staying with the patient's immediate communication longer and more intensely usually gains more understanding than is achieved either by a defense focus or a genetic focus on what isn't said. And Whitehead describes the affect-amplifying effects encountered in the deep strata of the unconscious:

Every time we make therapeutic contact with our patients we are engaging profound processes that tap into essential life forces in our selves and in those we work with. . . . *Emotions are deepened in intensity and sustained in time when they are intersubjectively shared.* This occurs at moments of *deep contact.* (2005, p. 624, emphasis added)

As previously discussed, a central tenet of regulation theory dictates that the interpersonal resonance within an intersubjective field triggers an amplification of state. The resultant cocreated increased arousal (metabolic energy) allows for hypoaroused dissociated unconscious affects to be intensified and thereby experienced in consciousness as a subjective emotional state. This bottom-up interactive regulation enables the affect beneath conscious awareness to be intensified and sensed in both. Thus the "potential beginning" of an unconscious affect (Freud, 1915/1957) is intersubjectively energized into emergence. According to Fosha (2003), the initiating mechanism of the change process is the alteration of "defense-dominated functioning" and "the state transformation leading to the visceral experience of core affective phenomena within an emotionally engaged therapeutic dyad" (p. 519).

As in all attachment dynamics, the dyadic amplification of arousal–affect intensity that is generated in a resonant transference–countertransference context facilitates the intensification of the felt sense in both therapist and patient. This same interpersonal psychobiological mechanism *sustains* the affect in time; that is, the affect is "held" within the intersubjective field long enough for it to reach conscious awareness in both members of a psychobiologically attuned therapeutic dyad. It should be noted that this affect charging-amplifying process includes an intensification of both negative and positive affects in an intersubjective field.

But more than empathic affect attunement and deep contact are necessary for further therapeutic progression. At the psychobiological core of the intersubjective field is the attachment bond of emotional communication *and* affect regulation. The clinician's psychobiological interactive regulation–repair of dysregulated, especially unconscious (dissociated), bodily based affective states is an essential therapeutic mechanism. Recall Bucci's (2002) proscription that the threatening dissociated affect must be sufficiently regulated. Sands notes that "Dissociative defenses serve to regulate relatedness to others. . . . The dissociative patient is attempting to stay enough in a relationship with the human environment to survive the present while, at the same time, keeping the needs for more intimate relatedness sequestered but alive" (1994, p. 149).

Due to early learning experiences of severe attachment failures, the patient accesses pathological dissociation in order to cope with potential dysregulation of affect by anticipating trauma before it arrives. In characterological dissociation, an autoregulatory strategy of involuntary autonomic disengagement is initiated and maintained to prevent potentially dysregulating intersubjective contact with others. But as the patient continues through the change process, he or she becomes more able to forgo autoregulation for interactive regulation when under interpersonal stress. Fosha (2005, p. 527) stresses this important principle: "Dyadic affect regulation is a process that is central, not only in infancy, but from the cradle to the grave, *a fortiori* when we are faced with (categorical) emotions of such intensity that they overwhelm us, in the moment seeming beyond the capacity of our available resources to handle (i.e., that being the definition of trauma)." Similarly, Ogden and her colleagues conclude:

> Interactive psychobiological regulation (Schore, 1994) provides the rela-
> tional context under which the client can safely contact, describe, and even-
> tually regulate inner experience. . . . Rather than insight alone, it is the
> patient's experience of empowering action in the context of safety provided
> by a background of the empathic clinician's psychobiologically attuned in-
> teractive affect regulation that helps effect. . . . change. (2005, p. 22)

This interactive affect regulation occurs at the edge of the regulatory boundaries of both high and low arousal in the intersubjective fields. In such work, Bromberg warns, "An interpretative stance . . . not only is thereby use-less during an enactment, but also escalates the enactment and rigidifies the dissociation" (2006, p. 8), and Maroda offers the caveat, "Interpretations giv-en when affect is needed amounts to anti-communication, resulting in the patient getting worse" (2005, p. 138). A therapeutic focus on regulating not only conscious but unconscious (dissociated) affect highlights the conclusion that implicit nonverbal affective factors, more than the explicit verbal cogni-tive (insight) ones, lie at the core of the change process in the treatment of more severely disturbed patients. At the most fundamental level, the inter-subjective work of psychotherapy is not defined by what the clinician does for the patient or says to the patient (left-brain focus). Rather, the key mech-anism is *how to be with the patient*, especially during affectively stressful moments when the patient's implicit core self is dis-integrating in real time (right-brain focus).

Note the similarity of working at the right-brain regulatory boundaries in the heightened affective moment of enactments to Lichtenberg's "disciplined spontaneous engagements" that occur within "an ambience of safety":

> *Spontaneous* refers to the [therapist's] often unexpected comments, gestures,
> facial expressions, and actions that occur as a result of an unsuppressed emo-
> tional upsurge. These communications seem more to pop out than to have
> been planned or edited. The [therapist] may be as surprised as the patient.
> By engagement, we refer to communications and disclosures that are more
> enactments than thought-out responses. (2001, p. 445)

Tronick's "moments of meeting," a novel form of engagement of the thera-peutic dyad, also occur at the regulatory boundaries:

> The [therapist] must respond with something that is experienced as specific
> to the relationship with the patient and that is expressive of her own experi-
> ence and personhood, and carries her signature. . . . It is dealing with "what

is happening here and now between us." The strongest emphasis is on the *now* because of the affective immediacy. . . . It requires spontaneous responses . . . [which] need never be verbally explicated, but can be, after the fact. (2007, p. 436)

According to Greenberg and Paivio (1997), reexperiencing the traumatic experience in therapy, with the safety and security provided by an empathic, supportive therapist, gives the person a new experience: specifically, the clinician's interactive regulation of the patient's communicated dysregulated right-brain hyperaroused and hypoaroused affective states. In support of this model current experimental researchers report: "As suggested in clinical practice, it is necessary to 'revisit' an emotionally distressing memory before it can be controlled" (Depue, Curran, & Banich, 2007, p. 218).

This dyadic psychobiological mechanism of the psychotherapeutic change process is described by Adler:

Because people in a caring, i.e., empathic relationship convey emotional experiences to each other, they also convey physiological experiences to each other, and this sociophysiologic linkage is relevant to the understanding the direct physiologic consequences of caring in the doctor–patient relationship—*for both parties.* (2002, p. 885, emphasis added)

He further argues that the therapeutic relationship—the interaction between the patient's emotional vulnerability and the therapist's emotional availability—represents a prime example of how individuals in an empathic relationship coregulate each other's autonomic activity. More specifically, the therapeutic relationship can act as "the antithesis of the fight-flight response"; and "the experience of feeling cared about in a relationship reduces the secretion of stress hormones and shifts the neuroendocrine system toward homeostasis" (Adler, 2002, p. 883). Adler argues that in this way social bonds of attachment embedded in the therapeutic relationship reduce stress-induced arousal.

Ongoing episodes involving therapeutic interactive regulation of affective arousal impact the patient's activation threshold of a right-brain stress response to a social stressor. Bromberg observes that the processing becomes "safer and safer so that the person's tolerance for potential flooding of affect goes up" (2006, p. 79). As a result:

The patient's threshold for triggering increases, allowing her increasingly to hold on to the ongoing relational experience (the full complexity of the here and now with the therapist) as it is happening, with less and less need to dissociate; as the processing of the here and now becomes more and more immediate, it becomes more and more experientially connectable to her past. (p. 69)

Effective work at the regulatory boundaries of right-brain low and high arousal states ultimately broadens the windows of affect tolerance, thereby allowing for a wider variety of more intense and enduring affects in future intersubjective contexts. LeDoux offers an elegant description of this advance of emotional development:

> Because emotion systems coordinate learning, the broader the range of emotions that [an individual] experiences the broader will be the emotional range of the self that develops. . . . And because more brain systems are typically active during emotional than during nonemotional states, and the intensity of arousal is greater, the opportunity for coordinated learning across brain systems is greater during emotional states. By coordinating parallel plasticity throughout the brain, emotional states promote the development and unification of the self. (2002, p. 322)

Growth-facilitating experiences cocreated at the regulatory boundaries thus promote the "affective building blocks" of enactments (Ginot, 2007, p. 317). The patient's increased ability to consciously experience and communicate a wider range of positive and negative affects is due to a developmental advance in the capacity to regulate affect. This further maturation of adaptive self-regulation is, in turn, reflected in the appearance of more complex emotions that result from the simultaneous blending of different affects, and in an expansion in the "affect array" (Schore, 1994).

Psychotherapy of attachment pathologies and severe personality disorders must focus on unconscious affect and the survival defense of pathological dissociation, "a structured separation of mental processes (e.g., thoughts, emotions, conation, memory, and identity) that are ordinarily *integrated*" (Spiegel & Cardeña, 1991, p. 367). Overwhelming traumatic feelings that are not regulated cannot be adaptively integrated into the patient's emotional life. This dissociative deficit specifically results from a lack of integration of the right hemisphere, the emotional brain. But effective therapy can positively alter the developmental trajectory of the deep right brain and facilitate the *integration* between cortical and subcortical right-brain systems. This enhanced interconnectivity allows for an increased complexity of defenses of the emotional right brain—coping strategies for regulating stressful affect that are more flexible and adaptive than pathological dissociation. These improved coping strategies in turn enhance the further maturation of the right hemisphere core of the self and its central involvement in "patterns of affect regulation that *integrate* a sense of self across state transitions, thereby allowing for a continuity of inner experience" (Schore, 1994, p. 33).

Concordant with this model of the change mechanism of psychotherapy, Fosha (2005) describes a "state in which affective and cognitive processes are seamlessly *integrated*, the core state that follows the experience of core affect is optimally suited for the therapeutic integration and consolidation that translate deep in-session changes into lasting therapeutic results" (p. 523). In this state of transformation "our view opens up: the entirety of the emotional landscape is visible, and it is evenly illuminated" (p. 523), and adaptive resources, resilience, and mindful understanding are available to the individual. Fosha speculates that this "wide angle lens" is "a capacity centrally mediated by the prefrontal cortex and the orbitofrontal cortex, the ultimate neuro-integrators of the meaning of personal experience (Schore, 2003a; Siegel, 2003)," and it generates "a cohesive and coherent autobiographical narrative" (p. 523). The latter is "primarily mediated by the right hemisphere' prefrontal cortex" (p. 523).

The increased resilience of unconscious strategies of stress regulation that results from an optimal psychotherapeutic experience represents an experience-dependent maturation of "the right hemispheric specialization in regulating stress- and emotion-related processes" (Sullivan & Dufresne, 2006, p. 55). Studies now indicate that the right hemisphere, which is dominant for autobiographical memory (Markowitsch et al., 2000), provides access to a triggering mechanism that initiates autonomic sympathetic and parasympathetic reactions to socioemotional signals (Spence et al., 1996). The regulation of emotional stress is essentially mediated by higher right cortical regulation of lower arousal systems, autonomic structures, and peripheral organs. Indeed, anterior areas of the right hemisphere are involved in the control of autonomic activation (Aftanas et al., 2005), and right orbitofrontal (ventromedial) cortical activity acts to regulate the sympathetic nervous system (Critchley et al., 2000; Hilz et al., 2006).

In a neuroanatomical description that echoes Fosha's description of the "wide angle lens" of the orbitofrontal core state, current studies conclude, "the rich connections of orbitofrontal cortex endow it with a panoramic view of the entire external environment, as well as the internal environment associated with motivational factors" (Barbas, 2007, p. 239). According to Barbas, frontal medial and orbitofrontal cortices, which are associated with appreciation of emotions, project to hypothalamic autonomic centers, which innervate brainstem and spinal autonomic autonomic structures. The latter, in turn, innervate peripheral organs whose activity is markedly increased in emotional arousal

(Barbas et al., 2003). It is now established that "the peripheral physiological arousal and action tendencies associated with emotion are implicit in the sense that they occur automatically and *do not require conscious processing to be executed efficiently*" (Lane, 2008, p. 217, emphasis added). Note that the left-brain explicit verbal system that analytically processes interpretations is never directly involved in regulating sympathetic nervous system activity. Both secure attachment experiences and effective psychotherapy increase the complexity of the right-brain affect-regulating system.

The right hemisphere continues its growth spurts over the stages of the lifespan, thereby allowing for therapy-induced plasticity in the system. The structural changes that occur from effective psychotherapy occur in descending right cortical top-down pathways from orbitofrontal and ventral medial prefrontal cortices to the amygdala and hypothalamus, thereby providing a more effective mechanism of prefrontal control of the autonomic nervous system, and thus in processes underlying the recognition and expression of emotions. The psychotherapy of patients with attachment pathologies, who all too frequently experience traumatic fearful states of arousal, directly impacts and potentially alters right-lateralized dysregulations of the fear/terror system, driven by the subcortical right amygdala, which specializes in fear conditioning (Baker & Kim, 2004) and "unseen fear" (Morris et al., 1999). Importantly, prefrontal areas that inhibit emotional memories and suppress emotional reactivity are lateralized predominantly to the right hemisphere (Depue et al., 2007). The observations of Phelps et al. (2004) directly relate to the learning process of the psychotherapy context:

> Understanding how fears are acquired is an important step in our ability to translate basic research to the treatment of fear-related behaviors. Understanding how learned fears are diminished may be even more valuable. . . . The amygdala may play an important role in extinction learning as well as acquisition and that ventromedial prefrontal cortex my be particularly involved in the retention of extinction learning. (p. 903)

Efficient functions of the right-brain implicit self are essential for the reception, expression, and communication of socioaffective information; the unconscious regulation of physiological, endocrinological, neuroendocrine, cardiovascular, and immune functions; subjectivity/intersubjectivity; trust and empathy; and an affective theory of mind. Hartikainen et al. summarize the critical role of nonconscious emotion processing for human survival:

> In unpredictable environments, emotions provide rapid modulation of behavior. From an evolutionary perspective, emotions provide a modulatory

control system that facilitates survival and reproduction. Reflex-like reactions to emotional events can occur before attention is paid to them. . . . Neuropsychological evidence supports a right hemispheric bias for emotional and attentional processing in humans. (2007, p. 1,929).

At the outset of this chapter I asserted that the emerging paradigm shift is highlighting the primacy of affect in human development, psychopathogenesis, and treatment. A large body of research in the neuroscience literature suggests a special role for the emotion-processing right hemisphere in empathy, identification with others, intersubjective processes, autobiographical memories, own body perception, self-awareness, self-related cognition, as well as self-images that are not consciously perceived—all essential components of the therapeutic process (see Schore & Schore, 2008, for references).

A fundamental theme of this work is that bodily based right-brain affect, including specifically unconscious affect, needs to be addressed in updated psychotherapeutic interventions. Even more than the patient's late-acting rational, analytical, and verbal left mind, the growth-facilitating psychotherapeutic relationship needs to directly access the regulatory boundaries and deeper psychobiological strata of both the patient's and the clinician's right-brain minds. Alvarez (2006) asserts, "Schore points out that at the more severe levels of psychopathology, it is not a question of making the unconscious conscious: rather it is a question of restructuring the unconscious itself" (p. 171).

Earlier I suggested that the right hemisphere is dominant in the change process of psychotherapy. Neuroscience authors now conclude that although the left hemisphere is specialized for coping with predictable representations and strategies, the right predominates not only for organizing the human stress response (Wittling, 1995), but also for coping with and assimilating novel situations (Podell et al., 2001) and ensuring the formation of a new program of interaction with a new environment (Ezhov & Krivoschekov, 2004). Indeed,

> the right brain possesses special capabilities for processing novel stimuli. . . . Right-brain problem solving generates a matrix of alternative solutions, as contrasted with the left brain's single solution of best fit. This answer matrix remains active while alternative solutions are explored, a method suitable for the open-ended possibilities inherent in a novel situation. (Schutz, 2005, p. 13)

Recall that resilience in the face of stress and novelty is an indicator of attachment security. Therapeutic changes in the patient's internal working model, encoding strategies of affect regulation, reflect structural alterations within the right brain.

The functions of the emotional right brain are essential to the self-exploration process of psychotherapy, especially of unconscious affects that can be integrated into a more complex implicit sense of self. Both optimal development and effective psychotherapy promote more than cognitive changes of the conscious mind, but an expansion of the right-brain implicit self, the biological substrate of the human unconscious.

6

Emotion as Integration

A Possible Answer to the Question, What Is Emotion?

Daniel J. Siegel

IN THIS CHAPTER WE WILL explore the fundamental question, "What is emotion?" As you read this collection of words, it may become apparent that the approach of this entry is different from the usual stance of a professional text: I will be directly addressing you in order to efficiently, and hopefully effectively, dive into the subjective nature of how we experience feelings. People use the term *emotion* in so many different and often seemingly conflicted ways. For this reason, from the outset, I'd like to suggest that you consider the usual English use of this term, *emotion*, as perhaps more problematic than it is helpful. You may wonder if the suggestion here is that emotion per se does not exist. And this is exactly the point: what is "per se" about the notion of emotion? What—in actual reality—is this absolutely real experience we have that in our language usage evokes the term *emotion* or *emotional* or other similar derivatives of the root word, *emotion*?

As a contributing author and one of the coeditors of this volume, and as the Founding Editor of the Norton Series on Interpersonal Neurobiology of which this book is a part, I feel particularly motivated to take this opportunity to invite you to try out this perhaps new way of communicating complex ideas: We will be honoring our subjective experience as much as we pay respect to our "objective" data of science. As historians of science know, science itself is a human endeavor, an unfolding story based on empirical explorations that use hypotheses and concepts to categorize and often quantify aspects of our perceived reality. Science has advanced our understanding of the world, and ourselves, in important ways that organize our view in a manner that subjective internal reflection alone could not have done. But, on the other hand, reflection on the subjective nature of our lives can also uniquely illuminate the nature of reality, especially that of the human mind, in ways that science cannot. Though subjective reflection is different from objective observation, both have important contributions to make to our deep understanding of the nature of emotion, the mind, human development, and the cultivation of well-being. In this way, we can attempt to integrate these two useful ways of knowing about reality into an inclusive approach that honors both points of view.

If this chapter can elicit in you a new and expanded perspective on the concept of "emotion," then the goal of this project will be met. Ultimately you will synthesize your own point of view; now and here I'd like to invite you to consider expanding your notion of what "emotion" is. We can journey together in addressing the ways in which our collective views, our scientific and subjective stories of "emotion," color our thinking and our actions.

Subjectivity, Science, and Story

Right now you have an inner world of subjective experience. No matter how many types of brain scans or other forms of technology we develop, such as functional magnetic resonance imaging (fMRI) and the quantitative electroencephalography (qEEG), we have a nonquantifiable inner world of our subjective reality. The truth is that we actually do not know how neural firing and subjective experience create each other. Though some scientists may posit a unidirectional flow from neural activity to subjective mental life, such an assumption may be only partially true. It also can be said with solid evidence that our subjective internal mental life uses the brain's activity to create itself. When you think of this morning's breakfast, you are seeing these words and experiencing the flow of energy and information that evokes a neural firing pattern in the seeing and in the recalling. Ultimately, neural firing and mental activity mutually influence each other. The important point here is that no one—not scientists, Nobel Prize winners, taxi drivers, or philosophers—actually know how it is that the physical property of neural firing and electrical activity somehow influence the creation of subjective mental life—or vice versa. We have identified correlations between brain areas and mental processes. But these are just that: correlations of timing and not explanations of mechanisms of how this process occurs. And so we need to keep an open mind about brain–mind relations and not carry lingering prejudices about the nature of causal direction: Each influences the other.

So what happens when, given the opportunity, we ask scientists or clinicians or the general unsuspecting public about what emotion is? As with the examination of science and subjectivity, I have been struck by the numerous and conflicting stories that actually emerge. Emotion has been described by various therapists as "the feelings we have inside," "the ways the body influences the mind," and the "motivation to do something, to act, to 'evoke motion.'" Some neuroscientists have suggested that emotion is the way in which soma shapes psyche through the input of physiological states. Others have proposed that emotional circuits coordinate and synchronize neural firing patterns. Developmental researchers sometimes view emotion as the glue that binds an individual across phases of growth. Social researchers may see emotion as that which connects people to each other in dyads, families, or larger groupings. The response of nonprofessionals is often initiated with a pause and then the use of ideas such as a "feeling" or a "mood" or a "reaction." Each of these views carries some truth for the speaker, but clearly the term *emotion* does not have a precisely shared meaning even for those who use the concept in their daily work.

In this chapter I am going to ask you to take a step back from what you've learned from daily living, from clinical practice, and from science in order to take a perhaps fresh look at this familiar word, *emotion*. It also may be helpful to gain some distance from the stories embedded in your mental models of the mind, of how the mind works, or what the mind is, so that we can attempt to see the world of feelings from a more basic or "bottom-up" perspective. The outer layer of the brain that is most evolved in mammals is the neocortex. This outer bark of the brain is structured such that incoming perceptual data rise up into the cortical six-layered columns and are met, straight on, by the "top-down" flow of information coming from prior learning as it passes downward from the higher cortical layers. It is here, at the crashing of these two streams of information flow, where one can imagine we shape our perception of reality. It is also likely that this bottom-up shaping by top-down flow is how stories, in part, mold our vision and create our knowledge of how things are. These mental models shape our perception and form the architecture of language that both expands and constrains the way we see the world. In many ways, not grasping on to judgments—a fundamental part of mindfully approaching a topic—is the way we loosen the influence of the top-down constraints that keep us from seeing the world with fresh eyes. These are the fresh eyes we will need in this chapter as we dive into the pursuit of an open view of what emotion is.

What Is Emotion???

If you say, "I had an emotional experience today," what exactly do you mean by that? And would someone else know what you meant by your use of the term *emotional*? We might guess that, yes, we all share some gut sense of what that statement means. And if I tell you this story, what would you think: I left a group of colleagues at lunch to go to my office to take a conference call. As I walked to the counter to pay the bill, I had a nonemotional experience. What does that mean? Well, you might say, nothing "emotional" happened. Okay. Now—what does *that* mean? And then if I said that on my short walk to the counter to pay, a woman called out my name and said, "Dan, is that you? I'm Sara Smith." Is this an emotional experience? If I didn't know Sara—or if I did, how might that fact make this moment emotional? Well, it turns out that Sara was the widow of my first psychotherapist—and, in fact, earlier today this is exactly what happened. She was sitting at lunch with her granddaughter, and I decided to be late to the conference call in order to take this unique emotional moment and connect with her and let both of them know what a wonderful man and therapist Dr. Smith had been for me. Sara's eyes welled up with tears and her granddaughter looked both proud and longing. I also felt a huge wave of sensations in my body, eyes filling, a feeling of sadness and gratitude and appreciation that Sara had stopped me and a feeling of transformation, of being different than when I first headed for the counter to pay the bill. This sense of transformation had an almost indescribable quality that the arrangement in my being was now different; somehow I was changed, and I'd likely be able to mark that moment in my life within memory as a significant event, something I might reflect on years later, or in a story I'd tell to others, perhaps you. Transformation feels as if some basic architecture is being remodeled rather than just new furniture being put in the house or moved from room to room. There is some deep structural change, even if quite subtle, that alters the backbone of existence. I would not be the same since this experience; something in me had changed, some awareness of the passage of time, of the therapy with Dr. Smith, of the changes in him, of his illness, his death, of all of our mortality, of the youthful glint in his granddaughter's eyes, the sadness in Sara's.

And so meeting the two women in the restaurant was emotional. We might all agree on that. Here the term *emotion* and its derivatives are reflecting something very powerful, something universal, something we even can agree upon in using the term in this example. But what makes this encounter emotional? What *is* emotion?

This story raises a first issue: Emotion is not a noun, but rather, a verb. It may be useful to sit with this thought that emotion is a verb for a moment. Emotion-related words and concepts are active processes, not fixed entities. Seeing emotion as a verb opens our mind to a fluid, moving mechanism that acts, changes, transforms.

Okay. But what is emotion, even if it is a verb? We can turn to a variety of views and summarize the various approaches from science and clinical experience and say that there actually is little firm agreement, even among some of the scientists and clinicians contributing to this volume, on how the word *emotion* actually is defined. Depending upon the larger story of the particular discipline of science, emotion can be seen as a process that links people together (anthropology, sociology), a fundamental part of the continuity that connects a person across development (attachment research, developmental psychology, developmental psychopathology), or a way that the body proper—our somatic physiology—is connected to the brain and coordinated within its various layers (neuroscience with its branches in affective and social neuroscience especially).

You may notice that there is an inherent side issue embedded in each of these differing stories of science. The term *consilience* refers to the search for common principles across distinct disciplines. After trying to find some summation across the sciences so that I could finish writing *The Developing Mind* (1999), I felt frustrated with this lack of convergence in definitions. It seemed that I would never be able to finish writing the book or the chapter with an overview of emotion given that there was no agreement on what emotion is. I even felt like the project would fall apart, or I'd be destined to try to continue to write it for yet another 5 years, threatening a sense of well-being in my marriage (in my head) and my sense of equilibrium. This was an emotional moment indeed. Surely something as basic as emotion had to have some common definition that we could all come to some sort of agreement upon. Fortunately, one concept—not identified directly but pointed to indirectly by each of the various disciplines—began to become clear in the journey to discover what emotion might actually be. The consilient finding that emerged from that effort is that of "connection" or "linkage" of different elements into a functional whole. *The linguistic term we use for the linkage of differentiated parts into a functional whole is the word integration.*

Though science and subjectivity narrate the story of "emotion" in very different ways, we can see that the consilient scientific view may indeed be the common, though not stated, perspective that *emotion is integrative.* What this means, literally, is that emotion, emotional processes, emotional regulation, emotional relationships, emotional experiences, emotionally meaningful events, emotional development, and emotional well-being each involve integration. It isn't even that emotion leads to integration. What I am suggesting is that emotion *is* integration. In this way, for example, an emotional experience is one that shifts our state of integration. Emotional development promotes integration. Emotional well-being reveals an integrated individual. We can increase integration in cases of emotionally meaningful events and when we feel emotionally well. Similarly, we can decrease integration when we are emotionally distraught or emotionally unwell. Emotion is the shifting in integrative states: Sometimes integration is enhanced, sometimes diminished. Herein we can see the verb nature of emotion: a shift in the state of integration.

This proposal is, yes, a bunch of words making yet another story, one that explains and doesn't describe. This is a consilient story, finding the hidden but shared views from separate disciplines and is one interpretation of the science and of our subjective descriptions. I ask myself, "Dan, why did you put this narrative perspective in now when you were building up this whole view of the importance of bottom-up direct description of experience and there you go, giving a top-down mental model?" Why didn't I save this for later in the chapter? I'm not sure. But stay with me for now—perhaps this view of emotion as integration, the linkage of differentiated components of a system—will help to expand and illuminate other stories we may have. And even the feeling inside of me now as I type is something like this: I felt a fear that you'd jump ship, saying "This chapter is just weird, what a waste of time," and so I wanted to throw in now, near the beginning, the essence of the chapter, the take-home message, so that you would feel more comfortable staying with the experience, thinking it to be worthwhile enough to stick with it. I am making an emotional appeal, an invitation to link your mind with mine, to integrate us together. Even this "emotional appeal" can be restated as an "integrative appeal." I think if I were reading this, my own logical circuits would welcome this concluding finding here, in the beginning, and then I'd feel readier for becoming more vulnerable to raw, direct experience: I'd have a logical framework within which I could abandon logic temporarily. And so there is an emotional reason I've put the punch line of the story in at this point: I want to invite you to integrate this idea into your perspective. It's like the old saying that you have to believe it to see it. Once the pattern can be stated, we can see the image in the picture. Without the identification of the pattern, its underlying organization remains invisible to us beneath the layers of seemingly disparate dimensions of this thing called *emotion*.

For my students and for myself in the last decade, this approach of translating the use of the commonly used but ill-defined noun *emotion* as the verb of *integration* has been extremely powerful. One aim of this chapter—side by side with the invitation to explore direct experience together—is to propose a precise definition of the term *emotion*: Emotion (verb) is integration. Emotional experiences involve dynamic shifts in integration. Such a new perspective actually helps us see what is meant by the term and what we can do to promote "emotional well-being."

Let's go forward and see how you feel as we go.

Being Mindful of Emotion

In this chapter I'm asking you to consider trying to be mindful—to be open-minded, intentional, and awake—about emotion. This means that we intentionally seek to notice the categories that shape our preconceived ideas of how we structure our perceptions. We avoid premature categorizations, come to an experience with an emergent sense of novelty and freshness, and remain attentive to our state of intention and the specific focus of awareness. This mindful stance gives us the possibility to see more directly the true nature of reality, accepting that much of what shapes our perceptions lies beneath the radar of our conscious awareness. Such a mindful awareness also enables us to become freer from the linguistic categorizations that constrict our view of the world. Being mindful of emotion entails identifying old beliefs and not grasping on to these perspectives so that we can see things as they are with more clarity, vividness, and detail. Naturally much of what goes on in our bodies, including our neural processes in the brain itself, is not a part of conscious awareness. Yet an openness to these physiological experiences is an intentional stance we can take: open to whatever arises, aware of the limited nature of consciousness and of linguistic-based explanations, pausing before making judgments, and being receptive rather than reactive.

Even with an open stance embracing reflection on the inner realm of experience, our nonconscious stories can still shape how we perceive the target of our attention—in this case, the experience of emotion. Becoming mindful entails more than just simply being aware. As we focus attention, say, on our experience of what is meant by the word, *emotion*, we can let the layers of prior learning that filter our experience also enter awareness. In this way the inner thoughts, perceptual biases, and interpretations of raw experience into the language of explanation become a focus of our attention. But here is a helpful distinction along our journey. Notice the difference in the inner experience that emerges when you see these two similar words: *description* versus *explanation*. You can try to describe your experience, what if feels like, the timing of what comes up when, where you experience things in your body, in the "space of the mind," or even in your interpersonal relationships. These are the common "what, when, where, and how" elements of description distinct from the more predominant linguistically organized left hemisphere's favorite pursuit, exploring "why." The left side of our cortex appears to specialize in the cause–effect explanations of syllogistic reasoning that is so coveted in science, and in schools, and perhaps in modern society in general. For now let's leave aside the whys of the *explanation* of cause–effect connections, this essence of left-dominant syllogistic reasoning. Here we will dive into description. If we are lucky, we may also move into the realm of a more open definition of what emotion actually is. Ultimately we will interweave the fullness of our experience in both left and right hemisphere perceptual modes to attain an integrated sense of our inner worlds.

Let me suggest that in the Norton Series—including this richly diverse edited volume, *The Mindful Brain* (Siegel, 2007), and *The Developing Mind* (Siegel, 1999)—there are plenty of scientific explanations and references to fill a left hemisphere's dream of exploring the "why." As the experience within the reading of those published works is already available, here in this chapter we will try to stick more closely to experience, use a descriptive role for words initially, and then see if broader concepts can then mindfully emerge as an explanatory framework. Let's just try to speak directly to each other here: me to you and you to me, by way of my imagining your possible response to these experiences and notions.

The Science and Story of Emotion

If you are continuing to read on, then I imagine you are game for the experience of looking straight into face of this question, "What is emotion." Some readers may have stopped early on in this chapter, seeking a more logic-focused, science-based, linguistic view. I am hoping that you will find that though this may be different from the usual approach, the unfolding experience of this chapter will be well worth the risk. And what is the risk? How are we vulnerable when we try to describe direct experience rather than rely on logical explanation? One risk is that we have to be honest with ourselves. Another is that we have to be open to what is, rather than relying on what has been defined by others. Our cortices are structured to organize perception based on prior learning. Being open to new learning, to examining an old term like *emotion* with fresh eyes, takes intentional focus and purposeful energy. Let's see how direct experience and description unfold in our quest to answering the question, "What is emotion?"

If sensing direct experience requires inward reflecting, what if looking inward leads us to come up with nothing? What if we peer inside and we en-counter emptiness? Or what shall we do if we sense pain, or confusion, or just plain cardboard boring bland unexciting run-of-the-mill dull internal layers of drab blanched hues of a meaningless existence? These are more of the risks of a direct-experience approach. Better to just rely on some experts' opinions, leaning on the data and group consensus, rather than the riskier process of peering inside and seeing with new eyes. Wouldn't it be "safer" to just stick to the science? Isn't it more comfortable or noble to have research backing us up than saying something like, "I have a sensation in my belly that washes over my awareness in ways I can barely articulate." And is that sensation emotion?

Integration and the Subjective Feeling of Feelings

Consider a time when you felt emotional in the recent past. What was the experience like for you? How did your state of being impact others at the time? What happened before you became emotional? What was the outcome of that emotional experience?

These questions could be asked about a minor event, like seeing a sunset—or not seeing one. My wife called me on the phone last night and asked if I'd like to come to watch the sun set over the sea near where we live. Our son had just gone out, and I assumed he had taken the car that he and I share. In fact, I had just been thinking of finally getting a car of my own after 2 years of rid-ing my bike to work while he drove his sister to school. So I said "no" to my wife, telling her that I could not go to see the sunset as I had no car. It turned out that both she and our son saw what they both said was one of the most gorgeous sunsets of their lives. On this plane, right now, as I am typing these words to you, I just looked out the window on my way to teach in Vancouver, and I am seeing a fabulous explosion of reds, blues, and purples as the Earth turns and the sun goes down. Right now I feel quite emotional. What is the emotion? In many ways, there are no words to define what I am feeling with normal English. I could say something like: nostalgia for the present with a sense of longing to connect to my wife and son and share with them an aware-ness of the passage of time in the glorious hues of nature's rainbow. And what would that tell you? What is this "emotion," as I am now feeling it? Well here is an elaboration of the story that puts it into a connection with this chapter's timing: When I realized that the car had actually been there in the driveway for me to take, I was frustrated with myself for assuming I'd had no means to get over to the beach. I had not been open to how things were but made a judgment, clung to a previously established expectation. I was not mindful.

This whole tale is one of integration and the lack of it: I could not share the romantic experience with my wife, felt absorbed in my own preoccupations about the car so that I didn't check on its actual availability, and my internal desire to share that transition of day to night with my wife was unmet. And the next day I was to leave for a trip to Canada. This was an emotional experience as it was filled with issues about integration—or lack of it. She as a differentiated person could not be linked to me. Integration was impaired. And so we can see this experience as another illustration of "emotion" as occurring when our state of integration is significantly altered—either raised or diminished.

Beyond such a subtle emotional experience, we often can draw on more intense traumatic events from the past to explore the recollection of emotion. Here we see how the feeling of an experience that is overwhelming blocks our sense of internal coherence. We feel distraught, blocked, terrified, shattered. In this shattering of our internal state, various elements of memory are literally separated from each other. Perceptual modalities can be isolated, such as sight from hearing, touch from smell. In interpersonal trauma we can feel betrayed as the individual with whom we expect to rely upon hurts us or neglects us. Such betrayal is, at its heart, impaired interpersonal integration.

A clinical example may illustrate this idea. A 25-year-old patient who recently came to therapy to deal with her anxiety about her new boyfriend arrived on her third visit highly distressed. After initially dating and then becoming romantically involved with him, she felt hesitant to move forward as he pressed for her to become physically intimate. On a rainy evening the night before our appointment, at his apartment she felt herself "slipping away" and became lost in what felt like a dream: She had the sensations of being sexually assaulted and became disoriented, confused as to where she was, lost in a flashback of an event she could not recall. I saw her on the following day and in the session she seemed disheveled, distant, disorganized. As her recollections of the night before unfolded, she returned to a state of immersion in a terrifying set of painful physical sensations. In this traumatic recall, her usual sense of time and self were distorted—disintegrated—as the usually linked elements of her consciousness and memory were unraveling. This "emotionally distressful" flashback was filled with elements of dis-integration—in memory, in her awareness of time and space, in her ability to be in the present moment. This was an emotionally significant moment in her life, in her therapy, and in her stepping into the integrative process of healing.

The definition of emotional experience as shifts in integration also reveals for us that something "emotional" occurs when integration is enhanced. When our internal state reaches more highly integrated configurations, we can have an "emotionally meaningful experience." My encounter with my old thera-pist's widow and granddaughter reveals such an experience. Also, when the dis-integrating effects of trauma or grief are healed, we can see that integra-tion is enhanced. Healing is integration; psychotherapy is facilitated integra-tion catalyzed by the relationship between two people. As we shall soon see, integration is at the heart of a coherent mind and living a harmonious life. In this way, we can see that we tend to use the term *emotion* or *emotional* for mo-ments when the state of integration is altered—when the degree of differen-tiation and/or linkage of components in a system such as the brain or our relationships is changed—and we are changed as a result.

Imagine someone with whom you feel emotionally close. What does that relationship actually entail that leads you to use this descriptive term? For many, such meaningful and rewarding relationships involve the essence of two people being intertwined. We feel safe and seen. Feeling safe comes along with being receptive and relaxed, open to others and to our own experience as it unfolds. Being seen gives a feeling of being real, of being connected, of not being alone. When we are safe and seen, when we have the sense of "feeling felt" and being psychologically held in mind by another, we develop a sense of inner security. In many ways, we have linked the differentiated mind of another within our own: We have integrated a secure relationship into the fabric of our psyche.

The opposite of these states of emotional closeness can be subtle or severe. They can include feeling unsafe and closed off, guarded, and well-defended. When we are not seen, we can come to feel isolated and alone. If we are not seen at a moment of intense arousal—of joy and excitement or sadness, fear, anger, or distress—then we can come to feel a state of shame. Our eye gaze turns away and there can be a heaviness in the chest and nausea in the belly. We may even have an internal thought of ourselves as being defective and unlovable. Clinically we may see this set of sensations as the state of shame in which a specific coordination of physiological processes coalesce within that "emotional state." These categorical emotions serve to organize our system—even into synchronized states of impaired overall integration. I know this may sound contradictory, so bear with me. The categorical emotions—the classic states of fear, anger, disgust, joy, surprise, sadness, and shame—have charac-teristic neural firing patterns that become manifest and organized. These are cohesive affective states: They stick together. Yet we can have certain states—for example, shame—actually restrict our degrees of freedom. So while these emotions are organizing our system, and thus changing our degree of integra-tion, in this case they are diminishing the level of integration achieved. Such diminishments can be proposed to include the uncomfortable emotions that may serve to paralyze our thinking, distort our perceptions, imprison our behaviors. For those of us with shame, these enslavements of self-concept and other-directed interactions lock us into rigid patterns of behavior, and we become stuck. Within therapy, the underlying sense of a defective self can emerge and become the direct focus of attention.

Here we see that fixed patterns of thought, perception, feeling, and action organize a way of being into "unhealthy" patterns derived from past experiences of impaired integration. The persistent organization of these states makes them seem to be *cohesive*—a state not to be confused with that of the integrative state of *coherence*. In cohesion, elements stick together and may or may not be adaptive. These can be seen as our self states, our repeating states of mind, and our categorical emotions described above. In the case of the cohesive state of shame, rigidity is the result. With increased integration emerges a state of coherence marked by a sense of fluidity and flexibility. The differentiation of two people who then come together as a functional whole, a "we," illustrates such a coherent harmony of an integrated system.

And love as an emotion? Yes, we can even see love as a form of integration. When we feel love for another, our whole being longs for connecting ourselves with that person in mind and in body. We show affection through touch, through the resonance of two minds, through the expression of our intention of good will, with the sharing of loving kindness. These are each reflections of enhanced integration.

The Emotional River That Flows between Chaos and Rigidity

Let's review the essential proposal that *emotion is integration*. We can suggest that whenever the terms *emotion* or *emotional* are used in their various combinations, the individual is very likely referring to shifts in the process of integration—the linkage of differentiated elements of a system to each other. Naturally people do not tend to think of the process of emotion as integration. Instead, we think of the sensations that wash over us, that fill our awareness, that are the topic of conversations, the focus of therapy, the stuff of novels and cinema. But I'd like to suggest that you consider the term *emotion* and its use in your own experience. Does this translation of emotion as integration work for you? When an experience is emotional, do you notice that the degree of integration in the system you are in is changing—that it is either enhanced or diminished? In this way emotion is a window into something changing. Psychotherapy is inherently an emotional opportunity in that we can help promote lasting change through the cultivation of integration in a person's life. But what are these changes of emotion? How do we know if they are good, bad, or irrelevant? Science offers us an underlying framework that both describes and explains the centrality of integration in the functioning of systems such as minds, brains, relationships, families, schools, and communities. Complexity theory offers a mathematical view into these questions and into the importance of integration. When an open system is capable of chaotic behavior, we call this a complex dynamical system. Such complex systems include clouds, a mind, a brain, or a relationship. They are called *nonlinear* in that small inputs can lead to large and unpredictable changes in the system. As such, nonlinear systems move through time, and their behavior is governed by a self-organizational process. Self-organization moves the system toward maximizing complexity. This odd and nonintuitive idea can be made more accessible when we read the details of this complexity theory's predictions: When a system links its differentiated elements together, it achieves maximal complexity. Herein lies the central role of integration as it moves the system in a unique state. With this integrative state of maximal complexity the system is the most flexible, adaptive, and stable. When I first read that, I fell off my chair and thought, "What an eloquent definition of well-being!" If we read on, we find that this flow toward maximal complexity occurs with integration and actually achieves the qualities we can remember with the acronym FACES: flexible, adaptive, coherent, energized, and stable.

And so this perspective yields a working definition we can consider of emotional well-being as an integrated system. And what happens when integration is lowered, when maximal complexity is not being promoted? When the system is not integrated, it reveals rigidity, chaos, or both. For example, if we are emotionally distressed, integration is decreased and we move into states of rigidity, chaos, or both. Even a random dive into the *Diagnostic and Statistical Manual of Mental Disorders* (DSM) reveals that any symptom of an "emotional disorder" has this profile. Such a review suggests that we could see integration as the heart of well-being that creates a flexible and adaptive state. This flow of a coherent mind is a river bounded by rigidity on one side and chaos on the other—giving us a new approach toward the evaluation of emotional health. We take "the pulse" of integration by assessing rigidity–chaos parameters in a person's or relationship's life. Individuals at various moments of their lives and in various settings reveal chaos and/or rigidity or they reveal the harmony of a FACES flow. Chaos might be seen as unstable affective outbursts, intrusive thoughts, impulsive behaviors. Rigidity can be revealed as repeating patterns of inflexible thinking or behaving, stuck ways of relating to others, self-destructive habits. Combinations of chaos and rigidity can be revealed in disturbances of self-regulation and in functions such as thinking or controlling attention.

And what does an integrated system look like? At the heart of this integrated FACES flow is the term *coherence*, which itself is an acronym for its own characteristics: connected, open, harmonious, engaged, receptive, emergent (something fresh and new), noetic (a sense of authentic knowing), compassionate, and empathic. These qualities help describe the nature of a life well lived, a feeling of exuberance and vitality, a state of flexibility and openness. This is the harmonious flow of an integrated system.

In contrast, consider times when you may have felt emotionally unwell. What was the sense of those states? For me, perhaps through the biased and distorting lens of my own top-down story of emotion as integration, such moments fit into this view of chaos and/or rigidity. The experience and concept are these: An integrative state moves like a river with a coherent and harmonious flow bounded on either side by the banks of chaos or rigidity. Trauma is a good example of an impairment in integration—a blockage to emotional well-being. As we saw in the example of the 25-year-old patient, described above, unresolved states can be prone to intrusive memories and images. We can also experience a shutting down into rigid states of avoidance and withdrawal. In many ways, unresolved trauma reveals a mind moving outside the central integrative flow of coherence. But what is actually flowing in this flow of well-being?

The FACES Flow of Integration

Emotional health can be seen as a form of resilience in which an integrated system—our nervous system, our relationships, our minds—moves in a particular flow. As we've seen, this flow can be described as flexible, adaptive, coherent, energized, and stable—that is, FACES. Certain regions of the brain participate in creating such an integrated state that links widely separated areas to each other. These regions are, literally, integrative in that they physically connect distinct, often anatomically distant, areas to one another via synaptic linkages. Of note: It is the integrative regions that also play a role in self-regulation, and it is also these integrative areas that may continue to grow into our adulthood. And further, childhood trauma and neglect have been found to impair the growth of the integrative fibers of the brain.

An important example of a regulatory integrative region is the front-most part of the frontal lobe of the neocortex: the prefrontal cortex just behind our foreheads. The middle area of this prefrontal region literally links the energy and informational flow from the cortex with the subcortical limbic, brainstem, and somatic regions. The prefrontal region also creates representations of other minds, of other nervous systems' states, so that we can add the social to this list. Linkage of social, somatic, brainstem, limbic, and cortical representations into a functional whole is a wonderful example of what we mean by the term *neural integration*.

And here we see that the neural regions considered essential for executive functions and for self-regulation are inherently integrative. We can propose that integrative regions—ones that link widely distributed and differentiated areas to each other—permit a coordination and balance to be achieved in the nervous system. "Affect regulation" is achieved via the coordination and balance of various areas of our nervous and social systems through the integrative fibers of the brain. Coordination involves the synchronous layering of firing in the nervous system to enable complex functions to be achieved. Balance implies the raising of some regions' activities with the simultaneous diminishment of others. Examples of this coordination and balance in the nervous system include the function of the middle prefrontal area in balancing the accelerating sympathetic branch of the autonomic nervous system with the decelerating parasympathetic/brakes branch. Across the hemispheres, the integrating fibers of the corpus callosum enable the homologous—or matching—areas of the right to mutually inhibit the firing of that area in the left hemisphere. With coordination and balance, integrative regions contribute to the regulatory functions of our brains, bodies, and relationships with each other.

This perspective on integration also raises an important dimension of our internal experience. We have considered the idea that emotion is a verb, not a noun. Integration is an active, changing process that moves through time. It is composed of two fundamental dynamic processes: differentiation of components of a system and then their linkage together in time. This layering of connection and interconnection permits coordination and balance to move a system through time as it achieves a dynamic and harmonious flexibility in its functioning. This is how integration can be seen as the heart of health—in a body, a brain, a mind, a relationship, or a group such as a community or a society. When we "emotionally process" something within any of these levels of experience, we are altering the state of integration of our system.

The Undefined Mind

But what elements of the system are differentiated and linked? We can sense a flow of something, but what is it? Notice how you feel when you read this word: *YES!* What do you notice in your experience? Now read this and see if you feel anything different: *NO . . . No . . . No. . . .* You may sense a difference in the quality of energy flowing through you. So energy flow, something even physicists are challenged to define but that we can feel directly, is part of the dynamic of integration. And what else? *Yes* and *no* have information embedded in them. They are linguistic symbols of something other than themselves. You may have experienced various bodily sensations when reading the words, then images, feelings, and even thoughts. These are various experiences that have information in them, such as that of an image or a word-based thought. If you saw red when you read "No," you should know that there is no red in your head, just the informational representation of the color.

We now come to a central element of this whole approach: the mind. Here is a strange and embarrassing research finding: The mind has not been defined in the training of over 95% of 77,000 therapists I've surveyed in lectures around the globe. In each of our various disciplines of mental health practice there is an odd absence of definition: What is the "mental" or even the "health" of what we are practicing? In interpersonal neurobiology we have had the opportunity to learn that a working definition of the mind can be a useful starting point: *The mind can be defined, in part, as a relational and embodied process that regulates the flow of energy and information.* This definition was of use to a study group of over 40 scientists gathering for 4 years to study the relationship between mind and brain. These individuals represented over a dozen sciences and found this working definition relevant in their individual pursuits. And in clinical practice, this definition offers us a shared starting point with which to define the entity we focus upon and to even then propose what a healthy mind might be.

As energy and information flow within the body–brain and relationships, various degrees of differentiation and linkage occur. Integration is a dynamic process of the mind that emerges as differentiated elements of this flow are linked together. In this way, emotion, clarified as integration, reveals how our feelings are the music of the mind—the fundamental pattern of energy and information flow that is at the heart of our subjective lives. We can propose that a healthy mind comes from an integrated flow in which the music of our minds achieves a state of harmony and coherence.

Types of Emotion/Integration

You may be wondering, "What does Dan do with issues such as those universal affects Darwin described over 100 years ago?" or "What about that whole business of motivational states and emotion that Jaak Panksepp and Steve

Porges so beautifully describe?" And how about the work of affect regulation embedded within relational aspects of emotional communication eloquently described by Allan Schore, Ed Tronick, and Colwyn Trevarthen? And the clinical work of pioneers such as Diana Fosha, Pat Ogden, and Marion Solomon in using these ideas of attachment, the body, and the centrality of emotion in the therapeutic process? (Please see this volume's chapters for these individuals' most current thinking on these and other related topics).

Here is one way in which we can approach these important questions. In common language, the term *emotion* often evokes the connotation of one of the seven basic states Darwin indeed described over a century ago. These are sometimes called the categorical emotions and include the familiar feelings of joy, surprise, fear, anger, sadness, disgust, and shame we discussed earlier in this chapter. These are also called the "universal" affects because the expression of these internal states—the affects—has been identifiable in cultures throughout the world. When a finding is universal, we sometimes view it as a hardwired, innate, genetically determined feature. Other basic universal affects that reveal a common internal state could also include states such as pride, confusion, rage, and betrayal. There are many states an individual is capable of experiencing that can be readily detected by other people.

How do we view such universal affective expressions in light of the proposal of this chapter that emotion *is* integration? Here is the idea: Each of these categorical emotions reveals the way in which we create common pathways of neural firing that link together states of activation into a functional whole we call an emotional state of mind. For example, the specific neural firings that cluster together for anger are different from those areas that link together for joy or for sadness. Each categorical emotion is created by a form of integration—the linkage of differentiated circuits—that is characteristically present for that particular state. A categorical emotion reflects this organized shift in the system's state of integration. We can even see how particular states of mind in one person can be perceived and then instantiate a similar state in the physiological response of another person. This basic form of affective resonance may be the underlying mechanisms by which two differentiated people become linked. But notice that we do not become the other person: Integration is not the same as homogenization. Each person can retain a sense of individuation even in the face of intimate interconnection. Through mirror properties inherent in our nervous systems, we come to resonate with each others' states, not become carbon copies. We then take the information from this altered state of interpersonal integration and access it through our insula, the passageway from the subcortical world from which affects arise to the cortical correlates of consciousness. It is through this flow from cortical perceptual mirror neuron activities to sub–cortical limbic–brainstem–bodily resonance and then back up to cortical representation that we come to feel the feelings of others, to be aware of our own internal state as a reflection of the internal world of another. As we take this vital subcortical data upward with interoception, the insula enables our prefrontal regions to receive the basic information needed to create images of the other's point of view in something we call empathic imagination. In this way, the linkage through affective perception of body to body, cortex to subcortex, subcortex back to cortex, enables the highly complex integrated state of empathy to be achieved.

We can see that the sharing of affective states, of emotional resonance, is a fundamental form of integration. Such resonance occurs with subtle nonverbal expressions of our internal state and how they come to be perceived by others, creating interpersonal integration. And even categorical emotions, with their internal states of neural net firing and their external affective expressions, are highly cohesive states that can be shared between people, identified, and labeled. As differentiated circuits are linked together, the degree of arousal can motivate us to action; hence we have *e-motion*, in which integrative firing motivates us to move, to act, to behave in particular ways. If I am walking down the street and not much is happening, but then I see an old friend and feel a sense of surprise and joy, my state of integration has shifted, and I am now "emotional," and it was an "emotionally meaningful experience."

I went for a walk this Thanksgiving with an old friend and in the course of our long seaside stroll, he began to cry profusely as we discussed issues about the meaning of life and decision points in our development. At that point, the discussion indeed induced a shift in integration—and hence was emotionally meaningful. At any point of change, there is also the risk of shifting out of the harmonious FACES flow of maximizing complexity with integration. In this incident, my friend moved toward chaos. He said that before the tears came, he also had found himself shutting down—becoming rigid—in our discussion of meaning and development and our looking deeply into our life's journeys. As our energy and information flow across time, we are in a dynamic process in which states of differentiation and linkage are forever changing. As we share those states and their dynamic shifts, as we blend the music of our minds with each other, we become open to unpredictable shifts that remind us we are all complex nonlinear systems in perpetual flux. When those states move in significant ways, we have an "emotional moment." Along that time of change, though, we can move through periods of disequilibrium in which the flow of the system moves away from complexity and into rigidity, chaos, or shimmering in combinations of both.

As my friend and I continued the walking and the talking, we explored just this issue. Staying present within awareness through the moments that unfold within rigidity or chaos enable those states to move in their natural process toward an inherent push the mind exerts for integrative complexity. This movement directly describes the experience of affect regulation and its fundamental interpersonal nature. *Because the mind's energy and information flow is both embodied and relational, regulating this flow is both neural and interpersonal.* We achieve new levels of integrative complexity by engaging in our internal and interpersonal worlds with the courage to transform our present state. Rather than this being just another early morning walk, my friend and I were both transformed because of the integrative nature of the talk. You might call this an "emotional walk" and, now that we've come this far in our journey together, I think we could agree that this is synonymous with a shared experience of integrative transformation. This is the natural path of healing, one that my friend and I could experience in the safety of each other's company.

But sometimes our paths get stuck and we find ourselves in the rut of rigidity and/or chaos as an engrained pattern in our lives. Whether we have a formal DSM diagnosis (which, startlingly, fits this notion of chaos and/or rigidity throughout its pages) or our own unique blend of movement in some personalized stuck fashion, we can now view how emotional health depends upon integration.

The Music of the Mind: Our Basic or Primary Emotions

In *The Developing Mind* I suggest that one nomenclature for processes involving the idea of "emotion" is to consider the mind's basic mechanisms like the primary colors of the rainbow. In that text the mind is defined as an embodied and relational process that regulates the flow of energy and information. This energy and information flow is happening all the time, and its texture, the music of the mind, can be considered "primary emotion." The layers of processing that occur include the following outline. (1) Attention is alerted such that the direction of energy and information flow is oriented in a specific pattern. This is called *primary orientation*. (2) Once the mind is focused in a particular way, the brain rapidly assesses whether this thing being attended to is "good" and should be amplified, or "bad" and to be avoided. This can be called *appraisal* and is the initial way in which meaning is created by the evaluative circuits of the brain. (3) As orientation and appraisal unfold, a layered process of *arousal* ensues in which the brain integrates itself—links differentiated regions together—to carry out effective information processing and behavioral enactment. Such arousal can lead to the classic universal emotional states described earlier, or to a unique configuration of firing that clusters differentiated regions together in a one-of-a-kind way (this one-off state is the more common experience). When we significantly shift integrative states, we would say that we have had an "emotional" experience. Because arousal itself is not a unitary process, the various energy levels and drives toward reward satisfaction can have layered degrees of engagements in our many states of mind.

With the less frequent universal states of categorical emotion and the more common unfolding of unique states of mind, we have a shared notion: Integration is being significantly altered. As the mind regulates energy and information flow within the body and between and among people, we can see that the dynamic process is the *state of mind*. Explored in great detail in *The Developing Mind* (1999), elaborated in *The Mindful Brain* (2007), and applied in therapy in *Mindsight* (in press), these states of mind can be shaped by the focus of our attention. In many ways, secure interpersonal relationships and mindful awareness harness a particular receptive state of mind that promotes integration and facilitates the flexible, adaptive, coherent, energized, and stable qualities of the flow of integration.

Integration, Mindsight, and Psychotherapy

Naturally this discussion of emotion as integration raises the fundamental question of what the transformative process of psychotherapy does to promote "emotional well-being." If our proposal is true that emotion is integration, then we can take a fresh look at psychotherapy in general, and at specific forms of interventions, including evidence-based approaches in particular, to see if there would be a consilience among treatment modalities that work. In my own personal journey over this last decade teaching to a wide array of therapeutic associations, it has been both rewarding and informative to see that the concept of integration has been welcomed and accepted as a valid mechanism that illuminates the underlying efficacy of the work of a broad range of groups focusing on individual, couples, family, and group therapeutic settings. From psychodynamic therapy to EMDR, Adlerian to family systems work, seeing integration at the heart of well-being illuminates the various mechanisms beneath these seemingly disparate approaches.

Meta-analyses of psychotherapy reveal that it is the "nonspecific" psychotherapeutic relationship that is the most robust feature leading to transformation in psychotherapy. When we look at these criteria in detail, it becomes clear that each of them—from the therapeutic alliance to empathy to openness to feedback—reveals an aspect of integration at work. Let's recall that *integration* is a very specific concept, not some California New-Age anything-goes term (I think I can say this as a native Californian still residing here). Integration is the linkage of differentiated parts. Within the common features of the therapeutic relationship, for example, alliance is the way in which two people align their goals; empathy is the means by which the therapist is receptive to the internal state of the patient and focuses attention on that shared state; through openness to feedback the therapist honors the input from the valued perspective of the client so that there is an explicit recognition that there is no "immaculate perception" and that the therapist and patient/client are collaborative partners in the journey toward healing. These aspects of the therapy each involve a process called "mindsight," in which we nurture our innate capacity to perceive our own mind and the mind of others. In this way, at the heart of effective therapy may be the capacity to cultivate our human ability for empathy and insight as we promote kinder relationships—both interpersonally and with ourselves. Mindsight is an internally and interpersonally integrative process.

Beyond these important integrative aspects of the therapeutic relationship, we can also propose that effective psychotherapy of any sort creates lasting change by altering the synaptic connections in the brain. We can call this the way we SNAG the brain: <u>s</u>timulate <u>n</u>euronal <u>a</u>ctivation and <u>g</u>rowth. As we join with the patient/client, the joint focus of attention stimulates neuronal firing. This state of shared focus alters neural activation such that neurons that fire together wire together in specific ways that harness higher states of integration. It isn't just that we are saying, "Let's go out and change the brain willy-nilly." Instead, we can propose that such SNAGing promotes healing by literally activating anatomically and functionally distributed neuronal groupings and linking their simultaneous firing in a way that leads to growth in integrative neuronal fibers. These neuronal pathways are called *interneurons* in more localized regions, or they may be of longer length and interconnecting more widely separated and differentiated regions. These latter integrative neurons are found in various areas such as the prefrontal cortex, the hippocampus, the corpus callosum, and the cerebellum. In research paradigms and in clinical settings we would seek to explore the ways in which the growth of these and other integrative fibers enables the systems of the person (body, mind, relationships) to achieve the FACES flow as a way of being. Markers of nonintegration—chaos and/or rigidity—would be our guideposts as we seek to identify and promote patterns in enhanced well-being through the integrative state of harmony and coherence.

One overall perspective we could propose is that interpersonal communication that honors the differentiated experiences of each person and then links them together is "integrative communication." This type of communication links differentiated minds as energy and information are passed back and forth between two or more people. We can view this energy and information flow between and among people as stimulating energy and information flow within each person in a way that is itself integrative. That is, disparate regions of the individual's nervous system distributed throughout the whole body— what we can simply call the *Brain* (with a capital *B*)—is in this state of mind linking differentiated areas together. In this manner, integrative communication facilitates integrative neuronal firing.

In the field of neuroplasticity, we have come to understand that patterns of neuronal firing lead to the activation of genetic material, such that protein is produced and new synapses are formed, old ones strengthened, and even neuronal stem cells are stimulated to grow into synaptically interwoven mature neurons. Based on a wide array of scientific findings and their consilient analysis, we could propose that integrative communication activates neuronal firing that is integrative and produces the conditions to promote the growth of integrative fibers in the nervous system. That's our proposal for effective therapeutic mechanisms of action in a nutshell. The result is a change in the Brain of each individual involved. This is how "emotionally therapeutic" relationships are at their core integrative as they SNAG the Brain.

The Triangle of Well-Being and Domains of Integration

This proposal of emotion as integration leads to the natural question, "Is there a way to organize an approach to psychotherapy with integration at its core?" The answer is "yes," and what follows is a very brief outline of such an approach. A chapter of *The Mindful Brain* (Siegel, 2007) and an entire book, *Mindsight* (Siegel, in press), are devoted to this approach and offer clinical examples illustrating each of the nine domains of integration described below. In this chapter, space considerations allow us to touch only lightly on the general notion of these areas.

To begin we need to propose a "triangle of well-being" which helps us envision the issues involved in integration. The triangle is essentially a metaphoric way of viewing energy and information flow. On one point of the triangle is the Mind: the regulation of energy and information flow. Another point is Relationships: the sharing of energy and information flow. And the third point is the "Brain" (or the distributed nervous system throughout the whole body), which embraces the neural mechanisms of energy and information flow. These are three irreducible elements. There is no need to create only one element.

Instead, this regulation, sharing, and physical mechanism of energy and information flow can be seen as the essence of human experience. When we focus on well-being, we can think of a coherent Mind, empathic Relationships, and a flexible and adaptive nervous system, the integrated Brain. Each of these reflects a state of integrated energy and information flow.

A psychotherapist armed with this triangle of well-being can enter the system of the individual or couple or family at any point: Relationships, Mind, or Brain. Each basic element mutually influences the others. By examining layers of chaos and/or rigidity, the evaluation process assesses the nature of integration in various domains. Therapeutic strategic planning is an emergent process embedded within this evaluation and the relationship between therapist and client/patient(s). At least nine domains can be articulated as a helpful framework for approaching the SNAGging of the system—that is, the way in which we inspire clients/patients to rewire their nervous systems, create coherence in mind, and compassion and empathy in their relationships.

These domains of integration, described in richer detail in the texts named above, can then serve to orient areas of focus within therapy.

The *integration of consciousness* involves the linkage of differentiated aspects of attention into a state of mindful awareness in the moment. A virtual tripod is constructed in which the camera of the mind's awareness is then able to offer a more vivid, richer, detailed, and clearly focused picture of objects of attention, including the fabric of the mind itself. This reflective tripod consists of three o's: openness to what is; objectivity that the objects of attention are not the totality of one's identity, and observation of the self as the experiencer of events.

These formal facets of mindfulness overlap with aspects of our psychotherapy goals. At the heart of such reflective practice is an integrative process in which the mind is open to what is, rather than being enslaved by prior learning and the consequent distortion of experience into what should be or what was. One stunning overlap uncovered in the journey to understand mindful awareness and its possible correlations with neural integration, secure attachment, and psychotherapy has been the following list of processes: (1) bodily regulation; (2) attuned communication; (3) affective balance; (4) fear modulation; (5) response flexibility; (6) self-understanding or "insight"; (7) empathy; (8) morality; and (9) intuition. This list was generated by working with a patient who had suffered a severe blow to her forehead resulting in damage to the middle portions of her prefrontal cortex. This region is profoundly integrative, and this array of middle prefrontally mediated processes—from bodily function to morality—are created by way of neural integration.

These are examples of what we mean by the FACES flow of flexibility, adaptability, coherence, energy, and stability.

The first eight elements of this list are also the independently proven outcomes of secure parent–child attachment (the last one, intuition, has not yet been studied in this context). Could this be a coincidence? Or could these be an example of what we in interpersonal neurobiology propose? Secure relationships are filled with integrative communication that promotes the growth of integrative fibers in the nervous system. It turns out that this list is also both the outcome and the process of mindful practice. Further, after asking thousands of psychotherapists, I can also state that this is a commonly held "wish list" for the outcome of effective psychotherapy and for a description of mental health. Teaching recently to early educators in Alaska, I was also told by a tribal elder that many points on this list have been the highlight of what the spiritual leaders of the Inuit culture have been teaching over the last 5,000 years as the essence of wisdom and well-being.

Vertical integration entails the linkage within awareness of our energy and information flow across the vertical plane, as we link somatic processes into cortically mediated awareness. *Horizontal integration* involves the linkage of the differentiated processing of the right and left sides of the brain. These anatomically oriented domains of integration entail bringing into awareness often-disparate elements of our information flow and honoring each of them. For example, in body-centered work we bring the sensations of the body up into cortically mediated awareness as a form of vertical integration. In narrative-based work, we enable the logical, linear, linguistic left hemisphere to draw upon the imagistic, holistic, nonverbal, bodily, autobiographical, and stress-reducing mechanisms of the right hemisphere. A coherent narrative can be seen to emerge from a bilateral form of horizontal integration.

Differentiated elements of neural firing embed experience into synaptic connections in something we call "memory." In many ways, memory is the way an experience in the past alters the way the mind functions in the present and the future. In research terms, "implicit" memory forms the basic building blocks of how an experience becomes embedded in the brain in the form of perceptual, affective, behavioral, and bodily memory. Without the integrative coordination of the hippocampus, these implicit puzzle pieces of memory remain isolated from each other. With the integration of the master puzzle-piece assembler, the hippocampus, we then have the emergence of factual and autobiographical forms of what is called "explicit" memory. With such *integration of memory*, we now know that when something is brought into awareness as a fact or as a sense of self from the past, it feels as if we are recalling something.

Memory integration refers to the ways in which we connect implicit memory into its more interwoven factual and autobiographical forms.

In *narrative integration,* the additional process of a "narrator" creates meaning as we harness this mental function that enables clusters of lived experience to be witnessed from afar. This witnessing self offers an important vantage point from which new decisions and perspectives can be derived to lift a person out of automatic pilot. Without narrative integration, we may be no more than passive observers of an ongoing drama. With narrative integration, we become the active authors of our own living story as it unfolds.

The brain has over 100 *billion* neurons with hundreds of *trillions* of connections among them. If the on–off firing patterns of the brain somehow correlate with our subjective experience of mind, then we could state that there is an estimated 10 times 10, 1 million times (i.e., 10 to the millionth power) of possible states of mind. What, then, does *state integration* actually entail? These clusters of neural firing patterns develop engrained profiles that are repeated across time. State integration refers to at least two dimensions of the linkage of these differentiated states of firing. The first dimension is within a given state. Some states of mind have an internal coherence that makes them stable and effective. An example might be a tennis-playing state of mind. Other states may be incoherent and prone to movement toward chaos and/or rigidity. Someone who was betrayed by a tennis teacher who sexually abused him or her would be an example of an incoherent state of tennis-playing. Unresolved states of trauma or loss are examples of impaired state integration.

A second dimension of state integration effects a linkage of information and energy flow across states, rather than within them. We have different motivational circuits that function to achieve different goals. Life is a heterogeneous mixture of needs and goals and states of mind that effectively (or not) carry out the internal processing and external behavior to meet those needs. Owning the complexity of human life is a part of honoring these different states and moving toward collaboration rather than believing that one state should dominate another.

Interpersonal integration also honors the unique states within different individuals. Integrative communication enables us to be open to the internal states of another, make sense of the other's needs, and then respond in a timely and effective manner. This contingency is found in all cultures and serves to promote a highly integrative state between two people: Each individual's differences are respected (i.e., differentiation is promoted) and his or her internal worlds are connected (i.e., linkage is promoted). This interpersonal integration is the heart of well-being in our relationships with each other.

The final two domains of integration bring us to some basic existential questions of human life. In *temporal integration* we embrace the issues raised by the passage of time. Three elements emerge in the ways in which the past, present, and future can be integrated. The first relates to the drive for certainty in the face of the reality of uncertainty. As this natural push to know and to predict the outcome of events meets face to face with life's lessons about the ultimate unpredictability and unknowable nature of how events unfold, we are faced with the first aspect of temporal integration. Allowing the drive for certainty to exist while we embrace authentically the reality of uncertainty is the challenge of linking differentiated aspects of our mental life.

A second aspect of temporal integration involves the idea and longing for permanence: that things we love and cherish remain forever. Yet reality hits us head on with the truth that nothing is permanent. Resolving this tension evokes the ability to honor our drive for permanence but to also welcome the unavoidable reality of transience in life.

Finally, our third dimension of temporal integration focuses on our drive for immortality in the face of the reality of death. So much of human life is spent on avoiding the reality of our mortality or driving us to various explanations of the nature of life and death. Temporal integration enables us to invite all of these longings of the mind—for immortality, permanence, and certainty—and their counterparts in solid reality—mortality, impermanence, and uncertainty. Time is the common dimension here, as we use our cortical machinery to represent life across time, we come to sense these central existential issues. Running from them, avoiding the challenges of temporal integration, throws us into patterns of chaos and/or rigidity in our effort to deny reality.

The ninth domain of integration moves us beyond our individual sense of a bodily and time-defined self as we come to feel a part of a larger whole. *Transpirational integration* refers to the ways in which we come to embrace the importance of a personal identity and coherent life history, linking us across all the previous eight domains of integration. But as we "across-breathe" or "transpire" through these domains, what seems to occur is a dissolving of the illusion of a wholly separate self. The previously rigid definition of a self that is contained within a body in this century of life on Earth seems to melt away as a sense of belonging to a much larger whole emerges. This belonging seems to happen naturally, without any effort or intention. Instead the top-down enslavements of a narrowly defined sense of self give way and in their place emerge a common description of a much larger self, a fuller mind, a sense of belonging to a larger whole.

The practical implication of this transpirational integration is that people seem to experience a widening in their sense of connection. Taking part in movements to help improve local communities, larger efforts at helping people they've never met, or feelings of commitment to helping the planet in ways that none of us alive today may come to enjoy—each of these ways of being a part of a larger whole seem to appear naturally.

Discussing emotion as integration, as we link our individual sense of self with its own unique, differentiated history to the selves of others now, in the past, and also in a future we will never directly see, we come to realize our "emotional ties" to a much larger whole. This is perhaps the essence of emotional health for our planet: We come to see that we are all interconnected, each a part of the other, part of one living, breathing organism we call life on Earth. Perhaps with a movement toward integration we can feel the sense of compassion and ease that emerge from such states of well-being—for us, here and now, and for future generations who will receive this message through our words, our relationships, and our integrative efforts to heal our world.

7

Emotion and Recognition at Work

Energy, Vitality, Pleasure, Truth, Desire & The Emergent Phenomenology of Transformational Experience[1]

Diana Fosha

"When the mind regards itself and its own power of activity, it feels pleasure: and that pleasure is greater in proportion to the distinctness wherewith it conceives itself and its own power of activity."
  —de Spinoza (1677/2005, Part 3, Proposition LIII; emphasis added)

"One [sculpture] drew her more than the others. It didn't mean it was better made; only that it had something special about it that worked particularly well for her. . . . *The sense that came through of the author. Wasn't that what made any work of art effective?* You got little sidelong glimpses of a soul, *and, if it resonated in a certain way with your own, you wanted more."*
  —Block (2003, pp. 223, 228–229; emphasis added)

ALONG WITH SUFFERING, psychopathology brings with it an energy crisis: There is a shrinking of the sphere of life lived with zest, a depletion of resourcefulness, and a growing restriction of the inner and outer lives of the individuals

---

1. This chapter is dedicated to Allan Whiteman in recognition of, and gratitude for, his being precisely who he is.

so afflicted (all of us at moments, some of us when moments develop into patterns and grooves). That is why a fundamental goal of the experiential therapies, along with ameliorating symptoms and relieving suffering, is to restore vitality and energy—the fuel for life.

This chapter is devoted to something as basic to the therapeutic process as the air we breathe: the process of transformation. It explores how, through a transformational process rooted in emotional experience, suffering can morph into flourishing, contraction can be motivationally reversed, and a reorientation toward growth can be achieved.

Emotions are, par excellence, vehicles of change; when regulated and processed to completion, they can bring about healing and lasting transformations. The experiential therapies, or the ABTs (affective balance therapies), as Panksepp (Chapter 1, this volume) calls them, make active use of emotions to that end. Accelerated experiential dynamic psychotherapy (AEDP; Fosha, 2000, 2002, 2003, 2005) is one such ABT.

The phenomenology of the transformational process that is unfolded here declared itself in the course of AEDP work with emotion in the context of an emotionally engaged therapeutic relationship. We discovered that not only does the processing of emotions release the adaptational resources contained within them, but also that the exploration of the *experience* of transformation activates a nonlinear, nonfinite *transformational spiral* (Fosha, in press). Elucidating the phenomenology of emotion-based transformational experience is the unifying thread of this chapter and its first theme.

The second theme involves the discovery that positive affects, positive interactions, and the process of healing transformation are organically intertwined. Positive, attuned, dyadic interactions are the constituents of healthy, secure attachments and the correlates of neurochemical environments conducive to optimal brain growth (Panksepp, 2001; Schore, 2001; Trevarthen, 2001a). Positive affects are the constituent phenomena of physical health, mental health, resilience, and well-being (Fosha, in press; Fredrickson & Losada, 2005). And AEDP work has revealed that the transformational process—when moving in the direction of healing—is accompanied moment to moment, by positive somatic/affective markers (Fosha, 2004; Fosha & Yeung, 2006; Russell & Fosha, 2008; Yeung & Cheung, 2008).

And yet change, even healing change, however much desired and sought, poses a challenge. For it to be palatable, change must be balanced with identity, adaptation with homeostasis. Emotions bring a piece of the world to us and into us, providing unprecedented opportunities for growth. But emotions must be regulated so that their yield can be woven into the fabric of the self. Lest we provoke an affective autoimmune response, the "new" that emotions bring must, in one way or another, acquire some flavoring of the familiar that will make them recognizable to the self as self. This is where the *recognition process* comes in (Sander, 2002). If emotion is our way into difference, expansion, and growth, then recognition is our way back into the self. The dialectic of emotion–accommodation and recognition–assimilation in emotion-based healing transformations is the chapter's third theme.

Transformance, the term for the overarching motivation for transformation that pulses within us (Fosha, 2008), is the fourth. Innate dispositional tendencies toward growth, learning, healing, and self-righting are wired deep within our brains and press toward expression when circumstances are right. Unlike the conservative motivational strivings under the aegis of resistance, which, in the long run, consume and drain psychic energy, transformance-based motivational strivings, when actualized, are energizing and vitalizing. The work on emotion and recognition and their role in transformational work is located within the context of transformance.

One last theme: At the nexus of neuroscience and clinical process lie phenomena. The phenomenological sensibility informs both clinical and conceptual aspects of this work, with the goal of extending the work on the phenomenology of emotion (Darwin, 1872/1965; James, 1890/1950, 1902; Tomkins, 1962) to include the positive affective phenomena associated with the cascading transformational processes. A commitment to descriptive phenomenology can thus substantively contribute to the emergent conversations among clinicians, scientists, developmentalists, and practitioners of Sino-Indo-Tibetan contemplative practices (Bushell, Olivo, & Theise, in press; Davidson & Harrington, 2002; Davidson, Kabat-Zinn, Schumacher, Rosenkrantz, et al., 2003; Fosha, in press), trumping territorial battles fought through different traditions of terminology that impede rather than foster progress.

This chapter builds on previous work on bodily rooted affective change processes and their role in experiential therapy (e.g., Gendlin, 1996; Greenberg & Paivio, 1997; Greenberg, Rice, & Elliott, 1993; Levine, 1997; McCullough Vaillant, 1997; Ogden et al., 2006), including my own previous writings (Fosha, 2003, 2004, 2005). However, whereas earlier work focused on the processing of overwhelming emotion to completion to resolve trauma and emotional suffering, this chapter focuses on *the processing of transformational experience* to consolidate and enhance therapeutic gains and promote flourishing.

- Part I introduces the constituent elements of the discussion: transformance, emotion, and recognition.
- Part II summarizes key aspects of AEDP, the lens through which the emotion-based transformational process is being viewed.

- Part III is devoted to the dynamics and phenomenology of the emotion-based transformational process.
- Part IV deals with the crisis that healing transformation can engender and its resolution through the metaprocessing of transformational experience.
- Part V is a case example illustrating the crisis that even positive transformations can bring and how it can be resolved.
- The concluding comments explore how the adaptive benefits of the transformational process increase through the energy and vitality associated with the emergent, limitless nature of the positive affective phenomena that characterize it.

Thus we will see how the emotion-based transformational process, in the context of dyadic safety and recognition, has within it the answer to the energy crisis that psychopathology creates.

Part I: On Transformance, Emotion, and Recognition

In the section that follows, the term *transformance* is introduced to name and honor the powerful motivational thrust that exists within us, a force toward healing that has long been ignored given our field's obsession with psychopathology. Agents of transformation, emotion, and recognition are explored as its agents, intertwined processes, the yin and yang of transformation.

On Transformance

Transformation is fundamental to our natures. Deep in our brains, there for the awakening and activation in facilitating environments, lodge wired-in dispositions for self-healing and self-righting (Doidge, 2007; Emde, 1983; Gendlin, 1996; Sander, 2002; Siegel, 2007) and for resuming impeded growth (Ghent, 1990; Grotstein, 2004; Winnicott, 1960/1965). *Transformance* is my term for the overarching motivational force that strives toward maximal vitality, authenticity, adaptation, and coherence, and thus leads to growth and transformation (Fosha, 2008). Naturally occurring affective change processes, such as emotion, dyadic affect regulation, and the empathic recognition of the self (Fosha, 2002), are manifestations of transformance-driven processes.

Transformation is the motivational counterpart of resistance. Whereas resistance is fueled by dread and the desire to avoid bad feelings, transformance is driven by hope and the search for the vitalizing positive experience. Resistance drives processes that achieve safety in the short run but eventuate in languishing, deterioration, and immobility; transformance drives processes that involve risk taking in the short run but eventuate in flourishing, resilience, health, and longevity (Fredrickson & Losada, 2005; Loizzo, in press). Wired for transformance, we naturally seek contexts in which we can surrender to our transformance strivings.

Key to the notion of transformance is its appetitive nature. "The brain . . . is not an inanimate vessel that we fill; rather it is more like a living creature with an appetite, one that can grow and change itself with proper nourishment and exercise" (Doidge, 2007, p. 47). We fulfill transformance strivings because we are wired to do so. When we do so, it feels good. And because it feels good, we want to do so more. The brain, motivated to learn from experience, responds plastically, for plasticity and motivation are linked (Doidge, 2007). Positive affects—that is, the reward aspect of enacting transformance strivings—light up the way. Whether we are talking about the secretion of dopamine and acetylcholine, or of oxytocin, or about the down-regulation of the amygdala as states of fear are replaced with exploratory states (Schore, personal communication, July 23, 2008), the brain registers and marks the positive nature of the experience and seeks to reengage it. In the process, we change and grow.

Finally, crisis and intense emotional suffering, *when experienced in conditions of safety*, can be a great boon to transformance strivings: The alchemy of transformance strivings together with the drive to relieve distress is an unbeatable mix for change.

On Emotion

Emotion theory and affective neuroscience (Damasio, 1994, 1999; Darwin, 1872/1965; Davidson et al., 2000; Panksepp, 1998a, Panksepp, Chapter 1, this volume; Tomkins, 1962, 1963) offer an account of change intrinsic to the experience of the *categorical emotions*, universal phenomena generated in the subcortical regions of the brain. Each categorical emotion—fear, anger, joy, sadness, disgust—plays a powerful role in survival. As Schore (2001, p. 21) says, "emotions [are] the highest order direct expression of bioregulation in complex organisms."

Emotion is fundamentally linked with change (Damasio, 1999). Our psychobiological response to conditions that violate expectations, emotions are the stuff that tells *us about us in relation to that change.* They come on board to register that something has changed, for good or bad, and that it behooves us—if we're interested in survival—to attend to that change and deal with it. In Damasio's words, "For certain classes of clearly dangerous or clearly valuable stimuli in the internal or external environment, *evolution has assembled a matching answer in the form of emotion*" (1999, p. 55; emphasis added). Motivation is intrinsic to emotion. Each emotion contains within it the pulse toward its own completion. Each categorical emotion is associated with a set of *adaptive action tendencies,* evolutionarily dedicated to endowing our bodies with the resources to contend with the situation that evoked the emotion to begin with (Frijda, 1986). Emotion is the experiential arc between the problem and its solution: Between the danger and the escape lies fear. Between novelty and its exploration lies joyful curiosity. Between the loss and its eventual acceptance lies the grief and its completion.

In addition to the unlocking of emotion-specific resources, release of the adaptive action tendencies is also accompanied by energy and vitality, which further bestow access to broadened thought–action repertoires and resilience (Fredrickson, 2001). Linked with adaptation, emotions are "ancestral tools for living" (Panksepp, Chapter 1, this volume). And, for us humans, they are also beacons of authenticity and organismic truth (Grotstein, 2004). But emotions are forces to contend with, which unless regulated, threaten to overwhelm us (McCullough, Kuhn, Andrews, Kaplan, Wolf et al., 2003; Osimo, 2002). According to Damasio (1999):

> A spontaneous smile that comes from genuine delight or the spontaneous sobbing that is caused by grief are [*sic*] executed by brain structures located deep in the brain stem under the control of the cingulate region. We have no means of exerting direct voluntary control over the neural processes in those regions. . . . We are about as effective at stopping an emotion as we are at preventing a sneeze. (p. 49)

Because of their suddenness, power, and invulnerability to fakery and voluntary control, we often experience emotions as foreign, as other, as external to us as "a clap of thunder or a hit" (Winnicott, 1960/1965, p. 141). Indeed, aloneness in the face of overwhelming emotions and the resultant need to ward them off for self-protection (with short-term benefits and long-term devastating consequences) and central in AEDP's conceptualization of how psychopathology develops. The questions become: How can we contend with emotions in a way that is progressive and transformance-informed rather than dread-driven and stopgap in its action? How can we make use of the transformational power of emotions and integrate their potentially profound gifts into our repertoires of self and relationships?

Enter recognition. For it is the process of recognition that holds the key to how to keep going forward, riding the river of emotion without needing to apply the damming counterforce of resistance. Recognition, as we are about to see, is the progressive alternative to resistance.

On Recognition

If emotion is what happens when we register a departure from the expected, recognition is the internal experience we have when something clicks into place—not so much "aha!" as "yes." Hart (1991) writes:

> There is an internal landscape, a geography of the soul; we search for its outline all our lives. . . . *Those who are lucky enough to find it* ease into it like water over a stone, onto its fluid contours, and *are home.* . . . We may go through our lives happy or unhappy, successful or unfulfilled, loved or unloved, without ever standing cold with the shock of *recognition,* without ever feeling the agony as the twisted iron in *our soul unlocks itself and we slip at last into place.* (p. 3; emphasis, added)

Recognition, specific and precise, occurs when there is "a moment of fittedness" (Sander, 2002, p. 19).[2] My usage of recognition includes, but goes beyond, the relational experience of being known: It refers to all experiences that occur whenever there is a match, a "click" between something inside and something outside, however *inside* and *outside* are subjectively defined.

In this chapter I am writing about recognition in two ways: as formal process and as receptive experience. Recognition as a receptive experience—that is, the felt sense of *feeling recognized,* is discussed later in the contexts of the transformational process and the clinical case.

Recognition as a process (Sander, 1995, 2002; see also, Lyons-Ruth, 2000) allows us to connect (1) the basic principles of organismic functioning (how we are wired) with (2) the emotion-based transformational processes through which we move when we self-right, heal, learn, and grow. Moment to moment, recognition is accompanied by and expressed through *vitality affects* (Stern, 2000), "spontaneous physiological rhythms that are manifest in arousal fluctuations, which are in turn expressed in fluctuating psychobiological affective states" (Schore, 2001, p. 21). These vitality affects have *positive somatic/affective markers* (e.g., deep sighs, fleeting smiles, head nods, sideways head tilts); they tell us that the transformational process is on track (Fosha, 2004).

---

2. By contrast, the moment that evokes emotion is a moment of *nonfittedness,* if you will, when the internal and the external do not match. Emotion arises when there is a violation of expectancy and the self has to reckon with it.

Recognition in the "how we are wired" sense is foundational to experiences that serve transformance strivings—that is, all *affective change processes* (Fosha, 2002). The developing self, actualizing its transformance strivings through the individual's engagement with some transformational process, becomes increasingly self-initiating and motivated to continue along this flow of experience. "It is how we feel our way along in unscripted relational transactions" (Lyons-Ruth, 2000, p. 92). It is this precise experience that guides the moment-to-moment, bottom-up processing of AEDP and other therapies that locate healing within the individual.[3]

This organismic recognition process occurs in experiential therapy when the moments of fittedness occur between the individual and some process in a dyadically co-constructed environment of safety. Recognition is always "dyadic" in that it involves two things fitting together, but it is not necessarily relational or interpersonal: the fit can be between self and other,[4] but it can also be between self and self, or self and process, or self and experience. The "click" occurs between what is felt as "me" and "not me," in a way that feels right and allows what was felt as "not me" to eventually become integrated into "me."[5]

A string of such moments of fittedness means that the individual is engaged in a transformational process. The flow of energy and vitality is enhanced, new phenomena and actions emerge, and the experience of what emerges thus becomes further motivating—a source of agency, direction, and self-initiative (Ghent, 2002; Sander, 2002). What Schore (2001) calls the "positively charged curiosity that fuels the burgeoning self's exploration of novel socioemotional and physical environments" is *"a marker of adaptive . . . mental health"* throughout the lifespan, not only in infancy (p. 21, emphasis added).

---

3. The use of recognition to guide the therapeutic process *assumes* that defensive blocks and inhibitory affects (e.g., anxiety, shame, guilt, fear) that scramble access to somatically based affective experience have been dealt with and that their impact is thus minimized. This is the stuff of technique and accounts for a large part of clinical writing, including my writing (e.g., Fosha, 2000). Howver, in this chapter, technique is not discussed, just assumed, or as it is said in the law, stipulated.

Nonetheless, it is necessary to make this point because recognition can accompany many phenomena that are the result of defensive and inhibiting affects and thus will not unleash healing transformational processes. Shunning people feels right to a schizoid person, and not getting out of bed can feel right to a depressed person, but recognition experiences that mark, reinforce, and amplify resistance-driven strivings are not the ones under discussion here. Nor are the techniques for transforming such experiences. What is under discussion are recognition experiences that mark, reinforce, and amplify transformance-driven strivings, to which the individual already has access.

4. See Fosha (2005) about recognition in the context of an encounter between True Self and True Other.

5. My hypothesis is that my "recognition processes" are similar to, or overlap with, what Panksepp and Northoff (2008) call self-related processing and Trevarthen (Chapter 2, this volume) calls the intrinsic motive formation (IMF).

Emotion and Recognition in Transformation

"The human mind," Dan Siegel tells us, "emerges from patterns in the flow of energy and information within the brain and between brains" (1999, p. 2). Emotion and recognition are two mechanisms that bring information and energy into the system. Emotions enlarge us as we face the environmental challenges that give rise to them, and recognition transforms us as we make seemingly foreign experiences our own. Through both moments of recognition and the activation of the adaptive action tendencies of emotion, along with new information, tremendous vitality and energy are released and made available to the organism.

Additionally, the balance of emotion and recognition processes allows the transformance strivings to go forward through the dialectical interplay of *emotion as accommodation*, through which we change our schemas to reflect new experiences, and *recognition as assimilation*, through which the new is integrated with already existing schemas. In the process of transformation, it is the psyche's system of checks and balances.

Part II: On AEDP, Its Healing Orientation, and Dyadic Affect Regulation

AEDP, which I and my colleagues developed and are developing (Fosha, 2000, 2002, 2003, 2004, 2005, 2006b, 2008, in press; Fosha & Yeung, 2006; Frederick, 2009; Gleiser et al., 2008; Lamagna & Gleiser, 2007; Prenn, 2009; Russell & Fosha, 2008; Tunnell, 2006; Yeung & Cheung, 2008), is the model and practice that informs these ideas on emotion-based transformation.[6]

Healing from the Get-Go

AEDP understands healing as a biologically wired-in process with its own phenomenology and dynamics, fundamentally different and separate from the process involved in repairing psychopathology (i.e., fixing what is broken). In AEDP, healing is not just the outcome of successful therapy, but rather a process to be activated from the get-go, as demonstrated in a published DVD of an initial session (Fosha, 2006a).

---

6. AEDP is a complex theoretical and clinical model of treatment. Only those aspects of the model that are most salient to the matters at hand are discussed here. For a comprehensive account, especially topics related to clinical issues and technique, the interested reader is invited to go to Fosha, 2000, 2003, 2008, and also to the AEDP website at *www.aedpinstitute.org*.

Most systems of psychotherapy regard the resistance-driven repetition of psychopathogenic patterns in the therapeutic situation as inevitable and believe that the corrective emotional experience comes in the scenario having a different ending (Alexander & French, 1946/1980). In AEDP, however, the repetition scenario is not seen as the inevitable shaper of the patient–therapist relationship. Accordingly, we don't just seek a new ending: From the outset we are also seeking a new beginning.

Aiming *to lead with* a corrective emotional experience (Fosha, 2000), we seek to facilitate conditions conducive for the entrainment of the transformance forces that are always present in people as dispositional tendencies. How we meet the patient, from the first encounter, will constitute the "features of sensitivity to initial conditions" (Sander, 2002, p. 16), and will have a lot to do with whether transformance or resistance strivings will be in ascendance. "Attachment decisively tilts whether we respond to life's challenges as opportunities for learning and expansion of the self or as threats leading to our constriction of activities and withdrawal from the world" (Fosha, 2006b, p. 570).

In AEDP, it is not sufficient that attachment operate implicitly, working as the background hum against which experience takes place. The patient's *experience* of the attachment relationship needs to be a major focus of therapeutic work (Fosha, 2006b). Thus, the processing of *receptive affective experiences* (i.e., experiences of being on the receiving end of what is subjectively felt as care, empathy, affirmation, or recognition) is as assiduously pursued as that of any other class of affective phenomena. Such receptive affective experiences are often described in terms of bodily sensations of warmth, melting, tingling, stirring, or relaxing. One patient said that her therapist's empathy felt like "warm liquid honey down her esophagus" (Osiason, personal communication, May 1, 2004). Receptive affective experiences form the substrate for many of the metatherapeutic processes that are discussed below.

The stance of AEDP is attachment based and sprinkled liberally with intersubjective delight in the patient. Following Lyons-Ruth (2007), Trevarthen (2001a), and Tronick (2003), who regard attachment motives for care and protection as different from intersubjective motives for companionship and pleasure, the stance of AEDP is conceived as having two strands. In the *attachment* strand, we meet all signs of pain, suffering, and fear with empathy and dyadic affect regulation, broadcasting our willingness to help. In the *intersubjective* strand, we focus on, and delight in, the quintessential qualities of the self of the patient; the therapist's delight *in* and *with* the patient is a powerful antidote to his or her shame (Hughes, 2006; Trevarthen, 2001a).

AEDP accomplishes the processing of heretofore unbearable emotion through three characteristic methods, all of which rely on the moment-to-moment tracking of fluctuations in affective experience: *dyadic affect regulation*, which is privileged here, since the rest of the chapter addresses the other two; *processing adaptive emotional experience to completion* (which AEDP shares with other experiential treatments—see Fosha, Paivio, Gleiser, & Ford, 2009; Gleiser et al., 2008; Greenberg & Paivio, 1997; Johnson, Chapter 10, this volume; Ogden, Chapter 8, this volume); and the *metatherapeutic processing of transformational experience*. The first and last are among AEDP's original technical contributions.

Dyadic Affect Regulation

AEDP understands psychopathology as resulting from the individual's unwilled and unwanted aloneness in the face of overwhelming emotions. The fundamental tenet that the patient not be left alone with overwhelming emotions is actualized through the process of dyadic affect regulation, AEDP's application and extension to the clinical situation of the developmental work of Beebe (Beebe & Lachmann, 1994, 2002) and Tronick (1989, 2003).

The process of dyadic affect regulation of emotion and relatedness proceeds through countless iterations of cycles of attunement, disruption, and repair. By means of the moment-to-moment affective communication that occurs through nonverbal, right-brain-mediated processes, the dyadic partners establish coordinated states, marked by positive affects. Because the experience of attunement is a pleasurable one, the coordinated state becomes a desired goal and is thus motivating.

Resilience-engendering dyads minimize the amount of time spent in negative emotions associated with stress and misattunement, and maximize the time spent in the coordinated states; the positive affects characterizing the latter correlate with neurochemical brain environments most conducive to growth and learning (Lyons-Ruth, 2007; Schore, 2003a, 2003b). In such dyads, the negative affect associated with disrupted attunement is a motivational spur toward repair and the restoration of coordination (Tronick, 1989).

Disruption occurs when one partner's experiences cannot be coordinated by the dyad. If attunement is the state in which self and other naturally resonate, to the delight of both, disruption is the realm of being on disturbingly different wavelengths. All the stuff excluded so as to maintain the previously coordinated state comes roaring back. In the disruption, the separateness and uniqueness of the self declares itself. However, if the disruption is repaired, it then becomes a major source of transformation.

Successful repair results in the establishment of a new, expanded coordinated state wherein differences can be encompassed and integrated; achieving that state is a vitalizing energizing human experience. "The flow of energy expands as states of brain organization in the two partners expand their complexity into new and more inclusive states of coherent organization" (Sander, 2002, p. 38). The achievement gives rise to new emergent phenomena that transform and expand the shared experience as well as the experience of each dyadic partner, reflecting how being together changes each of them (Beebe & Lachmann, 1994, 2002; Fosha, 2001, 2003; Hughes, 2006; Tronick, 2003; see also, Tronick, Chapter 4, this volume).

As we see below, dyadic affect regulation operates in both the *processing of emotional experience* and the *metaprocessing of transformational experience.*

Part III: The Emotion-Based Transformational Process

The notion of state is important here: Each state is characterized by a specific set of phenomena, which can reflect radically different capacities and ways of engaging and processing (cf. Porges, Chapter 2, this volume, for the ANS underpinnings for different states and their respective implications for what psychological functions are and are not likely to be entrainable). Crucially for the therapeutic enterprise as Tronick notes, "an individual's state of consciousness generates actions and intentions" (Tronick, in press). Thus the motivational characteristics of each state have very different implications for psychotherapeutic effectiveness.

Four States and Three State Transformations

Four states bridged by three state transformations (see Figure 7.1) characterize the transformational process.

STATE ONE—PHENOMENA THAT NEED TRANSFORMING:
STRESS, DISTRESS, AND SYMPTOMS
Characteristic of the state of affairs that brings the patient to treatment, State One phenomena result from strategies that have long stopped being adaptive and that have instead led either to Axis I problems (e.g., depression, anxiety, posttraumatic stress disorder [PTSD]), or to Axis II patterns and attendant problems in living and functioning. Characterized by the lack of regulated access to bodily based adaptive core affect, State One phenomena also result from the dominance of defenses and inhibiting affects such as shame and fear, which constitute strategies that block or scramble access to the individual's primary (i.e., core) affective experience. Dysregulation, by being disorganiz-

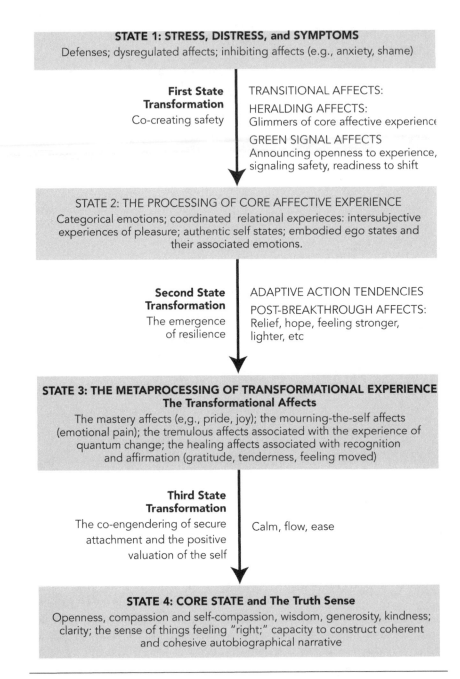

STATE 1: STRESS, DISTRESS, and SYMPTOMS
Defenses; dysregulated affects; inhibiting affects (e.g., anxiety, shame)

First State
Transformation
Co-creating safety

TRANSITIONAL AFFECTS:
HERALDING AFFECTS:
Glimmers of core affective experience
GREEN SIGNAL AFFECTS
Announcing openness to experience,
signaling safety, readiness to shift

STATE 2: THE PROCESSING OF CORE AFFECTIVE EXPERIENCE
Categorical emotions; coordinated relational experieces: intersubjective
experiences of pleasure; authentic self states; embodied ego states and
their associated emotions.

Second State
Transformation
The emergence
of resilience

ADAPTIVE ACTION TENDENCIES
POST-BREAKTHROUGH AFFECTS:
Relief, hope, feeling stronger,
lighter, etc

STATE 3: THE METAPROCESSING OF TRANSFORMATIONAL EXPERIENCE
The Transformational Affects
The mastery affects (e,g., pride, joy); the mourning-the-self affects
(emotional pain); the tremulous affects associated with the experience of
quantum change; the healing affects associated with recognition
and affirmation (gratitude, tenderness, feeling moved)

Third State
Transformation
The co-engendering of secure
attachment and the positive
valuation of the self

Calm, flow, ease

STATE 4: CORE STATE and The Truth Sense
Openness, compassion and self-compassion, wisdom, generosity, kindness;
clarity; the sense of things feeling "right;" capacity to construct coherent
and cohesive autobiographical narrative

FIGURE 7.1
The 4 states and 3 state transformations of the transformational process

ing, likewise prevents reliable, direct contact with somatically rooted experience.

But also invariably present in State One are glimmers—sometimes significantly more than glimmers—of transformance strivings and the patient's self-at-best.

• *The first state transformation.* As the influence of defenses and inhibiting affects diminishes, core affective experience rises. The first state transformation reflects the disruption of old, dysfunctional patterns as a result of the new experiences generated by the therapeutic dyad. We seek to amplify the glimmers of affect that herald previously warded-off intense emotional experiences by staying with the patient, so that he or she does not feel alone. *Green-signal affects, transitional affects,* and *heralding affects* signal the first state transformation and draw the therapist's attention to a critical window of therapeutic opportunity to facilitate the entrance into core affect (State Two).

Green-signal affects, the manifestation of vitality affects marking the operation of recognition processes, are positive somatic/affective markers of increases in the feeling of safety and willingness to take the next step. This increase can be expressed somatically (e.g., a deep exhale, a head nod) and/or through verbal expressions of readiness, hope, trust, or curiosity. The *heralding affects* evidence lowered defenses and "herald" the coming online of core affective experience; we see affective glimmers—eyes fill with tears, body tone shifts noticeably, breathing deepens or becomes more rapid, language becomes more direct, imagistic, evocative. The patient will say something like "I don't know why, but I keep having an image of this little girl." The therapist seizes on those changes and works with them to *midwife* (Osimo, 2001) the emergence of the next state. The *transitional affects* are a mix of the old and the new: here, right-brain experiencing is ahead of left-brain control, leading to a sense of destabilization, of being a bit "out of kilter." It is not uncommon to see a mix of some anxiety with some emergent core affective experience, one side of the body expressing defense (left arm holding oneself), the other side expressing the emergent emotion (right hand in a fist).

STATE TWO—CORE AFFECTIVE PHENOMENA:
THE PROCESSING OF EMOTIONAL EXPERIENCE

With defenses and inhibiting affects largely out of the way, the patient is in touch with body-rooted emotional experience, most notably, the categorical emotions, which are closely related to Panksepp's (Chapter 1, this volume) seven emotional primes. With the sense that even intense emotions are welcome and can be dyadically handled, emotional processing work can be launched. The conscious self surrenders to the organismic wisdom of the

deeper self and lets go; the brake is released, permitting access to a deep somatically rooted core affective experience pressing for expression.

State Two dyadic affect regulation has patient and therapist working together to help the patient fully experience and process subcortically initiated
and right-brain-mediated emotional experiences so that the seeds of healing
contained in such experiences can be released. Grief, rage, fear, joy, disgust,
and so on, can now come to the fore, and the individual's access to them, once
unlocked, is deepened and regulated, using the positive somatic/affective
markers of the process of recognition to stay on track, moment to moment.
The emergence of *adaptive action tendencies* and the *postbreakthrough affects* (e.g.,
feeling relieved, lighter, clearer, stronger) mark the end of the wave of processing one categorical emotion to completion.

• *The second state transformation.* The coming up and out of the wave of emotion is invariably positive and indicates the arrival of the second state transformation, where there is authentic relief and clarity. Patients speak of being "soft
of heart and open," in the words of one. There is a definite shift in the somatic sensory experience, frequently in the area of the "heart" or as warmth or
energy emerging from the "gut level."

By the end of the wave of processing emotional experience to completion,
the self is back in the driver's seat: *Vitality affects* come to the fore, releasing
enormous energy and thus providing fuel for adaptive action. The very experience of processed emotion activates resources essential to the resolution of
the problem requiring the person's heightened attention in the first place—
that is, *the adaptive action tendencies* associated with that emotion. The individual's
new responses reflect access to new emotional information—about the self,
the other, the situation—that was not accessible prior to the full experience of
the emotion. Even when the categorical emotion is itself negative and/or painful, as in the case of anger, for example, the affective experience following the
release of the adaptive action tendencies (e.g., strength, power, assertiveness)
is experientially highly positive and energizing.

STATE THREE—THE PROCESSING OF TRANSFORMATIONAL EXPERIENCE:
METATHERAPEUTIC PROCESSING AND THE TRANSFORMATIONAL AFFECTS[7]

What in most therapies is often seen as a natural endpoint marks the entry into
another round of experiential work for AEDP. The focus shifts to the *metather-*

---

7. John Gottman and his colleagues (Gottman, Katz, & Hooven, 1997) have developed a similar idea
of the meta-emotions (i.e., emotions about emotions) but in a different context. They are exploring the
problematic aspects of emotion about emotions that cause problems and symptoms, whereas I am exploring the expansive aspects of emotions about emotion in the context of transformational experience.

apeutic processing of the patient's *experience* of transformation. If in State Two we processed emotional experience associated with trauma, loss, disappointment, and other charged disruptions in the patient's world, in State Three we metaprocess transformational experience and the (good) havoc it wreaks in the patient's self. In this way, metaprocessing is mindfulness (Ogden, Chapter 8, this volume; Siegel, 2007) applied to transformational experience.

Metatherapeutic processing, or *metaprocessing* for short, is a quintessential contribution of AEDP, stemming from the discovery that focusing on the experience of transformation itself unleashes a transformational process, through which changes are consolidated, deepened and expanded. It is here that we encounter recursive, cascading transformational phenomena.

Both meta-affective and metacognitive, metaprocessing uses alternating waves of (right-brain-mediated) experience and (left-brain-mediated) reflection to integrate the fruits of intense emotional experience into the personality organization; concomitantly, it generates more positive phenomena associated with health, resilience, and expanding well-being, thus enlarging the sphere of transformational experience, all the while exploring it. That is the nature of the transformational spiral set in motion by the metaprocessing of transformational experience and the expanding energy and vitality it makes available to the individual.

Fundamental to metatherapeutic processing is awareness of how the self registers the transformational experience via *receptive affective experiences*, which usually operate silently and register in terms of sensations (e.g., safety and care as warmth and relaxation). The body's reaction to the experience of quantum change, that is, big, discontinuous and rather sudden and unexpected, change activates *"the healing vortex"* (Fosha, 2006b; Levine, 1997; Yeung, 2003, personal communication, August 4)—for example, oscillations, vibrations, currents, streamings, temperature swings, and other receptive affective experiences associated with the self's experience of the disruption of quantum transformation.

Metatherapeutic processing of the just-completed affective experience evokes phenomenologically distinct *transformational affects* (mastery affects, emotional pain, the healing affects, and the tremulous affects), each associated with a specific metatherapeutic process. The four metatherapeutic processes (underlined) and their respective transformational affects (in italics) are as follows:

1. <u>Mastery</u> evokes the *mastery affects*, the "I did it!" of therapy, the feelings of joy, pride, and confidence that emerge when fear and shame are undone.
2. <u>Mourning the self</u> is accompanied by *emotional pain*, which is grief for the

self, a painful but liberating experience of empathy for what one's self lost, either due to the limitations of others and/or to one's own chronic defensive functioning.

3. Traversing the crisis of healing change evokes *the tremulous affects*, as fear/excitement, startle/surprise, curiosity/interest, even a feeling of positive vulnerability, can be maintained during the emergent explorations with the support and holding of the therapeutic relationship.

4. The affirming recognition of the self and its transformation evokes *the healing affects*, which include gratitude and tenderness toward the other, as well as feeling moved, touched, or emotional within oneself.

If State Two processing of emotional experience is like a wave, State Three processing of transformational experience is like a spiral. Each new experience, once explored, becomes the platform for the next round of exploration. Each new attainment becomes a platform for the next reaching. This spiraling enlarges the sphere of experience within the context of a safe attachment, allowing ever-expanding exploration. Through explicitly exploring the experience and meaning of what has just gone on for each partner, and sharing it with one another, we also further strengthen attachment security, which is rooted in the successful traversing of difficult experience together.

• *The third state transformation.* The state-shift markers that signal the completion of State Three and the emergence of core state are calm, clarity, and tremendous openness. The stress of State One and the emotional tumult of States Two and Three are over. The storm has passed. The wind has died down. The sky is clear and the air is fresh. Breathing is deep and slow. Life is good. The metatherapeutic transformational spiraling leads to a profoundly satisfying, deeply felt state of ease, flow, and relaxation. These affects herald the availability of core state, the fourth state of the transformational process, as viewed through the lens of AEDP.

STATE FOUR: CORE STATE AND THE TRUTH SENSE

In the highly integrated *core state*, the patient has a subjective sense of "truth" and a heightened sense of authenticity and vitality; almost always, so does the therapist. The defining qualities of core state overlap with qualities characteristic of resilient individuals and also with those cultivated by contemplative and spiritual practices—wisdom, compassion for self and others, generosity, vibrant well-being, equanimity, confidence, creativity, naturalness, enhanced initiative and agency, a sense of the sacred, more.

Core state refers to an altered state of openness and contact wherein individuals are deeply in touch with essential aspects of their own experience. Experience is intense, deeply felt, unequivocal, and declarative; sensation is heightened, imagery is vivid, focus and concentration are effortless. Anxiety, shame, guilt, or defensiveness are absent; there is no pressure to speak, yet the material moves easily. Self-attunement and other-receptivity easily coexist. Mindfulness—the capacity to take one self, one's world, and one's own unfolding experience as objects of awareness and reflection—prevails. In this "state of assurance" (James, 1902), the patient contacts a confidence that naturally translates into effective action. The patient's true self declares itself. In Hart's (1991) words: "A stillness descended upon me. I sighed a deep sigh, as if I had slipped suddenly out of a skin. I felt old, and content. The shock of recognition had passed through my body like a powerful current" (pp. 26–27).

The affective marker for core state is the *truth sense.* The truth sense is a vitality affect whose *felt sense* is an *aesthetic experience of rightness,* the rightness of one's experience.[8] The truth sense is the felt manifestation of the internal experience of core state: deep relief at felt correctness, and the calm that settles in when a picture that's been crooked comes into alignment. There is an internal experience of coherence, cohesion, completion, and essence (Grotstein, 2004).

Through the transformational process we hope to foster the patient's—and our own—greatest degree of experiential contact with emotional truth. Often, the most powerful work can be done when both patient and therapist are in core state (which is not unusual), and therefore fully able to move back and forth between compassion and self-compassion, wisdom and generosity, and True-Self/True-Other[9] relating. The result is the patient's capacity to generate a coherent and cohesive autobiographical narrative—the single best predictor of security of attachment and resilience in the face of trauma (Main, 1999).

The Arc of Transformation

The emotion-based transformational process, unfolding through the directional thrust of emotion, moment to moment kept on a progressive track by vitality affects signaling the operation of recognition processes, describes an arc: A psychoevolutionary perspective at one end is organically linked with aesthetics, spirituality, and the quest for personal truth at the other. The experiential processing of emotions shaped by eons of evolution naturally culminates in experiences of aliveness, hope, faith, clarity, agency, simplicity, compassion, coherence, and both truth and beauty.

---

8. This is not about being right, but about things that *feel* right.
9. True-Self/True-Other relating (Fosha, 2005) is AEDP's version of Buber's (1965) I/Thou.

Part IV: The Crisis of Transformation[10]

We have established that emotion, a powerful agent of change, is synonymous with disruption (Damasio, 1999), but that, when regulated and processed through to completion, bestows great adaptive advantages on the individual. The *experience* of transformation, itself an agent of (further) transformation, when first registered, also represents a disruption, a perturbation of the status quo, and, as such, a challenge to familiar identity. It too is a vehicle for growth, but only if the crisis it engenders is successfully traversed.

Whereas the categorical emotions frequently arise in potentially aversive circumstances, the crisis of transformation always takes place in the context of change for the better, often the fulfillment of changes fervently wished for. But transformation requires letting go of the familiar, which even when painful, is comfortable because known. Here, and in the case that follows, we look at what happens when "the new"—the good "new"—evokes resistance[11] as it presents a threat to established identity.

Although transformation is a psychic crisis, it is not an external crisis. With a certain amount of therapeutic improvement already under one's belt, further change seems discretionary, not as essential to survival. The motivation of intense psychic distress, which initially brings the patient to treatment and functions as a spur to exploration, is absent. If anything, things are good. In these conditions, disruption is not so lightly undertaken. When dread or reticence is palpable, it is important that we acknowledge to the patient that transformation and change are disruptions, which, however desirable, can nevertheless be scary.

Since change can be like trauma (especially for those with a history of trauma—i.e., we do not know what will happen), how then does the new get to have an impact on us so that we can grow? Here we return to the concept of recognition and the dialectic of accommodation and assimilation. To reprise: If emotion is the disruption that forces us accommodate to new aspects of reality, recognition is the process by which we assimilate the new and fold it back into ourselves. Recognition, and the familiarity it paradoxically marks, is the progressive alternative to the regressive pull of resistance in the face of transforming change.

---

10. Mega-thanks to Carrie Ruggieri and her brilliant reporting of my presentation of this material to the NYC AEDP Seminar Series. Witnessing my work transformed through the light of her perception and experience—which momentarily rendered it as other—provided me with the experience of recognition and the ability to fold it back into myself with expanded understanding and all the vitality and energy emergent from such experiences.

11. The interested reader is invited to compare this patient's reaction to transformation with three other published cases in Fosha (2006, 2008) and Russell & Fosha (2008).

The patient traverses the arc of crisis and resolution through a dynamic process of emotion/disruption and recognition/reclaiming. Distinct, specific emotions—the *transformational affects*—mark this upheaval. The *tremulous affects* arise in response to the crisis of healing change: They emerge in the wake of receptive affective experiences that register the suddenness and magnitude of the change. The tremulous affects have the self almost literally shaking with vulnerability. The *healing affects*, on the other hand, emerge in the wake of receptive affective experiences of recognition, here recognition in the second sense, as felt experience. The emergence of the healing affects signals that the resolution of the crisis of transformation is on its way. Together, the tremulous affects and the healing affects are examples of what William James phenomenologically described as "the melting emotions and the tumultuous affections associated with the crisis of change" (1902, p. 328).

As we have been discussing, recognition is an intrinsically dyadic process, a moment of meeting between self and something else. In the case that follows, the recognition involves a moment of meeting between self and self, with the therapist as midwife. We now meet Dennis.

Part V. Clinical Case: The Searing Light of Transformation

Dennis is a divorced, devoted father of four and at the beginning of treatment a highly successful professional in a high-stress occupation. Depressed and anxious, he initially sought treatment because of distress over the disrespect he tolerated in both personal and professional relationships, and for his difficulties standing up for himself in the face of exploitation. At the time of this session, he is in his early 50s, and a year and a half into his second course of treatment, the first having been disrupted by his substance abuse.

Much of his early trauma (significant neglect and physical, emotional, and occasional sexual abuse) has been processed. No longer depressed and much less anxious, he has made progressive changes in his personal and professional life, and has developed better strategies for regulating stress. Having substantially decreased his drinking and smoking, he is becoming increasingly invested in his self-care.

Dennis is scaffolded by the therapeutic dyad as he moves from his opening struggle with irritation and resistance to the click of recognition and the emergent phenomena it yields—new meanings, wonder, zest in going forward—to avail himself of the full healing embodied in transformational experience. The exchanges transcribed below reveal the microdynamics of the affective change process that emerge when the transformational spiral is set in motion by the metaprocessing of transformational experience,[12] which in this particular session, is phenomenologically replete with experiences of intense light.[13]

Note: The italics in parentheses describe the nonverbal aspects of the interaction, and bracketed comments in bold are commentary on the process. The designation [**Click**] is shorthand for the "click of recognition slipping into place."

A committed patient captured by the process and enthusiastic by nature, nevertheless, at the beginning of this session, Dennis is feeling otherwise.

Vignette 1: Weariness, Irritation, and Resistance in the Face of Change

PATIENT: I feel sort of spent . . . I'm at a sort of pause in the process . . . like, uh, I've sort of had enough . . .

THERAPIST: I'm listening . . .

PATIENT: I have nothing in mind . . . feels like the work has been done. Now what? . . . I don't know . . . maybe my feeling of the plateau or pause is a subtle feeling of irritation.

When the session begins, the patient is visibly struggling. A bit fatigued, he feels he has reached a plateau in his therapy. Long, sometimes very long, pauses punctuate his narrative. In the pauses, there is nothing in his "mind," but plenty in his body. The therapist's stance is open, interested, patient, calm, and encouraging.

PATIENT: I don't even know if irritation is the right word . . . but kind of a . . . resistance . . .

THERAPIST: So the resistance, I mean, I want to honor it. It is saying something. I don't exactly understand it, but I think it has something to do with things being good . . .

PATIENT: Yeah.

THERAPIST: I could be wrong, but . . . something to do with new things . . . [a **platforming statement**[14]] . . . you know what I'm saying?

---

12. The "sort ofs" and the "I don't knows" from both patient and therapist document the process of emergence and bottom-up language (language whose goal is to capture the felt sense of an experience).

13. William James (1902), in his brilliant disquisition on transformational experience, reported the prevalence of *photisms*, phenomena having to do with light, in transformational experiences.

14. Platforming statements are verbal attempts to capture the emotional experience that precedes them. The results of a cocreated process, they reflect the therapist's experience and subjectivity, but whether they are deemed right or wrong depends on whether they feel right to the patient. The proof is in what follows. It appears that the establishment of a platform based on what has already happened becomes the platform for the patient's recognition experience, which, in turn, becomes the platform for the next round.

PATIENT: (*moved, slowing down now*) . . . I do (*long pause*) . . . You know, uh . . . I am really very accustomed to my life's miseries. [**Click**]

The therapist's integrative comment reframes the resistance as a fear of the good and the new. The patient, having done so much in the treatment already, is afraid of what's next. The reframe allows a dropping down, followed by the click of recognition. The "resistance" starts to part.

Vignette 2: Something Searing; a Sideways Glance

PATIENT: In our work I have had a real feeling of a break in the misery and (*moved*) uh . . . it's a bit searing . . . [**Note the photism of "searing," a light so intense, it burns.**] . . . a bit too much. It's weird, new and unsettling . . . I'm accustomed to my misery (*pause*). . . . I think I switch off the feeling of hope and joy. I do . . .

THERAPIST: So what is it about hope and joy and not having misery as a constant companion . . . what is it about that? You say "It's searing!" "Searing"— what's that like?

PATIENT: (*halting, emotional*) You know, those moments of breakthrough that we had before felt very full . . . and were around relationships with my parents and so on, and my family

THERAPIST: Uh-huh . . .

PATIENT: I had a tremendous feeling of just, even though Freud said you can't ever clear out the swamp, I had a feeling of clearing out the swamp. . . . And it felt real. . . .

THERAPIST: Uh-huh . . .

PATIENT: (*pause, halting speech*) . . . But yet, and as I try to respond to "Stay with that searing feeling" . . . it's almost like I can't quite look at it squarely. . . . Even when I tell you that it's searing, I sort of feel like I'm standing on the edge of something and I can only look sideways at it [**beautiful articulation of hard-to-articulate emergent experience**].

THERAPIST: Right . . . and what's that like? The sense of looking at it sideways?

PATIENT: It's subtle . . .

THERAPIST: I'm thinking that it's meaningful . . . and that there are two parts of the look away, you know . . . . One has to do with the sideways glance and the sense that there is something very searing about all these changes . . . and the other is a little bit . . . of a sense of a . . . and again it's subtle, of avoidance, like you're avoiding me . . . is sort of how it feels [**the new platform**].

PATIENT: I feel afraid (*voice shaking, tremulous affects*). [**Click**]

THERAPIST: (*soft empathic voice*) I know . . .

PATIENT: (*voice shaking, tremulous affects*) I feel afraid of what comes next . . . uh . . . I don't know quite how to start to explore, so . . . I feel like . . . uh . . . a bunch of stuff is going to happen to me and I am afraid of it. [**Click**]

THERAPIST: Yes, yes.

PATIENT: (*tremulous affects*) I can almost barely not . . . I mean, I want to turn away from the fear, it doesn't provoke me to investigate. . . . And yeah, I think do feel a little bit of avoidance. [**Click**]

The therapist's loving/interested/curious acceptance of the patient's "resistance" that is, his inclination toward avoidance, triggers the forces of transformance. The patient, who had been somatically vibrating in vagueness, is now able to start to take hold of his experience. Note how often the "click" of recognition follows a platforming statement and rapidly becomes a new platform for the next round of exploration. With each click of recognition, there is an energetic shift: release of tension, less anxiety, more access to internal experience. Where a minute before, "fear" and "avoidance" were the just-barely-grasped, they are now the platform for launching the next round of exploration.

In terms of phenomenology, *"searing"* is Dennis's receptive affective experience of transformation, which tells us how intense it is, and how disruptive. Once that is articulated, the tremulous affects come online. True to their nature, they are poised between avoidance and exploration in response to the novelty of transformational experience. In the next vignette, the patient, having experienced and articulated his fear, says "I don't really want to do something new . . . I do and I don't."

Vignette 3: Anxiety

PATIENT: I don't really want to do something new . . .

THERAPIST: Right.

PATIENT: I do and I don't . . . yeah.

THERAPIST: And I can almost *feel* you uncomfortable.

PATIENT: Yeah, I feel uncomfortable . . . yeah.

THERAPIST: I see the discomfort in your shoulders and . . .

PATIENT: Yeah . . . I feel physically uncomfortable.

THERAPIST: Where? Where and how?

PATIENT: I get this nervous leg thing. . . . When I was a kid in high school, I had this feeling of nervous legs. You know, anxiety . . . almost wanting to jump out of my skin, literally having to get up and walk and move around because. . . . I'm not feeling it like I did when I was 15, but I feel uncomfortable that way.

I encourage Dennis to stay with his somatic experience. This next portion of the session is quiet, intensely inward, as he reflects on the treatment, held by the therapist's calm, patient waiting.

Vignette 4: Surrender—at a Loss, Needing Help

PATIENT: It was very workmanlike up till now. . . . There were things that I needed to articulate, wanted to articulate, old hurts. . . . We picked up where we left off and really got it done. . . .

THERAPIST: We did it. Right. Right.

PATIENT: We did it. I came to our sessions with feelings and thoughts all mixed together and wanted to talk about them . . . and now, I don't know, I feel a little bit at a loss . . . like I need your help to ask questions . . . like I've sort of run out of my own introspection. . . . I had things to tell you before and I told you (*belly laugh*) . . . and now I don't know what to say.

THERAPIST: Right . . . right, but there is something . . .

PATIENT: I have discomfort . . . and it's not really taken a shape.

The next round of emergent emotional experience is announcing itself. It is hard to capture the fullness of somatic experiencing going back and forth between patient and therapist. Held by the therapeutic dyad, having moved through resistance and avoidance, the patient now surrenders to his experience. No longer fighting it, accepting of his vulnerability, he reaches out: "I need your help to ask questions." And he is met. Together, we are tolerating the discomfort of not knowing and striving to speak the bottom-up language of emotional experience (Prenn, 2009). It is that that keeps us on track as we go forward, riding the transformational spiral.

Vignette 5: Working with Emergent Experience—"On the Edge of My Vision Is. . ."

THERAPIST: Can you let yourself be in this discomfort and be with me? And let me be with you as you feel it? [**Dyadic affect regulation: It is "we" who are on this journey . . . he is not alone.**]

PATIENT: (*open, vulnerable*) Yeah . . . Yeah, I can.

THERAPIST: What's that like?

PATIENT: OK . . . (*staying with feeling, long pensive silence, puzzled expression . . . then a big smile*) You know how you sense something in an anticipatory way . . . a coincidence or a sixth sense? . . . That's what's in there with the discomfort . . . As I sit here with the discomfort feeling . . . I also have this feeling of something at the edge of my vision [**emergent phenomenon**].

THERAPIST: Uh-huh . . . [**nonverbally maintaining dyadic connection**]

PATIENT: (*said with the wonder of unfolding discovery*) It's not that I don't want to look at it, it's that it's just always just at the edge of my vision . . . [**Click! Something inchoate can now be articulated.**]

THERAPIST: It's like even if you turn your head, it's just at the edge of your vision, that's the nature of it . . . Stay with me . . . (*moves forward, leaning close to the patient*)

PATIENT: I have the sense that there's something there . . . I don't know what to do next . . .

THERAPIST: (*said tenderly*) But it touches something in you.

PATIENT: Yeah (*very tender, deep feeling, tears in his eyes; a pause . . . dyadic head nodding*).

THERAPIST: Just notice what's happening.

PATIENT: I was actually thinking something very particular. In the last 10 or 15 minutes I've just not even had many words . . .

THERAPIST: Right.

PATIENT: I've just been sitting here feeling this sort of discomfort and [this] something not seen. But the particular thought that I just had was . . . for a long time now, I am doing a bunch of stuff so that I don't attend to this, to this thing that's outside the edge of my vision. . . . I don't know, it's a very weird feeling that going out drinking, and smoking cigarettes, and watching a lot of television are all things that in and of themselves are not particularly appealing, but that I do them to fill time or to avoid . . . or not to see what is on the edge of my vision. [**Click**]

THERAPIST: Right . . . Right . . . Wow!!

PATIENT: (*long pause, pensive tone when he speaks*) Hmmm. I don't know.

THERAPIST: I don't know either, and again, and we're sort of like dealing in intangibles, but I am . . . I am physically or emotionally getting something about how much trepidation you have. . . . And really really appreciating your awareness. . . . Something came in a particular way, a sense of all of these activities as filler . . . and in a way (*smiles*), it occurs to me that you're . . . you're in big trouble.

PATIENT: (*rueful, light laughter*) I know.

THERAPIST: We've resolved all this stuff that's been very much part and parcel of your experience, you've gotten rid of your job with its insane pressures. You're starting to do more and more healthy things for yourself, you're getting rid of the drinking, and of the bad eating, and the smoking. . . . So, it's like "Oh! Oh!" . . . I'm joking a little, but you know, I'm actually not primarily joking . . .

PATIENT: I like the expression "and now I'm in bigggg trouble " (*laughing*). . . . It reminded me of that Far Side cartoon with the dog on a unicycle, on a high wire, doing a juggling act, saying, "I just realized something; this is fun but I'm an old dog and this is a new trick" (*both patient and therapist laugh*).

THERAPIST: What happened when I said "You're in trouble!"?

PATIENT: (*speaks in halting, moved voice, tears breaking through*) I thought that what's on the edge of my vision is . . . the person who I am supposed to be, the person who I was always meant to be (*healing affects*), who I just can't seem to get to. Which is a strange feeling for a middle-aged man to feel [**Big click! Wow!**].

The breakthrough brings in an extraordinarily coherent and poignant recognition: "What's on the edge of my vision is. . . . the person who I was always meant to be, who I just can't seem to get to."

We're in a new place, the tremulous affects successfully tilted toward exploration. From this point forward, the patient is in a heightened state of emotional experience, in direct contact with deep transformational experience, against which he is no longer defending. Surrendering to his experience, he is carried along by the power of the new emotional understanding and the emergent transformational emotions that vitalize it—no fatigue in sight.

Vignette 6: First Happiness, Then Insight

PATIENT: (*moved, speaking haltingly, as if he is finding out what he is thinking as he is saying it*) That's what's on the edge of my vision. It's a . . . (*long pause*) . . . if I let go of all the shit I carry around with me . . . it's not fear exactly . . . I get this feeling . . . I used the word "searing." . . . There is this brilliant possibility and just the thought of it . . . I don't know . . .

THERAPIST: Just the thought of it . . . just stay with it. And notice.

PATIENT: You know, there is fear . . .

THERAPIST: Yeeees, but there is something else too.

PATIENT: (*nods his head*) I think that . . . (*tears; crying now; healing affects*)

THERAPIST: Make room.

PATIENT: (*speaking through tears*) I have let go of a lot of little chunks of misery. . . . But now I think that there is this possibility of letting go of all of it. . . . That's what this feels like.

THERAPIST: Can you let yourself have the feeling you have?

PATIENT: (*filled with wonder*) Yeah. I feel . . . (*moved*). . . . I don't feel sad. . . . My eyes are filled with tears but . . . what a thought!!! . . . . That misery is like this carapace that I can take off like a great big scab. . . . What's searing is that it feels so happy. . . . (*healing affects*). . . . Actually, that's just what it feels like— like a scab that would come off, that the misery is one great big thing, all of it . . .

THERAPIST: . . . that's sheddable.

PATIENT: That's sheddable (*overcome with tears, trembling voice; healing affects*). I nev- er thought of that before . . . I never had that feeling before . . . that misery is something that's sheddable. That's why it felt so exquisite. I can take it off and put it aside. (*He makes a motion of taking off and putting aside.*) I could take every- thing off and put it aside . . . every bad feeling. . . . And the searing, painfully joyful thought is that . . . is that you might be able to do that (*crying, moved; healing affects; long pause*) . . . There is something about this idea of just picking up this hard skin and shedding it that makes me feel very happy. . . . But it feels very new. . . . You know, I think the swamp is the wrong metaphor.

THERAPIST: Yes, right. Very much so . . . we're in a very different place . . . this sort of searing light.

PATIENT: Yeah . . . light . . . (*slow dyadic head nodding, long pause*)

PATIENT: I think what's searing is the unfamiliarity of . . . is the brightness of the glimpse . . . [photism] . . . that might be possible. . . . It's almost like a physical shrugging off of something . . . deciding that I might be able to do that. That's what seems to be painful or that's what's emotional . . . 'cuz I hugged my misery to me for a long time.

Note the declarative tone and clarity: Whereas emergent experience is halting and tentative, fully felt emotional experience has clarity and force. Its vitality powers new meaning that emerges with each new cycle of the spiral.

Vignette 7: A Figure of Light

PATIENT: I was thinking of this movie *Cocoon*. [Some conversational description: Aliens take off their human "suits" . . . underneath, they are sheer light.] When I was . . . uh . . . feeling all that feeling, I had the sense of stepping out of something and just being a figure of light. [**photism**]

THERAPIST: Wow . . . it's so moving and so beautiful.

PATIENT: I just never had that thought before . . . that I could be happy basically. . . . Before, I thought that I could be happy if *this* happened, or I could be happy if *that* happened. But I never thought I could leave my all misery behind me.

THERAPIST: . . . and be yourself.

PATIENT: I mean . . . I don't know what it's going to be like not to carry around misery all the time, but I am willing to give it a try (*laughing*).

Vignette 8: Tears of Possibility

PATIENT: This is the possibility of letting go of all the misery. . . . It feels real, like something I could do. I don't know that I will do it, it's just the discovery that it is possible.

THERAPIST: Right . . . and that this thing that was at the edge of your vision was the self that you were meant to be.

PATIENT: Yeah . . . (*moved, tears*)

PATIENT: It just feels very beautiful. . . . (*Breakthrough of healing affects—sobs. Then, lifts head, lifts eyes; dyadic sighs; calmer now, tone of wonder, light filled eyes*) How strange, it's not sadness at all.

THERAPIST: It's not sadness.

PATIENT: It's not . . . You know, before [referring to earlier sessions], a lot of the emotion I felt were tears of sorrow for the wounded little boy. But this, this is tears of. . . . these are tears of possibility.

The patient cries deep sobs of happiness. His face is straight on, relaxed and open, with full eye contact when not overcome by crying. After the wave of tears, a deep calm comes into the room. It ushers in core state.

Vignette 9: Sweetness: Metaprocessing What Just Took Place

THERAPIST: How do you feel?

PATIENT: I don't feel tired . . . I feel relaxed.

THERAPIST: What do you notice in your legs?

PATIENT: (*smiles*) A warmth here (*pats his heart with his hand*).

THERAPIST: What's that like?

PATIENT: It's sweet. Like a good pear when you're hungry and thirsty at the same time.

Vitality affects, energy, and relaxation are the result of metaprocessing transformational experience. And in the next vignette come calm and deep insight.

Vignette 10: Narrative and Solid Assurance

PATIENT: You know, moments of discovery come with this feeling, and I felt it on previous occasions, and felt that "Well, this too will pass." . . . Except that I came back to tell you that it stayed with me . . . that glimpse of what I have seen more squarely just now feels very solid. [I have the] expectation it will stay with me. That this moment isn't just the flush of an experience

THERAPIST: Right. But rather . . . [**bridging statement**]

PATIENT: . . . but rather a point of departure after something left behind.

THERAPIST: Uh-huh.

PATIENT: Something very powerful about your encouraging me, encouraging *us*, to be uncomfortable together. And it was very powerful. It's so odd because it starts out feeling like it's going to go nowhere . . .

THERAPIST: Right

PATIENT: You know, I described it as irritated. There's a frustration, not even knowing what to do about it. . . . It's almost like I needed your encouragement to be patient . . .

THERAPIST: . . . to let something sort of settle or to trust yourself somehow.

PATIENT: Yeah. Yeah. It's pretty cool.

It is somehow fitting that the patient ends this session with "cool." It's the expression of his assimilating the enlightenment he just experienced into his familiar everyday self–or, in the felicitous vision of Ruggieri,[15] of his going "from a being of light back into a man in denim."

The experience of quantum transformation evokes the tremulous affects, a trembling before the new, poised between fear and excitement. Then, the mo-

---

15. In an e-mail to AEDP listserv.

ments of recognition, the moments when something slips into place, give rise to the healing affects. What feels foreign to the self, even scary, earlier in the process, just minutes later comes to be experienced as core, fundamental to one's self. New meanings and potentials for new ways of being are thus fueled by the positive vitality affects released.

Spirals and Positive Affects: Emergent Phenomena with a Mind of Their Own

The motivations that emerge from the dynamic features of the transformational process give rise to phenomena that are felt by the experiencer to rise unbidden, as if possessed of a mind of their own. These phenomena arise naturally during the metaprocessing of transformational experience in the context of a dyadic environment where the patients feel safe and known. Via the dialectic of emotion and recognition, the yields of the transformational process fuel the transformance strivings of the organism with vitality, energy, and the accessing of resources needed for the energetic pursuit of life: for growth, learning, and flourishing. If pathology drains and dissipates vitality and energy, recognition and emotion (when regulated and processed to completion) are fundamental constituents of transformational processes that keep on keeping on.

Fredrickson (2001) differentiates between the *negative emotions*, for survival, and the *positive emotions*, for expansion of capacities and growth. In parallel fashion, we could say that emotion-processing work is for dealing with changes in one's world, whereas transformation-processing work is for dealing with changes in one's self. The categorical emotions necessarily narrow our focus to the challenges most salient for survival. By contrast, positive emotions broaden it and lead to the enhancement and expansion of our repertoires, which in turn, motivate and fuel exploration. New thoughts, choices, and, most importantly, new capacities arise spontaneously and lead to new pursuits and experiences, which, accompanied by positive affect, bring more energy into the system and recharge the spiral yet again.

It is not just that attachment injuries are healed, trauma transformed, or depression lifted. Patients get better, but this is not about restoration to baseline: It is about the activation of new resources and capacities, which could have never been imagined, much less predicted, at the outset. As new experiences and meanings become integrated into the self, they motivate and organize new directions. The system acquires a new set goal.

Even if, content-wise, the potent motivational strivings that are emergent features of the transformational process cannot be described in advance, for there is nothing a priori about them, they *can* be described dynamically and phenomenologically (see Fosha, 2005, in press; Russell & Fosha, 2008). We are in the realm of phenomena best described within the framework of nonlinear dynamic systems theory. The basic quality of emergent experience is a surrender to experiences of flow, of being "in the zone," of things coming to us unbidden, arising fully formed, at times almost not bearing the mark of personal authorship. Mozart said that he didn't feel like a composer as much as an *amanuensis*, someone taking dictation from a source outside the self. We have the experience of being a vehicle for these phenomena, not vice versa, thus the sense of their having a mind of their own.

Fredrickson's (2001) research focuses on the constituents of resilience and the comparative responses to stress of resilient and nonresilient individuals. Resilience in the face of stress involves a capacity to maintain positive affects and to recover quickly from negative affects without relying on denial. This definition echoes what security-engendering mothers promote in their children (Schore, 2003a, 2003b), and what yogic contemplative practices promote (Davidson et al., 2003; Loizzo, in press). Such resilience, and the positive affects that are intrinsic to it, correlates highly with cardiac health, longevity, happier marriages, fewer colds, and just about everything good that you can think of (Fredrickson & Losada, 2005; Harker & Keltner, 2001).

These positive emotional transformational processes are, by their very nature, recursive processes, whereby more begets more. This is not a satiation model or a tension reduction model, but rather an appetitive model. Desire comes in the doing. The more we do something that feels good, the more we want to do more of it. In Ghent's (2002) words:

> Just as motivational systems lead to the emergence of new capacities and functions, so too do *new capacities beget new motivational derivatives* in an ever more complex developmental spiral. . . . The acquisition of a new capability is itself a perturbation that destabilizes the existing state of motivational organization. To the extent that the use of the new capacity provides pleasure and satisfaction, diminishes pain or distress, and, in some way, enhances survival, there will, barring inhibitory circumstances, emerge a new need to execute and develop the capacity. *Functional capacities acquire a new feature— the need to exercise that capacity and expand its range.* (emphasis added).

As we exercise our new capacities, they become part and parcel of who we are, new platforms on which to stand and reach for the next level. Thus, recursive cycles of healing transformation and emergent phenomena give rise to new transformational cycles and new phenomena, and those to the new capacities that translate into broadened thought–action repertoires. We are only beginning to understand and harness the plasticity that is in our brains, as Doidge makes clear in his book, *The Brain That Changes Itself*:

> Many tastes we think "natural" are acquired through learning and become "second nature" to us. We are unable to distinguish our "second nature" from our "original nature" because our neuroplastic brains, once rewired, develop a new nature, every bit as biological as our original. (2007, p. 102)

Although transformance strivings are wired in, we are not born with a drive to do ballet or fix cars or edit books on emotion. (If Michael Phelps, to date the greatest swimmer in the history of the Olympics, had never gone anywhere near a pool, we have no idea what, if anything special, he would have done.) But when transformational activities are satisfying and pleasurable *and* marked by recognition processes, doing them makes us become who we feel ourselves to be. Even in the patient–therapist dyad: When it works, it seems like the only dyad that could have worked. Same for a session like the one related above: How it unfolded has the coherence of inevitability, though in fact, there was nothing inevitable about it.

Our second and third and fourth natures come to feel as natural and fundamental to us as the wired-in categorical emotions. Positive emotions provide both the motivation and the fuel for that rewiring, broadening and building what we deem "self" and bringing us full circle—but on a spiral. For we are not the self, the "me," we started with: In the process of traveling, not only our destination but our point of departure has also changed.

ACKNOWLEDGMENTS
    I wish to thank Cindy Hyden for her resonant editorial help.

8

Emotion, Mindfulness, and Movement

Expanding the Regulatory Boundaries of the Window of Affect Tolerance

Pat Ogden

IN RECENT YEARS psychotherapy has begun to shift its emphasis from models of cognitive development to the "primacy of affect" in an intersubjective context, redefining psychotherapy as the "affect communicating cure" rather than the "talking cure" (Schore & Schore, 2008). Affect regulation and emotional processes are highlighted as central to psychopathology and thus to psychotherapy practice (Dorpat, 2001; Fosha, 2000; Goleman, 1995; Schore & Schore, 2008). Most current treatment models emphasize the resolution of unresolved emotions of painful past experiences and the expansion of the affect array. Therefore, prime targets of therapeutic intervention include a wide range of dysregulated and/or unintegrated emotions. The patient has often warded off these emotions, perceiving them as overwhelming, frightening, or too intense, until, within the context of an attuned therapeutic dyad, they are engaged, regulated, explored, fully experienced, and transformed.

That said, a direct, exclusive, or even primary focus on emotional processing can initially present difficulties in working with those patients who typically experience an overwhelming flood of emotions, a lack of emotion, or the same emotion over and over. Direct attention to emotions in such instances may exacerbate dysregulation and/or reinforce maladaptive emotional patterns. Affect might be best regulated, rather, through an exclusive focus on bottom-up or sensorimotor processing interventions that challenge these tendencies, promote stabilization, and pave the way for future efficacious processing of emotions. As we shall see, such sensorimotor processing interventions go beyond simple body awareness interventions ("What do you notice in your body? How do you experience that in your body?") by using body sensation and movement to address and change how information is *processed* on a bodily level ("Follow that sensation of tingling: what happens next in your body? Feel the tension in your shoulder . . . sense the movement that wants to happen there; what happens as you slowly execute that movement?").

From the specific vantage of an approach that privileges the regulation and processing of sensorimotor experiences, as such, this chapter explores the nature of procedural learning, trauma- and attachment-related issues, and the interface between emotions and the body, clarifying when and how to emphasize sensorimotor processing, when to emphasize emotional processing, and how to integrate the two. The use of directed mindfulness to work with procedural tendencies and to both deepen and enhance emotional processing is highlighted as well. I discuss theory and technique for working at the regulatory boundaries of the window of affect tolerance, as the patient's arousal, both emotional and physiological, begins to challenge his or her integrative capacity, and I include an exploration of play and positive affect.

Procedurally Learned Physical Tendencies

Procedural learning involves the learning of processes—the "how" rather than the "what" or "why." Commencing in infancy (Tulving & Schacter, 1990), procedural habits are formed gradually and incrementally as certain reactions to particular internal or external stimuli are engaged repeatedly over time. Once learned, these procedural internal actions (those that often cannot be observed: cognitive, emotional, and some physiological) and external actions (those that can be observed: physical and behavioral) are reliable and enduring. For example, skills such as riding a bike persevere over time and typically do not significantly diminish with disuse; similarly, tendencies such as the experience of shame, accompanied by physical tightening and withdrawing in the face of criticism, also persist long after the situations that originally elicited these reactions are over.

As powerful determinants of current actions, procedural learning encompasses habitual responses, skills, and conditioned behaviors (Schacter, 1996) formed by repeated iterations of movements, perceptions, cognitions, and emotions (Grigsby & Stevens, 2000). Although many kinds of actions that are procedurally learned can be initiated voluntarily (e.g., as tying one's shoes), procedural learning does not "require conscious or unconscious mental representations, images, motivations or ideas to operate" (Grigsby & Stevens, 2000, p. 316). It is characterized by automatic, reflexive performance, becoming an even more potent influence because of its relative lack of verbal articulation, thus rendering most procedural behavior unavailable for thoughtful reflection.

Stimulus-related procedurally learned tendencies—that is, tendencies to respond automatically (on cognitive, emotional, and sensorimotor levels) and in characteristic ways to particular conditions—foster an anticipation of actions that were adaptive in the past long after environmental conditions have changed. A patient who was sexually abused by her father remained chronically tense in childhood in expectation of abuse; as an adult, the muscular tension remained, a physical tendency that was exacerbated at the thought of an intimate relationship, and which contributed to her chronic sense of impending danger and affect dysregulation. Aggravated by internal and environmental reminders of the past, such tendencies take precedence when other actions would prove more adaptive to current reality. Although this same patient desperately longed for a mate, her muscular tension and accompanying fear precluded the openness and trust necessary to pursue an intimate relationship.

Procedurally learned physical tendencies can be viewed as "a statement of . . . psychobiological history and current psychobiological functioning" (Smith, 1985, p. 70) that complements and corresponds with emotional tendencies. Formed to help us cope with early trauma and maximize the resources of our attachment relationships, these actions are initially adaptive, but over time become habits that are often maladaptive for current situations. They manifest as either primarily *trauma-related* or primarily *attachment-related* tendencies. Trauma-related tendencies stem from overwhelming experiences that cannot be integrated and typically solicit subcortical animal defensive mechanisms and dysregulated arousal. Maladpative attachment-related tendencies stem from experiences with early childhood caregivers that caused emotional distress but that did not overwhelm the child. *Attachment trauma* ensues when these experiences *are* overwhelming and perceived as dangerous, such that animal defensive responses and extreme or prolonged dysregulation ensue. Although maladaptive attachment tendencies and trauma-related tendencies are interconnected experiences that mutually influence each other and cannot be teased apart in actuality, recognizing the primary indicators of each helps clinicians prioritize emotional or physical tendencies pertaining to either trauma or attachment. These clinical choices become paramount in an integrative therapeutic approach.

Trauma-Related Physical Tendencies

Trauma, as defined here, refers to exposure to events that represent a real or perceived threat to safety and/or existence and thus elicit subcortical mammalian, or animal, defenses that are not mediated by the cortex; in fact, they actually *disable* cortical activity when engaged. These defenses can be loosely categorized into three general subsystems, all of which arose as ways of preserving survival: (1) *relation-seeking actions*, (2) *mobilizing defenses* that organize overt action, and (3) *immobilizing defenses* that engender a lack of physical action.

RELATION-SEEKING ACTIONS

Relation-seeking actions include behaviors relating to the attachment system, such as the "attachment cry" that is instinctively stimulated in children when they feel distressed, and is also activated in adults in times of stress and threat. The attachment cry, designed to elicit the help and protection of an attachment figure, is to be distinguished from attachment-related actions designed to secure and maintain enduring relationships. Underlying attachment is the "social engagement system," mediated by the ventral parasympathetic branch of the vagus nerve, a relation-seeking system that fosters interaction with the environment (Porges, 1995, 2001a, 2001b, 2004, 2006a; cf. Chapter 2, this volume) because it governs parts of the body used in relational contexts: eyelid opening (e.g., looking), facial muscles (e.g., emotional expression), middle ear muscles (e.g., extracting human voice from background noise), laryngeal and pharyngeal muscles (e.g., prosody), and head tilting and turning muscles (e.g., social gesture and orientation) (Porges, 2003, p. 35).

Social engagement can also sometimes manage, modulate, and even disarm or neutralize an interpersonal threat, as illustrated by a patient's appeal to a perpetrator's empathy by "talking him down," thus activating his social engagement system and deactivating fight and predatory actions. This is a complex, sophisticated action that requires some ability to either dissociate one's own mammalian defenses temporarily or to override them consciously, whereas the attachment cry is a more primitive, basic defensive response that does not require interaction with the source of threat.

MOBILIZING DEFENSES

If relational strategies fail to ensure safety, the mobilizing defenses of fight or flight mediated by the sympathetic nervous system are engaged. Blood flow to large muscle groups is increased to prepare the body to take strong overt actions to ensure survival. When escape seems possible, flight is the instinctive defense of choice (Fanselow & Lester 1988; Nijenhuis et al., 1998; Nijenhuis et al., 1999) and can be conceptualized as both running away from danger and running toward safety. When aggression appears likely to be effective or when the victim feels trapped, the fight response is typically provoked. In addition to these instinctive defenses of fight and flight, mobilizing defenses can also include procedurally learned actions such as those used to operate a motor vehicle, which involve a complexity of automatic movements (e.g., turning the steering wheel, pressing the brakes) that can be executed without thought in the event of a potential accident.

IMMOBILIZING DEFENSES
When mobilizing defenses prove ineffective or maladaptive, such as in instances when a fight response might provoke more violence from the perpetrator or when the perpetrator and attachment figure are one and the same, passive avoidance or immobilization behaviors are the only remaining survival strategies (Allen, 2001; Misslin, 2003; Nijenhuis et al., 1998; Nijenhuis et al., 1999; Rivers, 1920; Schore, 2007). There seem to be at least three types of immobilizing defenses: (1) the sympathetically mediated freeze response (alert immobility), (2) the parasympathetically mediated feigned death response (floppy immobility), and (3) submissive behavior.

• *Alert immobility.* The freeze response is characterized by a highly engaged sympathetic system, possibly combined with arousal of the parasympathetic (dorsal vagal) system (Siegel, 1999); stiff, tense muscles; increased heart rate; and a feeling of paralysis coupled with hyper attentiveness. This "alert immobility" (Misslin, 2003, p. 58) may appear as complete stillness except for eye movement and respiration.
• *Floppy immobility.* "Feigned death" or "floppy immobility" (Lewis et al., 2004) is powered by the parasympathetic dorsal branch of the vagus nerve. Characterized by limp musculature, behavioral shutdown, slowed heart rate, and/or fainting (Lewis et al., 2004; Porges, 2001a, 2004, 2005; Nijenhuis et al., 1998, 1999; Scaer, 2001; Schore, 2007), this defense variant occurs as a "last resort" when all else has failed. With profound inhibition of motor activity (Misslin, 2003), coupled with little or no sympathetic arousal, this hypoaroused condition is a shutdown state that reduces engagement with the environment and may be accompanied by anesthesia, analgesia, and muscular–skeletal retardation (Krystal, 1988; Nijenhuis et al., 1999).
• *Submissive behaviors.* This type of passive avoidance "aim[s] at preventing or interrupting aggressive reactions" (Misslin, 2003, p. 59). Characterized by movements such as avoiding eye contact or lowering the eyes, crouching, and bowing the back before the perpetrator, submissive behaviors may include an

automatic obedience to the demands of the aggressor. Such behavior is often characterized by a mechanistic compliance or "robotization" (Krystal, 1978) and usually involves a lack of protest against abuse (Herman, 1992).

These mammalian defensive strategies are designed to increase safety and assure survival. However, they become liabilities when they are used repeatedly and automatically, because they turn into inflexible procedural tendencies rather than adaptive responses to immediate threat. Traumatized individuals tend to experience reminders of past trauma as indicating current danger, which sets off these bottom-up animal defensive subsystems again and again. Eventually, they become default behaviors over other, more adaptive actions. For example, habitual submissive behaviors, characterized by mechanistic obedience, can lead victims to respond to perceived threat with resignation, compliance, and acquiescence. One patient repeatedly allowed a relative who was her childhood perpetrator into her home, knowing that abuse would follow. Children whose dorsal vagal tone increased as the only defensive option to childhood abuse tend to become easily hypoaroused as adults, often characterized by a slumped, collapsed posture and/or flaccidity in the musculature. Action tendencies related to freeze are characterized by muscular tension and "agitated immobility" and typically include a "chronic state of hypervigilance, a tendency to startle, and occasionally panic" (Krystal, 1988, p. 161).

Habitual engagement of mobilizing defenses of fight, flight, and relation-seeking actions also impair adaptive functioning. These active defenses are invariably accompanied by hyperarousal and muscular constriction. Patients with a tendency toward "fight" responses typically report tension in the arms, shoulders, jaw, and back; patients with reliance on relation-seeking actions tend to overuse clinging and proximity-seeking behaviors; patients with dysregulated flight responses often exhibit fleeing behaviors, such as precipitously leaving social situations or the therapist's office or running away, as well as subtler flight actions such as turning, twisting, ducking imaginary objects, or backing away. For example, a patient who witnessed the collapse of the World Trade Centers afterward found herself beginning to run for cover whenever she heard a plane overhead.

For patients with dissociative disorders, these animal defensive strategies may manifest as discrete "parts" of the self, each with its own particular somatic tendencies (Ogden et al., 2006; van der Hart et al., 2006). One patient, after years of therapy, explained, "This [the tension and angry thrust of her jaw] is the part that fights, and this [the collapse in her spine and loss of energy in her arms] is the part that submits, and when I don't even feel my body, that is the part that just isn't there any more." In therapy, this patent initially reported feelings of "going crazy," reflecting an inability to understand her internal dissociative system and the adaptive function of the animal defensive responses gone awry in her current nonthreatening context. As for most patients, it was important for her to learn through therapy that, even though not adaptive in her current life, each animal defensive response was adaptive at the time of the abuse. It is not the defensive responses themselves but their overactivity and inflexibility that contribute to chronic affect dysregulation and pathology in traumatized individuals.

Attachment-Related Physical Tendencies

Early relational dynamics are the blueprints for the child's developing cognition, affect array, regulatory ability, and physical tendencies (e.g., the way the child learns to move, hold his or her body, and engage particular gestures and facial expressions). From interactions with attachment figures, the child forms internal working models (Bowlby, 1988) that are encoded in procedural memory and become nonconscious strategies of affect regulation (Schore, 1994) and relational interaction. Both attachment- and trauma-related issues ensue from traumatogenic environments where the attachment figure and perpetrator are one and the same, but attachment-related issues also stem from non-life-threatening childhood experiences with caregivers (e.g., inadequate parental attention; harsh, inconsistent, insensitive, or fault-finding parenting) that cause emotional distress but are not perceived by the child as physically dangerous or life threatening.

When an attachment relationship has induced negative emotions and negative cognitions, physical tendencies also ensue, preventing integrated, free-flowing, spontaneous movement. For example:

> If a child grows up in a family that values high achievement and is encouraged to "try harder" at everything she undertakes, her body will shape its posture, gesture, and movement around this influence. If this value is held at the expense of other values, such as "you are loved for yourself, not for what you do," the child's musculature will probably be toned and tense. The body will be mobilized to "try harder." A child who grows up in an environment where trying hard is either discouraged or maladaptive, and where everything she achieves is undervalued, might have a sunken chest, limp arms, and shallow breath reflecting a childhood experience of not feeling assertive and confident, of "giving up." It may be difficult for this child to mobilize consistent energy or sufficient self-confidence to complete a difficult task. (Ogden et al., 2006, p. 10)

These physical tendencies in turn reinforce chronic negative emotions and cognitive distortions and constrict affect array, whereas an aligned, erect, but relaxed posture, full breathing, and supple tonicity support adaptive affect regulation and array and a positive sense of self.

The physical tendencies of secure and insecure childhood attachment histories are visible in our adult patients. Adults who are securely/autonomously attached demonstrate the capacity to interactively regulate (Schore, 1994), reflected in context-appropriate physical action tendencies that enable seeking suitable contact and proximity to others: reaching out, moving toward and away, and setting adaptive boundaries. These tendencies reflect a capacity to ask for and use help when their own capacities are ineffective or overwhelmed (Fosha, Paivio, Gleiser, & Ford, 2009; Ogden et al., 2006; Schore, 1994). Additionally, these individuals are able to utilize autoregulatory strategies independent of relational contexts, which manifest in physical tendencies such as full breathing, grounding (being aware of the legs and feet, their weight, and their connection to the ground) and centering (being aware of the core of their body and their bodily sense of self).

People with insecure-avoidant attachment histories routinely shun situations that stimulate attachment needs and prefer to autoregulate under stress by withdrawing from others. Often becoming uncomfortable, awkward, or even dysregulated when executing simple actions such as reaching out with the arms and moving toward others, they may find pushing-away motions more familiar and less disturbing. Joey had grown up "tough" with an alcoholic father who could abide no weakness in his son. During the course of therapy, I asked Joey to experiment by simply reaching out with his arm as if to reach for another person. He said that he immediately wanted to "back away," and that he would rather push out than reach out. When he eventually did reach out, he said, "This feels like jumping off a cliff; I don't know how to do this," and his body mirrored his words in its tension, slight leaning back, stiff movement of his arm, reaching with locked elbow, palm down. His nonverbal bodily message was that he was uncomfortable and did not expect a safe, empathic reception.

Others with avoidant histories may experience low autonomic arousal as well as decreased muscular tonicity, finding it easier to passively withdraw than take action that would promote interactions with others (Cozolino, 2002). Jeanie said that relationships were "for other people," not for her. When she explored reaching out in therapy, her body drooped and her reaching was partial and weak. She failed to extend her arm fully—her elbow remained pinned to her side—and the gesture lacked energy and conviction. She said, "What is the point? No one will respond." The lack of tonicity and vitality in the act of reaching echoed her words: Both reflected a paucity of empathic parental attention and care.

These avoidant patterns contrast with those of patients with insecure-ambivalent histories, who typically have a tendency toward enmeshment, clinging behavior, and increased affect and bodily agitation at the threat of separation from an attachment figure. Usually quite comfortable with reaching out, such patients may experience intolerance for distance corresponding with a tendency to cling, grasp, and a failure to literally "let go." When Carmen experimented with reaching, she leaned forward eagerly, reaching out toward her therapist with a full extension of her arm, taking a step forward as she did so. Preoccupied with the emotional and physical availability of her therapist, she said she wanted to move even closer and became agitated and irritated when her therapist instead suggested she might explore reaching out from increased distance, interpreting the suggestion as indicative of her therapist's unavailability.

When the attachment figure is also a threat to the child, a confusing and contradictory set of behaviors ensues that can be conceptualized as the result of simultaneous or alternating stimulation of attachment and defense systems (Lyons-Ruth & Jacobvitz, 1999; Main & Morgan, 1996; Steele, van der Hart, & Nijenhuis, 2001; van der Hart et al., 2006). When the attachment system is stimulated, the individual instinctively seeks proximity and engagement, but during proximity, which is perceived to be threatening, the defensive subsystems of flight, fight, freeze, hypoarousal/feigned death, or submissive behaviors are mobilized. Therapists may be baffled by the paradoxical responses of their patients to relational contact. For example:

> Lisa frequently complained that "no one is there for me" and begged her therapist for more contact: to sit closer, to hold her hand if she cried, to call to see how she felt during the week. Yet, in sessions, Lisa consistently seated herself in such a way that she was facing away from the therapist and orienting toward the floor and sofa, and her body stiffened when the therapist moved her chair closer at Lisa's request. Proximity-seeking emerged in her verbal communication, while avoidance was communicated physically: Her body held back the approach, avoiding even eye contact. (Ogden et al., 2006, p. 53)

Lisa, like most patients with unresolved attachment trauma, was torn between her desperate need for relationship and her profound fear of it. Lisa had a mother who was a source of safety and comfort but who also tended to have fits of rage, during which she would vent her anger toward Lisa in physical and emotional abuse. Over time, Lisa's ability for adaptive emotional regulation and social engagement were sacrificed as sympathetic (i.e., mobilization) or dorsal vagal (i.e., immobilization) defenses predominated over ventral vagal tone (i.e., social engagement), and her postures and gestures associated with fear blended with and contradicted those physical movements of seeking relationship.

Emotions and the Body

Both trauma- and/or attachment-related physical tendencies influence, and are influenced by, emotion. Neuroscience has taught us that emotions and the body are mutually dependent and inseparable in terms of function (Damasio, 1994; Frijda, 1986, LeDoux, 1996; Schore, 1994). Darwin (1859/1897) proposed that emotional responses themselves comprise a set of postures and other motor behaviors that may denote an immediate emotional response to current stimuli or a habitual, chronic emotional state relevant to the past but triggered by current conditions. Damasio (1994, 1999) pointed out that emotions have two somatic components: interoception and expression. *Interoception* is usually invisible to others, being experienced as an internal subjective awareness as the sensory nerve receptors (interoceptors) receive and transmit sensations from stimuli within the body. The "primary emotional [sensations] reflect the non-verbal sensation of shifts in the flow of activation and deactivation—the flow of energy and evaluations of information—through the system's changing states" (Siegel, 1999, p. 125). In contrast, postures, facial expressions, and gestures outwardly *express* internal emotional states, communicating these states to others. Finally, emotions are commonly described as critical motivators of action, signals that orient us to important environmental stimuli (Krystal, 1978; van der Kolk et al., 1996) and serve as "drives or deterrents for most of our actions" (Llinas, 2001, p. 155).

However, both action and interoception are also precursors to, and to some degree, determinants of, emotion. A variety of studies demonstrates the impact of posture and other movements on the experience, interpretation, and expression of emotion. Subjects who received good news in a posture in which the spine was slumped reported feeling less proud than subjects who received the same news in a posture in which the spine was upright (Stepper & Strack, 1993). Schnall and Laird (2003) showed that subjects who practiced postures and facial expressions associated with sadness, happiness, or anger were more likely to recall past events that contained a similar emotional valence as that of the one they had rehearsed, even though they were no longer practicing the posture. Similarly, Dijkstra, Kaschak, and Zwann (2006) demonstrated that when subjects embodied a particular posture, they were likely to recall memories and emotions in which that posture had been operational. Thus, gestures, facial expressions, and posture are not only reflections of emotion but actively participate in the subjective experience of emotion and in our interpretation of our experiences. A slumped posture may tell us that our self-esteem is low or that we are depressed, whereas an erect, upright posture may inform us that we are feeling good; a mouth turned up in a smile both contributes to and reflects feelings of happiness, contrary to a mouth turned down in a frown.

Action may even precede the emotion, especially when we are threatened: "We react automatically, and only later (even if it is only a split second later) do we realize there is danger and feel afraid" (Hobson, 1994, p. 139). Actions are immediately followed by the brain's appraisal to determine the meaning of the sensation, action, and situation, and only then are the sensations interpreted as a sense of peril (Siegel, 1999). Thus, like posture and action, interoception informs us about, and is the result of, emotion. The sensation of tension in the jaw, shoulders, or arms not only conveys to us that we are angry but also serves to sustain the anger; a tingling sensation may be the result of a frightening experience and also tells us that we are afraid; the jittery sensation of butterflies in the stomach both results from and is causative of feelings of nervousness or excitement. These internal sensations equally reflect and stimulate the postures, gestures, and facial expressions that are the outward signs of emotional states.

Nina Bull's (1945) extremely relevant theory that "motor attitude" precipitates emotion, which only then leads to behavior, highlights the impact of the way we hold our bodies on how we feel. She defines motor attitude as "the preliminary motor set, or posture of the body" that precedes and paves the way for particular emotions, which, in turn, motivate the physical action. Bull posits that "we feel angry as a result of *readiness* to strike, and feel afraid as a result of *readiness* to run away, and not because of actually hitting out or running" [p. 211, emphasis added]. Bull goes on to say that even preceding the motor attitude is a "predisposition," the latent neural organization—a procedurally learned tendency—to execute particular motor attitudes, emotions, and overt actions.

Bull's theory encompasses one very important difference from the idea that emotion is the result of and follows action (e.g., "I am afraid because I run"), a theory that Bull (1945, p. 210) believes "failed to differentiate between attitude and action, the . . . idea that feeling comes before behavior could find no place in [this] scheme." Damasio (1999) recognized this point in his description of awareness of emotion being only part of what is meant by emotions:

The bodily sensations and physiological changes may reflect "dispositional tendencies" that appear similar to Bull's "motor attitude." Porges (Chapter 2, this volume) writes that neurophysiology determines the coming together of emotional expression and visceral states, because changes in the nervous system contribute to muscle activity, including facial expression and movements of the legs, arms, and trunk. Hurley (1999) takes this one step further by describing the continual feedback loops of emotion, perception, cognition, and behaviors, asserting that none precedes the others. The above concepts correlate well with Lane and Schwartz's (1987) structural developmental model that categorizes the capacity to be aware of and describe emotions in the self, as well as in the other, in terms of five stages: physical sensations, physical action tendencies, single emotions, blends of emotions, and blends of blends of emotions.

This section would not be complete without reference to "emotional operating systems" (Panksepp, 1998a) or "action systems" (Ogden et al., 2006; van der Hart et al., 2006). These evolutionarily prepared psychobiological systems, each with its characteristic emotional valence, stimulate us to form close attachment relationships (motivated by love, longing, distress upon separation, and, when threatened, fear); explore (characterized by interest and curiosity); play (characterized by joy and laughter); participate in social relationships (motivated by feelings such as affection and conviviality); regulate energy (through eating, sleeping, etc.); reproduce (governed by lust and sexual drive); and care for others (motivated by emotions such as tenderness and compassion) (Bowlby, 1969/1982; Cassidy & Shaver, 1999; Fanselow & Lester, 1988; Lichtenberg, 1990; Lichtenberg & Kindler, 1994; Marvin & Britner, 1999; Panksepp, 1998a; van der Hart et al., 2006).

Action systems most likely form an evolutionary basis for procedural tendencies. As a particular action system is aroused, particular physical tendencies are stimulated that correspond with the emotions characteristic of that system. For example, the curiosity of the exploration system manifests in seeking and orienting movements that enable the investigation of novelty. The play system, characterized by laughter, involves a variety of movement patterns: tilting of the head; relaxed, open posture; nonstereotyped movements that change quickly (Beckoff & Byers, 1998; Beckoff & Allen, 1998; Brown, 1995; Caldwell, 2003; Donaldson, 1993). The caregiving system manifests in "subtle, warm, and soft" (Panksepp, 1998a, p. 247) behavior as the caregiver attunes voice, behavior, and touch to the needs of the person for whom he or she is caring. A wide variety of social behaviors accompany social communication, including gestures, facial and bodily expressions, and vocalizations. The reproduction system incorporates particular movement sequences characteristic not only of sexual behavior but also of courtship and flirting: eye contact, smiling, vocalizations that are both of a higher pitch and augmented volume, and exaggerated gestures (Cassidy & Shaver, 1999). As these actions, designed to fulfill the purpose of their related action system, are repeatedly executed, procedural tendencies related to the arousal of that system are formed.

Trauma-Related Emotional Tendencies

To reiterate, animal defensive strategies and their corresponding emotions stimulated by threat are adaptive in the moment of immediate peril, but both tend to become inflexible tendencies in people with posttraumatic stress disorder (PTSD) and other trauma-related disorders. Once danger is assessed, emotional arousal, now commonly interpreted as terror or anger, serves to support instinctually driven animal defensive strategies (Frijda, 1986; Hobson, 1994; Rivers, 1920). These dysregulated emotions tend to persist for traumatized individuals, who are characterized as suffering not only from "feeling too much" but also from "feeling too little" (van der Kolk, 1994). Sympathetically mediated mobilizing defenses entail an amplification of subjective emotional states—feeling too much—which is very different from the dampening and deadening of subjective emotional states—feeling too little—that typically accompany the immobilizing hypoarousal defense (Ogden et al., 2006; van der Hart et al., 2006). Fear and terror corresponding with flight responses may become chronic, repeatedly triggered by conditioned stimuli. Those with a dysregulated "fight" defense may be emotionally reactive, angry, or violent, at the mercy of bouts of rage with minimal provocation. Patients who favor a freeze response report helplessness and panic associated with feeling paralyzed, whereas "feigned death" and submissive responses, accompanied by increased dorsal vagal tone, herald a subjective detachment from, or absence, of the emotions, as indicated by patients who report, "I just wasn't there; I didn't feel anything." Chronic immobilizing responses provoke feelings of helplessness, loss of internal locus of control, lessening of self-worth, and an inability to be effectively assertive (Krystal, 1988). Blaming themselves, patients then succumb to shame and further feelings of inadequacy and despair, particularly if they fail to understand that a lack of assertion is often the result of a tendency to depend upon immobilizing defenses for safety and not merely a psychological shortcoming.

The dissociative tendencies of traumatized individuals may also engender distinct emotional states corresponding with different internal dissociative parts of the self. As van der Hart et al. (2006, pp. 98–99) note: "Discrete alternations of affect (as well as accompanying thoughts, sensations, and behavior) may accompany switches among various dissociative parts of the personality because they may each encompass different affects and impulses." Patients with dissociative disorders may experience further affect dysregulation as a result of conflicting emotions among various parts of the personality: One may be aggressive, another fearful, while yet another desperately seeks proximity and attachment (van der Hart et al., 2006). It is also important here to note that parts interact with each other internally: As one part engages in an attachment cry, a fight part may be stimulated, which in turn evokes flight or freeze among other parts, etc. These various parts of the personality, with their accompanying emotions and physical action tendencies, may routinely intrude unbidden upon the daily functioning of survivors, adding profoundly to their distress and dysregulation.

Failing to adequately integrate emotion arousal and adaptive action over time, patients may experience emotions as urgent calls to explosive, dysregulated action or complain of depression lack of action and motivation, or alternate between bouts of impulsive action and stagnation. Trauma-related emotions tend to remain constant over time and are exacerbated by current internal and external triggers, causing survivors to endlessly relive the emotional tenor of previous traumatic experiences.

Attachment-Related Emotional Tendencies

Trauma-related emotions, described above, interface with equally powerful attachment-related emotions that are the result of "both the relational processing in intense affective experiences and the long-term consequences of internalizing the dyadic handling of such experiences" (Fosha, 2000, p. 42). Particular emotional tendencies are found with each attachment category; these tendencies interface with, but are distinguished from, the powerful emotions that correspond with trauma-related animal defenses.

Those with insecure patterns develop habitual emotions and expressions that are defenses that minimize or block frightening or aversive affects (Fosha, 2000; Frijda, 1986). These relational defensive emotions and their functions are to be distinguished from those corresponding with animal defenses activated under perceived conditions physical danger and life threat. The relational defenses are most likely built on animal defenses, but they are much more sophisticated psychologically, being the result of a "higher-order consciousness" that includes the concept of a sense of self and a conceptual grasp of past, present, and future (Edelman, 1999). The affects associated with relational defenses limit the negative impact of painful emotions that evoked inadequate or inappropriate regulation and empathy from caregivers. In adult patients, these patterned emotions may be experienced as familiar and habitual, circular, endless and without resolution, and they go hand in hand with physical tendencies related to attachment (described above).

Individuals with insecure–avoidant attachment histories typically dismiss signals of internal distress and minimize emotional needs. Having lost hope that communicating negative emotions would elicit caregiving to regulate them, such individuals may fail not only to communicate emotions but to even experience them. Dependent on autoregulation and parasympathetic (dorsal vagal) dominance (Cozolino, 2002; Schore, 2003a) to self-regulate, emotional experience is thus curtailed (Cassidy & Shaver, 1999). This "overregulation" indicates a reduced capacity to experience both positive and negative emotions (Schore, 2003). Having lost access to strong emotions, as well as to a broad range of affect array, such patients typically present with a flat affect. Affective experience has been forfeited in favor of functioning, leading to "isolation, alienation, emotional impoverishment, and at best, a brittle consolidation of self" (Fosha, 2000, p. 43).

In contrast, the emotionality of patients with insecure-ambivalent attachment histories stems from the childhood experience of an undependable caregiver whose attention could be obtained only intermittently by clingy, needy behavior and increased emotionality. The amplified signaling for attention leads to escalating distress (Allen, 2001), which results in increased emotional reactivity in adulthood, an inability to modulate distress, and a vulnerability to underregulatory disturbances (Schore, 2003a). Preoccupied with internal emotional states, such patients are prone to dysregulated affect blended with high anxiety (Fosha, 2000). Relating a problem in her marriage to her therapist, Carmen tearfully leaned forward, gestured dramatically, her face exceedingly expressive and insistent on eye contact, wrapped up in her own distress and expression rather than in genuine contact, and unaware of her intrusion upon the physical "boundary" of her therapist or her therapist's discomfort with Carmen's "too close" proximity. Instead of enhancing interpersonal connection, the emotionality of this pattern sabotaged authentic contact.

The individual with a disorganized/disoriented attachment history grew up with attachment figures that provoked extremes of low (as in neglect) and high (as in abuse) affects that tend to endure over time (Schore & Schore, 2008). Experiencing high sympathetic tone—intense alarm, higher cortisol levels, and elevated heart rate—vacillating with increased dorsal vagal tone—slowed heart rate and shut down (Schore, 2001)—these infants, and later adults, are left with an inability to effectively auto- or interactively regulate.

They suffer from rapid, dramatic, exhausting, and confusing shifts of intense emotional states, from dysregulated fear, anger, or even elation, to despair, helplessness, shame, or flat affect. These commonly become enduring patterns of various dissociative parts, some of which avoid interactive regulation, and some of which avoid autoregulation, and most of which are good at neither.

In contrast to those with insecure attachment histories, individuals with a history of secure attachment typically demonstrate a degree of "affective competence" that includes "being able to feel and process emotions for optimal functioning while maintaining the integrity of self and the safety-providing relationship" (Fosha, 2000, p. 42). However, although the attachment figures of the securely attached child provide adequate regulation and repair, nevertheless particular emotional responses are commonly favored over others even in the best of families. The habitual interpretation of emotional arousal in predictable ways leads to biases toward certain emotions. For example, Jim, securely/autonomously attached and successful and content in his marriage and his job, habitually interpreted sensations of emotional arousal as frustration and anger, having grown up in a family that minimized vulnerable emotions of sadness, hurt, and disappointment. He had narrowed his affect array in order to "fit into" his family, and the emotions of sadness and grief remained unacknowledged and unresolved. In contrast, Leslie demonstrated an affinity for sadness, avoiding feelings of anger or outrage—a tendency developed in a family that favored the more vulnerable feelings over more aggressive and assertive ones. To maximize the availability of her caregivers, Leslie suppressed feelings of anger. These emotional tendencies are also accompanied and sustained by somatic tendencies that limit the individual's range of affect, but which do not necessarily indicate insecure histories.

Patients with both secure and insecure attachment histories exhibit patterns of decreased affect array related to innate action systems as a result of responses of early attachment figures to the arousal of these systems. Some patients with excessively serious parents have trouble playing; others who grew up in overly protective environments are uncomfortable with the curiosity of exploration; some are awkward and self-conscious in groups; still others seem unable to experience adequate empathy to motivate effective caregiving behavior; and some whose attachment figures frowned on flirtations behavior remain stilted and awkward during courtship. Important components of therapy include noting physical and emotional tendencies related to the arousal of various actions systems, helping patients work through the emotional pain when the arousal of particular systems has evoked disapproval or danger, and then cultivating the suppressed emotions and actions related to each system.

A Note on Play and Positive Affect

The capacity for play and positive affect is typically diminished or absent in patients who have come to associate positive affect with vulnerability to ridicule, disapproval, disdain, or even danger. A broad variety of positive affect states depend upon the ability to regulate a wide range of arousal, which, in childhood, is facilitated by the caregiver's sensitive, attuned responses to both positive and negative affect. The "good enough mother" (Winnicott, 1945) actively engages with her infant, repeatedly pairing high arousal states with interpersonal relatedness, play, and pleasure, while also helping the child to recover from negative states of distress, fatigue, and discomfort. Thus, " Affect regulation is not just the reduction of affective intensity, the dampening of negative emotion. It also involves an amplification, an intensification of positive emotion, a condition necessary for more complex self-organization" (Schore, 2003a, p. 78).

Play and other positive affective states cannot develop in the shadow of threat and danger, or under the scrutiny of a strict, disapproving, or overly serious attachment figure. They depend upon the subjective experience of safety and comfort, but for many patients, competing states of uneasiness or fear impede these states. Qualities of spontaneity, vitality, pleasure, and flexibility, as well as the trust and resonance required to engage in a deeply satisfying intimate relationship, are precisely the traits that are incompatible with trauma-related procedural learning. Many attachment-related tendencies formed when caregivers were not playful themselves, were overly critical of normal childhood foibles and ebullience, or unduly emphasized achievement, order, and etiquette rather than spontaneity and fun, interfere with positive affect and playfulness.

Many patients have become more accustomed to actions and goals that have to do with avoiding pain and fear than with seeking out positive affect. Preoccupied with the possibility of danger, criticism, or rejection, they have not learned to attend to things, people, or activities that might bring them pleasure. Such clients report that they do not know their own preferences— what activities would bring them pleasure, satisfaction, joy, or other feelings of well-being, what they are curious about or interested in, or what sensory stimuli feel good or meaningful to them (Migdow, 2003; Resnick, 1997).

Trauma- and attachment-related physical tendencies are typically inflexible and lack spontaneity. Movements characteristic of nonplayful or overly serious interactions tend to be constrained, stereotyped, rigid, agitated, or nervous (Beckoff & Byers, 1998; Brown, 1995). In some cases, such as that of the patient who complained of being scattered, impulsive and incapable of commitment, uncontained and impetuous, flitting movements reflected procedural tendencies. In treatment, explorations that increase the patient's ability for play and positive affect can mitigate maladaptive procedural tendencies. The therapist tracks the bodily responses evoked by the patient's narrative, alert not only to indications of trauma- and attachment-related procedural tendencies, but also to expressions characteristic of social engagement, positive affect, and play. These may be observed in a relaxed, open body posture, a tilting of the head (Beckoff & Allen, 1998; Caldwell, 2003; Donaldson, 1993), expressive gestures, or movements that shift quickly and are nonstereotyped (Goodall, 1995). Even early on in therapy, patients may experience short-lived moments of pleasure, playfulness, and resonant connection with the therapist that include particular nonverbal gestures, postures, and movements, such as a spontaneous increase in proximity and gesture, enhanced social engagement, eye contact, and relaxed, mobile facial expressions (Beckoff & Allen, 1998). The therapist meticulously watches for incipient spontaneous actions and affects—the beginning of a smile, meaningful eye contact, a more expansive or playful movement—that indicate positive affect, and capitalizes on those moments by participating in kind and/or calling attention to them and expressing curiosity, enabling the moment to linger. Encouraging simple joy, humor, and lightheartedness that accompany play behavior and the feelings of competence, joy, peace, love, and the authentic expression of other positive affects can counter the often arduous work of therapy and help patients expand their regulatory boundaries to include intense positive emotions as well as negative ones.

Directed Mindfulness and Treatment

To discover and change procedural tendencies, the therapist is interested not only in the narrative or "story," but in observing the emergence of procedural tendencies in the here and now of the therapy hour. Through the practice of mindfulness, patients learn to notice rather than enact or "talk about" these tendencies. Therapist and patient together "study what is going on, not as disease or something to be rid of, but in an effort to help the client become conscious of how experience is managed and how the capacity for experience can be expanded" (Kurtz, 1990, p. 111). Because mindfulness is "motivated by curiosity" (Kurtz, 1990, p. 111), it "allow[s] difficult thoughts and feelings [and body sensations and movements] simply to be there, to bring to them a kindly awareness, to adopt toward them a more 'welcome' than a 'need to solve' stance" (Segal et al., 2002, p. 55). Mindfulness also includes labeling and describing experience using language (Kurtz, 1990; Ogden et al., 2006; Siegel, 2007). Such nonjudgmental observation and description of internal experience engages the prefrontal cortex in learning about procedural tendencies rather than enacting them (Davidson et al., 2003). Since emotions and procedural tendencies are the purview of the right hemisphere (Schore, 2003a), whereas language is the purview of the left hemisphere, mindfulness may serve to promote communication between the two hemispheres (Neborsky, 2006; Siegel, 2007).

Mindfulness is an activity that is similar to, but different from, the concept of "mentalizing"—the process by which we make sense of the contents of our own minds and the minds of others (Allan, 2008; Fonagy et al., 2002). Although the process of mentalizing can be conscious, involving explicit reflective functioning, it often occurs automatically, without thought or deliberation. Such "implicit" mentalizing is influenced by many factors, including the posture, sensation, and movement of the body as well as chronic and acute emotional states. For example, the mentalizing of an individual whose body is constricted and tense is different from that of an individual whose body is tension free; the mentalizing of one whose spine is slumped and shoulders rounded forward is different from that of another whose spine is erect and shoulders square. Through mindfulness, we become aware of such procedural tendencies as contributing to implicit mentalizing. Then mentalizing can become more explicit as these implicit phenomena are brought into consciousness and reflected upon. Mindful is also useful in changing procedural tendencies so that implicit mentalizing becomes more adaptive and responsive to current life situations instead of the past.

Definitions of mindfulness usually describe being open and receptive to "whatever arises within the mind's eye" (Siegel, 2006) without preference. "Directed mindfulness" (Ogden, 2007) is an application of mindfulness that directs the patient's awareness toward particular elements of present-moment experience considered important to therapeutic goals. When patients' mindfulness is not directed, they often find themselves at the mercy of the elements of internal experience that appear most vividly in the forefront of consciousness—typically, the dysregulated aspects, such as panic or intrusive images, which cause further dysregulation, or their familiar attachment-related patterns. An example of nondirected mindfulness would be a general question to a dysregulated patient such as, "What is your experience right now?" An example of directed mindfulness that guides a patient's attention toward meeting the goal of becoming more grounded would be, "What do you notice in your body right now, particularly in your legs?" The patient likely will report that she cannot feel her legs, which paves the way for generating sensation and movement in her legs by bringing her attention to them, thus promoting the therapeutic goal of groundedness. Directing mindfulness toward emotions or the body makes it possibly to utilize precise interventions targeted at emotional processing—the experience, articulation, expression, and integration of emotions—as well as sensorimotor processing—the experience, articulation, expression, and integration of sensations and physical actions.

Expanding the Regulatory Boundaries of the Window of Affect Tolerance

The "window of affect tolerance" refers to an optimal arousal zone within which emotions can be experienced and processed effectively. Hyper- or hypoaroused states exceed the window of affect tolerance and are not conducive to the efficacious processing and resolution of emotional states. Trauma and maladaptive attachment tendencies will narrow the window of tolerance, and it is essential to expand these boundaries (see Figure 8.1).

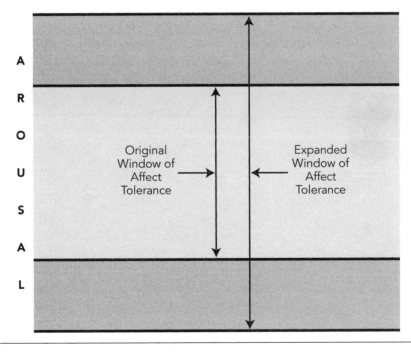

FIGURE 8.1
The window of affect tolerance.

Expanding the patient's regulatory boundaries involves experiencing and expressing core emotions, integrating dissociated or masked emotions, increasing the capacity for positive affect, and challenging physical procedural tendencies with new actions. Although these emotions and new actions are sometimes intense and painful, they also have a sense of aliveness, novelty, and richness and serve to connect patients with deeper layers of their emotional array. The activation and processing of these emotions leads to new resources, energy, and meaning (see also Fosha, Chapter 7, this volume; Trevarthen, Chapter 3, this volume).

The regulatory boundaries of the window of affect tolerance are challenged and expanded in psychotherapy as patients execute new, empowering physical actions, impossible during an actual traumatic event, or perform previously ineffective relational actions that foster attachment, connection, and interpersonal resonance, or engage the variety of actions that encourage and reflect positive affect (see Figure 8.2). Core affects are supported by the elab-

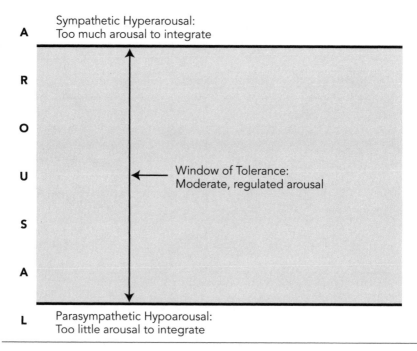

A Sympathetic Hyperarousal:
Too much arousal to integrate

R

O

U Window of Tolerance:
Moderate, regulated arousal

S

A

L Parasympathetic Hypoarousal:
Too little arousal to integrate

FIGURE 8.2
Expanding the regulatory boundaries of the window of affect tolerance.

oration of corresponding physical actions: Adaptive anger is supported by increased alignment of the spine, a degree of physical tension, and the capacity to push away or strike out; joy, by an uplifting of the spine and expansive movement; empathy, by a softening of the face and chest, and perhaps a gentle reaching out; play, by a tilt of the head, and spontaneous, rapid changes in movement.

However, venting the associated *patterned* emotions often exacerbates procedural tendencies, repeats the past, and thus fails to expand the regulatory boundaries. Thus, it is important that therapists assess the nature or source of a patient's emotional arousal: patterned, procedural tendencies that include dysregulated animal defensive responses, trauma-related hyperarousal or emotional tendencies; habitual emotions stemming from attachment history; or an authentic emotional response that expands the affect array, finishes unfinished business, reclaims emotions that have been dissociated, devalued, or suppressed, or increases positive affect tolerance.

Bromberg (2006) states that "retelling is reliving" and that while therapists must "try not to go beyond the patient's capacity to feel safe in the room, it is inevitably impossible for him to succeed, and it is because of this impossibility that therapeutic change can take place" (p. 24). Work with strong, authentic core emotions and new physical actions can precipitate excessive arousal that surpasses the patient's integrative capacity. These new emotions and actions typically cause arousal to escalate to the borders of dysregulation and require attentive and sensitive regulation by the therapist, who assures that arousal is high enough to expand the window, but not so high as to sacrifice integration. On the other hand, if patients' emotional and physiological arousal consistently remains in the middle of the window of tolerance (e.g., at levels typical of low fear and anxiety states), they will not be able to process past experience or expand their physical and emotional capacities because they are not in contact with traumatic or affect-laden attachment tendencies in the here and now of the therapy hour. Thus, as Bromberg states, therapy must be "safe but not too safe" in order to expand the window of affect tolerance.

Therapist and patient must continuously evaluate the level of arousal and the patient's capacity to process at the regulatory boundaries of the window of tolerance. Once arousal is at the regulatory boundaries, it is imperative to avoid stimulating additional emotional or physiological arousal and to avoid continuing with physical actions that cause further dysregulation at the expense of integration, working instead at the boundary with intention toward integration.

Working with Trauma-Related Tendencies

The overarching aim of trauma therapy is integration. At the beginning of therapeutic work with traumatized individuals, arousal typically becomes dysregulated (i.e., exceeds the patient's window of tolerance) both by the relationship and by articulation of the traumatic events. Abreaction and expression of trauma-related emotion that takes place far beyond the regulatory boundaries of the patient's window of affective tolerance is not encouraged because it does not promote integration (van der Hart & Brown, 1992). But through attending *preferentially and exclusively* to sensorimotor processing when arousal is at the edge of the window of tolerance, patients learn that the overwhelming arousal can be brought back to the window. This can be done independent of any particular emotional or cognitive content. Noticing and changing somatic tendencies in the present to the exclusion of emotions and content limit the information to be addressed to a tolerable amount and intensity that can be integrated, facilitates affect regulation, and paves the way for future work with strong emotions without causing excessive dysregulation.

The first task of therapy is to teach patients particular skills that serve to return their arousal to within the window of tolerance. After years of celibacy, Marcia, a sexual abuse survivor, began to explore sexual intimacy with her boyfriend, which in turn triggered bottom-up dysregulation. She reported in therapy, "My body's gone amuck! I can't sleep, I can't eat!" Asked by her therapist to "notice what happens inside" (an open-ended, general mindfulness directive), Marcia reported panic and trembling, an awareness that exacerbated her dysregulation. Marcia's therapist then used directed mindfulness by asking Marcia to pay attention only to her body sensation, thus excluding descriptions of emotions and content: "Let's just focus on your body: Feel the panic as body sensation—what does it feel like in your body?" Marcia directed all her attention to the sensation of trembling, using sensation vocabulary (e.g., tingling, traveling, shaking, calming down) rather than emotion vocabulary (e.g., scared, ashamed, panicked, anxious) to describe her somatic experience to her therapist. To encourage Marcia to describe the progression of these sensations until the sensations themselves subsided, her therapist continued to use directed mindfulness: for example, "Stay with that sensation of trembling—what happens next in your body? How does the sensation change?" Gradually, the sensations settled, the trembling abated, and Marcia's arousal returned to her window of tolerance.

Directed mindfulness can also help patients discover empowering, mobilizing defenses. In 1925 Janet wrote about his observation that traumatized patients are unable to execute empowering actions, or "acts of triumph" (p. 669).

When patients first turn their attention to the body, they typically become aware of disempowering, immobilizing defenses rather than triumphant actions. But as they learn to extend and refine their mindfulness of the body, they nearly always discover the impulses to fight or flee that were inhibited, for the sake of survival, during the original traumatic events but remain concealed within the body. These empowering actions often first reveal themselves in preparatory movements—the barely perceptible physical actions that occur prior to the full execution of a larger movement.

For example, as Marcia first talked about the abuse she had suffered as a child, she was aware only of the collapsed feeling in her body and a tendency toward hypoaroused responses: spacing out, feeling "nothing." However, as she continued to explore body sensations, she noticed a slight tightening in her jaw, tension that seemed to travel down her neck into her arms. Eventually, Marcia reported a small movement in her fists, a curling that seemed indicative of a larger aggressive movement. As she was directed by her therapist to feel the tension and to see what her body "wanted to do," Marcia became aware of impulses to strike out, and she slowly executed this motion against a pillow held by her therapist. Upon the completion of that movement, Marcia also reported the impulse to escape, experienced as a tightening of the muscles of her legs, which was executed through standing and experiencing her ability to walk away from unwanted stimuli.

Working with such physical acts of triumph is interwoven with working with patterned emotions and eventually with adaptive new emotional responses. At one point, as Marcia remembered her father coming into her bedroom when she was a child, her hands came up in a protective gesture, but then her hands suddenly drew in toward her body. Asked to notice this movement, Marcia expressed being ashamed, an aversive emotion that corresponded with impulses to curl up instead of protecting herself through pushing motions. As Marcia followed the impulse to curl up, she was able to experience her feelings of shame with her empathically regulating therapist, who not only facilitated Marcia's emotional expression but also the realization that the abuse was not her fault. However, this was only a step in Marcia's process, for the empowering "act of triumph" of pushing away remained incomplete and unexecuted. Thus, upon the settling of her emotional arousal, the therapist asked her to return to recalling the moment when her father came into her bedroom when she was a child and discover what her body "wanted to do," again facilitating not only somatic awareness but somatic *processing*. This time, Marcia reported a feeling of anger—contrary to her usual pattern of helplessness, shame, and fear—accompanied by tension in her arms, which proved to be the nascent mobilizing defense that she had, wisely, abandoned during the abuse. This time, Marcia was able to sustain directed mindfulness toward the anger and her somatic experience, both of which supported the execution of a new action as opposed to the repetition of submission and shame.

In previous therapy, Marcia had repeatedly expressed tendencies of shame and helplessness, but her propensity to dissolve into tears interfered with more adaptive emotional and physical responses such as anger and assertive action. Once she discovered her anger at what had happened and was able to execute her acts of triumph, she reported a core feeling of "being safe in my skin" and "more like myself than I've ever experienced." As she and her therapist shared their deep appreciation for these gains, Marcia began to cry softly. She expressed deep grief at the loss of the innocent trust in her father that she had treasured as a young girl. These very powerful emotions were accompanied by another surge of arousal, challenging the regulatory boundaries of her window of tolerance, but, as she sobbed, her therapist's empathic voice and interactive regulation kept Marcia from further escalation, resulting in an expansion of her window of affect tolerance and sense of competency. Afterward, Marcia reported that that she felt a new sense of fluid movement and an overall softening and receptivity in her body.

Treatment of Attachment-Related Tendencies

Aversive attachment-related affects, such as shame or defenses that mask or suppress a deeper emotion, recapitulate early affect-laden interactions with caregivers and limit affective experience, array, and expression. These emotions typically formed as successful strategies for meeting needs where direct authentic emotional communications proved unsuccessful, have a repetitive quality, and often disguise and defend against a deeper level of feeling. Geared to these needs, patterned emotions are used manipulatively (unconsciously, not maliciously) to influence the actions of others by stimulating guilt or sympathy or eliciting attention, help, empathy, freedom from pressure, privacy, or connection. Instead of venting these patterned emotions unawares, it is important to help patients both discover their function and experience the underlying or authentic or "core" affects (Fosha, 2000). Core affects provide a sense of deep contact and comfort with the self and the self in relationship: the experience and expression of the emotional pain unmasked of the defensive emotion, and the joy, pride, love, and deep resonance in the dyadic context.

Jim was quick to anger, expressing frustration and irritation at the slightest provocation. When this patterned response emerged as he was talking about his wife's criticism of him, his therapist asked him to focus on the somatic tendencies that correlated with the emotion. He first reported tension in his jaw, arms, and shoulders and expressed additional feelings of anger. The therapist empathically reflected his affect but also directed continued mindfulness toward his body rather than his emotions. As Jim refrained from expressing the anger and stayed aware of his body, he noticed tension in his chest. Recognizing this sensation as different from the physical tendency accompanying his characteristic anger, the therapist directed Jim to focus on that tension, notice its parameters, and to exaggerate it slightly (intending to raise the signal of a more core emotion). Jim reported that his heart hurt, and he spontaneously recalled a memory of his parents strongly ridiculing him for failing to successfully help his younger sister with her homework. The tension around his heart increased, and the therapist again asked him to stay aware of his body and to find the words that seemed to accompany the tension. Jim said softly, "I can't show my hurt—I have to be tough," and with those words, the underlying emotion of hurt and disappointment masked by the pattern of irritation and anger, emerged and deepened. The therapist's empathic resonance provided the opportunity for complete expression of this underlying, defended core affect and allowed Jim to cultivate new, more adaptive emotional responses. Over time, Jim was able to express a variety of core emotions and also learned to engage in new, more adaptive physical actions. He practiced softening the area around his heart to enable connection with more vulnerable emotions: He placed his hands gently over his heart, consciously relaxed his chest, and used his breath to soften his chest. He learned to become mindful of physical actions indicative of anger and frustration, such as tension in his jaw, arms, and shoulders, and to discern if these represented fixed reaction patterns or adaptive responses to the present moment.

Awakening and Regulating Play and Positive Affect

The therapist's encouragement of a wide variety of positive affects and their physical actions expands the boundaries of the window of tolerance and offers the potential for increasing the capacity for social engagement and trust in relationship. In the context of sensitive attunement and collaboration, the patient can learn to become more curious and mindful of internal experience in response to the thought, remembrance, or engagement of play and positive affect, to the movements that express them, or to spontaneous moments of playful interaction and positive affect with the therapist.

Joan reported to her therapist that she is often told she is "too serious" and that her husband complains of her inability to enjoy herself. These observations were corroborated by her bodily communications: Joan's body was stiff, pulled in, awkward in its rigidity, telegraphing a nonverbal message to "keep away" emotionally and physically. The tension across her hunched shoulders, a lack of movement and freedom in her upper body, and a plodding quality to her gait echoed Joan's feeling that she was accustomed to great hardships. Though Joan wistfully spoke of wishing that she could experience greater enjoyment in life, she also reported a sense of discomfort and even alarm when she attempted to be less serious or more playful. Having grown up with a maternal caregiver who was strict, somber, anxious, and depressed and who provided little protection from the frightening behavior of an alcoholic father, we can infer that, as an infant and child, Joan experienced inadequate soothing of her states of distress and a loss of playful, positively toned mother–child interactions.

Initially, the therapist's attempts to help Joan embody the flexible, unstereotyped movements characteristic of positive affect ignited procedurally learned animal and attachment defensive tendencies. As Joan began to explore expressive, playful movements, she reported tension and constriction in her body that told her to expect ridicule or even danger. Her therapist taught her how to practice a mobilizing defensive response of pushing away, utilizing the tension in a gesture of boundary setting and protection. This movement was practiced again and again, gradually fostering a sense of safety and mastery that alleviated her fear and frozen immobilization.

Eventually, Joan's therapist asked her what kind of posture and movements her body would want to make in a context of enjoyment, fun, and safety, and Joan reflected that those actions would be free, spontaneous, and expressive— qualities that challenged her usual restrained, stiff demeanor. In a carefree, playful manner, the therapist executed such movements (tilting of the head, dancing motions with legs and arms) at Joan's instruction, first modeling them for her and then asking her to explore mirroring these movements. Initially, Joan giggled, but then again reported that these playful actions felt frightening, and she felt the impulse to curtail the movements and return to her habitual tension. But since much work had already been done with regard to her fear and the corresponding physical tendencies, her therapist remained empathically playful, helped her sense the safety of the here and now, encouraged her to maintain eye contact, and also reminded her of her newly learned ability to set boundaries and say "no." With this support, Joan was able to explore spontaneous, relaxed, expressive movements characteristic of positive affect.

Over the course of therapy, Joan and her therapist practiced a variety of movements that facilitated positive affect, such as comparing Joan's plodding gait with a bouncy, "head up" walk, exchanging her hunched shoulders and rounded spine for an upright, shoulders-down posture that encouraged eye contact and engagement with others. With continued practice, Joan's more integrated posture and expressive actions as well as positive affects became more natural and accessible, and her movements became increasingly unpredictable, unforced and complex, occurring without prompting from her therapist. While her emotional arousal increased during many moments of experiencing a variety of positive affects (playfulness, joy, elation, mastery, pride, reception of the therapist's positive regard, deep resonance and even love between therapist and patient), high arousal was paired with positive affect, in marked contrast to her usual coupling of high arousal with negative affect, danger and hypervigilance. Over time, experiencing and enhancing positive affects and amplifying their accompanying movements challenged Joan's procedural tendencies, fostered resilience and buoyancy, stimulated social engagement, and expanded her window of tolerance.

Conclusion

Underscoring the relationship between affect, the body, and the brain, Ratey (2002) writes: "When we smile we feel happier and when we feel happier we smile. . . . The feedback between layers or levels of the brain is bidirectional; if you activate a lower level, you will be priming an upper level, and if you activate a higher level, you will be priming a lower level" (p. 164). Clinicians can utilize the feedback between emotions, sensation, and physical action to therapeutic advantage by integrating direct work with movement and body sensation into their skill base. Although addressing emotions (and cognitions) is essential in treatment, it is no substitute for the meticulous observation of procedurally learned physical tendencies or the thoughtful interruption of them that teaches patients to use their own movement, posture, and sensation to regulate arousal and expand their own affect-regulating capacity. The successful accomplishment of previously feared or unfamiliar actions in the context of an attuned social engagement with the therapist, along with appropriate processing of previously feared or unfamiliar core emotions, serve to develop more adaptive relational capacities, strengthen both interactive and autoregulatory abilities, and expand the regulatory boundaries of the window of tolerance. A comprehensive integration of work with emotion and elaboration of physical actions maximizes therapeutic possibility and, over time, inspires patients to engage a wider range of life-enriching behaviors and affects.

9

Emotion in Romantic Partners

Intimacy Found, Intimacy Lost, Intimacy Reclaimed

Marion Solomon

PEOPLE MEET, BOND, AND become wired together in ways that affect them at both neurological and psychological levels. Emotions play a fundamental role in that process. In secure relationships emotions are vehicles for communicating and solidifying attachment bonds. In contrast, couples come into therapy with narratives about their problems that often cover a deep well of disowned emotions, unmet dependency needs, and emotional pain. When deep core emotions are inaccessible and emotional needs remain unmet, powerful dysregulated feelings often interfere with the ability to self-regulate or repair injuries. As we witness growing numbers of people seeking therapy for relationship problems, it is clear that many partners fail to give and receive the very things that are essential for maintaining a secure attachment—empathy, listening, touching, dyadic resonance, a sense of seeing and being seen by each other, and ultimately, an opportunity to be in touch with core emotions while remaining present with each other.

Research has shown that the brain is a dynamic, connective, and socially seeking organ (Siegel, 1999). There is a neurological need for secure attachments. Attachment bonds provide a sense of safety and emotional availability in times of distress that remain constant from early childhood throughout the lifespan. Behavior, arousal, emotion regulation, and awareness are all organized simultaneously through an interactive process that helps to solidify emotional bonding and enable safe exploration of the environment. In every subsequent relationship throughout the lifespan, feelings arise subcortically that influence the process of reasoning and decision making. When negative feelings arise around repeated, unresolved attachment failures, defenses against emotional pain become locked in, while exploration and new behavioral repertoires feel unsafe.

The neural circuitry underlying emotional bonds is now being mapped out as clinical psychologists, developmental experts, and neuroscientists increasingly collaborate and integrate the important knowledge that is rapidly becoming available. In recent years, neuroscience has given us knowledge of the brain's plasticity and the transmitter circuits that can be altered and redirected by our thoughts, feelings, beliefs, relationships, and external life conditions (Doidge, 2007; Siegel, 2007). Based upon knowledge of how the circuits in the brain affect and are affected by past experiences, coloring perceptions of current relationships, it is possible to understand why people who meet, fall in love, and get married can later come to see each other as the cause of anxiety, distress, and danger (Solomon & Tatkin, in press). New situations reengage old memory patterns. In milliseconds, subcortical processes merge past and present emotional reactions. Feelings arise that can influence the processes of reasoning and decision-making.

Intimate relationships can create growth and change or, alternatively, can become locked into destructive patterns of interaction. This chapter explores ways to recognize and change locked-in, painful interactions between partners and shows how emotions and their regulation—or lack thereof—play a role both in the dysregulation and the healing of these patterns. Current neuroscience research uncovering ways to reengage mind, brain, memory, and cognition informs clinical interventions that can help intimate partners perceive and respond to each other's emotions and behaviors in new ways.

The Social Brain: Emotions and Attachment

Research confirms a high correlation between early attachment categories and adult attachment patterns (Main, 2000). From before birth throughout the lifespan, brain, body, and nervous systems are wired together in interaction with the environment, with cascades of emotion setting off chemical reactions that affect the developing mind (Siegel, 1999). Arousal levels, awareness, and behavior are all organized simultaneously in the brain through this interactive process. Individual psychic life originates in this interactional field. The eye-to-eye, skin-to-skin contact between baby and caretaker first regulates and organizes the experience of inner states (Schore, 2001).

Stern (2000) identifies various senses of self that are organized through interactions with "self regulating others." We discover ourselves through the reflection in the eyes of another (Winnicott, 1958). At the same time that we learn the extent to which we can depend on another to keep us safe, we develop our own unique patterns of relating. These become internal working models that shape all future relationships (Bowlby, 1969/1982).

If we are touched, nurtured, and held in safety, we learn to depend on others, and a secure mode of attachment develops. In a secure attachment there is an attunement, understanding, and acceptance of us as we are, rather than as what we are supposed to be to obtain the love of the other person. Through positive emotional interactions (mother and baby, intimate partners), we are likely to feel known, loved, and worthy. In relationships that work well, each feels enhanced by the interactions with the other. When things go well, a working model of secure attachment and positive affective interactions will shape our expectations as we enter new situations. This early influence does not guarantee a happy marriage, nor does an insecure early attachment mean an adult life bereft of good relationships. But a secure attachment does make it easier to cope with the stresses that invariably arise in a long-term committed relationship.

For intimacy to occur, the *care-seeking system* (Cassidy, 1999, p. 123), the caregiver's part of the attachment system, has to be functioning well. John Bowlby's concept of a "secure base" (Ainsworth, Blehar, Waters, & Wall, 1978) may be seen as a platform from which to explore Main's (2002) description of "earned secure attachment." Research shows that a good relationship can alter earlier disturbed attachment patterns. Treboux and Crowell (2001) studied adult attachment representations across two ordinary life events: marriage and becoming a parent. Their research found that these transitions could serve as catalysts to change in Bowlby's internal working models (Bowlby, 1969/1982). Indeed, over a period of 5 years, a secure adult relationship has been found to be associated with changed responses on the Adult Attachment Interview, from insecure to "earned secure" (Main, 2002). This finding confirms other research demonstrating that connections among neurons can be directly altered and shaped by current experience, thanks to the neural plasticity of the brain (Schore, 2003a, 2003b; Siegel, 2007).

Secure attachment facilitates comfort with autonomy. Securely attached people both seek care and give care that the other wants. *Giving care* means being available to an adult romantic partner in stressful times. It means recognizing when the other needs care and doing what is necessary to provide it. It means being loving, being respectful of the truth of another, and accepting a range of ways of being and feeling. In Cassidy's (1999) words:

"This need to be seen is as primary in the bonds of significant adult attach-ments as in the infant–caretaker bond. What is required is the ability to trust that others are available to respond sensitively when we are in the midst of troubling experiences and disturbing emotions. No life is without its stres-sors. One thing is certain for all of us; there will be times when the heart and mind will be hurt. Life for everyone involves times when at our innermost core we experience fear, sadness, anger, grief. At such times a person desires nurturing and loving care in a primary attachment relationship. It is here that a relationship is tested, and security that the other can be depended upon is confirmed, or not." (p. 130)

Only after a sufficient number of interactions in which security of attach-ment is tested, and in which the signal for comfort and safety is met positively, do mental representations develop of the other as loving, responsive, and sen-sitive, and of the self as loveable and worthy. The positive emotional interac-tions that emerge in the wake of successfully repaired ruptures are crucial (Fosha, 2000,[1] 2003; Schore, 1994; Tronick, 2007) because they are part and parcel of the representations that are the basis of secure working models of self and other. These internal working models carry the person, child, or adult through the many normal failures of attunement, followed by reparative expe-riences. When this happens, the relationship becomes a healing emotional bond, "a haven in a heartless world" (Lasch, 1995).

An important aspect of trust necessary for a well-functioning intimate rela-tionship is a belief that the self is valuable and worthy of being loved. This belief also grows out of the bonds of secure attachment. When, through re-peated responsive emotional interactions, a positive internal model of the other meets a positive internal representational model of the self, we have the necessary and sufficient conditions for intimacy. When these conditions are lacking, relationships suffer.

How Defenses Against Painful Emotions Endure as Lifelong Patterns

The affective reactions of people with unresolved early traumas often create dysfunctional attachment patterns in adult intimate relationships. Studies show a high correlation between childhood care received and adult care given

---

1. See, in particular, Fosha's Self–Other–Emotion configuration, a version of the internal working model with emotion regulation integrated within (pp. 118–126).

to a romantic partner Cassidy & Shaver, 1999). Attachment disturbances result from repeated separations, prolonged stress, or traumatic experiences in our early bonds. Unless recognized and resolved through a reparative relationship, the protective defenses that felt necessary for physical or psychic survival become wired in and affect relationships throughout a lifetime. Reemergence of intense feelings in later situations can distort the ability to respond appropriately. When strong emotions arise and are not regulated within the containment and safety of a secure attachment, it becomes difficult to distinguish between impulses of anger, the arousal of anxiety, and early-learned defenses against frightening or painful affect. These defenses, which have been incorporated into the internal working model, are triggered in each new relationship. Partnerships are tested repeatedly. This process occurs as if on autopilot, without conscious awareness or planning, because it has been wired into the brain.

Because affective response patterns are encoded at a subcortical level, emotions, defenses, and enactments remain stored in implicit memory (Siegel, 1999). An interpersonal event triggers emotional arousal that causes temporal loss—a kind of time travel in which past and present merge. The current situation and current person take on the characteristic of one or more people from the past. Partner and mother (or father) may blend at that moment, setting the stage for defensive reaction on both sides and the emergence of the "marriage monster" (Tatkin, personal communication, September 27, 2003). We will see this dynamic later, in the case of Ted and Robin.

Couples generally seek therapy when they are caught in repetitive, bewildering, painful patterns of interaction. They both have a narrative explanation of problems between them, each viewing the problems as lying within the other. Yet, as they describe their dissatisfaction and discomfort in the relationship, their account often reflects self-blame and inadequacy. When pressed to clarify, a partner may express numbness, bodily pain, or vague feelings of something being wrong. The therapist must be aware of the transferences between partners as well as transference reactions to the therapist. Many people come into therapy fearing that joint sessions are a dangerous territory in which they will be blamed, or in which shameful or humiliating feelings will emerge, uncovering a needy, fearful, undefended self.

Couples typically interact with each other from a conscious verbal level, while activated subcortical emotional underpinnings remain out of awareness. The conscious verbal narratives on which partners tend to rely are a product of left-brain cortical functions that provide a narrative of problems presented in ways that protect the speaker against deep shame or guilt. Sometimes partners convince each other, or the therapist, that the cause of the problem is sex, money, work, poor communication, extended family, etc. These may be real problems, but they often are overlays of hidden deep emotional issues.

The very young child uses whatever defenses are available, including denial, dissociation, projection of emotion to others, and a myriad of defenses designed to protect him or her from being overwhelmed by dangerous emotions. The emotions are particularly frightening and painful if there is no one present to understand or give comfort. What often appears to be high anxiety may be an "overlay," a defensive reaction covering hidden core emotions. What appears to be pathological enactment may be an attempt to share with another person emotions that are too primitive for words. When there has been severe trauma, the person may try to create certain feelings in another, so that he or she, too, knows what is too unbearable to feel. With emotions and defenses such as these, enactments are tests to see if this person understands and is strong enough and cares enough to contain the emotions that are too painful for the defender to endure. Relationships with partners and with therapists are tested repeatedly to see if, finally, there is someone who can provide the healing attachment that has been needed for so long. Often it takes years to trust the other when toxic emotions are present.

Actions and words that seem to make no sense when listening to explanations of the difficulties may become much more understandable when the therapist helps partners pay attention to the emotional undercurrents of the surface narratives. This is the path toward the warded-off emotions that previously felt too overwhelming. This type of intervention is best done in the moment during the session when one or both partners experience the emerging emotional content as uncomfortable, threatening, and unexplainable. The goal is to make the sessions a safe holding environment for containment and detoxification of hurtful emotions. These emotions are not only hidden from others, but even more, hidden from the self—terrifying affect around extreme vulnerability related to abandonment, intensely rageful feelings around neediness unfilled and unfulfillable—emotions too shameful to face.

Mary Main (2002) reported studies indicating that a 5-year relationship with a secure partner can change an insecure to a secure attachment. Still more research must be done to determine what happens to toxic emotions in a secure adult relationship. Videotapes of couple therapy sessions showcase how frozen emotions seem to thaw, solidly entrenched walls begin to melt, and partners relax and begin to say when they are hurt or frightened in moments of interaction.[2] The healing impact of what happens when core emo-

---

2. Videotapes of couples presented by Susan Johnson, Stan Tatkin, Marion Solomon, and John Gottman, at "Anatomy of Intimacy" conferences, University of California, Irvine.

tions that hold the emotional truth (Fosha, Chapter 7, this volume) come to the fore is illustrated in the clinical work with Ted and Robin.

Understanding the Interactional Experience

An important part of understanding and containing the interactional experience of the partnership is awareness of what is happening in the here and now at times when strong emotion surges to the surface and needs to be addressed. The therapist's ability to pay attention to physiological and emotional reactions in both partners, as well as in him- or herself, provides vital information to help all involved understand the process of the relationship in the moment. Patterns that are repeated over time become wired in the brain and body. New experiences can alter the brain and nervous system, but couples in distress often have difficulty generating novel experiences. Instead, their interactions during conflict tend to be noncontingent and repetitive. People become stuck in their own habitual patterns and enlist those close to them to play out a complementary part. Instead of hearing what the other is saying, each resorts to rigid communication scripts in which difficulties are never resolved. What we often see in therapy with couples is the partners' frustrated and failed efforts to find a better way to feel safe, worthy, and loved.

If either partner views him- or herself as unlovable and unworthy, based upon messages embedded in the brain early in life, the result may predispose him or her to painful encounters with others and repeated selection of disparaging or unavailable partners. *This unfortunate consequence may be due less to a masochistic desire for pain and more to a constant seeking for repair:* "Maybe this potential mate, who reminds me of someone important early in my life, will understand my needs, and will love me, treat me with care, soothe my wounds, be the healing relationship I need." We tend to select partners who have similar or complementary emotional wounds, each yearning for and testing the ability of anyone to know them at their darkest core and still love them. Like the tendency to press on an injury in an arm or a leg, we press repeatedly on emotional wounds (Cassidy, 1999).

Every therapist working with couples, or with individuals who have experienced repeated relational problems, has seen this pattern. Sometimes the individual therapist listens to his or her patient's description of a mate and wonders how he or she can live with such a "monster." Family therapists have described the transformation of a patient's narrative from "dream lover" to "worst nightmare" (Behry, 2007).

Case Example: Ted and Robin

I received an urgent call from Ted, a former patient, requesting a joint session with his wife, Robin. I had last heard from him almost 2 years before, when he had written from Las Vegas saying that they were going to get married and life was wonderful. Now he said they must come in right away because he, enraged and fed up, was about to pack up and leave her, much as he had left his first wife.

Ted and I had worked together for almost 4 years after he was divorced by his wife of two decades and then unceremoniously retired from a prestigious job. Left with a deep well of hurt and distrust, he was suspicious that employees in the new business he started would leave and take his ideas with them, and that women were interested in him only for the money in his golden parachute; he could not even fully trust therapy because he paid for it, " just as I would for a prostitute," he said disdainfully.

I knew Ted had had many early attachment problems. We seemed to have recreated together the unavailable parent–angry child experience he had lived through growing up. He was often angry at me and the process of therapy. He hated to stop at the end of a session, became enraged when vacations came up, and complained because I wouldn't talk very long when he called me at night. It seemed at times that we were in a war zone, even as he sat quite properly looking me in the eyes and talking about his life; the war was taking place inside, in the sessions, and he needed me to stay connected while he went through it.

The work of repair began in the therapeutic relationship. When feelings arose during the sessions, he learned to stop, pay attention to his body, and breathe. I gave him feedback about how our work affected me and made sure to match my breathing, body posture, and facial expression to his rhythms; sometimes, when I found that my mind was wandering, I commented on our "losing each other." When I pointed out that we had an impact on one another, he went from being upset with me for withdrawing to checking in with himself to see where *he* was when I was not connecting.

While we were going through some very difficult encounters in session, his business relationships improved, his agitation in the supermarket checkout line diminished, he overcame his fear of traveling by airplane, and he was able to sit through a movie without having to get up two or three times "to escape." He continued to date, but relationships were short-term, ending whenever a woman expressed interest in getting closer.

When Ted met Robin something changed. He no longer talked about the empty feeling inside, the rages, the sense of being lost, the "black monsters" that filled his dreams, or the wish to find a woman who "won't drive me crazy." Ted was in the ecstatic stage of falling in love. ("For the first time, I know what joy feels like.")

The brain in love produces a wonderful sense of timelessness and euphoria that involves little thought but much emotion (Bartels & Zeki, 2000; Fisher, 2004). Millions of neural networks are activated, and the brain centers that mediate emotions, sexuality, and the self begin to expand and reorganize. Romantic love involves surges of dopamine and norepinephrine, neurotransmitters that drive the reward system and are closely akin to those involved in addiction.

The romance was quite one-sided at the beginning. Robin told Ted that she was still recovering from the death of her fiancé in an automobile accident a year before and was not ready for a relationship. Her reticence seemed to make Ted desire her even more; he sent her flowers every day. He kept asking me how to get her more interested, becoming angry at me ("Who needs you anyway?") for not giving him advice on "matters of the heart," since I had written books about relationships, then calling me at 10:00 at night ("Robin is driving me crazy").

When Ted called Robin, she would take days to return his call. As was the case with his friendships of childhood, he had to do all the work to have a relationship. But when her friends, who met him, encouraged her to date him and to begin living again, he was elated, asserting that this was the kind of woman he wanted—strong, independent, worthy in so many ways. He proposed to her a few weeks after they'd met. Robin dated him but held him off until they went out on the 1-year anniversary of their meeting: Although she seemed very far away while they walked on the beach and watched the sun set, by the end of the evening she "dropped the word marriage" into the conversation.

When shortly thereafter they came to the office for their first couple session, I could understand why Ted was so enamored. Robin was a striking, almost 6-foot-tall woman in her mid-30s, with blond hair pulled back in a chignon. They made a very appealing-looking couple. I found myself drawn into their drama—his pushing to marry, her need to maintain a distance— even as I tried to uphold the therapeutic stance espoused by Wilfred Bion (1977), one "without memory or desire."

I asked them to tell me about what was happening in their relationship. Robin responded by explaining about the death of her fiancé and how she was not ready to move as quickly as Ted wanted to ("I think sometimes that we could get married, but I wish he would give me more room"). When I asked if she could focus on her unresolved feelings for a moment, she said she had difficulty getting to them, and when I suggested she take a moment to check what was happening in her body and see if any thoughts, sensations, or emotions came up, she said, "Nothing right now." Finally, when I observed that the loss of her fiancé had obviously been very traumatic for her and inquired as to how she felt about discussing, in the joint session, something that could bring up a lot of emotions, she replied that being emotional had never been part of her repertoire.

Knowing that open-ended questions about her emotions were not likely to result in any helpful dialogue, I focused on some specific questions about her history and her early relationships. For example, I asked her if she recalled to whom she had felt closest when she was very young. I asked if she recalled who was there, if anyone, when she fell down or hurt herself in some way. Utilizing some of the other questions developed by Mary Main (2006) for her research in the Adult Attachment Interview (AAI) and by Stan Tatkin (2007) in his extension, AAI Questions to Couples, I continued with questions such as, "Who put you to bed at night?"[3] She seemed comfortable answering only those questions for which she could give factual answers.

I asked Robin for three words that described the relationship with her mother when she was a very young child. She said "loving," "kind," and then couldn't think of a third word. I asked her if she could give me examples of what about her mother was loving. She said that her mom "was always at home . . . She was a housewife." She said that her mother "was not like a lot of my friends' mothers." When I asked her to tell me some incidents that would be examples of "kind," she said, "Mom would put down what she was doing if I needed her." I asked her if there was anything more, and she added, "I was a good girl and didn't ask for very much. . . . I read a lot, and whenever I asked for books, Mom took me to the store and let me pick whatever books I wanted." Mostly she had difficulty giving a coherent narrative about her relationship with either of her parents.

I thought of Robin as having been a solitary young girl with an avoidant attachment pattern. She differed from Ted, who had also experienced solitude when he was young, but hated it. He had ambivalent feelings of wanting to desperately connect, but he couldn't bear the intense emotions that came up when people disappointed him.

In our next conjoint session I asked to hear more about how their relationship had evolved. I knew Ted had come into Robin's life when he sought to

---

3. This is an elaboration of the AAI, modified by Dr. Stanley Tatkin and seen in videotapes of his training seminars.

add the computer company she ran to his business conglomerate. She said she found his interest in taking her out on a date quite exciting: "He wouldn't take no for an answer, and I loved the attention, but something about him scared me. It took a while before I went out with him, and then things went a little faster than I planned." She had wondered about her mixed feelings a year later when she and Ted were watching the sun set together. She could not understand herself or why she talked to him about getting married. "It just came out of me, but I wasn't ready yet."

She talked about memories that keep coming up of her dead fiancé. I noted to myself that she never mentioned his name. There seemed to be something not real going on—a smokescreen, I thought. I suggested that instead of exploring her emotions, perhaps she could spend a few minutes paying attention to her breathing and notice what was happening in her body as we talked about the shock of her fiancé's accidental death. Each time another memory came up of times and places they had been together, she seemed overwhelmed by grief. She recalled an early beach dinner with Ted when she kept remembering another time, another beach, and another man in her life, and was having difficulty saying goodbye. There had been many such scenes in her mind over the past 2 years. Her emotions were sparked every time something reminded her of her fiancé. That's why she kept Ted at a distance, she explained.

I asked what she had hoped to get out of the joint session. Robin went back to their 1-year anniversary and the sunset walk on the beach. It had been the first time she did not think of her dead fiancé, she said; perhaps it was time to get married. Ted, she added, is a wonderful, kind, generous man. I wondered how Ted felt on hearing this. I also felt protective toward him, as I did not get the sense that Robin was anywhere near ready to experience love for anyone. Ted just said, "Yes. Let's get married."

Robin mentioned that she had been very anxious about coming to sessions with him, having only ever talked to a therapist one time. I asked her to tell me about it, and she said it was when she was a teenager and was having family trouble; afterward the therapist spoke to her parents and they immediately pulled her out of therapy. When I asked to hear more, Robin agreed to tell me in a session alone, and we set a date, but because I could feel her discomfort and reluctance to go on, I offered to refer her to another therapist so that she could talk privately about some of the things going through her mind. She was quiet for a moment, then said, "No. This will be fine." But she canceled and reset the time of our session twice.

It was clear that that the distancing behavior of which Ted complained was a long-term avoidant attachment pattern. As I learned from what Robin hesitantly told me when she finally did come in, she was raised by a mother who was dismissing of any emotional needs and a father whose interest in business left neither time nor inclination to notice the needs or feelings of his wife or two young daughters. Her mother had had three miscarriages in effort to give her husband what he made clear he really wanted, a son to inherit his business empire. Robin got all the clothes and toys that she asked for but none of the love she yearned for.

Robin tried repeatedly to get her father's attention and at age 13 thought she was succeeding when her father began to invite her on business trips. But she found his behavior inappropriate and pushed him away when he made sexual advances toward her. She tried to talk to her mother, who suggested that she might be imagining things and sent her to the therapist she saw for one session, whereupon Robin was sent off to boarding school and never returned home. (She has wondered why the therapist didn't report her father. "Maybe she didn't believe me either.") She went on to university and graduate school and moved across the country to thrive in the field of emerging technology. She became much more comfortable when she began talking about her work.

I brought her back to discussing her family by asking how her parents felt about her achievements; immediately, her body seemed to bend over. That was particularly evident when she talked about her relationship with her father, so I asked her to notice what was happening in her body at that moment. She said, "I want to curl up and die." I said I could see that she was in great pain. She clutched at her throat and nodded. When I asked her to pay attention to any words, feelings, or images her throat was holding, she looked ready to burst into tears but said nothing, nor did I; after a few minutes she turned her head away and began to cry.

Robin and I spent the rest of the session talking about the shame she feels when she thinks about her family. She said she just closes down when she thinks about her father. She knows that she is angry with her mother for continuing to live with him and also perhaps for exposing her sister to molestation. I asked if she had ever discussed the subject with her sister, and she said she had not. In fact, she expressed surprise to be talking about it now, as it had been a closed part of her life.

People have not been that safe: "I trusted machines and animals," Robin said. ("It's one of the good things I got from my father," she said. "He is a computer whiz, one of the first in the tech field.") She earned her living designing computer systems for a successful small company she started with a classmate shortly after graduation. When her partner suggested that they merge their lives as well as their business, they got engaged, remaining so for 6 years because, despite his repeated requests, Robin said she never felt ready to marry. When he died so suddenly, she realized how much she had loved him and thought about her loss constantly.

I asked Robin what she wanted to do. She said she wasn't sure but Ted was probably the best shot she would have to get married: "We have a lot in common. It would probably be a good idea." While I wondered if marriage on that basis would work, I said only that she should take whatever time she needed before deciding; meanwhile, I suggested that therapy for her might be helpful and gave her the name of a colleague.

Ted made it clear when I met with him that he did not agree with my message about not rushing into marriage when there were many unresolved issues. He had no qualms and, like Robin, was not asking for my advice. He did not believe they needed any more joint sessions to discuss things, reported that Robin really felt good after her session with me, and said she would call the therapist I referred her to if she wanted to talk more.

She didn't call. They got married in Las Vegas and sent me a picture of the two of them, arms around each other, looking straight into the camera; it was a typical wedding shot but it made me wonder if they ever looked into each other's eyes. The next time I heard from them was 2 years later when Ted called again in great distress. I made an appointment to meet with him the first hour that I had available.

"What went wrong this time?" Ted opened by asking, feeling as though he was back in his first marriage. In a way, he was. Robin's distancing had always been part of their relationship, such that even when they made love he never felt that he had her fully with him. Now their sexual relationship had become nonexistent, and that was particularly painful for Ted because sexuality was a place where he could experience repressed emotions and express unmet needs from childhood "and yet feel like an adult." Sex was one place where he could safely allow himself to be touched, held, soothed, made to feel potent. Ted and Robin's pattern of pursuit–avoidance seemed to be turning into a series of angry, sometimes explosive, battles. I suggested a double session of couple therapy to see if we could sort out what was happening between them.

At first, each had lots to say about what was wrong with the other. I told them they used too many words and needed to slow down. I asked them to look at each other and take some deep breaths, then to look into each other's eyes and see if they could tune into what the other might be experiencing. Both expressed discomfort while doing the exercise in the session: Robin felt very uncomfortable with Ted "staring" at her; Ted was afraid of doing something wrong and failing in my eyes. Halfway through the double session Robin said she needed a bathroom break. I commented that her body might be telling her that the tension was too high, and I suggested they both take 10 minutes.

When we reconvened, I explained a little about what I thought might be going on at levels that were out of conscious awareness. Their issues were in the emotional rather than the thinking parts of their brains, I said. They might need to "hold the emotion at bay long enough to use the cortical functions that enable us to see what is happening between the two of you." They might do better being mindful of the reactions in their bodies and the emotions that come up as we explore their relationship.

Ted was unable to describe the emotion and could only express feelings of anxiety, an overlay to core affect. Robin, too, had a defense system that protected against emotions. Watching her respond in the session, I noted that when strong affect arose, she quickly moved to a "blank face" stance, a kind of freeze response (Porges, 2006b) that Tronick (2007) has described as one of the most distressing characteristics of attachment failure in the earliest bonds between infant and caretaker. The "still face" certainly set off alarms in Ted.

As I watch such locked-in partners, I try to pair my own cortical abilities with my physical and emotional reactions during the session, remaining aware of my body and regulating my arousal. Sometimes I am aware that my thoughts about what is happening during intense sessions serve to down-regulate my arousal.

Midnight Musings on the Case of a Complex Couple

So what was happening with Ted and Robin, two vulnerable people who were each dealing with the repercussions of early attachment failures? I found myself thinking about our work together at night, wondering *how* I could help them, *if* I could help them. There were times when I despaired that nothing I did would be able to break their mutually painful pattern.

It is possible for a therapist who has some grounding in attachment theory and affective neuroscience to see these principles in action in the relational patterns and reflexive defenses—the substrate of behavior—that are unique to each partner. Sometimes, though not always, this knowledge provides the therapist with a solid base from which to help partners heal old wounds. They can do so—heal old wounds—by bringing up not only the strong emotions but also the sense of failure and shame that makes strongly felt things hard to talk about.

Ted had learned unique ways to use his cortex to control hyperactive emotional reactions and to "think out of the box" in his business decisions. Robin had never been able to trust because her implicit memory system would become flooded by danger messages whenever she got too close to someone in an intimate relationship. Her amygdala was functioning overtime, forcing her to put walls around herself to ward off intrusions. Both of their attachment patterns were on autopilot, with little or no input coming from a thoughtful prefrontal cortex. The romantic feelings that Ted had felt from the moment he had met Robin, and her thought that she loved Ted when she agreed to marry him, had nothing to do with the "collusion" course on which they found themselves. Their early attachment patterns had everything to do with it.

At the beginning of the relationship, each of them looked to the other as an island of safety in a dangerous world. There is always a yearning to find someone who loves us, attunes to us, and provides a reparative experience for early traumatic attachments (Johnson, 2004). Unfortunately, Ted and Robin had selected what was most familiar to them, which allowed them to reenact their respective past attachment failures. They then defended against the pain inflicted by the other. Each felt too vulnerable to express dependency needs to the other (Solomon, 1989), nor could either acknowledge vulnerability, but instead defended against it.

Robin's pattern of avoidance caused her to withdraw whenever Ted's demands for more closeness encroached on her carefully maintained boundaries. Ted's history of insecure attachment made him pursue closeness while fearing being injured again. When he is able to talk about his old angry feelings, he gains some relief. Despite his intense physical and emotional reactions, he does not act out his rageful feelings, but he is often left with a precarious feeling of instability. He has always had an underlying yearning for another who would be available, understanding, and accepting of his deeply hidden, cut-off emotions. He believed that his uncontrolled emotions caused the end of his first marriage. This insight gave him the incentive initially to seek treatment and to do the work required to change; that is, to *experience* emotions rather than to be driven by them. In individual therapy he found a place to express his feelings and then, slowly, to experience intense primitive affect without being pushed away by the other person. He saw that nobody was destroyed by the feelings that came up in the therapy sessions. Using imagery and learning to mindfully connect to emotions as they arose, he faced parts of himself that he had never been able to touch. Slowly he began changing his pattern with colleagues and friends.

When he married Robin, her danger messages signaled her to avoid Ted's pressure for greater closeness. His sexual and emotional frustration swelled into an angry barrage of venomous feelings. She was extremely uncomfortable with any sexual demands and did what she had learned to do with her father's sexual advances; she distanced herself more. She kept telling Ted that she wanted him to love her for who she is, not for what he can get from her sexually. He responded by explaining to her that he feels the most loving after they have sex, and if she wants to demonstrate that she loves him, sex is the best way for her to show it.

Robin countered that love and sex are different things. She knew that after they made love, he seemed much calmer the next day. But that made her feel he was just using her for sex because he felt better. She had no understanding of the calming effects of oxytocin flowing through the brain following orgasm, as well as during intense bonding/attachment experiences. Her feeling was that when he pressured her for sexual relations, even as he saw she was not ready for it, she became an object to be used, not someone he loved.

Each talked, hoping to be understood; neither heard the message of the other. Underlying the conflicting narratives of each were painful experiences from their early childhood. What was unresolved was being replayed without conscious thought, with the hope that this time, what went wrong in childhood would be made right.

Two days before Ted's call, there was a turning point in their relationship. Their oft-repeated dialogue about sex and love had come to a head. Ted was describing his sense of rejection. He said that he became very angry on the anniversary of the day they had met. Ted bought Robin diamond earrings and told her that he was going to take off 2 weeks for the holiday in Paris for which she had been asking. Robin was warm and loving at their dinner in a fine restaurant. Upon returning home, Robin said that she was exhausted and fell asleep immediately upon going to bed. Ted said nothing about it the next day, but was cold and distant.

In their therapy session Ted said that he had learned to control his emotions when he got angry, and so said nothing to Robin. No matter what he does to draw her closer, he said, she clearly wants nothing to do with him sexually. He cannot stay married to Robin, seeing that she does not love him. His anger grew as he talked about ending the marriage. Robin had a "deer in headlights" look. She said that Ted's anger frightens her, and that she always walks into another room when he gets like that. The office was filled with emotion that felt ready to burst. I said that they both looked like they were in tremendous pain, and that I knew it is very hard for them to hear each other. I talked calmly about what I saw happening in each of them. Robin was experiencing the sense of danger that she has lived with for a long time. Ted was feeling the rejection that has been a life-long problem. The way they each protect themselves becomes the problem for the relationship. When strong feelings arise, and they cannot hear each other's pain, the therapist must provide empathic attunement to modulate the intense dysregulated emotion.

As I talked, I watched them for signs that they had calmed down enough to hear me, and possibly to hear one another. When each was nodding about something I'd said, I asked the two of them to turn their chairs toward each other and just maintain eye contact. I suggested that as they look at each other, they should be aware of what they were feeling. After a short while, Robin began to cry. But she didn't talk. After a few minutes, she said, "I think I want to leave now." I said, "I'm sure you feel like running away, but that is because what is coming up for you is so painful that you have had to push it away, as you've done for a long time. Just sit with the feeling and don't say anything," I suggested. Here again, the important work is to contain the toxic emotions and help partners remain present to whatever comes up, rather than allowing them to find ways to run, do battle, or freeze their emotions. "I want to be there with Ted," she said finally. "I say to myself that I have to, but sometimes I just can't." Again she was silent, as the tears seemed to want to come out against her will.

"Do you sometimes remember back to your father when you feel pressured by Ted?" I asked her. "No . . . yes. . . . It's all very confusing."

"Ted," I asked, "How much has Robin told you about why she has so little contact with her parents?"

"She told me that her father came on to her. She is always uncomfortable when she sees her parents. She doesn't like to talk about it. She says, 'It's history, it's over.'"

I asked Robin if she could share what happened when her father tried to molest her. I said, "I think it is very important, and that it is affecting you more than you let yourself realize." Robin cried harder, and said only that it was "all confusing. " She had told her mother, and then told "the lady" that her mother took her to, but no one had believed her. They had sent her away!

"What did you tell the therapist to whom your mother took you about your father trying to molest you?" I asked.

"He didn't *try* to; he *did* it to me!" The shocking words came tumbling out. "He hurt me, and he told me that I could never tell anyone. And that no one would listen anyway. He was right, and they sent me away. I don't like to get too close. I get afraid." Robin continued for several minutes, speaking, then silently crying. There it was, the truth of what had happened to her and all the emotion she was keeping locked up inside.

"And you've had to hold that in all these years," I said. "Your father raped you, and you were punished by being sent away."

"So that's why you always freeze up," said Ted. "I didn't know. I would never hurt you."

"But you do when you get angry and then get silent on me."

Ted reached over to Robin and put his arm on her shoulder. She put her arms around him and he held her close.

They had a lot of work to do to heal this relationship and themselves. But the secret that had kept Robin distant from the men in her life was now understood as a traumatic experience on which she could work. Her emotions led the way: They led the way to distance when unregulated, and they led the way to closeness when regulated. Her talking to Ted about what had happened to her, and her asking him to understand and help, opened a door to connection for him.

It has been 7 years since Ted called for help on his marriage. Ted and Robin are still married. There are times when they have difficulties and call for a "tune-up." But they have learned to connect emotionally. Their initial fears have receded. They hug each other often, look into each others eyes when they talk, and have found a way to meet their different sexual needs. Robin said the last time we met that her biggest disappointment is that they have not yet succeeded in having children.

From Intimate Enemies Into Intimate Partners: The Process of Conjoint Therapy

Watching partners interact in stressful moments during a conjoint session conveys much more information about the dynamics of their relationship than stories told by one partner to an individual therapist. By observing which of them talks first, how the other responds, whether they resolve things or move toward solution or agree to disagree, whether they respond to each other with criticism or resort to dismissing or become defensive, whether there are signs of Gottman's (1999) "Four Horsemen"—criticism, contempt, defensiveness, stonewalling—or not, the couple therapist can gather reliable indicators of how each partner operates in the relationship.

Partners who complain that there is no communication may be communicating constantly about things that the other doesn't want to hear (or see). The therapist can comment on nonverbal cues—for example, the smile when anger might be an appropriate reaction, the foot shaking up and down while a partner is talking—not by way of accusation but toward identifying some important information. This information forms a foundation for understanding how each learned to operate in the world and how each handles issues such as closeness and distance, power and control.

When couples like Ted and Robin seek help for their relationship, their conscious narratives of what is wrong rarely touch the underlying defensive/ protective dynamic that may be causing problems between them. It is here that therapists must intervene to facilitate the necessary changes and improve the relationship. The work requires enhancement of positive emotions and positive emotional interactions to build secure attachments.

One of the most powerful forces identified in the psychoanalytic literature is that of transference—the putting of old faces on new people. This happens on both sides between patient and therapist, and it happens in every powerful relationship between people. It was clear that Ted and Robin both experienced early attachment failures. Each was wired to defend against the pain that had occurred in early key relationships. Each molded the relationship to make the other into the "marriage monster" (Tatkin, personal communication) against which he or she defended. Old expectations and ways of avoiding the pain of unresolved separation and loss were recreated. Their pain and their defenses were evident in their muscles, throat, face, and everything else driven by the autonomic nervous system. During sessions, Robin's body became stiff as her throat tightened and her voice became hoarse when we focused on areas that brought up feeling. Ted alternated between tears and agitation, his body shaking as he tried to sit motionless. This restrained shaking reminded me of earlier discussions when he talked of holding himself back from throwing a brick through a store window when he became angry.

Whereas many psychotherapists are trained to attune to sensorimotor responses in patients and to their own reactions that arise in response to patients in the therapeutic setting, most marital partners have little understanding of what the body does with strong emotions that are kept out of conscious awareness. When transference-like responses occur between intimate partners, the tendency is for each to develop narratives that help to explain "why I feel so agitated, enraged, or anxious with this person with whom I am engaged." Rarely does anyone ask him- or herself, in the midst of an argument with a mate, "What is happening here between us that is making my partner so upset or withdrawn?" Instead, defense and attack patterns take over the interaction. The same arguments occur repeatedly with no resolution. They don't really know about the emotional undercurrents that are stirring them up. But teaching couples to ask that question and attend to the bodily reactions that accompany whatever arises can be a powerful way to dislodge those entrenched patterns and make room for more fulfilling interactions.

Limbic and Cortical Structures

Ted's and Robin's narratives about their relationship and the specific incidents we were discussing came from areas of the brain specializing in narratives, in explicit systems that are more linear. On the other hand, strong emotional reactions arise from more primitive areas specializing in nonverbal, implicit systems that are nonlinear. When faced with a threat, the brainstem and limbic areas become activated. Within milliseconds there is a discharge of adrenaline and other excitatory hormones. Higher functions of the prefrontal cortex, the "chief executive officer" (Behry, 2007) of the brain that helps to soothe the mind, regulate the body, and reengage in thoughtful reasoning, are overtaken by the emotional fear circuits.

The amygdala is one of the structures in the brain that processes perceptions and thoughts and tags them with the warning, "Be afraid, be very afraid!" Located near the brain's center, this almond-shaped bundle of neurons evolved long before evolution of the seat of conscious awareness, the neocortex. When faced with too much threat, hyperactivity in the amygdala may disrupt normal processing through the nearby hippocampus and up into higher cortical areas. In instances such as these, some people react in a self-protective manner, uninterested in relationship continuity or integrity, and unable to accurately sequence events later on. This is because the hippocampus, a horn-like structure that processes and transfers short-term memory into long-term memory and which is largely responsible for putting experiences into context, place, and sequence, is offline during threatening times (Hebb, as cited in Siegel, 1999).

Fear is undoubtedly one of the earliest of the emotions that developed in the evolution of humankind. *In experiences perceived as dangerous, a threat response that surfaces instantly can be lifesaving.* Messages that are immediately transmitted to the body create a sense of distress and preparation for fight or flight.

It is this process that can turn intimate partners into intimate enemies. The joint wiring that began in a state of romantic love and continues throughout an intimate relationship, creates a deep knowing, an empathy that is not necessarily used for benign or positive purposes. Who can be more hurtful than a mate who knows your most sensitive areas and vulnerabilities and chooses to use them as a weapon? The result can be what Kohut (1984, p. 210) described as "the stuff of which the breakup of marriages, accompanied by the undying hatred of the marital partners for each other . . . is made."

We are on the cutting edge of developing new models of treating couples that help to detoxify the destructive power of emotion and, as we saw with Ted and Robin, establish earned security in the relationship through reclaiming the healing power of well-regulated emotions. We are beginning to know

252 The Healing Power of Emotion

more and more about the processes that can help turn intimate enemies back into the intimate partners.

Treatment Methods for Reclaiming Emotions

- *Provide a place of safety for painful emotions to be experienced without the danger usually associated with discussion of feelings.*

When couples have presenting problems that never seem to be resolved, what is fundamentally wrong may not be the presenting problems but fear of their own and each other's emotions. The therapist models new ways of reacting in the present when intense emotion and defense arise as remnants of past trauma. It may be necessary to slow down the action: "Ted, can we stop for a moment? Just before you got so angry, your face and eyes looked as though you were holding back intense sadness. Can we go back to that moment and talk about how it was for you when Robin said that she is so frightened of you that she thinks about running away?"

Partners are encouraged to resist the impulse to react to fear or rage with fight, flight, freeze, or dissociation. These are among the hallmark indicators of early-disrupted attachment that become wired in as patterns that shape adult intimate relationships. Here is where the therapist can be most effective by paying attention to what is happening in the moment. The therapist again slows down the action between partners, encouraging each to be aware of the feelings of both by commenting on one or the other's body position or facial gestures, or on anything that is happening in the here and now of the session.

The goal is to contain the feelings rather than try to get rid of them or defend in ways that elicit destructive reactions. With the therapist's help, partners can learn (1) to ask themselves if their perceptions are accurate for the present situation; (2) to take time-outs when emotions are overwhelming; (3) to question whether their behavior is getting them what they want; (4) to honor/understand the meaning of what is happening in terms of what happened in the past; and (5) to try out new ways of responding.

- *Attend to the affective and physiological reactions of each member of the couple, especially in response to one another.*

The therapist must keep a stance that is attuned to, and equidistant from, both partners. This positioning avoids the danger of one member of the couple becoming the identified patient and the other being "here to help." Couples often fall unconsciously into this pattern: Each partner has slowly taken on a role in the relationship that is familiar from early history and advanced by the history of interactions between them.

To make sure that both experience their emotions as being held and contained, it is necessary to include both of them in comments. For example, after the foregoing question to Ted: "Robin, I noticed that you were hardly breathing when Ted started talking about how you close down when he tries to initiate sex. Can we talk about that old sense of numbness you've mentioned and see if you are experiencing it right now?"

When there are indications of traumatic attachments, sessions are designed to develop the reflective function of the prefrontal cortex. But first, emotions have to be experienced, not avoided. This requires a therapeutic milieu in which each of the partners feels safe enough to allow emotions that come up to be seen. The therapist notices tears that are held back and comments on the pain, and the shame, of needs unmet or thwarted; he or she comments on anger that must be held back and offers opportunities to look at underlying hurt, sadness, fear; he or she looks, with both partners, at their discomfort and avoidance of saying things that create problems the moment they walk out of the office.

In the case of Ted and Robin, when emotions come up now, Robin is able to attune to Ted and recognize the difference between his anger and his anxiety. Ted has begun to understand the difference between Robin's avoidant responses toward him and her memory of hurt and terror around sex. To create the climate for change between them, it was necessary to help each touch and stay with core emotions while encouraging mindful awareness and contingent communication.

- *Attend to one's own emotions and physiological reactions and consider occasional mindful self-disclosure.*

I came to rely on sensations in my body and on emotions that arose in me as well as on what I saw in the reactions in Ted and Robin when their interactions went awry and emotions felt toxic. To get to that island of safety that would provide a milieu for healing and growing together, I found it helpful to risk sharing some of my own responses and asking if they fit anything either of them was experiencing. Sometimes the therapist's responses will not fit, but the treatment can withstand therapists' incorrect comments if they are posed as questions or qualified ("I'm not sure, but I wonder if . . ."). Often, trusting one's own feelings and reactions is the path to addressing the unconscious reactions between partners in the moment of the session.

- *Engage the neocortex, foster positive affects, and encourage positive action.*

The therapist's stance here is that "partners are not sick; they are stuck" (Johnson, 2003a). When the emotional system is under chronic stress, the brain structures that allow clear cognitive processes are deactivated. Too often partners do not have access to the tools with which to talk about their history of built-up resentment. The goal is to get them thinking about the relationship rather than staying with the resentment or with the fear or anxiety many people carry into new situations. Therapists, using their own personal resources (humor, storytelling, analytical thinking), can develop interventions that enhance the reflective function of the prefrontal cortex in those with whom they work.

It is important to help partners understand how protective mechanisms that evolved early in life, out of necessity, may have negative repercussions when reenacted in current relationships. If they develop an ability to view one another with this understanding and with "mindsight,"[4] they are less likely to become critical of the necessary survival traits in each other. Moreover, identifying their respective unique patterns of attachment can sometimes take the couple's problems out of the realm of blame and shame.

- *Learn the techniques of the "social engagement system" and engage it.*

The social engagement system (Porges, 2001b, 2003, 2006a, 2006b; see also, Chapter 2, this volume) is a neurobiologically based construct that describes the intricate functioning of the numerous neural pathways involved in coordinating autonomic activity with social behavior. As defined by Porges (2006a), the construct of the social engagement system integrates links among various anatomical and neural components and describes the way in which they support adaptive strategies for dealing with the environment, including fight/flight/freeze responses when the environment is experienced as a threat. The system is comprised of circuits involved in the regulation of visceral states, including heart rate and the muscles of the face and head (Denver, 2004). Outside of conscious awareness, the nervous system evaluates risk in the environment and regulates the expression of adaptive behavior based on learned history of what to do when stress and fear arise.

Positive social engagement requires a neuroception (see Porges, Chapter 2, this volume) of safety and the formation of strong bonds that stand the test of time. For couples like Ted and Robin, whose attachment histories are perme-

---

4. Siegel (2007) describes *mindsight* as the ability to be with and see the other person.

ated with fear and defenses against being hurt, the therapeutic work requires an exploration of patterns that have developed between them—stress and fear-producing avoidance and distancing in Robin, while Ted continues in pursuit because the terror of isolation is an unbearable recreation of his past. Their troubled relationship might have continued for years in that state, if they had remained unable to engage in mutual caregiving, yet each too afraid of aloneness to end it.

Treatment focuses first on helping each partner recognize, without shame or blame, how common it is for patterns developed earlier in life to play out in the current relationship. Building on that basic foundation, there are a variety of ways to enhance positive emotions and positive emotional interactions. For example, the therapist can give homework assignments to maintain continuity of the work between sessions: "Keep a notebook handy and write down the times that you feel hurt by your partner or list the things that you appreciate about your partner." Another option: "Write down the things that you believe will make your partner feel good. Share your lists with each other and check out their accuracy."

- *Help partners develop mutual regulation.*

Therapists must help partners understand that the purpose of intimate relationships in our time and culture is not what it was in historical times, mutual survival, but rather, mutual regulation and positive emotional contact, and that emotional feelings are the result of our evolutionary heritage, not a sign of immaturity or pathology. When partners feel "felt" by one another, a new kind of secure attachment (Main, 2002) develops that helps each grow stronger individually. Partners can be encouraged to recognize and respect the value of meeting their deep dependency needs and of talking about their needs for positive emotional contact.

When partners learn to practice skills that enhance connection while protecting individual boundaries, the result is mutual regulation—interdependence with differentiation (Solomon, 1994). Ed Tronick (2007, p. 9) suggests that each partner affects the other's self-regulation during the process of mutual regulation: "Each individual is a self-organizing system that has its own states of consciousness—states of brain organization—which can be expanded into more coherent and complex states in collaboration with another self-organizing system." Tronick sees this expansion as a way of enhancing the therapeutic relationship, as both therapist and patient create and transform unique therapeutic states of consciousness through mutual and self-regulation. In the same way, intimate partners in conjoint therapy can explore and develop new paths to create and transform their relational states. The ultimate goal is to facilitate earned secure attachment (Main, 2002).

Conclusion

We now better understand why people who meet, fall in love, and get married later can come to see each other as the cause of anxiety, distress, and danger. Each relationship throughout life carries the remnants of earlier interactions. People such as Robin and Ted, who experience frequent breaches in the attachment system, live in a state of anxiety in their intimate relationships. Many day-to-day interactions trigger a threat response, along with the anticipation of an empathic failure, frustration, criticism, punishment, and/or withdrawal. Any interactional moment can recreate in each partner a spark of neuronal activation, which serves as a reminder of memories that remain unthought and of separation and loss in times of emotional need.

And we are now also beginning to better understand how couples who come to see each other as the cause of anxiety, distress, and danger can reclaim their intimacy and can come to trust each other and rely on being able to help one another. When couples such as Ted and Robin seek help for their relationship, their conscious narratives of what is wrong rarely touch the underlying defensive/protective dynamic that may be causing problems between them. Therapists can intervene to facilitate the necessary changes and improve the relationship by (1) creating safety, (2) undoing defensive patterns, and (3) facilitating the airing, sharing, and regulating of long-denied core emotions. The work also requires enhancement of positive emotions and emotional interactions to build secure attachments. We are on the cutting edge of developing new models for treating couples that help to detoxify the destructive power of emotion and to establish earned security in the relationship through reclaiming the healing power of well-regulated emotions.

10

Extravagant Emotion

Understanding and Transforming Love Relationships in Emotionally Focused Therapy

Susan Johnson

WILLIAM JAMES DESCRIBED emotions as "adaptive behavioral and physiological response tendencies called forth directly by evolutionarily significant situations" (1894). In one of the most evolutionarily significant situations of all—the creation and maintenance of emotional bonds between sexual partners—emotions are front, center, and often extreme. To create significant and lasting change, the discipline of couple therapy has to find a way to deal with, regulate, and harness the force of nature that is raw emotion to move distressed partners in the direction of stable, positive, and emotionally satisfying connection.

In the past this was deemed an impossible task. For many years couple therapists dedicated themselves to persuading distressed couples to minimize or replace their emotions with reason, insight, negotiation skills, and pragmatic problem solving. Bowenian, behavioral, and solution-focused approaches, in particular, moved in this direction. But, strong emotion in primary relationships is hard to get around and is suppressed only at great cost. The good news is that we no longer need to do this. We now have the scientific knowledge necessary to be able to use the considerable power of emotion to transform key emotional perceptions, signals, and the key ways partners engage each other in the situations that define a love relationship. Rather than fearing its disruptive potential, we can now harness the extravagant transformational power of emotion. We can create an emotionally intelligent couple therapy.

Such a therapy would first need to fit with what we know about the emotional variables in relationship distress and satisfaction. Secondly, it would need to reflect the new scientific clarity about the nature of emotion in general. And, thirdly and more specifically, it would need to be based on a theory of love that offers a guide to the extravagant and compelling emotions of love and how they define our relationships. Fourth, it would also need to provide a clear map of change processes that outlines the ways in which interventions address dysfunctional emotion and also uses emotional experience and expression to create change in cognitive, behavioral, and interactional patterns. These four requirements have been addressed in the current literature on emotionally focused therapy for couples (EFT; Johnson, 2004, 2005, 2008b). This chapter further explores EFT as such a therapy.

The model of EFT is well validated. Meta-analyses describe a recovery rate of 70–73% and an 86% significant improvement rate in distressed couples treated with EFT (Johnson, Hunsley, Greenberg, & Schindler, 1999), and there is evidence that results are stable even with high-risk couples (Clothier, Manion, Gordon Walker, & Johnson, 2001). There is also evidence of effectiveness with traumatized and depressed partners. EFT is used with many different kinds of couples (e.g., working class, less educated and executive couples, gay and "straight" couples) and across cultures (e.g., with Asian, Latino, Northern European, Japanese, and North American couples). There is also a number of studies validating the process of change documented in the EFT model. All studies of EFT are listed on the EFT website at *www.eft.ca*.

How Crucial Is Emotion in Defining the Quality of Romantic Relationships?

For the general public this is a moot point. A sense of emotional connection—of loving and being loved—is the main expectation for people involved in long-term partnerships (Coontz, 2005). Research on marriage has also made it clear that variables such as conflict containment are not at the "heart" of these relationships. Huston and colleagues, in a study of the trajectory of newly wed couples, found that, after 5 years, emotional responsiveness was the most powerful predictor of satisfaction (Huston, Caughlin, Houts, Smith, & George, 2001). In general, positive emotion seems to be the best predictor of marital satisfaction and stability (Gottman, Coan, Carrere, & Swanson, 1998), whereas facial expressions of negative emotion, especially fear on the face of the husband and angry contempt on the face of the wife, have been found to be powerful predictors of the negative future trajectory of marital relationships (Gottman, 1994). Habitual negative ways of expressing one's emotions create stable destructive patterns in interactions—for example, critical angry blaming on the part of one spouse, followed by an avoidance of emotional expression and withdrawal by the other. This pattern, in particular, is a powerful predictor of divorce (Gottman, 1994).

There appears to be a consensus in the relationship field that how partners regulate their emotions and thus how they engage with their loved one on an emotional level is a key determinant of relationship quality. Emotion and emotional communication are organizing or "leading elements" in human social systems (Johnson, 1998). In a circular fashion, emotional signals organize the relationship dance, and patterns of responses in this dance then shape emotional realities and responses.

It is also becoming increasingly clear that partners are the hidden regulators not only of each other's emotional lives, but of each other's physiology. Recent research into the neurobiology of emotion tells us that in close relationships we are engaged in a "neural duet" (Goleman, 2006), where partners impact each other's cardiovascular, immune, and endocrine systems. We also know that loneliness can increase blood pressure to the point where the risk of heart attack and stroke is doubled (Hawkley, Masi, Berry, & Cacioppo, 2006), and in men and women with congestive heart failure, the state of the patient's marriage is as good a predictor of survival after 4 years as the severity of symptoms and degree of impairment (Coyne et al., 2001). Moreover, the more belligerent and contemptuous partners' conflicts are, the higher the levels of stress hormones tend to be and the more depressed the immune system. These effects seem to directly impact processes such as wound healing (Kiecolt-Glaser et al., 2005). Emotional signals are the music of the dance between intimates. The music shapes each person's emotional and physical response, guides each partner's moves, and pulls for complementary moves from the other.

What Is Emotion?

Any effective couple therapy must not only contain powerful negative emotions, but also systematically shape positive emotions and use them to foster responses such as compassion, caring, and the longing for connection that are vital in a loving relationship. Understanding the general nature of emotion is essential. First, emotion is not a primitive, irrational response or simply a sensation or a "feeling." It is a high-level information-processing system that integrates a person's awareness of innate needs and goals with feedback from the environment and predicted consequences of actions (Frijda, 1986). It is comprised of the following elements (Arnold, 1960):

• *Initial, rapid, unconscious appraisal of environmental cues as they relate to key survival imperatives and an orientation to relevant cues.* Emotion orients and directs us to focus on what is important in our environment. People who cannot access emotion due to brain injuries cannot make rational decisions and choices (Damasio, 1994). They become caught in pondering all possible possibilities because they have no internal compass to orient them to what they want and need—to give them a felt sense of what matters to them.

• *Body responses.* The word *emotion* comes from the Latin word *emovere*, meaning to move. Emotion "moves" us physically and mentally. Both the initial appraisal and body response occur extremely fast, without cognitive mediation, whereas the more reasoning part of the brain, the frontal cortex, integrates information at a slower pace. This is especially true in fear reactions, for which immediate response is vital and can mean the difference between life and death.

• *Cognitive reappraisal.* The meaning of cues and sensations is considered and evaluated and this meaning linked and integrated into cognitive frameworks.

• *Action priming.* Emotion motivates and primes us for action in a rapid and compelling manner (Tomkins, 1962, 1963). Anger, for example, often primes assertion of needs and fear often primes flight or freeze responses. For the couple therapist it is important to note that the signals that arise as a result of this process then communicate to others our inner state and intentions. Affective expression also organizes the interpersonal reflex or action tendency of the other.

This kind of information is directly relevant for a therapist. In EFT, for example, the therapist can work with these elements to "unpack" a particular emotional response and then to reframe the whole into a new construction. An example of this process is given later in this chapter.

There seems to be general agreement (Ekman, 2003) that the core emotions, which can be universally recognized from distinct facial configurations, are the following: anger, sadness, fear, joy, surprise and excitement, disgust and shame. These emotions appear to be universal and to be associated with specific neuroendocrine patterns and brain sites (Panksepp, 1998a). Emotions often have "control precedence" (Tronick, 1989), easily overriding other cues and behaviors, especially in important relationships with those on whom we depend the most. As John Bowlby (1980), the father of attachment theory, states:

The most intense emotions arise during the formation, the maintenance, the disruption and renewal of attachment relationships. The formation of a bond is described as falling in love, maintaining a bond as loving someone, and losing a partner as grieving over someone. Similarly, threat of loss arouses anxiety and actual loss gives rise to sorrow; while each of these situations is likely to arouse anger. The unchallenged maintenance of a bond is experienced as a source of security and the renewal of a bond as a source of joy. Because such emotions are usually a reflection of the state of a person's affectional bonds, the psychology and the psychopathology of emotion is found to be in large part the psychology and psychopathology of affectional bonds.

Emotion can be differentiated into at least three levels: (1) adaptive, primary, or core; (2) secondary or reactive, as when we feel the prick of fear but ignore it or deal with it by leaping into angry defensiveness; and (3) instrumental, as when we express emotion to manipulate others (Greenberg & Johnson, 1988). Primary emotions can also become maladaptive when they are overlearned and based on overwhelming traumatic experience (Greenberg & Paivio, 1997). Secondary reactive emotions tend to hide primary responses, to obscure the original response, and to take interactions between intimates in a negative direction. EFT advocates evoking the primary-attachment-oriented emotions to shift habitual negative response patterns that reflect secondary emotional responses by, for example, exploring the primary despair and fear that underly a blaming partner's apparent chronic anger. When this primary kind of fear is expressed, it elicits a different response from the partner and begins to shift stuck negative interactional patterns.

Emotion in the Context of Love Relationships

Couple therapists need more than a general understanding of emotion. They need to understand how emotions work in, and help to define, close relationships. This understanding has to address specific issues. For example:

When is positive emotional engagement particularly essential in a close relationship?

How do we understand the powerful emotional dramas that characterize love relationships?

What do we make of the habitual differences in emotional expression between partners?

Attachment theory (Bowlby, 1969/1982, 1988; Johnson, 2003a) offers the therapist an invaluable guide to such issues by helping to define features of love relationships, set treatment goals that are relevant and meaningful, and map out the best ways to intervene. It offers the couple therapist a compass in the change process. More than this, in the last 15 years the work on adult attachment (Cassidy & Shaver, 1999; Rholes & Simpson, 2004; Mikulincer & Shaver, 2007) has validated and expanded original formulations of attachment theory and made it clear that this theory is, at one and the same time, a theory of intrapsychic affect regulation and a systemic theory of relatedness. A sense of secure connection to a loved one can help us keep our emotional balance, rather than becoming flooded with overwhelming emotion or suppressing emotions to the point where we are numb and unable to use them as a guide or to flexibly attune to our partner. As Schore notes (1994, p. 244), contact with a supportive, safe attachment figure "tranquillizes the nervous system." A safe relationship promotes optimal affect regulation, and vice versa (Fosha, 2000).

The role of attachment in affect regulation can be seen in a study by Coan, Schaefer, and Davidson (2006). Women were placed in a magnetic resonance imaging (MRI) machine and told that when a light flashed, they would sometimes be shocked on their feet. Researchers could then see how the brain lit up in response to this stressor. Being left alone in the machine maximized the stress response and the subjective experience of pain from the shocks. However, when a stranger held a woman's hand, the stress response and pain intensity lessened. The most significant decrease occurred when a spouse was present to hold the woman's hand. This effect was directly proportional to the women's experience of the positive quality of their connection with this partner. The research on attachment in adults is consistent in finding that a sense of secure connection to a loved one fosters the ability to deal with extreme negative emotions—for example, emotions arising from trauma such as imprisonment as a prisoner of war (Solomon, Ginzburg, Mikulincer, Neria, & Ohry, 1998). A sense of secure connection also helps people process more everyday emotional experiences and to process emotion in a way that promotes positive relationship behaviors, such as confiding or assertiveness (Levy & Davis, 1988).

Attachment Theory

Attachment theory states that seeking and maintaining emotional contact with significant others is an innate, primary, motivating principle in human beings across the lifespan. Dependency is then an innate part of being human rather than a childhood trait that we outgrow. A sense of connection with an attachment figure is an innate survival mechanism. The emotional, physical, or representational presence of attachment figures provides a sense of comfort and security, whereas the perceived inaccessibility of such figures creates distress. A sense of secure emotional connection with another is the natural antidote to anxiety and vulnerability. Positive attachments create *a safe haven* that offers a buffer against the effects of stress and uncertainty (Mikulincer, Florian, & Weller, 1993) and an optimal context for the continuing development of a mature, flexible, and resourceful personality. Secure attachment also offers a *secure base* from which individuals can explore their universe and adaptively respond to their environment. This secure base promotes the confidence necessary to risk, learn, and continually update models of self, others, and the world so that adjustment to new contexts is facilitated. Safe connection with an attachment figure strengthens the ability to stand back and reflect on oneself, one's behavior, emotional responses, and mental states (Fonagy & Target, 1997). Securely attached individuals are better able to take emotional risks, to reach out to and provide support for others, and to cope with conflict and stress. Their relationships tend to be happier, more stable, and more satisfying than those of people with insecure attachments.

Secure attachment complements self-confidence and autonomy (Feeney, 2007). Secure dependence and autonomy are two sides of the same coin, rather than dichotomies (see also Hughes, Chapter 11, this volume, and Solomon, Chapter 9, this volume), as often presented in the couple and family literature. Security is associated with a more coherent, articulated, and positive sense of self (Mikulincer, 1995). The more securely connected we are, the more separate and different we can be. Health in this model means maintaining a felt sense of interdependency, rather than attempting to become "self-sufficient" and maintaining boundaries with others. The building blocks of secure bonds are emotional accessibility and responsiveness. An attachment figure can be physically present but emotionally absent. If there is no perception of emotional accessibility or engagement, an emotional process of separation distress results. In attachment terms, any response (even anger) is better than none.

Emotion is central to attachment, and this theory provides a guide for understanding and normalizing many of the extreme emotions that accompany distressed relationships. Theorists such as Panksepp (1998a; see also, Chapter 1, this volume) suggest that loss of connection with an attachment figure induces a particular kind of fear—a primal panic. This concept fits with Bowlby's belief that isolation is *inherently* traumatizing for human beings. Any form of threat to the individual or the relationship activates attachment emotions and needs. Attachment needs for comfort and connection then become particularly salient and compelling, and attachment behaviors, such as proximity seeking, are activated. A sense of connection with a loved one is a primary inbuilt emotional regulation device. Attachment to key others is our "primary protection against feelings of helplessness and meaninglessness" (McFarlane & van der Kolk, 1996, p. 24).

If attachment behaviors fail to evoke comforting responsiveness and contact from a loved one, a prototypical process of angry protest, clinging, depression, and despair occurs, culminating eventually in grieving and emotional detachment. Depression is a natural response to loss of connection. Bowlby viewed anger in close relationships as often being an attempt to make contact with an inaccessible attachment figure, and he distinguished it from the anger of hope, where a viable response is expected from the other, and the anger of despair, which becomes desperate and coercive. In secure relationships protest at perceived inaccessibility is recognized and accepted (Holmes, 1996). An attachment-oriented therapist views many extreme emotional responses in distressed couples as primal panic or secondary reactive emotions to this panic. This approach differs from other perspectives, wherein these responses might be seen as signs of immaturity, a lack of communication skill, a personality flaw, or a sign of "enmeshment" in the couple's relationship.

In this theory, ways of regulating primary attachment emotions are finite, and individual differences in emotional regulation and expression are predictable. In secure relationships the connection to the partner is used as a form of comfort and creates a sense of emotional homeostasis. In insecure relationships there are only limited ways of coping with a negative response to the questions: "Are you there for me?" "Will you respond when I need you?" "Can I depend on you?" "Do you value me and the connection with me?"

Insecure attachment responses are organized along two dimensions: anxiety and avoidance (Fraley & Waller, 1998). When the connection with an irreplaceable other is threatened, attachment emotions, particularly anxiety, can become hyperactivated. Attachment behaviors become heightened and intense; anxious clinging, pursuit, and even aggressive attempts to obtain a response from the loved one escalate. Even when the loved one responds, the response may not be completely trusted, and a heightened emotional sensitivity to relationships cues may remain. This response can be momentary or it can become chronic and develop into a habitual way of dealing with emotions and engaging the partner.

The second strategy for dealing with the lack of safe emotional engagement, especially when hope for responsiveness has been lost, is to try to deactivate the attachment system and suppress attachment emotions and needs, focusing on external tasks and avoiding attempts at emotional engagement. Unfortunately, the suppression of affect is hard work and ineffective, often resulting in increased physiological arousal and tension in both partners (Gross, 2001). If this affect regulation style becomes generalized, it effectively cuts off the person from an awareness of his or her emotional responses and needs and shuts out the partner. These two basic affect regulation strategies— (1) the *anxious heightening of emotion* eliciting hypervigilant clinging behaviors, and (2) the *detached avoidance*—tend to pull for confirming responses from a partner. A third strategy, *fearful avoidant*, (Bartholomew & Horowitz, 1991), wherein a partner clings and then, when closeness is offered, avoids, is associated with traumatic attachments wherein others are both the source of, and solution to, fear (Johnson, 2002).

The anxious and avoidant strategies were first identified via experimental separations and reunions between mothers and their infants. Some infants were able to modulate their distress on separation, to connect with their emotions and process them so as to give clear signals to the mother, and to accept her calming, reassuring contact when she returned. Then, confident of her responsiveness if she was needed, they returned to exploration and play. These children were viewed as *securely attached*. Others became extremely distressed on separation and clung or expressed anger to the mother on reunion. They were difficult to soothe and seemed to swerve between one reactive negative emotion and another. They were viewed as *anxiously attached*. A third group showed signs of significant physiological distress but showed little emotion at separation or reunion. The infants in this group focused on tasks and activities and were seen as *avoidantly attached*. These styles are "self-maintaining patterns of social interaction and emotion regulation strategies" (Shaver & Clarke, 1994, p. 119). Although these habitual forms of engagement can be modified by new relationships, they can also mold current relationships and so become self-perpetuating.

These strategies impact many key relationship behaviors because they sculpt the nature of emotional engagement with others. Research has found that secure attachment is linked to more positive and intense positive emotion and less frequent and intense negative emotion, such as anger in key, relationships. Shaver and Mikulincer (2007, p. 450) note that people who are securely attached can "reappraise situations, construe events in relatively benign terms, symbolically transform threats into challenges, hold onto an optimistic sense of self-efficacy and attribute undesirable events to controllable, temporary, or context dependent causes." In brief, these individuals have learned that distress is manageable.

Attachment affect regulation strategies also predict key relationship behaviors, such as responses to conflict and responses to seeking and giving support. Those with a secure style are generally happier and better able to reach out for and provide support (Simpson, Rholes, & Nelligan, 1992; Simpson, Rholes, & Phillips, 1996), and they have closer, stabler and more trusting, satisfying relationships (Collins & Read, 1990; Simpson, 1990). They can better acknowledge and communicate their needs and are less likely to be verbally aggressive or withdraw during problem solving (Senchak & Leonard, 1992). Research suggests that partnerships containing at least one secure partner are more harmonious and have fewer conflicted interactions (Cohn et al., 1992).

Strong emotion in attachment relationships also cues associated internal working models of self and other. Secure attachment is characterized by a working model of self that is worthy of love and care and is confident and competent and a model of others as dependable and worthy of trust. These models of self and other, distilled out of a thousand interactions, are not one-dimensional cognitive schemas: rather, they are saturated with emotion and translate into procedural scripts for how to create relatedness. More specifically, they reflect how emotion is regulated within specific relationships (Fosha, 2003). Emotion is an organizing force in working models rather than an outcome of them. Working models are formed, elaborated, maintained, and, most important for the couple and family therapist, revised through emotional communication (Davila, Karney, & Bradbury, 1999). In fact, to be optimally useful, they must be constantly revised as changes occur in interpersonal contexts.

Attachment theory outlines the basic human responses, particularly those needs and fears that structure long-term bonds. It offers a new and comprehensive understanding of romantic love (Johnson, 2008c) and a map identifying pivotal, emotionally "hot" events that seem to define relationships and in which individual identities are shaped. Attachment theory provides a way to identify key recurring moments of palpable emotional disconnection, wherein reactive emotions spark negative cycles, such as demand and withdraw, which then take over the relationship. It also identifies key positive moments of bonding that restore connection, create new positive emotions, and provide an antidote to negative cycles. This theory helps us understand when strong emotional impasses prevent the renewal of connection and how to use emotion in the service of restoring trust after an injury. These events, called attachment injuries, occur when partners experience abandonment and betrayal at times of intense need (Johnson, Makinen, & Millikin, 2001; Makinen & Johnson, 2006).

In summary, attachment theory provides the couple therapist with a clear set of goals, a focus, a compass to navigate the process of change, and a language for the emotion-laden dilemmas and stuck places that cripple love relationships.

Emotionally Focused Interventions

EFT is a humanistic constructivist approach (Neimeyer, 1993) combining a Rogerian model of working with emotion with a systemic structural model of changing interactions. EFT uses emotion in the way that Bowlby suggested it be used (1991): as a primary source of information to the self and to others about needs and motives and as a primary route to connecting with attachment figures.

In general, the EFT therapist tracks, accesses, and evokes emotion as a source of information about people's needs and fears and how these "move" partners and so structure the relational dance. The therapist also helps clients to shift their habitual ways of regulating their emotions in interactions with their spouse; for example, by expressing anger indirectly through criticism and hiding softer emotions such as fear. The therapist helps clients unfold and restructure key emotional experiences that may be marginalized in their awareness, such as, for example, the experience of loss and abandonment that fuels rage or the sense of hopelessness underlying expressions of apathy or numbness. The therapist also uses primary "soft" attachment emotions, such as sadness, to shape new responses that are crucial to secure attachment, such as the ability to assert needs or ask for comfort and caring. The EFT therapist assumes that it is not simply naming or reframing negative emotions that is crucial for change; rather, a new experience of core attachment emotions, which then organizes new interactional responses, is necessary.

The goals of EFT are sequential. First, we seek to reprocess and restructure the negative emotions that constrain interactive response and create stuck cycles of insecurity in a couple relationship. Second, we seek to create new positive emotions and responses to one's partner that turn the relationship into a safe haven and a secure base. The change process moves through three stages: (1) negative cycle deescalation, (2) restructuring of attachment interactions, and (3) consolidation.

Rather than list the steps and interventions of EFT or describe this model in detail (Johnson 2004, 2008a), here I focus on key change events in EFT to show how negative emotional responses are reprocessed in destructive demand–withdraw cycles and how emotion is restructured to elicit positive responses to one's partner.

James and Sarah have been married for 25 years. James has always struggled with depression and with a lack of confidence in himself. Sarah is a strong woman who has battled multiple sclerosis for years, volunteers in her community, and helps with her grandchildren whenever she can. James's therapist has suggested that his depression will not change, even if he attains the promotion he is seeking at work, unless his marriage improves. When I ask him how he seems the problem, he mutters that it is probably about how useless he is and how he cannot ever please his wife. Sarah explodes with frustration and talks about how he shuts her out and ignores her for days. James asks me, in a curt, tight voice, for exercises he can do to make his wife happy. She cannot ask for comfort but makes demands in a critical way. He cannot respond consistently but goes into his shell to protect himself and deal with his attachment fears. She then feels deserted and becomes enraged.

Once a safe alliance has been established, and the negative cycle is clear, I reframe the problem between the partners in terms of this cycle that leaves them both alone and helpless. As an EFT therapist, I now use my knowledge of the elements of emotion to open up James's response to his wife and access more primary emotions, using reflection, evocative questions, and small, specific but brief interpretations.

THERAPIST: So, James, can we stay here for a moment, please? You see the problem in terms of how "useless" you are and that you cannot please Sarah? (*He nods.*) How do you feel as you say this?

JAMES: Oh, I don't "feel" anything. I think she has these standards, and I always get a failing grade here. (*He begins to strike his leg with the flat of his right hand.*)

THERAPIST: That must be very hard, to see yourself as "useless," to never feel that you can please your wife? (*His face softens a little here.*) You feel that way a lot. Can you remember a moment just recently when that was very present for you? [The therapist homes in on the moment when strong emotions arise and key negative interactions take place.]

JAMES: Yes, last night. I actually asked her how she was feeling and she said, "Well, it took you long enough to ask. Why don't you just come and hold me instead of sitting over there asking me that question." I am wrong before I even start.

THERAPIST: [focusing in on the initial appraisal that begins the process] So, you were trying to show concern? (*He nods.*) But somehow the message you got was that you were already off base, on the path to failure, yes? That is hard, demoralizing. How do you feel as you talk about this right now? [The therapist asks questions to evoke the specific emotional response and increase emotional engagement in the moment.]

JAMES: It makes me angry, actually. Whatever I do, she is going to sit there with her gavel and robe. I will hear that I have blown it. [He offers the secondary reactive emotion of anger, which is what his wife usually sees.]

THERAPIST: So you make an attempt to reach out to your wife. You get the message that you are not doing it right. You get mad, decide there is no point and then? (Links secondary emotional response to his actions in the negative cycle.]

JAMES: I just give up. I went upstairs and played around on the computer, and we didn't talk all evening. I guess you would call it "withdrawing." (He opens his hands as if he is letting something fall.)

THERAPIST: You get the message that you have "blown it," and you give up— and I notice that you open your hands as if letting something go. (Therapist repeats the cue that contains the attachment threat.) Then what? You go away and try to calm yourself?

JAMES: I just try to numb out—distract myself, I guess.

THERAPIST: How does it feel to say this right now: "I get mad for a moment but then I just give up and numb out"? Something about the message that you have "blown it" is very hard to hear.

JAMES: (in a very soft voice) Don't know, I'm just mad, you know. (He sighs deeply.)

THERAPIST: (in a soft, low, evocative voice) You are feeling mad right now as you say "I give up, numb out," and you sigh and open your hands as if the relationship were slipping through your fingers? (He nods very slowly.) How does your body feel right now as we talk about this? [Therapist attempts to expand James's awareness of emotion by focusing on body cues.]

JAMES: I don't want to talk about this. I feel heavy, weak, kind of defeated. I always feel that way. I'm used to it.

THERAPIST: And is that when this sense of being "useless" comes up—that you are useless? You can never please Sarah? There is a moment of anger, a kind of protest, and Sarah sees this and plugs into it, but this is just for a moment. Then you feel this heaviness, that you will always blow it, never get it right. You say to yourself that you are useless—not good enough—a failure—yes? [Therapist moves into the cognitive meaning he makes of his emotional experience—his model of self and other.] That must be very hard.

JAMES: Yes. (in a bitter edgy voice) I get that I am a big fat failure with her. And it's like there is nowhere to turn. So I just hunker down and go inside myself.

Maybe that is what she means when she says that I shut her out. (*He begins to rub his eyes with his hands.*)

SARAH: Yes. And then we get into that terrible circle where I get meaner and push you more, and you move even further away. [Sarah links all this to their negative cycle; often the therapist makes this kind of connection.]

THERAPIST: What happens to you, James, when you say to yourself, "I can't please Sarah. I'm useless, a big fat failure"? I notice that you are stroking your face. Maybe that is soothing?

JAMES: I don't want to cry. (*He tears up.*) I don't want to feel this. I feel so small, sort of ashamed of myself.

THERAPIST: Yes. You go away to hide all the shame and the sadness that your feel when you hear that message, that you are somehow failing with Sarah.

JAMES: I think I have lost her already. And that is scary too.

THERAPIST: Yes. Can you tell her, James, can you turn and tell Sarah, "I reach out and it doesn't work, and then you might see a flash of anger but inside I'm hurting—all this sadness, shame, fear of losing you—don't know what to do with that, so I numb out on you?"

JAMES: (*He turns to Sarah and smiles.*) It's like she said. (*They laugh.*) But no, seriously, in these times I just hear that I'm useless—useless to you. And that is so hard, so scary. So I give up on us and I go away. Can you understand that?

SARAH: Yes, I understand.

THERAPIST: And how do you feel about James as he says this?

SARAH: I feel closer to him. I respect that he is taking this risk. I don't want him to feel this bad.

In this excerpt, the therapist, through her empathy-laden explorations/interventions has (1) "discovered" with James his primary underlying emotions, (2) linked them to his steps in the relationship dance, and (3) had him express these feelings in such as way as to expand this dance into a new kind of connection with his partner. The therapist focused on the elements of emotion outlined by Arnold (1960) to unpack James's emotional world and allow him to show new aspects of himself to his partner. If necessary, the partner is supported to connect with and not dismiss this new view of his or her lover. This work allows for the reframe that James does not move away out of rage or indifference, but that he does so out of a sense of hopelessness and helplessness. In this mapping out of emotional experience and responses, secondary reactive emotions (i.e., his anger and numbing) are contained and placed in a larger context. New emotions—his fear and helplessness—are accessed to set up new and more positive interactions.

Key Change Events in Sessions

In the best sessions of EFT ("best" as assessed by the therapist and the couple), particular change events occur in the restructuring stage that are associated with stable recovery from distress (Bradley & Furrow, 2004). Successful events are associated with therapists asking questions that evoke primary emotions— for example, "When your wife turns and says [whatever is the issue], what happens? I know you get angry, but in the second before you feel that anger?"— and heightening these emotions to create powerful expressions of attachment needs. A new construction of key emotional experience leads to a new kind of connection with the partner. The first of these change events occurs when more withdrawn partners *engage with their primary emotions and assert their needs* in a way that connects them with their lover. (They too yearn for love and close- ness.) The second and more dramatic of these is *blamer softening*: Previously blaming partners reach for their now more available lovers and ask for their attachment needs to be met from a position of vulnerability, that is, in a man- ner that elicits caring from these other partners. At these moments both part- ners are accessible and responsive. In a *softening*, blaming partners essentially do what secure partners can do when they are distressed—that is, they listen to their own attachment feelings and needs, express them congruently and coherently, ask for what they need, take in and trust the offered comfort of the other, and internalize a sense of felt security and safety in the relationship. In these sessions, the elements in the blaming partner's emotional experience are ordered and made into a coherent whole so that this person's attachment needs are clear.

At the end of such an event, Sarah tells her James, "I get so desperate for you to respond to me that I just try to bulldoze you. Then I don't even see it when you are trying to be there. I'm just so scared. I can't feel this alone all the time. You told me you wanted me to step out of the judge's chair and give you a chance. I want to know that you won't leave me standing here all by myself. Hurting. It is so hard to ask you, but I want you to see my softer side and hold me. Can you hold me?"

These events are turning points in a relationship. This is where the clear expression of newly formulated emotions pulls for new and more loving re- sponses from the other partner. The couple then have an expanded range of emotion. Partners are able to move past narrow, secondary emotional responses such as irritation or numbing out, and they have a new ability to regulate their deeper emotions, such as abandonment fears, shame, and anticipated rejection. They develop an ability to share these emotions with each other to create positive connection. In this process both partners then learn that separation distress is manageable and resolvable. Disconnection can then be experienced as merely unpleasant, rather than potentially catastrophic. Furthermore, new emotion generates new cognitions, such as more generous attributions about the intentions of the other, new images of self, and new frames for relationship problems. Sarah says, "I believe that he wants to be there for me. I guess we just got so very stuck. The ways we had of protecting ourselves just scared the hell out of the other person. We have to help each other feel safe. Give each other the benefit of the doubt. I know that when he reassures me, it moves me deep in my heart. And I start to feel better about myself too. If he loves me, then I must be okay."

The Role of Emotion in Key Change Events

These change events are very powerful, and partners experience them as key bonding moments that transform their relationship. Beginning therapists often ask why this kind of heightening of emotion and these "hot" enactments are necessary, because, after all, clients find them challenging. The new neuroscience of emotion can help us understand the power of these events and become more precise in our interventions. In the beginning, the practice of EFT was crafted from observing videotapes and gradually grasping and systematizing the moves and moments that led to change. The therapist did what worked, without always knowing why or how things changed.

In these events, therapists first help partners reprocess and deepen key emotions, repeating cues, sensations, emotional images, and emotional action tendencies and linking them into a coherent framework of attachment needs and behavioral responses. Second, therapists routinely guide couples into enactments and insist that partners look at each other when expressing deep emotion, even if this is difficult for a partner to do. This difficulty with direct eye contact is also often apparent during events where partners are focusing on the forgiveness of injuries. Therapists try to ensure that deep emotions are expressed directly and poignantly to the other spouse and that only then, after emotion is heightened, does the therapist help clients formulate needs and reach for the other partner. It has become more and more apparent that these vital enactments in the second stage of EFT are especially powerful for those who were traumatized by attachment relationships or life events, because they create not only improvement in trauma symptoms but also a new and more positive sense of self. They seem to be curative even when the emotional risks involved appear to be high.

New thinking and research on emotion in relationships help us understand more precisely what happens in these change events and how to mine them so that they transform the dancers and the dance. Some of this knowledge is very specific. For example, when people speak of their emotional response in terms of "hurt," this refers to a mixture of anger, sadness, loss, and fear and involves a cognitive sense of being devalued as a person and as a relationship partner (Feeney, 2005). This kind of information helps therapists capture a client's experience and connect with parts of this experience that may be less accessible or less well articulated. We can also move to a more general level and examine how some of the new science of emotion and relationships applies here.

Resonance and Mirror Neurons

Physicists speak of "resonance" as a sympathetic vibration between two elements that allows these elements to suddenly synchronize signals and act in a new harmony. This kind of resonance, in the form of a mutual coordination, can be seen between infant and mother in free play. The timing of responses is exquisite, facial expressions are synchronized, emotions are shared, and the intentions of the other are anticipated. There is a correspondence, a flow that is beyond empathy and has been suggested as the source of a deep intimacy or intersubjectivity (Trevarthen, 1980; Stern, 2004) between attachment figures. Each person's mind and emotion are attuned to the other's. Each person knows the other's mind and recursively knows that he or she exists in this mind. Some modern theorists speak of this kind of connection as a human need over and beyond that of secure attachment, but it is also equally possible to see this kind of connection as the flowering of the attachment process and an integral part of it. As Fonagy has suggested (Fonagy & Target, 1997), secure attachment is knowing that you exist in the mind of the other. Partners in softening episodes appear to resonate with each other in this fashion, to be totally present and able to synchronize moves and responses in an entirely new way. This is not just calming but also intensely rich and rewarding.

But how do we "feel" the other? How do we obtain this "felt sense" of secure, evolving connection. Neuroscience suggests that when we watch another move and act with intentionality, mirror neurons in our brains mimic the movement and action so that we feel this in our own bodies. This finding illuminates the process of empathizing with another or imitating another. Mirror neurons appear to be part of our "wired-to-connect" heritage that primes us to reach out for and connect with others. For a moment, we share minds and a common world.

For the EFT therapist, it is essential to direct people to slow down and look directly at their partner when this partner is expressing a powerful emotion. In the process of creating forgiveness, for example, the injured party has to look in the other's face and see that his or her pain is "felt," that it impacts the offending partner. Without this level of connection, which potentially activates mirror neurons, apologies tend to be simply empty words. When partners, with the therapist's help, can safely focus their attention on the other and resonate with him or her, a natural wellspring of empathy and sensitive caring often appears even in those who, on a cognitive level, do not know "how" to be close and how to respond in a loving way. This kind of connection can be an entirely new experience for many partners, and it can only occur when the therapist provides safety and also actively structures risk taking and emotional engagement. Manageable stress stimulates the brain, creates new connections among neurons, and appears to create new cognitive integrations and hence new behaviors. Science is helping us fill in the blanks in accepted mechanisms of change in therapy, giving new meaning to the much-used phrase, a "corrective emotional experience."

The Physiological Impact of Key Change Events

The neurochemical base of attachment is also becoming clearer and helping us understand the powerful impact of key change events such as *softenings*. Research shows that in moments of responsive emotional engagement our brains are flooded with the "cuddle hormone" oxytocin (Carter, 1998). This neurotransmitter is produced only by mammals and is associated with states of calm, joy, and contented bliss. It seems to create a cascade of pleasure and comfort and appears to be the physiological basis of the safe haven that Bowlby outlined in his theoretical writings.

Researchers discovered the power of oxytocin when they compared the mating habits of two different kinds of prairie voles (Carter, Devries, & Getz, 1995). In one species, males and females are monogamous, rear their young together, and form lifelong bonds; in the other, males and females mate promiscuously and leave offspring to fend for themselves. The faithful rodents produce oxytocin, but their promiscuous cousins do not. When scientists give monogamous voles a chemical that counteracts oxytocin, these voles mate but do not bond with their partners. However, when researchers give the same rodents extra oxytocin, they bond tightly whether they mate or not.

In humans, oxytocin is released when we are proximal to, or in physical contact with, an attachment figure, especially during moments of heightened emotion, such as orgasm and breastfeeding. Kerstein Uvnas-Moberg (1998), a Swedish neuroendocrinologist, discovered that merely thinking about loved ones can trigger a release of oxytocin. The administration of oxytocin also appears to increase the tendency to trust and interact with others. Oxytocin reduces the release of stress hormones such as cortisol and so is beginning to be viewed as a hormone with real significance for the cardiovascular system (Gutkowska, Janowski, Mukaddam-Daher, & McCann, 2000). We are starting to understand the physiology that literally links the heart, the traditional metaphor for love and longing, with key interactions with loved ones who can soothe and comfort us.

These findings help explain the pattern found in EFT clinical practice and research that once distressed partners learn to emotionally connect and reach out to each other, speaking their attachment needs, new transforming moments occur. Partners return to these moments again and again, thus creating new patterns of emotion regulation and interpersonal engagement. When couples can create these moments, they have the tools with which to repair times of disconnection and create a safe haven within the relationship. This ability, developed by the couple, provides a way to understand the low relapse rate found in EFT outcome research.

Creating a Coherent Whole

Research on emotion suggests that it is not easy to modify powerful emotional responses, especially fear. As LeDoux (1996) points out, fear, once conditioned, is almost indelible. This is perhaps because nature favors false positives over false negatives where matters of threat and survival are at stake. The link between trigger and response can be weakened, but the emotional system does not allow data to be removed easily. However, to the great relief of psychotherapists, it does allow new additions that then create variations (Ekman, 2003). This perspective fits very well with the EFT therapist's respect for a client's presenting emotional response. There is no attempt to "get rid of" this emotion. On the contrary, it is validated and then developed further, so that, for example, anger recedes and the threat that is a vital part of that anger comes to the forefront. However, for the key emotions that guide interactions to be modified or expanded, it is also necessary for this emotion to be given specific meaning, in that it is placed in a clear interpersonal context and emotion, cognition, and response tendency can then be integrated into a new whole. Once the client can so order difficult emotions, they become easier to tolerate and are able to be expressed in a more positive way.

This process meshes with the research on secure attachment conducted by Mary Main and her colleagues (Main, Kaplan, & Cassidy, 1985). This research, based on clients' ways of describing their relationships with attachment fig-ures—mostly figures from their past, especially parents—suggests that the es-sence of attachment security is not what happened to these clients in these relationships, per se, but rather how they processed these experiences. Secure clients are able to talk about painful events in an engaged manner with con-gruent affect and are able to create a coherent story out of these events. They can stay with their emotions, reflect on them, and form clear interpretations of these past events. Those who are more insecure either, if avoidant, minimize the emotional impact of attachment experiences and create detached inter-nally inconsistent narratives, or, if anxious in their attachment style, become overwhelmed by emotions, cannot maintain a focus, digress, become vague, or oscillate between differing perspectives and emotions. Insecurity involves an inability to integrate emotion, cognition, and expressive responses and thus interferes with the ability to maintain a coherent, consistent sense of connec-tion and caring.

In a beginning couple therapy session, Doug, an anxiously attached man who experienced abuse in his childhood, states, "I don't know why I feel so mad at these little things, but I love her so much, she is everything to me. And I say to myself, 'That's it, if she isn't going to listen then maybe I am better off out of here.' I get so jazzed up. This is the only relationship I have ever had that meant anything. Don't you think that she has a sleep problem? Now if she slept better, maybe I wouldn't get so mad, or if she could just ignore my anger, then it would be better. But then it is never going to work between us anyway. So I just get mad or shut down." His ambivalence about connection and in-ability to formulate an integrated coherent response to his attachment needs and to his wife are key in maintaining his relationship distress.

A large part of key change events is not only the heightening of emotion and its expression to the partner, but the creation of a coherent experience within the client whereby emotion, behavior, and cognition are formed into a coherent, congruent, and integrated whole with the guidance of the therapist. In a softening session, Gail, a previously mercurial critical partner, is finally able to put all the elements of her emotion, which she elaborated in previous sessions, into an integrated whole. At the end of the session, she can feel in-tensely and can also reflect on her experience and stay open to Ed, her partner. She states:

"I don't feel angry right now. I feel more of those scary feelings we have talked about. Part of me wants to keep you away and test you to see if you really care, just like I used to do in the past. Then all you see is this controlling, angry person. And I might even look kind of cool right now. But inside I have that sense of feeling small and not wanting you to see how helpless I feel. But I do feel this helplessness. (*She weeps.*) This is so hard. I do believe that you want to be there for me. And I understand now how we have hurt each other in this pattern we got caught in. But it is a risk for me to talk like this, to feel this. I am so afraid that if I ask you, if I let you see how much I need you, you will not respond. Then I will feel more alone, so alone. That aloneness is so cold, cold like death. I want to ask you. I need to know that you will turn to me, hold me. (*in a soft, voice, leaning toward him*) Can you hold me?"

Here Gail is able to integrate emotion and cognition, past and present, inner experience and outer expression, and consider her partner's perspective at the same time. This makes her message clear and makes it easier for Ed to attune to her and to respond. The role of the therapist is to actively link new emotion, cognition, models of self and other, and a shift in interactional moves into a mosaic of meaning and experience that supports a shift to more secure relating. The practice of EFT has evolved to include more deliberate reflection, repetition, summarizing, and linking of these different elements to create this coherence of mind and experience.

A Final Note

As mentioned previously in this chapter, the traditional concept of a corrective emotional experience as being an essential element of change in psychotherapy (both individual and couple) is now being elucidated by many different findings in various areas of psychology. What might be the key elements of such an experience and how might it be "corrective"?

First, emotion must come online; it must be aroused. Second, it must be attended to; the therapist plays a key role here in directing attention to different aspects of experience. Third, the client's emotional "soup," which includes more surface reactive emotions and more primary emotions, must be explored and ordered. This step involves more than clarifying and ordering of content; the process of experiencing—that is, how experience is structured from moment to moment and emotion regulated—must be included. A client becomes aware, for example, of different levels of emotion and coping mechanisms, such as habitual numbing and a felt sense of what this numbing conceals from view.

Fourth, as the client's emotional soup is explored, a network of associated cognitions and inherent action tendencies emerge. Key cognitions,—especially about the nature of the self, the needs of the self, and the nature of relationships with others—are often accessible only when a client is deeply engaged emotionally. The structure and logic of different aspects of experience and how they interconnect are then elucidated. New emotions are also aroused, such as grief for the needs that have never been spoken or met. A new sense of agency is accessed as the client becomes aware of the manner in which he or she has actively created, and is now recreating, his or her inner reality. New insights and new motivations are then born out of this process.

Fifth, as previously discussed, all of the above is integrated into a new coherent whole where models of self and other can be revised and new responses become possible. This restructuring, once considered to be metaphorical, now appears to be literal. There is more and more evidence that new neural and synaptic pathways are laid down in the brain by new experience. The anatomy of the brain, not just the details of its wiring, has been shown to change, for example, in London taxi drivers, who show a growth in the posterior of their hippocampus associated with their years of experience storing increasingly detailed spatial maps of this city (Maguire et al., 2000). Therapy, such as cognitive–behavioral therapy for obsessive–compulsive disorder, has been shown in positron emission tomography (PET) scans to engage different brain circuitry and thereby foster a client's ability to resist habitual compulsions (Schwartz, 1998). The concept that significant new experience in therapy can reprogram the brain is intriguing. Repetitive and patterned activation lays down neural organization during development (Rueda, Posner, & Rothbart, 2005), and there is more and more evidence of the neuroplasticity of the adult brain as it responds to, and processes, new experience (Schwartz & Begley, 2002).

The therapist is essential to this process in many ways: as a guide directing attention, as an active surrogate processor of significant experience, and as a source of support and safety so that the therapy experience does not become overwhelming. Interesting questions to consider are:

- In the client's processing of an emotional experience, when does the therapist exert the most corrective influence?
- Does the therapist act as a top-down surrogate processor for and with a client, perhaps helping to provide a cognitive reappraisal, a new meaning for already existing emotional realities?
- Does the therapist help to activate and draw attention to physiological sensations, nonverbal cues, cognitive and emotional shifts—in fact to the "felt sense" of the client's experience, as neural circuits are firing and

being challenged, thereby exerting influence in a bottom-up manner and changing perception?

It is clear that the social proximity of a close other, a trusted therapist or an attachment figure, can influence the perception of threat in the brain and reduce anxiety, thereby changing the essential nature of key emotional experiences as they occur. Coan (2007) suggests that social affect regulation is a relatively bottom-up process as opposed to solo affect regulation, which is more top down, and, since it happens later in the process of experiencing and requires more effort, less efficient. The empathic presence of the therapist, found to be so crucial to change even in cognitive therapies (Castonguay et al., 1996), then allows for a new engagement with experience *as it occurs and is being encoded in the brain.* In turn, neural circuits are shaped and reshaped as they are challenged (Coan, personal communication, June 24, 2008).

In couple therapy, the potential for a corrective emotional experience is heightened considerably by the ease with which emotion may be activated in the ongoing drama with the other partner and by the use of new interactions with this partner to generate both new experiential inputs and new reappraisals of familiar experience. When both partners then send clearer and more coherent emotional signals and so create a closer and more attuned interpersonal dance, they literally are able to shape a new and transformative emotional world for each other.

On a more general note, new understandings of our inner emotional life and the new science of relationships (Berscheid, 1999) are coming together in ways that would have been unimaginable only a few decades ago. The great unknowns—the nature and importance of emotion and the nature of adult bonding—that impact formulations of the change process in couple and individual therapy are enigmas no longer. Even the facilitation of relatively complex emotional responses, such as compassion for others, is able to be systematically addressed. For example, attachment research finds that accessing images of loving attachment figures reliably primes softer emotions such as compassion for others (Milkulincer et al., 2001; Mikulincer, Shaver, Gillath, Nitzberg, 2005). Change is now possible with couples whose emotional responses are extreme and cycles of interactions are rigid and infused with the echoes of past traumas (MacIntosh & Johnson, 2008). In couple therapy, we can now systematically create attunement and compassionate responsiveness, but only if we know how to enlist the most powerful force in human behavior—emotion.

11

The Communication of Emotions and the Growth of Autonomy and Intimacy within Family Therapy[1]

Dan Hughes

THE FAMILY LIES AT THE crossroad of human development. Whether we focus on the creative activities and aspirations of the autonomous individual or on the loving connections of individuals as couples, or as members of the community and the culture, we might best turn to the family to understand the context in which human beings develop. Many fields of human research, including those that focus on the structure and functioning of the human brain, are increasingly demonstrating that the choice between autonomy and intimacy is false: When that is the only choice, it is the result of the failure of the family to facilitate the development of its members. Optimal family functioning, along with optimal neurological functioning, considers autonomy and intimacy, as well as self and other, to be two sides of the same coin. The family is entrusted with the responsibility of nurturing both sides, and when it does its job well, these dichotomies fade.

Interwoven with autonomy and intimacy, extending into each and reflecting the energy—the vitality—of their interactions, are the emotions. Emotions represent the various forms of specific energy that move within one mind or between minds within relationships. Anger and joy, fear and love, guilt and excitement are here-and-now experiences that bring the individual—and the

My gratitude to Diana Fosha for her clear and illuminating suggestions and questions and enthusiastic support. Thanks for this, for AEDP, and for your presence.

relationships between individuals—to life. Without emotion, both the individual and the relationship would be characterized by inertia and indifference. Emotions carry direction, meaning, and purpose in the development of the individual and the relationship. With anger, one is more likely to be motivated to right a wrong. With the joyful experience of nature, one is likely to be motivated to take a trip to the Grand Canyon. Sadness—when shared—is likely to become lessened. Pleasure—when shared—is likely to become larger. Our emotions create and reflect the ebbs and flows, the peaks and valleys of our life's journeys. And our emotions, being as "contagious" as they are, invite others to join us on our journeys.

This chapter focuses more on the communication of emotions than on emotions themselves. Through the communication of emotions, we create an opening that makes our own inner life clear to the other person. As emotion is expressed nonverbally, its background affective tone becomes apparent. The nonverbal expression of affect conveys its intensity, urgency, and animated features. When the other resonates with this nonverbal expression, matching it in a synchronized rhythm and degree of intensity, the two individuals move forward on the same path. The sense of being deeply understood by the other, of feeling "felt" by the other, comes through such matching. Dan Stern (1985) calls this living process "attunement." Colwyn Trevarthen (personal communication, May 27, 2008) refers to the same joined affective state as "synrhythmia." It is hard to imagine how to develop and maintain emotional intimacy without the continuous presence of such *ongoing experiences of shared affect.* Such experiences are at the core of intersubjectivity, whose central role in the rich emotional life of the family is explored in this chapter.

Yet frequently the family is seen as the context in which a great deal of human suffering occurs. Within the family rage and terror, despair and shame, unresolved grief and loss all occur much too frequently among individuals who call each other "my family." Such human pain is often generated by individuals who find emotional communication to be too difficult and too frightening to be easily done. Such communication—when expressed in a reactive manner—often leads to attacks on both the other and the self. Similarly, such communication—when continuously avoided—often leads to increased isolation and loneliness, rather than emotional intimacy. And yet, when such emotional communications are able to express core experiences of self while remaining open to similar experiences in other family members, the family best fosters full human development. In families that cherish open emotional communication, children are nourished and thrive, their parents experience deep satisfaction, and together, they experience meaning and joy.

Intersubjectivity—whereby family members influence one another through the sharing of their emotional experiences—lies at the core of successful family communication and relationships. More specifically, intersubjectivity refers to the interpersonal process whereby the subjective experience of one member of the dyad or group has an ongoing impact on the subjective experience of the other(s), and vice versa. It is inherently a reciprocal process. All members of the family are influenced by the subjective experience of one another, without sacrificing the integrity and inherent validity of the experience of any. While being aware of one's own experience, one is also open to the experience of the other person. Intersubjective experiences are nonauthoritative: They are not based on asymmetric power or on a power differential. Within intersubjective experiences, one member of the dyad does not dominate the other. The authority of the parent is not based on devaluing the experience of the child. For the experience of one person to be seen, understood, and valued, the other person does not have to be made into an object that is lacking in valued subjective experience.

Intersubjectivity involves three central components: joined affect (attunement), joined awareness, and joined intentions (Trevarthen, 2001a; Stern 1985, 2004). Emotional communications are at the core of intersubjectivity. (I am using the term *affect* to refer to the background energy of experience—what Dan Stern [1985] refers to as "vitality affect." *Emotion* refers to the specific "categorical affects" of Stern [1985], such as anger, excitement, joy, shame.) The emotions that are associated with the events of our lives are central in organizing our experiences of these events and integrating them into our narrative. Communicating the emotions (along with the thoughts, intentions, and other qualities of our inner lives) associated with these events with an attachment figure often facilitates this integration.

Emotions tend to be the focus of these communications because they are often harder to accept. They are apt to place stress on the relationship, lightning rods that draw conflict and defensiveness. Yet, when we are able to successfully share our emotional experience with a trusted other, we are better able to regulate these emotions because the other is now being experienced as if he or she had been there with us in the event. We are then better able to reflect on the experience and to make sense of it.

Intersubjective experiences that have the greatest power to facilitate the development of family members are characterized by an unconditional acceptance of the experience of the other. Within the atmosphere created by acceptance, family members are deeply curious about the experiences of one another, they come to know the inner lives of each other, and they resonate with the other's experience with a tone of lightness and empathy. Their curiosity about each other is not meant to control the other but rather to better know—and hopefully love—the other.

Within the context of direct, open, reciprocal emotional communications, children are very likely to develop a secure attachment with their parents. Through the safety inherent in such an attachment, children are able to begin to explore who they, their parents, and the larger world, are. With attachment security, they are very likely to be able to regulate, identify, and express the full range of their emotional experiences. At the same time, they are very likely to be able to reflect on these experiences so that they "make sense" in the context of their life. Over time, with the ongoing development of emotional and reflective functioning, they are able to organize their life's journey—their autobiographical narrative—in a coherent and comprehensive manner. New events need not be denied or distorted in order to be integrated into their narrative. Children who develop attachment security tend to become adults who manifest such a coherent narrative. In this manner, the optimal interpersonal process is interwoven with the optimal intrapersonal process.

Within the context of emotional communications, the meaning of the event becomes more organized, the autobiographical narrative becomes more coherent, and the experience of intimacy carries safety, joy, and discovery into our lives. This chapter attempts to summarize this developmental process as well as briefly explore how the family therapist may utilize the intersubjective communications that occur within the session to make use of the power of emotions to facilitate transformations within both the individual and the family.

Our knowledge of the world develops incrementally through the lived experience of events along with the ability to reflect on these experiences. Upon reflection, we become better able to describe the event, notice other events with which an event is often associated, and understand cause–effect patterns in the sequence of events. Our knowledge moves from the specific to the general and back again. We come to understand qualities in the event that are unique to it, and qualities that are common to other events. To be effective, the clinician needs to be able to perceive what is unique to the client and what features are common to other individuals and families in similar situations. To be effective, the researcher needs to perceive what is common among events as well as the manner in which one feature is crucial in causing the sequence of patterns that is occurring. The clinician and researcher have complementary knowledge that enables each to better understand the patterns that are occurring within both the individual and within similar individuals and groups.

This complementary knowledge is even more crucial when the subject of our understanding involves the lived experience of family members who are engaged in ongoing nonlinear interactions with one another. The unique sequences that are occurring need to be understood well if the most appropriate and unique interventions to best guide these sequences are to occur. Yet the universal qualities of intersubjective experience need also be understood if clinicians are to be able to identify features of the experience that are lacking and that are central in the maladaptive patterns that are occurring within the family. The findings of child development and neuroscience will be joined with clinicians' experiences in developing their empirical interventions. The findings of clinicians will be joined with researchers' hypotheses in developing their experimental interventions.

The Developmental Impact of Intersubjective Experience

Colwyn Trevarthen (2001a) and Daniel Stern (2000) have contributed greatly to our understanding of the role of intersubjective experience in human development. Their theories and research, in turn, have received convincing support from findings that derive from neurological research (e.g., Schore, 2003b; Siegel, 1999). Trevarthen, Stern, and others have proposed that development is greatly facilitated when the infant's emotional and behavioral expressions are noticed and sensitively responded to with contingent expressions from his caregiver. The caregiver's expressions are also supported and facilitated by the infant's contingent responses. The reciprocal quality of these interactions enables the infant to develop a sense of agency through having an impact on the caregiver, as well as to begin to understand his or her own expressions by experiencing how the caregiver experiences these expressions. He comes to organize his experience of both self and other through experiencing the caregiver's experience of both. When the caregiver experiences interest, joy, love, and delight while interacting with the baby, in turn the baby comes to experience him- or herself as being interesting, joyful, lovable, and delightful. When the caregiver experiences annoyance, disgust, and boredom while interacting with the baby, in turn the baby comes to experience him- or herself as being annoying, disgusting, and boring.

Thus, the flowing, rhythmic, affective states of the infant become, in part, increasingly organized into specific emotional experiences of self. These emerging emotions regarding aspects of self (e.g., delightful or disgusting; brave or scared) are most often forming within the templates generated by parents' emotional experiences of these selfstates. These emotional states of the infant develop within intersubjective experiences and initially have a central *receptive* quality to them: the infant's emerging emotional experiences are being organized around the parents' emotional experience of him or her. For optimal emotional development, the individual needs to be able to actively modify and assimilate these receptive, intersubjective emotions. As children mature, they are better able to do so, especially when their parents convey their emotional experience of them in a manner that values their autonomy. This is likely to happen when the parents' intersubjective stance is characterized by playfulness, acceptance, curiosity, and empathy.

These emerging emotional patterns are easily seen within the parent–infant "dance" when both members of the dyad are engaged in an affectively rich interaction characterized by much reciprocal eye contact, matching facial expressions and voice prosody, with congruent movements and gestures. The rhythms and intensity of these elaborate nonverbal communications are equally matched. These patterns remain present and become even more elaborate and sophisticated as infants become toddlers, then 8-year-olds, and then adolescents. Children continue to be greatly affected by their parents' emotional experience of their affective expressions of their own inner life. Parents tend to give meaning to these expressions, and these meanings have an impact—for better or worse—on the meanings that children give to their expressions of their own inner life. In a reciprocal manner, children give meaning to their parents' expressions, and that meaning has an impact on the parents' emotional experience of their own functioning as parents.

Intersubjective communications involve nonverbal and (frequently) verbal expressions, that reveal the individual's affective, reflective, and intentional states. When there is congruence between nonverbal and verbal expressions, there tends to be clarity with regard to the inner lives (thoughts, emotions, wishes, intentions, perceptions) of those communicating. When the nonverbal expressions are at odds with what is expressed verbally, however, there is great risk of miscommunications and faulty assumptions regarding the inner life of interactants. These situations are the context in which many family conflicts originate.

Experiences between parent and child are described as *intersubjective* because they refer to how the subjective experience of an event by one member influences the subjective experience of that event by the other member. If the "event"—for example, an exuberant arm movement and synchronized vocal expression by the infant—is experienced by the parent as revealing of the infant's healthy initiatives and interests, then the infant is likely to experience that aspect of his or her developing self as something to enjoy and even encourage. However, if the same event is experienced by the parent as representing a willful and selfish attitude, then the infant is likely to experience that aspect of his or her developing self as being something to inhibit, hide from the parent, and disavow within the self. Finally, if the same event is not noticed by the parent, the infant is less likely to notice him- or herself engaged in that manner (see John Bowlby's [1980] concept of "defensive exclusion"). The very same influence occurs within intersubjective experiences throughout the life cycle. Maintaining an openness to the receptive emotions that are emerging from within intersubjectivity creates both the deep joy as well as the sharp conflicts inherent in our attachment relationships.

Within intersubjectivity, participants hold some degree of awareness of both their own experience as well as the experience of the other. In giving expression to their own experience, they are immediately aware of the impact of their experience on the other, and they allow their experience and its expression to change to better match this perceived impact. Their intention is to communicate with the other, to deepen mutual understanding or resolve a conflict, not for the other to submit to their experience. In short, intentions are congruent; there is similarity of purpose in their interactions. All three— affect, cognition, and intention—are "in synch." When individuals are so engaged, each is likely to be functioning within the "core state" described by Fosha: "The core state is marked by effortless focus and concentration, ease and relaxation, a subjective sense of clarity, purity, even truth, and often remarkable eloquence" (2000, p. 142). The same subjective experience is likely to be present in the entrainment process of the social engagement system (see Porges, Chapter 2, this volume).

When we are speak of intersubjective experiences, we often include a description of moments when the parent and infant are "absorbed" by each other. Those are the moments when they gaze deeply into each other's eyes, time seems to "stand still," and neither appears to be aware of anything except the other. Such moments of absorption typically occur less frequently as the child develops. But when they do occur, the attachment is again strengthened. Empathy with and understanding of the inner life of the other becomes deeper. Acceptance—not judgment—pervades the relationship, and each is again more open to being influenced by the other. Both feel safe enough to be open to the emotional expression of the other's experience, and the intersubjective impact on each of them becomes strong again. Each again trusts the intentions of the other that lie behind the behaviors—even those behaviors that generate conflicts. During these *moments of absorption*, both the individuals and the relationship are transformed.

There is a lovely cycle within the intersubjective experience that begins when the emotional expression of an event by one member of the dyad is met by the other with the attitude of acceptance, curiosity, and empathy. When the emotional expression is met with that attitude, the experience of both (i.e., knowing and being known) is unique and rich. Both become absorbed by the experience. The original emotional expression and its reception by the other is now transformed into a joint emotional experience of deep engagement that, in turn, may be transforming to each. Each now knows the other in a more profound manner, while each is equally known by the other. Both are absorbed in their shared, living moment. In short, the original emotional expressions serve as bridges into the worlds of each other. The emerging experience of emotional absorption serves as a transforming experience for both within their newly shared world.

All experience involves an affective component that might range from being very mild to very extreme, as well as from being positive to negative. Children (and their parents) often experience events with a specific response involving emotions such as joy or excitement, anger or fear, pride or shame. When these emotions become intense, the individual is at risk of experiencing dysregulated emotion that may become expressed in impulsive outbursts; diffuse hyperactive behaviors; frightened, withdrawn, or repetitive actions; or passive, dissociative states. When children have a relationship with parents that is characterized by attachment security, they are much more likely to be able to regulate their own intense emotional states (Sroufe, Egeland, Carson, & Collins, 2005). Because they express their experience to their parents, and the parents' own emotional state remains regulated, which enables children to regulate their own emotion. Parents' emotional states co-regulate the emotions of their children. When such intersubjective experiences occur frequently enough, children gradually are able to autoregulate similar emotional states when parents are not present.

However, if parents respond to children's intense emotional states with rejection, ridicule, or indifference, then children are at risk of having even greater difficulty in regulating their emotional states. If children's emotional states cause their parents to become dysregulated emotionally by eliciting fear, shame, or rage, then children are at great risk of not being able to develop autoregulation skills; these children frequently demonstrate impulsive and emotionally volatile reactive behaviors and/or pervasive dissociation in response to events associated with a wide range of emotions. In these families, emotional communication leads either to a dysregulation of emotion, or it causes the family members to avoid emotional topics in order to prevent such dysregulation.

When emotional regulation does not develop well, a person is often forced to defend against certain experiences of events that are likely to elicit specific emotions. The subjective experience of an emotion consists of interwoven affective, cognitive, intentional, and perceptual components. When one aspect of emotional experience is difficult to integrate into the experience of the event, the experience itself becomes poorly organized and is often not able to be brought into the person's narrative in a coherent manner. Thus the emotions associated with those events become dysregulating, often leading to dissociative and/or impulsive reactions, or they are rigidly avoided. Significant events in a person's life then may become triggers for such reactions. Family life becomes a place of threat and disorganization, not safety and open exploration of self and other.

Within families characterized by attachment security, parents are able to provide the safety required for a child to begin to autoregulate the full range of affective states, including those involving very intense emotions. The parent welcomes the child's emotional communications as an opportunity to better understand the inner life of his or her child. As the emotion is accepted, the child is then able to experience the event more deeply, on an intersubjective level. The child can then cocreate the meaning of the event with the active participation of the parent's reflective mind and affective heart in the event with him or her. The meaning of the event as it is emerging is also being accepted by the parent, and then by the child.

The continuous, evolving, impact of the communication on both enables participants to achieve a much greater understanding of, and empathy for, how each is experiencing the event. It is when the expression of emotions precludes an openness to the emotion of the other that emotional "communications" lead to conflicts that cause dysregulation or to separations that cause avoidant withdrawal rather than reflection.

Thus, within the intersubjective context, parents may still express anger at their children's behavior, but their *intention* is to communicate the impact that the behavior has had on them in order to deepen reciprocal understanding and facilitate relationship repair. Their intent is not to force compliance and use their children as objects for venting anger.

Lacking intersubjectivity in the communication, the other is an "object" and each person's intention is to change the "object" so that he or she experiences the event in the same manner as the self does. The intent is to "control" the inner life of the other and to force compliance to one's own inner life. In such situations, there is no communication since the subjective experience of each is not recognized, understood, or valued. Differences in thoughts, emotions, and motives are not seen as signs of healthy individuation but rather as signs of potential problems and faulty values. In such situations, domination and control become appealing.

In families characterized by attachment security, parents accept that their children's inner life reflects an emerging self that needs to be accepted, welcomed, and cherished, not controlled. When control is necessary (e.g., when a child is about to hit a neighbor's child with a stick), parents restrict their expectations and limit setting to the behavior itself rather than to the thoughts, feelings, and motives that led to the behavior. After limiting the behavior, these parents demonstrate interest in the emotions, thoughts, and intentions that led to the behavior through an attitude of acceptance, curiosity, and empathy. When children experience such an attitude, they are more likely to share their inner life and to be receptive to allowing the experience of their parents to influence their own experience—and possibly their future behaviors as well.

When parents attempt to control and force changes in their children's inner life, the message is, the "self" of the child is deficient. When children experience that message, they are very likely to also experience shame, fear, sadness, and anger. Furthermore, these emotions are likely to elicit a defensive response whereby children protect their inner life from their parents, are less open to new experiences, and are less ready to share their inner life with their parents in the future. If this sequence leads children to adopt a more secretive stance about what they think, feel, and intend to do, then their parents will have less influence over the development of their inner life. Subsequently, the children will be less able to take advantage of the more extensive experiences and loving guidance of their parents—and their inner life will suffer for this deficit.

Thus emotional communication, when it exists in an intersubjective stance characterized by acceptance, curiosity, and empathy, fosters greater understanding and empathy for the experience of both self and other, and facilitates further emotional awareness, regulation, and integrated expression within each member of the dyad. Each member is both expressive of self and receptive to the other at the same time. When emotional communication exists in a judgmental, closed, and defensive stance, it often leads to further emotional dysregulation, no increase in reflective functioning, and greater conflict that is unresolved. Within the intersubjective context, emotional communication facilitates an increase in both the coherence of the self as well as the emotional intimacy of the relationship.

Family Therapy

Bringing clarity and an intersubjective stance to the dysregulated emotional communications among family members is a central task of the family therapist. The therapist explains and models that the subjective experience of every family member needs to be accepted (through a nonjudgmental stance) both cognitively (through open, reflective curiosity) and emotionally (through empathy). By focusing on these emotional expressions, the therapist is able to begin the process of enabling emotional communications to become more effective means of increasing family safety and reciprocal understanding, as well as repairing conflicts and misunderstandings that are occurring. By so doing the confusion often associated with emotional communications is reduced and the invalidation of experience that often is associated with such confusion is prevented (Hughes, 2004, 2006, 2007, 2009).

The attachment-focused family therapist delves deeply into the *affective–reflective* and *intentional experiences* of each family member and shows, through his or her own affective–reflective and intentional communications, that the creative, autonomous experiences of the individual within the family can be celebrated and cherished, while at the same time, celebrating the collaborative, nurturing, safe, and intimate environment in which each family member can thrive. The family therapist never loses sight of the reality that the emotional strength of the family is interwoven with the unique, autonomous strengths of each member. Nor does he or she lose sight of the reality that the family is the strongest when each family member feels safe enough to give expression to his or her own strengths and vulnerabilities.

Characteristics of Family Therapy

Attachment-focused family therapy has the following features:

1. *Intersubjective engagement.* Attachment-focused family therapists experience each family member positively and openly communicate their experience (nonverbally and verbally). Therapists' experience of family members enables those individuals, in turn, to experience themselves differently. Therapists are not ambiguous in their expression of their experience, and they do not adopt a "neutral stance." They are able to experience each family member positively even though parents and children may be quite angry with each other. Family members experience greater safety, and each experiences self more positively. Therapists' more positive experience of individual family members allows each to see the others in a move positive light, and—if he or she is feeling safe—to reexperience the others.

At times, the actions of a family member may elicit a negative affective response within the therapist. At this point, he or she is seldom likely to share this response with the client. Rather, the therapist is likely to explore the client's comment more deeply. Often a therapist's annoyance in response to a client's comment indicates that the therapist needs to understand the client's inner life—thoughts, feelings, and intentions—more fully through heightened curiosity in order to experience empathy and greater understanding for his or her behavior.

The therapist's positive experience of clients is not based on a selective perception that intentionally disregards any challenging personal behaviors. Rather, it is founded upon a gentle but relentless persistence to understand what lies under clients' behaviors and generates their expressions. In so doing, the therapist is likely to discover that each family member is doing the best that he or she can. The therapist will also discover that he or she is coming to deeply care for each unique person—with all of his or her strengths and vulnerabilities—within each unique family.

The therapist, too, is affected by the intersubjective. The parent and child's experience of him or her affects his or her experience of self-as-therapist (and, at times, self-as-person). The parent and child then learn how *their* experience of the therapist affects him or her, which in turn changes their experience of themselves. And so on. The therapist sets the tone of the resonating quality of the dialogue by participating in the intersubjective context with a receptive and open attitude that is characterized by *playfulness, acceptance, curiosity,* and *empathy* (PACE).

2. *Affective–reflective (A-R) dialogue.* When communications are the most transforming, the affective component—the energy and emotional content of the message—is interwoven with a reflective quality. The *affective component* of the therapist's communications enables the recipients to experience the message safely, and the experience of safety enables the recipients to be more receptive to what is being said. This is the nonverbal, background affective tone—the vitality affect—that conveys the therapist's *intent* to help the family members understand each other's current experiences while understanding the therapist's experience. The *reflective component* conveys the therapist's experience of the event being explored *while, at the same time,* communicating his or her deep interest in and understanding of the other's experience of that event. The therapist's thoughts are often directed toward the deeper meanings of the event—the intentions that may lie under the behavior, as well as the intentions that lie under the surface intentions (e.g., he took the money in order to make his mother angry; he wanted to make his mother angry in order to confirm his belief that she does not like him). The experiences are understood and valued in order to effect a resolution of the conflict. The therapeutic intention is to arrive at a mutual understanding and resolution, not to dominate or intimidate the other. Therapists' strive to hold their mind open to the experience of the other while, at the same time, communicating their own experience.

Therapists need to hold their mind open to perceiving the experiences of the family members when therapists communicate their experience of each family member in the dialogue. If there is any deficiency in A-R dialogue, therapists need to point it out in order to ensure that the dialogue maintains its intersubjective nature. To do so, therapists also need to be present intersubjectively, with joined affect, cognition, and intentions.

The following is an example of the therapist's active role in facilitating the flow of A-R dialogue. In this example, the therapist works to help a child "make sense of" his experience of anger toward his mother, while also working to ensure that his mother will be open to her child's experience as it is emerging. Often at the beginning of such sequences the child's or parent's communications are characterized by an intensity that suggests strong anger or distress. The parent and child are focused on their own immediate emotions and associated thoughts and are not receptive to either the subjective context of their own experience or the experience of the other. *The therapist matches the vitality of these expressions and, in so doing, often generates the necessary momentum and reciprocity of the dialogue.* As the rhythm of the dialogue moves participants into the experience of each other, the therapist focuses on going beneath the surface to uncover thoughts, feelings, self-intentions, or the perceived intentions of the other that are central to the experience. In so doing, the therapist is facilitating an exploration of one member's experience, and then focuses on generating an open dialogue between parent and child regarding their joint experiences. At this level of exploration, there is no "right" or "wrong." This nonjudgmental stance enables both members to share subjective experiences without impulsive attacks on the other or defensive efforts to protect the self. The therapist facilitates an emotional expression that fully communicates the inner life of both members without sacrificing the inner life of either.

SON (Dave, 10 years old): She never lets me do anything!

THERAPIST (Arthur): Never? Never! Wow! If that's how it seems to you, no wonder you get upset!

SON: She doesn't!

THERAPIST: I hear you, Dave! It seems to you that she never lets you do anything! Why would that be Dave, why wouldn't she ever let you do anything?

SON: I don't know! Ask her!

THERAPIST: I do want your mom's experience, Dave. First I want your guess. If she never wants you to do what you want . . . why would that be?

SON: Because she doesn't care about what I want!

THERAPIST: You think that she doesn't care about what you want!

SON: No, she doesn't!

THERAPIST: Wow! If that is her reason for saying "no" to you—that she just does not care about what you want to do . . . that what you want is not important to her . . . I can see why that would really get you upset!

SON: It does!

THERAPIST: Wait, Dave! Have you ever told her that? That you think she just does not care about what is important to you!

SON: It's not what I think! It's what *is*!

THERAPIST: So you can read her mind? Or did she tell you that what is important to you is not important to her? That what is important to you does not matter to her?

SON: She did say that!

THERAPIST: What did she say?

SON: That I could not see my friend!

THERAPIST: That's telling you what she did not want you to do then, Dave. That's not saying that she does not care that it is important to you to see him.

SON: So?

THERAPIST: So you're just guessing about her reason for saying no, Dave. Why not tell her what you guess is her reason?

SON: What?

THERAPIST: Say, "Mom, sometimes I think that you say 'no' to me because it just does not matter to you what is important to me."

SON: Why?

THERAPIST: Because I want to know if she says that your guess is right. And I think that it would be good for you to know what she thinks about it too.

SON: (*to Mom, with voice tone similar to therapist's tone*) Sometimes it doesn't seem to me that you care whether or not something is important to me. You just don't care.

MOM (Linda): Dave, I'm sorry that you think that's why I say "no" to you sometimes. I can see why you'd get real mad at me if I said "no" because I didn't care that something was important to you.

SON: That's what it seems like to me.

MOM: I'm sorry, Dave. I have to be clearer about my reason. I do care if something is important to you. When I think that, I want to let you do it, and there has to be what I think is a really good reason before I say "no."

SON: Then why do you say "no"?

MOM: Oh, different reasons. Sometimes I think that you have too much going on and need some down time at home . . . or I want you to take care of something first. But I feel badly when I know you really want to do something and I say "no." I don't like saying that when it's really important to you. I feel great inside when I can see that you are happy with what's going on.

SON: I know, Mom.

MOM: I think you're telling me and Arthur that sometimes you don't know. You're not sure if I care about what you want—and how much—when I make my decisions. Thanks for telling us, Dave. Thanks for helping me to maybe do better next time. I'm glad you've been honest about this. Your words helped me a lot.

SON: It's OK, Mom. I do know you care.

MOM: I'm glad. I'm glad you know. I really, *really* do care.

Linda's responses expressed great empathy and understanding for her son's inner life. The therapist had held a few meetings with Linda and her husband before Dave was brought into the sessions in order to enhance Linda's awareness of the value of such communications and even to coach her in her choice of words.

3. *Interactive repair and its initiation.* When a family comes for therapy because of significant difficulties with emotional communication, there are likely to be many examples of these difficulties throughout the treatment sessions. Often the difficulties have, at their core, family members' ignorance of how to engage in interactive repair. When behaviors are interpreted by one family member as placing the relationship with another member of the family at risk or diminishing the other member's value, these behaviors often elicit intense anger or withdrawal in the other—neither of which is likely to lead to relationship repair. The therapist must take the lead in facilitating both the repair of the relationship that has been stressed by the immediate dialogue and the ability of family members to engage in relationship repair at home.

The therapist works from the assumption that the initial steps toward repair are the responsibility of the parent, not of the child, regardless of the nature of the conflict that led to a break in their relationship. The parent serves as the attachment figure for the child, not vice versa. By initiating repair, the parent is communicating to the child that the relationship is more important than specific conflicts or behaviors. The parent is also communicating that he or she has the skills and commitment to maintain the continuity of the relationship under whatever circumstances emerge. Some of these skills can be enhanced by the therapist's modeling, using PACE, how to address differences or inconsistencies evident in any area of the parent–child relationship or in the emerging communications in the treatment session itself.

The therapist facilitates repair by experiencing the intersubjective breaks in the dialogue and then addressing these breaks. Therapists accept these breaks, not judging them to be "wrong" or searching for someone to blame for the break, but by exploring the reasons for the breaks by helping family members become aware of differences in their experiences of the immediate discussion and/or the past event being discussed. Therapists can facilitate an A-R dialogue about the preceding dialogue segment that caused the intersubjective break. Or they may focus on family members' difficulty with interactive repair and explore reasons for those difficulties or ways to maintain an A-R dialogue when varying experiences are being expressed.

When the "emotional communication" is characterized by escalating anger followed by withdrawal, its value is minimal and, most likely, there has been some damage to the continuity of the relationship. In individual treatment, where the expression of emotion functions to convey more fully and clearly aspects of the client's inner life to both the client and the therapist, the impact of these expressions on the person referred to (and who is not present) need not be considered (at least not at that time). However, in family therapy, the expression of emotion functions both to communicate inner life and to influence the other who *is* present in the session. Thus, the need to facilitate reciprocal communication of emotions must not be forgotten. Any positive value of an emotional expression can be lost quickly if it has a negative impact on the ability of two people to reestablish an emotional connection.

The following is an example of a therapist addressing the lack of repair in a conflict between a father, John, and his 14-year-old son, Robert. The therapist needs to be cautious about (1) becoming embedded in the content of the conflict and becoming a "judge" as to who was right, and (2) embarking on problem-solving strategies. When a conflict is not followed by relationship repair, the therapist's first priority is usually to facilitate that needed repair and then focus on whether or not such lack of repair is a pattern that often undermines the relationship. *Developing an awareness of the need for repair, of the parent's responsibility to initiate it, and of the skills needed to be successful at it is much more important than the specific conflict.*

SON (Robert, 15 years old): (*to therapist*) I just don't know why he won't let me. It's my money!

DAD (John): How many times do I have to tell you! You know why!

SON: You are so clueless!

DAD: Keep talking to me that way and it will just get worse for you!

SON: Whatever!

THERAPIST: You both are showing some big anger toward each other now. When this happens at home, where does it usually lead?

DAD: We usually just go our separate ways and calm down. Keeping at it only tends to make it worse.

THERAPIST: And after you've calmed down?

DAD: Usually we just let it go.

THERAPIST: Because?

DAD: If one of us brings it up again, it generally just leads to another round of anger.

THERAPIST: Any problems with that approach?

DAD: I don't know. Maybe one of us really doesn't let it go . . . and it comes out later.

THERAPIST: And my guess is that you really don't feel that close for awhile. And maybe you then avoid that topic, since it most always leads to anger and then distance from each other, with both of you tense and isolated.

DAD: That's the way it's always been. But we get over it.

THERAPIST: Yeah, eventually. How about if we try to find another way, though, with less anger, tension, and isolation?

DAD: OK.

THERAPIST: Robert?

SON: I guess.

THERAPIST: Let's start with you, John. Help me understand where your anger came from when Robert asked you again about buying the computer.

DAD: How many times do I have to tell him?

THERAPIST: I hear your anger coming back. Is this what happens at home? The anger comes back?

DAD: Yeah.

THERAPIST: I need to understand it more deeply, John. Why do you get angry when your son asks you a number of times for the same thing?

DAD: He just won't accept my decision.

THERAPIST: And what does that mean to you?

DAD: It means that he wants his own way!

THERAPIST: And in wanting his own way, does that mean anything about his relationship with you?

DAD: It means that he doesn't accept my authority as his father.

THERAPIST: Ah! And what does that mean, if he doesn't accept your authority?

DAD: It means . . . I don't know.

THERAPIST: Do you think that it might mean that Robert does not value you as a dad the way that you want him to?

DAD: I guess that's one way of saying it.

THERAPIST: That sometimes Robert does not want to rely on your judgment, to accept what you think is best for him.

DAD: That's right, he doesn't.

THERAPIST: And what does that mean, if Robert doesn't rely on you very much?

DAD: Like I said, that my authority isn't that important to him.

THERAPIST: I wonder if it also means to you that your place in his life is less than you wished it were. If he relied on your judgment more, maybe it would seem that you were more important to him. Maybe even that he wanted to be closer to you.

DAD: I don't know if I'd go that far. He *is* 15.

THERAPIST: And he's moving away from you in various ways. He's moving toward being an adult. And maybe you're not sure what place he will want you to have in his life when he is an adult—whether or not he will want to be close to you . . . whether or not you're important to him.

DAD: Maybe you're right. Sometimes I do think that he wants too much independence. I'm not against that, I just want . . . to still be his father.

THERAPIST: And when he argues with you about your decisions for him, seems like you experience it as your not being very important to him anymore.

DAD: Maybe I do. It seems what is happening is what I was afraid would happen all along. I was never close to my dad. I always wanted it to be different between me and my son than what it was between me and my dad. And I'm not sure that it will be.

THERAPIST: So you two have a conflict, which seems to you to be due to your son's not wanting a close relationship with you in which he relies on you . . . and that leads to withdrawing from each other . . . which leads to your doubting that your son does want to be close with you . . . and it begins to look like how it was between you and your dad.

DAD: That's about it.

THERAPIST: Why not tell him that?

DAD: What?

THERAPIST: Why not tell him that sometimes when he questions your decision, you begin to think that he might not value you that much anymore . . . that it's a step toward you two becoming more and more distant as he gets older. And that upsets you. You want to be close to your son regardless of how old he is.

DAD: She's right, son. Sometimes when we argue, I do think that you don't want my ideas for you as to what's best, and even that we're not as close as we used to be. And I worry that we're going to drift apart, just like I did with your grandpa.

SON: That's not it, Dad.

THERAPIST: Wait a second, Robert. Your dad mentioned his worry to you about your relationship with each other. Did you know that he worried about that?

SON: No.

THERAPIST: How do you feel about your dad hoping that you two stay close, no matter how old you get and where you are?

SON: I want that too. It's just that sometimes, Dad, it seems like you don't want me to grow up . . . like I have to stay a kid and rely on you all the time and never decide anything for myself. I love you, Dad, but I want to be able to make my own decisions much more than you let me.

DAD: I love you too, son. I just want what's best for you.

SON: I know, Dad. But sometimes I think that your letting me make my own decision—even when I make a mistake—is what's best.

DAD: Maybe you're right, Robert. Maybe you are. Let me think about that computer some more.

SON: Thanks, Dad.

THERAPIST: Great dialogue, you two. Once you got behind the anger and saw each other's fears and wishes, it seemed to be so much easier to see how important you are to each other. The strength of your relationship was no longer lost in your anger.

4. *PACE.* During the dialogue the therapist strives to maintain an attitudinal stance that is characterized by the qualities of playfulness, acceptance, curiosity, and empathy. By *playfulness* I am not suggesting that therapists look for reasons to joke about family issues and minimize the seriousness of the themes being explored. Rather, I am suggesting that they convey a lightness in their explorations and experiences of the family themes that suggests that they are confident that the issues can be resolved. This quality of playfulness also clearly implies that the issues are not a threat to the safety of the members. Playful-

ness at times finds a humorous side to an interaction or event—humor that conveys the presence of a positive or "redeeming" quality to the issue.

Acceptance is the foundation for providing safety to the dialogue. Acceptance conveys a strong message that the intent of the dialogue is to *explore* and *communicate* experiences, not to evaluate them. Within the context of acceptance each member feels free to attend to his or her own experience, often to the extent that he or she better understands the experience. This individual is then in a position to communicate more clearly about the experience, which is crucial for "making sense" of the behaviors that are leading to the family discord. The nonjudgmental tone of the exploration ensures that all family members will feel safe in sharing aspects of their inner lives. Behaviors can be evaluated; the thoughts, emotions, intentions, perceptions, and memories that lie beneath them are not.

Curiosity refers to the open stance whereby each member is encouraged and assisted in exploring his or her inner life more fully and openly. There are no preconditions about what members "should" think, feel, want, or perceive. It is a "not-knowing" stance unburdened by assumptions that today's experience must be similar to yesterday's experience. Uncovering a reason for a particular behavior is often only the first step. Curiosity leads that person to look underneath that reason for another, and another, if necessary, searching for reasons that reflect aspects of the narrative. These reasons reflect the strengths and/or vulnerabilities that lie under any problem or defense.

Curiosity is not simply a receptive stance regarding the emotional expressions of the family members. It is also a very active stance that leads clients into their inner lives. This lead taking is often crucial for individuals who do not habitually hold a self-reflective stance. While leading, therapists hold no assumptions about what they will "find." Their open-ended questions are both invitations to self-discovery as well as the means by which the discoveries are more likely to be made. Curiosity *does not* involve a "rational" uncovering of facts. Curiosity *does* involve an active, reflective stance that leads to the cocreation of experience. And it reflects the therapist's deep fascination with the personhood of the other.

Whereas curiosity primarily lies within the reflective component of the dialogue, *empathy* lies primarily within the affective component. Curiosity is the cutting edge of empathy. *Empathy deepens the understanding created by curiosity by affectively joining with the person in the experiences that are being uncovered.* Combining with curiosity, empathy does not lose its perspective of the event, and so it ensures that the intersubjective quality of the experience will be present and able to facilitate a reexperience of the event by the clients. *Therapist empathy often serves to coregulate the emotions associated with the stressful events or conflicts so that clients are able to more fully reflect on the events and experience them more deeply.* Within the context of the therapist's empathy, family members are often able to begin to experience empathy for each other and for themselves.

5. *Narrative flow.* Within the safety and creative exploration of the A-R dialogue, facilitated by PACE, family members are often now able to participate, fully and spontaneously, in the intersubjective experience of coregulating emotions and cocreating new experiences within and among each other. The nature of the A-R dialogue often creates a momentum that invites and welcomes further contributions that tend to make the narrative under focus more understandable and coherent. The forward momentum of the dialogue enables family members to share experiences that they would otherwise never feel safe enough to disclose. The dialogue frequently creates a joint experience of "storytelling" that seems to encourage all to contribute. This tone conveys clearly that within this intersubjective process of exploring, sharing, and even cocreating experiences, the experiences all have equal value and importance. It is not a search for who is "right," since that term has no place in the experiential realm. Experiences simply are, they are never "right" or "wrong."

Within such a narrative flow, emotional communication occurs more safely and spontaneously. Expressions of anger, sadness, fear, or shame are accepted as representing a feature one family member's experience. In this context, when the child expresses anger, the parent is less likely to respond defensively and more likely to understand and experience empathy for his or her child's anger and the distress that it may represent.

The therapist ensures that the dialogue does not drift into areas of disorganized distractions or repetitive criticism. The therapeutic task is to assist family members in creating their joint and separate stories; the therapist must focus on the plots, the underlying narratives, that give meaning to the behaviors of the various family members.

6. *Moments of absorption and transformation.* When the therapy dialogue begins to convey frequent intersubjective qualities, the therapist is often able to facilitate "moments of absorption" in which the parent and child experience each other in the depth of the relationship—much like how they experienced each other when the child was an infant. In speaking of "moments of absorption," I am building upon the "moments of meeting" described by Dan Stern (2004) and colleagues with the Boston Change Process Study Group. The "meeting" that I wish to facilitate between parent and child begins with an act of reciprocal discovery and is immediately followed by rich joint affective experiences wherein time stands still and nothing else exists beyond the other at that moment in time. The meeting is intersubjectivity at its most complete,

similar to that between a parent and infant, though with a greater reciprocal reflective component. It is not a meeting over tea "but a bold swinging—demanding the most intensive stirring of one's being—into the life of the other" (Buber, 1965, p. 81).

At these moments the therapist encourages open, affective, vulnerable, and empathic communication between parent and child while they (often) gaze into each others eyes. Such moments of absorption activate the depth of confidence and trust within the child that is described as "attachment security" and leaves both parent and child receptive to the contingent intersubjective expressions of the other. Time and space are experienced differently and the relationship becomes transformed, leading to the transformation of each. Because they are absorbed in each other, the emotional communications being expressed have a much deeper impact on both. Differences in subjective experience are much easier to accept and repair, if necessary, within the experience of mutual love that is generated by these moments. (There are many similarities between moments of absorption and the transformational affects presented by Fosha, 2000; see also, Fosha, Chapter 7, this volume.)

Therapists are aware that when a family comes for treatment, emotional closeness is not likely to have been experienced by family members for some time. The confidence and openness that reflect attachment security are likely to be weak or nonexistent. When the therapist is able to maintain the flow of intersubjective dialogue, there are likely to be opportunities to encourage moments of absorption that may be transforming for family members. Often family members have "ah-ha" experiences with each other in which they seem to experience the other in a deeper way. Parents are often able to experience the strengths and vulnerabilities of their child, which they previously had not noticed. Children are often able to experience their parents' love, commitment, and compassion for them in ways that they previously had not noticed. To the therapist, it often appears that the parent and child are discovering each other as well as the depth and importance of their relationship in ways that they had not experienced, possibly for years. During moments of absorption between parent and child, they have a strong emotional experience of intimacy wherein they are lost in each other's gaze while spontaneously showing a soft and joyful smile and reaching out to touch the other. These moments often seem to be mildly disorienting in that both parent and child seem to suddenly remember that they are in the therapist's office, and they then look at the therapist with a mixture of pride, joy, and possibly mild embarrassment that their emotional intimacy was witnessed by him or her.

These moments of meeting and absorption are often transforming to both parent and child, and to their relationship. The conflicts and experiences of separateness suddenly disappear and the lived experience of their relationship enables each to see the other with an open and loving gaze. The event that precipitated the conflicts are now experienced as representing mild differences of opinion or misperceptions. That event is now easier to accept, understand, and probably respond to differently. More importantly, however, is the probability that similar conflicts and differences in the future are more likely to be experienced as simply representing the ebb and flow that occurs when autonomy and intimacy—both highly valued—move along together within the family.

For example, early in the family treatment of a 10- year-old girl and her parents, both mother and daughter became aware that although there was ongoing anger between them that existed on the surface, underneath was a similarly intense stream of fear and sadness over their lack of emotional intimacy. After they smiled and acknowledged their tears, the therapist asked them to hold hands and look into each other's eyes. Mom was asked to tell her daughter what she saw in her daughter's eyes.

MOM: I see my lovely child. I see her determination and strength, and also her goodness and gentleness. I see my daughter who is so special to me. I see the person who is much more than her anger. I feel so sorry that at times I have not seen my daughter the way I see her now. My wonderful daughter. (*Mom pulled her daughter to her and they swayed back and forth on the couch.*)

THERAPIST: (*to daughter*) Would you look into your mom's eyes for a moment and tell me what you see in her eyes?

DAUGHTER: I see her . . . loving me. I see that she loves me. She seems very happy. (*Mother and daughter then stare into each other's eyes for a minute, become tearful, and then begin to laugh, get quiet again, smile warmly at each other, and then laugh again.*)

THERAPIST: You two seem to be remembering your life together when you were mother and baby and there was nothing else. You seem to be feeling a bit of that again right now—that special time, that you might have forgotten for awhile.

MOM: Yes, maybe I did. But never again. Never again (*hugs her daughter again*).

Following this interchange, the father was asked for his experience of his wife and daughter, and he spoke glowingly about his love for them both and his joy in their relationship.

This moment of absorption for these three family members transformed the nature of their subsequent conflicts and relationship repair. Disagreements did not seem to matter as much for either. Attachment security became a vital reality again and served as a safe context in which conflicts—differences in subjective experiences—came and went without causing significant stress to the relationship.

Summary

Emotional communications within a family characterized by attachment security generate a resonating tone that carries vitality into the family dialogues. This resonance enables the unique subjective experiences of each member to contribute to the family tapestry. Differences in experiences bring a rich diversity to the developing family history and are not a threat to the safety of the members. Differences that create conflict or doubt are often quickly repaired, enabling autonomy and intimacy to develop together.

Emotional communications within a family that comes for treatment often are reactive, one-directional expressions meant to intimidate and win submission. Or they are rigidly avoided in order to maintain a false front of family harmony.

The family therapist is wise to engage this family intersubjectively, with joined affect, awareness, and intention, in a reciprocal, nonlinear dialogue wherein all participants can engage in the very A-R dialogues that will lead the family into the type of emotional communications that can be transforming. In these communications, the intention is to convey one's own experience while at the same time being receptive to the experience of the other. These communications enable family members to influence each other—to have a positive impact on each other or to resolve conflicts with each other—without ignoring anyone's perspective.

The family therapist also is aware of the value of assisting parent and child in remembering and reexperiencing those moments of meeting and absorption that characterized their first years together. Such moments were transforming in the development of both parent and child then, and they can also be transforming now. When he or she does facilitate such moments, the therapist—who is also participating in the dialogue intersubjectively—is transformed by the experience. The emerging intimacy and autonomy of the family members is likely to have an impact on him or her as well.

References

Adamec, R. E., Blundell, J., & Burton, P. (2003). Phosphorylated cyclic AMP response element bonding protein expression induced in the periaqueductal gray by predator stress; its relationship to the stress experience, behavior, and limbic neural plasticity. *Progress in Neuro-Pharmacology and Biological Psychiatry, 27*, 1243–1267.

Adamec, R. E., & Young, B. (2000). Neuroplasticity in specific limbic system circuits may mediate specific kindling induced changes in animal affect: Implications for understanding anxiety associated with epilepsy. *Neuroscience and Biobehavioral Reviews, 24*, 705–723.

Adler, H. M. (2002). The sociophysiology of caring in the doctor–patient relationship. *Journal of General Internal Medicine, 17*, 883–890.

Adolphs, R. (2002). Trust in the brain. *Nature Neuroscience, 5*, 192–193.

Aftanas, L. I., Savotina, L. N., Makhnev, V. P., & Reva, N. V. (2005). Analysis of evoked EEG synchronization and desynchronization during perception of emotogenic stimuli: Association with autonomic activation processes. *Neuroscience and Behavioral Physiology, 951–957.*

Alcaro, A., Huber, R., & Panksepp, J. (2007). Behavioral functions of the mesolimbic dopaminergic system: An affective neuroethological perspective. *Brain Research Reviews, 56*, 283–321.

Ainsworth, M.D.S., Blehar, M. C., Waters, E., & Wall, S. (1978). *Patterns of attachment: A psychological study of the strange situation.* Hillsdale, NJ: Lawrence Erlbaum.

Aitken, K. J. (2008). Intersubjectivity, affective neuroscience, and the neurobiology of autistic spectrum disorders: A systematic review. *Keio Journal of Medicine, 57*(1), 15–36.

Aitken, K. J., & Trevarthen, C. (1997). Self–other organization in human psychological development. *Development and Psychopathology, 9*, 651–675.

Alexander, F., & French, T. M. (1980). *Psychoanalytic therapy: Principles and application.* Lincoln, NE: University of Nebraska Press. (Original work published 1946)

Alexander, P. C. (1993). Application of attachment theory to the study of sexual abuse. *Journal of Consulting and Clinical Psychology, 60*, 185–195.

Allan, J. *Mentalizing.* Retrieved May 20, 2008, from http://www.menningerclinic.com/resources/Mentalizingallen.html.

Allen, J. G. (2001). *Traumatic relationships and serious mental disorders.* Chichester, UK: Wiley.

Allen, J. G., Console, D. A., & Lewis, L. (1999). Dissociative detachment and memory impairment: Reversible amnesia or encoding failure? *Comprehensive Psychiatry, 40*, 160–171.

Allman, J. M., Watson, K. K., Tetreault, N. A., & Hakeem, A. Y. (2005). Intuition and autism: A possible role for Von Economo neurons. *Trends in Cognitive Sciences, 9*, 367–373.

Alvarez, A. (2006). Some questions concerning states of fragmentation: Unintegration, under-integration, disintegration, and the nature of early integrations. *Journal of Child Psychotherapy*, 32, 158–180.

Arnold, M. B. (1960). *Emotion and personality*. New York: Columbia University Press.

Baker, K. B., & Kim, J. J. (2004). Amygdalar lateralization in fear conditioning: Evidence for greater involvement of the right amygdala. *Behavioral Neuroscience*, 118, 15–23.

Ball, W., & Tronick, F. (1971). Infant responses to impending collision, optical and real. *Science*, 171, 818–820.

Barbas, H. (2007). Flow of information for emotions through temporal and orbitofrontal pathways. *Journal of Anatomy*, 211, 237–249.

Barbas, H., Saha, S., Rempel-Clower, N., & Ghashghaei, T. (2003). Serial pathways from primate prefrontal cortex to autonomic areas may influence emotional expression. *BMC Neuroscience*, 4, 25.

Bargh, J.A., & Chartrand, T.L. (1999). The unbearable automaticity of being. *American Psychologist*, 54, 462–479.

Barrett, L. F. (2006). Are emotions natural kinds? *Perspectives on Psychological Science*, 1, 28–58.

Bartels, A., & Zeki, S. (2000). The neural basis of romantic love. *Neuroreport*, 11(17), 3829–3834.

Bartholomew, K., & Horowitz, L. M. (1991). Attachment styles among young adults: A test of a four category model. *Journal of Personality and Social Psychology*, 61, 226–244.

Bateson, M. C. (1979). The epigenesis of conversational interaction: A personal account of research development. In M. Bullowa (Ed.), *Before speech: The beginning of human communication* (pp. 63–77). Cambridge, UK: Cambridge University Press.

Bazhenova, O. V., Stroganova, T. A., Doussard-Roosevelt, J. A., Posikera, I. A., & Porges, S. W. (2007). Physiological responses of 5-month-old infants to smiling and blank faces. *International Journal of Psychophysiology*, 63, 64–76.

Beauregard, M., Levesque, J., & Bourgouin, P. (2001). Neural correlates of conscious self-regulation of emotion. *Journal of Neuroscience*, 21, RC165.

Beckoff, M., & Allen, C. (1998). Intentional communication and social play: How and why animals negotiate and agree to play. In M. Beckoff & J. Beyers (Eds.), *Animal play: Evolutionary, comparative, and ecological perspectives* (pp. 97–114). New York: Cambridge University Press.

Beckoff, M., & Byers, J. (1998). *Animal play: Evolutionary, comparative, and ecological perspectives*. New York: Cambridge University Press.

Beebe, B., Jaffe, J., Feldstein, S., Mays, K., & Alson, D. (1985). Inter-personal timing: The application of an adult dialogue model to mother–infant vocal and kinesic interactions. In F. M. Field & N. Fox (Eds.), *Social perception in infants* (pp. 217–248). Norwood, NJ: Ablex.

Beebe, B., & Lachmann, F. M. (1994). Representation and internalization in infancy: Three principles of salience. *Psychoanalytic Psychology*, 11(2), 127–165.

Beebe, B., & Lachmann, F. M. (2002). *Infant research and adult treatment: Co-constructing interactions*. Hillsdale, NJ: Analytic Press.

Beebe, B., Stern, D., & Jaffe, J. (1979). The kinesic rhythm of mother–infant interactions. In A. W. Siegman & S. Feldstein (Eds.), *Of speech and time: Temporal speech patterns in interpersonal contexts* (pp. 23–34). Hillsdale, NJ: Erlbaum.

Behry, W. (2007). *A knightmare in shining armor*. (Unpublished manuscript).

Berlyne, D. E. (1960). *Conflict, arousal, and curiosity*. New York: McGraw-Hill.

Bernstein, N. (1967). *Coordination and regulation of movements*. New York: Pergamon Press.

Berscheid, E. (1999). The greening of relationship science. *American Psychologist, 54,* 260–266.

Bion, W. (1972). *Attention and interpretation.* New York: Basic Books.

Bisson, J. I., Ehlers, A., Matthews, R., Pilling, S., Richards, D., & Turner. S. (2007). Psychological treatments for chronic post-traumatic stress disorder: Systematic review and meta-analysis. *British Journal of Psychiatry, 190,* 97–104.

Block, L. (2003). *Small town.* New York: William Morrow.

Bodkin, J. L., Zornberg, G. L., Lucas, S. E., & Cole, J. O. (1995). Buprenorphine treatment of refractory depression. *Journal of Clinical Psychopharmacology, 16,* 49–57.

Bollas, C. (1987). *The shadow of the object: Psychoanalysis of the unthought known.* New York: Columbia University Press.

Bowlby, J. (1980). *Loss.* New York: Basic Books.

Bowlby, J. (1982). *Attachment* (2nd ed.). New York: Basic Books. (Original work published 1969)

Bowlby J. (1988). *A secure base: Parent–child attachment and healthy human development.* New York: Basic Books.

Bowlby, J. (1991). Postscript. In C. Murray Parkes, J. Stevenson-Hinde, & P. Marris (Eds.), *Attachment across the life-cycle.* New York : Routledge.

Bradley, B. S. (2009). Early trios: Patterns of sound and movement in the genesis of meaning between infants. In S. Malloch & C. Trevarthen (Eds.), *Communicative musicality: Exploring the basis of human companionship,* pp. 263–280. Oxford: Oxford University Press.

Bradley, B., & Furrow, J. (2004). Toward a mini-theory of the blamer softening event: Tracking the moment to moment process. *Journal of Marital and Family Therapy, 30,* 233–246.

Bradshaw, G. A., & Schore, A. N. (2007). How elephants are opening doors: Developmental neuroethology, attachment, and social context. *Ethology, 113,* 426–436.

Bråten, S. (1998). (Ed.). *Intersubjective communication and emotion in early ontogeny.* Cambridge, UK: Cambridge University Press.

Bråten, S., & Trevarthen, C. (2007). Prologue: From infant intersubjectivity and participant movements to simulations and conversations in cultural common sense. In S. Bråten (Ed.), *On being moved: From mirror neurons to empathy.* Amsterdam/Philadelphia: Benjamin Publishing.

Brazelton, T. B. (1979). Evidence of communication during neonatal behavioural assessment. In M. Bullowa (Ed.), *Before speech: The beginning of human communication* (pp. 79–88). Cambridge, UK: Cambridge University Press.

Brazelton, T. B. (1993). *Touchpoints: Your child's emotional and behavioral development.* New York: Viking.

Brazelton, T. B., & Nugent, J. K. (1995). *Neonatal behavioural assessment scale* (3rd ed.). London: MacKeith Press.

Bromberg, P. M. (2006). *Awakening the dreamer: Clinical journeys.* Mahwah, NJ: Analytic Press.

Brown, S. (1995). Through the lens of play. *Revision, 17,* 4–14.

Brown, S. (2000). The 'musilanguage' model of music evolution. In N. Wallin, B. Merker, & S. Brown (Eds.), *The origins of music,* pp. 271–300. Boston: The MIT Press.

Bruner, J. S. (1968). *Processes of cognitive growth: Infancy* (Heinz Werner Lectures). Worcester, MA: Clark University Press (with Barri).

Bruner, J. S. (1990). *Acts of meaning.* Cambridge, MA: Harvard University Press.

Buber, M. (1965). *The knowledge of man.* New York: Harper & Row.

Bucci, W. (2002). The referential process, consciousness, and sense of self. *Psychoanalytic Inquiry, 22,* 766–793.

Bull, N. (1945). Towards a clarification of the concept of emotion. *Psychosomatic Medicine, 7*, 210–214.

Burgdorf, J., & Panksepp, J. (2006). The neurobiology of positive emotions. *Neuroscience and Biobehavioral Reviews, 30*, 173–187.

Burgdorf, J., Wood, P. L., Kroes, R. A., Moskal, J. R., & Panksepp, J. (2007). Neurobiology of 50-kHz ultrasonic vocalizations in rats: Electrode mapping, lesion, and pharmacology studies. *Behavioral Brain Research, 182*, 274–283.

Busch, F. N., & Milrod, B. L. (2004). Nature and treatment of panic disorders. In J. Panksepp (Ed.), *Textbook of biological psychiatry* (pp. 345–366). New York: Wiley.

Bushell, W., Olivo, E. L., & Theise, N. D. (Eds.) (in press). *Longevity, Regeneration, and Optimal Health: Integrating Eastern and Western Perspectives.* New York: Annals of the New York Academy of Sciences.

Caldwell, C. (2003). Adult group play therapy. In C. Schaefer (Ed.), *Play therapy with adults* (pp. 301–316). Hoboken, NJ: Wiley.

Cannon, W. B. (1929). Organization for physiological homeostasis. *Physiological Reviews, 9*, 399–431.

Cannon, W. B. (1929). Organization for physiological homeostasis. *Physiological Reviews 1X*, 399–431.

Carretie, L., Hinojosa, J. A., Mercado, F., & Tapia, M. (2005). Cortical response to subjectively unconscious danger. *NeuroImage, 24*, 615–623.

Carter, C. S. (1998). Neuroendocrine perspectives on social attachment and love. *Psychoneuroendocrinology, 23*, 779–818.

Carter, C. S., Devries, A. C., & Getz, L. L. (1995). Physiological substrates of mammalian monogamy: The prairie vole model. *Neuroscience. Behavioral Review, 19*, 303–314.

Casagrande, M., & Bertini, M. (2008). Night-time right hemisphere superiority and daytime left hemisphere superiority: A repatterning of laterality across wake–sleep–wake states. *Biological Psychology, 77*, 337–342.

Cassidy, J. (1999). Attachment and intimacy? In J. Cassidy & P. R. Shaver (Eds.), *Handbook of attachment: Theory, research, and clinical applications.* New York: Guilford Press.

Cassidy, J., & Shaver, P. (Eds.). (1999). *Handbook of attachment: Theory, research, and clinical applications.* New York: Guilford Press.

Castonguay, L., Goldfried, M. R., Wiser, S., Raue, P., & Hayes, A. (1996). Predicting the effect of cognitive therapy for depression: A study of unique and common factors. *Journal of Consulting and Clinical Psychology, 64*, 497–504.

Clothier, P., Manion, I., Gordon Walker, J., & Johnson, S. M. (2001). Emotionally focused interventions for couples with chronically ill children: A two year follow-up. *Journal of Marital and Family Therapy, 28*, 391–399.

Coan, J., Schaefer, H., & Davidson, R. (2006). Lending a hand. *Psychological Science, 17*, 1–8.

Cohn, D. A., Silver, D. H., Cowan, C. P., Cowan, P. A., & Pearson, J. (1992). Working models of childhood attachment and couple relationships. *Journal of Family Issues, 13*, 432–449.

Collins, N. L., & Read, S. J. (1990). Adult attachment, working models, and relationship quality in dating couples. *Journal of Personality and Social Psychology, 58*, 644–663.

Condon, W. S., & Sander, L. S. (1974). Neonate movement is synchronized with adult speech: Interactional participation and language acquisition. *Science, 183*, 99–101.

Coontz, S. (2005). Marriage—a history: From obedience to intimacy or how love conquered marriage.

Coyne, J., Rohrbaugh, M. J., Shoham, V., Sonnega, J., Nicklas, J. M., & Cranford, J.

(2001). Prognostic importance of marital quality for survival of congestive heart failure. *American Journal of Cardiology, 88*, 526–529.

Cozolino, L. L. (2002). *The neuroscience of psychotherapy.* New York: Norton.

Craig, A. D. (2005). Forebrain emotional asymmetry: A neuroanatomical basis? *Trends in Cognitive Science, 9*, 566–571.

Critchley, H. D. (2005). Neural mechanisms of autonomic, affective, and cognitive integration. *Journal of Comparative Neurology, 493*, 154–166.

Critchley, H. D., Elliott, R., Mathias, C. J., & Dolan, R. J. (2000). Neural activity relating to generation and representation of galvanic skin conductance responses: A functional magnetic resonance imaging study. *Journal of Neuroscience, 20*, 3033–3040.

Critchley H. D., Wiens, S., Rotshtein, P., Ohman, A., & Dolan, R. J. (2004). Neural systems supporting interoceptive awareness. *Nature Neuroscience, 7*, 189–195.

Crucian, G. P., Hughes, J. D., Barrett, A. M., Williamson, D.J.G., Bauer, R. M., Bowres, D., et al. (2000). Emotional and physiological responses to false feedback. *Cortex, 36*, 623–647.

Damasio, A. (1994). *Descartes' error: Emotion, reason, and the human brain.* New York: Grosset/Putnam.

Damasio, A. (1999). *The feeling of what happens: Body and emotion in the making of consciousness.* New York: Harcourt, Brace.

Daniels, D., Miselis, R. R., & Flanagan-Cat, L. M. (1999). Central neuronal circuit innervating the lordosis-producing muscles defined by transneuronal transport of pseudorabies virus. *Journal of Neuroscience, 19*, 2823–2833.

Darrow, C. W. (1943). Physiological and clinical tests of autonomic function and autonomic balance. *Physiological Reviews, 23*, 1–36.

Darwin, C. (1965). *The expression of emotion in man and animals.* Chicago: University of Chicago Press. (Original work published 1872)

Davidson, R. J., & Cacioppo, J. T. (1992). New developments in the scientific study of emotion: An introduction to the special section. *Psychological Science, 3*, 21–22.

Davidson, R. J., & Harrington, A. (Eds.) (2002). *Visions of compassion: Western scientists and Tibetan Buddhists examine human nature.* New York: Oxford University Press.

Davidson, R. J., Jackson, D. C., & Kalin, N. H. (2000). Emotion, plasticity, context, and regulation: Perspective from affective neuroscience. *Psychological Bulletin, 126*, 890–909.

Davidson, R. J., Kabat-Zinn, J., Schumacher, J., Rosenkrantz, M., Muller, D., Santorelli, S. F., et al. (2003). Alterations in brain and immune function produced by mindfulness. *Psychosomatic Medicine, 65*(4), 564–570.

Davila, J., Karney, B., & Bradbury, T. N. (1999) Attachment change processes in the early years of marriage. *Journal of Personality and Social Psychology, 29*, 1383–1395.

Davis, K. L., Panksepp, J., & Normansell, L. (2003). The affective neuroscience personality scales: Normative data and implications. *Neuro-Psychoanalysis, 5*, 21–29.

Decety, J., & Chaminade, T. (2003). Neural correlates of feeling sympathy. *Neuropsychologia, 41*, 127–138.

Denver, J. W. (2004). *The social engagement system: Functional differences in individuals with autism.* Unpublished doctoral dissertation, University of Maryland, Baltimore.

Depue, B. E., Curran, T., & Banich, M. T. (2007). Prefrontal regions orchestrte suppression of emotional memories via a two-phase process. *Science, 317*, 215–219.

De Quervain, D. J. (2008). Glucocorticoid-induced reduction of traumatic memories: Implications for the treatment of PTSD. *Progress in Brain Research. 167*, 239–247.

de Spinoza, B. (1677/2005). *Ethics.* (E. Curley, Trans.). London: Penguin Classics.

Diener, M. J., Hilsenroth, M. J., & Weinberger, J. (2007). Therapist affect focus and patient outcomes in psychodynamic psychotherapy: A meta-analysis. *American Journal of Psychiatry, 164,* 936–941.

Dijkstra, K., Kaschak, M. P., & Zwann, R. A. (2006). Body posture facilitates retrieval of autobiographical memories. *Cognition, 102*(1), 139–149.

Dissanayake, E. (2000). *Art and intimacy: How the arts began.* Seattle: University of Washington Press.

Doidge, N. (2007). *The brain that changes itself: Stories of personal triumph from the frontiers of brain science.* New York: Penguin Books.

Donald, M. (2001). *A mind so rare: The evolution of human consciousness.* New York: Norton.

Donaldson, F. (1993). *Playing by heart: The vision and practice of belonging.* Deerfield Beach, FL: Health Communications.

Donaldson, M. (1978). *Children's minds.* Glasgow: Fontana/Collins.

Donaldson, M. (1992). *Human minds: An exploration.* London: Allen Lane/Penguin Books.

Dorpat, T. L. (2001). Primary process communication. *Psychoanalytic Inquiry, 3,* 448–463.

Draghi-Lorenz, R., Reddy, V., & Costall, A. (2001). Re-thinking the development of "nonbasic" emotions: A critical review of existing theories. *Developmental Review, 21*(3), 263–304.

Draijer, N., & Langeland, W. (1999). Childhood trauma and perceived parental dysfunction in the etiology of dissociative symptoms in psychiatric inpatients. *American Journal of Psychiatry, 156,* 379–338.

Eckerdal, P., & Merker, B. (2008). "Music" and the "action song" in infant development: An interpretation. In S. Malloch & C. Trevarthen (Eds.), *Communicative musicality: Narratives of expressive gesture and being human* (pp. 241–262). Oxford, UK: Oxford University Press.

Edelman, G. M. (1999). *The remembered present: A biological theory of consciousness.* New York: Basic Books.

Ekman, P. (1980). Biological and cultural contributions to body and facial movement in the expression of emotions. In A. Rorty (Ed.), *Explaining emotions.* Berkeley, CA: University of California Press.

Ekman, P. (2003). *Emotions revealed.* New York: Henry Holt.

Ekman, P., Levenson, R. W., & Friesen, W. V. (1983). Autonomic nervous system activity distinguishes among emotions. *Science, 16,* 1208–1210.

Ekman, P., & Oster, H. (1979). Facial expressions of emotion. *Annual Review of Psychology, 20,* 527–554.

Emde, R. N. (1983). The pre-representational self and its affective core. *Psychoanalytic Study of the Child, 38,* 165–192.

Ezhov, S. N., & Krivoschekov, S. G. (2004). Features of psychomotor responses and interhemispheric relationships at various stages of adaptation to a new time zone. *Human Physiology, 30,* 172–175.

Fanselow, M., & Lester, L. (1988). A functional behavioristic approach to aversively motivated behavior: Predatory imminence as a determinant of the topography of defensive behavior. In R. Bolles & M. Beecher (Eds.), *Evolution and learning* (pp. 185–212). Hillsdale, NJ: Erlbaum.

Feeney, B. C. (2007). The dependency paradox in close relationships: Accepting dependence promotes independence. *Journal of Personality and Social Psychology, 92,* 268–285.

Feeney, J. (2005). Hurt feelings in couple relationships. *Personal Relationships, 12,* 253–271.

Feldman, C. (2002). The construction of mind and self in an interpretive community. In J. Brockheimer, M. Wang, & D. Olson, (Eds.), *Literacy, narrative, and culture.* London: Curzon.

Feynman, R. (1965). *The character of physical law.* Cambridge: MIT Press.

Field, T. (1992). Infants of depressed mothers. *Development and Psychopathology, 4,* 49–66.

Field, T., Healy, B., Goldstein, S., Perry, S., Bendell, D., Schanberg, S., et al. (1988). Infants of depressed mothers show "depressed" behaviour even with non-depressed adults. *Child Development, 59,* 1569–1579.

Fifer, W. P., & Moon, C. M. (1995). The effects of fetal experience with sound. In J.-P. Lecanuet, W. P. Fifer, N. A. Krasnegor, & W. P. Smotherman (Eds.), *Fetal development: A psychobiological perspective* (pp. 351–366). Hillsdale NJ: Erlbaum.

Fisher, H. E. (2004). *Why we love: The nature and chemistry of romantic love.* New York: Henry Holt.

Fonagy, I. (2001). *Languages within language: An evolutive approach.* Philadelphia: John Benjamins.

Fonagy, P., Gergely, G., Jurist, E. L., & Target, M. (2002). *Affect regulation, mentalization and the development of the self.* New York: Other Press.

Fonagy, P., & Target, M. (1997). Attachment and reflective function: Their role in self-organization. *Development and Psychopathology, 9,* 679–700.

Fosha, D. (2000). *The transforming power of affect: A model for accelerated change.* New York: Basic Books.

Fosha, D. (2001). The dyadic regulation of affect. *Journal of Clinical Psychology/In Session, 57*(2), 227–242.

Fosha, D. (2002). The activation of affective change processes in AEDP (accelerated experiential-dynamic psychotherapy). In J. J. Magnavita (Ed.), *Comprehensive handbook of psychotherapy: Vol. 1. Psychodynamic and object relations psychotherapies* (pp. 309–344). New York: Wiley.

Fosha, D. (2003). Dyadic regulation and experiential work with emotion and relatedness in trauma and disordered attachment. In M. F. Solomon & D. J. Siegel (Eds.), *Healing trauma: Attachment, trauma, the brain and the mind* (pp. 221–281). New York: Norton.

Fosha, D. (2004). "Nothing that feels bad is ever the last step": The role of positive emotions in experiential work with difficult emotional experiences. *Clinical Psychology and Psychotherapy, 11,* 30–43.

Fosha, D. (2005). Emotion, true self, true other, core state: Toward a clinical theory of affective change process. *Psychoanalytic Review, 92*(4), 513–552.

Fosha, D. (2006a). *Accelerated experiential dynamic psychotherapy with Diana Fosha, Ph.D.* Systems of Psychotherapy APA Video Series # 4310759. Available online at *www.apa.org/videos/4310759.html.*

Fosha, D. (2006b). Quantum transformation in trauma and treatment: Traversing the crisis of healing change. *Journal of Clinical Psychology/In Session, 62*(5), 569–583.

Fosha, D. (2008). Transformance, recognition of self by self, and effective action. In K. J. Schneider (Ed.), *Existential-integrative psychotherapy: Guideposts to the core of practice* (pp. 290–320). New York: Routledge.

Fosha, D. (in press). Positive affects and the transformation of suffering into flourishing. W. C. Bushell, E. L. Olivo, & N. D. Theise (Eds.), *Longevity, regeneration, and optimal health: Integrating Eastern and Western perspectives.* New York: Annals of the New York Academy of Sciences.

Fosha, D., Paivio, S. C., Gleiser, K., & Ford, J. (2009). Experiential and emotion-focused therapy. In C. Courtois & J. D. Ford (Eds.), *Complex traumatic stress disorders: An evidence-based clinician's guide* (pp. 286–311). New York: Guilford Press.

Fosha, D., & Yeung, D. (2006). AEDP exemplifies the seamless integration of emotional transformation and dyadic relatedness at work. In G. Stricker & J. Gold (Eds.), *A casebook of integrative psychotherapy* (pp. 165–184). Washington, DC: American Psychiatric Assoiacation Press.

Fraley, C., & Waller, N. G. (1998). Adult attachment patterns: A test of the typological model. In J. A. Simpson & W. S. Rholes (Eds.), *Attachment theory and close relationships* (pp. 77–114). New York: Guilford Press.

Frederick, R. (2009). *Living like you mean it: Use the wisdom and power of your emotions to get the life you really want.* San Francisco: Jossey Bass.

Fredrickson, B. L. (2001). The role of positive emotions in positive psychology: The broaden-and-build theory of positive emotions. *American Psychologist, 56,* 211–226.

Fredrickson, B. L., & Losada, M. (2005). Positive affect and the complex dynamics of human flourishing. *American Psychologist, 60*(7), 687–686.

Freeman, W. J. (2000). Emotion is essential to all intentional behaviors. In M. D. Lewis and I. Granic (Eds.), *Emotion, development, and self-organization: Dynamic systems approaches to emotional development* (pp. 209–235). Cambridge, UK: Cambridge University Press.

Freud, S. (1957). The unconscious. In J. Strachey (Ed. & Trans.), *The standard edition of the complete works of Sigmund Freud* (Vol. 19, pp. 159–205). London: Hogarth Press. (Original work published 1915)

Freud, S. (1961). New introductory lectures on psycho-analysis. In J. Strachey (Ed. & Trans.), *The standard edition of the complete works of Sigmund Freud* (Vol. 22, pp. 1–183). London: Hogarth Press. (Original work published 1933)

Freud, S. (1964). An autobiographical study. In J. Strachey (Ed. & Trans.), *The standard edition of the complete works of Sigmund Freud* (Vol. 19, pp. 227–234). London: Hogarth Press. (Original work published 1925–1926)

Frijda, N. (1986). *The emotions.* Cambridge, UK: Cambridge University Press.

Fukkink, R. G. (2008). Video feedback in widescreen: A meta-analysis of family programs. *Clinical Psychology Review, 28,* 904–916.

Gadea, M., Gomez, C., Gonzalez-Bono, E., R., & Salvador, A. (2005). Increased cortisol and decreased right ear advantage (REA) in dichotic listening following a negative mood induction. *Psychoneuroendocrinology, 30,* 129–138.

Gainotti, G., Caltarirone, C., & Zoccolotti, P. (1993). Left/right and cortical/subcortical dichotomies in the neuropsychological study of human emotions. *Cognition and Emotion, 7,* 71–93.

Galin, D. (1974). Implications for psychiatry of left and right cerebral specialization: A neuropsychological context for unconscious processes. *Archives of General Psychiatry, 31,* 572–583.

Gallese, V. (2003). The roots of empathy. The shared manifold hypothesis and the neural basis of intersubjectivity. *Psychopathology, 36,* 171–180.

Gallese, V. (2005). Embodied simulation: From neurons to phenomenal experience. *Phenomenology and the Cognitive Sciences, 4,* 23–48.

Gallese, V., Keyers, C., & Rizzolatti, G. (2004). A unifying view of the basis of social cognition. *Trends in Cognitive Sciences, 8:9,* 396–403.

Gellhorn, E. (1964). Motion and emotion: The role of proprioception in the physiology and pathology of the emotions. *Psychological Review, 71,* 457–472.

Gendlin, E. T. (1996). *Focusing-oriented psychotherapy: A manual of the experiential method.* New York: Guilford Press.

Ghent, E. (1999). Masochism, submission, surrender: Masochism as a perversion of surrender. In S. A. Mitchell & L. Aron (Eds.), *Relational psychoanalysis: The emergence of a tradition* (pp. 211–242). Hillsdale, NJ: Analytic Press.

Ghent, E. (2002). Wish, need, drive: Motive in light of dynamic systems theory and Edelman's selectionist theory. *Psychoanalytic Dialogues, 12*(5), 763–808.

Gibson, E. J. (1988). Exploratory behavior in the development of perceiving, acting, and the acquiring of knowledge. *Annual Review of Psychology, 39,* 1–41.

Ginot, E. (2007). Intersubjectivity and neuroscience. Understanding enactments and their therapeutic significance within emerging paradigms. *Psychoanalytic Psychology, 24,* 317–332.

Gingrich, B., Liu, Y., Cascio, C., Wang, Z., & Insel, T. R. (2000). D2 receptors in the nucleus accumbens are important for social attachment in female prairie voles (*Microtus ochrogaster*). *Behavioral Neuroscience, 114,* 1, 173–183.

Gleiser, K., Ford, J. D., & Fosha, D. (2008). Exposure and experiential therapies for complex posttraumatic stress disorder. *Psychotherapy: Theory, Research, Practice, Training, 45*(3), 340–360.

Goleman, D. (1995). *Emotional intelligence: Why it can matter more than IQ.* New York: Bantam Books.

Goleman, D. (2006). *Social intelligence: The new science of human relationships.* New York: Bantam Press.

Gomes-Pedro, J., Nugent, J. K., Young, J. G., & Brazelton, T. B. (Eds.). (2002). *The infant and family in the twenty-first century.* New York: Brunner-Routledge.

Goodall, J. (1995). Chimpanzees and others at play. *Revision, 17,* 14–20.

Gottman, J. (1994). An agenda for marital therapy In S. M. Johnson & L. S. Greenberg (Eds.), *The heart of the matter: Perspectives on emotion in marital therapy* (pp. 256–296). New York: Brunner/Mazel.

Gottman, J. (1999). *The seven principles for making marriage work.* New York: Crown.

Gottman, J., Coan, J., Carrere, S., & Swanson, C. (1998). Predicting marital happiness and stability from newlywed interactions. *Journal of Marriage and the Family, 60,* 5–22.

Gottman, J., Katz, L. F., & Hooven, C. (1997). *Meta-emotions: How families communicate emotionally.* New York: Erlbaum.

Grabner, R. H., Fink, A., & Neubauer, A. C. (2007). Brain correlates of self-regulated originality of ideas: Evidence from event related power and phase-locking changes in the EEG. *Behavioral Neuroscience, 121,* 224–230.

Granic, I., & Patterson, G. (2006). Toward a comprehensive model of antisocial development: A dynamic systems approach. *Psychological Reviews, 133*(1), 101–131.

Gratier, M., & Apter-Danon, G. (2008). The musicality of belonging: Repetition and variation in mother–infant interaction. In S. Malloch & C. Trevarthen (Eds.), *Communicative musicality: Narratives of expressive gesture and being human* (pp. 301–327). Oxford, UK: Oxford University Press.

Gratier, M., & Trevarthen, C. (2008). Musical narrative and motives for culture in mother–infant vocal interaction. *Journal of Consciousness Studies.*

Gray J. A. (1971). *The psychology of fear and stress.* New York: McGraw-Hill.

Greenberg, L. S. (2008). Emotion coming of age. *Clinical Psychology: Science and Practice, 14,* 414–421.

Greenberg, L. S., & Johnson, S. M. (1988). *Emotionally focused therapy for couples.* New York: Guilford Press.

Greenberg, L. S., & Paivio, S. C. (1997). *Working with emotions in psychotherapy.* New York: Guilford Press.

Greenberg, L. S., Rice, L. N., & Elliott, R. (1993). *Facilitating emotional change: The moment-by-moment process.* New York: Guilford Press.

Gregg, T. R., & Siegel, A. (2001). Brain structures and neurotransmitters regulating aggression in cats: Implications for human aggression. *Progress in Neuro-Psychopharmacology and Biological Psychiatry, 25,* 91–140.

Grigsby, J., & Stevens, D. (2000). *Neurodynamics of personality.* New York: Guilford Press.

Gross, J. (2001). Emotion regulation in adulthood: Timing is everything. *Current Directions in Psychological Science, 10,* 214–219.

Grotstein, J. S. (2002). *The haunting presences who dwell within us and the nature of their stories: A vitalistic approach to unconscious phantasies.* Paper presented at the first meeting of the International Association for Relational Analysis and Psychotherapy, New York City.

Grotstein, J. S. (2004). The seventh servant: The implications of a truth drive in Bion's theory of "O." *International Journal of Psychoanalysis, 85,* 1081–1101.

Gupta, R. K., Hasan, K. M., Trivedi, R., Pradhan, M., Das, V., Parikh, N. A., et al. (2005). Diffusion tensor imaging of the developing human cerebrum. *Journal of Neuroscience Research, 81,* 172–178.

Gutkowska, J., Janowski, M., Mukaddam-Daher, S., & McCann, S. (2000). Oxytocin is a cardiovascular hormone. *Brazilian Journal of Medical and Biological Research, 33,* 625–633.

Halliday, M.A.K. (1975). *Learning how to mean: Explorations in the development of language.* London: Arnold.

Ham, J., & Tronick, E. (2009). Relational psychophysiology: Lessons from mother–infant physiology research on dyadically expanded states of consciousness. *Psychotherapy Research,* 1–14.

Harker, L., & Keltner, D. (2001). Expressions of positive emotions in women's college yearbook pictures and their relationship to life outcomes across childhood. *Journal of Personality and Social Psychology, 80,* 112–124.

Harrison, A., & Tronick, E. (2007). Contributions to understanding therapeutic change: Now we have a playground. *Journal of the American Psychoanalytic Association, 55*(3), 891–897.

Hart, J. (1991). *Damage.* New York: Columbine Fawcett.

Hart, S., & Legerstee, M. (Eds.). (in press). *Handbook of jealousy: Theories, principles, and multidisciplinary approaches.* Hoboken, NJ: Wiley Blackwell.

Hartikainen, K. M., Ogawa, K. H., Soltani, M., & Knight, R. T. (2007). Emotionally arousing stimuli compete for attention with left hemispace. *NeuroReport, 18,* 1929–1933.

Hawkley, L., Masi, C. M., Berry, J., & Cacioppo, J. (2006). Loneliness is a unique predictor of age related differences in systolic blood pressure. *Journal of Psychology and Aging, 21,* 152–164.

Heath, R. G. (1996). *Exploring the mind–body relationship.* Baton Rouge, LA: Moran.

Heilman, K. M. (1997). The neurobiology of emotional experience. *Journal of Neuropsychiatry and Clinical Neurosciences, 9,* 439–448.

Henry, J. P. (1993). Psychological and physiological responses to stress: The right hemisphere and the hypothalamo–pituitary–adrenal axis, an inquiry into problems of human bonding. *Integrative Physiological and Behavioral Science, 28,* 369–387.

Herman, B. H., & Panksepp, J. (1981). Ascending endorphinergic inhibition of distress vocalization. *Science, 211,* 1060–1062.

Herman, J. (1992). *Trauma and recovery.* New York: Basic Books.

Hess, W. R. (1954). *Diencephalon: Autonomic and extrapyramidal functions.* Orlando, FL: Grune & Stratton.

Hesse, E., & Main, M. M. (1999). Second-generation effects of unresolved trauma in nonmaltreating parents: Dissociated, frightened, and threatening parental behavior. *Psychoanalytic Inquiry, 19,* 481–540.

Hesse, E., & Main, M. M. (2006). Frightened, threatening, and dissociative parental behavior in low-risk samples: Description, discussion, and interpretations. *Development and Psychopathology, 18,* 309–343.

Hilz, M. J., Devinsky, O., Szczepanska, H., Borod, J. C., Marthol, H., & Tutaj, M. (2006). Right ventromedial prefrontal lesions result in paradoxical cardiovascular activation with emotional stimuli. *Brain, 129,* 3343–3355.

Hinde, R. A. (1979). *Towards understanding relationships.* London: Academic Press.

Hobson, J. (1994). *The chemistry of conscious states.* New York: Back Bay Books.

Hofer, M. A. (1970). Cardiac respiratory function during sudden prolonged immobility in wild rodents. *Psychosomatic Medicine, 32*, 633–647.

Holmes, J. (1996). *Attachment, intimacy and autonomy: Using attachment theory in adult psychotherapy.* Northdale, NJ: Jason Aronson.

Holstege, G., Bandler, R., & Saper, C. B. (Eds.). (1996). *The emotional motor system.* Amsterdam: Elsevier.

Holstege G., Georgiadis, J. R., Paans, A. M., Meiners, L. C., van der Graaf, F. H., & Reinders, A. A. (2003) Brain activation during human male ejaculation. *Journal of Neuroscience, 23*, 9185–9193.

Holt, R. (1967). The development of the primary process: A structural view. In R. Holt (Ed.), *Motivation and thought* (pp. 344–384). New York: International Universities Press.

Hoppe, K. D. (1977). Split brains and psychoanalysis. *Psychoanalytic Quarterly, 46*, 220–244.

Howard, M. F., & Reggia, J. A. (2007). A theory of the visual system biology underlying development of spatial frequency lateralization. *Brain and Cognition, 64*, 111–123.

Hughes, D. (2004). An attachment-based treatment of maltreated children and young people. *Attachment and Human Development, 6*, 263–278.

Hughes, D. (2006). *Building the bonds of attachment* (2nd ed.). Lanham, MD: Jason Aronson.

Hughes, D. (2007). *Attachment-focused family therapy.* New York: Norton.

Hughes, D. (2009). *Attachment-focused parenting.* New York: Norton.

Huston, T. L., Caughlin, J. P., Houts, R. M., Smith, S. E., & George, L. J. (2001). The connubial crucible: Newly-wed years as predictors of delight, distress, and divorce. *Journal of Personality and Social Psychology, 80*, 237–252.

Ikemoto, S., & Panksepp, J. (1999). The role of nucleus accumbens dopamine in motivated behavior: A unifying interpretation with special reference to reward-seeking. *Brain Research Reviews, 31*, 6–41.

Insel, T. R., & Young, L. J. (2001). The neurobiology of attachment. *Nature Reviews Neuroscience, 2*, 129–136.

Izard, C. (1977). *Human emotions.* New York: Plenum Press.

Jackson, J. H. (1931). *Selected writings of J.H. Jackson: Vol. I.* London: Hodder & Soughton.

Jaffe J., Stern D. N., & Peery J. C. (1973). Conversational coupling of gaze behavior in prelinguistic human development. *Journal of Psycholinguistic Research, 2*, 321–330.

James, W. (1894). The physical basis of emotion. *Psychological Review, 101*, 205–210.

James, W. (1902). *The varieties of religious experience: A study in human nature.* New York: Penguin Classics.

James, W. (1950). *The principles of psychology: Vol. 2.* New York: Dover. (Original work published 1890)

Janet, P. (1925). *Principles of psychotherapy.* London: George Allen & Unwin.

Johnson, S. M. (2002). *Emotionally focused couple therapy with trauma survivors: Strengthening attachment bonds.* New York: Guilford Press.

Johnson, S. M. (1998). Listening to the music: Emotion as a natural part of systems theory. *Journal of Systemic Therapies, 17*, 1–17.

Johnson, S. M. (2003a). Paper & videotape presented at the Anatomy of Intimacy conference, University of California, Irvine.

Johnson, S. M. (2003b). Attachment theory: A guide for couple therapy. In S. M. Johnson & V. Whiffen (Eds.), *Attachment processes in couples and families* (pp. 103–123). New York: Guilford Press.

Johnson, S. M. (2004). *The practice of emotionally focused couples therapy: Creating connection* (2nd ed.). New York: Brunner-Routledge.

Johnson, S. M. (2005). Emotion and the repair of close relationships. In W. Pinsof & J. Lebow (Eds.), *Family psychology: The art of the science* (pp. 91–113). New York. Oxford University Press.

Johnson, S. M. (2008a). Attachment and emotionally focused couple therapy: Perfect partners. In J. Obegi & E. Berant (Eds.), *Clinical applications of adult attachment* (pp. XX–XX). New York: Guilford Press.

Johnson, S. M. (2008b). Emotionally focused couple therapy: Creating connection. In A. S. Gurman (Ed.), *The clinical handbook of couple therapy* (4th ed., pp. 107–137). New York: Guilford Press.

Johnson, S. M. (2008c). *Hold me tight: Seven conversations for a lifetime of love.* New York: Little, Brown.

Johnson, S. M., Bradley, B., Furrow, J., Lee, A., Palmer, G., Tilley, D., et al. (2005). *Becoming an emotionally focused couple therapist: The workbook.* New York Brunner/Routledge.

Johnson , S. M., & Greenberg, L. S. (1988). Relating process to outcome in marital therapy. *Journal of Marital and Family Therapy, 14,* 175–183.

Johnson, S. M., Hunsley, J., Greenberg, L. S., & Schindler, D. (1999). Emotionally focused couples therapy: Status and challenges. *Clinical Psychology, Science, and Practice, 6,* 67–79.

Johnson , S. M., Makinen, J., & Millikin, J. (2001). Attachment injuries in couple relationships: A new perspective on impasses in couples therapy. *Journal of Marital and Family Therapy, 23,* 135–152.

Jung, C. G. (1946). *The psychology of the transference* (R.F.C. Hull, Trans.). London: Routledge & Kegan Paul.

Keay, K. A., & Bandler, R. (2001). Parallel circuits mediating distinct emotional coping reactions to different types of stress. *Neuroscience and Biobehavioral Reviews, 25,* 669–678.

Kestenberg, J. (1985). The flow of empathy and trust between mother and child. In E. J. Anthony & G. H. Pollack (Eds.), *Parental influences in health and disease* (pp. 137–163). Boston: Little, Brown.

Kiecolt-Glaser, J. K., Loving, T. J., Stowell, J. K., Malarkey, W. B., Lemeshow, S., Dickinson, S., et al. (2005). Hostile marital interactions, proinflammatory cytokine production, and wound healing. *Archives of General Psychiatry, 62,* 1377–1384.

Kirmayer, L. J. (2004). The cultural diversity of healing: Meaning, metaphor and mechanism. *British Medical Bulletin, 69,* 33–48.

Kohut, H. (1984). *How does analysis cure?* Chicago: University of Chicago Press.

Krystal, H. (1978). Trauma and affects. *Psychoanalytic Study of the Child, 33,* 81–116.

Krystal, H. (1988). *Integration and self-healing: Affect, trauma, alexithymia.* Hillsdale, NJ: Analytic Press.

Kugiumutzakis, G. (1998). Neonatal imitation in the intersubjective companion space. In S. Bråten (Ed.), *Intersubjective communication and emotion in early ontogeny* (pp. 63–88). Cambridge, UK: Cambridge University Press.

Kühl, O. (2007). *Musical semantics* (European Semiotics: Language, Cognition, and Culture, No. 7). Bern: Peter Lang.

Kurtz, R. (1990). *Body-centered psychotherapy: The Hakomi method.* Mendicino, CA: LifeRhythm.

Lachmann, F., & Beebe, B. (1996). Three principles of salience in the organization of the patient-analyst interaction. *Psychoanalytic Psychology, 13,* 1–22.

Lamagna, J., & Gleiser, K. (2007). Building a secure internal attachment: An intra-relational approach to ego strengthening and emotional processing with chronically traumatized clients. *Journal of Trauma and Dissociation 8*(1), 25–52.

Lamb, Porges, S. W., et al. (Eds.). *Attachment and bonding: A new synthesis.* Cambridge, MA: MIT Press.

Lane, R. D. (2008). Neural substrates of implicit and explicit emotional processes: A unifying framework for psychosomatic medicine. *Psychosomatic Medicine, 70,* 214–231.

Lane, R. D., Ahern, G. L., Schwartz, G. E., & Kaszniak, A. W. (1997). Is alexithymia the emotional equivalent of blindsight? *Biological Psychiatry, 42,* 834–844.

Lane, R. D., & Schwartz, G. E. (1987). Levels of emotional awareness: A cognitive-developmental theory and its application to psychopathology. *American Journal of Psychiatry, 144,* 133–143.

Langer, S. (1942). Philosophy in a new key. Cambridge, MA: Harvard University Press.

Langley, J. N. (1921). *The autonomic nervous system.* Cambridge, UK: Heffer & Sons.

Lanius, R. A., Williamson, P. C., Bluhm, R. L., Densmore, M., Boksman, K., Neufeld, R.W.J., et al. (2005). Functional connectivity of dissociative responses in posttraumatic stress disorder: A functional magnetic resonance imaging investigation. *Biological Psychiatry, 57,* 873–884.

Larsen, J. K., Brand, N., Bermond, B., & Hijman, R. (2003). Cognitive and emotional characteristics of alexithymia: A review of neurobiological studies. *Journal of Psychosomatic Research, 54,* 533–541.

Lasch, C. (1977). *Haven in a heartless world.* New York: Basic Books.

Leckman, J. F., Grice, D. E., Boardman, J., Zhang, H., Vitale, A., Bondi, C., et al., (1997). Symptoms of obsessive–compulsive disorder. *American Journal of Psychiatry, 154,* 911–917.

LeDoux, J. (1996). *The emotional brain: The mysterious underpinnings of emotional life.* New York: Simon & Schuster.

LeDoux, J. (2002). *Synaptic self: How our brains become who we are.* New York: Viking.

Lee, D. N. (2005). Tau in action in development. In J. J. Rieser, J. J. Lockman, & C. A. Nelson (Eds.), *Action as an organizer of learning and development* (pp. 3–49). Hillsdale, NJ: Erlbaum.

Legerstee, L. (2005). *Infants' sense of people: Precursors to a theory of mind.* Cambridge, UK: Cambridge University Press.

Leite-Panissi, C. R., Coimbra, N. C., & Menescal-de-Oliveira, L. (2003). The cholinergic stimulation of the central amygdala modifying the tonic immobility response and antinociception in guinea pigs depends on the ventrolateral periaqueductal gray. *Brain Research Bulletin, 60,* 167–178.

Lenzi, D., Trentini, C., Pantano, P., Macaluso, E., Iacoboni, M., Lenzi, G. I., et al. (in press). *Neural basis of maternal communication and emotional expression processing during infant preverbal stage: Cerebral cortex.*

Levine, P. (1997). *Waking the tiger: Healing trauma.* Berkeley, CA: North Atlantic Books.

Levy, M. B., & Davis, K. E. (1988). Love styles and attachment styles compared. *Journal of Social and Personal Relationships, 5,* 439–471.

Lewis, L., Kelly, K., & Allen, J. (2004). *Restoring hope and trust: An illustrated guide to mastering trauma.* Baltimore, MD: Sidran Institute Press.

Lewis, M. D. (2005). Bridging emotion theory and neurobiology through dynamic systems modeling. *Behavioral and Brain Sciences, 28,* 169–194.

Lichtenberg, J. D. (1990). On motivational systems. *Journal of the American Psychoanalytic Association, 38*(2), 517–518.

Lichtenberg, J. D. (2001). Motivational systems and model scenes with special reference to bodily experience. *Psychoanalytic Inquiry, 21,* 430–447.

Lichtenberg, J. D., & Kindler, A. R. (1994). A motivational systems approach to the clinical experience. *Journal of the American Psychoanalytic Association, 42*(22), 405–420.

Llinas, R. (2001). *I of the vortex: From neurons to self.* Cambridge, MA: MIT Press.

Loewald, H. W. (1986). Transference-countertransference. *Journal of the American Psychoanalytic Association, 34,* 275–287.

Loewenstein, R. J. (1996). Dissociative amnesia and dissociative fugue. In L. K. Michaelson & W. J. Ray (Eds.), *Handbook of dissociation: Theoretical, empirical, and clinical perspectives* (pp. 307–336). New York: Plenum.

Loizzo, J. (in press). Optimizing learning and quality of life throughout the lifespan: a global framework for research and application. In W. C. Bushell, E. L. Olivo, & N. D. Theise (Eds.), *Longevity, regeneration, and optimal health: Integrating Eastern and Western perspectives.* New York: Annals of the New York Academy of Sciences.

Lyons-Ruth, K. (2000). "I sense that you sense that I sense . . .": Sander's recognition process and the specificity of relational moves in the psychotherapeutic setting. *Infant Mental Health Journal, 21*(1–2), 85–98.

Lyons-Ruth, K. (2005). The two-person unconscious: Intersubjective dialogue, enactive representation, and the emergence of new forms of relational organization. In L. Aron & A. Harris (Eds.), *Relational psychoanalysis* (Vol. 2, pp. 2–45). Hillsdale, NJ: Analytic Press.

Lyons-Ruth, K. (2007). The interface between attachment and intersubjectivity: Perspective from the longitudinal study of disorganized attachment. *Psychoanalytic Inquiry, 26*(4), 595–616.

Lyons-Ruth, K., & Jacobvitz, D. (1999). Attachment disorganization: Unresolved loss, relational violence, and lapses in behavioral and attentional strategies. In J. Cassidy & P. Shaver (Eds.), *Handbook of attachment: Theory, research, and clinical applications* (pp. 520–554). New York: Guilford Press.

Lonstein, J. S., & Stern, J. M. (1998). Site and behavioral specificity of periaqueductal gray lesions on postpartum sexual, maternal, and aggressive behaviors in rats. *Brain Research, 804,* 21–35.

MacIntosh, H. B., & Johnson, S. (2008). Emotionally focused therapy for couples and childhood sexual abuse survivors. *Journal of Marital and Family Therapy, 34,* 298–315.

MacIntosh, H. B., & Johnson, S. M. (in press). Emotionally focused therapy for couples and childhood sexual abuse survivors. *Journal of Marital and Family Therapy.*

Maguire, E. A., Gadian, D. G., Johnsrude, I. S., Good, C. D., Ashburner, J., Frackowiak, R.S.J., & Frith, C. (2000). Navigation–related structural change in the hippocampi of taxi drivers. Proceedings of the National Academy of Sciences of the United States of America, 97, 4398–4403.

Mahler, M. S., Pine, F., & Bergman, A. (1975). *The psychological birth of the human infant.* New York: Basic Books.

Main, M. (1999). Attachment theory: Eighteen points with suggestions for future studies. In J. Cassidy & P. R. Shaver (Eds.), *Handbook of attachment: Theory, research and clinical applications* (pp. 845–888). New York: Guilford Press.

Main, M. (2000). The organized categories of infant, child, and adult attachment: Flexible vs. inflexible attention under attachment-related. *Journal of the American Psychoanalytic Association, 48*(4), 1055–1096.

Main, M., & Goldwyn, R. Adult attachment scoring and classification system. Unpublished manual. Department of Psychology, University of California at Berkeley.

Main, M., Kaplan, N., & Cassidy, J. (1985). Security in infancy, childhood, and adulthood: A move to the level of representation. In I. Bretherton & E. Waters (Eds.), *Growing points in attachment theory and research. Monographs of the Society for Research in Child Development, 50,* (serial no 209) 66–106.

Main, M., & Morgan, H. (1996). Disorganization and disorientation in infant strange situation behavior: Phenotypic resemblance to dissociative states. In L. Michelson & W. J. Ray (Eds.), *Handbook of dissociation: Theoretical, empirical, and clinical perspectives* (pp. 107–138). New York: Plenum Press.

Makinen, J., & Johnson, S. M. (2006). Resolving attachment injuries in couples using emotionally focused therapy: Steps toward forgiveness and reconciliation. *Journal of Consulting and Clinical Psychology, 74,* 1005–1064.

Malloch, S. (1999). Mother and infants and communicative musicality. In Deliègel (Ed.), *Rhythms, musical narrative, and the origins of human communication: Musicae Scientiae, Special Issue* (pp. 29–57). Liège, Belgium: European Society for the Cognitive Sciences of Music.

Malloch, S., & Trevarthen, C. (2008). *Communicative musicality: Exploring the basis of human companionship.* Oxford, UK: Oxford University Press.

Mancia, M. (2006). Implicit memory and early unrepressed unconscious: Their role in the therapeutic process (How the neurosciences can contribute to psychoanalysis). *International Journal of Psychoanalysis, 87,* 83–103.

Markowitsch, H. J., Reinkemeier, A., Kessler, J., Koyuncu, A., & Heiss, W.-D. (2000). Right amygdalar and temperofrontal activation during autobiographical, but not fictitious memory retrieval. *Behavioral Neurology, 12,* 181–190.

Maroda, K. J. (2005). Show some emotion: Completing the cycle of affective communication. In L. Aron & A. Harris (Eds.), *Revolutionary connections: Relational psychoanalysis: Vol. II. Innovation and expansion* (pp. 121–142). Hillsdale, NJ: Analytic Press.

Martindale, C., & Hasenfus, N. (1978). EEG differences as a function of creativity, stage of the creative process, and effort to be original. *Biological Psychology, 6,* 157–167.

Marvin, R., & Britner, P. (1999). Normative development: The ontogeny of attachment. In J. Cassidy & P. Shaver (Eds.), *Handbook of attachment: Theory, research, and clinical applications* (pp. 44–67). New York: Guilford Press.

Marwick, H., & Murray, L. (2008). The effects of maternal depression on the "musicality" of infant-directed speech and conversational engagement. In S. Malloch & C. Trevarthen (Eds.), *Communicative musicality: Narratives of expressive gesture and being human* (pp. 281–300). Oxford, UK: Oxford University Press.

McCullough, L., Kuhn, N., Andrews, S., Kaplan, A., Wolf, J., & Hurley, C. L. (2003). *Treating affect phobia: A manual for short-term dynamic psychotherapy.* New York: Guildford.

McCullough Vaillant, L. (1997). *Changing character: Short-term anxiety-regulating psychotherapy for restructuring defenses, affects, and attachment.* New York: Basic Books.

McFarlane, A. C., & van der Kolk, B. A. (1996). Trauma and its challenge to society. In B. A. van der Kolk, A. C. McFarlane, & L. Weisaeth (Eds.), *Traumatic stress: The effects of overwhelming experience on mind body and society* (pp. 24–45). New York: Guilford Press.

Meadows, M., & Kaplan, R. F. (1994). Dissociation of autonomic and subjective responses to emotional slides in right hemisphere damaged patients. *Neuropsycholgia, 32,* 847–856.

Merker, B. (2005). The liabilities of mobility: A selection pressure for the transition to consciousness in animal evolution. *Consciousness and Cognition, 14*(1), 89–114.

Merker, B. (2006). Consciousness without a cerebral cortex: A challenge for neuroscience and medicine. *Behavioral and Brain Sciences, 30,* 63–134.

Merker, B. (2008). The ritual foundations of human uniqueness. In S. Malloch & C. Trevarthen (Eds.), *Communicative musicality: Narratives of expressive gesture and being human* (pp. 45–59). Oxford, UK: Oxford University Press.

Migdow, J. (2003). The problem with pleasure. *Journal of Trauma and Dissociation, 4,* 5–25.

Mikulincer, M. (1995). Attachment style and the mental representation of the self. *Journal of Personality and Social Psychology, 69,* 1203–1215.

Mikulincer, M., Florian, V., & Weller, A. (1993). Attachment styles, coping strategies, and posttraumatic distress: The impact of the Gulf War in Israel. *Journal of Personality and Social Psychology, 64,* 817–826.

Mikulincer, M., Gillath, O., Halvey, V., Avihou, N., Avidan, S., & Eshkoli, N. (2001). Attachment theory and reactions to others needs: Evidence that the activation of attachment security promotes empathic responses. *Journal of Personality and Social Psychology, 81*, 1205–1224.

Mikulincer, M., & Shaver, P. (2007). *Attachment in adulthood: Structure, dynamics, and change.* New York: Guilford Press.

Mikulincer, M., Shaver, P., Gillath, O., & Nitzberg, R. A. (2005). Attachment, caregiving, and altruism: Boosting attachment security increases compassion and helping. *Journal of Personality Social Psychology, 89*, 817–818.

Minagawa-Kawai, Y., Matsuoka, S., Dan, I., Naoi, N., Nakamura, K., & Kojima, S. (2009). Prefrontal activation associated with social attachment: Facial-emotion recognition in mothers and infants. *Cerebral Cortex, 19*, 284–292.

Misslin, R. (2003). The defense system of fear: Behavior and neurocircuitry. *Clinical Neurophysiology, 33*(2), 55–66.

Mlot, C. (1998). Probing the biology of emotion. *Science, 280*, 1005–1007.

Mollon, P. (1996). *Multiple selves, multiple voices: Working with trauma, violation, and dissociation.* Chichester: Wiley.

Morris J. L., & Nilsson, S. (1994). The circulatory system. In S. Nilsson & S. Holmgren (Eds.), *Comparative physiology and evolution of the autonomic nervous system* (pp. 193–246). Switzerland: Harwood.

Morris, J. S., Ohman, A., & Dolan, R. J. (1999). A subcortical pathway to the right amygdale mediating "unseen" fear. *Proceedings of the National Academy of Sciences, 96*, 1680–1685.

Moskal, J. R., Kroes, R. A., Otto, N. J., Rahimi, O., & Claiborne, B. J. (2006). Distinct patterns of gene expression in the left and right hippocampal formation of developing rats. *Hippocampus, 16*, 629–634.

Murray, L., & Cooper, P. J. (Eds.). (1997). *Postpartum depression and child development.* New York: Guilford Press.

Murray, L., & Trevarthen, C. (1985). Emotional regulation of interactions between two-month-olds and their mothers. In T. M. Field & N. A. Fox (Eds.), *Social perception in infants* (pp. 177–197). Norwood, NJ: Ablex.

Murray, L., & Trevarthen, C. (1986). The infant's role in mother–infant communication. *Journal of Child Language, 13*, 15–29.

Nadel, J., Carchon, I., Kervella, C., Marcelli, D., & Réserbat-Plantey, D. (1999). Expectancies for social contingency in 2-month-olds. *Developmental Science, 2*, 164–173.

Nadel, J., & Muir, D. (2005). (Eds.). *Emotional development.* Oxford, UK: Oxford University Press.

Nagy, E. (2008). Innate intersubjectivity: Newborns' sensitivity to communication disturbance. *Developmental Psychology.*

Nagy, E., & Molnár, P. (2004). *Homo imitans* or *Homo provocans?* Human imprinting model of neonatal imitation. *Infant Behaviour and Development, 27*(1): 54–63.

Nathanson, D. L. (1996). Interview with Donald Nathanson. Available online at *www.behavior.net/column/nathanson.*

Neborsky, R. J. (2006). Brain, mind, and dyadic change processes. *Clinical Psychology: In Session, 62*(5): 523–538.

Neimeyer, R. A. (1993). An appraisal of constructivist therapies. *Journal of Consulting and Clinical Psychology, 61*, 221–234.

Nelson, E. E., & Panksepp, J. (1998). Brain substrates of infant–mother attachment: Contributions of opioids, oxytocin, and norepinephrine. *Neuroscience and Biobehavioral Reviews, 22*, 437–452.

Niedenthal, P. M. (2007). Embodying emotion. *Science* 316(5827): 1002–1005.

Nijenhuis, E.R.S. (2000). Somatoform dissociation: Major symptoms of dissociative disorders. *Journal of Trauma and Dissociation, 1,* 7–32.

Nijenhuis, E.R.S. (2004). *Somatoform dissociation: Phenomena, measurement, and theoretical issues.* New York: Norton.

Nijenhuis, E.R.S., & van der Hart, O. (1999). Forgetting and reexperiencing trauma: From anesthesia to pain. In J.Goodwin & R. Attias (Eds.), *Splintered reflections: Images of the body in trauma* (pp. 35–69). New York: Basic Books.

Nijenhuis, E.R.S., Vanderlinden, J., & Spinhoven, P. (1998). Animal defensive reactions as a model for trauma-induced dissociative reactions. *Journal of Traumatic Stress, 11,* 243–260.

Nijenhuis, E.R.S., van Dyck, R., et al. (1999). Somatoform dissociation discriminates among diagnostic categories over and above general psychopathology. *Australian and New Zealand Journal of Psychiatry, 33*(4), 511–520.

Nitschke, J. B., Heller, W., Palmieri, P. A., & Miller, G. A. (1999). Contrasting patterns of brain activity in anxious apprehension and anxious arousal. *Psychophysiology, 36,* 628–637.

Northoff, G., Henzel, A., de Greck, M., Bermpohl, F., Dobrowolny, H., & Panksepp, J. (2006). Self-referential processing in our brain: A meta-analysis of imaging studies of the self. *Neuroimage, 31,* 440–457.

Northoff, G., & Panksepp, J. (2008). The trans-species concept of self and the subcortical–cortical midline system. *Trends in Cognitive Sciences, 12,* 259–264.

Numan, M., & Insel, T. R. (2003). *The neurobiology of parental behavior.* New York: Springer-Verlag.

Ogawa, J. R., Sroufe, L. A., Weinfield, N. S., Carlson, E. A., & Egeland, B. (1997). Development and the fragmented self: Longitudinal study of dissociative symptomatology in a nonclinical sample. *Development and Psychopathology, 9,* 855–879.

Ogden, P. (2007). *Beneath the words: A clinical map for using mindfulness of the body and the organization of experience in trauma treatment.* Paper presented at Mindfulness and Psychotherapy Conference, Los Angeles, CA.

Ogden, P., & Minton, K. (2000). Sensorimotor psychotherapy: One method for processing trauma. *Traumatology, 5,* 149–173.

Ogden, P., Minton, K., & Pain, C. (2006). *Trauma and the body: A sensorimotor approach to psychotherapy.* New York: Norton.

Ogden, P., Pain, C., Minton, K., & Fisher, J. (2005). Including the body in mainstream psychotherapy for traumatized individuals. *Psychologist–Psychoanalyst, 25*(4), 19–24.

Ogden, T. (1994). The analytic third. Working with intersubjective clinical facts. *International Journal of Psychoanalysis, 75,* 3–19.

Ohnishi, T., et al. (2004). The neural network for the mirror system and mentalizing in normally developed children: An fMRI study. *NeuroReport, 15,* 1483–1487.

Osborne, N. (2009a). Towards a chronobiology of musical rhythm. In S. Malloch & C. Trevarthen (Eds.), *Communicative musicality: Narratives of expressive gesture and being human* (pp. 545–564). Oxford, UK: Oxford University Press.

Osborne, N. (2009b). Music for children in zones of conflict and post-conflict. In S. Malloch & C. Trevarthen (Eds.), *Communicative musicality: Exploring the basis of human companionship* (pp. 331–356). Oxford, UK: Oxford University Press.

Osimo, F. (2001). *Parole, emozioni e videotape: Manuale di psicoterapia breve dinamico-esperienzale (PBD-E).* Milano: FrancoAngeli.

Osimo, F. (2002). Brief psychodynamic therapy. In J. J. Magnavita (Ed.), *Comprehensive Handbook of Psychotherapy, Vol. 1: Psychodynamic and Object Relations Psychotherapies* (pp. 207–238). New York: Wiley.

Osimo, F. (2003). *Experiential short-term dynamic psychotherapy: A manual.* Bloomington, IN: Authorhouse.

Panksepp, J. (1985). Mood changes. *Handbook of clinical neurology: Vol. 1. Clinical neuropsychology* (pp. 271–285). Amsterdam: Elsevier Science Publishers. New York: Norton.

Panksepp, J. (1998a). *Affective neuroscience: The foundations of human and animal emotions.* New York: Oxford University Press.

Panksepp, J. (1998b). The periconscious substrates of consciousness: Affective states and the evolutionary origins of the self. *Journal of Consciousness Studies, 5,* 566–582.

Panksepp, J. (2001). The long-term psychobiological consequences of infant emotions: Prescriptions for the 21st century. *Infant Mental Health Journal, 22,* 132–173.

Panksepp, J. (2003). Trennungsschmerz als mogliche ursache fur panikattacken—neuropsychologische Uberlegungen und Befunde. *Personlichkeitsstorungen: Theorie und Therapie, 7,* 245–251.

Panksepp, J. (2004a). The emerging neuroscience of fear and anxiety disorders. In J. Panksepp (Ed.), *Textbook of biological psychiatry* (pp. 489–520). New York: Wiley.

Panksepp, J. (Ed.) (2004b). *Textbook of biological psychiatry.* New York: Wiley.

Panksepp, J. (2005a). Affective consciousness: Core emotional feelings in animals and humans. *Consciousness and Cognition, 14,* 19–69.

Panksepp, J. (2005b). On the embodied neural nature of core emotional affects. *Journal of Consciousness Studies, 12,* 161–187.

Panksepp, J. (2006). Emotional endophenotypes in evolutionary psychiatry. *Progress in Neuro-Psychopharmacology and Biological Psychiatry, 30,* 774–784.

Panksepp, J. (2007a). Can play diminish ADHD and facilitate the construction of the social brain? *Journal of the Canadian Academy of Child and Adolescent Psychiatry, 10,* 57–66.

Panksepp, J. (2007b). Neuroevolutionary sources of laughter and social joy: Modeling primal human laughter in laboratory rats. *Behavioral Brain Research, 182,* 231–244.

Panksepp, J. (2007c). Neurologizing the psychology of affects: How appraisal-based constructivism and basic emotion theory can coexist. *Perspectives on Psychological Science, 2,* 281–296.

Panksepp, J. (2008a). The affective brain and core-consciousness: How does neural activity generate emotional feelings? In M. Lewis, J. M. Haviland, & L. F. Barrett (Eds.), *Handbook of emotions* (pp. 47–67). New York: Guilford Press.

Panksepp, J. (2008b). Play, ADHD, and the construction of the social brain: Should the first class each day be recess? *American Journal of Play, 1,* 55–79.

Panksepp, J. (2008c). The power of the word may reside in the power of affect. *Integrative Psychological and Behavioral Science, 42,* 47–55.

Panksepp, J. (2009). Primary process affects and brain oxytocin. *Biological Psychiatry, 65,* 725–727.

Panksepp, J. (in press). The evolutionary sources of jealousy: Cross-species approaches to fundamental issues. In. S. L. Hart & M. Lagerstee (Eds.), *Handbook of jealousy: Theories, principles, and multidisciplinary approaches.* New York: Wiley-Blackwell.

Panksepp, J., & Burgdorf, J. (2003). "Laughing" rats and the evolutionary antecedents of human joy? *Physiology and Behavior, 79,* 533–547.

Panksepp, J., Burgdorf, J., Beinfeld, M. C., Kroes, R., & Moskal, J. (2007). Brain regional neuropeptide changes resulting from social defeat. *Behavioral Neuroscience, 121,* 1364–1371.

Panksepp, J., Burgdorf, J., Gordon, N., & Turner, C. (2003). Modeling ADHD-type arousal with unilateral frontal cortex damage in rats and beneficial effects of play therapy. *Brain and Cognition, 52,* 97–105.

Panksepp, J., & Gordon, N. (2003). The instinctual basis of human affect: Affective imaging of laughter and crying. *Consciousness and Emotion, 4,* 197–206.

Panksepp, J., & Harro, J. (2004). The future of neuropeptides in biological psychiatry and emotional psychopharmacology: Goals and strategies. In J. Panksepp (Ed.), *Textbook of biological psychiatry* (pp. 627–660). New York: Wiley.

Panksepp, J., Lensing, P., Leboyer, M., & Bouvard, M. P. (1991). Naltrexone and other potential new pharmacological treatments of autism. *Brain Dysfunction, 4*, 281–300.

Panksepp, J., & Moskal, J. (2008). Dopamine and SEEKING: Subcortical "reward" systems and appetitive urges. In A. Elliot (Ed.), *Handbook of approach and avoidance motivation* (pp. 67–87). Mahwah, NJ: Erlbaum.

Panksepp, J., Normansell, L. A., Cox, J. F., & Siviy, S. (1994). Effects of neonatal decortication on the social play of juvenile rats. *Physiology and Behavior, 56*, 429–443.

Panksepp, J., Normansell, L. A., Herman, B., Bishop, P., & Crepeau, L. (1988). Neural and neurochemical control of the separation distress call. In J. D. Newman (Ed.), *The physiological control of mammalian vocalizations* (pp. 263–300). New York: Plenum Press.

Panksepp, J., & Northoff, G. (2009). The trans-species core self: The emergence of active cultural and neuro-ecological agents through self-related processing within subcortical–cortical midline networks. *Consciousness and Cognition, 18*, 193–215.

Panksepp, J., & Trevarthen, C. (2009). Motive impulse and emotion in acts of musicality and in sympathetic emotional response to music. In S. Maloch & C. Trevarthen (Eds.), *Communicative musicality*. Oxford, UK: Oxford University Press.

Panksepp, J., & Zellner, M. (2004). Towards a neurobiologically based unified theory of aggression. *International Review of Social Psychology, 17*, 37–61.

Papoušek, H., & Papoušek, M. (1977). Mothering and cognitive head start: Psychobiological considerations. In H. R. Schaffer (Ed.), *Studies in mother–infant interaction: The Loch Lomond symposium* (pp. 63–85). London: Academic Press.

Papoušek, H., & Papoušek, M. (1987). Intuitive parenting: A dialectic counterpart to the infant's integrative competence. In J. D. Osofsky (Ed.), *Handbook of infant development* (2nd ed., pp. 669–720). New York: Wiley.

Papoušek, M. P. (1996). Intuitive parenting: A hidden source of musical stimulation in infancy. In I. Deliège & J. Sloboda (Eds.), *Musical beginnings: Origins and development of musical competence* (pp. 88–112). Oxford, UK: Oxford University Press.

Papoušek, M. P. (2007). Communication in infancy: An arena of intersubjective learning. *Infant Behavior and Development, 30*, 258–266.

Pavlicevic, M., & Ansdell, G. (2009). In S. Malloch & C. Trevarthen (Eds.), *Communicative musicality: Exploring the basis of human companionship* (pp. 357–376). Oxford: Oxford University Press.

Pavlov, I. P. (1927). *Conditioned reflexes*. London: Oxford University Press.

Payne, K. (2000). The progressively changing songs of humpback whales: A window on the creative process in a non-human mammal. In N. Wallin, B. Merker, & S. Brown (Eds.), *Origins of music* (pp. xx–xx). Cambridge, MA: MIT Press.

Pessoa, L., McKenna, M., Gutierrez, E., & Ungerleider, L. G. (2002). Neuroprocessing of emotional faces requires attention. *Proceedings of the National Academy of Sciences (USA), 99*(11), 458–463.

Pfaff, D. W. (1999). *Drive: Neurobiological and molecular mechanisms of sexual behavior*. Cambridge, MA: MIT Press.

Phelps, E. A., Delgado, M. R., Nearing, K. I., & LeDoux, J. E. (2004). Extinction learning in humans: Role of the amygdala and vmPFC. *Neuron, 43*, 897–905.

Pincus, D., Freeman, W., & Modell, A. (2007). A neurobiological model of perception. Considerations for transference. *Psychoanalytic Psychology, 24*, 623–640.

Pipp, S., & Harmon, R. J. (1987). Attachment as regulation: A commentary. *Child Development 58*, 648–652.

Podell, K., Iovell, M., & Goldberg, E. (2001). Lateralization of frontal lobe functions. In S. P. Salloway, P. F. Malloy, & J. D. Duffy (Eds.), *The frontal lobes and neuropsychiatric illness* (pp. 83–89). Washington, DC: American Psychiatric Association.

Porges, S. W. (1995). Orienting in a defensive world: Mammalian modifications of our evolutionary heritage—a polyvagal theory. *Psychophysiology, 32,* 301–318.

Porges, S. W. (1997). Emotion: An evolutionary by-product of the neural regulation of the autonomic nervous system. *Annals of the New York Academy of Sciences, 807,* 62–77.

Porges, S. W. (1998). Love: An emergent property of the mammalian autonomic nervous system. *Psychoneuroendocrinology, 23,* 837–861.

Porges, S. W. (2001a). Is there a major stress system at the periphery other than the adrenals? In D. M. Broom (Ed.), *Dahlem workshop on coping with challenge: Welfare in animals including humans* (pp. 135–149).

Porges, S. W. (2001b). The polyvagal theory: Phylogenetic substrates of a social nervous system. *International Journal of Psychophysiology, 42,* 123–146.

Porges, S. W. (2003). Social engagement and attachment: A phylogenetic perspective. *Roots of Mental Illness in Children, Annals of the New York Academy of Sciences, 1008,* 31–47.

Porges, S. W. (2004). Neuroception: A subconscious system for detecting threats and safety. Zero to Three. Retrieved August 8, 2005, from *bbc.psych.uic.edu/pdf/neuroception.pdf.*

Porges, S. W. (2006). The role of social engagement in attachment and bonding: A phylogenetic perspective. In C. S. Carter, L. Ahnert, K. E. Grossman, S. B. Hardy, M. E. Lamb, S. W. Porges, and N. Sachser (Eds.). *Attachment and bonding: A new synthesis.* Cambridge, MA: The MIT Press.

Porges, S. W. (2007). The polyvagal perspective. *Biological Psychology, 74,* 116–143.

Porges, S. W., Doussard-Roosevelt, J. A., & Maiti, A. K. (1994). Vagal tone and the physiological regulation of emotion. *Monograph of the Society for Research in Child Development, 59,* 167–186.

Porges, S. W., Doussard-Roosevelt, J. A., Portales, A. L., & Greenspan, S. I. (1996). Infant regulation of the vagal "brake" predicts child behavior problems: A psychobiological model of social behavior. *Developmental Psychobiology, 29,* 697–712.

Prenn, N. (2009). I second that emotion! On self-disclosure and its metaprocessing. In A. Bloomgarden & R. B. Menutti (Eds.), *The psychotherapist revealed: Therapists speak about self-disclosure* (pp. 85–99). New York: Routledge.

Preter, M., & Klein, D. F. (2008). Panic, suffocation false alarms, separation anxiety, and endogenous opioids. *Neuro-Psychopharmacology and Biological Psychiatry, 32,* 603–612.

Price, J. L. (2005). Free will versus survival: Brain systems that underlie intrinsic constraints on behavior. *Journal of Comparative Neurology, 493,* 132–139.

Rapaport, D. (1951). *Organization and pathology of thought.* New York: Columbia University Press.

Ratey, J. (2002). *A user's guide to the brain: Perception, attention, and the four theaters of the brain.* New York: Vintage Books.

Raz, A. (2004). Anatomy of attentional networks. *Anatomical Records, 281B,* 21–36.

Recordati, G. (2003). A thermodynamic model of the sympathetic and parasympathetic nervous systems. *Autonomic Neuroscience: Basic and Clinical, 103,* 1–12.

Reddy, V. (2005). Feeling shy and showing off: Self-conscious emotions must regulate self awareness. In J. Nadel & D. Muir (Eds.), *Emotional development* (pp. 183–204). Oxford, UK: Oxford University Press.

Reddy, V. (2008). *How infants know minds.* Cambridge, MA: Harvard University Press.

Reddy, V., & Trevarthen, C. (2004). What we learn about babies from engaging with their emotions. *Zero to Three, 24*(3), 9–15.

Resnick, S. (1997). *The pleasure zone: Why we resist good feelings and how to let go and be happy.* Berkeley, CA: Conari Press.

Rholes, W. S., & Simpson, J. A. (2004). *Adult attachment: Theory, research, and clinical implications.* New York: Guilford Press.

Richards, M.P.M. (1973). The development of psychological communication in the first year of life. In J. S. Bruner & F. J. Connolly (Eds.), *The growth of competence* (pp. xx–xx). New York: Academic Press.

Richter, C. P. (1957). On the phenomenon of sudden death in animals and man. *Psychosomatic Medicine, 19,* 191–198.

Rivers, W. (1920). *Instinct and the unconscious: A contribution to a biological theory of the psychoneuroses.* Cambridge, UK: Cambridge University Press.

Rizvi, T. A., Ennis, M., Behbehani, M. M., & Shipley, M. T. (1991). Connections between the central nucleus of the amygdala and the midbrain periaqueductal gray: Topography and reciprocity. *Journal of Comparative Neurology, 303,* 121–131.

Rizzolatti, G., & Arbib, M. A. (1998). Language within our grasp. *Trends in the Neurosciences, 21,* 188–194.

Robarts, J. Z. (2009). Supporting the development of mindfulness and meaning: Clinical pathways in music therapy with a sexually abused child. In S. Malloch & C. Trevarthen (Eds.), *Communicative musicality: Exploring the basis of human companionship* (pp. 377–400). Oxford: Oxford University Press.

Robb, L. (1999). Emotional musicality in mother–infant vocal affect and an acoustic study of postnatal depression. In Deliègel (Ed.), *Rhythms, musical narrative, and the origins of human communication* (pp. 123–151). Liøge, Belgium: European Society for the Cognitive Sciences of Music.

Roelofs, K., Keijers, G.P.J., Hoogduin, K.A.L., Naring, G.W.B., & Moene, F. C. (2002). Childhood abuse in patients with conversion disorder. *American Journal of Psychiatry, 159,* 1908–1913.

Rotenberg, V. S. (2004). The ontogeny and asymmetry of the highest brain skills and the pathogenesis of schizophrenia. *Behavioral and Brain Sciences, 27,* 864–865.

Rueda, M. R., Posner, M. I., & Rothbart, M. K. (2005). The development of executive attention: Contributions to the emergence of self-regulation. *Developmental Neuropsychology, 28,* 573–594.

Russ, S.W. (2000–2001). Primary-process thinking and creativity: Affect and cognition. *Creativity Research Journal, 13,* 27–35.

Russell, E., & Fosha, D. (2008). Transformational affects and core state in AEDP: The emergence and consolidation of joy, hope, gratitude, and confidence in the (solid goodness of the) self. *Journal of Psychotherapy Integration, 18*(2), 167–190.

Ryan, J. (1974). Early language development: Towards a communicational analysis. In M.P.M. Richards (Ed.), *The integration of a child into a social world* (pp. 185–213). Cambridge, UK: Cambridge University Press.

Ryan, R. (2007). Motivation and emotion: A new look and approach for two reemerging fields. *Motivation and Emotion, 31,* 1–3.

Safran, J., & Muran, C. (2003). Negotiating the therapeutic alliance. A relational treatment guide. New York: Guilford.

Sander, L. W. (1977). The regulation of exchange in infant–caregiver systems and some aspects of the context-contrast relationship. In L. A. Rosenblum (Ed.), *Interaction conversation and the development of language.* New York: Wiley.

Sander, L. W. (1995). Identity and the experience of specificity in the process of recognition. *Psychoanalytic Dialogues, 5,* 579–594.

Sander, L. W. (2002). Thinking differently: Principles in process in living systems and the specificity of being known. *Psychoanalytic Dialogues, 12*(1), 11–42.

Sands, S. H. (1994). What is dissociated? *Dissociation, 7*, 145–152.

Sano, K., Mayanagi, Y., Sekino, H., Ogashiwa, M., & Ishijima, B. (1970). Results of stimulation and destruction of the posterior hypothalamus in man. *Journal of Neurosurgery, 33*, 689–707.

Sarkar, J., & Adshead, G. (2006). Personality disorders as disorganization of attachment and affect regulation. *Advances in Psychiatric Treatment, 12*, 297–305.

Sato, W., & Aoki, S. (2006). Right hemisphere dominance in processing unconscious emotion. *Brain and Cognition, 62*, 261–266.

Saugstad, L. F. (1998). Cerebral lateralization and rate of maturation. *International Journal of Psychophysiology, 28*, 37–62.

Scaer, R. C. (2001). The neurophysiology of dissociation and chronic disease. *Applied Psychophysiology and Biofeedback, 26*(1), 73–91.

Schacter, D. L. (1996). *Searching for memory: The brain, the mind, and the past.* New York: Basic Books.

Schechter, D. S. (2004). How post-traumatic stress affects mothers' perceptions of their babies: A brief video feedback intervention makes a difference. *Zero to Three, 24*(3), 43–49.

Schnall, S., & Laird, J. D. (2003). Keep smiling: Enduring effects of facial expressions and postures on emotional experience and memory. *Cognition and Emotion, 17*(5), 787–797.

Schore, A. N. (1991). Early superego development: The emergence of shame and narcissistic affect regulation in the practicing period. *Psychoanalysis and Contemporary Thought, 14*, 187–250.

Schore, A. N. (1994). *Affect regulation and the origin of the self.* Mahweh, NJ: Erlbaum.

Schore, A. N. (1997). Interdisciplinary developmental research as a source of clinical models. In M. Moskowitz, C. Monk, C. Kaye, & S. Ellman (Eds.), *The neurobiological and developmental basis for psychotherapeutic intervention* (pp. 1–71). New York: Jason Aronson.

Schore, A. N. (1999). Commentary on emotions: Neuro-psychoanalytic views. *Neuro-Psychoanalysis, 1*, 49–55.

Schore, A. N. (2001). The effects of relational trauma on right brain development, affect regulation, and infant mental health. *Infant Mental Health Journal, 22*, 201–269.

Schore, A. N. (2002a). Advances in neuropsychoanalysis, attachment theory, and trauma research: Implications for self psychology. *Psychoanalytic Inquiry, 22*, 433–484.

Schore, A. N. (2002b). Dysregulation of the right brain: A fundamental mechanism of traumatic attachment and the psychopathogenesis of posttraumatic stress disorder. *Australian and New Zealand Journal of Psychiatry, 36*, 9–30.

Schore, A. N. (2003a). *Affect dysregulation and disorders of the self.* New York: Norton.

Schore, A. N. (2003b). *Affect regulation and the repair of the self.* New York: Norton.

Schore, A. N. (2003c). Early relationship trauma, disorganized attachment, and the development of a predisposition to violence. In M.F. Solomon & D.J. Siegel (Eds.), *Healing trauma: Attachment, trauma, the brain, and the mind* (pp. 107–167). New York: Norton.

Schore, A. N. (2005a). Attachment, affect regulation, and the developing right brain: Linking developmental neuroscience to pediatrics. *Pediatrics in Review, 26*, 204–211.

Schore, A. N. (2005b). A neuropsychoanalytic viewpoint: Commentary on paper by Steven H. Knoblauch. *Psychoanalytic Dialogues, 15*, 829–854.

Schore, A. N. (2007). Review of *Awakening the dreamer: Clinical journeys* by Philip M. Bromberg. *Psychoanalytic Dialogues, 17*, 753–767.

Schore, A. N. (in press). Attachment trauma and the developing right brain: Origins of pathological dissociation. In P. F. Dell & J. A. O'Neil (Eds.), *Dissociation and the dissociative disorders: DSM-V and beyond.* New York: Routledge.

Schore, J. R., & Schore, A. N. (2008). Modern attachment theory: The central role of affect regulation in development and treatment. *Clinical Social Work Journal, 36,* 9–20.

Schuengel, C., Bakersmans-Kranenburg, M. J., & van IJzendoorn, M. H. (1999). Frightening maternal behavior linking unresolved loss and disorganized infant attachment. *Journal of Consulting and Clinical Psychology, 67,* 54–63.

Schutz, L. E. (2005). Broad-perspective perceptual disorder of the right hemisphere. *Neuropsychology Review, 15,* 11–27.

Schwartz, J. M. (1998). Neuroanatomical aspects of cognitive behavioral therapy in obsessive compulsive disorder: An evolving perspective on brain and behavior. *British Journal of Psychiatry, 173,* Supplement 35, 39–45.

Schwartz, J. M., & Begley, S. (2002). *The mind and the brain: Neuroplasticity and the power of mental force.* New York: Harper Perennial.

Segal, Z., Teasdale, J., & Williams, M. (2002). *Mindfulness-based cognitive therapy for depression.* New York: Guilford Press.

Selby, J. M., & Bradley, B. S. (2003). Infants in groups: A paradigm for study of early social experience. *Human Development, 46,* 197–221.

Selye, H. (1936). A syndrome produced by diverse nocuous agents. *Nature, 138,* 32.

Selye, H. (1956). *The stress of life.* New York: McGraw-Hill.

Senchak, M., & Leonard, K. (1992). Attachment styles and marital adjustment among newly wed couples. *Journal of Social and Personal Relationships, 9,* 51–64.

Shaver, P., & Clarke, C. L. (1994). The psychodynamics of adult romantic attachment. In J. Masling & R. Bornstein (Eds.), *Empirical perspectives on object relations theory* (pp. 105–156). Washington, DC: American Psychiatric Association.

Shaver, P., & Mikulincer, M. (2007). Adult attachment strategies and the regulation of emotion. In J. J.Gross (Ed.), *Handbook of emotion regulation* (pp. 446–465). New York: Guilford Press.

Shewmon, D. A., Holmes, D. A., & Byrne, P. A. (1999). Consciousness in congenitally decorticate children: Developmental vegetative state as self-fulfilling prophecy. *Developmental Medicine and Child Neurology, 41,* 364–374.

Shuren, J. E., & Grafman, J. (2002). The neurology of reasoning. *Archives of Neurology, 59,* 916–919.

Siegel, A. (2005). *The neurobiology of aggression and rage.* Boca Raton, FL: CRC Press.

Siegel, D. J. (1999). *The developing mind.* New York: Guilford Press.

Siegel, D. J. (2003). An interpersonal neurobiology of psychotherapy: The developing mind and the resolution of trauma. In M. F. Solomon & D. J. Siegel (Eds.), *Healing trauma: Attachment, trauma, the brain, and the mind* (pp. 1–54). New York: Norton.

Siegel, D. J. (2007). *The mindful brain.* New York: Norton.

Siegel, D. J. (in press). *Mindsight.* New York: Bantam Books.

Siegel, D. J., & Hartzell, M. (2004). *Parenting from the inside out.* New York: Tarcher.

Simpson, J. A. (1990). The influence of attachment style on romantic relationships. *Journal of Personality and Social Psychology, 59,* 971–980.

Simpson, J. A. (1999). Attachment theory in modern evolutionary perspective. In J. Cassidy & P. R. Shaver (Eds.), *Handbook of attachment: Theory, research, and clinical applications* (pp. 115–140). New York: Guilford Press.

Simpson, J. A., Rholes, W., & Nelligan, J. (1992). Support seeking and support giving within couples in an anxiety provoking situation: The role of attachment styles. *Journal of Personality and Social Psychology, 62,* 434–446.

Simpson, J. A., Rholes, W. S., & Phillips D. (1996). Conflict in close relationships: An attachment perspective. *Journal of Personality and Social Psychology, 71,* 899–914.

Siviy, S. M., & Panksepp, J. (1987). Juvenile play in the rat: Thalamic and brain stem involvement. *Physiology and Behavior, xx,* 39–55.

Smith, A. (1982). Of the nature of that imitation which takes place in what are called the imitative arts. In W.P.D. Wightman & J. C. Bryce (Eds.). *Essays on philosophical subjects* (pp.176–213). Indianapolis: Liberty Fund. (Original work published 1777)

Smith, A. (1984). *Theory of moral sentiments.* Indianapolis: Liberty Fund. (Original work published 1759)

Smith, E. (1985). *The body in psychotherapy.* Jefferson, NC: McFarland.

Solms, M., & Turnbull, O. (2002). *The brain and the inner world.* New York: Other Press.

Solomon, M. (1989). *Narcissism and intimacy: Love and marriage in an age of confusion.* New York: Norton.

Solomon, M. (1994). *Lean on me: The power of positive dependency in intimate relationships.* New York: Simon & Schuster.

Solomon, M., & Tatkin, S. (in press). *Love and war in intimate relationships: How the mind, brain, and body interact.* New York: Norton.

Solomon, Z., Ginzberg, K., Mikulincer, M., Neria, Y., & Ohry, A. (1998). Coping with war captivity: The role of attachment style. *European Journal of Personality, 12,* 271–285.

Spence, S., Shapiro, D., & Zaidel, E. (1996). The role of the right hemisphere in the physiological and cognitive components of emotional processing. *Psychophysiology, 13,* 112–122.

Spiegel, D., & Cardeña, E. (1991). Disintegrated experience: The dissociative disorders revisited. *Journal of Abnormal Psychology, 100,* 366–378.

Spitzer, C., Barnow, S., Freyberger, H. J., & Joergen Grabe, H. (2007). Dissociation predicts symptom-related treatment outcome in short-term inpatient psychotherapy. *Australian and New Zealand Journal of Psychiatry, 41,* 682–687.

Spitzer, C., Wilert, C., Grabe, H-J., Rizos, T., & Freyberger, H. J. (2004). Dissociation, hemispheric asymmetry, and dysfunction of hemispheric interaction: A transcranial magnetic approach. *Journal of Neuropsychiatry and Clinical Neurosciences, 16,* 163–169.

St. Clair, C., Danon-Boileau, L., & Trevarthen, C. (2007). Signs of autism in infancy: Sensitivity for rhythms of expression in communication. In S. Acquarone (Ed.), *Signs of autism in infants: Recognition and early intervention* (pp. 21–45). London: Karnac.

Steele, K., van der Hart, O., & Nijenhuis, E.R.S. (2001). Dependency in the treatment of complex PTSD and dissociative disorder patients. *Journal of Trauma and Dissociation, 2,* 79–116.

Stepper, S., & Strack, F. (1993). Proprioceptive determinants of emotional and nonemotional feelings. *Personality and Social Psychology, 64*(2), 211–220.

Stern, D. N. (1971). A micro-analysis of mother–infant interaction: Behaviors regulating social contact between a mother and her three-and-a-half-month-old twins. *Journal of American Academy of Child Psychiatry, 10,* 501–517.

Stern, D. N. (1974). Mother and infant at play: The dyadic interaction involving facial, vocal and gaze behaviours. In M. Lewis & L. A. Rosenblum (Eds.), *The effect of the infant on its caregiver* (pp. 187–213). New York: Wiley.

Stern, D. N. (1977). *The first relationship.* Cambridge, MA: Harvard University Press.

Stern, D. N. (1993). The role of feelings for an interpersonal self. In U. Neisser (Ed.), *The perceived self: Ecological and interpersonal sources of self-knowledge* (pp. 205–215). New York: Cambridge University Press.

Stern, D. N. (1999). Vitality contours: The temporal contour of feelings as a basic unit for constructing the infant's social experience. In P. Rochat (Ed.), *Early social cognition: Understanding others in the first months of life* (pp. 67–90). Mahwah, NJ: Erlbaum.

Stern, D. N. (2000). *The interpersonal world of the infant: A view from psychoanalysis and development psychology* (2nd ed.). New York: Basic Books.

Stern, D. N. (2004). *The present moment in psychotherapy and everyday life.* New York: Norton.

Stern, D. N., & Bruschweiler-Stern, N. (1997). The birth of a mother: How the motherhood experience changes you forever. New York: Basic Books.

Stern, D. N., Hofer, L., Haft, W., & Dore, J. (1985). Affect attunement: The sharing of feeling states between mother and infant by means of inter-modal fluency. In T. M. Field & N. A. Fox (Eds.), *Social perception in infants* (pp. 249–268). Norwood, NJ: Ablex.

Stern, D. N., Jaffe, J., Beebe, B., & Bennett, S. L. (1975). Vocalization in unison and alternation: Two modes of communication within the mother–infant dyad. *Annals of the New York Academy of Science, 263,* 89–100.

Stern, D. N., Sander, L., Nahum, J. P., Harrison, A. M., Lyons-Ruth, K., Morgan, A. C., et al. (1998). Non-interpretive mechanisms in psychoanalytic therapy. *International Journal of Psychoanalysis, 79,* 903–921.

Stern, J. M. (1997). Offspring-induced nurturance: Animal–human parallels. *Developmental Psychobiology, 31,* 19–37.

Stolorow, R. D., Brandchaft, B., & Atwood, G. E. (1987). *Psychoanalytic treatment: An intersubjective approach.* Hillsdale, NJ: Analytic Press.

Suler, J. R. (1989). Mental imagery in psychoanalytic treatment. *Psychoanalytic Psychology, 6,* 343–366.

Sullivan, R. M., & Dufresne, M. M. (2006). Mesocortical dopamine and HPA axis regulation: Role of laterality and early environment. *Brain Research, 1076,* 49–59.

Sun, T., Patoine, C., Abu-Khalil, A., Visvader, J., Sum, E., Cherry, T. J., et al. (2005). Early asymmetry of gene transcription in embryonic human left and right cerebral cortex. *Science, 308,* 1794–1798.

Sur, M., & Rubenstein, J. L. (2005). Patterning and plasticity of the cerebral cortex. *Science, 310,* 805–810.

Suter, S. E., Huggenberger, H. J., & Schachinger, H. (2007). Cold pressor stress reduces left cradling preference in nulliparous human females. *Stress, 10,* 45–51.

Symonds, L. L., Gordon, N. S., Bixby, J. C., & Mande, M. M. (2006). Right-lateralized pain processing in the human cortex: An fMRI study. *Journal of Neurophysiology, 95,* 3823–3830.

Szyf, M., McGowan, P., & Meaney, M. J. (2008). The social environment and the epigenome. *Environmental and Molecular Mutagenesis, 49,* 46–60.

Tatkin, S. (2003). Marital therapy: The psychobiology of adult primary relationships Part I.

Tatkin, S. (2007). Using the strange situation to understand and predict separation and reunion behaviors. University of California at Los Angeles, Department of Family Medicine, David Geffen School of Medicine.

Taylor, G. J., Bagby, R. M., & Parker, J.D.A. (1997). *Disorders of affect regulation: Alexithymia in medical and psychiatric illness.* Cambridge, UK: Cambridge University Press.

Thayer, J. F., & Lane, R. D. (2000). A model of neurovisceral integration in emotion regulation and dysregulation. *Journal of Affective Disorders, 61,* 201–216.

Theoret, H., Kobayashi, M., Merabet, L., Wagner, T., Tormos, J. M., & Pascual-Leone, A. (2004). Modulation of right motor cortex excitability without awareness following presentation of masked self-images. *Cognitive Brain Research, 20,* 54–57.

Tomkins, S. S. (1962). *Affect, imagery, and consciousness: Vol. 1. The positive affects.* New York: Springer.

Tomkins, S. S. (1963). *Affect, imagery, and consciousness: Vol. 2. The negative affects.* New York: Springer.

Treboux, D., & Crowell, J. (2001, April). *Are AAI classifications stable across phases of adult development?: Transitions to marriage and to parenting.* Symposium presented at the biennial meeting of the Society for Research in Child Development, Minneapolis.

Trevarthen, C. (1977). Descriptive analyses of infant communication. In H. R. Schaffer (Ed.), *Studies in mother–infant interaction: The Loch Lomond symposium* (pp. 227–270). London: Academic Press.

Trevarthen, C. (1979). Communication and cooperation in early infancy. A description of primary intersubjectivity. In M. Bullowa (Ed.), *Before speech: The beginning of human communication* (pp. 321–347). Cambridge, UK: Cambridge University Press.

Trevarthen, C. (1980). The foundations of intersubjectivity: Development of interpersonal and co-operative understanding of infants. In D. Olson (Ed.), *The social foundations of language and thought* (pp. 316–342). New York: Norton.

Trevarthen, C. (1985). Neuroembryology and the development of perceptual mechanisms. In F. Falkner & J. M. Tanner (Eds.), *Human growth* (2nd ed., pp. 301–383). New York: Plenum Press.

Trevarthen, C. (1986). Form, significance, and psychological potential of hand gestures of infants. In J-L. Nespoulous, P. Perron, & A. R. Lecours (Eds.), *The biological foundation of gestures: Motor and semiotic aspects* (pp. 149–202). Hillsdale, NJ: Erlbaum.

Trevarthen, C. (1989). Motives for culture in young children: Their natural development through communication. In W. Koch (Ed.), *The nature of culture* (pp. 80–119). Bochum, Germany: Brockmeyer.

Trevarthen, C. (1993a). The function of emotions in early infant communication and development. In J. Nadel & L. Camaioni (Eds.), *New perspectives in early communicative development* (pp. 48–81). New York: Cambridge University Press.

Trevarthen, C. (1993b). The self born in intersubjectivity: An infant communicating. In U. Neisser (Ed.), *The perceived self: Ecological and interpersonal sources of self-knowledge* (pp. 121–173). New York: Cambridge University Press.

Trevarthen, C. (1996). Lateral asymmetries in infancy: Implications for the development of the hemispheres. *Neuroscience and Biobehavioral Reviews, 20*(4), 571–586.

Trevarthen, C. (1998). The concept and foundations of infant intersubjectivity. In S. Bråten (Ed.), *Intersubjective communication and emotion in early ontogeny* (pp. 15–46). Cambridge, UK: Cambridge University Press.

Trevarthen, C. (1999). Musicality and the intrinsic motive pulse: Evidence from human psychobiology and infant communication. In Deliège (Ed.), *Rhythms, musical narrative, and the origins of human communication: Musicae Scientiae, Special Issue* (pp. 157–213). Liège, Belgium: European Society for the Cognitive Sciences of Music.

Trevarthen, C. (2001a). Intrinsic motives for companionship in understanding: Their origin, development and significance for infant mental health. *Infant Mental Health Journal, 22*(1–2), 95–131.

Trevarthen, C. (2001b). The neurobiology of early communication: Intersubjective regulations in human brain development. In A. F. Kalverboer & A. Gramsbergen (Eds.), *Handbook on brain and behavior in human development* (pp. 841–882). Dordrecht, The Netherlands: Kluwer.

Trevarthen, C. (2002). Origins of musical identity: Evidence from infancy for musical social awareness. In R.A.R. MacDonald, D. J. Hargreaves, & D. Miell (Eds.), *Musical identities* (pp. 21–38). Oxford, UK: Oxford University Press.

Trevarthen, C. (2005a). Action and emotion in development of the human self, its sociability and cultural intelligence: Why infants have feelings like ours. In J. Nadel & D. Muir (Eds.), *Emotional development* (pp. 61–91). Oxford, UK: Oxford University Press.

Trevarthen, C. (2005b). Stepping away from the mirror: Pride and shame in adventures of companionship—reflections on the nature and emotional needs of infant intersubjectivity. In C. S. Carter et al. (Eds.), *Attachment and bonding: A new synthesis* (pp. 55–84). Cambridge, MA: MIT Press.

Trevarthen, C. (2008a). Human biochronology: On the source and functions of "musicality." In R. Haas & V. Brandes (Eds.), *Proceedings of the Mozart and science conference* (pp. xx–xx). Vienna: Springer.

Trevarthen, C. (2008b). The musical art of infant conversation: Narrating in the time of sympathetic experience, without rational interpretation, before words. In M. Imberty & M. Gratier (Eds.), *Narrative in music and interaction: Musicae Scientiae, Special Issue* (pp. 15–48). Liège, Belgium: European Society for the Cognitive Sciences of Music.

Trevarthen, C. (2009). Infant consciousness. In T. Bayne, A. Cleermans, & P. Wilkin (Eds.), *Oxford companion to consciousness* (pp. 372–375). Oxford: Oxford University Press.

Trevarthen, C., & Aitken, K. J. (1994). Brain deselopment, infant communication, and empathy disorders: Intrinsic factors in child mental health. *Development and Psychopathology, 6*, 599–635.

Trevarthen, C., & Aitken, K. J. (2001). Infant intersubjectivity: Research, theory, and clinical applications. *Journal of Child Psychology and Psychiatry and Allied Disciplines, 42*(1), 3–48.

Trevarthen, C., & Aitken, K. J. (2003). Regulation of brain development and age-related changes in infants' motives: The developmental function of "regressive" periods. In M. Heimann (Ed.), *Regression periods in human infancy* (pp. 107–184). Mahwah, NJ: Erlbaum.

Trevarthen, C., Aitken, K. J., Vandekerckhove, M., Delafield-Butt, J., & Nagy, E. (2006). Collaborative regulations of vitality in early childhood: Stress in intimate relationships and postnatal psychopathology. In D. Cicchetti & D. J. Cohen (Eds.), *Developmental psychopathology: Vol. 2. Developmental neuroscience* (2nd ed., pp. 65–126). New York: Wiley.

Trevarthen, C., & Daniel, S. (2005). Rhythm and synchrony in early development, and signs of autism and Rett syndrome in infancy. *Brain and Development, 27*, (Suppl.) S25–S34.

Trevarthen, C., Delafield-Butt, J., & Schögler, B. (in press). Psychobiology of musical gesture: Innate rhythm, harmony, and melody in the movements of narration. In A. Gritten & E. King (Eds.), *Music and gesture—2*. Aldershot, UK: Ashgate.

Trevarthen, C., & Hubley, P. (1978). Secondary intersubjectivity: Confidence, confiding, and acts of meaning in the first year. In A. Lock (Ed.), *Action, gesture and symbol: The emergence of language* (pp. 183–229). New York: Academic Press.

Trevarthen, C., Murray, L., & Hubley, P. (1981). Psychology of infants. In J. Davis & J. Dobbing (Eds.), *Scientific foundations of clinical paediatrics* (2nd ed., pp. 235–250). London: Heinemann Medical Books.

Trevarthen. C., & Reddy, V. (2007). Infant consciousness. In T. Bayne, A. Cleermans, & P. Wilkin (Eds.), *Oxford companion to consciousness*. Oxford, UK: Oxford University Press.

Tronick, E. Z. (1980). On the primacy of social skills. In D. B. Sawin, L. O. Walker, & J. H. Penticuff (Eds.), *The exceptional infant: Vol. 4. Psychosocial risks in infant-environmental transactions* (pp. 144–158). New York: Brunner/Mazel.

Tronick, E. Z. (1989). Emotions and emotional communication in infants. *American Psychologist, 44*, 112–119.

Tronick, E. Z. (1998). Interactions that effect change in psychotherapy: A model based on infant research. *Infant Mental Health Journal, 19*, 1–290.

Tronick, E. Z. (2003). "Of course all relationships are unique": How co-creative processes generate unique mother–infant and patient–therapist relationships and change other relationships. *Psychoanalytic Inquiry*, *23*, 473–491.

Tronick, E. Z. (2004). Why is connection with others so critical? Dyadic meaning making, messiness and complexity govern selective processes which co-create and expand individuals' states of consciousness. In J. Nadel & D. Muir (Eds.), *Emotional development* (pp. xx–xx). New York: Oxford University Press.

Tronick, E. Z. (2007). *The neurobehavioral and social emotional development of infants and children.* New York: Norton.

Tronick, E. Z. (in press). *The psychobiology of pleasure.*

Tronick, E. Z., Als, H., Adamson, L., Wise, S., & Brazelton, T. B. (1978). The infant's response to entrapment between contradictory messages in face-to-face interaction. *Journal of the American Academy of Child Psychiatry*, *17*, 1–13.

Tronick, E. Z., & Weinberg, M. K. (1996). Infant affective reactions to the resumption of maternal interaction after the still-face. *Child Development*, *67*, 905–914.

Truex, R. C., & Carpenter, M. B. (1969). *Human neuroanatomy* (6th ed.). Baltimore, MD: Williams & Wilkins.

Tulving, E., & Schacter, D. L. (1990). Priming and human memory systems. *Science*, *247*, 301–306.

Tunnell, G. (2006). An affirmational approach to treating gay male couples. *Group*, *30*(2), 133–151.

Turner, M. (1996). *The literary mind: The origins of thought and language.* New York: Oxford University Press.

Tutte, J. C. (2004). The concept of psychical trauma: A bridge in interdisciplinary space. *International Journal of Psychoanalysis*, *85*, 897–921.

Tzourio-Mazoyer, N., De Schonen, S., Crivello, F., Reutter, B., et al. (2002). Neural correlates of woman face processing by 2-month-old infants. *Neuroimage*, *15*, 454–461.

Uvnas-Moberg, K. (1998). Oxytocin may mediate the benefits of positive social interaction and emotions. *Psychneuroendocrinology*, *23*, 819–835.

Van der Hart, O., & Brown, P. (1992). Abreactions re-evaluated. *Dissociation*, *3*, 127–140.

Van der Hart, O., Nijenhuis, E., et al. (2004). Trauma-related dissociation: Conceptual clarity lost and found. *Australian and New Zealand Journal of Psychiatry*, *38*, 906–914.

Van der Hart, O., Nijenhuis, E., & Steele, K. (2006). *The haunted self: Structural dissociation and the treatment of chronic traumatization.* New York: Norton.

van der Kolk, B. A. (1994). The body keeps the score: Memory and the evolving psychobiology of posttraumatic stress. *Harvard Review of Psychiatry*, *1*, 253–265.

van der Kolk, B. A., McFarlane, A., & Weisaeth, L. (1996). *Traumatic stress: The effects of overwhelming experience on mind, body, and society.* New York: Guilford Press.

Vanhoutte, P. M., & Levy, M. N. (1979). Cholinergic inhibition of adrenergic neurotransmission in the cardiovascular system. In C. M. Brooks, K. Koizumi, & A. Sato (Eds.), *Integrative functions of the autonomic nervous system* (pp. 159–176). Tokyo: University of Tokyo Press.

van IJzendoorn, M. H. (1995). Adult attachment representations, parental responsiveness, and infant attachment: A meta-analysis on the predictive validity of the adult attachment interview. *Psychological Bulletin*, *117*, 387–403.

van Lancker, D., & Cummings, J.L. (1999). Expletives: Neurolingusitic and neurobehavioral perspectives on swearing. *Brain Research Reviews*, *31*, 83–104.

Wallin, N., Merker, B., & Brown, S. (Eds.). (2000). *The origins of music.* Cambridge, MA: MIT Press.

Watt, D. F. (2003). Psychotherapy in an age of neuroscience: Bridges to affective neuroscience. In J. Corrigall & H. Wilkinson (Eds.), *Revolutionary connections: Psychotherapy and neuroscience* (pp. 79–115). London: Karnac.

Watt, D. F., & Panksepp, J. (2009). Depression: An evolutionarily conserved mechanism to terminate separation-distress?: A review of aminergic, peptidergic, and neural network perspectives. *Neuropsychoanalysis, 11,* 5–104.

Whitehead, A. N. (1929). *Process and reality: An essay in cosmology.* Cambridge: Macmillan University Press.

Whitehead, C. C. (2005). Neo-psychoanalysis: A paradigm for the 21st century. *Journal of the Academy of Psychoanalysis and Dynamic Psychiatry, 34,* 603–627.

Wigram, T., & Elefant, C. (2009). Therapeutic dialogues in music: Nurturing musicality of communication in children with autistic spectrum disorder and Rett syndrome. In S. Malloch & C. Trevarthen (Eds.), *Communicative musicality: Exploring the basis of human companionship* (pp. 423–445). Oxford: Oxford University Press.

Winnicott, D. W. (1945). Primitive emotional development. In *Collected papers: Through pediatrics to psycho-analysis* (pp. 145–146). New York: Brunner Mazel.

Winnicott, D. W. (1958). The capacity to be alone. *International Journal of Psycho-Analysis, 39,* 416–420.

Winnicott, D. W. (1965). Ego distortion in terms of true and false self. In *The maturational processes and the facilitating environment* (pp. 140–152). New York: International Universities Press. (Original work published 1960)

Winnicott, D. W. (1989). *Playing and reality.* New York: Routledge. (Original work published 1982)

Winston, J. S., Strange, B. A., O'Doherty, J., & Dolan, R. J. (2002). Automatic and intentional brain responses during evaluation of trustworthiness of faces. *Nature Neuroscience, 5,* 277–283.

Wittling, W. (1995). The right hemisphere and the human stress response. *Acta Physiologica Scandinavica, 161* (Suppl. 640), 55–59.

Woodworth, R. S. (1928). Dynamic psychology. In C. Murchison (Ed.), *Psychologies of 1925.* Worcester, MA: Clark University Press.

Yeung, D., & Cheung, C. (2008). *The rainbow after: Psychological trauma and accelerated experiential dynamic psychotherapy.* Hong Kong: Ming Fung Press.

Ziabreva, I., Poeggel, G., Schnabel, R., & Braun, K. (2003). Separation-induced receptor changes in the hippocampus and amygdala of *Octodon degus:* Influence of maternal vocalizations. *Journal of Neuroscience, 23,* 5329–5336.

Zeedyk, M. S. (Ed.). (2008). *Making contact: Promoting social interaction for individuals with communicative impairments.* London: Jessica Kingsley.

Zlatev, J., Racine, T. P., Sinha, C., & Itkonin, E. (2008). *The shared mind: Perspectives on intersubjectivity.* Amsterdam: John Benjamins.

Zoia, S., Blason, L., D'ottavio, G., Bulgheroni, M., Pezzetta, E., Scabar, A., et al. (2007). Evidence of early development of action planning in the human foetus: A kinematic study. *Experimental Brain Research, 176,* 217–226.

Index

AIR POLLUTION

VOLUME III
Sources of Air Pollution and Their Control

ENVIRONMENTAL SCIENCE

An Interdisciplinary Monograph Series

EDITORS

DOUGLAS H. K. LEE
National Environmental Health Sciences Center
Research Triangle Park
North Carolina

E. WENDELL HEWSON
Department of Meteorology and Oceanography
The University of Michigan
Ann Arbor, Michigan

C. FRED GURNHAM
Department of Environmental Engineering
Illinois Institute of Technology
Chicago, Illinois

ARTHUR C. STERN, editor, AIR POLLUTION, Second Edition. In three volumes, 1968

In preparation

L. FISHBEIN, W. G. FLAMM, and H. L. FALK, CHEMICAL MUTA-GENS: Environmental Effects on Biological Systems

R. E. MUNN, Biometeorological Methods

AIR POLLUTION

SECOND EDITION

Edited by

ARTHUR C. STERN

Department of Environmental Sciences and Engineering
School of Public Health
University of North Carolina
Chapel Hill, North Carolina

VOLUME III

Sources of Air Pollution and

Their Control

1968

ACADEMIC PRESS New York London

ACADEMIC PRESS, INC.
111 Fifth Avenue, New York, New York 10003

United Kingdom Edition published by
ACADEMIC PRESS, INC. (LONDON) LTD.
Berkeley Square House, London W1X 6BA

LIBRARY OF CONGRESS CATALOG CARD NUMBER: 67-31042

Second Printing, 1970

PRINTED IN THE UNITED STATES OF AMERICA

This volume is dedicated
to Dick, Bob, and Mark

List of Contributors

Numbers in parentheses indicate the pages on which the authors' contributions begin.

DONALD F. ADAMS (243), Research Division, College of Engineering, Washington State University, Pullman, Washington

SEYMOUR CALVERT (457), School of Engineering and Air Pollution Research Center, University of California at Riverside, Riverside, California

KNOWLTON J. CAPLAN (359), Carter-Day Company, Minneapolis, Minnesota

STANLEY T. CUFFE (191), Control Agency Development Program, National Air Pollution Control Administration, Arlington, Virginia

SIDNEY EDELMAN (553), Environmental Health Branch, Public Health Division, Office of the General Counsel, Department of Health, Education, and Welfare, Washington, D.C.

HAROLD F. ELKIN (97), Sun Oil Company, Philadelphia, Pennsylvania

RICHARD B. ENGDAHL (3), Battelle Memorial Institute, Columbus, Ohio

W. L. FAITH (269), Consulting Chemical Engineer, San Marino, California

MELVIN W. FIRST (291), School of Public Health, Harvard University, Boston, Massachusetts

F. E. GARTRELL (535), Tennessee Valley Authority, Chattanooga, Tennessee

DON R. GOODWIN (191), Abatement Program, National Air Pollution Control Administration, Durham, North Carolina

CHAD F. GOTTSCHLICH (437), Selas Corporation of America, Dresher, Pennsylvania

AUSTIN N. HELLER (191), Department of Air Pollution Control, New York, New York

R. W. HURN (55), Bartlesville Petroleum Research Center, U.S. Bureau of Mines, Bartlesville, Oklahoma

K. IINOYA (409), Department of Chemical Engineering, Kyoto University, Sakyo-Ku, Kyoto, Japan

JOHN A. MAGA (797), California Air Resources Board, Sacramento, California

vii

JOHN S. NADER (813), Chemical and Physical Research and Development Program, National Air Pollution Control Administration, Cincinnati, Ohio

KENNETH W. NELSON (171), Department of Hygiene and Agricultural Research, American Smelting and Refining Company, Salt Lake City, Utah

C. ORR, JR. (409), School of Chemical Engineering, Georgia Institute of Technology, Atlanta, Georgia

HAROLD J. PAULUS (521), School of Public Health, University of Minnesota, Minneapolis, Minnesota

JEAN J. SCHUENEMAN (719), Division of Air Quality Control, Maryland State Department of Health, Baltimore, Maryland

WILLIAM E. SEBESTA (143), Republic Steel Corporation, Cleveland, Ohio

ARTHUR C. STERN (319, 601), Department of Environmental Sciences and Engineering, School of Public Health, University of North Carolina, Chapel Hill, North Carolina

VICTOR H. SUSSMAN (123), Pennsylvania Department of Health, Harrisburg, Pennsylvania

AMOS TURK (497), Department of Chemistry, The City College of the City University of New York, New York, New York

Preface

This second edition is addressed to the same audience as the previous one: engineers, chemists, physicists, physicians, meteorologists, lawyers, economists, sociologists, agronomists, and toxicologists. It is concerned, as was the first edition, with the cause, effect, transport, measurement, and control of air pollution.

So much new material has become available since the completion of the two-volume first edition, that it has been necessary to use three volumes for this one. Volume I covers three major areas: the nature of air pollution; the mechanism of its dispersal by meteorological factors and from stacks; and its effect upon plants, animals, humans, materials, and visibility. Volume II covers the sampling, analysis, measurement, and monitoring of air pollution, and can be used independently of the other two volumes as a text or reference on the chemical analysis of air pollutants. Volume III covers four major areas: the emissions to the atmosphere from the principal air pollution sources; the control techniques and equipment used to minimize these emissions; the applicable laws, regulations, and standards; and the administrative and organizational procedures used to administer these laws, regulations, and standards. The concluding chapter of Volume III discusses air pollution literature sources and gives guidance in locating information not to be found in these volumes. Volumes, I, II, and III were prepared simultaneously, and the total work was divided into three volumes to make it easier for the reader to use.

To improve subject area coverage, the number of chapters was increased from the 42 of the first edition to 54. The scope of some of the chapters, whose subject areas were carried over from the first edition, has been changed. Every contributor to the first edition was offered the opportunity to prepare for this edition either a revision of his chapter in the previous edition or a new chapter if the scope of his work had changed. Since ten authors declined this offer and three were deceased, this edition includes 32 of the previous contributors and 28 new ones.

The new chapters in this edition are concerned chiefly with the chemical analysis of air pollutants and pollution problems of specific industries not covered previously. The decision to expand coverage of chemical analysis of air pollutants was based on the demise of Morris B. Jacobs (an author in the first edition), who, in his lifetime, had authored a succession of books, each of which, in its turn, became the standard work on air pollutant sampling and analysis. It is hoped that Volume II will fill the gap created by the stilling of his prolific pen. Even with the inclusion in this edition of the air pollution problems of additional industrial processes, many are still not covered in detail. It is hoped that the general principles discussed in Volume III will help the reader faced with problems in industries not specifically covered.

Because I planned and edited these volumes, the gap areas and instances of repetition are my responsibility and not the authors'. As in the first edition, the contributors were asked to write for a scientifically advanced reader, and all were given the opportunity of last minute updating of their material.

As the editor of a multiauthor treatise, I thank each author for both his contribution and his patience, and each author's family, including my own, for their forbearance and help. Special thanks are due my former secretary, Nancy Sue Myers, who carried sixty times the burden of all the other authors' secretaries combined. In this task, Lucy Trainor helped her carry the load. I should also like to thank my former superiors in the U.S. Department of Health, Education, and Welfare for having permitted my participation and that of so many of my former National Air Pollution Control Administration colleagues.

ARTHUR C. STERN

Chapel Hill, N.C.
August, 1968

Contents

Part VII. SOURCES OF AIR POLLUTION

32. Stationary Combustion Sources

Richard B. Engdahl

33. Mobile Combustion Sources

R. W. Hurn

34. Petroleum Refinery Emissions

Harold F. Elkin

35. Nonmetallic Mineral Products Industries

Victor H. Sussman

36. Ferrous Metallurgical Processes

William Sebesta

37. Nonferrous Metallurgical Operations

Kenneth W. Nelson

38. Inorganic Chemical Industry

Austin N. Heller, Stanley T. Cuffe, and Don R. Goodwin

39. Pulp and Paper Industry

Donald F. Adams

40. Food and Feed Industries

W. L. Faith

Part VIII. CONTROL METHODS AND EQUIPMENT

41. Process and System Control

Melvin W. First

42. Efficiency, Application, and Selection of Collectors

Arthur C. Stern

43. Source Control by Centrifugal Force and Gravity

Knowlton J. Caplan

44. Source Control by Filtration

K. Iinoya and C. Orr, Jr.

45. Source Control by Electrostatic Precipitation

Chad F. Gottschlich

46. Source Control by Liquid Scrubbing

Seymour Calvert

47. Source Control by Gas–Solid Adsorption and Related Processes

Amos Turk

48. Nuisance Abatement by Combustion

Harold J. Paulus

49. Water Pollution Potential of Air Pollution Control Devices

F. E. Gartrell

Part IX. AIR POLLUTION CONTROL

50. Air Pollution Control Legislation

Sidney Edelman

51. Air Pollution Standards

Arthur C. Stern

52. Air Pollution Control Administration

Jean J. Schueneman

53. Public Information and Education

John A. Maga

54. Air Pollution Literature Resources

John S. Nader

Appendix

Contents of Other Volumes

VOLUME I.   AIR POLLUTION AND ITS EFFECTS

VOLUME II.   ANALYSIS, MONITORING, AND SURVEYING

Part IV.   Analysis of Pollutants

Part V.   Air Quality and Meteorological Monitoring

AIR POLLUTION

VOLUME III
Sources of Air Pollution and Their Control

Part VII
SOURCES OF AIR POLLUTION

32 Stationary Combustion Sources

Richard B. Engdahl

I. Introduction

A characteristic of civilization since its beginning has been the combustion of fuel for useful heat. More recently, combustion has been used extensively for thermal power generation—practically always accompanied by emissions to the atmosphere of smoke, ash, odors, noxious and benign gases. After the Industrial Revolution transformed many ways of life, the smoking industrial chimney came to be widely accepted as a welcome sign of the new prosperity. Then, slowly, as living in industrial smoke became almost intolerable, industrial centers, one by one, began breaking free from acceptance of the tradition that smoke is a necessary concomitant of prosperity. St. Louis, Pittsburgh, and then, Los Angeles led the way.

Although much fuel has been used wastefully, and some of it even sent unburned into the air, economic pressures have resulted in vast improvements in the efficiency of most fuel-burning equipment. Reduction in air pollution has occurred as a result. For the benefit of all who are directly concerned with fuel economy, it must be emphasized that clear flue gas emanating from a chimney does not automatically mean high efficiency. Probably the most wasteful fuel-burning installations operating today are those which have clear effluents, but in which the fuel gases are needlessly diluted with tremendous volumes of air which carry wasted heat away from the point of release.

II. Fly Ash

Incombustible solid portions of fuels which are too small to settle out in the combustion chamber naturally escape suspended in the high-velocity flue gases. If they are not then captured by effective collectors, they are carried out to the atmosphere as fly ash. Fly ash is rarely homogeneous; it is usually made up of a large number of inorganic compounds widely found in the mineral matter of the earth's crust. In suspension burning, such as with pulverized coal and in spreader stokers and incinerators, the high temperature often fuses the ash into rough, solid, or hollow spheres. Because of incomplete combustion, the fly ash from carbonaceous fuel combustion will often contain unburned carbon.

Table I shows the range of chemical characteristics of typical fly ash from various plants using pulverized coal. The fly ash produced by any one steam plant, where coal from a given producing area is burned year after year, can exhibit a much smaller range in chemical composition. For example, at one large utility generating station, the major fly ash

TABLE I

TYPICAL RANGES OF CHEMICAL
COMPOSITION OF FLY ASH FROM
PULVERIZED COAL-FIRED PLANTS[a]

Constituent	Range, % by weight
Silica, SiO_2	34–48
Alumina, Al_2O_3	17–31
Iron oxide, Fe_2O_3	6–26
Calcium oxide, CaO	1–10
Magnesium oxide, MgO	0.5–2
Sulfur trioxide, SO_3	0.2–4
Loss on ignition, carbon	1.5–20

[a] From Minick (1).

constituents showed the following range of values over a 2-year period: silica, 44.6–48.0%; alumina, 24.1–27.7%; and loss on ignition, 2.9–4.0% (1). Fly ash has a mass-median diameter of approximately 15 μ, with 30–40% being less than 10 μ (1a). Many tons of captured fly ash are being utilized in roads, dams, fill, and other applications (2).

III.   Gases

Compared with the large amounts of the innocuous gases released from the usual combustion processes—namely, carbon dioxide, nitrogen, and oxygen—only small amounts of other gases are usually emitted. The most common of these are: sulfur dioxide, sulfur trioxide, carbon monoxide, nitric oxide, nitrogen dioxide, aldehydes, and other hydrocarbons.

A. SULFUR OXIDES

Most of the sulfur in burning fuels appears in the resulting exhaust gases as sulfur dioxide and sulfur trioxide. In the case of coal and residual oil, a small amount of the sulfur remains in the ash residue as sulfates. Some field measurements of SO_2 emission deviate widely from that theoretically expected from computations based on the sulfur content of the fuel fired (3), apparently because of the difficulty of obtaining well-mixed gas samples in practical combustion equipment.

Despite the comparatively small amout of sulfur trioxide produced (4), its presence is important because it drastically raises the dew point

of flue gas and readily forms sulfuric acid mist with atmospheric moisture. Under some atmospheric conditions this mist converts a usually
colorless plume to a conspicuous bluish-white haze. After many hours or
days in the atmosphere, all of the SO_2 emitted is first oxidized to SO_3,
then H_2SO_4 which, in turn, is eventually converted to sulfates which
settle or are washed out of the air by rainfall.

Gumz (5) has assembled data on SO_2—SO_3 ratios from Johnstone (6)
and other as follows:

Pulverized fuel, wet bottom	0
Pulverized fuel, dry bottom	0 to 0.008
Solid fuel beds	0.016 to 0.029
Small oil furnaces	0.032 to 0.074
Large oil furnaces	0.005 to 0.040

Recent measurements by Cuffe et al. (7) on dry-bottom and on wet-
bottom furnaces gave ratios from 0 to 0.0825. Smith (8) assembled a
large number of results on oil-fired furnaces which show the same range
of ratios.

Reduction of excess air to almost stoichiometric proportions has been
shown by Glaubitz (9) to reduce the SO_3 produced by oil-fired furnaces.
The major advantages of the technique are elimination of corrosion and
deposits on the boiler surfaces, and reduction of heat lost in the exhaust
gases. Unusually precise control of air-fuel ratio and excellent mixing
are required to prevent formation of smoke. Figure 1 from Niepenberg
(10) shows the effect of oxygen in the waste gases on the conversion of
SO_2 to SO_3. A possible disadvantage of low excess air is suggested by the
finding of Jefferis and Sensenbaugh (11) that an increase in CO_2 from
13.1 to 14.7 was accompanied by a 7-fold increase in particulate emission.
Fauth and Schüle (11a) have shown that with most burners in medium-

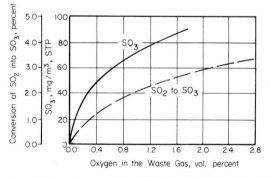

FIG. 1. Formation of SO_3 and conversion of SO_2 into SO_3 plotted against oxygen in flue
gas (measured values) when burning heavy oil.

sized oil-fired furnaces, there is a close relationship between carbon monoxide emission and soot emission. The advantages of low excess air operation seem also possible when burning pulverized coal; but as yet, no means for the necessary precise combustion control have been developed.

The general status of the formation of SO_3 is summarized by the following excerpts from a chapter entitled "Oxides of Sulfur in Boilers and Gas Turbines" (12).

Sulfur trioxide can be formed by three mechanisms: (1) dissociation of sulfates in fuel beds (13), (2) combination of SO_2 and atomic oxygen produced by the flame (4), and (3) catalytic oxidation of SO_2 (14). The accumulated evidence of many investigations points to the fact that the first two mechanisms can play at most only a small part in SO_3 production. Most of the SO_3 seems to result from some catalytic action. The chief catalytic agent is generally considered to be Fe_2O_3 formed on the various steel surfaces. Other materials such as fly ash, silica, and alumina may also catalyze the oxidation of SO_2 to SO_3. In oil-fired systems the V_2O_5 and vanadates present would be expected to be particularly active in producing SO_3 catalytically.

Both coals and residual oils contain sulfur, and in some course of the combustion process the bulk of this sulfur is oxidized to SO_2. Generally, about 5 percent of the sulfur appears as SO_3 but it is not clear as yet how much of this is produced during the combustion process and how much by later oxidation of the SO_2. In coal-fired systems, the highest concentration of SO_3 is produced by stoker firing and the least by cyclone firing. Factors which can cause the SO_3 content of the flue gases to be high include: (1) a low quantity of fly ash, (2) a moderate amount of excess combustion air, and (3) high sulfur content of the coal.

In oil-fired systems the ash content is relatively small, whereas the sulfur content of a residual oil is of the same order of magnitude as that in coal. Consequently, the role of sulfur is accentuated in oil-fired systems. The SO_3 content of the gas stream increases with the sulfur content of the oil, the flame temperature, the rate of firing, and the amount of excess air (15).

The acid dew point is commonly used as a measure of the SO_3 content of flue gases, and lies between 140 and 360 °F, depending on the SO_3 concentration. The dew point has been shown to increase with the sulfur content of the fuel, the water vapor content of the flue gases, and the amount of excess air. The dew point can be lowered by any device that inhibits SO_3 formation or removes it from the flue gases. Successful methods of reducing the dew point have depended on the use of materials that would physically adsorb SO_3, would combine with atomic oxygen, or would combine with SO_3. Physical adsorption is achieved by such agencies as pulverized-coal ash, or silica, metal oxides, and carbon smokes. Nitrogen-containing bases have been most effective for removal of atomic oxygen from the gas stream. Various additives have successfully combined with SO_3 to eliminate the acid dew point. Of these additives only dolomite, magnesium oxide, and ammonia seem to combine the requisite features of economy, efficiency, and ease of handling that make a practical additive. The possibility of inhibiting SO_3 formation or of poisoning catalytic surfaces seems promising, but as yet has not been thoroughly investigated.

Jenkinson and Firminger (15a) have recently summarized British experience with fuel additives to control SO_2, smut, and oil sludge formations. Hedley (*15b*) has made an extensive analysis of the available data on SO_3 formation, concluding that much more data on reaction rates are needed before the predominant mechanism of formation can be specified. Merryman and Levy (*15c*) have explored the kinetics further.

1. *The Control of Sulfur Oxides Emission from Combustion Sources*

Table II shows the sources of sulfur oxides which are emitted primarily from combustion in the United States (*15d*) and Great Britain (*15e*). Most of the U.S. low-sulfur coal reserves [Table III (*15f*)] are both (a) low rank sub-bituminous and lignite, and (b) located west of the Mississippi River. A large part of U.S. low-sulfur coal production is committed to the metalurgical coke and export markets. Most of the high-sulfur residual fuel oil burned in the U.S. is imported. A technology exists for reducing the sulfur content of residual fuel oil (see Chapter 34, Volume III).

Of the many processes for SO_2 removal from flue gases now under active investigation, the nearest to practical use appears to be the addition of limestone, dolomite, lime, or any other reactive metal oxide to the coal in the pulverizing mill, or, as a powder, to the furnace. These will combine with sulfur oxides in the furnace to form calcium, magnesium, or other metallic sulfates which can be removed from the flue gas along

TABLE II

SULFUR DIOXIDE[a] EMITTED OVER UNITED STATES (*15d*),
GREAT BRITAIN (*15e*), AND WEST GERMANY (*15ee*)

	U.S. 1966	Great Britain[b] 1945	West Germany 1962
Power generation—coal	11.9	1.1	1.4
Power generation—oil	1.2	—	
Other coal combustion	4.7	3.3	
Other oil combustion	4.4	0.5	
Smelting of ores	3.5	—	
Oil refining operation	1.5	—	
Coke processing	0.5	0.1	
Sulfuric acid manufacturing	0.5	—	
Coal refuse banks	0.1	—	
Refuse incineration	0.1	—	
Miscellaneous sources[c]	0.1	0.1	
	28.6	5.1	—

[a] In millions of tons.

[b] Total for 1963 was 3.4.

[c] Natural gas, LPG, pulp and paper mills, chemical manufacture, etc.

TABLE III
SULFUR CONTENT OF FUELS IN UNITED STATES

| Sulfur (%) | Coal, 1964 (%) | | | | Residual fuel oil, 1965 (%) Total usage |
	Production	Electric utility usage— bituminous	Total reserves	Reserves (east of Mississippi River)	
<1.0	41	19	65	20	23
1.1–3.0	33	60	15	37	72
>3.0	26	21	20	43	5
Total	100	100	100	100	100

with the fly ash and the uncombined rock dust; and disposed of as a solid waste. Where the furnace is followed by a dry dust collector, sulfur removal appears to be less than 50% even when stoichiometric quantities of dolomite are added. However, when the furnace is followed by a wet scrubber (Fig. 2), over 95% sulfur oxides removal has been demonstrated. (*15g, 15gg*) Much work is underway to learn more about the influence on this process of rock composition, size, point and rate of introduction, furnace time–temperature relationships, scrubber design, and other variables.

The remaining processes under development have in common that they (a) treat the flue gas after it has left the principal heat exchange surface (There are advantages in removing the sulfur oxides from the

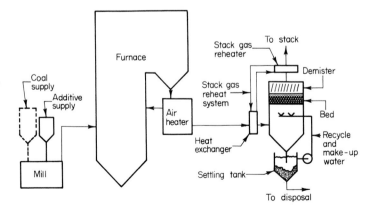

FIG. 2. System for SO₂ recovery by limestone injection followed by scrubbing (*15g*).

gases at a relatively high temperature so that they may be less corrosive when they pass through low-temperature heat-exchange surfaces); and (b) yield a useful by-product, rather than a waste. The by-product can be variously sulfur, concentrated sulfur dioxide, sulfuric acid, ammonium or other sulfate. The more advanced of these processes are the following:

1. *The catalytic oxidation process* (*15h, 15i*) using a vanadium oxide catalyst to produce a 70–80% sulfuric acid (Fig. 3) or ammonium sulfate (Fig. 4).

2. *The char sorption process* (*Reinluft*) (*15j*) which successively adsorbs and desorbs sulfur oxides from an activated char (coke) made within the process from make-up additives of coal to produce 40–50% SO_2 (Fig. 5) (*15k*). Other char processes include the Lurgi "Sulfacid" wet-char sorption system and Japanese processes (Hitachi, Ltd. and Tokyo Electric Power Company) which yield dilute sulfuric acid (*15l*).

3. *The metal oxide sorption process* (alkalized alumina) which absorbs sulfur oxides at 625 °F on alkalized alumina which is regenerated with producer gas with the release of H_2S and COS which is converted to elemental sulfur in a Claus reactor (Fig. 6) (*15m*). Other metal oxide sorption processes include (a) the Japanese DAP-Mn process of Mitsubishi Heavy Industries, Inc., and the Chuba Power Company which uses manganese oxide and produces ammonium or calcium sulfate

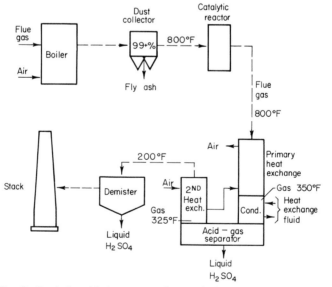

FIG. 3. Catalytic oxidation process for producing sulfuric acid (*15h*).

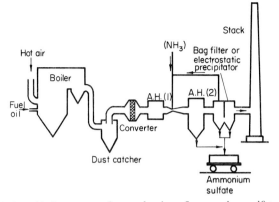

FIG. 4. Catalytic oxidation process for production of ammonium sulfate (15i). A.H. indicates air heater.

(15n), (b) the German "Grillo" process which uses a combination of metal oxides, and (c) the German "Still" process which uses a regenerable lignite ash.

4. *Liquid scrubbing processes* which include the water scrubbing processes of the 1930's (15j); lime water (15o) and ammoniacal liquor processes (15p); and current bench-scale processes involving molten salts or organic liquids.

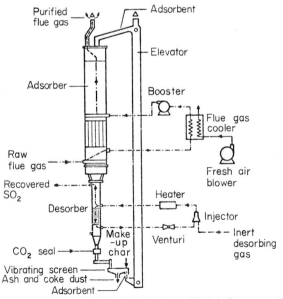

FIG. 5. British pilot plant for investigation of Reinluft process (15j).

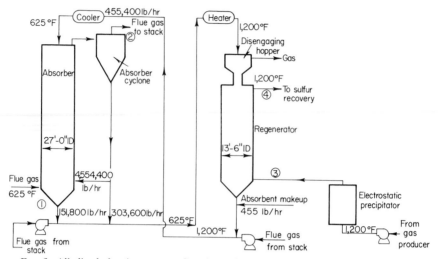

FIG. 6. Alkalized alumina process flowsheet (flue gas from 800-MW plant); amounts of solids flow are the total for 6 units (*15mm*).

| | | | | Total gas flow (6 units), volume percent | | | | | | | Million |
Stream	N_2	O_2	CO_2	H_2O	H_2	CO	SO_2	SO_3	H_2S	CH_4	C_2H_6	scfh
1	76.2	3.4	14.2	6.0	—	—	0.2	Trace	—	—	—	87.3
2	76.5	3.3	14.2	6.0	—	—	Trace	—	—	—	—	87.0
3	47.4	—	5.0	1.4	16.6	26.2	—	—	0.4	2.6	0.4	1.8
4	47.4	—	29.6	4.0	4.3	1.6	—	—	10.1	2.6	0.4	1.8

B. NITROGEN OXIDES

The oxides of nitrogen—nitric oxide (NO) and nitrogen dioxide (NO_2)—are always formed when atmospheric nitrogen and oxygen are heated to a high temperature in a flame. Ermenc (*16*) measured the yields of NO at various furnace wall temperatures, as shown in the tabulation:

Furnace wall temp. (°F)[a]	Yield of NO (%)
2800	0.26
3000	0.41
3200	0.77
3400	1.30
3600	1.55
3800	1.75

[a] Flame temperature was estimated to be 300 °F above wall temperature.

If the hot products of combustion cool slowly enough, the nitrogen oxides formed in the flame will decompose to oxygen and nitrogen. In the usual combustion apparatus, the heat of combustion is transferred for some useful purpose as rapidly as possible. When this happens the nitrogen oxides are fixed in the exhaust gas.

The range of concentrations of oxides of nitrogen emitted by various equipment has been assembled by Tow (17) as follows:

Power plants (gas- and oil-fired)	400–700 ppm
Other boilers and heaters	100–500 ppm
Incineration	50–150 ppm

Extensive measurements (18) in Los Angeles in 1959 on emissions of oxides of nitrogen from small stationary sources indicated much lower concentrations than those given by Tow. The maximum concentration found in incinerators of capacities up to 1000 lb/hour was 90 ppm, with an average of 43 ppm. Gas-fired boilers under 500 hp averaged emissions of 0.14 pound nitrogen oxides per million Btu (70 ppm). Similar oil-fired boilers averaged 0.49 pound per million Btu (250 ppm).

Faith (19) has estimated that 15–35% of the nitrogen oxides in Los Angeles come from gas and fuel burning. The balance are assumed to be from automobile exhaust. Thomas and St. John (20) estimated from measurements at Menlo Park, California, that approximately equal contributions come from automobiles and natural gas uses.

The production of NO in large water-walled, oil-fired boilers has been shown to be affected by air admission, burner location, and direction (21–22a). The principle here is that if the combustion process can be distributed and made more uniform without impairing its function, then hot spots will be minimized and the formation of NO from overheating will be reduced.

C. Carbon Oxides

Theoretically, when carbon is burned perfectly in air, the resulting dry flue gas is about 21% carbon dioxide and 79% nitrogen, by volume. Most actual fuels contain hydrogen; hence, the resulting flue gas is a mixture of carbon dioxide, water vapor, and nitrogen.

There are 2300×10^9 tons of CO_2 in the atmosphere and about $150,000 \times 10^9$ (23) tons dissolved in the sea. The great increase in the use of carbonaceous fuels has resulted, over the years, in the release of 200×10^9 tons of carbon dioxide to the air. This is approximately 10% of the amount of carbon dioxide in the atmosphere. All of the fuel used in the world today produces about 9.0×10^9 (24) tons of carbon dioxide per year. Photosynthesis is estimated to use up about 60×10^9 tons per year but respiration and decaying vegetation and animal life returns carbon dioxide to the atmosphere at about the same rate. The present average atmospheric concentration of carbon dioxide is approximately 300 ppm, and combustion processes are now raising it at the rate of about 1 ppm per year (25, 26).

Although speculation on the possibly deleterious effects of CO_2 on the earth's climate is becoming increasingly imaginative, one place where deliberate massive increases in CO_2 are becoming common is in commercial greenhouses. Whereas the normal atmospheric concentration is about 300 ppm (0.03 volume percent), intensive growth on a bright day in a nearly closed greenhouse may use up the available atmospheric CO_2, with the result that photosynthesis becomes temporarily limited by the lack of CO_2. The most common method of making up this lack in greenhouses is by CO_2 enrichment through the combustion of carbonaceous fuels, usually oil or gas—discharging the CO_2, H_2O, N_2 mixture directly into the greenhouse. The sulfur content of the fuel must be below 0.1%, and there must be even less aldehydes and ethylene produced to avoid plant damage. Greenhouse atmospheric CO_2 concentrations achieved through these means range up to 3000 ppm (0.3 volume percent), or 10 times normal. The results are spectacular, both in increased yields and shortened time for maturing (27). The concentrations used are well below the threshold limit value of CO_2 for humans— 5000 ppm for 8-hour exposure.

Stationary fuel burners emit no CO if combustion is at maximum efficiency. Carbon monoxide itself is a fuel with a heat value of 4347 Btu per pound—hence, if formed, it should be burned in the furnace. Carbon monoxide is usually formed when insufficient oxygen is present where the carbon is burning. The total oxygen supply may be ample, even excessive; but, if mixing of air and fuel is poor, CO may form. Smith and Gruber (28), surveying data which they judged old and no longer representative, found that coal-fired large boilers emit from 0.005 to 0.044 pound per million Btu input, or about 0.2 to 1.1 pounds per ton of 13,000 Btu coal. From an air-pollution standpoint, CO from large stationary furnaces is rarely a problem (28a) because if such a plant emits significant quantities, the resulting loss in efficiency would be unacceptable to the owner. Carbon monoxide is more likely to be an air pollution problem from the totality of automotive and household sources in a community.

D. Hydrocarbons

Smith and Gruber (28) show single-atom hydrocarbons and aldehydes from industrial units as ranging from 0.001 to 0.010 pound per million

Btu input and from 0.00006 to 0.0002 pound per million Btu input, respectively. They estimate that typical emissions are less than these values. They point out that the polynuclear hydrocarbon content of particles from large coal-fired units changes very little, if any, in passing through dust-collection equipment, thus leading them to conclude that these emissions are in extremely fine particles.

E. SMOKE

Smoke is a submicron particulate aerosol, from a combustion source, which obscures vision. It may, and usually does, contain comparatively little particulate matter by weight. However, it may appear to be an impenetrable mass because of the light-scattering properties of materials in the size range 0.3 to 0.5 μ (29). On the other hand, the effluent from a stack emitting a much larger tonnage of large particles, say 100 μ, may appear clear because such particles do not scatter light and, moving at high speed, they may be invisible. Smith and Gruber (28) conclude from the extensive measurements of Hangebrauck et al. that "no direct relationship seems to exist between the total particulate loading and the opacity of the smoke plumes." Nevertheless, dense smoke plumes are undesirable in populated areas.

A source of large particle emission is the accumulation of fine particles of smoke and fly ash on boiler heating surfaces and their subsequent flaking-off as agglomerates. Within a few hours of operation the insulating effect of these deposits reduces heat transfer to such an extent that their removal is necessary by a process called "sootblowing." Most of the agglomerates thus removed are so coarse that they are readily collected in conventional collectors. Particulate emissions from oil-fired units are more than doubled during sootblowing (7).

A word should be said here about the time-worn practice of judging the smoking tendencies of furnaces on the basis of furnace volume or flame travel. If mixing is at all times as thorough as possible, the time needed to complete burning is a function of gas velocity and furnace volume. However, a furnace with good mixing will need much less volume than one with poor mixing. Hence, unless the degree of mixing is specified, comparison of furnace volumes may be nearly meaningless. Unfortunately, no criterion for mixing has been established. Expressed in another way, a furnace may be smoking because of poor mixing rather than because of inadequate furnace volume. This is not to say that related criteria, such as heat-release rate and Btu per cubic foot of furnace volume, may not be of value in rating the behavior of ash in various furnaces. But because heat-release rates have some validity in predicting ash behavior, there is no reason for using these criteria for evaluating smoke tendencies.

IV. Gas-Burning Sources

Gas-fired equipment generally is found to produce a minimum of air pollution, although poor burning conditions may at times result in small, though objectionable, emissions of carbon monoxide, organic gases, and vapors. Solid particulate pollutants are produced with gas fuels in only two situations: first, when combustion-air supply to a high temperature zone is deliberately or inadvertently restricted—carbon black or soot is then produced as a dense black smoke; and second, residual solids are initially present in the fuel gas, as in the case of blast furnace and certain other process gases. If the particles are incombustible, they will emerge from the flame as solids.

A. FUEL GASES

Fuel gas composition and characteristics vary widely. Natural gas is primarily methane. Manufactured and coke-oven gas are about half hydrogen and one-third methane. Producer and blast furnace gases are mostly incombustible nitrogen with the combustible part being carbon monoxide with some hydrogen. For a thorough tabulation of the composition of approximately 100 different examples of fuel gas of many different types, consult "Gas Engineers Handbook" p. 2/18–2/19, The Industrial Press, New York, 1965.

B. GAS BURNERS

Common usage has named the device for mixing gas and air the "burner." If burning actually occurred in most burners, it would be an alarming indication that the system was not operating properly; the burner parts might be damaged through overheating. Nevertheless, the mixing role of the burner is essential to completing combustion without leaving unburned residual gases. In general, gas burners achieve their purpose extremely well, and the amount of unburned gases lost in the flue gases is usually too small to be detected by conventional combustion gas analysis.

Most small gas burners are atmospheric burners, so defined because they use the entraining force of a jet of raw gas to induce the inward flow of atmospheric (primary) air for mixing in the burner. Secondary air is usually induced to flow into the combustion chamber at essentially atmospheric pressure, by action of the draft, or thermal head, provided by the combustion system itself. Virtually all of the many varieties of gas burners and associated appliances available in the United States normally operate with negligible amounts of unburned gas loss because of the rigid test requirements which they must meet to receive the approval of the American Gas Association. The design and characteristics of atmospheric burners have been extensively developed (*30*).

Industrial gas burners may be of the atmospheric type or power-driven; in the latter, the air and intense mixing are provided by a blower. Because both types are readily designed for practically complete combustion, air pollution from them is usually slight. Oxides of nitrogen, though present, are, with present knowledge, unavoidable, and the amounts of sulfur dioxide and trioxide produced depend only on the amount of sulfur in the fuel.

C. Air–Gas Ratio

Theoretically, combustion gases require a definite amount of oxygen for complete combustion, depending on their composition. Table IV shows the theoretical air requirements of typical fuel gases. Because of imperfections in even the best of mixing, it is usually impracticable to fire a fuel stoichiometrically, i.e., with only the amount of air theoretically required. Instead, it is necessary to supply an excess of air to assure that any pockets of incompletely mixed fuel and air will nevertheless have sufficient air for complete combustion. Consequently, some of the total air supplied is unused; this is called excess air. For each practical burning situation there is a relation between the percentage of excess air and the amount of unburned fuel leaving the furnace. Usually, with automatic gas-fired equipment, it is practicable to maintain the excess air below 25% without producing appreciable unburned gases (*30a*).

TABLE IV
AIR REQUIRED FOR COMBUSTION
OF SOME TYPICAL FUEL GASES

Fuel gas	Amount (ft^3 air/ft^3 gas)
Natural	9.8
Liquefied petroleum	29.5
Manufactured	4.9
Coke oven	4.9
Blast furnace	0.7
Producer	1.0
Sewage	6.3

D. Combustion Chamber

When an approved atmospheric burner is given access to ample air supply, combustion is practically perfect over a wide range of operating conditions. When the normal flame is enclosed within a chamber which

TABLE V

OXIDES OF NITROGEN AND ALDEHYDES IN PRODUCTS OF COMBUSTION
FROM NATURAL GAS-FIRED APPLIANCES[a]

Appliance	Nitrogen oxides (as NO_2)		Aldehydes	
	ppm	lb/10^6 Btu	ppm	lb/10^6 Btu
Bunsen burner	21	0.07	2	—
Range, top burner	22	0.03		—
Range, oven	15	0.05	11	0.02
Water heater, 20 gal	25	0.05	—	—
Water heater, 100 gal	45	0.09	8	0.01
Floor furnace	30	0.07	3	0.005
Forced-air furnace	50	0.09	—	—
Steam boiler (10^7 Btu/hr)				
Low fire	40	0.14	5	0.01
High fire	90	0.16	—	—
Industrial burners[b]	216	—	49	—
Boilers and process heaters[c]	—	0.21	—	0.0028

  [a] From Vandaveer and Segeler (33).
  [b] Stanford Research Institute (33b). Additional effluents from industrial gas burners are: ammonia, 0.5 ppm; acids, 30 ppm; sulfur dioxide, 4 ppm.
  [c] Los Angeles County Air Pollution Control District (33c).

neither impedes air flow nor limits the natural flame, completeness of combustion is unchanged. However, if air flow is impeded, or if the combustion chamber walls block the normal flame path, or are considerably cooler than the flame, incomplete combustion will result; and appreciable amounts of carbon monoxide, aldehydes, and other organic gases may be produced. Here again, the approval requirements of the American Gas Association have been effective in virtual elimination of unsuitable combustion systems in appliances.

Few data are available on the amounts of unburned gases produced by gas-fired equipment (Tables V and VI). Tebbens *et al.* (31) have shown that as many as 16 aromatic hydrocarbons may be produced by the incomplete combustion of natural gas, but that "in contrast, complete combustion does not result in any of these hydrocarbons."

Estimates made in 1954 of unburned gases produced by all domestic, commercial, and industrial uses of natural gas in the Los Angeles basin (18) indicated that the acids and organics emitted were of the order of 30–50% greater than the aldehydes produced. It was also estimated that the weight of nitrogen oxides produced was about 3 times the weight of aldehydes. In England, measurements showed (32) that blue flames produced nitrogen oxide in the amount of 50 ppm, while yellow flames produced 50–100 ppm.

Other unburned gases may be found in minute quantities where a gas has been accidently or deliberately burned with a deficiency of air, such as in providing a special controlled atmosphere for chemical or metallurgical processing. Vandaveer and Segeler (33) report formaldehyde, acetaldehyde, other aldehydes, organic acids, and methyl alcohol when burning natural, coke oven, or butane gas under various conditions of air deficiency. In most gas-burning installations (33a) these would not be produced; but where controlled atmosphere furnaces are vented without afterburning or where, because of maladjustment or improper maintenance, the air-fuel ratio of ordinary burners is other than optimum, such emissions may be significant.

Fuel gases often contain trace amounts of sulfur, as hydrogen sulfide, carbon disulfide, mercaptans, or other organic sulfides. When natural gas occurs without these sulfur compounds, it is common, for safety reasons, to add mercaptan or other sulfur-bearing odorizers to the gas in the amount of 1 to 3 grains per 1000 ft^3 so that leaks of the gas will not go unnoticed (34). Attempts to distribute natural gases containing H_2S in amounts as high as 100 grains per 1000 ft^3 (0.016% by volume) have encountered trouble, not from air pollution, but from corrosion in the utilization equipment. However, manufactured gases contain from 20 to 200 grains of organic sulfur per 1000 ft^3 (35). Faith (36) assumed that natural gas in Southern California contained 400 grains of sulfur per 1000 ft^3, which was assumed to produce 1 pound of SO_2 per billion Btu. This value resulted in an estimate of 0.34 tons of SO_2 emitted to the Los

TABLE VI

TYPICAL RANGES OF EMISSIONS FROM NATURAL GAS-FIRED
INDUSTRIAL AND COMMERCIAL EQUIPMENT[a]

Equipment	Carbon monoxide (%)	Aldehydes (ppm)	Oxides of nitrogen (ppm)	Particulates (grains/ft³ at 12% CO₂)
Scotch marine boilers	0.000–0.2	2–7	8–56	0.0028–0.0079
Fire tube boilers	0.000–0.1	4	35–37	0.0025–0.051
Water tube boilers	0.000–0.2	3–11	16–127	0.0034–0.0082
75-gal water heater	0.001	2	46	0.03
Space heater	0.0	2	19	0.01
Bake oven	0.000	6	20	0.062
Industrial ovens, indirect	0.000	3–6	16–34	0.002–0.009
Ceramic kilns, indirect	0.000–0.04	2–7	3–66	0.0051–0.023

[a] From Chass and George (33a).

Angeles atmosphere per day by all gas uses, which is small compared with other sources.

All of the sulfur compounds in fuel gases can be considered to form sulfur dioxide and sulfur trioxide in burning. When burning gas containing 120 grains of organic sulfur per 1000 ft^3, Maconochie (37) found 0.00146% SO_2 by volume in the flue gas. SO_3 was also found in the unusually high amount of 28% of the SO_2; this is a much higher proportion than was reported by Johnstone (6). Barrett *et al.* (37a) showed that excess air affects SO_3 formation.

Strong sensations of acrid odor or eye irritation, or smoke, accompanying the emission of flue gases from gas-fired equipment are sensitive signals that combustion is incomplete and that burner adjustment is needed.

V. Oil-Fired Furnaces

The combustion of oil for heating purposes is a growing source of petroleum-based pollutants. Where appreciable unburned fuel is emitted, it is attributable to inappropriate oil or equipment.

A. Fuel Oils, Furnaces, and Burners

The variation in composition of crude oils is considerable, although increased flexibility in refining methods has minimized its effect on the behavior of the derived fuels. Crudes contain thousands of hydrocarbon compounds which are classified roughly as paraffins, napthenes, aromatics, resins, and asphalt. Those crudes which contain predominantly paraffins are called paraffinic. Those predominantly composed of napthenes are napthenic. Most crudes are intermediate or mixed. Depending on the composition of the crude, the refining process may involve various combinations of fractional distillation, thermal and catalytic cracking, and chemical processing.

Most of the ash and sulfur in fuel oil may be assumed to be emitted as pollutants. Since all crudes contain some sulfur, desulfurization is a step which is important in reducing the air pollution potential of the resultant fuels. A study of the costs of desulfurization of residual oils (38) concluded that reduction to 0.5% sulfur would cost the refiners 40 to 65 cents per barrel, enough to price residuals out of many markets, compared to higher sulfur fuels.

As may be inferred from Table VII (38a) there is considerable overlapping in properties among the different oils. Depending on economic,

TABLE VII

FUEL OIL CHARACTERISTICS AFFECTING AIR POLLUTION[a]

	Maximum ash (%)	Maximum sulfur (%)
No. 1, a distillate oil intended for pot-type burners requiring this grade	—	0.05
No. 2, a distillate oil for general purpose domestic heating	—	1.0
No. 4, an oil for burner installations not equipped with preheating facilities	0.10	No limit[b]
No. 5, a residual type of oil for burner installations equipped with preheating facilities	0.10	No limit[b]
No. 6 (also known as Bunker C), an oil for use in burners equipped with preheaters permitting high viscosity fuel	—	No limit[b]

[a] From "Specification for Fuel Oils" (38a).
[b] To be specified if required for special purpose.

technical, or geographic conditions, the composition of the specific grades can vary widely. Hence, two oils of the same grade may not necessarily perform equally well. If an oil is high in paraffins, the temperature of the flame will cause them to decompose readily into lighter and more volatile fractions which burn easily. On the other hand, aromatics do not readily decompose and, at the temperatures at which they do, cracking will occur which can produce tar, smoke, and soot. To a lesser extent, the olefins may crack and form compounds which are hard to burn. The principal burner types which have been evolved have, on the whole, demonstrated a capability for coping with the many possible variations in oils (38b). However, some burners are limited in this capability, as will be pointed out.

Residual fuels may be considered as colloidal dispersions of high molecular weight solids in an oil medium. These solids produce cokelike particles in the course of combustion (39). Given sufficient residence time at high enough temperature (39a), these particles will burn to completion (39b). However, if their burning is arrested, emission of fine coke dust will result. The emission rate of fly ash from high-ash fuel oil is appreciable and may be comparable to that emitted from some forms of solid fuel-fired apparatus. In some instances, which to date have been rare, it has been necessary to use dust-separating equipment such as cyclone (39a) or bag collectors (40, 40a) or electrostatic precipitators on residual oil-burning installations to meet local requirements.

TABLE VIII

CLASSIFICATION OF OIL BURNERS ACCORDING TO APPLICATION AND
LIST OF POSSIBLE POLLUTANTS

Burner type	Applications	Oil type usually used	Defects which may cause odors and smoke
Domestic[a]			
Pressure atomizing	Residential furnaces, water heaters	No. 1 or 2	Increased viscosity of oil; nozzle wear; clogged flue, gas passes, or chimney; dirt clogging air inlet; oil rate in excess of design
Rotary	Residential furnaces, water heaters	No. 1 or 2	Increased viscosity of oil; clogged nozzle or air supply; oil rate in excess of design
Vaporizing	Residential furnaces, water heaters	No. 1	Fuel variations; clogged flue gas passages, or chimney; clogged air supply
Commercial, Industrial			
Pressure atomizing	Steam boilers, process furnaces	No. 4, 5	Oil preheat too low or too high; nozzle wear; nozzle partly clogged; impaired air supply; clogged flue gas passages; poor draft; overloading
Horizontal rotary cup	Steam boilers, process furnaces	No. 4, 5, 6	Oil preheat too low or too high; burner partly clogged or dirty; impaired air supply; clogged flue gas passages; poor draft; overloading
Steam atomizing	Steam boilers, process furnaces	No. 5, 6	Oil preheat too low or too high; burner partly clogged or dirty; impaired air supply; clogged flue gas passages; poor draft; overloading; insufficient atomizing pressure
Air atomizing	Steam boilers, process furnaces	No. 5	Oil preheat too low or too high; burner partly clogged or dirty; impaired air supply; clogged flue gas passages; poor draft; overloading; insufficient atomizing pressure

[a] Commercial standard CS-75 established by U.S. Dept. of Commerce requires that all oil burners labeled as complying with the standard shall have smoke-free combustion.

Table VIII lists the types of oil burners which are commonly available, the types of pollutants which may be expected from them, and the defects in operation which create most of these pollutants. Probably the greatest cause of air pollution from oil burning is overloading, or firing in excess of the design firing rate. Systems which have been chronically neglected frequently become gradually overloaded because of growing heat requirements while, at the same time, the attention of owners and operators is drawn to seemingly more urgent problems in a plant. The obvious solution is regular attention by competent and responsible personnel, or if this has been neglected, a repair program plus a load survey; and, if necessary, added capacity, then regular attention.

Impingement of an oil flame on a cool solid surface can partially quench the flame and cause incomplete combustion with the release of hydrogen, hydrocarbons, carbon monoxide, and soot. This again can be a result of overloading, which may cause the flame envelope to be larger than that for which the combustion chamber was originally designed.

B. POLLUTANTS FROM OIL BURNING

Table IX shows the results of measurements in Los Angeles on the unburned gases which may escape from conventional oil-burning systems (41). Table X shows some typical emissions (42) from residential oil burners in European practice when burning kerosene. For a pressure burner burning gas-oil, the authors show the stack solids ranging from a low of 0.65 mg/m^3 for good, continuous burning; to 6.5 mg/m^3 for poor, intermittent burning. Burroughs (42a), quoting the unpublished work of Scott, shows, for unadjusted residential burners on No. 2 fuel oil, emissions ranging from 4 to 200 mg/m^3.

Figure 7, from Wingfield (42b), shows the data of Sambrook relating stack solids to Bachrach smoke number for domestic oil burners (42c). Also shown are the more recent data of Hunt and Biller (42d).

Burners are mechanical devices and, hence, may be expected to wear and drift out of adjustment. Therefore, periodic maintenance and adjustment must be provided to assure continuing clean performance (43–44b). It is common to judge a well-run burner system on the basis of the absence of smoke or aldehyde odor in the flue gases. Analytical techniques will detect aldehydes in concentrations as low as 0.5 ppm. The threshold of odor perception of most aldehydes is of the same order, less than 1 ppm. Thus, if an oil-burning system emits appreciable odor, causes eye irritation, or smokes, there is generally little justification for measurement of emissions, because something is wrong in atomization, mixing, or burning, and should be corrected.

TABLE IX
EMISSIONS FROM VARIOUS INDUSTRIAL AND COMMERCIAL OIL-FIRED EQUIPMENT[a]

Equipment	Rated size (hp)	Oil rate (ghp)	Oil properties API gravity	S (%)	Ash (%)	Excess air (%)	Sulfur Dioxide Measured ppm	Measured lb/hour	Calculated lb/hour	SO₃ (ppm)	CO (%)	Aldehydes (as formaldehyde) (ppm)	Nitrogen oxide (as NO₂) (ppm)	Particulates (grains SCF at 12% CO₂)	(mg/m³ at 12% CO₂)
							Number 2 Fuel Oil								
Firetube boiler	60	9	31	1.05	0.02	65	355	1.4	1.37	1.6	0.01	9	47	0.069	158
Scotch marine boilers	300	39.6	35	0.29	0.01	220	7	2.2	—	0	0	6	14	0.142	325
	200	21.0	34	0.97	0	210	11	2.3	—	5.6	0.02	52	21	0.14	320
	350	85.3	33	0.42	0	94	17	7.2	—	0	0	3	72	0.014	32
Water tube boiler	100	6.1	29	0.71	0	290	98	0.5	0.64	1.4	0.002	5	36	0.071	163
	200	9.7	35	0.55	0	370	trace	—	—	0	0.002	8	55	0.10	229
	245	23.1	33	0.21	0.07	115	102	1.3	—	0.5	0.002	7	33	0.041	94
Oil heater	—	5.2	34	0.80	0	120	138	0.4	—	2.8	0.002	11	34	0.073	167
							Number 1 Fuel Oil								
Scotch marine boiler	150	15.3	40	0.09	0	150	28	0.5	0.19	1.7	0.001	5	20	0.038	87
Ceramic kiln	—	10.0	45	trace	0	21	0	0	—	0	0.04	3	27	0.004	9
	—	20.0	45	trace	0	373	trace	—	—	0	0	3	20	0.038	87
							Heavy Fuel Oil								
Firetube boiler	120	36.3	16	1.0	0	68	414	7.5	5.3	4.7	0.003	7	368	0.074	169
Scotch marine boiler	125	23.1	11	1.78	0.18	180	264	5.0	7.4	3.2	0	9	128	0.11	252
Water tube boiler	245	99.4	11	0.44	0.13	43	397	17.3	83.0	0.4	0	8	387	0.064	146
	425	160.0	8	3.06	0	110	700	75.0	10.4	6.7	0.001	4	275	0.28	640
	460	80.5	12	0.78	0.12	107	362	17.6	55.5	2.2	0	7	199	0.039	89
	500	248.0	15	1.39	0.04	92	594	79.0	55.5	3.6	0	17	256	0.045	103
	580	57.5	13	1.30	0.03	95	640	21.0	12.2	2.2	0	8	206	0.060	137
	870	168.0	9	1.94	0.03	73	344	27.2	55.5	1.2	0	48	256	0.096	220

[a] From Chass and George (41). Standard Conditions at 60F and 14.7 psia.

TABLE X

Measurements of Unburned Hydrocarbons and Other Gaseous Pollutants in Flue Gases from Three Types of Domestic Burners for Good and Bad Conditions[a]

Boiler output (kcal/h)	Burner	Combustion	Operating conditions				Gaseous and condensable pollutants	
			Smoke no. (Bacharach scale)	CO_2 (% vol)	CO (ppm vol)	NO_2 (ppm vol)	Aldehydes (as HCHO) (ppm vol)	Total unburned hydrocarbons (ppm vol)
20,000	Fan-assisted pot	Good	2[b]	7.7	35	<20	4	16
		Bad	6-7	9.8	60	<20	14	24
10,000	Wallflame	Good	<1	13.6	60	<20	3	15
		Bad	1-2	13.9	8,000	<20	25	55
10,500	Pressure atomizing	Good	2-3	8.5	Not detected	—	3	6
		Bad	8-9	10.2	60	—	10	17

[a] All results were obtained when operating on kerosene-type fuel.
[b] 5 at start of firing cycle.

25

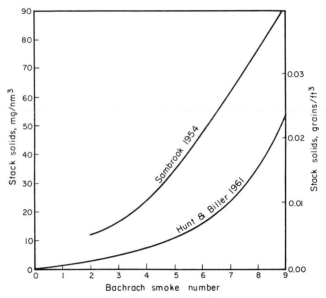

Fig. 7. Relation of solids emission to smoke for domestic oil burners.

Acid smuts form by agglomeration of smoke particles on the inside of chimney surfaces, particularly when uninsulated or poorly designed chimneys are operated at low loads or at temperatures below 275 °F. This eventually forms a heavy layer, highly acidified by adsorption of the sulfur oxides present. When there is an increase in flue gas temperature or velocity, the deposits flake off and are carried as large flakes out of the chimney to be deposited nearby. Increasing combustion chamber temperature reduces such deposits. Insulation of the chimney has been shown to practically eliminate these deposits (44c).

C. Oil Additives

Occasionally, proprietary products are brought forth with claims to reduce pollution from oil burners (45). Although some metallic oxides are known (46) to provide beneficial effects by reducing the ignition temperature of carbon, as in soot, data regarding their effects on the "cleanness" of combustion are not available. Until such data are obtained, abatement of objectionable pollution from fuel-oil burning can best be achieved through means previously indicated in this section. Some work has been done on addition of calcium and magnesium salts to fuel or furnace to react with the sulfur oxides (46a) to reduce fireside corrosion.

An objectionable feature of the use of metallic oxides as "soot removers" is that they cause an increase in particulate emission. This occurs because the ignition of fluffy carbon deposits on heat transfer surfaces of a boiler results in increased gas temperatures and localized turbulence. Thus, portions of the burning soot are blown free of the surface and are carried out of the stack before burning is complete.

The rapid expansion of the use of large stationary gas turbines for electric power generation in populated areas has called attention to their light smoking tendencies. Current work has shown some success in eliminating this smoke by means of combustor changes and by the addition of up to 150 ppm of manganese in the fuel oil in the form of an oil-soluble organic additive (*46b, 46c, 46d*). Work so far indicates that as smoking increases, additive effectiveness decreases and that improvements in oil atomization plus refinements in combustor air admission give most promise for smoke elimination.

VI. Solid Fuels

Utilization of solid fuels has been, in the past, frequently associated with various degrees of smoke emission. The advent of completely automatic equipment to replace hand-firing methods has greatly reduced and, in most cases, eliminated smoke from solid fuels. Increasingly widespread enforcement of air pollution control ordinances has caused users of solid fuels either to install practically smoke-free equipment or to use the more easily utilized, but often more costly fluid fuels. In many applications of solid fuels, provisions for fly ash collection must be made to keep the final solids emission within the limits of local ordinances.

Sulfur dioxide emission continues to be a problem when burning most coals because economic means have not been found to remove all of the sulfur which, in most coals, is about equally divided between organic and pyritic sulfur (*46e*). Ultrafine grinding followed by subsequent processing has not shown economic promise in reducing the sulfur content.

A. Volatile Content

Table XI lists the principal solid fuels in the approximate order of increasing volatile content. Volatile content is defined as that portion of the moisture-free fuel which is driven off when a sample is heated to 1750 °F in a closed crucible. Volatiles in coal are a complex mixture of hydrocarbons and organic materials, some of which may decompose to form smoke plus other organics, when heated to high temperatures in a deficiency of air. In the days of hand firing, volatile content was widely

TABLE XI

SOLID FUELS IN ORDER OF INCREASING VOLATILE CONTENT, LISTING SUITABLE FIRING EQUIPMENT FOR EACH CATEGORY

	Volatile content on dry basis (%)	Typical moisture content as fired (%)	Typical ash (%)	Typical sulfur (%)	Automatic firing equipment best suited to minimize air pollution[a]
High-temperature coke	2	5	15	2	Any fixed or traveling fuel bed
Anthracite	5	5	10	0.5	Pulverized firing or traveling grate
Low-temperature coke	10–15	5	15	2	Any fixed or traveling fuel bed, cyclone furnace
Low-volatile bituminous coal	20	5	7	1	Pulverized firing, any fixed or traveling fuel bed, underfeed stoker, cyclone furnace
Medium-volatile bituminous coal	30	5	10	2	Pulverized firing, traveling grate, underfeed stoker, cyclone furnace
Subbituminous coal	35	25	5	1	Pulverized firing, traveling grate, underfeed stoker, spreader stoker
High-volatile bituminous coal	40	5	10	2	Pulverized firing, traveling grate, underfeed stoker, cyclone furnace
Lignite	40	30	5	1	Pulverized firing, traveling grate, underfeed stoker, spreader stoker
Bagasse	40	50	2	0	Spreader stoker
Wood	80	25	1	0	Spreader stoker

[a] Dust collector may be necessary to ensure compliance with local ordinances.

TABLE XII

POLYNUCLEAR HYDROCARBONS EMITTED BY BITUMINOUS COAL WITH VARIOUS FIRING METHODS[a]

	Pulverized firing	Cyclone	Spreader stokers		Chain-grate stoker	Underfeed stokers			Hand-fired
Benzo(*a*)pyrene	0.04–0.13	0.49	0.04	0.057	0.082	22	0.26	8.4	880
Pyrene	0.20–0.40	2.25	0.23	1.30	0.860	35	3.70	17	1,320
Benzo(*e*)pyrene	0–0.58	0.87	0.13	0.770	0.290	17	0.510	11.9	220
Perylene	0–0.15	0.07				3.5			132
Benzo(*ghi*)perylene	0.02–1.42	0.44				9.9		1.28	660
Anthanthrene	0–0.02					0.64			198
Coronene	0–0.15	0.01	0.02	0.057		0.73		2.64	66
Anthracene						1.9			880
Phenanthrene			0.11	0.790		22	2.2	64	2,200
Fluoranthene		0.17				83.9	7.1	103	2,200
Benz(*a*)anthracene					1.50	8.6		1.23	

Type of unit

[a] From Smith and Gruber (*69*). Figures are pounds per million-million Btu input.

used as a rough index of the smoke-forming tendency of a solid fuel. However, with modern automatic firing equipment, smoke is almost completely eliminated regardless of the volatility of the fuel used.

B. HAND FIRING

The only instances in which hand firing of high-volatile fuels has been acceptably and smokelessly accomplished has been in small domestic equipment utilizing the downdraft principle (47). In contrast to burning in the open fireplace or in the conventional stove or furnace, where the hot products of combustion rise upward through fresh fuel that is fired on top of the incandescent bed, the downdraft principle causes a downward flow of air and gases. Complete combustion is readily attained with a wide variety of fuels. The method produces practically no fly ash. Unfortunately, successful application of this principle has been limited to small units, owing to problems of fuel flow and of heat transfer through the fuel mass in large ones.

Many hand-firing methods have been devised with the aim of achieving smokeless operation of the conventional overfeed fuel bed, in which air flows upward, counter to the downward flow of fuel. Generally, these so-called smokeless methods provide for fresh fuel to be fired over only a portion of the burning fuel bed. They are variously called the alternate, side-bank, or coking methods. However, application of these methods usually requires more frequent firing than if the entire surface is covered. Also, in firing a large furnace by such means, considerable muscular effort and skill are required for firing in such a way as always to leave a major portion of the fuel bed uncovered. Consequently, unless the fireman is extremely conscientious and skilled, these methods reduce, but do not practicably eliminate smoke and unburned gases. Actually, rising costs of labor have probably been as effective as air pollution abatement in causing general replacement of hand-fired equipment by automatic firing methods. Brief studies on a single overfeed warm-air furnace, hand-fired with bituminous coal, gave, when smoke varied between 40 and 80% opacity, benzo(a) pyrene of 6000 μg per pound fuel, whereas almost all other fuels and firing methods gave less than 100 μg and one gave less than 1 μg (48, 48a) (see also Table XII).

C. OVERFIRE AIR JETS

Jets of air over the fuel bed, sometimes induced into the furnace by jets of high pressure steam, have been used for over a hundred years (49) to abate smoke from solid fuel-fired furnaces. The action of the jets is to cause intense mixing of the stratified streams of air and burning gas which usually flow upward from a solid fuel bed. Methods for application of overfire jets have been thoroughly described (*50*, *51*), and data have been obtained on their effects on some types of firing systems.

D. UNDERFEED STOKERS

Overfeed fuel beds have been shown to be inherently smoky in operation because burning gases rise through fresh fuel, thus resulting in rapid devolatilization of the new fuel in a zone having a deficiency of oxygen. On the other hand, underfeed beds are inherently smoke free. The air and fresh fuel flow concurrently, usually upward; hence, the zone of ignition, which is near the point of maximum evolution of combustible gases, is supplied with ample air, well mixed, which promotes complete combustion.

Because high velocity jets of burning gas escape through fissures in the underfed fuel bed, some fly ash will be produced. Measurements on small- and medium-sized underfeeds show particle emissions ranging from 0.24 to 0.68 pound per 1000-pound flue gas at 50% excess air (*48*). At burning rates of 40 lb/ft²/hour (approximately 500,000 Btu/ft²/hour), the amount of fly ash may be great enough to require dust collectors to clean the flue gases. Data on dust emission are available for two large multiple-retort stokers. Measurements on one unit, made in 1932 (*52*), showed emissions ranging from 0.3 to 1.5 grains/ft³ for burning rates of between 25 and 45 lb/ft²/hour. Later measurements on a similar unit using low-volatile coal (*53*) showed emissions of 0.2 to over 1.5 grains/ft³ for approximately the same range of burning rates. The amounts of unburned gases which escape from underfed stokers have been shown, in limited tests, to be low when operation is smokeless; moderately high when smoky (*48*).

The usual underfeed stoker is better suited for caking coals than for noncaking or free-burning coals because the volatiles are released more slowly from caked masses than from a porous bed of coals, Consequently, there is the possibility of smoke from misapplication of coal to such equipment, but no data are available on the amount of pollution which can result from such a condition. Flue-gas analyses on a single retort-underfeed stoker applied to a small industrial boiler showed no carbon monoxide, hydrogen, methane, ethane, or illuminants within the limits of detection of the combustion gas analyzer used, i.e., 0.1%, even when smoke was produced deliberately by firing a coarse, uniformly sized coal (*54*).

E. Traveling-Grate Stokers

The traveling grate is usually applied to the burning of anthracite, subbituminous and weakly caking bituminous coal, lignite, and occasionally, coke. Generally, it works best with noncaking fuels because air distribution is most uniform through a uniform bed of noncaked masses. For many years, mixing of the burning gases above the traveling grate was achieved by the use of elaborate suspended arches which forced the upward flow of flame into a narrow throat walled by incandescent refractory. However, the recent trend has been to use only rear arches or simple open furnaces and to attain mixing by means of high-velocity jets of secondary air directed from a number of nozzles located in one or more of the furnace walls. These are effective in eliminating smoke which may result from poor mixing (55). Zoned control of the air admitted to various portions of the fuel bed is an effective means for reducing smoke and fly ash emission.

Measurements on a single power-generating traveling-grate stoker, operating near rating, showed negligible hydrocarbon emissions even with smoke between 20 and 40% opacity, but particulate emission was 0.99 pound per 1000 pounds gas at 50% excess air (48).

Vibrating-grate stokers move the coal slowly across the furnace by means of small, rapid oscillations of the grate. Fly ash may be slightly higher than on traveling-grate stokers because of increased agitation of the fuel bed.

F. Spreader Stokers

The spreader stoker employs either a mechanical spreader or jets of steam or air to throw the solid fuel into the furnace, where it falls on a grate that is traveling or stationary. Essentially, it employs overfeed burning, an inherently smoky method, plus suspension burning, an inherently smoke-free fly ash-producing, method. Overfire jets have been found essential to smoke-free operation.

Figure 8 shows the effect of burning rate on dust emission from a spreader stoker (56) when the dust was measured ahead of the dust collector. The two upper curves indicate that, without a dust collector, dust emission at all burning rates would be well above most commonly used limitations on fly ash in the flue gas. Overfire jets reduce dust emission significantly but not enough to meet most ordinances. On the other hand, the cluster of points in the lower right of the figure are dust-emission data after the collector for a similar unit (57) having a dust collector of high efficiency. The separate lower curve shows emission from large underfeed stokers having no collectors (58).

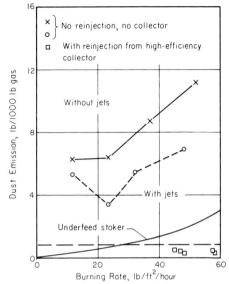

Fig. 8. Effect of burning rate, overfire jets, and collector efficiency on dust emission from spreader stokers and one large underfeed stoker burning eastern bituminous coal (56–58).

As a part of extensive studies in Germany on a number of different fuels, boilers, and firing systems, Kuhlman (59) found that spreader stokers in firetube boilers emitted little more flue dust, about 1.8 kg per metric ton of steam generated, than hand firing or traveling grates, about 1.3 kg per metric ton. The former figure is roughly equivalent to 30 pounds of dust per short ton of coal fired, 1.2 pounds per million Btu, or 1.4 pounds per 1000-pound flue gas.

Smoke is characteristic of most spreader stokers if they are operated at less than approximately 25% of full load, because low furnace temperature causes incomplete suspension burning. Accordingly, a spreader stoker-fired system should be supported by suitable auxiliary heat-generating means so that at low plant loads the stoker can either be operated to carry all of the load or be shut down completely. Modulating controls have been shown to help reduce dust emission (60).

The unburned gases emitted by spreaders are extremely low when operation is smokeless, similar to values characteristic of pulverized-coal firing.

G. Pulverized-Fuel Firing

An outstandingly successful effort to bring some of the advantages of the fluid fuels to solid fuel utilization has been the suspension burning of fine coal in large quantities. The coal is pulverized to a median size of 50μ, which permits rapid combustion. The success of increasingly larger pulverized coal-fired furnaces has led many to attempt small applications such as in residences, apartments, and small commercial plants—with uniform lack of commercial success. The principal causes for these failures have been the high cost of fuel preparation and distribution, and the problem of fly ash accumulation and disposal.

The largest single use of coal in the United States is in pulverized coal-fired boilers for electric power-generating stations. In these plants combustion is closely controlled so that it can safely be assumed that modern well-run plants of this type emit rather small percentages of unburned gases. Measurements by Sherman (61) of combustion in pulverized coal flames showed measureable amounts of methane and hydrogen near the burner only, but none leaving the furnace (using methods sensitive to 0.2%). Such furnaces characteristically emit 50–80% of the ash fired in the coal in the form of fine fly ash; hence, all modern plants of this type are equipped with high efficiency dust collectors. This has resulted in the collection annually in the United States of an estimated 20 million tons of uniformly sized, low combustible content fly ash, which is finding increasing markets as cement additives, in road building, and other areas (62). But of the total production, about 16 million tons are discarded because no market has yet been found for it.

In the process of combustion, the individual particles of coal become heated, which causes them to become plastic. Simultaneously, the rising temperature causes the volatile portion of the coal to be vaporized. As the vapor forces its way out of the softened particles, the latter become puffed into irregularly shaped, porous masses called cenospheres (63), which may be 2–5 times as large as the original particles. Then, as the cenospheres solidify to char, and as burning continues, the gas in the particles is released. Much of the ash is carried away by the ambient gases in the form of minute particles much smaller than the original coal particle. The remainder of the ash in the cenosphere may remain as a fragile, lacy, hollow sphere of fused minerals. The nature of the residual particle depends somewhat on the coal type and furnace conditions, but primarily on the composition and mode of distribution of the ash in the coal, which usually is quite complex.

The fly ash emission characteristics of the two principal types of furnaces, slag-tap and dry-bottom, are distinctly different, although closely comparable data to show this difference are not available. The slag-tap furnace is designed with the deliberate intention of causing molten ash particles to accumulate on the lower walls and floor of the furnace. The liquefied ash then flows slowly down the walls and out of the furnace bottom through a slag tap. Depending on the composition and flow characteristics of the ash, about 50% of the ash in the coal leaves a slag-tap furnace as fly ash (64). Measurements on one large slag-tap furnace showed that 70% of the ash left the furnace in the gases (65,66). A significant innovation in the disposal of collected fly ash by "refiring" has been successfully applied to some slag-tap furnaces (67). Measurements (65) on one boiler using reinjection showed that as the total ash flow to the furnace was increased, the percentage of the ash retained by the furnace stayed at 30%.

The dry-bottom furnace is designed to cool all of the residual ash particles below their melting point before they strike the furnace walls or heat absorbing surfaces. Measurements indicate (65) that approximately 60–80% of the ash fired leaves a dry-bottom furnace as fly ash.

Many modern utility plants using pulverized coal have installed dust collectors of such high efficiency that the net emission is well below the limits permitted by most air pollution ordinances. This practice, largely unheralded, and carried out especially by large utilities, is a farsighted recognition of their self-selected role as good neighbors. This is done in anticipation of the years to come when even remote plants will have new neighbors, and community atmospheric standards will have become more stringent as the population density increases.

Nearly all of the sulfur in pulverized coal appears as SO_2 or SO_3 in the flue gases. Partial desulfurization of the fuel in elaborate coal-cleaning plants at coal mines is widely practiced, but the amount of residual sulfur oxides is frequently great enough to be objectionable. Numerous attempts to remove the oxides from the gases have failed economically owing to the high costs of handling the large gas volume diluted by oxygen, nitrogen, and CO_2 (68) (see Chapters 46 and 47). The most successful economic "solution" to the problem so far has been the use of tall chimneys ranging in height from 400 to 1000 feet (see also Chapter 8, Vol. I).

TABLE XIII

COMBUSTIBLE GASES EMITTED BY BITUMINOUS COAL WITH VARIOUS FIRING METHODS[a]

	Pulverized firing	Cyclone	Spreader stoker	Chain-grate stoker	Underfeed stoker	Hand-fired
Single atom hydrocarbon	1–10	—		5	36–120	730
Carbon monoxide	5–44	—	29	510	160–1100	3500
Formaldehyde	0.1–0.25	0.17	0.06	0.14	0.21–0.38	—

[a] From Smith and Gruber (69). Data in pounds per billion Btu input.

Because of the excellent mixing and burning conditions in pulverized coal-fired furnaces, the combustion of volatile matter is excellent and the very low emission rates of hydrocarbons (48a) are of the same order as those from typical fluid-fuel burners. Table XII (69) shows polynuclear-hydrocarbon emissions from bituminous coal by pulverized and other firing methods. The total polynuclear-hydrocarbon emissions from any unit are generally less than one-millionth the rate of sulfur dioxide emissions from the same unit. Table XIII shows gaseous emissions from the same equipment (69). Small scale laboratory experiments on pulverized coal indicate that near-stoichiometric combustion significantly reduces the formation of nitrogen oxides but that flue-gas recirculation is ineffective (69a).

H. Cyclone Furnaces

A highly effective method for large-scale firing of coal is the cyclone furnace (70). It fires crushed coal, nearly as fine as pulverized coal, into a water-cooled, refractory-lined, cylindrical chamber which discharges gases nearly horizontally into a water-tube boiler. Combustion is so intense that a small portion of the molten ash coating the wall of the chamber is vaporized, as was shown by careful ash balances on an early cyclone (71). Approximately 85% of the ash fired is retained as molten slag; hence, the fly ash load is much lower than with pulverized coal

TABLE XIV
EMISSION OF NITROGEN OXIDES[a]

Type of unit	Pounds per million Btu input
Pulverized coal	
Vertical firing	0.38
Corner firing	0.95
Front wall firing	0.68
Horizontal opposed firing	0.65
Cyclone	2.5
Stoker:	
Spreader stoker	0.65
Commercial underfeed	0.30
Residential underfeed	0.36
Hand-fired	0.11

[a] From Hangebrauck et al. (48) and Cuffe and Gerstle (72).

(71a). However, the ash which does escape the cyclone is extremely fine (71b), hence, difficult to collect; but high efficiency of collection has been shown to be feasible (71).

Possibly because of the rapid cooling effect of the cyclone wall, the nitrogen oxides produced are higher than by other methods. Table XIV (72) shows the emission of nitrogen oxides from various bituminous coal-fired units.

VII.   Incinerators

Incineration of private or community waste has traditionally been carried out at points as remote as conveniently feasible from inhabited areas or structures, because incinerators have often been obnoxious to the optic and olfactory senses. This has come about because "waste disposal is generally a financially unrewarding act, and engineers and community officials responsible for management of wastes have tended to respond to this attitude in a negative manner. In general, they have apologized for the fact that waste handling systems cost anything at all. But there is a growing awareness that waste management is worth whatever it costs within the framework of honest engineering and sound public health practice; and that the cost is the price man must pay for the benefits of a modern urban-industrial-agricultural society" (73).

Increasing population density has increased the incineration load, while at the same time reducing the number of available remote locations for community incinerators, and strengthening the requirements for clean, inoffensive operation. Consequently, incinerator design is gaining increasing attention, and is now in a state of flux more than at any time in the past. Basically, the principle of incineration is unchanged: the employment of combustion to convert combustible waste, primarily cellulose, into two odorless gases, carbon dioxide and water vapor, leaving only a small fraction of the charge, usually about 10–20%, as a solid, easily disposable ash. Table XV shows the waste classifications suggested by the Incinerator Institute of America (74).

A. Large Industrial and Municipal Incinerators

Stephenson and Cafiero (75) have tabulated data on over 200 American incinerators built since 1945 which indicate that many of them are of the batch type. Often these are characterized by uncertain control of combustion conditions at certain parts of the cycle. An increasing number of new installations, however, incorporate continuous flow of refuse, with a consequently improved opportunity to control combustion.

TABLE XV

Classification of Incinerator Fuels Suggested by
Incinerator Institute of America[a]

Classification of wastes		Approximate composition by weight (%)	Moisture content (%)	Incombustible solids (%)	Heat value of refuse as fired Btu/lb	Recommended min. burner input per pound waste, Btu/hour
Type	Description					
0	Trash	Trash 100	10	5	8500	0
1	Rubbish	Rubbish 80 Garbage 20	25	10	6500	0
2	Refuse	Rubbish 50 Garbage 50	50	7	4300	1500
3	Garbage	Garbage 65 Rubbish 35	70	5	2500	3000
4	Animal solids and organic wastes	Animal and human tissue	85	5	1000	8000 (5000 primary) (3000 secondary)
5	Gaseous, liquid or semiliquid wastes	Variable	Variable	Variable	Variable	Variable
6	Semisolid and solid wastes	Variable	Variable	Variable	Variable	Variable

[a] From Incinerator Institute of America (74).

In general, no large incinerators can meet a reasonably restrictive dust limit standard without the use of an efficient dust collection system. Construction costs usually force the designer to use high burning rates which inevitably result in entrainment of fly ash. Large quantities of excess air moving at moderately high velocity are usually used to keep refractories from overheating (76), but this procedure also results in entrainment of dust by the gases. Waste-heat recovery is generally costly but simplifies the problem of hot-gas cleaning, and will rightly receive increasing attention as incinerator engineering advances.

Rose and others (77) have shown in an experimental incinerator that certain operating factors such as chamber temperature, burning rate, proportion of overfire air, and uniformity of feed are predominating factors. All of these are affected somewhat by design, but largely by operation. Few of the available data are directly comparable among themselves, owing to the great variation of local design and operating factors. Discussing the extensive measurements he made on municipal incinerators, Rehm (78) reported: "Exit dust loadings from municipal incinerators tested to date, when operated with force draft air, at rated capacity and without benefit of fly ash collection systems, range from 1.30 to 3.00 lb per 1000 lb flue gas adjusted to 12 percent CO_2. Most of the test results are in the order of 2.00 to 2.7 lb per 1000 lb flue gas, adjusted to 12 percent CO_2. Actual exit dust loadings (unadjusted) for these conditions ranged from 0.25- to 1.20-grains per standard cubic foot, 32 °F, 29.92 in Hg." These data indicate a range of emissions of 10–26 pounds per ton of charge. In contrast to these data are some reported by Kanter and others (79) on two municipal incinerators of 6000 and 9000 pound per hour capacity, operated at 90% capacity, and emitting only 0.106 and 0.246 grains per standard cubic foot, or 5.7 and 8.1 pounds per ton of charge, respectively.

Subsequently, Jens and Rehm (80) have reported the results of 17 tests on a two-furnace, rocking-grate municipal plant rated at a total of 300 tons per 24-hour day and having a wetted vertical baffle type of dust separator, with an efficiency of about 50%. The stack particulate emissions from this combination ranged from 0.679 to 1.40 pounds per 1000 pounds gas corrected to 50% excess air. These correspond to 7.57 and 9.20 pounds emission per ton of charge, respectively (Table XVI).

Data on gaseous emissions from incinerators are even fewer than the particulate data. Feldstein and others (81) have presented a few data (Table XVII) from the application of a long-path, infrared technique. The effect of an afterburner in completely eliminating most hydrocarbon gases is clearly shown. Data from Los Angeles (82) show that large municipal incinerators there emit 2.5 pounds of nitrogen oxides per ton of charge. In contrast, the lowest emission from large utility boilers is 100 pounds per ton of fuel. Table XVIII (83) shows polynuclear-hydrocarbon emission from medium and large units.

B. Dust Collection for Large Incinerators

Traditionally, large incinerators have been equipped with so-called secondary, combustion, expansion, settling, or subsidence chambers, in which combustion supposedly was completed and dust settled out of the hot gases before their discharge to the community atmosphere. These were popular with designers because they collected the large particles which were characteristic of wood- and paper-burning operations. These particles, when emitted to the surroundings, were readily traceable despite generally high rates of dust deposition from many other sources. However, these chambers were ineffective in trapping fine particles. Such tremendous advances have been made in the reduction of fly ash from other sources through the application of pollution-abatement equipment that incinerators must now employ means which will be equally effective.

There is some indication (84) that modification of old expansion

TABLE XVI

PARTICULATE EMISSIONS FROM INCINERATORS WITH VARIOUS GRATES AND LOW PRESSURE DROP DUST COLLECTORS[a]

	Tons per day	Pounds dust per 1000 pounds gas corrected to 50% excess air	Dust collector type	Emission Pounds per ton charged						Size of particulate Percent less than	
				Furnace outlet			Stack				
				Max.	Min.	Aver.	Max.	Min.	Aver.	10μ	5μ
Traveling grate	250		Dry settling chamber	18.9	7.7	12.4	—	—	9.8	23.0	17.5
Reciprocating grate	250		Wetted steel baffle chamber	36.6	17.3	25.1	16	8.5	11.8	26.8	20.8
Rocking grate	120		Wetted vertical refractory baffle	11.0	6.1	9.1	11.5	4.9	8.2	38.1	31.9
Rocking grate[b]	273	0.708	Wetted vertical steel baffle	—	—	—	—	—	11.4		
	465	1.025	Wetted vertical steel baffle	—	—	—	—	—	19.4		

[a] From Jens and Rehm (80).
[b] From Walker and Schmitz (80a).

TABLE XVII

CONCENTRATIONS OF TYPICAL GASEOUS EFFLUENTS FROM INCINERATORS[a]

| | Concentration (ppm) | | | | | | | |
| | Single chamber | | Multiple chamber | | | | | |
	No after-burner	No after-burner	After-burner off	After-burner on	After-burner off	After-burner on	After-burner on	After-burner on
Methane	314	340	40	0	40	0	0	0
Acetylene	355	520	5	0	50	0	0	0
Ethylene	20	27	5	0	52	0	0	0
Other hydrocarbons[b]	60	75	5	0	85	0	0	0
Carbon monoxide	520	570	165	—	3900	150	10	10
Nitrogen dioxide	—	—	10	6	70	160	8	10
Nitrous oxide	—	—	—	—	—	40	75	100

[a] From Feldstein et al. (81).
[b] Corrected for the presence of methane, ethylene, acetylene, propylene.

chambers by means of wetted impingement baffles and water-covered floors will increase their efficiency. However, they are unlikely to be sufficient for the increasingly stringent particulate emission regulations being promulgated in densely populated areas.

Where space limitation, or the need for extreme cleanliness requires, water scrubbers or metallic multicyclones preceded by cooling sprays have been successful. However, both systems require induced-draft fans and automatic controls, and wet systems require water treatment to minimize water pollution by the plant discharge. Also, where metallic parts are employed in warm, moist gases, corrosion is often severe. In Europe, many installations employ electrostatic precipitators to assure clean effluent (85). Table XIX shows data (86) on emissions from four European units.

C. SPECIAL INDUSTRIAL INCINERATORS

Incinerators for a large variety of specialized industrial wastes are generally fired with ample amounts of auxiliary fuels to assure high temperature, and thus, complete decomposition of the wastes. In some cases scrubbers are required to minimize atmospheric contamination. Examples are oil- and gas-fired crematories, oil- and gas-fired sewage sludge incinerators, and incinerators for radioactive wastes. Automobile-burning incinerators have recently come into use for removing combustible materials from scrapped cars. Usually these employ fuel-fired afterburners to burn unburned gases. Coleman (86a) has summarized the products of combustion of some plastics.

TABLE XVIII

POLYNUCLEAR HYDROCARBON EMISSION SUMMARY—INCINERATION SOURCES[a]

Type of unit	Sampling point	Benzo(a)pyrene		Micrograms per pound of refuse charged									
		(μg per 1000 m³)[b]	(μg per pound)[c]	Pyrene	Benzo(e)-pyrene	Perylene	Benzo-(ghi)-perylene	Anthan-threne	Coronene	Anthra-cene	Phenan-threne	Fluoran-thene	Benz(a)-anthra-cene
Municipal													
250-ton/day multiple chamber	Breeching (before settling chamber)	19	0.075	8.0	0.34				0.24			9.8	0.37
50-ton/day multiple chamber	Breeching (before scrubber)	2,700	6.1	52	12		34		15		18	4.6	
	Stack (after scrubber)	17	0.089	2.1	0.58		0.63		0.63			3.3	0.15
Commercial													
5.3-ton/day single chamber	Stack	11,000	53	320	42	3.1	90	6.6	21	47	140	220	4.6
3-ton/day multiple chamber	Stack	52,000	260	4200	260	60	870	79	210	86	59	3900	290

[a] A blank in the table for a particular compound indicates it was not detected in the sample.

[b] Micrograms per 1000 m³ of flue gas at standard conditions (70 °F, 1 atm).

[c] Micrograms per pound of refuse charged.

TABLE XIX
PARTICULATE EMISSIONS FROM SOME LARGE EUROPEAN INCINERATORS[a]

Incinerator type	Installation	Maximum fly ash emission grams/1000 m³	Method of dust collection	Equivalent U.S. measure lb/1000 lb
Rotary kiln plus reciprocating grate	Paris	0.3–0.5	Wet	0.232–0.386
Reversing inclined grate	Munich	0.382	Electrostatic	0.296
Rotary drum plus inclined grate	Duesseldorf	0.0505	Electrostatic	0.039
Inclined rocking grate plus slagging chamber	Hamburg	<0.15	Electrostatic	0.116

[a] From Stabenow (86).

The ancient practice of open-pit burning has been greatly improved (87), although its problem of fly ash emission from high-ash wastes remains unsolved. The virtue of the open-pit incinerator is that it is effectively cooled by direct radiation to the sky; hence, costly refractories are unnecessary. The improvement has been to add flame agitation to the pit by means of a row of 2- to 3-inch diameter high-velocity jets of air spaced on 6-inch centers aimed downward at an angle from one side of the pit opening. An intense vortex of flame is thus induced in the pit with such thorough mixing of air and combustible that smoke is readily eliminated. However, if the solid or liquid waste is high in finely divided ash content, the intense mixing helps to lift a major portion of the fine ash out of the chamber with the clear exhaust gases. Thus, beyond some still unknown limiting ash content, the pit incinerator will need an exhaust gas cleaner so positioned as to capture and clean essentially all of the gas, but yet leaving the pit uncovered so as to give good radiant cooling.

A common sight in lumber processing areas is the tall conical steel "teepee" sawdust burner topped by a hemispherical screen to quench glowing cinders which are lifted from the crude burning pile centered in the base of the burner. Without controlled flow of fuel and air and without good mixing of the burning gases, these burners usually give off smoke and fly ash (87a). A study by Boubel et al. (88), showed a variation in particulate emission from waste wood burners of 1–20 pounds per ton burned. Tepees also are used for general refuse disposal with generally higher emissions than sawdust because of the heterogeneity of the material. Some components of smoke from sawdust have been measured (*88a*).

The sulfate liquor recovery boiler in the paper industry and the bagasse burner in the sugar industry are examples of waste disposal units which recover waste heat from the process and, in the case of sulfate liquor, also recover valuable chemicals. The value of the fine chemical dust which is carried out of the sulfate recovery furnace is such that electrostatic precipitators are generally used for its collection (*89*).

D. DOMESTIC INCINERATORS

The ubiquitous backyard bonfire of earlier years in America has given way in many large cities and suburbs to the wire basket or perforated barrel type of trash burner. These obnoxious and ineffective eyesores have, in some areas, been superseded by simple steel or concrete incinerators which, though constituting some improvement, have been convicted of a significant contribution to air pollution in Los Angeles County (*90*) and have, therefore, been banned from the scene in that community.

Likewise, the slightly more sophisticated indoor incinerator which boasts simply a firebox, a door, a grate, and a flue connection has been shown to be intolerable for urban use, particularly when burning food wastes (*91*). As a result of long and vigorous activity by the American Gas Association (*92*), gas-fired afterburner-type incinerators for indoor and outdoor use are being approved by the A.G.A. Laboratories (*93*).

Tables XX and XXI (*94*) show comparative data from many sources on gaseous and particulate emissions of various incinerators and other common stationary combustion sources. Of particular interest is the relatively low nitrogen oxide emission from *all* incinerators.

E. FLUE-FED INCINERATORS

The concentration of population in tall urban apartment buildings has dictated the development and installation of central basement incinerators which receive waste from chutes from the floors above. The single-flue type uses the same flue to receive the waste and discharge the gases. The double-flue unit permits much better control since feed and exhaust are separate. Still the random feed and intermittent burning of garbage and paper in such devices has long been a source of odor annoyance in large cities. Afterburners have shown some success in abating such odors (*95*). Fly ash from flue-fed units is considerable (*96*). However, the development of means to control and clean the exhausts from these devices may be so costly as to inhibit the expansion of their

TABLE XX

Comparison of Stack Emissions from Gas-Fired Incinerators and Other Stationary Combustion Sources
(Particulate Matter and Smoke)

Source	Particulate matter (including tarry organic materials)					Emission rate (lb/ton burned)	Smoke compliance with USASI[c] smoke requirements
	Grains/ft³				Emission rate, lb/1000 lb flue gas, 50% excess air		
	At standard temperature and pressure			At 500 °F 50% excess air			
	Actual	12% CO₂	50% excess air				
Gas-fired domestic incinerators							
AGA prototype, shredded paper	0.017–0.019	—	0.042–0.053	0.023–0.028	0.079–0.097	3.4–3.8	Yes
AGA prototype, USASI domestic wastes	0.005–0.018	—	0.011–0.048	0.006–0.026	0.021–0.090	0.9–4.3	Yes
AGA prototype, other refuse mixtures	0.008–0.017	—	0.026–0.037	0.014–0.020	0.048–0.069	1.6–2.2	–
New manufacturers units, shredded paper	0.013–0.095	—	0.055–0.410	0.030–0.222	0.104–0.766	3.5–27.7	Yes
New manufacturers units, USASI wastes	0.006–0.012	—	0.020–0.048	0.011–0.026	0.038–0.090	2.0–5.6	Yes
Older units, shredded paper	0.039–0.132	—	0.155–0.520	0.084–0.282	0.290–0.972	7.0–26.4	No
Older units, USASI domestic wastes	0.019–0.097	—	0.215–0.971	0.122–0.526	0.421–1.815	11.8–27.2	Yes
Municipal incinerators							
Glendale, Calif., with scrubber	0.035–0.060	0.22–0.30	0.22–0.30[a]	0.12–0.16[a]	—	—	—
Glendale, Calif., without scrubber	0.128–0.347	0.25–1.22	0.25–1.22[a]	0.14–0.66[a]	—	—	—
Nine units in Los Angeles County	0.105–0.596	0.242–0.860	0.24–0.86[a]	0.13–0.47[a]	—	3.34–17.8	—
Milwaukee, Wis., with scrubber	0.159–0.239	—	0.290–0.405	0.149–0.208	0.510–0.736	—	—
Milwaukee, Wis., without scrubber	0.403–0.598	—	0.690–0.993	0.354–0.509	1.265–1.860	—	—
Alhambra, Calif., with spray chambers	0.568	—	—	—	—	23	—
Three units in Calif., with scrubber	0.05–0.24[b]	—	—	—	—	—	—
Three units in Calif., without scrubber	0.05–0.40[b]	—	—	—	—	—	—
Municipal, with wet dust collector	0.034	—	0.161	0.083	0.277	—	—
Municipal, without collector	0.235	—	1.630	0.836	2.850	—	—
Other incinerators							
Single chamber	0.75	—	—	—	—	31	—
Wood waste	—	—	—	—	—	20	—
Back yard, 6 ft³ paper	—	—	—	—	—	150	—
Back yard, 6 ft³ trimmings	—	—	—	—	—	415	—
Experimental multiple chamber	0.24–0.47	—	—	—	—	0.96–8.6	—
Commercial	0.039	—	0.246	0.126	0.426	—	—
Industrial	0.060	—	0.576	0.296	1.013	—	—
Domestic	0.118	—	0.461	0.236	0.798	—	—
Gas- and oil-fired heating units							
Large gas-fired industrial units	—	—	—	—	—	3	—
Large oil-fired industrial units	—	—	—	—	—	10	—

[a] Estimated from corresponding values of grains per standard cubic foot at 12% CO₂.

[b] Much higher values were obtained by an alternate method of measurement.

[c] United States of America Standards Institute.

TABLE

COMPARISON OF STACK EMISSIONS FROM GAS-FIRED INCINERATORS

Combustion source	Aldehydes (as formaldehyde)			Nitrogen oxides (as nitrogen dioxide)		
	mg/m³	ppm	lb/ton	mg/m³	ppm	lb/ton
Gas-fired domestic incinerators						
AGA prototype, shredded paper	10–26	8–21	0.9–2.3	11–25	6–13	1.0–2.2
AGA prototype, USASI[a] domestic wastes	10	8	0.8	0.8	15	2.1
AGA prototype, other refuse mixtures	21–27	17–22	1.2–3.1	42–46	22–24	2.6–3.8
New manufacturers units, shredded paper	5–82	4–67	0.7–15.9	4–13	2–7	0.3–2.6
New manufacturers units, USASI domestic wastes	31–49	25–40	—	4–9	2–5	—
Older units, shredded paper	30–59	24–48	0.3–0.4	9	5	0.6–0.8
Older units, USASI domestic wastes	6–37	5–30	5–6	6	1–3	0.6–2
Municipal incinerators						
Glendale, Calif., with scrubber	1–11	1–	—	45–108	24–58	—
Glendale, Calif., without scrubber	1–27	1–22	—	110–173	58–92	—
Alhambra, Calif., with spray chamber	60	49	1.1	120	64	2.1
Three units in Calif., with scrubber	11–33	9–27	—	—	—	—
Three units in Calif., without scrubber	1–58	1–47	—	—	—	—
Other incinerators						
Single chamber	—	—	0.03–2.7	—	—	3.9–4.6
Wood waste	44	34	1.8	33	17	1.3
Backyard (Battelle), paper and trimmings	930	760	29	<3	<1.5	<0.1
Backyard, 6 ft³, paper	60	49	2.1	13	7	0.5
Backyard, 6 ft³, trimmings	125	102	5.7	13	7	0.6
Backyard, 3 ft³, mixed rubbish	—	—	5.1	—	—	10.6
Experimental multiple chamber	—	—	—	89–171	47–91	1.6–2.9
Gas- and oil-fired heating units						
Large gas-fired industrial units	60	49	2	410	215	14
Gas-fired steam boiler, low fire	6	5	0.5	75	40	6
Gas-fired steam boiler, high fire	—	—	—	170	90	7
Large oil-fired industrial units	75	61	2.4	800	390	26

[a] United States of America Standards Institute.

use. There seems to be merit in the development of suitable closed containers for transport of waste to large municipal incinerators.

Table XXII shows gaseous and solid emissions from three flue-fed incinerators in sixteen-story apartment buildings (97). Table XXIII shows data on the average composition of gaseous emissions, obtained from three typical tests.

VIII. Fires

A. OPEN FIRES

The occasional accidental burning of outdoor stores of lumber, sawdust, scrapped cars, tires, textiles, and open dumps is adequate evidence

XXI

AND OTHER COMBUSTION SOURCES (GASEOUS EMISSIONS)

Organic acids (as acetic acid)			Ammonia			Hydrocarbons (as hexane)		Sulfur oxides (as sulfur dioxide)			Carbon monoxide
mg/m³	ppm	lb/ton	mg/m³	ppm	lb/ton	ppm	lb/ton	mg/m³	ppm	lb/ton	ppm
—	—	—	<4	<5	—	—	—	—	—	—	100
17	7	1.8	<4	<5	—	0.7	0.3	5	2	—	200–400
—	—	—	—	—	—	—	—	—	—	—	—
—	—	—	<4	<5	—	—	—	—	—	—	200–400
—	—	—	<4	<5	—	—	—	—	—	—	200–1000
—	—	—	4	5	—	—	—	—	—	—	—
42	17	6.6	4	5	—	4.7	2.5	—	—	—	—
—	—	—	—	—	—	—	None	—	—	—	<1000
—	—	—	—	—	—	—	None	—	—	—	<1000–3000
35	14	0.6	20	29	0.3	—	—	95	36	1.9	—
—	—	—	—	—	—	—	—	0–84	0–32	—	<1000–12,000
—	—	—	—	—	—	—	—	29–157	11–60	—	<1000
—	—	2.0–3.9	—	—	0.33–0.5	—	None	—	—	1.4–2.3	—
11	5	0.4	0.8	1	0	—	—	3	1	0.15	—
—	—	—	45	65	1.8	—	—	—	—	—	5500–27,000
44	18	1.5	3	4	0.1	—	—	90	34	1.2	—
—	—	—	100	140	4.4	—	—	0	0	0	—
—	—	27.4	—	—	—	—	—	—	—	—	—
—	—	—	—	—	—	—	0.00–2.5[b]	—	—	—	<700–2000
75	30	2.5		0.4	0.6	—	—	10	4	0.3	—
—	—	—	—	—	—	—	—	—	—	—	—
—	—	—	—	—	—	—	—	—	—	—	—
900	365	30		0.4	0.6	—	—	2000	750	60	—

[b] Hydrocarbons were determined with a hexane-sensitized infrared analyzer.

TABLE XXII
EMISSIONS FROM FLUE-FED INCINERATOR[a]

Source	Particulates, lb/ton charged	Noxious gases, lb/ton charged
Basic incinerator	26.2	49.6
With overfire jets added	15.8	32.2
With jets and gas burner added	10.2	14.6
With scrubber only added	2.6	38.8
With overfire jets and scrubber added	1.8	25.2

[a] From Kaiser et al. (97).

TABLE XXIII

COMPOSITION OF NOXIOUS GASES OF BASIC
FLUE-FED INCINERATOR OF TABLE XX

Component	Pounds per ton charged
Aldehydes, as formaldehyde	4.6
Ammonia	0.4
Esters	21.5
Nitrogen oxides, NO_2	0.1
Organic acids, as acetic acid	22.4
Phenols, as phenol	0.1
Sulfur dioxide	0.5
	49.6

that pollution in urban areas would be intolerable if such fires were widespread and continuous. Most of these materials will burn smokelessly if supplied with sufficient air, properly mixed. However, if combustible material is piled on the impervious ground, there is little chance of air entering the hot zone in sufficient quantities; hence, the usual tower of long flame over the center of the pile, terminating in black smoke from incomplete combustion.

In recent measurements of gases collected by a conical hood suspended over open fires, Gerstle and Kemnitz (97a) found that carbon monoxide and particulate emissions were released as follows:

	CO (lbs/ton)	Particulates (lbs/ton)
Municipal refuse	85	16
Landscape refuse	65	17
Auto components	125	100

Gaseous hydrocarbon emissions paralleled the carbon monoxide concentrations and averaged 30 pounds per ton of material burned for all tests. The organic acid concentrations averaged about 15 pounds per ton of material fired. Formaldehyde concentrations varied from 0.095 pound per ton for municipal refuse to 0.006 pound per ton for the landscape refuse.

Highest values for nitrogen oxides occurred during the initial burning period when temperatures were high. After the initial intense burning period of about 10 minutes, concentration dropped off rapidly.

Emissions of polynuclear hydrocarbons for municipal or landscape refuse were comparable to emissions from small commercial incinerators. For auto components, the concentrations were comparable to those for small coalburning furnaces.

In the case of piled coal, where air filtering into the pile may create enough oxidation to cause spontaneous ignition within the pile, air flow into the pile soon becomes insufficient to keep up with the rate of gas evolution, and noxious smoke results.

Gob-pile fires result when air can flow readily through the many interstices in large piles of low-combustible refuse from coal preparation plants at mines. Slow oxidation occurs, heat is liberated, then higher temperatures develop until ignition occurs. These fires have been shown to be preventable by compacting and sealing of the pile by means of clay or other fine sealing material so that air cannot flow into the pile (98).

Field burning after harvest is a common source of annoying air pollution (99), particularly when the grass, stubble, and soil are moist. The validity of the practice is controversial. One view, that of a Kansan, is: "The reason for field burning by farmers during the spring (to a lesser extent in the fall) is entwined in the realm of agricultural folklore, but the practice is frowned upon by agronomists as well as highway safety personnel and public health officials. Plowing or discing this material into the soil would be beneficial from both an agricultural and an air pollution standpoint" (100). An opposing view (101) from Oregon: "Reasons for burning following harvest are: (1) to control plant diseases, (2) to eliminate surface organic matter which utilizes nitrogen during decomposition, and (3) to promote quick return of nutrients to the soil." Meland and Boubel (102) observed that visible pollution is appreciably lessened if the grass is very dry. This may explain why field burning is uncommon in the moist areas; that is, the smoke from the deliberate burning of moist grass and stubble may have long ago been found to be so intolerable that no amount of justification could be marshaled to support traditional burning in those areas. Once more the question arises of how much value we place on clear air; if we value it highly, then alternative and, perhaps, more costly means are justified for controlling diseases, weeds, insects, and to provide ample soil nitrogen and minerals.

B. FIREPLACES

The often-welcome odor of a wood-buring fireplace and the artist's cherished plume rising over a forest lodge are evidence enough that some pollution results from the incomplete surface burning which takes place in the coal- or wood-fired open fireplace. In England, this common means of heating for comfort has been shown to be a major source of urban air pollution. Excellent research has been done in England (*103*), both to improve the low efficiency of fireplaces and minimize the emission of tar and soot. Abandonment of the cheery glow of the open fire may never come. In fact, in the gadget-ridden modern American home the open fireplace persists, often in gaudy, prefabricated, all-metal splendor, not so inefficient, but still as smoky as it was when Franklin sought to improve upon it with his stove in the late eighteenth century.

REFERENCES

1. L. J. Minick, *Am. Soc. Testing Mater., Proc.* **54**, 1129–1164 (1954).
1a. Anonymous, "Criteria for the Application of Dust Collectors for Coal-Fired Boilers." Ind. Gas Cleaning Inst., New York, 1967.
2. J. P. Capp, *Combustion* **37**, 36–40 (1966).
3. W. S. Smith, *U.S. Public Health Serv., Publ.* **999-AP-2**, 26 (1963).
4. P. H. Crumley and A. W. Fletcher, *J. Inst. Fuel* **29**, 322–327 (1956).
5. W. Gumz, H. Kirsch, and M. T. Mackowsky, "Schlackenkunde," p. 353. Springer, Berlin, 1958.
6. H. F. Johnstone, *Univ. Illinois Bull., Eng. Expt. Sta., Bull.* **228** (1931).
7. S. T. Cuffe, R. W. Gerstle, A. A. Orning, and C. H. Schwartz, *J. Air Pollution Control Assoc.* **15**, 59–64 (1965).
8. W. S. Smith, *U.S. Public Health Serv., Publ.* **999-AP-2**, 29 (1963).
9. F. Glaubitz, *Combustion* **7**, 31–35, 25–27 (1963).
10. H. Niepenberg, *J. Fuel Heat Technol.* **14**, 34–36 (1966).
11. G. C. Jefferis and J. D. Sensenbaugh, *Mech. Eng.* **82**, 111 (1960) (abstr.).
11a. V. Fauth and W. Schüle, *Staub* **27**, 257–265 (1967).
12. H. H. Krause, "A Review of Available Information on Corrosion and Deposits in Boiler and Gas Turbines," Chapter 2. Am. Soc. Mech. Engrs., New York, 1959.
13. M. T. Mackowsky, *Mitt. Ver. Grosskesselbestizer* **38**, 16–22 (1955).
14. W. F. Harlow, *Trans. ASME* **80**, 224 (1958).
15. D. R. Anderson and F. P. Manlek, *Trans. ASME* **80**, 1231–1237 (1958).
15a. J. R. Jenkinson and J. Firminger, *J. Fuel Heat Technol.* **14**, 29–35 (1967).
15b. A. B. Hedley, *J. Inst. Fuel* **40**, 142–151 (1967).
15c. E. L. Merryman and A. Levy, *60th Ann. Meeting Air Pollution Control Assoc., Cleveland, Ohio, 1967* Paper No. 67-161.
15d. F. A. Rohrman, J. H. Ludwig, and B. J. Steigerwald, "SO$_2$ Emissions to U.S. (1966)," Memorandum, National Center for Air Pollution Control, U.S. Public Health Service, Cincinnati, Ohio, 2 pp., 1967.
15e. A. Parker, *Proc. 5th World Power Conf., Vienna,* (1956).
15ee. A. A. Roussel, and H. Stephany, *Proc. Intern. Clean Air Congr. London, Part I,* 29–34 (1966).
15f. H. Perry and J. A. Decarlo, *Mech. Eng.* **89** (4), 22–28 (1967).
15g. A. L. Plumley, O. D. Whiddon, F. W. Shutko, J. Jonakin, Paper at American Power Conference, Chicago, April, 1967.
15gg. K. Wickert, *Mitt. Ver. Grosskesselbesitzer* **83**, 74–82 (1963).
15h. R. F. Bovier, *Proc. Am. Power Conf.* **26**, 138–146 (1964).
15i. R. Kiyaura, *J. Air Pollution Control Assoc.,* **16**, 488–489 (1966).
15j. T. T. Frankenberg, *Mech. Eng.* **87**, 36–41 (1965).

15k. H. Kettner, *Bull. World Health Organ.* **32,** 421–429 (1965).

15l. K. Tanaka, "Desulfurization of Stack Gas," Resources Research Institute, Kawaguchi, Saitame, 1966.

15m. D. Bienstock, J. H. Field, and J. G. Myers, *Trans. ASME,* **86,** 353–360 (1964).

15mm. D. Bienstock, J. H. Field, S. Katell, and K. D. Plants, Paper 65-16, Air Pollution Control Association, Toronto, 1965.

15n. M. Y. Atsukawa, Y. Nishimoto, K. Matsumato, "Dry Process Sulfur Dioxide Removal Method," Mitsubishi Heavy Industries, Ltd., Technical Review, January, 1967.

15o. R. Lessing, *J. Soc. Chem. Ind.* **57,** 373–388 (1938).

15p. A. L. Kohl, and F. C. Riesenfeld, "Gas Purification," McGraw-Hill Book Co., New York (1960).

16. E. D. Ermenc, *Chem. Engr. Progr.* **52,** 149 (1956).

17. P. S. Tow, *J. Air Pollution Control Assoc.* **7,** 234–240 (1957).

18. "Emissions of Oxides of Nitrogen from Stationary Sources in Los Angeles County," Repts. No. 1 and 2. Los Angeles County Air Pollution Control District, Los Angeles, California, 1960.

19. W. L. Faith, *Air Pollution Found. (Los Angeles), Rept.* **2,** 8 (1954).

20. M. D. Thomas and G. A. St. John, *J. Air Pollution Control Assoc.* **8,** 277 and 2349 (1958).

21. G. C. Jefferis and J. D. Sensenbaugh, *Am. Soc. Mech. Engrs., Preprint* **59-A-308** (1959).

22. D. H. Barnhart and E. K. Diehl, *J. Air Pollution Control Assoc.* 397–406 (1960).

22a. D. Bienstock, R. L. Amsler, and E. R. Bauer, *J. Air Pollution Control Assoc.* **16,** 442–445 (1966).

23. "Implications of Rising Carbon Dioxide Content of the Atmosphere," Conf. Rept. Conserv. Found., New York, 1964.

24. H. W. Seuss, *Bull. At. Scientists,* **17,** 374 (1961).

25. G. A. Callendar, *Weather* **4,** 310 (1949).

26. G. N. Plass, *Am. Scientist* **44,** 302 (1956).

27. S. H. Wittwer and W. Robb, *Econ. Botany* **18,** 34–35 (1964).

28. W. S. Smith and C. W. Gruber, *U.S. Public Health Serv., Publ.* **999-AP-24,** 21 (1966).

28a. A. A. Orning, J. F. Smith, and C. H. Schwartz, *Am. Soc. Mech. Engrs., Paper* **64-WA/FV-2** 1964.

29. H. L. Green and W. R. Lane, "Particulate Clouds, Dusts, Smokes, and Mists," p. 96. Spon, London, 1957.

30. L. Schnidman, "Gaseous Fuels," 2nd ed., p. 283. Am. Gas Assoc., New York, 1948.

30a. G. R. Fryling, ed., "Combustion Engineering," rev. ed., pp., 19–21. Combustion Eng., Inc., New York, 1966.

31. B. D. Tebbens, J. R. Thomas, and M. Mukai, *A.M.A. Arch. Ind. Health* **14,** 413–425 (1956).

32. Joint Research Committee, Repts. 28 and 35. Institution of Gas Engineers and Leeds University.

33. F. E. Vandaveer and C. G. Segeler, *Ind. Eng. Chem.* **37,** 816–820 (1945); see also correction *Ind. Eng. Chem.* **44,** 1833 (1952).

33a. R. L. Chass and R. E. George, *J. Air Pollution Control Assoc.* **10,** 34–43 (1960).

33b. Stanford Research Institute, "The Smog Problem in Los Angeles County," p. 130. Stanford Res. Inst., Menlo Park, California, 1954.

33c. Los Angeles County Air Pollution Control District, "Emissions in the Atmosphere from Petroleum Refineries," Rept. No. 7, p. 23. Los Angeles, California, 1958.

34. L. Schnidman, "Gaseous Fuels," 2nd ed., p. 358. Am. Gas Assoc., New York, 1948.

35. L. Schnidman, "Gaseous Fuels," 2nd ed., p. 95. Am. Gas Assoc., New York, 1948.
36. W. L. Faith, *Air Pollution Found. (Los Angeles) Rept.* **2, 8** (1954).
37. J. E. Maconochie, "The Deterioration of Domestic Chimneys." Consumer's Gas Co., Toronto, Canada, 1952.
37a. R. E. Barrett, J. D. Hummell, and W. T. Reid, *Trans. Am. Soc. Mech. Engrs. for Power,* **87,** 165–172 (1966).
38. Anonymous, *Oil Gas J.* **63,** 35 (1965).
38a. Specification for Fuel Oils, *Am. Soc. Testing Mater.,* Std. D-396-64T (1965).
38b. G. Wentink, *Staub* **27,** 173–176 (1967).
39. W. Sacks, *Trans. ASME* **76,** 375 (1954).
39a. H. A. Belyea and W. J. Holland, *Proc. 59th Ann. Meeting Air Pollution Control Assoc., San Francisco, 1966* Paper No. 66-56.
39b. L. K. Rendle, *J. Inst. Fuel* **37,** 26–30 (1964).
40. A. E. Gosselin, *Proc. Am. Power Conf.* **26,** 128–137 (1964).
40a. H. C. Austin and W. L. Chadwick, *Mech. Eng.* **82,** 63–66 (1960).
41. R. L. Chass and R. E. George, *J. Air Pollution Control Assoc.* **10,** 34–43 (1960).
42. B. G. Gills and E. L. Howe, *Schweiz. Arch. Angew. Wiss. Tech.* **31,** 119–216 (1965).
42a. L. C. Burroughs, *Fuel Oil Oil Heat* pp. 43–46 and 92–96 (1963).
42b. S. L. Wingfield, *Proc. Intern. Clean Air Cong., Part II, London,* 14–15 (1966).
42c. B. Gills and E. L. Howe, *Proc. Intern. Clean Air Conf., Part I, London,* 37–43 (1966).
42d. R. A. Hunt and R. E. Biller, *Proc. API Res. Conf. Distillate Fuel Combust.,* API Publication No. 1541, Paper No. 61-6, Chicago, 1961.
43. "Handbook of Oil Burning." Oil Heat Inst. of America, New York, 1951.
44. W. S. Smith, *U.S. Public Health Serv., Publ.* **999-AP-2** (1962).
44a. G. Schremaun, *Staub* **25,** 450–457 (1965).
44b. W. Hess, *Staub* **25,** 460–465 (1965).
44c. B. G. Gills and B. Lees, *J. Inst. Fuel* **39,** 29–33 (1966).
45. Anonymous, *Pollution Atmosphere, Paris,* **8,** 295–318 (1966).
46. P. N. Nicholls and W. T. Reid, *U.S., Bur. Mines, Bull.* **404** (1937).
46a. L. M. Exley, A. E. Tamburrino, and A. J. O'Neal, Jr., *Power* **110,** 69–73 (1966).
46b. S. M. DeCorso, C. E. Hussey, and M. J. Ambrose, "Smokeless Combustion in Oil-Burning Gas Turbines," *Am. Soc. Mech. Engrs., Paper* **67-PWR-5** (1967).
46c. F. F. Davis, Jr., "Smoke Abatement in Gas Turbines for Industrial Use," *Am. Soc. Mech. Engrs., Paper* **67-PWR-4** (1967).
46d. W. G. Taylor, "Smoke Elimination in Gas Turbines Burning Distillate Oil," *Am. Soc. Mech. Engrs., Paper* **67-PWR-3** (1967).
46e. R. E. Zimmerman, *Chem. Eng. Progr.* **62,** 61–66 (1966).
47. B. A. Landry and R. A. Sherman, *Am. Soc. Mech. Engrs., Paper* **48-A-119** (1948); see *Mech. Eng.* **71,** 47 (1949) (abstr.).
48. R. P. Hangebrauck, D. J. von Lehmden, and J. E. Meeker, *J. Air Pollution Control Assoc.* 267–278 (1964).
48a. E. K. Diehl, F. du Breuil, and R. A. Glenn, *ASME J. Eng. Power* **88,** 1–7 (1966).
49. E. D. Benton and R. B. Engdahl, *Trans. ASME* **69,** 35 (1947).
50. "Application of Overfire Jets to Prevent Smoke in Stationary Plants." Bituminous Coal Research, Pittsburgh, Pennsylvania, 1944 (revised 1957).
51. W. Gumz, *Combustion* **22,** 39–48 (1951).
52. A. C. Stern, *Combustion* **5,** 35–47 (1933).
53. C. E. Miller, *Proc. Midwest Power Conf.* **9,** 97 (1949).
54. R. B. Engdahl and J. H. Stang, *Natl. Engr.,* May (1947).
55. "Applications of Overfire Jets to Prevent Smoke in Stationary Plants." Bituminous Coal Research, Pittsburgh, Pennsylvania, Vol. 21, 1944 (revised 1957).
56. W. C. Holton and R. B. Engdahl, *Trans. ASME* **74,** 207–215 (1952).

57. C. Morrow, W. C. Holton, and H. L. Wagner, *Trans. ASME* **75,** 1363 (1953).
58. P. H. Hardie and W. S. Cooper, *Trans. ASME* **56,** 833–849 (1934).
59. A. Kuhlman, *Staub* **24,** 121–131 (1964).
60. E. J. Boer and C. W. Porterfield, *Am. Soc. Mech. Engrs., Paper* **53-S-26** (1953) (unpublished).
61. R. A. Sherman, *Trans. ASME* **56,** 401–410 (1934).
62. J. P. Capp, *Combustion* **37,** 36–40 (February, 1966).
63. H. H. Lowry, ed., "Chemistry of Coal Utilization," Vol. 2, p. 1550. Wiley, New York, 1945.
64. "Steam," 37th ed., p. 18-7. Babcock & Wilcox, New York (1955).
65. S. T. Cuffe, R. W. Gerstle, A. A. Orning, and C. H. Schwartz, *J. Air Pollution Control Assoc.* **14,** 353–362 (1964).
66. S. T. Cuffe, R. W. Gerstle, A. A. Orning, and C. H. Schwartz, *J. Air Pollution Control Assoc.* **15,** 59–64 (1965).
67. F. J. Feeley, *Trans. ASME* **78,** 1747 (1956).
68. A. C. Monkhouse and H. E. Newall, *Brit. Chem. Eng.* **1,** 99–100 (1956).
69. W. S. Smith and C. W. Gruber, *U.S., Public Health Serv., Publ.* **999-AP-24** (1966).
69a. A. D. Bienstock, R. L. Amsler, and E. R. Bauer, *J. Air Pollution Control Assoc.* **16,** 442–445 (1967).
70. A. E. Grunert, L. Skog, and L. S. Wilcoxson, *Trans. ASME* **69,** 619 (1947).
71. V. L. Stone and I. L. Wade, *Mech. Eng.* **74,** 359–368 (1942).
71a. C. T. Smith, *Am. Soc. Mech. Engrs., Paper* **59-SA-53** (1959).
71b. Anon., "Design Criteria for the Application of Dust Collectors to Coal-Fired Boilers," Industrial Gas Cleaning Institute, Rye, New York, 1967.
72. S. T. Cuffe and R. W. Gerstle, "Summary of Emissions from Coal-Fired Power Plants." A.I.H.A., Houston, Texas, 1965.
73. Environmental Pollution Panel "Restoring the Quality of Our Environment," Report of Presidential Committee (headed by J. W. Tukey). The White House, Washington, D.C., 1965.
74. Incinerator Standards. Incinerator Inst. of America, New York, 1966.
75. J. W. Stephenson and A. S. Cafiero, *Proc. Natl. Incinerator Conf., New York,* pp. 1–38. Am. Soc. Mech. Engrs., New York, 1966.
76. R. B. Engdahl and J. D. Sullivan, *Am. Soc. Testing Mater. Bull.* p. 182 (1959).
77. A. H. Rose, R. L. Stenburg, M. Corn, R. A. Horsley, and D. R. Allen, *J. Air Pollution Control Assoc.* **8,** 297 (1959).
78. F. R. Rehm, *J. Air Pollution Control Assoc.* **6,** 199–206 (1957).
79. C. V. Kanter, R. G. Lunche, and A. P. Fudurich, *J. Air Pollution Control Assoc.* **6,** 191–198 (1957).
80. W. Jens and F. R. Rehm, *Proc. Natl. Incinerator Conf., New York,* pp. 74–83. Am. Soc. Mech. Engrs., New York, 1966.
80a. A. B. Walker and F. W. Schmitz, *Proc. Natl. Incinerator Conf., New York,* pp. 64–73. Am. Soc. Mech. Engrs., New York, 1966.
81. M. Feldstein, J. D. Coons, H. C. Johnston, and J. E. Yocom, *Am. Ind. Hyg. Assoc. J.* **20,** 374–378 (1959).
82. J. L. Mills, K. D. Leudtke, P. I. Woolrich, and L. B. Perry, "Emissions of Oxides of Nitrogen from Stationary Sources in Los Angeles County," Rept. No. 3. Los Angeles County Air Pollution Control District, Los Angeles, California, 1961.
83. C. V. Kanter, J. L. Mills, K. D. Leudtke, R. M. Ingels, H. Linnard, and P. Newmark, "Emissions of Oxides of Nitrogen from Stationary Sources in Los Angeles County," Rept. No. 4. Los Angeles County Air Pollution Control District, Los Angeles, California, 1961.
84. R. D. Ellsworth and R. B. Engdahl, *J. Air Pollution Control Assoc.* **7,** 43–48 (1957).

85. R. L. Bump, *Proc. Natl. Incinerator Conf., New York*, pp. 161–166. Am. Soc. Mech. Engrs., New York, 1966.
86. G. Stabenow, "Report on Observations of European Incinerator Installations and Their Performance," Sub-Committee. Am. Soc. Mech. Engrs., New York, 1963 (unpublished).
86a. E. H. Coleman, *Plastics (London)* **24**, 416–418 (1959).
87. E. S. Monroe, *Proc. Natl. Incinerator Conf., New York*, pp. 226–23(Am. Soc. Mech. Engrs., New York, 1966.
87a. T. E. Kreichett, *U.S. Public Health Serv., Publ.* **999-AP-28** (1966).
88. R. W. Boubel, M. Northcraft, A. Van Vhet, and M. Popovich, *Oregon State Coll., Eng. Expt. Sta., Bull.* **39** (1958).
88a. W. Fiddler, R. C. Doerr, A. E. Wasserman, and J. M. Salay, *J. Agr. Food Chem.* **14**, 659–665 (1966).
89. O. de Lorenzi, ed., "Combustion Engineering," p. 28-8. Combustion Eng. Co., New York, 1947.
90. J. E. Yocom, G. M. Hein, and H. W. Nelson, *J. Air Pollution Control Assoc.* **6**, 84–89 (1956).
91. L. T. Bissey, *Gas Age* **102**, 30–31 (1948).
92. F. E. Vandaveer, *J. Air Pollution Control Assoc.* **6**, 90–97 (1956).
93. D. W. Skipworth, G. M. Hein, and H. W. Nelson, *Am. Gas Assoc., Res. Bull.* **78** (1958).
94. G. M. Hein and R. B. Engdahl, "A Study of Effluents from Domestic Gas-Fired Incinerators," p. 23. Am. Gas Assoc., New York, 1959.
95. R. J. Reed and S. M. Truitt, *J. Air Pollution Control Assoc.* **4**, 109–117 (1954).
96. E. R. Kaiser, J. Halitsky, M. B. Jacobs, and L. C. McCabe, *J. Air Pollution Control Assoc.* **9**, 85 (1959).
97. E. R. Kaiser, J. Halitsky, M. B. Jacobs, and L. C. McCabe, *J. Air Pollution Control Assoc.* **10**, 183 (1960).
97a. R. W. Gerstle and D. A. Kemnitz, "Atmospheric Emissions from Open-Burning." *J. Air Pollution Control Assoc.* **17**, 324 (1967).
98. V. H. Sussman and J. J. Mulhern, *J. Air Pollution Control Assoc.* **14**, 279–284 (1964).
99. M. Feldstein, S. Duckworth, H. C. Wohlers, and B. Linsky, *J. Air Pollution Control Assoc.* **13**, 542–545 and 564 (1963).
100. D. F. Metzler, G. S. Strella, and L. C. Doughty, "The Air Resources of Kansas," p. 48. Kansas State Board of Health, Topeka, Kansas, 1962.
101. J. R. Hardison, *Proc. 24th Ann. Meeting Oregon Seed Growers League, 1964* pp. 93–96.
102. B. R. Meland and R. W. Boubel, *Proc. 59th Ann. Meeting Air Pollution Control Assoc., San Francisco, 1966* Paper No. 66-9.
103. L. L. Fox, *J. Inst. Fuel* **25**, 267 (1952).

GENERAL REFERENCE

Since the completion of this chapter, pertinent material has been published in Chapters 8 and 9 of the "Air Pollution Engineering Manual, Los Angeles APCD" (J. A. Danielson, ed.), PHS Publ. 999-AP-40, DHEW, Cincinnati (1967). Additional material will be published in the National Air Pollution Control Administration's publications: "Control Technology for Particulate Air Pollutants," and "Control Technology for Sulfur Oxides Air Pollutants."

33 Mobile Combustion Sources

R. W. Hurn

I. Introduction

Mobile combustion sources include automobiles, trucks, busses, railroad locomotives, aircraft, and marine vessels. Of these, the automobile is now, and for the foreseeable future will continue to be, the dominant source of air pollutants in this category. Pollutants from these sources contain both toxic compounds and organic materials that are not in themselves objectionable but which react in the atmosphere to form smog. In addition, objectionable smoke and odor, separately or together, may accompany other exhaust emissions.

II. Atmospheric Pollutants from Gasoline-Powered Equipment

Technically, it is useful to treat internal-combustion engine-powered vehicle emissions according to their origin within the vehicular system.

1. Exhaust emissions—pollutants that are present in the exhaust gas stream as it is discharged into the atmosphere.
2. Evaporative emissions—vapors lost directly to the atmosphere from the fuel tank, carburetor, or any other part of the fuel system.
3. Crankcase blow-by—gases and vapors that under pressure escape the combustion chamber past the engine pistons and enter the crankcase.

A. EXHAUST EMISSIONS

Complete oxidation of hydrocarbon fuel yields only carbon dioxide and water as the products of chemical combination. When air is used as the source of the oxygen, some of the nitrogen and oxygen combine at the temperatures normally reached in the combustion process to form nitric oxide. Under the conditions of combustion in an internal combustion engine, other products also are formed. These include carbon monoxide, hydrogen, and partially oxidized materials primarily in the aldehyde family (1–3). Some fuel passes through the engine unburned and, additionally, under the thermal stress of the combustion process, some of the fuel is chemically rearranged by cracking or synthesizing reactions. The effect of this rearrangement is primarily to produce lighter fragments of the fuel molecule.

Particulate and nonvolatile matter invariably accompany the gases even when not present in visible quantity.

Both absolute and relative concentrations of combustion products are influenced by numerous factors. Some of the more prominent factors include: ratio of the weight of air to the weight of fuel (air–fuel ratio) in the cylinder at the time of combustion; ignition timing; absolute charge density; combustion chamber geometry; and variable engine parameters such as speed, load, and engine temperatures.

Of these factors the air–fuel ratio has the most fundamental significance and in practice exerts the major influence in establishing the relative properties of the principal combustion products. For a given amount of fuel, a given, precise amount of air is required for complete combustion according to the fundamental relationship:

$$C_x H_y + (x + 1/4y)\ O_2 \rightarrow x\ CO_2 + 1/2y\ H_2O$$

If less than the "correct" amount of oxygen (air) is included in the mixture, it is said to be "rich," i.e., rich in fuel. If excess oxygen is included, the mixture is "lean," i.e., lean or deficient in fuel. The chemically correct mixture—that mixture in which the carbon, hydrogen, and oxygen are in balance according to the equation above—is called the stoichiometric mixture. This stoichiometric mixture requires about 14 1/2 pounds of air per pound of a typical gasoline, i.e., a 14.5:1 air–fuel ratio. A 12:1 air–fuel ratio is considered to be decidedly rich; a 17:1 ratio is quite lean. Combustion of rich mixtures produces carbon monoxide and tends to result in residual fuel in the exhaust, either unburned or only partially burned. Lean mixtures produce much less CO and, in general, lower concentrations of unburned hydrocarbon. However, if the mixture that is supplied an engine is made excessively lean, flame will not propagate through it properly, the engine will misfire, and emissions in all categories may rise quite high. The air–fuel ratio and combustion product relationships are illustrated in Figs. 1 and 2.

Ignition timing also has great influence upon the combustion process. It governs the time available for combustion to occur before the process is disturbed by cooling in the expansion stroke or exhaust blowdown. Both air–fuel ratio and ignition timing are readily adjustable, both in design specifications and field tune-up adjustments.

1. Carbon Monoxide

Ideally, as shown in Figs. 1 and 2, gasoline engines could be made to operate with CO levels near zero. Although the zero limit is not a reasonable target, less than 1/2% CO is a reasonable goal.

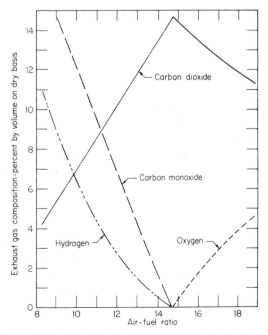

FIG. 1. Relationship of combustion products to air–fuel mixture (*3b*).

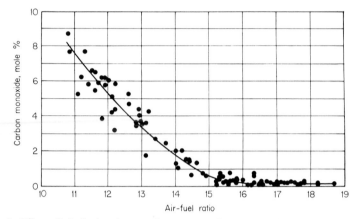

Fig. 2. Effect of air-fuel ratio on exhaust gas carbon monoxide concentration. Three engines. From Hagen and Holiday (3a).

For 1968 model* vehicles with air–fuel ratios on the rich side of stoichiometric, carbon monoxide concentrations range as high as 7% in the composite of exhaust discharged in transit over a "typical" urban driving route. With air–fuel ratio adjusted at or near stoichiometric and other engine parameters given optimal adjustment, the CO concentration in a composite sample of exhaust from some 1968 U.S.-made vehicles can be reduced to under 1 1/4%. This low level of CO emission is achieved in 1968 vehicles only with some sacrifice in auto driveability or other engine performance. Advances in engine design beyond 1968 are expected to achieve low CO emission without sacrificing driveability and performance.

Typically, concentrations of CO in emissions are high during the engine idle mode and decrease as engine speed is increased outside of the idle range. The total or overall emission of CO is therefore significantly influenced by the amount of idle and low-speed operation included in a vehicle's duty cycle. This relationship is reflected in the dependence of CO upon average route speed (Fig. 3).

2. Unburned Hydrocarbons

Concentrations of unburned hydrocarbons are influenced by air–fuel ratio (A/F) in the same manner as CO is influenced, i.e., lowest emission levels are associated with an air–fuel ratio near stoichiometric. Further, as with CO, higher levels of hydrocarbon emission are associated with

* In the United States, automobiles introduced in the late summer or fall of a year (e.g., 1966) are called the next year's (e.g., 1967) model.

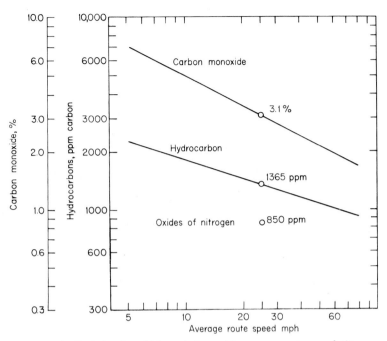

FIG. 3. Variation in vehicle emissions with average route speed (3).

idle and low-speed operation. This relationship is illustrated by the dependence of hydrocarbon emission levels upon route speed (Fig. 3). For the national average urban route speed of 25 mph,* emissions from the 1966 nonequipped** U.S. automobile population† contain an average of about 1400 ppm of hydrocarbon. This corresponds to about 3.3% of the amount of fuel supplied to the engine. Somewhat lower emission levels are found for U.S. vehicles manufactured since 1962. The reduction has resulted from engineering refinements that have involved leaner fuel mixtures and improved carburetion and mixture distribution.

Exceptionally high values of hydrocarbon in the exhaust, e.g., several

---

* Based on findings by the U.S. Bureau of Highways in a 7-year study of vehicle operations in 22 states from which it has been estimated that the average trip in urban driving is 8 miles driven in 19.2 minutes. In average service a vehicle makes 3 1/4 such trips per day.

** The nonequipped category excludes new automobiles sold in the State of California in model years 1966 and 1967; these vehicles were modified or fitted with accessory equipment to limit emissions of certain pollutants.

† Mostly 1956–1966 vehicles.

thousand ppm, usually are indicative of cylinders occasionally or continually misfiring (i.e., not firing); each such event causes a cylinderful
of raw unburned fuel–air mixture to be discharged through the exhaust
valve.

3. Oxides of Nitrogen

This pollutant is generated first as nitric oxide (NO) with conversion
to nitrogen dioxide (NO_2) subsequent to the combustion event. Other
nitrogen oxides (4, 5) are involved in much lesser amounts; the aggregate of the variable mixture, including NO and NO_2, is commonly designated as NO_x. The initial combination of nitrogen with oxygen occurs
only at relatively high combustion temperatures and then only if free
oxygen is present. Thus, factors that tend to increase combustion temperature, and/or to increase oxygen availability, also tend to increase
NO_x emission. Consistent with this chemical behavior, air–fuel ratio is
found to be the dominant influence upon NO_x emissions, and highest
emissions are associated with air–fuel ratios slightly on the lean side of
stoichiometric. This relationship is illustrated in Fig. 4. Other factors

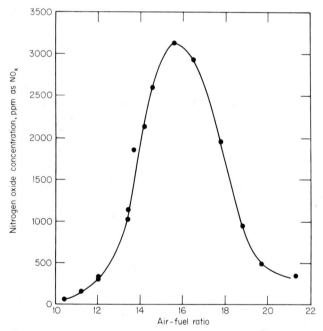

FIG. 4. Influence of air-fuel ratio on concentration of NO_x in exhaust gas. Each point
the average of three determinations. Adapted from Jackson (5a).

relevant in NO_x generation are engine compression ratio, spark timing, and intake air temperature and humidity.

Levels of NO_x emissions in typical urban traffic range between 800 and 3000 ppm with the overall average near the lower value. High speeds and heavy accelerations produce the major portion of the NO_x and therefore the total amount of the pollutant produced in any locality is markedly influenced by driving practice within that locality.

4. Partial Oxidation Products (6)

Relatively little is known about this class of pollutants, which includes aldehydes, alcohols, esters, ketones, and acid derivatives. They often are found at total concentrations between 50 and 100 ppm in the composite of "typical" exhaust. Formaldehyde and acetaldehyde are most prominent. Sampling and analytical procedures for these materials are not reliable and there is reason to believe that they may be quantitatively more important than generally recognized. In addition to formaldehyde and acetaldehyde, some higher aldehydes and acrolein are found. All of the class—formaldehyde- and acroleinlike compounds in particular— are objectionable because of odor and irritant properties. Additionally, they are photochemically active.

In general these products are intermediates in the oxidation process and may be associated with incomplete combustion. They appear in copious quantity in the exhaust from misfiring engines and it may be reasonably assumed that malfunctioning automobiles are a source of significant quantities of these objectionable materials. Further clarification of the auto as a source of these important pollutants must await results of research.

5. Particulate Matter

Exhaust emissions produce large numbers of extremely fine particles with approximately 70% by count in the size range of 0.02–0.06 μ. On a weight distribution basis, however, particles less than 1.0 μ in size account for less than 5% of the total weight of the exhausted particulate matter. Examination indicates that these particulate materials (7, 8) consist of both inorganic compounds and organic compounds of high molecular weight. The quantity of particulate material produced in the exhaust varies between 0.22 and 3.2 mg/gm of gasoline burned, with an average emission rate of 0.78 mg/gm of gasoline burned.

The most significant fractions of the automotive particulate emission are lead compounds resulting from the use of tetraethyl lead as a fuel additive to provide the antiknock characteristics necessary for present-

TABLE I

COMBUSTION-RELATED VEHICULAR EMISSIONS

	Emissions[a]			
	Blow-by		Exhaust	
Component	Concentration	Wt. (lb/day)	Concentration	Wt. (lb/day)
Carbon monoxide	Trace	Nil	3.12%	4.160
Oxides of nitrogen	Trace	Nil	850 ppm	0.202
Hydrocarbons				
Paraffins				
C_1–C_5	3150 ppm	0.033	130 ppm	0.034
C_6 and heavier	4780 ppm	0.072	155 ppm	0.073
Olefins				
C_2–C_4	230 ppm	0.001	500 ppm	0.079
C_5 and heavier	1420 ppm	0.017	30 ppm	0.012
Aromatics				
Total less benzene	5150 ppm	0.089	190 ppm	0.100
Benzene	270 ppm	0.003	75 ppm	0.029
Acetylenes	60 ppm	0.001	285 ppm	0.036
Total hydrocarbon	15060 ppm	0.216	1365 ppm	0.363

[a] Mass emissions calculations based upon 31.0 ft³/min, STP average exhaust gas flow rate or 71.0 ft³/mile, STP. Adapted from Rose 1966 (3).

TABLE II

CONTRIBUTION OF THE VARIOUS ENGINE MODES TO THE TOTAL OF EXHAUST HYDROCARBON EMISSION EXCLUDING WARM-UP[a]

Mode	Percent of total[b] contributed by each mode (± Standard Error)	
	Vehicles without emission control	Vehicles with emission control
Idle	5 ± 1	3 ± 1
0–25 Accelerate	20 ± 3	24 ± 6
30 Cruise	7 ± 2	9 ± 2
30–15 Decelerate	13 ± 5	8 ± 6
15 Cruise	4 ± 1	3 ± 1
15–30 Accelerate	32 ± 5	35 ± 8
50–20 Decelerate	19 ± 6	17 ± 8
Number of vehicles tested	50	76

[a] Data contributed by General Motors Engineering Staff, Michigan.

[b] Composite of exhaust emissions produced during the seven modes of a hot cycle as prescribed by U.S. Federal Standards for certification of 1968 vehicles.

day high-compression engines. Approximately 70–80% of the lead burned in the engine is exhausted to the atmosphere over normal 20,000 to 30,000 mile driving periods of mixed urban and suburban driving. The remaining 20–30% portion of the lead is retained in the engine and exhaust system, or scavenged into the engine lubricating oil, in approximately equal amounts.

The total amount of lead discharged from the engine for any given operation is proportional to the concentration of tetraethyl lead in the ingested fuel, but the composition and particle size distribution appear to be independent of this variable. The composition of the lead exhausted is principally in the form of mixtures of $PbCl \cdot Br$, alpha and beta forms of $NH_4Cl \cdot 2PbCl \cdot Br$ and $2NH_4Cl \cdot PbCl \cdot Br$. Changes in the sulfur content of the gasoline and the addition of phosphorus-containing gasoline additives caused no significant change in the particle size distribution or quantity of lead exhausted to the atmosphere. Phosphorus-containing compounds to a limited extent alter the chemical composition of the lead emitted.

Principal combustion products, concentration levels, mass emissions of these materials, and contributions of the various engine modes to the total hydrocarbon are summarized in Tables I and II.

B. EVAPORATIVE EMISSIONS

Emissions in this category can be estimated as roughly accounting for from 10 to 30% of the hydrocarbon in vehicular emissions. The estimate is uncertain because techniques for measuring evaporative emissions involve large uncertainties. However, even at the lower limit of the estimate, these losses are significant. Included in the evaporative emissions (9–12) are losses from the fuel tank and from the carburetor. Fuel tank losses consist primarily of the more volatile fractions of gasoline displaced from the vapor space above the liquid fuel in the gas tank. These losses occur primarily as a result of temperature changes in the tank fuel and in the vapor volume, which induce a pumping action alternately admitting air into and expelling vapor from the tank. Depending upon the direction of temperature changes, tank fill, and tank agitation, the vapors may be discharged at any time, with the vehicle either operating or stationary.

Fuel volatility, maximum tank temperatures, and the breadth of temperature "swings" markedly affect the magnitude of these losses. Tank temperatures are elevated during vehicle operation. The magnitude of this temperature elevation varies within wide limits because ambient

TABLE III

EVAPORATIVE LOSS—MASS EMISSIONS

	Hydrocarbons (lb/day)	
Components	Tank loss	Carburetor-soak loss
Paraffins		
C_1–C_5	0.039	0.029
C_6 and heavier	0.010	0.040
Olefins		
C_2–C_4	0.001	0.001
C_5 and heavier	0.013	0.016
Aromatics		
Total less benzene	0.003	0.004
Benzene	0.002	0.001
Total	0.068	0.091

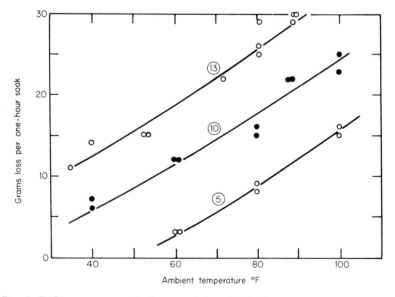

FIG. 5. Carburetor evaporative loss—variation with fuel vapor pressure and with ambient temperature. Numbers in large circles are Reid vapor pressure. From Muller, Kay, and Wagner (10).

temperature, tank configuration, location of the tank with respect to components of the exhaust system, and the flow pattern of the heated air that passes underneath the vehicle, all significantly affect tank fuel heating. For U.S.-made vehicles operated in a 70°–90° F ambient temperature, tank fuel temperature is raised by about 10° during a typical 15-mile trip.

Losses from the carburetor occur primarily during the periods after a hot (i.e., fully warmed-up) engine is stopped. During vehicle operation the carburetor and fuel in the carburetor remain at about the temperature of the air under the hood. But when underhood air flow is stopped by stopping the engine, the carburetor absorbs heat from the hot engine components and the temperature of the gasoline in the float bowl is raised. The temperature rise typically is on the order of 50°–80° F or well into the boiling range of any gasoline. Appreciable amounts of fuel are distilled from the carburetor bowl under these conditions, and the vapor escapes through various carburetor vents and openings.

Lesser magnitudes of loss from the carburetor occur during vehicle operation as a result of vapor loss through external carburetor vents. However, these losses are small, and a trend toward internal venting in the design of carburetors has largely removed operating losses at the carburetor as a significant source of vehicular emissions.

Evaporative losses and effects of temperature and fuel volatility are summarized and illustrated in Table III and Fig. 5.

C. CRANKCASE BLOW-BY (13)

Beginning with the model year 1963, this category of vehicular emissions has been totally controlled in U.S.-made automobiles. That is, engine design has been such as to prevent loss of blow-by from the engine system—accomplished by recycling the blow-by gas from the crankcase into the engine air or air-mixture intake. However, a large, albeit steadily diminishing, section of the auto population remains uncontrolled in this respect.

With the uncontrolled vehicle, crankcase blow-by accounts for about one-fifth of the hydrocarbon in all vehicle emissions. Vehicles with badly worn engines may discharge blow-by in much larger quantity to account for up to one-third or more of the total for those vehicles. Experimental evidence fully establishes that the blow-by gases are primarily, i.e., about 85%, carbureted fuel-air mixture that flows past the piston (and piston ring seal) during the compression stroke and prior to passage of flame through the mass. The remainder, comprising about 15% of the blow-by gas, is made up of combustion products. Therefore, any blow-by that is discharged to the atmosphere is rich in hydrocarbon. Concentration of unburned material in these gases varies between 5000 and 12,000 ppm of hydrocarbon, depending primarily upon cylinder and ring conditions that govern the proportion of blow-by from the compression and expansion strokes. Effective control of this source in older cars is feasible, but the cost may be unacceptable when measured against the total worth of an older vehicle.

D. Chemical Composition and Photochemical Reactivity of Hydrocarbon Emissions

The terms "photochemical reactivity" and "reactive" are used here in a broad sense. In this context, all olefins, all aromatics except benzene, and all paraffins having a molecular weight above that of hexane are assumed to be "reactive"; all other hydrocarbons are assumed to be "nonreactive." More precise reactivity value assignments have been made (Table IV) and are recommended for use in any definitive work

TABLE IV
Photochemical Reactivity of Hydrocarbons

Hydrocarbon or family	Reactivity	
	G-M (14)	USPHS (18)
Paraffins (C_1–C_3)	0	0 (C_1–C_5)
Acetylenes	0	0
Benzene	0	0
Monoalkyl benzenes	2	3
Paraffins (C_4 and heavier)	2	1 (C_6 and heavier)
Ortho- and paradialkyl benzenes	2	6
Cyclic paraffins	2	1[a]
Ethylene	5	4
Metadialkyl benzenes	5	6
Aldehydes	5	6[a]
1-Olefins	10	7
Diolefins	10	6
Tri- and tetraalkyl benzenes	10	6
Internally bonded olefins	30	8
Cycloolefins	100	8[a]
Internally bonded olefins with substitution at the double bond	100	8

[a] Value assigned by author interpolating source data.

that involves prediction or assessment of photochemical reactivity of vehicular emissions on the basis of hydrocarbon content.

While these reactivity values provide useful guidance, it should be noted that they were derived from laboratory experiments in which all interactions are not yet adequately understood. Further study involving atmospheric systems will be required for reliable assessment of the true photochemical effect of the constituent pollutants.

1. Unburned Hydrocarbons (14–18)

The C_5-and-heavier unburned hydrocarbons in the exhaust reflect the composition of the fuel that is burned; but the C_4-and-lighter components primarily result from fuel cracking during the compression-combustion cycle, and therefore do not mirror the fuel composition. Ironic as it seems, the more reactive species of the unburned hydrocarbons have their origin in the engine. Quantitatively, about two-thirds of the reactive material is of such origin; and this two-thirds portion contributes up to three-fourths of the total reactivity of the unburned hydrocarbon (Table V).

Air–fuel ratio, ignition timing, and driving cycle affect the composition of the hydrocarbon component of exhausts, but each exerts its respective influence through an effect upon combustion temperature and combustion efficiency. The severe high-temperature combustion associated with lean mixture yields quantitatively less total hydrocarbon, but a higher percentage of it will be photochemically reactive. A parallel effect (toward higher emission reactivity) is found in any influence that tends to increase combustion severity. Thus, ignition timing for minimal total emissions, carburetor adjustment for lean idle, or change in driving cycle to include a greater percentage of time in the power or cruise modes will each decrease the total, but increase the specific reactivity, of the hydrocarbon emissions.

2. Evaporative Emissions

Both tank and carburetor evaporative emissions (19, 20) involve only fuel components unmodified by any combustion process or thermal stress. Therefore the composition of these emissions corresponds exactly to that portion of the fuel evaporated and, correspondingly, the reactivity of evaporative losses varies with fuel composition.

In order to understand the significance of volatility and fuel composition on the reactivity of evaporative emissions, it is necessary to understand the manner in which fuel evaporates. As temperature of a gasoline

TABLE V

PRINCIPAL HYDROCARBONS IN EXHAUST—ORIGIN AND CONTRIBUTION TO
PHOTOCHEMICAL REACTIVITY

Most prominent on basis of concentration	Percent of total hydrocarbons
Ethylene	19.0
Methane	13.8
Propylene	9.1
Toluene[a]	7.9
Acetylene	7.8
1-Butene, i-butene, and 1,3-butadiene	6.0
p-, m-, and o-xylene[a]	2.5
i-Pentane[a]	2.4
n-Butane[a]	2.3
Ethane	2.3
Total	73.1

Most prominent on basis of reactivity	Percent of total reactivity
Ethylene	17.6
Propylene	16.9
1-Butene, i-butene, and 1,3-butadiene	11.3
2-Methyl-2-butene[a]	8.5
t- and c-2-butene	7.9
Toluene[a]	5.4
p-, m-, and o-xylene[a]	3.7
Propadiene and methylacetylene	2.2
t- and c-2-pentene[a]	2.2
2-Methyl-2-pentene[a]	1.9
Total	77.6

[a] Fuel components—others are products of fuel cracking or rearrangement in the engine. Adapted from Jackson 1966 (*16*).

in a simple container* is raised, and vapor driven off, the cumulative amount of vapor that is evaporated will depend upon the temperature attained (Fig. 6). Different gasolines have different distillation curves with the shape depending upon the relative amounts of volatile and heavy components. The material first evaporated will be rich in low molecular weight hydrocarbons, such as butanes and pentanes.

Tank losses involve primarily the more volatile front-end components that typically have low olefin content and conversely, high paraffin content. As a result only 20–40% of tank losses are reactive. Carburetor

* The evaporation or "distillation" process is influenced by any configuration of the container that causes a portion of the vapor to condense and return to the liquid.

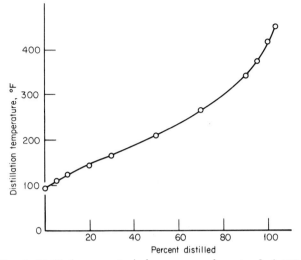

FIG. 6. Distillation curve typical summer grade motor fuel, U.S.

losses cut deeper into the gasoline boiling range and include relatively more olefins and reactive paraffins. From 50 to 70% of these losses are included in the reactive category.

Fuel volatility markedly affects the total *quantity* of evaporative losses, while the *reactivity* of these losses is most prominently influenced by the composition of the volatile front-end components. Therefore, adjustments in either, or both, of these factors provide opportunity for altering the amount and pollution-related significance of evaporative emissions.

III. Automotive Emissions Control

A. EXHAUST EMISSIONS

Exhaust, or tailpipe, emissions that are subject to control include unburned hydrocarbons, carbon monoxide, and nitric oxide. Emission levels of unburned hydrocarbons and carbon monoxide can be reduced through either more efficient oxidation in primary combustion, or in further oxidation after the combustion event. Unfortunately, measures that give favorable results upon hydrocarbons and carbon monoxide may adversely affect nitric oxide concentrations. Methods to reduce nitric oxide are therefore discussed separately.

1. *Hydrocarbon and Carbon Monoxide Control (21–24)*

Early engineering attempts to reduce emissions of hydrocarbon and CO were centered upon the development of equipment to be added to or incorporated in the exhaust systems and to act upon and further oxidize the pollutants. Both direct-flame afterburners (Fig. 7) and mufflers or "converters" (Fig. 8) charged with an oxidation catalyst were included in the early development.

Catalytic exhaust oxidation systems typically employ about 4–10 pounds of catalyst. Either a driven air pump or air-aspiration system is incorporated to provide approximately 30% additional secondary air injected into the exhaust stream ahead of the catalyst. Such systems have been found to remove as much as 95% of the photochemically re-active hydrocarbon and to reduce carbon monoxide concentrations to well below 1%. These values refer to the composite of exhaust produced over a typical city-suburban driving cycle.

The catalyst systems would appear to be inherently expensive. At its present stage of development a reliable system for a typical U.S.-made vehicle in the 250–300 in.³ engine displacement category would cost an initial $75–$90 and require an annual maintenance expense of half that amount. Moreover, the catalysts that have been offered have been found to have inadequate service life, generally losing effectiveness after 6,000–12,000 miles of accumulated short and medium-trip service. Additionally, catalysts that are available at reasonable cost are susceptible

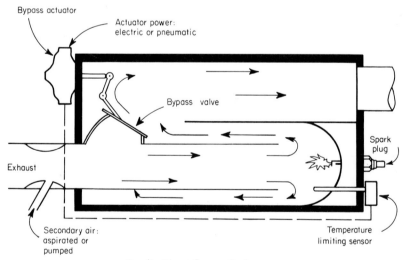

Fig. 7. Direct-flame afterburner.

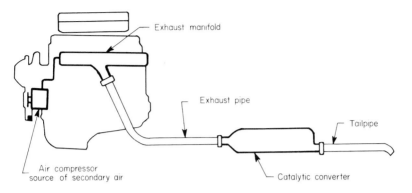

Fig. 8. Catalytic converter system.

to lead fouling and this susceptibility constitutes one of the major problems in the development of a satisfactory catalyst system.

Another problem inherent in catalytic conversion is protection against excessive temperature. Few, if any, known catalysts suitable for automotive use retain catalytic activity after exposure to temperatures in excess of 1800° F and it is difficult to limit catalyst temperature below this value during periods of prolonged deceleration, misfire, or other engine malfunction. Protective devices can be installed to bypass exhaust around the catalyst bed before excessive temperatures are reached, but the bypass procedure has the inherent disadvantage that the converter is made inoperative at a time when large amounts of objectionable pollutants are presented to it.

Several systems employing oxidation catalysts were successfully developed to the point of qualifying under State of California 1965 standards (25), but none of the qualifying devices were selected for use on U.S. automobiles. Presumably, they were not used because all (1) were too expensive initially, (2) would require excessive maintenance, and (3) have unacceptably short service life of less than 12,000 miles.

It is not yet clear whether the lead or the temperature limitations on catalyst life predominate. If the former is the case, one obvious route to an acceptable catalytic converter is the use, nationally, of nonleaded gasoline. The cost of so doing is discussed in Chapter 34.

After the unsatisfactory experience in adaptation of catalytic conversion to emission control, it appears unlikely that catalysts will play a significant role in emissions control before the 1970's. At that time catalytic oxidation may find a place in exhaust clean-up devices for exacting, low-level (possibly below 50 ppm hydrocarbon) emissions control. In cases of such application it appears likely that catalysts would be used in conjunction with other measures that would serve to reduce hydrocarbon concentration ahead of the catalytic device to well below 200 ppm.

Early developments of the direct-flame afterburner involved self-contained units separate and distinct from the engine. The device was unsatisfactory largely because of inability to sustain combustion in the afterburner during periods of low emissions. Experience in the early work suggests that for an afterburner to operate satisfactorily without fuel addition, heat must not be rejected from the exhaust prior to the afterburning process. This suggests that the combustion gases be discharged directly from the exhaust ports into the afterburner. In applying this concept, the afterburner logically takes a configuration that has come to be known as an exhaust manifold reactor; the conversion process is referred to as exhaust system oxidation.

Utilizing the exhaust as a reactor system, the oxidation of hydrocarbons and carbon monoxide can be continued in time beyond the primary combustion process provided (1) thermal energy of the exhaust is conserved, (2) sufficient residence time is provided for oxidation, and (3) secondary oxygen is supplied with adequate mixing. These requirements are partially met in manifold air injection systems that were introduced in cars sold in the State of California beginning with the model year 1966. A typical installation is shown in Fig. 9.

Design targets for emissions levels to be met with such manifold air injection systems were 275 ppm hydrocarbon measured as hexane, and 1-1/2% CO over an extended service life. These targets are realized only in part. On the average, new units supplied in the 1966 and 1967 period only marginally qualified, and performance in controlling emissions at the levels called for was not maintained by the average vehicle

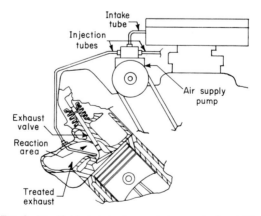

FIG. 9. Manifold air-injection emission control system.

surveyed in 1966–1967. Factors contributing to performance deterioration include:

1. Changes in carburetion due to intake system deposits and mechanical instability of parts and adjustments (particularly the idle adjustment).
2. Mechanical failure in air injection system components.
3. Ignition timing change resulting from wear and mechanical instability.
4. Combustion chamber deposit buildup and spark plug fouling.

A simplified approach to emissions control involves only modification of the engine without addition of secondary air to the exhaust. Such engine modification systems (EMS) incorporate features to (1) maintain good combustion and prevent hydrocarbon discharge during idle and deceleration, (2) provide generally more uniform fuel–air mixture to all cylinders, and (3) operate at air–fuel ratios near stoichiometric and avoid overenrichment in accelerator pump and power jet actions. Compared with engineering practices prevalent prior to 1966, the EMS approach incorporates:

1. Higher idle speed with retarded ignition timing.
2. Modified ignition timing oriented toward less advance for low speed accelerations and providing spark advance during decelerations.
3. Earlier choke release—choking modulated closer to lean limit.
4. Overall leaner mixture ratios, including idle.

In addition to these design features, the EMS concept involves the following which are being incorporated in varying degree in current automotive design.

1. Aerodynamically cleaner intake manifolding coupled with more efficient fuel atomization to improve fuel–air mixing and promote uniform mixture distribution. Continuous addition of heat from the exhaust to the intake mixture is utilized in some designs to assist in mixture control.

2. Alteration of combustion chamber geometry to reduce flame quench, to avoid pockets that tend to trap hard-to-ignite mixtures, and generally to remove interferences to flame sweeping the combustion volume.

3. Closer manufacturing tolerances for carburetion and ignition system components and for final engine adjustments.

4. Measures to prevent or to minimize engine adjustments drifting from factory set points after delivery into customer use.

Positive fuel metering systems offer good potential for achieving improved mixture control and for reducing both evaporative (fuel system) and exhaust emissions. Thus far, complexity and performance deficiencies have generally negated any advantage to be gained over the venturi carburetor. However, one such system was introduced commercially in 1968 and further development in this design area is probable.

Technical evolution can be expected to yield EMS systems producing exhausts with emissions reduced to within the vicinity of 180 ppm hydrocarbon and 1% CO. Advance beyond that point using EMS alone is unpredictable.

Prototypes of emission-control systems to reduce hydrocarbon and CO below 50 ppm and 1/2%, respectively, employ exhaust air oxidation in conjunction with engine modification. These advanced systems are distinguished primarily by an exhaust manifold designed to provide thermal insulation of the exhaust prior to air addition, efficient and rapid air-exhaust mixing, and increased residence time for the mixture at elevated temperature.

2. *Oxides of Nitrogen Control*

The concentration of nitrogen oxides (*26, 27*) in exhaust is most heavily influenced by peak combustion temperatures and by oxygen availability at the fixation temperature (*4*). Reduction in either reduces NO_x levels, and the effects are additive. Altering these combustion parameters therefore affords an approach to control over NO_x emission levels.

In one such approach to NO_x control, a portion of the exhaust gas is reintroduced to the cylinder intake charge. This serves both to reduce peak combustion temperature—the inert diluent serves as a heat sink—and to reduce absolute oxygen concentration throughout the combustion event. Reductions of NO_x of up to 90% are readily achieved by this method, referred to as exhaust gas recirculation. Mechanical features of one exhaust recirculation system are shown in Fig. 10.

For recirculation to result in NO_x reduction approaching 90%, up to 30% exhaust gas must be used in the intake charge. Obviously, introducing inert material decreases maximum power available from the engine, and therefore the percentage of exhaust in the intake flow is reduced as the throttle opening approaches full. Also, inasmuch as NO_x levels are low at idle and low-speed cruise, the percentage of exhaust is also decreased under those conditions.

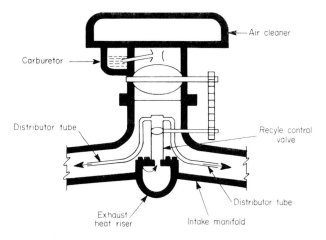

FIG. 10. Exhaust gas recirculation for NO_x control. From Daigh and Deeter (27).

NO_x emissions can be controlled by the action of a reducing catalyst on the exhaust stream. However, the only system known to be effective utilizes a copper catalyst to reduce NO in the presence of CO. The method holds little promise for controlling NO_x because conditions that are favorable to it are adverse to other emission-control objectives. A catalyst used to control NO_x emissions would likely be subject to the same temperature and fouling restraints as has been discussed with respect to oxidation catalysts.

3. *Exhaust Emission Goals*

The goal in establishing current, i.e., 1968 and earlier, vehicular emissions standards was to reduce, or roll back, the total of such emissions to some formerly existing level. Quite obviously if the total pollutant quantity is to remain at the same reduced level (or in some cases reduced still further) while the *number* of individual emitting units is increased, the allowable amount per unit will be progressively decreased. Projecting this philosophy, the ultimate goal for the present century is for discharge of objectionable pollutants to be essentially nil (per vehicle) in comparison with present standards. For the 1970–1980 decade the pattern of *approach* to the ultimate pollution-free exhaust is more relevant to this discussion.

The following resumé reflects current emission standards and goals for further reductions.

EXHAUST EMISSION GOALS

	Hydrocarbons (ppm as hexane)	Carbon monoxide (%)	Nitrogen oxides (ppm)
Averages from 1962 MVPCB[a] survey in Los Angeles	900	3.2	1000
Present California and U.S. national standards for new cars	275	1.5	Not specified
U.S. standards—1970,[b] avg.	180	1.0	Not specified
Suggested national objectives[c] for:			
1975 model cars	50	0.5	250
Ultimate	25	0.25	100

[a] Motor Vehicle Pollution Control Board (California), now Air Resources Board.

[b] The 1970 U.S. national standards (27a) specify permissible vehicle emissions in terms of weight. These are, for passenger cars and light duty vehicles as follows:

> hydrocarbon: 2.2 gm per vehicle mile
> carbon monoxide: 23 gm per vehicle mile

The 1970 values in the table represent, roughly, concentrations that correspond to the permissible weights of the respective emissions in the volume of exhaust discharged per "average" mile by a typical 4000 lb U.S. passenger vehicle.

[c] The Automobile and Air Pollution: A Program for Progress Report of the Panel on Electrically Powered Vehicles. U.S. Department of Commerce Technical Advisory Board, Part I, Oct. 1967. Part II, Dec. 1967.

Hydrocarbon levels specified in the foregoing are referred to measurement by nondispersive infrared absorption in hexane vapor. The measurement loses practical significance at the 50 ppm level and it is probable that by 1975 the specification will have been changed to one covering photochemically reactive hydrocarbons. There exists no consensus regarding appropriate and realistic goals for reactive hydrocarbons; nevertheless, the author suggests a 1975 goal of less than 20 ppm (molar basis) reactive hydrocarbon to be accompanied by no more than 20 ppm total aldehydes. The goals cited above for CO and NO_x appear realistic except that there may be doubt concerning both need for and feasibility of NO_x control at a level below 250 ppm. Further information on health and atmospheric effects involving the oxides of nitrogen are required to resolve the question.

While the emissions goals are discussed above in terms of *concentration,* it is the *quantity* or *amount* that is directly relevant to the pollution effect and standards proposed for the U.S. for 1970 are based upon weight. Therefore the goals above may be reinterpreted in like terms but with progressive reductions little changed from those indicated above.

B. EVAPORATIVE EMISSIONS

Control of evaporative emissions (28,29) has been considered by regulatory bodies in the United States since as early as 1964 but no controls were applied through 1967. In 1966, the state of California proposed a limit of 6 gm per day loss from the fuel tank plus, in effect, a 2 gm loss from the carburetor per vehicle trip. This proposed limit was subsequently enacted in 1968. Also in 1968, the U.S. set forth its 1970 national standard under which fuel system losses would be limited to 6 gm during a test to simulate (a) one diurnal temperature cycle, (b) one "average" vehicle trip, and (c) the subsequent 1-hour "hot soak" period. In consideration of problems in implementing the 1970 U.S. standard, its application was deferred until 1971.

In general, evaporative emissions can be reduced by reducing fuel volatility; however, any marked change in the volatility characteristics of motor gasoline from world-wide 1968 levels involves serious problems and penalties in fuel manufacturing. Furthermore, a decrease in fuel volatility below the 8–12 pound Reid vapor pressure range, now commonly used in temperate climates throughout the world, aggravates problems of fuel mixture distribution in carbureted engines. Any move toward use of fuels with generally reduced vapor pressures will therefore require compensating development in design of carburetors and intake manifolds. Features and factors in carburetor and induction system design for fuels with reduced vapor pressure include (1) means to add heat and thermostatically control the temperature of the intake air, (2) highly atomized fuel—efficient air–fuel mixing, and (3) attention to intake manifold design to minimize fuel–air separation and to promote and maintain a uniform and homogeneous carbureted mixture.

Evaporative losses may also be reduced by attention to mechanical design. Large areas of exposed liquid surface contribute to high fuel tank losses and these losses are notably aggravated by heat sources (such as mufflers) in close proximity to the fuel tank. Carburetor losses are also adversely influenced by having the carburetor coupled to or near elements of the engine that reach and remain at elevated temperature after the engine is shut down.

Although evaporative emissions controls have not been applied in any United States vehicles produced commercially prior to 1968, several control concepts are technically feasible. Features of these control systems include:

1. Design for minimal fuel system temperatures.
2. Design for minimal surface area of exposed liquids.

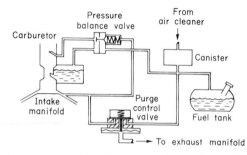

FIG. 11. Fuel system evaporation-loss control device. From Clarke *et al.* (*28*).

3. Reduction in volume of the liquid retained in the fuel system exposed to elevated temperatures during engine shutdown.
4. Automatic fuel drains.
5. Vapor capture during engine shutdown with recycle into the intake system upon restarting.

All except the last of these concepts are intended to minimize the amount of fuel, vapor or liquid, that is released from the fuel system proper. Vapor recycle is intended to intercept vapors that are released into the induction system before they are freed into the underhood compartment. These vapor-capture systems employ some retention element, such as charcoal or foamed polyurethane, that presents a large surface area on which to adsorb and temporarily retain the hydrocarbon vapors. Such systems incorporate features to purge, i.e., desorb, the hydrocarbon from the trap into the intake system of the automobile when air flow is restarted. One problem of the adsorption/desorption emission-control system involves overenrichment of the engine air–fuel mixture during the desorption period. Some degree of control over this factor is exercised by the use of a valve that controls the rate at which hydrocarbons are desorbed back to the engine. A schematic of an emission-control system operating on the adsorption/desorption principle is shown in Fig. 11.

Although evaporative emission-control systems were not commercially employed as late as 1968, the technical feasibility of controlling this source of pollutants has been demonstrated. There appears little doubt that starting about 1971, automotive engine and vehicle designs will incorporate features to prevent fuel-system evaporation losses.

C. CRANKCASE BLOW-BY (*30, 31*)

Crankcase emission-control systems vary greatly in detail, but basically all provide for returning the blow-by gases to the air intake system of the engine. A typical system is shown schematically in Fig. 12. In this system the crankcase blow-by is vented through a tube leading to a flow-modulating valve which is connected to the intake manifold immediately below the carburetor. Typically, the valve is designed so that it restricts flow at high vacuum and permits free flow at low vacuum. With this provision, high ventilation rates parallel the large volume of blow-by associated with high speed, high power, low vacuum engine operation. With high manifold vacuum when blow-by rate is low, the modulating valve restricts flow to a correspondingly low value.

In simplified systems the crankcase is totally closed and blow-by gases are vented into the engine air cleaner to be entrained with the intake air. Such systems sacrifice good crankcase ventilation but generally provide effective control over crankcase emissions.

Inasmuch as the recirculated blow-by gases carry high concentrations of hydrocarbons, these gases tend to enrich the intake mixture. This enrichment should be recognized and appropriately compensated by correction to the primary fuel metering.

D. TESTING FOR CERTIFICATION AND INSPECTION OF VEHICLES

Standardized test procedures are required for regulatory purposes and are indispensable aids in effective experimental research and development. Therefore it is significant that experimental research in depth has been devoted to developing test procedures appropriate to vehicle emission measurement. These procedures should:

1. Provide that the vehicle be operated through a pattern of varied speeds and loads, with appropriate sequence and duration in each

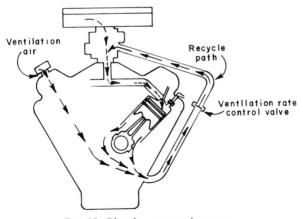

FIG. 12. Blow-by gas recycle system.

mode to approximate patterns found in typical or average metropolitan usage. Alternatively, the pattern of test operation must be shown to yield emissions suitably like those produced in operating the vehicle over a typical metropolitan route.

2. Provide for a test environment that is reasonable in comparison with ambient conditions that may prevail whenever and wherever vehicular emissions constitute a pollution problem.

3. Provide for suitable methods of measuring and differentiating emissions that are significant as air pollutants. This provision properly encompasses exhaust sample collection, and, subsequent to measurement, appropriate evaluation of the test data.

A fuel specification is prerequisite to these basic provisions inasmuch as fuel composition (including volatility) can influence both actual and measured values of emissions, and not necessarily in the same degree.

Certification of control systems additionally requires a procedure for accumulating service under uniform controlled duty conditions to determine durability of the system in service.

Procedures for use in certifying automotive equipment for compliance with permissible emission criteria were first drawn by the State of California in 1961. The California procedures, with amendments, subsequently served as the basis, or model, for U.S. test and certification procedures adopted in 1966 and applicable to new vehicles and new vehicle engines beginning with the 1968 model year. Details of the procedures are given in the text of regulations published in the *Federal Register,* Vol. 31, No. 61, March 30, 1966, Part II—Title 45, Subtitle A, Part 85. (For 1970 and later models see Vol. 33, No. 108, June 4, 1968, Part II.)

Briefly hydrocarbon and CO emissions are determined from data obtained on exhaust gases produced while the vehicle is operated on a chassis dynamometer through a cycle of operations repeated seven times. The basic cycle is as follows:

1. Beginning at idle, idle engine for 20 seconds.
2. Accelerate 0–25 mph in 11.5 seconds.
3. Continue acceleration 25–30 mph in 2.5 seconds (data from this 25–30 acceleration is not read).
4. Cruise at 30 mph for 15 seconds.
5. Decelerate from 30 to 15 mph in 11 seconds.
6. Cruise at 15 mph for 15 seconds.
7. Accelerate from 15 to 30 mph in 12.5 seconds.
8. Continue acceleration from 30 to 50 mph in 16.5 seconds (data from this 30–50 acceleration is not read).
9. Decelerate from 50 to 20 mph in 25 seconds.

10. Continue deceleration from 20 to 0 mph in 8 seconds
    (data from this 20–0 deceleration is not read).
    Cumulative time in the cycle is 137 seconds.

On the first cycle the idle period at start is for a period of 40 seconds in neutral. For all other cycles, idle periods are for 20 seconds in gear.

The sequence, or cycle, is repeated seven times for a complete test; the first four cycles provide warm-up data; the last two provide "hot cycle" data. No information is taken from the fifth cycle.

Concentrations of both CO and hydrocarbon are determined by continuous measurement in nondispersive infrared analyzers (the hydrocarbon detector is sensitized with n-hexane). CO_2 also is measured in order that all measurements may be referred to a standard dry exhaust mixture containing 15% ($CO + CO_2$). The concentrations of the respective emissions are determined for each of the modes for which data are taken. Details are given in the regulation cited, but roughly, the procedure is to obtain the time-averaged concentration registered during each of the modes.* Each value so determined is then weighted according to the following factor assigned the mode:

Idle—0.042; 0 to 25 accel.—0.244; 30 cruise—0.118; 30 to 15 decel.—
0.062; 15 cruise—0.050; 15 to 30 accel.—0.455; 50 to 20 decel.—0.029.

The total of values so weighted (for the respective emissions) produces the value for the cycle. The average of the respective weighted values for the first four warm-up cycles and the average of values for the last two cycles are combined in the ratio .35 (average warm-up value) plus .65 (average hot value) to yield the computed seven-mode cycle emission values.

The test procedure yields single values for hydrocarbon and carbon monoxide concentrations but certification is based on acceptability of emission data on groups of test vehicles. In like manner, U.S. certification requires that data be obtained on several vehicles at intervals of no less than 4000 miles for a total per vehicle of not less than 50,000 miles. Mileage for the durability tests is accumulated over routes representative of urban driving with an average speed of 32 mph. Approved city routes or a closed test track driving schedule are used in the durability mileage accumulation.

A satisfactory procedure for determining evaporative loss from the carburetor has not been established. Various methods that have been

---

* And corrected by the factor $15/(CO + CO_2)$ for all except deceleration modes which are to be corrected by the factor $15/(6HC + CO + CO_2)$. CO and CO_2 as percent, HC as percent n-hexane.

used include (1) plugging all external openings and trapping vapors at the air intake. (2) sweeping the carburetor throat with air to entrain evolving vapors and subsequently recapturing the material for measurement, (3) directly measuring residual volumes in the carburetor bowl, and (4) taking gravity (or density) measurements upon fuel in the carburetor bowl before and after the period of loss and relating the change to the amount of fuel evaporated. The latter two methods require that modifications be made upon and access provided to the fuel system components and therefore the methods are not feasible for tests that involve large numbers of vehicles. Some variation of vapor entrainment, recovery, and measurement will therefore probably evolve as the accepted procedure for measuring evaporative loss from the carburetor or fuel intake system.

Vapor evolved from the fuel tank of a vehicle is readily captured by forcing the escaping vapor through either a charcoal trap or a cold trap. Weights before and after vapor recovery reveal the loss from the tank.

Evaporative loss from all sources may be determined by effectively confining the vehicle in a closed cell and monitoring change in the hydrocarbon concentration in the air contained therein.

In the United States, an evaporative loss standard applicable in 1971 would utilize vapor recovery test techniques combining method (1) above with direct fuel tank trapping (27a).

Each of the procedures for evaporative loss measurement is utilized to some extent in research and development that will continue through 1970. Standardization may be expected near the end of that period.

IV.   Atmospheric Pollutants from Diesel-Powered Equipment

As a source of pollution the diesel engine is notorious for smoke and odor of its exhaust. Because these characteristics involve primarily esthetic values, there have been few attempts (and a notable lack of success) in applying objective measurement to them. The diesel emissions problem is therefore ill-defined and only grossly measured. For that reason the following discussion is general in character; wide latitude in assigned values and other technical liberties in the text are properly interpreted by the reader as deficiencies in knowledge concerning both the nature and the quantity of pollutants in diesel exhausts.

A. NATURE OF DIESEL EMISSIONS

In addition to smoke and odor, diesel exhausts carry significant concentrations of unburned hydrocarbons, nitric oxides, oxygenated compounds, and in some cases, carbon monoxide (*32–35*). The concentration levels of pollutants as emitted from the diesel engine are deceptively low if compared with similar data from auto exhausts. This is because diesel engines are operated with an unthrottled air intake and induct large quantities of excess air that dilute the combustion products. Comparable dilution does not occur with spark-ignited engines that operate with the intake throttled and with fuel metered proportional to air flow to maintain the air–fuel ratio within a narrow range of values.*

If concentration data for diesel exhausts are to be meaningful, they must be expressed with reference to a standard mixture—logically near stoichiometric. In practice, this correction involves multiplying the actually determined values by factors that vary from about 15 for products produced during idle to 1 1/4 to 3 (depending upon scavenging air, if used) for products produced at full load. An assumption of 15% total for CO and CO_2 in the "standard" exhaust mixture is reasonable, and normalization of other values to the 15% $(CO + CO_2)$ value will yield corrections of the magnitude indicated above. Values so corrected are appropriate for comparison with automotive data.

B. Fuel and Engine Effects on Diesel Emissions

Concentrations of pollutants in diesel exhausts vary enormously depending upon engine type, speed, and load (Table VI). Viewed broadly, the values for diesel emissions bracket values for automotive emissions averaged over a traffic cycle. The general pattern is that concentrations of pollutants in diesel exhaust decrease with load while the absolute values are dependent upon both speed and load in a manner not yet reliably defined.

The available experimental data are inadequate to permit satisfactory generalizations concerning influences of fuel and engine parameters upon diesel emissions (*36*). Experience in the Bartlesville Petroleum Research Center suggests a surprising lack of any correlation between fuel quality or its predominant hydrocarbon character, and concentration levels of any of the objectionable emissions.

Design of the diesel engine affects principally smoke and odor and these are discussed separately in following paragraphs. However, the 4-cycle diesel would appear to be inherently a somewhat lower hydrocarbon emitter than an air-scavenged 2-cycle diesel with its quenching blowdown. The limited data that are available suggest this to be true,

---

* Even with secondary air injected into the exhaust, the dilution of automotive exhausts is minor compared with dilution by excess air in diesels under all except full-load conditions.

TABLE VI

DIESEL EMISSIONS BOTH "AS MEASURED" AND CORRECTED FOR
DILUTION BY EXCESS AIR

(Steady-state, engine dynamometer tests)[a,d]

| | Rated speed | | | | | | Idle | |
| | Full load | | Half load | | No load | | | |
Emissions	As measured	Ad-justed[b]	As measured	Ad-justed[b]	As measured	Ad-justed[b]	As measured	Ad-justed[b]
Two-cycle engine, No. 2 fuel								
Unburned hydrocarbon:								
ppmC by gas-liquid[c]								
chromatography	467	1,148	605	2,530	530	5,094	401	6,275
Weight, 10^{-4} lb/min	48.5	—	62.7	—	54.8	—	11.2	—
Percent by weight of								
fuel supplied	0.797	—	1.68	—	0.305	—	3.51	—
Formaldehyde, ppm	13	32	8.1	33.5	7.3	70.2	11	160
NO_x, ppm	622	1,530	392	1,618	147	1,414	210	3,057
CO, %	0.1	0.25	0.03	0.12	0.03	0.29	0.03	0.42
CO_2, %	6.0	14.8	3.6	14.9	1.53	14.7	1.0	14.56
O_2, %	12.9	—	16.6	—	19.5	—	20.5	—
Air rate, lb/min	21.3	—	21.7	—	21.6	—	5.87	—
Fuel rate, lb/min	0.608	—	0.372	—	0.180	—	0.032	—
Number of tests reported	6		6		6		6	
Four-cycle Engine, No. 2 fuel								
Unburned hydrocarbon:								
ppmC by gas-liquid								
chromatography	29	39	68	198	73	884	104	1,637
Weight, 10^{-4} lb/min	2.0	—	5.2	—	5.2	—	3.5	—
Percent by weight of								
fuel supplied	0.028	—	0.136	—	0.559	—	1.22	—
Formaldehyde, ppm	4.3	6.0	6.8	19.5	1.8	21.8	6.8	109
NO_x, ppm	921	1,280	493	1,415	109	1,319	119	1,916
CO, %	0.2	0.28	0.03	0.09	0.03	0.36	0.03	0.48
CO_2, %	10.6	14.7	5.2	14.9	1.21	14.6	0.9	14.5
O_2, %	5.79	—	13.9	—	18.8	—	20.29	—
Air rate, lb/min	14.13	—	15.65	—	15.06	—	6.89	—
Fuel rate, lb/min	0.704	—	0.381	—	0.094	—	0.028	—
Number of tests reported	4		6		6		6	

[a] Hydrocarbon values reported in the table were derived from gas-liquid chromatography data. Corresponding measurements by total-hydrocarbon flame-ionization measurements averaged from about 25 to 50% higher as referred to calibrations for automotive emissions. GLC responses were referred to calibrations made with hydrocarbons in the diesel boiling range and, of the two sets of data, are believed to be the more reliable.

[b] Concentration values as read normalized to $(CO + CO_2)$ concentration = 15%.

[c] ppmC, carbon-atom concentration, equivalent to: (ppm mole basis) (average number of carbon atoms per molecule).

[d] From Hurn and Seizinger (32).

but, as of this publication, the comparison remains a conjecture. Also unknown is the difference in emissions characteristics between designs using, respectively, open or precombustion chamber injection. Nonetheless, one may speculate that the precombustion process with its fuel-rich character may offer reduced NO_x emissions. Other effects are not so readily deduced.

The hydrocarbon portion of diesel exhaust includes both fuel com-

TABLE VII

HYDROCARBON DISTRIBUTION IN DIESEL EMISSIONS[a]

(Steady-state, engine dynamometer tests)

	Rated speed			
	Full load	Half load	No load	Idle
Two-cycle engine, No. 2 fuel				
C_1–C_5[b]	153	77	65	26
C_6–C_8[b]	1.1	0.4	1	1
C_9–C_{12}[c]	133	163	166	163
C_{13}–C_{15}	106	186	179	151
C_{16}–C_{18}	56	136	95	51
$C_{19}+$	18	43	24	9
Total	467	605	530	401
Number of tests reported	6	6	6	6
Four-cycle engine, No. 2 fuel				
C_1–C_5[b]	22	10.3	18.3	19
C_6–C_8[b]	4.7	2.2	6.6	3.3
C_9–C_{12}[c]	2.0[d]	21	20.0	39
C_{13}–C_{15}	—	19	17	29
C_{16}–C_{18}	—	12	8	10
$C_{19}+$	—	4	3	4
Total	29	68	73	104
Number of tests reported	4	6	6	5

[a] Emissions by gas-liquid chromatography, ppmC.

[b] Data based on two tests.

[c] Molecular weight distribution C_{10} and higher is reported only as a loose classification. More precisely, the components would be described as "C_x n-paraffins and other material eluted with or nearest the C_x n-paraffin." GLC separations were made with a nonpolar column; therefore, the elution order of the components may be assumed to have followed boiling point.

[d] Emissions measured as $C_{10}+$.

ponents and light, i.e., low molecular weight, cracked products. Fuel components predominate in the mixture of fuel and cracked products except in exhausts produced at or near full load in engines that are inherently low emitters (Table VII). Portions of the combustion products —the unsaturated hydrocarbons—are photochemically reactive, and some or all of the unfractured fuel components may also be reactive. Experiment with automotive fuel components has shown that both heavy paraffins and most aromatics (i.e., those in motor fuels) are photochemically reactive. Therefore, lacking more definitive information on hydrocarbons in the diesel boiling range, it can only be assumed that the heavy hydrocarbons in diesel exhausts also are reactive as atmospheric pollutants.

The overall contribution of diesel exhausts to photochemical air pollution is now and through at least 1970 will continue to be minor in the mobile source category. Beyond 1970 with reductions in automotive emission becoming effective, the balance may change significantly; almost without question the diesel will become relatively more important as a source of photochemical pollutants.

C. Diesel Smoke

Diesel smoke (37–41) is placed in three categories for technical treatment-(1) black, (2) blue, and (3) white. Black smoke results from incomplete combustion of the fuel due to fuel injection irregularity or to overfueling the engine.* Blue smoke results from excessive oil consumption and unequivocally indicates an engine problem. White smoke represents unburned fuel fog and generally is associated with cold engine operation. Of the three types of diesel smoke, only the black variety represents a significant problem of widespread proportion in emissions control.

1. Smoke Measurement

European countries have relied principally upon instrumental measurement methods while in the U.S., dependence is primarily upon subjective methods, i.e., an observer's judgment. However, visual assessment is only as good as the observer's judgment, which is highly variable and greatly affected by gas velocity and by the background against which the smoke is viewed. In the U.S. the Ringelmann chart is widely used as a visual reference standard (see Chapter 29).

Two types of instruments are used for smoke measurement—one type responsive to light interruption (extinction or obscuration) by the smoke particles and the other utilizing particle filtration or deposition upon suitable media. Photocells sensitive to light, either transmitted through a smoke column or reflected from a smoke-soiled filter element (depending upon the type of meter), ordinarily are used to measure the smoke effect (Figs. 13 and 14). The Hartridge-B.P. smoke meter is the

---

* As fuel delivery to a diesel engine is increased, the exhaust typically will darken as the quantity of fuel injected approaches the maximum amount that can be burned utilizing the amount of oxygen present in the air charge. The point of significant darkening, the smoke point, varies with engine type but generally occurs with fuel delivery about 20% below the stoichiometric value.

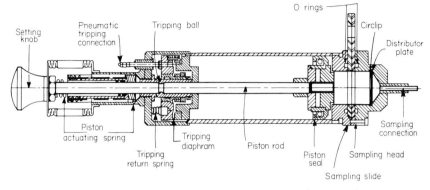

FIG. 13. Bosch smoke sampler. From Vulliamy and Spiers (*37*).

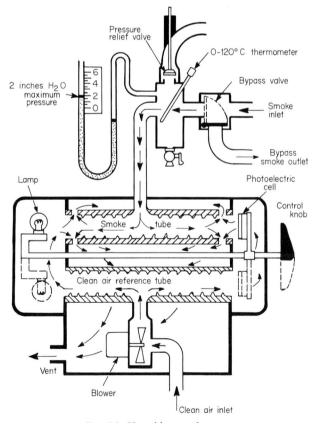

FIG. 14. Hartridge smoke meter.

most widely used of the light-extinction type. The Bosch spot meter is the most widely used example of the filtration type. Both are in common use in Europe. Both are used also in the United States, where, in addition, the Von Brand filter-paper smoke meter is used. Instead of the paper disk used in the Bosch meter, the Von Brand utilizes a moving tape that continuously changes the smoke-deposition surface. This meter is therefore adaptable to continuous smoke measurement although, depending upon tape speed, it inherently smooths or averages transient changes in smoke values.

Strenuous objection has been raised to the instruments commonly used for smoke measurement on the grounds that none respond in a manner that can be correlated with human response. In order to overcome this objection, the U.S. Public Health Service has sponsored development of a light-extinction smoke meter in which a collimated light beam is used. This reduces scatter effects that account for much of the difference between instrumental and human responses. An instrument of this type is specified in standards adopted by the United States for 1970 (27a).

Each of the smoke meter types has advantage in one or more applications. The light-extinction types are well suited for laboratory and stationary use and for continuous monitoring to reveal rapid changes during engine transients. The filter type can be very simple and is well suited for use on the road (see also Chapter 51).

2. Control of Diesel Smoke

Diesel smoke is controlled primarily by (1) proper maintenance, and (2) restricting power extracted from the engine to a value below the smoke point. In addition, smoke may be suppressed through use of fuel additives.

White smoke—or unburned fuel—is excepted from this discussion. It is a problem only in cold-start operations and does not constitute a major pollution problem.

Blue smoke is corrected by correcting excessive lubricating oil consumption. Because it generally is in the operator's interest to avoid the cause of blue smoke, the problem tends to have a built-in incentive for correction.

Excessive black smoke can result from fouled injectors or other malfunction that causes faulty fuel injection. Good maintenance practice and rapid correction of engine casualties is the obvious approach to control of these problems. Unfortunately, well-maintained diesel engines also discharge black smoke at power settings well below the maximum power available from the engine. Moreover, objectionable smoke generally is encountered with increased power before specific fuel consumption becomes excessive (Fig. 15). Therefore the load that is permissible with a given engine typically is governed by the onset of heavy smoking. Throttle or fuel rack stops often are used to limit the quantity of fuel injected to a value corresponding to a predetermined smoke-limited power level.

Engines are rated by the manufacturer for use at power levels below which heavy smoking occurs (Fig. 15). There is, however, no general agreement on criteria for an acceptable smoke level. Such criteria and appropriate instrumentation are recognized world-wide as pressing needs in further developing diesel power technology. The technical problems are not serious, and standardized smoke measurement and acceptance criteria probably will materialize by 1970.

While both engine design and fuel properties affect diesel smoking characteristics, the dominant factors in excessive smoke are poor engine (or injector) maintenance and overfueling. Engine selection and engine maintenance are therefore prime factors in diesel smoke control.

Metals, particularly barium-base materials used as a fuel additive, are highly effective in suppressing diesel smoke. The mechanism of smoke suppression is unknown. However, metal additives are known to decrease the ignition temperature of soot particles, and it is reported that their use reduces the tendency of smoke particles to agglomerate.

Although the latter effect may be present, data not yet published indicate the primary influence to be the metal's catalytic effect on soot burning with little effect upon its formation. The smoke suppressant

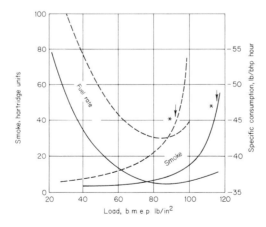

FIG. 15. Diesel smoke and fuel rate—variation with engine power. ——— direct injection engine, 1500 rpm; – – – – indirect injection engine, 1750 rpm; * manufacturer's power rating.

additives (SSA) typically are oil-soluble, fully miscible, metal/organic liquids. About 0.10 to 0.20 weight percent of the metal itself is required for appreciable improvement in smoke emission. As supplied, the SSA is used at about 1/4 to 1/2 volume percent concentration.

Use of the fuel additive can under favorable conditions reduce smoke from heavy black to negligible; or, in terms of power, can permit extraction of 10–20% more power without excessive smoke than would be permissible with untreated fuel. The additive material is inherently expensive because of its high metal content. Its use in commercial service is a question of economic balance between the cost of the additive and the cost of either increased engine size or engine derating.

All smoke suppressant additive materials have high ash content that in sustained use may cause problems with some engines. Effects of the additive on engine emissions other than smoke appear to be negligible.

The toxicity of smoke suppressant additive materials discharged to the atmosphere in exhaust gases is being studied intensively but is not yet adequately assessed. Evidence from the studies previously cited shows barium to be discharged primarily as barium sulfate, in which form the metal has very low toxicity. With regard to the availability of sulfur for the sulfate conversion, almost all diesel fuels contain more than is required. Only 0.01 to 0.03% sulfur is required for stoichiometric conversion of a barium smoke suppressant additive used at 1/4 to 3/8% concentrations. The potential toxicity of this additive resides in that portion of the barium exhausted in forms other than sulfate.

D. DIESEL ODOR

While diesel smoke has received the bulk of regulatory attention around the world, the offensive odor (42) of diesel exhaust has probably drawn more criticism from the general public. Although the two are commonly associated, as attests the phrase "diesel smoke and odor," this generalized association is misleading. Discernible odor almost always accompanies any visible smoke, but virtually clear exhaust may carry highly offensive odors. The specific odorants in diesel exhaust have been neither isolated nor identified but are commonly associated with the broad family of oxygenates. Odor identification is being studied intensively (43).

In an attempt to associate factors in engine design with the odor problem, one finds no reliable technical basis for judgment. Consensus as judged by the author is that, of engines in general use in the United States, the 2-cycle air-scavenged engine presents the most serious problem of malodorous emissions. Of the engine modes, acceleration following idle and the high-torque/mid-speed-range modes tend to produce the more malodorous exhausts. Combustion quenching, poor air utilization, and partial oxidation of unburned fuel in the exhaust system are suspect as contributing to generation of odorants associated with the above factors.

Objectionable odor has not been reliably associated with any one or any combination of fuel factors; therefore fuel specification as yet offers no approach to odor abatement. Fuel additives, purporting to inhibit diesel odor, are offered commercially, but results of large-scale field and carefully controlled laboratory trials of odor inhibitors are yet inconclusive. Odor masking agents added to the fuel are effective in substituting presumably "pleasing" odors for unpleasant ones. Unfortunately, however, a reception that is initially favorable to the substitute odor may, upon repeated exposure, turn unfavorable. Pilot trials of masking agents in city bus operations have not produced encouraging results.

Oxidation catalysts used under favorable conditions effectively reduce the intensity and the objectionable character of diesel exhaust odor. To be effective, however, catalysts tested thus far must be operated within a range of temperatures higher than temperatures readily maintained in all duty in which diesel engines are employed and in which exhaust odor is a problem.

Catalytic odor control systems combining the muffler and catalyst container in a catalytic muffler have been used and development effort continues. Results in terms of engineering problems, cost, and real gain in improved exhaust odor quality are inconclusive and will not be reliably established before 1970.

Experimental study of combustion odor is seriously handicapped by lack of acceptable methods for measuring and evaluating odor; suitable reference odors are needed but are not available. Synthesized odor standards and human panel evaluation procedures have been subjects of significant experimental studies in the period 1964 through 1968. However, both standards and procedures are undergoing such rapid and significant change that reference to them would serve little purpose. In short, the problem of odor from moving pollution sources is little understood and corrective measures are not revealed. The subject is being experimentally studied intensively—in breadth and in depth—by both public and private interests, and significant new information can be expected.

V. Gas Turbines

Gas turbines operate with fuel mixtures that, overall, are extremely lean compared with the mixture ratios used in spark-ignited piston en-

gines. Assuming efficient combustion, turbine emissions of CO and unburned hydrocarbon would be expected to be quite low.

Emissions levels of other pollutants, NO_x and oxygenates, are dependent upon parameters of a specific system, and generalizations in
the case of the turbine are hazardous in the absence of extensive experience. Nonetheless, it has been widely assumed that the gas turbine could
be developed to have emissions characteristics favorable in all categories.
It remains to be demonstrated that such an objective can be realized.

Abatement of smoke from mobile oil-burning gas turbines should follow methods being developed for stationary turbines (see Chapter 32).

A. AUTOMOTIVE

A very limited number of automotive gas turbines have been produced for field trial. Instrumental measurements and subjective assessment of exhaust from these units have revealed no evident pollution
problems. However, measurements made upon the highly diluted exhausts must be much more refined before automotive turbine exhausts
are satisfactorily evaluated.

B. AIRCRAFT

Emissions from gas turbines of aircraft jet engines were measured
by engineers at Bartlesville in 1962 and again in 1967. Data were taken
using commercial jet engines in the 10,000–16,000 pound thrust category operated in airline overhaul test facilities. As in the case of the
automotive gas turbine, sampling and measurement techniques are inadequate and estimates may involve uncertainty equal at least to the
estimate. The principle aircraft turbine gaseous emissions are summarized and estimates given in Table VIII. Overall, aircraft cannot be
considered a significant source of pollution but may present local nuisances or aggravate area pollution in the vicinity of airport operations.

In addition to the gaseous emissions summarized in Table VIII, aircraft turbines present a smoke problem that in the late 1960's had become serious at major airports in the United States and Europe. Intense
jet engine smoke was first associated with water injection used for power
boost on takeoff, but dry engines, subsequently developed, have retained the smoke problem. Fuel characteristics markedly influence
smoke generated in can combustors. Aromatic hydrocarbon aggravates
the problem and aromatics in jet fuel is generally limited to a maximum
of 25% in order to control carbon deposition. While this specification
is not directed toward visible smoke, per se, some measure of smoke
control is realized. In general, the problem of jet aircraft engine smoke

TABLE VIII
AIRCRAFT TURBINE EMISSIONS[a]
(15,000 pound Thrust Category Engine)

Engine mode	Hydrocarbon		NO_x		Aldehydes	
	Concentration (ppmC)	Mass (lb/hour)	Concentration (ppm)	Mass (lb/hour)	Concentration (ppm)	Mass (lb/hour)
Idle	150	20	5	2	5	2
Cruise	5	2	50	45	1	1.5
Takeoff	2	1	5	5	Trace	Nil

[a] Values in this table are estimates intended only to show orders of magnitude. No comparable published data are available, therefore estimates are by the author using unpublished data from tests with less than ten engines.

is not well understood and solutions are unknown. Experimental investigation is being continued with further attention to the design of can combustors and fuel injectors, to air utilization, and to fuels and fuel additives for smoke abatement.

REFERENCES

1. W. A. Daniel and J. T. Wentworth, Gen. Motors Eng. J. **10**, No. 1, 14–20 (1963).
2. W. A. Daniel, SAE (Soc. Automotive Engrs.) Trans. **76**, 774–795 (1968).
3. A. H. Rose, Jr., "A Summary Report of Vehicular Emissions and Their Control," presented to Am. Soc. Mech. Engrs., New York, 1966.
3a. D. F. Hagen and G. W. Holiday, S.A.E. (Soc. Automotive Engrs.) "Vehicle Emissions" Technical Publication Series 6, 1964 p. 206.
3b. A. H. Rose, Jr., "Air Pollution," (A. Stern, ed.), Vol. 2, Academic Press, 1st ed., 1962 p. 41.
4. E. S. Starkman and H. K. Newhall, SAE (Soc. Automotive Engrs.) Trans. **74**, 826–838 (1966).
5. State of California, "The Oxides of Nitrogen in Air Pollution," Dept. of Public Health, Bur. of Air Sanitation, Berkeley, California, 1966.
5a. M. W. Jackson, S.A.E. (Soc. Automotive Engrs.) "Alcohol in Motor Fuels" Special Publication 254, 1964 p. 11.
6. K. J. Hughes, R. W. Hurn, and F. G. Edwards, in "Third International Gas Chromatography Symposium" (N. Brenner, J. E. Callen, and M. D. Weiss, eds.), pp. 171–182. Academic Press, New York, 1962.
7. D. A. Hirschler, L. F. Gilbert, F. W. Lamb, and L. M. Niebylski, Ind. Eng. Chem. **49**, No. 7, 1131–1142 (1957).
8. R. W. Gates, "Particulate Matter in Automobile Exhaust," Stanford Res. Inst. Rept. No. 2. Menlo Park, California, 1955.
9. T. O. Wagner, Proc. Am. Petrol. Inst., Sect. III **46**, 401–406 (1966).

10. H. L. Muller, R. E. Kay, and T. O. Wagner, *SAE (Soc. Automotive Engrs.) Trans.* **75**, 720–730 (1967).
11. W. F. Deeter and R. G. Jewell, *Proc. Am. Petrol. Inst. Sect. III* **46**, 427–441 (1966).
12. D. T. Wade, *SAE (Soc. Automotive Engrs.) Trans.* **76**, 811–823 (1968).
13. P. A. Bennett, C. K. Murphy, M. W. Jackson, and R. A. Randall, *S.A.E. Trans.* **68**, 514–528 (1960).
14. J. D. Caplan, *S.A.E. (Soc. Automotive Engrs.), Preprint* No. 650641 (1965).
15. The British Petroleum Company Limited, "Influence of Fuel Composition on Spark Ignition Engine Emissions," Tech. Mem. No. 110,123. BP Res. Centre, Middlesex, England, 1965.
16. M. W. Jackson, *SAE (Soc. Automotive Engrs.) Trans.* **75**, 672–689 (1967).
17. L. A. McReynolds, H. E. Alquist, and D. B. Wimmer, *SAE (Soc. Automotive Engrs.) Trans.* **74**, 902–911 (1966).
18. A. P. Altshuller, *J. Air Pollution Control Assoc.* **16**, No. 5, 257–260 (1966).
19. G. D. Ebersole and L. A. McReynolds, *SAE (Soc. Automotive Engrs.) Trans.* **75**, 731–746 (1967).
20. J. C. Mulac, R. L. McCafferty, and W. A. P. Meyer, *Proc. Am. Petrol. Inst., Sect. IV* **46**, 442–457 (1966).
21. M. Patrick Sweeney, *J. Air Pollution Control Assoc.* **15**, No. 1, 13–18 (1965).
22. E. W. Beckman, J. O. Sarto, and W. S. Fagley, *SAE (Soc. Automotive Engrs.) Trans.* **75**, 557–570 (1967).
23. G. W. Niepoth and S. H. Mick, *Gen. Motors Eng. J.* **13**, No. 3, 20–29 (1966).
24. E. N. Cantwell and A. J. Pahnke, *SAE (Soc. Automotive Engrs.) Trans.* **74**, 930–954 (1966).
25. J. A. Maga and J. R. Kinosian, *S.A.E. (Soc. Automotive Engrs.), Preprint* No. 660104 (1966).
26. R. A. Baker, Sr. and R. C. Doerr, *J. Air Pollution Control Assoc.,* **14**, No. 10, 409–444 (1964).
27. H. D. Daigh and W. F. Deeter, *Proc. Am. Petrol. Inst., Sect. III* **42**, 643–656 (1962).
27a. Federal Register, Vol. 33, No. 108, June 4, 1968, Washington, D.C. "Control of Air Pollution from New Motor Vehicles and New Motor Vehicle Engines."
28. P. J. Clarke, J. E. Gerrard, C. W. Skarstrom, J. Vardi, and D. T. Wade, *SAE (Soc. Automotive Engrs.) Trans.* **76**, 824–842 (1968).
29. F. L. Hartley, C. C. Moore, and J. B. Gregory, *J. Air Pollution Control Assoc.* **10**, No. 2, 143–146 (1960).
30. G. R. Fitzgerald, *Proc. 55th Ann. Meeting Air Pollution Control Assoc., Chicago, 1962* p. 25.
31. S.A.E. Engine Committee, "Crankcase Emission Control Test Code," S.A.E. Handbook Suppl. J900. Soc. Automotive Engrs., New York, 1965.
32. R. W. Hurn and D. E. Seizinger, *Proc. Am. Petrol. Inst., Sect. III* **45**, 127–132 (1965).
33. J. R. Kinosian, J. A. Maga, and J. R. Goldsmith, "The Diesel Vehicle and Its Role in Air Pollution," State of California, Dept. of Public Health, Bur. of Air Sanitation, Berkeley, California, 1962.
34. J. Harkins and J. K. Goodwine, *J. Air Pollution Control Assoc.* **14**, No. 1, 34–38 (1964).
35. R. C. Schmidt, R. Kamo, and A. W. Carcy, *SAE (Soc. Automotive Engrs.) Trans.* **75**, 102–109 (1967).
36. G. McConnell and H. E. Howells, *SAE (Soc. Automotive Engrs.) Trans.* **76**, 598–615 (1968).
37. M. Vulliamy and J. Spiers, *SAE (Soc. Automotive Engrs.), Preprint* No. 670090 (1967).
38. D. W. Golothan, *SAE (Soc. Automotive Engrs.) Trans.* **76**, 616–640 (1968).

39. A.P.C.A. Vehicular Exhaust Committee, *J. Air Pollution Control Assoc.* **13,** No. 6, 290–291 (1963).
40. C. O. Miller, *S.A.E. (Soc. Automotive Engrs.), Preprint* No. 670093 (1967).
41. I. Glover, *J. Inst. Petrol.* **52,** No. 509, 137–160 (1966).
42. J. O. Savage, "The Diesel Engine Exhaust Problem with Road Vehicles," Publ. S302. Diesel Engrs. and Users Assoc., London, 1965.
43. L. R. Reckner, W. E. Scott, and W. F. Biller, *Proc. Am. Petrol. Inst., Sect. III* **45,** 133–147 (1965).

34 Petroleum Refinery Emissions

Harold F. Elkin

I. Introduction

As of January, 1967 (*1*), there were 261 refineries in the United States capable of processing 10.5 million barrels of crude oil daily (Table I). During the period 1960 to 1967, total U.S. crude processing capability increased 5% despite a 10% reduction in the number of refineries, indicating a gradual trend toward larger installations. Processing facilities at these refineries represented an investment of roughly $11.4 billion (*2*).

In 1966 (*3*), liquid petroleum products and natural gas supplied 73% of the total fuel energy requirements of the United States. U.S.-refined products represented approximately half of the total energy furnished from oil and gas.

TABLE I
Survey of Operating Refineries in the U.S.[a]
State capacities as of January 1, 1967[b]

State	No. plants	Crude capacity b/cd	Crude capacity b/sd	Vacuum distillation	Thermal operations	Catalytic cracking—b/sd Fresh feed	Catalytic cracking—b/sd Recycle	Catalytic reforming	Hydrogen treating	Alkylation	Production capacity—b/sd Polymerization	Lubes	Coke (tons)	Asphalt
Alabama	5	20,770	22,320	11,500	—	—	—	—	—	—	—	—	—	11,350
Alaska	1	20,000	NR	—	—	—	—	—	—	—	—	—	—	—
Arkansas	6	85,730	89,400	44,875	16,650	31,000	8,700	17,240	27,000	5,900	500	4,675	420	9,800
California	31	1,429,050	1,497,410	644,070	513,925	388,500	174,375	328,220	515,230	60,690	3,450	26,330	6,455	88,410
Colorado	4	39,500	42,765	9,400	13,200	15,500	8,500	10,300	8,000	—	1,500	—	—	1,470
Delaware	1	140,000	150,000	90,700	42,000	62,000	44,000	45,000	88,000	5,000	5,100	—	1,200	—
Florida	1	3,000	3,000	2,400	—	—	—	—	—	—	—	—	—	1,500
Georgia	2	8,600	10,000	—	—	—	—	—	—	—	—	—	—	6,700
Hawaii	1	35,000	NR	—	—	13,000	13,000	—	—	3,800	—	—	—	555
Illinois	12	683,800	714,095	231,440	124,820	279,030	110,915	173,125	321,125	44,695	8,785	5,700	1,235	34,355
Indiana	11	500,525	518,500	196,900	88,150	208,000	68,100	94,700	154,900	28,700	3,100	10,950	2,040	29,900
Kansas	12	360,250	376,860	96,600	39,800	136,900	81,600	74,400	68,500	29,520	2,550	4,000	1,175	21,700
Kentucky	3	126,425	130,000	46,000	21,000	42,400	9,500	24,000	30,500	—	4,400	—	—	9,400
Louisiana	14	903,950	940,325	303,100	110,600	368,500	116,500	153,150	73,400	61,400	9,500	25,815	2,825	17,500
Maryland	2	19,400	20,500	8,000	—	—	—	—	—	—	—	—	—	11,900
Michigan	9	150,700	158,315	52,500	23,700	54,000	31,150	34,850	58,250	7,850	1,900	—	430	9,500
Minnesota	3	106,100	110,300	16,000	22,000	40,100	14,500	17,700	40,000	6,200	2,000	—	1,200	9,000
Mississippi	5	152,400	164,500	69,775	6,700	48,000	31,000	35,700	20,500	12,100	—	—	320	18,860
Missouri	1	72,400	73,850	35,000	14,300	36,000	18,000	14,000	20,000	4,600	2,200	—	400	20,000
Montana	9	116,325	123,435	32,350	15,150	35,300	30,200	20,540	66,010	3,600	1,725	—	250	15,825
Nebraska	1	3,000	3,100	—	1,300	—	—	875	—	—	25	—	—	—
Nevada	1	2,000	2,000	—	—	—	—	—	—	—	—	—	—	—

TABLE I (Continued)

State	No. plants	Crude capacity b/cd	b/sd	Vacuum distillation	Thermal operations	Catalytic cracking Fresh feed	Recycle	Catalytic re-forming	Hydrogen treating	Alkylation	Polymerization	Lubes	Coke (tons)	Asphalt
New Jersey	6	491,000	520,375	246,245	45,945	230,445	93,780	71,945	184,155	21,835	7,775	8,000	850	47,400
New Mexico	6	36,070	38,635	9,800	1,600	10,400	7,400	7,150	3,300	3,000	—	—	—	2,430
New York	2	72,500	75,000	31,600	4,500	27,500	13,000	17,500	21,500	2,450	1,000	—	—	10,500
North Dakota	2	52,000	55,000	—	1,500	20,500	10,300	8,200	10,800	2,400	1,440	—	—	—
Ohio	11	474,700	498,545	145,700	60,900	174,400	97,400	100,400	142,850	28,485	6,520	4,200	1,100	39,520
Oklahoma	13	429,910	444,620	139,210	75,000	174,150	84,825	80,470	73,990	26,855	6,675	11,650	1,420	16,850
Oregon	1	8,700	9,500	9,500	—	—	—	—	—	—	—	—	—	5,900
Pennsylvania	13	648,695	683,500	308,070	85,750	242,200	110,960	150,700	231,100	26,600	8,680	26,330	—	14,500
Rhode Island	1	11,000	13,000	5,000	—	—	—	—	—	—	—	—	—	8,000
Tennessee	1	22,000	23,000	11,500	—	10,000	5,000	—	—	1,600	350	—	—	3,500
Texas	48	2,736,300	2,865,935	934,945	284,555	1,112,365	375,865	628,010	1,019,465	178,815	22,285	78,860	2,635	50,400
Utah	5	108,550	112,755	30,000	—	42,000	19,250	18,300	8,000	7,525	700	—	—	2,850
Virginia	1	43,600	45,000	—	14,000	25,000	15,000	8,100	23,100	—	2,500	—	900	—
Washington	5	191,000	201,320	60,605	8,100	78,775	32,610	28,690	83,445	15,135	4,220	—	—	5,100
West Virginia	2	6,850	7,300	2,000	700	—	—	2,350	2,500	—	—	1,750	—	—
Wisconsin	2	25,500	27,000	13,000	—	5,000	5,000	3,000	6,900	1,100	—	—	—	4,000
Wyoming	7	114,300	123,445	48,800	6,445	40,825	18,060	18,445	50,290	4,770	2,005	1,070	140	14,115
Total	261	10,451,600	10,952,495	3,886,585	1,642,290	3,953,235	1,649,935	2,187,060	3,352,810	595,045	110,885	209,330	24,995	542,850

[a] From reference (1).

[b] For state totals, calendar-day figures reported by some companies were converted to stream-day basis.

99

Energy consumption in the United States is expected to increase by more than 50% by 1980 (4), with petroleum supplying a large share of the increase. A domestic demand of 18 million barrels a day (5) of petroleum products is predicted by that time.

II. Oil Refining Technology

Because of the technological intricacy of petroleum refining processes, an understanding of air pollution control techniques is necessarily dependent on a general knowledge of oil industry manufacturing operations. Descriptions and flow diagrams for commercial refining processes as well as capabilities of the various operations for each refinery are readily available in the literature (6). However, this information is difficult to keep up to date because of the changing nature of the industry.

Although each modern refinery is unique in design and contains a composite of many processes employing a multitude of towers, vessels, piping, valves, tubes, exchangers, and storage tanks, the operations can be classified into four basic procedures—separation, conversion, treating, and blending (7).

Crude oil is initially separated into its various components or fractions, e.g., gas, gasoline, kerosine, middle distillates such as diesel fuel and fuel oil, and heavy bottoms. Since these initial fractions seldom conform to either the relative demand for each product or to its qualitative requirements, the less desirable fractions are subsequently converted to more salable products by splitting, uniting, or rearranging the original molecular structure. Separation and conversion products are subsequently treated for removal or inhibition of undesirable components. The refined base stocks may then be blended with each other and with various additives to develop the most useful products.

Individual refineries differ widely, not only as to crude oil capacity, but also as to the degree of processing sophistication employed. Simple refineries may be confined to crude separation and limited treating (Fig. 1). Intermediate refineries may add catalytic or thermal cracking, catalytic reforming, additional treating, and manufacture of such heavier products as lube oils, and asphalt (Fig. 2). Complete refineries, generally large in capacity, include crude distillation, cracking, treating, gas processing, manufacture of lube oils, asphalts, waxes, as well as gasoline upgrading processes such as catalytic reforming, alkylation, or isomerization (Fig. 3).

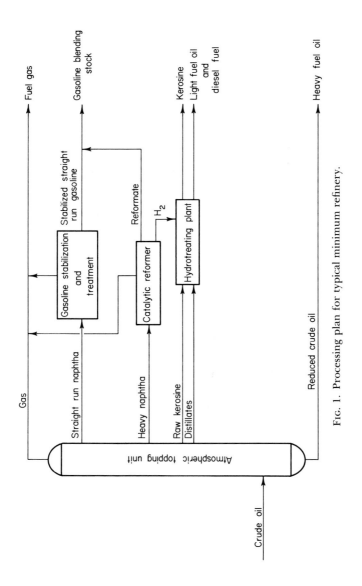

FIG. 1. Processing plan for typical minimum refinery.

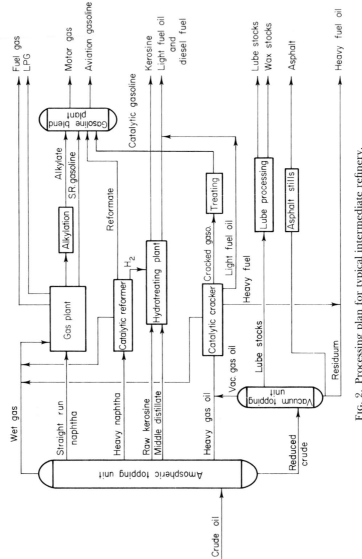

FIG. 2. Processing plan for typical intermediate refinery.

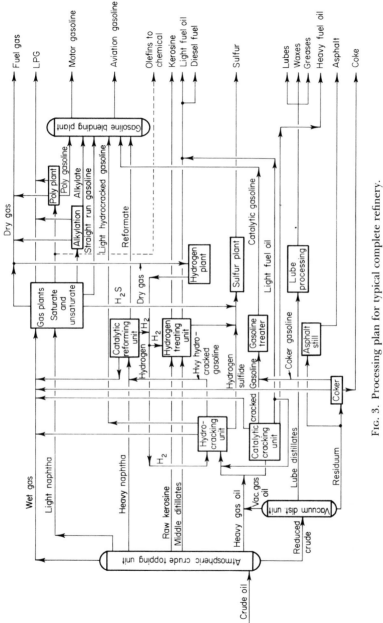

FIG. 3. Processing plan for typical complete refinery.

A. SEPARATION

Crude oil is a mixture of many different hydrocarbons combined with small quantities of sulfur, oxygen, nitrogen, and traces of other elements. Distillation is employed to separate crude oil into its various components with different boiling ranges such as wet gas, gasoline, kerosine, fuel oil, middle distillate, lube distillate, and heavy bottoms. The relative quantity of these "straight-run" products is determined by the composition of the original crude oil. Depending on the completeness of the particular refinery, these initial products may be treated and sold as feedstock for subsequent processing. The crude oil is distilled by heating in furnaces followed by vaporization and separation in fractionating towers. Heavy fractions of the original crude may be subsequently vaporized by steam or vacuum distillation.

B. CONVERSION

Conversion processes are employed to increase the yield of the more desirable products such as gasoline and, conversely, to reduce the quantity of fractions with a currently lesser consumer demand, such as middle distillates. Product volume requirements can fluctuate, and processing flexibility can provide for shifts in demand. In addition to shifting the product distribution, conversion processes also upgrade component quality. The most familiar technique is cracking, whereby relatively heavy hydrocarbon molecules are split under heat and pressure to produce smaller, lower-boiling hydrocarbons. Cracking by catalytic action is still the most significant conversion process employed. U.S. refineries have catalytic cracking facilities for approximately 50% of the total crude capacity. Catalytic cracking yields additional "synthetic" gaseous hydrocarbons, gasoline, and reduced quantities of heavy fuel oil. Coke deposits which form on the catalyst, usually an alumina-silicate, are burned off in separate regeneration vessels. Earlier catalytic processes employed fixed-bed or once-through catalysts. Moving-bed and fluid-bed systems are now commonly used.

Hydrocracking, cracking in the presence of a high hydrogen partial pressure, is experiencing rapid growth. Hydrocracking complements catalytic cracking and adds flexibility in meeting seasonal product volume demand fluctuations. This process is characterized by high liquid yields of saturated isomerized products.

Virtually supplanted by catalytic cracking and hydrocracking, some thermal cracking units are still operating. Coking (severe cracking) and visbreaking (mild cracking) are still useful forms of thermal cracking.

Catalytic reforming is a rearrangement of molecular structure to produce higher quality gasoline and large quantities of hydrogen. Polymerization combines two or more gaseous olefins (unsaturated hydro-carbons), while alkylation joins an olefin and an isoparaffin (branched-chain hydrocarbon) to form liquid hydrocarbons in the gasoline range. Isomerization alters the arrangement of the atoms in a molecule to form branched-chain hydrocarbons for higher octane fuel. These processes utilize catalysts such as phosphoric, sulfuric, and hydrofluoric acid; platinum; and aluminum chloride.

C. TREATING

Crude oil may contain small quantities of impurities, such as sulfur and certain trace amounts of metals. Sulfur in oil generally occurs as sulfides, mercaptans, polysulfides, and thiophenes. A substantial portion of the domestic crude in the United States contains over 0.5% sulfur, and perhaps 10% of the crude contains about 2% sulfur. Imported crudes vary similarly over a wide range of sulfur content. Over recent years, the sulfur content of available crudes has generally increased, although new sources of low-sulfur crude have been discovered and exploration has continued vigorously. While sulfur removal from basic crude is neither technically nor economically feasible at this time, de-sulfurization of products and intermediate stocks has come into·wide use except for residual fuel where costs thus far have been uneconomic as discussed below. Desulfurization of products is practiced because of the effect on product quality, catalyst sensitivity, odor, and corrosivity.

Both physical and chemical procedures are available for treating products and feedstocks. Physical methods include electrical coalescence, filtration, absorption, and air blowing. Chemical methods include acid treatment of hydrocarbon streams to remove sulfur and nitrogen com-pounds, sweetening processes to oxidize mercaptans to disulfides, solvent extraction such as removing sulfur compounds with strong caustic, and the use of additives to oxidize mercaptans to disulfides.

Solvent extraction for removal of aromatics is also widely practiced. The lighter aromatics are extracted from gasoline boiling-range material for sale as petrochemicals, and heavier aromatics are extracted from fuel oil and lube oil fractions for quality improvement.

The use of hydrogen for desulfurization of petroleum products has become widespread. The hydrogenation converts organic sulfur com-pounds into hydrogen sulfide for subsequent disposal or recovery. The extracted hydrogen sulfide is generally converted and recovered as elemental sulfur or burned to sulfur dioxide in plant boilers when the quantities do not justify recovery. This process also converts gum-form-ing hydrocarbons and diolefins into stable compounds. Hydrogen re-quired for the process is commonly furnished by catalytic reforming units and is frequently supplemented by generated hydrogen from processes such as steam-methane reforming.

D. Blending

The relatively few base and intermediate stocks are blended in innumerable combinations to produce over 2000 finished products including liquefied gases, motor and aviation fuels, lubricating oils, greases, waxes, and heating fuels. Rigorous specifications as to vapor pressure, viscosity, specific gravity, sulfur content, octane number, initial boiling point, etc. must be satisfied, depending on the product.

E. Desulfurization

Recent considerations have focused attention on the technology available and progress to date in desulfurizing petroleum products.

A retrospective cost study (8) completed for the period 1946–1965, indicated that U.S. refiners invested some $582.6 million to reduce the sulfur content of fuel products. An additional $103.6 million was invested for sulfur removal in natural gas processing facilities. Of these expenditures, 48.4% were allocated for hydrotreating, 11.8% for hydrocracking, 18.4% for catalytic cracking and 21.4% for extraction and conversion. In addition to these capital costs, an estimated $159.5 million annually was spent for operating these facilities.

During the same period, 1946–1965, industry expenditures for research and development directed toward sulfur reductions totaled $123 million, of which $30.3 million was spent for research on desulfurization of residual fuels. As of the 1966 survey date, research and development expenditures were estimated at $11.8 million annually.

These expenditures have had a significant impact in reducing the total fuel sulfur content which could otherwise have contributed to atmospheric pollution even though the average sulfur content of crude charged has increased slightly as shown in the following tabulation:

Fuel	Average sulfur content wt %	
	1950	1965
Motor gasoline	0.084	0.042
Kerosine	0.20	0.084
Heating oils	0.37	0.27
Diesel fuels	0.65	0.36
Residual fuel oil	1.19	1.47
Crude oil	0.72	0.76

Even though residual fuel oil has increased in weight percent sulfur, the volume produced in the U.S. has decreased from 20.3% to 8.1% of crude charged between 1950 and 1965. This reduction in liquid output resulted in a net 20% decrease in total weight of sulfur in residual fuel produced by domestic refineries.

Residual fuel oil has received considerable study as the principal remaining petroleum product which generally contains a substantial sulfur content. Residual fuel oil is customarily a marginal product. Specifications are generally concerned with flash point, viscosity, and a maximum limit on sediment and water. Residual fuel sulfur content depends not only on the properties of the crude but also on the degree of processing that each of the blend components has received.

Hydrogen treating at high pressure in the presence of a catalyst is thus far the most feasible means of effecting a significant degree of sulfur reduction for most refinery stocks. Hydrodesulfurization processes for treating gasolines, middle distillates, and lubricating oils are in extensive use at this time. Extension of this technology toward residual oils has proved costly, and has found only limited application at this writing although certain commercial processes are available. Processing a high sulfur residual oil through a hydrodesulfurization unit converts this feedstock into a "synthetic crude" with a full range of materials ranging from gas and distillates down to a true residual fraction. The various fractions can be utilized for sale, as feedstocks for other units, and in part for blending with the reduced volume residual from the desulfurization step.

A 1964 study (9) suggested an approximate cost of $0.40–0.65 per barrel for desulfurizing typical West Coast U.S. residual fuels from a typical initial sulfur content of 1.5% down to 0.5% sulfur content.

A 1967 study (10) determined the approximate costs for desulfurizing residual fuel oil produced in Caribbean refineries which have supplied 85% of the residual fuel imported into the United States. The principal crude charged to these refineries originates in Venezuela. Based on a "typical" 281,500 barrel per day Caribbean refinery producing 161,600 barrels of residual oil, or 57% of crude charge, the study considered reductions from an initial 2.6% sulfur in the residual fuel. Reduction to 2% sulfur would require an additional facilities investment of approximately $45 million and would result in an incremental cost in the order of $0.30 per barrel. Reduction down to 1% sulfur would require double this investment and cost approximately $0.72 per barrel on an equivalent Btu basis. Desulfurization to a 0.5% sulfur level could require an investment in the order of $100 to $150 million and would result in incremental costs per barrel of $0.90–$1.00 on an equivalent Btu basis. Since no desulfurization processes have been employed on residuals with the high metals content of typical Caribbean oils or in the large scale examined in this study, there are areas of uncertainty in this evaluation, particularly in achieving sulfur levels below 1%. Metals content, which varies with crude type, has an adverse effect on catalyst life and thereby influences processing costs.

Factors influencing residual fuel sulfur content include the sulfur content of the crude oil prior to processing, availability of low sulfur crude and blending stocks and whether all residual fuel produced at a particular refinery has to meet a single sulfur specification of whether two or more sulfur levels are produced.

F. Lead Antiknock Additives

Inquiries on the feasibility and economics of producing motor gasoline in the U.S. without lead antiknock additives prompted a study of this subject in 1967 (11). This study concluded that, to maintain gasoline volume without lead with similar antiknock and performance qualities as leaded fuels would require an investment of some $4.24 billion by U.S. refiners. This figure would represent $42\frac{1}{2}\%$ of the current gross investment in domestic refining equipment. Added manufacturing costs would range from 1.8 to 4.7 cents per gallon, depending on refinery size, existing processing and, to a lesser extent, location, and would average somewhat over 2 cents per gallon. Processes such as high severity reforming, aromatic extraction, alkylation, olefin disproportionation, isomerization, naphtha steam cracking, and hydrocracking were included in the technology available for application by the study. Total crude oil processed would increase approximately 5.5%, largely due to the extra energy consumed in the additional refining processing. The impact on construction would be substantial as the required new facilities would be approximately double the present annual building capability of U.S. process equipment erectors. The unleaded gasolines of equivalent octane value would be considerably higher in aromatic content and somewhat lower in olefins than conventional leaded fuels.

III.   Type of Emissions

The estimation and evaluation of refinery atmospheric emissions is an immensely complicated project. Individual refineries vary greatly as to the character and quantity of emissions. Controlling factors include crude oil capacity, type of crude processed, type and complexity of the processing employed, air pollution control measures in use, and the degree of maintenance and good housekeeping procedures in force. Refinery emissions may be classified as smoke and particulate matter, hydrocarbons, and other gaseous compounds, principally oxides of sulfur and nitrogen, but also including malodorous vapors. The technology of emission evaluation and abatement has been established through the cooperative efforts of the industry and regulatory authorities, particularly in the Los Angeles area (12–15) (Table II).

While the quantitative aspects of refinery emissions are generally considered by type of equipment, the major refining operations offer a guide as to the type of releases that are encountered. In crude separation the use of barometric condensers in vacuum distillation can release noncondensable hydrocarbons to the atmosphere. Regeneration of catalyst in cracking by controlled combustion can release unburned hydrocarbons, carbon monoxide, ammonia, and sulfur oxides although these gases are now commonly rendered less objectionable through the use of CO boilers. Catalyst handling systems can also be the source of discharge of catalyst fines, but conventional mechanical or electrical separation equipment has proved successful for control of this material.

The molecular rearrangement processes—alkylation, reforming, polymerization, and isomerization—are significant in that they handle volatile hydrocarbons; and tight equipment such as valves and pumps

TABLE II

POTENTIAL SOURCES OF SPECIFIC EMISSIONS FROM OIL REFINERIES[a]

Emission	Potential sources
Oxides of sulfur	Boilers, process heaters, catalytic cracking unit regenerators, treating units, H_2S flares, decoking operations.
Hydrocarbons	Loading facilities, turnarounds, sampling, storage tanks, waste water separators, blowdown systems, catalyst regenerators, pumps, valves, blind changing, cooling towers, vacuum jets, barometric condensers, air-blowing, high pressure equipment handling volatile hydrocarbons, process heaters, boilers, compressor engines.
Oxides of nitrogen	Process heaters, boilers, compressor engines, catalyst regenerators, flares.
Particulate matter	Catalyst regenerators, boilers, process heaters, decoking operations, incinerators.
Aldehydes	Catalyst regenerators.
Ammonia	Catalyst regenerators.
Odors	Treating units (air-blowing, steam-blowing) drains, tank vents, barometric condenser sumps, waste water separators.
Carbon monoxide	Catalyst regeneration, decoking, compressor engines, incinerators.

[a] From reference (7).

TABLE III
ESTIMATED DAILY REFINERY EMISSIONS[a]

Substance	Without controls	After rigorous controls	
		1958	1966
Hydrocarbons	100	14	7
Nitrogen oxides	4	4	4
Sulfur dioxide	145	20	5
Sulfur trioxide	>3	<1	[b]
Carbon monoxide	220	[b]	13
Particulate matter	14	<2	[b]
Ammonia	<1	<1	<1[b]
Aldehydes	<1	<1	<1[b]
Organic acids	<1	<1	<1[b]
Aerosols	<1	[b]	<1

[a] Los Angeles refinery emissions, tons per 100,000 barrels crude capacity.

[b] Not reported or assumed value.

NOTE: Emissions from combustion of fuels not included in above totals.

becomes of greater emission control importance than in the heavier oil processes yielding fuel oils, lubes, or asphalts.

Pollution aspects of treating operations are concentrated on methods of disposing of the spent chemicals and extracted impurities such as spent acids, spent caustics, and hydrogen sulfide. Air agitation and blowing, vessel vents, drains, valves, and pump seals are possible sources of loss or leakage of sulfur oxides and hydrocarbons in any of the above processes or handling procedures.

Before considering individual emission sources, an overall estimation of refinery releases will be of interest. The following data is interpolated from the exhaustive studies in Los Angeles where control procedures have achieved a degree of completeness that is as unique as the local climatic conditions that motivated their adoption (14, 16, 17). Estimated refinery contaminants, before the rigorous controls of the 1950's, are compared with the relatively complete containment of the Los Angeles refineries which process over 700,000 barrels per day of crude oil (Table III).

RELATIVE SIGNIFICANCE OF EMISSIONS

As would be expected, refineries and refining areas vary considerably in the degree of control of the above emissions. The extent and need for control depend on local meteorological and topographical conditions, size and type of plant, quantity and height of release, and proximity to community activity. Most refineries have facilities to reduce hydrocarbon and sulfur emissions to an economic level, and many so-called air pollution control measures are customarily included by refiners as accepted good conservation practices. Few, if any U.S. refineries discharge emissions to the extent of the "Without Controls" column in Table III.

Conversely, the high degree of containment accomplished in the Los Angeles refineries is probably unmatched in other refining areas. The acute photochemical smog problem in southern California, which had its origin in the unique local meteorology, actuated an intensive control program over a decade ago which effectuated numerous rules and regulations, many of which apply specifically to oil industry operations.

Although all petroleum vapors have been subject to control in Los Angeles refineries, a relatively low percentage of these hydrocarbons are believed to participate significantly in the chemical reactions associated with air pollution manifestations (7). At this writing, most paraffins, naphthenes, benzene, and acetylene (18) are considered essentially as slow or nonreactive photochemically (see also Chapter 18). Hydrocarbon emissions in amounts normally released by refinery operations are invisible, have no offensive odor, are nontoxic, are relatively inert, and not all of them enter into photochemical smog reactions.

Only the olefinic or unsaturated hydrocarbons and certain aromatics (18) have been demonstrated to react rapidly enough in the atmosphere to participate in the complex photochemical reaction mechanism involving nitrogen oxides and resulting ozone in the presence of ultraviolet light from the sun. A survey of Los Angeles refineries indicated that olefins represented only 6.5% of the total hydrocarbon evaporation loss (19, 20), the remainder consisting principally of the relatively inert paraffins. Los Angeles refinery survey data for 1966 (17) classifies only 10–12% of the remaining uncontrolled hydrocarbons emitted to the atmosphere as "high reactivity." Similarly, of the total 700 tons per day of Los Angeles refinery hydrocarbon and other organic gas emissions prevented from being discharged to the atmosphere, 12% are classified in the "high reactivity" category. The significance of the Los Angeles refinery abatement effort must therefore be qualified by the high proportion of low or nonreactive hydrocarbons controlled by this program. (Reactive hydrocarbons in the southern California atmosphere, as elsewhere, originate principally from incomplete combustion and evaporation of fuel in unmodified motor vehicles and to a lesser extent from the use of organic solvents. Controls for these sources are discussed elsewhere in this text. See Chapters 32 and 33.)

Emissions of gaseous contaminants other than hydrocarbons, principally oxides of sulfur and nitrogen, originate mainly from combustion sources. Emissions of sulfur oxides result from the sulfur content of the crude oil being charged to the plant and the type of processing employed. Most of the original crude sulfur content is driven into the hydrocarbon gas and heavy fuel fractions during distillation, cracking, and other processing. Hydrogen sulfide in light hydrocarbon fractions and fuel gas can be extracted prior to burning. Process waste waters can likewise be stripped of hydrogen sulfide. The extracted hydrogen sulfide can be recovered as elemental sulfur.

Along with hydrocarbons and sulfur oxides, refineries discharge relatively small quantities of carbon monoxide, nitrogen oxides, aldehydes, organic acids, ammonia, and particulate matter. The technology of dust control by mechanical means has been well established and is in extensive use. The other miscellaneous discharges originate from combustion reactions in boilers, process heaters, and catalyst regeneration units.

IV. Source and Control

Refinery atmospheric emissions and control procedures are customarily considered by types of equipment employed rather than by refinery process operation (20a).

A. Storage Tanks

Hydrocarbon vapors may be released through a number of mechanisms in storage tanks, including tank breathing due to temperature changes, direct evaporation, and displacement during filling. The principal source of potential loss is from crude oil and light distillate products. The hydrocarbon content of crude oil is substantially saturated and, as explained above, is not believed to be involved in the photochemical smog complex. Light distillates have considerable value and are normally controlled to a practical economic level. Vapor conservation storage may involve tanks with floating roof covers, pressurized tanks, and connections to vapor recovery systems. The development of low-cost plastic covers may make conversion of conventional cone-roof storage to vapor conservation storage more attractive.

B. Catalyst Regeneration Units

Coke formed on the surface of catalysts during catalytic cracking, reforming, and hydrogenation is burned off in regenerating vessels by controlled combustion. Flue gases from regenerators may contain catalyst dust, carbon monoxide, hydrocarbon (principally methane), and sulfur and nitrogen oxides. The catalyst dust may be controlled by mechanical or electrical collecting equipment. The carbon monoxide and unburned hydrocarbons are generally dispersed in the atmosphere, but may be eliminated by burning in a waste heat boiler which also generates additional steam.

C. WASTE WATER SEPARATORS

Waste water gravity separators are commonly used to trap and recover oil discharged to the sewer system from equipment leaks and spills, shutdowns, sampling, process condensate, pump seals, etc. Depending on the quantity and type of oil in the sewers, some hydrocarbon vapors may evaporate from the drainage and separator system. If this vaporization is sizable and control is indicated, the front end of the separators may be covered. Catch basin liquid seals, manhole covers, and good housekeeping practices will likewise control drainage system vapor losses.

D. LOADING FACILITIES

While most petroleum products leave the refinery through pipelines with no emission to the atmosphere, loading into tank trucks, tank cars, and drums can result in hydrocarbon vapor loss by displacement or evaporation. Careful operation to minimize spillage, and vapor collection and recovery equipment will control vapor loss from this operation.

E. PIPELINE VALVES

The typical refinery contains a maze of piping, mostly above grade. The effects of heat, pressure, vibration, and corrosion may cause leaks in valved connections. Depending on the product carried and the temperature, the leaks may be liquid, vapor, or both. Regular inspection and prompt maintenance will correct vapor loss from this source.

F. PUMPS AND COMPRESSORS

Hydrocarbons can leak at the contact between the moving shaft and stationary casing in pumps and compressors. Asbestos or other fibers are packed around the shaft to retard leakage from shaft motions. Mechanical seals, consisting of two plates, perpendicular to the shaft, forced tightly together, are also used. Wear can cause both packed and mechanical seals to leak product. Inspection and maintenance, sealing glands under pressure, and use of mechanical seals in light hydrocarbon service are useful control measures.

G. Blowdown Systems, Flares, and Shutdowns

Refinery process units and equipment are periodically shut down for maintenance and repair. Since these turnarounds generally occur about once a year, losses from this source are sporadic. Hydrocarbons purged during shutdowns and startups may be manifolded to blowdown systems for recovery, safe venting, or flaring. Vapors can be recovered in a gas holder or compressor and discharged to the refinery fuel gas system. Flares should be of the smokeless type, utilizing either steam or air injection. Design data for smokeless flares are readily available from combustion equipment manufacturers and in industry technical manuals (21).

H. Boilers and Process Heaters

Refineries depend on boilers and heaters to supply high pressure steam at elevated temperatures. Fuels may include refinery or natural gas, heavy fuel oil, and coke, often in various changing combinations. Sulfur oxides in the flue gas are, of course, a result of the sulfur in the fuel feed. Nitrogen oxides and small quantities of hydrocarbons, organic acids, and particulate matter are also present. Sulfide stripping of fuel gas prior to burning and selective blending of fuels may be employed to control sulfur emissions. Normally, good combustion practices will control smoke and particulate matter.

Stacks on boilers and heaters are elevated to improve atmospheric dispersion and further diminish resulting ground-level concentrations of gases such as sulfur dioxide, and nitrogen oxides.

I. Miscellaneous

Various other miscellaneous emission sources, usually of lesser significance, will be found in refinery operations. Pressure relief valves may be manifolded into vapor recovery or flare systems to control leakage and relief discharge. Steam-driven vacuum jets, employed to induce negative pressure in process equipment, may discharge light hydrocarbons with the exhaust steam. These gases may be vented and burned in an adjacent boiler or heater firebox.

Fumes from air blowing operations may be consumed by incineration or absorbed by scrubbing. Gases from spent caustic and mercaptan disposal may be burned in fireboxes.

Hydrogen sulfide and mercaptans are the principal potential pollutants that may cause odors. These gases can be released from process steam condensates, drain liquids, barometric condenser sumps, sour volatile product tankage, and spent caustic solutions from treating operations.

Odorous compounds in steam condensates can be removed by stripping with air, flue gas, or steam and offensive gases can be burned in furnaces or boilers. Drain liquids can be collected in closed storage systems and recycled to the process. Barometric condensers are being replaced by more modern surface condensers, and the noncondensables may be burned in process heaters or in a separate incinerator.

Spent caustic can be degasified, neutralized with flue gas and/or stripped before disposal. Sulfides can also be removed from sour process water and spent caustic solutions by air oxidation to thiosulfates and sulfates.

Refinery waste gases that contain hydrogen sulfide are generally scrubbed with appropriate solutions for extraction of the sulfide by nonregenerative or heat-regenerative procedures. In the former method, the waste gases are scrubbed with a caustic solution, producing a solution of sodium sulfide and acid sulfide. As described above, the spent caustic may be oxidized by air blowing or sold. Vent gas from the blowing operation should be burned.

Heat-regenerative methods involve scrubbing sour gases with various types of amine, phenolate, or phosphate solutions which absorb hydrogen sulfide at moderately low temperatures and release it at higher temperatures. These methods are cyclic and consist of an absorption step, in which the hydrogen sulfide is scrubbed from the absorbing solution at approximately 100 °F, followed by a regeneration step in which the solution is reactivated for use by heating it to its boiling point to drive off the hydrogen sulfide. The released hydrogen sulfide is then burned or oxidized to form sulfur.

Refinery process changes may have the net effect of reducing overall emissions to the atmosphere. Examples of such process changes include substitution of hydrogen treating for chemical treatment of distillates, use of harder catalysts to reduce attrition losses, and regeneration of spent chemicals for reuse.

V. Estimation of Quantities

When an accurate estimate of refinery atmospheric emissions is required, there is no substitute for in-plant field testing, preferably by

TABLE IV
Emission Factors Developed from Los Angeles Survey[a]

Combustion sources	Units of emission factor — Pounds per	Emission factors					
		Hydro-carbons	Aldehydes as HCHO	Carbon monoxide	NO_x as NO_2	Ammonia as NH_3	Particu-late matter
Boilers and process heaters	Bbl of fuel oil burned	0.14	0.025	Neg.	2.9	Neg.	0.8
Boilers and process heaters	1000 cu ft of gas burned	0.026	0.0031	Neg.	0.23	Neg.	0.02
Compressor internal comb. engine	1000 cu ft of gas burned	1.2	0.11	Neg.	0.86	0.2	—
Fluid bed cat. cracking unit[d]	1000 bbl of fresh feed	220.	19.	13,700	63.	54.	[b]
Moving bed cat. cracking unit[d]	1000 bbl of fresh feed	87.	12.	3,800	5.0	5.0	[c]

[a] Data adapted from reference (7).
[b] With electrical precipitators: 0.0009% of catalyst circulated; without electrical precipitators: 0.005% of catalyst circulated.
[c] With centrifugal separators: 0.002% of catalyst circulated.
[d] Before CO waste heat boiler.

plant personnel familiar with the equipment and operations involved. Although on-site evaluation programs can be complicated, time-consuming, and costly, they are required for reliable determination of the highly variable emission rates from such contributing elements as tank evaporation, catalytic cracking regeneration, vacuum jet exhausts, and air blowing operation.

The purpose of the survey should be clearly defined in order to establish the extent and depth of the evaluation. If a rough order-of-magnitude appraisal is indicated, available data from neighboring or similar refining operations may be extrapolated to the operations of the plant under consideration. However, emission data on which to base the need for control should always be developed by actual in-plant appraisal.

Before any effort is made to apply survey results from one refinery study to another, the many variables of type of crude run, processes employed, existing status of control facilities, and procedures must be carefully considered. Despite apparent similarities between refineries, experienced judgment is required to establish the necessary basis of comparison and avoid misleading correlations.

When it is determined to employ comparative refinery emission data in a particular study, the information developed by the Los Angeles Joint Project study will be useful (7, 8, 15). Comparisons of refinery emissions on the basis of crude capacity or fuel consumption can be grossly misleading and are not recommended. Very rough estimates of total hydrocarbon emissions by type of equipment and capacity can be developed from the above study. However, hydrocarbon losses from refineries may range from 0.1 to 0.6% by weight of crude throughput, depending on the complexity of refining procedures and the employment of abatement facilities.

The Joint Project Study has developed average emission factor data (7, 15) for various discharges including hydrocarbons, particulate matter, and nitrogen oxides which, when judiciously applied to specific refinery sources, will provide an estimate of the magnitude of emissions. Actual in-plant surveys should accompany such estimates to develop reliable data. The reader is referred to Tables IV and V for information on typical petroleum refinery emission and loss factors.

VI. Economics of Control

The economics of air pollution control are a function of specific sources and methods of control in individual refineries. It has become industry-wide practice to include pollution control equipment and costs

TABLE V
HYDROCARBON LOSS FACTORS DEVELOPED FROM LOS ANGELES SURVEY[a]

Evaporation sources	Units of emission factor	Emission factor
	Pounds of hydrocarbon per	
Pipeline valves	Valve per day	0.15
Vessel relief valves	Valve per day	2.4
Pumps seals	Seal per day	4.2
Compressor seals	Seal per day	8.5
Cooling towers	Million gal of cooling water circulated	6.0
Blowdown systems	1000 bbl of refining capacity	5–300[b]
Vacuum jets	1000 bbl of vacuum distillation capacity	0–130[b]
Process drains	1000 bbl of waste water processed	8–210[b]
Storage tanks	Tank per day	c
Other sources	1000 bbl of refinery capacity	10.0

[a] Data adapted from reference (7).
[b] Range of values.
[c] For computation method, see Luche and Deckert (22).

as an integral part of new process and equipment design. A well-designed new plant may have a satisfactory pollution control posture incorporated in original construction that will obviate additional expenditures for many years. An older refining operation, particularly with encroaching community development, may require relatively high expenditures to correct an objectionable condition.

Partial economic return may be realized when pollution control facilities recover such components as hydrocarbons, sulfur, and catalyst. The amount of this return will, of course, be a function of the value of the material recovered, capital investment for equipment, amortization period, interest rates, maintenance, and operating expenses. In general, rates of return on pollution control expenditures do not approach those for normal processing installations. In some cases, processing revisions have been combined with plant modernization steps, resulting in modest economic return. More frequently, little or no payout results from pollution control installations. In extreme cases, an existing operation may even be discontinued or replaced with newer equipment at great cost. Odor and particulate matter control are particularly unattractive categories for economic justification. However, the amount expended is not always an accurate measure of the effectiveness of air pollution controls. Relatively small expenditures for process alterations and for supporting good operating and housekeeping procedures may result in significant improvements, whereas excessively large sums may be required to comply with unduly restrictive limits established without full consideration of economic justification.

Some order of magnitude of U.S. refiners' expenditures for air pollution control was reported (23) in an industry-wide survey in 1966. U.S. refiners reported expenditures of over $200 million for air pollution control facilities during the 10-year period through 1966. Built-in air pollution controls incorporated in the design of new processing units, not included in the above reported expenditures, are also increasing and have been variously estimated to add 3% to capital costs for new facilities.

The cumulative totals and trends for refinery control facilities by types of emissions are shown in Table VI.

Sulfur compound control expenditures include sulfide removal from waste waters and gases and for sulfur recovery units. Hydrocarbon combustion expenditures included installations of carbon monoxide waste heat boilers, combustion of off gases from process units as well as vapors stripped from treating units and asphalt-blowing operations plus improved boiler combustion, coker blowdown, and improvements in flaring systems. Hydrocarbon recovery expenditures covered the incremental cost of floating roofs on new and existing tankage plus the installation of vapor recovery systems on tankage and loading racks and from covered oil separators. Also included are costs for vapor recovery systems to reduce waste gas flaring and for mechanical seals on centrifugal pumps.

Smoke and particulate matter costs were charged to improved mechanical cyclones, electrostatic precipitators, improved catalyst handling equipment, smokeless flares, stack heaters for plume reduction and additional height on stacks for dispersion. Odor and fume control expenditures were allocated for such facilities as sludge recovery and sour gas scrubbing systems.

Although refinery emission control can initially prove economically attractive as certain obvious hydrocarbon vapor, sulfur and particulate discharges are recovered, increasing containment of these and other releases rapidly diminishes in payout. This is illustrated in Table VII prepared from the above-described survey (23).

Table VII summaries $85.3 million in U.S. refinery air pollution control expenditures on which payout data were available for the period 1961–1965. As shown, expenditures with a "good" payout diminished over 50% during this period. During the same period, air pollution control expenditures which had a "poor" or no payout doubled. Since overall expenditures had increased by 50% during this period, the trend toward poor and marginal return projects becomes obvious.

TABLE VI
TREND IN EXPENDITURES BY TYPES OF EMISSIONS[a]

Year	Sulfur com- pounds	Hydro- carbons (com- bustion)	Hydro- carbons (recovery)	Smoke and particu- lates	Odors and fumes	Total
1956	$ 6,154	$ 4,977	$ 5,325	$ 2,150	$ 1,171	$ 19,777
1957	6,154	4,977	5,325	2,150	1,171	19,777
1958	4,087	2,235	7,628	449	981	15,380
1959	2,693	3,640	3,124	2,780	1,091	13,328
1960	4,495	2,230	7,152	780	1,047	15,704
1961	5,560	1,501	6,497	3,437	4,381	21,376
1962	1,474	6,143	2,501	5,257	3,046	18,421
1963	2,191	3,829	4,012	2,109	2,711	14,852
1964	4,230	4,515	2,421	3,868	2,030	17,064
1965	1,795	5,497	2,700	3,840	2,101	15,933
1966	7,901	6,959	3,821	5,361	9,368	33,410
Total	$46,734	$46,503	$50,506	$32,181	$29,098	$205,022

[a] From reference (23). In thousands of dollars.

Apart from abating obvious major emission sources and implementing good conservation practices, it can be seen that economic prudence suggests that attention be directed principally toward those types and sources of emissions causing a defined problem in a particular community. Similarly, application of control techniques with marginal or no payout should not be arbitrarily imposed in localities without a specific identifiable need for control of the particular emission category.

TABLE VII
TREND IN RELATIVE PAYOUT OF
CONTROLS (23)

	Total of expenditures (in $1,000) for which payout was:		
Year	Good	Fair	Poor or none
1961	9,433	5,357	6,079
1962	7,880	4,087	6,044
1963	5,785	4,253	4,490
1964	3,892	6,373	6,250
1965	4,412	6,288	4,728
1966	4,443	16,357	11,929

REFERENCES

1. Survey of Operating Refineries in the U.S., *Oil Gas J.* **65,** No. 14, 180 (1967).
2. "Annual Analysis of the Petroleum Industry." Chase Manhattan Bank, New York, 1965.
3. "Crude Petroleum and Petroleum Products," *U.S. Bur. Mines, Monthly Petrol. Statement Mar. 20, p. 26 (1967).*
4. "Energy R & D and National Progress; Findings and Conclusions," p. 3. U.S. Interdepartmental Energy Study Group, Washington, D.C., 1966.
5. C. F. Luce, Under Secretary, U.S. Dept. of the Interior, Remarks made to the Independent Petroleum Association of America, May 5, 1967.
6. "Process Handbook," *Hydrocarbon Process, Petrol. Refiner* **45,** No. 9 (1966).
7. "Atmospheric Emissions from Petroleum Refineries; a Guide for Measurement and Control," Public Health Serv. Publ. No. 763. U.S. Div. Air Pollution, Washington, D.C., 1960.
8. "The Economic Impact of Sulfur Removal," Report to the American Petroleum Institute by the Pace Company, Houston, 1967.
9. "The Economics of Fuel Oil Desulfurization." U.S. Div. Air Pollution, Washington, D.C., 1964 (Study by the Bechtel Corporation).
10. "Desulfurization of Caribbean Residual Fuel Oils," Report by the Bechtel Corporation to the American Petroleum Institute, 1967.
11. "The Economics of Manufacturing Unleaded Motor Gasoline," Report by Bonner and Moore Associates to the American Petroleum Institute, 1967.
12. "Atmospheric Emissions for Petroleum Refineries; a Guide for Measurement and Control," Public Health Serv. Publ. No. 763. U.S. Div. Air Pollution, Washington, D.C. 1960.
13. Technical Progress Report, "Control of Stationary Sources," Vol. I, Chapter VI. Petrol. Ind., Los Angeles County Air Pollution Control District, Los Angeles, California.
14. "Emissions to the Atmosphere from Petroleum Refineries in Los Angeles County," Joint District, Federal, and State Project, Final Rept. No. 9. Los Angeles County Air Pollution Control District, Los Angeles, California, 1958.
15. M. Mayer, "A Compilation of Air Pollution Emission Factors for Combustion Processes, Gasoline Evaporation, and Selected Industrial Processes." U.S. Public Health Serv., Washington, D.C., 1965.
16. S. S. Griswold, G. Fisher, and C. V. Kanter, *Proc. Natl. Conf. Air Pollution, Washington, D.C., 1958* pp. 140–146. Washington, D.C. [see *U.S., Public Health Serv. Publ.* **654** (1959)].
17. "Air Pollution Data for Los Angeles County." Los Angeles County Air Pollution Control District, Los Angeles, California, 1967.
18. E. R. Stephens, E. F. Darley, and F. R. Burleson, *Proc. Am. Petrol. Inst., Sect. III* 47 (1967).
19. "Air Pollution and Smog," *Air Pollution Found. (Los Angeles)* (1960).
20. W. L. Faith, *Ind. Wastes* **5,** No. 4 (1960).
20a. "Air Pollution Engineering Manual, Los Angeles APCD" (J. A. Danielson, ed.), Chapters 10 and 11, PHS Publn. 999-AP-40, DHEW, Cincinnati (1967).
21. D. H. Stormont, *Oil Gas J.* **63,** No. 48 (1965).
22. R. G. Lunche and I. S. Deckert, "Hydrocarbon Losses from Petroleum Storage Tanks," Air Pollution Eng. Rept. Los Angeles County Air Pollution Control District, Los Angeles, California, 1956.
23. "Manual on Disposal of Refinery Wastes," Vol. II. Am. Petrol. Inst. (to be published).

35 Nonmetallic Mineral Products Industries

Victor H. Sussman

I.   Introduction

The conversion of naturally occurring minerals into salable products involves the employment of various operations and processes. Operations are concerned with physical alteration, and processes are concerned with chemical alteration. Certain unit operations are common to practically all mineral production procedures. Table I lists air pollution control techniques applicable to these unit operations.

II.   General Operations

A. Mining

1. *Deep Mining*

Air pollution problems may be created by the discharge of deep mine ventilation air. Such problems are infrequent and easily controlled, most often by relocating the discharge vent.

TABLE I

MINERAL PRODUCTION OPERATIONS CHECK LIST

Operation	Control techniques
A. Mining	
Open pit and quarry roads	Paving; periodic oiling, watering, $CaCl_2$ cover, and/or cleaning; covering trucks to prevent spillage.
Blasting	Controlling size of blast, using water sprays immediately after blasting and blasting only when wind direction and other meteorological conditions are such that "neighborhood dusting" will not occur. Using "blasting mats."
Drilling	Wet drilling or local exhaust ventilation
B. Transportation and storage	
Conveyor belts	Enclosure and local exhaust ventilation or wet spray—with special attention given to control at transfer points.
Elevators	Enclosure and local exhaust ventilation.
Discharge chutes	Telescoping chutes to permit discharge point to be close to surface of pile. Spray or local exhaust ventilation at discharge point.
Storage piles	Enclosure (silos, bins, etc.); covers (plastic coating, tarpaulin, clay, vegetation); wind breaks (trees, barricades).
C. Size reduction	
Crushing and grinding	Enclosure and local exhaust ventilation. Wet sprays and/or exhaust hoods at mill inlet and outlet. Where possible employ wet operations.
D. Concentration, classification and mixing	Enclosures and local exhaust ventilation. Where possible employ wet operations
E. Drying	When possible use indirect dryers. Exhaust dryer to suitable collector. Classification prior to drying to remove fines.

2. Open-Pit Mining

Particulate matter produced during open-pit mining operations is usually discharged directly to the atmosphere, rather than being captured by a local exhaust ventilation system, and is thus difficult to control. Many open-pit mining operations have an indefinite operating life which may make the installation of a fixed dust collecting system economically impractical. Therefore, dust control should be based upon prevention, at the point at which the contaminants are generated, by wet methods and portable equipment for dust suppression. Drilling, blasting, ore handling operations, and wind erosion are responsible for most of the particulate matter emissions produced during open-pit mining (1).

B. Transportation and Storage

Mineral producers in the United States handle approximately 3 billion tons of ore and waste a year. Scientific materials handling techniques and automation have reduced air pollution from these operations. Reducing the number of transfers and the period of time required for each should be the first consideration in a materials handling air pollution abatement program.

Loading and unloading, conveyor belt discharge and transfer, and stockpiling operations can produce particulate matter emissions. Local exhaust ventilation and wet sprays can effectively control these emissions.

Lack of attention to wind erosion of stockpiles has often created an "air pollution control paradox." If the dust collected from air pollution control devices is promiscuously piled in open areas, wind erosion of these piles can cause as serious air pollution as that which would have been caused by emission from the operations had they originally not been controlled.

Gaseous emissions can be produced by evaporation of materials from storage piles. Also, there is the possibility of reaction between materials in storage piles. An example of this is the emission of hydrogen sulfide from aggregate produced from blast furnace slag. Hydrolysis occurs when the hot slag is quenched with water during production and when rain falls on a slag storage pile. The hydrolysis of the calcium sulfide in the slag results in the formation of hydrogen sulfide:

$$CaS + H_2O \rightarrow H_2S + Ca(OH)_2$$

C. Size Reduction

Size reduction operations are commonly classified as either crushing or grinding, according to the size range of feeds and the size reduction ratio achieved. Crushing operations usually involve feed sizes of from 20 to 60 inches and size reduction ratios of from 3:1 to 10:1. Grinding, pulverizing, and disintegrating operations usually involve feed sizes of from 0.05 to 0.5 inches and reduction ratios of from 10:1 to 50:1. Jaw, gyratory, cone, pan, roll, and rotary crushers and ball, pebble, rod, tube, ring-roller, hammer and disk mill grinders are commonly used. Various types of crushers and grinders (2) are usually operated in series (often close-circuited with a classifier) to obtain desired size reduction (Fig. 1).

Dust is discharged from crusher and grinder inlet and outlet ports. For most effective dust control, crushers and grinders should be enclosed and provided with exhaust ventilation discharging to a suitable collector. Hoods at inlet and outlet ports are inefficient since they require the use of large quantities of air to "reach out" and capture dust;

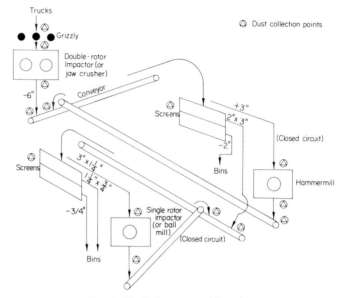

FIG. 1. Typical stone crushing plant.

and ambient air currents can easily interfere with the flow of dust from the source to the hood. Information on enclosure design and ventilation requirements is available (3–6).

Although generally not as effective as local exhaust ventilation, wet sprays can be used to control dust emissions from crushing, grinding, and other mineral production operations (7). Wet grinding should be substituted for dry grinding operations, when there is no objection to obtaining a product in slurry form.

D. Classification, Concentration, and Mixing

Following size reduction operations, ores are generally size classified, concentrated (i.e., separated from gangue by wet or dry processes) and/or mixed to obtain a desired size consistency or composition. Local exhaust ventilation systems have been specifically designed to control dust emissions from these operations (3). Dry concentration operations, e.g., mechanical separation by magnetic, inertial, or electrostatic forces (8), screening and inertial classification equipment, all generate significant amounts of dust. Unenclosed screening operations at quarries can produce dust concentrations in excess of 10 mg/m³ in residential areas adjacent to the operations (9). Screens should be enclosed and provided with exhaust ventilation (10). The area of openings in the enclosures should be kept to a minimum. Inlet face velocities through enclosure openings should be sufficient to prevent the escape of dust. Velocities of 100–200 feet/min have been found to be sufficient, in most cases. Exhaust from the ventilation system should be discharged through an efficient collector.

Dry mixing operations (11) should be enclosed and ventilated in a manner similar to screens. Loading and discharge ports should be enclosed and connected to an exhaust ventilation system.

E. DRYING

Wet mixes, slurries, and filter cakes are dried in either direct or indirect dryers. In direct dryers, the wet material is brought into direct contact with the hot gases. In indirect dryers, heat transfer takes place through the dryer wall (12). Direct drying operations are used most often in mineral production. Direct drying usually creates more air pollution than indirect drying. Hot gases remove dust and gases from the material being dried.

III.   Specific Processes

A. COAL PREPARATION

The equipment and processes involved in coal preparation are similar to those used in the beneficiation of most mineral ores. Wet processes do not, in themselves, cause air pollution problems. But when the wet product must be dried to facilitate transportation, significant air pollution problems can occur. A by-product of the operations, coal refuse, presents a major problem in storing so as to prevent air and water pollution. The construction of large coal-burning power stations near "mine mouths" has resulted in a close physical and operational association between coal preparation plants and power stations. In the absence of a practical system to remove sulfur oxides in flue gases, coal preparation is the prime method for reducing these emissions. In order to fully evaluate the air pollution problems associated with the combustion of coal, consideration must be given to available coal preparation techniques.

The major air pollution problems associated with coal preparation procedures are gaseous emissions from ignited coal refuse disposal areas, dust from refuse and coal storage piles, and particulate matter from coal dryers and de-dusting operations.

1. *Cleaning and Drying*

Coal preparation (coal cleaning) operations involve the processing of run-of-mine coal to produce a salable product. Run-of-mine coal contains impurities in varying amounts and ranges in size from fines to pieces having equivalent diameters of over 10 feet. The primary purpose of a preparation plant is to crush the coal, remove impurities, and classify the product into standard sizes.

There are four principal coal cleaning techniques (*13*).

a. Cleaning at the Mine Face. This technique is being used less because of the increased use of mechanical mining methods. The removal of unwanted material, usually manually, at the mine face has the advantages of reducing the amount of material which must be transported to the preparation plant, reducing the amount of refuse produced at the plant, and thus reducing the size of coal refuse piles.

b. Picking by Hand or by Mechanical Means. Hand picking, the earliest method used, is usually employed in combination with mechanical methods, e.g., shaking tables.

c. Froth Flotation. This is a common ore preparation method in which fine coal particles attach themselves to foam bubbles, while heavier particles of slate do not.

d. Gravity Concentration. This mechanical cleaning method is based upon the difference in the specific gravities of coal and slate or shale. An appropriate separating medium (either liquid, gas, or fluidized solid—or a combination of these) is used to segregate the heavy and light particles.

After wet process cleaning operations, the coal is usually subjected to thermal drying (*14, 15*). Mechanical coal drying (*16*) usually does not create significant air pollution. Thermal drying usually involves the combustion of coal and the passage of the combustion gases through a bed of wet coal. The size consistency of the coal being dried and the velocity of the gases through the bed are major factors in determining the air pollution potential of the plant. Emissions include products of combustion and entrained coal fines.

The use of inertial collectors and wet scrubbers, or packed towers, in series, can provide efficient control of emissions. Fabric collectors are not usually used because of fire hazard. High efficiency cyclones, a venturi scrubber, and a demister installed on a thermal dryer reduced particulate matter from 2 to 0.04 grains per standard cubic foot (*17*).

Controlling operating procedures and providing for proper maintenance of equipment are the most important factors in preventing air pollution from thermal dryers. Even with the best air pollution control equipment, consideration must be continually given to:

1. Not overloading the plant. Increase in the rate or moisture content of coal feed will require an increase in the rate, and thus velocity through the bed, of drying gases, which will increase particle entrainment from the bed.

2. The prevention of clogging of ducts, cyclone, and other equipment by caked coal fines. This can usually be prevented by maintaining proper gas velocities through equipment and insulating (or heating, by using a portion of the combustion gases) surfaces on which condensation may take place.

2. Coal Refuse Disposal

From 20 to 50% of the raw coal processed in a cleaning plant is rejected as refuse. Refuse is piled into banks, either near the mine or near the preparation plant, having a base area of from an acre or less to hundreds of acres. The piles vary in height from 20 to 300 feet. Many piles contain millions of tons of refuse.

Coal refuse piles ignite either through spontaneous combustion, carelessness, or deliberate action. Studies have been conducted on the oxidation and resultant heating of coal refuse (18, 19). The oxidation of the carbonaceous and pyritic material in coal refuse is an exothermic reaction. The temperature of a coal refuse pile, or portions of the pile, will increase when the amount of air circulating in the pile is sufficient to cause oxidation, but insufficient to allow for the dissipation of heat. The temperature of the refuse increases until its ignition temperature is reached. Mine timbers, vegetation, or household refuse in the pile may act as kindling. The most recent nationwide study (20) indicates that there are approximately 500 burning piles in 15 states, approximately 150 in Pennsylvania and 200 in West Virginia.

Significant concentrations of H_2S and SO_2 have been measured in communities adjacent to burning refuse piles (21). While passing through the pile, the products of combustion react with each other and with materials in the pile (partially combusted pyritic and carbonaceous material) to form a number of noxious gases including carbon monoxide, ammonia, hydrogen sulfide, oxides of sulfur, and carbon disulfide. The extent and nature of air pollution from coal refuse piles and control techniques have been described by Sussman and Mulhern (22).

Proper construction, including compaction and sealing to prevent the circulation of air within refuse piles, will prevent ignition (23). Harrington and East (24) list five methods of controlling a burning coal refuse dump:

1. Digging out the fire or isolating the fire area by trenching.
2. Pumping water onto the fire area and immediate vicinity.

3. Applying a blanket or cover of incombustible material, such as limestone dust, shale dust, or slag dust over the fire area.
4. Injecting a slurry of rock dust or other incombustible material into the fire area through drill holes; grouting with cement is also practiced.
5. Spraying water over the fire area.

Additional techniques being studied include (25):

1. Removing burning refuse from the pile and extinguishing it by compaction and the use of water sprays. Preliminary estimates indicate that the cost of this procedure is approximately $.50/ton of refuse.
2. Sealing the surface of burning piles with plastic foam.
3. Using hydraulic mining "cannons" to remove and extinguish burning sections.
4. Using explosives to loosen the pile, and then extinguishing it with water sprays.

B. CEMENT PRODUCTION

Approximately 361,000,000 barrels of portland cement were produced in the United States in 1964 (26). Production is expected to increase at the rate of about 5% per year, with the trend toward larger plants (27). Major concentrations of cement plants in the United States are in eastern Pennsylvania; the Birmingham, Alabama area; the St. Louis and Kansas City, Missouri areas; central Texas; California, and the Pacific Northwest.

All portland cement is made by either the wet process or the dry process. In 1964 there were 110 wet process plants in the United States with a total capacity of over 285 million barrels per year. During the same year there were 69 dry process plants with a total capacity of approximately 200 million barrels per year.

To produce one barrel of cement, weighing 376 pounds, approximately 600 pounds of raw materials (not including fuel) are required (27). The raw materials required to make cement may be divided into those supplying the lime component (calcareous), the silica (siliceous), the alumina (argillaceous), and the iron component (ferriferous).

The major steps in the production of portland cement are quarrying, crushing, grinding, blending, clinker production, finish grinding, and packaging (Fig. 2). The operations prior to, and subsequent to, clinker production were discussed in Section II. Detailed descriptions of both wet and dry production operations are contained in the "Pit and Quarry Handbook and Purchasing Guide" (27). The major difference between

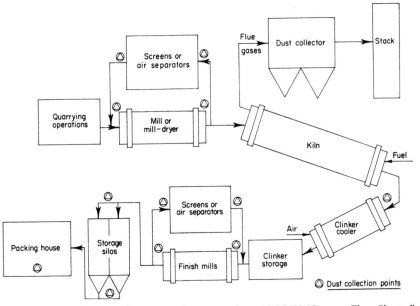

FIG. 2. Flow diagram of cement plant operations. (ACGIH "Process Flow Sheets," August 1960.)

the wet and dry processes is that in the wet process, the raw materials, i.e., the charge to the kiln, are ground to form a slurry, whereas in the dry process the free moisture content is reduced to less than 1% prior to or during raw grinding. In the dry process, the kiln feed may be dried in a rotary dryer or in combined drying and grinding units in which drying is accomplished in a separate compartment within the grinding unit.

The kiln is the major source of emissions from a cement plant. The rotary kiln used in most United States plants is a steel cylinder with a refractory lining. Kilns may be as small as 6 feet in diameter by 60 feet in length or as large as 25 feet in diameter by 760 feet in length. The kiln is erected horizontally with a gentle slope of 3/8 to 3/4 inch per foot of length and rotates on its longitudinal axis.

The kiln feed, commonly referred to as "slurry" for wet process kilns or "raw meal" for dry process kilns, is fed into the upper end of the revolving sloped kiln. As the feed flows slowly toward the lower end, it is exposed to increasing temperatures. During the passage through the kiln (1–4 hours), the raw materials are heated, dried, calcined, and finally heated to a point of incipient fusion (about 2900 °F), a temperature at which a new mineralogical substance, called clinker, is produced. In the lower portion of the kiln, coal, fuel oil, or gas is burned to pro-

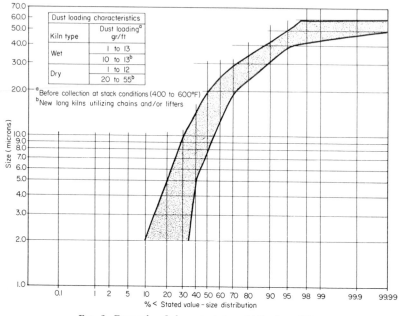

Fig. 3. Example of characteristics of kiln dust (26).

duce a process temperature of 2600° to 3000 °F. The combustion gases pass through the kiln counterflow to the material and leave the kiln, along with carbon dioxide driven off during calcination, at a temperature of from 300° to 1800 °F, depending on the kiln length and the process used.

Figure 3 indicates typical dust loading characteristics of gases leaving kilns. Kiln emissions for the wet process range from 15 to 50 pounds of dust per barrel of cement produced, with 28 pounds of dust per barrel of cement produced being a typical value. In the dry process, the losses range from 22 to 87 pounds of dust per barrel of cement produced, with 45 pounds of dust per barrel of cement being a typical value (28).

1. Emission Control Techniques

There are some unique aspects of cement production operations which warrant special consideration.

a. *Storage Silos.* Storage silos are under slight pressure as a result of material displacing air during the filling operation. In modern installations displaced dust-laden air is vented to a bag-type dust collector. This is especially true for silos with pneumatic loading and circulating systems.

b. Rotary Dryers. Dust concentrations of 5 to 10 grains per cubic foot of rotary dryer discharge gas prior to treatment can normally be expected. A heavier dust concentration may be expected in dryers utilizing kiln exit gases (waste-heat dryers), due to the dust carry-over from the kilns.

The rotary dryer, like the rotary kiln, is a major source of dust generation in a cement plant and requires a collecting system designed for higher temperatures. Systems in common use generally include multicyclones or other type mechanical collectors, electrostatic precipitators or combinations thereof. Where cloth filters are applied to drying operations, they must be the glass fiber type suitable for temperatures above 250 °F.

c. Clinker Cooler. The clinker coming from the kiln is normally cooled in rotary drum, shaking, inclined, horizontal or traveling-grate coolers. When a rotary drum cooler is used, cooling air induced through it may be utilized in the kiln as secondary combustion air, whereas the air drawn through the grate cooler is in excess of the quantity that can be used as secondary combustion air in the kiln. However, this excess can be used for drying purposes or can be discharged to the atmosphere. Since only 10–15% of the dust from a clinker cooler is below 10μ in size, mechanical collectors may be used to capture dust emissions.

2. *Kiln Operation (Clinker Production)*

A typical dry process kiln operating at a burning rate of 3000 barrels of clinker per day will use 150 tons of coal and approximately 900 tons of solid raw material to produce 540 tons of clinker and 4320 tons of kiln gas. It can readily be seen that the kiln gases far outweigh the other materials handled and that this is one reason dust collection equipment and auxiliaries represent such a large capital expenditure in a cement plant (*29*).

Some degree of control of dust from kiln operation may be obtained by adjusting operating conditions and kiln design to keep dust within the kiln. Reducing gas velocities within the kiln (some of the newer designed kilns have larger diameters at the feed end), modification of the rate and location of feed introduction, and hanging a dense curtain of lightweight chain at the discharge end of the kiln appear to have some effect on reducing the amount of dust discharged.

The weight-rate of dust emission from kilns is of such a magnitude that efficient collection is required, irrespective of the location or size of the plant. Since most of the kiln dust is usually smaller than $10~\mu$ in size, inertial collectors alone are not adequate for efficient control. Electrostatic precipitators or fabric filters (often in series with inertial collectors) can effectively collect fine kiln dust. The development of siliconized glass fabric has made it practical to use fabric filters to remove dust from hot kiln gases. Fabric filters have been used successfully on both wet and dry processes.

The weight of kiln dust per unit weight of clinker produced varies, depending upon the type of process (wet or dry), operating conditions, and whether or not collected dust is reintroduced to the kiln. A 4000 bbl/day wet process plant can produce 60 tons/day of kiln dust. A 90% efficient collection system would only reduce emissions to 6 tons/day. This would create an air pollution problem, even if the plant were located in a rural area. At present, some manufacturers will guarantee least 99.5%+ collection efficiency, and this is the range usually required to prevent air pollution problems.

In the Lehigh Valley, Pennsylvania, area there are presently 16 cement kilns equipped with 99%+ efficient collectors. Dust loadings from these units average 0.02 grains/scf.

Because of the number of plants in the area (12 plants having a total capacity of over 31,000,000 bbl/year) dustfall rates of over 35 tons per square mile per month are being recorded in areas adjacent to efficiently controlled kilns (30).

3. Handling Collected Dust

Considerable progress has been made in developing techniques to reintroduce collected kiln dust into the kiln. Reintroduction methods vary from plant to plant and may consist of one or a combination of the following.

1. Mixing with the raw feed either prior to or at the kiln charging end.
2. Dust return by scoop feeders located in front of the chain system.
3. Leaching dust with large volumes of water, mechanical dewatering, and introducing the resultant slurry into the kiln feed, onto the chain system, or into the kiln as raw feed. Leaching is one method employed to control the alkalinity of feed dust (see below).
4. Introducing dust into the burning zone (insufflation), often through the fuel pipe. The high temperature at the burning zone causes the dust to sinter.

The characteristics of collected dust, such as degree of calcination, alkalinity, sulfur content and fineness, are important considerations in determining if reintroduced kiln dust will adversely affect clinker quality, kiln operation, or dust collector efficiency. The percentage of alkali permissible in finished cement is limited by ASTM specification. Very fine collected dust usually has a high alkali content and often cannot be introduced into the kiln without pretreatment. The coarser dust captured by primary inertial collectors is usually low in alkali content and can be directly introduced. The introduction of very fine partially calcined dust can increase the undesirable mud ring-forming qualities of the raw feed. The introduction of very fine high alkali dust with the raw feed increases the tendency of the kiln dust to blind fabric collectors.

Collected kiln dust which cannot be reintroduced into the kiln may be used as a substitute for agricultural limestone, fertilizer, or mineral filler. If collected dust cannot be reused, it is often disposed of in abandoned quarries or storage piles. When stored in this manner, the dust piles should be covered, enclosed, or sprayed with water to form a surface crust.

C. Asphaltic Concrete

A flow diagram of an asphaltic concrete plant is shown in Fig. 4. Aggregate (gravel, rock, and sand) is proportioned and charged to a rotary dryer and heated to about 300°–350 °F. The dried aggregate is screened, transferred to storage bins, and introduced into a mill where it is mixed with hot asphaltic oil.

Air pollution sources include the rotary dryer, transfer points, bucket elevators, screens, weighing and mixing operations, storage piles, plant roads and sometimes the boiler facility. The dryer is the major source of dust emissions. Dust control systems usually include hoods and enclosures connected to a local exhaust ventilation system which discharges to mechanical collectors and scrubbers in series. Tests on dust loadings from asphaltic concrete plants have indicated that multiple centrifugal scrubbers can provide efficient control (31). It has been estimated that the basic processing equipment for a 200,000 pound per hour plant costs approximately $150,000 and a scrubber for the plant costs $10,000 (32).

A direct oil-fired dryer (24 feet long, 60 inch diameter; capacity: 50 to 60 tons/hour, approximate moisture reduction: from about 12% to 0.5%) requires 11,830 cfm exhaust ventilation capacity. Associated with this dryer, the hot elevator requires 1000 cfm, vibrating screens 2000 cfm, bins 1500 cfm and scales 1500 cfm (33). Tests for dust loadings from this type of equipment indicate a wide variation depending primarily upon the aggregate size consistency (31, 34). Scrubber stack emissions increase linearly with an increase in the amount of minus 200-mesh material charged to the dryer. Dust and particulate emissions from the scrubbers usually average around 0.2 pound per ton of product produced. If no scrubbers are used, the dust and particulate emission averages around 5 pounds per ton of product produced (28).

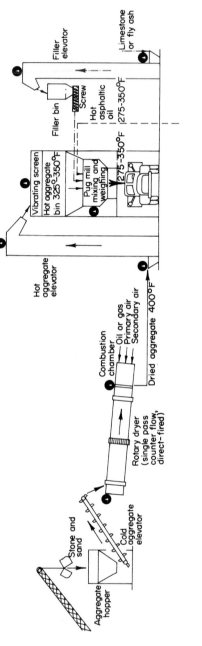

Fig. 4. Flow diagram of asphalt (paving) plant operations. (ACGIH "Process Flow Sheets," February 1959.)

Stone and sand

Aggregate hopper

Cold aggregate elevator

Rotary dryer (single pass counter-flow, direct-fired)

Combustion chamber
Oil or gas
Primary air
Secondary air
Dried aggregate 400°F

Hot aggregate elevator

Vibrating screen
Hot aggregate bin 325°-350°F

Pug mill mixing and weighing 275°-350°F

Filler bin
Screw
Hot asphaltic oil 275-350°F

Filler elevator

Limestone or fly ash

Dust control points

D. Concrete Batching

Concrete batching plants (28) are generally simple arrangements of steel hoppers, elevators, and batching scales for proportioning rock, gravel, and sand aggregates with cement for delivery, usually in transit mixer trucks. Aggregates are usually crushed and sized in separate plants and are delivered by truck or belt conveyors to ground or other storage from which they can be reclaimed and placed in the batch plant bunkers. Dust control procedures for these operations are described in Section II.

By careful use of sprays, felt, or other filter material over breathers in the cement silos, and canvas curtains drawn around the cement dump trucks while dumping, dust losses can be controlled. Aggregate stocks in bunkers should be wet down with sprays to prevent dusting. With careful operation, losses in these plants can be held to about 0.025 pound of dust per cubic yard of concrete. Uncontrolled plants have emissions of about 0.2 pound of dust per cubic yard of concrete handled.

E. Glass and Ceramics Manufacturing

The ceramic industries (35–37) make products from common minerals, mostly silicates, employing high temperature processes. Manufacturing operations for the production of refractories, glass, porcelain enamel, abrasives, whiteware, pottery, brick, and tile involve crushing, grinding, classifying, screening, proportioning and firing, baking or fusion of materials in kilns or smelting furnaces at temperatures averaging 1000 to 1700 °C. Ceramic processes may require the fusion of such simple materials as sand, soda, lime, and borax to produce glass, or of complicated mixtures of sodium silico-fluoride, zirconium oxide, titanium oxide, fluorspar, refractories, and fluxes to produce porcelain enamel.

The following types of emissions are common to most ceramic processing operations:

a. Dusts. To obtain rapid reaction, raw materials are usually of a fine particle size. Gas turbulence within direct-fired furnaces during charging can cause dust to become gasborne. Gasborne dust should be limited not only to prevent its emission with the combustion gases but also to prevent caking of the fines on the furnace walls and checkers which requires downtime for cleaning. In indirectly heated units, although dust from the charge cannot get into the flue gas, it can contaminate the workroom air which is usually vented to the atmosphere through roof ventilators. Dust emissions may be controlled by modifying charging techniques, i.e., charging raw materials in a wet or pelletized form. The use of calcium silicate instead of calcium carbonate and soda ash eliminates the production of carbon dioxide and thus turbulence in the batch. This reduces the amount of particulate matter picked up by combustion gases and discharged to the stack. The use of electric melting furnaces also reduces the amount of particulate matter discharged by eliminating the combustion gases which sweep through the furnace and cause fine particles from the batch to become gasborne.

b. Gases and Fumes. During the firing cycle, materials such as silicates, halogen-bearing compounds, and carbonates react to form fumes and gaseous mixtures of carbonates, nitrates, chlorides, and fluorides. Gases and fumes liberated during the firing cycle usually must be rapidly removed from the firing chamber so as not to affect the finished product. Emissions of these gases and fumes from large furnaces can cause air pollution problems. Recent tests at a large fused silica furnace showed emissions of over 200 pounds/hour of HCl, with downwind concentrations approaching 1 ppm. These emissions caused significant vegetation damage in the area of the plant. Wet scrubbers, usually required to be corrosion resistant, have effectively controlled such gaseous furnace emissions. Special designs, usually of higher pressure drop, are required if control of fumes is also required.

c. Products of Fuel Combustion. It is often necessary to use soft coal to impart certain desired color characteristics to brick. Heavy smoke usually occurs during oven startup. By using gas or oil during oven startup periods and changing to soft coal later in the heating cycle, it is possible to obtain the desired brick color with a significant reduction in air pollution.

During curing operations smoke-producing fuels or smoke-producing firing techniques are sometimes employed to create a reducing atmosphere in ovens. Secondary combustion chambers in ovens or afterburners in stacks are used to control the resultant smoke emissions. Consideration should be given to modifying raw materials so that desired product characteristics may be obtained by curing in a smokeless atmosphere.

F. Asbestos Processing

The special biological effects resulting from occupational exposure to asbestos dust have been recognized since the late 1920's. Recent studies have been conducted with respect to nonoccupational community exposures to asbestos dust (38–40). Milling and manufacturing operations can cause air pollution problems.

1. *Milling*

Fiber production from ore presents unique problems in air pollution control because of the large amounts of dust produced by milling equipment and the large amounts of air used in these operations. Milling operations vary, depending upon the type of rock to be processed. The basic operations usually are crushing and drying the ore, fiber separation, and grading.

Primary and secondary crushing, close-circuited with vibrating screens (Fig. 1), is used to prepare mine rock for drying and milling. The crushed rock is dried in vertical or rotary dryers to remove surface moisture. Dryer gas temperatures vary between 200° and 350 °F. Emissions are usually controlled by a wet-type dynamic precipitator. Because of possible plugging, fabric collectors are not often employed.

After drying, the ore may be subjected to additional crushing before being processed to separate fibers. During milling the fiber is released from the ore, fluffed up, and separated by aspiration (*41*). Shaking screens release the fiber and the lighter fibers are aspirated through an air exhaust hood and duct system to cyclone-type collectors, while coarse rock particles and unopened bundles of fiber cascade over the end of the screens and fines drop through the screens. This extraction process is repeated several times over a series of successively finer mesh screens, each treating the fines from the previous screen. The unaspirated overs from these screens go through fiberizers to release and open up the rest of the fiber and these products are also fed to aspirating screens. An asbestos mill may use several hundred screens. A variety of crushing machines are used, such as cone, gyratory, hammermill or disk type. Fiberizers are often of local design based essentially on hammermill principles, but are generally run at slower speeds than the usual type hammermill.

The fibers recovered from the various milling stages are cleaned and graded to market specifications. This involves another series of screening operations with fiber aspiration, using shaking type screens or special forms of revolving trommel screens and various types of air separators. Fractions of the various sizes obtained from these operations may be blended to produce a wide range of fiber grades, before being conveyed to bins from which they are drawn off to mechanical packing or bagging machines.

Large quantities of dust are generated during dry asbestos milling. However, pneumatic transport is an inherent process component so that only a fraction of the total air moving capacity in a mill is provided exclusively for dust control. About 75 tons of process air may be handled for each ton of asbestos fiber produced, supplemented by an additional 25 tons of air exhausted for dust removal at nonaspirated screens, belt conveyors, bucket elevators, rock and fiber bins, graders, hoppers, and pressure-packing machines. Central air handling and filtering systems usually provide for combined process and dust control air (42).

Fabric collectors are placed in series following the cyclone collectors which are part of the process equipment.

2. Product Manufacturing

Chrysotile, a hydrous magnesium silicate having the theoretical formula $3MgO \cdot 2SiO_2 \cdot 2H_2O$, is the most often used type of asbestos. Asbestos fiber is used to manufacture textiles (safety clothing, curtains, lagging cloth, brake linings, clutch facings), cement products (pipes, sheets, shingles), plastics (as filler), and many other products. The asbestos cement industry is the principal consumer of chrysotile asbestos— on a world-wide basis, approximately two-thirds of the asbestos produced is used to manufacture cement products.

Because of the awareness of the industry to the occupational health aspects of asbestos, processing and handling equipment is routinely equipped with local exhaust ventilation systems. These systems usually discharge to a fabric filter collector—or a wet scrubber, if moisture in the exhaust gases may cause filter plugging (43, 44).

Conventional stack sampling and general atmospheric sampling techniques cannot be employed to evaluate emissions from asbestos processing operations. Air quality standards, which are not entirely firm, are based upon a particle count for asbestos dust.

IV. Conclusion

Experience has shown that many air pollution problems associated with mineral processing are caused by overloading or not operating process equipment at design capacity. Also, the importance of good plant "housekeeping" cannot be overstressed. Overloading kilns, dryers, and furnaces results in higher gas velocities which tend to pick up more dust and overload collectors. Many air pollution problems can be abated or substantially reduced by modifying operations—changing techniques and material handling procedures; providing for proper equipment maintenance—hopper clean-out, enclosure and duct-work repair; and good "housekeeping"—clean roadways, enclosed storage piles, and vacuum sweeping systems. In selecting dust collectors, it is important to consider the size consistency and other characteristics of the collected dust which will permit recovery in a usable form. The size consistency is usually the most important factor in determining if recovered mineral dust can be reintroduced into the process or directly become a salable product. The proper selection and arrangement of collectors (often placing two or three types in series to fractionate the dust stream) will often permit recovery of some of the dust in a usable form.

REFERENCES

1. F. G. Anderson, R. L. Evans, and R. G. Peluso, *U.S., Bur. Mines, Inform. Circ.* **8130** (1962).
2. A. L. Stern, *Chem. Eng.* **69** (25), 129–146 (1962).
3. American Conference of Governmental Industrial Hygienists, "Industrial Ventilation, A Manual of Recommended Practice," 6th ed., Committee on Industrial Ventilation, Lansing, Michigan, 1960.
4. W. C. L. Hemeon, "Plant and Process Ventilation." Industrial Press, New York, 1955.
5. D. M. Anderson, *Ind. Med. Surg.* **33,** 68–72 (1964).
6. R. T. Pring, J. F. Knudsen, and R. Dennis, *Ind. Eng. Chem.* **41,** 2442–2450 (1949).
7. C. B. Schuder, *Power Eng.* **59,** 74–77 (1955).
8. J. H. Perry, ed., "Chemical Engineer's Handbood," 3rd ed., pp. 1072–1095. McGraw-Hill, New York, 1950.
9. Files, Div. Air Pollution Control, Pennsylvania Dept. of Health, Harrisburg, Pa., March, 1966.
10. Committee on Industrial Hygiene of the American Iron and Steel Institute, "Steel Mill Ventilation," pp. 37 and 38. New York, 1965.
11. J. H. Perry, ed., "Chemical Engineer's Handbook," 3rd ed., pp. 1195–1231. McGraw-Hill, New York, 1950.
12. J. H. Perry, ed., "Chemical Engineer's Handbook," 3rd ed., p. 799. McGraw-Hill, New York, 1950.
13. D. R. Mitchell, "Coal Preparation," 2nd ed., p. 820. Am. Inst. Mining Met. Engrs., New York, 1950.
14. H. R. Brown, C. J. Dalzell, E. Hartman, G. J. R. Toothman, and C. H. Schwartz, *U.S., Bur. Mines, Rept. Invest.* **5198** (1956).
15. H. A. Schrecengost and M. D. Childers, *U.S., Bur. Mines, Inform. Circ.* **8258** (1965).
16. F. X. Feney, *Coal Age* **19** (9), 78–88 (1965).
17. Files, Stack Test. Pennsylvania Dept. of Health, Harrisburg, Pa., 1966.
18. J. W. Myers, "Control of Fires in Coal-Mine Refuse Piles." U.S. Bureau of Mines, 1955 Pittsburgh, Pa. (unpublished manuscript, on open file).
19. W. L. Nelson, "Report of Investigation of Fundamental Aspects of the Spontaneous Heating of Coal," portions of report published in *J. Air Pollution Control Assoc.* **6,** 105–110 (1956).
20. R. W. Stahl, *U.S., Bur. Mines, Inform. Circ.* **8209** (1964).
21. Community Air Sampling Files. Pennsylvania Dept. of Health, Harrisburg, Pa., 1959–1966.
22. V. H. Sussman and J. J. Mulhern, *J. Air Pollution Control Assoc.* **14,** 279–284 (1964).
23. Technical Coordinating Committee T-4 Coal Report, *J. Air Pollution Control Assoc.* **6,** 105–110 (1956).

142 VICTOR H. SUSSMAN

24. D. Harrington and J. H. East, Jr., *U.S., Bur. Mines, Inform. Circ.* **7439** (1948).
25. Pennsylvania Department of Mines and Mineral Industries, Harrisburg, Pennsylvania, private correspondence (1966).
26. Unless otherwise indicated, information for this section was obtained from S. T. Cuffe (personal communication, Div. Air Pollution, U.S. Public Health Serv., Robert A. Taft Sanit. Eng. Center, Cincinnati, Ohio, 1966) related to a pending P.H.S. publication "Atmospheric Emissions From Portland Cement Manufacture."
27. R. Rick, ed., "Pit and Quarry Handbook and Purchasing Guide," 57th ed. Pit & Quarry Publ., Chicago, Illinois, 1964.
28. M. Mayer, "A Compilation of Air Pollutant Emission Factors for Combustion Processes, Gasoline Evaporation, and Selected Industrial Process." U.S. Public Health Serv., Cincinnati, Ohio, 1965.
29. R. J. Plass, *Proc. Electrostatic Precipitation Seminar, Pennsylvania State Univ. 1960.*
30. E. Doherty, "Annual Report." Lehigh Valley Air Pollution Control, Northampton, Pa., 1965.
31. R. M. Ingels, N. R. Shaffer, and J. A. Danielson, *J. Air Pollution Control Assoc.* **10**, 29–33 (1960).
32. "Air Pollution Control—Hearings Before the Committee on Public Works," S.432, S.444, S.1009, S.1040, S.1124, and H. R. 5618, p. 445. United States Senate, Washington, D.C., 1963.
33. W. A. McKim and D. E. Bonn, *Roads Streets* **102**, (8), 172–175 (1959).
34. G. L. Allen, F. H. Viets, and L. C. McCabe, *U.S., Bur. Mines, Inform. Circ.* **7627** (1952).
35. M. Bozsin, *J. Air Pollution Control Assoc.* **16**, 332–333 (1966).
36. W. C. L. Hemeon, *Am. Ceram. Soc. Bull.* **28**, 94 (1949).
37. E. F. Wilson, *Glass Ind.* **41**, 202–203, 236–239 (1960).
38. H. E. Whipple, *Ann. N.Y. Acad. Sci.* **132**, Art. 1, 184–246 (1965).
39. F. Wagler, *Ges. Hyg. Grenzgebeite (Berlin)* **8**, 246–255 (1962).
40. V. D. Redaksie, *S. African Med. J.* **37**, 629–630 (1963).
41. J. C. Kelleher, *Asbestos* **27**, No. 3, 2–10; No. 4, 3–10; No. 5, 6–12 (1945).
42. L. Rispler and C. R. Ross, "Flow Sheet for Milling of Asbestos Ores," ACGIH Process Flow Sheets, ACGIH, Cincinnati, Ohio, 1961.
43. H. E. Whipple, *Ann. N.Y. Acad. Sci.* **132**, Art. 1, 322–334 (1965).
44. B. F. Postman, *Am. Ind. Hyg. Assoc. J.* **23**, 67–74 (1962).

GENERAL REFERENCE

Additional pertinent material is in Chapters 7 and 11 of "Air Pollution Engineering Manual, Los Angeles APCD" (J. A. Danielson, ed.), PHS Publn. 999-AP-40, DHEW, Cincinnati (1967); and will be published in the National Air Pollution Control Administration's publications: "Control Technology for Particulate Air Pollutants," and "Control Technology for Sulfur Oxides Air Pollutants."

36 Ferrous Metallurgical Processes

William Sebesta

I. Coke Production

During the last half of the eighteenth century, iron ores were reduced to cast iron by means of small stack furnaces which resembled blast furnaces as we now know them today. Usually they were short truncated cones constructed of stone in an area where the three basic materials for the manufacture of iron were prevalent, namely, iron ore, limestone, and charcoal, the form of carbon used at that time for reducing iron ores. Charcoal was made by local woodcutters, in the area where the wood was cut, and the carbonizing of the wood was accomplished by igniting a large earth-covered pile of cut wood. This provided the controlled burning necessary to produce charcoal of the desired quality (*1*).

Later there was developed, evidently from applying these same basic carbonizing principles to coal, a brick dome-shaped oven in which coke was made. Since the shape of this brick furnace resembled a beehive, they became known as beehive coke ovens. Usually a group of these units was constructed, most often near the supply of the coal. Row orientation of these units was used since the production line system began to be applied to coke production. Two, back to back rows of beehive ovens were usually constructed, but alternated in their lines so that any oven could be loaded by a charging car operating on one set of tracks running above and between both lines. Raw coal was charged into the still-hot oven, leveled, and some was allowed to burn to provide the heat to drive off the volatile matter from the remainder. The finished charge was then quenched with water. The quenched coke from these ovens was loaded into railroad cars which ran on depressed tracks situated alongside the wharves (cooling docks) outside of the two rows of ovens. The process of making coke by beehive ovens was eventually replaced by the by-product ovens we know today.

By-product ovens are usually constructed in groups called batteries. They consist of a block of many long, narrow firebrick ovens with heating chambers made of similar brick located between the ovens, so that a battery of ovens is a huge block of coking cells separated from an intricate system of combustion chambers. The fuel used to heat coke ovens may be blast furnace gas, coke oven gas, or natural gas, each fuel requiring a different set of burner adjustments. None of the coal being coked is burned to provide heat for the coking operation.

The carbonization of the coal begins soon after crushed and sized coal is loaded into red-hot ovens. The gaseous products and condensates are conveyed continuously via the large collecting mains from the coke oven battery to an adjacent by-product plant. Usually each oven has a steam jet aspirator which aids in conveying the gaseous carbonization products into the collecting main.

The charging holes on the top of the battery are closed almost immediately after charging to minimize escape of gas or dust into the atmosphere. Spacing of the charging holes, and sleeves on the charging car hoppers, have been used to minimize such emissions. Smoothness of operation and the physical characteristics of the coal being used aid in the reduction of these emissions. Most operators attempt, through door maintenance programs and operating procedures, to further reduce the escape of gas through the charging holes.

In the by-product plant, tar, benzene, naphtha, and other commercial products are segregated and separately removed from the coke oven gas. The by-product recovery plant has processes similar to those in petroleum refineries (see Chapter 34) and chemical plants (see Chapter 38). The cleaned gas, having a medium heating value, is customarily used as fuel in boilers and other furnaces, including those of the coke oven. Since sulfur has an undesirable influence in steelmaking, the steel industry has always endeavored to use materials with low sulfur content. Therefore, low sulfur coal is used for coke making. Coke oven gas usually contains some sulfur-bearing compounds derived from the sulfur in the coal (2).

After the coking period, the incandescent coke is pushed from the oven into a quenching car where burning in air takes place. This car is a large special-type railroad car with perforated sides, which is used to carry the flaming coke to an area where a huge quantity of water is sprayed onto the coke to quench it, i.e., extinguish its incandescence. During this operation, which stops the burning of the coke, large quantities of steam are generated. It is usually performed in a quenching tower. The quiescent coke is then conveyed to a cooling wharf where the coke is spread out so that the excess water may drain away. After cooling, the coke is sized in a plant similar to that for screening rock and ores (see Chapter 35).

II. Sinter Production

The sintering process was developed because of the increasing amount of fines in available ores. With higher blast furnace production rates, the resulting increased gas velocities tend to carry out of the blast furnace dust which then has to be captured by the blast furnace dust-collection system. Hauling ore fines, which later are wasted, adds to material cost. The cost of disposing of these fines is greater than the cost of recovery. Other steel plant fines, such as coke breeze and scale, are also available. The sintering process fuses some collected dusts, fine ore, coke fines, and scale into a stable mass called sinter, which is satisfactory for blast furnace use.

A uniform blend of the available and necessary materials is fed to the sintering machine (Fig. 1) which is a continuous line of cast-iron pallets moving over a series of wind box chambers. The wind box is connected to the exhaust system of the sinter plant. The mixture of fines is ignited

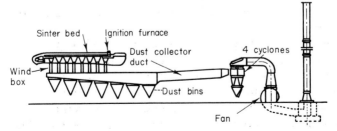

FIG. 1. Sintering machine and associated dust collection system.

and the draft of air moves the combustion process down through the bed, fusing the materials in the bed into a clinker. The flue gases, which carry unreacted ore, coke, and ash particles, customarily pass through dust collectors before discharge to the atmosphere.

Most sintering operations are equipped with sinter coolers. The air drawn through the bed of discharged sinter is also passed through dust collectors before discharged to the atmosphere. Collected dusts are returned to the sinter process.

Sinter Plant Emissions and Their Control

About 20 pounds of dust may result per ton of sinter. The dust concentration in a sinter plant stack will vary with the amount of air being drawn through the sinter bed. The chemical composition of the dust will vary with the type of materials being processed in the plant. One would expect that the dust would be quite high in iron oxides. Its particle size can be expected to be large. One British investigator reported as follows: Larger than 420 μ—3.7%; larger than 178 μ—26.3%; larger than 76 μ—63.1%; and smaller than 76 μ—36.9% (3); another reported: smaller than 1000 μ, 87 to 95%; smaller than 100 μ, 38 to 65%; smaller than 10 μ, 4 to 19%; and smaller than 2 μ, 0.3 to 4% (4).

The wind box gases from the sinter bed are usually drawn through dust control equipment before being directed to the stack. Cyclones, miniature cyclone clusters, electrostatic precipitators, baghouses, and venturi scrubbers have been used with varying degrees of success.

III.   Iron Production

Most iron produced in blast furnaces is either transported as molten iron to steelmaking furnaces or cast into pigs for the foundry trade. A blast furnace of today is a large complex of boiler plate, refractories, dust collectors, and air-moving equipment. The blast furnace itself is a large steel stacklike chamber, lined with refractory materials, into which iron ore, coke, and limestone are fed at the top and reacted with large amounts of hot air to produce molten iron and by-products (slag and blast furnace gas). The blast furnace gas, after cleaning by dust collectors, is burned in the blast furnace stoves, or under boilers for steam to drive the turbo-compressors that furnish the wind for blast furnace operation. The air handled by these compressors is heated by passage through the above-noted stoves before being fed into the blast furnace. Stoves are huge networks of firebrick with small openings between the bricks. The blast furnace gas burned in stoves must be relatively clean or plugging of the brick checkerwork will result.

The boilers require clean fuel gas. Therefore, blast furnace gas is usually cleaned to better than 0.10 grains of particulate matter per standard cubic foot of gas at 60 °F and 30 inches of Hg.

The particulate matter, which is carried out of the blast furnace by the high velocity gas stream, is removed from the gas by a series of collection devices, dry cyclones, and wet scrubbers before the gas is used as fuel in any of the above processes.

Blast furnaces are sometimes "sick" and the burden (charge) slips (shifts) irregularly in a violent manner. The resulting rush of gas causes abnormal pressures to occur in the furnace and relief valves at the top of the furnace pop open as a safety measure to protect the furnace. When this occurs, there are brief spurts of dusty gas into the atmosphere to relieve the excessive pressure in the blast furnace.

Technological advances are decreasing the frequency and severity of slips. Blast furnace burdens are being controlled to make them more permeable. To minimize sudden slips of the blast furnace burden, some operators follow the practice of controlled periodic bleeding of the furnace top pressure. By reducing the pressure on the top of the furnace, the pressure differential across the burden is increased and a controlled slip occurs. Allowing the blast furnace burden to shift or slip down periodically permits more uniform descent of the materials within the furnace and minimizes sudden surges or slips.

Some blast furnace operators increase the weights on the relief valves to prevent them from opening so often. It has been found that a slight increase of blast furnace pressure has not been detrimental. To minimize the occurrence of slips during periods when the furnace may be prone to slips, some operators reduce the wind on the furnace periodically, to allow adjustment of the furnace burden with little chance of opening the relief valves.

Operators usually usefully consume all the blast furnace gas produced.

POTENTIAL BLAST FURNACE EMISSIONS AND THEIR CONTROL

As blast furnace gas leaves the top of the furnace (Fig. 2), it carries a dust content of 12 grains/ft^3 or less, STP. A good primary dust collector will clean the gas down to about 3 grains/ft^3. Collector efficiencies may range from 50 to 80% depending upon the type of ores used, the blast volume, and the operational pressure of the furnace. The pressure drop through a collector of this type will vary from 0.5 to 1.0 inches of water.

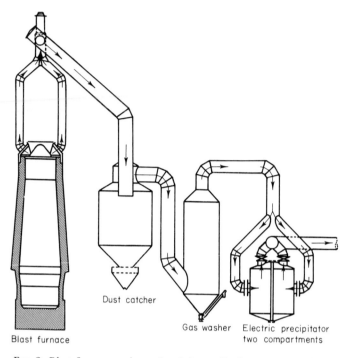

Fig. 2. Blast furnace and associated dust collection system (typical).

After the primary dust catcher, the blast furnace gas is usually sent through a primary wet washer. Modern designs of these clean the gas down to a dust content of 0.05–0.15 grains/ft³, STP. The gas pressure loss through such units may run 10–15 inches of water.

Following these units, blast furnace gas is, in some cases, still further cleaned by electrostatic precipitators. With inlet gas of 0.25 grain/ft³, STP, dust content, clean gas of 0.010 grain/ft³ can be expected. All this remaining dust is not, of necessity, emitted to the air, since some is re-

TABLE I

COMPOSITION OF PARTICULATE EMISSIONS FROM BLAST FURNACES
(in percent)

Fe₂O₃	FeO	Silicates as SiO₂	Al as Al₂O₃	Ca as CaO	Mg as MgO	Cu as CuO	Zn as ZnO	Mn as MnO	C	Loss on ignition	Reference
25.6	NR[a]	19.3	10.0	7.1	1.1	3.4	4.5	7.9	9.6	NR	(5)
23.5	7.15	14.3	3.5	13.8	2.5	NR	NR	2.38	NR	11.42	(6)
2.0	10.75	25.0	10.0	16.1	7.0	NR	NR	2.70	NR	19.35	(6)

[a] NR = not reported.

TABLE II

PARTICLE SIZE DISTRUBITION OF BLAST FURNACE DUST RETAINED BY EACH OF
THREE DUST COLLECTORS IN SERIES (5)

Size range (μ)	Dust catchers		Spray tower		Disintegrator	
	Inlet dust loading[a]	Collection efficiency, [3](%)	Inlet dust loading[a]	Collection efficiency, (%)	Inlet dust loading[a]	Collection efficiency, (%)
>700	0.040	100	—	—	—	—
700 > 100	8.000	100	—	—	—	—
100 > 90	0.050	100	—	—	—	—
90 > 80	0.700	68	0.222	100	—	—
80 > 70	0.785	58	0.329	97	0.0080	100
70 > 60	0.423	59	0.175	96	0.0087	100
60 > 50	0.351	67	0.111	94	0.0065	100
50 > 40	0.712	56	0.311	97	0.0096	100
40 > 30	1.250	56	0.540	98	0.0087	100
30 > 20	1.820	59	0.740	98	0.0152	100
20 > 10	1.890	40	1.140	96	0.0405	92
<10	1.970	25	1.490	88	0.1850	98
Overall efficiency, %		72.6		94.4		98.0

[a] Grains/ft^3 (STP).

tained in the stoves in which the gas is burned. The dust composition will be influenced by the type of materials charged into the furnace (5, 6) (Table I).

The particle size of blast furnace dusts also varies with the type of materials charged, wind volumes, and working pressure of the furnace (Table II).

IV.   Steel Production

A. BESSEMER CONVERTERS

This converter process has been gradually replaced by other steel-making methods. In 1966, Bessemers produced only 0.4% of the steel produced in the United States. The type of refractory material and slag determines whether the process is acid or basic (1, 7).

The blowing cycle of an acid Bessemer converter is divided into three periods. In the first period, iron oxide (Fe_2O_3) is formed by the reaction of iron with oxygen in the blowing air. This reaction produces heat, and as the heat increases, silicon and manganese, which also have an affinity for oxygen, begin reacting, forming SiO_2 and MnO; and the Fe_2O_3 reaction decreases. When the SiO_2 and MnO reactions are taking place, a large reddish-brown flame issues from the mouth of the converter. This period is called the silicon blow and lasts about 4 minutes.

During the second period, known as the carbon blow, the carbon in the pig iron reacts with oxygen to form carbon monoxide. The carbon monoxide flame, which leaves the mouth of the vessel during this cycle, is yellowish-white and up to 30 feet long. A fume is generated from the droplets of metal that are shot into the air during this cycle of the blow. When the carbon portion of the blow ends, the flame shortens and dies. Following the carbon blow, there is a period called the afterblow which completes the cycle.

In the basic Bessemer process, the principal difference from the acid process described above is that, during the afterblow, the phosphorus contained in the charge is converted to P_2O_5 and is combined with the slag.

A disadvantage of the Bessemer is its small batch size. Yields are not comparable to the open hearth process.

Bessemer Converter Emissions and Their Control

Kosmider *et al.* (8) conducted tests on a 20-ton converter, finding that the dust concentration in an attached stack varied from 0.132 grains/ft³ to 0.393 grains/ft³, and that, because the dust particle sizes were of the order of 0.5 to 2.0 μ, special equipment would be necessary to clean the exhaust gases. With steam addition to the blowing gas, practically no brown smoke was formed.

Dehne (9) conducted many experiments at Duisburg-Hushinger on a 36-ton Thomas unit. This converter discharged into a stack. Particle size measurements of the emissions indicated that the diameter of the fume particles were between 0.03 to 0.15 μ. A number of wet scrubbers and dry collectors were tried unsuccessfully.

Meldau and Laüfhutte (10) measured the particle size distribution in the waste gas stream from a bottom blown converter during the four-minute dephosphorization blow. With an air blast, the sizes ranged from 0.03 to 1 μ, with the mean being between 0.12 and 0.15 μ. With oxygen enrichment, the particle size at the edge of the flame was between 0.06 and 0.18 μ, with a mean of 0.12 μ.

O'Mara (11) indicated that with a Bessemer rated at 25 to 30 tons per heat and two or three cycles per hour, with a 10 to 15 minute blow, the emission would be about 10 grains/ft³ or between 15 to 20 pounds per ton of steel produced. Other references (11a, 11b) have estimated a 20 pounds per ton of steel emission rate for this size converter. Lower emission concentrations of 0.15 to 0.40 grains/ft³ have been quoted (*11c*) and another investigator suggested grain loadings of 0.8 grains/ft³ (*11*).

Recent research work in the United States (*7*) has been performed on a pilot plant scale acid Bessemer converter to evaluate the degree of smoke suppression with various processing changes. The dust concentrations observed averaged about 0.50 pounds of particulate matter per 1000 pounds of exhaust gases. This is equivalent to about 0.27 grains/ft³.

B. Open Hearth Furnaces

The open hearth process may be a disappearing means of steel manufacture. The basic oxygen furnace is assuming a greater role in total steel production, and the open hearth system may be phased out as has been happening to the Bessemer converter.

In open hearth furnaces (Fig. 3) the flame sweeps across a molten pool of material in the hearth. The furnace consists of a hearth, over which there is a brick arch roof, brick conduits at each end of the furnace for the removal of hot gases, checker chambers (brick-filled rooms) for heat exchange, and firebrick tunnels to a stack for exhausting of combustion gases to the atmosphere (*1, 12*).

Each complete charge of the furnace, known as a heat of steel, consists of scrap metal, limestone, and pig iron (molten blast furnace iron, or cold pig iron, if molten iron is not available). Some iron ore or other

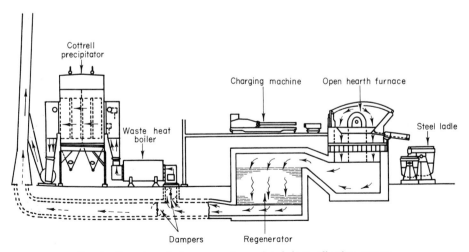

FIG. 3. Open hearth furnace and associated dust collection system.

source of iron oxide may also be added. First, the limestone and scrap are charged into the furnace through the doors on one of the long sides of the furnace. Natural or mixed fuel gases and hot combustion air (drawn through the hot checkerworks) create flame over the hearth until the temperature of the charged contents climbs to and above their melting point.

After the scrap has melted, molten pig iron (if available) is poured into the furnace from a large ladle. The charge begins to boil (work) and becomes a uniform mass of molten iron. The carbon of the iron combines with the oxygen of the iron ore and the air, and is carried off as gas. The calcined limestone combines with other impurities of the mass and forms a slag on top of the bubbling metal pool. During the refining, a melter keeps constant watch of the furnace contents. Since the finished steel is to meet certain specifications, sufficient carbon, phosphorus, sulfur, and other impurities must be removed from the molten bath of metal. Periodically, samples of the bath are taken and are rushed to a nearby laboratory for immediate testing. When a test shows that a heat is not developing satisfactorily, a melter may make additions to aid the furnace toward the desired reaction. Conditions within the furnace—temperature, pressure, and the flow of fuel and air—can be regulated from a control panel located on the charging floor. When the refining is completed, the heat of steel is tapped. A plug in the taphole at the rear of the furnace is punctured, and the white-hot molten steel runs into a ceramic-lined ladle with a shower of sparks.

Various alloying elements, as required by specifications, are added to the receiving ladle during this furnace-tapping operation. The entire refining takes about 8 to 10 hours. In some furnaces the process may be speeded up by the use of an oxygen lance which expedites the removal of carbon from the molten metal.

The temperature of the gases leaving the open hearth stacks varies depending upon the degree of heat recovery used. The gases are passed through checker chambers and other temperature-reducing equipment before being directed into air pollution control facilities. The outlet gas temperatures (without dust collection equipment installed) are high, 1600 °F, and therefore must be reduced before control equipment can be applied. Cooling of the gases by water evaporation has inherent difficulties, namely, condensation, corrosion, and no change in total volume after cooling to operational temperature.

Waste heat boilers are frequently used both to recover heat and to reduce outlet gas temperature.

Open Hearth Furnace Emissions and Their Control

Open hearth fume consists predominantly of iron oxides. Other constitutents of the emission are related to the raw materials used in the process. The analysis of the scrap available may influence the characteristics of the emissions. The emission concentration is dependent upon process characteristics at various times during the heat cycle. The particle spectrum varies considerably; one may find particles as small as 0.001 μ in the effluent.

Many investigators of the open hearth process, whether it be the regular or the oxygen-lanced practice, have found by chemical analysis of the collected dusts (be it from air sampling in the stacks or analysis of the collected material) that the dust is predominantly the most oxidized form of iron (*12–18*) (Table III). During the lime boil portion of a heat, the percent of iron oxide may be less. Strauss (*15*) in his studies of a 200-ton oxygen-lanced open hearth furnace, found that iron oxide averaged about 50% of the total particulate matter over most cycles, but was above 60% during the working period and ore boil, and reached 80% during the periods of oxygen lancing.

Composite dust samples taken over a complete heat show that a large number of the particles, about 50%, are less than 5 μ in size; however, the spectrum of particle sizes varies considerably during the heat (*16,*

TABLE III
COMPOSITION OF PARTICULATE EMISSIONS FROM OPEN HEARTH FURNACES (%)

Period of heat	Fe_2O_3	FeO	Silicates as SiO_2	Al as Al_2O_3	Mn as MnO	Ca as CaO	Mg as MgO	P as P_2O_5	Reference
Charging of scrap	66.71	1.56	4.49	5.10	2.62	4.19	2.51	NR	(*13*)
Charging of pig iron	74.20	NR[a]	2.41	2.64	2.30	3.30	2.40	NR	(*13*)
Melting	71.50	NR	3.14	1.97	2.26	3.80	1.84	NR	(*13*)
Boil	72.64	NR	3.56	2.60	2.33	3.78	2.00	NR	(*13*)
Location									
Ohio	61.3–61.8	NR	1.08–2.56	0.23–1.92	0.30–0.70	0.30–1.43	Trace	0.73–0.97	(*14*)
Great Britain (1959)	88.3	NR	3.77	1.35	NR	6.48	1.70	0.23	(*15*)
Pennsylvania (1961)	89.07	1.87	0.89	0.52	0.63	0.85	0.5	0.47	(*12*) (*16*)
Pennsylvania (1962)	88.70	3.17	0.92	0.67	0.61	1.06	0.39	1.18	(*17*)
Canada (1964)	90.0–96.5	NR	1.16–1.56	0.15–0.44	0.56–0.71	0.68–1.06	0.32–0.44	0.14–0.28	(*18*)

[a] NR = not reported.

TABLE IV
PARTICLE SIZE DISTRIBUTION OF EMISSIONS FROM OPEN
HEARTH FURNACES (%)

$<5\,\mu$	5–$10\,\mu$	10–$20\,\mu$	$>20\,\mu$	Reference
50%	Balance		Few	(19)
46%	22%	17%	15%	(16)
50–55	25–30	15–20	Bal	(17)

17, 19) (Table IV). Bishop (16) found that, whereas 46% of the particles in a composite sample (for one complete heat) were less than 5 μ in size, about 77% of the particles collected during the lime boil period were less than 5 μ. This was also confirmed by the appearance of the stack discharge from the control equipment, which seemed to be more visible during this period even though the collection efficiency of the venturi scrubber was as satisfactory as during other periods of the heat.

TABLE V
PARTICULATE EMISSION LOADING OF EFFLUENT GASES FROM OPEN HEARTH FURNACES
WITHOUT DUST COLLECTION EQUIPMENT

Furnace type (hot metal or cold scrap)	Furnace size (net), tons	Gas volume (cfm, STP)	Dust loading, range	Average grains/ft^3 (STP)
Cold	60	14,400	0.1 –2.0	0.69
Cold	100	NA^a	0.01–0.08	NA
Cold	NA	NA	0.04–0.18	NA
Hot	110	20,000	0.02–0.07	0.04
Hot	NA	NA	0.1 –1.4	0.43
Hot O$_2$ lanced	NA	NA	0.07–0.4	0.25^b
Hot	NA	NA	0.11–1.26	0.5^b
Hot O$_2$ lanced	205	40,000	0.1 –1.2	0.6^b
Hot	225	33,000	0.5 –2.5^c	0.43
Hot	250	18,000 to 60,000	0.1–2.0	0.5
Hot	250	NA	0.11–0.34	NA
Hot	275	33,500 to 61,800	0.10–0.31	NA
Hot O$_2$ lanced	330	37,700	0.8 –2.5	NA

^{a} NA = Data not available.

^{b} Estimated by the reviewers.

^{c} Range data are from an earlier reference than the average data; therefore, the average figure is probably more accurate.

TABLE VI

PARTICULATE EMISSION LOADING OF EFFLUENT GASES FROM OPEN HEARTH FURNACES
WITHOUT DUST COLLECTION EQUIPMENT

Furnace size (net tons)	Gas volume (cfm, STP)	Stage of heat, dust loading, grains/ft^3 (STP)					
		Charging	Melt-down	Hot metal	Ore and lime boil	Working and refining	Refer-ence
60	14,400	0.87	0.51	d	NR	0.34	(12)
NR[a]	NR	0.11	0.11	0.33	0.43[b]	0.66	(12)
NR	33,500–61,800	0.27	0.54	0.39	0.60	0.19	(12)
205	about 40,000	0.35	0.35	0.45	0.82[c]	0.87[c]	(12, 16)
NR	NR	0.17	NR	d	0.18	0.18	(12)
NR	NR	0.24	0.23	0.25	0.25	0.40	(12)
NR	NR	NR	0.22	0.95	0.66	0.22	(19)
270	52,000	0.56		0.61		0.18	(18)
						0.11	

[a] NR = not reported.   [c] Roof lances used; with high-purity oxygen.
[b] Average of 3 determinations.   [d] Only cold scrap.

Emission characteristics are usually related to various operational factors (Tables V and VI) and vary so widely that it is often difficult to determine whether or not there is a fume collection system on an open hearth stack. The most nearly correct fume loading in open hearth stack gases may be that reported by Bishop (3, 19); namely, 0.43 grains/ft^3 for an entire heat. Another useful figure is 7–12 pounds of dust and fume per ton of steel produced in open hearth furnaces (3).

The use of oxygen in open hearths does not increase the dust emission by a large amount, although it may appear to do so. When consideration is given to the increased amount of steel produced in unit time, the increase in emission rate per ton of steel produced is small. There may be some influence of the use of oxygen on the particle size distribution but, in both open hearth systems, there are inherent factors in favor of the generation of small and large particles which probably lead to the presence of agglomerates before the dust leaves the stack.

Various means of controlling emissions have been attempted: dry electrostatic precipitators, baghouses, and high-energy scrubbers. Most dry control equipment cannot tolerate temperatures greater than 500 °F; in fact, baghouses for the control of particulate matter may be damaged when gas temperatures exceed 300 °F. In some instances, the presence of moisture may be detrimental to the durability of the bag fabric.

Oxygen-lanced open hearths have had a number of fume collection methods applied. Where adequate waste heat boilers were available (or spray cooling was used alone or as a supplement to the waste heat boilers), electrostatic precipitators have been applied. One fiberglass baghouse installation has been attempted for the control of fume from a 380-ton open hearth. Such installations have been successful, but considerable maintenance and improved operational techniques may be necessary. The duct velocities must be constantly watched, and where dust begins to settle out in inaccessible areas, innovations must be developed. Where no waste heat boilers were available and were impractical to add, venturi scrubbers have been applied.

C. ELECTRIC ARC FURNACES

An electric arc steel furnace consists of a cylindrical steel shell with a dishlike bottom lined with refractory materials. For pouring finished molten steel, the furnace tilts on rocker supports which ride on tracks mounted on a concrete foundation. The roof of an electric furnace is like an inverted dish made from a large steel ring and filled with firebrick to form a dome. During construction, three large round holes are left in the roof for the carbon electrodes to be lowered into the furnace. Electric arcs between the tips of these electrodes melt the steel scrap, which is charged into the furnace. The electrodes are incandescent at their tips, gradually burn up, and are added to as necessary by means of connecting adapters.

The roofs of these furnaces are replaced periodically. Early furnaces were charged through a door in the side, and the roof remained stationary. Newer furnaces have roofs which raise and electrodes which withdraw upward, both of which then swing away from the furnace. This procedure facilitates charging the furnace from the top by means of large buckets. The charging buckets have leaflike bottoms which are pivoted by means of cables to cause the scrap charge to drop into the furnace shell. Usually, two separate charges are required to properly fill a furnace. These furnaces are ideal for use of bulky, lightweight scrap.

1. Electric Arc Furnace Emissions and Their Control

The basic construction of electric furnaces may create air pollution control problems that are difficult to solve. With the necessary electrodes atop an electric furnace and the requirement for access to the top or side of the furnace for bucket charging of scrap, design of an effective hooding and fume collection system for the emissions during the various heat stages requires considerable ingenuity. The exhaust ductwork must withstand the temperature involved and provide sufficient clearance from the electrical components to prevent unwanted arcing or grounding. The emission rate varies and is dependent upon scrap quality, the sequence of adding materials to the furnace, the meltdown rate and the refining procedure. Dust from electric furnace operations may have such characteristics as high angle of repose, high electrical resistivity, difficult wettability, and strong adhesion to bag fabrics. These characteristics may lead to extensive difficulties in the operation of the collection equipment. At one installation, it was about 15 years before changes and improvements in the original design achieved adequate fume control.

Such problems may require constant vigilance of the process to assure satisfactory operation of the dust collection system. Proper hooding is a necessity. Conditioning of hot gases (precooling) may be required. Control equipment such as scrubbers, fabric collectors, and electrostatic precipitators have been used with variable results.

The dust which occurs when steel is being processed in an electric furnace results from the exposure of molten steel to the extremely high temperatures. Electric furnace fume escapes from the furnace roof, where the electrodes penetrate the roof, as well as from the side doors. There have been several exhaust systems developed to collect the generated fume. Each system has some advantages, but also some undesirable effects. Some steels cannot tolerate infiltration of air into the furnace.

The methods of fume collection used are: (1) direct exhaust from the furnace through an elbow in the roof or a tap into the side wall of the furnace; (2) collection of the fumes as they leave the furnace shell at the electrodes and doors; (3) collection of the escaping fumes by means of a hood above the furnace; and (4) exhausting the fumes from the building to prevent escape to the outside atmosphere. Although method (1) involves handling the least air, furnace operating practice may not permit the system to be used at all times, and means for cooling the gases are necessary before the dust can be collected by most control methods. Each other method, in the order (2), (3), and (4), requires the handling of increasing volumes of air, but high temperature gases are not required to be handled in methods (3) and (4). For electric furnace emissions, venturi scrubbers and electrostatic precipitators have their separate characteristics.

The analysis of the generated fume (*20–28*) (Tables VII and VIII) will vary with the type of materials and furnace practices prevailing.

The fume concentration in grains per cubic foot of effluent gas from electric furnace operation is quite indefinite because this type of steel melting furnace is not directly attached to a stack. Concentration will be greatest for method (1) (above), least for method (4), with methods (2) and (3) intermediate. Wide variations in rate of fume generation may be attributable to the following factors: type of furnace process, furnace size, formulation of charge, quality of scrap, cleanliness of scrap, sequence of charge additions, meltdown rate, metal refining procedure, and pouring temperature.

TABLE VII

COMPOSITION OF PARTICULATE EMISSIONS FROM ELECTRIC ARC FURNACES
(in percent)

| Component | Reference | | | | | | |
	(20)	(21)	(22)	(23)	(24)	(25)	(26)
Fe_2O_3	19–44	59.33	85.6		50.55	23.95	
FeO	4–10	11.43				9.66	
Fe			4.7	25.0			
Total Fe	10–36						35.0
Si	2–9	6.05	3.9	2.0	5.76	3.76	5.5
(as SiO_2)							
Al	1–13	2.76[a]		3.0	5.85	0.47	
(as Al_2O_3)							
Ca	5–22	1.68		6.0	2.60	15.41	9.8
(as CaO)							
Mg	2–15	3.13		2.0	7.78	15.25	6.6
(as MgO)							
Mn	3–12	2.74	3.3	4.0	12.22	2.75	
(as MnO)							
Ni	0–3	NR[b]				0.62	3.2
(as NiO)							
Zn	0–44	2.96		37.0			
(as ZnO)							
Alkalies	1–11	NR				11.25	
P	<1	NR	0.4	0.5	0.64	Trace	
(as P_2O_5)							
S	<1	NR			Trace	0.64	
C	2–4	NR				1.60	
Cu	<1	1.18		0.2			
(as CuO)							

[a] Includes TiO_2.
[b] NR = not reported.

TABLE VIII

PARTICLE SIZE DISTRIBUTION OF EMISSIONS FROM
ELECTRIC ARC FURNACES (%)

Size range (μ)	Reference		
	(23)	(27)	(28)
0–3			18%
0–5	71.9%	67.9%	
3–11			64
5–10	8.3	6.8	
11–25			7
10–20	6.0	9.8	
>25			11
20–44	7.5	9.0	
>44	6.3	6.5	

Effects of furnace process or furnace size on fume generation are not obvious in the data surveyed. No significant difference in fume formation in acid and basic processes is apparent. Some (12, 38) have stated that the quantity of fume per ton of metal processed increases with furnace size, but this relationship has not been found in the data (12) surveyed by the author.

The quality of the scrap charged is of extreme importance since the inclusion of large quantities of lower boiling nonferrous metallic impurities in the melt inevitably leads to high concentrations of oxides of these metals in the fume.

Fume generation may be affected further by the sequence of charge additions to the furnace. Metal oxide fumes from the melt are normally decreased after slag additions because of the slag blanket formed. Impurities may then be included within the slag rather than vaporized to the furnace atmosphere.

The rate of fume release appears to reach a peak during the boil and refining periods. In general, the reduction of carbon content of the charge by materials other than oxygen in air may tend to reduce the rate of fume generation.

D. BASIC OXYGEN FURNACES

This process is also known as the oxygen-blown steelmaking process. Several types of vessels are in use throughout the world using this principle. Basically, it is a variation of previous pneumatic steelmaking processes that involved air. The present system employs oxygen of much greater purity (95% or better). The oxygen is blown onto or into the bath in a suitable vessel or furnace.

The importance of oxygen in converting molten iron to steel has been recognized for some time but only recently have means of producing large quantities of high-quality oxygen been available at a low enough cost. The process, as it exists today, was developed to full scale operation in the early 1950's at Linz-Donawitz, Austria from which it began to be known as the L-D process. In Europe, the process was designed to use pig iron produced from local ores high in manganese and low in phosphorus, which were not suitable for air-blown processes. At the end of 1967, there were in operation oxygen steelmaking plants throughout the world with an annual capacity of more than 110 million tons. More plants of this nature are in the planning stages.

There are three basic designs used throughout the world to make steel by this method. They are the basic oxygen process, the Stora-Kaldo process, and the rotor process.

1. *Basic Oxygen Process*

The major installations in the United States consist of large pear-shaped vessels which are lined with special brick (Fig. 4). The vessel is fixed in a holder ring which can rotate 360° to facilitate all steps of the operation. Initially, the vessel is charged with scrap steel when it is in

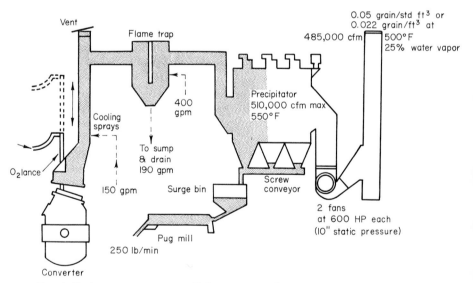

FIG. 4. Basic oxygen converter (L-D process) and associated dust collection system (typical).

an inclined position with its mouth slightly above the horizontal. Next the vessel is tilted further upward and a charge of molten pig is added. The vessel then is rotated until it is upright and, with the mouth of the vessel under the fume hood, the oxygen lance is lowered into it and the reaction begins.

The refining period consists of almost one-half hour of blowing considerable amounts of oxygen against the surface of the metal in the vessel. The reaction which converts the crude molten iron into steel generates considerable particulate emission. At the end of the blow, the lance is withdrawn and the vessel is rotated enough for a test sample to be taken from it for analysis. Depending upon the results of the analysis, refining may either be continued or concluded. The vessel is then ready for tapping into a nearby brick-lined steel pouring ladle.

The vessel is tapped through a small hole on its side to minimize the amount of slag run into the steel ladle. After molten steel is poured into the ladle, alloying materials are added to the ladle to produce the desired analysis. The slag remaining in the vessel is poured into thimbles for disposal elsewhere.

2. *The Stora-Kaldo Process*

This process, which uses a vessel similar to that used in the L-D process, is a Swedish development, but in it the vessel is not stationary in its ring (*1*). The vessel is charged with scrap, lime, and hot metals in the tilted position. After charging, the fume hood is moved in place and oxygen lancing is begun. In this process the fume collection hood is not directly over the vessel but moves in from the side to fit over the mouth of the vessel, which is inclined only slightly above the horizontal. There are two vessels in one plant in the United States, but other installations exist in England, Sweden, and France. The reaction between the oxygen and carbon is basically the same as in the basic oxygen process described above.

3. *The Rotor Process*

This process, which was developed in Germany, consists of a cylindrical vessel mounted on rollers which enable it to rotate in a horizontal plane (*1*). The vessel is longitudinal, open at both ends, and is lined with ceramic materials. The raw materials are added at the same end into which the oxygen lance is inserted. The other end is for the discharge of fume-laden gases. The vessel is tapped by means of a hole at one sector of the waste gas end. The operations within the vessel are similar to those described above.

4. Basic Oxygen Furnace Emissions and Their Control

Particulate emissions and the gases evolved from these several designs of furnaces are conducted through large ducts where, after combustion of any combustible gases, they are cooled, humidified (if necessary), and drawn through dust collection devices before being exhausted to the atmosphere through a fan and an appropriate stack.

The generated fume and dust from basic oxygen furnaces is controlled by several methods of dust collection. Electrostatic precipitators, high-energy venturi scrubbers, and baghouse systems have been applied. Most of the major installations in the United States involve the use of electrostatics and venturis. In most present control installations, the gases, particularly carbon monoxide, leaving the oxygen converter vessel are allowed to burn completely to carbon dioxide in the hood above the vessel. This creates greater volumes of gases to be handled, but eliminates subsequent explosion hazards, especially with the use of the electrostatic precipitator. In Japan, the combustion of carbon monoxide is suppressed, smaller volumes of gases are handled, the iron particles separated from the gas are in the reduced form, and the collected, clean gas is stored for use as fuel in boilers and other units. This is called the OG process.

Dust concentrations at the mouth of the converter may be greater than 20 grains/ft^3. The efficiency of collection units applied is usually greater than 95%. Humidity is an important factor in the acceptable operation of electrostatic precipitators, whereas, with scrubbers, the effect of humidity is insignificant.

The analysis of collected dust (29–31) (Tables IX and X) will vary according to operating practices. Gaw (30) indicated that BOF dust size distribution is as follows: less than 0.5 μ, 20%; 0.5–1.0 μ, 65%; and 1.0–15 μ, 15%.

TABLE IX

COMPOSITION OF PARTICULATE EMISSIONS FROM BASIC OXYGEN FURNACES
(in percent)

Total Fe	FeO	Fe$_3$O$_4$	Metallic Fe	Fe$_2$O$_3$	Si as SiO$_2$	Ca as CaO	Mg as MgO	P as P$_2$O$_5$	Mn as MnO	Cu as CuO	S	C	Reference
71.7	51.4	27.1	7.6	6.6	1.5	1.5	0.6	0.23	4.1	0.1	0.07	0.06	(29)
	1.5			90.0	1.25	0.4	NR[b]	0.3	4.1				(30)
83.1[a]					1.2	4.6	NR	NR	NR				(31)

[a] As iron dusts.

[b] NR = not reported.

TABLE X
PARTICLE SIZE DISTRIBUTION OF EMISSIONS FROM
BASIC OXYGEN FURNACES
(in percent)

Size range (μ)	OG dust	L-D dust
>40	31	19.8
30–40	12.7	13.1
20–30	29.2	39.0
15–20	10.1	7.0
10–15	11.0	9.3
5–10	4.0	10.5
<5	2.0	1.3

E. REHEATING FURNACES

Reheating is used to bring semifinished steel up to rolling temperature. Large tunnellike furnaces are used. Cold steel ingots are charged from one end, are skidded along rails in the furnace and moved through zones of increasing temperatures. After the ingot has been heated to rolling temperature, it is pushed out onto a table for transfer to the rolling area.

Reheating furnaces are quite efficient. They usually burn natural or mixed gas, and elaborate controls are used to assure satisfactory combustion. This operation is not an important source of air pollution. Particulate matter emission is essentially dependent on the particulate matter concentration of the fuel gas used for heating.

F. SCARFING

Scarfing is a method of surface preparation of semifinished steel to minimize the surface defects that develop when ingots are processed in a blooming mill to reduce them to appropriate shape and size for heating and rerolling into finished steel for shipment to fabricators. This process, which removes the seams or flaws from the billets by an oxygen-gas flame, generates an iron oxide fume which is entrained in low-temperature air. Steel quality and inspection experience determine which grades of steel are conditioned in this manner. The rate of evolution of fume is affected by the steel analysis and amount of metal removal required, and can vary widely. The volume of air handled is dependent upon the dimensions of the billets handled. High pressure water jets also are used in the scarfing machine to flush away the scale and generated slag from this conditioning operation. Considerable particulate matter is entrapped by these water sprays and it is not likely that such material becomes airborne. The considerable water used also creates a highly humid exhaust. The fume which remains is small, its size probably depends upon the steel and scarfing practice involved. Emission concentrations reported for two United States installations have been low—0.016 to 0.122 grains/ft³. Others (32) have reported brief emission concentrations of 0.4 grains/ft³. No particle size data has been published on this operation.

V. Foundry Operations

The handling and cleaning of sand and castings may result in dust escaping. Some odors may be generated by the pyrolysis of the oils and resins used in cores and molds. Dust or odorous gases of this nature are generally confined within exhaust ventilating systems and are discharged to the atmosphere through baghouses, scrubbers, or incinerators (see Chapters 41 and 48). However, the principal air pollution problem of ferrous foundries is caused by the melting of the iron or steel prior to pouring the molten metal into the molds. In grey or ductile iron foundries the melting is done in cupolas or electric melting furnaces. In steel foundries, the molten steel comes from open hearth or electric arc furnaces. These latter have already been discussed in Sections IV,B and IV,C.

A. Cupolas

The cupola (33) is the major source of molten iron for the production of castings. It is usually a simple vertical cylinder made of boiler plate, lined with firebrick to withstand the 3000 °F temperature. Close to the base are combustion air inlets (tuyeres). At the front also, near the base, is a taphole from which the metal and slag flows. Near the top, approximately 20 feet above the base, is a charging door through which the coke (fuel), limestone (flux), and cold metal are charged.

In operation, the doors at the base of the cupola are closed and inside the cupola, a layer of sand is rammed over the door openings to protect the joints from heat and molten iron. Initially, a bed of coke is placed on the sand bottom, filling the cupola to a height of 4 to 6 feet. After the bed of coke has begun to burn properly, alternate layers of coke, flux and metal are charged into the cupola until it is filled up to the charging door. Combustion air is forced in through the tuyeres causing the coke to burn and melt the iron. As the layer of coke burns and a layer of metal has melted, the alternate layers above descend, allowing room for more material to be charged through the charging door. Molten iron flows out through the taphole in a continuous or intermittent stream.

In many foundries, the air used in the cupola blast is preheated in order to produce a faster melting rate and better fuel economy. There are two types of hot-blast systems. The one which involves the use of an externally fired preheater, similar to a residential heating unit, has no effect on cupola emissions. The other, which is a recuperative type, uses a closed-top cupola and recovers some potential heat from the cupola effluent gases. With this system, the effluent gases, which contain CO, are burned in a combustion chamber raising the temperature in this zone to about 1700 °F (33). These gases are then directed through a distributing chamber which usually consists of a series of heat exchanger tubes, similar to boiler flues, then through a secondary distributing chamber. The incoming blast air is forced past the other side of the tubes, counter-current to the flow of hot combustion gases within the tubes, thus both preheating the blast air and cooling the effluent gases. Some of the heavier particles are dropped out of the gases into the heat exchanger hopper.

Cupola Emissions and Their Control

It is questionable whether sampling procedures used to date for evaluating cupola emissions give an accurate or reproducible picture of such variables as weight of solids discharged and particle size of the discharged solids.

TABLE XI

DUST AND FUME DISCHARGE FROM GRAY IRON CUPOLA

Particle size (wt. %)	Reference				
	(35)	(35)	(36)	(36)	(34)
0–5 μ	1–15	17.2	18.1	23.6	4–10
5–10 μ	1–15	8.5	6.8	4.3	2–15
10–20 μ	1–15	10.1	12.8	4.8	4–15[a]
20–44 μ	15–25	17.3	32.9	9.5	5–15[b]
>44 μ	40–65	46.9	29.3	57.9	45–85[c]

[a] Particle size range = 10–24 μ.
[b] Particle size range = 25–49 μ.
[c] Particle size range = larger than 50 μ.

As much as 24% by weight of solids emitted by three cupolas in Los Angeles County was smaller than 10 microns in particle diameter, and a maximum of 74% was coarser than 325 mesh (43 microns) (Table XI). If it is merely desired to prevent the deposition of cinders and coarse dust on the foundry roof, a cupola stack washer will trap the offending material. However, a simple washer may not collect all of the intermediate and fine solids, instead permitting a major fraction to pass through and escape into the atmosphere.

Only electrostatic precipitators, high energy scrubbers, and cloth filters are capable of removing the extremely fine particles from cupola gases. There are several installations employing completely automatic, tubular, cloth-filter-type dust collectors using synthetic filter bags in conjunction with cooling of the hot gases prior to filtration. The primary difficulty in their use arises from poor control of inlet gas temperature. When it is too high the bags burn out; when it is too low, the fabric blinds from condensation of water vapor.

Electrostatic precipitators have failed to consistently attain high collection efficiencies due to the wide variation of gas stream conditions. To satisfactorily apply electrostatic precipitation to foundry-cupola-fume collection, it is essential to determine the temperature at which the peak resistivity of the fume occurs, and to design the gas-conditioning system to provide a gas temperature well away from that at which the resistivity reaches its maximum. Because of the difficulty of accomplishing this, no new electrostatic precipitation installations have been made within the last several years.

Regardless of whether electrostatic precipitators or baghouses are used as the means of gas cleaning, it is necessary to maintain efficient secondary combustion in the cupola stacks, e.g. in a recuperative preheater of the type described in the preceeding section. Otherwise, the operation of the gas-cleaning equipment is adversely affected. Maintaining a reducing atmosphere in the cupola stack will allow unburned oil vapor and tarry matter, as well as coke fines and other combustibles, to be carried over into the gas cleaning equipment. The secondary combustion process does, however, cause the volume of the gases to be treated to increase in volume. Hence, a system requiring secondary combustion must be designed to handle greater gas volumes per unit time or capacity.

B. Electric Melting Furnaces

The particle-size range and other characteristics of electric furnace fume are quite uniform. Typical fume from an electrical steel melting furnace has a particle size range of 0.01 to 2.0 microns (Table XII).

TABLE XII
TYPICAL DATA ON FURNACE GASES[a]

Type furnace	Capacity (tons/hour)	Product	Stack gas volume SCF/lb charge	Stack loss-solids			Particle size-weight		Reference
				Grains/SCF	Lb/hour	Lb/ton charge	Micron	%	
Arc furnace	3–6	Steel castings	120–180	0.4		6–8	−0.5	95	(38)
	50–75	Steel ingots			198	12			
Arc furnace		Steel castings		1.0[b]			0.5	90	(39)
Arc furnace	3	Steel castings		0.35–0.57[b]					(40)

[a] From reference (37).
[b] At stack temperature.

The extremely fine particle size and great surface of electric furnace fume results in discharge to the atmosphere of a plume that may not meet the visibility restrictions in some air pollution codes, even when weight requirements are met. The concentration of particulate in the effluent air from an electric-furnace fume control system may have to be less than 0.05 grain per cubic foot of air if an emission is to satisfy an equivalent opacity restriction. There does not appear to be a consistent relationship between the weight concentration of the emission and its equivalent opacity. During certain periods of the melt cycle, the emission rate may increase greatly.

There have been several electrostatic precipitator installations to control pollution from larger furnaces. As in the case with cupolas, it is necessary to determine the resistivity of the furnace fume and to cool the gases to the point of minimum resistivity.

There are about 50 installations employing cloth filter collectors for the control of electric-furnace emissions. Cloth collectors generally result in an effluent nearly free from visible particulate. The principle difficulty in applying them to electric-furnace fume control is estimation of the proper exhaust volume to accomplish:

1. Adequate fume control at the furnace.
2. Sufficient cooling at the furnace to protect the exhaust system into which the hot furnace gases are drawn.
3. Optimum gas temperature at the collector to protect the filter medium used.

The level of activity within the furnace determines the volume and temperature of gases entering an electric-furnace fume-control system. This level of activity is related to the power input to the furnace and the metallurgical reactions which take place during various phases of the melt. A furnace with high melt-down rate and/or prolonged oxygen lancing needs more ventilation and cooling air than the same size furnace operated at a lower melting rate and/or without oxygen lancing. Carrying this concept further, a duplexing furnace, for example, a furnace charged with molten iron, may need less air and create lower exhaust gas temperatures than would a similar furnace melting steel scrap.

Where a single furnace, with reasonably short melting cycles, is exhausted, an intermittent type baghouse may be employed and the collected fume can be shaken from the filter bags whenever the furnace roof is swung out for charging or back charging. If several furnaces are attached to the same fume collection system, continuous automatic baghouses are needed in which one compartment at a time shuts down for bag cleaning while other compartments continue in operation. However, if the operation of furnaces is staggered, the exhaust capacity per furnace may be minimized because of the tempering effect of cooler gases from one furnace on the hotter gases from another. Continuous automatic cleaning equipment is required on duplexing furnaces where hot charging and continuous pouring serve to minimize furnace downtime.

Three principal methods for electric furnace ventilation are those described in Section IV,C,2. Comparisons have shown that roof-mounted hoods and direct shell tap ventilation require approximately the same total quantity of air, so long as the roof is air cooled by both methods. Where an overhead canopy is employed, two to three times more air must be handled.

REFERENCES

1. H. E. McGannon, ed., "The Making, Shaping and Treating of Steel," 8th ed. U.S. Steel Corp., Pittsburgh, Pennsylvania, 1964.
2. A. D. Brandt, *Iron Steel Engr.* **36,** 103–108 (1959).
3. A. H. Meadley and J. G. Colvin, *Iron Steel Inst. (London), Spec. Rept.* **61** (39), 1958.
4. P. A. Youngs, K. H. Pearson, and C. O. Beale, *Blast Furnace, Coke Oven, Raw Mater. Comm., Proc.* **20,** 299–316 (1961).
5. R. F. Jennings, *J. Iron Steel Inst.* **164,** 305–325 (1950).
6. B. S. Belyaoski, *Stal'* **21,** 938–939 (1961) (in English).
7. A. R. Orban, J. D. Hunmall, and G. G. Cocks, *J. Air Pollution Control Assoc.* **11,** No. 3, 103–113 (1961).
8. H. Kosmider, H. Neuhaus, and H. Kratzenstein, *Stahl Eisen* **74,** No. 17, 1045–1054 (1954) (English Transl.).
9. W. Dehne, *Stahl Eisen* **77,** No. 1, 553–562 (1957) (English Transl.).
10. R. Meldau and D. Laüfhutte, *Arch. Eisenhuettenw.* **27,** No. 3, 149–152 (1956) (H. Brutcher Transl. No. 3770).
11. R. F. O'Mara, *Iron Steel Engr.* **30,** 100–106 (1953).
11a. M. W. Thring and R. J. Sarjant, *Iron & Coal Trades Rev.* **174,** 731–734 (1957).
11b. F. S. Mallette, *Proc. Inst. Mech. Engrs. (London)* 168, No. 22, 595–628 (1954).
11c. R. J. Sarjant, *Iron & Steel (London)* **32,** 185–190 (1959).

12. Air Pollution Aspects of the Iron & Steel Industry, Tech. Assistance Branch, Div. Air Pollution, Dept. of Health, Education, and Welfare, U.S. Public Health Serv. (a review prepared for the U.S. House of Representatives), Taft Sanit. Eng. Center, Cincinnati, Ohio Public Health Service Publication No. 999-AP-1, 1963.

13. Y. V. Krasovitski, *Stal'* **21**, 622–626 (1961) (in English).

14. K. Guthmann, *Iron & Steel (London)* **27**, 538–541 (1954).

15. W. Strauss and M. W. Thring, *J. Iron Steel Inst. (London)* **193**, 216–221 (1959).

16. C. A. Bishop, W. W. Campbell, D. L. Hunter, and M. W. Lightner, *J. Air Pollution Control Assoc.* **11**, 83–87 (1961).

17. R. L. Schneider, *J. Air Pollution Control Assoc.* **13**, 348–354 (1963).

18. A. C. Elliott and A. J. Lafreniere, *J. Air Pollution Control Assoc.* **14**, 401–406 (1964).

19. C. A. Bishop, *Blast Furnace Steel Plant* **40**, 1448–1453 (1952).

20. W. W. Campbell and R. W. Fullerton, *J. Air Pollution Control Assoc.* **12**, 574–576 and 590 (1962).

21. M. N. Kaibicheva, *Stal'* **20**, 658–661 (1960) (in English).

22. I. H. Douglas, *Iron Steel Inst. (London), Spec. Rept.* **83**, 144–149 (1963).

23. R. S. Coulter, *Iron Age* **173**, 107–110 (1954).

24. H. W. Peterson, *Elec. Furnace Steel, Proc.* **14**, 262–271 (1956).

25. R. T. Pring, *Air Conditioning, Heating, Ventilating* **58**, 45–49 (1961).

26. G. A. Pettit, *J. Air Pollution Control Assoc.* **13**, 607–609 and 621 (1963).

27. E. O. Erickson, *Elec. Furnace Steel, Proc.* **11**, 156–160 (1953).

28. H. Dok, *J. Air Pollution Control Assoc.* **5**, 23–26 (1955).

29. M. Yukawa and K. Okaniwa, *Iron Steel Engr. Yearbook* pp. 991–997 (1962).

30. R. G. Gaw, *Iron Steel Engr.* **37**, 81–85 (1960).

31. E. R. Watkins and K. Darby, *Iron Steel Inst. (London), Spec. Rept.* **83**, 24–35 (1963).

32. S. E. Specht and R. W. Sickles, *Air Repair* **4**, 137–140 and 170 (1954).

33. APCA Information Reports, *J. Air Pollution Control Assoc.* **11**, 4 (1961).

34. "Foundry Air Pollution Problems," *Foundry* **95** (3), pp. 136–142 (1967).

35. A. J. Grindle, "Cupola Emission Problem & Its Solution," Paper presented at semi-annual meeting, East-Central Section of APCA, Harrisburg, Pa. 1953.

36. H. R. Crabaugh, A. H. Rose, Jr., and R. L. Chass, *J. Air Pollution Control Assoc.* **4**, 3 (1954).

37. "Foundry Air Pollution Control Manual," American Foundrymen's Society. Second Edition, 1967.

38. G. L. Allen, F. H. Viets, and L. C. McCabe, Bureau of Mines Information Circular 7627, U.S. Govt. Printing Office, 1952.

39. J. M. Kane, American Society of Mechanical Engineers. Pittsburgh Regional Conference, April 24, 1950.

40. V. E. Zang, American Institute of Mining and Metallurgical Engineers, Electric Furnace Steel Conference, Pittsburgh, 1952.

37 Nonferrous Metallurgical Operations

Kenneth W. Nelson

I. Introduction

Nonferrous metals production has been important in the development of the science, if we may call it that, of air pollution. Smelting processes attain high temperatures. Dusts, fumes, and gases are generated in the normal course of winning a virgin metal from its ores or concentrates.

Most of the copper, lead, and zinc in the earth's crust occurs as sulfide minerals. The constituent sulfur is oxidized at one or more smelting steps and is evolved as sulfur dioxide. In the early days SO_2 was vented with combustion gases into flues and from stacks high enough only to provide adequate draft for furnaces. To prevent operations from creating a smoke nuisance, smelters were established in isolated areas. As the scale of operations increased, however, and as lands near smelters were inhabited and cultivated by farmers, smelter smoke created problems.

In 1905, Haywood of the U.S. Department of Agriculture examined plants grown near smelters and showed that foliage injured by effluent gases had a higher sulfate content than noninjured samples (1). In 1915 the Selby Smelter Commission reported the results of its study of the effects of smoke from the Selby smelter located on the northeast shore of San Francisco Bay (2). The study group measured the effects of different concentrations of SO_2 on vegetation and clearly demonstrated that some growing plants are more sensitive to the gas than is man. The Commission's report is a classic in air pollution literature.

In 1914 the American Smelting and Refining Co. established a department of agricultural investigations for systematic research into the effects of smelter effluents and means of their control. Much of the first work on differences in sensitivity of various species of plants was done by that department. In 1928 one of the members, M. D. Thomas, invented an automatic instrument for detecting, measuring, and recording low concentrations of SO_2. The Thomas Autometer is now widely used for monitoring. The earlier scientific contributions of O'Gara (3) and of Thomas' contemporaries and colleagues have also been noteworthy (4–6).

Injury to crops and trees by SO_2 from smelters has been the basis for much protracted and costly litigation. Court-ordered shutdowns of California smelters prompted the establishment of the Selby Smelter Commission. Since then there have been numerous lawsuits by farmers and, in one instance, the United States was the complainant. It was claimed that smoke from the Consolidated Mining and Smelting Co. at Trail, British Columbia, was crossing the U.S.–Canadian border and causing damage to forests. The International Joint Commission began hearings on the matter in 1928. Not until 1941 did the Trail Smelter Arbitral Tribunal come to a final decision and set up a regime under which the smelter was required to operate.

Some smelter owners have felt that a few farmers asked for damages allegedly caused by smoke when crop losses were actually caused by poor farming practices or unfavorable weather. Habitual claimants were referred to as "smoke farmers" and their actions forced smelting companies to keep detailed records of SO_2 concentrations in potentially affected farm areas and to inspect crop conditions regularly through the growing season.* A typical program designed to protect the interests of the farmers as well as those of the company has been described by Davis (7).

While SO_2 from the smelting of copper, lead, and zinc has been the principal pollutant of interest in nonferrous metallurgy, gaseous and particulate fluorides from aluminum smelting also have been of concern. A significant difference between the two types of pollution is that the fluoride problems first came to attention because of adverse effects on grazing animals rather than effects on vegetation. Agate (8) reported that fluorosis was common among cattle and sheep grazing downwind from an aluminum plant operated near Fort William, Scotland.

II. Copper

A. MINING, MILLING, AND CONCENTRATING

Both open-pit and underground mining are practiced (see also Chapter 35). Open-pit operations are conducted successfully with ores containing less than 1% Cu. Costs of operating underground mines are higher, and such mines usually must have a somewhat better grade of ore. The greater proportion of copper ore from U.S. mines is taken from the low-grade, open-pit type.

Copper ores are handled in tremendous quantities. Mills processing 500 tons or more per hour are not unusual. Enormous jaw, gyratory, and cone crushers are used to reduce large boulders to pebble-sized pieces.

---

* An amusing bit of doggerel printed in a Tacoma newspaper 40 years ago tells the story (by "W. C. H." from the files of the late Paul H. Ray, Salt Lake City, Utah):

The Joke Is on the Smelter

If the horses have the glanders,
    If the turkeys have the roup,
If the deadly hawk is flying
    Into his chicken coop.

The farmer has his inning,
    The matter is no joke
For he traces down his losses
    Direct to smelter smoke.

The frost may blight the melons,
    The crows may get his corn,
And the pigs may have the cholera,
    His cow a crumpled horn.

The farmer grabs his pencil
    He charges all to smoke,
He swiftly sends his little (?) bill,
    And thinks it is a joke.

The water in the stream dries up,
    The south wind blasts his fields,
His daughter has the whooping cough,
    His wheat it fails to yield.

But the farmer's never troubled,
    He banks his wealth in town,
He never feels the want of cash,
    Till the smelter closes down.

Separation of the traces of copper-bearing minerals from the mass of waste is essential to economic recovery of the metal. Crushed ore is ground wet in ball or rod mills to produce a thin slurry. The slurry plus a variety of flotation reagents is piped to flotation cells where air is beaten into the mixture. A copper-rich froth is formed and skimmed off. Solids in the froth are dewatered by settling and filtration and are shipped to a smelter. The concentrate contains 20–30% Cu.

B. Smelting

Copper sulfide concentrates received at the smelter are normally roasted in multiple hearth roasters to remove moisture, to burn off part of the contained sulfur, and to preheat the material before smelting (Fig. 1). In recent years the roasting step has been eliminated at many smelters.

Roaster calcines or wet concentrates are charged into large reverberatory furnaces where copper in the form of oxides, sulfides, and sulfate is converted to cuprous sulfide. Some iron, calcium, magnesium, and aluminum—all as silicates—are removed in the form of a viscous slag.

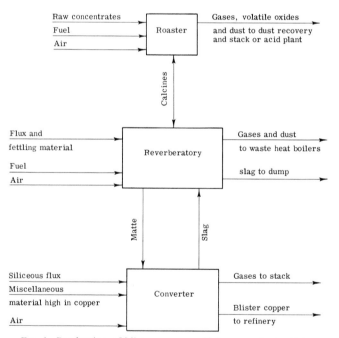

Fig. 1. Production of blister copper sulfide concentrates (8a).

Copper matte, a mixture of cuprous and ferrous sulfides, is tapped off into large ladles and transferred to converters. Siliceous fluxes are added to the matte in the converter and air is blown into the hot, molten mass through tuyeres. Iron and other impurities form a silicate slag on top of the denser cuprous sulfide. The slag is poured off at intervals and charged back to the reverbs. Further blowing of the converter oxidizes the sulfur—leaving free copper according to the equation:

$$Cu_2S + O_2 \rightarrow 2\ Cu + SO_2$$

Copper is then poured off and transferred to a holding furnace for deoxidizing and casting as slabs of blister copper—about 98.5% pure; or as shaped anodes for shipment to a refinery.

C. Refining

A small percentage of domestic copper leaves the smelter refined enough by special furnace treatment to be used directly in certain applications. The bulk of the copper is intended for electrical uses, however, and must be highly purified. Mere traces of certain impurities greatly reduce copper's electrical conductivity.

Anodes of blister copper—so named because of its rough surface—are arranged alternately, face to face with thin sheets of pure copper in large tanks. The sheets are the cathodes of the multiple electrolytic cells to be formed in each tank. The tanks are nearly filled with a dilute solution of copper sulfate and sulfuric acid. A low voltage current passes between anodes and cathodes, causing solution of copper from the anodes and deposition on the cathodes. Trace metals present in the impure anode either dissolve in the circulating electrolyte or settle to the bottoms of the tanks as a black sludge called anode mud or slimes. The slimes may contain selenium, tellurium, gold, silver, platinum, and palladium. All these elements may be associated with copper in its ores.

D. Emissions and Controls

Dust is a problem in underground mines in spite of wet collaring and drilling. Free silica in country rock may be appreciable and pose a health risk. Ventilation must be provided to keep dust concentrations down to safe levels. In most instances power ventilation is also necessary to remove nitrogen oxides and carbon monoxide from blasting and to control heat and humidity.

Although dust and blasting gases are eventually discharged from the mine, there is no significant contribution to community air pollution. The concentrations of dust particles are low—of the order of 5 millions of particles per cubic foot of air. Blasting gases are absent except during the short period of blasting and then are highly diluted by the large volume of ventilating air constantly being moved through the mine.

Open-pit mining may create localized dustiness near operating drills, power shovels, and other equipment. But it is standard practice to use water while drilling and to wet down ore and waste piles, when necessary, before loading the material into trucks or railway cars for transport from the mine. Roadways are sprinkled to reduce dusting.

Blasting, properly done, disperses surprisingly little dust in open-pit mining. Nitrogen dioxide may be produced from explosions of ammonium nitrate—fuel oil (ANFO) or other ammonium nitrate combinations. When the air in the pit is cool in relation to air at the brim of the pit, as on a summer morning, blasting may create a visible cloud of $NO_2-N_2O_4$. Viewed from a distance of several hundred feet, the cloud looks formidable. But tests have shown the nitrogen oxide concentration to be less than 30 ppm. The gases dissipate in minutes.

Ore-crushing generates considerable dust. Water is used to wet the ores but it must be applied judiciously to avoid difficulties such as overwetting, build-ups of mud on conveyor belts and pulleys, and clogging of chutes. Furthermore, as ore passes through successive crushing stages new, dry surfaces are exposed and dust is readily abraded from them. Wetting, therefore, must usually be supplemented by appropriate exhaust ventilation for good dust control. Because dust burdens in ventilating air may be heavy, effluents may be neighborhood nuisances unless effective collectors are incorporated in the exhaust systems.

The flotation process itself creates no dust problems but waste material, or tailings, issuing as a sandy slurry from the flotation plant may do so. The slurry is channeled into ponds from which water, free of settleable solids, may be recovered. As the solids accumulate, a tailings dump covering many acres is formed. Surface drying of the dump and high winds may result in localized dust storms. Keeping the dump wet is an effective means of control. Planting and cultivation of ground cover and shrubs to act as windbreaks are also successful.

The high temperatures attained in roasting, smelting, and converting cause volatilization of a number of the trace elements which may be present in copper ores and concentrates. The raw waste gases from these processes contain not only these fumes but also dust and SO_2 (Table I). Roasting drives off a portion of any arsenic, antimony, and lead as the oxides. More of those elements plus bismuth and some selenium and tellurium may be eliminated as fume in the reverberatory furnace. They also to some extent become incorporated into furnace slag.

The stronger oxidizing conditions of converting effect almost com-

TABLE I

EMISSIONS FROM COPPER ROASTERS, REVERBERATORY FURNACES,
AND CONVERTERS[a]

	Waste gas (m³)	Raw gas	
		Dust content (gm/m³)	SO₂ content (%)
Roasters	1300[b]	15	2–8
Reverberatory furnaces	2000[b]	4	—
Converters	10,000[c]	12	to 8

[a] Clean Air Guide 2101, Kommission Reinhaltung der Luft, Verein Deutscher Ingenieure, VDI—Verlag GmbH, Dusseldorf, West Germany. January, 1960.

[b] Per ton of concentrates.

[c] Including extraneous air per ton of charge.

plete removal of the remaining volatile elements except selenium and tellurium. Nickel, cobalt, and the precious metals are also not volatilized significantly and remain dissolved in the crude copper.

The value of the volatilized elements, as well as air pollution considerations, dictates efficient collection of fumes and dusts from process off-gases. Balloon flues in which gases move at low velocities serve as gravity collectors of the larger particles and provide low resistance ducting for the large volumes of combustion gases and ventilating air that must be moved. Cyclones may be used also. For collection of the finer particulates, electrostatic precipitators are most often used. Collection efficiencies up to 99.7% for copper dust and fume are attained by careful conditioning of flue gases.

Cleaned hot flue gases are vented to the atmosphere via tall stacks for maximum dispersion and dilution of contained sulfur dioxide. A major proportion of the gas may be used to produce sulfuric acid. Not all of it is used for this purpose because the SO_2 concentration in gases available from some sources within the smelter may be too low for efficient catalytic oxidation to SO_3 by presently available commercial processes. To make sulfuric acid, SO_2 concentration in the gas should be 4–8%.

Utilization of SO_2 reduces the potential air pollution problem associated with copper smelting; hence acid production would seem to be an obvious and simple solution. The facts are that acid plants require heavy capital investment and substantial operating costs, which, for profitable operation of the recovery plant, must be returned by sale of the product.

There may not be a local market for acid. Distances to demand areas and consequent shipping charges may be prohibitive for smelter acid to compete with plants using Frasch sulfur as a source of SO_2. Each copper smelter is unique in some ways, and the addition of an acid plant may or may not be economical.

The idea of recovering sulfur dioxide from smelter gases is an attractive one, and a large number of processes have been described in the technical and patent literature. An excellent summary of them is given in a report by the Ontario Research Foundation (9). So far as major copper smelters are concerned, however, none of the processes, other than direct conversion to sulfuric acid, has yet proved practicable. Tall stacks, up to 828 feet, as at El Paso, Texas, are depended upon for dispersion and dilution of SO_2 to keep ground level concentrations to a minimum. The effectiveness of high smelter stacks was shown by Hill *et al.* in 1944 (10) and has been emphasized recently by Smith (11).

Monitoring stations at selected points around a smelter are helpful in carrying out a "Sea Captain" method of controlling SO_2 emissions. This technique makes use of measurements of meteorological conditions and an expert evaluation of them. If conditions are unfavorable for adequate dispersion of gas, or are predicted to be unfavorable, SO_2-emitting operations are curtailed. Forecasting is not perfect, however, and the detection of significant SO_2 at ground level by an automatic instrument may be the first indication that dispersion and dilution are not adequate. Telemetering of detector information to the smelter control center permits immediate curtailment action to be taken. If there are multiple sources of SO_2 in a given area in the same direction from a detecting station, smelter control by monitoring is hampered.

Electrolytic copper refining operations, by their nature, do not create significant air pollution. In tank houses traces of electrolyte mist are generated by splashing of liquid as it is circulated by gravity and pumps among the tanks. Repeated tests by the author have shown acid mists to be within the ACGIH* limit of 1.0 mg H_2SO_4 per cubic meter of air.

In one part of the copper refining process called electrolyte purification there is the possibility of arsine evolution. The copper content of electrolyte becomes very low during purification, and hydrogen is produced at the cathode. If traces of arsenic are carried in the solution, arsine, AsH_3, will be evolved in sufficient amounts to be dangerous to men working in the vicinity. Hence, exhaust ventilation of purification tanks is essential. Purification tanks are few in number compared to the total number of tanks in a refinery and so are easily isolated and ventilated.

* American Conference of Governmental Industrial Hygienists.

Treatment of slimes for recovery of silver, gold, selenium, tellurium, and traces of other elements usually entails fusion and oxidation in a furnace of appropriate size. Some selenium is volatilized during the process and is captured as the furnace gases pass successively through a wet scrubber and an electrostatic precipitator. The latter removes mists which escape the scrubber.

III. Lead

A. Mining, Milling, and Concentrating

Most lead ores are mined underground. Crushing, grinding, and concentrating follow the same general pattern as the processing of copper ores. Lead ores, however, are richer. The run of the mill contains between 6 and 10% Pb. The lead mineral of greatest importance is galena, PbS. Traces of silver and other metals usually are present in lead ores and they accompany the lead in the ore concentrate. (See also Chapter 35.)

B. Smelting

The sulfur content of lead concentrates is reduced by sintering them on Dwight-Lloyd sintering machines (Fig. 2). Moistened concentrate–flux mix is fed to an endless belt of cast iron grate sections. The charge is ignited, burns under forced draft, and is finally discharged from the machine as grates flip over at the head pulley of the belt. The charge is now a loosely fused mass of material called sinter. It may be crushed, mixed with other materials such as flue dusts, and sintered a second time, or it may be fed directly to the blast furnaces. In addition to eliminating most of the sulfur from PbS concentrates, the sintering procedure prevents dust losses which would occur if concentrates were smelted directly. Also, it creates a more porous raw material to facilitate smelting.

A mixture of sinter, iron, and coke is charged into blast furnaces. Contact with free carbon and carbon monoxide at high temperatures reduces lead compounds to metallic lead. A mixture of molten lead and siliceous slag accumulates in the hearth of the furnace and is tapped off, either continuously or intermittently. Gravity separation of the lead from the slag takes place in heavily insulated settlers. Slag is allowed to overflow from the top into slag pots for transport to the dump or to a fuming furnace for zinc recovery.

As it is tapped periodically from the settlers, the crude lead is at red heat and contains considerable amounts of dissolved impurities which become insoluble as the metal cools. Hence the hot lead is transferred

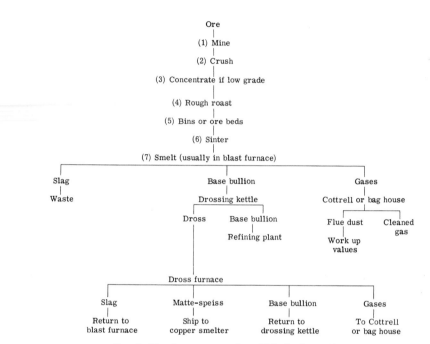

FIG. 2. Usual treatment of a sulfide lead ore (*8a*).

to holding kettles for cooling and subsequent skimming of impurities from the surface. At this stage the metal is about 95 to 99% pure and is further refined on the premises or cast into blocks for shipment to a refinery.

C. REFINING

Lead bullion is purified by a number of different processes. The Parkes process consists, in broad outline, of heating under oxidizing conditions in a reverberatory furnace for removal of arsenic, antimony, and tin (softening), dissolving zinc in softened lead in kettles, cooling, and skimming of a silver-rich zinc crust (desilverizing), and removing dissolved zinc by vacuum distillation (dezincing). If bismuth is present, it is removed by treatment with calcium and magnesium (debismuthizing).

The Harris process employs treatment with molten sodium hydroxide and sodium nitrate as a substitute for furnace softening. Arsenic, antimony, and tin, if present, are separated as sodium salts.

The Betts process is electrolytic and produces pure lead cathodes plus a slime containing impurities derived from the crude lead bullion.

An important part of lead refining is the recovery of silver and gold. Zinc crust collects both metals. The crust, containing a considerable percentage of entrained lead, is heated in graphite or clay retorts to distill off the zinc. The residual bullion is transferred to cupel furnaces for separation of lead. This is done by means of an air blast directed on the molten bullion. The litharge (PbO) produced is molten and is carefully decanted as it accumulates on the surface. Doré metal (Ag-Au) is the final product of cupellation and is tapped off for further treatment.

D. Emissions and Controls

Dust problems in the mining, milling, and concentrating of lead are the same as those outlined for copper.

Hot gases from the lead concentrate sintering process carry dust and the oxide fume of volatile metals such as antimony and zinc (Table II). Also, some lead is volatilized and oxidized. Dust and fume are recovered from the gas stream by settling in large flues and by precipitation in Cottrell treaters or filtration in large baghouses.

Collection efficiencies are up to 96% for precipitators and 99.5% for baghouses.

Sulfur dioxide derived from sintering is not concentrated enough to be used directly by presently available commercial processes for sulfuric acid production. It is possible, however, by recirculation of gases or updraft sintering to build up to the SO_2 concentration sufficiently to permit economic production of H_2SO_4 or liquid sulfur dioxide from

TABLE II

EMISSIONS FROM LEAD SINTERING, BLAST FURNACES, AND REVERBERATORY FURNACES[a]

		Raw gas	
	Waste gas (m^3)	Dust content (gm/m^3)	SO_2 content $(\%)$
Sintering	3000[b]	2–15	1.5–5
Blast furnaces	15,000–50,000[c]	5–15	—
Reverberatory furnaces	100–500[d]	3–20	—

[a] Clean Air Guide 2285, Kommission Reinhaltung der Luft, Verein Deutscher Ingenieure, VDI—Verlag GmbH, Dusseldorf, West Germany, September, 1961.

[b] Per ton of sinter.

[c] Per ton of coke.

[d] Per ton of charge.

a portion of the gases. A practicable process for liquid SO_2 production at a lead smelter has been described by Fleming and Fitt (12).

Because the sulfur proportion in galena, PbS, is only 13.4%, the total amount of by-product SO_2 theoretically available from lead smelting is considerably less than from copper or zinc smelting for equivalent rates of metal production. A 5000-ton per month lead plant thus would have in theory only 670 tons of sulfur available for about 2000 tons of H_2SO_4 per month. Acid plants would therefore be relatively small and perhaps uneconomic in a particular set of circumstances. Low SO_2 potential, on the other hand, diminishes the dispersion problem and the necessity for SO_2 recovery.

Lead blast furnace gases, after cooling, are amenable to treatment in large baghouses having several chambers, each of which will contain hundreds of bags. A common size of bag used is 18 inches by 30 feet. Wool has been traditionally used for the bags, and the service lives in many cases have been remarkable; continuous service for 20 years has been recorded. Synthetic materials, including glass fibers, are competing successfully with wool because of superior resistance to high temperatures.

Lead refineries have baghouses for recovery of fume from softening furnaces and cupeling furnaces. Zinc oxide fume released during distillation of zinc from zinc-silver skims may be captured by a local exhaust ventilation system and passed into the flue serving cupel furnaces.

IV.   Zinc

A. MINING, MILLING, AND CONCENTRATING

The processes used for zinc are essentially the same as for copper and lead (see also Chapter 35). The bulk of zinc ore contains zinc as sphalerite, ZnS, which is separated as a concentrate from accompanying minerals by selective flotation. Concentrates contain about 60% Zn.

In recent years, an important source of raw material for zinc metal has been zinc oxide from fuming furnaces. Zinc as an impurity in lead smelting is recovered from lead blast furnace slag by heating the slag to high temperatures and blowing pulverized coal and air through it. Zinc is reduced, volatilized, reoxidized and is collected as ZnO in bag filter units. The baghouse product is passed through a rotary kiln to reduce the lead content by volatilization and to increase the density of the material for easier handling and shipping.

B. ROASTING AND RETORTING

For efficient recovery of zinc, sulfur must be removed from concentrates to less than 2%. This is done by roasting. Multiple hearth or Ropp roasting may be followed by sintering; or double-pass sintering may be used alone (Fig. 3).

The liberation of zinc from roasted concentrates involves simple heating of a mixture of roast and coke breeze to about 1100 °C. Simultaneous reduction of zinc from the oxide to the metal and distillation of the metal take place. Zinc vapor passes from the heated vessel into a condenser where it condenses to a liquid which is drained off at intervals into molds.

Reduction and distillation of zinc may be done as a batch process in banks of cylindrical retorts—the Belgian retort process—or in continuously operating vertical retorts. Gas is the preferred fuel, hence most smelters are located in natural gas fields. Electric distillation furnaces are used to a small extent.

A spectroscopically pure zinc is produced by a continuous fractional distillation process developed by the New Jersey Zinc Co.

A process for simultaneous smelting of roasted lead and zinc concentrates has been developed within the past decade by the Imperial Smelting Corp. The process makes use of carbon monoxide generated from coke to reduce lead and zinc oxides in a sealed shaft furnace. Lead bullion accumulates in the furnace bottom and acts as a collector for copper, silver, and gold. Zinc passes as a vapor out the top of the furnace into condensers in which a shower of molten lead is continuously main-

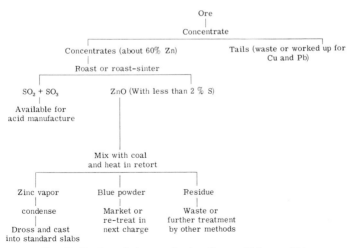

FIG. 3. Outline of zinc production from sulfide ore (8a).

tained. Zinc vapor is condensed quickly to a liquid which dissolves in the molten lead. Outside the condenser the lead-zinc solution is cooled and a 98% pure zinc floats to the surface and overflows into containers. The cooled lead is pumped back to the condensers (*13*).

C. Leaching and Electrolysis

Zinc of high purity may be produced from roasted concentrates from densified zinc oxide from fuming furnaces, or from impure metallic zinc, by solution in sulfuric acid, removal of impurities from the solution by appropriate chemical treatment, and finally electrolysis of the purified electrolyte.

Electrolysis is done in tanks containing alternating anodes of lead and cathodes of aluminum. Pure zinc is deposited on the cathodes and later stripped from them by hand. The zinc is then melted in a small reverberatory furnace and cast into slabs or other forms for shipment.

D. Emissions and Controls

Dust, fume, and SO_2 are evolved from zinc concentrate roasting or sintering (Table III). Particulates are caught in conventional baghouses or Cottrells. Sulfur dioxide attains concentrations of 6–7% in roaster gases and may be converted directly into sulfuric acid or vented from tall stacks. An interesting and very successful process for recovery of zinc roaster SO_2 as well as of the more dilute SO_2 from lead roasting has been developed at Trail, British Columbia, by the Consolidated Mining and Smelting Co. Inexpensive hydroelectric power for ammonia synthesis permits the absorption of SO_2 from the gas streams and the

TABLE III

Emissions from Zinc Sintering and Horizontal Retorts[a]

		Raw gas		
	Waste gas (m³)	Dust content (gm/m³)	% Particles < 10 μ	SO₂ content (%)
Sintering	4000[b]	10	100	4.5–7
Horizontal retorts	12,000–18,000[c] 96,000–144,000[d]	0.1–0.3	100	

[a] Clean Air Guide 2284, Kommission Reinhaltung der Luft, Verein Deutscher Ingenieure, VDI—Verlag GmbH, Dusseldorf, West Germany. September, 1961.
[b] Per ton of ZnS.
[c] Waste flue gas per ton of Zn.
[d] Condenser waste gas (including extraneous air) per ton of Zn.

eventual production and marketing of ammonium sulfate as a fertilizer. Steps in the process are outlined in Fig. 4.

In zinc distillation by the retort process small holes are left in vapor condensers to vent gases from charged retorts as they are heated. When the temperature becomes high enough for zinc vapor to distill over, some vapor escapes from the hole and ignites spontaneously. The total

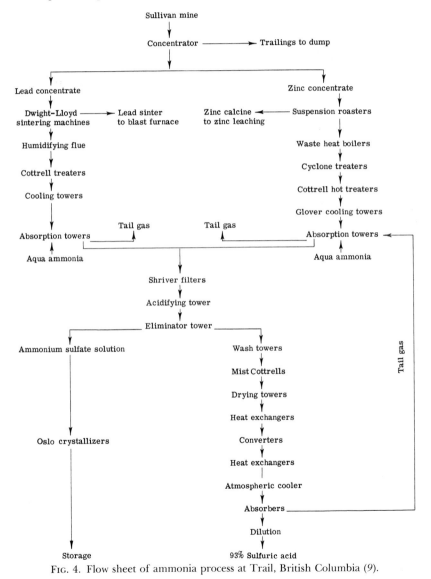

FIG. 4. Flow sheet of ammonia process at Trail, British Columbia (9).

zinc oxide fume so produced is appreciable. It is carried by convection currents up the fronts of the condenser banks and out to atmosphere with combustion gases through ridge ventilators of the furnace buildings. A distinctive characteristic of the zinc retort plant is a flag of white ZnO fume. The actual fume concentrations are low and the cost of its collection would not be compensated for by the value of the recovered material.

Leaching and electrolysis do not emit significant amounts of particulates or gases. Tanks in which leaching and electrolyte purification are done are covered and ventilated to prevent worker exposure to possible toxic gases or mists. The electrolytic process itself does disperse some electrolyte mist because of gas evolution, but this is a problem only within the confines of the tank houses.

V. Aluminum

A. Mining and Ore Treatment

Bauxite is the base ore for aluminum production. It is a hydrated oxide of aluminum associated with silicon, titanium, and iron, and contains 30–70% Al_2O_3.

Most bauxite ore is purified by the Bayer process. The ore is dried, ground in ball mills, mixed with sodium hydroxide solution, and autoclaved for several hours to dissolve the Al_2O_3 as sodium aluminate, $NaAlO_2$. By settling, dilution, and filtration, iron oxide, silica, and other insoluble impurities are removed. Aluminum hydroxide is precipitated from the diluted, cooled solution—the reaction being initiated or "seeded" by introduction of a small amount of freshly precipitated $Al(OH)_3$. The precipitate is filtered, washed, and calcined to produce pure alumina, Al_2O_3. (See also Chapter 35.)

B. Electrolysis

Commercial recovery of aluminum from the oxide is accomplished by a unique electrolytic process discovered simultaneously in 1886 by Hall of this country and Heroult of France. Alumina is dissolved in a fused mixture of fluoride salts and dissociated electrically into metallic aluminum and oxygen. Fused natural or synthetic cryolite ($3NaF \cdot AlF_3$) with about 10% fluorspar and 5% dissolved alumina is contained in carbon-lined cells or pots. Heavy carbon anodes are immersed in the mixture to within about 2 inches of the cathode, a heel of molten aluminum covering the carbon lining. A heavy electric current between anode and cathode reduces Al_2O_3 to Al which accumulates and is drawn off at intervals into crucibles. Alumina is steadily fed onto the top of the molten electrolyte to replace that which has been decomposed. Crucible aluminum is skimmed of dross, has alloying metals added to it, and is charged into holding furnaces before being cast out as salable ingot.

C. EMISSIONS AND CONTROLS

Calcining of aluminum hydroxide for the production of alumina entails mechanical dust dispersion (Table IV). The valuable dust is recovered from kiln effluents by electrostatic precipitation preceded by cyclone-type collectors.

Oxygen liberated in electrolytic cells attacks carbon anodes, producing CO_2 and mechanically dispersing some carbon dust. Thermal and chemical action in the cells also evolves some alumina dust, and both particulate and gaseous fluorides. The various effluents are collected by ventilation hoods over the cells.

Aluminum plants using carbon anodes which have been baked before mounting in cells may have dry dust collectors to remove particulates from collected effluents, scrubbers for removal of gaseous fluorides, and stacks for final dispersion of scrubbed gases. Plants employing the Soderberg method of forming and baking carbon electrodes in place on the cells may omit dry collection and scrub all effluents directly. Tarry hydrocarbons from the baking carbon electrode mixture interfere with the operation of dry collectors.

Spillage of fluoride-containing waste gases from aluminum pot lines

TABLE IV

EMISSIONS FROM CALCINING ALUMINUM HYDROXIDE AND FROM CLOSED ELECTROLYTIC CELLS USING SODERBERG ELECTRODES[a]

		Raw gas	
	Waste gas (m^3)	Dust content (gm/m^3)	Fluorine content (gm/m^3)
Calcining aluminum hydroxide	3000[b]	300–400	—
Closed electrolytic cells using Soderberg electrodes	2000–3000[c]	0.08–0.12	0.040

[a] Clean Air Guide 2286, Kommission Reinhaltung der Luft, Verein Deutscher Ingenieure, VDI—Verlag GmbH, Dusseldorf, West Germany. September, 1961.

[b] Per ton of Al_2O_3.

[c] Including extraneous air. Waste gas per cell in cubic meters per hour.

into the pot room and then out roof monitors has released sufficient fluorides at some plants to require the installation of scrubbers to wash the air leaving the roof monitors.

Aluminum chloride or chlorine gas is used to treat aluminum in holding furnaces, to flux and to degas the molten metal. Aluminum chloride is volatile, subliming at 180 °C. It reacts with hot moist air to form a highly visible "smoke" cloud. Electrostatic precipitation, scrubbing, and condensation of the volatilized salt are effective means of control.

VI.   Secondary Copper, Lead, Zinc, and Aluminum

A. SOURCES

Scrap provides an important source of metals for the market. Copper in substantial tonnage is recovered from electrical cable and automobile radiators. About 85% of the lead used in automobile batteries is collected by scrap dealers and eventually sold to secondary lead smelters. Zinc comes from galvanizing baths and die-cast scrap. Aluminum is recovered mostly from industry-generated scrap, but aircraft assemblies and even pots and pans may be used. Economics governs the flow of material in and out of the secondary plant.

B. RECOVERY PROCESSES

Scrap may be converted directly to usable metal by simple melting and casting into salable ingots. More often, scrap of similar composition is melted together and its composition is adjusted by removal or addition of some constituent elements. When the right proportions of each are present, the charge is cast out. Brass, type metal, babbitts, and solders are produced in this way.

Insulation is stripped or burned from electrical cable and the copper wire is melted and cast into anodes for direct conversion by electrolysis into refined copper.

Lead battery plates are charged into reverberatory furnaces with coke and fluxes for smelting. The product is an antimonial lead bullion which will be refined to pure lead or adjusted in composition for sale as an alloy.

Zinc scrap is commonly refined by distillation from retorts, the vapor being condensed to a liquid and cast into slabs, or condensed directly from the vapor state to a powder of controlled particle size.

Aluminum alloys are melted in reverberatory furnaces and adjusted in composition by drossing, chlorination, and addition of alloying metals.

C. Emissions and Controls

Emissions from secondary metal processes are similar to those from primary metallurgical operations except that little or no sulfur dioxide is evolved, and, in general, smaller quantities of metal oxide dusts and fumes are produced. There are no sulfides in secondary metal furnace charges as there are in primary smelting furnaces, and only small amounts of sulfur are used to kettle-refine lead-base alloys.

Lead oxide is volatilized from secondary lead smelting. Zinc oxide fume is a by-product of zinc-alloy distillation and of brass furnace operation. Baghouses, more commonly, and electrostatic precipitators are successfully used for collection.

Chlorination of molten aluminum in secondary refining furnaces produces aluminum chloride fume which creates a high-opacity white cloud when it comes in contact with moist air. Properly designed scrubbers or condensers are effective control devices. One successful installation has been described by Donoso (14).

VII.   Nonferrous Foundries

A. Alloys and Operations

Brass, bronze, and zinc die-casting metal are the principal alloys used. Brasses contain 60–65% copper; the other major constituent is zinc. Lead or tin or both may be present.

Bronzes usually contain 85–90% copper with small amounts of aluminum, zinc, tin, manganese, silicon, and phosphorus—singly or in combination. Alloy names are misleading. Manganese bronze, for example, may contain only 0.25% Mn.

Zinc die-casting metal is about 95% high-grade zinc, 4% aluminum, plus traces of other metals.

Copper base alloys are melted in rotary, reverberatory induction furnaces or in small crucibles and are poured at bright red heat into molds. After the castings have solidified they are shaken from molds, and finished.

Zinc die-cast alloy is melted in kettles and poured or injected at a temperature of 775°–825 °F into permanent dies.

B. Emissions and Controls

Metal fume will be evolved during the melting and casting of alloys if the temperatures are high enough for volatile constituent elements to have appreciable vapor pressure, and if no intermetallic compounds are formed. For example, zinc is fairly volatile and will be vaporized from molten brass and oxidized, producing visible white ZnO fume. The higher the temperature and the greater percentage of zinc in the alloy, the more copious the fume. Copper in the brass, on the other hand, will not be volatilized significantly because its vapor pressure is very low at the melting point of brass.

Zinc die-casting alloy is used with no metal fume evolution.

Shakeout of castings from sand molds is a dusty operation and may be conducted under hoods or over downdraft gratings. Dust loadings in ventilating air range from 0.25 to 1.0 grain per cubic foot. Collection of up to 97% of such material is effected with wet or dry centrifugal collectors, up to 99+% with dry fabric type collectors (15).

REFERENCES

1. J. K. Haywood, *U.S. Dept. Agr., Bur. Chem. Bull.* **89** (1905); *U.S., Bur. Mines, Bull.* **537** (1954) (abstr. No. 1231).
2. J. A. Holmes, E. C. Franklin, and R. A. Gould, *U.S., Bur. Mines, Bull.* **98** (1915).
3. P. J. O'Gara, *Met. Chem. Eng.* **17,** No. 12 (1917).
4. G. R. Hill and M. D. Thomas, *Plant Physiol.* **8,** 223 (1933).
5. M. D. Thomas, J. O. Ivie, J. N. Abersold, and R. H. Hendricks, *Ind. Eng. Chem., Anal. Ed.* **15,** 287 (1943).
6. M. D. Thomas, R. H. Hendricks, and G. R. Hill, *Proc. 1st Natl. Air Pollution Symp., Pasadena, Calif., 1949* p. 142.
7. C. R. Davis, *Pay Dirt,* No. 326, p. 5, C. F. Willis, Phoenix, Arizona, 1966.
8. J. N. Agate *et al., Med. Res. Council Memo.* **22** (1949); quoted by P. Drinker, *J. Roy. Inst. Public Health Hyg.* **20,** 307 (1957).
8a. C. R. Hayward, "An Outline of Metallurgical Practice," 3rd ed. Van Nostrand, Princeton, New Jersey, 1952.
9. Ontario Research Foundation, "The Removal of Sulphur Gases from Smelter Fumes." B. Johnson, Toronto, 1949.
10. G. R. Hill, M. D. Thomas, and J. N. Abersold, *Proc. 9th Ann. Meeting Ind. Hyg. Found., Pittsburgh, 1944* p. 11.
11. M. F. Smith, *Proc. 3rd Natl. Conf. Air Pollution, Washington, D.C., 1966* p. 151.
12. E. P. Fleming and T. C. Fitt, *Ind. Eng. Chem.* **42,** 2249 (1950).
13. P. J. Callahan and T. D. Parker, *Chem. Eng.* **74,** 159 (1967).
14. J. J. Donoso, *Proc. 40th Ann. Conv. Smoke Prevent. Assoc. Am., Toronto, 1947* p. 39.
15. J. M. Kane, *Am. Foundryman 19,* 34 (1951).

GENERAL REFERENCE

Additional pertinent material is in Chapter 6 of "Air Pollution Engineering Manual, Los Angeles APCD" (J. A. Danielson, ed.), PHS Publn. 999-AP-40, DHEW, Cincinnati (1967); and will be published in the National Air Pollution Control Administration's publications: "Control Technology for Particulate Air Pollutants," and "Control Technology for Sulfur Oxides Air Pollutants."

38 Inorganic Chemical Industry

Austin N. Heller, Stanley T. Cuffe, and Don R. Goodwin

I. Introduction

This chapter discusses the air pollution aspects of the manufacture of eight principal inorganic acids and alkalies, phosphate fertilizers, ammonium nitrate, and the two halogens, bromine and chlorine (Table I).

Significant recent changes in technology of process operations and related improvements in abatement devices will be considered. Of the major inorganic chemical processes, the phosphate fertilizer components have had the greatest growth since 1959, and presage an even greater ratio of growth in the next 5 to 10 years. The increasing air pollution potential of these manufacturing processes requires frequent periodic assessment to establish a basis for process improvement and more efficient effluent control.

II. Hydrochloric Acid

Hydrochloric acid is produced in the United States by three processes: (1) the reaction of sulfuric acid and common salt; (2) by-product recovery from chlorination of organic compounds; and (3) the synthesis of hydrogen and chlorine (2-4).

In 1965 estimated production of hydrochloric acid was 80% by by-product recovery and 10% each by the salt process and chlorine–hydrogen synthesis (Table I). This contrasts with 74% from by-product recovery (5) in 1959 and none in 1934 (2).

A. Salt Process

The salt process involves two reactants, common salt (NaCl) and 60° or 66° Baumé sulfuric acid. The products of the reaction are hydrogen chloride, sodium bisulfate (NaHSO$_4$), and the normal sulfate (Na$_2$SO$_4$). The equations involved are:

$$NaCl + H_2SO_4 \rightarrow HCl + NaHSO_4 \tag{1}$$

$$NaCl + NaHSO_4 \rightarrow HCl + Na_2SO_4 \tag{2}$$

$$2NaCl + H_2SO_4 \rightarrow 2HCl + Na_2SO_4 \text{ (salt cake)} \tag{3}$$

TABLE I
PRODUCTION TRENDS OF MAJOR INORGANIC CHEMICALS[a]
(IN SHORT TONS)

Chemical	1966 (est.)	1965 (preliminary)
Ammonium nitrate		
Fertilizer, solution[b]	2,140,000	2,000,000
Fertilizer, solid	2,415,000	2,300,000
Explosive and other uses	549,000	410,000
Bromine	21,000	20,414
Chlorine gas[c]	6,946,000	6,400,000
Hydrochloric acid, total (100% HCl)	1,505,000	1,368,000
From salt and acid	150,000	145,000
From chlorine	139,000	140,000
By-product and other	1,216,000	1,015,000
Hydrofluoric acid (100%)	244,000	220,000
Calcium oxide (lime),		
sold and used by producers	16,000,000	15,500,000
Nitric acid	5,337,000	4,950,000
Phosphate rock	30,800,000	27,500,000
Phosphoric acid, total (100% P_2O_5)	3,950,000	3,450,000
From phosphorus	1,070,000	1,020,000
From other sources	2,880,000	2,430,000
Sodium carbonate		
Synthetic	5,073,000	4,928,000
Natural	1,755,000	1,510,000
Total[d]	6,828,000	6,438,000
Sodium hydroxide		
Liquid	7,342,000	6,796,000
Solid	553,000	540,000
Sulfuric acid		
Total gross	27,169,000	24,225,000
Chamber process	1,330,000	1,325,000
Contact process, gross	25,839,000	22,900,000
Contact process, new	24,660,000	21,910,000
Spent acid used in fortification	1,179,000	990,000

[a] Includes data for government-owned, but privately operated plants.
[b] Excludes amounts converted to solid.
[c] Includes amounts liquefied.
[d] Includes amounts used to manufacture caustic soda, sodium bicarbonate, and finished light and dense soda ash.

In this process, salt and sulfuric acid are indirectly heated in a closed system furnace (usually Mannheim) to 1400°–1600 °F (Fig. 1). Modern furnaces are kept under negative pressure (−0.05 to −0.50 inches of water). Entrained solids in the exhaust gases are controlled by dust control equipment such as settling chambers and cyclones.

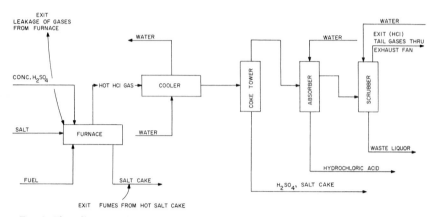

FIG. 1. Flow diagram of the salt process for the manufacture of hydrochloric acid, noting potential air pollution sources.

The gases evolved, 30–70 volume % hydrogen chloride, are cooled to about 100 °F and purified prior to passing to a water absorber. Different types of absorbers have been used, but, in the main, a packed tower system or a cooled absorption tower followed by a packed tail gas tower or falling film type tower are used. The gas stream from the absorption system is then vented through a tall stack.

Air Pollutant Emissions and Their Control

Losses of hydrogen chloride may occur in the exhaust gases from the furnace, the hot salt cake, or the tail gases (*2, 3*). Furnace losses in older units may occur at the doors, particularly if they are hand operated. Control usually consists of hooding the doors and scrubbing the exit gases with water. In the more modern furnaces, control is exercised by maintaining a very slight negative pressure in the muffle. The potential loss of hydrogen chloride from the hot salt cake, usually removed from the oven at about 1000 °F, can be controlled by cooling the cake in a water-cooled screw conveyor prior to dumping.

Tail gas is passed through a tails tower (stoneware packed) where the residual HCl is absorbed countercurrently with feed water or recycled dilute hydrochloric acid. The concentration of the exiting acid is 20% or less. There are some installations that use several tail towers in series to reduce the hydrogen chloride loss to a range of 0.1 to 0.3% by volume (*6*).

Upsets in the absorption system due either to improper temperature control or insufficient feed water can usually be corrected quickly with minor adjustments. In the case of cooled tower absorption systems, the addition of water to the tail tower of the absorption system may be automatically controlled. The temperature of the tail tower acid exit is correlated with the strength of the product acid from the absorber. Control of water addition to the tail tower is usually gauged by product acid strength and tower temperature.

B. By-product Hydrogen Chloride

Hydrogen chloride in the exit gases from the chlorination of organic substances is normally contaminated with chlorine, air, organic products, and moisture. The exact nature of the impurities depends upon the initial reactants. The separation of hydrogen chloride from the effluent gas mixture differs for each case.

In the chlorination of methane, for example, the effluent gas contains methane, chlorine, chlorinated products and hydrogen chloride (Fig. 2). This mixture is treated in an absorber using a carbon tetrachloride–chloroform absorbing solution. A mixture of hydrogen chloride and methane escapes from the top of the tower, and is called the major gas stream. Hydrogen chloride, chlorine, and some of the tower chlorinated products stripped from the absorbing solution are called the minor gas

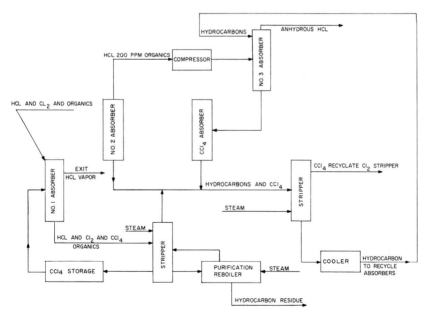

Fig. 2. Flow diagram of the by-product process for manufacture of hydrochloric acid, noting potential air pollution sources.

stream, and are contacted with hot water in an adiabatic absorber producing 15% acid. The escaping gases, containing hydrocarbons, chlorine, water vapor, and hydrogen chloride, are neutralized, dried, compressed, and distilled. The 15% acid is cooled in an intercooler and fed into a water-cooled absorption column, where it contacts the major gas stream to produce 20° Baume acid (about 30%). The escaping gases, containing methane, water vapor, and some hydrogen chloride are neutralized, dried, compressed, and recycled to the reaction.

Air Pollutant Emissions and Their Control

Hydrogen chloride recovery from the chlorination of organic chemicals has been the subject of many patents (7–11). Each process described is peculiar to the reactants used and is reflected in the composition of the off-gases to be scrubbed. In many cases the neutral gas streams are recovered efficiently by countercurrent washing with water in either a packed or bubble plate tower (12–14). Present trends (3) favor one or more cooled absorption towers (falling film type) followed by packed adiabatic tail gas scrubbers. The weak acid (about 20%) from the tail gas scrubber is returned to the primary absorption towers. Higher pressures than atmospheric may also be used to increase recovery of acid.

C. SYNTHETIC HYDROGEN CHLORIDE

Production of hydrochloric acid by the synthetic method is used where high purity hydrochloric acid is required. The acid produced by this method has shown a steady decline, 150,000 tons in 1966 vs. 184,304 tons in 1959.

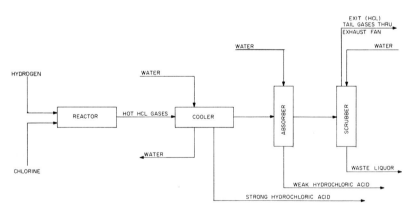

Fig. 3. Flow diagram of the synthetic process for the manufacture of hydrochloric acid, noting potential air pollution sources.

Hydrogen is burned (*3, 4*) with chlorine in a reactor to produce a high purity hydrogen chloride gas (98–99.7%) (Fig. 3). Product gas purity is dependent on the purity of the raw materials. The absorption and recovery of acid is similar to those previously stated. The exit gas composition will depend upon the method (*3, 5*) required to remove impurities in the acid.

III. Hydrofluoric Acid

In 1966 approximately 244,000 tons of anhydrous hydrofluoric acid were produced in 15 plants located in 10 states (*15*). Plants range in size from 10,000 to 35,000 tons per year (*16*). More than 75% of hydrofluoric acid production is used captively by the aluminum and fluorocarbon industries. Commercial users include the Atomic Energy Commission, the petroleum industry (for use as an alkylation catalyst), and manufacturers of fluorides. All hydrofluoric acid is manufactured by the fluorspar–sulfuric acid process.

FLUORSPAR–SULFURIC ACID PROCESS

Acid grade fluorspar and 93–99% sulfuric acid are the basic raw materials in the manufacture of hydrofluoric acid. Acid grade fluorspar contains about 98% calcium fluoride and a maximum of 1% silicon di-

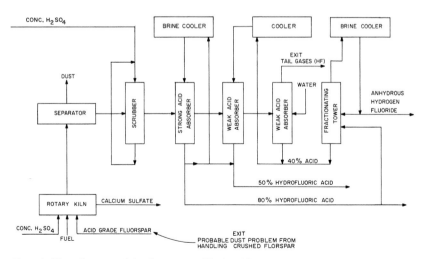

FIG. 4. Flow diagram of the fluorspar-sulfuric acid process for hydrofluoric acid, noting potential air pollution sources.

oxide, 0.03% sulfur, 1% calcium carbonate, and 0.1% moisture. Approximately 97% of the ground fluorspar will pass through a 170-mesh screen.

One mole fluorspar to 1.2 moles sulfuric acid are fed continuously into a rotary kiln heated to 250–350 °F (15) (Fig. 4). The hydrogen fluoride gas stream evolved from the kiln also contains water vapor, sulfur dioxide, silicon tetrafluoride, hydrogen sulfide, sulfuric acid, spar, and calcium sulfate. A scrubbing system removes the solids, condenses the water and sulfuric acid, and returns the mixture to the kiln. The purified hydrogen fluoride gases leave the scrubbing system and pass through a series of absorption and cooling towers, recovering most of the hydrogen fluoride. The crude hydrofluoric acid obtained from the condensers is distilled to anhydrous hydrofluoric acid (17). Yields from calcium fluoride vary from 85 to 92% depending on the purity of the sulfuric acid and fluorspar (15–18).

Air Pollutant Emissions and Their Control

The major potential source of air pollutants are the tail gases which contain trace quantities of hydrogen fluoride, sulfur dioxide, hydrogen sulfide, and fluosilicic acid fumes (17). Another probable source of dust is in the handling and sizing of fluorspar.

The exit gases from the kiln pass through a scrubbing system which removes most of the sulfuric acid mist and dust. Scrubbing systems used include cyclone and scrubber combinations, packed absorption towers, and shell-and-tube precondensers—all using concentrated sulfuric acid as the scrubbing agent (15, 19, 20). After recovery of the hydrogen fluoride, the gaseous silicon tetrafluoride and the remaining hydrogen fluoride are removed by a water scrubber to form a weak solution of fluosilicic acid (15).

Caustic soda scrubbers have also been used on the tail gases (19). In addition, scrubbing with water ejectors has provided excellent results in eliminating damage to nearby vegetation. These units help maintain vacuum on the entire system, thus minimizing emissions to the atmosphere (20).

IV. Phosphoric Acid

Orthophosphoric acid production has increased rapidly due to the increased demand for phosphate fertilizer. Wet process phosphoric acid has increased from 1,577,000 tons of P_2O_5 in 1962 to 2,837,119 tons of P_2O_5 in 1965 (*21, 21a*). There are about 41 plants producing wet process phosphoric acid owned by 34 companies in the United States (*23*). Many new plants are being constructed.

Furnace process phosphoric acid has increased steadily over the years but has not approached the rapid growth of wet process phosphoric acid production. Production of furnace acid has increased from 870,000 tons P_2O_5 in 1962 to 1,007,941 tons P_2O_5 in 1965 (*21a*). In the United States there are about 31 plants producing furnace phosphoric acid operated by 8 companies.

Superphosphoric acid is a relatively new form of phosphoric acid produced commercially to meet the demand for higher analysis phosphate fertilizers (*26, 27*). Less than 5% of the total phosphoric acid produced is superphosphoric acid. Production has increased sharply from less than 3000 short tons in 1958 to 178,000 in 1966 (estimated).

A. WET PROCESS

Basically the production of phosphoric acid by the wet process involves the decomposition of phosphate rock with a mineral acid (Fig. 5). Either sulfuric, nitric, or hydrochloric acid may be used. The latter two are not commercially significant at the present time. Most phosphoric acid plants use a concentrated process sulfuric acid (93–98%). The phosphate rock is normally ground to a size which allows 50–55% to fall through a 200-mesh screen (*24*).

Crushed phosphate rock is contacted with sulfuric acid in a series of agitated vessels or compartments. The reaction continues as the mixture passes through the reaction system. From the last reaction com-

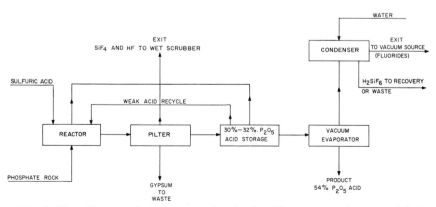

FIG. 5. Flow diagram of wet process phosphoric acid process, noting potential air pollution sources.

partment the slurry passes to a continuous rotary filter where the gypsum is separated, washed to recover weak acid, and then discharged to waste. The filtrate is 30–35% P_2O_5 orthophosphoric acid which is then concentrated in evaporators to a final strength of 50–55% P_2O_5. The principal reaction is:

$$Ca_3(PO_4)_2 + 3H_2SO_4 + 6H_2O \rightarrow 2H_3PO_4 + 3CaSO_4 \cdot 2H_2O \tag{4}$$

Air Pollutant Emissions and Their Control

The primary air pollutants of physiological importance are the fluorides. Carbon dioxide, silicon tetrafluoride, and some hydrogen fluoride are evolved from the reaction system (*24*). There is also a small fluoride emission from the filters, but this is usually not significant except in a large plant with several filters. Emissions from the acid evaporators will depend on the type of equipment utilized. If direct contact or submerged combustion evaporation is used there will be a considerable emission of phosphoric acid mist together with fluorides and hydrogen fluoride gas. If, as is modern practice, vacuum evaporation is used, about 30–40% of the fluorine originally present in the rock will be removed in the barometric condenser as a solution of hydrofluosilicic acid (*24*).

Most modern wet process phosphoric acid plants provide a complete collection system through one scrubber. Fumes from the reaction tanks, filter, storage tanks, and slurry tanks are vented to the atmosphere through a low-pressure-drop wet scrubber. Emission from a system of this type should be about 0.05 to 0.10 pounds F per ton of P_2O_5 produced. The scrubber efficiency should be $>99\%$ (*21*).

B. FURNACE PROCESS

In a typical installation liquid phosphorus and air are introduced into a cylindrical combustion chamber (Fig. 6), where the phosphorus burns according to the reaction:

$$P_4 + 5O_2 \rightarrow 2P_2O_5 \tag{5}$$

The gases leave the combustion chamber, consisting of P_2O_5 and steam, nitrogen, oxygen, and nitrogen oxides, and pass into a hydration tower where the P_2O_5 is hydrated to orthophosphoric acid. The hydrated acid is passed through a water spray absorbing tower where an acid of about 85% H_3PO_4 is produced. The reaction in the hydration tower is:

$$P_2O_5 + 3H_2O \rightarrow 2H_3PO_4 \tag{6}$$

Much of the acid produced is used in food materials and must be treated

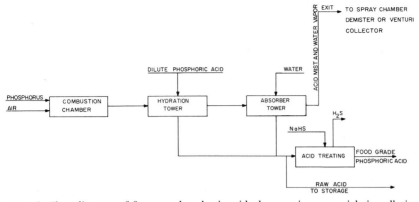

FIG. 6. Flow diagram of furnace phosphoric acid plant, noting potential air pollution sources.

with NaHS to remove traces of lead and arsenic ions. These metallic ions are precipitated as insoluble sulfides which are removed by filtration.

Air Pollutant Emissions and Their Control

The primary pollutant is acid mist from the absorber tower discharge. Venturi scrubbers and packed towers have been used to control acid mist. High pressure drop wire mesh mist eliminators and glass fiber mist eliminators are being operated at 99.9% efficiency. Emission of P_2O_5 is in the range of 0.3 to 5.0 pounds of P_2O_5 per thousand pounds of elemental phosphorus (P_4) burned (25).

Absorber tower off-gases will also contain nitrogen oxide. Recent tests indicate the concentration to be in the order of 10 ppm (25).

The acid treating plant has an intermittent emission of hydrogen sulfide from the unreacted H_2S in the treating tank. An odor problem can be eliminated by alkaline scrubbing or venting this gas, through a suitable flashback device, to the furnace, where hydrogen sulfide will be oxidized to sulfur dioxide.

C. SUPERPHOSPHORIC ACID PROCESS

Superphosphoric acid ($>70\%$ P_2O_5) was first made by the Tennessee Valley Authority by concentrating electric furnace phosphoric acid. It is now also made by dehydrating wet process phosphoric acid (28).

In the production of superphosphoric acid from elemental phosphorus, phosphorus is burned with air under the same conditions as

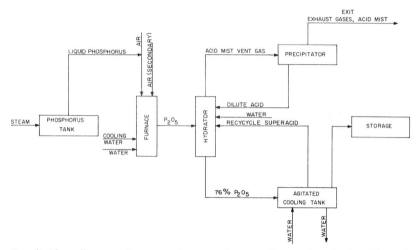

FIG. 7. Flow diagram of process for manufacture of superphosphoric acid, noting potential air pollution sources.

in the furnace acid process, with one major difference (Fig. 7). In the hydrator, the combustion gas is cooled with water or dilute acid sprays. About half of the P_2O_5 drops out of this vessel as superphosphoric acid, the rest leaves as acid mist at 200 °F, and is collected as less concentrated acid in an electrostatic precipitator; other types of mist collectors such as a venturi scrubber or a packed tower can also be used in this step. The dilute acid is sprayed back into the hydrator, and the effluent gas from the precipitator is vented to the stack.

Superphosphoric acid flows from the hydrator at about 300 °F to a combination cooling and agitating tank. Temperature is maintained at 200 °F. Product acid overflows to a sump and the stream for recycle is withdrawn and pumped to the hydrator.

Superphosphoric acid is also made from dehydration of the normal 50–55% acid. Most of the work on these processes is highly confidential and little data are available.

Air Pollutant Emissions and Their Control

The primary pollutant emitted is the phosphoric acid mist which is not removed by the mist eliminator. The acid mist can be assumed to be equal to or less than that vented in the furnace process and is related to the efficiency of the precipitator. The off-gases will also contain nitrogen oxides. Data are not available about its concentration.

The process for manufacturing superphosphoric acid from wet process acid operates at high vacuum which tends to limit emissions. Emissions of fluorine and P_2O_5 to the atmosphere can be controlled to satisfy the most stringent air pollution ordinances (25a).

V. Nitric Acid

Nearly all of the nitric acid manufactured today comes from the catalytic oxidation of ammonia. About 75% goes into the manufacture of ammonium nitrate which is used primarily as a fertilizer, and only secondarily in commercial explosives. Substantial quantities of nitric acid are used for nitrating organic compounds and as a component of rocket fuels. The production of nitric acid, 100% basis, has increased sharply from 400,000 tons in 1941 to 4,950,000 tons for 1965, slightly more than a 10-fold increase in two decades (1, 6).

The ammonia oxidation process is the most economical commercial process used today in the manufacture of nitric acid. Other processes such as the electric arc, the Wisconsin or nuclear fixation, have not proved to be economically competitive with ammonia oxidation. The future trend is toward the construction of larger ammonia oxidation plants with capacities of 500 or more tons of nitric acid (100% basis) per day.

A. PRESSURE PROCESS

In the pressure process a preheated mixture of 90% air and 10% ammonia, by volume, is passed through a catalytic converter containing five platinum-rhodium wire gauzes at about 750 °C (1650 °F) and 112 psig (Fig. 8). The conversion of ammonia to nitric oxide and water is about 95% complete at these conditions. The remaining 5% is lost through dissociation and side reactions. The resulting hot nitric oxide-air-water vapor mixture (about 10% nitric oxide) is cooled and passed through a cyclone separator before entering the base of the absorber. Condensate, which is 40–50% nitric acid, enters the column at an intermediate point. Fresh make-up water enters the top of the column and secondary air enters the bottom of the column to provide oxygen for conversion of nitric oxide to nitrogen dioxide in the absorber.

Unabsorbed gas, principally nitrogen, leaves the absorption tower at a tower temperature of about 85 °F and is passed through an entrainment separator. The tail gas is then heated by heat exchange with the hot process gases and is recovered in a centrifugal expander which drives the air compressor. The gas leaving the expander is then dis-

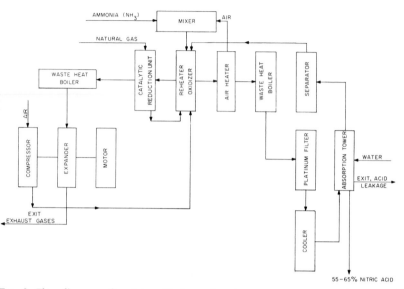

Fig. 8. Flow diagram of a nitric acid plant using the pressure process, noting potential air pollution sources.

charged to the atmosphere. If desired, the reheated tail gas may be passed through a catalytic reduction unit before entering the centrifugal expander to further reduce the oxides of nitrogen before venting.

B. COMBINATION PRESSURE PROCESS

In the combination pressure process, the oxidation of ammonia occurs at pressures from atmospheric to about 30 psig. The resulting oxides of

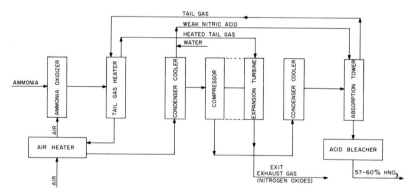

Fig. 9. Flow diagram of a nitric acid plant using the combination pressure process, noting potential air pollution sources.

nitrogen are then cooled and compressed to about 30 to 50 psig before being absorbed (Fig. 9). This system provides the benefits of lower maintenance, lower catalyst loss, and higher conversion efficiency obtained by operating the ammonia converter at low pressures, with the benefits obtained by high pressure absorption. Acid strengths of up to 70% have been obtained (31). In the United States, such plants are not common. With the advent of acid-resistant steel alloys able to withstand elevated pressures, and the need for higher strength nitric acid, the atmospheric pressure plant became outmoded (32).

C. Concentration Processes

The major portion of the 55–65% nitric acid produced by the ammonia oxidation process is consumed at this strength. Concentration either to fuming nitric acid or USP grades (95–99%) is accomplished by distillation in the presence of a dehydrating agent such as concentrated sulfuric acid. A 70–75% magnesium nitrate is also used, but to a limited extent.

The process consists of feeding strong sulfuric acid and 60% nitric acid to the top of a packed dehydrating column where it flows downward countercurrent to ascending vapors (Fig. 10). Concentrated nitric acid leaves the top of the column as 98% vapor containing a small amount of NO_2 and O_2 resulting from the dissociation of nitric acid. The vapors pass to a bleacher and countercurrent condenser system

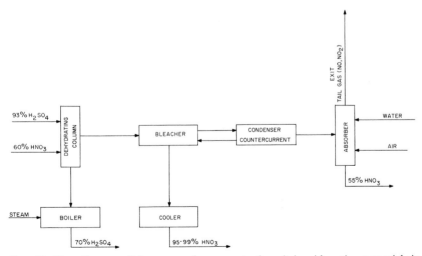

Fig. 10. Flow diagram of the process for concentrating nitric acid, noting potential air pollution sources.

to effect condensation of strong nitric acid and the separation of the oxygen and nitrogen oxides. These cooled, noncondensable gases flow to an absorption column for recovery of the nitrogen oxides as weak nitric acid, in much the same manner as in the pressure process nitric acid plants. Auxiliary air is added to the bottom of the column and inert gases and unreacted nitrogen oxides are vented to the atmosphere from the top of the column (32).

Air Pollutant Emissions and Their Control

The primary source of atmospheric emissions from nitric acid processes is the absorption tower. The unabsorbed oxides of nitrogen are largely in the form of nitric oxide and nitrogen dioxide. Trace amounts of nitric acid mist are also present. Emissions of nitrogen oxides may range from 0.1 to 0.69 volume percent with an average of 0.37%. Concentrations of 0.13 to 0.19 volume percent in the tail gas produce a definite reddish-brown color (32). Loss to the atmosphere from nitric acid concentrators may vary from 0.5 to 0.7% of the strong acid produced (32).

Emissions of nitrogen oxides may vary widely with changes in plant operation and with faulty equipment. The main plant operating variables which affect tail gas concentrations adversely are: insufficient air supply to the system; low pressure in the system, especially in the absorber; high temperatures in the cooler-condenser and absorber; the production of an excessively high strength product acid; and operation at high throughput rates. Faulty equipment to be considered includes such items as improperly operating compressors and pumps, and leaks between rich and lean nitrogen oxide gas streams.

The emission of nitrogen oxides may be reduced by absorption, adsorption, catalytic reduction and flaring, which may be summarized as follows:

1. Absorption in water where the nitrogen oxide content as NO_2 is high, i.e., 2–8%. This approach is suitable for recovery and reduction of nitrogen oxides from nitration or nitric acid oxidation processes (32). Where the concentration of oxides of nitrogen is less than 1% by volume, such as from nitric acid manufacturing plants, water absorption may not be very effective.

2. Treatment of the tail gases with nitrogen dioxide followed by cooling and absorption in ammonium bicarbonate. A solution of ammonium nitrite, ammonium nitrate, and ammonium carbonate or bicarbonate is formed (34, 35).

3. Absorption in waste caustic ammonia liquor (36).

4. Absorption with dry oxides of lime to produce mixed fertilizers (37).

5. Absorption with a suspension of lime in an aqueous solution of calcium nitrate and calcium nitrite (38).

6. Absorption in water as the first stage and sodium hydroxide as the second stage, yielding nitrite and nitrate salts (32). Disposition of the by-product salt solution must be taken into account.

7. Nitrogen dioxide may be removed by adsorption in activated charcoal or silica gel. These methods have not been used commercially for reducing emission of nitrogen oxides (32, 33).

8. The catalytic reduction system especially can be used in the pressure ammonia oxidation process. It can only be used when the absorber tail gas is of uniform composition and flow, under pressure, and can be reheated by heat exchange to the necessary reduction system feed temperature. Efficiencies above 90% may be realized, and also may be economically feasible. The system is as follows:

In operation, the tail gases from the absorber are heated to 800° to 1000 °F and are mixed with a hydrocarbon fuel (natural gas) prior to entering the catalytic reduction system in which these reactions take place (15, 30, 32):

$$\text{hydrocarbon} + O_2 \rightarrow H_2O + CO_2 \tag{7}$$

$$\text{hydrocarbon} + NO_2 \rightarrow H_2O + NO + CO_2 \tag{8}$$

$$\text{hydrocarbon} + NO \rightarrow H_2O + N_2 + CO_2 \tag{9}$$

In all cases, the product gases are passed through waste heat boilers and then to a power recovery gas turbine at about 800–1000 °F. The effluent gas from the turbine is discharged to the atmosphere at about 500 °F.

A wide range of fuels may be used in a converter to reduce nitrogen oxides, such as hydrogen, natural gas, coke oven gas, and carbon monoxide; in one case ammonia has been used. The final choice is largely an economic one.

Due to material temperature limitations, a two-stage reduction system may be required for complete nitrogen oxide removal if a large excess of oxygen is initially present. Concentrations of about 3% oxygen may be removed per stage, when burning natural gas; and about 4%, using hydrogen.

Normally, a colorless effluent is accepted as an indication of proper operation. This, however, is misleading from an air pollution standpoint. In one known case in which 1% methane was reacted with a tail gas containing 1100 ppm NO_2, 1900 ppm NO, and 4% O_2, the exit gases contained 260 ppm NO_2 and 2300 ppm NO (38). The exit gas was nearly colorless but its nitrogen oxides content was reduced only slightly.

A large nitric acid plant equipped with a catalytic tail gas reduction unit uses no outside power after start-up. The heat generated in the oxidation of ammonia and in catalytic reduction combine to provide the energy to drive the air compressor (15). Flaring will destroy the oxides of nitrogen and provide a colorless emission. For intermittent discharges of 1% or more, flaring may be a satisfactory abatement method (32).

VI.   Sulfuric Acid

Sulfuric acid is made by either the chamber process or the contact process. In 1965 about 95.7% of all sulfuric acid in the United States was manufactured by the contact process, in about 165 contact plants. The 60 chamber plants account for the balance of U.S. production. No new chamber plants have been built since 1956. Chamber plants rarely produce acid above 60° Baume, whereas the product of the contact plants is between 98% and 100% acid. This product can be either diluted to lower concentrations or fortified with sulfur trioxide to yield fuming acid.

Raw materials vary from elemental sulfur, pyrites, by-product sulfur dioxide, or hydrogen sulfide emanating from many manufacturing and refining processes. Elemental sulfur accounts for about 75% of all raw materials used in American sulfuric acid production. Substantial quantities of "fresh clean acid" are made by regeneration or decomposition of spent acid from petroleum refineries or other chemical processes.

Both processes start with the burning of the sulfur or sulfur-bearing material to produce sulfur dioxide. In commercial practice sulfur is melted and burned in a stream of dry air to produce a gas containing 8–12% sulfur dioxide at a temperature from 1400° to 1800 °F. Where other raw materials are used, such as iron pyrites, acid sludges from refinery operations, smelter off-gases, etc., the gas produced contains less sulfur dioxide than when sulfur is used, and more dust and other impurities. Purification includes dust removal, cooling, scrubbing, filtering, and drying.

A. CHAMBER PROCESS

Hot sulfur dioxide gases, 425°–600 °C, from the sulfur burner, ore roaster, or other sulfur dioxide-producing equipment are introduced

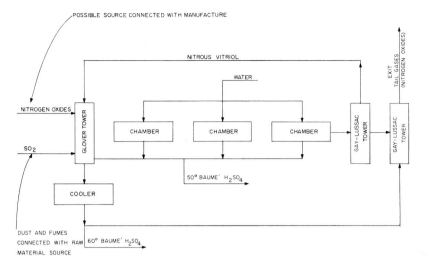

FIG. 11. Flow diagram of chamber process in the manufacture of sulfuric acid, noting potential air pollution sources.

into the base of a Glover tower (Fig. 11). If the sulfur dioxide gases are dirty, an electrostatic dust precipitator or cyclone dust collector precedes the Glover tower. In the Glover tower the gases pass countercurrently to cool nitrous vitriol (72.8% H_2SO_4) from the Gay-Lussac towers. The hot (100°–140 °C) Glover or "tower" acid (60° Baumé) is cooled and a portion is fed back to the Gay-Lussac tower. In the Glover tower the sulfur dioxide is oxidized in the presence of oxides of nitrogen to sulfur trioxide, which combines with water vapor to form sulfuric acid. The chemical reactions are complex and not yet fully understood.

The gases from the Glover tower mix at the top of the tower with oxides of nitrogen, generated by an ammonia oxidation unit. At this stage about 10% of the sulfur dioxide is oxidized to sulfur trioxide. The mixed gases (SO_2, SO_3, N_2, NO, NO_2, N_2O_3, and steam) leave the Glover tower at a temperature of 70°–110 °C and pass to the lead chamber. At this point the major portion of the sulfur dioxide is oxidized by catalysis with oxides of nitrogen to sulfur trioxide, and hydrated to sulfuric acid. In the chambers, water or dilute acid is injected by means of sprays, and the sulfuric acid formed condenses on the lead walls, runs to the floor, and is collected. This chamber acid (62–68% H_2SO_4) is pumped to the Glover tower where it is concentrated and the nitrogen oxides are removed.

The gases leaving the chamber, which contain little sulfur dioxide, nitrogen oxide and mist, enter the bottom of the Gay-Lussac tower countercurrent to cold (35 °C to 40 °C) 60° Baumé (77.7%) sulfuric acid.

The oxides of nitrogen are stripped out, forming nitrous vitriol containing 1–2.5% N_2O_3 by weight. The nitrous vitriol is pumped to the top of the Glover tower. The stripped tail gases from the Gay-Lussac towers then pass to the discharge stack.

The chemical reactions describing the chamber process are:

$$2NO + O_2 \rightarrow 2NO_2 \tag{10}$$

$$NO_2 + SO_2 + H_2O \rightarrow H_2SO_4 + NO \tag{11}$$
$$\text{(98–99\% conversion)}$$

Air Pollutant Emissions and Their Control

Exit gases are composed of nitrogen, sulfur dioxide, nitrogen oxides, moisture, acid mist, and mechanically entrained acid spray.

In sulfur burning plants (40), sulfur dioxide emissions vary from less than 0.1% to 0.2% by volume. When other raw materials are used, emissions may be twice as high. Emissions of oxides of nitrogen vary usually from 0.1% to 0.2% by volume expressed as NO_2. Concentrations of acid mist, composed of sulfuric acid and dissolved nitric oxides, vary from zero to about 30 mg per standard cubic foot of exit gas. Reductions of 40% of the sulfur dioxide and 25% of the nitrogen oxides discharged from the Gay-Lussac tower using a water scrubber are reported (40). Other methods of control of Gay-Lussac tail gases are (1) use of water sprays (2) use of weak nitric acid which is then used as a spray in first chamber, (3) scrubbing in packed towers coupled with electrostatic precipitation, and (4) using venturi scrubbers with water or sodium carbonate solution.

B. CONTACT PROCESS

The basic contact process uses a catalyst to convert sulfur dioxide to sulfur trioxide from which sulfuric acid is formed upon hydration (Fig. 12).

In this process, the dried gas mixture, which contains 7 – 10% sulfur dioxide (depending on the source of SO_2) and 11–14% oxygen, is preheated and passed through a catalytic converter, usually platinum, or vanadium pentoxide, to form sulfur trioxide. The conversion of SO_2 to SO_3 is about 96–97%. The temperature varies from 500° to 600 °C in the second part. The latter is selected to obtain an optimum equilibrium constant related to maximum conversion at minimum cost. Contact time in the converter is about 2–4 seconds.

The converter gases are cooled to about 100 °C and passed through an oleum tower for partial absorption of the sulfur trioxide. The resid-

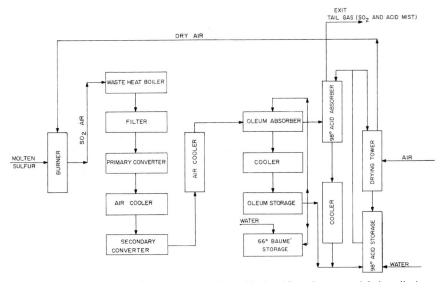

Fig. 12. Flow diagram of contact process for sulfuric acid, noting potential air pollution sources.

ual gases are passed over a second tower where the remaining sulfur trioxide is scrubbed with 98% sulfuric acid. The remaining unabsorbed gases are discharged via a stack to the atmosphere.

The basic reactions are:

$$2SO_2 + O_2 \xrightarrow{\text{catalyst}} 2SO_3 \tag{12}$$

$$SO_3 + H_2O \longrightarrow H_2SO_4 \tag{13}$$
$$\text{(92–96\% yield (sulfur))}$$

Air Pollutant Emissions and Their Control

The major source of emissions from the contact sulfuric acid plant (*40*) is the waste gas from the absorber exit stack. This discharge contains sulfur dioxide, sulfur trioxide, nitrogen, oxygen, and H_2SO_4 mist. Minor additional quantities of sulfur dioxide and sulfur trioxide are released from storage tanks, tank cars, acid concentrators, and leaks in process.

The concentration of SO_2 in the discharge gas ranges from 0.13 to 0.54% by volume; the acid mist (H_2SO_4) varies from 1.1 to 48 mg per standard cubic foot.

Operating factors controlling emissions are: (1) method of manufacture of sulfur dioxide; (2) temperatures in converters; (3) percent SO_2 in feed gases; and (4) percent of operating plant capacity being used.

In the main, manufacturing controls will reduce emissions. However, such control devices as two-stage knitted wire mesh filters (*40, 41*) report 82–99% mist removal with 1.5 to 2.0 inch pressure drop (water). Electrostatic precipitators have a reported efficiency of 99% of the acid mist only (*42*). There are many methods to reduce SO_2 in the exit gases, such as scrubbing with alkali, chemical absorption with ammonia to give ammonium sulfite, and subsequent stripping to yield an exit gas containing less than .03% SO_2 (*39, 40, 43*).

C. BAYER DOUBLE-CONTACT PROCESS

There are two basic differences in the double contact process when compared to the usual contact process (Fig. 13). These are: (1) an intermediate absorption stage before further contact and (2) a higher concentration of SO_2 in the feed gas used in the process; 10% SO_2 instead of about 7% SO_2 when pyrites are used, and 13.4% SO_2 instead of about 10% SO_2 when elemental sulfur is used as the raw material.

In the double contact process the reaction is interrupted after 90% of the SO_2 has been converted to SO_3. The SO_3 is removed in the first absorption stage (intermediate absorption) and the remaining mixture of SO_2 and air is once more reacted (contacted) and passed through the final absorption tower. By removing the SO_3 in the first stage, the approach to equilibrium is increased, which permits further reaction and thereby increases the conversion of the SO_2 to SO_3.

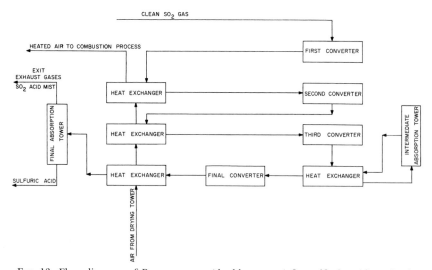

FIG. 13. Flow diagram of Bayer process (double contact) for sulfuric acid production showing gas phase flow, noting potential air pollution sources.

Theoretically, the double contact process allows the degree of conversion to be increased from about 98% for the usual contact process to about 99.8% for double contact (*44*).

Air Pollutant Emissions and Their Control

After the intermediate absorption, the temperature at which the contact catalyst responds is 50 °C lower than in the usual contact process. This reduces SO_2 in the exit gases by 50% of that in the usual contact process.

The increase in yield for the double contact process reduces the emissions from 2000 ppm of SO_2 for an efficient contact plant to 500 ppm of SO_2 for a double contact unit. Acid mist in the exit gas will require the same type of control as used in the usual contact process.

VII. Calcium Oxide (Lime)

In 1965, about 10 million tons of lime were produced in the United States by 101 commercial lime plants operating in 33 different states (*45*). Although there are presently more vertical kilns than rotary kilns, it is estimated by the National Lime Association that in 1965 80% of all commercial lime tonnage is derived from rotary kilns, 17% from vertical kilns, and the remaining 3% from other types such as fluo-solid processes (*46*). Soda ash manufacturers are the largest single consumers of lime (*15*). Dolomitic limestone is used principally to produce hydrated lime for building construction, while dead burned dolomite is employed for metallurgical purposes.

CALCINATION OF LIMESTONE PROCESS

Lime (CaO) is produced by burning (calcining) various types of limestone in continuous rotary or vertical kilns. Small size limestone (0.25 to 2.5 inches) is usually burned in rotary kilns, while lump limestone (4–8 inches) is usually calcined in vertical pot or shaft kilns. The calcining zone of either type of kiln is heated to about 2100 °F to dissociate the calcium carbonate into lime (calcium oxide) and carbon dioxide.

In the operation of a shaft kiln (Fig. 14) the limestone is conveyed to the top of the kiln and dropped into a hopper where it is preheated by slowly rising kiln gases. As the stone passes down into the calcining section, lime is formed and carbon dioxide liberated. If carbon dioxide is to be recovered, the kiln off-gases are piped under slight vacuum to compressors. The kilns are heated by coal, oil, or gas in such a manner

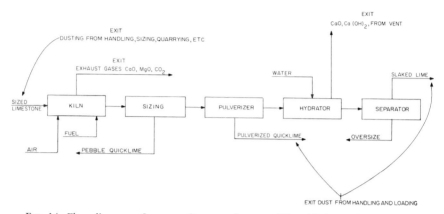

FIG. 14. Flow diagram of process for manufacture of lime (CaO), noting potential air pollution sources.

that the product is not contaminated. The calcined lime drops to a cooling zone where incoming combustion air partially cools the hot lime. The kiln doors are opened at intervals to discharge the lime, which is further cooled prior to packaging as lump lime, or is crushed and screened to yield pulverized lime. Some of the quicklime is slaked to the hydrated form and aged in dustproof bins prior to packaging in bags.

Large rotary kilns will produce over 300 tons/day of lime using a heating time of about 3 hours per charge. The temperature of gases leaving rotary kilns fired with pulverized bituminous coal range from 600 °F for a 6-foot diameter by 300-foot kiln to 1350 °F for a kiln 6 feet in diameter by 80 feet in length (46). Rotary kilns produce 3.37 pounds of lime per pound of coal.

Air Pollutant Emissions and Their Control

The major source of airborne dust from lime manufacturing operations is the exit flue gases from lime kilns. Other sources of dust include (1) blasting operations in open pit quarries, (2) primary and secondary limestone crushing operations, (3) screening crushed limestone for size separations, (4) lime conveying-transfer points, (5) lime hydration, and (6) pulverizing, bagging, and bulk loading of limestone.

Dust emissions from vertical lime kilns are usually lower than those from rotary kilns because of the larger size of the limestone feed, lower gas velocities, and the relative absence of abrasion of the charge when passing through the vertical kiln. Because of charge abrasion and high gas velocities, the dust generated by rotary lime kilns ranges from 5 to 15% by weight of lime produced (46). A vertical lime kiln releasing

33,500 ft³ of gas per minute had a dust content of 0.9 grain/ft³. Ninety percent of the particles were under 100 μ, 50% under 30 μ, and 10% under 10 μ. A rotary lime kiln, on the other hand, released 26,000 ft³ of gas per minute with a dust loading as high as 8 grains/ft³. Fifty percent of these particles were under 25 μ and 10% under 10 μ (47).

The exit gases from modern rotary lime kilns, ranging in temperature from 600° to 1800 °F, usually pass first through multicyclone dust collectors for recovery of coarse particulate. From 65 to 85 weight percent of the dust in the kiln exit gases is recovered in this primary collection system. This primary dust is often disposed of in waste dumps, used as landfill, or applied to farm land as a soil conditioner. It is usually wetted before hauling or mixed with water and pumped as a slurry. The more efficient control systems used for collection of dust from rotary kilns include electrostatic precipitators, glass fabric filters, or wet scrubbers used alone or in combination with centrifugal collectors.

Wet scrubbing systems serving rotary kilns are reported to operate with collection efficiencies of 95–98% and with exit dust concentrations ranging from 0.02 to 0.07 grains/ft³ of stack gas (46, 47). Venturi scrubbers have a reported efficiency of 99 weight percent with a relatively low-pressure drop (6 to 8 inches of water) when heavy slurries are used as a scrubbing liquor (48). Impingement baffle scrubbers have reported lime dust collection efficiencies of 97–99% (49). The concentration of lime dust from an electrostatic precipitator serving a rotary kiln was 0.2 grain/ft³ of stack gas; while that from a glass fabric filter, also serving a rotary kiln, was 0.001 grain/ft³ of exit gas (46). Although wet scrubbers serving rotary kilns have operated efficiently, a dust collection system consisting of a centrifugal collector, settling chamber, and scrubber was reported to operate unsatisfactorily when serving a vertical kiln (50). The replacement of this system with a 25,000 cfm reverse jet tubular type baghouse resulted in the collection of an additional 20 tons of lime dust per day. The charging of vertical lime kilns using tipper buckets can also create a significant dust nuisance problem. A well-designed kiln top and distribution mechanism can reduce these emissions significantly.

During the hydration of lime, steam-laden air sweeps the dust from the hydration pan into the exit gas stack. Since the dust is easily wetted, it can be collected efficiently by a water scrubbing tower. Part of the water from the spray tower is fed to the hydrator as a hydrated lime slurry. The concentration of particulate emissions from the hydrator scrubber ranges from 0.01 to 0.07 grain/ft³ of stack gas (46).

Water spray or mechanical-type collectors serving primary or secondary crushers have reported exit dust grain loadings ranging from

0.02 to 0.05 grain/ft³ of air. Concentrations of lime dust in exit gases from multicyclone collectors serving lime conveyor transfer points range from 0.2 to 0.8 grain/ft³ of air. An exit grain loading of less than 0.01 grain/ft³ of air is reported from a fabric filter serving a lime distribution system, a hydrate packer and loader. A high concentration of dust, 2 grains/ft³ of exit gas, from a multicyclone collector serving a pulverized limestone dryer is also reported (46).

VIII.   Sodium Carbonate (Soda Ash)

Soda ash (sodium carbonate) is manufactured by three processes: (1) Solvay process (ammonia-soda), (2) natural or Lake Brines process, and (3) electrolytic soda ash process. In 1965, about 5,000,000 tons of soda ash were produced by the Solvay process in nine plants located east of the Rocky Mountains (15, 51). These plants range in size from 550 to 2600 tons/day capacity. Four plants located in California and Wyoming manufactured soda ash by the Lake Brines process, while one plant in Texas utilized the electrolytic soda ash process. Since the Solvay process accounts for over 80% of the total production of soda ash, the natural and electrolytic processes will not be discussed.

SOLVAY PROCESS

Ammonia, coke, limestone (calcium carbonate), and salt (sodium chloride) comprise the basic raw materials for manufacturing soda ash. The salt brine is first purified of calcium, magnesium, and other heavy metal ions by precipitation. This is accomplished in a series of absorbers with ammonia and carbon dioxide from waste process gases.

In the Solvay process, purified salt brine (15 °C) is contacted with ammonia in an absorber (Fig. 15). The ammoniated brine from the absorber is pumped to two carbonating towers in series, in which it first contacts lean carbon dioxide gases from the lime kiln and then rich carbon dioxide from the bicarbonate calciner. Sodium bicarbonate is formed in the towers. The lean carbon dioxide from the carbonating towers and the ammonia from the absorbers are passed to the brine purification system for recovery. The slurry from the carbonating towers is filtered under vacuum and the bicarbonate cake conveyed to a sealed rotary kiln. The vacuum filtrate is passed to an ammonia still and the carbon dioxide and ammonia gases are piped to the bottom of the carbonating towers. The bicarbonate cake is heated to about 175 °C in the rotary kiln and the released rich carbon dioxide gases are trans-

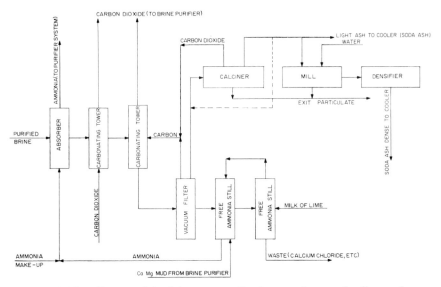

FIG. 15. Flow diagram of the Solvay process for the manufacture of sodium carbonate (soda ash), noting potential air pollution sources.

ferred to the carbonating tower. The product soda ash is cooled and conveyed to storage and packaging.

The vacuum filtrate is pumped to a series of two ammonia stills. The recovered free ammonia is returned to the absorber with some make-up ammonia (usually 0.35–0.5% of the final soda). The fixed ammonia in the filtrate is treated with milk of lime, while the ammonia released is also returned to the absorbers. The effluent from the fixed still, which is essentially calcium chloride, is either sent to a waste disposal area or to a calcium chloride recovery plant.

Air Pollutant Emissions and Their Control

The major potential source of air pollution from the manufacture of soda ash is the release of ammonia. Ammonia recovery is reported to be 99.8% via the tower absorbers. Only about 5% of the overall 0.2% loss of ammonia is accounted for in the vent gases from the brine purification system. Intermittent losses of ammonia can also occur during the unloading of tank trucks or tank cars into storage tanks. The installation of a vacuum type unloading system prevents the release of ammonia fumes and precludes possible paint damage to nearby buildings.

Sources of dust emission include rotary dryers, dry solids handling, and the processing of lime. Rotary dryers heated by coal-fired furnaces often result in smoke and fly ash problems. The conversion from coal to gas-fired furnaces will markedly reduce this problem, and can result in overall savings due to reduced maintenance costs and a reduction in the labor requirements for coal and ash handling (50). Mechanical dust collection equipment is still needed, however, for the collection of soda ash in the effluent gases from the dryer.

Dust emissions of fine soda ash also occur from conveyor transfer points, air classification systems, loading into tank cars and trucks, and during packaging. In one plant, the dust generated from these sources was handled unsatisfactorily by combination cyclone-wet washers. The replacement of the cyclone-wet spray systems with reverse-jet fabric filter dust collectors eliminated the dust nuisance problem, and resulted in the collection of 6 tons/day of dense soda ash previously discharged to the atmosphere (50).

The particulate emissions and methods of control for airborne dust from lime kilns are detailed in Section VII.

IX.   Sodium Hydroxide (Caustic Soda)

Sodium hydroxide is manufactured by both the lime-soda and electrolytic processes as a coproduct in the manufacture of chlorine. While caustic soda was produced primarily by the lime-soda method early in this century, the electrolytic process took the lead in the late 1930's. In 1964, only five soda-lime caustic plants were still operating in the United States and the electrolytic process had captured 95% of the caustic production. The greater demand for chlorine has been responsible for this transition.

A. Electrolytic Process

In the electrolytic process sodium chloride, obtained from natural brines, mines, or the evaporation of seawater, is either dissolved in water or concentrated to produce a saturated solution (Fig. 16). After treatment to remove impurities, the hot brine is fed into electrolytic cells at a rate sufficient to maintain a constant level in the cells.

There are two types of cell used in the United States—the mercury cell and the diaphragm cell, which are described in detail in Section XII.

In the diaphragm cell, 10–12% caustic, containing salt impurities, is produced and later concentrated in multiple effect evaporators to produce the standard 50%, commercial grade, caustic soda. As the caustic concentrates, the salt settles out and is removed for recycle to the cells.

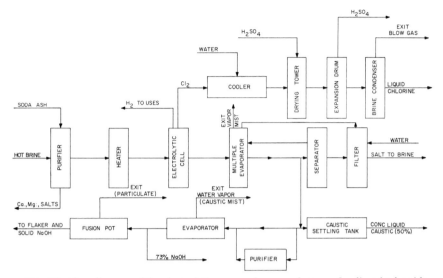

FIG. 16. Flow diagram of the electrolytic process for manufacture of sodium hydroxide, noting potential air pollution sources.

To produce virtually salt-free 50% caustic for rayon manufacture, liquid-liquid extraction with ammonia is often employed. Additional evaporators will produce the 73% caustic. This is often followed by oil-fired fusion pots or Dowtherm-heated evaporators which are used to obtain anhydrous caustic.

The mercury cell usually produces nearly 50% caustic that can be marketed directly. It is notably pure and salt free.

Air Pollutant Emissions and Their Control

Caustic manufacture by the electrolytic method presents minor air pollution problems. Some caustic mists may be emitted from the fusion pots and grinders of anhydrous caustic flakes. In addition, emissions of ammonia from the ammonia scrubber in caustic purification have been reported as 1.5 pounds of ammonia per 100 tons of anhydrous caustic purified (*51a*).

Control efforts would include the use of water scrubbers for dust problems.

B. Lime-Soda Process

In the continuous lime-soda process (Fig. 17) a 20% solution of sodium carbonate (soda ash) is treated with calcium hydroxide (milk of

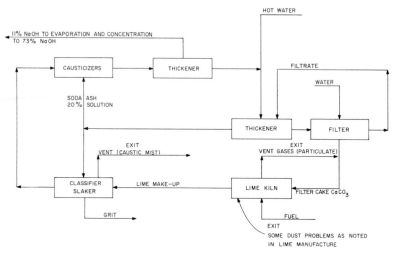

FIG. 17. Flow diagram of lime-soda process for sodium hydroxide, noting potential air pollution sources.

lime) to precipitate calcium carbonate and form a weak caustic liquor. The chemical reaction, which is carried out at about 85 °C, is:

$$NaCO_3 + Ca(OH)_2 \longrightarrow 2NaOH + CaCO_3 \qquad (14)$$
$$(88\text{--}90\% \text{ yield})$$

The slurry of precipitated calcium carbonate and weak caustic liquor is then fed to a series of multitray thickeners, where, by continuous countercurrent decantation and filtration, a 10–12% caustic soda solution and a calcium carbonate cake are obtained. The calcium carbonate cake is burned in a kiln to produce lime for reuse in the process. The carbon dioxide evolved is also used in process in integrated soda ash plants.

The clear liquor from the first thickener contains 11% sodium hydroxide and 1.7% sodium carbonate. This weak solution is concentrated to a 50% solution in multiple-effect evaporators. The sodium carbonate in solution precipitates out during and after concentration. The precipitate is removed by a thickener and filter and is pumped back to the causticizer. The overflow from the thickener is either stored for sale or concentrated further (usually in single effect evaporators) to 73% caustic soda. As with the electrolytic caustic, further dehydration to the anhydrous form is accomplished in fusion pots and packaged as a solid or flake.

Air Pollutant Emissions and Their Control

The most serious pollution source arises from lime kiln dust and carbon dioxide, which may also be considered a pollutant if it is not recovered for process uses. Minor sources include soda ash and anhydrous caustic handling and flaking operations. Dust control equipment for the lime kiln was discussed in Section VII,A.

X.   Phosphate Fertilizers

A. PHOSPHATE ROCK PREPARATION

Phosphate rock preparation involves benefication to remove impurities, drying to remove moisture, and grinding to improve reactivity.

In the United States phosphate rock is mined principally in Florida, the mountain states (Idaho, Montana, Wyoming, Utah), and Tennessee. New mines are opening in North Carolina. It is estimated that a total of 27 million tons was produced in the 1965–1966 fertilizer season (*22*). Mining of phosphate rock in the United States is done primarily by strip mining. In Florida, which provides about 70% of the production, the rock is found as a phosphate rock matrix about 20 feet in depth, lying beneath an overburden normally averaging 15 feet thick.

Usually, direct fired rotary kilns, 25–100 feet long, 8–10 feet in diameter, are used to dry phosphate rock (Fig. 18). These dryers use natural gas or fuel oil as fuel and are fired countercurrently. From the dryers,

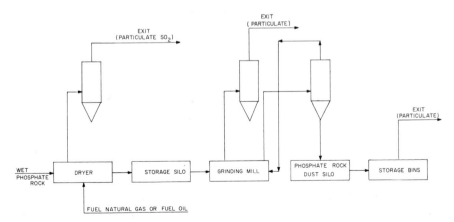

FIG. 18. Flow diagram of phosphate rock storage and grinding facilities, noting potential air pollution sources.

the material may be ground before storage and is finally conveyed to large storage silos. Air-swept ball mills are preferred for grinding phosphate rock.

Air Pollutant Emissions and Their Control

Although there are no significant emissions from phosphate rock beneficiation plants, emissions may be expected from drying and grinding operations. These emissions consist primarily of fine rock dust, but some sulfur dioxide may be present in the dryer exhaust from the combustion of the sulfur in the fuel. Phosphate rock dryers are usually equipped with dry cyclones followed by wet scrubbers. Particulate emissions are usually higher when drying pebble rock than concentrate. Because of its larger size, pebble rock usually has small adherent particles of clay and slime which, upon drying, are blown to the collectors or the atmosphere.

Phosphate rock grinders are a closed system except for vents to the atmosphere to control moisture. Because of the extremely fine 200-mesh particle size, considerable quantities of dust can be emitted from phosphate rock grinders with the vented air. For this reason, fertilizer plants are normally provided with baghouse collectors which will reduce atmospheric emissions from phosphate rock grinding to about 1 pound of dust per day per grinder. Other points of emission in a phosphate rock grinding and preparation plant are transfer points on conveying systems and discharge points at storage hoppers and silos. These can be provided with hoods and an exhaust system to collect the dust. One example is a bag collector, installed on top of a holding bin with dust pickup points not only from the bin but from the conveyor and weigh scale, with a capacity of 4,000 cfm and an efficiency of greater than 99% (52).

B. NORMAL SUPERPHOSPHATE PRODUCTION

Normal superphosphate is the term applied to the fertilizer produced by reacting sulfuric acid with phosphate rock. Normal superphosphate contains from 16 to 21% phosphoric anhydride (P_2O_5).

Past practice has been to locate the plants near the consumer, which means that the phosphate rock is shipped from the mining area to the plant. There are today over 200 normal superphosphate plants throughout the United States. Production and the total number of plants has declined slowly in recent years as more concentrated P_2O_5 products have been developed to meet the high analysis requirements. Production in 1966 was estimated to be 1.07 million tons (22).

While there have been developments and refinements, the three basic steps in the production of normal superphosphate have remained the same over the years (Fig. 19). Sulfuric acid and rock are intimately mixed (22, 53), dropped into a den, held for sufficient time to allow the slurry mixture to set into a solid porous form and stored to permit the acidulation to go to completion (54). Plants are described as batch or continuous, depending upon the type of den used. Over 75% of U.S. plants use the batch process. The most common type of plant uses a pan mixer capable of mixing a 2-ton batch of material. Its normal charge is 5 parts rock to 4 parts acid, which is mixed for 1–3 minutes in the mixer and then dropped into a batch den. Dens commonly used in this country have a capacity of about 40 tons, but others are available with capacities up to 300 tons. The mixing operation is practically continuous and an experienced operator can easily make 40 tons per hour of superphosphate (54).

The cone mixer developed by the Tennessee Valley Authority has come into use in many plants because of its low capital expense, low maintenance cost, and simple operation. This type of mixer can be used with either a batch or continuous den.

Depending upon the type of den, the mixture may be held from 30 minutes up to overnight before being transferred to storage. Some dens operate automatically with a cutting wheel which shaves the solidified mass from the den; others must be emptied by a drag line, by a crane, or by hand. Continuous dens are essentially slow-moving conveyor belts which permit the mixture of acid and rock to solidify before reaching the end of the belt. A cutting knife slices the solidified material from the belt. It is then carried to storage. Normal superphosphate as it comes from the dens is uncured and must be held in a curing building for up to 6 weeks to permit the acidulation reaction to go to completion.

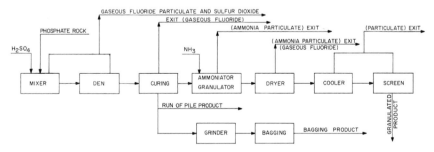

Fig. 19. Flow diagram of normal superphosphate plant, noting potential air pollution and sources. Control devices are not shown.

Simplified equations showing the reactions in the acidulation of phosphate rock are as follows:

$$3[Ca_3(PO_4)_2]CaF_2 + 7H_2SO_4 \rightarrow 3[Ca(H_2PO_4)_2] + 7CaSO_4 + 2HF \tag{15}$$

$$4HF + SiO_2 \rightarrow SiF_4 + 2H_2O \tag{16}$$

Following the curing period, three alternates are available: (1) the product can be ground and bagged for sale; (2) the cured superphosphate can be sold directly as run of pile product; or (3) the material can be granulated for sale as granulated superphosphate or granular mixed fertilizer.

For the latter alternative, normal superphosphate is blended with some or all of the following ingredients—ammonia, sulfuric acid, phosphoric acid, triple superphosphate, potash. Steam or water is added, if needed, to aid in granulation. The mixture is then passed through a rotary dryer where either natural gas or fuel oil dries the granulated product so that it will retain its form. From the dryer the material passes through a rotary cooler which removes sufficient moisture to eliminate the chance of the pellets binding together. From the cooler the product moves to storage bins for sale as a bagged or bulk product.

Air Pollutant Emissions and Their Control

The gases released from the acidulation of phosphate rock contain silicon tetrafluoride, carbon dioxide, steam, and sulfur oxides (55). The emission of sulfur oxides is a recent discovery and appears to arise from the reaction of phosphate rock and sulfuric acid (56). From 20 to 38% of the total fluoride in the phosphate rock is evolved in the acidulation and curing operation (53, 57). Curing building emissions are not usually controlled in normal superphosphate plants.

Fluoride concentration in the uncontrolled discharge from a normal superphosphate acidulation plant will average between 1 to 3 gm/ft³, STP (58). Usually the effluent gases will also contain from 6 to 10 mg of particulate per standard cubic foot of stack gas (59).

Until recently, it had been the practice to absorb the volatized fluorine compounds released from the acidulation plant in a water scrubber and run the solution to waste. This is still practiced in a few plants. Usually these scrubbing towers are locally designed and made of wood. Removal of silicon tetrafluoride is a relatively easy matter, and usually these scrubbers are quite effective as long as they are provided with sufficient water sprays. Water eductor scrubbers are also used quite frequently. These have the advantage of providing their own motive force to move the gases from the mixer and den through the scrubber without a separate fan. Efficiencies, based upon total fluorides, of 92–97% are claimed for these scrubbers (59). With the recent advent of fluoridation of municipal water supplies, there has been a trend toward recovering the fluorine from the water scrubbers as a solution of about 25% fluorsilicic acid. Vent gases from a granulator-ammoniator may contain particulates, ammonia, silicon tetrafluoride, hydrofluoric acid, ammonium chloride, and fertilizer dust. Emissions from the dryer will include gaseous and particulate fluorides, ammonia, and fertilizer dust. Some emissions will also contain sulfur oxide, especially if high sulfur oil is used as fuel to the dryer. Emissions from the cooler will contain primarily fertilizer dust, and may also include traces of the aforementioned pollutants.

Emissions from granulation plants are handled in many ways. In some remote plants, the granulator effluent is emitted directly to the atmosphere. In others the effluent may pass through a wet scrubber or it may be combined with the discharge from the dryer and collected in the dryer collector. Normally the dryer and cooler gas streams are passed through cyclone collectors. Up to 5% of the fertilizer may be carried to the cyclones in this form (60). Frequently, secondary collectors of either the wet scrubber or bag collector type are used (51a).

Emissions from the cyclone collector may range between 0.4 to 1.4 pounds of dust per 1000 pounds of gases (61). Emissions from secondary collectors will depend on their efficiency, which may range from 90 to 99%.

C. TRIPLE SUPERPHOSPHATE PRODUCTION

Triple superphosphate is the popular name for the product resulting from the reaction between phosphate rock and phosphoric acid. The product generally contains 40–49% P_2O_5, which is about $2\frac{1}{2}$ times the P_2O_5 usually found in normal superphosphate. Production has increased steadily over the years and triple superphosphate is now the most important source of P_2O_5 available in this country. There were approximately 16 plants in the United States, with a capacity of about 5.3 millions tons per year at the end of 1965 (22). There are indications that the growth of ammonium phosphate production will tend to retard the rate of increase in production capacity of triple superphosphate.

Unlike normal superphosphate, the production of triple superphosphate is usually a continuous operation in large plants located near phosphate rock deposits. The phosphate rock is ground to a fineness between about 80% through a 100-mesh screen and 95% through a 200-mesh Tyler screen (60). Although either furnace or wet process

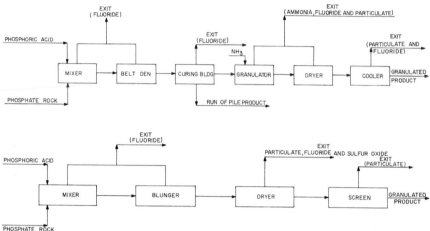

FIG. 20. Flow diagram for production of run of pile and granular triple superphosphate, noting potential air pollution sources.

phosphoric acid may be used as the acidulant, at the present time wet process acid is used almost exclusively. Concentrated acid with a P_2O_5 content of 50–55% is used. Fluoride content of wet process acid may be as high as 1–2%.

There are two major processes used in the production of triple superphosphate. The first uses a mixing cone to achieve intimate contact between the acid and rock. The resulting mix falls to a conveyor belt which moves the material to the curing building. On its way to the curing building the mix is passed through several mixers or blungers to aid in the contact of the rock and acid as well as to release fluorine vapors. Fluoride containing fume is collected along the entire length of the belt by a tight hood over the belt, the blungers, and the mixer. After curing for 30–60 days, the product can be sold as run of pile (ROP), or it can be granulated in separate equipment.

With the increased demand for granulated products, a second process was designed to produce granulated fertilizer directly. In one commercial process, the acid and phosphate rock are placed in mixing tanks, fed through a blunger for intimate mixing and release of some of the effluent gases, and then dried in a rotary dryer using oil or gas as fuel. The product is a directly granulated material which is rather hard and dense and normally not amenable to ammoniating (Fig. 20).

Air Pollutant Emissions and Their Control

Most triple superphosphate is of the nongranular type. The exit gases from a plant producing the nongranular product will contain considerable quantities of silicon tetrafluoride, some hydrogen fluoride, and a small amount of particulates. Usually low-pressure-drop wet collectors are used to reduce the fluorine content. Emission from one typical plant with a wet scrubber averaged 0.14 pound of fluoride per ton of product (62). Plants of this type retain the triple superphosphate in the curing building for 6 weeks to allow completion of the acidulation reaction. It has been estimated that emissions from curing buildings may be about 1.5 to 3 pounds of fluoride per ton of ROP superphosphate produced (62). Some companies are being required by local ordinances to seal their curing buildings and recirculate the building air through water scrubbers to reduce the emissions of fluoride.

In cases where ROP triple superphosphate is granulated or mixed as a granulated-mixed fertilizer, one of the greatest problems is the emission of dust and fumes from the dryer and cooler. Granulation plants of this type are usually equipped with cyclones and, in more progressive plants, have a water scrubber or even a bag collector. Emissions include silicon tetrafluoride, hydrogen fluoride, ammonia, particulate matter, and ammonium chloride. Fluoride emissions from ROP granulation plants will be about 0.05-0.1 pound fluoride per ton of product (62). Less fluorides are emitted in ROP granulation than by the direct granulation process.

In direct granulation plants the vessels used for initial contact between the phosphoric acid and the dried rock are vented through wet scrubbers to remove silicon tetrafluoride and hydrogen fluoride. Fluoride emission from the wet scrubber ranges from 0.03 to 1.56 pounds of fluoride per ton of product (62). Screening stations and bagging stations are a source of fertilizer dust emissions in this type of process.

D. DIAMMONIUM PHOSPHATE PRODUCTION

Ammonium phosphate production has not been separately reported, but can be estimated by noting that 16-48-0* fertilizer had a production of about 201,000 short tons in the year 1962–1963. This was a 33% increase over the preceding year. 18-46-0 fertilizer was consumed at the rate of 175,000 tons during the same year. This was a 116% increase over the preceding year (23). In the United States, ammonium phosphate is displacing, or at least retarding, the growth of triple superphosphate production. The primary reason is the higher plant food content and the lower shipping cost per pound of P_2O_5. There are today in the United States about 48 diammonium phosphate plants owned by 39 companies. Many new plants are being installed.

In the manufacture of diammonium phosphate the initial reaction

*16% nitrogen, 48% P_2O_5, 0% potassium.

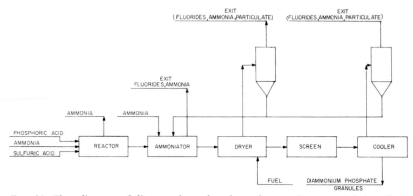

Fig. 21. Flow diagram of diammonium phosphate plant, noting potential air pollution sources.

between ammonia and phosphoric acid takes place in an acid brick-lined reactor tank (Fig. 21). Both fresh acid and acid that recycles from the gas scrubbers are used as feedstock. In many plants some 93% sulfuric acid is used to control the analysis of the final product. The relative amounts of phosphoric and sulfuric acid usually depend on the purity of the incoming phosphoric acid. The product of the reactor is pumped as a slurry to a TVA rotary ammoniator. In the ammoniator additional ammonia is sparged underneath the mixing bed to achieve a final mole ratio of 1.8 to 2.0. While the equipment is rotating, agglomeration takes place and the ammoniation is completed. Diammonium phosphate granules are discharged from the ammoniator to a rotary dryer, thence through a screening station and a rotary cooler to storage. Some ammonium phosphate is recycled back to the ammoniator for product control. The basic reaction involved in the process is given by:

$$2NH_4 + H_3PO_4 \rightarrow (NH_4)_2HPO_4 \qquad (17)$$

Air Pollutant Emissions and Their Control

The major pollutants from diammonium phosphate production are fluoride, particulates, and ammonia. Dust-producing areas are the cage mills, where oversized product from the screens is ground before being recycled to the ammoniator. Dust from these points is usually vented through cyclone collectors and then to either an impingement or a venturi scrubber. Vent gases from the reactor and ammoniator tanks, which contain high quantities of ammonia, are usually scrubbed with acid to recover the residual ammonia.

Fluoride emissions in diammonium phosphate production will range from 0.10 to 0.40 pounds of fluoride per ton of P_2O_5 produced (62). Little data is available on ammonia emissions. These may be significant in many cases, but usually are carefully controlled since loss of product is involved.

E. GRANULATION

Granulation is a method of processing that has been widely adopted as a means of improving the storage and handling properties of fertilizer materials and mixtures by increasing their normal particle size to material that will largely be retained on a 16-mesh sieve and which includes particles in the range of 1 to 4 mm in diameter. Some superphosphate and mixed fertilizers have a narrower particle size range, and occasionally an appreciable portion of a semigranular or granular product passes a 16-mesh sieve. Fertilizers in this general particle size range are classed as granular whether they are agglomerates of smaller particles, or are produced by either the mechanical disintegration of larger masses, or the mechanical removal of small particles. Conversely, the terms nongranular and powdered fertilizer do not necessarily relate to an extremely finely divided powder but rather to a material that has not been processed to increase its normal average particle size.

After the introduction of granular normal superphosphate to the market in 1935, granulation practice in the U.S. advanced very little for the next 15 years (63). It was not until 1950 (64) that the first plant (Iowa Plant Food Manufacturing Co.) to incorporate the ammoniator technique for granulation of a mixture directly to grade became operative. There has been great advance since then. Although no recent statistics are available, it can be assumed that more than 50% of the fertilizer produced is in the granular form (29).

In the granulation of ammonium phosphate fertilizer, a gypsum-acid slurry is obtained by bypassing the filter in a phosphoric acid plant (Fig. 22). Ammonia is introduced into this slurry and into acidulated phosphate from the acidulation tank. The mixture then flows to the dryer. From the dryer the product is screened. Large lumps are crushed and recycled to the granulator along with the fines passing the screens (65).

Many types of equipment are used in the granulation step to apply a slurry coating to undersized particles. These include twin shaft pugmills or blungers, rotating drums, etc. (29, 66).

Air Pollutant Emissions and Their Control

Water scrubbers of various types are used for recovery of ammonia and ammonium salts, which are then recycled to the process. The

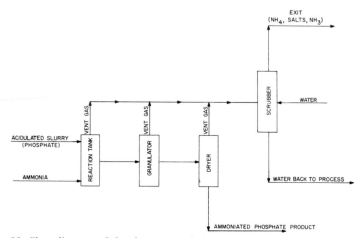

FIG. 22. Flow diagram of the slurry granulation process in the manufacture of fertilizer, noting potential air pollution sources.

greater portion of the ammonia is recovered. However, ammonium salts are not easily recovered due to their very fine size. They can be recovered by high-pressure-drop venturi-type scrubbers and effluent dust loadings can be reduced to 0.05 grains/ft³, STP.

In nonslurry granulation, part or all of the neutralization reaction is carried out in the granulation vessel. The number of sources of air pollution is reduced by elimination of the reaction tanks. This method of granulation is widely used for mixed fertilizers based on superphosphate (67).

F. Bulk-Dry Blending, and Mixing

In the early days of the mixed fertilizer industry mechanical dry mixing was the general practice. With the advent of ammoniators in the early 1930's the practice of dry mixing declined and the use of ammoniating solutions became popular as a means of incorporating low-cost nitrogen by chemical reaction of ammonia with superphosphate. When granulation became the established practice in the industry, sulfuric and phosphoric acid became important raw materials for fixing ammonia and for furnishing heat of reaction in mixed granulation processes. However, for a number of reasons, the industry has resumed "bulk-dry blending," an unfortunate choice of words because most mixed fertilizers are blended in bulk during early stages of processing. Present practice, mainly used in the central area of the U.S. (29), involves the mixing of dry granular materials such as ammonium sulfate, concentrated superphosphate, and potassium chloride in small plants and transporting the product in bulk to the farmer. The granular product, and bulk delivery of the product direct to the farmer, distinguish present day bulk-dry blending from the dry mixing operation of a generation ago.

The chief advantage of dry-bulk blending is service to the customer. The custom mixer uses the production point as the distribution point. Material comes in by rail, is mixed, and sent directly to the user.

Air Pollutant Emissions and Their Control

Most emissions occur at loading and unloading points. Cyclones and bag filters are used to reduce emissions and are quite effective (*18*). Recovery can be above 99% with properly designed equipment. Loading and unloading equipment design, and proper maintenance of this equipment to prevent leakage at these points is important in keeping emissions to a minimum.

XI. Ammonium Nitrate

Until the end of World War II, ammonium nitrate was important mainly for its use in munitions and commercial explosives. Ammonium nitrate is now a principal ingredient of inorganic fertilizers and is the leading source of nitrogen for fertilizer use (*68*). Total production of ammonium nitrate in 1965 was 2 million tons.

Commercial processes for the manufacture of ammonium nitrate depend almost entirely on the neutralization of nitric acid with ammonia in liquid or gaseous form (Fig. 23). Synthetic ammonia, as the anhydrous

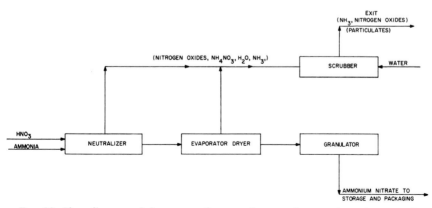

FIG. 23. Flow diagram of the process for manufacture of ammonium nitrate, noting potential air pollution sources.

liquid, and nitric acid produced from the oxidation of ammonia are used.

Essentially three steps are involved in producing ammonium nitrate: neutralization, evaporation of the neutralized solution, and control of the particle size and characteristics of the dry product.

A. NEUTRALIZATION

Direct neutralization is practiced when pure reactants are used in an aqueous medium. The reaction of ammonia with nitric acid is strongly exothermic; both reactants are volatile at the resulting elevated temperatures. This condition must be controlled to prevent loss of materials. Usually a slight excess of nitric acid, the less volatile of the two reactants, is maintained during neutralization.

B. EVAPORATION

Procedures vary depending on the water content of the reactants and the control of temperatures. In methods formerly in wide use, the neutral ammonium nitrate solution was evaporated to a high degree of concentration, with subsequent cooling and granulation of the product. Other processes carry the evaporation to a lesser degree of concentration and complete the separation of the solid ammonium nitrate by crystallization or, more frequently, by continuous evaporation in specially designed apparatus.

C. CONTROL OF PARTICLE SIZE AND PROPERTIES

Various procedures, such as graining, flaking, and spraying, have been practiced over the years to obtain nitrate particles or grains for the final product. The method that has been adopted by the great majority of plants constructed since the end of World War II is called prilling (69).

Synthetic, gaseous, ammonia is reacted with nitric acid in aqueous medium. The neutralized solution is brought to a concentration of about 95% NH_4NO_3 through utilization of the heat of reaction. This highly concentrated solution, at a temperature of 130°–135 °C, is then sprayed or otherwise introduced into a tall tower of resistant material so that it falls in the form of spherical droplets. The tower may be as high as 100–200 feet to allow the drops to solidify during fall. The moisture of the solid drop is not greatly reduced in the solidification step but remains enclosed in the crusted particle. Its moisture is then successively reduced in a series of dryers first to around 2%, then to about 0.2%. The final product consists of firm, dry pellets of relatively small diameter.

D. CONTINUOUS VACUUM CRYSTALLIZATION PROCESS

This process was developed by the Tennessee Valley Authority, and a large plant was constructed.

Sufficient ammonia gas is introduced below the surface of a body of aqueous nitric acid, so that the resulting solution is slightly acidic. The solution then flows to the neutralizers where it initially contains about 56% NH_4NO_3, and is maintained in boiling condition by reaction heat. It is then charged to vacuum evaporators operating in parallel. The heat for evaporation is furnished from by-product steam from the neutralizers and the liquor leaves the evaporators at a concentration of about 79% NH_4NO_3, about 1% under saturation.

The solution then goes to a number of vacuum crystallizers where further concentration takes place at a temperature of about 36 °C and a pressure of 25 mm Hg. The crystals are removed from the bottom of the crystallizer and pass to centrifuges which bring the water content down to 1–2%. The water content is further reduced to around 0.05% in a rotary dryer. The highest temperature reached in the process is 60°–65 °C, at which point the material is discharged from the dryer.

E. STENGEL PROCESS

This process claims the advantage of lower equipment requirement and savings in the evaporation step, brought about by preheating the reactants prior to the neutralization step. Heated ammonia gas and pre-heated nitric acid solution are caused to flow continuously into a packed, tubular reactor where ammonium nitrate is formed, with vaporization of water. The mixture of molten ammonium nitrate and steam passes to a cyclone separator from which the molten material, containing 0.1–0.2% water flows out at the bottom. The steam leaves at the top. The original Stengel process caused the molten nitrate to solidify by cooling onto a cooled conveyor belt. The sheet of solid material could be broken up into particles, e.g., by flaking. Desirable particle size and characteristics may also be obtained by the prilling method.

Air Pollutant Emissions and Their Control

The main emissions in the aforementioned processes occur in the neutralization and drying operations. By keeping the neutralization process on the acidic side, losses of ammonia and nitric oxides are kept at a minimum. In the prilling process losses are dependent upon the velocity of the air in the prilling tower. Total fines lost from the process can be kept to less than 1% of equivalent process raw materials. Some losses are due to the nitrous oxides present in the feed acid. This can be reduced by purchase of nitric acid with no more than 0.1% nitrous acid. Water scrubbers are used in most cases to recover ammonia and ammonium nitrate dust entrained in the vent gases. Water is recycled in scrubbers and returned to process.

XII.   Chlorine

In 1964, approximately 6 million tons of chlorine were produced in the United States (70) by 69 plants (71). Ninety-five percent of the chlorine tonnage in this country is produced by two electrolytic methods—the diaphragm and mercury cell processes. All other processes, such as the fused salt and the nitric acid-salt processes account for the remaining 5%.

Chlorine is used principally in the manufacture of chlorinated hydrocarbons and organics, pulp and paper bleaching, and in the purification of municipal water supplies. In 1966 estimated production of chlorine was 6,946,000 tons.

ELECTROLYTIC PROCESS

The major raw material needed for electrolysis is brine, obtained from rock salt, underground brine pools, or concentrated seawater. Most new chlorine installations are located near the brine sources because of the high shipping costs of salt. Brine impurities include calcium, magnesium, and iron sulfates. These must be removed from the brine to ensure high cell operating efficiencies.

The electric energy requirements for electrolysis are large, amounting to 2500–4000 kilowatt hours per ton of chlorine produced (72).

Of the two major types of electrolytic cells produced in this country, the diaphragm cell accounts for about 70% of the output (Fig. 24). Consisting of two graphite electrodes, a diaphragm covering the cathode serves to separate the reaction products—chlorine and sodium hydroxide—while allowing the brine to diffuse to the cathode and the hydroxyl ions to diffuse to the anode. Purified, saturated brine (26.5% NaCl) is fed continuously to the anode compartment, where hot, wet chlorine gas is produced. Sodium hydroxide and gaseous hydrogen are liberated at the cathode. The caustic-brine solution is withdrawn from the cathode compartment and sent to the caustic evaporators for salt separation and concentration to either 50% or 73% solutions. (See Section IX,A.) Hydrogen from the cathode is usually burned to gain its heat of combustion, although some plants utilize the by-product hydrogen for organic hydrogenation or the synthesis of hydrochloric acid.

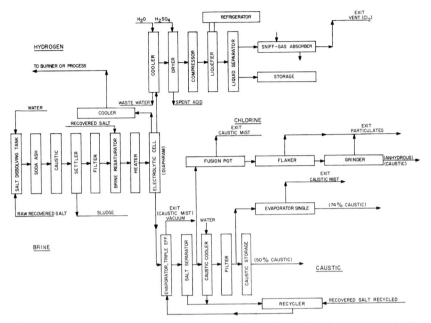

FIG. 24. Flow diagram of diaphragm cell installation for sodium hydroxide and chlorine manufacture, noting potential air pollution sources.

The chlorine cell gas is saturated with water vapor at 50 °C and contains about 98% chlorine. The remaining 2% is hydrogen, carbon dioxide, and air. Direct-contact water scrubbers cool the hot gas and condense the water vapor. Sulfuric acid drying towers next remove residual moisture. The dried chlorine gas then passes through fiber mist eliminators to remove brine and sulfuric acid mists from the process stream (73). Sulfuric acid sealed compressors raise the pressure of the gaseous chlorine to 50 or 60 pounds per square inch. It is then liquefied by refrigeration. The liquid chlorine then is stored and shipped in 55-ton tank cars or 1-ton cylinders to the chlorine consumer.

The mercury cell is not used as extensively in the United States as it is in Europe. Unlike the diaphragm cell, only chlorine is produced directly in the mercury cell anode, while the sodium ion forms an amalgam with the moving mercury cathode. This amalgam is then transferred to a decomposer where the amalgam reacts with water to produce gaseous hydrogen and caustic solution. Separation of the caustic from the brine prevents transfer of heavy metal brine impurities and thus ensures high quality sodium hydroxide.

Chlorine gas from the mercury cell is dried, cooled, and liquefied using essentially the methods described for diaphragm cells.

Air Pollutant Emissions and Their Control

The major source of gaseous chlorine from the electrolytic production of chlorine is the liquefaction vent gases. Other sources include: (1) tank car, cylinder, and barge loading operations, whereby liquid chlorine displaces chlorine-laden vapors from the empty containers; (2) dechlorination of weak brine cell liquor in preparation for recycle to the cell; and (3) occasional equipment failure, such as that of chlorine compressors, which necessitates the disposal of moderate amounts of chlorine cell gas.

The liquefaction of chlorine by compression and cooling recovers about 85–95% of the chlorine. The remaining chlorine is present in the residual vent gases by virtue of its vapor pressure at liquefaction temperatures. The residual or "sniff gas," (also called "blow gas") contains carbon dioxide, hydrogen, air, and chlorine.

Recent improvements in chlorine liquefaction techniques have yielded liquefaction efficiencies as high as 99% (74). One such technique, for instance, involves second-stage liquefaction at lower temperatures with air dilution to prevent buildup of hydrogen beyond the 4–5% explosive limit. Such improvements not only add to overall process efficiencies and economics but also decrease the chlorine content in the sniff gas.

Typical sniff-gas concentrations, however, will vary from 20 to 50% by volume, and may represent as much as 8% of a plant's total chlorine production (75). Exact sniff-gas composition will depend upon liquefaction pressure, temperature, and the chlorine concentration of the incoming gas stream. For an uncontrolled 125-ton/day plant, sniff-gas losses could mean a potential emission rate ranging from 1 to 6 tons per day (76). With such obvious economic benefits to be realized from chlorine recovery, a number of direct uses for sniff gas have been found: (1) production of hydrochloric acid; (2) chlorination of organic and inorganic compounds; and (3) chlorination of cooling tower water to prevent algae buildup. Not all installations, however, are capable of

TABLE II
Chlorine Sniff-Gas Recovery and Removal Systems

System	Reference
1. Water scrubber and desorber	76–78
2. Caustic and/or lime scrubber	79, 80
3. Carbon tetrachloride absorber and desorber	75, 78, 81, 82
4. Silica gel adsorber and desorber	83
5. Brine absorber	84

finding in-plant uses for the sniff gas, so that absorption and scrubbing systems are required. Table II lists some sniff-gas recovery or treatment systems, reported in the literature and in patents.

In chlorine recovery systems using water as the absorptive medium, a rubber-lined steel blow-gas tower filled with ceramic packing contacts the vent gas countercurrently at liquefier pressures. The chlorine-rich water is then returned to the direct-contact cooler where the scrubber water cools the chlorine cell gas. The action of the hot cell gas releases the absorbed chlorine, while a steam heating section, at the bottom of the cooler, completes the chlorine stripping. Chlorine emissions from one water absorber vent gas have been reported at 0.5–1.0% chlorine by volume for a blow-gas composition of 15% chlorine (77). Because the water absorber does not remove all of the vent gas chlorine, even at high pressures, it is common practice to conduct the water scrubber vent gases to tall stacks for dispersion or to a caustic or lime scrubber for complete absorption.

A much simpler system, one that involves treatment of the sniff gas only, employs a caustic scrubber to react chlorine with sodium hydroxide. The reaction products are bleach, salt, and water:

$$Cl_2 + 2NaOH \rightarrow NaOCl + NaCl + H_2O \tag{18}$$

Since caustic is often found in excess near chlorine plants, it represents an inexpensive approach to the blow-gas problem. The main disadvantage of the caustic scrubber arises from the disposal of bleach-salt solutions. Some plants dispose of this waste in nearby rivers or streams. In a more acceptable manner, one plant plans to send the effluent to a treatment plant (77a). Chlorine emissions from the caustic scrubber are virtually nil, provided that caustic flow rates and concentrations are maintained. Caustic mist eliminators should be employed on the gas outlets. Lime solution may also be used to replace caustic as a scrubbing liquor.

Another blow-gas recovery system employs carbon tetrachloride to absorb chlorine at pressures of 100 psig, and a separate steam-heated stripper to boil off pure chlorine and regenerate the solvent. Chlorine gas from the stripper is then recycled to the liquefaction gas stream or returned to chlorine-consuming processes in the plant.

Since carbon tetrachloride can absorb 10 to 12 times more chlorine than water, recovery of the chlorine is much more complete. However, carbon tetrachloride losses have been reported at 30 pounds per ton of recovered chlorine (78). The use of other organic solvents for the absorption of chlorine has also been reported in the patent literature (78a).

Other chlorine vent gas recovery systems include: (1) use of silica gel as an adsorbent under pressure, and recovery of chlorine by degassing at low pressure; and (2) absorption in cell brine. Neither method has gained wide acceptance in the industry.

Other sources of air pollution from chlorine plants are tank car and container filling operations in which chlorine losses may amount to 2% of chlorine production (78). In most plants, these vent gases are piped to the blow-gas recovery scrubber and are used there or in other in-plant processes, such as chlorination.

In mercury cell plants, it is common practice to dechlorinate the depleted brine before resaturation by using successively (1) acidification with hydrochloric acid; (2) vacuum flash towers operating at about 70 °C and 50% atmosphere; and (3) air-blowing packed towers. Free chlorine from the first two processes is returned to the cell chlorine manifold, while the air-blower vent gases are sent to the sniff-gas disposal units.

Where convenient hypochlorite outlets, such as paper mills, exist, air blowing the brine directly and absorbing the evolved chlorine in caustic is employed (78a).

An infrequent pollution problem in chlorine plants arises when a compressor failure occurs. Moderate amounts of cell chlorine are usually disposed of using the existing sniff-gas disposal systems mentioned above.

XIII.   Bromine

The principal use of bromine is the production of antiknock compounds for gasoline. The 1950 production of bromine was 98.5 million pounds (68). Production in 1965 was 20,414 tons. Ninety-nine percent of the world's commercially available bromine is in seawater. Other sources of bromine are closed basins such as Searles Lake, containing 0.085% bromine, and commercial brines in Michigan and Arkansas (0.05–0.30% bromine).

In all bromine production processes, the reactions require: (1) oxidation of bromide to bromine; (2) removal of bromine by vaporization from solution: (3) condensation of the vapor; and (4) purification. Only chlorine is used for oxidation to bromine. Bromine removal requires driving out bromine vapors with a current of air or steam. Steam is suitable only when the raw material contains 0.1% or more of bromine, but air is more economical when the percentage is less.

Steam Process for Natural Brines and Bitters

Raw brine is preheated to 90 °C then passed to a chlorinator—a tank lined with resistant material and packed with rings (Fig. 25). A portion

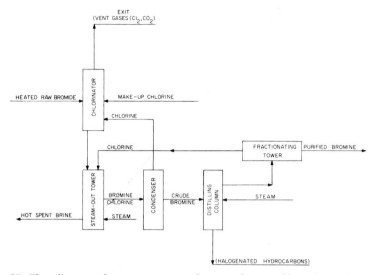

FIG. 25. Flow diagram of steam-out process for manufacture of bromine, noting potential air pollution sources.

of the total chlorine used is introduced into the chlorinator. Brine is then passed to the steam-out tower at the top, and flows down through the packing. Steam is introduced into the bottom. The remainder of the chlorine is introduced above the steam inlet to prevent escape of chlorine into the outgoing brine. The brine is then neutralized with lime.

Halogen-laden vapor passes through the condenser to the gravity separator. The noncondensible gases Br_2 and Cl_2 are returned to the bottom of the chlorinator tower so that they may be recovered; gases, such as CO_2, escape from the chlorinator. The water layer from the separator, saturated with chlorine and bromine, is returned to the steam-out tower. Crude bromine collects at the bottom of the separator, and then passes through a trap to a distilling column, where higher boiling halogenated hydro-carbons are removed from the bottom and free halogens are boiled off at the top. The vapors are cooled in the reflux condenser, from which chlorine is recycled to the steam-out tower, while bromine proceeds to a fractionating column for purification.

Although raw brine is nearly neutral, it contains small amounts of reducing substances which produce HCl when chlorine is introduced to the brine. This acid must be neutralized to prevent corrosion of pumps and heat exchangers.

The bromine manufacturing process is strictly controlled. There is little waste of chlorine. The surplus is continually returned to the towers and the amount consumed is essentially that needed to replace the bromides or react with reducing substances. Better than 95% of available bromine is recovered from the brine (3). The system is designed so that pumping of wet halogens is not required.

Air Pollutant Emissions and Their Control

Very little chlorine is lost in the chlorinator and most losses, if they occur, are during start-ups and shutdowns, or in leakage in storage, piping, or venting. Most emissions can be eliminated by proper process feed control in the chlorinator.

REFERENCES

1. *Chem. Eng. News* **43,** 100–107 (1965).
2. R. W. Shreve, "The Chemical Process Industries," 1st ed. McGraw-Hill, New York, 1945.
3. R. W. Shreve, "The Chemical Process Industries," 2nd ed. McGraw-Hill, New York, 1957.
4. R. E. Kirk and D. F. Othmer, "Encyclopaedia of Chemical Technology," 2nd ed. Vols. 2, 7, 9, 10, 12, and 13. Wiley (Interscience), New York, 1951.
5. Bureau of Census, Dept. of Commerce, Washington, D.C., 1960.
6. W. L. Faith, D. B. Keyes, and R. L. Clark, "Industrial Chemicals," Wiley, New York, 1957.
7. T. Hooker, U.S. Patent 2,841,243 (1953).
8. D. H. Campbell, U.S. Patent 2,717,199 (1955).
9. J. W. Latchum, Jr., U.S. Patent 2,433,996 (1948).
10. L. A. Meyers, U.S. Patent 2,490,454 (1949).
11. J. W. Spranger and A. Peschko, U.S. Patent 2,558,011 (1951).
12. M. Sitenfield, *Purdue Univ., Eng. Bull., Ext. Ser.* **30,** 53–62 (1949).
13. J. E. Siebold, U.S. Patent 2,545,314 (1951).
14. C. J. Tobraty, R. J. Moore, R. D. Barnard, and R. H. Meyer, *Chem. Eng. Progr.* **49,** 611–616 (1953).
15. W. L. Faith, D. B. Keyes, and R. L. Clark, "Industrial Chemicals," 3rd ed., pp. 426–433. Wiley, New York, 1965.
16. *Chem. Eng. News* **42,** 25–26 (1964).
17. A. J. Rudge, "The Manufacture and Use of Fluorine and its Compounds." Oxford Univ. Press, London and New York, 1962.
18. *Ind. Chemist* **37,** No. 435, 379–383; No. 436, 315–318 (1961).
19. W. R. Rogers and K. Muller, *Chem. Eng. Progr.* **59,** 85–88 (1963).
20. H. W. Zabel, *Chem. Ind.* **66,** 508–509 (1950).
21. K. K. Huffstutler and W. E. Starnes, *Proc. 54th Ann. Meeting Air Pollution Control Assoc., New York, 1961* Paper No. 9.
21a. Census of Manufacturers, Industrial Inorganic Chemicals, Bureau of Census, U.S. Department of Commerce, Washington, D.C., 1963.
22. A. J. Piombino, *Chem. Week* **95,** 109–132 (1964).
23. E. C. Houston, "The Phosphate Industry in the United States." Tennessee Valley Authority, 1965.
24. W. C. Weber and F. W. Edwards, *Proc., Fertilizer Soc. Soc. Anal. Chem.* **67,** 39 (1961).
25. "Atmospheric Emissions from Thermal Process Phosphoric Acid Manufacture,"

Cooperative Study Project. Mfg. Chemists, Assoc. and U.S. Dept. of Health, Education, and Welfare, Public Health Serv., Washington, D.C., 1968 (in publication).

25a. Anonymous, *Chem. Eng.* pp. 94, 96, May 11, 1964.

26. M. M. Striplin, Jr., *Chem. Eng.* p. 160, 1961.

27. J. J. Pike, *Chem. Eng.* **74**, 194 (1967).

28. *Chem. Eng.* **68**, 112–114 (1961).

29. U.S. Department of Agriculture and T.V.A., "Superphosphate: Its History, Chemistry and Manufacture," Agri. Res. Serv., 1964.

30. P. Drinker and T. Hatch, "Industrial Dust," 2nd ed. pp. 213–239, McGraw-Hill, New York, 1954.

31. G. Drake, *Brit. Chem. Eng.* **8**, 12–20 (1963).

32. "Atmospheric Emissions from Nitric Acid Manufacturing Processes," Cooperative Study Project, Mfg. Chemists' Assoc. and U.S. Dept. of Health, Education, and Welfare, Public Health Serv., Div. Air Pollution, Cincinnati, Ohio 1965.

33. M. D. Peters, *Chem. Eng.* **62**, 197–200 (1955).

34. H. Rudorfer and K. Kremsey, Austrian Patent 184,922 (1956).

35. R. Schonbeck, Austrian Patent 188,723 (1957).

36. H. R. L. Streight, *Can. J. Chem.* **36**, 3–11 (1958).

37. V. M. Kakabadze and I. L. Kakabadze, *Akad. Nauk Gruzen, USSR* No. 5, pp. 549–556 (1957) (In Russian), see *Chem. Abstr.* **52**, 13284c (1958).

38. H. C. Andersen, W. J. Green, and D. R. Steel, *Ind. Eng. Chem.* **53**, 199–204 (1961).

39. H. C. Hosphord, *Air Pollution Smoke Prevent. Assoc. Am., Proc.* **45**, 65–69 (1952).

40. "Atmospheric Emissions from Sulfuric Acid Manufacturing Processes," U.S. Dept. of Health, Education, and Welfare, Public Health Serv., 1965.

41. O. D. Massey, *Chem. Eng.* **7**, 143 (1959).

42. K. H. Roll, *Air Repair* **1**, 6–10 (1952).

43. C. Lawler, *J. Air Pollution Control Assoc.* **7**, 29–31 (1957).

44. W. Moller and K. Winkler, *Proc. 60th Ann. Meeting Air Pollution Control Assoc., Cleveland, Ohio, 1967*, Paper No. 67–115.

45. "Commercial Lime Plants in the United States and Canada." Natl. Lime Assoc., Washington, D.C., 1965.

46. C. J. Lewis, *Proc., Ann. Conv. Natl. Lime Assoc., Phoenix, Arizona* **64**, (1966).

47. S. S. Blackmore, *57th Ann. Meeting Air Pollution Control Assoc., Houston, Texas, 1964* Paper No. 11.

48. T. T. Collins, Jr., *Tappi* **42**, 9–13 (1959).

49. F. Gibaldi, *Rock Prod.* **58**, 126–134 (1955).

50. F. B. Kaylor, *J. Air Pollution Control Assoc.* **15**, 65–67 (1965).

51. *Chem. Eng. News* **43**, 51–118 (1965).

51a. H. C. Twiehaus and N. J. Ehlers, *Chem. Ind.* **63** (2), 230–233 (1948).

52. H. O. Grant, *Chem. Eng. Progr.* **60**, 53–55 (1964).

53. K. D. Jacob, *Am. Soc. Agron., Monograph* **3**, 454 (1954).

54. W. H. Waggaman, "Phosphoric Acid. Phosphates and Phosphatic Fertilizers," A.C.S. Monograph Ser., 2nd edition. Am. Chem. Soc., Washington, D.C., 1952.

55. A. V. Slack, *et al.*, "Superphosphate—Its History, Chemistry, and Manufacture." U.S. Govt. Printing Office, Washington, D. C., 1964.

56. K. A. Sherwin, *Trans. Inst. Chem. Engrs. (London)* **32**, Suppl., 172 (1954).

57. K. D. Jacob, *et al., Ind. Eng. Chem.* **34**, 722–728 (1942).

58. K. T. Semrau, *J. Air Pollution Control Assoc.* **7** (1957) (a review).

59. R. L. Webb, *Farm Chem.* **29** (7), 29–30 (1960).

60. V. Sauchelli, "Chemistry and Technology of Fertilizers," A.C.S. Monograph Ser. Am. Chem. Soc., Washington, D.C., 1960.

61. Anonymous, *Farm Chem.* **27** (9), 15–16 (1958).
62. K. K. Huffstutler and W. E. Starnes, *Proc. 59th Ann. Meeting Air Pollution Control Assoc., San Francisco, 1966* Paper No. 66-8.
63. B. Ober and E. H. Wright, U.S. Patent 1,947,138 (1934).
64. *Agr. Chem.* **31,** 36 and 93–94 (1950).
65. G. F. Moore and T. Beer, U.S. Patent 2,963,259 (1957).
66. C. K. Perry, "Chilton Kirpatrick Perry's Chemical Engineer's Handbook," 4th ed., McGraw-Hill, 1963.
67. Tennessee Valley Authority Report, "Ammoniator-Granulator-Granular Diammonium Phosphate." Tennessee Valley Authority, 1960.
68. R. E. Kirk and D. F. Othmer, "Encyclopedia of Chemical Technology," 2nd ed., Vol. 11, 1963.
69. "Modern Chemical Processes," Vol. 3. Reinhold, 1954.
70. "Chlorine Production in the United States." The Chlorine Institute, Inc., 1965.
71. "Chlor-Alkali Producers and Chlorine Repackagers in North America." The Chlorine Institute, Inc., 1965.
72. D. W. F. Hardie, "Electrolytic Manufacture of Chemicals from Salt," p. 18, Oxford Univ. Press, London and New York, 1959.
73. J. H. Nichols and J. A. Brink, Jr., *Chem. Eng.* **71,** 221–222 (1964).
74. H. A. Sommers, *Chem. Eng. Progr.* **61,** 94–109 (1965).
75. R. C. Sutter, *J. Air Pollution Control Assoc.* **7,** 30–31 (1957).
76. T. Hooker, *et al.,* U.S. Patent 2,750,002 (1956).
77. H. W. Bryson, *Oregon State Coll., Eng. Expt. Sta., Circ.* **29,** 147–149 (1963).
77a. Anonymous, *Chem. Age* **80,** 635–644 (1958).
78. Anonymous, *Chem. Eng.* **64,** 6 (1957).
78a. J. S. Sconce, "Chlorine: Its Manufacture, Properties and Uses," 1962.
79. Verein Deutscher Ingenieure, Kommission Reinhaltung der Luft, "The Restriction of Chlorine Gas Emissions," VDI 2103, p. 5. Federation of the Chemical Industry, Frankfurt/Main, 1960.
80. F. H. Cady, "A Kraft Mill Chlorine Gas Recovery Scrubber," Weyerhaeuser Company, Pulp and Paperboard Div., Everett, Washington.
81. F. Molyneux, *Chem. & Process Eng.* **43,** 267–275 (1962).
82. R. E. Hulm, U.S. Patent 2,765,873 (1956).
83. R. Wynkoop, U.S. Patent 2,800,197 (1955).
84. G. P. Henegar, *et al.,* U.S. Patent 3,052,612 (1962).

GENERAL REFERENCE

Additional pertinent material is in Chapter 11 of "Air Pollution Engineering Manual, Los Angeles APCD" (J. A. Danielson, ed.), PHS Publn. 999-AP-40, DHEW, Cincinnati (1967); and will be published in the National Air Pollution Control Administration's publications: "Control Technology for Particular Air Pollutants," and "Control Technology for Sulfur Oxides Air Pollutants."

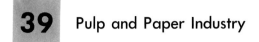

39 Pulp and Paper Industry

Donald F. Adams

I. Introduction

Three major processes, mechanical, semichemical, and chemical, are used in the preparation of cellulose wood pulp. The chemical processes inherently have the greatest potential for air pollution. Of the various commercially developed chemical processes, only the sulfate (kraft) and sulfite methods will be considered since they represent the most-used chemical methods.

The 1966 total world production of wood pulp by all processes was approximately 95,646,000 short tons (*1*). Ten countries have an annual production in excess of 1 million tons, representing nearly 89% of the world production. In five of these countries, representing approximately 74% of the world production, 47% of pulp production was by the kraft process; 24% was mechanical pulp; and 16% was sulfite. In the United States, kraft pulp accounted for more than 63% of the total production. Most of the new chemical pulp production facilities under construction or in the design stage will use the kraft process.

Chemical pulp is obtained by cooking the raw material, usually wood, with appropriate concentrations of chemicals in a digester under controlled conditions of temperature, pressure, and time. During cooking (digestion) the wood lignins, carbohydrates, organic acids, resins, etc., are dissolved in the cooking liquor, leaving a mass of impure cellulose fibers. The pulp, after washing to remove the adhering cooking chemicals, may then be formed directly into unbleached sheets of desired thickness, or subjected to purification and bleaching with oxidants, such as Cl_2 or ClO_2, and then formed into bleached sheets with the required whiteness. These steps are common to all chemical pulp production processes.

Simplified descriptions of the chemical methods of pulping are provided to permit an understanding of the complex interdependence of types and quantities of air emissions and process modifications. Detailed descriptions of these pulping methods are available in the literature (2, 3).

II. Kraft Pulping Process

A. Sources of Emissions

In the kraft process, wood chips are cooked at elevated temperature under pressure with a solution of sodium sulfide and sodium hydroxide (white liquor). The spent cooking liquid (black liquor) is separated from the cellulose fiber. The fiber is then washed, and bleached if necessary to produce the desired product, and formed into sheets. The remainder of the process involves recovery and regeneration of the cooking chemicals. Odorous and particulate emissions are potential by-products from many of the process steps. Figure 1 presents a generalized flow sheet of the process.

1. *Digestion*

Gases are continually evolved during the digestion of the wood chips with alkaline sodium sulfide. The concentration of the chemicals are usually maintained within a "sulfidity" range of 15–25%—the percentage representing that portion of the sodium ions present as sodium sulfide. The remaining sodium ions are coupled with hydroxide ions.

During digestion, some cellulose is demethylated and reacts with sulfide to yield mercaptan and methyl sulfide. Hydrogen sulfide also may be produced. The build-up of head pressure in the digester is intermittently relieved to the atmosphere, thereby contributing small volumes of volatile sulfur and turpentine compounds to the atmosphere. The types and quantities of sulfur compounds produced are dependent upon the cooking variables of chemical concentration, tem-

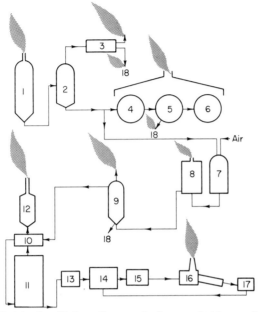

FIG. 1. Simplified kraft mill flow diagram. 1, digester; 2, blow tank; 3, blow heat recovery; 4, washers; 5, screens; 6, dryers; 7, oxidation tower; 8, foam tank; 9, multiple-effect evaporator; 10, direct evaporator; 11, recovery furnace; 12, electrostatic precipitator; 13, dissolver; 14, causticizer; 15, mud filter; 16, lime kiln; 17, slaker; 18, sewer.

perature, pressure, time, and species of wood being pulped. Isopropyl mercaptan has been reported from the pulping of eucalyptus (4, 5) and other wood (6).

In at least two laboratories, research is under way which will correlate the digestion parameters of chemical concentration, time, pressure, temperature of cook, and species of wood with the quantity and types of sulfur compounds produced (7, 8). Considerable work still remains if all of the many commercially pulped species are to be studied in detail.

Upon completion of the cook, the entire contents of the vessel are blown into a tank. When this happens, the head gas and steam are released suddenly to the atmosphere, emitting a large volume of odorous gases, similar in composition to relief gases.

These intermittent releases of digestion gases, which characterize the batch digestion process, do not occur in the newer continuous digestion process in which malodorous gases and steam are bled off at a low, continuous rate, which should simplify the application of deodorization techniques.

In some plants, before emission to the atmosphere, the digester gases are passed through a heat exchanger (blow heat recovery), condensing the higher boiling sulfur-containing and turpentinelike compounds into an aqueous stream. Odor subsequently may be evolved into the atmosphere from this stream during its reuse as warm water, or downriver from the point of discharge. Odorous, noncondensable gases escape from the blow heat recovery system, unless collected and treated.

2. Washing

The cellulose pulp is washed to remove black liquor. Some occluded volatile sulfur compounds are lost from the residual black liquor and usually are exhausted through roof vents above the washers.

3. Evaporation

The weak black liquor, containing 13–15% solids, is next concentrated to 60–70% solids in multiple-effect evaporators or a combination of multiple-effect and direct contact evaporators. North American practice leans heavily toward increasing the total solids to the 50% level in multiple-effect evaporators and completion of the evaporation to the 65% solids level by direct contact between the black liquor and hot recovery furnace gases in disk or cascade direct-contact evaporators. Northern European practice relies heavily upon multiple-effect evaporators alone to concentrate the liquor to the 65% solids level.

Considerable quantities of methyl mercaptan, methyl sulfide, and hydrogen sulfide leave the multiple-effect evaporators through the barometric leg of the jet condenser. Hot furnace gases strip volatile sulfur compounds from the strong black liquor during direct contact evaporation, particularly in the absence of black liquor oxidation.

4. Chemical Recovery

The carbonaceous material in concentrated black liquor is burned (oxidized) in a recovery furnace, and the cooking chemicals in the liquor are regenerated through reduction of the sulfur compounds to a molten liquid smelt of sodium sulfide and sodium carbonate which is removed from the furnace for reuse. Variable quantities of odor are generated, depending upon the mode of operation of the furnace. As much as 10–1000-fold variations in hydrogen sulfide emission rates may be encountered in furnaces operating between design capacity and overload, adequate and insufficient secondary combustion air or furnace temperature (Fig. 2). Equally important factors influencing hydrogen sulfide

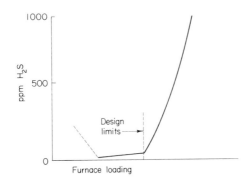

FIG. 2. Relation between H_2S production and furnace loading.

emission are the shape of the combustion chamber and the placement of the secondary air inlets.

The primary malodorous constituent is hydrogen sulfide plus some methyl mercaptan and as yet unidentified partial oxidation products of organic sulfur-containing compounds. A number of nonsulfur organic compounds have been identified, but are nonodorous (9). Under conditions of efficient oxidation, sulfur dioxide is the primary sulfur-containing waste product and does not contribute significantly to the atmospheric odor problem. Much of the sulfur dioxide may be retained in the alkaline smelt as sodium sulfite. The particulate matter in the flue gas from a recovery furnace is sufficiently great to require the use of dust control equipment.

An unusual type of nuisance pollution may result when iron shot is circulated in the "economizer" heat exchanger for the purpose of preventing build-up of salt cake on its interior surfaces. Iron particles may erode from the shot and become entrained in the flue gas. If these particles deposit on painted surfaces in the neighborhood, they leave undesirable brown spots. A magnetic flue gas cleaner is used to collect these small iron particles.

5. Lime Kiln

The recovery furnace smelt, consisting of sodium carbonate and sodium sulfide, is dissolved in water to produce "green" liquor. Dissolving may produce an alkali mist and some odor. The "green" liquor is then causticized with calcium hydroxide to yield "white" liquor—a solution of sodium hydroxide and sodium sulfide. The solid calcium carbonate is removed by clarification and filtration and is then calcined in a lime kiln to regenerate calcium oxide, which, when slaked with water, produces the calcium hydroxide needed for causticizing. Minor

TABLE I

TYPICAL GASEOUS EMISSION RANGES FROM KRAFT PULPING IN PARTS PER MILLION[a]

	H_2S	CH_3SH	CH_3SCH_3	$(CH_3S)_2$
Recovery furnace flue gas				
Electrostatic precipitator	0–100	2.5–12	1–5	8–80
	360–1,350	0–205	0	38
	130–935	60–1,400	125	ND[b]
Venturi scrubber	0–300	0–117	13	109
Digester gas—No treatment				
Continuous	59	41,200	2,880	30
Batch	0–295	1,530–36,800	190–13,500	53
Batch	0	36,600	├———— 8,940[c] ————┤	
Batch	0–137	0–52,000	ND	ND
Black liquor oxidation				
Without digester or evaporator gas	0	0–45	0–45	0–107
With digester or evaporator gas	0	12–32	0–659–924	800–5,600
Lime kiln	0–600	0–480	0–374	0–720
Dissolving tank without control	0	0–136	0–580	0–320
Evaporators				
Direct contact	0–895	0–374	0–24	0–91
Multiple effect	2,000–9,160	186–1,860	8–42	237–1,790
Multiple effect	0–24,150	0–36,700	0–5,500	0–2,780
Multiple effect	(10 lb/ton)	ND	ND	ND
Multiple effect	├———— 8,700[d] ————┤		├——— 1,500[c] ———┤	

[a] From Hisey and other authors (4–6, 11–15).
[b] Not determined.
[c] Composite analysis for all organic sulfides.
[d] Composite analysis for H_2S and CH_3SH.

quantities of hydrogen sulfide may escape from the lime kiln and dust control equipment on the kiln effluent gases is required to minimize lime losses.

6. Estimation of Emission Losses

The magnitude of losses of sulfur from a given plant may be roughly determined by examination of the chemical replacement required to maintain the "sulfidity" and alkalinity of the cooking liquor. A "sulfidity" of 20% indicates an approximate ratio of five equivalents of sodium to one of sulfur. Since neither chemical losses in the washing process, nor particulate losses from the recovery furnace change the usual 5:1 ratio, any change in the ratio of sodium to sulfur makeup requirements provides a measure of the magnitude of volatile sulfur losses to the

TABLE II
AIR POLLUTION CONTROL METHODS IN USE

| Sources | Methods | |
	Malodorous gases	Particulates
Digester blow and relief	Incineration	
	Heat recovery	
	Alkaline scrubbing	
	Chlorine scrubbing	
	Black liquor oxidation	
Washers	Chlorination	
	Incineration	
Multiple-effect evaporators	Black liquor oxidation	
	Incineration	
	Alkaline scrubbing	
	Chlorine scrubbing	
Direct contact evaporators	Secondary scrubbing	
	Heat recovery	
Recovery furnace		
Primary treatment	Maintain adequate	Electrostatic
	secondary oxygen	precipitator
	Operate within design	Venturi
	capacity	scrubber
	Black liquor oxidation	
	Tall stacks	Tall stacks
Secondary treatment	Heat recovery	Heat recovery
	Secondary scrubbing	Secondary scrubbing
Foul condensates	Acidification, air	
	stripping and	
	incineration	
	Oxidation by aeration	

atmosphere. Chemical replacement varies widely from mill to mill and most frequently requires the addition of 50–100 pounds of sodium sulfate, including possibly some elemental sulfur, per ton of pulp produced (*10*). This makeup requirement has a sodium-to-sulfur equivalent ratio of 1:1 or less, thereby indicating the magnitude of volatile sulfur losses. As air quality improvement becomes a part of the pulping process, the ratio of sodium to sulfur in the chemical makeup shifts toward the ideal of 5:1 through substitution of sodium carbonate or sodium hydroxide for sodium sulfate and elemental sulfur.

There is little published information describing the extent and type of sulfur compounds lost from the various steps in the pulping process. Typical available data have been condensed and are presented in Table I.

Table II outlines methods which are being used by the kraft industry to minimize gaseous and particulate emissions. Single methods or combinations of methods may be used to control each indicated source. For example, a two-stage secondary scrubber might involve a first-stage chlorine spray followed by an alkaline spray with heat and chemical recovery from the scrubber liquor.

B. Control of Gaseous Emissions

The major odor control processes used by the kraft industry include: black liquor oxidation, Cl_2 oxidation, air oxidation, combustion, scrubbing, absorption, and waste heat recovery.

1. *Black Liquor Oxidation*

Sodium sulfide and volatile sulfur compounds in hot black liquor will react with atmospheric oxygen in a suitable tower to form stable, nonvolatile compounds, thereby minimizing the release of malodors from the multiple-effect and direct-contact evaporators. Although the chemistry of the oxidation is still obscure, sulfides are apparently converted to thiosulfates or sulfites, and methyl mercaptan is oxidized to dimethyl disulfide. Both countercurrent and cocurrent oxidation systems are in use. Noncondensable digester gases are sometimes fed into the oxidation tower to be fixed in the black liquor, although the effectiveness of this technique has not been adequately substantiated with analytical data.

The spent air issuing from the oxidation tower may contain variable amounts of dimethyl sulfide or dimethyl disulfide. If the towers are overloaded, increasing amounts of hydrogen sulfide and methyl mercaptan also may be carried into the atmosphere.

A comparison of the emission types and rates from six oxidation towers, three of which were fed with air only and three with a mixture of air and noncondensable gases from digesters and evaporators, indicated that the gases emerging from the latter towers were heavily ladened with dimethyl sulfide and dimethyl disulfide. Methyl mercaptan reacts in an alkaline solution with an oxidizing agent such as oxygen, yielding dimethyl disulfide. These data also indicated that the total sulfur emission from these oxidation towers was greater than the inlet sulfur concentration. Thus an additional treatment is required to avoid air pollution from the oxidation tower. It is obvious, under these conditions, that an economic loss of sulfur may result from the introduction of sulfur gases into oxidation towers (6).

Collins (16) provided a comprehensive review of the status of black liquor oxidation up to 1953. Landry (17) discussed the practice and development of black liquor oxidation with particular reference to the problem of the production of large volumes of foam from black liquor coming from the pulping of resinous southern pine wood, as compared with low foam production from less resinous wood such as fir, hemlock, etc. Foaming has been minimized by several southern mills by oxidizing concentrated black liquor from which the soaps have been skimmed and by using oil or mechanical foam breakers. Ricca (18) studied the oxidation of black liquor with pure oxygen in an effort to minimize foam production from southern black liquor. The high cost of oxygen makes this technique economically unsound.

The oxidation of black liquor after evaporation is being used in some southern mills (19) with minimum foam production. This technique does not reduce the quantities of malodorous compounds stripped from the evaporators, but does reduce sulfur losses from the recovery furnace.

Harding and Hendrickson (20) have described a method of "foam fractionation" producing complete oxidation of the sulfides in weak black liquor with a concomitant increase in the recovery of tall oil fractions in a concentrated form.

Murray studied the influence of temperature in the oxidation tower upon the chemical reactions taking place (21). Below 140 °F, elemental sulfur was produced and subsequently reverted to sulfide and thiosulfate during evaporation of the oxidized liquor. The sulfide ions then reacted with carbonic acid produced from the flue gas in the direct evaporator, forming H_2S, which was stripped from the liquid.

The Swedish AB Mörrums Bruk mill combines black liquor oxidation with treatment of the digester and evaporator gases, followed by a final cleanup with waste chlorine-containing bleach liquor (Fig. 3). The

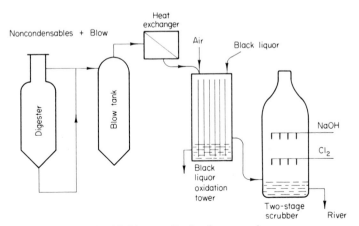

FIG. 3. AB Morrum Bruk odor control system.

digester relief and blow gases first pass through a blow tank and a hot water accumulator. Noncondensable digester gases are combined with similar gases from the multiple-effect evaporators and are fed into three British Columbia Research Council oxidation towers that are arranged in series. A constant gas (air and noncondensable gases) volume is always fed into the BCRC system, although the ratio of air to noncondensable gases will vary markedly, depending upon whether or not a blow is in progress. The exhaust gases from the oxidation towers are given a final cleanup in a two-stage spray contactor The gases first pass through a spray of acid, chlorine-containing waste water from the bleaching process. No additional chlorine is added to the first-stage spray water. The second-stage spray uses alkaline waste water from the brownstock washers. Additional caustic may be added to maintain the pH between 11 and 12 in the second stage. The efficiency of this system is being studied by Ruus (14).

In Nettingsdorf, Austria, oxidation is accomplished by forcing compressed air countercurrent to the black liquor in a system of tubes. The oxidation equipment is reported to be significantly smaller than conventional units using air at atmospheric pressure.

2. Combustion

Malodorous sulfur-containing compounds may be converted to sulfur dioxide by combustion. Large volumes of malodorous air–gas mixtures have been used as a partial source of combustion air for the lime kilns, recovery furnaces, and special odor destruction furnaces. Safety measures such as flame arrestors, safety pop valves, and gas holding tanks are required to prevent flashbacks or explosions in the ducting. Combustion techniques have been applied with varying degrees of success throughout the kraft industry in North America, Europe, and other parts of the world.

The Weyerhaeuser system utilizes a low-pressure gas accumulator (Vaporsphere) as a surge tank for collection of digester relief and blow gases. This spherical steel tank has a lightweight fabric diaphragm attached inside at the middle. The gas enters at the bottom and is retained under the diaphragm which "floats" up and down on the gas cushion (22). The gas inflow rate ranges between 30–100 cfm and the outflow is adjusted to equal the net gas flow generated from each cooking cycle. This eliminates the explosion hazard by preventing dilution of these gases with air. The gases are fed into the lime kiln, and just prior to injection into the furnace they are diluted with air to a ratio of more than 50:1. Oxidation of the sulfide is complete when incinerated at 1400 °F.

The Nettingsdorf, Austria, odor abatement system is based on in-cineration in a specially designed burner. The essential features of the system included (1) minimizing the dilution of the malodorous gas streams with air, and (2) a self-sustaining combustion furnace. An automatic valving arrangement on the digester prevents air from mixing with and diluting the relief and blow gases. The resultant volume of the gas stream is small and will sustain combustion. The upper section of the small cylindrical furnace is packed with firebrick that, during op-eration, reaches a temperature of approximately 1650 °F. The gas burner nozzle is surrounded by a heat exchanger circulating cold water to cool the incoming gas line below the ignition point. A water trap is located between the digester and the burner as a further safety device to prevent flashback. The flow of gas into the burner is controlled by two water tanks. Gravity feed from the upper tank forces the gas at a constant rate into the furnace from the lower storage tank.

Cartiera Vita Mayer & Co. has an integrated odor abatement system based upon incineration (23) (Fig. 4). The digester relief and blow gases pass through a series of surface and direct heat exchangers to recover heat, remove condensable compounds from the gas stream, and mini-mize the volume of the digester gases to be handled by the burner. The foul condensates from the digesters and evaporators are acidified to a pH below 6 by sulfuric acid waste from the chlorine dioxide plant. The acidified liquid is then fed into the top of a packed stripping tower. A small volume of air is blown up through the tower, and the stripped gases are combined with the noncondensable gases from the heat

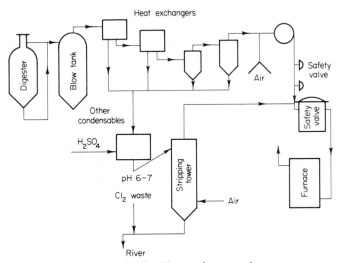

FIG. 4. Carteria Vita Mayer odor control system.

exchangers, and burned in the recovery furnace. The liquid effluent from the stripping tower is treated with chlorine-containing waste liquid from the bleach plant, and discharged into the river. Three safety devices minimize the danger of explosion of these gases in the ducts and furnace. Explosion vents are sealed with waterproof paper designed to break should the pressure exceed a critical value. Second, the velocity of the gas through the ducts is maintained at 4–5 times flame propagation speed. Finally, there is a hydraulic check valve in the duct near the furnace that closes if the velocity of the gas drops below 1.5 times flame propagation velocity. A somewhat similar system is used in St. Gaudens, France, following the Vita Mayer design.

3. *Chlorine Oxidation*

Chlorine reacts with hydrogen sulfide, methyl mercaptan, dimethyl sulfide, and dimethyl disulfide, under appropriate conditions and with varying efficiency, to yield less odorous or nonodorous products. The design of effective reacting devices depends primarily upon the nature of the malodorous gas to be treated. Recovery furnace gases containing up to 12% carbon dioxide in the range of 300 °F are difficult to treat, as are gas streams that contain water-insoluble dimethyl sulfide and dimethyl disulfide.

Although chlorine oxidation of H_2S can progress equally well under acidic or alkaline conditions in a static system, low H_2S absorption rates, and stripping of absorbed H_2S and Cl_2, are experienced in an acid–chlorine scrubbing system (24). Also, oxidation rates are much slower in the gaseous, than in the liquid, phase. Thus, practical chlorine oxidation systems usually include a final alkaline cleanup stage.

Providing adequate alkalinity to maintain the system pH above 8 for complete neutralization of the carbon dioxide in the recovery furnace gas would be costly. Plit and Dol (25) found that the rate of absorption of hydrogen sulfide was much more rapid than the rate for carbon dioxide when mixtures of these gases are passed rapidly through an alkaline scrubbing tower. Thus the alkali requirement should be significantly less than that theoretically required for the carbon dioxide present.

Systems designed primarily for recovery of additional heat from recovery furnace gases have been designed utilizing two-stage scrubbing, the first stage operating under acid conditions, followed by an alkaline stage to pick up the stripped and unabsorbed chlorine and malodors from the first stage. Any odor reduction achieved by this means is usually considered to be secondary to the recovery of heat or particulates.

The relatively small mill of Lorento and Peña Pobre, Mexico treats the digester gases and condensates first with air in the presence of water, then with chlorine, and finally with a caustic solution. A similar treatment procedure, known as the "TLT" method, is applied to the recovery furnace gases. The chlorine requirement for the treatment of the gases from these two sources ranges from 1.8 to 3.4 kg/ton of pulp (26).

Local air pollution complaints arose from the discharge of foul condensates into the river near Äänekoski, Finland. A chlorine treatment system was developed in which these condensates are treated with 4–4.5 tons of Cl_2 per day—1.5 tons of which is obtained from the waste bleach effluent and sludge from the production of hypochlorite. An additional 3–3.5 tons of chlorine per day is added to the system to complete the oxidation. Weekly evaluation of the odor of the river water at five sampling sites has indicated odor removal in all but the closest site. The raw waste liquid stream contains approximately 7 kg of H_2S and 8.4 kg of methyl mercaptan per hour. These data indicate the presence of other chlorine-consuming materials in the liquid stream, since the chlorine consumption is more than twice the theoretical demand of the sulfur present. The addition of chlorine to the waste water stream is automatically controlled with redox instrumentation.

Gas-phase chlorination of hydrogen sulfide, mercaptans, and alkyl sulfides and disulfides from the recovery furnace, digester, evaporator, lime kiln, and dissolver emissions have been studied. The reaction products were identified by gas chromatography. In the gas phase the only significant reaction was the oxidation of methyl mercaptan to dimethyl disulfide. Hydrogen sulfide was not appreciably oxidized. No significant reduction in odor potential was achieved by gas phase chlorination (26a).

4. Oxidation by Air or Ozone

Variable results have been reported when foul water is contacted with air. Biological oxygen demands have been reduced in some applications, and other studies have shown 0–50% reduction in the chlorine demand of the effluent liquid. Insufficient data are available to predict the degree of odor reduction to be obtained through aeration of foul waters.

Ozone has been proposed (27) for the oxidation of pulp mill odors. Analytical data substantiating the destruction of these malodors by gas phase reaction with ozone have not been published. Subjective evaluation by sensory perception techniques is subject to question because of the known inhibitory effect of ozone upon the sense of smell.

Catalytic oxidation of pulp mill odors has also been considered. The major difficulty appears to be related to the particulate loading of the malodorous gases, and the poisoning of the catalyst by these materials.

5. *Scrubbing*

At Husum, Sweden, evaporator noncondensable gases are scrubbed in a Venemark washer in which a full cone jet of weak causticized liquor from lime mud washing is sprayed into the top of the washer, and the evaporator gases pass downward, concurrently with the liquid, over vertical, roughened plates. Two washers are used in parallel for the initial scrubbing of the total gas volume. The gaseous effluent from the first stage then passes through a second stage, single Venemark washer. The recovered sulfur is returned to the process.

In this same plant, flue gases from the recovery furnace first enter an economizer at approximately 616 °F, emerge at 257 °F, pass through an electrostatic precipitator, and then go to a three-stage washer which reduces the exit flue gas temperature to 149°–176 °F. Cold water is introduced into the second stage, is circulated back to the first stage, and is then sent to hot water storage tanks at approximately 198 °F. Weak, waste chlorine-containing water from the bleach plant is used in the third stage and is then sewered. The flue gas is discharged to the atmosphere just above its dew point. The first two stages of this system recover approximately 60 kg sulfur/hour, which is returned to the process in the causticizing department.

The evaporator noncondensables from Fiskeby AB are scrubbed in a Venemark washer using white liquor. Approximately 2 kg sulfur/ton of pulp are recovered. This liquor is returned to the white liquor makeup.

A. Ahlström Osakeyhito has developed a "Warkaus" venturi for

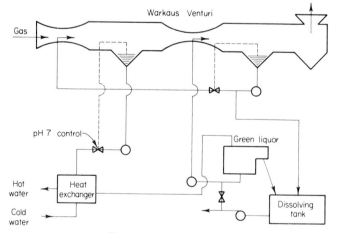

FIG. 5. Warkaus venturi.

scrubbing large volumes of gases, and recovering heat and chemicals (Fig. 5). The distinctive features of this venturi include a larger than usual throat, giving negligible pressure loss, and injection of the scrubbing liquid at the same speed and direction as the gas flow. The power requirements are reportedly quite low, normally being 0.3–0.8 kw/1000 m³/hour. In practice, two to three stages of scrubbing are utilized, and a variety of scrubbing liquids have been used in different installations. Recovery flue gas temperatures can be reduced to 122°–140 °F in a two-stage scrubber, and, if the water is not recirculated, to 104°–122 °F.

A two-stage Warkaus venturi scrubber is used on the recovery furnace at Äänekoski, Finland. Weak white liquor is introduced into the second stage, and then enters the first stage. The pH is maintained between 8 and 8.5. A portion of the scrubbing liquor returns to the dissolving tank. Approximately 11 tons of 100% NaOH makeup are required per week to maintain the pH of the scrubbing liquor. The flue gas exit temperature ranges from 140°–160 °F.

Flue gases in Pori, Finland, are scrubbed in a two-stage Warkaus venturi using green liquor. The overflow from the scrubbing liquor storage tank goes to the dissolving tank. The pH of the circulating liquor is maintained in the range of 6.8–7.0 pH. The exit flue gas temperature ranges from 140°–160 °F.

Odor emissions from the brownstock washers in one Swedish mill are minimized by use of "Rauma Repola" enclosed pressure washers in which the pressurized air is reused. The malodorous vapors arising from the brownstock washers at another Swedish mill are collected and mixed with chlorine-containing gases from the bleaching process and exhausted to the atmosphere through a separate stack.

6. Stripping

"Bergstrom" towers have been used successfully to strip and concentrate for subsequent treatment sulfur-containing compounds from foul condensate waters. The condensates enter the top of the packed tower, and hot recovery furnace flue gases enter the bottom, stripping the volatile sulfur compounds from the water. Modifications of this technique involve acidification of foul waters with waste sulfuric acid, and stripping with air. The gaseous effluent may then be burned, or scrubbed with chlorine-containing water.

7. Absorption

The Korsnas AB plant at Marmavorke has a system for scrubbing the digester gases with warm (95 °F) white liquor to collect hydrogen sulfide and methyl mercaptan. The unabsorbed gases then pass through an activated charcoal bed to remove dimethyl sulfide and dimethyl disulfide. The charcoal is periodically steam stripped, the organic sulfides condensed and sold.

8. Waste Heat Recovery

Much of the progress in odor abatement in northern Europe has come as a by-product of heat recovery. The relatively low cost of fuel in North America, as compared with northern Europe, is argued as a major deterrent to the application of Scandanavian heat recovery practices in North America. A second difference reported is the higher average temperatures in available water supplies in North America. Furthermore, recovery furnaces in northern Europe generally operate within their design capacity. Thus the sulfur compounds in the black liquor are oxidized to SO_2 under conditions of 2–6% excess oxygen, without danger of overheating. Such oxidation to SO_2 produces a significant reduction in odor when compared with combustion of the black liquor under reducing conditions, in an overloaded furnace, from which H_2S is the primary sulfur-containing combustion product.

In the process of recovering heat from the furnace flue gases, additional salt cake is collected, and malodorous, sulfur-containing compounds are condensed and returned to the process. Likewise, additional heat recovery from digester and evaporator gases reduces the total volume of noncondensable, malodorous gases, as well as trapping condensable, malodorous compounds in a liquid stream. These gases can subsequently be stripped from the condensates into small volumes of air for incineration, or can be collected in an alkaline scrubbing system and returned to the process (28). Collins and Collins (29) presented an early review of the recovery of heat and chemicals from the kraft recovery furnace gases.

A preliminary analysis of the total process heat requirement and heat loss from the recovery furnace in a typical Pacific Coast mill has indicated that 23–28% of this waste heat could be recovered utilizing typical Scandanavian heat recovery practice. The heat recovered would save approximately $300,000 now spent annually for natural gas (30) to provide an equivalent quantity of heat. A. Ahlström Osakeyhito estimates that the intial capital investment for a two-stage Warkaus heat recovery system for the above mill might approximate $400,000–500,000. The annual operational cost would approximate $100,000. The net annual saving of approximately $200,000 would apply toward equipment amortization. The potential saving in recoverable chemicals has not been considered in these figures.

Another Pacific Coast mill has reportedly installed a waste heat recovery unit on their recovery furnace. Early estimates indicate an actual saving of approximately 30% in Btu's as reflected by decreased purchases of natural gas. Collins (29) has independently proposed an integrated odor control and heat recovery system.

9. Dispersion

Diffusion of the remaining odorous gases from a pulp mill located at the bottom of a 140-foot valley near Milan, in the center of a 25 square mile area having a population of approximately 180,000, is accomplished by piping the flue gases to the valley rim, where they are exhausted to the atmosphere through a 260-foot chimney discharging the gases 400 feet above the valley floor (23). The mill is increasing its production capacity, and a new chimney, approximately 400 feet high, will be built to discharge the flue gases at 540 feet above the valley floor.

10. Production of Useful Chemicals

Goheen (31) described the production of dimethyl sulfide (DMS) from black liquor. Dimethyl sulfide can be oxidized to dimethyl disulfide and dimethyl sulfone. These compounds are finding increasing use as solvents and reactants. Dimethyl sulfoxide has a potential medical application in the reduction of muscular and joint pains through topical application.

11. Discussion of Kraft Odor Abatement Systems

An evaluation of the cost and effectiveness of a particular design for the reduction of odorous emissions from digestion, evaporation, and black liquor combustion must include an analysis of complex interrelations, which produce a given sulfur equilibrium within the mill under one set of operating conditions, and a new equilibrium following introduction of one or more odor control techniques. For example, the collection and return of a significant fraction of volatile sulfur compounds previously lost to the atmosphere from the multiple-effect evaporators would reduce the percentage of sulfur lost from the system. Although there would be a lower percentage sulfur loss, it is conceivable that the total sulfur loss would not decrease, because of the resultant higher sulfidity.

Likewise, an attempt to abate odors from the digester and evaporator gases, by passing them through the black liquor oxidation tower, could result in odor contributions to the atmosphere because the tower might thereby become overloaded. Also, by virtue of decreased oxidation of the liquor resulting from substitution of a portion of the design air volume by an equivalent volume of reducing gases, the odor contribution to the atmosphere from the subsequent direct contact evaporation of the black liquor could also be increased. Even though malodorous gases stripped from such an overloaded oxidation tower might be treated with chlorine to reduce the odor contribution to the atmosphere, the primary objective of black liquor oxidation—increased sulfur recovery—is minimized because the volatile sulfur stripped from the tower is not returned to the pulping process. Many other examples of the interrelationships among the various pulping steps can easily be envisioned.

Unfortunately, there is a dearth of analytical data on the atmospheric losses of the major classes of sulfur-containing compounds from uncontrolled processes and from the wide variety of available control processes. The problem is further complicated by process differences among mills. It is hoped that the development of direct gas chromatographic analysis of gaseous emissions will soon provide an objective means for evaluation of the odor contribution from the various pulping processes, process modifications, process variables, and control techniques.

Each of the odor reduction techniques needs to be studied objectively under many operating conditions, in several mills, using different species of woods and process modifications to improve our understanding of the mechanisms and value of these techniques. This is particularly true of (1) black liquor oxidation variations, the passing of variable volumes of foul gases to the oxidation tower, keeping the total gas input at a constant volume, etc., (2) chlorine oxidation of foul gases with various types of scrubbing systems, (3) operating parameters in the black liquor recovery furnace, (4) secondary scrubbers following the electrostatic precipitators, and (5) heat recovery as an odor control measure.

Incineration is the most direct and effective method of odor destruction, although it does not provide for chemical recovery. At least three major incineration techniques have been described and are in use in the industry. For any given plant, the most effective and economical odor reduction system will undoubtedly reflect a well-planned integration of the many techniques currently in piecemeal use, including improved recovery furnace operation through proper loading, design and placement of secondary air jets to provide adequate oxygen; secondary scrubbing of the furnace gases for additional heat, odor, and particulate recovery; black liquor oxidation; and incineration or scrubbing of evaporator and other malodorous gas streams. Malodorous-containing waste water will also be treated by aeration or chlorination before discharge to the receiving water.

Late in 1967 two major U.S. boiler manufacturers delivered their first "no-contact evaporator" (31a) or "air contact evaporator" (31b) recovery furnaces to the kraft industry. The former system—similar to Scandinavian systems—concentrates the black liquor to 60% in multiple-effect evaporators. The combustion gases are cooled in a vertical tube economizer before entering an electrostatic precipitator. In the latter, gases flow through the recovery furnace in the normal manner and through an economizer. Air is heated in the economizer by the flue gases, routed to the direct contact evaporator and thence into the recovery furnace. In this way, any nonoxidized emissions are directed back into the furnace where they are incinerated.

These techniques are still in the development stage. However, the early test data indicate that these systems should provide a significant contribution to odor reduction from the recovery furnace stack.

C. CONTROL OF PARTICULATE EMISSIONS

Early attempts to minimize particulate emissions were rather inefficient by modern technological standards. Such procedures as filtration through wetted wood chips or straw were utilized. Modern equipment includes electrostatic precipitators, venturi scrubbers, wet cyclones, and demister pads. Demisters are particularly useful above the recovery furnace smelt-dissolving tanks. Venturi scrubbers and electrostatic precipitators are the principal types of collectors used for the collection of salt cake from recovery furnace effluent gases. The collection efficiencies for electrostatic precipitators average 95%, with capital investment and maintenance relatively high, and operating costs relatively low. Venturi scrubbers have efficiencies of the order of 85%, low capital investment and maintenance, and high operating costs. Some heat recovery is obtained; and gain or loss of volatile sulfur compounds may be experienced with a venturi scrubber depending upon whether black liquor oxidation is practiced and other process variables. More recently, scrubbers have been used to provide secondary collection following precipitators. Such scrubbers are effective for reduction of both particulate and gaseous emissions and may be integrated into a comprehensive system of heat recovery (28).

The economics of salt cake recovery are well established, since approximately 150 pounds of particulate salt cake leaves the recovery furnace per ton of pulp produced. With an average collection efficiency of 90% it is thus possible to save approximately $2 per day per ton of pulp produced. Salt cake collection efficiencies above 95% will be required to meet air quality standards presently enacted by some states and control districts.

III. Sulfite Pulping Process

A. SOURCES OF EMISSIONS

1. *Digestion*

The active cooking chemicals in the sulfite process are sulfur dioxide, sulfurous acid, and a bisulfite of an alkaline base such as calcium, sodium, ammonium, or magnesium. The cooking liquor contains an excess of sulfurous acid, and is therefore acidic. The liquor is prepared by burning sulfur to form sulfur dioxide, and then cooling the gas to minimize SO_3 formation and improve absorption. The cooled gas is reacted with the appropriate alkaline solution, or suspension, to produce the desired composition and strength of cooking acid. Cooking is accomplished in acid-resistant-brick-lined steel, or stainless steel digesters.

During the initial period of digestion of the wood chips, pressure must be relieved because 2–3 times the required amount of chemical is used. This relief reduces the sulfur dioxide content during the period of initial temperature rise. The relief sulfur dioxide is recycled to "build up" the cooking acid. Relief is minimized when using a soluble base cooking acid.

2. *Chemical Recovery*

The substitution of other bases such as sodium, magnesium, or ammonium for calcium hydroxide has technical advantages, in some cases, even though the cost of a soluble base is approximately 4–5 times greater per ton of pulp than calcium base. The recovery of cooking chemicals from a lime-base liquor is severely hampered by calcium insolubility and scale formation in evaporators. Liquor recovery must be practiced in the soluble base processes to compensate for the higher chemical cost. To maximize the economic recovery of chemicals from the soluble base processes, effective gas and solid phase recovery systems are required. This, in turn, minimizes air and water pollution. All of these factors must be balanced against the usual stream pollution problem encountered in the cheaper calcium base process in which approximately 200–300 pounds of sulfur, 150–210 pounds of lime, and 2500 pounds of organics per ton of sulfite pulp are sewered to receiving waters. The BOD loading of waste calcium-base sulfite liquor may vary anywhere from 450 to over 1000 pounds of oxygen per ton of pulp.

Some success has been achieved in the disposal of waste calcium sulfite liquor as a fuel. In the Ramen process, partially concentrated, 30% solids liquor is sprayed into 2000 °F stack gas; the water is evaporated; and a dry powder is produced which is used for fuel. The gas leaving the cyclone powdered fuel collector is further cooled and scrubbed prior to discharge into the atmosphere to minimize air pollution. In the Rosenblad process the liquor is evaporated to 50–55% solids in multiple-effect evaporators. Scaling is minimized by interchanging the flows of liquor and steam on an 8-hour basis to remove the scale through wide changes in evaporator wall temperature.

Concentrated spent sulfite liquor is used as road binder, flotation agent, and drilling mud. Useful products may be produced from the spent liquor, including ethanol, vanillin, and fodder yeast. The economics of chemical production from spent liquor are carefully balanced against the market demand, the cost of recovery vs. the cost of alternate production methods, the heat value of the liquor, the urgency for stream quality improvement, the cost of raw materials, etc.

B. Control of Emissions

Steam and gas from the blowing of the digester contents are carried off from the blow pit or tank by a suitable stack. Provision should be made for condensing the steam and SO_2 coming from the blow pit or tank. One 800 ton per day mill reports a net annual saving of more than $260,000 in this manner (32). The typical odor from sulfite digestion is generally sweeter, and has a higher olfactory detection threshold, than kraft digester odors. The daily emission of odors to the atmosphere is significantly lower than from kraft mills. Some SO_2 vegetation injury has been observed in the vicinity of sulfite mills, and has usually been traced to plant accidents or equipment malfunction.

IV. Analytical Methods

A. Stack and Field Sampling

Early sampling and analysis techniques proposed by Felicetta et al. (33), and Bialkowsky and De Haas (34), were either lengthy and involved, or provided only total sulfur values. A manual for the sampling and analysis of kraft mill recovery gases, developed and recently improved by Hendrickson and co-workers (35), is simpler and more straightforward. The stack effluent is sampled isokinetically through a heated line and manifold. Particulates are removed in a paper thimble, dried, and weighed. Gases are collected in two absorption trains. Hydrogen sulfide and alkyl mercaptans are trapped in 10% cadmium chloride solution; sulfur dioxide is fixed in sodium tetrachloromercurate (TCM) solution; alkyl sulfides and disulfides are collected in benzene, and total sulfur is determined. Hydrogen sulfide is determined iodometrically at a pH of 0.8. The total sulfide and mercaptide is determined iodometrically on a second aliquot at 3 M HCl concentration. Sulfur dioxide is measured colorimetrically using the modified West and Gaeke method designed to prevent interference from oxides of nitrogen. The combined alkyl sulfides are determined by bromate-bromide titration.

Progress is being made in the application of gas-liquid chromatography to the analysis of stack gases. Early work (36, 37) utilized thermal conductivity detectors and concentrated the gases on silica gel at Dry Ice-acetone temperature or in ethylbenzene. Direct injection of unconcentrated samples was limited to a minimum initial concentration of approximately 500 ppm. The advent of more sensitive ionization detectors (38), and sulfur-specific detectors, permits the detection of compounds present in the parts per million to parts per billion concentration range. Gas chromatography has been successfully applied to the analysis of the organic compounds present in kraft mill gases using flame ionization detectors and Triton X-305 columns (7, 14). The increased sensitivity provided by a modification of a commercially available coulometric detector (39) permits detection of a few parts per billion of total sulfur compounds in the ambient air. This "sulfur-specific" bromide coulometric detector has been successfully used to provide a complete source gas analysis for the five major types of sulfur compounds in 12 minutes using a Triton X-305 column and temperature programming (39a).

Sampling and analysis of ambient concentrations of H_2S and SO_2 use essentially the same techniques that are recommended for stack sampling, the primary difference being the longer sampling time required to accumulate sufficient concentrations to be detected by the colorimetric techniques. The major difficulty still facing the gas chromatographic analysis of sulfur compounds at concentrations found in the ambient air is the loss of these low concentrations on the column packing when attempting chromatographic separation prior to microtitration (39b).

Lead acetate-impregnated tiles have been studied to assess their effectiveness as a long-term measure of average hydrogen sulfide air concentrations (40). These studies indicated a maximum of an 8-hour useful lifetime of a tile, and that they must be protected from light and air movement to avoid excessive fading.

The usefulness of a daily report of odor intensity by a corps of untrained observers has been demonstrated over a period of years by the Lorento a Peña Pobre mill. Trends toward increased or decreased numeric odor intensity response correlate well with changes in control techniques, production methods, and species of wood used (40a).

An intensive, short-term odor survey was conducted by the U.S. Public Health Service using high school science students as untrained observers (*11*). The detection of odor was primarily related to time of day and season of the year. A public opinion questionnaire was also used in this survey to evaluate the "awareness" and "concern" of a sampling of residents. The degree of response appeared to vary directly with social status, civic pride, length of residence in the community, and occupational prestige of the household head.

B. INSTRUMENTAL METHODS

The Titrilog, a continuous coulometric titration instrument, has been used by one West Coast mill to monitor the H_2S levels in their recovery furnace gases. The Titrilog is no longer manufactured and has been replaced by the Barton 286 which operates on a similar principle. Another mill has adapted the Rubicon analyzer for continuous analysis of H_2S in furnace gases. In this instrument, hydrogen sulfide reacts with a lead acetate-impregnated cellulose acetate film and the darkening is measured photometrically. These instruments require the removal of particulates and water prior to analysis.

The Barton 286, equipped with a series of selective liquid scrubbers, has been successfully used to determine individually the concentrations of sulfur dioxide, hydrogen sulfide, mercaptans, alkyl sulfides, and alkyl disulfides in process gas emissions from the recovery furnace, evaporators, and lime kiln (*40a*).

A continuous recording instrument for measuring H_2S concentrations in flue gases based on ultraviolet absorption (after conversion to SO_2) has been described by Risk and Murray (*41*). The analyzer has a selection of full-scale values between 300 and 2500 ppm H_2S, and has monitored flue gases continuously for over 2 months with only two short interruptions for routine maintenance.

A number of investigators have independently proposed that H_2S should be the compound to be measured for control of recovery furnace operations, rather than the usual "CO-CO_2-combustibles" measurement. Certainly if air pollution is to be held at a minimum, the furnace must be operated in a manner to hold H_2S production to a minimum.

Lead-impregnated filter tapes in sequential samplers, particularly those samplers providing for a continuous readout of the increase in lead sulfide color as H_2S is sampled, may be used for ambient air H_2S measurement. Considerable difference of opinion exists as to the stability of the developed lead sulfide spots upon storage (*11, 42*). Thus the continuous readout sampler should minimize the possible errors due to bleaching of the color during storage. Unfortunately, lead sulfide is claimed to be light sensitive. Thus even the continuous readout instrument may be subject to error. Additional research will be required to resolve the questions raised by Sanderson *et al.* (*42*).

The bromine coulometric microtitration gas-liquid chromatographic cell may also be used for direct analysis of the total gaseous sulfur content of the atmosphere by substituting approximately 176 ml/minute of air for the chromatograph carrier gas. Sensitivity is below 5 ppb, which is below the olfactory threshold (*43*). Sulfur dioxide can be selectively removed from a complex atmospheric mixture of sulfur compounds by prior filtration through a sodium bicarbonate-impregnated membrane filter (*44*).

A sequential, preselective filter system has been developed to provide a continuous, stepwise analysis for mixtures of sulfur-containing gases, including sulfur dioxide, hydrogen sulfide, mercaptans, alkyl sulfides, and alkyl disulfides. Particulates are first removed from the sampled air with an MSA electrostatic precipitator which is modified to eliminate ozone production. The particulate-free air is then sequentially sampled through five chemically impregnated membrane filters (*43*).

C. Needed Research

Much of the progress toward effective odor abatement is dependent upon the ease and accuracy with which the analytical chemist can identify and quantify the compounds from various sources, and establish the efficiencies of control equipment and techniques. Simplified analytical methods are available for the analysis of H_2S, SO_2, mercaptans, and alkyl sulfides and disulfides in source gases and in the atmosphere. Odor reduction techniques may now be studied in terms of their effectiveness under different operating parameters, the mechanisms involved, and the comparative economics of the various systems. For example, we need information concerning the efficacy of (1) different techniques for black liquor oxidation, (2) the passing of variable volumes of foul gases to the black liquor oxidation tower while keeping the total gas input at a constant volume, (3) chlorine oxidation of foul gases in various types of scrubbing systems, (4) operating parameters in the black liquor recovery furnace, (5) secondary scrubbers following the electrostatic precipitators, and (6) heat recovery as an odor control measure. The ultimate solution to the kraft odor problem may be attained through the development of a new pulping process which does not require sulfur.

V. Conclusion

Julson (*45*) has stated that the future of pulp and paper enterprises "if they are to be successful—depend not only upon the continuing satisfaction of (the) customers and a favorable profit situation. They also depend upon the manner in which we manage the soil, the forests, the air and the waters upon which (we) must depend year after year. This is not purely altruistic, it is a matter of vital self-interest to our future growth and progress." It is hoped that the information provided here will stimulate further thought and action to further improvement of air quality.

REFERENCES

1. "The Seventeenth Annual World Review," *Pulp & Paper* **41**, No. 29 (1967).
2. J. N. Stephenson, ed., "Pulp and Paper Manufacture. Preparation and Treatment of Wood Pulp," Vol. I. McGraw-Hill, New York, 1950.
3. J. P. Casey, "Pulp and Paper," Vol. I. Wiley (Interscience), New York, 1952.
4. W. O. Hisey, *Tappi* **34**, 1–6 (1951).
5. H. A. Reid, *Proc. Australian Pulp Ind. Tech. Assoc.* **3**, 479–500 (1949).
6. D. F. Adams, D. M. Jungroth, and B. L. Blymyer, "Survey of Kraft Mill Gaseous Emissions Using Gas Chromatographic Techniques," Tech. Bull. No. 16. Natl. Council for Stream Improvement, New York, 1962.
7. D. K. Andersson, Institute for Cellulose Technology, Stockholm, 1964, personal communication.
8. I. B. Douglass, Department of Chemistry, University of Maine, 1964, personal communication.
9. E. R. Hendrickson, C. G. Walker, and V. D. Chapnekar, *Am. Ind. Hyg. Assoc. J.* **24**, 121–126 (1963).
10. J. H. Stacie and R. G. Guide, *Tappi* **46**, 141–144 (1963).
11. "A Study of Air Pollution in the Interstate Region of Lewiston, Idaho, and Clarkston, Washington," Publ. No. 999-AP-8. U.S. Dept. of Health, Education and Welfare, Public Health Service, 1964, Cincinnati, Ohio.
12. H. O. V. Bergström, *Pulp Paper Mag. Can.* **54**, No. 12, 135–140 (1953).
13. P. A. Kenline, *Robert A. Taft Sanitary Eng. Center, Tech. Rept.* **A62-9** (1962).
14. L. Ruus, Waste Water Laboratory, Stockholm, private communication, 1964.
15. E. Vannemark, *Svensk Papperstid.* **64**, 800–801 (1961).
16. T. T. Collins, Jr., *Paper Trade J.* **136**(12), 37–40 (1953); **136**(13), 19–24 (1953).
17. J. E. Landry, *Tappi* **46**, 766–772 (1963).
18. P. M. Ricca, Ph.D. Dissertation, University of Florida (1962).
19. G. Hawkins, *Paper Trade J.* **146**, 38–39 (1962).
20. C. I. Harding and E. R. Hendrickson, *J. Air Pollution Control Assoc.* **14**, 491–499 (1964).
21. F. E. Murray, *Tappi* **42**, 761–767 (1959).
22. G. A. Hansen, *J. Air Pollution Control Assoc.* **12**, 409–413 (1962).
23. P. Ghisoni, *Tappi* **37**, 201–205 (1954).
24. G. A. Jensen, D. F. Adams, and H. Stern, *J. Air Pollution Control Assoc.* **16**, 248–253 (1966).

25. I. G. Plit and V. I. Dol, *Tr. Dnepropetr. Khim.-Technol. Inst.* **6,** 155 (1958).
26. K. G. Trobeck, W. Lenz, and A. Tirado, *Tappi* **42,** 425–432 (1959).
26a. W. Lenz and A. Tirado, *Paper Trade J.* **150**(34), 64–68 (1966).
27. W. E. Cromwell, *Ind. Eng. Chem.* **51,** 83-4A (1959).
28. D. F. Adams, *Tappi* **48,** 83A-87A (1965).
29. T. T. Collins, Jr. and R. H. Collins, *Paper Ind. Paper World* **29,** Part I, 1608–1611 (1948).
30. G. A. Jensen and D. F. Adams, "Preliminary Estimate of Recoverable Heat from the Kraft Pulping Process," Res. Rept. 65/1-24. College of Engineering, Research Division, Washington State University, 1965.
31. D. W. Goheen, *Tappi* **47,** 14A, 18A, 22A, and 26A (1964).
31a. W. J. Darmstadt, Babcock & Wilcox, Barberton, Ohio, personal communication.
31b. R. H. Dowhan, Combustion Engineering, Inc., personal commdnication.
32. N. A. Lea and E. A. Christoferson, *Chem. Eng. Progr.* **61,** 89–93 (1965).
33. V. F. Felicetta, Q. P. Peniston, and J. L. McCarthy, *Tappi* **36,** 425–432 (1953).
34. H. W. Bialkowsky and G. G. De Haas, *Pulp Paper Mag. Can.* **53,** 99–105 (1952).
35. E. R. Hendrickson, "A Method for Measuring the Concentration of Sulfur Compounds in Process Gas Streams," Tech. Bull. No. 28. Natl. Council for Stream Improvement, New York, 1965.
36. D. F. Adams, R. K. Koppe, and D. M. Jungroth, *Tappi* **46,** 602–608 (1960).
37. G. C. B. Cave, *Tappi* **46,** 1–20 (1963).
38. D. F. Adams, R. K. Koppe, and W. N. Tuttle, *J. Air Pollution Control Assoc.* **15,** 31 (1962).
39. D. F. Adams, G. A. Jensen, J. P. Steadman, R. K. Koppe, and T. J. Robertson, *Anal. Chem.* **38,** 1094–1096 (1966).
39a. D. F. Adams and R. K. Koppe, *J. Air Pollution Control Assoc.* **17,** 161–165 (1967).
39b. R. K. Koppe and D. F. Adams, *Environ. Sci. Tech.* **1,** 479–481 (1967).
40. E. F. Gilardi and R. M. Manganelli, *J. Air Pollution Control Assoc.* **13,** 305–309 (1963).
40a. G. N. Thoen, G. G. DeHaas, and R. R. Austin, Atmospheric Pollution Technical Bulletin, No. 35, Natl. Council for Stream Improvement, New York, 1968.
41. J. B. Risk and F. E. Murray, *Can. Pulp Paper Ind.* **17,** No. 10, 31–34 (1964).
42. H. P. Sanderson, R. Thomas, and M. Katz, *J. Air Pollution Control Assoc.* **16,** 328–330 (1966).
43. D. F. Adams, W. L. Bamesberger, and T. J. Robertson, *J. Air Pollution Control Assoc.* **18,** 145 (1968).
44. J. B. Pate, J. P. Lodge, Jr., and M. P. Neary, *Anal. Chim. Acta* **28,** 341–348 (1963).
45. J. O. Julson, *Paper Ind.* **46,** 621–623 (1964).

40 Food and Feed Industries

W. L. Faith

I. Introduction

Food for man, and feed for animals, are primarily products of agriculture. But between the farm or ranch and the ultimate consumer there often are a variety of intermediate processing steps, such as refining, preservation, and product improvement, as well as considerable handling in storage, packaging, and shipping. Historically, these intermediate steps have collectively made up the food and feed industry. In modern technology, the several processing and handling steps are so influenced by agricultural practices that the industry includes all operations from soil preparation to the grocery cart. The air pollution problems of the industry are basically of a dual nature, dust and odor. In this chapter, the two problems are discussed separately inasmuch as abatement methods to be invoked are quite dissimilar. On the other hand, control methods suitable for one product are often suitable for several others.

II.   Crop and Animal Production

In many air pollution control jurisdictions it is common practice to exempt agricultural operations from air pollution control regulations. However, the separation of agricultural from industrial operations is becoming more obscure every year. Preferential treatment of agriculture is difficult to defend and will soon disappear. Important agricultural practices that contribute to air pollution are: soil preparation, crop spraying, weed burning, orchard smudging, fruit and vegetable harvesting, and animal production.

A. Soil Preparation

Whenever natural soil is disturbed so as to produce a dry powder, a latent dust problem is created. The problem becomes particularly bothersome in low rainfall areas during periods of high winds. The conversion of range land in western Kansas and Oklahoma to wheat land in the 1920's led to the devastating dust storms of the early 1930's. The dust was carried by the wind as far as the eastern seaboard of the United States. In the source area, farm homes and outbuildings were inundated with waves of sand and only a hardy few withstood the siege. The "dust bowl" was eventually reclaimed by adoption of contour plowing practices (only short stretches of furrows in the direction of the wind) and establishment of windbreaks.

Even in areas with lower wind speeds, soil tilling on marginal land releases great quantities of dust during plowing, harrowing, and planting. Dust raised by high winds in some agricultural areas virtually paralyzes automotive transportation at times and leaves a fine powder in the air for days after a blow. To alleviate this condition, several counties in California have passed ordinances restricting the time when plowing and cultivation may be done, or the type of cultivation equipment that may be used.

Another agricultural practice that results in severe dust storms is typified by the practices of asparagus growers in the delta region of the San Joaquin and Sacramento Rivers in California. At harvest time, irrigation is suspended and the fine, powdery, peat soil is mounded around the plants to produce white asparagus. Winds sweeping through the area produce severe dust storms, and again the fine particles remain in the atmosphere for days (1). The only solution appears to be a change in agricultural practices.

The application of fertilizers and soil conditioners, both organic and inorganic, may also create localized dust problems. Powdery materials become airborne much more readily than granular fertilizers. Some fertilizers are also highly odorous.

B. INSECTICIDE SPRAYING

Agriculture has always been dependent to a great extent on pest control, but present extensive use of pesticides far exceeds the practices of only 20 years ago. On large farms it is common practice to apply agricultural dusts and sprays by means of aircraft. If the aerosol is toxic and drifts away before settling on the plants, a hazard to men, animals, and other crops may ensue. Fortunately drift can be minimized or even eliminated by limiting application to periods of low winds or by use of "particulated" sprays.

When first introduced, the herbicide, 2,4-dichlorophenoxyacetic acid (2,4-D) in volatile ester form sometimes drifted considerable distances from the point of application and injured sensitive crops. Ten thousand acres of cotton were damaged in Texas by 2,4-D sprayed from airplanes on rice fields 15–20 miles away. Middleton et al. (2) estimated 1 gm of 2,4-D could mark all the cotton plants on 25 acres and 15 gm could injure them permanently. Volatile esters are seldom used any more, having been replaced by nonvolatile compounds.

C. WEED BURNING

One common method of weed abatement is open burning, a familiar practice along highways and railroad rights-of-way. Similarly, entire fields of noxious weeds are often burned in some localities. The resulting smoke is usually just a nuisance, but indiscriminate burning has occasionally caused severe illness as when volatile irritant oils from burning poison ivy have contacted sensitive people driving through a smoke cloud which was drifting across a highway.

Closely related to weed burning is the agricultural practice of burning straw and stubble after a grain crop has been harvested. Sugar cane fields are often burned off (in a similar manner) after harvesting. So are potato vines and peanut vines. Other agricultural refuse disposed of by open burning includes straw stacks, manure piles, tree trimmings, sometimes entire dead fruit trees. In Louisiana, swamp grass is burned to allow muskrat trapping.

Extensive experiments have been carried out at the University of California at Riverside (3) to determine the nature and amount of emissions from the open burning of dried grasses, fruit prunings, and brush. The principal pollutant emitted was smoke; gaseous emissions were more variable.

Several methods of coping with the agricultural burning problem have been tried. In Los Angeles County the practice has been banned. Even when entire citrus groves are uprooted, the trees must be cut into short lengths and hauled away to sanitary landfill sites. In some other California counties, burning is permitted only when wind speed and other meteorological conditions are suitable to rapid dispersion of the smoke. Burning of weeds along rights-of-way is unnecessary, inasmuch as herbicides may be used effectively. Cutting, hauling and burying is also an acceptable but expensive alternative.

D. SMUDGING ORCHARD CROPS

In many areas, fruit trees must be protected from frost at least a few nights of the year. One of the methods often used is called "smudging," the production of black smoke by burning heavy oil in pots. Smoke from smudge pots was a serious problem in the citrus belt of southern California in the early twentieth century. Orange and lemon growers believed that smoke was desirable to prevent the sun's rays from striking the fruit after a frosty night. On cold nights oil was burned in open pans, and discarded rubber tires were piled up and fired. The resulting smoke pall had to be seen to be believed.

Eventually it was learned that heat rather than smoke was protecting the fruit, so less smoky heaters were developed. In 1947, Los Angeles County banned the use of all orchard heaters, except certain approved types "of such design that not more than one gram per minute of unconsumed solid carbonaceous matter is emitted" (4). In adjacent San Bernardino County, emission of solid carbonaceous matter is restricted to 1/2 gm/min, except for specified heaters in which maximum burning rate is limited so as to prevent solid emissions in excess of 1 gm/min (5).

A recent census of orchard heaters in San Bernardino County (6) showed over 500,000 heaters for which permits have been issued. In many groves orchard heaters are being replaced by wind machines, in which a rotating horizontal propeller mounted on a vertical pole draws warm air from upper levels to mix with cold air near the ground, thus preventing frost formation.

Use of smudge pots and smoking heaters is not restricted to citrus groves. Stockman and Hildebrandt (7) measured the particulate matter in the air of Yakima Valley (Washington) during periods when smudging was being used to protect apple, peach, and similar fruit trees. Suspended particulate matter reached values of 240 gm/m³ in contrast to normal values of 40 to 50. Tape sampler results exceeded 10.4 cohs/1000 feet on several occasions, in sharp contrast with a normal value of 0.5 cohs.

E. FRUIT AND VEGETABLE GROWING

A common problem in fruit and vegetable districts is odor from plant waste allowed to remain on the ground. Old cabbage leaves remaining on the ground in warm, wet weather after harvest are particularly prone to develop obnoxious odors. Dropped fruit causes a similar problem. Even when rotten fruit is gathered and hauled away, mere dumping is not a solution to the problem. The material should be covered with earth. Obviously, good housekeeping applies to agriculture as well as to the home.

F. ALFALFA DEHYDRATION (8)

The dehydration and grinding of alfalfa to produce alfalfa meal is an especially dusty operation commonly carried out in rural communities.

Wet, chopped alfalfa is fed into a direct-fired rotary dryer where it meets hot combustion gases at 1800°–2000 °C (Fig. 1). The dried alfalfa particles are carried with the combustion gases into an air cooler, then to a collecting cyclone from which hot moist air, carrying some odorous dust, escapes. The collected particles are then ground to meal and bagged. Even with cyclones on the grinder and bagger, considerable dust is lost (the overall dust loss may be as high as 7%). The use of cloth collectors after the grinder and bagger cyclones can reduce the total losses to 1.0–1.5% without further control of the primary cooler cyclone.

G. ANIMAL PRODUCTION

The feeding of cattle, sheep, and hogs for weight gain often produces a noxious odor problem. Considerable feeding is done on the farm, but commercial feeding, particularly of cattle, is a rapidly growing industry.

1. Cattle Feed Yards

In U.S. feedlots, 10 million cattle are on feed. Farm lots may have 100 or less cattle, whereas commercial feedlots may have populations varying from 3200 to 32,000 head during the peak season.

Cattle are brought from the range to a feedlot where each animal eats

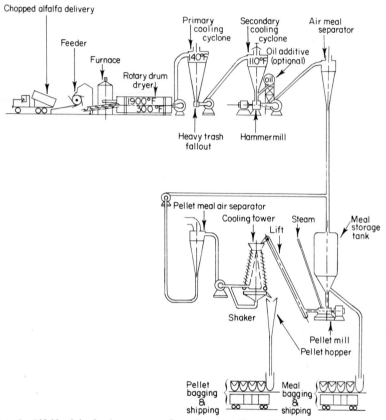

FIG. 1. Alfalfa dehydrating process flow diagram. From "Air Pollution from Alfalfa Dehydrating Mills" (8).

25 pounds of a balanced ration every day for 150 days. During the stay in the feedlot the average animal gains 1 pound in weight for each 8–10 pounds of feed. In a commercial lot, the average 1000-pound animal will produce 26 pounds in total excreta each day, of which 15 pounds is urine. Accordingly, the potential for an atmospheric odor problem is ever present.

Control of the feedlot odor problem depends primarily on sanitation and housekeeping. If the pens are paved with either concrete or asphalt, a continuous program of pen cleaning and manure removal is necessary. In the summer, daily removal of manure should be practiced. Paved areas should also have good drainage to prevent pooling. Lots following these practices can accommodate one animal for each 80 ft² of lot.

In arid and semiarid regions, and on farms, feedlots often have earth floors. Here manure need not be removed so frequently inasmuch as moisture does not build up in the pen. Generally the manure dries and does not emit a putrefactive odor if it is not allowed to remain wet or to form a crust. Pooling or wet areas must not be allowed to develop, particularly around mangers and water troughs.

As the dry manure builds up on the pen or corral surface, it may be kept relatively odorless by scarifying with a spring-tooth cultivator to allow penetration by sun and air. When the manure becomes too deep for adequate scarifying it should be removed (at least three times a year). It also has been found that odor levels following manure removal and scarifying can be kept to a minimum by spraying the lot with a 1% solution of potassium permanganate so that each treatment amounts to 20 pounds $KMnO_4$ per acre (9). Earth-floor lots should allow 300 ft^2 floor area for each animal.

Stockyard pens should be subject to the same sanitation and space requirements as cattle feed yards. It is usually recommended that they be paved.

Another problem of unpaved corrals in dry areas is dusting if too much manure is allowed to build up. Cattle begin to move around ("play") in the early evening and stir up very fine manure dust. Areas downwind receive the brunt of the dust. Careful spraying of a limited amount of water into the lot by means of fog nozzles can correct the situation.

Nearly all feedlot operations have tried the use of odor counteractant sprays at one time or another. If the yard practices good sanitation methods, odor counteractants may be helpful; if sanitation is poor, odor counteractants are useless and an unnecessary expense.

Whatever the kind of feedlot, manure disposal is usually a difficult economic problem. In a few localities it may be dehydrated and sold for fertilizer use. Generally, it is easier spread on adjacent agricultural land or buried. If necessary it may be incinerated. Composting has proved satisfactory in some instances (10). Experimental work has also been done on lagooning.

2. Hog and Sheep Pens

The keeping of hogs and sheep in an urban community is difficult to justify and is usually prohibited. Still, with housing tracts invading rural areas, hogs often become neighbors to suburbanites.

Usually, sheep and hog odors are more offensive than cattle odors. Pens should be located indoors, well-ventilated and lighted. Floors should be of concrete and have good drainage. The pens should be cleaned and manure removed on a daily basis. Only in this way can sheep and hog pens be acceptable.

3. *Poultry and Egg Production*

Generally, the raising of poultry and production of eggs are not important contributors to air pollution. Nevertheless two rather specialized problems have arisen, one in connection with poultry ranches, the other with egg production.

The poultry ranch problem is well illustrated by the troublesome problem of dust clouds around turkey ranches. Several hundred large flocks of turkeys (over 50,000 birds) are kept in the San Joaquin and Sacramento Valleys of California on relatively small acreages of land. These ranches soon become barren of vegetation, so at feeding time when thousands of turkeys run across the ground flapping their wings, great clouds of dust, feathers, and feces rise into the air. Under stable atmospheric conditions these clouds may persist for more than a day. Public health authorities are concerned not only with the dust nuisance, but the risk of allergic reactions and transmission of bacterial and virus infections. In some locations it has been claimed that dust from poultry ranches has settled on nearby vegetation and reduced yields.

At egg ranches, the problem is odor. The birds are kept inside houses in small cages. Manure droppings fall to the ground under the houses. Unless the droppings dry rapidly or are removed frequently, or continually, odors develop and flies are attracted. One California rancher has used a composting process to control odor (*11*).

III. Dust from Food and Feed Processing

Wherever in the food and feed industries a dry powder is produced or handled, there is a potential for air pollution from dust. Principal operations in this category are grain milling (flour, feed, malt, etc.), drying operations (sugar and starch), mixing of dry feeds and foods, coffee roasting, and related shipping, packaging, and conveying operations.

A. Grain Milling

All grain milling operations involve disintegration of the dried grain followed by a series of sizing, separating, and mixing processes. Inasmuch as all these processes involve handling fine dust particles in an airstream, a potential dust problem always exists. Even before the milling operation begins, the grain must be delivered, unloaded from cars, cleaned, stored, and brought from storage to the processing site.

Of all these operations the dustiest is the loading and unloading of boxcars, ships, trucks, and barges. Proper control involves loading and unloading in enclosed or semienclosed areas operated under negative pressure to prevent the escape of dusty air. Baffles to contain dust and to direct air flow are useful in lessening dust losses during unloading. Finally, any exhausted airstream must be sent through cyclone collectors, and possibly baghouses, if complete air cleaning is required.

The use of special bulk feed and grain cars is highly recommended. These cars have discharge hopper bottoms, sectional compartments, and top spout openings, all of which reduce dust emissions.

Prior to processing, the grain is always cleaned by passing it over a series of scalpers (to remove tramp iron and other large objects), screens (to separate weed seeds, small stones, soil, etc.) and aspirators (where an airstream blows out chaff, grain hairs, pollen, mold spores, parts of insects and other lightweight contaminants). Uncleaned grains usually contain 3% dockage, of which 90% is removed during the cleaning operation.

Cleaning leads to another major problem, disposal of the collected dust. Regardless of final disposition by the salvager, it must be loaded into dust cars, a difficult and extremely dusty operation. Again, cyclones and baghouses are required if dust is to be controlled. Air-cloth ratio ranges from 3 to 5 ft^3 per square foot of cloth.

1. Milling of Wheat

The milling of wheat flour entails the following steps after the grain is cleaned (12):

1. Blending of various grades of wheat in a mixer.
2. Scalping, screening, and aspirating the grain for a final cleaning.
3. Washing grain to toughen outside bran layer so it will separate easily.
4. Rolling, screening, and sifting grain in a series of operations to yield flour.
5. Additional processing as desired, e.g., bleaching, enrichment, etc.
6. Packaging.

The only air pollution problem of any consequence is the movement of the raw grain, as discussed previously. All emissions from the milling operation are well contained within the building itself by use of a closed cleaning system and recycle of air from cloth-type filters (air-cloth ratios 3:1 to 4:1).

The chief dust problem specific to the flour-milling operation is the loading of chaff and middlings into rail cars.

2. *Milling of Other Grains*

Secondary to the milling of wheat is the milling of a variety of other grains, e.g., corn, rice, oats, barley, buckwheat, and rye. As in the case with wheat, the major dusty operations are loading and unloading cars, and cleaning the grain. Buckwheat and rye are milled in a manner quite similar to wheat. The other grains are processed by modified methods directed to separating the hulls, germ, and bran from the endosperm. In the case of rice an endosperm of maximum grain size is desired. Inasmuch as the processing of all these grains involves grinding and separation of fine or lightweight material, cyclone separators are attached to nearly every piece of separation equipment. If the dust loss becomes a nuisance, the cyclones are backed up with cloth collectors.

Barley malting is a specialized process in which cleaned barley grain is germinated to increase its content of the enzyme, diastase. When the desired amount of diastase has formed, the germination is stopped by drying the malt in a rotary kiln. The dried malt is separated from sprouts and other waste material and shipped to breweries or food manufacturers.

Even though the grain is cleaned prior to malting, continual handling of the malting grain releases dust all through the process. It is captured in cyclone collectors and sold as animal feed.

The wet milling of corn yields cornstarch and its derivatives as end products. It is called wet milling because the corn is soaked (steeped) in a water solution of sulfur dioxide prior to the subsequent separations, and because water is used in large quantities in nearly every step of the process. Grain handling and finished product drying and blending are the only dust problems of note.

B. Drying and Mixing Operations

Whenever a powder or dry crystalline product is desired as the result of a wet process, the final operation is drying. In the corn wet-milling process, for instance, the final wet products are a starch cake and a gluten cake. Similar cakes result from the wet processing of grain sorghum or various roots, e.g., potatoes, cassava (tapioca), and sago.

In any event, washed starch (or gluten) is fed to a rotary or belt dryer where it meets warm air usually in a countercurrent fashion. Some fine dried particles are picked up by the airstream and blown from the dryer. Usually the product is sufficiently valuable to warrant capture in a cyclone or bag collector. Similar equipment is used in the drying of sucrose (cane sugar) and dextrose (corn sugar).

In the past 15 years, spray drying operations have become widespread in the food industry. Here a water slurry is sprayed under considerable pressure into a chamber where dry air evaporates the moisture from the spray droplets before they meet the side or floor of the chamber. The dryer is so designed and operated that the resulting dried powder is uniform in size, denatured only slightly, if at all, and readily soluble. Among the more common products are milk powder, coffee, tea, corn syrup solids, starches, potatoes, eggs, cheese, fruit and vegetable powders, etc.

All dryers use cyclone collectors to collect the fine particles that do not settle in the dryer chamber (usually conical in shape). Dust losses are normally less than 0.1% of product. If necessary, the cyclone can be backed up with a cloth collector, unless the powder is hygroscopic. In the latter case, a wet scrubber may be used.

After a product is dried, it is often blended with other dry products to form a dry food mix. In the United States, the manufacture of dry food mixes which require a minimum of preparation before serving is a

TABLE I

RECOMMENDED AIR–CLOTH RATIOS FOR FOOD PRODUCTS

| | Ratio of ft³ of air to ft² of cloth | |
Material	Recommended	Range
Alfalfa dust (cold)	6:1	—
Beef scrap dust (dried)	5:1	4:1 to 6:1
Blood (animal, dried)	5:1	4:1 to 6:1
Coffee (ground)	4:1	3:1 to 5:1
Coffee (spray-dried)	3.5:1	2:1 to 4:1
Cornstarch	2.5:1	2:1 to 3:1
Cottonseed meal	4:1	3:1 to 5:1
Egg albumen (dried)	3:1	3:1 to 4:1
Feed	4:1	4:1
Fiber	4:1	4:1 to 5:1
Flour (roll suction)	3:1	3:1
(other)	4:1	4:1
Grain dust	4:1	3:1 to 5:1
(elevator)	5:1	4:1 to 6:1
Milk (powdered, whole)	2.5:1	2.5:1
(powdered, nonfat)	3:1	3:1
Soybean flour	3:1	3:1
Sugar	2:1	2:1
Yeast (dried)	3:1	3:1

rapidly expanding business. Among these convenience foods are cake and cookie mixes, puddings, gelatin desserts, pie crusts, hot and cold cereals, soft drink powders, soups, dehydrated vegetables, etc. Processing entails drying, grinding and pulverization, mixing, conveying and packaging, all operations that produce dust (usually 10–100 μ particle size). Recovery for economic reasons is almost universal. Both cyclones and cloth collectors are used. Recommended air–cloth ratios for various food products are shown in Table I.

IV. Odors from Food and Feed Processing

Nearly every food and feed contains proteinaceous or nitrogenous material. As soon as proteins leave the life cycle they begin to decompose by one mechanism or another until ultimately their nitrogen content is returned to the soil or to the sea as nitrate. Then it is available for plant growth and life's nitrogen cycle begins again.

In the course of protein decomposition, highly odoriferous materials containing nitrogen or sulfur or both are formed. These intermediates of the putrefaction process are the source of most odors around food processing plants. Wherever concentrated proteins, such as meat or fish, are handled, odors are a continuing and obvious problem. Further, almost all animal and vegetable waste contains some protein, so that wherever animal or vegetable waste is discarded, obnoxious odors may develop. Most of the odoriferous gases are amines, e.g., mono-, di-, and trimethylamine, triethylamine, putrescine, cadaverine, indole, and skatole.

Under some conditions starches and sugars may ferment to produce highly unpleasant fatty acids, e.g., butyric, valeric, and caproic acids. Where sulfur is involved in the biological species, highly unpleasant sulfur compounds may escape, such as mercaptans, thiols, mercaptoacetic acid, allyl isothiocyanate, and hydrogen sulfide. The odor threshold level of many of these compounds is less than 1 ppb.

The most important segments of the food industry from an odor standpoint are the meat and meat products industry, fish processing, and disposal of fruit and vegetable wastes.

A. MEAT AND MEAT PRODUCTS

1. Meat Packing

Meat packing plants or abattoirs usually consist of 10 sections:

1. Holding yards and pens
2. Killing floor
3. Hide room
4. Casing room

5. Paunch and intestinal content removal
6. Coolers
7. Trimming and boning
8. Pickle room
9. By-product processing
10. Smoke-oven operations

The control of odors from holding yards and pens are similar to those discussed in Section II,G,1. Some odors arise from the hide room, casing room, and paunch removal area. Odors from the casing area are from manure and the sour, partly digested foodstuffs of the intestine. Further decomposition must be prevented by good sanitation practices. The air from the room should also be treated before it is exhausted to the atmosphere. Some believe a water wash is adequate. Scrubbing the air with a potassium permanganate solution is much more effective.

Waste water treatment facilities may also produce obnoxious odors if good sanitation methods are not practiced. Common causes of odors are decomposition of screened solids (if not disposed of daily), low flow rates in trickling filters, and spring thawing of stabilization ponds when the ice cover first disappears.

2. Inedible Fat Rendering

By-product processing presents the most difficult of all the odor problems of the meat industry, and the paramount process of all is inedible fat rendering. The fat rendering industry is widely noted for odor problems for good reasons. The process involves the application of heat to the raw material (meat scrap, intestines, bones, etc.) in order to remove water, disintegrate the bone tissue, and release fat or tallow.

In a typical rendering system, (Fig. 2) meat scrap and other animal

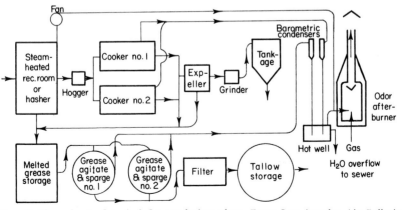

FIG. 2. Flow sheet of typical fat rendering plant. From Los Angeles Air Pollution Control District (12a).

residues are ground to a hamburgerlike consistency and charged to horizontal, steam-jacketed kettles. During the cooking process, fat cells are broken down to water, grease, and proteinaceous solids. The solids are then separated from the grease, which may subsequently be purified to produce tallow. Odors are emitted through the entire process, beginning with the raw material storage bins.

The major area odor problem of the rendering plant is caused by the high volume of odorous gases delivered from the cooker. Catalytic and direct flame afterburners, a variety of scrubbers, and several odor masking agents have all been used for odor control. Potassium permanganate solutions have been found to be especially effective in scrubbers. In a 20,000 cfm scrubber using a 1–2% KMnO$_4$ solution, the chemical cost was $8.40 per day.

Another cooker odor control system, said to be in successful operation in two plants, replaces the multiple condensers normally used with a condenser-deodorizer. Vapors from the cooker enter the bottom of the condenser tangentially, then go to a centrifugal separator, to a spray chamber, and through a bed of activated carbon to remove odors and thence to a vacuum ejector. All of these operations are incorporated in a single unit.

Localized odor problems of an objectionable nature are related to transportation and storage of the raw material. Bacterial decomposition of animal tissue begins at the death of the animal and putrefaction progresses rapidly with time and elevated temperatures. Just the dumping of a "ripe" load of offal can create a problem. If, then, the material is held over a weekend before processing, a highly obnoxious problem develops. To alleviate the problem, all plant air should be exhausted through control equipment. The use of refrigeration during offal transport and storage would also be effective. Obviously, good housekeeping is also required.

3. Smoke Oven

Smoke from ovens and smoke houses used for curing meat is sometimes objectionable because of both smoke and odor. In Los Angeles County, regulations are extremely strict, and smoke houses cannot comply without the addition of smoke and odor control equipment. One installation required a water scrubber, a low-voltage electrostatic precipitator, and an afterburner. In this case, the air pollution control equipment cost $42,000 whereas the basic oven cost only $18,000 (13). In many operations a water scrubber followed by an afterburner is satisfactory.

B. Fish Processing

The canning, dehydration, and smoking of fish, and the manufacture of fish oil and fish meal are the important segments of the fish industry. Odors emanate from the fishing boats and raw storage through all processing steps, e.g., cooking, pressing, screening, centrifuging, drying, and waste disposal. Principal malodorants are acrolein, oil decomposition products, hydrogen sulfide, ammonia, butyric and valeric acids, and trimethylamine (14).

Odor control entails passing gaseous process effluents and exhaust air from processing areas through control equipment which will either destroy the odorous gas or absorb it. Some of the methods used are activated carbon adsorbers, scrubbing with chlorinated water or some other oxidizing solution, catalytic combustion, incineration, and the use of masking and counteraction agents.

In Europe, water scrubbing is the principal control method in fish meal plants. If the scrubbed gases are low in volume they are sent through a boiler; if high in volume chlorine is added. Odor counteractants are also used. Failure to use incineration in European practice probably reflects the high cost in fuel. Generally the use of chlorine is not favored for fish meal plants in the United States, but chlorine dioxide at 100–150 ppm in scrubber water is said to be effective. Nevertheless, one tuna processing plant in California is effectively using chlorinated seawater to treat cooker effluent gases.

Fish smoking is subject to the same problems as the smoking of meat (q.v.).

In many areas fish waste is still dumped into the harbor nearby. Often current flow is sufficient to carry the waste out to sea for dispersal, but wherever stagnant conditions exist, solids settle to the bottom, break down anaerobically, and emit highly odorous gases. Fortunately, more and more municipalities are requiring plants to treat their liquid wastes before disposal.

C. Fruit and Vegetable Processing

The most important processes for the preservation of fruits and vegetables are canning, dehydration, and quick-freezing. The only important air pollution problem is related to the disposal of hulls, leaves, rinds, pods, cuttings, etc. If held too long these materials decay and produce revolting odors.

Water pollution regulations prohibit sending the waste to streams unless it has been processed to reduce biological oxygen demand (BOD). One method commonly used to reduce BOD is digestion of the cannery waste in either anaerobic or aerobic lagoons. Even the best-operated lagoon has upsets during which period odorous gases (hydrogen sulfide, mercaptans, fatty acids, amines, and other nitrogenous gases) are evolved. If the upsets are only occasional, odor-counteracting or masking agents may be released on the downwind side of the lagoon. If the condition persists, addition of a nutrient, precipitation of excess sulfide, or reestablishment of the active organism may be required. Some food processors have replaced lagoons with spray irrigation plots to advantage. The National Canners Association is currently studying methods of composting (15).

Leaves, stalks, and cuttings can sometimes be disposed of odorlessly in adequately designed incinerators. Sanitary landfill is an alternate method.

D. Miscellaneous Food Odors

One action that commonly nettles food manufacturers is public complaint about odors normally considered to be pleasant, e.g., the odor of baking bread, coffee being roasted, or melting chocolate. Nevertheless, many who encounter these odors continually don't like them, so some sort of control is in order. The operation receiving the most attention is coffee roasting.

1. *Coffee Roasting Industry*

Emphasis on control of coffee roasters (16) rises not only from characteristic odor emissions, but also from emissions of smoke and particulate matter (dust and chaff).

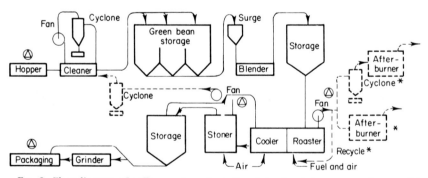

Fig. 3. Flow diagram of coffee roasting plant. ⊿, points of emission; ---, usual or possible control; *, alternate control possibilities. From U.S. Dept. of Health, Education, and Welfare (16).

TABLE II

PARTICULATE EMISSIONS FROM THE COFFEE ROASTING PROCESS[a]

Processes	Concentration (grains per standard cubic foot)	Pounds solids per 1000 pounds green beans	Condensed tar (%)	Control equipment
Direct-fired roaster	0.193	1.12	81	Cyclone
Indirect-fired roaster	0.127	0.58	36	Cyclone
Cooler	0.036	0.29	—	None
Stoner	0.097	0.37	—	None
Stoner and cooler combined	0.017	0.16	27	Cyclone

[a] From U.S. Dept. of Health, Education, and Welfare (16).

In a typical coffee roasting operation (Fig. 3), green coffee beans are freed of dust and trash by dropping the beans in a current of air. The dust and chaff removed may be recovered in a cyclone collector. The cleaned beans are air-blended and sent to a batch or continuous roaster where they contact hot combustion gases. Time and temperature are important variables. During the roasting, moisture is driven off, the beans swell, and certain chemical changes occur that give the roasted beans their typical color and aroma. When the roasting has reached a certain color the beans are quenched, cooled, and stoned (heavy particles removed in an airstream). Particulate emissions from the roasting process are shown in Table II. As indicated in the table, cyclone collectors are adequate to control particulate emissions.

Smoke and odor pass through the cyclones. In one "smokeless roaster," a damper system recirculates the combustion gases through the gas flame of the roaster to eliminate smoke and odor. Additional fuel consumption of 40% is required. Smoke and odor control may also be accomplished by an afterburner in the roaster stack, but fuel requirements are increased 100–150% over that of a conventional roaster.

Similar dust and odor problems may be expected in the manufacture of instant (spray-dried) coffee, and in the incineration of spent coffee grounds. Cyclones, wet scrubbers, and afterburners are adequate for control.

2. Spices and Condiments

The milling of a variety of barks, bulbs, leaves, buds, fruits, roots, and seeds to produce spices and condiments can lead to strong and pungent odors. Subsequent mixing and packaging operations also contribute their share. These operations are carried out in an isolated portion of the food processing plant to prevent odors from contaminating other food products. Exhaust air is commonly run through activated carbon filters to abate the odor present.

V. Feed Manufacture

A. MIXED FEEDS

Nearly all grain handling and grain processing operations involve by-product material which eventually ends up in animal feed, e.g., cracked grain from elevators and cleaning operations, bran middlings and shorts from flour milling, bran and fiber from the milling of minor grains; gluten and steepwater solids from corn wet milling; spent grain and distillers' solubles from the fermentation industry; beet pulp from the beet-sugar industry. In addition, by-products of the meat packing and milk industries also end up in animal feeds. Alfalfa, molasses, calcium salts, and phosphates are further constituents.

Unloading the bulk grains and grain products from box cars and transporting them to bins is the chief dust-producing operation of the industry. Alfalfa is particularly dusty and must be handled carefully.

After the raw materials are unloaded, the grain and other granular material is ground in a hammer mill, then mixed—usually in continuous operations. When molasses is added, a batch mixing process is normally used. In either case the mixtures are later moistened with steam and forced through dies to produce pellets.

Both the grinding and mixing operations are dusty, but the dust may be adequately controlled with cyclones or cloth collectors.

The principal problem during pelleting is emission of odors. The odors are particularly strong and unpleasant when feeds contain large quantities of tankage and bone meal. The only solution is treating the exhausted air in scrubbers or incinerators, or passing it through a bed of activated charcoal.

B. BY-PRODUCT FEEDSTUFFS

Air pollution problems accompanying the recovery of by-product feedstuffs are those inherent in the manufacture of the main food product. Whenever the by-product is high in protein value, it is dried, ground, and sold as a high-protein feed, or mixed with low protein by-products (chaff, hulls, bran, etc.) to increase the feed value of the latter. Among the more important high-protein feeds are corn gluten meal, oil-seed meals, dried distillers' solubles, fish meal, and various animal residues (blood, tankage, etc.).

Corn gluten meal is a by-product of the wet milling of corn, a process in which whole grain corn is steeped in a dilute sulfurous acid solution and subsequently separated into starch, fiber, gluten, and corn germ. Sulfur dioxide is emitted throughout the wet-separation process and sometimes causes an in-plant problem, but the comparatively small quantities reaching the ambient atmosphere are rapidly dispersed.

In some of the older plants the gluten is concentrated by settling in open tanks prior to filtration and drying. If it is allowed to stand too long in the wet state or if spillage is not controlled, putrid odors may develop. Rapid handling of gluten liquors and good sanitation practice have solved the odor problem in modern plants.

Some of the gluten meal is mixed with coarse and fine fiber (hulls and bran) and other low-protein by-products to make a lower-grade feed than the meal itself. Drying and handling of the final feed produces dust which may be controlled by cyclone collectors, or cloth collectors when necessary.

Oil-seed meals, e.g., cottonseed meal, flaxseed meal, safflower seed meal, are by-products of the recovery of vegetable oils by pressing or solvent extraction. Excessive loss of solvent vapors during extraction or subsequent steaming of the meal may produce a localized odor problem. Usually the solvent is valuable enough to warrant recovery by condensation or adsorption on activated charcoal. Subsequent processing of the oil may also release odorous material.

Brewers' grains, distillers' dried grains, and distillers' solubles are all by-products of the brewing and distilling industry. Air pollution may arise from (1) raw material preparation, (2) the fermentation process, and (3) solid and liquid waste disposal. Fermentation odors are usually not strong enough to be objectionable. If they are, vent gases or air from the vicinity of the source may be passed through scrubbers or activated carbon adsorbers. Dust and odors from feed dryers may be controlled by means previously described.

VI. Allied Industries

In addition to food and feed, a variety of agricultural products and food industry by-products are converted to other articles of commerce. Wherever spoilage (protein and carbohydrate decomposition) takes place there is potential for an odor problem. Wherever the material is ground, or where dust or other fine material is handled or processed, there is potential for a dust problem. The problems may be abated by methods similar to those described for food and feed products. The more important agricultural process operations where a potential for air pollution exists include glue and gelatin manufacture; leather tanning, particularly liming and bating; curing of hides and pelts; cotton ginning; wool scouring, and combing; degreasing; hair recovery and cleaning; feather utilization; tobacco curing and manufacture of tobacco products.

REFERENCES

1. "Clean Air for California," p. 17. California Dept. of Public Health, Berkeley, Calif. (1955).
2. J. T. Middleton, A. S. Crafts, R. F. Brewer, and O. C. Taylor, *Calif. Agr.,* **10**, No. 6, 9 (1956).
3. E. F. Darley, F. R. Burleson, E. H. Mateer, J. T. Middleton, and V. P. Osterli, *J. Air Pollution Control Assoc.* **16**, 685–690 (1966).
4. "Rules and Regulations," p. 33. Los Angeles County Air Pollution Control District, Los Angeles, California, 1958.
5. "Rules and Regulations," p. 13. San Bernardino County Air Pollution Control District, San Bernardino, California, 1958.
6. Annual Report, p. 30. San Bernardino County Air Pollution Control District, San Bernardino, California, 1964.
7. R. L. Stockman and P. W. Hildebrandt, "The Air Pollution Aspects of Orchard Heating in the Yakima, Washington Area." Washington State Dept. of Health, Seattle, Washington, 1961.
8. "Air Pollution from Alfalfa Dehydrating Mills," *Robert A. Taft Sanitary Eng. Center, Tech. Rept.* **A60-4,** (1960).
9. W. L. Faith, *J. Air Pollution Control Assoc.* **14**, 459–460 (1964).
10. J. S. Wiley, *Compost Sci.* **5**, No. 2, 15–16 (1964).
11. R. C. Hartman, *Compost Sci.* **4**, No. 1, 26–28 (1963).
12. M. E. McLouth and H. J. Paulus, *J. Air Pollution Control Assoc.* **11**, 313–317 (1961).
12a. "Control of Stationary Sources," Vol. 1, Tech. Progr. Rept. Los Angeles Air Pollution Control District, Los Angeles, California, 1960.
13. R. L. Chass, *in* "Proceedings of National Conference of Air Pollution," p. 277. U.S. Dept. of Health, Education, and Welfare, Public Health Service, Washington, D.C., 1963.
14. L. C. Mandell, *Proc. 54th Ann. Meeting Air Pollution Control Assoc., New York, 1961* pp. 1–12.
15. W. W. Rose *et al., Compost Sci.* **6**, No. 2, 13–25 (1965).
16. "Air Pollution in the Coffee Roasting Industry," Public Health Serv. Publ. No. 999-AP-9. U.S. Dept. of Health, Education, and Welfare, U.S. Public Health Serv., Div. Air Pollution, Cincinnati, Ohio, 1964.

GENERAL REFERENCE

Additional pertinent material is in Chapters 7 and 11 of "Air Pollution Engineering Manual, Los Angeles APCD" (J. A. Danielson, ed.), PHS Publn. 999-AP-40, DHEW, Cincinnati (1967).

Part VIII
CONTROL METHODS AND EQUIPMENT

41 Process and System Control

Melvin W. First

I. Introduction

Hatch has wisely pointed out (*1*) that "Prevention of community air pollution from industrial operations starts within the factory or mill." Resort to air and gas cleaning devices to eliminate or reduce emissions of air polluting substances and to tall discharge stacks to disperse and dilute offensive substances to acceptable ground level concentrations becomes unnecessary when process and system control is effective in preventing the formation and release of air pollutants.

Even when gas cleaning and atmospheric dispersion must be used as final steps, process and system control is a means of minimizing the quantities of substances entering clean-up systems and, ultimately, being discharged to the atmosphere. Process and system control will concentrate contaminants in the smallest possible volume of air. This is important as the cost of control equipment is based principally on the volume of gas that must be handled and not on the amount or concentration of the substances that must be removed. Also, most air and gas removal equipment is more efficient when handling higher concentrations of contaminants, all else being equal.

Current estimating practice for construction costs of tall stacks is $1000 per foot for the first 600 feet and $2500 for each additional foot. Thus a 1000 foot stack would be estimated to cost approximately $1.6 million. Much process and system control can be built into a process for sums of this magnitude.

Reduction of air-polluting emissions by process and system control is an important adjunct to air and gas cleaning technology and to atmospheric dispersion, as well as an important technique when it can be used as the only control measure. The present trend toward rapid adoption of restrictive emission limitations and air quality standards makes it essential that all methods of air pollution control be utilized to the maximum possible degree in areas where the air environment is threatened with excessive pollution.

II. Elimination of Air Pollution Emissions

A. Substituting Products

Offensive substances often may be eliminated entirely from processes which are causing air pollution by substituting materials which perform equally well in the process but which discharge innocuous products to the atmosphere or none at all. When this method of air pollution control can be applied, it usually produces very satisfactory pollution control at trivial cost. The numerous new chemical products that enter the commercial market annually make it worthwhile to maintain a continuing search for substitute materials of low pollution potential, even when past searches have failed.

A typical example for industry of a product change controlling an air pollution problem is substitution of a cold-setting synthetic resin for rubber in the manufacture of paint brushes. Before this change, it was necessary to vulcanize the rubber bond at the base of the bristles for a period of many hours, causing severe odor nuisances in the vicinity of the factory from the emission of sulfur-containing volatile products. The cold-setting resins selected as rubber substitutes produce no odors and completely eliminate air-polluting emissions from this operation.

In the field of transportation, there is considerable interest in electric battery power as a substitute for the internal combustion automobile engine although a great deal of technological development and innovation must precede the widespread use of electric vehicles for commuting and intra-urban family use. A battery-powered automobile would be virtually pollution free, in contrast to emissions from conventional automobiles of carbon monoxide, nitrogen and sulfur oxides, and a long list of organic compounds.

Little technological effort is required to substitute low sulfur for high sulfur fuels for the production of heat and power, but these desirable fuels have limited availability. Complete freedom from sulfur oxides and other gaseous emissions associated with the burning of fossil fuels for heat and power may be obtained by changing to water power and nuclear fuels, but there appears to be little prospect that these two sources of electricity will be able to satisfy the demand for the foreseeable future.

B. CHANGING PROCESS

Process changes can be as effective as product substitution in eliminating air-pollution emissions. The chemical and petroleum refining industries have undergone radical changes in processing methods which emphasize continuous automatic operations, often computer controlled, and completely enclosed systems that minimize release of materials to the atmosphere. It has been found possible, and often profitable, to control loss of volatile materials by condensation and reuse of vapors, (e.g., condensation units on volatile petroleum product storage tanks), and recycling noncondensible gases for additional reactions (e.g., polymerization and alkylation of gaseous hydrocarbons to produce gasoline).

Other examples are: (1) The development of ultra-high voltage systems for long distance transmission of electricity has made it economically feasible to substitute distant water-powered turbines for urban fuel-burning steam stations. (2) The use of liquid and gaseous fertilizer chemicals, e.g., anhydrous ammonia, applied by injection into the earth instead of being spread across the surface as finely divided powders subject to wind entrainment, reduces pollution. (3) A substantial reduction in oxidation of SO_2 to SO_3, by reducing excess air from 15 to 20% to less than 1% when burning fossil fuels, has eliminated sulfuric acid emissions, but the absence of excess air tends to result in greater soot production.

III. Minimizing Emissions of Gaseous and Gasborne Wastes

A. GROUND-LEVEL, WIDE AREA POLLUTION SOURCES

Although primary emphasis is usually placed on emissions from stacks, polluting substances may enter the air in other ways, usually at or near ground level and often over extended areas. Both situations tend to restrict natural atmospheric dilution and create severe local pollution problems. For example, sulfite process pulp mills often discharge odorous liquid wastes into streams that slowly release offensive substances to the air by degassing or volatilization for many miles downstream. Areas subjected to air pollution by this means may be larger than from a tall stack, with the added disadvantage of not being relieved, even intermittently, by changes in wind direction. Treatment of this waste liquor prior to discharge to a river, by removal of volatile and putrescible fractions, will reduce its air pollution potential to a level that can be met by the natural cleansing capabilities of the stream.

Similar considerations apply to air pollution from open dump burning. This, also, is an extensive source that releases at ground level intensely offensive airborne substances that sweep across large land areas without substantial dilution. Substitution of sanitary landfilling for open dump burning eliminates air pollution from this operation. When sanitary landfill sites are unavailable, modern, high temperature, central-station incinerators equipped with dust removal equipment minimize air-polluting emissions from the disposal of solid wastes.

B. Good Building Construction, Plant Layout, and Housekeeping

Open storage piles of chemicals, such as sulfur and bauxite, and minerals, such as sand and clay, are often local pollution sources during dry, windy weather. The application of persistent surface coatings such as wetting agents and plastics, combined with supplementary spraying during dry weather, is effective for suppression of dust from inactive storage piles of coal and similar granular materials. For active piles of crushed stone, sand, etc., the continuous application of water, with or without wetting agents, is an important control measure, especially for elevated conveyor belts handling pulverized products. Enclosed storage buildings, widely used for the curing of phosphate fertilizers, eliminate loss of particulate matter by wind erosion.

Industrial operations may be controlled to minimize the production and release of air pollutants with the aid of careful building construction, plant layout, and housekeeping. These precautions are of especial importance for all processes that handle food or inedible putrescible material. The traditional "offensive trades" (slaughtering, rendering, leather tanning, and pig farming) earned this designation because they frequently cause severe odor nuisance. The application of modern sanitary science can prevent this from occurring in most of these industries, although the virtual impossibility of deodorizing garbage-fed pig colonies has resulted in their complete disappearance from the out-skirts of most cities.

Food processing plants are usually under strict sanitary surveillance by health and agricultural authorities but processing of animal products for other than human consumption is not similarly supervised. When these operations are conducted under primitive sanitary conditions, they result in the release to the air of offensive substances. The production from trash fish and gurry (fish remains after filleting) of fish meal (for animal feed supplements) and fish oils (for soap, paint, and varnish) has been associated with air pollution wherever a plant is located near a population center. Using ice to halt the deterioration of fish during storage is not an industry practice so that fish are often in an advanced state of decomposition when oil and meal processing begins.

The principal processing steps (see also Chapter 40) are grinding the raw fish, cooking to separate oil, drying the nonoil, nonsoluble residues and grinding them to obtain a storable, oil-free whole-fish product. All these processes, including raw fish storage, give off airborne products that cause air pollution. These emissions may be minimized by proper plant design and maintenance: First, all floors, walls, and fixtures in the plant should be smooth, hard, and impervious to water so that they may be hosed down to prevent fish scraps from lodging in cracks and crevices to putrefy. Second, scrupulous cleanliness is required to pre-vent accumulation of wastes. Cleaning water should contain a few parts per million of residual chlorine to discourage microbiological activity and all surfaces should be pitched to drain to sumps for treatment of the cleaning water. Third, seawater condensers—most of these plants are located on the shore for easy transfer of fish from boats to plant—should be used in the steam vents of the fish cookers to minimize the escape of condensible gases and vapors from the kettles. Fourth, steam-heated shell driers should be used in preference to direct-fired units to minimize local overheating and scorching of the meal and the discharge of malodorous burnt protein decomposition products with the moist flue gases. Attempts have been made to reduce fuel consumption in direct-fired fish meal driers by recycling a fraction of the discharged gases through the heating flame, but this results in burning and charring of the airborne dust and produces extremely unpleasant odor problems.

All of these recommended practices minimize the amounts of gases, vapors, and particles generated by, and emitted from, the processing vessels and make it possible to treat the remaining air pollutants by direct flame incineration or hypochlorite scrubbing in an economical and technically satisfactory manner. Proper plant construction, careful equipment maintenance to prevent breakdown of essential control equipment, and sanitary operation give good air pollution control results when combined with residual gas cleaning.

Rendering plants that produce fats and meal by similar processes offer the same opportunities for minimizing air-polluting emissions by correct plant design, selection of suitable processing equipment, and sanitary operation. Tanning of hides, production of glue and gelatin, and many other necessary manufacturing operations are dependent on similar techniques to reduce pollution levels.

C. Process Modification and Material Substitutions

1. *Industry*

Substantial benefits and economies may be realized even when process modifications and material substitutions merely reduce air pollution emissions, rather than completely eliminating them. For example, a change in the steel industry from raw ore to briquetted or pelleted sintered ore has greatly reduced dust production during ore handling and helped reduce blast furnace "slips" which result in emission to the atmosphere of enormous amounts of uncleaned blast furnace gas when the safety dampers open and allow the gases to bypass the dust collectors.

Abnormally large emissions to the atmosphere result from operating certain kinds of production equipment at excessive rates. For example, the output of the rotary sand and stone drier controls the production rate of hot mix asphalt plants (see also Chapter 35). When hot gas velocity through the drier is increased above the design rate, to improve drying capacity, the quantity of dust carried out increases in greater proportion than the increase in gas volume. This relationship, unfavorable from the air pollution standpoint, occurs because in the range of viscous particle flow, i.e., particles less than 100 μ diameter, the size of particles entrained is related to the square of the diameter whereas the weight of dust entrained is related to the cube of particle diameter. Because this industry customarily uses scrubbers having a collection efficiency that is relatively insensitive to changes in dust loading, the weight discharged to the atmosphere increases in proportion to the dust load carried out of the rotary drier.

Many air pollution problems caused by the hot mix asphalt paving industry in cold climates stem from the traditional practice of postponing maintenance procedures until winter shutdown. This means that the machinery progressively declines in effectiveness from startup time in early spring until seasonal shutdown in late autumn. By the time the dry, windy autumn months arrive, considerable unrepaired damage has occurred to dust collectors, exhaust systems, and equipment enclosures which results in excessive and unnecessary air pollution. Additional examples of industrial process and component changes to reduce air pollution have been noted by Rose *et al.* (2). These include substitution of bauxite flux for fluorine-containing fluorspar in open hearth practice and the use of borate salts as a substitute for elemental sulfur, used as an antioxidant and flux when casting molten magnesium metal. Both changes result in decreased emission of air pollutants.

2. *Transportation*

The amount of carbon monoxide and hydrocarbons produced by well-maintained, well-tuned engines is only a small fraction of the quantity emitted from those that have not been given proper maintenance. In only a very few communities are automobiles which trail dense clouds of blue smoke ordered off the highways until suitable maintenance procedures have been taken to eliminate excessive emissions.

Injection of air into the hot exhaust manifold of a gasoline engine to continue the combustion of carbon monoxide and hydrocarbons that was halted in the cylinders by the depletion of oxygen represents an equipment modification designed to minimize the emission of polluting substances by the automobile (see also Chapter 33). Modifications to carburation and ignition produce similar results. The long-term durability of these devices has yet to be determined and installing them only on new automobiles, though logistically and politically defensible, leaves the largest emission sources (e.g., older cars) untouched.

Changes in automotive use patterns by the entire urban community could play a decisive role in controlling air pollution. These include: (1) enlargement and improvement of urban mass transportation systems to reduce the need for bringing private vehicles into the city, (2) speeding traffic flow to decrease average trip time and to take advantage of decreased contaminant emission rates at higher speeds, and (3) encouraging, by taxation policy, the use of small, low-horsepower vehicles which emit less contaminants per mile of travel. These kinds of solutions for vehicle pollution obviously require public support and long-range urban planning. Although difficult to achieve, pollution control plans of this nature hold promise of substantial relief because they produce fundamental alterations of contaminant generation patterns.

3. Agriculture

Air pollution arising from agricultural operations may be minimized by a number of techniques (see also Chapter 4, Vol. I, and Chapter 40). Spraying for insect and weed control (by terrestrial and aerial methods) should be conducted during windless weather to confine the spread of insecticides and weed control chemicals to the intended areas. The damage that may be caused by imprudent spraying is demonstrated by the fact that 1 gm of 2,4-dichlorophenoxyacetic acid (2,4-D) can mark all cotton on 25 acres and 15 gm can injure this amount of cotton permanently. In one aerial spraying incident, 10,000 acres of rice were damaged by 2,4-D 15–20 miles downwind of the spraying site.

Dust storms originating in the midwestern prairies of the United States during the 1930's were a severe local problem and ultimately obscured the sun thousands of miles distant. These dust storms were the result of poor farming techniques. Present-day agricultural practices in these same regions are designed to prevent land erosion and have been effective in reducing airborne dust from this source to an acceptable level.

In recent years, the pollen content of urban atmospheres has been reduced by greater weed control on nearby farms and by routine weed eradication activities of highway and public works departments. Although pollen travels long distances by wind action, often the greatest annoyance is produced by pollen emitted locally.

4. Fuel Burning for Space Heating, Steam, and Power

Particulate emissions from burning coal, especially from pulverized coal, have been significantly reduced as a result of coal washing that reduces the ash content of run-of-mine coal. In a modern pulverized coal-burning furnace, approximately 80% of the coal ash finds its way into the flue gas. Reductions in ash content by washing are reflected in corresponding decreases in the amount of fly ash produced. Electrostatic precipitators are now used routinely in modern coal-burning stations to collect fly ash. As they are purchased for large, new stations with a guarantee that they will collect 99.5% of the fly ash in the flue gases, emissions to the atmosphere are related directly to the ash content of the coal, and reductions in incombustible residue by coal washing result in lower particulate emissions.

Coal washing also results in a reduction in the sulfur content of coal and an additional reduction occurs in the pulverizer. For some coals, sulfur reduction by washing and pulverizing may reach as high as 40%;

whereas for others, the decrease in sulfur may be insignificant. The physical state and chemical nature of the sulfur compounds that are present determine the result. When sulfur is present principally in the form of organic compounds that are intimately mixed with coal, little or no sulfur reduction may be obtained by coal cleaning techniques. Satisfactory sulfur removal processes that are applicable to most of the available coal deposits are still being sought. It has been found technologically possible, but costly, to remove sulfur from oil at the refinery (see also Chapter 32). Methods of stretching limited supplies of low sulfur fuel are: (1) blending high and low sulfur grades, (2) storing low sulfur fuel and issuing it for use as a substitute for a high sulfur fuel when unfavorable weather conditions reduce the natural processes of atmospheric dilution and dispersion, (3) requiring high efficiency flue gas SO_2 cleaning systems for large fuel users so they may burn high sulfur fuels safely, and then allocating the limited supply of low sulfur fuel to the large numbers of small users who discharge flue gases close to ground level and cannot operate flue gas SO_2 cleaning systems economically.

It is well to recall that similar problems were faced and resolved when limitations on the volatile content of coals used for commercial and industrial purposes were instituted in the United States many years ago to assist in reducing smoke and soot emissions. Following the 1952 London air pollution disaster, Britain adopted similar prohibitions for domestic fuels in areas designated as "smokeless zones" and the number of communities affected by this rule is gradually being extended.

Technological improvements in heat transfer equipment, turbine generators, and furnaces have resulted in a reduction in the pounds of coal needed to generate a kilowatt of electricity from 1.4 pounds (12,000 Btu/lb) in 1927 to only slightly more than 0.7 pound today. This extraordinary reduction in fuel requirements results in an equal reduction in the emission of sulfur gases and other contaminants to the atmosphere per unit of electricity produced.

The technology to reduce pollution effects from emissions associated with space heating includes: (1) increasing the efficiency of space heating by better insulation of buildings so that less fuel is required to produce a given indoor temperature, (2) providing heat to groups of buildings from a single source in the form of steam, hot water, or electricity, (3) gasifying solid or liquid fuels and use of the resulting gas for space heating, and (4) reducing emissions from space heaters by improved combustion efficiency, tighter fuel specifications with respect to ash, sulfur, viscosity, etc., and limitation of allowable fuels.

IV.   Concentration of Air Pollutants at the Source for Effective Treatment Prior to Release to the Atmosphere

A. Sources of Contaminants

Off-gases result from diverse manufacturing steps. Many are generated in totally enclosed processes. Frequently, these off-gases contain volatile or entrained waste products that the process is designed to remove as a manufacturing step. Processes for drying a wide variety of products, from sand to fish meal, place the moist product in intimate contact with a stream of warm, dry air so that excess water may be extracted and carried off in the effluent gases. Were water the only product carried out of a drier, no air pollution problems would result. However, other less innocuous volatile substances and entrained particles are also carried out of the processing vessel. The minimum volume of drying air and maximum drying temperature are determined by the amount of moisture to be removed and the heat-resistant properties of the materials being dried. It is therefore generally impossible to reduce the volume of gases needing cleaning or atmospheric dilution. Many process tail gases contain valuable products in concentrations too low to make recovery economically worthwhile. Nonetheless, these lean tail gases often represent concentrated air pollution sources. In the manufacture of nitric acid the tail gases contain approximately 0.2–0.3% NO_x when operating under ideal conditions. The price of nitric acid does not justify additional NO_x removal so that these tail gases are customarily discharged to the atmosphere through tall stacks. If this source of air pollution is to be eliminated, special gas cleaning devices must be installed to remove the nitrogen oxide before release of the waste gases to the atmosphere. Similar considerations apply to the recovery of tail gases from sulfuric acid manufacturing and many other processes.

Pollution also originates from the discharge of local exhaust ventilation systems installed to protect workers and prevent in-plant damage. Included are systems which ventilate open surface tanks, crushing and grinding operations, high temperature melting of metals and minerals, curing of elastomers, and use of products containing volatile solvents. As pollution controls may add as much as 40% to the capital cost of electric arc furnace equipment, it is not surprising that efforts are made to minimize the size and cost of collection systems. This is accomplished by enclosing the furnace in a closely fitting exhaust hood to prevent the escape of fumes and by water-cooled hoods and ducts to prevent damage to the apparatus from the high temperatures that are generated. However, some electric furnace operators have elected, for easy access to their furnaces, to leave them unhooded, and permit dust, fumes, and heat to rise to the roof of the factory building before collection and cleaning. To keep dusts, fumes, and temperatures in the working zone at levels tolerable for the employees, the number of factory air changes per hour must be maintained at high rates, and the volumes of air that must be handled are an order of magnitude greater than with hooded furnaces utilizing local exhaust ventilation. The air, however, is at lower temperature, so that ordinary ductwork may be used to conduct it from the roof monitors to the equipment which cleans it before discharge to the atmosphere.

These two systems of controlling the escape of dust and fumes from electric arc furnaces illustrate the advantages and disadvantages of each method. The trend toward automation to increase production rates and reduce labor costs makes manual access to the processing equipment less important than formerly. The very considerable cost of high performance dust collection equipment for submicron-sized fume particles, now required to meet most air pollution codes, is an important force tending to favor the use of local exhaust ventilation systems designed to concentrate the materials evolved from the process into the least possible volume of air.

B. EFFECT OF CONTAMINANT CONCENTRATION ON ATMOSPHERIC DISPERSION

After contaminants have been discharged to the atmosphere for dilution and dispersion, it makes relatively little difference at some distance downwind whether the polluting substances were emitted in concentrated or dilute form as downwind ground level concentration will be proportional to mass rate of emission rather than to concentration in the effluent gas. When hot gases are discharged with little or no dilution by cool air, benefits may be obtained from increased effective stack height. This favors the use of process enclosures that conserve gas temperature and minimize discharge volume. On the other hand, when gases are already cool, greater effective stack height may be obtained by increasing the volume and velocity of the stack discharge, as by adding dilution air. Generally, however, greater increases in effective stack height may be obtained by modest temperature elevations of the stack discharge than by large increases in volume rate and velocity of discharge. Only when those subjected to pollution are very close to the emission source may substantial benefits be obtained from diluting stack discharges with clean air to reduce the concentration of contaminants. For this situation, the laws governing the behavior of air jets are more applicable than the accepted atmospheric diffusion equations which become fully effective only when the stack emission has assumed the speed and direction of the wind and has reached reasonable density equilibrium with the atmosphere. In most cases, local exhaust ventilation of processes that produce contaminants is preferable to general factory ventilation and concentrated exhaust streams are more easily cleaned than dilute ones. Therefore, properly designed and installed local exhaust systems are an important aspect of process control to minimize the emission of contaminants to the atmosphere.

C. PRINCIPLES OF LOCAL EXHAUST HOOD DESIGN

1. Dispersive Forces and Control Velocities

Local exhaust hoods are designed to create a controlled air velocity which will prevent the escape of contaminants from an exhaust-ventilated enclosure to the general workroom air, or to draw inward, or capture, contaminants generated at a distance from the hood face. The air velocity which will just overcome dispersive forces, plus a suitable safety factor, is known as the "control velocity." Control velocity is adjusted to the least air flow rate that gives satisfactory results to keep gas volumes to a minimum and contaminant loadings to a maximum in order to reduce cost and increase the effectiveness of air and gas cleaning operations. Optimum control velocities are determined by a number of factors which include the nature of the process and the dispersive properties of the immediate environment. When complete enclosure of a process is possible, as shown in Fig. 1 (3), the control velocity is the average velocity through the open hood face.

The control velocity must be great enough to overcome disruptive

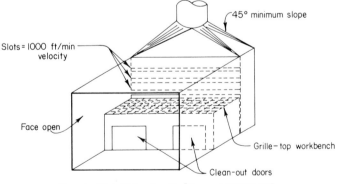

FIG. 1. Metallizing booth [From ACGIH (3)].

air turbulence generated by (1) movement of work pieces into and out of ventilated enclosures, e.g., lowering and raising workbaskets during solvent degreasing, (2) man and machine traffic in the immediate vicinity of the exhaust hood, and (3) air currents from open windows, loading platforms, and mechanical heating and ventilating equipment. Air currents generated by most of these sources seldom exceed 100 ft/min near hoods, but air currents that sweep into the workroom from nearby open doors and windows may reach several times this value. Therefore, operations requiring local exhaust ventilation should be placed in areas that are protected from drafts if minimum control velocities are to be effective. Control velocities of 100–150 ft/min usually are adequate to prevent loss of contaminant to the general room atmosphere.

a. Rotary Machines. Other sources of disruptive air currents may be found inside the exhaust ventilation enclosure itself. Grinding wheels and high speed lathes behave as low efficiency centrifugal fans, i.e., the rotating parts act as fan blades. Depending on peripheral speed and roughness, the fan effect may generate high speed air currents that are difficult to confine and require high control velocities. The movements of bucket conveyor scoops inside conveyor housings act as paddle wheels to impart velocity to the air in contact with them.

b. Percussive Machines. Drop forge hammers compress hot air between the hammer and anvil and "squirt" air out horizontally at high velocity just before impact. These intermittent high velocity jets entrain gases, die lubricants, and fragments of metal scale and must be counteracted by a continuous inward flow of air at a velocity that exceeds the dispersive properties of the machine. There is little or no theory that can be used to determine control velocities for these and similar situations. Although rules of thumb and experience are the principal guides for estimating the velocity and direction of air currents generated by such machines, the behavior of jets in free air (Fig. 2) is of assistance in explaining the observed phenomena (4). At first (zone 1), the jet travels outward as a column of air which retains its initial cross-sectional dimensions and velocity. After a distance equal to about four or five jet diameters, the jet begins to entrain the quiescent atmosphere in contact with it. This results in an enlargement of the jet cross section (zone 2) and a reduction of velocity as energy is transferred to the entrained air. During this phase, which covers a distance of about eight jet diameters, center line velocity decreases as the square root of the distance of travel. In the last phase (zone 3), velocity decreases more rapidly with distance and the cross section spreads more rapidly until, after 25–100 jet diameters, it degenerates into generalized turbulence. To apply jet theory to evaluate the magnitude of the air currents generated by a drop

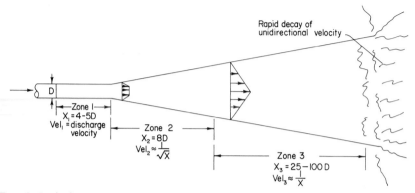

FIG. 2. Jet in free air. D = diameter of jet opening; X = centerline distance of flow zone.

forge hammer, all that is needed is knowledge of the cross section and speed of the hammer. If a two-foot square hammer descends at the rate of 1000 ft/min, it displaces air at the rate of 4000 cfm. As the hammer nears the anvil and the height of the cross section through which displaced air can escape sideways becomes very small, high horizontal air velocities result. For example, when the distance between hammer and anvil decreases to 1 inch, the instantaneous ejection velocity of the displaced air in all four directions becomes 4000 cfm/4 × 2(feet) × 1/12 (feet) = 6000 ft/min. Horizontal jet velocities become increasingly larger as the hammer approaches the anvil, but theory indicates that persistence of the jet and transference of momentum to the surrounding air are influenced by the absolute size of the jet. Therefore, velocity increases during the final instant are less effective in creating disruptive air currents than are the somewhat lower velocities associated with jets of larger cross section. From Fig. 2, it is possible to estimate jet velocity at various distances from the bed of the forge and to determine the control velocity that will be needed to confine the air contaminants generated by the forge. Although the airborne products generated during the forging of iron and steel have little air pollution significance, the processing of powdered beryllium and other highly toxic metals by this fabrication technique requires careful design and construction of local exhaust systems.

c. Particle Projection. Not only are particles entrained by dispersive air currents generated in machines, but in many instances they are given substantial acceleration. This is the case with grinding wheels. The peripheral velocities of large, high speed grinding wheels exceed 20,000 ft/min and particles are discharged tangentially from the surface of the wheel at speeds that approximate those of the wheel surface. Fine particles, i.e., those in the Stokes' law range, move through air in laminar flow and rapidly attain the speed and direction of the air currents which entrain them. This is especially true for particles in the respirable size range, i.e., less than 10 μ diameter. For these particles, control velocities scarcely greater than those needed to contain the air currents generated by the fan effect of the wheel are all that will be needed to capture them. Large particles generated by coarse-grained grinding wheels may be projected many feet because of the momentum imparted by the wheel, but they settle from the air under gravitation force so rapidly that they represent only a plant housekeeping problem and have little significance for air pollution. According to Drinker and Hatch (5), a 2-mm particle thrown into the air from a grinding wheel with an initial velocity of 10,000 ft/min travels 70 feet before its speed is reduced to the point where the residual travel is in the streamlined flow range, whereas a 10-μ particle having the same initial velocity comes to rest in still air within a distance of less than 2 inches and a 1-μ particle travels only about 400 μ in still air before coming to rest. Therefore, it may be concluded that control of turbulent air currents generated by grinding wheels and similar contaminant-producing machines is of greater importance in the design of local exhaust hoods and the selection of control velocities than the dynamic projection velocity or distance of travel of particles independent of entraining air movement.

d. Falling Granular Materials. During free fall, materials such as crushed stone, sand, and finely divided powders of diverse origin entrain air that is expelled at the bottom of the drop. This air separates explosively and at high velocity from the granular material with which it was mixed and, in turn, entrains large fractions of the finest dust. This dust-laden air must be released from the storage bin, transfer station, or pile into or onto which the granular material has been deposited. If this air and its entrained dust is released directly to the atmosphere, pollution results. For control, the dust-laden air must be conducted to dust collecting devices with a minimum amount of induced air. Required local exhaust velocities and air volumes are determined from a knowledge of the amount of air entrained during the free fall of the granular materials.

Air displacement is related to the rate of flow of material, the height of fall, and the size and shape of the granular material. Measurements by Pring *et al.* (6) show that the induced air volume is roughly proportional to the cube root of the weight rate of granular material flow and inversely proportional to the diameter of the granules. Drinker and

Hatch (5), using the observations of Chirico (7) for crushed rock falling in chutes, showed that the ratio

$$\frac{Q}{(Wh^2)^{1/3}}$$

has a value between 4.7 and 7.8 for fall distances (h) from 10 to 30 feet, material flow rates (W) from 1230 to 6660 lb/min, air displacements (Q) from 300 to 2570 cfm, and material sizes ranging from fine to coarse. Though far from precise, this empirical relationship provides a basis for estimating the order of magnitude of the induced air flows that must by overcome by controlling air flows during conveying of granular materials.

Free fall air entrainment is modified by the degree of enclosure of the dropping stream and the ease with which air can enter and leave the enclosure. Modification of materials handling equipment (Fig. 3) is capable of reducing the height of fall of materials to very low levels, thereby minimizing air displacement and entrainment of fine dust.

e. Gas Diffusion. Gaseous contaminants that must be confined for air pollution control purposes possess diffusive properties which cause them to migrate in all directions from the point of release. The rate at which one gas, i.e., a contaminant, diffuses through another, i.e., the air, is related to temperature, pressure, and the molecular weights and volumes of the gases. Viles (8) examined the relative importance of diffusion as a dispersive force in laboratory fume hoods and concluded that when control velocities are adequate to prevent contaminant losses from drafts and traffic-induced turbulence, no escape of fumes occurs because of the diffusive properties of even highly volatile materials.

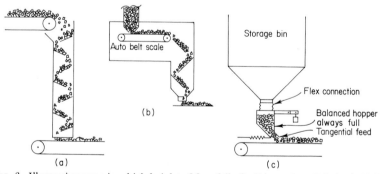

Fig. 3. Illustrating ways in which height of free fall of solids can be minimized. (a) Stone ladder in vertical chute. (b) Sloping surfaces taking material from continuous weighing machine. (c) Balanced secondary hopper below storage bin with tangential feed of material onto belt.

f. Hot Processes. Heat sources within a local exhaust enclosure generate convective air currents whose upward velocity is proportional to the rate of heat transferred to the surrounding air and the height of rise of the heated air. When hot gases rise through a confining enclosure which acts as a chimney, the vertical velocity of rise is proportional to the square root of the difference in weights of the heated air column and the weight of an equal column of the surrounding ambient air—the so-called "stack" or "chimney" effect. However, when a column of hot air rises in a free atmosphere, it entrains the surrounding cooler air in the manner of a low velocity jet—cooling and spreading laterally as it rises. This is a much more complex system to define and analyze than the hot chimney and only approximate solutions are available. Hemeon (9) has suggested the following approximate formula for estimating the quantity of air flow (Q) induced by the presence of a hot body inside a ventilated enclosure:

$$Q = 29H^{1/3}A^{2/3}X^{1/3} \tag{1}$$

where

Q = cubic feet per minute
H = heat loss from the hot body, Btu/min
A = cross-sectional area of hot body, ft^2
X = height of rise of hot air column, feet

Control velocities for hot processes must take into account the large volumes of air heated by the hot body or else part of the induced air will spill out of the enclosures.

2. Hood Design

Although complete enclosure of a process which emits dusts, fumes, vapors, and gases results in the least possible exhaust volume and minimizes the difficulties of preventing air pollution, many processes cannot be enclosed. For these processes, local exhaust velocities must be generated at a distance from the source to entrain and remove contaminants. Unlike air jets, which retain a substantial fraction of their initial discharge velocity at distances as great as 100 jet diameters from the point of discharge, exhaust velocities decrease rapidly with distance from the source of suction [Fig. 4, from Alden (10)]. The reason for this difference is that whereas a jet retains its cross section almost unchanged for many jet diameters downstream, a suction opening draws its air from all directions simultaneously and creates quasispherical or cylindrical surfaces of equal flow that rapidly decrease in velocity as the distance from the suction opening increases. In Fig. 4, lines of equal velocity

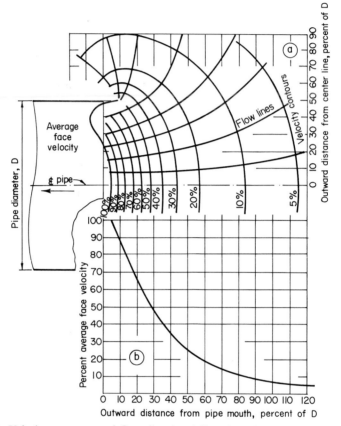

FIG. 4. Velocity contours and flow directional lines in radial plane of circular suction pipe [From Alden (10)].

at graduated distances from a round suction opening (expressed in multiples of the pipe diameter) are shown as percent of suction opening face velocity. The stream lines are shown perpendicular to the spherical envelopes of equal velocity. As may be seen, control velocity falls off very rapidly in free air.

The relationship between suction opening face area (A), total exhaust volume rate (Q), and velocity (V) at a distance (X) out along the center line from the suction opening (for round, square, and rectangular cross sections with side ratios up to 1:3) was determined by DallaValle (11) to be:

$$V = \frac{Q}{10X^2 + A} \tag{2}$$

Velocity at a distance is somewhat higher than would be calculated from a theoretical point source of suction; and the larger the suction opening, the less the velocity falls off with distance. This is because real exhaust hoods, both simple and flanged, have finite dimensions that impede the flow of air from areas to the rear of the opening (Fig. 5).

The velocity distribution outward from a long exhaust slot—the usual exhaust ventilation arrangement for controlling losses from downdraft tables (Fig. 6a) and open surface tanks (Fig. 6b) (characteristic of electroplating, solvent degreasing, and similar operations)—corresponds only approximately to a theoretical cylinder of equal velocity enveloping a line source of suction in space. This is because the surface of the table or the liquid, and the finite dimensions of the exhaust hood, profoundly modify the stream lines—in effect, drawing air from an area having the approximate shape of a half or quarter cylinder. This suggests that flanged hoods, which restrict air flow from all areas except those immediately in front of the suction opening, may be used effectively to reduce the exhaust volume needed to generate satisfactory control velocities.

Overhead, canopy-type, exhaust hoods have application for many potential contaminant-emitting operations including paint dipping,

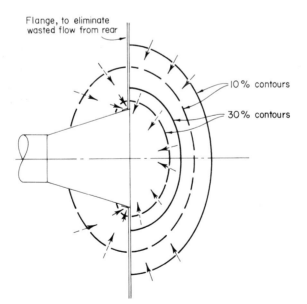

Fig. 5. Relative position of contours for flanged and simple hoods. (- - -) Plain hood. (—) Flanged hood. Note outward displacement of contours for flanged hood.

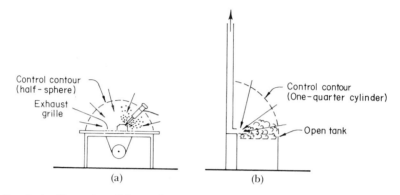

FIG. 6. An illustration of the confining effect of adjacent plane surfaces on the pattern of air flow into exhaust hoods. (a) A downdraft hood on bench, with work surface acting as a confining plane. (b) Exhaust slot along back of tank draws air from only a quarter cylinder because of confining vertical wall and horizontal tank surface.

metal pickling, and a variety of hot processing steps that emit gases, vapors, and aerosols. Figure 7 shows the velocity contour around a typical canopy hood over a dip tank. The entire open perimeter of the hood must be used when calculating the air volume needed to produce appropriate control velocities. This is seldom less than 100 cfm per square foot of opening. When the nature of the work permits, erection of side enclosures, shown in Fig. 8, results in savings from two sources: (1) the open face area across which control velocity must be maintained is substantially reduced and (2) lower control velocities are possible as the emitting source is well shielded from drafts and turbulence. The laboratory fume hood is basically a canopy hood enclosed on three

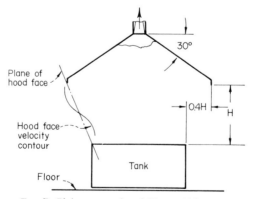

FIG. 7. Plain canopy hood [From Alden (10)].

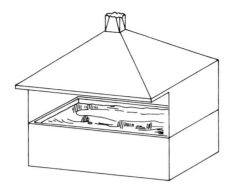

FIG. 8. Canopy hood with side enclosures [From Alden (*10*)].

sides. Its effectiveness for retaining fumes at low air flow rates is indicated by commonly recommended face velocities as low as 70–80 ft/min when chemicals of low toxicity are used.

Additional exhaust hood shapes for a variety of commonly encountered industrial operations that produce dusts and fumes are shown in Figs. 9 through 12.

D. PRINCIPLES OF EXHAUST SYSTEM PIPING

1. *Conveying Velocity*

Pipes that carry particulate contaminants from exhaust hoods must be sized to prevent settlement, most likely to occur in long horizontal pipe runs. Particle conveying velocities suitable for horizontal runs will be satisfactory for other, less critical, parts of the system, also. Although it is possible to calculate theoretical minimum conveying, or transport, velocities based on a knowledge of particle size, shape, specific gravity, and dust loading, calculated values have been shown to be inadequate. Therefore, higher velocities, based on experience, are employed. Conveying velocities of 3500 to 4500 ft/min are recommended for mineral dusts (the higher velocities for small diameter ducts); 2500 to 3500 ft/min for plastic and rubber dust and for many substances of vegetable origin such as coffee, beans, and grain; and 1500 to 2500 ft/min for cotton lint, wood sander dust, and similar fluffy materials.

Considerations of conveying velocity are absent when the exhaust system carries only gases and vapors. For this service, duct diameters may be selected on the basis of minimizing the total cost of the system over its predictable lifetime. Savings on installation cost by selecting small diameter ducts and high pipe velocities may be offset within a few

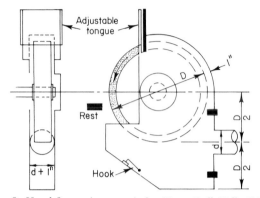

FIG. 9. Hood for stationary grinder [From DallaValle (11)].

years by the higher annual power costs associated with the greater pressure drop characteristic of high velocity systems. Duct velocities of 2000 to 3000 ft/min have been found economical for systems of moderate size that handle only gases and vapors. When designing large systems, it is generally advisable to account for all expense items and then optimize the size of the system for minimum total cost. Maximum duct velocities are usually based on the erosive properties of aerosol particles, such as silica and rock dust, and on the high noise characteristics of air movers when total system pressure drop exceeds 10–12 inches water gage. Alden (10) notes that "The elbows of a conveying system handling a heavy tonnage of abrasive materials will cut through in 12 months or so while the piping will last about twice as long."

2. Materials of Construction

Galvanized steel sheet, in thicknesses from 16 to 24 gage, is the most common construction material for exhaust piping—up to a 42 inch

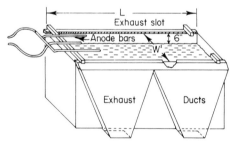

FIG. 10. Lateral slots for chrome plating tank [From DallaValle (11)].

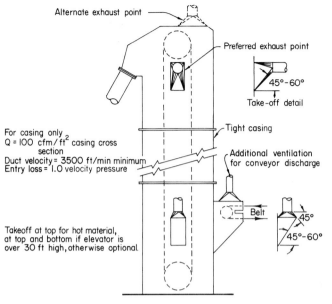

Alternate exhaust point

Preferred exhaust point

45°-60°

Take-off detail

Tight casing

For casing only
$Q = 100$ cfm/ft^2 casing cross
section
Duct velocity = 3500 ft/min minimum
Entry loss = 1.0 velocity pressure

Additional ventilation
for conveyor discharge

Takeoff at top for hot material,
at top and bottom if elevator is
over 30 ft high, otherwise optional.

Belt

45°

45°-60°

Belt speed   Volume
Less than 200 fpm – 350 cfm/ft of belt width. Not less than 150 cfm/ft of opening
Over 200 fpm   – 500 cfm/ft of belt width. Not less than 200 cfm/ft of opening

FIG. 11. Bucket elevator ventilation [From ACGIH (3)].

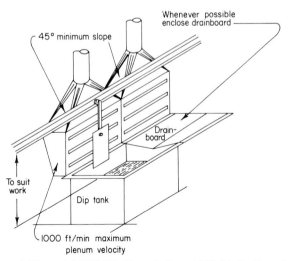

Whenever possible
enclose drainboard

45° minimum slope

Drain-
board

To suit
work

Dip tank

1000 ft/min maximum
plenum velocity

FIG. 12. Dip tank [From ACGIH (3)]. Slot velocity = 2000 ft/min. Entry loss = 1.78 slot
velocity pressure + 0.25 duct velocity pressure.

diameter for light service and up to 24 inches for the transport of abrasive particles. Longitudinal crimped and soldered pipe seams are commonly used. The interior of the seam is hammered flat to give smooth inner surfaces that will not interfere with the flow of air or collect materials. Long pipe runs are assembled from smaller sections with telescoping joints that have the small end of each section oriented to face downstream and thereby offer least resistance to flow. Heavier piping is constructed of welded iron sheet and sections are joined with bolted flanges or by circumferential welding of the ends. Provision must be made for the expansion and contraction of long straight runs of all-welded piping that occurs when temperature changes.

Rigid polyvinylchloride (PVC) and glass-reinforced polyester piping are used extensively for hood and piping construction when corrosive gases and vapors are to be handled. Generally these materials are assembled into gastight, seamless systems by chemical bonding techniques. Centrifugal blowers, gas cleaning devices of many types, and discharge stacks made from these two materials are also available for severe corrosive conditions. For example, rigid PVC and glass-reinforced polyester structures have almost entirely replaced metal and wood in exhaust ventilation systems for electroplating service. When a temperature greater than about 300 °F is associated with corrosive contaminants, stainless steels, and metals such as titanium and tantalum must be used as construction materials.

3. Pipe Fittings

To reduce air flow resistance and the tendency of abrupt changes in direction and internal roughness to collect dusts, fibers, etc., with eventual plugging of the system, pipe fittings should be constructed with smooth, unobstructed internal surfaces throughout. This may be accomplished by using (1) long sweep elbows; a 90° elbow having a centerline radius of two pipe diameters has less than one quarter the air flow resistance of a miter elbow, (2) gradual merging of branch ducts and mains; a branch joining a main at an included angle of 30° has one-seventh the energy loss of a tee joining at 90°, and (3) gradual duct expansions and constructions; an abrupt expansion has more than 3 times the energy loss of a gradual, twenty-degree expansion of the same cross-sectional change.

The high negative pressures developed in most local exhaust ventilation systems make it essential that air leakage into the systems be eliminated if adequate control velocities are to be maintained. Careful attention must be paid to sealing of longitudinal pipe seams, the joints between duct sections, and duct fittings. The flimsy metal gages and S-type joints that are commonly employed in low pressure supply air systems are certain to fail when employed for exhaust ventilation service. There is no practical way of sealing the multiple openings which characterize this method of construction or the additional leaks which occur as a result of flexure of thin-walled ducts when subjected to high negative pressure. Certain fittings, such as slide dampers, are likely to leak excessively when constructed in the customary manner. For exhaust ventilation service, special attention to airtight construction is required for every component of the system.

4. Blowers

Good practice in the design of local exhaust ventilation systems calls for blowers to be the last component before the discharge stack. This arrangement makes it possible to keep most of the system (and usually all of it located within workrooms) under negative pressure so that leakage, if any, will be inward. If maintained under positive pressure, contaminant-laden air would spurt out into the workroom atmosphere through cracks and leaks in the system. When an air cleaner is used to remove particulate matter or acid gases, it should be placed immediately upstream of the blower to protect it from the erosive and corrosive effects of the contaminants. Recommended methods for balancing the various branches of complex exhaust systems and for calculating the system volumetric air flow rate and resistance are illustrated and explained in detail in a number of accepted texts on this subject. These include Drinker and Hatch (5), Alden (10), the ACGIH publication "Industrial Ventilation" (3), the ASHRAE Guide (12), and the USA Standard Z9.2 (13). With this information, it is possible to select a blower having the required delivery rate and static pressure characteristics.

5. Discharge Stacks

Discharge stacks from exhaust ventilation systems should extend high enough above the roof of the building in which they are installed, as well as above nearby structures, to be out of the zone of influence of turbulence wakes that tend to turn the stack effluent groundward. Similar unfavorable downward flow effects are created when stacks are equipped with devices such as rain caps and goose necks for preventing the entry of rain. Not only do such devices direct the discharge downward, and thereby eliminate all beneficial effects that might be gained from the increased effective stack height associated with upward dis-

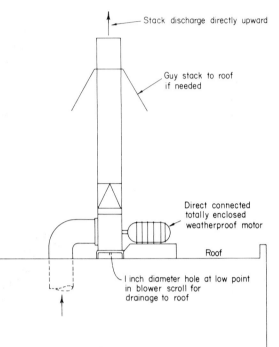

FIG. 13. Exhaust stack and blower.

charge velocity and the buoyancy of elevated gas temperature, but they are, in fact, unnecessary for protection against rain because when the system is in operation, no precipitation can penetrate the upward air current emerging from a vertical, uncapped stack. When the system is shut down, the small amount of precipitation that collects in a stack (for example, a 1-inch rain will deposit less than 5 gallons of water in a 36-inch diameter stack) can be drained away by any one of several arrangements, such as the one illustrated in Fig. 13, which shows a free-standing stack supported on a centrifugal blower casing which has been rotated to the correct upward discharge position. Drainage is accomplished through a 1-inch diameter hole drilled in the bottom of the scroll casing of the blower. The motor shown is a direct-connected, totally enclosed, weatherproof unit, thereby eliminating the need for a V-belt drive and a motor-drive weather housing.

V. Utilizing Untapped Air Resources

Air pollution is primarily an urban phenomenon and results from the crowding together of large numbers of people who produce and consume the numberless products and services that contribute to the contamination of the atmosphere. It has been estimated (*14*) that two-thirds of the population in the United State now lives on less than 9% of the land area and that by the end of this century more than three-fourths of a much larger population will be living on this same space. This means that the number of cubic feet of air available to each city dweller for operating his automobile, heating his home, producing his electricity, manufacturing the products he consumes, burning the refuse from these products, and breathing, is already limited and will continue to shrink. However, the atmosphere over the other 91% of the United States is being utilized at far less than its natural capacity and the 70% of the world covered by oceans is being used hardly at all.

These untapped air resources are utilized effectively when, for instance, mine-mouth coal-burning generating stations produce electricity in remote, lightly populated areas and send it many hundreds of miles to crowded urban centers for consumption without adding to the existing pollution load from vehicles and other activities that cannot be relocated. This, and similar practices, should not subject a small, local population in a remote area to excessive air pollution as a substitute for exposing a large urban population. Rather, the largely unused atmospheric resource at the mine-mouth location should be capable of diluting emissions from a single power station without exceeding recommended air quality criteria designed to protect even the most sensitive element in the local population.

Some measure of air pollution control may be obtained by staggering work hours. This would avoid overburdening the assimilative capabilities of the atmosphere during peak traffic hours and under-utilizing the full air resource during off-peak hours. Other projects are under study to utilize a greater percentage of the atmospheric resource. Under one such plan, waste collections would be transported to docks and transferred to an ocean-going vessel (*15*). When loaded, the vessel would put to sea, burn the wastes, and discharge the residue into deep holes in the ocean floor. Studies are under way to determine the biological effects of incinerator residue on marine species; and meteorological measurements and analyses are under way over offshore waters to locate ideal burning sites that will avoid the movement of stack discharges to the shore under all weather conditions. Preliminary cost analyses indicate that this method of waste handling compares favorably with land-based incineration. Convenient dumping grounds, that is, holes in the ocean floor, located offshore of coastal cities, already approved by the United States Coast Guard and Army Engineers, are adequate for handling the residue from ship incinerators for a hundred or more years. It appears practical, therefore, to utilize the vast assimilative capacity of ocean waters and the ocean atmosphere to solve a troublesome urban problem. Studies show that this can be done without polluting the environment, decreasing the recreational use of the waters, or interfering with commercial and sport fishing.

It is already quite clear that all available methods that are designed to minimize the production and emission of contaminants must be employed to the maximum possible extent if pollution of the environment of an overpopulated, overcongested world is to be avoided in the future. An important element of environmental pollution control is the wise use of as large a fraction of the total environment as may be accomplished.

ACKNOWLEDGMENT

The author wishes to thank Professor T. Hatch for his kind permission to reuse material which he presented in the first edition of this book.

REFERENCES

1. T. Hatch, in "Air Pollution" (A. C. Stern, 1st ed.), Vol. 2, p. 211. Academic Press, New York, 1962.
2. A. H. Rose, Jr., D. G. Stephan, and R. L. Stenburg, "Prevention and Control of Air Pollution by Process Changes or Equipment," SEC TR A58-11. Robert A. Taft Sanitary Eng. Center, Cincinnati, Ohio, 1958.
3. American Conference of Governmental Industrial Hygienists, Committee on Industrial Ventilation, "Industrial Ventilation, A Manual of Recommended Practice," 9th ed. A.C.G.I.H., Lansing, Michigan, 1966.
4. A. Koestel, ASHVE Trans. 60, 385 (1954).
5. P. Drinker and T. Hatch, "Industrial Dust," 2nd ed. McGraw-Hill, New York, 1954.
6. R. T. Pring, J. F. Knudsen, and R. Dennis, Ind. Eng. Chem. 41, 2442 (1949).
7. F. N. Chirico, unpublished data referred to by Drinker and Hatch (5).
8. F. J. Viles, Jr., College Univ. Business 22, No. 6, 41 (1957).
9. W. C. L. Hemeon, "Plant and Process Ventilation." Industrial Press, New York, 1954.
10. J. L. Alden, "Design of Industrial Exhaust Systems for Dust and Fume Removal," 3rd ed. Industrial Press, New York, 1959.
11. J. M. DallaValle, "Exhaust Hoods." Industrial Press, New York, 1952.
12. American Society of Heating, Refrigerating and Air Conditioning Engineers, Guide and Data Book, "Fundamentals and Equipment." A.S.H.R.A.E., New York, 1967.
13. United States of America Standards Institute, USA Standard, "Fundamentals Governing the Design and Operation of Local Exhaust Systems," Z9.2-1960. New York, 1960.
14. Environmental Pollution Panel, President's Science Advisory Committee, "Restoring the Quality of Our Environment." The White House, Washington, D.C., 1965.
15. L. Silverman, Am. Public Works Assoc., Rept. 31, No. 7, 2 (1964).

Additional pertinent material is in Chaps. 3, 6, 7, and 11 of "Air Pollution Engineering Manual, Los Angeles APCD" (J. A. Danielson, ed.), PHS Publn. 999-AP-40, DHEW, Cincinnati (1967); and will be published in the National Air Pollution Control Administration's publication "Control Technology for Particulate Air Pollutants."

42 Efficiency, Application, and Selection of Collectors

Arthur C. Stern

CONVERSION FACTORS USED IN COLLECTOR TECHNOLOGY[a]

Multiply	By	To get
Btu/hour input	10^{-7}	megawatts of steam-generated electricity (approx.)
stnd cu ft/sec	mol wt × 9.3	pounds of gas/hr
stnd cu ft/min	mol wt × 0.155	pounds of gas/hr
grains/stnd cu ft	1.89	pounds/1000 lb gas[b]
grains/stnd cu ft	2300	milligrams/stnd cu m
grains/stnd cu ft	2.30	grams/stnd cu m
grains/stnd cu ft (adjusted to 50% excess air)	2.20	pounds/10^6 Btu input
grams/stnd cu m	0.435	grains/stnd cu ft
grams of gas/stnd cu m	24.2×10^3/mol wt	ppm by vol

(Continued)

319

CONVERSION FACTORS USED IN COLLECTOR TECHNOLOGY[a] (*Continued*)

Multiply	By	To get
megawatts of steam-generated electricity	10^7	Btu/hr input (approx.)
micrograms of gas/stnd cu m	0.0242/mol wt	ppm by vol
milligrams of gas/stnd cu m	24.2/mol wt	ppm by vol
milligrams/stnd cu m	4.35×10^{-4}	grains/stnd cu ft
ppm by vol	mol wt $\times$ 41.3 $\times$ 10^{-6}	grams of gas/stnd cu m
ppm by vol	mol wt $\times$ 0.0413	milligrams of gas/stnd cu m
ppm by vol	mol wt $\times$ 41.3	micrograms of gas/stnd cu m
ppm by vol	10^{-4}	percent by vol
percent by vol	10^4	ppm by vol
pounds of gas/hour	6.48/mol wt	stnd cu ft/min
pounds of gas/hour	0.108/mol wt	stnd cu ft/sec
pounds/1000 lb gas[b]	0.53	grains/stnd cu ft
pounds/1000 lb gas[b] (adjusted to 50% excess air)	1.18	pounds/10^6 Btu input
pounds/10^6 Btu input	0.45	grains/stnd cu ft (adjusted to 50% excess air)
pounds/10^6 Btu input	0.85	pounds/1000 lb gas[b] (adjusted to 50% excess air)

[a] Reference 6, pp. 2433–2434 (J. R. Garvey).
[b] mol wt = 29.

KEY: m = meter; mol wt = molecular weight; stnd = standard at 70 °F and atmospheric pressure.

I.   Efficiency of Collectors

The most common way of expressing dust collector or gas scrubber performance is efficiency (η), which is usually stated in percent.

$$\eta(\text{in percent}) = \frac{100C}{A} = \frac{100C}{B + C} = \frac{100(A - B)}{A} \qquad (1)$$

where

A = the entering loading or concentration
B = the leaving loading or concentration
C = the amount caught in or retained by the collector
    (all expressed in the same units)

It also follows that where a collector discharges to the atmosphere, the formula for the amount discharged is

$$B = \frac{(100 - \eta)A}{100} \qquad (2)$$

Determinations based only upon entering and leaving concentration may be on a mass, particle count, radioactive particle disintegration, or staining basis per unit volume or per unit time. The expressions involving the amount caught in the collector are usually only on a mass basis.

A. FRACTIONAL EFFICIENCY

In collectors for particulate matter, the efficiency of collection can vary with particle size; this introduces the additional concept of fractional efficiency, i.e., the efficiency with which particles in a specified size range are collected. By using a subscript x to denote reference only to particles within the specified range x, Eqs. (1) and (2) can be written in terms of η_x, A_x, B_x, and C_x.

Where the spectrum of particle sizes in the entering concentration is completely encompassed by n size ranges for each of which the collection efficiency and percentage of the mass or count of dust therein is known, the overall efficiency may be computed (1) by:

$$\eta = \eta_1 \left(\frac{A_1}{A}\right) + \eta_2 \left(\frac{A_2}{A}\right) + \cdots + \eta_n \left(\frac{A_n}{A}\right) \tag{3}$$

$$\eta = \frac{1}{\left[\dfrac{C_1}{\eta_1 C} + \dfrac{C_2}{\eta_2 C} + \cdots + \dfrac{C_n}{\eta_n C}\right]} \tag{4}$$

$$\eta = 100Y/(Y+1) \tag{5}$$

where $\quad Y = \left[\dfrac{\eta_1 B_1}{(100 - \eta_1)B} + \dfrac{\eta_2 B_2}{(100 - \eta_2)B} + \cdots + \dfrac{\eta_n B_n}{(100 - \eta_n)B}\right]$

Where η is overall efficiency and η_x is efficiency for size range x, both efficiencies expressed in percent:

$$\frac{A_x}{A} = \frac{(100 - \eta)}{(100 - \eta_x)} \frac{B_x}{B} = \frac{\eta}{\eta_x} \frac{C_x}{C} \tag{6}$$

$$\frac{B_x}{B} = \frac{(100 - \eta_x)}{(100 - \eta)} \frac{A_x}{A} = \frac{\eta(100 - \eta_x)}{\eta_x(100 - \eta)} \frac{C_x}{C} \tag{7}$$

$$\frac{C_x}{C} = \frac{\eta_x}{\eta} \frac{A_x}{A} = \frac{\eta_x(100 - \eta)}{\eta(100 - \eta_x)} \frac{B_x}{B} \tag{8}$$

In the foregoing discussion and equations, the subscript x can be used not only to denote a particle diameter range, but also a range of values of any other parameter affecting collector efficiency, such as, for instance, the terminal velocity range of the dust.

B. Penetration, Decontamination Factor, and Index

For extremely high efficiency collectors, efficiencies expressed in percentages such as 99.99 or 99.999% become awkward to use, and, as a consequence, for efficiencies over 99% it is convenient to use other methods of expressing efficiency. The simplest of these is penetration (P), which, in percent, is:

$$P = 100 - \eta \qquad (9)$$

Alternately, efficiency may be expressed as the decontamination factor (DF):

$$DF = \frac{A}{B} = \frac{1}{1 - (\eta/100)} \qquad (10)$$

The decontamination factor equivalent to a percentage efficiency of 99.999 is 10^5. The logarithm to the base 10 of the decontamination factor is known as the decontamination index. Using the previous example, this index becomes 5.0.

C. Efficiencies Based upon Particle Count or Soiling Index

Efficiency may also be based on the reduction in particle count effected by the collector or by the relative quantities of gas, before and after passage through the separator, necessary to produce equal soiling of a standard filter paper. Efficiencies based on mass, particle count, and soiling are comparable only for an aerosol in which all particles are of only one size and have identical characteristics. Although this can be approximated in the laboratory, it cannot in the field. In the real situation, aerosols which must be collected include particles differing as to size, shape, surface area, density, and mass, as well as optical and electrostatic properties.

Assuming constant particle density and spherical shape, mass is proportional to the cube, and soiling to the square of the particle diameter. Therefore, efficiency based on mass is invariably higher than that based upon soiling, which in turn should be higher than that based upon particle count.

As an example, assume a dust which for every thousand 1-μ particles has a hundred 10-μ particles and one 100-μ particle. Next assume two collectors, one which separates all particles larger than 10 μ; the other, all particles larger than 1 μ. Applying the second and third power proportionalities noted above, the collection efficiencies of these two collectors by mass, soiling, and particle count are shown in the tabulation.

| | Efficiency (%) | | |
Collector	Mass basis	Soiling basis	Count basis
Collects all above 10 μ	91	48	0.09
Collects all above 1 μ	99.9	95	9

D. EFFECT OF NONISOKINETIC SAMPLING ON EFFICIENCY

These same hypothetical collectors and the same hypothetical dust can be used to show the apparent efficiency that would be erroneously measured by nonisokinetic sampling from the inlet gas stream of the particles larger than 10 μ (even though the sampling of 10 μ and smaller particles were accurate). The apparent results for 50% over- or under-sampling in the inlet gases of particles larger than 10 μ would be as shown in the tabulation.

| | Mass efficiency, (%) | | |
Collector	Over-sampling	True	Under-sampling
Collects all above 10 μ	48	91	160
Collects all above 1 μ	52	99.9	183

This example stresses the importance of accurate sampling of particles over 10 μ in the inlet gas stream if erroneous mass efficiency measurements are to be avoided. The possibility of this type of error is much less when sampling the outlet gases from a collector, since the outlet gases are generally free of large particles. Because of this, in installations where the catch for a given time interval can be weighed accurately (i.e., to within 1%) there is less chance for error in basing efficiency on catch weight and output sampling than on other bases. This problem does not arise in pilot plant testing where accurately known weights of dust are fed to the collector.

E. OTHER SOURCES OF ERRONEOUS EFFICIENCY TEST RESULTS

Measured efficiencies higher than true efficiencies, including tests showing over 100% efficiency, can also result from dust, built up within the system prior to test, augmenting hopper collection during the test. The reverse can occur if the buildup occurs during tests where hopper collection is one of the factors used in efficiency calculation. Basing performance estimates upon samples brought to a test collector in a drum introduces similar possibilities for error, the most important of which is the use of material collected by a method which allowed an appreciable proportion of the original fines to escape. The ultimate extension of this error is to present for test material collected by a collector with a fractional efficiency curve similar to, or poorer than, that of the collector being evaluated.

Although some standard test dusts and aerosols have been developed for the testing of air filters, none have received acceptance for testing devices intended to remove particles from process or combustion effluents prior to their discharge to the ambient air. However, a standard dust for the calibration of the centrifugal classifier (Bahco) used for the determination of terminal velocity distribution according to Section 4.02 of the American Society of Mechanical Engineers Power Test Code 28 (1965)—"Determining the Properties of Fine Particulate Matter" is available for $5.00 from the chairman of the Power Test Code Committee #28, c/o ASME, 345 East 47th Street, New York, 10017. This Power Test Code covers test methods for terminal velocity distribution, specific gravity, sieve analysis, bulk electrical resistivity, moisture content, loss on ignition, water soluble content, water soluble sulfate content, bulk density, and specific surface of fine particulate matter. German practice with respect to measurement of dust collector performance is to be found in V.D.I. 2066 "Performance Measurements of Dust Collectors." (7).

F. Effect of Particle-Size Analysis Techniques on Fractional Efficiency

1. Sedimentation and Elutriation Techniques

The determination of fractional efficiency of separators is subject to errors of interpretation which are inherent in the procedures commonly used for particle-size analysis in dust collector testing. Almost invariably, the sampling procedure involves first the concentration in a sampling device of aerosol particles originally dispersed in a gas stream, and second the redispersal of the concentrated sample in the manner required by the size analysis technique employed. More likely than not, the state of agglomeration of the redispersed material will differ from that of the original aerosol. For instance, the original aerosol may have consisted of agglomerates of small particles or of large particles "coated" with adhering small particles. If this sample is redispersed in a liquid medium for size analysis by sedimentation, these agglomerates probably will be broken up so that the size analysis will tend to indicate a finer sized aerosol than was actually being treated in the separator. This would make most forms of separator appear better in fractional performance than they actually are. The same situation exists where separators are rated by laboratory or pilot scale tests on samples of material redispersed into a gas stream from a drum or carton of the material. Here the process of redispersal quite likely injects a preponderance of aggregates into the gas stream, and, if size analysis of the material in the drum or carton (as well as from samplers or the separator hopper) involves liquid redispersal, the fractional efficiency will appear better than it actually is.

The opposite situation may also occur, i.e., where the particles in the gas stream are not agglomerated, but where, after sampling, they are redispersed into an airstream for size analysis by air elutriation or classification. Since, in this case, the redispersed aerosol may have a high proportion of agglomerates, the fractional efficiency curve will make the separator appear poorer than it really is. This situation can also occur in tests of collectors using particle generators of the atomizing or condensing types which produce aerosols with minimum agglomerates. Performance against real (partially agglomerated) aerosols will tend to be better than against such test aerosols.

In many dusts there is specific gravity variation among particles of the same diameter. In such cases sedimentation or elutriation techniques assign the same "size" classification to a wide range of particle diameters, surface areas, and volumes, thereby making such "size" classes invalid for the determination of separator fractional efficiency.

2. Particle-Counting Techniques

Redispersion of a composite aerosol sample onto a microscope slide may show the sample in a state of agglomeration different from that in either the gas from which it was collected or the composite prior to redispersal on the slide. Samples precipitated directly onto optical microscope slides or electron microscope films preserve the actual state of aerosol agglomeration. However, analyses of both redispersed and precipitated slides yield size distributions proportional to the "diameter" of the particles and, for most practical applications, require arbitrary conversion to a mass basis.

Where no attempt is made to convert microscope size distributions to a mass basis, the sizing of several hundred particles is usually considered sufficient to establish the distribution. However, where conversion to a mass basis is intended, a much larger number of particles must be counted to ensure inclusion of the correct proportion of the larger particles that each weigh the same as from a thousand to a million of the smaller particles measured.

Light-scatter pulse-counting techniques yield size distributions proportional to the surface area of the particles and therefore also require arbitrary conversion to mass size distribution to be compatible with sedimentation, elutriation, and sieve data.

Conversion from a surface area or diameter basis to a mass basis, and vice versa, involves assumptions as to particle shape, density, and porosity that are discussed in Chapters 3 and 21. For additional insight into these matters, the reader is referred to texts on particle-size analysis and fine particle statistics (2).

3. Terminal Velocity Basis of Data Presentation

Because of these conversion difficulties, it has been proposed that instead of using particle-size efficiency curves to express fractional efficiency, such data be presented as particle terminal velocity efficiency curves. Where the particles must be redispersed to measure terminal velocity, all the problems previously noted with regard to redispersal still remain to cast doubt on the interpretation of the resultant data. This is true even where a method for separating the influent aerosol into terminal velocity classes without redispersal is used, if a method requiring particle redispersal must be used to size the hopper collection or the effluent aerosol.

In some collector types, the large particles in the effluent gases are agglomerates which were not present in the influent gases but were created in the collector. Rating such collectors on a settling velocity basis would show the collector to be poorer on large particles and better on fine particles than it really is.

There is obviously no one correct way to determine fractional efficiency. The best one can ask for is that in comparing collectors, each be tested in like manner with regard to sampling and particle-size analysis and that the methods used neither penalize nor inflate performance data of one to a greater extent than the others.

G. Effect of Inlet Loading on Efficiency

In collectors of the filter type, there is very little variation of efficiency with inlet dust loading although inlet loading greatly affects the rate of increase of pressure drop across the collector. In electrostatic precipitators, the ability to handle large increases in inlet loading is a function of the ability of the plate and rapping system to unload the increased dust quantity into the hopper without greater reentrainment into the gas stream than when handling smaller quantities of dust in the same equipment. If the system does not have this ability, efficiency will decrease with increased inlet loading. In the case of cyclone collectors, there is a significant increase in efficiency with inlet loading. A serious error in cyclone specification can result if the prospective user erroneously assumes that the high efficiencies obtained against the extremely high inlet loadings that characterize fluidized catalyst recirculation systems will also be found in applications of the identical cyclone to the much lower inlet loading applications more commonly encountered. Specification of collectors of all types should, therefore, be based upon test data on inlet loadings comparable to those in the proposed installation.

H. GUARANTEED EFFICIENCY

Collectors are frequently built for a new plant or unit under construction for which the gas flow rates, temperature, composition, density, and viscosity as well as the aerosol concentration, size distribution, composition, shape, and density are all designers' estimates. Once the plant is in operation, the real values for these variables become evident and may differ somewhat from design values. Efficiency and pressure drop guarantees based upon design values must then be checked by acceptance tests based upon test conditions different from those anticipated. Failure to meet guaranteed performance may involve both penalty payments and noncompliance with air pollution control regulations. Overperformance may involve both bonus payments and excess operating costs. The equations for converting from test to guarantee conditions must be based upon the physical laws governing the performance of the equipment and, preferably, should be specified in the contract. Corrections for gas temperature, pressure, density, and viscosity are fairly straightforward. As an example, the correction from test condition a, to guarantee condition b, for pressure drop h in cyclone collectors when there are differences in gas flow rate Q, gas density ρ_g, and gas temperature T (absolute), is:

$$\frac{h_a}{h_b} = \frac{Q_a^2 \rho_{ga}}{T_a} \cdot \frac{T_b}{Q_b^2 \rho_{gb}} \tag{11}$$

The corrections to pressure drop for differences in gas viscosity μ, particle density ρ_P, and particle size are negligible for cyclones, and that for dust loading is empirical.

Pressure drop and fan horsepower will be different for a bare collector and the same collector plus its housing, ductwork, and straightening vanes. The changes in housing, ductwork, or vanes needed to meet efficiency guarantees may cause pressure drop and power guarantees to be exceeded. The correction to efficiency of cyclone collectors for changes in gas conditions is:

$$\frac{100 - \eta_a}{100 - \eta_b} = \left(\frac{Q_b}{Q_a}\right)^{0.5} \cdot \left(\frac{\rho_p - \rho_{gb}}{\rho_p - \rho_{ga}}\right)^{0.5} \cdot \left(\frac{\mu_a}{\mu_b}\right)^{0.5} \tag{12}$$

The correction for change in gas temperature is made by appropriately correcting density and viscosity for the temperature change.

Efficiency correction factors based upon substantial differences in aerosol characteristics are much more difficult to develop. Corrections for difference in dust loading are empirical. Those associated with particle size and density form the basis for fractional efficiency curves. Among the most troublesome corrections are those for derivative characteristics of aerosol composition such as their electrical resistivity, wettability, and agglomerating properties.

Frequently collectors as initially tested fail to meet their guaranteed efficiency. This is not surprising, since the initial test represents the first time reality replaces designers' assumptions. The equipment supplier now faces the task of making changes in the equipment which will raise its efficiency to that guaranteed. These changes should preferably be systematic ones based on previous experience with such situations rather than a series of cut-and-try desperation alterations. Depending upon collector type, the kinds of changes tried include changes in gas flow pattern, velocity, temperature, humidity, or composition; in liquid flow patterns, rate, pressure, quantity, or composition; in voltage, current or wave form; in construction materials, dimensions or configuration; and in operating cycle or procedure. Since changes in the collector itself are costly and involve interruptions in plant operation, tests on a small-scale model (3), usually made of transparent plastic, are helpful in selecting those to be tried on the collector itself. Although models were originally used for improving equipment already in operation, they are now often built and tested while the full-scale equipment is still in the design stage so that the improvements discovered may be incorporated into the construction of the collector. German practice with respect to guaranteed performance is in VDI 2260 "Performance Guarantees for Dust Removers" (7).

I. Series Operation of Collectors

Collectors are used in series, the primary collector preceding the secondary collector, for the following main reasons:

1. The primary collector may act as a precleaner to prevent plug-

ging the secondary collector or to take out of the gas a heavy loading of large particles so that the secondary collector has to treat only a lighter loading of smaller particles.

The addition of a primary collector as a precleaner adds pressure drop and cost, and is warranted only where performance of the secondary collector is known to be inadequate without a primary collector of the type proposed. Where an inertial precleaner precedes a fabric filter, the over-all pressure drop will be greater for the combination than for the filter alone.

2. The primary collector may act as an agglomerator to build up the size of the particles presented to the secondary collector so that they are in the size range the latter can efficiently collect. There is argument in steam power plant circles as to which collector should precede in an electrostatic-precipitator multiple-cyclone combination. The proponents of locating the precipitator ahead of the cyclones argue that the precipitator acts as an agglomerator, particularly during soot-blowing. The secondary cyclones also catch material re-entrained from collecting electrodes by the scouring action of the flue gases or during electrode rapping, thereby allowing higher flue gas velocity and more vigorous rapping. Those favoring cyclones ahead of precipitators argue that removing the coarser particles by cyclones reduces the dust load on the precipitator so that it will operate more efficiently and operate with less rapping and dust loss due to rapping.

Actually, the presence of some coarse particles is advantageous to precipitator operation since they help sweep finer particles to the collecting electrodes and since an admixture of coarse particles in the precipitated dust layer prevents too tight packing of the finer particles on the electrodes, thus improving shake-off during rapping.

3. In a series arrangement, the secondary collector may act as a reserve collector in the event of malfunction in the primary collector. This application is particularly to be found in fluidized catalytic cracking processes in petroleum refineries, where several identical cyclones may be used in series, so that there are tertiary and higher order collectors. Then any plugging of the dip legs (which discharge the collected particulate matter by gravity) of one or more preceding cyclones transfers to the subsequent cyclone in the series whose dip leg is working the function of primary collector until the dip legs of the preceding ones are cleared and once again made to discharge freely.

4. A primary collector may act as a fire protection device by preventing a source of ignition such as incandescent particles, or readily combustible material such as cotton lint, from entering the secondary collector.

5. Series collectors may be used to classify materials in a mixture,

i.e., one separator may remove a reusable or soluble material, the other a waste material.

6. A primary collector may act as a plenum chamber from which several secondary collectors may be operated in parallel.

7. A primary collector may act as a concentrator so that there are two exit gas streams from it, one with a small gas flow and a high particle loading, the other with a large gas flow and a low particle loading. Either or both of the exit gas streams may go to secondary collectors. A collector acting as concentrator may also discharge separated particles in addition to the two exit gas streams.

Efficiency Computations for Series Operation of Collectors

To compute efficiency for series operation of collectors, two efficiencies must be known:

η_p = efficiency of primary collector on incoming dust load
η_s = efficiency of secondary collector on dust leaving primary collector

For straight series operation the combined efficiency η is expressed:

$$\eta = \eta_p + \eta_s(100 - \eta_p) \tag{13}$$

Where the primary collector acts only as a concentrator to split the gas into two outlet streams, one dirtier and one cleaner than the influent stream, and no dust is removed from the primary collector, removal being effected only from the dirtier gas stream by the secondary collector, η_p is considered "efficiency as a concentrator," and the computation becomes:

$$\eta = \frac{\eta_p \eta_s}{100} \tag{14}$$

One special case is that for the collector with a purged dust hopper, i.e., a hopper which is placed under suction by a bleed line going to a secondary collector, for which the equation is:

$$\eta = \eta_p + \frac{Z\eta_p}{100}\left(\frac{\eta_s}{100} - 1\right) \tag{15}$$

where Z = per cent of dust collected by primary collector which leaves hopper in purge to secondary collector

Another special case is that for the skimmed collector, i.e., one which has a normal dust hopper but in which the cleaned gas stream is split into two streams, one dirtier and one cleaner than the average, for which the equation is:

$$\eta = \eta_p + \frac{X\eta_s}{100} \left(1 - \frac{\eta_p}{100}\right) \tag{16}$$

where $X =$ percent of dust leaving primary collector which goes to secondary collector

J. TEMPERATURE REDUCTION OF INFLUENT GASES

One problem common to all collector types is the handling of gases initially at high temperature. The alternatives are to treat them at the initial high temperature in a unit adapted to service at that temperature or to reduce the temperature by radiation-convection cooling, evaporative cooling, dilution with cooler air or gases, or by a combination of these methods. Temperature reduction increases the choice of collector types that can be considered and, for those types applicable at the initial high temperature, allows the use of a less costly version at the lower temperature. Electrostatic precipitators and inertial collectors can be designed for temperature as high as the metal structures will allow, whereas fabric filters are limited to temperatures the fabric will withstand.

Both evaporative and dilution cooling benefit by some inherent radiation-convection cooling, but a radiation-convection cooling installation may be used without evaporative or dilution cooling. Pure dilution cooling increases the gas volume to be treated; the other methods, including most combination methods, decrease the gas volume as well as the temperature. It has been concluded (4) that there is no economic justification for dust removal at any temperature higher than 750 °F where air pollution control is the prime consideration. An exception to this is where the dust removal device precedes a process for removing a gaseous pollutant, such as SO_2, from the gases prior to their discharge to the atmosphere. Since several of the more promising processes for removing SO_2 from flue gas are most efficient when the gases are both clean and hot, there may be justification in such situations for dust removal at temperatures higher than 750 °F.

In certain cases, even though collectors of a class can be designed for higher temperature operation, optimum performance is obtained at a somewhat lower temperature. Thus the optimum conditions for the electrical precipitation of fumes from open hearth furnaces and converters (including enriched air and oxygen processes) is in the range 270 °–360 °F and with a moisture content of not less than 10% (5).

When gases are cooled prior to collection, the cooling may destroy the buoyancy of the gases. When a wet collector is used with hot gases, any evaporated water may add an objectionable steam plume to the gases as they come to earth. The required collection efficiency may well have been chosen on the assumption of a certain minimum diffusion of the plume before reaching earth. Thus, by allowing the plume to come to earth before adequate diffusion, a local problem may be created despite the efficiency of the collection process.

II.   Selection of Collectors*

A. CONTROL EQUIPMENT TYPES

Control equipment may be classified into several general types: filters, electrical precipitators, cyclones, mechanical collectors (other than cyclones), scrubbers, adsorbers, and equipment in which the contaminant is burned as the means for its control. This latter category includes afterburners, catalytic combustion, and similar apparatus. Some equipment combines elements of more than one type. Thus there are cyclones in which a liquid is sprayed, and there are scrubbers in which cyclonic action is employed to remove the liquid droplets. Packed bed filters, operated wet, and packed bed scrubbers are alike in construction, the difference being that when the device is designed to remove particulate matter it is a filter and when it is designed to remove a gas or vapor phase contaminant it is considered a scrubber. Equipment of different types are frequently used in series and sometimes incorporated into the same equipment housing. Thus filters commonly incorporate an integral settling chamber, a form of mechanical collector.

1. Filters

Devices for removal of particulate matter from gas streams by retention of the particles in or on a porous structure through which the gas flows are filters. The porous structure is most commonly a woven or felted fabric, but can include pierced, woven, or sintered metal, and beds of a large variety of substances such as vegetable fibers, metal turnings, coke, slag wool, sand, etc. Unless they are operated wet to keep the interstices clean, filters in general improve in retention efficiency as the interstices in the porous structure begin to be filled by collected particles and as the particles collected themselves form a porous structure of their own, supported by the filter and having the ability to intercept and retain other particles. This increase in retention efficiency is accompanied by an increase in pressure drop through the filter. Therefore, to pre-

---

* This section is adapted from material prepared by the author for Vol. II of the American Industrial Hygiene Association Air Pollution Manual.

vent decrease in gas flow through the filter either the gas-moving equipment must be able to cope with the increased pressure drop without loss of flow rate or the filter must be either continuously cleaned or periodically cleaned or replaced.

In special applications, filters are used to remove gas or vapor by reaction with the particulate matter retained on or in the porous structure.

2. Electrical Precipitators

Devices in which one or more high intensity electrical fields are maintained to cause particles to acquire an electrical charge and to cause the charged particles to be forced to a collecting surface are electrical precipitators. The collecting surface may be either dry or wet. Since the collecting force is applied to only the particles, not to the gas, the pressure drop of the gas is only that of flow through a duct having the configuration of the collector. Hence pressure drop is both very low and does not tend to increase with time. In general, collection efficiency increases with length of passage through an electrical precipitator. Therefore, additional precipitator sections are employed in series to obtain higher collection efficiency.

3. Cyclones

Devices in which organized vortex motion created within the collector provides the force to cause particles to be propelled to locations from which they may be removed from the collector are called cyclones. They may be operated either wet or dry. They may either deposit the collected particulate matter in a hopper, or concentrate it into a stream of carrier gas that flows to another separator, usually of a different type, for ultimate collection. As long as the interior of the cyclone remains clean, pressure drop does not increase with time. Up to a certain limit, both collection efficiency and pressure drop increase with flow rate through a cyclone; beyond that limit only pressure drop continues to increase with flow rate increase. Cyclones are frequently used in parallel, seldom in series.

4. Mechanical Collectors (Other than Cyclones)

This category includes devices which collect particulate matter by gravity or centrifugal force but which do not depend upon a vortex, as in the case of cyclones. These devices include settling chambers, baffled chambers, louvered chambers and devices in which the carrier gas–particulate matter mixture passes through a fan in which separation occurs. In general, collectors of this class are of relatively low collection efficiency. They are frequently used as precleaners preceding other types of collectors.

5. *Scrubbers*

Devices in which contact with a liquid introduced into the collector for the purpose of such contact as the prime means of collection are scrubbers. Scrubbers are primarily employed to remove gases and vapor phase contaminants from the carrier gas, but are sometimes used to remove particulate matter. The liquid may either dissolve or chemically react with the contaminant collected. Methods of effecting contact between scrubbing liquid and carrier gas include: spraying the liquid into open chambers, or chambers containing various forms of baffles, grillage or packing; flowing the liquid into these structures over weirs; bubbling the gas through tanks or troughs of liquid, and utilizing gas flow to create droplets from liquid introduced at a location of high gas velocity. The liquid can frequently be recirculated to the scrubber after partial or complete removal of the collected contaminant from the liquid. In other cases all or a part of the liquid must be discarded to waste. In general, as long as the interior elements of the scrubber remain clean, pressure drop does not increase with time. Usually pressure drop increases with increasing gas flow rate. The relationship between collection efficiency and gas flow rate depends upon design, generally tending to increased efficiency, provided the liquid feed keeps pace with gas flow, and that carry-out of liquid with the effluent gas is effectively prevented.

6. *Adsorbers*

Devices in which contaminant gases or vapors are retained on the surface of the porous media through which the carrier gas flows are adsorbers. The media most commonly used is activated carbon. The design of an adsorber is similar to that of a filter for particulate matter in that the gas flows through a porous bed. However, in the case of an adsorber, the porous bed is frequently protected from plugging by particulate matter by preceding it with a filter so that the gases passing through the adsorption bed are free of particles. In true adsorption, there is no irreversible chemical reaction between the adsorbent and the adsorbed gas or vapor. The adsorbed gas or vapor can therefore be driven off the adsorbent by heat, vacuum, steam, or other means. In some adsorbers, the adsorbent is regenerated in this manner for reuse. In other applications the spent adsorbent is discarded and replaced with fresh adsorbent. Pressure drop through an adsorber which does not handle gas contaminated by particulate matter, should not increase with time, but should increase with gas flow rate. The relationship between retention efficiency and gas flow rate depends upon design.

7. *Equipment in Which the Contaminant is Burned as the Means for Its Control*

In devices of this class, combustible organic contaminants are burned by the oxygen in the carrier gas to products of as complete combustion as possible. In some cases, combustion takes place on the surface of a catalyst; in others no catalyst is necessary. Combustion is rarely used for particulate contaminants, but mostly for contaminant organic gases and vapors.

B. GENERAL PRINCIPLES

Collector selection involves two basic steps: first, the choice from among all collector types of those which will meet the technical requirements of the process; and second, the choice from among those meeting the requirements, of the type which will do the job at lowest overall cost. The technical requirements are set forth in terms of the carrier gas and the contaminants it carries. With respect to the carrier gas, one must know its physical and chemical properties, its rate of flow and variations of these properties with changes in both rate of flow and time. With respect to the contaminants, one must also know their physical and chemical properties, their concentration or loading in the carrier gas and variations in both loading and properties with flow rate and with time.

The principal physical properties of the carrier gas and the contaminant are related to their chemical composition. It is not necessary that the chemical composition be precisely known if the physical characteristics are known. However, when collectors selected on the basis of assumed physical properties do not work, it is sometimes necessary to precisely determine chemical composition in order to know what changes to try so as to make the collector work properly.

The prime physical properties of the carrier gas, temperature and pressure, are usually independent of chemical composition unless constituents are reacting exothermally or endothermally. The major properties dependent upon chemical composition of the carrier gas are density, viscosity, humidity, reactivity, combustibility, toxicity, and electrical and sonic properties. Many of these latter depend upon temperature and pressure as well as chemical composition. If reactivity is construed as including solubility and adsorbability, the above list of properties applies as well to the contaminant as to the carrier gas.

In the special case where the contaminant is a particulate solid, there is an additional group of physical properties related to the size, shape, density, and surface properties of the particulate. These properties are of concern both when the particulate is suspended in the gas stream, and after its collection when they affect the flow and packing properties of the collected material.

When the process is in operation, but without a collector, and the need is to select a collector to add to the process, many of these properties can be measured using accepted techniques. For some of the properties mentioned, there are no accepted techniques. Basic properties are not always translatable into a measure of the ease with which the pollutant may be collected. In these instances, tests must be devised for the specific collection technique being considered. Examples of these latter are those for electrical resistivity of dust and for the retentivity of gases in adsorbents. These tests are designed to provide a direct measure of "collectibility" by a given technique, and do not rely on measurement and interpretation of more basic physical properties. When the process is on the drawing board and the collector is to be specified as part of the plant design, the prime recourse is to experience on similar plants and processes. Where such experience does not exist, one must compute those properties such as carrier gas viscosity, density, humidity, reactivity, and combustibility from basic physical principles. However, methods are not yet sufficiently refined for the advance computation of many of the properties, such as those of the particulate phase, which are necessary for equipment design and selection.

When experience does not exist on a particular process, it is frequently possible to base design upon a closely parallel process for which design information exists. To provide a margin for error in the assumptions made, it is wise in such cases to incorporate a safety factor in the design so that changes required to improve collection efficiency after the plant goes into operation will not necessitate major reconstruction. Such safety factors include the initial provision of motors larger than the minimum horsepower computed, of ducts, pipes, and casings of ample dimensions, etc.

C. Properties of the Carrier Gas

1. Composition

As was previously noted, gas composition is important only as it affects its physical and chemical properties. The chemical properties are important to the extent that there may be chemical reaction between the gas, the contaminant, and the collector—its structure or its contents. One common example of reaction between gas components and equipment is where gases containing sulfur oxides and water vapor corrode metallic parts of collectors.

2. *Temperature*

The two principal influences of temperature are on the volume of the carrier gas and on the materials of construction of the collector. The former influences the size and cost of the collector and the concentration of the contaminant per unit of volume, which, in turn, is a factor where concentration is itself the driving force for removal. Viscosity, density, and other gas properties are temperature dependent.

Adsorption processes are generally exothermic and are impracticable at higher temperatures, the adsorbability being inversely proportional to the temperature (when the reaction is primarily physical and is not influenced by accompanying chemical reaction). Similarly in absorption (where gas solubility depends on the temperature of the solvent) temperature effects may be of significance if the concentration of the soluble material is such that appreciable temperature rise results. In combustion as a means for contaminant removal, the gas temperature affects the heat balance, which is the vital factor in the process. In electrostatic precipitation, both dust resistivity and the dielectric strength of the gas are temperature dependent.

Wet processes cannot be used at temperatures where the liquid would either freeze, boil, or evaporate too rapidly. Filter media can only be used in the temperature range within which they are stable.

3. *Pressure*

In general, carrier gas pressure much higher or lower than atmospheric pressure requires that the control equipment be designed as a pressure vessel. Some types of equipment are much more amenable to being designed into pressure vessels than others.

Pressure of the carrier gas is not of prime importance in particulate collection except for its influence on gas density, viscosity, and electrical properties. It may, however, be of importance in certain special situations such as where the choice is between high efficiency scrubbers and other devices for collection of particulate. The available source pressure can be used to overcome the high pressure drop across the scrubber and thereby reduce the high power requirement which often limits the utilization of scrubbers. In absorption, high pressure favors removal and may be required in some situations.

4. *Viscosity*

Viscosity is of importance to collection techniques in two respects. First, it is important to the removal mechanisms in many situations (inertial collection, gravity collection, and electrostatic precipitation). Particulate removal techniques often involve migration of the particles through the gas stream under the influence of some removal force. Ease of migration decreases with increasing viscosity of the gas stream. Second, viscosity influences the pressure drop across the removal equipment and thereby becomes a power consideration.

5. *Density*

Density appears to have no significant effect in most real gas cleaning processes although the difference between particle density and gas density appears as a factor in the theoretical analysis of all gravitational and centrifugal collection devices. Particle density is so much greater than gas density that the usual changes in gas density have negligible effect.

6. *Humidity*

Humidity of the carrier gas stream may be important to the selection or performance of control equipment in any of several basically different ways. High humidity may lead to caking and blocking of inertial collectors, caking on filter media, or corrosion. In addition, the presence of water vapor may influence the basic removal mechanism in electrostatic precipitation and greatly influence resistivity. In catalytic combustion it may be an important consideration in the heat balance which must be maintained. In adsorption it may tend to limit the capacity of the bed if water is preferentially or concurrently adsorbed with the contaminant. Even in filtration it may influence agglomeration and produce subtle effects. Carrier gas humidity limits the utilization of evaporative cooling to cool gases prior to collection. In situations where humidity is a serious problem for one of the above reasons, scrubbers or absorption towers may be particularly appropriate devices.

7. *Combustibility*

The handling of a carrier gas which is flammable or explosive will require certain precautions. The most important of these precautions is to be sure that the carrier gas is either above the upper explosive limit or below the lower explosive limit with respect to any air admixture that may exist or occur. The use of water scrubbing or absorption may be an effective means of minimizing the hazards in some instances. Electrostatic precipitators are impractical where they tend to spark and may thereby ignite the gas.

8. *Reactivity*

A reactive carrier gas presents special problems. In filtration, for example, the presence of gaseous fluorides may eliminate the possibility of high temperature filtration using glass fiber fabrics. In adsorption, carrier gas must not react preferentially with the adsorbents. For example, silica gel is not appropriate for adsorption of contaminants when water vapor is present as a component of the carrier gas stream. Also, the magnitude of this problem may be greater when one is dealing with a high temperature process. On the one hand, devices involving the use of water may be eliminated from consideration if the carrier gas reacts with water. On the other hand, scrubbers may be especially appropriate in that they tend to be relatively small and require small amounts of material of construction so that corrosion-resistant components may be used with lower relative increase in cost.

9. *Toxicity*

When the carrier gas is toxic or irritant, special precautions are needed in the construction of both the collector, the ductwork, and the means of discharge to the atmosphere. The entire system up to the stack must be under negative pressure and the stack must be of tight construction. Since the collector is under suction, special means such as "airlocks" must be provided for removing the contaminant from the hoppers, if collection is by a dry technique. Special precautions may be required for service and maintenance operations on the equipment.

10. *Electrical and Sonic Properties of the Carrier Gas*

Electrical properties will be important to electrostatic precipitation in that the rate or ease of ionization will influence removal mechanisms.

Generally speaking, intensity of Brownian motion and gas viscosity both increase with gas temperature. These factors are important gas stream characteristics which relate to the "sonic properties" of the stream. Increases in either property will tend to increase the effectiveness with which sonic energy can be used to produce particle agglomeration.

D. FLOW CHARACTERISTICS OF THE CARRIER GAS

1. *Flow Rate*

The rate at which a carrier gas must be treated depends on its rate of evolution from the process, its initial temperature, and the means by which it is cooled, if cooling is used. These factors fix the rate at which gases must be treated and therefore the size of removal equipment and the rate at which gas passes through it. For economic reasons it is desirable to minimize the size of the equipment. Optimizing the size and velocity relationship involves consideration of two effects: (1) reduction in size results in increased power requirements for handling a given amount of gas because of increased pressure loss within the control device and (2) the effect of velocity on the removal mechanisms must be considered. For example, higher velocities favor removal in inertial equipment up to the point of turbulence but beyond this, increased velocity results in decreased efficiency. In gravity settling chambers, flow velocity determines the smallest size that will be removed. In venturi scrubbers, efficiency is directly proportional to velocity through the system. In absorption, velocity varies film resistance to mass transfer. In filtration, the resistance of the medium will often vary with velocity because of changes in dust cake permeability with flow. In adsorption, velocity across the bed should not exceed the maximum which permits effective removal. Optimum velocities have not generally been established with certainty for any of the control processes because they are highly influenced by the properties of the contaminant and carrier gas as well as the design of the equipment. Certain generalizations are possible, however. In gravity settling changers, flows are generally limited to 10 ft/sec to minimize reentrainment. For adsorption on activated carbon, velocities through the beds range from 20 to 120 ft/min. For conventional fabric filters, filtration velocities range from $1\frac{1}{2}$ to 3 ft/min.

2. *Variations in Flow Rate*

Rate variations result in velocity changes and thereby influence equipment efficiency and pressure drop. Various control techniques have differing ability to adjust to flow changes. In situations where rate variations are inescapable, it is necessary to: (1) design for extreme conditions, (2) employ devices that will correct for flow changes, or (3) use a collector which is inherently positive in its operation. Filtration is most adapted to extreme rate variations because it presents a positive barrier for particulate removal. This process is, however, subject to pressure drop variations and generally the air moving equipment will not deliver at a constant rate when pressure drop increases. In most other control techniques variations in flow will result in change in the effectiveness of removal unless the equipment has been designed for the least desirable flow condition.

One means for coping with rate variation is the use of two collectors in series, one which improves performance with increasing flow (e.g., multicyclone) and one whose performance decreases with increasing flow (e.g., electrostatic precipitator).

3. Changes in Carrier Gas Properties with Variations in Flow Rate

Variations in flow rate are of two main types: those where merely more or less of the same carrier gas flows and those where variations in flow are caused by process changes which also cause variation in the composition or temperature of the carrier gas. Since many carrier gas properties change when composition and temperature changes, equipment selection must give these changes recognition.

4. Changes in Properties with Time

This is the more general case of that just discussed. It recognizes that there are processes where flow rate remains reasonably uniform over a process cycle but where gas composition goes through a cyclic variation. The problems are essentially the same as when there is variation of both composition and rate.

5. Relationship to Air Mover Characteristics

Control techniques that result in progressively increasing collector pressure loss with time will require that consideration be given to the effect of such changes on air mover selection. Fabric filters are perhaps the best illustration of this effect. Accumulation of dust cake during the filtering cycle results in increased resistance to flow. The increase in resistance generally reduces centrifugal fan output. Where the resultant flow variation cannot be tolerated by the process, positive displacement blowers or other special precautions must be employed.

E. GENERAL PROPERTIES OF THE CONTAMINANT

1. Composition

In general, the composition of the contaminant is important only as it affects physical and chemical properties and the chemical properties are, in turn, important mainly as they affect physical properties. As a separate consideration, composition directly affects the use or value of the collected material which in turn frequently dictates the kind of collection device required. Thus, if the collected material is to be used in process or shipped dry, a dry collector is indicated, and if the collected material is of high intrinsic value, a very efficient collector is indicated.

a. Change in Composition with Time. Just as the carrier gas composition can change throughout a cyclic process, so can the composition of the contaminant. In the secondary smelting of aluminum, the period of evolution of extremely fine $AlCl_3$ fume lasts for only a few minutes of the 8–16 hours of the total cycle. Since chemical and physical properties vary with composition, a collector must be able to cope with cyclic composition changes.

2. Loading

Loading influences different types of collectors in different ways. Thus cyclone efficiency increases markedly at high dust loadings. Conversely, extremely high loading may overtax hopper, rapper, or shaker capacity. Processes such as sonic agglomeration are quite sensitive to changes in loading.

a. Changes in Loading with Time. Contaminant loading from many processes varies over a wide range for the operating cycle. Ten to one variation in loading is not uncommon. One example of such a process is the open hearth furnace; another is soot blowing in a steam boiler.

b. Changes in Contaminant Loading with Carrier Gas Flow Rate. A prime example of a process in which loading increases rapidly with flow rate is fly ash in flue gas from a stoker-fired coal furnace. An increase in flue gas flow rate is the result of an increase in upward velocity of air through the coal bed and increased gas velocity in the furnace, both of which increase the carry-over from the fuel bed into the gas stream.

3. Contaminant Phase

In most air cleaning operations, the contaminant to be removed will not undergo change of phase at temperatures near those normally existing in conventional collection equipment (unless such change of phase is related to the actual removal mechanism as it is in absorption where gaseous pollutants are put into solution). However, in some situations determination of the temperature at which the gas should be cleaned may depend on the relationship between temperature and phase of the contaminant. For example, aluminum chloride is evolved from operations concerned with removal of magnesium from reprocessed aluminum. This aluminum chloride exists as a vapor at temperatures in excess of about 360 °F. Since this change of phase takes place at temperatures which commonly exist in many types of control equipment, selection and control of the operating temperature is obviously critical. Change of phase with change in carrier gas temperature has been used as a means for the selective removal of the fumes of different metals in different banks of collectors assembled in series. In this application, the gas in the first collector bank is at a high enough temperature that only one metal fume is condensed to the particulate phase and collected, the fumes of all other metals present in the gas being still in the vapor phase. A drop of temperature between the first and second collector bank condenses another metal fume which is then collected in the bank, and so forth until all metals present have been removed as a fume in an appropriate collector bank.

F. Specific Properties of the Contaminant

1. Solubility

Solubility of contaminant is important to absorption, adsorption, and scrubbing. In absorption, the degree of solubility is one indication of the ease of removal of the contaminant. In adsorption, solubility may be important to the ease with which the adsorbent may be regenerated. In scrubbing to remove particulate, solubility will provide a secondary removal mechanism to aid the basic separating forces.

2. Sorbability

The sorbability, or ease with which a contaminant can be removed by absorption or adsorption techniques, is a function of a number of more basic properties. Generally adsorption is defined as the process whereby gases, vapors, or liquids are exposed to and concentrated on the surface or in the pores of a solid. Absorption is a similar process where the sorbent may be either liquid or solid and the combination is more permanent because it is accompanied by chemical reaction (which may be reversible) between the contaminant and the sorbent. The more basic properties of temperature, pressure of the system, chemical composition of contaminant and sorbent, solubility, as well as undefined properties such as the nature of the surface forces on adsorbing solids, are of controlling importance in any given situation.

3. Combustibility

Generally, it is not desirable to use a collection system which permits accumulation of "pockets" of contaminant when the contaminant collected is explosive. Systems handling such materials must be protected against accumulation of static charges. Electrostatic precipitators are not suitable because of their tendency to spark. Wet collection by scrubbing or absorption methods may be especially appropriate. However, some dusts such as magnesium are pyrophoric in the presence of small amounts of water. In combustion (with or without a catalyst), explosability must be considered.

4. *Reactivity*

Certain obvious precautions must be taken in the selection of equipment for the collection of reactive contaminants. In filtration, selection of the filtering media may present a special problem. In adsorption, certain situations require that the adsorbed contaminant react with the adsorbent so that the degree of reactivity will be important. For uses where scrubbers are considered, aggravation of corrosive conditions must be balanced against the savings possible because of the fact that corrosive-resistant construction requires relatively small amounts of material.

5. *Electrical and Sonic Properties*

The electrical properties of the contaminant may influence the performance of any of several collector types. Electrical properties are considered to be a contributing factor influencing the buildup of solids in inertial collectors. In electrostatic precipitators, the electrical properties of the contaminant are of paramount importance in determining collection efficiency and influence the ease with which it is removed by periodic cleaning. In fabric filtration, electrostatic phenomena may have direct and observable influence upon the process of cake formation and the subsequent ease of cake removal. In spray towers or other forms of scrubber in which liquid droplets are formed and contact between these droplets and contaminant particles are required for particle collection, the electrical charge on both particles and droplets is an important process variable. The process is most efficient when the charges on the droplet attract rather than repel those on the particle. Sonic properties are significant where sonic agglomeration is employed.

6. *Toxicity*

The degree of contaminant toxicity will influence collector efficiency requirements and may necessitate the use of equipment which will provide ultrahigh efficiency. Toxicity will also affect the means for removal of collected contaminant from the collector and the means of servicing and maintaining the collector. However, toxicity of contaminant does not influence the removal mechanisms of any collection technique.

7. Contaminant Size, Shape, and Density

a. General. Size, shape, and density are the three factors that determine the magnitude of forces resisting movement of a particle through a fluid. These forces are a major factor in determining the effectiveness of removal by means of inertial collectors, gravity collectors, venturi scrubbers, and electrostatic precipitators. In fact, this force is a prime consideration for any device, except fabric filters, in which particulate is collected. In every instance, this force is balanced against some removal force which is applied in the control device and the magnitude of the net force tending to remove the particle will determine the effectiveness of the equipment. Even in the case of filters, size and shape of particle influence both collection efficiency and pressure drop.

The only analogous situation in gaseous removal is found in adsorption where minimum molecular weight relates to the adsorbability of the gas. Generally, molecular weights must be in excess of 40–45 before the contaminant can be effectively adsorbed.

b. Size Distribution. Since size has the previously discussed importance to the ease with which individual particles are removed from the gas stream, it is apparent that size distribution will largely determine the overall efficiency of a particular piece of control equipment. Generally, the smaller the size to be removed, the greater the expenditure that will be required for power or equipment or both. To increase the efficiencies obtainable with scrubbers it is necessary to expend additional power either to produce high gas stream velocities as in the venturi scrubber or to produce finely divided spray water. Cyclones will require that a larger number of small units be used for higher efficiency in a given situation. Both the power cost (because of the increased pressure drop) and equipment cost (for a multiple unit installation) will be increased. Higher efficiencies for electrostatic precipitators will require that a number of units be used in series. Generally there is an approximately inverse logarithmic relationship between outlet concentration and the size of collection equipment. A precipitator giving 90% efficiency must be doubled in size to give 99% efficiency and tripled in size to give 99.9% efficiency.

8. Hygroscopicity

Hygroscopicity is not specifically related to any removal mechanism. However, it may be a measure of how readily particulate will cake or tend to accumulate in equipment if moisture is present. If such accumulation occurs on a fabric filter, it may completely blind it and prevent gas flow.

9. *Agglomerating Characteristics*

Collectors are sometimes used in series with the first collector acting as an agglomerator, the second as the collector of the particles agglomerated in the first one. Carbon black collection is an example of a process where extremely fine particles are first agglomerated so that they may be made practicably collectable.

10. *Flow Properties*

These properties are mainly related to the ease with which the collected dust may be discharged from the collector. Extreme stickiness may eliminate the possibility of using equipment such as fabric filters. Hopper size depends in part on the packing characteristics or bulk density of the collected material.

11. *Catalyst Poisoning*

The presence of traces of metals such as mercury, lead, and zinc will make catalytic combustion impractical even though effluent stream characteristics are such that it would otherwise be a suitable technique. Other than by mechanical attrition, catalysts are deteriorated by four other phenomena associated with stream content or condition: (1) surface coating of the granular structure by particulate contaminants within the gas stream, (2) coating by particulate products of oxidation, (3) chemical reaction with gaseous components of the stream, and (4) bed temperature levels which will cause sintering of the catalyst.

G. DISCUSSION

In general, collectors handle as dust between 0.25 and 3.0% by weight of the solid material being processed.

In selecting a collector, one of the principal choices is between wet and dry collectors. Wet systems range between those using 100% makeup water and those with elaborate works for separating the particulate matter from the water so the water may be reused with only minimum addition of makeup water. This same range is involved when dry collectors are used with hydraulic transport of particulate matter from the hoppers to the point of disposal. The factors to be weighed in considering a wet system include solubility of the aerosol, ultimate pH of the scrubbing liquid, its corrosion and erosion potential, special metals or protective coatings necessary to cope with these problems, availability of makeup water, disposal and treatment of waste water, space required for liquid-handling equipment. Some types of wet systems can also separate aerosols and scrub gaseous pollutants simultaneously from a waste gas stream.

Among the other factors to be considered are:

1. Operating life of collector components. Fabric filters require periodic replacement. Electrostatic precipitator elements need protection against condensation if corrosive-gas water-vapor mixtures near the dew point are processed. Cyclones can have holes worn in them by abrasive erosion.

2. Leakage between "dirty" and "clean" compartments. In fabric filters and multiple cyclones a pressure differential exists between the dirty and clean sides of the separator. Any leakage between the two, which bypasses the normal flow path through the fabric or the cyclone, will carry aerosol into the clean compartment, thereby reducing overall efficiency. In fabric filters the most important sources of bypass flow are rips and tears through the fabric itself or its sewn seams and the fabric-to-metal connections required to allow easy fabric replacement. In multiple cyclones, in addition to gasket leakage, there is the possibility of backflow of gas and dust from the dust hopper into the dust discharge opening if there is partial or complete stoppage of the gas inlet to a unit.

3. Uniformity of aerosol distribution across the inlet duct. Electrostatic precipitators require elaborate measures to ensure such uniformity; inertial collectors are less dependent, and fabric filters least dependent on such uniformity to maintain design efficiency.

III. Application of Collectors*

The status of control technology and collector application is given in Tables I (p. 350) and V (p. 357). Collector characteristics and performance are shown in Tables II (p. 355) and III (p. 356). Collector costs are shown in Tables II and IV (p. 356), Figs. 1–4 (pp. 348–349).

German practice in the operation and maintenance of collectors is found in V.D.I. 2264 "Operation and Maintenance of Dust Collectors" (7). Some reasons for unsatisfactory operation of dust removal plants is discussed by Pistor (9).

* Additional pertinent material is in the "Air Pollution Engineering Manual, Los Angeles APCD" (J. A. Danielson, ed.), PHS Publn. 999-AP-40, DHEW, Cincinnati (1967); "Air Pollution Manual, Part II," American Industrial Hygiene Assn., Detroit (1968); and will be published in the National Air Pollution Control Administration's publications: "Control Technology for Particulate Air Pollutants," and "Control Technology for Sulfur Oxides Air Pollutants."

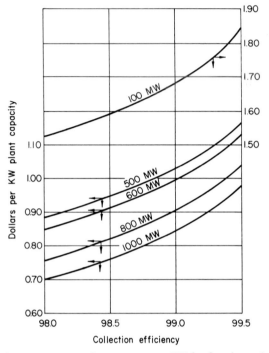

FIG. 1. Approximate average equipment cost per KW for fly ash precipitators. Erected price = 1.68 × F.O.B. Ash removal system = 0.13 per KW (6, p. 2642).

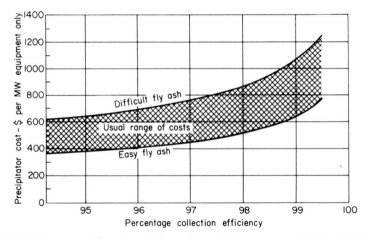

FIG. 2. Base cost of fly ash precipitator for a 1000 megawatt unit (6, p. 2643).

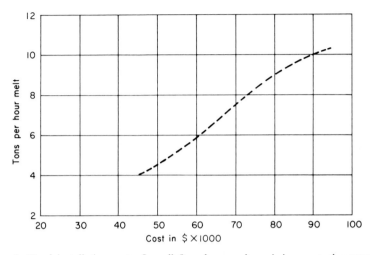

FIG. 3. Total installation cost of small foundry cupola emission control system. Wet collectors or dry mechanical collectors (6, p. 2644).

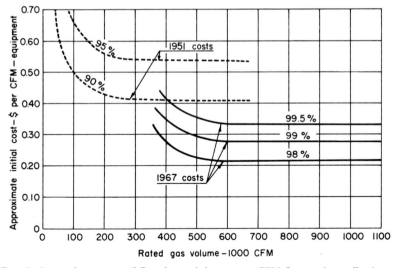

FIG. 4. Approximate cost of fly ash precipitators per CFM for varying collection efficiencies (6, p. 2645).

TABLE I

STATUS OF CURRENT TECHNOLOGY IN THE CONTROL OF EMISSIONS TO THE ATMOSPHERE[a]

Source	Particulates		Sulfur oxides		Carbon monoxide		Others		Remarks
	C	NC	C	NC	C	NC	C	NC	
Domestic and commercial heating plants:									
Coal fires (not hand fired)	(b)		X			X	Smoke	NO_x	CO not of major concern.
Oil fired	(b)		X			X	Smoke	NO_x	Control of SO_x only by switching to low sulfur fuel.
Gas fired					X			NO_x	Control of CO by good combustion.
Industrial heating plants:									
Coal fired	X			X	X		Smoke	NO_x	Control of particulate during soot blowing needed.
Oil fired	(b)			X	X		Smoke	NO_x	Partial control of NO_x is possible.
Gas fired					X			NO_x	Partial control of NO_x is possible.
Electric generating plants:									
Coal fired	X		X		X		Smoke	NO_x	Control of particulate during soot blowing needed.
Oil fired	X		X		X		Smoke	NO_x	Partial control of NO_x is possible.
Gas fired					X			NO_x	Partial control of NO_x is possible.
Hand-fired coal burning furnaces	X				X		Smoke	NO_x	Controlled by elimination of hand firing of coal which may be a hardship on low-income households.
Incinerators:									
Domestic; commercial; industrial:									
Single chamber		X			X			Smoke; organics	Can be controlled by eliminating single-chamber incinerators.
Multiple chamber	X						Smoke; organics		More effective control of particulate emissions is needed.
Municipal	X						Smoke; organics		
Auto body and scrap wire	X						Smoke; organics		
Mineral industry:									
Cement	X							NO_x	Particulate control difficult for old plant.
Insulation	X							NO_x; odors uncontrolled in some glass wool plants	
Glass manufacturing	X						Fluorides	NO_x	Can control fluoride and visible emissions by raw material control.
Frit	X							NO_x	

350

Source					Remarks
Phosphate fertilizer	X		Fluorides; ammonia		Fluoride control difficult on older plants and certain processes.
Asphalt concrete batching	X			Odors; NO_x	Fugitive dust control difficult at older plants.
Concrete batching	X				
Carbon black:					
Furnace black	X			NO_x	SO_x may be a problem and cannot be controlled.
Channel black		X		NO_x	
Coal cleaning	X				Older plants often difficult to control.
Charcoal manufacturing	[c]			Organics; smoke	
Ceramics	X			Fluorides; NO_x	Fluorides from decomposition of certain clays.
Refractories	X			NO_x; fluorides, if in raw material	
Rock and gravel processing	X				Fugitive dust difficult to control.
Metallurgical industry:					
Iron and steel:					
Coke plants:					
Slot type	X	X	NH_3, benzol, toluol, organics	Odors	Emissions from charging and discharging ovens. Old plants are very difficult to control.
Beehive	X	X		Organics; odors	Completely noncontrolled.
Blast furnace	X	X		NO_x	CO used as fuel.
Sintering plants	X	X	Fluorides	NO_x	Control difficult on older plants.
Open hearths	X		Fluorides	NO_x	Being phased out.
Oxygen lance open hearths	X	X		NO_x	
Basic oxygen	X			NO_x	Replacing basic open hearth.
Electric furnaces	X			NO_x	Emissions not controlled during tilting and charging.
Scarfing	[c]			NO_x	
Grey iron cupola:					
Production	X	X	Organics	NO_x	
Jobbing	[c]	X	Organics	NO_x	
Ferroalloys	X			NO_x	
Aluminum:					
Reduction	X		Fluorides	Carbonaceous matter	Fluoride control poor in Soderberg furnaces.
Secondary operations	X		Chlorine		
Smelting:					
Lead ores	X			NO_x	
Zinc ores	X			NO_x	
Copper ores	X			NO_x	

NOTE: See footnotes at end of table, p. 354.

KEY: C—Control technology generally available; NC—Control technology not generally available; CO—Carbon monoxide; HC—Hydrocarbons; SO_x—Sulfur oxides; NO_x—Nitrogen oxides.

TABLE I (Continued)

Source	Particulates		Sulfur oxides		Carbon monoxide		Others		Remarks
	C	NC	C	NC	C	NC	C	NC	
Refining:									
Zinc	X							NO_x	⎫ Particulate control at small scrap reclaiming
Brass	X							NO_x	⎬ operations is economically burdensome.
Taconite plants	X							NO_x	⎭
Petroleum industry:									
Petroleum refining:									
Separation (crude distillation, etc.)							HC, H_2S		
Conversion:									
Catalytic cracking	X				X		H_2S	NO_x	
Reforming							H_2S		
Treating							Odors		Odors often noticeable.
Blending							HC		
Petroleum production							HC		
Petroleum marketing:									
Bulk plants							HC		
Service stations							HC	HC	Partial control possible.
Solvent evaporation:									
Drycleaning							Solvents	Solvents[b]	Recovered.
Paint spraying	X							Solvents[b]	Generally uncontrolled.
Industrial storage							Solvents		Breathing losses usually uncontrolled.
Degreasing							Solvents	NO_x	
Bake oven								Water vapor	Water vapor controlled in Europe. Some odors detectable at <1 ppb.
Kraft pulpmills:									
Digesters	X						Sulfur compounds		
Smelt tank	X						Sulfur compounds		
Lime kiln	X		X				Sulfur compounds		
Recovery furnace	X		X		X		Sulfur compounds	Sulfur compounds; NO_x	Control of odorous sulfur compounds usually not satisfactory.

Source		Sulfides, odors	Sulfur compounds and odors.	
Evaporators				
Oxidation towers				
Chemical industry:				
Sulfuric acid	X	Sulfuric acid mist	NO$_x$ (chamber process)	Better control of SO₂ desirable.
Nitric acid		NO$_x$		
Hydrochloric acid		HCl, solvents		
Phosphoric acid		Fluorides; phosphoric acid mist.		Flouride control often difficult. Particulate control difficult for submerged combustion acid evaporation.
Hydrofluoric acid		HF		
Chlorine		Cl$_2$		Cl₂ leaks are hard to control at old plants. Well-developed technology and mammoth plants.
Ammonia (synthetic)		NH$_3$ organic bases		
Lime	X		NO$_x$	
Soda ash:				
Ammonia soda	X	NH$_3$		
Trona	X			
Caustic soda:				
Lime-soda				Practically obsolete (see chlorine plants).
Electrolytic	X	Cl$_2$		Odor from Cl₂ distillation tower bottoms if exposed.
Polyethylene		HC		Tight process system.
Polyvinyl chloride		HCl, vinyl chloride, vinylidene chloride, vinyl acetate.		Tight process system.
Alum	X	Mists		Old plant controls may be poor.
Paint and varnish	X	Odors, solvents	NO$_x$	Old plant controls difficult. Often have odors.
Synthetic rubber		HC, solvents, odors		Odor control only fair.
Rubber tire manufacturing	X	Odors		
Oil bodying operation	X		Odors	
Formaldehyde	X	Methanol, formaldehyde, HC.		Tight system.
Methanol (synthetic)		Benzene, toluene, odors		Tight system.
Phenol (synthetic)	X			
Rayon		Sulfides, carbon disulfide odors.		Odor control only fair.

NOTE: See footnotes at end of table, p. 354.

KEY: C—Control technology generally available; NC—Control technology not generally available; CO—Carbon monoxide; HC—Hydrocarbons; SO$_x$—Sulfur oxides; NO$_x$—Nitrogen oxides.

TABLE I (Continued)

Source	Particulates		Sulfur oxides		Carbon monoxide		Others		Remarks
	C	NC	C	NC	C	NC	C	NC	
Insecticides:									
Chlorinated	X						Cl₂; HCl	Odors	Some are supertoxic.
Phosphorus type	X							Odors	Some are highly toxic. Nonpersistent.
Carbamates	X								Partial control of odor possible.
Soap and detergent	X							Odors	
Phosgene							Cl₂ and phosgene		Highly toxic. Tight system; mainly captive use.
Phthalic anhydride	X						Odors		
Food processing and agriculture:									
Cotton ginning	X							Pesticides	Some gins have cost problems. Incineration of cotton trash of concern in regard to arsenic.
Alfalfa dehydrating	X							Odors; NO_x	Often unsatisfactory.
Feed and grain mills	X								
Flour mills	X								
Meat smoking	X						Odors; smoke		
Starch manufacturing	X								
Fish processing	X						Odors	Odors	Cl₂ scrubbers. Partial control of odors possible.
Coffee roasting	X						Odors	NO_x	Fume burners.
Rendering							Odors		Complete odor control difficult.
Agricultural burning:									
Fields		X						Organics, odors	
Forests		X						Organics, odors	
Crop spraying							Drift	Many insecticides and herbicides.	Hazardous to life unless carefully done.

[a] Reference (6), pp. 2274–2277 (J. H. Ludwig)

[b] Emission control is possible but cost is unacceptably great compared to capital investment of plant or or as a factor in cost of finished products or in relationship to the ability of persons responsible for control to bear the costs.

NOTE.—Nitrogen oxides (NO_x) are always formed in high-temperature combustion. Amounts vary with conditions. Feasible means for adequate control of emissions are not available.

KEY: C—Control technology generally available; NC—Control technology not generally available; CO—Carbon monoxide; HC—Hydrocarbons; SO_x—Sulfur oxides; NO_x—Nitrogen oxides.

354

TABLE II

APPROXIMATE CHARACTERISTICS OF DUST AND MIST COLLECTION EQUIPMENT (8)

Equipment type	Relative cost[a]	Smallest particle collected (μ)[b]	Pressure drop (inches H_2O)	Power used[c] $\left(\dfrac{kw}{1000 \text{ ft}^3/\text{min}}\right)$	Remarks
A. Settling chambers					
1. Simple	1	40	0.1–0.5	0.1	Large, low pressure drop, precleaner
2. Multiple tray	2–6	10	0.1–0.5	0.1	Difficult to clean, warpage problem
B. Inertial separators					
1. Baffle chamber	1	20	0.5–1.5	0.1–0.5	Power plants, rotary kilns, acid mists
2. Orifice impaction	1–3	2	1–3	0.2–0.6	Acid mists
3. Louver type	1–3	10	0.3–1	0.1–0.2	Fly ash, abrasion problem
4. Gas reversal	1	40	0.1–0.4	0.1	Precleaner
5. Rotating impeller	2–6	5	—	0.5–2	Compact
C. Cyclones					
1. Single	1–2	15	0.5–3	0.1–0.6	Simple, inexpensive, most widely used
2. Multiple	3–6	5	2–10	0.5–2	Abrasion and plugging problems
D. Filters					
1. Tubular	3–20	<0.1	2–6	0.5–1.5	High efficiency, temperature and humidity limits
2. Reverse jet	7–12	<0.1	2–6	0.7–1.5	More compact, constant flow
3. Envelope	3–20	<0.1	2–6	0.5–1.5	Limited capacity, constant flow possible
E. Electrical precipitators					
1. One-stage	6–30	<0.1	0.1–0.5	0.2–0.6	High efficiency, heavy duty, expensive
2. Two-stage	2–6	<0.1	0.1–0.3	0.2–0.4	Compact, air conditioning service
F. Scrubbers					
1. Spray tower	1–2	10	0.1–0.5	0.1–0.2	Common, low water use
2. Jet	4–10	2	—	2–10	Pressure gain, high velocity liquid jet
3. Venturi	4–12	1	10–15	2–10	High velocity gas stream
4. Cyclonic	3–10	5	2–8	0.6–2	Modified dry collector
5. Inertial	4–10	2	2–15	0.8–8	Abrasion problem
6. Packed	3–6	5	0.5–10	0.6–2	Channeling problem
7. Rotating impeller	4–12	2	—	2–10	Abrasion problem

[a] Including necessary auxiliaries.   [b] With 90–95% efficiency by weight.   [c] Includes pressure loss, water pumping, electrical energy.

355

TABLE III
MECHANICAL COLLECTORS[a,b]

	Percent of particles < 10 μ in size	Efficiency range (%)
1. Fly ash (power)		
(a) Spreader Stoker fired boilers	20	90–95
(b) PC fired boilers	42	75–90
(c) Cyclone fired boilers	65	55–65
2. Nonmetallic minerals (mechanical collectors used as primary stage where collector catch a part of process).		
(a) Cement (kilns & process)	40	70–80
(b) Asphalt plant (Bit. mix)	10	80–95
(c) Lite Weight aggregate (kiln)	30–40	80–90
(d) Refractory Clays (kiln)	40–50	70–80
(e) Lime (kiln)	40–50	75–80
(f) Fertilizer plant (Process equipment)	40	80–85
3. Steel (Ore beneficiation)		
(a) Pelletizing (vertical shaft and rotary kiln)	10–40	80–95
(b) Foundry (general)	10–40	80–95
4. Chemical process (drying, calcining)	10–40	80–95
5. Incinerators (municipal)	20–40	65–75
6. Coal processing (thermal drying)	10	90–97
7. Petroleum (cat cracking process)	18	99+
8. General industrial application (in plant)	10–60	65–95

[a] Reference (6), pp. 2640–2641 (E. L. Wilson).

[b] Mechanical Collectors with broad range of equipment available will not meet all code requirements, therefore, efficiencies identified herein will cover the general range of efficiency expected on various applications.

TABLE IV
RULE-OF-THUMB COSTS OF TYPICAL COLLECTORS OF
STANDARD MILD STEEL CONSTRUCTION[a]

	Equipment cost	Erection cost	Yearly maintenance and repair cost
Type of collector	Dollars per cubic feet per minute		
Mechanical collector	0.07–0.25	0.03–0.12	0.005–0.02
Electrostatic precipitator	0.25–1.00	0.12–0.50	0.01–0.025
Fabric filter	0.35–1.25	0.25–0.50	0.02–0.08
Wet scrubber	0.10–0.40	0.04–0.16	0.02–0.05

[a] Reference (6), p. 2633 (E. L. Wilson).

TABLE V
Use of Particulate Collectors by Industry[a,b]

Industrial Classification	Process	Electrostatic precipitator	Mechanical collector	Fabric filter	Wet scrubber	Other[c]
Utilities and industrial power plants	Coal	⊕	⊕	—	—	—
	Oil	⊕	⊕	—	—	—
	Natural gas		——not required——			
	Lignite	⊕	⊕	—	—	—
	Wood and bark	+	⊕	—	+	—
	Bagasse	—	⊕	—	—	—
	Fluid coke	⊕	+	—	—	+
Pulp and paper	Kraft	⊕	—	—	⊕	—
	Soda	⊕	—	—	⊕	—
	Lime kiln	—	—	—	⊕	—
	Chemical	—	—	—	⊕	—
	Dissolver tank vents	—	⊕	—	—	+
Rock Products	Cement	⊕	⊕	⊕	+	—
	Phosphate	⊕	⊕	⊕	⊕	—
	Gypsum	⊕	⊕	⊕	⊕	—
	Alumina	⊕	⊕	⊕	+	—
	Lime	⊕	⊕	+	—	—
	Bauxite	⊕	⊕	—	—	—
	Magnesium oxide	+	+	—	—	—
Steel	Blast furnace	⊕	—	—	⊕	+
	Open hearth	⊕	—	—	+	+
	Basic oxygen furnace	⊕	—	—	⊕	—
	Electric furnace	+	—	⊕	⊕	—
	Sintering	⊕	⊕	—	—	—
	Coke ovens	⊕	—	—	—	+
	Ore roasters	⊕	⊕	—	+	—
	Cupola	+	—	+	⊕	—
	Pyrites roaster	⊕	⊕	—	⊕	—
	Taconite	+	⊕	—	—	—
	Hot scarfing	⊕	—	—	+	—
Mining and metallurgical	Zinc roaster	⊕	⊕	—	—	—
	Zinc smelter	⊕	—	—	—	—
	Copper roaster	⊕	⊕	—	—	—
	Copper reverb.	⊕	—	—	—	—
	Copper converter	⊕	—	—	—	—
	Lead furnace	—	—	⊕	⊕	—
	Aluminum	⊕	—	—	⊕	+
	Elemental phosphorus	⊕	—	—	—	—
	Ilmenite	⊕	⊕	—	—	—
	Titanium Dioxide	+	—	⊕	—	—
	Molybdenum	+	—	—	—	—
	Sulfuric acid	⊕	—	—	⊕	⊕

NOTE: See footnotes at end of table, p. 358.

TABLE V (*Continued*)

Industrial Classification	Process	Electrostatic precipitator	Mechanical collector	Fabric filter	Wet scrubber	Other[c]
	Phosphoric acid	—	—	—	⊕	⊕
	Nitric acid	—	—	—	⊕	⊕
	Ore beneficiation	+	+	+	+	+
Miscellaneous	Refinery catalyst	⊕	⊕	—	—	—
	Coal drying	—	⊕	—	—	—
	Coal Mill vents	—	+	⊕	—	—
	Municipal incinerators	+	⊕	—	⊕	+
	Carbon black	+	+	+	—	—
	Apartment incinerators	—	—	—	⊕	—
	Spray drying	—	⊕	⊕	+	—
	Machining operation	—	⊕	⊕	+	+
	Hot coating	—	—	—	⊕	⊕
	Precious metal	⊕	—	⊕	—	—
	Feed and flour milling	—	⊕	⊕	—	—
	Lumber mills	—	⊕	—	—	—
	Wood working	—	⊕	⊕	—	—

[a] Reference (6), pp. 2637–2638 (E. L. Wilson).

[b] ⊕ = most common; + = also used.

[c] Other = Packed towers, mist pads, slag filter, centrifugal exhausters, flame incineration, settling chamber.

REFERENCES

1. A. C. Stern, *Trans. ASME* **59**, FSP, 289 (1937).
2. C. Orr, Jr. and J. M. DallaValle, "Fine Particle Measurement, Size, Surface and Pore Volume." Macmillan, New York, 1959; G. Herdan, "Small Particle Statistics." Elsevier, Amsterdam, 1953.
3. E. F. Wolf, H. L. von Hohenleiten, and M. B. Gordon, *Proc. Intern. Clean Air Conf., London, 1959* p. 239. Natl. Soc. Clean Air, London, 1960.
4. P. W. Spaite, D. G. Stephan, and A. H. Rose, Jr., *J. Air Pollution Control Assoc.* **11**, 234 (1961).
5. J. E. Sayers, *J. Inst. Fuel* **33**, 542 (1960).
6. Hearings before the Subcommittee on Air and Water Pollution of the Committee on Public Works, U.S. Senate, 90th Congress, 1st Session, S.780—Air Pollution—1967 (Air Quality Act) Part 4, March 15–18, 1967, U.S. Govt. Printing Office, Washington, D.C. (1967).
7. Richtlinien-Kommission Reinhaltung der Luft, Verein Deutcher Ingenieure, Dusseldorf, West Germany.
8. D. G. Stephan, *Modern Castings* **38** (1), 75 (1960).
9. R. Pistor, *Staub* **26** (11) (Nov. 1966), (p. 41, English Transl.), Clearinghouse for Scientific and Technical Information, U.S. Dept. of Commerce, Springfield, Va. #CFSTI-TT66-51159/11.

43 Source Control by Centrifugal Force and Gravity

Knowlton J. Caplan

I. Introduction

Particles suspended in a gas possess inertia, momentum, and are acted upon by gravity. These properties may be used to create centrifugal forces acting on the particle if the gas stream is forced to change direction. Centrifugal force is the primary mechanism of particle collection in cyclone separators and in most types of dust collection equipment loosely classed as "inertial separators." Inertia of particles and centrifugal forces also play a part in filtration, scrubbing, and other methods of gas cleaning, but other mechanisms are also important in such equipment.

The cyclone collector is widely used and cyclone theory is the basis for many inertial separator designs. The cyclone is simple, inexpensive, has no moving parts, and can be built of any reasonable material of construction. If the gas cleaning problems do not require high efficiency—viz., nontoxic, coarse, low-value dusts—the collection efficiency of properly designed cyclones is frequently adequate. Disappointing cyclone installations are usually due to overoptimistic estimates of efficiency. Also, because cyclones can be constructed of so many materials, they are frequently used under severe service conditions where erosion, corrosion, or plugging would create problems with any type of equipment. The basic purpose of this chapter is to further the proper application of cyclones and related equipment.

Solid or liquid particulates settle slowly through gas under the influence of gravity. Settling chambers utilizing this mechanism are practical only for relatively coarse material, and have high space requirements.

II. Cyclone Collector

A. Definition

A cyclone collector is a structure without moving parts in which the velocity of an inlet gas stream is transformed into a confined vortex from which centrifugal forces tend to drive the suspended particles to the wall of the cyclone body.

B. Types of Cyclones

The necessary elements of a cyclone consist of a gas inlet which produces the vortex; an axial outlet for cleaned gas; and a dust discharge opening. The various arrangements of these elements lead to a classification system of types (Fig. 1A–D):

A. The common cyclone, tangential inlet with axial dust discharge.
B. Tangential inlet with peripheral dust discharge.
C. Axial inlet through swirl vanes, with axial dust discharge.
D. Axial inlet through swirl vanes, with peripheral dust discharge.

C. Mechanism of Cyclone Operation

1. *Properties of the Vortex*

The common cyclone will be used as the basis for describing the cyclone vortex. The gas entering the tangential inlet near the top of the

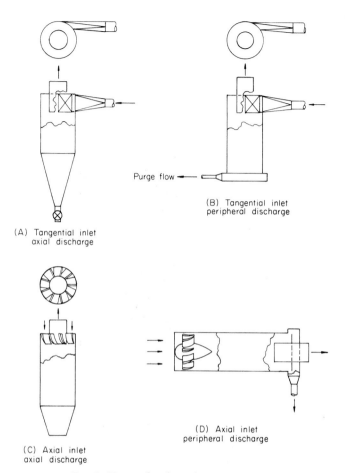

(B) Tangential inlet
peripheral discharge

(A) Tangential inlet
axial discharge

(D) Axial inlet
peripheral discharge

(C) Axial inlet
axial discharge

FIG. 1. Types of cyclones in common use.

cylindrical body creates a vortex or spiral flow downward between the walls of the gas discharge outlet and the body of the cyclone. This vortex, called the "main vortex," continues downward even below the walls of the gas outlet, and at some region near the bottom of the cone, the vortex reverses its direction of axial flow but maintains its direction of rotation, so that a secondary or inner vortex core is formed traveling upward to the gas outlet (Fig. 2).

The tangential velocity of gas in the vortex (V_t) increases as the radius decreases from the radius of the cylindrical body (R_p) to a maximum at some intermediate radius; and from this intermediate point inward to the axis of the cylinder the tangential velocity decreases.

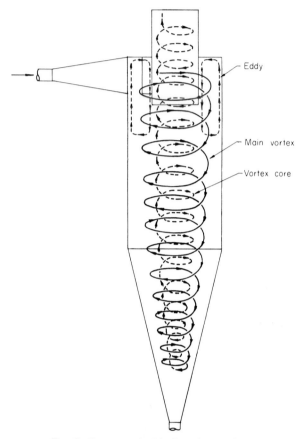

Eddy

Main vortex

Vortex core

FIG. 2. Vortex and eddy flows in a cyclone.

In the main vortex (*1*)

$$V_t = V_{tp} \left(\frac{R_p}{R}\right)^n \qquad (1)$$

where

V_t = tangential velocity at radius R, ft/sec
V_{tp} = tangential velocity at perimeter (body wall), ft/sec
R_p = radius of cyclone body, feet
R = radius, feet
n = exponent, dimensionless

For an ideal gas n would equal 1. Real values are between 0.5 and 1, depending upon the radius of the cyclone body and gas temperature.

The vortex core is generally smaller in diameter than the gas outlet. The radius of the core is between 0.2 and 0.4 times the radius of the gas outlet; and the radius of maximum tangential velocity is from 0.4 to 0.8 times the radius of the gas outlet (2).

In the annular space between the cyclone body and the gas outlet, near the top of the body where the tangential inlet enters, the tangential gas velocity increases uniformly from the body wall to the outlet wall and there is generally downward vortex flow. Because the radius of the

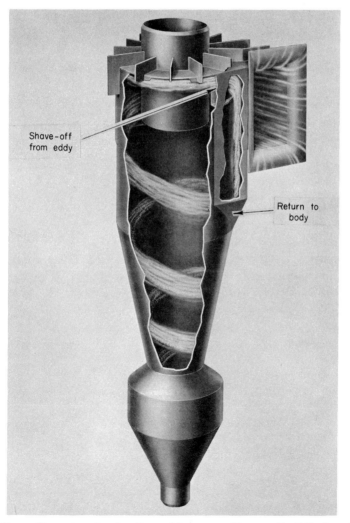

Fig. 3. Shave-off to reduce dust loss from eddy current. (Courtesy Buell Engineering Co.)

outlet is greater than the radius of maximum velocity, the gas does not attain the maximum velocity in the annulus that it can attain later in the main body of the cyclone. In addition, there is upward gas flow along the body wall surface near the top of the cylinder. This upward flow, known as an eddy, carries gas (and dust particles) up along the body wall, inward across the top, and downward along the gas outlet wall. From this point dust particles are lost into the gas outlet. The longer the gas outlet projection into the body, the more pronounced the eddy; elimination of the gas outlet protrusion, however, does not eliminate the eddy. Proprietary designs have been furnished to combat the effects of this eddy current as shown in Fig. 3. The axial inlet cyclone (Fig. 1) has no such eddy.

2. *Separation of Dust Particles in the Vortex*

Particulate matter is separated from the gas by centrifugal force which drives the particles toward the cyclone wall, across the stream lines of the gas flow. The radial force imparted to the particle is

$$F_s = \frac{M_p V_p^2}{gR} \tag{2}$$

where

F_s = separating force, pounds
M_p = particle mass, pounds
V_p = particle tangential velocity, ft/sec
g = gravitational constant, 32.2 ft/sec/sec
R = radius of rotation, feet

By assuming that the particle velocity is the same as the gas velocity in the tangential direction, and introducing the parameters for particle mass, the separating force becomes

$$F_s = \frac{\beta \rho_p D_p{}^3 V_{tp}{}^2 R_p^{2n}}{gR^{(2n+1)}} \tag{3}$$

where

ρ_p = particle density, lb/ft^3
D_p = particle diameter, feet
β = volume shape factor, dimensionless

It can be shown that the Stokes' law force resisting the motion of a particle through the gas in the particle size range 3–100 μ is

$$F_r = K\mu D_p u \tag{4}$$

where

F_r = frictional resistance to flow, pounds
K = proportionality constant, dimensionless
μ = gas viscosity, lb/ft-sec
u = particle velocity with respect to gas, ft/sec

Thus the separating force increases with the cube of the particle diameter but the resistance to particle flow toward the cyclone wall increases only linearly with the particle diameter. In any practical cyclone, the particulate matter is spread over the width of the dirty gas inlet, so that the radius of rotation, tangential velocity, and distance from the cyclone wall vary from the layer entering next to the outer wall of the cyclone to that nearest the wall of gas outlet. Therefore, the cyclone separator is a poor classifier and does not make a sharp size cut between particles separated and passed. Lapple (3) has presented an equation typical of those purported to permit calculation of the size particle which will be collected in a given cyclone. Many such equations have been proposed (1), and this is presented merely as typical, and to demonstrate the parameters involved.

$$D_{cp} = \sqrt{\frac{9 \, \mu W_i}{2 \, \pi N_e V_i (\rho_p - \rho)}} \qquad (5)$$

where

D_{cp} = "cut size," that size collected at 50% efficiency
μ = gas viscosity, lb/ft-sec
W_i = inlet width, feet
N_e = effective number of turns in cyclone (5 to 10 for typical cyclone)
V_i = gas inlet velocity, ft/sec
ρ_p = particle density, lb/ft^3
ρ = gas density, lb/ft^3

3. Discharge of Separated Dust

The application of centrifugal force to drive particles out of the gas stream toward the walls of a cyclone collector results in a concentrated dust layer swirling slowly down the walls of the cyclone body. The dust is yet to be finally separated from the gas stream. The purpose of the discharge is to retain the dust or liquid in a container and to prevent its reentrainment into the gas stream at the base of the vortex. The length and dimension ratios of the cyclone body and cone of course affect such reentrainment. Smoothness of the inner walls of the cyclone is essential to prevent small eddy currents which would bounce the dust layer out into the active zone of the vortex. Recirculation of gas or in-leakage of gas into the dust outlet will be harmful to attempts to discharge the dust without reentrainment, and conversely, a small purge flow of gas outward from the dust outlet will be helpful; similarly an air lock material discharge valve or dip leg is an aid to discharging dust without reentrainment.

Because the outlet duct for the gas discharge consists essentially of a cylinder to confine and conduct the vortex core out of the cyclone, any dust which escapes into this gas stream is still subjected to centrifugal forces and tends to be concentrated near the walls of the duct. Devices for skimming off the outside layer of this vortex can be employed to improve the overall efficiency of dust separation.

D. EFFICIENCY AND PRESSURE DROP OF CYCLONES

1. *General Conditions*

Cyclones **are** frequently divided into two classes, conventional and "high-efficiency." High efficiency cyclones merely have a smaller body diameter to achieve greater separating forces and there is no sharp dividing line between the two groups. High efficiency cyclones are generally considered to be those with body diameters up to about 9 inches.

Cyclones as a class of equipment provide the lowest collection efficiency as well as the lowest initial cost for devices in general commercial use to control particulate air pollution sources. Ranges of efficiency to be expected from cyclone collector installations are shown in Table I.

In general, efficiency will increase with increase in dust particle size or density, gas inlet velocity, cyclone body or cone length, and ratio of body diameter to gas outlet diameter. Conversely, efficiency will decrease with increase in gas viscosity or density, cyclone diameter, gas outlet diameter, and inlet width or inlet area.

TABLE I

EFFICIENCY RANGE OF CYCLONES

| Particle size range (μ) | Efficiency range (wt. % collected) | |
	Conventional	"High-efficiency"
Less than 5	Less than 50	50–80
5–20	50–80	80–95
15–40	80–95	95–99
Greater than 40	95–99	95–99

For a given cyclone arrangement, the resistance varies with the square of the air volume and therefore with the square of the inlet velocity. Since the velocity pressure or velocity head of a flowing gas also varies with the square of the velocity, it is convenient to express cyclone pressure drop in terms of the number of inlet velocity heads.

Unfortunately, changes in parameters which tend to increase collection efficiency also tend to increase pressure drop. The loss of pressure of the gas stream through the cyclone is on the order of one to four inlet velocity heads, with a resulting range of resistance from 1/4 to 8 inches water gage (wg). Most actual installations will show a resistance between 2 and 7 inches wg. Efficiency increases with increasing inlet velocity, but this increase is at a lower rate than the increase in pressure drop. In addition, for any practical installation there is a limiting value of inlet velocity above which turbulence causes a decrease in collection efficiency with further increase in inlet velocity.

The only practical upper limit to dust loadings occurs with the smaller body diameters of high efficiency cyclones, where as much as 10 to 15 grains per cubic foot of a fine or sticky dust may cause plugging of the narrow passages. For ordinary cyclones, there is no practical upper limit to the dust loadings and the efficiency increases with an increasing dust load. Even though the percent collected increases with increasing dust load, the total weight rate of contaminant discharged will be higher for higher inlet loadings because the efficiency increase is not nearly as rapid as is the increase in loading.

An extensive survey (*1*) was made of the various proposed equations for calculating cyclone pressure drops, and the most promising of these methods were tested against three different sets of field data which included 29 different cyclone installations. It was concluded that there was no known satisfactory method for predicting cyclone resistance from cyclone dimensions which was accurate over a wide range of different types of construction. For commercial units, pressure drop should be determined experimentally on a geometrically similar prototype. Where this is not possible, the following method developed by Alexander (*4*) is presented as being equivalent to other published methods and yielding results which are as good as can be obtained in the present state of the art.

According to Alexander, cyclone resistance is assumed to be a function of gas inlet area and outlet area in the form

$$\Delta P_c = \frac{C H_i W_i}{d_o^2} \tag{6}$$

where

ΔP_c = cyclone resistance, number of inlet velocity heads
C = proportionality constant
H_i = inlet height, feet
W_i = inlet width, feet
d_o = gas outlet diameter, feet

The proportionality constant C can be determined from

$$C = 4.62 \frac{R_o}{R_p} \left\{ \left[\left(\frac{R_p}{R_o} \right)^{2n} - 1 \right] \left(\frac{1 - n}{n} \right) + f \left(\frac{R_p}{R_o} \right)^{2n} \right\} \tag{7}$$

where

R_o = gas outlet radius, feet
R_p = body radius, feet
f = varies with n

n	0	0.2	0.4	0.6	0.8
f	1.90	1.94	2.04	2.21	2.40

The value of the exponent n can be determined from Fig. 4, and Eq. (7) has been reduced to graphical form in Fig. 5, p. 370.

2. Design Factors Affecting Efficiency and Pressure Drop

a. Body Diameter and Dimension Ratios. In the study of design parameters which affect efficiency and pressure drop, a typical cyclone has been selected as the starting point. The dimensions of the various body elements (Fig. 6) are based on the proportion of the dimension to the gas outlet diameter.

Starting with this design, a cyclone of higher efficiency and higher pressure drop could be designed by increasing the length of the cyclone, decreasing the inlet width, or increasing the ratio of body diameter to outlet diameter while at the same time providing a smaller body diameter.

The length of the cyclone body is of importance. An increase in length provides for a longer residence time of gas in the vortex and therefore for more revolutions or turns in the vortex. A very practical consideration involving the total length of the cyclone is that one of the most common defects leading to lower efficiency is reentrainment of dust into the vortex core from the region of the dust discharge port. The longer the cyclone below the gas outlet, the greater the opportunity for reentrained dust to be precipitated out of the vortex core before it enters the gas outlet.

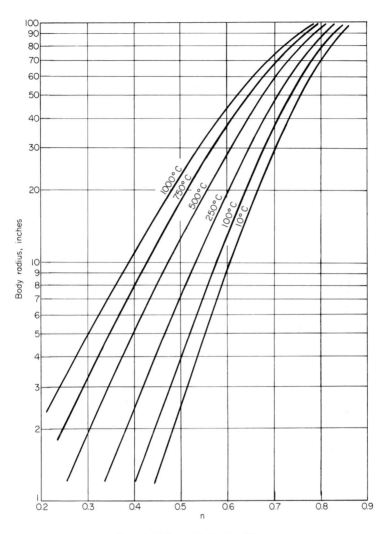

FIG. 4. Values of n in Eq. (7).

A number of investigators (4–7) have presented data or conclusions which are in substantial agreement that the height of the main vortex zone should be at least 5.5 times the gas outlet diameter, preferably more, perhaps up to 12 times the outlet diameter. The total length for the typical cyclone (Fig. 6) of 8 times the outlet diameter seems to meet these criteria. Contrary to general statements previously made, increasing the length of the cyclone without changing any other dimension

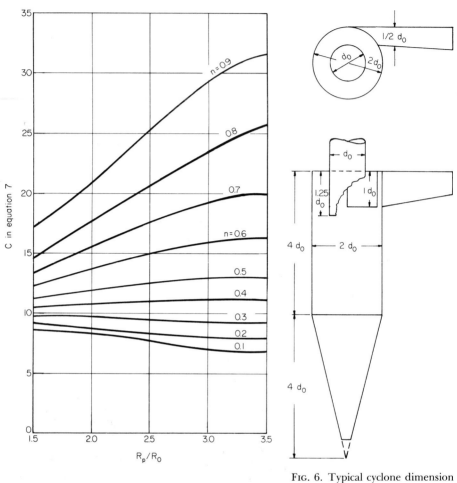

FIG. 5. Values of C in Eq. (7).

FIG. 6. Typical cyclone dimension ratios.

ratios will achieve an improvement in efficiency with no penalty in terms of increased pressure loss.

Increasing the ratio of the body diameter to the gas outlet diameter does show an increase in efficiency up to a ratio of about 3 with relatively small gain above that. On the other hand, there is a corresponding increase in pressure drop as this ratio increases so that the optimum ratio would appear to be between 2 and 3.

Theoretically, efficiency should continue to increase with a decrease in cyclone diameter, but this has not been proved in practice. In a very small cyclone, the gas outlet is dimensionally very close to the region where the dust is concentrated along the cyclone wall. Therefore any bouncing of large particles or local eddies caused by turbulence are more likely to result in accidental loss of dust to the gas outlet merely because the dimensions are so small. Furthermore, the corresponding dimensions of gas inlet and dust discharge are small, leading to practical difficulties with many industrial dust dispersions of a sticky nature.

b. Cone Design. The definition of a cyclone makes no mention of a cone. If a cone is present its design is important, but it is not necessary for a cyclone to have a cone. Neither is a cone essential to cyclone theory, since the main vortex will transform to the upflowing vortex core in a long cylinder without a cone. The various types of cyclones without a cone will be discussed later under the subject of dust discharge. However, a cone does serve the practical function of delivering the dust to a central point for ease in disposal, and forces the main vortex to transform to the vortex core in a shorter total length than would occur in a straight cylinder. In nature, the axis of a free vortex is frequently curved. A similar curvature or eccentricity of the vortex core has been observed in cyclone operation (8) and may amount to as much as one-fourth the gas outlet diameter. Theoretically, the diameter at the apex of the cone should be greater than one-fourth the gas outlet diameter to prevent the vortex core from touching the wall of the cone and reentraining collected dust. For cyclones of larger sizes, a cone apex of such dimensions may be unreasonable. This merely reemphasizes the need for adequate total cyclone length so that any dust reentrained at the cone apex may be separated again before it reaches the gas outlet.

c. Inlet Design. The design of the cyclone inlet is of critical importance to both cyclone efficiency and pressure drop. Unfortunately, little design data is available for the axial inlet type, since most cyclones of this design are proprietary. However, there has been much effort to experiment with the design of the tangential inlet to improve cyclone performance. The different types of common tangential inlets are shown in Fig. 7.

The helical inlet design is provided to impart a downward velocity to the gas to avoid interference between the incoming gas and the mass of gas already rotating in the annulus. Existing test data is conflicting as to whether or not this design actually does provide a lower pressure drop, and there is some indication that a lower efficiency is obtained. Most commercial cyclones do not have a helical inlet.

As the inlet gas enters the annular space between the cyclone body wall and the wall of the gas outlet duct, it undergoes a squeeze between the body wall and the rotating air mass already in the annulus. The involute inlet design has been developed to minimize the interference between these gas streams. Use of multiple involute inlets has the further ad-

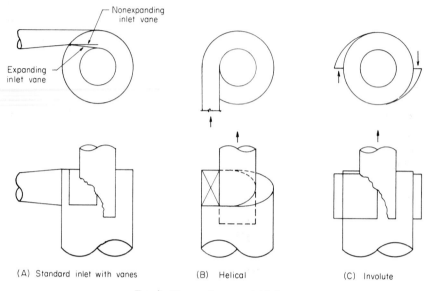

(A) Standard inlet with vanes   (B) Helical   (C) Involute

Fig. 7. Types of tangential inlets.

vantage that for the same inlet area and height, the inlet width is reduced.

No quantitative test data is available on the effects of multiple inlets on efficiency or pressure drop. However, in most practical cases, the multiple inlet designs involve small "high efficiency" cyclones where the inlet gas is taken from a plenum serving all inlets simultaneously. If practical, a bell-mouth inlet from the plenum to the cyclone inlets will reduce pressure loss and possibly improve efficiency.

The acceleration of gas associated with the previously described squeeze of gas entering the annulus is an important part of the total pressure loss of the cyclone. Inlet vanes (Fig. 7A) have been tried as a method of reducing this pressure loss. Nonexpanding inlet vanes result in one-half the pressure drop of the same cyclone without vanes; expanding vanes correspondingly in one-fourth the pressure drop. However, both of these types of inlet vanes decreased dust collection efficiency by preventing the formation of a vortex in the upper part of the annulus. Here again we are confronted with the dilemma of designs to decrease the pressure drop resulting in a corresponding decrease in efficiency. A cyclone is a device for the creation of a vortex, and it is the vortex that does the work in separating the particulate matter from the gas. Therefore it seems unwise to make modifications which are intended to, or which result in, suppressing the vortex.

The approach duct to a common cyclone is usually round, and if a proper inlet height-to-width ratio is to be obtained, the round duct must be transformed to a rectangular inlet. Such transformation should be gradual, if possible with a maximum included angle of 15° or less, in order to minimize shock losses if inlet velocity is increased from duct velocity. Similarly, if the inlet velocity is lower than the duct velocity, a gradual transformation will result in maximum static pressure regain. To conserve space an involute inlet can be used as shown in Fig. 7.

The orientation of the inlet duct is also important. If the inlet is downwardly inclined from the horizontal to a vertical axis cyclone, the pressure drop is increased and the efficiency is decreased (9). Although no supporting data is found, if is commonly assumed that an approach inclined upward will improve performance since it is the converse of the arrangement which decreased performance. It is also assumed that an elbow in the horizontal plane leading to a vertical axis cyclone will improve the cyclone performance if it is the same hand as the cyclone vortex, and will decrease performance if it is opposite hand.

d. Dust Discharge. It is essential in any cyclone design to remove the separated dust from the cyclone cone or body as immediately, completely, and continuously as possible. Many different schemes have been developed for accomplishing these results. The most simple system is a hopper or dust bin closed at the bottom and open at the top to the cyclone discharge. There will be a vortex in the bin as well as in the core. If this upflow is excessive, the normal discharge of dust is prevented. The vortex in the connection between the cyclone cone and dust bin can be suppressed by straightening vanes in the dust discharge pipe; or by baffles (disks or cones) installed about two dust discharge diameters above the apex of the cone so that there is approximately a 3-inch annular space between the edge of the baffle and the cone wall. An axial disk near the dust discharge is a trend toward the peripheral dust discharge cyclone design discussed later.

Another common method of minimizing upflow through the dust discharge pipe is to use some type of valve to prevent such flow. For most dust collection systems, where the negative pressure at the bottom of the cyclone is in the range of inches water gage, ordinary rotary valves are sufficiently gastight. If the negative pressure is higher, however, much better valving is required—usually a double set of valves which are capable of providing airtight closure in the presence of solids. Choke discharge screw conveyors may also be used at the bottom of a cyclone as a gas seal.

Various commercial designs of automatic flap valves are available, whereby the dust accumulates in the cyclone or in an intermediate position in the valve until its weight forces a counterweighted flap valve open. Since flap valves do not provide a positive closure, various mechanical improvements have been offered to upgrade their performance.

Cyclones inside of pressure vessels, for example in fluid catalytic crackers, may rely solely upon a full leg of dust, called a dip leg, to prevent reverse flow. Such dip legs are of course subject to plugging, and the location of the dip leg terminus so that the proper pressure relationships are obtained is frequently difficult. Dip legs are useful only where valves or other mechanisms would be inaccessible for service.

Since an inward flow of gas at the dust discharge is harmful, one method of correcting this situation is to install the cyclone at such a location in the system that it is under positive pressure with respect to the atmosphere or to the dust retention bin. Although this solves the problem of gas inflow at the dust discharge, it causes two other problems which may be of equal importance. First, the dust retention bin and disposal system may itself become a source of air pollution; second, such an arrangement requires the entire dust load to be handled by the fan, in many cases with excessive erosion or fan unbalance.

Inflow of gas at the dust discharge can also be prevented by installing an auxiliary fan to maintain a positive gas flow outward—commonly called "purge" flow. A purge flow of 10% of gas throughput may decrease dust emission from a relatively efficient cyclone by as much as 20–28% (6).

So many combinations of devices have been proposed and used at the dust discharge, with such varying degrees of success according to particular circumstances, that a summary evaluation of specific designs is impractical. However, the design of the dust discharge merits as much or more engineering attention as any other aspect of cyclone design. For successful operation, it is necessary to meet the criteria of immediate, complete, and continuous discharge of dust, with prevention of inflow, and if possible, inducement of outflow of gas through the dust discharge.

Peripheral discharge cyclones offer some advantages if dust discharge purge is to be used. With this design, the dust discharge area can frequently be made smaller than the dust discharge of a conventional cone bottom cyclone, with the result that the necessary volume of purge flow is reduced. A secondary advantage of purge flow is that the dust retention bin may be remotely located from the cyclone itself. In the Mark III Dunlab cyclone (Fig. 1B) the purge rate is normally 1% of the throughput (10). Another type of peripheral discharge, sometimes called "uniflow," has the gas and dust discharge at the same end. This has advantages in that there is no inlet eddy current and no reversal of gas flow in the axial direction. On the other hand, it requires higher purge rates, on the order of 25%, to attain high efficiency (5).

A method for skimming dust out of the eddy current at the inlet annulus has previously been described. The disposition of this small flow is of importance in connection with dust discharge. Some designs conduct the flow from the skimming slots to the dust bin under the bottom of the cyclone. The static pressure at the outer wall of the cyclone in the region of the annulus is higher than at any other zone, so the induced flow of gas to the dust bin would return upward from the dust bin through the main dust discharge, thus inducing an inflow of gas at a point where it is highly undesirable. It is preferable to make any connection from the slots in the annulus back into the body of the cyclone in the upper or central part of the main vortex zone. The pressure at the outer wall of the annulus is somewhat higher than at the wall lower in the body or cone. There is not much static pressure difference available to induce flow through such a skimming arrangement, but whatever flow is induced may be helpful and will not be harmful.

e. Gas Outlet Design. The eddy currents in the annulus of the cyclone require that the gas outlet have an extension into the body of the cyclone in order to minimize loss of dust through the gas outlet. The optimum length of the gas outlet extension has been determined (5) to be about one gas outlet diameter. It is also generally assumed that this extension should terminate slightly below the bottom of the gas inlet. The shorter the outlet extension into the cyclone, the lower the pressure drop attained. No outlet extension results in the lowest pressure loss, but dust collection efficiency under such circumstances will generally be unsatisfactory.

The gas flowing out of the gas outlet extension is in vortex flow, and therefore contains energy in excess of normal flow and also is continuing to separate dust from the stream by centrifugal force. Various devices have been developed for recovery of the pressure and energy in the outlet pipe. Those devices which consist of straightening vanes, baffles, etc., in or just below the gas outlet pipe achieve their energy recovery by suppressing the vortex; and as has been noted previously, this will also decrease the dust collection efficiency, and is undesirable. The most successful pressure recovery devices on the outlet are the involute scroll or the outlet drum as shown in Fig. 8. The involute scroll is designed as a conventional duct expansion wrapped around a circle, receiving the gases at high rotational velocity near the wall of the gas outlet pipe and converting the kinetic energy to static pressure by gradual expansion. The outlet drum operates somewhat as a cyclone in reverse tending to convert vortex flow back into linear flow. Outlet devices of this type can decrease the pressure drop of the cyclone from 5 to 10% without any detrimental effects on the dust collection efficiency.

The vortex in the gas outlet pipe also concentrates dust near the

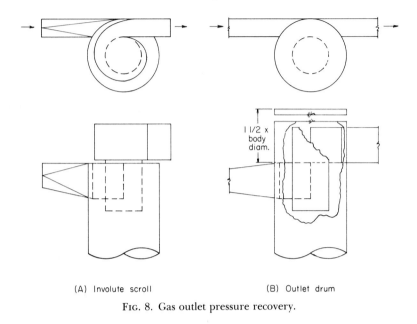

(A) Involute scroll   (B) Outlet drum

FIG. 8. Gas outlet pressure recovery.

wall of the outlet (*11*), and the installation of skimmers to shave off
the dust-rich layer can be used to further improve the collection efficiency. The practical problem is that there is no place in the cyclone
where the pressure relationships are proper so as to induce a flow from
a skimmer in this location to any place within the cyclone which will not
result in reentrainment of dust. The purge flow through such skimmers must be induced by a separate fan. The only practical further
treatment is to return it in a thin layer adjacent to the outer wall of the
inlet, or to handle the purge flow separately in smaller diameter cyclones
or some other type of high efficiency dust collector.

f. Effect of Internal Roughness. An extensive experimental and theoretical investigation of cyclone design and performance (*2*) resulted in the
conclusion that the wall friction in the cyclone was a negligible portion
of the pressure drop. The pressure drop is due almost entirely to the
vortex, and to the design of the inlet and gas outlet. Increased roughness
of the internal wall of the cyclone, probably by the inducement of local
eddy currents and increased local wall friction, reduces vortex intensity,
with the overall result that cyclone pressure drop is reduced. Dust
collection efficiency is also reduced.

An experiment (*12*) wherein coatings of sand particles of definite
sizes were applied to the wall of the cyclone showed that the cyclone

pressure drop was reduced from 8 inlet velocity heads with a smooth wall to 4.1 velocity heads with a heavy coating of sand of 0.5- to 1.0-mm particle size. Another experiment where 1/2-inch diamond mesh liner was applied to a cyclone collecting fly ash at 3500 ft/min inlet velocity showed a decreasing collection efficiency with an increase in the amount of internal area lined with diamond mesh, as shown in the tabulation.

Area lined (%)	Collection efficiency (%)
0	87.5
11.6	86.1
75.5	81.9
87.0	78.0

Roughness at the cyclone wall will cause local eddy currents to carry dust away from the wall and defeat any effort to concentrate it at the wall and separate it from the gas stream. All seams should be ground smooth on the inside or consist of carefully matched flanged joints. If access doors are provided in the cyclone body, they should be designed so that there is a minimum crack and so that the inner surface of the door is flush with the inner cyclone surface. A buildup of adhesive dust sticking to the internal wall surface, or erosive wear of the metallic surfaces, will also result in surface roughness. No data is available as to the quantitative effect of this degree of roughness. Certain types of cyclones are lined with erosion-resistant refractory linings, and if this lining were to fail, exposing the metal mesh or ties used to hold the lining in place, the effect on efficiency would almost certainly be quite large.

E. EFFECT OF OPERATING VARIABLES ON CYCLONE PERFORMANCE

1. *Flow Rate*

The pressure drop theoretically varies with the square of the flow rate and therefore with the square of the inlet velocity. This is the reasoning behind the expression of cyclone pressure drop in terms of the number of inlet velocity heads. Experimentally, deviations have been found (*1*). For example, the exponent of flow rate in a test of pressure drop on 13 different cyclone designs resulted in values ranging from 1.5 to over 2.0. However, out of the 13 designs, 8 of them exhibited exponents of flow rate in the range of 1.75 to 2.0. Unless there is test data to show otherwise, it is customary to assume that pressure drop varies with the square of flow rate.

Pressure drop through a given cyclone also varies with the properties of the gas, as will be discussed later.

Variation in flow rate also has a marked effect on efficiency. Efficiency increases with increasing flow rate up to some limiting velocity, above which the internal turbulence increases more rapidly than the separation, thus causing a decrease in efficiency with further increase in flow rate. This limiting velocity is not a troublesome problem in most practical designs, because it generally occurs at velocities above 4000–5000 ft/min, in a range where the pressure drop would be excessive anyway.

There is wide disagreement as to the quantitative relationship of efficiency with inlet velocity. In an analysis of all available data (1) the following conclusions were reached.

1. As inlet velocity is increased from zero, there is at first a substantially straight-line increase in efficiency. The slope of the line is steeper for larger particles and for small cyclones than it is for finer particles and larger cyclones. This straight line continues to about 70% of the maximum efficiency obtainable, after which the slope decreases rapidly. Cyclones are almost never used in this portion of the curve.

2. Following the initial portion of straight-line efficiency increase, the line gradually decreases in slope until it becomes essentially flat. The inlet velocity at which the curve becomes essentially flat is lower for small-diameter cyclones and large particles. In most cyclone applications, the flat portion of the curve is never reached.

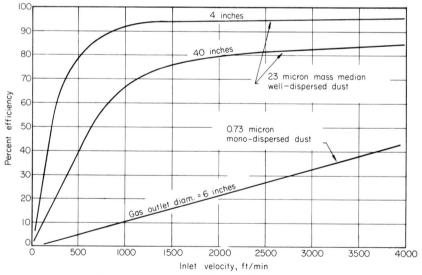

FIG. 9. Variation of efficiency with inlet velocity.

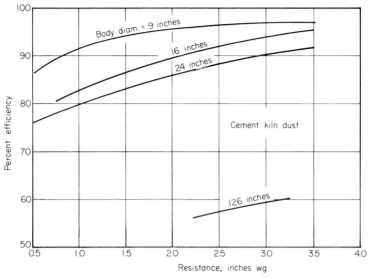

FIG. 10. Variation of efficiency with pressure drop.

3. In many practical installations, the variation of efficiency with inlet velocity is masked by an increase of particle size or an increase of dust loading with flow rate, both of which independently affect efficiency. Other variables, such as the presence or absence of agglomerates, also affect efficiency and frequently are affected by flow rate in a given installation.

4. Plots of cyclone efficiency vs. pressure drop are more useful for cyclone selection than are plots of efficiency vs. flow. Typical curves of the various parameters discussed are shown in Figs. 9 and 10.

5. Specific test data for the cyclone and dust in question is to be preferred over any other method of estimating. However, in the absence of such data, variation of efficiency with flow rate over short ranges of flow may be estimated by Eq. (8).

$$\frac{100 - \eta_a}{100 - \eta_b} = \left(\frac{Q_b}{Q_a}\right)^{0.5} \tag{8}$$

where

η_a = collection efficiency, weight percent at condition a
η_b = collection efficiency, weight percent at condition b
Q_b = flow, ft^3/min at condition b
Q_a = flow, ft^3/min at condition a

2. *Physical Properties of the Gas*

The pressure drop of a cyclone is affected by the temperature, density, and pressure of the gas as shown in Eq. (9).

$$h = \frac{KQ^2 p \rho_g}{T} \tag{9}$$

h = pressure drop, inches water gage
K = proportionality constant
Q = flow rate, ft³/min
p = absolute pressure, atmospheres
ρ_g = gas density, lb/ft³
T = absolute temperature °R

The viscosity of the gas through which the dust particle must be driven to the cyclone wall obviously will have an effect on collection efficiency. The viscosity of gases increases with increasing temperature and correspondingly the efficiency will decrease with increasing temperature, all other factors being constant. This has been verified by several experimenters.

On the basis of formulas for critical size of particles separated, the relation between efficiency and gas viscosity at constant flow rate may be estimated by Eq. (10).

$$\frac{100 - \eta_a}{100 - \eta_b} = \left(\frac{\mu_a}{\mu_b}\right)^{0.5} \tag{10}$$

where μ = viscosity at conditions a and b, any consistent units

Although the density of the gas is theoretically a factor in separation of particles, its value is so small compared to particle density that for most practical cases any variation in gas density is negligible. Of course, at very high pressure or density it should be taken into consideration. The relationship between efficiency and gas density may be estimated by Eq. (11).

$$\frac{100 - \eta_a}{100 - \eta_b} = \left(\frac{\rho_p - \rho_{gb}}{\rho_p - \rho_{ga}}\right)^{0.5} \tag{11}$$

where

ρ_p = density of dust particle, lb/ft³
ρ_g = density of gas at condition a and b, lb/ft³

3. *Properties of the Dust*

The properties of the dust to be collected represent the most important variable in cyclone efficiency, and are probably the most difficult to evaluate. Many physical properties of the dust will affect the efficiency, but the only ones that have been investigated quantitatively are particle size and particle density. Other physical and chemical properties which make the dust hard or easy to handle will also affect the practical aspects of cyclone operation. These aspects are discussed later in terms of erosion and fouling in cyclones.

The particle-size distribution of a dust should be expressed as a mass distribution if cyclone efficiency is to be considered on a weight basis. Manipulation of various types of particle-size distribution data, as well as the determination of particle size, are involved and complicated subjects which are referred to detailed discussions (*13, 14*).

A new standard method for determining the properties of dust has been published by the American Society of Mechanical Engineers as Power Test Code 28 (1965). This method standardizes the determination of fractional settling velocity of a dust, as well as the determination of particle specific gravity. Settling velocity, taking into account particle density and shape as well as particle size, is more meaningful in relation to cyclone efficiency than is particle size alone, because these additional factors also affect the separation of particles in the cyclone. Manipulation of fractional efficiency data to obtain total efficiency is identical whether the fractional size units are in terms of microns or settling velocity.

The advantages of the settling velocity method are:

1. It is more valid technically for cyclone collectors and other equipment dependent primarily on centrifugal or inertial forces.
2. The method of analysis is much more rapid, and requires less skill, than a microscopic determination of particle size.

The new method has not yet gained widespread acceptance, and during the changeover period, conversion may be made between micron particle size and settling velocity by a method also described in Power Test Code 28, which also requires a knowledge of the particle density and certain assumptions concerning particle shape.

Any realistic consideration of the effect of particle size on cyclone efficiency requires a fractional efficiency curve for the type of cyclone in question which can be obtained only from test data (Fig. 11). The fractional efficiency curve should also specify all the other factors affecting the performance such as the gas, temperature, pressure, dust load, nature of dust, true density of dust particles, and any unusual characteristics of the dust.

If the fractional efficiency curve of the cyclone and the size distribution of the dust to be collected are known, the overall collection efficiency may be calculated. Using the particle-size data in Fig. 12 and the

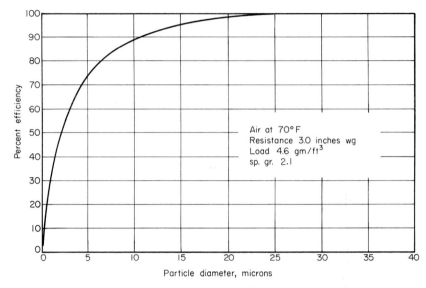

FIG. 11. Typical fractional efficiency curve.

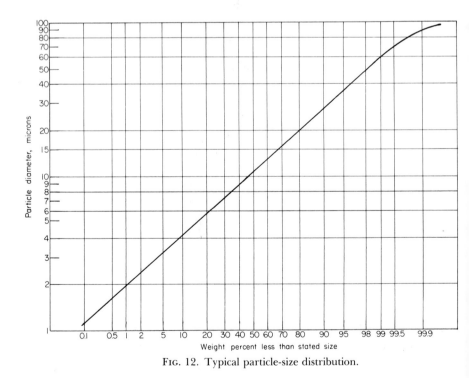

FIG. 12. Typical particle-size distribution.

TABLE II
Calculation of Overall Efficiency from Fractional Efficiency and Particle-Size Data

1 Weight percent less than size	2 Size (μ)	3 Efficiency for size
0.1	1.1	32
0.5	1.6	40
1.0	1.9	47
2.0	2.4	55
5.0	3.2	62
10.0	4.2	68
20.0	5.9	78
30.0	7.3	83
40.0	8.8	87
50.0	10.7	90
60.0	13.0	93
70.0	15.5	96
80.0	19.8	98
90.0	27.2	99.5
95.0	35.5	100
98.0	48.0	100
99.0	58.0	100
99.5	69.0	100
99.9	87.0	100

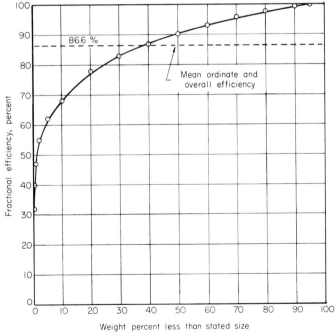

Fig. 13. Total efficiency graph (from Table II).

fractional efficiency curve of Fig. 11, the particle size corresponding to various intervals of the size distribution is tabulated (columns 1 and 2 of Table II). The corresponding efficiency for that particle size is taken from Fig. 11 and tabulated as column 3. Column 1 is plotted against column 3 as shown in Fig. 13. The area under the curve may be determined by graphical integration, and the mean ordinate determined. The mean ordinate represents the total dust collection efficiency of the cyclone for the size distribution of the dust considered.

Test data which gives the overall collection efficiency for a specified dust and does not give the fractional efficiency data is useful for extrapolation to other dusts only if the particle-size distributions and particle shapes of both dusts are closely similar. Corrections for other factors such as particle density, dust load, gas characteristics, etc., can be made. No correction can be made for differences in particle-size distribution if the fractional efficiency curve of the cyclone is not known.

In the absence of test data, cyclone efficiency may be only crudely estimated. A rough approximation of the efficiency may be obtained by determining the cut size [Eq. (5)] and assuming the overall collection efficiency will be equal to the cumulative percentage of the dust larger than the cut size.

The efficiency of cyclone dust collection is greater for particles of high density than for low density. Although theoretically the efficiency might be expected to vary as the square root of particle density, ex-

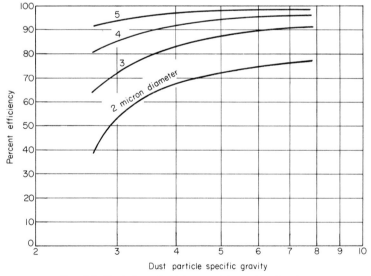

FIG. 14. Variation of efficiency with particle density.

perimental data (15) does not confirm this, as shown in Fig. 14. In all considerations of efficiency, it is the true density of the particle, and not the bulk density of the dust, that is of importance.

4. Dust Loading

Increased inlet dust loading to a cyclone causes the pressure drop to be lower and the efficiency to be increased. Apparently the pressure drop at a heavy dust load of 75–100 grains/ft³ will be in the range of 75–85% of that with essentially clean air. One author (16) gives an equation for this relationship as:

$$\Delta P_d = \frac{\Delta P_c}{0.013 \sqrt{C_i} + 1} \tag{12}$$

where

ΔP_d = pressure drop with dust load
ΔP_c = pressure drop with clean air
C_i = inlet dust concentration, grains/ft³

Dust collection efficiency increases with dust loading. At very high loadings, all cyclones have relatively high percentage efficiencies although the gas discharge still contains progressively higher dust loadings. Apparently the details of design become less important to efficiency as loading increases, but because erosion and plugging become more important factors, cyclones are designed to overcome those problems. Therefore, small-diameter cyclones are seldom used for very heavy dust loads.

At very high loadings, the movement of the larger dust particles toward the cyclone wall creates an air drag which also sweeps some of the finer particles in the same direction. In addition, there is some impaction of large particles on small particles. A less important reason is the fact that a higher inlet velocity is obtainable at the same pressure drop because the higher dust loading results in a lower pressure drop than would be the case with clean air. W. A. Baxter has developed the following equation from an analysis of 15 different studies of dust loading vs. collection efficiency.

$$\frac{100 - \eta_a}{100 - \eta_b} = \left(\frac{C_{bi}}{C_{ai}}\right)^{0.182} \tag{13}$$

where
η = efficiency at conditions a and b
C = inlet concentration at conditions a and b, grains/ft³

5. Parallel Cyclone Operation

Where high efficiency cyclones are used, it is customary to operate a number of them in parallel in order to achieve practical gas volume. If the number of cyclones in parallel is small, each cyclone should have its own inlet and its own dust bin. The inlet should be a well-designed duct branch from the dust collection header, arranged so as to provide relatively uniform distribution of gas and dust to each of the cyclones. The gas outlets may be direct to the atmosphere or may be manifolded together into a common duct.

When the number of cyclones in parallel is large, the only practical arrangement is to use a common inlet plenum chamber, a common dust bin, and a common outlet plenum chamber. Under such circumstances, new operating problems arise. To obtain efficiencies near those obtainable with a single tube of the same size, it is necessary to equalize the gas and dust load distribution to the cyclones to prevent backflow through individual cyclones, plugging of cyclones, or reentrainment from the dust bin. Although in many practical installations is has been observed that the efficiency of a bank of parallel cyclones is noticeably less than for an individual tube, if all these problems are prevented, it is possible to obtain essentially the same efficiency.

The inlet and outlet plenums and the dust bin should be designed so that the pressure relationship between these three chambers is essentially the same at all portions of the housing. High plenum velocities, poor manifold layouts, or variations in tube sizes or shape will cause excessive flow through some tubes and backflow through others. Obviously if backflow occurs from the dust bin up through the gas discharge opening of a tube, the collection efficiency of that tube will be nil.

If the dust discharge of any of the individual tubes should plug, that particular tube will begin to pass 100% of the dust entering its inlet. The dust outlet of tubes may be plugged by collected dust in the hopper below building up to that point. Therefore dust bin design should take into account the fact that the dust may not be uniformly deposited but may be banked up against one wall.

One of the ways of minimizing dust outlet plugging in parallel cyclone operation is to provide a small purge out of the dust collection hopper. This is accomplished by using a separate purge fan which returns the flow either to the common inlet plenum or to a separate collector. Purge rates in this application are usually about 5% of the total gas flow.

If it is necessary to valve off individual cyclones in a parallel arrangement in order to maintain efficiency at reduced gas loading, it is necessary to close both the inlet and the outlet in order to prevent entrainment of dust from the bin through the dust outlet and gas outlet. In a large

FIG. 15. Typical bank of small-diameter, high efficiency cyclones. (Courtesy Research-Cottrell, Inc.)

installation involving a number of plenums and hoppers, entire plenums should be valved off.

A typical arrangement of multiple, small-diameter high efficiency cyclones is shown in Fig. 15.

6. Series Cyclone Operation

The efficiency of two cyclone dust collectors operating in series on the gas flow is expressed by Eq. (14).

$$\eta = \eta_p + \eta_s(100 - \eta_p) \tag{14}$$

where

η = efficiency of the combination of both cyclones

η_p = efficiency of the primary cyclone

η_s = efficiency of the secondary cyclone (based on the inlet dust load to it)

Previous discussion has indicated the difficulty of calculating cyclone efficiency in the absence of test data. The calculation of the efficiency of the second cyclone in series is even more difficult. The second cyclone serves to separate particles which could have been but were not collected in the first cyclone owing to statistical distribution across the inlet, accidental reentrainment due to roughness or eddy currents, or reentrainment in the vortex core. The efficiency of the second cyclone will be less than that of the first cyclone. It is frequently assumed that the efficiency of the second cyclone is half that of the first in series. It has been shown (17) that the total collection efficiency of one cyclone, operated at an inlet velocity such that its pressure drop is equal to the total of two geometrically similar cyclones in series, is higher for the single cyclone than for the two in series. It is known that cyclones have a limit in ability to increase efficiency with increasing inlet velocity, so the range of velocities over which this relationship holds must also be subject to a similar limit.

Sometimes conditions prevail which make the use of series cyclones advantageous for practical reasons. Examples of such circumstances are:

1. Dust agglomerates which are fragile and subject to degradation of particle size at high velocities may be collected more advantageously in two cyclones in series at low velocities.

2. A primary large-diameter cyclone may be used to collect coarse material which would otherwise foul the smaller passages of more efficient small-diameter secondary cyclones.

3. If dependable operation is paramount, cyclones in series may be used so that a large degree of dust collection is maintained even if the dust outlet of the primary cyclone plugs. If this were to happen, the secondary cyclone then acts as a primary cyclone as far as collection efficiency is concerned. Three cyclones in series is the maximum number that has been used commercially, and this only under very severe service conditions as typified by fluid catalytic cracking.

Cyclone collectors are frequently successful when installed in series with other types of dust-collecting equipment. One of the most common applications is to install high efficiency cyclones ahead of electrostatic precipitators. In an installation of this kind, the cyclone exhibits an increased efficiency with an increase of gas load and/or dust loads; on the other hand, the precipitator shows an increase in efficiency with a reduced gas load or dust load. Thus the characteristics of the two types of equipment compensate for each other with a tendency to maintain a good efficiency over a wide range of gas flow and dust loading.

F. EROSION IN CYCLONES

Erosion in cyclones is caused by the impingement and rubbing of dust particles on the cyclone wall. Erosion is worse with high dust loadings, high inlet velocities, and large or hard dust particles. Any defect in cyclone design or operation which tends to concentrate dust moving at high velocity will accelerate erosion.

The areas most subject to erosive wear are those along welded seams or mismatched flange seams, near the bottom of the cone; and opposite the inlet. Surface irregularities at welded joints, and the annealing softening of metal adjacent to the weld will induce rapid wear in the weld region. Welded seams should be kept to a minimum, and heat-treated if necessary to maintain the hardness of the metal adjacent to the weld.

The importance of proper dust discharge has been stressed previously in discussions of efficiency. It is similarly important in preventing erosion. If dust is not effectively and continuously discharged from the bottom of the cone, a high circulating dust load is maintained in that region, leading to excessive wear of the cone. If the dust outlet should plug, the entire circulating dust load is conducted through the cyclone, including the gas discharge pipe, and it may cause erosive wear at any point.

Excessive wear of the cyclone shell opposite the inlet may occur, particularly if large particles are handled. This can be cured by the provision of removable wear plates of abrasive-resistant metal or rubber designed so as to be flush with the inside surface of the shell.

Combinations of dust loading and velocity which will, if exceeded, induce erosion have been shown in the tabulation (1).

Dust load (grains/ft³)	Velocity (ft/min)
0.3	7000
3.0	4000
3000	400

It has also been determined that typical dust particles smaller than the 5- and 10-μ range do not cause appreciable erosion.

It is possible to design a cyclone to reduce erosion by increasing the diameter of the cyclone body without increasing the diameter of the gas outlet. This results in reduced velocity at the body wall without reducing maximum velocities and separating force of the vortex. It also results in increased pressure drop. Consequently, at high loadings of abrasive dust, large-diameter cyclones are required to control erosion. For more moderate conditions, small-diameter cyclones have an advantage since they usually do not have seams or welds.

Erosion-resistant linings consisting of a troweled or cast refractory may be used. Such linings are usually 5/8 to 1 inch thick and must be supported by metal mesh or ties. It is necessary to maintain the integrity of such refractory linings to maintain efficiency and it is recommended that inlet velocities be kept below the range of 60–75 ft/sec if such linings are used.

G. Fouling in Cyclones

Fouling of cyclones results in decreased efficiency, increased erosion, and increased pressure drop. Fouling is generally found to occur either by plugging of the dust outlet or by the buildup of materials on the cyclone wall.

Dust outlets become plugged by large pieces of extraneous material in the system, by the overfilling of the dust bin, or by the spalling of material caked upon the walls of the cyclone. The valves used to discharge dust from the collection bin should not be smaller than 4 inches in most applications, and in all except the large pneumatic conveying or fluidized bed applications need not be larger than 14 inches. A vertical axis cyclone is somewhat less subject to plugging of the dust outlet because gravity helps to remove large objects through the discharge.

It is of utmost importance to prevent overfilling of dust hoppers, particularly under multiple banks of small-diameter cyclones. If a hopper has filled sufficiently to plug the outlets and later has been emptied, the dust plugs may remain in the outlets. In large-diameter cyclones, cleanout openings can be provided, but this is not practical for large banks of small-diameter tubes.

The buildup of sticky materials on the wall of the cyclone is primarily a function of the dust. In general, the finer and softer the dust, the greater the tendency to cake on the wall. Chemical and physical properties will also affect this behavior. Condensation of moisture on the walls of the cyclone will also contribute to the accumulation of material. In many cases, buildup of sticky material on the walls can be minimized by keeping the inlet velocity above 50 ft/sec. Smoothness of the cyclone walls is also important, and some applications have even used electro-polished walls to minimize the buildup of powdered milk or coffee dust.

The cure for excessive wall buildup frequently must be tailored to meet the particular circumstance. In one case, the removal of an inertial precleaner so as to permit the coarser material to also traverse the cyclone walls may present a cure; in another, periodically inducing a reverse gas flow from the dust bin by the introduction of compressed air to the bin may be successful. If wall condensation is the cause, it must be eliminated by insulation or other appropriate methods. In some cases, the use of water or other fluids is necessary to wash accumulations out of the tubes. As far as the design is concerned, the important features to minimize fouling are good removal of dust from the dust discharge, adequate size of dust bin discharge, prevention of dust bin overfilling, choice of proper inlet velocity, and prevention of wall condensation.

H. WET CYCLONES

1. Problems of Definition

Most types of commercial gas-cleaning equipment utilize, either accidentally or by design, more than one of the possible theoretical mechanisms for separating particulate matter. This leads to difficulty in classifying the numerous types of equipment. Cyclones and inertial separators, when operated wet, cannot avoid some droplet collision phenomena associated with wet scrubbers; and furthermore, various features of the construction or appurtenances may be modified to adapt the equipment to handling liquid or slurry. For the purposes of this discussion, however, wet cyclones are defined as equipment which meets the basic definition of a cyclone, and is handling liquid, whether in the form of droplet or mist contamination of the entering gas, or deliberately introduced sprays or flushing streams.

2. Droplet Collection

Cyclones are frequently used for removal of liquid droplet contamination of a gas stream. Practically 100% collection can be obtained for droplets of 100 μ and over, typical of entrainment from boiling liquids. Efficiency of well-designed wet cyclones range from 95 to 99% for reasonably light loadings of 5- to 50-μ droplets and 99% or more with heavy loadings of droplets over 50 μ.

Various proprietary designs of devices known as cyclone scrubbers consist of a primary device designed to wet the dust particles by impaction and a secondary cyclone serving to collect the droplet dispersion. These devices are usually considered scrubbers since the major objective in design is to wet the particles. Large amounts of power are required to achieve artificial droplet suspensions on the order of 100 μ in size, and the cyclone portion of such scrubbers is usually simple in design and effective in performance.

3. *Wet Operation for Dry Dust*

Cyclones operated wet for the collection of dry dust improve efficiency, prevent wall buildup and fouling, and reduce erosion. The efficiency is considerably higher because the dust particles are trapped in a liquid film and are not easily reentrained. The usual application of water to an otherwise dry cyclone consists of spraying countercurrent to the gas flow in the inlet duct, at water rates of from 5 to 15 gal/min per 1000 ft³/min capacity. Additional sprays may be installed in the duct upstream of the cyclone inlet if desired.

Care must be exercised to direct spray nozzle patterns and flushing streams so that no portion of the cyclone or duct is merely moist, since this condition will lead to caking and plugging. Troublesome areas will be the inlet duct, the dust discharge, and under some conditions, the gas outlet. If the cyclone is cone-bottom, swirl patterns in the lower part of the cone may concentrate the water streams, leaving unflushed areas between them, and auxiliary flushing may be needed.

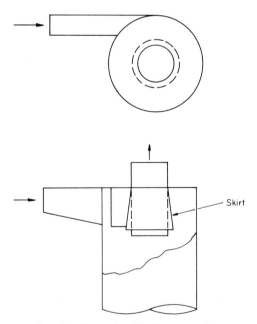

Fig. 16. Gas outlet skirt for wet cyclones.

4. *Preventing Reentrainment from Wet Cyclones*

Reentrainment from a wet cyclone is very deleterious to its efficiency, but is rather easily prevented. It is necessary to continuously and completely drain the liquid from the bottom of the cyclone in order to prevent the vortex core from shearing droplets off the axial peak of liquid, which would occur if it were retained in the bottom of the cyclone. If the tangential wall velocity is high enough, it can shear the film from the wall in droplets too small to be recollected. An inlet velocity of 150 ft/sec maximum is recommended for atmospheric air and water, and corresponding maximum tangential velocities for other combinations.

Excessively high liquid loadings sometimes give difficulty, probably because the vortex of gas is suppressed. The recommended solution for a problem of this nature is to reduce the inlet gas velocity or to install cyclones in series.

One of the most common causes of reentrainment from wet cyclones is the shearing of droplets from a liquid film which tends to creep along the walls to the gas outlet lip. A cylindrical or conical baffle installed around the gas outlet extension (as shown in Fig. 16) provides a point for the liquid to drop, or to be sheared off while still in the separating zone of the vortex.

Care should be taken to prevent the impingement of the inlet gas stream on such a skirt.

5. *Advantages and Disadvantages of Wet Operation*

The operation of cyclones as wet collectors for the removal of droplets, or even for the collection of dry dust, presents a number of advantages provided that the droplet size is sufficiently large and that reentrainment of liquid from the cyclone is prevented. The liquid droplets collect on the cyclone wall and form a continuous film which is less subject to reentrainment in the gas stream than is a dispersion of dry dust. In addition, liquid can be drained from any point in the cyclone bottom, thus permitting a location away from the axis of the vortex core. Gas flow into the liquid outlet can be completely prevented by a simple liquid leg seal. Under such conditions wet cyclones operate with a higher efficiency and less erosion and plugging difficulties than do dry cyclones.

The major disadvantage of wet cyclone operation is caused by the corrosion problem. If corrosive dusts or gases are handled, the presence of water usually makes the problem that much worse. Other fluids may be advantageous but are more expensive. The other disadvantage to the wet operation of cyclones is the additional cost of water, and the cost of recirculating or disposing of the contaminated water.

I. Scope of Cyclones in Field Use

1. Range of Efficiency

The range of efficiency of cyclones in field use is as shown in Table I. If operated wet, a conventional cyclone will yield efficiencies comparable to that of the high efficiency cyclone. For practical reasons, banks of multiple high efficiency tubes are seldom operated wet. Cyclones are frequently of great practical value in minimizing air pollution sources if the dust dispersion is not too fine and if the contaminant is not highly valuable, or highly toxic.

Efficiencies can be improved by design changes which usually result in higher pressure drop. No designs are available which yield a very high efficiency on very fine contaminant dispersions.

2. Range of Pressure Drop

Pressure drop through cyclones under field conditions usually ranges between one and four inlet velocity heads, corresponding to 1–7 inches water gage. Pressure drop increases with the square of the inlet velocity and efficiency also increases, but not as rapidly as pressure drop. All devices intended to minimize pressure drop result in decreased efficiency except those which recover the energy in the vortex flow leaving the gas outlet.

3. Range of Loading and Operating Conditions

Cyclones can be designed to handle any dust loads and the percentage collection efficiency increases with increasing dust loads. However, at loads above a few hundred grains per cubic foot, erosive and plugging conditions become severe and only large-diameter cyclones are practical. Cyclone efficiency decreases with a decreasing dust load, and cyclones are seldom applied to applications below 1 grain/ft³. The dust load entering a cyclone can be reduced by the installation of settling chambers or inertial traps upstream of the cyclone, but this is seldom found necessary in practice.

Cyclone dust collectors can be made of any reasonable material of construction and have no moving parts. Consequently, as a class, they can be designed to handle a wider range of chemical and physical conditions than most other types of collecting equipment. Sticky materials which tend to block the air passages or dust passages in cyclones present one of the main limiting factors in their application. Many such problems can be solved by operating the cyclone wet, and others may be solved by using large-diameter cyclones as a precleaner ahead of a bank of small-diameter high-efficiency tubes.

III.   Rotary Stream Dust Separator

A. DEFINITION AND DESCRIPTION

Although not conforming exactly to the definition of a cyclone collector, the recently developed rotary stream dust separator (drehströmungstauber) is basically akin to the cyclone in that it uses primarily centrifugal forces in a confined vortex, and is without moving parts. It may be defined as a cylindrical flow tube in which the main gas stream forms an inner vortex, opposed by a secondary outer vortex flowing in the same tangential direction but in the opposite axial direction, so that the combined centrifugal forces and radial gas flows concentrate the dust particles in an annular ring. A typical device is shown in Fig. 17. The bulk of the description and performance data given below is from Klein (*18*) with additional material from Nickel (*19*), Schaufler (*20*), and Schmidt (*21*).

B. MECHANISM OF OPERATION

The entering dusty gas passes through the annular space between the dobbas and the inside walls of the inlet port. The inside diameter of the inlet port increases slightly toward the open end, and the presence of the dobbas stabilizes the flow pattern and aids in establishing the inner vortex at a lower point in the tube. The outer vortex caused by the secondary air jets creates a vortex pattern of flow in the entering gas.

The secondary air jets, entering at a tangential angle near the top of the tube, create an outer vortex ("potential flow") with a downward axial component and an inward radial component. This potential flow creates an inner vortex ("rotational flow") in the same direction of rotation but with an upward axial component. The result of these forces is the concentration of the dust in an annular space, called the "mixed flow" region. This dust-rich layer is conducted downward, outside the lips of the inlet port, and into the dust bunker below (or withdrawn separately) as part of a purge flow, with a compensating return flow from the bunker to the dirty gas inlet.

The baffle ring at the top serves to block the portion of the uppermost jet flow that would otherwise escape from the top of the tube, and markedly improves the efficiency.

Typical dimensions of a 200-mm diameter experimental tube are shown in Fig. 18.

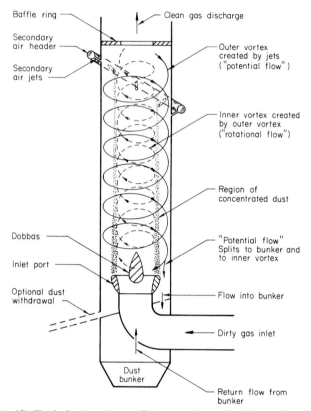

FIG. 17. Typical rotary stream dust separator and major gas flows.

C. Efficiency and Pressure Drop

Two pressures are involved—the pressure loss in the main gas stream, and the pressure required for optimum operation of the secondary air jets. For a 200-mm diameter unit handling 500 m³/hour (300 cfm) of dusty gas, the jet pressure used was 480 mm water gage, resulting (according to the investigators) in a total "equivalent" pressure drop of 200 mm (approximately 8 inches) water gage. Under these conditions, using various test dusts, the following efficiencies were obtained:

Particle size frequency maximum, microns	% Collection efficiency
2.5	92
5	95
10	98.5

Fractional efficiencies are stated to be 100% for 5-μ particles and 90% for 1-μ particles, of density 2.65 grams/cm³.

The efficiency variation with dust load is negligible over the range of 1 to 200 grains/m³ (0.4–88 grains/ft³). This is attributed to the fact that the dust is introduced near the zone of separation, and is separated in a space filled with well-defined and controllable flow patterns, without deleterious eddy currents.

The amount of bleed flow conducting the dusty concentrate out of the tube affects the efficiency. Again in the 200-mm diameter tube treating 500 m³/hour of gas, a bleed flow of 10 m³/hour (2%) resulted in 88% efficiency, while a bleed flow of 50 m³/hour (10%) yielded 92.5%. Further increases in bleed flow lowered efficiency, because the vortex patterns were upset.

The efficiency characteristics of a 200-mm and 500-mm diameter tube are essentially equal, but larger sizes (viz. 1000 mm diameter) show

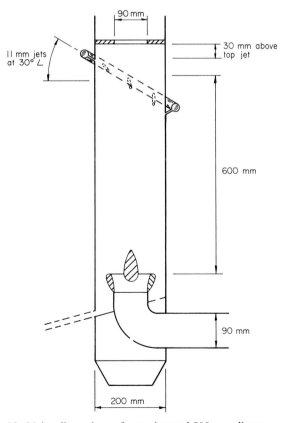

FIG. 18. Major dimensions of experimental 200-mm diameter tube.

a decreased efficiency. On "fine grain coal dust," 98% collection was obtained with 200 and 500 mm units, 97% with the 1000-mm unit. On a larger scale field trial, a 2000-mm diameter unit treated the cyclone discharge from the dry drum of a tar-macadam plant. The gas was at 200 °C, dust concentration 4–5 grams/m³, with a particle size maximum frequency of 2 μ and a maximum particle size of 12–15 μ. Collection efficiency was 90%.

D. Comparison with Conventional Cyclones

In terms of efficiency, the rotary stream dust separator appears to be definitely superior to conventional cyclones, and at comparable total power costs. The efficiency is in the range of the better wet scrubbers and ordinary applications of dry electrostatic precipitators. In spite of the fact that increasing body diameter is less harmful to efficiency than it is with cyclones, it is still deleterious; and the highest efficiency must be obtained with multiple-bank installations of small tubes. These, as with banks of small cyclones, must be designed for reasonably uniform distribution of pressure in the dirty gas plenum. Other problems of dust load distribution, etc., appear less difficult than with cyclones.

Another important advantage is the absence of erosion problems on the tube wall, and the absence of a need for smooth internal construction of the tube. Minor turbulence caused by welding beads, etc., has no detrimental effect.

On the other hand, the rotary stream separator does require a source of higher pressure secondary air, and presumably, therefore, a high pressure blower. Furthermore, for optimum performance the secondary air pressure and flow rate must be controlled in relation to the flow of primary gas; this could, on occasion, be an advantage, because by exercising such control, efficiency may be kept at a peak over a wide range of operating conditions.

IV. Gravity Settling Chambers (22)

A. Definition

A gravity settling chamber is a chamber large enough so that the gas velocity is reduced sufficiently to permit dust or droplets to settle out by the action of gravity. The chamber may contain horizontal plates to reduce the distance through which particles must settle. A settling chamber usually consists of a horizontal rectangular chamber with an inlet at one end and an outlet at the other, with or without horizontal plates.

B. THEORY

If the velocity in the settling chamber is low enough so that turbulence is minimized and the gas flow entering and leaving the chamber is well distributed, the performance is expressed by Eq. (15).

$$\eta = \frac{100 \ u_t L}{HV} \tag{15}$$

where

η = efficiency, weight percent of particles of settling velocity u_t
u_t = settling velocity of dust, ft/sec
L = chamber length, feet
H = chamber height, feet
V = gas velocity, ft/sec

Under the above assumptions and combining Stokes' law with Eq. (15), the minimum particle size that can be completely separated may be calculated by Eq. (16).

$$D_p = \sqrt{\frac{18 \ \mu H V}{gL(\rho_p - \rho)}} \tag{16}$$

where

D_p = minimum size particle collected at 100% efficiency
μ = gas viscosity, lb/ft-sec
H = chamber height, feet
V = gas velocity, ft/sec
g = gravitation constant, 32.2 ft/sec/sec
L = chamber length, feet
ρ_p = particle density, lb/ft^3
ρ = gas density, lb/ft^3

Horizontal plates in the settling chamber, arranged as shelves, reduce the vertical distance through which the particles must settle. The performance of such a chamber is given by Eqs. (17) and (18).

$$\eta = \frac{N u_t W L}{q} \tag{17}$$

$$D_p = \sqrt{\frac{18 \ \mu N q}{gWL(\rho_p - \rho)}} \tag{18}$$

where

N = number of plates
W = width of chamber, feet
q = gas flow rate, ft^3/sec
other units as in Eq. (15)

C. Applications

The gravity settling chamber has the advantage of utmost simplicity, and can be constructed of almost any material. However, the space required for such chambers is large, and they are seldom used to remove particles smaller than 40- to 50-μ diameter. Their most practical use is in removing very large particles as an aid or adjunct to more efficient subsequent gas cleaning equipment. The particles which can be removed by the settling chamber itself are seldom of air pollution significance.

Careful design of the settling chamber is necessary to provide good distribution of gas entering and leaving the settling chamber. The usual types of design include gradual transitions, splitters, or perforated distributing plates. The gas velocity in the chamber should generally be restricted to 600 ft/min or less in order to prevent excessive reentrainment. Settling chambers with horizontal plates offer greater efficiency in a smaller space but present difficult cleaning problems; probably the most effective method of cleaning is to flush the plates with water sprays.

V. Inertial Separators (22)

A. Definition

Inertial separators are devices which, by causing sudden changes in direction of the gas stream, cause particles to be separated by a combination of the inertia of the dust particle, impaction on a target, and centrifugal forces. The separated particles may be retained on the impaction target, separated into a dust bin, or separated in a dust-enriched side stream which is conducted to a secondary high efficiency dust collector.

The specific designs of collectors which employ such principles are legion. Most of the designs are proprietary, and they have corresponding advantages and disadvantages for particular applications.

B. Theory

Impingement or impaction separation occurs when the gas undergoes a sudden sharp change in direction of flow, the principles of which are illustrated in Fig. 19.

The target efficiency of impingement, defined as the fraction of particles in the field volume swept by the impinging target which will impinge on that target, has been determined for simple shapes as shown in Fig. 20 (23).

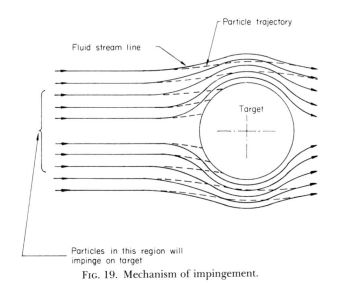

FIG. 19. Mechanism of impingement.

The separation number in Fig. 20 is defined as

$$N_s = \frac{D_p^2 V \rho_p}{18 \, \mu D_b} \tag{19}$$

where

N_s = separation number, dimensionless
D_p = particle diameter, feet
V = relative velocity gas to target, ft/sec
ρ_p = particle density, lb/ft³
μ = gas viscosity, lb/ft-sec
D_b = target diameter, feet (ribbon width)

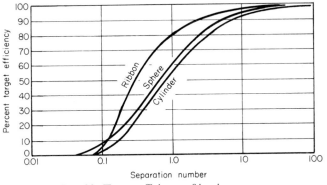

FIG. 20. Target efficiency of impingement.

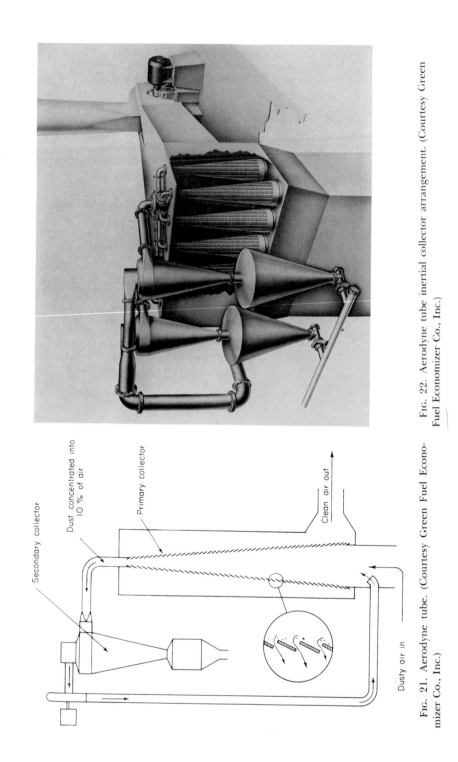

Fig. 21. Aerodyne tube. (Courtesy Green Fuel Economizer Co., Inc.)

Fig. 22. Aerodyne tube inertial collector arrangement. (Courtesy Green
Fuel Economizer Co., Inc.)

Secondary collector

Dust concentrated into
10 % of air

Primary collector

Clean air out

Dusty air in

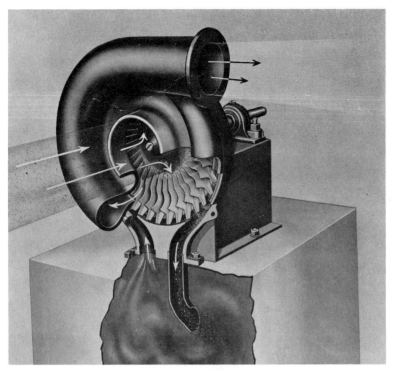

FIG. 23. Type D Rotoclone, a mechanical inertial collector. (Courtesy American Air Filter Co.)

FIG. 24. "Low draft loss" fly ash collector. (Courtesy Buell Engineering Company, Inc.)

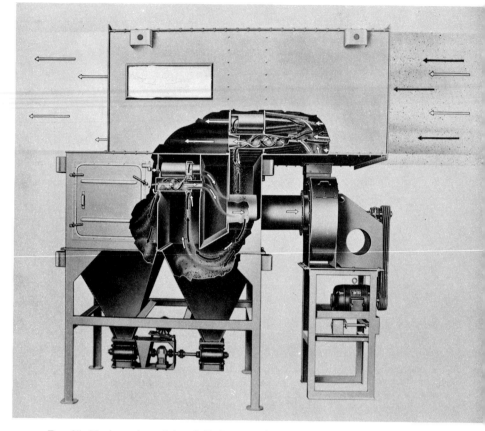

FIG. 25. Horizontal, peripheral discharge cyclones arranged for partial series operation. (Courtesy American Air Filter Co.)

The above illustrations and equations serve to demonstrate the relationship of the parameters involved in impingement. Higher target efficiencies will be obtained for larger or denser particles, small impinging targets, and higher relative velocities between particles and target.

Although the theory of impingement separation has been well developed (23–25), such theoretical approaches afford little practical information in evaluating the commercial inertial separators on the market. The most practical approach to efficiency and pressure drop considerations is the use of experimental data. Fractional size efficiency data and overall efficiency calculations may be handled in the same manner as previously described for cyclone separators.

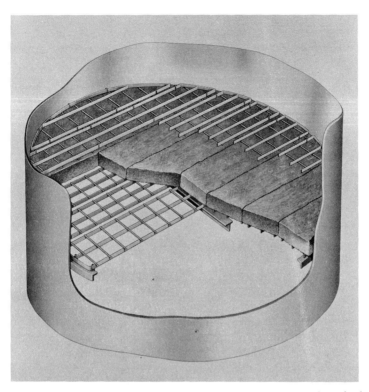

FIG. 26. York demister. Mist droplets removed by impaction on metal or plastic mesh. Tower or stack installation shown. (Courtesy Otto H. York Co., Inc.)

C. SOME COMMERCIAL TYPES

Commercial cyclone and inertial separators are furnished in a very wide variety of arrangements and combinations. Many of these have evolved in response to a particular need, and have advantages for such specific applications. Space does not permit a comprehensive review of all the commercially available equipment of this general type. A few selected examples, illustrating the wide range of combinations possible, are shown in Figs. 21–26.

D. RANGE OF PERFORMANCE

In general, the range of performance of inertial separators is similar to that of high efficiency cyclones. Particular designs may be more suited for particular applications because they may occupy less space, or may be specially designed to compensate for particular problems such as

TABLE III
REPRESENTATIVE PERFORMANCE OF CYCLONES AND INERTIAL SEPARATORS

Collector type	Process	Material	Air flow (ft³/min)	Pressure drop (inches wg)	Efficiency (weight percent)	Inlet load (grains/ft³)	Inlet mass median size (μ)
Series cyclones	Fluid catalytic cracking	Catalyst	40,000	High	99.98	2800	37.0
Special cyclone	Laboratory test	Fly ash	185	23.0	91.2	0.06	3.0
Special cyclone	Laboratory test	Micronized talc	185	23.0	83.9	5.6	2.3
Cyclone	Abrasive cleaning	Talc	2,300	0.33	93.0	2.2	—
Cyclone	Drying	Sand and gravel	12,300	1.9	86.9	38.0	8.2[a]
Cyclone	Grinding	Aluminum	2,400	1.2	89.0	0.7	—
Cyclone	Planing mill	Wood	3,100	3.7	97.0	0.1	—
Rotary stream separator	Test dust (2.65 sp. gr.)	—	300	8	100	0.4	5
					90	88	1
Rotary stream separator	Tar-macadam plant	—	—	—	90	2	2[b]
Inertial	Cyclone outlet	Sand and gravel	1,700	4.0	50.0	5.8	5.3[c]
Mechanical	Grinding	Iron scale	11,800	4.7	56.3	0.15	3.2[d]
Mechanical	Rubber dusting	Zinc stearate	3,300	9.0	88.0	0.6	1.7

[a] Outlet mass median size, microns = 3.2.
[b] Size frequency maximum.
[c] Outlet mass median size, microns = 1.8.
[d] Outlet mass median size, microns = 2.5.

erosion, necessity to minimize pressure drop, etc. In general, those without moving parts may be constructed of any reasonable material of construction, while those with moving parts must include considerations of stress and accelerated corrosion and erosion of the moving parts. Most inertial separators can be operated wet if desired, and under such conditions they exhibit a higher collection efficiency due to the same factors that operate in the case of cyclone dust collectors. A tabulation of representative data from various sources is shown in Table III.

REFERENCES

1. A. C. Stern, K. J. Caplan, and P. D. Bush, "Cyclone Dust Collectors." Am. Petrol. Inst., New York, 1955.
2. M. W. First, Fundamental Factors in the Design of Cyclone Dust Collectors, Ph.D. Thesis, Harvard University (1950).
3. C. E. Lapple, Ind. Hyg. Quart. 5, No. 11, 40–48 (1950).
4. R. McK. Alexander, Australasian Inst. Mining & Met. Proc. [N.S.] 152/3, 202–228 (1949).
5. A. J. ter Linden, Proc. Inst. Mech. Engrs. (London) 160, 233 (1949).
6. C. J. Stairmand, Trans. Inst. Chem. Engrs. (London) 29, 356–383 (1951).
7. F. B. Schneider, Gen. Elec. Rev. 53, 22–29 (1950).
8. F. Schulz, Eng. Digest 5, 49 (1948).
9. H. L. M. Larcombe, Mining Mag. (London) 77, 137–148, 208–217, 273–278, and 356–347, Sept.–Dec. (1947).
10. Bitum. Coal Res. 14, No. 1, 8–12 (1954).

11. L. Silverman *et al., U.S. At. Energy Comm. Contract* **AT-30-1,** Gen-238, Rept. NYO-1527 (1950).
12. K. Iinoya, *Mem. Fac. Eng., Nagoya Univ.* **5,** No. 2 (1953).
13. P. Drinker and T. Hatch, "Industrial Dust," 2nd ed. McGraw-Hill, New York, 1954.
14. K. T. Whitby, *Univ. Minn. Inst. Technol., Eng. Expt. Sta., Bull.* **32** (1950).
15. R. Dennis *et al., U.S. At. Energy Comm. Contract* **AT-30-1,** 841 Rept. NYO1583 (1952).
16. L. W. Briggs, *Trans. Am. Inst. Chem. Engrs.* **42,** No. 3, 511–526 (1946).
17. E. Feifel, *Schweiz. Bauztg.* **68,** 247–251 (1950).
18. H. Klein, *Staub* **23,** No. 11, 501–509 (1963).
19. W. Nickel, *Staub* **23,** No. 11, 509–512 (1963).
20. E. Schaufler, *Staub* **23,** No. 4, 228–230 (1963).
21. K. R. Schmidt, *Staub* **23,** No. 11, 491–501 (1963).
22. C. F. Gottschlich, "Gravity Inertial, Sonic and Thermal Collectors." Am. Petrol. Inst., New York, 1961.
23. S. K. Freidlander *et al.,* "Handbook on Air Cleaning." U.S. At. Energy Comm., Washington, D.C., 1952.
24. W. E. Ranz, *Penn. State Univ., Mineral Ind. Expt. Sta., Bull.* **66** (1956).
25. J. B. Wong *et al., J. Appl. Phys.* **26,** 244–249 (1955).

GENERAL REFERENCES

Additional pertinent material is in Chapter 4 of "Air Pollution Engineering Manual, Los Angeles APCD" (J. A. Danielson, ed.), PHS Publn. 999-AP-40, DHEW, Cincinnati (1967); and in Chapter 4 of "Air Pollution Manual. Part II." American Industrial Hygiene Assn., Detroit (1968); and will be published in the National Air Pollution Control Administration's publication: "Control Technology for Particulate Air Pollutants."

44 Source Control by Filtration

K. Iinoya and C. Orr, Jr.

Nomenclature

C_i Inlet mass concentration of aerosol particles, grains/ft³ or gm/m³ (1 grain/ft³ = 2.29 gm/m³)

C_k Cunningham slip correction factor for a fiber = $1 + (2\lambda/D_f)$ $[1.23 + 0.41\{\exp(-0.44 D_f/\lambda)\}]$

D Diameter, feet, meters, or microns

D_{ps} Specific surface diameter of particles, feet, meters, or microns

E Overall collection efficiency of a filter, percent or relative number

g_c Gravitational conversion factor, 32.2 ft lb-mass/(lb-force sec²) or 9.8 kg m/(kg-force sec²)

k Boltzmann constant $\left(=1.38 \times 10^{-23} \dfrac{\text{kg m}^2}{\text{sec}^2 {}^\circ\text{K}}\right)$

L Filter thickness, feet or meters

M Total dust loading on the filter, pounds or kilograms

m Collected dust loading on the filter, lb/ft² or kg/m²

Δp Pressure loss, lb-force/ft² or kg-force/m² (= mm H₂O) or in. H₂O

Re Reynolds number, $D_f u \rho_g/\mu$

t Time, seconds

T Absolute gas temperature, °K

u Average true gas velocity, ft/min or m/sec ($=u_s/\epsilon$)

u_s Superficial gas velocity, ft/min or m/sec

α Average specific resistance of collected particle layer, ft/lb or m/kg

ϵ Volumetric void or porosity, (always < 1)

λ Mean free path of gas molecules, feet or meters

μ Gas viscosity, lb/ft sec or kg/m sec

ρ Density, lb/ft³ or kg/m³

η Collection efficiency of a single fiber, percent or relative number

ζ_0 Coefficient of pressure loss for a clean filter medium, ft^{-1} or m^{-1}

Subscripts

f Fiber

g Gas

i With interference effect

o Filter medium only (initial condition)

p Particles

I. Introduction

Filtration is the oldest and generally one of the most reliable of the many methods by which dusts, mists, and fumes may be removed from gases. Filters are especially desirable for extracting particulate matter from gases produced by industrial operations since they generally give very satisfactory collection efficiencies with only moderate power consumption. Initial cost and upkeep expenditure may be either relatively low or comparatively high, however, depending on the size, density, and other properties of the matter to be collected.

Filters are most readily classified according to the nature of their filtering media. These different media may be broadly considered to be woven fabric or felt cloth, paper, fibrous mats, and aggregate beds.

II. Fabric Filters

Fabric filters, because they are capable of handling the high particle loads sometimes carried by process gases, are used extensively in industrial operations to recover valuable matter, as well as to control atmospheric pollution at the source. Such filters are commonly made in the form of a tubular bag or of an envelope slipped over a wire frame much in the manner of a pillowcase. In the bag filter the tubular sleeves range from 5 to 20 inches in diameter and may be as long as 44 feet. Particle-laden gas is usually introduced inside the tube as shown in Fig. 1 in such a manner as to allow the larger particles to settle, or be projected into, the dust hopper before the gas actually enters the tubes. In an envelope or panel filter, Fig. 2, the individual filters range from 18 inches to 3 feet wide and are only 1 to 2 inches thick. Gases pass from the outside inward in these units since the filters are prevented from collapsing by the inner framework. As in the bag filters, the panels are mounted in multiples. The structure enclosing a number of filter or tubular elements is called a baghouse.

Typically, fabric filters are employed in carbon black, cement, clay, and pharmaceutical plants, where retaining the product is a prime

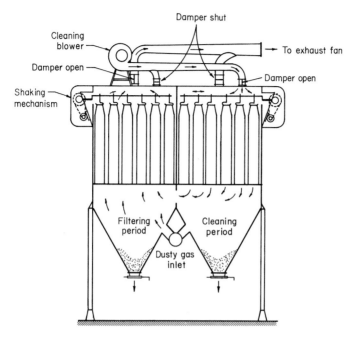

FIG. 1. Typical bag filter employing reverse flow and mechanical shaking for cleaning.

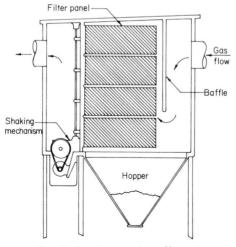

FIG. 2. Panel or envelope filter.

motive. In operations involving abrasives, irritating chemicals, and the like *(1–3)*, fabric filters are employed to control harmful or obnoxious emissions. They may also be employed in exhaust treatment facilities. For example, filters are utilized when solid alkaline additives, such as dolomite or limestone dusts, are introduced into oil-fired, power-plant exhausts *(4)* to reduce the SO_3 concentration, i.e., lower the acid dew-point.

A. Methods of Cleaning

The efficiency of a fabric filter increases as the particle layer collects on the fabric, but the accompanying rise in pressure across the filter sets practical limits for the deposit thickness. Bag and panel filters are therefore provided with manual, electric, or pneumatic mechanisms to dislodge periodically the collected material. In most installations the

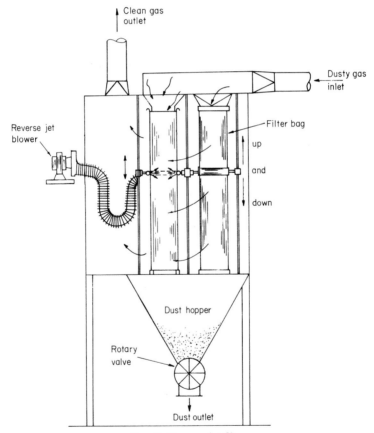

Fig. 3. Reverse-jet filter.

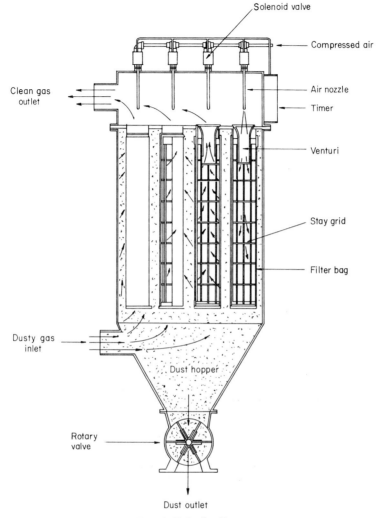

FIG. 4. Pulse-jet filter.

collecting medium is mounted directly over a hopper into which the particles may fall when the fabric is shaken. Shaking may be accomplished at fixed intervals of time or upon actuation by pressure-limiting devices. Filters are generally compartmentalized or installed in multiples so that the particle-laden gas may be made to bypass the compartment being cleaned by opening and closing appropriate dampers. Clean air from the outside, or other appropriate gas, may also be blown in the reverse direction into the compartment requiring cleaning (see Fig. 1). A cleaning cycle usually requires only a very few minutes.

Of the systems for cleaning filters continuously, one called the "reverse jet" and shown in Fig. 3, utilizes air emerging from a slit in a ring that encircles each bag. The ring moves vertically up and down the entire bag length (5). High velocity air streaming through the fabric removes the accumulated material from the inside surface of the filter. In this case the particle-laden gas enters the top of each bag. A thick felt is most satisfactory as the filtering medium. Another type, illustrated in Fig. 4, utilizes a pulsing air pressure provided by a single jet located above each filter bag. The transient pressure wave produced by the jet detaches the particles in this case. The frequency of the jet is adjustable to accommodate a wide range of dust loadings. In this type of equipment the particle-laden gas flows from the outside into each bag which is prevented from collapsing by an internal framework. Filters equipped with reverse jets or pulsing devices can handle, in some instances, gases at high rates of flow having high dust loadings without need of separate bypass units as in the case of filters cleaned by mechanical shakers. Shock waves have also been investigated for cleaning filters. Collapse cleaning of bags without any shaking motion is effective for some low-strength filter cloths. Other cleaning innovations (6) utilize low-frequency sound generators that cause the bags

TABLE I

SUPERFICIAL GAS VELOCITY EMPLOYED WITH REVERSE-JET AND
PULSE-AIR FILTERS IN TYPICAL APPLICATIONS[a]

Superficial velocity,[b] u_s (ft/min)	Application
15	Cake mix, cardboard dust, cocoa, livestock feeds, flour, grain, leather dust, sawdust, tobacco dust.
12	Asbestos, buffing dust, fibrous and cellulosic dust, foundry shakeout, gypsum, hydrated lime, perlite, rubber chemicals, salt, sand, sandblast dust, soda ash, talc.
10	Alumina, aspirin, carbon black, (finished) cement, ceramic pigments, clay and brick dust, coal, fluorspar, natural gum, kaolin, limestone, perchlorates, rock dust, ores and minerals, silica, sorbic acid, sugar.
9	Ammonium phosphate fertilizer, coke, diatomaceous earth, dry petrochemicals, dyes, fly ash, metal powder, metal oxides, pigments, plastic, resins, silicates, starch, stearates, tannic acid.
6	Activated carbon, molecular carbon black, detergents, fumes and other dispersed products directly from reactions, powdered milk, soaps.

[a] From Frey and Reinauer (10).
[b] Velocity of approach to the filter medium.

to vibrate and mechanical devices that impart a gentle oscillating motion to the top of each bag. These latter systems are especially applicable with glass fiber bags because they create a minimum of fiber abrasion and allow operation up to about 500 °F.

Longer bag life and more efficient filtration is obtained by careful attention to the cleaning schedule (7–9). A heavy deposit on the filter may put too much stress on the fabric, while too frequent agitation may lead to early rupture. Attention should also be given to the load retained by each portion of a filter. Obviously, uniform service from each portion of each filter element is desirable, but specific positions along a filter often show surprising irregularities in retention as well as cleaning characteristics. It is often found that napped cloth retains an increasing dust load with every cleaning cycle. Other weaves, however, rarely show this characteristic.

Superficial gas velocities of approach to the fabric in units equipped for mechanical shaking usually are between 2 and 10 ft/min, while velocities in continuous filtering units range from 6 to 15 ft/min as shown in Table I. The pressure loss in continuously operating tube filters remains relatively constant at an average value of about 4 inches of water; the resistance of periodically cleaned filters ordinarily ranges from about 1 to as much as 6 inches of water.

B. WEAVE AND FIBER CHARACTERISTICS

The selection of the best fabric for dust collection under any particular condition still largely requires trial-and-error testing even though fabrics have been under development for many years. Fabric weaves commonly employed in gas filtration are designated, as in Fig. 5, either plain, twill, or sateen. Twills and sateens are most frequently used. The performance of any fabric is greatly influenced by thread density, fiber composition, and the nap, i.e., the hairy or downy texture, of the cloth surface. The chief characteristics of filter cloth are listed in Table II. Cotton is the least expensive. Wool is rarely used now because synthetic fibers have been developed with superior properties. Silicone-coated glass fiber cloth is commonly employed in high-temperature applications. A colloidal graphite finish is reported to triple the endurance of silicone-treated glass filter bags used for cleaning hot gases (11). It withstands temperatures to 500 °F and usually gives an acceptably long life. Tetrafluoroethylene (Teflon) fiber is too expensive for many purposes while graphitized cloth is not sufficiently strong for many.

Filter life generally is greatly improved if operating temperatures are held below the limits indicated in Table II. Other factors upon which

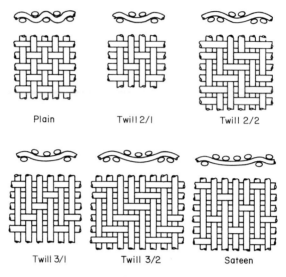

Plain   Twill 2/1   Twill 2/2

Twill 3/1   Twill 3/2   Sateen

FIG. 5. Filter cloth weaves.

fabric life depends are the frequency and manner of shaking, the characteristics of the particulate matter, the nature of the gas, and the care with which the installation is designed for the particular application (12, 12a). Because these vary widely, fabric filter life is difficult to assess; generally 6 months to 2 years of service is considered acceptable.

The electrostatic properties of both the dust and the collecting fabric influence filter performance (13–17). Fibers and fabrics conform to a triboelectric series as indicated in Table III, and dusts, likewise, can be classified in a similar series. The intensity of the charge developed on either the fabric or the dust, or both, depends upon the processing conditions, as well as on the nature of the materials themselves. The charge dissipation rate is an especially important property depending upon both the filter medium and the collected dust. The rate of charge loss by a fabric has, for example, a very marked influence on its cleaning ability. As yet, not enough is known about these factors to use them effectively in filter and baghouse design.

Although the filter material is an important factor in the operation, filtration is principally accomplished by the accumulated particle layer. Therefore, it inevitably is difficult to predict filter pressure loss and filter collection efficiency, these being nevertheless very important criteria in filter performance (16, 18, 19).

TABLE II
PROPERTIES OF FIBER MATERIALS

Fiber	Physical characteristics				Relative resistance to attack by			Other attribute
	Relative strength	Specific gravity	Normal moisture content (%)	Maximum usable temperature (°F)	Acid	Base	Organic solvent	
Cotton	Strong	1.6	7	180	Poor	Medium	Good	Low cost
Wool	Medium	1.3	15	210	Medium	Poor	Good	—
Paper	Weak	1.5	10	180	Poor	Medium	Good	Low cost
Polyamide (nylon)	Strong	1.1	5	220	Medium	Good	Good[a]	Easy to clean
Polyester (Dacron)	Strong	1.4	0.4	280	Good	Medium	Good[b]	—
Acrylonitrile (Orlon)	Medium	1.2	1	250	Good	Medium	Good[c]	—
Vinylidene chloride	Medium	1.7	10	210	Good	Medium	Good	—
Polyethylene	Strong	1.0	0	250	Medium	Medium	Medium	—
Tetrafluoroethylene	Medium	2.3	0	500	Good	Good	Good	Expensive
Polyvinyl acetate	Strong	1.3	5	250	Medium	Good	Poor	—
Glass	Strong	2.5	0	550	Medium	Medium	Good	Poor resistance to abrasion
Graphitized fiber	Weak	2.0	10	500	Medium	Good	Good	Expensive
Asbestos	Weak	3.0	1	500	Medium[d]	Medium	Good	—
"Nomex" nylon	Strong	1.4	5	450	Good	Medium	Good	Poor resistance to moisture

[a] Except phenol and formic acid.
[b] Except phenol.
[c] Except heated acetone.
[d] Except SO_2.

TABLE III

Electrostatic Charging Order of Filter Fibers[a]

Material	Relative charge generation
Wool	+20
Silicon-treated glass (filament and spun)	+15
Woven wool felt	+11
Nylon (spun)	+7 to +10
Cotton (sateen)	6
Orlon (filament)	+4
Dacron (filament)	0
Dynel (spun)	−4
Orlon (spun)	−5 to −14
Dacron (spun)	−10
Steel	−10
Polypropylene (filament)	−13
Acetate	−14
Saran	−17
Polyethylene (filament and spun)	−20

[a] From Frederick et al. (13–15).

C. Pressure Loss

Under normal conditions, gas flow through both the fabric and the collected particle matter is laminar in character (20–23). The pressure loss, being the sum of the loss due to the filter itself and the collected particles, may be written[1]

$$\Delta p = \Delta p_o + \Delta p_p = (\zeta_0 + \overline{\alpha}m)u_s\, \mu/g_c \tag{1}$$

The value of the pressure loss coefficient ζ_0 for a clean filter depends upon the fabric; it usually is negligibly small in practical applications. The value of the average specific resistance $\overline{\alpha}$ of a deposited particle layer depends upon the particle size, the volumetric voids of the layer, and the density of the particles. Values as indicated in Fig. 6 (24) are typical. The terms of Eq. (1) might then have values as follows: $\zeta_0 = 5 \times 10^7$/m, $\overline{\alpha} = 1.4 \times 10^{10}$ m/kg (see Fig. 6), $m = 0.13$ kg/m², $u_s = 0.02$ m/sec (=0.79 inch/sec), $\mu = 1.81 \times 10^{-5}$ kg/m sec (at 760 mm Hg and 20 °C), and $g_c = 9.8$ m kg/sec²kg. Substituted into the equation, these values result in a pressure loss of 69 kg/m² or 2.7 inches of water.

[1] See nomenclature for definition of symbols, p. 409.

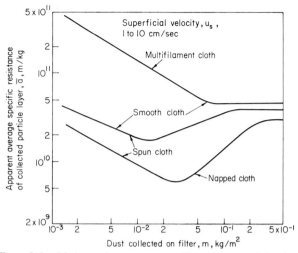

FIG. 6. Effect of the fabric on the average specific resistance of the dust layer [From Kimura and Iinoya (24)].

The change in pressure loss with particle collection may be obtained from the Kozeny-Carman relationship (24) written

$$\frac{d(\Delta p_p)}{dm} = \frac{180 \ \mu u_s}{g_c \rho_p D_{ps}^2} \frac{(1 - \epsilon_p)}{\epsilon_p^3}$$

(2)

where the apparent volumetric void ϵ_p is obtained from Fig. 7. For example, using the values of u_s and μ as above, $\rho_p = 2000$ kg/m³, $D_{ps} =$

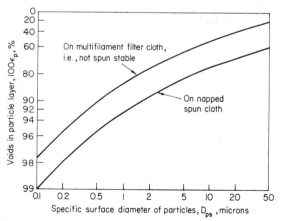

Fig. 7. Relation between specific surface diameter of particles to be collected and the voids of the collected particle layer [From Kimura and Iinoya (24)].

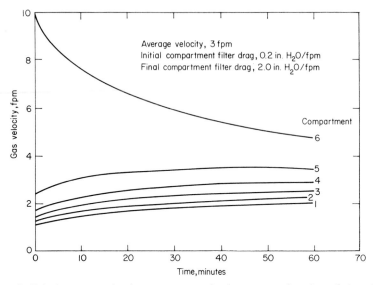

FIG. 8. Velocity pattern in six-compartment baghouse as a function of time [From Walsh and Spaite (9)].

0.38×10^{-6} m, and $\epsilon_p = 0.96$, Eq. (2) gives a value for $d(\Delta p_p)/dm$ of 1040 Kg/kg or 1040 mm of water per kg/m² of cloth area.

Typical gas flow behavior to be expected within a multicompartmented baghouse (9) is presented in Figs. 8 and 9. The term filter drag is employed on Fig. 8. The concept of drag in this case is analogous to re-

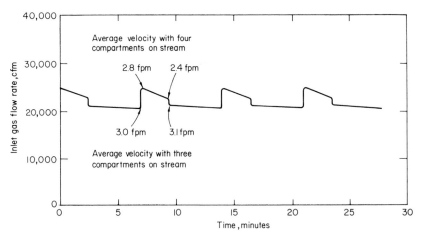

FIG. 9. Flow variation as a function of time in a four-compartment baghouse [From Walsh and Spaite (9)].

sistance in an electric circuit. It includes the resistance to flow of both the deposit and the filter medium, and is determined by dividing the pressure loss across the filter by the superficial gas velocity through the filter.

D. EFFICIENCY

Particle separation by fabric filters is more than a simple entrapping of the particles by single fibers, since the open spaces through such media are usually many times the size of the individual particles which are collected. Actually, separation with filters is poor until enough particles have been captured to form a bridge across the openings. Under the usual conditions of operation the particle layer will form in a matter of seconds, and once it has done so, separation efficiency will rise to values near 99% as indicated in Fig. 10. Efficiencies of 99.99% are not unknown (25). Failure to achieve very high collection efficiency is almost always due to excessive cleaning, torn bags, bypass leakage, or an excessive gas flow rate which produces holes within the deposited particle layer (26). Instantaneous efficiency values are, in theory, more meaningful than average efficiencies because the collection ability of a fabric generally increases with the dust deposit (26, 27).

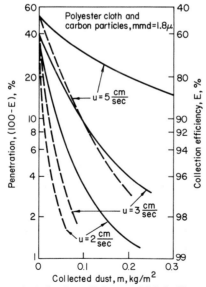

FIG. 10. Collection efficiency of fabric filters. The solid lines show cumulative collection efficiencies and the broken lines show instantaneous ones. mmd = mass median diameter.

The efficiency of mist removal by filters such as one of glass fiber is greatly increased if the cloth is treated with a silicone preparation to provide a water-repellent surface. A normally water-repellent plastic cloth, for example polytetrafluoroethylene, needs no treatment (28).

III.   Paper Filters

High efficiency filters employing paper as the collecting substrate, in addition to being used for sampling purposes as described in Chapter 16, find practical applications where radioactive dusts or bacterial particulates need to be collected (29, 30). Clean rooms, also called "white rooms," as used in pharmaceutical plants, in electronic instrument assembly areas, in operating rooms, etc., utilize paper filters to obtain air essentially free of particulates.

These filters are constructed upon frames of several sizes and are installed in airtight banks. Each filter element, or cell, has 10 to 15 times its apparent filtering area because the paper medium is arranged in accordionlike pleats, folds, or pockets. Paper filters cannot be cleaned and reused. When it becomes necessary to change them, the collecting medium is either replaced on the frame or both the frame and filter are discarded and new units are installed. The latter course is necessary, of course, when radioactive or pathogenic contaminants are collected.

The pressure loss through clean filter paper is described (31) by

$$\Delta p = \frac{(1 - \epsilon_f)}{\epsilon_f[0.034 + 0.601(C_k - 1)]} \frac{\mu L u_s}{D_f^2 g_c} \tag{3}$$

This equation shows, for example, that if $\epsilon_f = 0.875$, $D_f = 10^{-6}$ m, $L = 0.51 \times 10^{-3}$ m (=0.02 inch), $\mu = 1.81 \times 10^{-5}$ kg/m sec, $u_s = 0.0254$ m/sec (=1 inch/sec), $g_c = 9.8$ m kg/sec² kg, and $C_k = 1.16$ (corresponding to a D_f of 10^{-6} m), the pressure loss is 28.3 kg/m² or 1.1 inches of H_2O. In practice, the user rarely needs to compute the pressure loss of filter paper since the various manufacturers publish such data.

The pressure loss of a typical, clean, paper filter is relatively large compared to the pressure loss at the time of filter replacement as shown in Fig. 11. This is so because paper filters must have high initial resistances to ensure nearly complete collection throughout their entire lifetime.

Gas velocities with paper filters are generally of the order of 5 ft/min. Resistance is allowed to rise to about 1 to 2 in. of water before the filter is replaced (Fig. 11). The useful service time of a paper filter, if protected by a less expensive prefilter, ranges from 10^3 hours to 10^4 hours when filtering ordinary city air. This service time is often prolonged in clean-

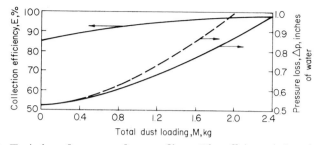

FIG. 11. Typical performance of paper filters. The efficiency is based on National Bureau of Standards atmospheric air stain test, using (solid lines) Cottrell precipitator dust with 4% linters fed at rate of 2 gm/min and (broken line) Cottrell precipitator dust without linters fed at rate of 2 gm/min.

room operations by use of high-efficiency prefilters and recirculation of the treated air.

The collection efficiency rating of paper filters (*32, 33*) depends on the method of evaluation. The best commercial cellulose-asbestos paper filters show 99.97% by weight collection efficiency for dioctyl phthalate (DOP) monodispersed aerosols having 0.3 μ diameter particles. A radioactive aerosol also affords a convenient means for measuring the efficiency of dry filter media (*34*). Table IV presents tests and results to be expected with which to judge the performance of paper filters (*35*).

TABLE IV

CODE FOR THE COLLECTION EFFICIENCY OF PAPER FILTERS[a]

Test aerosol	Measurement	If the collection efficiency is equal to or greater than indicated, the filter is:	
		Superior	Normal
Paraffin oil mist with all particles < 1 μ diam. and most of them between 0.3 and 0.5 μ diam.	Scattered light	99.7%	85%
Radioactively tagged aerosols below 0.3 μ diam.	^{228}Th radiation activity	99.95%	70%
Quartz dust with all particles < 10 μ diam. and most of them between 0.5 μ and 2μ	Scattered light	99%	95%
Paraffin oil[b]	Scattered light	No visible mist	Trace of mist

[a] From reference (*35*).

[b] Concentrated oil mist is fed to the filter with the lowest possible velocity (less than 0.1 cm/sec) and the filter is illuminated with a strong light (at least 500 watts). The exhaust stream is viewed against a black background.

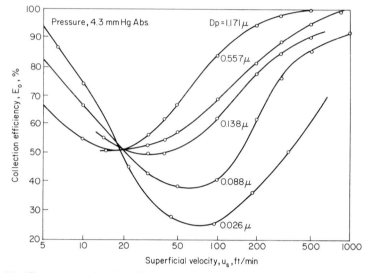

FIG. 12. Filter paper collection efficiency under reduced pressure [From Stern *et al.* (*36*)].

Diffusion accounts for much of the collection in high efficiency paper filters, as is evident from their performance under reduced pressure, Fig. 12 (*36*). Electric charging also contributes, for charged DOP aerosols with 0.25 to 0.55 μ diameter particles are more efficiently collected (*37*) by U.S. Army Chemical Corps No. 5 paper than are uncharged aerosols of otherwise similar characteristics.

IV. Fibrous Mats and Aggregate Beds

Fibrous-mat filters find their most extensive use in air-conditioning, heating, and ventilating systems, but high efficiency mat filters are also employed as aftercleaners and as roughing units to protect still more efficient equipment for pollution control purposes. Application of mat filters is always restricted, however, to conditions where only moderate dust concentrations are to be handled (*38*). They are usually constructed with fibers of natural substances, metal, glass, or plastic packed loosely into a frame, generally about 20 inches square and 1–4 inches thick. Superficial gas velocities employed with mats range from 50 to 600 ft/min and their pressure losses from 0.1 to 1 inch of water.

Metallized fibrous filters (*39*) have recently been introduced for high temperature applications. These so-called metallic-depth media are produced by metallizing a paper or other nonwoven substrate with a metal such as nickel. Filters of ceramic or mineral fibers withstand temperatures up to 1500 °F and will resist chemical corrosion (40–45).

Static, aggregate-bed filters are exemplified by the slag-wool filters (46) sometimes used with blast furnaces, coke filters for acid mist collection, and sand and glass-wool filters. All such filters give rather high collection efficiencies but they also exhibit high resistances, 5 to 10 inches of water (47–50). Perhaps the best-known application of an aggregate bed filter is in the destruction of sulfuric acid mists. "Coke boxes" for this purpose are usually lead-lined or tile chambers packed with 10 to 20-mesh coke through which the gas flow may be upward, downward, or horizontal. The acid flows from the filter as it is collected. When solid particulate matter is present, the life of a bed filter is inversely proportional to the loading. Such a filter can be reconstructed only by aggregate removal and cleaning or by replacing the aggregate.

Fixed-bed sand filters were employed at the Hanford, Washington, U.S. Atomic Energy Commission facility, beginning in 1948, to remove radioactive particles from exhaust gases. These filters were prepared with successively finer gradations of sand totaling between 6 and 7 feet deep in a large underground container. Initially built as an expedient solution to a problem, they consistently gave efficiencies of the order of 99.7% for submicron particles. They were, however, large and expensive. More recently, glass fiber beds have been installed instead of sand filters. These, treating air containing between 0.00002 and 0.0004 grains/ft^3 of particulate matter, have given efficiencies approaching 99.99%.

Gravel bed filters (51) are continuously useful at temperatures up to 660 °F and yield dust loadings in the cleaned gas of the order of 0.02 to 0.04 grains/ft^3. The pressure loss exhibited by gravel bed filters ranges between 2 and 6 inches of water for superficial gas velocities of 1 to 3 ft/sec.

A dynamic, aggregate-bed filter is one in which the aggregate is caused to move so as to permit continual regeneration. Fluidized and nearly fluidized beds have also been employed as filters (52).

Glass fiber filters apparently are quite effective collectors of hydrogen fluoride as well as of particulate materials (53). They have been found to collect up to 250 μg fluorine per square inch of filter area before losses through them reached 5%. Filters with a latex binder are less efficient in collecting hydrogen fluoride than those without a binder.

Porous solid plate or cylindrical filters of ceramic (54) or metal construction are used only for special purposes because of their greater expense.

A. METHODS OF CLEANING

Fibrous mat filters are most often discarded and replaced with new or cleaned ones when their pressure loss becomes excessive or when the flow rate through them becomes too low. However, the self-cleaning, automatic, viscous filter shown in Fig. 13 or a filter cleaned with water sprays (55) as indicated in Fig. 14 can be operated continuously. The automatic viscous filter is constructed of overlapping, hinged panels mounted so as to create a vertical curtain. The curtain travels on chains over top and bottom sprockets either at a continuous slow speed or intermittently under the control of an electric timer. In either case the rate of movement is such that one complete circuit is usually made in 24 hours. The gas to be cleaned passes through a double layer of filter panels. At the bottom point of their cycle the panels dip into an oil bath where agitation dislodges the accumulated matter, which falls to the bottom of the tank, forming a sludge that is periodically removed. The panels, cleaned and freshly oiled, upon rising return to their over-lapping position to form again a filtering curtain.

Some types of aggregate bed filters are equipped with circulating or vibrating mechanisms which serve to clean the media. The vibrating system (51) actually shakes the bed container, which is spring supported, and at the same time reverses the flow of gas. Shock wave cleaning has been successfully applied to a stainless steel filter collecting open hearth furnace fumes (56). Aggregate can, of course, be removed from the filter bed for cleaning, either continuously or batchwise.

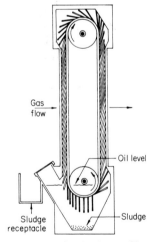

FIG. 13. Automatic viscous filter.

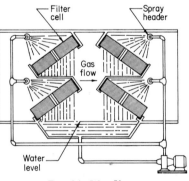

FIG. 14. Wet filter.

B. PRESSURE LOSS

A great many relationships for the resistance of fibrous mats have been proposed (57, 58). From a large quantity of experimental data on filters of glass and steel fibers, the empirical equation

$$\Delta p = \left(0.6 + \frac{4.7}{\sqrt{Re}} + \frac{11}{Re}\right) \frac{2\rho_g u^2 L(1 - \epsilon_f)}{\pi g_c D_f} \tag{4}$$

has been suggested. It is most satisfactory (59) for conditions of $10^{-3} < Re < 10^{-2}$ (laminar flow) and $0.93 < \epsilon_f < 0.98$. Here Re $(=D_f u \rho_g / \mu)$ is the Reynolds number, and all other quantities are expressed in consistent units. If $\epsilon_f = 0.95$, $L = 0.0254$ m $(=1$ inch), $D_f = 2 \times 10^{-5}$ m, $\rho_g = 1.20$ kg/m³, $\mu = 1.81 \times 10^{-5}$ kg/m sec, $u_s = 0.51$ m/sec $(=100$ ft/min). With u defined as u_s/ϵ_f, the Reynolds number will be 0.712 and the pressure loss indicated by Eq. (4) will be 31 kg/m² or 1.2 inches of water.

Open pore foam filters show little pressure increase during the dust-loading period. Their collection efficiency is similar to that of a glass fibrous mat if an apparent fiber diameter is derived from initial pressure loss data (60). The pressure loss across a homogeneously mixed, multi-component fiber filter is always lower than is the pressure drop across a filter composed of layers of the same components in the same weight fractions (61).

C. EFFICIENCY

The removal by fibrous filters of fine, uncharged particulate matter suspended in a gas stream is due to inertial effects, Brownian motion, and direct interception. While it is a simple matter to describe in general terms the characteristics and relative importance of these several factors, only by means of monodisperse aerosols is it possible to offer convincing experimental demonstration of their influences. Curves of efficiency plotted against velocity using monodisperse aerosols generally show a decrease in efficiency as the velocity increases. Diffusional effects decrease under the same conditions but inertia becomes steadily more important. Particles of approximately 0.1 μ diameter penetrate a mat filter more readily than any other because both inertial influences and Brownian diffusion are small (62) in this size range. A typical efficiency curve is shown in Fig. 15 with collection efficiency plotted against a nondimensional inertia parameter.

Electrostatic attraction will draw particles from the gas stream to the fibers if the two are oppositely charged. Even if only one of the materials, i.e., the particles or the fibers, is charged, an induced charge will be created on the other, producing a polarization force that results in at-

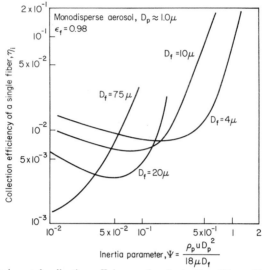

FIG. 15. Experimental collection efficiency of a single fiber [From Kimura and Iinoya (62a)].

traction and particle deposition (63). Electrostatic charge also influences particle agglomeration which increases the likelihood of particle entrapment. Charges may be developed through frictional effects during the filtering operation (64) even if not initially present. Applying electrostatic charges to the filter by means of embedded wires, for example, also enhances collection efficiency (65–68).

By no means all the particles that contact a fiber adhere to it. The adherence or nonadherence of particles upon impact depends, among other factors, upon the angle of impaction (69). Some of the unexplained filtration results may be due in part to the particles escaping capture on contact. Reentrainment always begins to be a significant factor after a certain dust load is accumulated on a mat. The particular condition under which this occurs depends primarily on the filter medium itself, the particles, and the gas velocity. It is not presently predictable.

A general correlation for the collection efficiency of a single fiber, neglecting gravitational and electrical influence but considering diffusion and direct interception (70–72), may be written

$$\eta_0 = \frac{6\left(\dfrac{kT}{3\,\pi\mu}\right)^{2/3}}{\left(\dfrac{\mu}{\rho_g}\right)^{1/6} D_f^{1/2} D_p^{2/3} u^{1/2}} + \frac{3D_p^2 u^{1/2}}{\left(\dfrac{\mu}{\rho_g}\right)^{1/2} D_f^{3/2}} \tag{5}$$

where all terms are expressed in consistent units. This equation, for example, indicates a single-fiber efficiency of 0.73% when $k = 1.38 \times 10^{-23}$ kg m²/sec °K, $T = 293$ °K, $\mu = 1.81 \times 10^{-5}$ kg/m sec, $\rho_g = 1.20$ kg/m³, $D_f = 2 \times 10^{-5}$ m, $D_p = 10^{-6}$ m, and $u = 0.537$ m/sec as for Eq. (4). Neighboring fibers, of course, exert an influence on the collection efficiency of any individual fiber (73). An experimentally derived expression that takes into account this influence is written (62a)

$$\eta_i = \eta_0 \left[1 + 10 \left(\frac{D_f u \rho_g}{\mu} \right)^{1/3} (1 - \epsilon_f) \right] \tag{6}$$

where the single fiber efficiency is multiplied by the Reynolds number to account for dynamic changes and by a porosity function to allow for variation in the filter itself. Equation (6), therefore, expresses the efficiency of a single fiber for collecting particles when other fibers are nearby. Using the value for η_0 as calculated by Eq. (5), $\epsilon_f = 0.95$, and other values as before, Eq. (6) gives this value to be 1.04%.

If the depth of the filter corresponds to less than a layer of 500 individual fibers, the initial efficiency of the filter, i.e., the efficiency at the beginning of use, becomes

$$E_o = 1 - \exp \left[\frac{-4(1 - \epsilon_f)L}{\pi D_f} \eta_i \right] \tag{7}$$

on the basis of the so-called log-penetration theory. The overall efficiency of a filter 1 inch thick (=0.0254 m) with other conditions as before is 56.8%, according to Eq. (7). Other experimental equations of the initial filter efficiency have been presented using specified parameters (74).

Since the collection efficiency of a mat gradually increases as dust accumulates, the cumulative collection efficiency, i.e., the average efficiency from time zero to time t, is a useful quantity. The efficiency at time t may be estimated from a dimensionless correlation involving the initial collection efficiency (75) expressed by

$$E = 1 - (1 - E_0) \exp \left[-50 \sqrt{\frac{(1 - \epsilon_f)}{\pi}} \frac{\mu C_i \eta_i}{\rho_g \rho_p D_p D_f} t \right] \tag{8}$$

This equation, using the conditions previously assumed and the calculated results with $C_i = 11.4 \times 10^{-6}$ kg/m³ (=5 $\times 10^{-3}$ grains/ft³), gives an efficiency of 84.3% when $t = 1$ hour and 99.7% when $t = 5$ hours. The cumulative efficiency is obtained by combining Eqs. (7) and (8).

Fibers having a noncircular cross section will behave somewhat differently from round fibers. In granular beds particularly the condensation of vapor on the grains and evaporation from their surfaces will have an influence (76). Very small particles—0.0015 μ in diameter, a size which actually classes them as atmospheric ions—are readily captured by filters (77). This behavior is due to the diffusion mechanism.

V. General Considerations

A. Precooling

Furnace and other process gases must often be cooled before filtering in order to protect the filter media and to ensure an economical filter life. One of three methods—cooling by radiation, convection, or waste heat boilers; addition of tempering air; and cooling with water sprays—or a combination of methods is usually employed.

Cooling by radiation, convection, or heat exchanger involves a considerable investment in equipment, requires a relatively large amount of space, and lacks flexibility with respect to the temperatures that can be attained. Admission of outdoor air permits precise regulation of temperature, when full modulating bleed-in dampers are used, and is just about the only method of cooling that is practical with gases having high moisture content. However, because the filter is required to handle a greater volume of gas owing to the tempering air, the filter must necessarily be larger and more expensive and the operating cost of the blower becomes greater. Therefore, the tempering air method is usually the most expensive one. Direct water spray cooling is feasible if the gas is dry. Water sprays may be used indirectly to cool the outside of radiation and convection surfaces when that method of cooling is employed. Cooling is generally more satisfactory if two or more of the above methods are employed in a single installation to supplement each other, thereby making possible better control. Assuming average construction and operating costs for each element, comparisons among the total estimated costs of the three cooling methods show that if a cotton cloth filter is used which limits the allowable temperature to about 210 °F and if the superficial gas velocity is taken as 10 ft/min, the spray cooling method will give the lowest cost. If, on the other hand, a glass cloth filter is used with an operating temperature of about 480 °F and an allowable superficial velocity of only 3 ft/min, the indirect heat exchanger may be the cheapest. An example of relative fan horsepower requirements for gas cooling is given in Fig. 16 (78). Two cases are

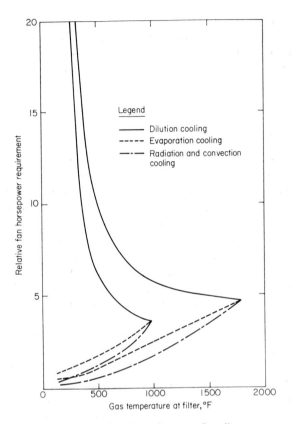

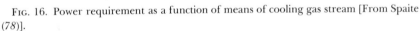

FIG. 16. Power requirement as a function of means of cooling gas stream [From Spaite (78)].

illustrated, one where the initial temperature is 1000 °F and one where it is 1800 °F. As indicated, the fan horsepower requirement for dilution cooling increases with the difference between the stream and cooling gas temperature. Heat exchanger cooling (radiation and convection) requires the lowest fan horsepower.

B. FIRE HAZARDS

Filtration of oxidizable substances can constitute a serious fire hazard. Sparks or accidental sources of ignition such as lighted cigarettes can be extremely dangerous. Fires in filtration units may quickly attain high temperatures unless the air flow is cut off and sprinkler systems or other fire control mechanisms are available to control the conflagration. Because of this, all large filter installations having this characteristic should be equipped with automatic devices for closing off the flow of air in case of fire, and should be provided with adequate sprinklers or carbon dioxide fire control apparatus. The use of spark arresters in ducts leading to filter units is recommended.

C. OVERALL COSTS

Compared to other particulate collectors, the filter usually exhibits a high maintenance cost, especially if the medium is of the throwaway type. In addition, the cost of the blower, motor, structural steel, piping, and installation, taken together, may exceed that of the basic filter unit. If the filter can be installed for pressure operation, i.e., with the blower located ahead of the filter, the initial cost may be less than if a suction-type installation is required. This is so because the physical dimensions of the filter housing can be slightly smaller and hence less expensive.

The initial cost of a reverse-jet filter is currently approximately $1.00 per cfm of capacity, which is comparable to that of an electrostatic precipitator. A fabric filter provided with intermittent mechanical cleaning costs between $0.30 and $0.60 per cfm which is approximately twice that of cyclone collectors. High temperature capability and the necessity of lower filtering velocity will, of course, make the initial cost greater. Cotton is the cheapest filter cloth, while fiber glass is usually the most expensive. The initial costs of fibrous mat filters are generally about one-tenth those of cloth filters, but their maintenance, including replacement charges, can easily reverse the situation.

Filter maintenance costs, exclusive of power costs, are usually around 10–30% that of the cloth filters themselves and may reach three times the initial installed costs for throwaway filters.

From the standpoint of construction and operating costs, the optimum superficial velocity for a filter cloth is usually between 5 and 10 ft/min, regardless of the operating temperature. This is so because lower velocities require larger filtering areas and greater initial cost while higher velocities are accompanied by greater pressure losses which give rise to higher operating cost. The actual superficial velocity is often set lower than the above figure in order to obtain a lower pressure loss, greater collection efficiency, and longer fabric life.

D. HUMIDITY

High relative humidities during warm seasons of the year have very little effect on the performance of most gas filtering units unless the collected particles are hygroscopic. Troubles are most likely to occur during the winter if filter units are located out of doors. In such cases, when gas comes from a humid operation at a temperature considerably higher than that outside, it is very likely that there will be condensation of moisture. While moisture of itself may render a filter's operation unsatisfactory, it can lead to even greater difficulties if freezing takes place. The possible effects of condensation should therefore, always be considered in designing and locating a filter.

REFERENCES

1. W. E. Ballard, *Rock Prod.* **65**(10), 61 (1962).
2. R. T. Pring, *Heating Ventilating* **49**(12) 97 (1952).
3. J. E. L'Anson, *et al.*, *Am. Foundryman* **23**(1), 61 (1963).
4. A. E. Gosselin, Jr., *J. Air Pollution Control Assoc.* **15**, 179 (1965).
5. K. J. Caplan, *Chem. Eng. Progr.* **50**, 409 (1954).
6. Anonymous, *Chem. Eng. Progr.* **56**(5), 126 (1960).
7. D. G. Stephan and G. W. Walsh, *Ind. Eng. Chem.* **52**, 999 (1960).
8. D. G. Stephan, P. T. Bohnslav, R. A. Herrick, G. W. Walsh, and A. H. Rose, *Am. Ind. Hyg. Assoc. J.* **19**, 276 (1958); **21**, 1 (1960).
9. G. W. Walsh and P. W. Spaite, *J. Air Pollution Control Assoc.* **12**, 57 (1962).
10. P. F. Frey and T. V. Reinauer, *Air Eng.* **6**(4), 30 (1964).
11. P. W. Spaite, J. E. Hagen, and W. F. Todd, *Chem. Eng. Progr.* **59**(4), 54 (1963).
12. C. A. Snyder and R. T. Pring, *Ind. Eng. Chem.* **47**, 960 (1955).
12a. W. Strauss, "Industrial Gas Cleaning." Pergamon Press, Oxford, 1966.
13. E. R. Frederick, *Chem. Eng.* **68**(13), 107 (1961).
14. E. Butterworth, *Mfg. Chemist* **35**(6), 66 (1964); **35**(2), 65 (1964).
15. L. Silverman, E. W. Conners, and D. M. Anderson, *Ind. Eng. Chem.* **47**, 952 (1955).
16. K. T. Whitby, D. A. Lundgren, A. R. McFarland, and R. C. Jordan, *J. Air Pollution Control Assoc.* **11**, 503 (1961).
17. D. A. Lundgren and K. T. Whitby, *Ind. Eng. Chem., Process Design Develop.* **4**, 345 (1965).
18. P. A. F. White and S. E. Smith, "High Efficiency Air Filtration." Butterworth, London and Washington, D.C., 1964.
19. J. L. Englesberg, *Ind. Eng. Chem.* **56**(10), 65 (1964).
20. K. Iinoya and M. Yamamura, *Chem. Eng. (Tokyo)* **20**, 163 (1956).
21. G. E. Cunningham, G. Broughton, and R. R. Kraybill, *Ind. Eng. Chem.* **46**, 1196 (1954).
22. C. N. Davies, *Proc. Inst. Mech. Engrs. (London)* **B1**, 185 (1952).
23. L. W. Rainard, *Textile Res. J.* **16**, 473 (1946); **17**, 167 (1947).
24. N. Kimura and K. Iinoya, *Chem. Eng. (Tokyo)* **29**, 166 (1965); abridged ed. in English **3**, 193 (1965).
25. R. Dennis, G. A. Johnson, and L. Silverman, *Chem. Eng.* **59**, 196 (1952).
26. K. Iinoya, "Sujin-sochi (Dust Collectors)," p. 200. Nikkan Kogyo Shinbun-sha, Japan, 1963.
27. K. Iinoya, "Funtaikogaku Handbook (Handbook of Power Technology)," p. 406. Asakura-shoten, Japan, 1965.
28. G. L. Fairs, *Trans. Inst. Chem. Engrs. (London)* **36**, 476 (1958).
29. E. Stafford and W. J. Smith, *Ind. Eng. Chem.* **43**, 1346 (1951).

30. P. A. F. White and S. E. Smith, *Research (London)* **13**, 228 (1960).
31. J. A. Wheat, *Can. J. Chem. Eng.* **41**, 67 (1963).
32. R. H. Collingbourne and H. E. Painter, *Intern. J. Air Water Pollution* **8**, 159 (1964).
33. R. F. Hounam, *Ann. Occupational Hyg.* **4**, 301 (1961).
34. J. K. Shrebowski and B. W. Sutton, *Brit. Chem. Eng.* **6**, 12 (1961).
35. *Staub* **23**, 21 (1963) [translation by J. P. Lodge, *J. Am. Assoc. Contamination Control* **4**(2), 10 (1965)].
36. S. C. Stern, H. W. Zeller, and A. I. Schekman, General Mill Inc. Rept. No. 1890 (1959) (for AEC); *J. Colloid Sci.* **15**, 546 (1960).
37. G. G. Goyer, R. Gruen, and V. K. LaMer, *J. Phys. Chem.* **58**, 137 (1954).
38. E. Landt, *Gesundh.-Ingr.* **77**, 139 (1956).
39. C. A. Rodman and J. A. Staricenka, *Mech. Eng.* **85**, 54 (1963).
40. L. Silverman, *Ind. Eng. Chem.* **49**, No. 7, 67A (1957).
41. L. Silverman, *et al., Ind. Wastes* **4**, 73 (1959).
42. C. E. Billings, C. Kurker, Jr., and L. Silverman, *J. Air Pollution Control Assoc.* **8**, 185 (1958).
43. C. E. Billings, L. H. Lebenbaum, C. Kurker, E. C. Hickey, and L. Silverman, *J. Air Pollution Control Assoc.* **8**, 53 (1958).
44. M. W. First, J. B. Graham, G. M. Butler, C. B. Walworth, and R. P. Warren, *Ind. Eng. Chem.* **48**, 696 (1956).
45. R. B. Norden, *Chem. Eng.* **66**(16), 158 (1959).
46. O. H. York and E. W. Poppele, *Chem. Eng. Progr.* **59**(6), 45 (1963).
47. R. E. Yoder and F. M. Empson, *Am. Ind. Hyg. Assoc. J.* **19**, 107 (1958).
48. J. A. Brink, Jr., *Chem. Eng.* **66**(23), 183 (1959).
49. L. Silverman, *Blast Furnace Steel Plant* **43**, 735 (1955).
50. L. Silverman and M. W. First, *Ind. Eng. Chem.* **44**, 2777 (1952).
51. H. L. Engelbrecht, *J. Air Pollution Control Assoc.* **15**(2), 43 (1965).
52. D. C. Scott and D. A. Guthrie, *Can. J. Chem. Eng.* **37**, 200 (1959).
53. M. R. Pack, *J. Air Pollution Control Assoc.* **15**, 166 (1965).
54. M. W. First and J. B. Graham, *Ind. Eng. Chem.* **50**, No. 6, 63A (1958).
55. M. W. First, R. Moschella, L. Silverman, and E. Berly, *Ind. Eng. Chem.* **43**, 1363 (1951).
56. C. E. Billings and L. Silverman, *Intern. J. Air Water Pollution* **6**, 455 (1962).
57. J. B. Wong, W. E. Ranz, and H. F. Johnstone, *J. Appl. Phys.* **27**, 161 (1956).
58. C. Y. Chen, *Chem. Rev.* **55**, 595 (1955).
59. N. Kimura and K. Iionya, *Chem. Eng. (Tokyo)* **23**, 792 (1959).
60. N. Kimura and K. Iionya, *Chem. Eng. (Tokyo)* **29**, 622 (1965).
61. L. A. Clarenburg and R. M. Werner, *Ind. Eng. Chem., Process Design Develop.* **4**, 293 (1965).
62. J. W. Thomas and R. E. Yoder, *A.M.A. Arch. Ind. Health* **13**, 545 (1956).
62a. N. Kimura and K. Iinoya, *Chem. Eng. (Tokyo)* **29**, 538 (1965).
63. V. Havlicek, *Intern. J. Air Water Pollution* **4**, 225 (1961).
64. A. T. Rossano and L. Silverman, *Heating Ventilating* **51**(5), 102 (1954).
65. R. D. Rivers, *ASHRAE, J.* **4**(2), 37 (1962).
66. J. W. Thomas and E. J. Woodfin, *Trans. AIEE* **78**, Part II, 276 (1959).
67. R. Flossman and A. Schuetz, *Staub* **23**, 443 (1963).
68. K. Iinoya, K. Makino, and N. Kimura, *Chem. Eng. (Tokyo)* **29**, 574 (1965).
69. T. Gillespie, *J. Colloid Sci.* **10**, 266, 289, and 299 (1955).
70. S. K. Friedlander, *Ind. Eng. Chem.* **50**, 1161 (1958).
71. R. E. Pasceri and S. K. Friedlander, *Can. J. Chem. Eng.* **38**, 212 (1960).

72. A. Aiba and T. Yasuda, *A.I.Ch.E. Journal* **8,** 704 (1962).
73. I. Gallily, *J. Colloid Sci.* **12,** 161 (1957).
74. R. G. Dorman, *Intern. J. Air Water Pollution* **3,** 112 (1960).
75. N. Kimura and K. Iinoya, *Chem. Eng. (Tokyo)* **28,** 39 (1964); abridged ed. in English **2,** 136 (1964).
76. N. Fuchs and A. Kirsch, *Chem. Eng. Sci.* **20,** 181 (1965).
77. J. Fortan, D. Blanc, and A. Bouville, *Health Phys.* **11,** 15 (1965).
78. P. W. Spaite, D. G. Stephan, and A. H. Rose, *J. Air Pollution Control Assoc.* **11,** 243 (1961).

GENERAL REFERENCES

Additional pertinent material is in Chap. 4 of "Air Pollution Engineering Manual, Los Angeles APCD" (J. A. Danielson, ed.), PHS Publ. 999-AP-40, DHEW, Cincinnati (1967); and in Chapter 5 of "Air Pollution Manual, Part II," American Industrial Hygiene Assn., Detroit (1968); and will be published in the National Air Pollution Control Administration's publication: "Control Technology for Particulate Air Pollutants."

45 Source Control by Electrostatic Precipitation

Chad F. Gottschlich

Nomenclature

A Cross-sectional area of dust layer, cm^2

A_R Resistivity constant characteristic of the material, ohm-cm

A_s Total collecting electrode surface, m^2

b Roughness factor

C Constant of integration, volts

D Particle diameter, meters

d Spacing between the discharge and plate electrodes, meters

E Electrical field strength, v/m

E' Activation energy required for conduction, joules

E_c Charging field, v/m

E_p Collecting field, v/m

E_s Minimum field strength required for corona discharge, v/m

h Average spacing between discharge electrodes, meters

I Electrical current, amperes

i Electrical current per unit length of the discharge electrode, amp/m

J $1.764 + 0.562e^{-0.785D/\lambda}$

K Ion mobility, m^2/v-sec

k Boltzmann's constant, 1.3805×10^{-23} joules/°K

K_0 Dielectric constant of a vacuum, 8.85434×10^{-12} coulombs²/joule-m

N Ion concentration, ions/m^3

p $\dfrac{3\xi}{\xi + 2}$

Q Volumetric flow rate, m^3/sec

q Electrical charge on a particle, coulombs

R_1 Discharge electrode radius, meters

R_2 Collecting electrode radius, meters

r Radial distance measured from the centerline of the discharge electrode, meters

T Absolute temperature, °K

t	Time, seconds	η	Precipitator collection efficiency, percent
V	Voltage difference between the electrodes, volts	λ	Mean free path of gas molecules, meters
V_c	Voltage difference across the corona, volts	μ	Absolute viscosity, poises
V_s	Corona starting voltage, volts	ξ	Dielectric constant, electrostatic cgs units
w	Particle drift velocity, m/sec		
x	Dust layer thickness, centimeters	ρ_B	Bulk resistivity, ohm-cm
ϵ	Elementary electronic charge, 1.5921×10^{-19} coulombs	σ	Space charge, coulombs/m^3

I. Introduction

The function of an electrostatic precipitator is the removal of particles (solid or liquid) from gaseous streams. This is done by passing the gas between a pair of electrodes—a discharge electrode at a high potential and an electrically grounded collecting electrode. The potential difference must be great enough so that a corona discharge surrounds the discharge electrode. Gas ions formed in the corona move rapidly, under the action of the electrical field, toward the collecting electrode, and transfer their charge to the particles by collision with them. The electrical field interacting with the charge on the particles then causes them to drift toward, and be deposited on, the collecting electrode.

When the particles are liquid droplets, the collected droplets coalesce on the collecting electrode and drip off the bottom of that electrode into a collecting sump. When the particles are solid, the dust layer that forms on the collecting electrode is removed by rapping to cause the deposit to break loose from the electrode. In effect, this returns the dust to the gas stream, but not in its original finely divided state. As a result of cohesive forces developed between the particles deposited on the electrode, the dust is returned as agglomerates which are large enough so that gravity will cause them to fall into dust hoppers below the electrodes. Reduced to its essentials, the electrostatic precipitator acts as a particle agglomerator combined with a gravity settling chamber.

The electrical mechanisms for precipitation of particles are: (1) supplying an electrical charge to the particles and (2) supplying the electrostatic force that causes the charged particles to drift toward the collecting electrode. In the usual industrial electrostatic precipitators, both are supplied simultaneously and the precipitator acts as a single-stage unit. Typical industrial precipitators are shown in Figs. 1 and 2. However, in the case of air conditioning applications and a few industrial applications, a two-stage precipitator is used in which the two mechanisms are separated. One set of electrodes supplies the electrical

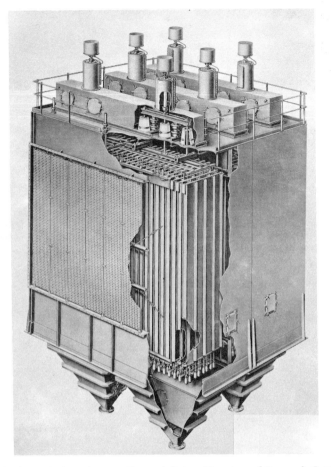

FIG. 1. A wire-and-plate electrostatic precipitator. (Courtesy of Research-Cottrell, Inc., Bound Brook, New Jersey.)

charge to the particles and a second set supplies the electrostatic force that precipitates the charged particles.

The essential components of the electrode system are a fine "wire" discharge electrode and an extended surface collecting electrode. Typical collecting electrode designs are shown in Fig. 3. Many designers currently prefer solid plates having triangular baffles (the Opzel plate) to reduce reentrainment of the dust by the gas stream. A substantial improvement in collection efficiency has been claimed (1). Although hereinafter referred to as a wire, the discharge electrode may take forms other than finely drawn wire. The usual electrode arrangements are: (1)

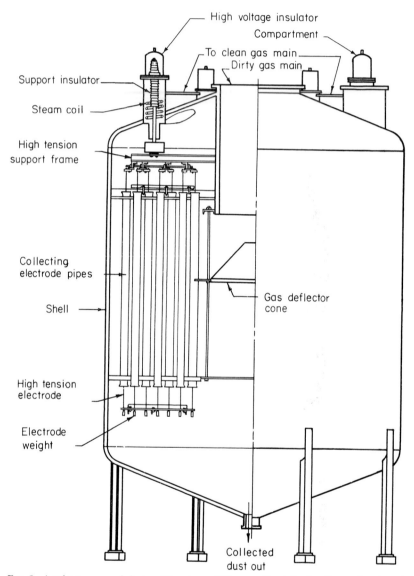

FIG. 2. A tube-type precipitator. (Courtesy of Western Precipitation Corp., Los Angeles, California.)

wires suspended along the centerline of vertical, tubular collecting electrodes and (2) vertical wires suspended midway between parallel-plate collecting electrodes.

The wires are suspended from an insulated hanger at the top and are kept under tension by weights attached to their lower ends. For the wire-

and-tube electrode system, the gas flow path is down around the outside of the tubes and then up through the inside of the tubes. For the wire-and-plate electrode system, the gas flow may also be vertically upward between the plates, but is usually horizontal between the plates.

The electrostatic precipitator is a high efficiency collector. The objective of visually clear stacks has made it necessary for many installations to operate at efficiencies of 98–99% and in some cases in the 99.5–99.9+% range. Units have been installed with capacities up to 3,000,000 cfm, gas temperatures up to 1200 °F, and pressures up to 150 psig. The draft loss is low, 0.1 to 0.5 inches of water. The electric power required to maintain the corona ranges from 50 to 500 watts/1000 cfm. These energy requirements are small compared to those for other gas cleaning devices. This is so primarily because the energy used for collection is applied directly to the particles. In other types of devices the energy is applied to the entire gas stream. Disadvantages of precipitators are higher first cost, larger space requirements, and a possible explosion hazard if the particles or the gas are combustible.

Over 60% of the installed capacity of precipitators in the United States is used for fly ash recovery. Lesser amounts are used in the following industries: 16% in metals, 10% in cement, 6% in paper, and 3% for chemicals. The remaining capacity is used mainly for the detarring of fuel gases and for carbon black recovery. Possible future applications, some of which are presently under development, include fine particle recovery for coal-burning gas turbines, fossil fuel gasification, fluid-bed reactors, magnetohydrodynamic power generation, and urban incinerators.

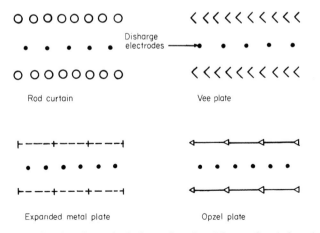

FIG. 3. Typical collecting electrode designs, plan view. The gas flow is from left to right.

II. Electrical Field and Particle Charging

The field strength, E, of the electrical field between the electrodes is defined as the derivative of the voltage, V, with respect to distance, r, i.e., the voltage gradient. The fundamental differential equation which describes the field distribution between a pair of electrodes is Poisson's equation. In its most general form it is expressed vectorially,

$$\nabla \cdot E = \frac{\sigma}{K_0} \tag{1}$$

where σ is the space charge, i.e., the quantity of electrical charge per unit volume of the space between the electrodes.

Since the wire-and-tube electrode arrangement is easier to analyze mathematically, it will be used to derive a number of the relationships involved in precipitator operation. The more important wire-and-plate electrodes will be discussed later. For the wire-and-tube electrodes with no space charge (i.e., no gas ions or charged particles in the space between the electrodes), Poisson's equation becomes, in cylindrical coordinates,

$$\frac{dE}{dr} + \frac{E}{r} = 0 \tag{2}$$

Integration of this equation yields

$$E = \frac{C}{r} \tag{3}$$

The constant of integration, C, can be determined from

$$V = -\int_{R_1}^{R_2} E \, dr \tag{4}$$

and is

$$C = \frac{V}{\ln R_1/R_2} \tag{5}$$

Equation (3) shows that the finer the discharge electrode, the greater will be the field strength at the surface of the electrode. At points distant from the discharge electrode, the field strength becomes small. This is the kind of field distribution that is required to produce a corona.

If a direct-current voltage greater than the corona starting voltage is applied to a wire-and-tube electrode system, ionization of the gas occurs, producing a corona confined to the region of high field strength, i.e., close to the wire. If the field distribution were more nearly uniform, as is that produced by parallel-plate electrodes, the corona would no

longer be confined and would become unstable, producing only sparking. In sparking, the gas ionizes in narrowly confined paths extending
from one electrode to the other, a condition not conducive to efficient
particle collection.

At very high gas temperatures the gas will also become ionized as a
result of the thermal collisions of the molecules. If this occurs to an
appreciable extent, the conductivity of the gas rises rapidly, resulting
in a sharp drop in the voltage that can be maintained between the electrodes. Thus, the region of appreciable thermal ionization puts an upper
limit to the temperature at which electrostatic precipitators may be
operated. The actual temperature depends upon the composition of
the gas, but in most cases is of the order of 1500 °F (2).

One has a choice of applying either a positive or a negative potential
to the discharge electrode. For industrial precipitators the negative potential is normally selected because, usually, higher voltages can be used
without excessive sparking. However, this is true only if the gas has elec-
tronegative constituents, such as oxygen, sulfur dioxide, water vapor,
and halogens, as is the case with most industrial gases. Although some
contradictory evidence exists (3), a negative corona seems superior up
to the highest temperatures investigated. This has been borne out by
the recent development of several high temperature precipitator applications (2).

Peek (4) has found experimentally that the field strength required to
form a corona (for wire-and-concentric-tube electrodes) must be at least

$$E_s = 31 \times 10^5 b \left(1 + \frac{0.0308}{\sqrt{R_1}} \right) \tag{6}$$

for air at 25 °C and 1 atm of pressure. The constant, b, is a "roughness
factor" which takes into account the nature of the wire surface; with increasing roughness, b decreases, and consequently E_s decreases.

By combining Eq. (6) with Eqs. (3) and (5) for the field distribution,
an equation for the corona starting voltage may be derived.

$$V_s = 31 \times 10^5 b \left(1 + \frac{0.0308}{\sqrt{R_1}} \right) R_1 \ln R_1/R_2 \tag{7}$$

This equation shows that to obtain the lowest possible starting voltage,
it is necessary to use a discharge electrode having the smallest radius of
curvature that other considerations, e.g., mechanical strength requirements, permit. If mechanical strength requirements make a large
diameter wire necessary, an electrode having a square rather than a
circular cross section is used. The sharp edges of the square wire correspond to a very small radius of curvature so that the square wire be-

haves like a round wire having a much smaller diameter. Spiked wires have also been used. The sharp points of the spikes make such electrodes effective in reducing the corona starting voltage.

Ionization occurs in the corona, producing an electrically neutral mixture of positive ions, electrons, and negative ions. Because the discharge electrode is usually negatively charged, the positive ions stream toward it, where they are neutralized. Positive ions are absent in the region outside the corona. In this outer region the electrons and negative ions are streaming toward the collecting electrodes. As they do so, many of them will strike and become attached to the dust particles by so-called electrical image forces. Pauthenier and Moreau-Hanot (5) found that the charge, q, accumulated on a spherical particle during a period of time, t, is

$$q = \frac{pED^2}{12 \times 10^8} \left[\frac{t}{t + \dfrac{4K_0}{N\epsilon K}} \right] \tag{8}$$

Equation (8) shows that a particle will achieve 91% of its ultimate charge in $40K_0/N\epsilon K$ seconds. Under normal conditions, this time is of the order of 10^{-2} seconds, which corresponds to a small fraction of the residence time of the gas in the precipitator field.

Ion bombardment, as discussed above, is the most important charging mechanism for dust particles having a diameter greater than about 2 μ. For particles smaller than about 0.2 μ, charging by ion diffusion becomes the controlling mechanism. ("Ion diffusion" means motion of the ions produced by thermal motion of the surrounding gas molecules, rather than motion caused by the electrical field.) For particles in the 0.2–2.0 μ range, both mechanisms are, of course, important. Since the particles are larger than 2 μ in most applications, ion diffusion is not an important mechanism for dusts normally encountered in electrostatic precipitators, except for some metallurgical fumes. However, as the demand for still cleaner industrial effluent gases continues, charging by ion diffusion will become more important.

In a precipitator, the space charge produced by the gas ions must be considered in the integration of the Poisson equation. Townsend (6) solved this problem in the course of an investigation of ion mobilities and obtained

$$E = \left(\frac{C^2}{r^2} + \frac{i}{2\pi K_o K} \right)^{1/2} \tag{9}$$

C is an arbitrary constant resulting from the integration and must be computed from Eq. (4).

Equation (9) can be simplified for certain special cases. For larger values of i and r, a convenient approximation of the equation is

$$E = \sqrt{\frac{i}{2\pi K_0 K}} \qquad (10)$$

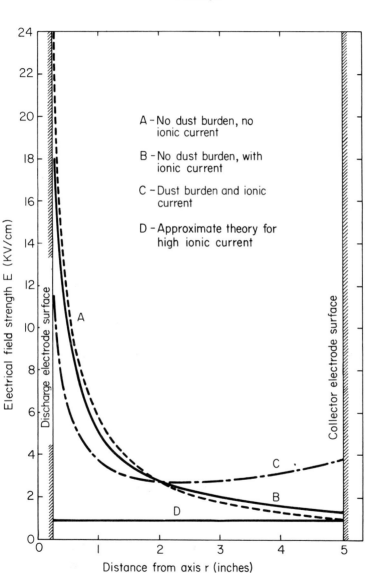

FIG. 4. Electrical field strength as a function of position in a wire-and-tube precipitator. [Courtesy of H. J. Lowe, D. H. Lucas, and the Institute of Physics, London (7).]

This equation does not apply in the vicinity of the discharge electrode, where the field strength is much greater. Figure 4 shows a comparison of the various field strength equations given [Curve A, Eq. (3); B, Eq. (9); D, Eq. (10)] with a more rigorous theory (Curve C).

Despite the drastic assumptions that have been made in the derivation of Eq. (10), Troost (8) has shown that it describes at least some of the behavior of precipitators with high accuracy. He made the assumption that there is a constant voltage drop, V_c, across the corona. The remainder of the voltage drop between the electrodes is accounted for by Eq. (10), i.e.,

$$V = V_c + (R_2 - R_1) \sqrt{\frac{i}{2\pi K_0 K}} \tag{11}$$

This equation shows that a plot of the total voltage drop V against the square root of the current per unit length of discharge electrode should be a straight line. Measurements made by Troost on a wire-and-tube precipitator confirmed his assumptions satisfactorily.

Additional measurements made by Troost, together with a semitheoretical argument, indicate that the field in a wire-and-plate precipitator is

$$E = \sqrt{\frac{2id}{\pi K_0 K h}} \tag{12}$$

This differs from Eq. (10) for wire-and-tube precipitators only by a geometrical factor.

The presence of dust in the gas alters the conclusions stated above because the dust contributes to the space charge. For a fixed voltage between the electrodes, the principal effect of the additional space charge is a reduction in the current (9). This is especially noticeable when it is possible to compare the current near the entrance with that near the exit of a precipitator. Very fine dusts can reduce the current almost to zero (10) with a resultant marked reduction in the charge acquired by the particles and in the collection efficiency.

III. Collection Efficiency

A. THEORETICAL EQUATIONS

The gas in a precipitator is normally flowing turbulently because the Reynolds number is usually high and because of the so-called "electric wind" effect. The "electric wind" is motion of the gas at right angles to the main gas flow, induced by the motion of the gas ions streaming from the discharge electrode to the collecting electrode. As a result of the turbulence, the collection efficiency equation takes on an exponential form first empirically determined by Evald Anderson in 1919 and then theoretically derived by W. Deutsch in 1922. One of the more recent derivations of the Anderson-Deutsch collection efficiency equation was made by Rose and Wood (11), who assumed that the turbulent mixing effect is intense enough so that the particle concentration is constant over any cross-sectional area at right angles to the main gas flow, and also implicitly assumed that there is no particle mixing in the direction of gas flow. As a first-order approximation to actual precipitator conditions, these are reasonable assumptions. One of the equivalent forms in which their equation can be expressed is

$$\eta = 100(1 - e^{-\frac{A_g w}{Q}}) \tag{13}$$

The equation shows that the efficiency, η, is related to precipitator size, the quantity of gas flowing per unit time, and the drift velocity of the particles toward the collecting electrodes.

On the reasonable assumptions that (1) the charge accumulated by a particle approaches a limiting value rapidly, (2) the fluid friction acting on the particle can be computed from Stokes' law together with the Cunningham correction factor (important for particles having diameters comparable to or smaller than the mean free path of the gas molecules), and (3) the terminal velocity of the particle drifting toward the collecting electrode is attained rapidly, the drift velocity can be computed from the equation

$$w = \frac{pDE_c E_p}{36 \times 10^7 \pi \mu}\left(1 + \frac{J\lambda}{D}\right) \tag{14}$$

For single-stage precipitators the charging field E_c and the collecting field E_p are approximately the same. For practical calculations they may be obtained from one of the simplified equations for field strength [Eq. (10) or (12)].

B. DUST REMOVAL

The accumulated dust must be removed periodically to maintain good collection efficiency. In light dust load applications such as air conditioning, the precipitator is cleaned by shutting it down and washing the dust off the electrodes. Since the dust load is light, this can be done at relatively infrequent intervals. With the heavy dust loads encountered in industrial precipitators, such a cleaning procedure is impractical.

Methods that are used industrially are: (1) a water film which washes the dust off the collecting electrode surface and (2) electrode rapping.

Electrode rapping is the most common method used. Rapping is carried out by tying groups of collecting plates together by means of a rapping bar passing through them. The end of the bar is periodically struck by a hammer to shake the dust loose. The hammer may be actuated by lifting it to a fixed position and then allowing it to swing against the rapping bar, or it may be spring-loaded and actuated pneumatically, electromagnetically, or by a motor-driven cam.

The frequency and intensity of the rapping cycle have an important effect on the collection efficiency of the precipitator. A high collection efficiency requires that the dust, when rapped loose from the collecting plate, should fall as coarse aggregates, so that the dust is not redispersed into the gas stream. Practical achievement of this is obtained by using frequent, gentle rapping. A rapping frequency of one impact per minute is typical in many applications. It is not desirable to clean the collecting plate electrode completely (12); allowing a layer of dust of 1/2–1 inch thickness to remain reduces reentrainment of the dust. Sproull (13) has observed that rapping in a direction normal to the collecting electrode dislodges the dust layer more easily than rapping parallel to the electrode.

C. REENTRAINMENT

In the theoretical derivations of equations for the collecting efficiency, reentrainment of the deposited dust is usually neglected. For liquid droplets this is proper, but for dry particles, reentrainment losses can markedly reduce the efficiency. There are a number of different causes of reentrainment, each with its own solution. Gas flow through the hoppers can sweep collected dust back into the gas stream. This is minimized by installing baffles in the hoppers to reduce the circulation of gas bypassing the electrodes through the hoppers and by careful elimination of all leaks that would allow the inflow of air by way of the hoppers.

Reentrainment during rapping is discussed in Section III,B.

The strongest force holding the dust on the collecting electrodes is electrostatic and is caused by the flow of current through the dust (14). If the resistivity of the dust is too low, not enough charge will be retained to produce a strong force. In fact, the dust may lose its negative charge completely, acquire a positive charge from the electrode, and then spring back off the plate. This effect is observed, for example, with larger fly ash particles that have undergone only partial combustion, and with carbon black particles. In the first case reentrainment is reduced by using high efficiency cyclone separators preceding the electrostatic precipitator to remove the coarser particles. In the second case the carbon black particles are too fine to be collected by cyclone separators and too conductive to be collected by electrostatic precipitators. However, precipitators act as excellent agglomerators, so that the coarser agglomerated particles produced can be collected in low-velocity cyclones.

Another example of the precipitator being used as an agglomerator is reported by Walker (15). The application is the recovery of "black-liquor" furnace fume. The experimental study indicated that the fume can be agglomerated through collection by, and resuspension from, precipitator electrodes. The coarser particles produced are then recoverable, at high efficiency, in a scrubber.

The flow of gas past the dust deposited on the collecting electrode, at typical velocities of 4–15 ft/sec, produces some reentrainment by erosion. The extent of this is sensitive to the design of the electrode. White and Baxter (1) have reported on experimental measurement of the relative effectiveness of the electrode designs shown in Fig. 3. They conclude that the Opzel plate is distinctly superior to the other designs because of its better shielding against reentrainment.

It is also important that the gas flow be distributed uniformly in the precipitator; otherwise, excessive velocities will occur in some parts with concurrent high reentrainment rates.

IV. Dust Resistivity and Conditioning

A. EFFECT OF RESISTIVITY

The resistivity of the dust layer which accumulates on the collecting electrode has been shown by many investigators (12, 16, 17) to have a marked effect on precipitator operation. Bulk resistivity, ρ_B, is defined by the equation

$$\rho_B = \frac{AV}{xI} \tag{15}$$

The resistivities for dusts normally encountered in industrial precipitator operation range from 10^{-3} ohm-cm for carbon black to 10^{14} ohm-cm for dry lime rock dust at 200 °F (17).

The effect of a resistivity below 10^3–10^4 ohm-cm is discussed in Section III,C.

If the resistivity is very high, more than 2–5×10^{10} ohm-cm, many investigators have observed the occurrence of a phenomenon known as back corona which severely reduces particle collection efficiency. Sproull and Nakada (17) and White (12) have shown that this results from the large voltage drop that develops across a layer of high resistivity dust. According to their description of the process, the dust layer is subjected to a continuous rain of negative ions and negatively charged dust particles. The charge that accumulates must be dissipated by a current flow through the dust layer. For a given current, the voltage drop across the dust layer will be proportional to the dust resistivity and the thickness of the dust layer. It was found that Ohm's law expressed in equation form,

$$V = \rho_B \frac{Ix}{A} \tag{16}$$

applied, except for the first few seconds of dust layer formation. Substituting numerical values in Eq. (16), for a dust of 10^{10} ohm-cm resistivity and a typical precipitator current density of 10^{-6} amp/cm^2, the voltage drop across a layer of dust 1 cm thick is 10 kv. This corresponds to a field strength of 10 kv/cm and is in the range in which ionization of the gas trapped in the dust, i.e., back corona, may occur.

B. Conditioning

Methods must be found to reduce the high field strength that builds up in the dust layer for high resistivity dusts if satisfactory operation of the precipitator is to be attained. Equation (16) shows that this can be done if either the resistivity or the current density can be reduced. However, Sproull and Nakada (17) point out that if the current density is reduced much below 2×10^{-8} amp/cm^2 the particles will not acquire enough charge to precipitate properly. The only alternative then is to find some method of reducing resistivity.

Resistivity can be reduced in many cases by spraying water or steam into the gas before it enters the precipitator. The water, or steam, is adsorbed on the dust particles to form a liquid surface film through which electrolytic conduction of the accumulated charge can occur.

In the case of dusts that do not readily adsorb moisture, chemical conditioning agents such as SO_3 (for basic dusts) and NH_3 (for acidic dusts) will increase the moisture adsorption capacity of the dust. Although the quantity of moisture required for conditioning is normally large, the quantity of the chemical conditioning agent required is strikingly small.

C. Effect of Temperature on Resistivity

The effect of temperature and moisture concentration on the resistivity of a lead fume from a sintering plant (18) is shown in Fig. 5. Quali-

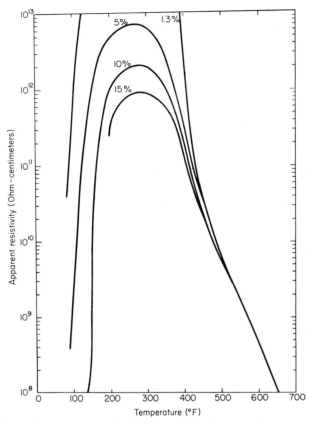

FIG. 5. Effect of temperature and volume percent moisture on the apparent resistivity of lead fume from a sintering plant. [Courtesy of W. A. Schmidt (*18*) and the American Institute of Mining and Metallurgical Engineers, New York.]

tatively, the resistivity curves that have been reported for other materials are similar in appearance to those for lead fume. The resistivity curve passes through a maximum as the temperature is increased, and decreases with increasing moisture concentration.

The general shape of these curves can be explained in the following way. As the temperature rises, less water can be adsorbed on the surface of the dust. The surface conduction path provided by the adsorbed water film is accordingly reduced and the resistivity of the dust rises. Near the maximum of the resistivity curves, so little water remains adsorbed on the surface of the solid that it seems reasonable to say that surface conduction becomes unimportant compared with conduction through the interior of the dust particle.

The dusts normally encountered in electrostatic precipitation are semiconductors. For such materials, the electrical conductivity is partly electronic, as in metals (except that the number of free electrons available is greatly reduced), and partly ionic, as in salt solutions. The temperature dependency of the semiconductor resistivity (18) is the same for both the electronic and the ionic mechanisms, and may be expressed by the equation

$$\rho_B = A_R e^{E'/kT} \tag{17}$$

As Eq. (17) shows, increasing temperature reduces the resistivity of the dust and accounts for the decreasing resistivity of dusts at high temperature.

Figure 5 reveals that at low temperatures and high humidities, and at high temperatures regardless of the humidity, the resistivity is below the level at which precipitation difficulties will be encountered, showing that temperature and humidity controls are essential.

V.   Pressure Drop and Gas Distribution

The electrostatic precipitator has an extremely low pressure drop because it consists of little more than a large box through which gases flow at a low velocity (19). To obtain the maximum advantage from the low pressure drop of the precipitator, care is required in designing the ducts leading from the sources of dusty gas to the precipitator in order to keep the duct pressure losses low as well. This requires minimizing the length and the number of bends in the duct and, in addition, using turning vanes in the bends to further minimize the pressure drop.

A uniform distribution of gas and dust entering a precipitator is essential to obtain the maximum collection efficiency; therefore, careful consideration must be given to proper gas distribution when a precipitator and its ductwork are being designed. The problem is complex and important enough so that some precipitator manufacturers build small-scale models of the precipitators and their ductwork to determine the best way to make the gas distribution uniform.

Two general methods are used to produce a uniform gas and dust distribution. The method employed in almost all modern precipitators is the use of a perforated plate in the inlet to the precipitator. Perforated plates are effective because the flow resistance that they produce tends to smooth out the gas flow approaching the plate.

The second method is the use of turning vanes in the duct bends. They are effective for two reasons: (1) they prevent the duct bends from

producing flow distortion and from centrifuging the dust to the outside radius of the bend, and (2) because of their controlled flow resistance, they also tend to smooth out the flow pattern of the gas approaching them.

VI. Energization

A. POWER SUPPLIES

A power supply to provide a reliable source of high-voltage direct
current is essential for the operation of an electrostatic precipitator. The
power supply consists of a transformer to step up the line voltage, followed by a rectifier to convert the alternating current to the required
direct current.

The maximum output voltage of the transformer ranges from 30,000
to 100,000 v, with the majority of units operating in the 40,000- to
65,000-v range. Control of the output voltage is provided by taps on the
primary which permit the transformer stepup ratio to be adjusted. In
addition, a ballast resistance is connected in series with the transformer
primary to suppress sparking in the precipitator. This is essential because efficient operation of the precipitator requires that it operate near
enough to the sparking voltage so that occasional sparks will occur. The
resistor prevents such sparks from lasting more than a moment because
the increased current resulting from the spark increases the voltage
drop across the resistor and thus reduces the voltage applied to the
precipitator.

Three types of rectifiers are used: mechanical, electronic, and solid
state (e.g., the silicon rectifier). The oldest is the mechanical rectifier
which is simply a synchronously driven switch. Although mechanical
rectifiers are cheap, rugged, and reliable, the present trend is away from
their use in new precipitator installations. The mechanical rectifier has
a number of disadvantages. The open arc produced by the switching
operation is noisy, produces nitrous oxides, and is an explosion hazard.
The electrical contacts require daily cleaning to maintain efficient operation. The mechanical rectifier also produces radio interference unless
properly shielded. It requires more space than do the electronic and
solid-state rectifiers.

Electronic rectifiers were not widely accepted until tube life became
great enough to make their use economically practical. Tube life now
ranges from about 12,000 to 20,000 hours of operation. The newer
electronic rectifiers use a saturable reactor transformer which has made

it possible to eliminate the ballast resistor and the transformer taps. A higher electrical efficiency results from the use of such a transformer and, furthermore, it lends itself well to the use of automatic voltage control of the precipitator.

The more recently developed silicon diode, introduced in 1956, has replaced the electron tubes in precipitators built after the late 1950's (20).

The kind of rectifier used has little effect on the performance of the precipitator, but the wave form of the rectified current can have an important effect. Half-wave rectified current is used almost exclusively for precipitators because, during the period of no current flow, sparking in the precipitator is quenched. This permits a higher operating voltage which produces a higher collection efficiency for the precipitator.

A further refinement in the control of current wave form has been discussed by White (12, 21). White uses a pulse generator in addition to rectifiers and transformers, so that the frequency, amplitude, and wave form of the rectified current can be controlled independently of the line frequency. The advantages claimed for this system are that control of the wave form permits higher operating voltages without increased sparking and that it permits a higher degree of high-voltage electrode sectionalization. Both factors lead to increased collection efficiency for the precipitator.

With most precipitators, the optimum operating voltage fluctuates widely and frequently. Automatic voltage control is used to continuously adjust the precipitator to this optimum voltage, thus producing a collection efficiency significantly higher than can be maintained with a manually controlled precipitator (22).

B. Sectionalization

If a large precipitator is energized by a single power supply, the collection efficiency is lower than would be expected from pilot scale measurements. The cause is that the sparking rate and intensity, at a fixed voltage, increase with increasing size. During each spark the electric current becomes concentrated in the spark channel. This deprives the rest of the precipitator of current. Also, because of the internal impedance of the power supply, the precipitator voltage falls during the spark. Both of these effects markedly reduce the efficiency. White (12) has discussed the solution of this problem in terms of dividing a large precipitator into a number of electrically independent sections, i.e., high-tension sectionalization. He has shown that while the optimum sparking rate (corresponding to maximum efficiency) is independent of the size of the precipitator energized by a single power supply, the actual spark-ing rate increases linearly. Also, since the internal impedance diminishes with increasing current rating of the power supply, the current that can flow during a spark can be larger and the time required to quench it becomes longer. Sectionalization overcomes these problems because of the smaller size of the individual power supplies. As the cost of the power supply increases with an increase in the number of independent electrical sections, there must be an optimum degree of sectionalization.

An additional advantage that results from sectionalization is that the voltage can be adjusted to suit the local conditions in the precipitator. In particular, the high dust concentrations at the inlet reduce the elec-tric current markedly relative to the outlet. Also, the sparking rate at the inlet is higher, for a given voltage. Thus, it is particularly desirable to use series sectionalization to match better the energization requirement to the local conditions. Parallel sectionalization is also needed in large precipitators to overcome the effect of uneven gas and dust distribution that still occurs, to some degree, in spite of efforts to make the flow uni-form. Although parallel sectionalization is useful, series sectionalization is more important. Usually from one to five series sections are used, the larger number being needed for higher efficiency precipitators. In terms of the number of sections needed relative to the volume of gas pro-cessed, there is a range of one-half to ten sections per 100,000 cfm.

REFERENCES

1. H. J. White and W. A. Baxter, Jr., *Mech. Eng.* **82,** 54 (1960).
2. A. B. Walker, H. J. Hall, and M. Robinson, personal communication, Research-Cottrell, Inc., Bound Brook, New Jersey, 1965.
3. C. C. Shale, *Combustion* **35,** 42 (1964); *Proc. 57th Ann. Meeting Air Pollution Control Assoc., Houston, Texas, 1964* Paper No. 64–8.
4. F. N. Peek, Jr., "Dielectric Phenomena in High Voltage Engineering." 2nd ed. McGraw-Hill, New York, 1920.
5. M. Pauthenier and M. Moreau-Hanot, *Electrician* **113,** 187 (1934).
6. J. S. Townsend, *Phil. Mag.* [6] **28,** 83 (1914).
7. H. J. Lowe and D. H. Lucas, *Brit. J. Appl. Phys.* **2,** 540 (1953).
8. N. Troost, *Proc. Inst. Elec. Engrs.* (*London*) **101,** Part II, 369 (1954).
9. P. Cooperman, *Trans. AIEE* **79,** Part I, 47 (1960); **82,** 324 (1963).
10. W. T. Sproull, *J. Air Pollution Control Assoc.* **13,** 617 (1963).
11. H. E. Rose and A. J. Wood, "An Introduction to Electrostatic Precipitation in Theory and Practice." Constable, London, 1956.
12. H. J. White, "Industrial Electrostatic Precipitation." Addison-Wesley, Reading, Massachusetts, 1963.
13. W. T. Sproull, *J. Air Pollution Control Assoc.* **15,** 50 (1965).
14. G. W. Penney and E. H. Klinger, *Trans. AIEE* **81,** Part I, 200 (1962).
15. A. B. Walker, *J. Air Pollution Control Assoc.* **13,** 622 (1963).
16. G. W. Penney, *Elec. Eng.* **70,** 1009 (1951).

17. W. T. Sproull and Y. Nakada, *Ind. Eng. Chem.* **43**, 1350 (1951).
18. F. Seitz, "The Modern Theory of Solids," 1st ed. McGraw-Hill, New York, 1940.
19. C. F. Gottschlich, "Removal of Particulate Matter from Gaseous Wastes: Electrostatic Precipitators." Am. Petrol. Inst., New York, 1961.
20. H. J. Hall, *Chem. Eng. Progr.* **59**, 67 (1963).
21. H. J. White, *Trans. AIEE* **71**, 326 (1952).
22. H. E. Van Hoesen, H. J. White, and H. J. Hall, *Trans. AIEE* **77**, Part I, 126 (1958).

GENERAL REFERENCES

Additional pertinent material is in Chap. 4 of "Air Pollution Engineering Manual, Los Angeles APCD" (J. A. Danielson, ed.), PHS Publ. 999-AP-40, DHEW, Cincinnati (1967); and in Chapter 7 of "Air Pollution Manual, Part II," American Industrial Hygiene Assn., Detroit (1968); and will be published in the National Air Pollution Control Administration's publication: "Control Technology for Particulate Air Pollutants."

46 Source Control by Liquid Scrubbing

Seymour Calvert

Nomenclature

a Particle radius (centimeters or feet)

a_μ Particle radius (microns)

a' Transfer area per unit volume of scrubber (ft²/ft³)

A Cross-section area (ft² or cm²)

B Width of flow channel (feet)

B_1 An empirical constant

B_p Packing factor

c Concentration of particles in gas (lb/ft³ or gm/cm³)

c_i Concentration of particles in inlet gas

c_o Concentration of particles in outlet gas

c_l Concentration of compound in the liquid (moles/ft³)

c_l^* Concentration in equilibrium with the gas (moles/ft³)

C_1, C_2 Empirical constants

C_{Ai} Concentration of diffusing component "A" at the interface (same units as q)

d_o Sauter (surface/volume ratio) mean drop diameter (microns)

D Diffusivity of transferring compound (cm²/sec), D_l, liquid; D_g, gas; D_A, component A; D_B, component B

D_c Diameter or width of collector (feet or centimeters)

$D_{c\mu}$ Diameter or width of collector (microns)

e Base of natural logarithms

E Particle collection efficiency of drop for particles of one size (fraction)

E_a Collection efficiency for particles of diameter "a"

E_a' Average over a velocity range

E_F Total particle collection efficiency of scrubber (fraction)

f Fractional approach to equilibrium in mass transfer; f_p, cocurrent; f_c, countercurrent

f' Velocity ratio $= \dfrac{v_r}{v_g}$

f_a' Velocity ratio for atomization

F Overall efficiency of mass transfer

F_a Force required for acceleration (pounds)

F_c Overall efficiency for countercurrent operation

F_p Overall efficiency for cocurrent (parallel) operation

g_c Gravitational acceleration $= 32.17$ (ft/sec^2)

G Gas flow rate (moles/hr-ft^3)

h Scrubber height (drop fall height) (feet)

H Henry's law constant (atm/mole fraction)

H' Henry's law constant (atm/mole/ft^3)

H_d Drop holdup (volume liquid/total volume)

k Mass transfer coefficient (lb. moles/hour-ft^2-atm)

k' Mass transfer coefficient (gm moles/sec-cm^2-atm)

k_g Mass transfer coefficient based on driving force between the gas and the interface
$\left(\dfrac{\text{lb mole}}{\text{hour-ft}^2\text{-atm}}\right)$
$= 7400 \, k_g' \left(\dfrac{\text{gm mole}}{\text{sec-cm}^2\text{-atm}}\right)$

k_l Mass transfer coefficient based on driving force between the liquid and the interface
$\left(\dfrac{\text{lb mole}}{\text{hour-ft}^2\text{-lb mole/ft}^3}\right) =$
$118 \, k_l' \left(\dfrac{\text{gm mole}}{\text{sec-cm}^2\text{-gm mole/cm}^3}\right)$

k^* Mass transfer coefficient with chemical reaction

K Inertial impaction parameter $= \dfrac{2v_r\rho_p a^2}{9\mu R_c}$

K_a Inertial impaction parameter at atomization velocity

K_{og} Mass transfer coefficient based on overall gas phase driving force (lb moles/hour-ft^2-atm)

K_{ol} Mass transfer coefficient based on overall liquid phase driving force $\left(\text{lb moles/hour-ft}^2 - \dfrac{\text{mole}}{\text{ft}^3}\right)$

L Liquid flow rate (moles/hour-ft^2)

L' Ratio of liquid to gas flow rates (gal/1000 ft^3)

L'' Liquid flow rate per unit of scrubber cross section (gal/min-ft^2)

L_s Water velocity based on superficial area (ft^3/sec-ft^2)

m Phase equilibrium constant $= \dfrac{y}{x}$ at equilibrium

M Mass (lb)

n Number of 360° turns taken by gas

n' An empirical constant

N Mass transfer flux—moles transferred per hour per ft^2 of transfer area

N_{OG} Number of mass transfer units—overall gas phase driving force

N_{TD} Number of dust transfer units (dimensionless)

p Partial pressure compound (atm), p_i, inlet; p_o, outlet

p^* Partial pressure in equilibrium with liquid (atm)

P Total pressure (atm)

P_A Partial pressure of compound A (atm)

ΔP Pressure difference (lb/ft^2 or inches H$_2$O)

ΔP_a Pressure difference due to acceleration (lb/ft^2)

$\Delta P_a''$ Pressure drop, in inches of water, as defined by Eq. (26)

ΔP_{VH} Pressure drop equivalent to one velocity head (lb/ft²)

P_t Penetration of collector by particles $= \frac{c_o}{c_i}$ (fraction)

q Concentration of reactive component in the bulk liquid

Q Volumetric flow rate (ft³/sec or m³/sec), Q_w, liquid; Q_g, gas

r Radius of drop (feet or centimeters)

r' Radius of drop (microns)

R Gas constant
$$= 82.057 \left(\frac{\text{atm-cm}^3}{\text{mole} - {}^\circ\text{K}} \right)$$

R_c Radius of particle collector (feet or centimeters)

Re Reynolds' number (dimensionless)

t Time (seconds)

t_g Contact time for gas (seconds)

t_l Contact time for liquid (seconds)

T Absolute temperature (°K)

u Velocity in the horizontal direction (ft/sec or cm/sec), u_d, u_g, and u_1 have similar meanings as v_d, v_g, and v_l (ft/sec) or (cm/sec)

v Velocity in vertical direction (ft/sec or cm/sec)

Δv Change in velocity

v_b Gas velocity based on open cross-sectional area (ft/sec)

v_d Drop or particle velocity relative to duct (ft/sec)

v_g Gas velocity relative to duct (ft/sec)

v_l Liquid velocity relative to duct (ft/sec)

v_r Drop velocity relative to gas

v_s Gas velocity based on superficial cross-sectional area (ft/sec)

v_t Terminal settling velocity

We Weber number (dimensionless)

x Mole fraction of compound in the liquid phase, x_i inlet, x_o outlet

x_A Mole fraction of compound A in the liquid

x^* Mole fraction of compound in the liquid phase at equilibrium with the gas contacting it

y Mole fraction of compound in the gas phase, y_i inlet, y_o outlet

y^* Mole fraction of compound in the gas phase at equilibrium with liquid contacting it

z Distance traveled by drop relative to duct.

z' Stopping distance of a drop (centimeters), z_1' initial position, z_2' final position

Z Height or length of scrubber (feet)

ρ Density (lb/ft³) or (gm/cm³), ρ_g, gas; ρ_1, liquid; ρ_p, particle

ρ_M Molar density (moles/ft³)

π 3.14159

σ Surface tension (dynes/cm)

μ Viscosity (poises or lb/sec-ft)

ψ Drag coefficient (fraction)

∞ At equilibrium—after infinite contact

I. Introduction

Source control by liquid scrubbing involves the removal of contaminants in either vapor or particulate state from an effluent gas stream (1–6). The transfer of contaminant requires the contacting of the gas and liquid and their subsequent separation into cleaned gas and contaminated liquid streams. For particulate matter, material transfer between the gas and liquid phases may be by a variety of mechanisms. For gaseous molecules, it is basically by diffusion. The particulate collection mechanisms active in scrubbers involve inertial, gravitational, electrostatic, thermal, and diffusional phenomena. Gaseous mass transfer proceeds by diffusion, moving from a region of high concentration to one of low concentration.

A stream of gas flowing past a solid wall wetted with liquid is shown in idealized fashion in Fig. 1. In the lower part of the diagram there is a plot of contaminant concentration vs. position in the liquid or gas stream. In the gas phase the concentration is highest at the center and lowest at the gas-liquid interface. This concentration gradient causes the movement of contaminant away from the highest potential because of turbulent and molecular diffusion.

Molecular diffusion is the transport of mass by the random movement of single molecules. Molecules move at the same velocity in all directions. If 1000 molecules cross a small plane area parallel to the interface from right to left (Fig. 1) in a given time, then the same number will cross from the opposite side of the plane. If the 1000 molecules crossing from the high concentration region (right side) include 10 contaminant molecules, then those crossing from the low concentration region will include a smaller number of contaminant molecules, say nine. There is thus, in this example, a net movement (diffusion) of one contaminant molecule to the left per element of area in each unit of time.

When turbulence exists, as is usually the case in contacting equipment, mass can also be transferred in relatively large pieces (eddies) of fluid. The effect is the same as for molecular diffusion: material is moved in

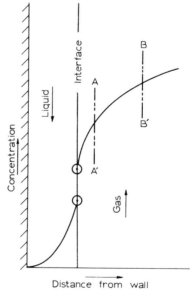

FIG. 1. Concentration vs. position in liquid and gas.

a direction down the concentration gradient but at a much higher rate than for molecular diffusion. Evidence of the higher rate for turbulent than for molecular diffusion is shown by the steeper gradient across the plane A-A' than across the plane B-B' in Fig. 1. Turbulence is damped out by a solid wall so that the eddying or mixing is much more intense in the middle of the gas stream than near the interface. As a result, local differences in concentration are evened out more rapidly in the turbulent core than in the quiescent laminar and transition regions of the flowing gas. Another way of looking at this is that a much higher concentration gradient is required for a given mass flux (mass transferred per unit of area per unit of time) for molecular diffusion than for turbulent diffusion.

Basically both diffusional transport mechanisms provide random motion of single molecules or groups of molecules, which tends to move material from regions of high concentration to regions of low concentration. This same random motion will result in the transfer of heat if there is a difference of temperature between the gas and the interface, and in the transfer of momentum if there is a difference of velocity. Turbulent transfer of heat and momentum are both more rapid than by molecular diffusion. The rate of transfer of momentum from the flowing gas to the gas-liquid interface and ultimately to the solid wall is the frictional force exerted by the fluid upon the wall.

While heat transfer might or might not be important in a given scrubber system, mass and momentum transfer always are. Mass transfer rate influences the efficiency of contaminant collection, while momentum transfer rate determines the amount of frictional pressure drop and, therefore, the power requirement. Efficiency is also dependent on the level of equilibrium between the gas and the liquid phases since this, by definition, describes the ultimate states of the two phases left in contact.

Capacity is generally determined by the flow rate at which the scrubber will become inoperable because of excessive or complete carry-over of liquid by gas, or at which pressure drop will become excessive. As a rule, the necessary height or length of the gas scrubbing path will increase with the efficiency required, and the necessary cross-sectional area will increase with the capacity required.

II. Gas Absorption

A. EQUILIBRIUM CONSIDERATIONS

The object of gas scrubbing for mass transfer is to get as much material as possible out of the gas and into the liquid at as low cost as possible.

TABLE I
HENRY'S LAW CONSTANTS FOR SEVERAL GASES IN WATER[a]

Gas	0 °C	5 °C	10 °C	15 °C	20 °C	25 °C	30 °C
H_2S	26.8	31.5	36.7	42.3	48.3	54.5	60.9
NO	16.9	19.3	21.8	24.2	26.4	28.7	31.0
N_2O	—	1.17	1.41	1.66	1.98	2.25	2.59
N_2	52.9	59.7	66.8	73.8	80.4	86.5	92.4
O_2	25.5	29.1	32.7	36.4	40.1	43.8	47.5
CO	35.2	39.6	44.2	48.9	53.6	58.0	62.0
SO_2	0.0056	—	0.007	—	0.014	—	0.016

[a] $H \times 10^{-3}$ (atm/mole fraction).

There are, however, physical or chemical equilibrium limits to the solubility of material in liquid that cannot be exceeded regardless of how intimate the contacting of phases or how long the time of contact.

The solution of SO_2 in water is an example of physical equilibrium, even though there is chemical interaction with the water and some heat of solution. The chemical reactions involved are reversible and rapid as compared to the rate of diffusion through the liquid. In contrast, the absorption of SO_2 in NaOH solution is a clear case of chemical reaction since the reaction is substantially irreversible and rapid at the temperature and pressure of the scrubber. Furthermore, the rate of absorption may be influenced by the chemical reaction rate or by the rate at which reactant (NaOH) can diffuse toward the interface to replace that which has been used up.

Gas solubilities in water can usually be described in terms of Henry's law,

$$P_A = Hx_A \tag{1}$$

especially for the low partial pressures that are encountered in air pollution control equipment (Table I).

B. CONTACTING SCHEME

The amount of mass transfer depends not only on the equilibrium relationship but also on the contacting scheme. If liquid enters the top of a vertical column so that it runs down and gas enters the bottom so that it passes upward through the column, the contacting scheme is said to be countercurrent, and the effluent gas has its last contact with the entering liquid. Were the gas also to enter the top and pass downward through the column, the contact would be cocurrent and the effluent gas would last contact the effluent liquid.

These processes may be followed in a graph (Fig. 2) in which y, the gas phase concentration (mole fraction) of the transferring component (e.g., SO_2), is plotted against x, the liquid phase concentration (mole fraction) of the same component. So as not to complicate the picture, it is assumed that the remaining constituents of the gas phase are insoluble and that those of the liquid phase are nonvolatile. The bulk compositions of the gas and liquid phase at any point in the column are shown by the operating line $(x_i, y_i) - (x_o, y_o)$ for cocurrent contact; and the operating line $(x_i, y_o) - (x_o, y_i)$ for countercurrent contact. The operating lines are defined, for the case of low concentration and nonvolatile

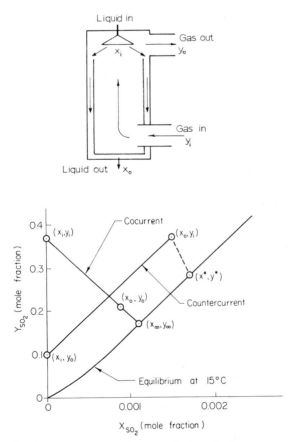

FIG. 2. Sketch of countercurrent column and plot of phase compositions showing operating and equilibrium lines.

solvent, by:

$$G(y_i - y) = L(x_o - x) \quad \text{for countercurrent} \tag{2}$$

and

$$G(y_i - y) = L(x - x_i) \quad \text{for cocurrent} \tag{3}$$

The slope of the operating line is L/G in both cases, but it is positive for countercurrent, and negative for cocurrent flow.

A variant in the contacting scheme is when one stream flows in a direction perpendicular to the other stream. This is called cross, or cross-current, flow. Examples of this are spray chambers in which the gas travels horizontally while spray drops fall vertically; and trays across which liquid flows horizontally while gas flows vertically. These situations are complicated to analyze and are generally treated with the simplifying assumption that one phase is completely and instantaneously mixed along any plane parallel to the flow of the other phase. Thus in a cross-flow spray chamber one could assume that the gas is completely mixed along any vertical plane with the result that the operating line for the liquid–gas contact along a plane would be a horizontal (constant y) line.

In a sieve plate column the overall fluid motion is either co- or countercurrent, but the motion on each plate is essentially crosscurrent. The situation along a vertical plane across the liquid flow path would be described approximately by a vertical (constant x) operating line. Combinations of these variations may occur in a single piece of equipment and any attempt to analyze carefully its performance requires that the liquid and gas flow paths be known and taken into account. Once the operating conditions are fixed, they, in conjunction with the equilibrium relationship, determine the ultimate performance possible. For a cocurrent scrubber (Fig. 2), no matter how long the phases are kept in contact or how efficient the device, the gas composition can never go below y_∞ or the liquid composition above x_∞. In a countercurrent scrubber, more efficient contact moves the operating line closer to the equilibrium line (the slope remains L/G). Ultimate performance would result when the operating line touches the equilibrium line which is equivalent to stating that the gas can never become leaner (or cleaner) than that in equilibrium with the inlet liquid for countercurrent flow, or with the outlet liquid for cocurrent flow. If L/G is less than m, i.e., y/x at equilibrium, for countercurrent contacting, the equilibrium limit is reached when the outlet liquid is in equilibrium with the inlet gas.

C. Approach to Equilibrium

The proper measure of scrubber performance is the degree to which the two streams approach the equilibrium limits noted above. Overall efficiency is the product of the fraction removed at equilibrium and the fractional approach to equilibrium. This equilibrium efficiency or fractional approach to equilibrium is defined in terms of the gas phase by:

$$f = \frac{y_i - y_o}{y_i - mx_i} \quad \text{for countercurrent} \tag{4}$$

and

$$f = \frac{y_i - y_o}{y_i - mx_o} \quad \text{for cocurrent} \tag{5}$$

Overall efficiency is defined as:

$$F = f\left(\frac{y_i - mx_i}{y_i}\right) = \frac{y_i - y_o}{y_i} \quad \text{for countercurrent} \tag{6}$$

and with x_o replacing x_i for cocurrent.

Mass transfer rate and contacting time are what determine equilibrium efficiency. Transfer rate may be described mathematically as:

$$N = k_g(p - p^*) = k_g P(y - y^*) \tag{7}$$

Equation (7) describes mass transfer in the gas phase in terms of the partial pressure driving force between the bulk of the gas phase and the liquid surface, and a coefficient which depends on how rapidly the transferring material diffuses through the gas phase. Mass transfer within the liquid phase is described by:

$$N = k_l(c_l^* - c_l) \tag{8}$$

For low concentrations we may use the approximation that:

$$c_l = x\rho_M \tag{9}$$

Thus:

$$N = k_l\rho_M(x^* - x) \tag{10}$$

Equations (7) and (10) can be used to define mass transfer rates if y^* or x^* are known. These equilibrium values are generally assumed to be those which exist just at the gas–liquid interface and are so shown in Fig. 2 where (x^*, y^*) is the interfacial condition corresponding to the point (x_o, y_i) in the scrubber.

In preference to using Eqs. (7) and (10), mass transfer relationships based on the overall driving force between the bulk phase compositions are used. The definitions for overall gas and liquid phase coefficients are:

$$N = K_{og}(p - H'c_l) = K_{ol}\left(\frac{p}{H'} - c_l\right) \tag{11}$$

These overall coefficients are related to the individual phase coefficients by the following equations when the operating and equilibrium lines are straight:

$$\frac{1}{K_{og}} = \frac{1}{k_g} + \frac{H'}{k_l} \tag{12}$$

and

$$\frac{1}{K_{ol}} = \frac{1}{k_l} + \frac{1}{H'k_g} \tag{13}$$

One or the other overall coefficient is used, depending on whether the absorption is gas phase or liquid phase resistance controlled.

Gas phase resistance controls when the gas is very soluble in the liquid. Liquid phase resistance controls when the gas is only slightly soluble in the liquid. It can be appreciated that when the capacity of the liquid is high the burden is placed upon the gas phase to maintain the transfer rate because the liquid can carry material away from the interface with ease. When the solubility is low the gas phase can easily keep the interface nearly saturated and the rate of transfer will depend on how rapidly the liquid can move material from the interface.

The significance of whether gas or liquid phase controls stems from the fact that gas phase transfer is much more rapid than liquid phase transfer. The type of equipment used and its size will, therefore, depend upon this fact. A method for the estimation of which phase controls can be based on a rearrangement of Eq. (12):

$$\frac{k_g}{K_{og}} = 1 + \frac{H'k_g}{k_l} \tag{14}$$

If k_g is nearly equal to K_{og}, the transfer is gas phase controlled and a ratio of $k_g/K_{og} \leqslant 1.1$ indicates a clear-cut case of this condition. At the other extreme, a ratio of 10 or greater is the criterion for liquid phase control. The ratio of transfer coefficients (k_g/k_l) is relatively constant (7). Therefore most of the variation in ($H'k_g/k_l$) is due to variation of H'. If H' is less than about 3.0, the system is gas phase controlled and if it is greater than about 3000 the liquid phase controls. This range of values will compensate for the probable extremes of transfer coefficients and is not large in relation to the variation in gas solubilities. Thus to a first approximation, the efficiency of a gas absorber can be related to solubility alone. A better definition of efficiency, in terms of both solubility and the ratio of liquid to gas, is discussed later.

1. Prediction of Coefficients

Mass transfer coefficients have been predicted and correlated by a variety of approximate methods, among which the "penetration theory" does as well as any other. It has the attractive virtues of permitting predictions to be made for new cases, and of providing a logical mechanistic model for conceptual purposes. This theory states that mass transfer from or to turbulent streams may be considered to be the consequence of many small elements of fluid transferring material to or from an interface for a short period of time. Before and after their time of contact with the interface, the fluid elements are thoroughly mixed with the main stream. Development of this idea with further assumptions (8) leads to the following equations:

$$k'_g = \left(\frac{2}{RT}\right)\left(\frac{D_g}{\pi t_g}\right)^{1/2} \tag{15}$$

and

$$k'_l = 2\left(\frac{D_l}{\pi t_l}\right)^{1/2} \tag{16}$$

Many substances have diffusivities in water of about 1.5×10^{-5} cm²/sec and in air of about 0.1 cm²/sec.

Taking a column packed with 1 inch Raschig rings as a typical device, the liquid and gas contact times are estimated as the time it takes either phase to move a distance of one packing diameter. Within the range of data given by Shulman (9) and at 50% of flooding, t_l ranges from 0.525 to 0.18 second. The gas contact time might range from 0.01 to 0.05 second. Using these approximations, we estimate:

$$k'_g = \left(\frac{2}{82.06 \times 298}\right)\left(\frac{0.1}{0.01\pi}\right)^{1/2} = 1.45 \times 10^{-4}$$

for a gas contact time of 0.01 second and 0.65×10^{-4} for $t_g = 0.05$. Similarly, we can estimate that the liquid phase coefficient k'_l would range from about 6.0×10^{-3} to 10×10^{-3}. Most design calculations and performance reporting are not on the basis of coefficients, but rather in terms of "transfer units." Equation (17) defines an overall gas phase transfer unit for the dilute gas case:

$$N_{OG} = \int_{p_o}^{p} \frac{dp}{p - Hx} = \frac{K_{og}a'ZP}{G} \tag{17}$$

The integral equal to the number of transfer units is a measure of the difficulty of transfer and is approximately equal to the change in composition divided by the average driving force for transfer. More complex forms must be used when the concentration of the transferring gas is greater than 5 or 10% (1) to account for changes in total gas flow rate and the effect of diffusion of inert species toward the interface.

Integration of Eq. (17) for constant L/G and H, and cocurrent flow, gives the following expression for equilibrium efficiency:

$$f_p = 1 - \exp - \left(\frac{K_{og}a'zP}{G}\right)\left(1 + \frac{HG}{PL}\right) \tag{18}$$

Overall efficiency for cocurrent operation is:

$$F_p = \frac{p_i - p_o}{p_i} = \left(\frac{1}{1 + \dfrac{HG}{PL}}\right)f_p \tag{19}$$

For countercurrent contact we have an implicit definition of equilibrium efficiency as:

$$N_{OG} = \frac{1}{1 - \dfrac{HG}{PL}}\ln\left[\left(1 - \frac{HG}{PL}\right)\left(\frac{1}{1 - f_c}\right) + \frac{HG}{PL}\right] \tag{20}$$

and the overall efficiency is:

$$F_C = \left(\frac{p_i - Hx_i}{p_i}\right)f_c \tag{21}$$

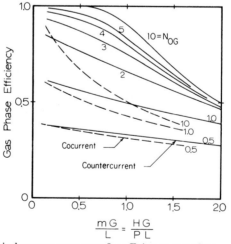

Fig. 3. Relationship between mass transfer efficiency, transfer parameter, and number of transfer units for cocurrent and countercurrent.

The efficiencies which are defined in Eqs. (18) through (21) are based on changes in gas composition and are referred to as gas phase efficiencies. Figure 3 is a plot of F_p and f_C vs. HG/PL with N_{OG} as the parameter. If we consider the case of countercurrent contact where the inlet liquid concentration is zero, then $F_C = f_C$ and Fig. 3 shows the overall efficiencies for the two modes of contact. We can see that for low efficiency, such as 0.5 transfer units will provide, there is little advantage of counter over cocurrent. For more difficult separations, such as 10 transfer units can provide, countercurrent contact is superior.

An estimate of the column height required for a desired efficiency can quickly be made with the help of Fig. 3. Economic operation is usually in the region of (HG/PL) between 0.5 and 1.0 for countercurrent. Thus, if we need 95% efficiency it will take something like 5 to 10 transfer units to do the job, depending on the amount of liquid we use to scrub the required gas volume. Since the column height per transfer unit generally runs from 1 to 4 feet, with 2 feet being a good average for approximation, we will need about 10 to 20 feet of packed height. The exact choice will depend on the economic balance between cost of tower and higher gas pumping power for more transfer units and the higher liquid pumping and purification costs for fewer transfer units.

2. Chemical Reaction

Higher gas absorption efficiency and greater absorbing capacity of the liquid phase can result from the use of a chemically reactive liquid. Components such as the ethanol amines, dimethyl aniline, and other organic compounds capable of forming weak complexes with contaminants such as H_2S, SO_2, and CO_2 can be used. Slurries (suspensions) of reactive or adsorptive particles in liquids, such as lime slurry for acid gas (10) and activated carbon slurry for adsorbable gases (11) may also be used.

The ultimate performance for a reactive liquid occurs when all "back pressure" of the transferring gas above the liquid is eliminated by the gas reacting with it instantly. If the concentration of the reactant is high enough and the reaction rate fast enough, Eq. (17) becomes:

$$N_{OG} = \int_{p_o}^{p_i} \frac{dp}{p} = \ln \frac{p_i}{p_o} \tag{22}$$

In addition to decreasing the number of transfer units, chemical reaction will also reduce the height of a transfer unit because of the increase in liquid phase mass transfer rate. One can get an idea of the possible benefit due to a chemical reactant from the following equation relating the liquid phase coefficient with chemical reaction to that for physical absorption.

$$\frac{k_l^*}{k_l} = \left[\left(\frac{D_A}{D_B}\right)^{1/2} + \left(\frac{D_A}{D_B}\right)^{1/2}\frac{q}{C_{Ai}}\right] \tag{23}$$

Equation (23) is valid for a very rapid second-order reaction and has been successfully applied to a few systems such as the absorption of H_2S in NaOH and KOH solutions. A coefficient 12 times that for physical absorption has been obtained with a hydroxyl ion concentration of about 1.0 (gm mole/liter) and the relationship was linear as indicated by Eq. (23).

Unfortunately, it is not presently possible to do much more in the way of predicting for absorption with chemical reaction. Some data are available for specific systems (1, 3, 5, 12) but there is no general method for predicting the complex combination of kinetic, transport, thermal, and concentration effects which are involved. If full-scale data are not available, small scale or pilot plant data must be used for reliable design.

D. METHOD OF CONTACT

Gas liquid contacting can be done in a variety of ways. It is helpful to classify them before discussing scrubbing equipment. The first point of distinction is whether the gas is dispersed and the liquid continuous, or vice versa. Bubbles of gas in a tank of liquid is a simple example of a dispersed gas system. One can enhance contacting in such a system by mechanical stirring or by adding baffling elements in the form of packing or plates. Packing elements may serve to spread the liquid out in thin films, to promote the stirring of the liquid as well as the gas phase, and to induce centrifugal forces on particles due to changing the direction of gas flow.

Dispersed liquid in the form of drops moving through gas is the inverse analogy to the bubbles in a tank system. Here too, one can enhance contacting by mechanical agitation and by the use of packing or baffles.

Generally, the liquid is a single phase but it is also possible to use a suspension of chemically reactive or absorptive particles. In this way one can utilize the properties of insoluble solids while retaining the advantages of fluid handling.

E. TYPES OF EQUIPMENT

Equipment for gas phase dispersed systems (1, 2, 13–15) is usually of the plate column type. Various forms of gas dispersing elements such as bubble caps, perforated plates, and variations are incorporated at one or more levels (stages or plates) in a vertical column. Usually, the scrubbing liquid is introduced at the top and runs down from stage to stage, either through downcomer pipes or by dripping through perforations. During operations the gas causes violent agitation of the liquid, forming a dense froth ranging from a few inches to a foot deep. A pressure drop of 2 or 3 inches of water per plate is common. Packed columns are the most common apparatus used for liquid-phase dispersal in gas absorption. The reason is that packing supports liquid contact area throughout the range of flow rates in countercurrent flow usually desired for gas absorption. Packing materials are continually being invented and range from dense packings such as rings, saddles, and spheres (Fig. 4) to low

FIG. 4. Photograph of common packing materials.

TABLE II
COMPARISON OF VARIOUS CONTACTING COLUMNS[a]

Plate or packing type	Plate liquid throughput		Efficiency, %		Flexibility		Hydraulic resist. at 85% of max. load (inches H_2O),	Plate spacing (inches)	Cost relative to bubble cap plate
	Low	Medium	At 85% of max. throughput	Over the practical loading range	% Throughput change at constant efficiency	Ratio of max. to min. loading			
Bubble cap[b]	1	1	80	60–80	80	5	3.2	16–32	1
Uniflux with S-shaped elements[b]	1.1	1.2	80–90	60–90	50	8	3.2	16–32	1/2
Valve type Flexitray (disk, valves)[c]	1.2	1.3	80	70–90	80	9	2.0	12–24	2/3
Value ballast Flexitray[c] (weighed disk valves)	1.2	1.5	80	70–90	80	9	2.0	12–24	2/3
West[d]	1.2	1.3	80	80	80	5	1.6	–8	1.1–1.2
Sieve[d]	1.2	1.4	80	70–90	55	3	1.6	16–32	2/3
Kaskade[b]	1.5	2	90	70–100	—	4	1.0	8–16	—
Jet	1.3	1.3	80	—	—	—	2.4	—	1/2
Kittel	1.4	1.1	90	70–90	40	3	1.2	12–24	—
Grid (no downcomers)[b]	1.2	1.4	75	60–80	10	3	1.2	12–24	1/2
Turbogrid[b]	1.5	2	70	60–80	10	2	0.8	8–16	—
Ripple (drip type)[b]	1.2	1.6	70	60–75	70	3	0.8	12–24	1/2
Spraypak packing	1.5	1.3	80	—	20	—	—	—	—
Pall rings	0.7	0.6	85	—	15	—	—	—	—

[a] From Aleksandrov and Skoblo (18).
[b] Good operation under flooding conditions.
[c] Operation under flooding conditions requires study.
[d] Poor operation under flooding conditions.

density fabrications of expanded metal, screen, and fibers. Also devices exploiting the characteristics of secondary and separated flows have been investigated for mass transfer and particle collection (*16, 17*). The choice of one packing material over another, or a packed tower instead of a plate column, will depend upon economics, the availability of suitable materials of construction, and design constraints such as limitation on pressure drop or tendency to become plugged. Larger diameter packed columns require special provisions for liquid distribution to counteract the channeling which develops as liquid flows down. Table II (*18*) provides some data for comparing several types of contacting columns.

The plates and packings listed in Table II are described in most chemical engineering texts (*1, 5*) and are characterized here in terms of several operating parameters. Plate liquid throughput is the rate relative to that on a bubble cap plate evaluated at low and medium gas throughput rates. Efficiencies, which were determined for distillation at 85% of the maximum throughput (gas rate) and over a practical range, indicate no great variation among the contactors. It must be borne in mind that plate efficiencies will be considerably lower for the absorption of low solubility gases. Flexibility means the ability of the plate to operate satisfactorily over a wide range of conditions. Hydraulic resistance is the gas phase pressure drop per plate at a flow rate of 85% of the flooding velocity. Note that at 0.5 inch of water pressure drop any of these devices would not be close to 85% of flooding. The remaining items in Table II are estimates of the usual range of plate spacings and approximate cost relative to bubble cap plates.

Spray contactors (Fig. 5) are devices whose basic mode of operation is the transfer of gas or particles to drops of liquid. Spray contactors are not well suited to countercurrent gas absorption, but are superior for particle collection without danger of plugging with accumulated mud. Liquid drops may be generated by spray nozzles or by the atomization of liquid by a high velocity stream of gas. Some scrubbers, such as the Doyle scrubber, whose action seems at first glance to be based on the impingement of gas on liquid or solid phase, may actually depend on impingement upon atomized drops torn from the liquid mass. The high energy gas-atomizing types such as flooded disk, wedge, orifice, and venturi scrubbers have been given more attention in recent years as the demand for high efficiency has grown.

F. CAPACITY

Pressure drop for gas flow through scrubbers is caused by friction with stationary surfaces and by the acceleration of liquid. Frictional loss

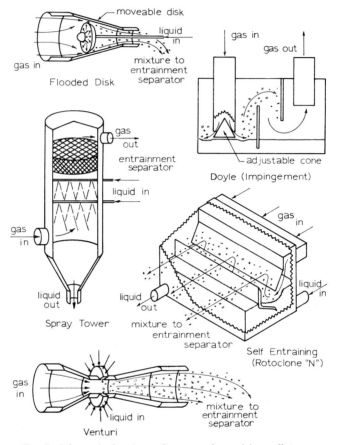

FIG. 5. Schematic drawings of spray and atomizing collectors.

is very dependent upon the geometry of the scrubber and must generally be determined experimentally. Acceleration loss is fairly insensitive to scrubber geometry and is frequently the predominant cause of pressure drop. It can be accounted for by use of Newton's law describing the force required to change the momentum of liquid at a given rate:

$$F_a = \frac{d(Mv)}{g_c\,dt} = \Delta P_a A \qquad (24)$$

If the liquid is introduced at a velocity, v_l, in the direction of gas flow, and finally attains the gas velocity, v_g;

$$\Delta P_a = \frac{(v_g - v_l)}{g_c A}\frac{dM}{dt} \qquad (25)$$

For pressure drop, $\Delta P_a''$, in inches of water, and water flow rate, L', in gallons per thousand cubic feet (mcf) of gas flow, the following dimensional equation is approximately equivalent to Eq. (25):

$$\Delta P_a'' = 5 \times 10^{-5}(v_g - v_l)^2 L' \tag{26}$$

The velocity squared term suggests that the pressure drop could be expressed in terms of velocity heads for comparison with the empirical correlation of data for venturi scrubbers (19–22) shown in Fig. 6. In terms of velocity heads for air of density 0.075 lb/ft³ and $v_l = 0$;

$$\frac{\Delta P_a}{\Delta P_{VH}} = \frac{\Delta P_a}{\dfrac{\Delta v^2 \rho_g}{2g_c}} = 0.22L' \tag{27}$$

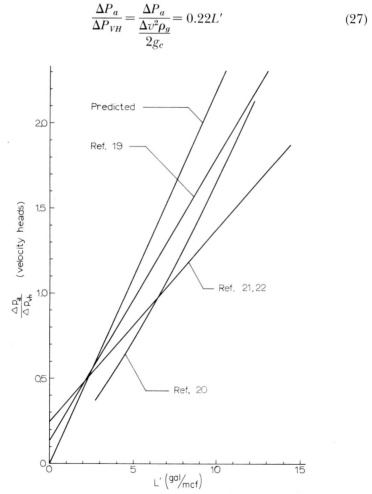

FIG. 6. Relationship between pressure drop and liquid flow rate for venturi scrubbers (mcf = 1000 cf).

Equation (27) predicts a higher pressure drop than experimentally measured except at low liquid rates, where the frictional losses for the gas alone are significant. At higher liquid rates it appears that 80–90% of the momentum of the liquid is lost rather than serving to recompress the gas. This is in keeping with the observation (23) that the pumping efficiency of an ejector venturi is generally less than 15%.

Frictional pressure drop through packed columns is dependent on many factors and there is no simple and exact relationship to define it. For specific information, one must consult manufacturers' data or such sources as Perry's Handbook (1). In a simplified form of the correlation given by Eckert (24) for contact between air and water, the conditions for pressure drop of 0.5 inches of water per foot of packed height are approximated by:

$$v_s^2 = \frac{B_1}{B_p}\left(28.6\,\frac{L_s}{v_s}\right)n' \tag{28}$$

The values of the constants are given in the following tabulation.

B_1	n'	$\left(\dfrac{28.6L_s}{v_s}\right)$ range
800	−0.2	0.03 to 0.1
375	−0.55	0.1 to 1.0
350	−1.2	1.0 to 4.0

The packing factor, B_p, is the ratio of packing surface to the cube of void fraction and ranges from 250 to 650 for 1/2-inch packings, 50 to 150 for 1-inch packings (Pall rings, saddles, and Raschig rings), 25 to 100 for 1½-inch packings, and 17 to 65 for 2-inch packings.

Flooding

Scrubber capacity is limited to the gas flow at which the amount of liquid carried over (entrained) by the gas becomes excessive, and at which flooding occurs, i.e., when not enough liquid will pass through the device so as to give proper operation. Flooding in countercurrent packed column operation will occur at a gas velocity about 1.5 times that which causes 0.5 inch H_2O pressure drop (24, 25).

Entrainment of liquid requires that the drop size be small enough and the gas rate high enough for the drops to be carried out. If the drops are already formed, as in a spray scrubber, the conditions for entrainment can be predicted simply from drop dynamics. When drops are not initially present or when gas velocity is high enough to shatter large drops, it is necessary to consider the atomization process.

A wide variety of gas-liquid atomization systems can be described by the Nukiyama-Tanasawa correlation (26) [Eq. (44)]. Another way of predicting the stable drop for a given gas velocity is to use the fact that drops will shatter at a critical value of the Weber number:

$$We = \frac{\rho_g u^2 r}{\sigma} \text{ (dimensionless)} \tag{29}$$

Experiments on the drop shatter of several liquids (27) give critical values of Weber number ranging from 5 to 12. If we use the properties of standard air and water with a critical Weber number of 5 and a drop radius of 0.1 cm, the required air velocity is 1820 cm/sec = 60 ft/sec. To shatter a 0.2 cm radius drop, which is on the order of raindrop size, would take an air velocity of about 42 ft/sec.

Comparison of the critical drop size, predicted by the Weber number criterion with the mean drop diameter predicted by Nukiyama and Tanasawa (see Fig. 11) for lowest water rate, shows that the former is much larger at low velocities. The two methods approach agreement at velocities higher than 300 ft/sec. Because the range of Nukiyama and Tanasawa's experiments went down to about 200 ft/sec, it is probably safer to use Goldshmid's Weber number criterion for velocities below about 100 ft/sec.

III. Particle Collection

A. MECHANISMS

While the number and variety of scrubber designs on the market is bewildering, there are only a few basic mechanisms operative and there is little concerning these which is unique to wet scrubbers. If we look closely at the available devices, we observe that in many of them the purpose of the liquid is to clean the solid surfaces which do the collecting. In the others, we observe that particles are captured by the liquid by the same mechanisms of inertia, electrostatic attraction, diffusion, thermal force, and sedimentation as are operative in dry systems. There is considerable variability among designs in the size and shape of the collection elements and in liquid velocity relative to that of gas. Surface forces can also be important (27) in determining the wetting of particles by the liquid. Vaporization or condensation can affect particle size and can exert a force on particles toward or away from the liquid surface because of vapor flow. Inertial force is the predominant mechanism in wet scrubbers generally, although diffusion becomes significant where the particle size is below 0.1 or 0.2 μ diameter.

B. Packed Beds

When packed bed scrubbers are operated in the gas phase continuous range (i.e., not flooded) their dust collection performance is usually unaffected by the liquid. A probable exception to this is extremely low density packing which serves to support and interrupt the fall of liquid and does not present as much area to the gas as does the liquid. Ribbon packings made of parallel rows of 1/8-inch wide × 0.01-inch thick metal set on 3/8-inch centers in the horizontal and vertical are an example (28) of packing which emphasizes the effect of liquid holdup.

Fibrous beds such as glass fiber mats, and wire mesh and screen are amenable to the design calculations of Chapter 44. Densely packed beds of large elements, such as the tower packings shown in Fig. 4, have only recently been studied in a definitive manner.

Experimental determination of particle (oil mist) collection for vertical and horizontal flow through beds of 1/2 inch, 1 inch, and $1\frac{1}{2}$ inch packings and 3–5 inch coke with bed depths up to 24 inches, in an 18 inch diameter bed, have yielded results (29, 30) which are consistent with an inertial collection mechanism. If we assume that the air negotiates a series of semicircular bends of width B and is completely mixed by turbulence at all levels in the bed, we obtain:

$$p_t = \exp - \left[\pi n \left(\frac{D_c v_b}{B v_s} \right) K \right] \tag{30}$$

in which the inertial impaction parameter, K, is defined by:

$$K = \frac{2 v_r \rho_p a^2}{9 \mu R_c} \tag{31}$$

If we estimate that the gas turns 1/2 of a circle for each packing diameter of bed depth, that $B = D_c/7$ as an approximation of the geometry, and that $v_s = 0.7 v_b$ in view of bed porosities running about 0.3, Eq. (30) can be put in more compact form:

$$P_t = \exp - C_2 \left(\frac{Z}{D_c} \right) K \tag{32}$$

With the above approximation, we would expect C_2 to be about 15, which compares well with the experimental values shown below:

	Packing	C_2
1/2 inch	Berl saddles, marbles, Raschig rings, and Intalox saddles	10.7
1 inch	Berl saddles, Raschig rings, and Pall rings	10.0

| $1\frac{1}{2}$ inches | Berl saddles, Raschig rings, and Pall rings | 12.0 |
| 3–5 inches | Coke | 100.0 |

There is a slight unexplained effect of gas velocity in the range of v_0 about 6 to 10 ft/sec for the 1-inch and 1 1/2-inch packings. Even with this, the spread of the data is about ±10% about the correlated efficiency. The high value of C_2 for coke is probably due to the small size of the gas flow passages in comparison to the coke.

C. SPRAYS

Particle collection by liquid drops may be under the influence of several mechanisms, but inertia is the force most commonly effective in scrubbers. Predicting scrubber performance requires that the interaction between a large population of drops and an aerosol be accounted for over the flight time of each drop. Given drop size, velocity, and concentration at each instant, one can apply the factors governing collection by single drops and sum up the contribution of the entire population of drops.

Inertial impaction efficiency for spherical collection elements, and liquid drops behaving much the same as solid spheres, has been studied by several investigators (27, 31, 32). While the data of Walton and Woolcock (32) are good for values of K larger than a few tenths, Goldshmid (27) elucidated some facts of importance for dealing with liquid drops and low values of K. He found that drop shape and oscillation have negligible effect on collection. Interfacial tension as measured by contact angle has an influence in the region of K between 0.1 and 0.4, with efficiency being lower for nonwetting combinations of particle and liquid—consistent with the observations of a crust being formed on the drop by nonwetting particles.

Of special significance for submicron particles was Goldshmid's discovery that particle collection on the back of the drop becomes substantial for low values of K. Figure 7 shows the collection efficiencies determined for monodisperse sulfur particles by water drops compared with Walton and Woolcock's experimental curve, and Fonda and Herne's theoretical curve. The absence of a critical value of K, below which efficiency is zero, is clear and is in contradiction to the published theory based only on collection on the front of the sphere.

A simple inertial model predicts a linear relationship between efficiency and K, but does not account for the different lines shown in Fig. 7, which probably are due to variation of transport into and retention in the wake of the drop as a function of particle size. This model also shows that

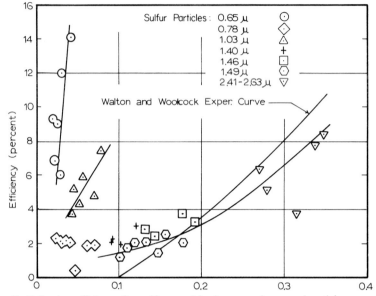

FIG. 7. Collection efficiency for sulfur particles by water drops vs. inertial parameter.

particles larger than about a micron will be spun out of the wake and not be captured on the rear of the drop—as is observed experimentally.

Whether or not this mechanism persists at the very high velocities (200 ft/sec) present in venturi scrubbers is a question of obvious importance for submicron particle collection. For the present, we will use the theoretical relationships of Fonda and Herne (31) as these give conservatively low values of efficiency.

Spray chambers are one of the simplest forms of scrubbers. There are

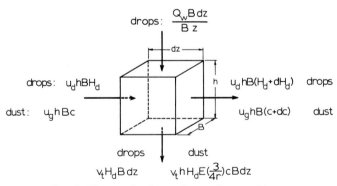

FIG. 8. Elemental volume of cross-flow scrubber.

two principal variants, cross-flow and counter-flow. Drop size and concentration are determined by the atomizing device, and are assumed to be known from performance data on the atomizer.

D. CROSS-FLOW

In the cross-flow case the spray will fall a distance h at a velocity v_t and will be approximately evenly distributed over a length z. The volume fraction of drops at any point, H_d, is given by a spray material balance for a differential slice of the scrubber (Fig. 8) as:

$$u_d hB \left[H_d - \left(H_d + \frac{dH_d}{dz} \, dz \right) \right] + \frac{Q_w B \, dz}{Bz} - v_t H_d B \, dz = 0 \qquad (33)$$

and if $\dfrac{dH_d}{dz} = 0$, then

$$H_d = \frac{Q_w}{v_t Bz} \qquad (34)$$

A material balance for dust over the same volume element gives:

$$u_g hBc - u_g hB \, (c + dc) - v_t hH_d E \left(\frac{3}{4r} \right) cB \, dz = 0 \qquad (35)$$

where the first term is the rate of flow of dust into the element, the second is the rate of flow out of the element, and the third is the rate of removal by collection on drops. Note that H_d ($hB \, dz$) is the total volume of drops in the element, that $(3/4r)$ is the ratio of drop cross-sectional area to volume, and that v_t times total drop area is the rate at which gas volume is swept by falling drops. Equation (35) simplifies to:

$$-\frac{dc}{c} = \frac{3H_d v_t E \, dz}{4r u_g} \qquad (36)$$

If it is assumed that the dust concentration is uniform across any plane perpendicular to the flow (perfect lateral mixing):

$$\ln \frac{c_i}{c_o} = \frac{3Q_w hE}{4Q_g r} \qquad (37)$$

or

$$E_F = 1 - \exp - \left(\frac{3Q_w hE}{4Q_g r} \right)$$

Efficiency increases with the height of drop fall, while the length of the gas flow path does not enter into Eq. (37).

E. Vertical Countercurrent Flow

For the case of a vertical countercurrent flow scrubber (Fig. 9) of height Z and cross-sectional area A, the spray and dust balances give:

$$H_d = \frac{Q_w}{(v_t - v_g)A} = \frac{Q_w}{v_d A} \tag{38}$$

$$-\frac{dc}{c} = \frac{3 v_t H_d E \; dz}{4 r v_g} \tag{39}$$

$$\ln \frac{c_i}{c_o} = \frac{3 Q_w v_t E Z}{4 Q_g r v_d} \tag{40}$$

or,

$$E_F = 1 - \exp - \left(\frac{3 Q_w E v_t Z}{4 Q_g r v_d}\right)$$

When the upward gas velocity is nearly equal to the settling velocity of the drops, the drop velocity relative to the scrubber wall is low, the holdup is high, and overall collection efficiency is higher. Thus a conservative design for counter-flow would minimize scrubber diameter in order to ensure maximum collection efficiency.

The equations for cross-flow and counter-flow (37 and 40) are similar, except for the ratio of (v_t/v_d), which defines the effect of relative velocity on drop holdup. The group $(3Q_w/4rQ_g)$, in practical units of $L' =$ gal/1000 ft³ and r' in microns, has the value:

$$\frac{3Q_w}{4Q_g r} = 30.5 \frac{L'}{r'} \tag{41}$$

The liquid spray rate required for a given performance may be calcu-

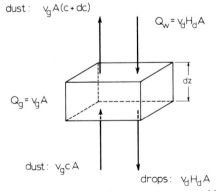

dust: $v_g A(c + dc)$

$Q_w = v_d H_d A$

$Q_g = v_g A$

dz

dust: $v_g c A$

drops: $v_d H_d A$

Fig. 9. Elemental volume of countercurrent scrubber.

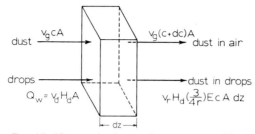

FIG. 10. Elemental volume of cocurrent scrubber.

lated from Eqs. (37), (40), and (41), if drop and dust sizes and densities are known.

F. COCURRENT FLOW

Cocurrent flow occurs in high velocity scrubbers such as the venturi, flooded disk, orifice, and other variations. The majority of these involve the atomization of the liquid by the high velocity gas stream. This case will be treated here (see Fig. 10). Liquid holdup and particle collection are described by Eqs. (38) and (39) as given for countercurrent flow. The particle concentration in a volume element of gas during the process of picking up some water, atomizing it, and accelerating the drops to zero relative velocity (i.e., $f' = 0$) can be described by the following two equations in which to avoid confusion with terminal settling velocity, v_r rather than v_{ts} is used to describe the drop velocity relative to the gas:

$$-\frac{dc}{c} = \frac{v_r}{v_g} \frac{Q_w}{(v_g - v_r)A} \left(\frac{3}{4r}\right) E_a \, dz \tag{42}$$

when $v_r = f'v_g$:

$$-\frac{dc}{c} = \frac{f'Q_w 3E_a \, dz}{v_g(1 - f')4rA} \tag{43}$$

We will assume that particles are collected only on atomized drops, and that these are formed in accordance with Nukiyama and Tanasawa's correlation:

$$d_o = \frac{585}{v_r} \sqrt{\frac{\sigma}{\rho}} + 597 \left(\frac{\mu}{\sqrt{\sigma\rho}}\right)^{0.45} \left(\frac{1000Q_w}{Q_g}\right)^{1.5} \tag{44}$$

which becomes for standard air and water:

$$d_o = \frac{5000}{v_r} + 29 \left(\frac{1000Q_w}{Q_g}\right)^{1.5} \tag{45}$$

we may also convert Eq. (45) to:

$$d_o = \frac{16,400}{v_g} + 1.45(L')^{1.5} \qquad (46)$$

This correlation does an adequate job of describing two-fluid atomization regardless of the geometric configuration of the atomizer. A solution of Eq. (45) for the region of most interest is plotted in Fig. 11 as mean drop diameter vs. air velocity, with liquid flow rate and predicted pressure drop as parameters. Air pressure drop is computed by means of Eq. (26).

Given this means for predicting drop size, we need still to know drop velocity and collection efficiency as a function of distance the drop travels, z. For this purpose the findings of Ingebo (33) on the acceleration of liquid drops by air drag are useful. His drag coefficient data are different from those for steady-state motion and are represented by:

$$\Psi = 27Re^{-0.84} \qquad (47)$$

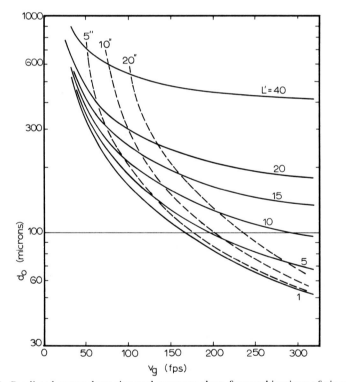

FIG. 11. Predicted water drop size and pressure drop for combinations of air velocity and water rate based on equations 26 and 46. Dashed line = predicted pressure drops. Solid line = water to air ratio.

The drag coefficients for the accelerating drop lie between the steady-state drag coefficients for laminar and turbulent flow. For simplification of equations we will use a linear approximation of Ingebo's data within the range of Reynolds' numbers of interest for atomizing scrubbers:

$$\Psi = \frac{55}{Re} \tag{48}$$

Unsteady drop motion due only to drag and inertial forces is described by equation 49 for drop motion relative to gas:

$$\int_{Re_1}^{Re_2} \frac{dRe}{\Psi Re} = \frac{3\rho_g(z_2' - z_1')}{8r\rho_l} \tag{49}$$

By substitution of Eq. (48) in (49) and integrating we obtain:

$$\frac{Re_1 - Re_2}{55} = \frac{Re_1(1 - f')}{55} = \frac{-3\rho_g z(1 - f')}{8r\rho_l f'} \tag{50}$$

By differentiation of Eq. (50) we obtain a relationship between dz and df' which may be substituted into Eq. (43) to give:

$$\frac{dc}{c} = \frac{E_a Q_w 4\rho_l r}{A55\mu} \, df' \tag{51}$$

and upon definite integration with E_a considered constant,

$$\ln \frac{c_0}{c_i} = -\frac{E_a Q_w 4\rho_l r}{A55\mu} \, f' \tag{52}$$

At this point it is well to consider some concrete numbers as related to the physical situation. If we use the properties of standard air ($\rho_g = 1.19 \times 10^{-3}$ gm/cm³ and $\mu_g = 1.8 \times 10^{-4}$ poise) and water ($\rho_l = 1.0$ gm/cm³), compute drop trajectories with drag coefficients given by Eq. (45), and use inertial impaction efficiencies for potential flow (31), we can compute the relationships shown in Fig. 12. This is a plot of collection efficiency vs. the dimensionless stopping distance of a drop, with the ratio of particle radius to drop radius as the parameter. We can estimate the dimensionless stopping distance from Eq. (50) with constants evaluated for air and water:

$$Re_1 - Re_2 = 4.9 \times 10^{-2} \left(\frac{z'}{D_c}\right) \tag{53}$$

If a drop has an initial Reynolds' number of 500 (equivalent to a 125 μ diameter drop at 200 ft/sec) and a final $Re = 0$, we estimate that $(z'/D_c) = 10,000$. In other words, the drop will travel 10,000 drop diameters before it attains the same velocity as the gas. As the drop acceler-

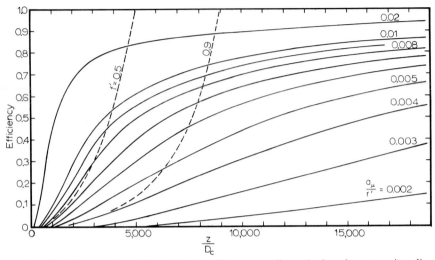

FIG. 12. Theoretical particle collection efficiency vs. dimensionless drop stopping distance with particle to drop size ratio as parameter $\left(\dfrac{z'}{D_c} = \dfrac{\text{stopping distance}}{\text{drop diameter}}\right)$.

ates, the z'/D_c corresponding to its velocity relative to the gas decreases and its collection efficiency decreases.

It will be shown later that atomization occurs at some value of f' less than 1.0 and would seem to be at about $f_a' = 0.4$ based on collection data. In other words, the liquid seems to be accelerated to about 1/2 the gas velocity before it shatters to final size. One could work in a representation of the change in E_a with relative velocity by assuming that it varies linearly with f' so that

$$E_a = \left(\frac{f'}{f_a'}\right) E_a' \tag{54}$$

If we substitute this in Eq. (51) and then integrate we will obtain:

$$\ln \frac{c_o}{c_i} = -\left(\frac{4Q_w\rho_l r'}{55A\mu}\right) E_a' \frac{f_a'}{2} \tag{55}$$

An exact solution of Eq. (51) can be obtained by a graphical integration utilizing the point values of E_a. This refinement, however, is hardly warranted in view of the inaccuracy of our knowledge of drop size, velocity, collection efficiency, and other factors.

A plot which is very convenient for estimating collection efficiency can be prepared by using Eqs. (26), (45), (55), and (56). On this one plot we can relate penetration, air velocity, water rate, pressure drop, and particle properties. The final forms of the relationships for standard air and water are:

$$K_a = \frac{2f_a' v_g \rho_p a^2}{9\mu R_c} = 7.5 f_a' \left(\frac{v_g}{D_{c\mu}}\right) (\rho_p a_\mu^2) \qquad (56)$$

$$\ln \frac{c_o}{c_i} = -[13{,}500(L') + 1.2L'^{2.5}v_g]E_a' \left(\frac{f_a'}{2}\right) \times 10^{-4} \qquad (57)$$

If we solve equation 57 for $f_a' = 0.4$ and E_a as 1.0, the results can be plotted as Fig. 13. This figure shows the effect of drop dynamics alone

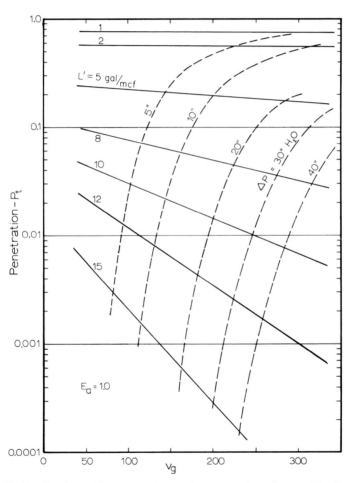

FIG. 13. Predicted particle penetration and pressure drop for combinations of air velocity and liquid rate with collection efficiency of 1.0.

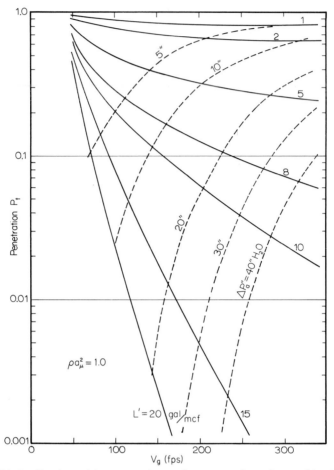

Fig. 14. Predicted particle penetration and pressure drop for combinations of air velocity and liquid rate with $\rho a_\mu^2 = 1.0$ and variable E_a.

and reveals the limit of performance of a cocurrent flow atomizing scrubber.

Plots for values of E_a less than 1.0 have been prepared for values of particle size parameter ρa_μ^2 equal to 0.25 and 1.0, (gm micron²/cm³). A value of $f_a' = 0.4$ and variable E_a, as in Eq. (55), were used in making Figs. 14 and 15. It is interesting to note on Fig. 15 that there are minima in the pressure drop curves indicating optimum water rates if fan horse-power is the main consideration. For the collection of larger particles as in Fig. 14, however, there are no minima and it appears that the more water the better, so far as air pressure drop goes. Useful data on venturi

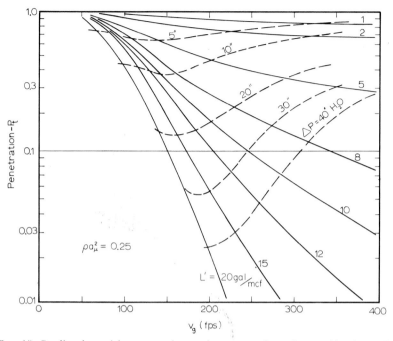

FIG. 15. Predicted particle penetration and pressure drop for combinations of air velocity and liquid rate with $\rho a_\mu^2 = 0.25$ and variable E_a.

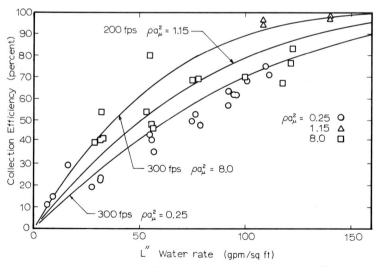

FIG. 16. Comparison of predicted and experimental collection efficiency.

scrubbers are scarce and it is not possible to do more than locate the preceding theory in an approximate position at this time. Figure 16 shows
some experimental data compared with predictions of efficiency as a
function of L' (gpm/ft²). This is a way of plotting which is not very sensitive to changes in air velocity.

The two sets of points for $\rho a_\mu^2 = 0.25$ and 8.0 are Ekman and Johnstone's data (22) for the collection of dioctyl phthalate (DOP) mist of
1.0 and 5.5μ mean diameter in an experimental venturi scrubber with
a 1 3/16-inch diameter throat at velocities ranging from 226 to 488
ft/sec, and water rates from 0.35 to 8.9 gal/mcf. The points for $\rho a_\mu^2 =$
1.15 are Brink's (19) data for the collection of phosphoric acid mist
(mean diameter = 1.7μ) in a venturi scrubber with a 6 inch × 34 inch
throat cross section at air velocities of about 200 ft/sec and water rates
of 8.9–11.8 gal/mcf.

The predictions are somewhat high for the 1.0μ DOP and low for
the 1.7μ acid mist. That we are not in a position to do much better will
become apparent after considering several points. Large venturi scrubbers give better performance than small ones and phosphoric acid is
more wettable than DOP, so the acid collection should be relatively
more efficient.

Examination of the experimental data shows that efficiency increases
slightly with increasing air velocity on this kind of plot while the prediction runs in the opposite direction. The most obvious explanation
for this is that f_a' must vary with air velocity—if not also with water rate—
and must be larger for higher air velocity. We may also note that the
predictions are based on average drop and particle sizes in addition to
several other simplifying approximations.

With its limitations, the foregoing is the only rational design method
available for atomizing scrubbers. It is clear that some careful study must
be given to this class of scrubbers and that it must include a definition
of the atomization process. We must also explore the diffusional collection range and the drop wake collection mechanism because particles
a few tenths of a micron diameter and smaller are collected at higher
efficiency than predicted for impaction.

Example

A venturi scrubber with a 6 × 12 inch throat is to be operated with
6000 cfm of air at 70 °F and 14.7 psig and with 60 gpm of water into
the throat. What will be its collection efficiency for 1.2-μ diameter particles with a density of 2.8 gm/cm³?

Solution: The air is nearly at standard conditions (60 °F and 14.7 psig) so that Eq. (57) may be used. We need to know the particle collection efficiency of a drop and for this we need the drop diameter. Given drop diameter, particle diameter, and density, and air velocity at atomization we could compute the collection parameter by means of Eq. (56). From a plot of collection efficiency vs. inertial parameter one could then obtain E_a. Alternatively, one can compute (z'/D_c) from Eq. (53) and then use Fig. 12 to find E_a. We will use the latter method simply to illustrate the nature of Fig. 12.

$$v_g = \frac{6000 \ (\text{ft}^3/\text{min})}{60 \ (\text{sec/min}) \ \dfrac{6 \ (\text{in}) \times 12 \ (\text{in})}{144 \ (\text{in}^2/\text{ft}^2)}} = 200 \ \text{ft/sec}$$

$$L' = \frac{60 \ (\text{gal/min})}{\dfrac{6000}{1000} \ (\text{mcf}^3/\text{min})} = 10 \ (\text{gal/mcf})$$

$$d_o = \frac{16{,}400}{200} + 1.45(10)^{1.5} \tag{46}$$

$$d_o = 82 + 45.5 = 127.5\mu$$

The initial Reynolds' number (at $v_g = 200$ ft/sec) is:

$$Re_1 = \frac{127.5 \times 10^{-4}(\text{cm})200(30.5)(\text{cm/sec})1.19 \times 10^{-3}(\text{gm/cm}^3)}{1.8 \times 10^{-4} \ (\text{poise})} = 515$$

Dimensionless stopping distance for $f_a' = 0.40$ is given by:

$$\frac{z'}{D_c} = \frac{515(0.4)}{4.9 \times 10^{-2}} = 4200$$

$$\frac{\text{particle radius}}{\text{drop radius}} = \frac{a_\mu}{r'} = \frac{0.6}{64} = 0.0094$$

From Fig. 12 we obtain

$$E_a = 0.54 \quad \text{at} \quad \frac{z'}{D_c} = 4200 \quad \text{and} \quad \frac{a_\mu}{r'} = 0.0094$$

We may now use Eq. (57) to compute collection efficiency for the scrubber.

$$\ln \frac{c_o}{c_i} = -[13{,}500(10) + 1.2(10)^{2.5}(200)](0.54) \left(\frac{0.4}{2}\right) \times 10^{-4}$$

$$\ln \frac{c_o}{c_i} = -[214,000](0.54)[0.2] \times 10^{-4} = -2.31$$

$$\frac{c_o}{c_i} = 0.099 = \text{fractional penetration}$$

$$\text{Collection efficiency} = 1 - 0.099 = 0.9 \text{ or } 90\%$$

IV. Power Requirement

A roughly constant relationship between collector efficiency and total power input has been observed for a number of types of collectors (34–36). For purposes of estimation, one can assume that any fan horsepower saved by the use of mechanical or liquid pressure atomizing devices will have to be expended in these devices.

The performance of any inertial collection device can be described by a log-log plot of number of particle transfer units vs. power input (36) and the expected relationship has been shown (17) to be of the following form:

$$N_{TD} = \ln \frac{c_i}{c_o} = C_1 \frac{v_t (Z \, \Delta P)^{1/2}}{D_c} \tag{58}$$

It is clear from Eq. (58) that the number of transfer units attainable at a given pressure drop will be most sensitive, next to collector diameter, to particle size (since v_t varies as a^2) and least sensitive to the equipment length. In order that N_{TD} be solely dependent on ΔP for a given dust size, there would have to be a nearly constant ratio of Z/D_c among the various types of equipment. One can only conclude at present that any observed constancy in this relationship is fortuitous.

V. Economics

Costs are the ultimate criterion of the optimum system in gas scrubbing, as in any industrial operation. One must decide whether one type of equipment is better than another when both are capable of the desired performance; whether to use less expensive equipment and more power; whether to use more expensive materials or to have higher maintenance costs; or whether to use a higher stack and less efficient collection equipment. The rationalization of these various trade-offs requires the use of a single method of evaluation: total cost.

Cost estimation methods range from quick and dirty predesign approximations to elaborate compilations of firm bids on completely designed systems. Even the latter will only give results with a probable error of between 7% over and 15% under actual capital costs. Other elements such as labor and maintenance will be more inaccurate. Nevertheless, a decision based on approximate costs is better than one based on no cost considerations. The situation is eased considerably because the comparison of cost estimates generated in the same way is likely to be more accurate than their absolute magnitudes and because sometimes the most doubtful items may contribute only a small fraction of the total cost.

The following list includes average capital investment costs in chemical plants.

1. Delivered equipment cost; updated to present is starting point for calculations.
2. Installed equipment cost is taken from publications or is computed as 1.43 times delivered cost.
3. Process piping = 30–60% of installed cost (item 2 above).
4. Instrumentation = 3–20% of installed cost, depending on amount of automatic control.
5. Buildings and site preparation = 10–30% of installed cost for outdoor and 60–100% for indoor plants.
6. Auxiliaries = 0–5% of installed cost for minor additions to 25–100% for new facilities.
7. Outside lines (i.e., not with the process) = 5–15% of installed cost for intermediate cases.
8. Fixed capital investment is the total of items 2 through 7 plus costs for engineering and construction, contingencies, and a size factor.

The methods presented here are those commonly used in the chemical process industry (37, 38) and can serve as a reasonable basis for preliminary decision making. It is important that all relevant items under the general headings of capital and operating costs be recognized and included. Capital investment covers the plant site and buildings, utilities, storage facilities, and emergency facilities, in addition to the process equipment cost. The amount of nonmanufacturing investment such as for site, shop, and warehouse facilities to be assessed against the project will depend upon circumstances such as whether it is a plant addition or a new plant. Process equipment costs include the basic collection equipment plus installation, piping, instrumentation, insulation, fans, foundations, and supporting structure and may be estimated by use of published data. The total system cost is the sum of items 2 through 7 in the list above. To this must be added cost for engineering and construction (20–60% of total system cost), contingencies (30% of total) and a size factor (0 for routine plants costing $2,000,000, 5–15% of total for routine plants costing $500,000 to $2,000,000 and 15–35% for experimental plants costing $500,000) to give the fixed capital investment. An overall average for fluid processes is that fixed capital investment is 4.74 times delivered equipment cost.

Costs for gas scrubbing equipment have been compiled from several sources and are presented in Fig. 17 and below. Gas absorber costs vary with diameter, height, type of internals, and materials. For purposes of comparison, the costs in Fig. 17 are for scrubbers conforming to the following specifications:

> Column diameter is based on atmospheric pressure air at 4 ft/sec superficial velocity; height based on 10 trays at 18-inch spacing or five transfer units at 4 feet/transfer unit; and steel construction with ceramic packing, if not otherwise specified. Costs are updated to autumn of 1965 by means of Marshall & Stevens Index, are based on data from references (*1, 31–33*), and are for installed scrubbers exclusive of fans, ductwork, supporting structure, utilities, etc.

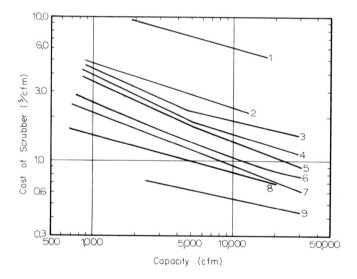

FIG. 17. Scrubber cost vs. capacity for several types. Types of scrubbers are 1, packed column, stainless shell; 2, packed column, steel shell; 3, bubble cap column, steel shell; 4, sieve plate column, steel shell, stainless plates; 5, turbogrid plate column, steel shell, stainless plates; 6, cyclone scrubber, steel; 7, venturi and disk scrubber, steel; 8, packed column, plastic (polyvinyl chloride); 9, spray scrubber, steel.

For extrapolation purposes one may use the following generalizations:

1. Equipment cost varies with about the 0.6 power of capacity.
2. Total plant cost varies with about the 0.7 power of capacity.
3. Costs may be updated by means of Marshall & Stevens Equipment Cost Index as published in "Chemical Engineering" magazine.
4. Cost variation with material can be computed as the cost for plain carbon steel equipment times a multiplying factor. These factors are: copper = 1.4, aluminum = 1.5, lead = 1.6, 304 stainless = 2.3, 316 stainless = 2.7, Monel or nickel = 3.0, Hastelloy = 3.5.

Examples

Some cost data for wet collectors obtained from a large steel company indicate the range for large installations. The following are on the installed cost basis.

High Energy Collectors

1. Venturi-type scrubber at an iron-making furnace (mainly dust):
   a. Unit installed in 1961 cost $2730 per thousand cfm capacity.
   b. Unit installed in 1964 at another plant cost $1000 per thousand cfm capacity.
   c. Unit installed in 1965 at a different plant, cost $3150 per thousand cfm capacity.
2. Venturi-type scrubber at steel-making (metallurgical) furnaces (mainly fume):
   a. Unit installed in 1964 cost $2920 per thousand cfm capacity.
   b. Unit installed in 1965 cost $4100 per thousand cfm capacity.

Medium Energy Collectors

Wet scrubbers installed at raw materials preparation plants (dust):
   a. Unit installed in 1961 cost $2250 per thousand cfm capacity.
   b. Unit installed in 1963 cost $1000 per thousand cfm capacity.
   c. A system involving four collectors at an operation similar to the above, date of installation not given, cost $1770 per thousand cfm capacity.

REFERENCES

1. J. H. Perry, ed., "Chemical Engineers' Handbook," 4th ed. McGraw-Hill, New York, 1963.
2. G. Nonhebel, "Gas Purification Processes." George Newnes Ltd., London, 1964.

3. A. L. Kohl and F. C. Riesenfeld, "Gas Purification." McGraw-Hill, New York, 1960.
4. N. A. Fuchs, "The Mechanics of Aerosols." Macmillan, New York, 1964.
5. J. E. Vivian and C. J. King, *Mod. Chem. Eng.* 1 (1963).
6. G. Seidell, "Solubilities of Inorganic and Metal Organic Compounds." Van Nostrand, Princeton, New Jersey, 1940.
7. S. Calvert and W. Workman, *Talanta* 4, 89 (1960).
8. S. Calvert and G. Kapo, *Chem. Eng.* Feb. 4, Mar. (1963).
9. H. L. Shulman, et al., *A.I.Ch.E. Journal* 1, 249 and 259 (1955).
10. R. Russell, M.S. Thesis, Case Institute of Technology (1962).
11. D. S. Mehta and S. Calvert, *Environ. Sci. Technol.* 1, 325 (1967).
12. A. Astarita and E. Gioia, *Chem. Eng. Sci.* 19, 963 (1964).
13. N. Gilbert, "The Removal of Particulate Matter from Gaseous Wastes." Am. Petrol. Inst., New York, 1961.
14. Iron and Steel Inst., "Proceedings on Fume Arrestment," Spec. Rept., p. 83. Williams Lea & Co. Ltd., London, 1964.
15. C. J. Stairmand, *Chem. Eng.*, No. 194, CE310 (1965).
16. S. Calvert and R. Hodous, *J. Air Pollution Control Assoc.* 12, 326 (1962).
17. S. Calvert and M. Taheri, *Brit. Chem. Eng.* 43, 254 (1966).
18. I. A. Aleksandrov and A. I. Skoblo, *Intern. Chem. Eng.* 2, 353 (1962).
19. J. A. Brink, Jr., and C. E. Contant, *Ind. Eng. Chem.* 50, 1157 (1958).
20. J. E. Yocum and S. Chapman, *Air Repair* 4, 154 (1955).
21. H. F. Johnstone and M. H. Roberts, *Ind. Eng. Chem.* 41, 2417 (1949).
22. F. O. Ekman and H. F. Johnstone, *Ind. Eng. Chem.* 43, 1358 (1951).
23. L. S. Harris, *J. Air Pollution Control Assoc.* 15, 302 (1965).
24. J. S. Eckert, *Chem. Eng. Progr.* 57, 54 (1961).
25. F. A. Zenz and R. E. Lavin, *Hydrocarbon Proc. Petrol. Refiner* 44, 121 (1965).
26. S. Nukiyama and Y. Tanasawa, *Trans. Soc. Mech. Engrs.* (*Japan*) 4, 86 (1938).
27. Y. Goldshmid and S. Calvert, *A.I.Ch.E. Journal* 9, 352 (1963).
28. F. Fun and S. Calvert, *58th Ann. Meeting Am. Inst. Chem. Engrs., San Francisco, 1965.*
29. S. Jackson and S. Calvert, *A.I.Ch.E. Journal* 12, 1075 (1966).
30. S. Calvert and S. Jackson, *Am. Ind. Hyg. Assoc. Meeting, Houston, 1965.*
31. A. Fonda and H. Herne, *Intern. J. Air Pollution* 3, 26 (1960).
32. W. H. Walton and A. Woolcock, *Intern. J. Air Pollution* 3, 129 (1960).
33. R. Ingebo, *NASA, Tech. Note* 3762 (1956).
34. C. E. Lapple and H. J. Kamack, *Chem. Eng. Progr.* 51, 110 (1955).
35. K. T. Semrau, C. W. Marynowski, K. E. Lunde, and C. E. Lapple, *Ind. Eng. Chem.* 50, 1615 (1958).
36. K. T. Semrau, *J. Air Pollution Control Assoc.* 10, 200 (1960).
37. C. H. Chilton, "Cost Engineering in the Process Industries." McGraw-Hill, New York, 1960.
38. F. C. Vilbrandt and C. E. Dryden, "Chemical Engineering Plant Design," 4th ed. McGraw-Hill, New York, 1963.
39. S. K. Friedlander, "Handbook on Air Cleaning—Particulate Removal." U.S. At. Energy Comm., Washington, D.C., 1952.

47   Source Control by Gas–Solid Adsorption and Related Processes

Amos Turk

I.   General Principles

The forces which hold atoms, molecules, or ions together in the solid state exist throughout the body of a solid and at its surface. The forces at the surface may be considered to be "residual" in that they are available for binding other molecules which come in contact or in very close proximity to it. Any gas, vapor, or liquid will, therefore, adhere to some degree to any solid surface. This phenomenon is called adsorption, or sorption, the adsorbing solid is called the adsorbent, or sorbent, and the adsorbed material is the adsorbate, or sorbate. A molecule which moves to and is held at the surface of a solid loses the energy of its motion; adsorption is therefore always an exothermic, or energy-releasing process. Since this chapter is concerned with control of air pollutant sources, only adsorption from the gaseous state is within its scope (1).

Adsorption is useful in air pollution control because it is a means of concentrating gaseous pollutants, thus facilitating their disposal, their recovery, or their conversion to innocuous or valuable products.

Some sorption processes are irreversible and very strongly exothermic. For example, part of the oxygen adsorbed on activated carbon at ambient temperatures is recoverable only as CO and CO_2; it is therefore concluded that chemical bonds have been formed between oxygen and

497

the adsorbent. A process of this type is called chemisorption. More important in practical air pollution control are phenomena in which adsorbates react with each other; the adsorbent, by serving as a concentrating medium, speeds up the reaction rate. Material in the adsorbed state may be especially reactive; the adsorbent then functions as a true catalyst. In some cases a specially selected catalyst or reactant is incorporated into an adsorbent prior to the use of the adsorbent as a gas purifier. The adsorbent is then said to be impregnated with the material. Such impregnation may increase the rate, capacity, or selectivity of the adsorbent for gas purification.

The quantity of material that can be adsorbed by a given weight of adsorbent depends on the following factors: (1) the concentration of the material in the space around the adsorbent, (2) the total surface area of the adsorbent, (3) the temperature, (4) the presence of other molecules in the environment which may compete for a place on the adsorbent, (5) the characteristics of the molecules to be adsorbed, especially their weight, electrical polarity, chemical activity, size, and shape, (6) the microstructure of the adsorbing surface, especially the sizes and shapes of its pores, and (7) the chemical nature of the adsorbent surface, including electrical polarity and chemical activity. Maximum capacity for adsorption of a given substance is favored by a high concentration of the substance in the space adjoining the adsorbent, a large adsorbing surface, freedom from competing substances, low temperature, and by aggregation of the substance in large molecules which fit and are strongly attracted to the receiving shapes of the adsorbent.

The net rate of adsorption of a substance depends on the rate at which molecules reach the adsorbing surface, the fraction of those making contact which are adsorbed, and the rate of removal of molecules from the surface (desorption). Therefore, to favor rapid adsorption, the adsorbing equipment should be designed with a view to providing ample duration of contact (detention time) between the gas to be purified and an adsorbent which is sufficiently retentive to the contaminants that are to be removed.

Disposal of pollutant gases that have been concentrated by adsorption may be effected in any of the following ways: (1) The adsorbent with its adsorbate may be discarded. Since even the saturated adsorbent is relatively nonvolatile, this step seldom involves difficult problems. An exception occurs when the sorbate is radioactive. (2) The adsorbate may be desorbed and either recovered, if it is valuable, or discarded. (3) The adsorbate may be oxidized on the adsorbent surface. If the adsorbent is not simultaneously oxidized, it may be recovered.

II. Adsorbents

A. ACTIVATED CARBON

Activated carbon (2) (also called active carbon, or activated charcoal) consists of particles of moderately to highly pure carbon which have a large surface area per unit weight or volume of solid. For use in a fixed bed for air or gas purification, the particles must be so sized that they impose little resistance to flow for a given sorption efficiency; the range of 4–20 mesh (U.S. Sieve Series) encompasses the predominant portion of carbon for such use. To minimize mechanical attrition during transportation and use, the activated carbon should be hard. Hardness is determined in part by the nature of the raw material used for manufacture of the activated carbon, and in part by the manufacturing process. Raw materials include coconut and other nut shells, fruit pits, bituminous coal, hard woods, and petroleum residues. Activated carbon from bone char is not used for gas purification. The extent and micropore structure of the carbon surface are of prime importance. Total surface area is in the order of several hundred thousand square feet per pound of activated carbon. The distribution of pore diameters is also determined both by the nature of the raw material and by the activating process; different carbons may differ in this characteristic to an extent which may demonstrably affect their performance. When the activated carbon surface is used as a site for oxidation of collected pollutants, the kindling temperature of the carbon is important; the higher the kindling temperature, the less is the carbon prone to oxidative attrition.

Activated carbon, consisting largely of neutral atoms of a single species, presents a surface with a relatively homogeneous distribution of electrical charge. As a result, there are no significant potential gradients of molecular dimensions on the surface which would selectively orient and bind polar in preference to nonpolar adsorbate molecules. Activated carbon is therefore effective in adsorbing molecules of organic substances with less selectivity than is exhibited by other, more polar sorbents. Activated carbon is effective in adsorbing organic molecules even from a humid gas stream. The water molecules, being highly polar, exhibit strong attractions for each other, which compete with their attractions for the nonpolar carbon surface; consequently the larger, less polar organic molecules are selectively adsorbed.

The total adsorptive capacity of a sample of activated carbon may be measured by its activity or retentivity for a standard vapor. The activity

TABLE I

TYPICAL SPECIFICATIONS FOR ACTIVATED CARBON
USED FOR AIR PURIFICATION

Property	Specification
Activity for CCl$_4^a$	At least 50%
Retentivity for CCl$_4^b$	At least 30%
Apparent density	At least 0.4 gm/ml
Hardness (ball abrasion)^c	At least 80%
Mesh distribution	6–14 range (Tyler Sieve Series)

^{a} Maximum saturation of carbon, at 20 °C and 760 torr in an air-stream equilibrated with CCl$_4$ at 0 °C.

^{b} Maximum weight of adsorbed CCl$_4$ retained by carbon on exposure to pure air at 20 °C and 760 torr.

^{c} Percent of 6–8 mesh carbon which remains on a 14-mesh screen after shaking with 30 steel balls of 0.25–0.37 inch diam. per 50 gm carbon, for 30 minutes in a vibrating or tapping machine.

is the maximum amount of a vapor which can be adsorbed by a given weight of carbon under specified conditions of temperature, concentration of the vapor, and concentration of other vapors (usually water). The retentivity is the maximum amount of adsorbed vapor which can be retained by the carbon after the vapor concentration in the ambient air or gas stream has been reduced to zero. Because an adsorbent may be required to retain its adsorbate even in pure air, the retentivity represents the practical capacity of the carbon in service.

Typical specifications for activated carbon to be used for air purification are given in Table I.

B. OTHER ADSORBENTS

All commercially important sorbents other than carbon are simple or complex oxides; their surfaces contain inhomogeneous distribution of charge on a molecular scale and hence are polar. These sorbents show considerably greater selectivity than does activated carbon, and overwhelmingly greater preference for polar than for nonpolar molecules. As a result, they are more useful than carbon when separations are to be made among different types of pollutants, but much less useful when overall decontamination of an airstream is to be accomplished. They are essentially ineffective for direct decontamination of a moist air or gas stream. Since the latter tasks greatly predominate in problems of control of air pollutant sources, polar sorbents are of less general applicability and will be considered only in brief outline.

1. *Siliceous Adsorbents*

These comprise the silica gels, fuller's, diatomaceous, and other siliceous earths, and synthetic zeolites or "molecular sieves." These materials are available in a wide range of adsorbent capacities per unit weight or volume of solid. At their best, their capacities are of the same order of magnitude as that of the most highly activated carbons. As previously stated, these materials also exhibit greater specificity of adsorption than do the activated carbons on the basis of preference for more polar molecules. In addition, the synthetic zeolites can be made with specified and uniform pore diameters, which give them outstanding properties of adsorbent specificity on the basis of size or shape of adsorbate molecules. Even this structural uniqueness, however, does not obviate the preference of the adsorbent for polar rather than nonpolar molecules; as a result, these materials will not absorb organic molecules, even of sizes which match their pores, from a moist airstream, the water molecules being adsorbed in preference.

2. *Metallic Oxide Adsorbents*

Since metals are less electrophilic than silicon, the metallic oxides are even more polar than the siliceous adsorbents. Metallic oxide adsorbents therefore serve as desiccants, catalyst carriers, or catalysts; they are never used directly for source control of airborne pollutants by physical adsorption. Activated alumina (aluminum oxide) is an example of this type of adsorbent.

C. ADSORBENT IMPREGNATIONS

The effectiveness of adsorbent impregnations may be related to any of the following modes of action:

1. The impregnant may be a reagent that chemically converts a pollutant to a harmless or adsorbable product. As an example, carbon may be impregnated with 10–20% of its weight of bromine. The adsorbed bromine will react with olefins whose molecules come in contact with the bromine-impregnated surface. If the olefin is ethylene, which causes significant plant damage and which, because of its low molecular weight, is not significantly removed from an airstream by physical adsorption alone, the reaction is chemical addition to form 1,2-dibromoethane. The brominated product is readily adsorbed and remains on the surface. When the bromine is chemically consumed, the sorbent system loses its effectiveness in removing ethylene from air streaming through it. Other chemical reagent impregnations include iodine for mercury vapor,

lead acetate for hydrogen sulfide, and sodium silicate for hydrogen fluoride.

2. The impregnant may be a catalyst that acts continuously. Since the only reacting materials available are the carrier gas (air) and the pollutant itself, the only reactions to be catalyzed are oxidation and decomposition. For continuous oxidative catalysis, limitations are imposed by the following factors: if activated carbon is the sorbent, a highly active oxidation catalyst will tend to make the carbon pyrophoric; if the catalyst activity is low, only easily oxidizable pollutants will be converted; if a nonoxidizable carrier is used, selection must be made from among the polar sorbents whose limitations were discussed above. Within this framework, applications of continuous oxidative catalysis have been made by using chromium, copper, silver, palladium, and platinum impregnations on activated carbon. The metal depositions are usually effected by *in situ* decomposition of complex salts which were used in the impregnating solutions. As a result, some of the deposited metallic catalyst probably remains in a chemically combined condition. The copper and silver oxidation catalysts are effective for readily oxidizable pollutants and have been designed for the removal of specific war gases (chloropicrin, lewisite), with relatively little attention to other applications. At ambient temperatures the impregnated carbon itself is stable to oxidation, but its kindling temperature is significantly lowered and hence it must be treated as a readily combustible substance. The noble metal impregnations are severely limited by their marked enhancement of the pyrophoricity of the carbon. Catalytic oxidations on nonoxidizable carriers are generally conducted at elevated temperatures; these are the processes of catalytic combustion described in Chapter 48. Some high temperature catalytic processes are also described in Section IV,B of this chapter.

When the pollutant character of a substance can be abated by decomposition, the acceleration of this action by a catalyst is a valid objective in source control. This application is limited to inherently unstable substances; most important among these are the molecules which contain oxygen-to-oxygen linkages: ozonides, peroxides, hydroperoxides, and ozone itself. Even the untreated surface of activated carbon acts as a catalyst for rapid decomposition of these substances; the effect is enhanced by any of a number of metallic oxide catalysts, such as manganese dioxide and cupric oxide.

3. Finally, the impregnant may be a catalyst which acts intermittently. This action would be applied to a pollutant that is first collected for an interval of time by physical adsorption. When the capacity of the sorbent has been used up, the temperature may be raised to initiate a catalytic

surface oxidation of the collected sorbate. If carbon is used as the adsorbent, the catalyst must not render it pyrophoric even at the highest operating temperature. Oxides of chromium, molybdenum, and tungsten have been used *(3)*.

III. Equipment and Systems

A. EQUIPMENT

1. *Design Principles*

The general requirements that sorption phenomena impose on equipment design *(4)* are (1) long enough duration of contact (detention time) between airstream and sorbent bed for adequate sorption efficiency, (2) sufficient sorption capacity to provide the desired service life, (3) small enough resistance to air flow to allow adequate operation of the air moving devices being used, (4) uniformity of distribution of air flow over the sorbent bed to ensure full utilization of the sorbent, (5) adequate pretreatment of the air to remove nonadsorbable particles which would impair the action of the sorbent bed, and (6) provision for renewing the sorbent after it has reached saturation. The action of a sorbent bed on a moving airstream as it affects system design is illustrated by the schematic "adsorption wave" in Fig. 1. Polluted air is moving through the

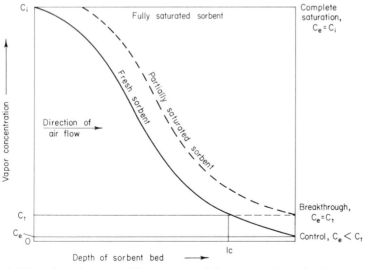

FIG. 1. The adsorption wave. Time pattern of the action of an adsorbent bed on a moving airstream.

bed from left to right. The vertical axis represents pollutant concentration (C) in contact with the bed at any depth l. If the initial concentration is C_i, then reduction to a desired concentration C_t (e.g., threshold for odor or toxicity) is accomplished initially within the "critical bed depth," l_c. If l exceeds l_c, the emergent concentration C_e will be less then C_t. The entire curve is being displaced to the right continuously with time, and the bed may be considered to have reached the breakthrough point when $C_e = C_t$. The bed reaches complete saturation when $C_e = C_i$.

Design requirements imposed by the objectives set forth above and by the nature of the dynamic adsorption wave are met by several types of equipment and of system arrangements.

2. Adsorbent Disposed on a Carrier

Considerable flexibility in sorbent bed design may be obtained when the sorbent, usually in the form of fine powder, is disposed on an inert carrier. The latter may be paper, organic, or inorganic textiles, or extruded plastic filaments. Papers have been developed that contain 50–

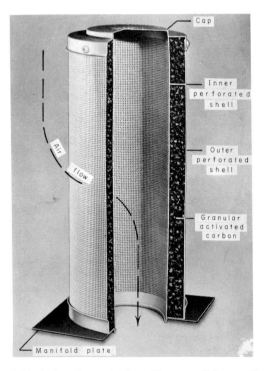

Fig. 2. Cylindrical thin-bed canister adsorber. (Courtesy of Connor Engineering Corp.)

75% carbon by weight; cellulose monofilaments extruded with activated carbon powder may effectively reach a level of about 80% of activated carbon. Even at best, however, the limitations in sorption capacity imposed by carriers, and their limitations of rigidity, have excluded such media from application to industrial source control of atmospheric pollution.

3. *Thin-Bed Granular Adsorbers*

The great advantage of thin-bed adsorbers (*4–7*) is the low resistance which they impose to air flow. Since even small differences in depth of thin-bed adsorbers constitute a significant portion of the total depth and may promote channeling, bed depth uniformity is important. Flat, cylindrical, and pleated bed shapes have been used. Beds may be retained by porous barriers, screening, or perforated sheet metal. Requirements for rigidity have led to the overwhelming use of perforated sheet metal retainers. Equipment is illustrated in Figs. 2, 3, and 4. Commerically available cylindrical canisters are designed for about 25 ft³/min of air; the larger pleated cells handle 750–1000 ft³/min, and cells comprising aggregates of flat bed components handle 2000 ft³/min.

FIG. 3. Pleated cell thin-bed adsorber. (Courtesy of Barneby-Cheney Co.)

FIG. 4. Aggregated flat cell thin-bed adsorber. The small test element located on the upstream side of the cell contains carbon that is to be analyzed after some period of service for degree of saturation, and thereby to predict the remaining capacity of the cell. (Courtesy of Connor Engineering Corp.)

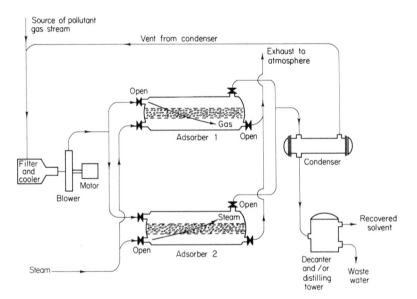

FIG. 5. Two-stage regenerative system. Adsorber 1 is adsorbing; adsorber 2 is steaming. After No. 1 is saturated and No. 2 is clean, their functions are reversed.

4. Thick-Bed Granular Adsorbers

These are used when large adsorbing capacity is needed. The concomitant increase in efficiency is generally not, in itself, sufficient justification for use of thick adsorbent bed equipment (8). Even with this type of equipment, reasonable bed uniformity is desirable for effective use of the sorbent. Adsorbers for regenerative systems (see below) are usually in the range of 1–3 feet in bed depth, with a downward gas flow to minimize bed lifting. Typical thick-bed adsorbers, such as are used in solvent recovery systems are shown in Figs. 5, 6, and 9.

5. Fluidized Adsorbers

When a gas is passed upward through a bed of granular adsorbent, the pressure drop imposed by the bed (see Fig. 10) is in opposition to its own weight (9). If the gas velocity is increased to a sufficient value, the pressure drop equals the weight of the bed and the solids begin to move. This motion is the beginning of fluidization. At higher gas ve-

FIG. 6. Thick-bed adsorbers used in a solvent recovery system. (Courtesy of Union Carbide Corp.)

locities, the granular adsorbent particles may be maintained in constant motion. The pressure drop required for fluidization depends on the bed depth and the densities of the gas stream and of the solid particles.

B. Systems

1. *Principles*

The contaminated air may be passed through the sorbent bed partially (the remainder being bypassed), completely (single-pass), or with some recirculation (multiple-pass) (*4*). Most frequently, however, a single pass is made through the adsorbent system, the decontaminated stream being released to atmosphere. Before the adsorbing step, however, the gas stream may have to be treated in any of the following ways: (1) Particles so gross that they may build up an obstructive coating on the adsorbent bed must be removed by filtration. (2) Sorptive capacity for the contaminant can be increased by any action that preconcentrates contaminants; this includes operating under increased pressure. (3) Moisture droplets, which may also act as an obstructant to gas adsorption, may be removed by electrical or mechanical means such as are elaborated in Chapters 43–45. As an alternative, the capacity of the carrier airstream for removing the droplets by vaporizing them may be increased by diluting the stream with ambient air if the relative humidity of the latter is low. Excessively high humidities may be reduced by cooling the air sufficiently with fin tube type coils so that condensation occurs and then by reheating the air until the relative humidity falls below about 50%. (4) If gas temperatures are too high, cooling may be needed. The usual objective is to reach a temperature of 100 °F or lower. High temperature reduces the capacity of the carbon and, to some extent, accelerates its rate of oxidation and thus reduces its service life and imposes greater difficulties of carbon recovery. Cooling by dilution with ambient air necessitates an increase in the size of the adsorbers and in the power cost for moving the air. Nonetheless, for thin-bed equipment, dilution is sometimes the most economical approach to cooling. The increased cost of larger adsorbers is partially compensated by a longer service life. (5) Excessively high concentrations are disadvantageous because they may approach the explosive range or because high heat of adsorption may cause an excessive carbon bed temperature. In such cases, dilution must be used to decrease the concentration.

The service life of the adsorbent is limited by its capacity and by the contaminating load. Provision must therefore be made for periodic renewal of the adsorbent. There is no satisfactory instrumentation to record or monitor the degree of saturation of an adsorber used to de-contaminate a humid gas stream. Weight gain is not a valid criterion for the purpose because moisture content of the adsorber is variable. Renewal of adsorbent must be made either on the basis of deterioration of performance (break-through) or according to a time schedule based either on previous performance history or on calculations of expected saturation, all relevant factors being known (see Section IV). If mechanically feasible, a representative element or portion of the adsorbent bed may be removed and chemically analyzed to determine the degree of saturation of the entire bed.

2. Nonregenerative Systems

In these systems the adsorbent is discarded or removed elsewhere for reactivation after its performance has deteriorated. Either thin (Fig. 7) or thick-bed equipment may be used, depending on factors previously described. A possible modification to ensure more complete use of the sorbent involves a two-stage bed (Fig. 8, dampers 2 and 3 open, air flowing to the right). When breakthrough occurs from the stage 2 bed, stage 1 is replaced, and air is made to flow to the left (dampers 1 and 4 open). Similarly, after each succeeding breakthrough, the "downstream" bed is replaced and the air flow is reversed. This system enables the sorbent to be used in the capacity range between breakthrough and complete saturations (Fig. 1), usually a significant fraction of its total capacity.

Nonregenerative systems are economically applicable for control of pollutant sources whose vapors are odorous but present either in low concentrations (i.e., under about 2 ppm) or only at intermittent intervals (e.g., laboratory exhaust systems), or both.

3. Regenerative Systems

a. Recovery of Sorbate. Regenerative systems provide for the on-site periodic recovery of the adsorbent and/or the adsorbate (8). Such systems may advantageously be used for removal of vapors from polluting sources in which concentrations are above about 1000 ppm (0.1%). The facilitated recovery of valuable organic matter, usually solvent, is generally the prime economic determinant. In operation, vapor-laden air, free from gross particulate matter and not warmer than about 100 °F, is driven through one or more thick-bed stages of activated carbon, and the effluent is released to the atmosphere. When the sorbent reaches a given level of saturation, the vapor-laden pollutant source is directed to another, fresh adsorber, so that pollution abatement is continuous. Meanwhile, the saturated bed is regenerated by blowing

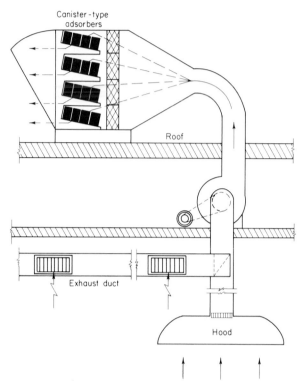

Canister-type
adsorbers

Roof

Exhaust duct

Hood

FIG. 7. Thin-bed exhaust purification system.

steam through it in a direction counter to that which the polluted air stream had taken. The mixture of effluent steam and desorbate is condensed; the desorbate may be recovered by decantation or distillation. Figures 5 and 6 illustrate such a cycling system. Figure 9 shows a scheme for a regenerative system designed to make full use of the sorbent's capacity. Absorber 1 is fresh and its effluent may be discharged to the atmosphere. Adsorber 2 is partly saturated, but its residual capacity may be used if its effluent is passed through a second stage (adsorber 3). The latter adsorber, having just been steamed, is simultaneously being cooled. The final adsorber (4) is undergoing reactivation. When the cycle is complete, the adsorbers change functions according to the schedule: 1→2; 2→4; 3→1; 4→3. Caution must be exercized, however, before any contaminated air stream is committed to a hot carbon bed. Such contact may promote decomposition or partial oxidation and thereby result in the discharge of odorous or irritating gases to the atmosphere. As an example, the action of hot activated carbon on

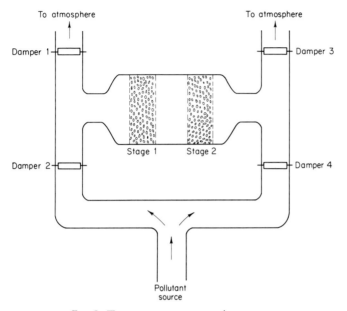

Stage 1 Stage 2

FIG. 8. Two-stage nonregenerative system.

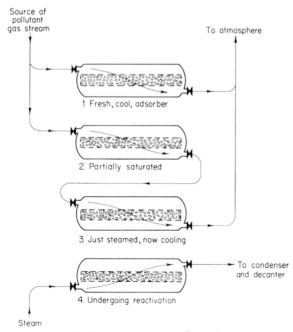

1. Fresh, cool, adsorber

2. Partially saturated

3. Just steamed, now cooling

4. Undergoing reactivation

FIG. 9. Four-stage regenerative system.

an airstream containing methylethyl ketone yields an objectionable effluent that contains acetic acid and other irritating oxidized components. In many cases, it is not necessary to have separate cooling and drying cycles because the vapor-laden air cools and dries the carbon bed so rapidly that there is always enough cool dry carbon to handle the adsorption. In such cases, the cooling wave travels through the bed considerably more rapidly than the adsorption wave. It is when the rates of travel of the two waves at high vapor concentrations are essentially equal, that precooling is necessary.

b. Destruction of Sorbate. The wide range of pollutant vapor concentration above about 2 ppm but less than about 1000 ppm is frequently unsuitable both for nonregenerative system operation, because of high costs for frequent sorbent replacement, and for sorbate recovery systems, because of the meager economic worth of the organic material recovered. In this range, a cycling system with oxidative destruction of the sorbate may be considered (3). In such a system, the absorbent is activated carbon which has been impregnated with a small amount of catalyst of only moderate activity. The carbon then serves as an ambient-temperature adsorbent, without catalytic action, until it becomes saturated with respect to the pollutant vapors in the airstream passing through it. At this point, instead of using steam desorption, reactivation is effected by warming the entering airstream to a temperature at which catalytic oxidation is initiated, and for sufficient time to permit complete oxidative destruction of all the adsorbate on the catalytic surface. An activated carbon with a high kindling temperature permits quantitative partition in oxidizing all the adsorbate but none of the carbon. Commercial carbons are available whose kindling temperatures are 350°–400 °C or more. Successive reactivations of this kind can be carried out without impairing the adsorptive nature of the carbon surface. The vapors desorbed during initial warming, before catalytic oxidation predominates, may be recycled to minimize their discharge to the atmosphere.

IV. Applications to Source Control

A. Effect of Process Variables

1. *Air Flow*

The rate of air flow is in inverse proportion to the detention time, or duration of contact, between airstream and sorbent bed. The possible effects of rapid air flow in uneven channeling through the sorbent bed,

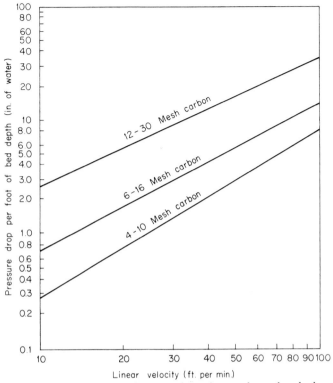

FIG. 10. Pressure drop vs. flow rate through granular carbon beds.

with resultant displacement or mechanical attrition, must also be considered. In the great majority of cases, however, the prime determinant of permissible flow rate is the pressure drop imposed by the sorbent bed on the moving airstream. Figure 10 presents pressure drop information as a function of flow rate for several typical granulations of activated carbon. Representative air flows in commercial sorption equipment range from about 25 ft/min in thin-bed adsorbers up to about 80 ft/min in the thicker solvent recovery beds.

The distribution of particle sizes in a granular adsorbent bed is an important factor in determining the bed efficiency. Adsorption efficiencies exceeding 95% can be attained in a well-packed bed of carbon granules in the 6–16 mesh size range, even with thin beds (0.5–0.7 inches) at lineal velocities of 30–50 ft/min and residence times approximating 0.03 seconds. For the thick beds used in recycling systems, lineal air velocities as high as 200 ft/min have been used without adversely affecting bed efficiencies. The limiting factor in such cases is usually the increased power costs for driving the air through the bed.

2. *Temperature*

The capacity of an adsorbent increases with decrease of temperature. As mentioned in Section III,B,1, temperatures above about 100 °F should be avoided. Excessive temperature fluctuations such as may be caused by process cycling are also disadvantageous because they may induce massive desorption during periods of temperature rise.

3. *Humidity*

Activated carbon will adsorb moisture from a humid airstream, but will release this moisture to the atmosphere during the process of adsorbing larger, less polar molecules such as are usually common to pollutant gas streams. The presence of some moisture, in fact, is desirable because the vaporization of the water from the carbon dissipates heat of adsorption and provides a more uniform bed temperature. The presence of a moderate amount of moisture in the airstream from a polluting source, therefore, is not significantly deleterious to the performance of gas-adsorbing activated carbon. When the relative humidity of the airstream exceeds about 50%, its detraction from the carbon's capacity begins to be significant, but is not necessarily disabling. At higher moisture contents, the loss of capacity and efficiency increases. This effect has been found to be largely independent of temperature in the ranges normally encountered.

4. *Vapor concentration*

The duration of service of the adsorbent is determined by the prevailing vapor concentration according to the relationship

$$t = \frac{6.43(10)^6 SW}{eQ_r M C_v} \tag{1}$$

where t = duration of adsorbent service before saturation (hours)
S = proportionate saturation of sorbent (fractional). Refer to Table II for typical maximum values (retentivities).
W = weight of adsorbent (pounds)
e = sorption efficiency (fractional)
Q_r = air flow rate through sorbent bed (ft^3/min)
M = average molecular weight of sorbed vapor
C_v = entering vapor concentration, ppm by volume

For a typical average retentivity value, in source control by adsorption, we may take $S = 0.20$ (see Table II). For a vapor with $M = 100$, and complete adsorption ($e = 1$), this relationship then reduces to Eq. (2).

TABLE II

RENTENTIVITY OF VAPORS BY ACTIVATED CARBON[a]

Substance	Formula	Molecular weight	Normal boiling point, °C	Approx. retentivity[a] in % at 20 °C 760 torr
Acetaldehyde	C_2H_4O	44.1	21	7
Amyl acetate	$C_7H_{14}O_2$	130.2	148	34
Butyric acid	$C_4H_8O_2$	88.1	164	35
Carbon tetrachloride	CCl_4	153.8	76	45
Ethyl acetate	$C_4H_8O_2$	88.1	77	19
Ethyl mercaptan	C_2H_6S	62.1	35	23
Eucalyptole	$C_{10}H_{18}O$	154.2	176	20
Formaldehyde	CH_2O	30.0	−21	3
Methyl chloride	CH_3Cl	50.5	−24	5
Ozone	O_3	48.0	−112	Decomposes to oxygen
Putrescine	$C_4H_{12}N_2$	88.2	158	25
Skatole	C_9H_9N	131.2	266	25
Sulfur dioxide	SO_2	64.1	−10	10
Toluene	C_7H_8	92.1	111	29

[a] Percent retained in a dry airstream at 20 °C, 760 torr, based on weight of carbon.

$$t = \frac{1.29(10)^4 W}{Q_r C_v} \tag{2}$$

Polymerizable vapors or vapor mixtures (e.g., phenol vapor with formaldehyde vapor) tend to deposit nondesorbable resins in the pores of the carbon, thus making such carbon useless for cycling systems that employ steam. (Since such resins are combustible, oxidative regeneration is not invalidated.) In cases where the polymerizing gases constitute a small fraction of the total, it may be worthwhile to remove them first. An example is caustic scrubbing of gases to remove small portions of phenolics from larger, recoverable quantities of solvents.

B. SPECIFIC PROCESSES

1. Deodorization of Odorous Emissions

Many odorants in low concentrations, such as 10^{-7} (100 ppb) or less, are detectable and objectionable. The deodorization of such gas streams by solid adsorption is, in many instances, an effective and economical procedure (10, 11). When odorous gases are discharged in high con-

TABLE III
PROCESSES WHICH INVOLVE ATMOSPHERIC DISCHARGE OF ADSORBABLE ODORS

Industry	Process
Food processing	Dehydration, canning, cooking, frying, baking, coffee roasting; processing of fish, poultry, and meats; handling and blending of spices; fat and scrap rendering and other waste digestions; fermentation processes.
Manufacturing and use of chemicals	Processes involving discharge to atmosphere of waste or recoverable by-product, solvent or plasticizer; loss of small quantities of highly odorous materials, as in manufacture of pesticides, glues, cements, adhesives, fertilizers, and pharmaceutical products (especially those extracted from natural sources such as glands, urine, and blood); paint and varnish production; release of odorous vapors by displacement from storage tanks during filling and transfer operations.
Miscellaneous processes	Gas odorizing sites, including containers, storage tanks, and odorant injection points; paper and pulp manufacturing; tannery operations; foundries; manufacturing of asphaltic products such as roofing; discharge of odorous exhausts from animal laboratories; and many others.

TABLE IV
STEPS IN THE REINLUFT PROCESS

Step[a]	Chemical or physical action
A. Flue gas, containing SO_2 and SO_3, enters the adsorber at 300 °F.	The SO_3 is adsorbed on the carbon; the SO_2 passes through.
B. The flue gas is drawn off, cooled, and returned to the adsorbent bed at a higher level.	Cooling of SO_2 from 300 °F to 220 °F.
C. The SO_2 is oxidized to SO_3, and sulfuric acid is produced. The sulfuric acid remains on the carbon.	$SO_2 + \frac{1}{2}O_2 \rightarrow SO_3$ $SO_3 + H_2O \rightarrow H_2SO_4$
D. The downward motion of the bed carries the carbon with sulfuric acid to the regenerator section (700 °F), where the sulfuric acid dissociates. Some of the SO_3 is recovered; some reacts with the carbon.	$H_2SO_4 \rightarrow SO_3 + H_2O$ $2SO_3 + C \rightarrow CO_2 + 2SO_2$
E. The product gas that leaves the regenerator at 300 °F is reheated to 700 °F and returned to base of the regenerator.	

[a] The letters A–E refer to steps shown in Fig. 11.

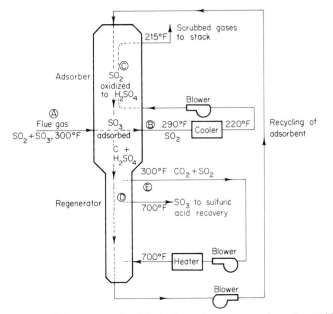

FIG. 11. The Reinluft process. Simplified schematic representation. (See Table IV.)

centration, even the effluents from reasonably efficient cleanup methods may still be objectionably odorous. Solid adsorption methods may then be used effectively as a final deodorizing stage.

Examples of unpleasant and pervasive odorous effluents discharged to the atmosphere, which can be controlled in a final cleanup stage by solid adsorption, include those shown in Table III.

2. Control of Gaseous Radioactive Emissions

The adsorption of radioactive substances follows the principles set forth for nonradioactive gases and vapors. Applications have been made in which activated carbon systems serve as active or standby installations to prevent the emission of radioactive gases from nuclear reactors or other sources (12, 13). Radon and radioiodine are examples of adsorbable radioactive gases.

3. Removal of SO_2 from Flue Gas

a. The Reinluft Process. This process (14) involves both adsorption and catalytic oxidation by means of a moving bed of activated carbon in a regenerative system. The separate steps involved are listed in Table IV and are illustrated in the flow diagram of Fig. 11.

b. The Alkalized Alumina Process. In this process (*14, 15*) flue gas that contains SO_2 and SO_3 is passed upward through a free or baffled falling bed, or a fluidized bed, of alkalized alumina at 625 °F. The composition of the adsorbent corresponds approximately to 56% Al_2O_3 and 37% Na_2O, the remaining portion being largely carbonates and sulfates. The actions that ensue are the oxidation of SO_2 to SO_3 and the conversion of SO_3 to sulfates by the alkalized alumina.

The spent adsorbent is transferred to a regenerator where it is treated with hydrogen or re-formed natural gas (CO, CO_2, and H_2) at 1200 °F. The adsorbed sulfates are thereby reduced to yield H_2S, CO_2, and H_2O. The H_2S is ultimately recovered as elemental sulfur (by the oxidation of some of the H_2S to SO_2, and the reaction of H_2S and SO_2 to yield sulfur).

c. The Catalytic Oxidation Process. Flue gas containing SO_2 is freed from particulate matter by being passed through a mechanical dust collector and then through a high temperature electrostatic precipitator (*14*). The cleaned gas then flows at 900 °F through a fixed bed of vanadium pentoxide which converts the SO_2 to SO_3 during a detention time of 0.3 seconds. This system thus is essentially a contact-process sulfuric acid plant. The exit gas is cooled to 200 °F and the resulting mist, when removed by an electrostatic precipitator or a filter type demister, is a 70% sulfuric acid solution.

d. The Dolomite Process. The addition of pulverized dolomite (calcium magnesium carbonate) or magnesite (magnesium carbonate) to the flue gases has been recommended as a method of reducing the content of SO_2 in the gases exhausted to the atmosphere (*16*). The dolomite powder promotes the air oxidation to SO_2 to SO_3 and thus functions essentially as a fluidized catalyst bed. The SO_3 reacts with the carbonates to produce sulfates,

$$CaCO_3 \rightarrow CaO + CO_2$$

$$SO_3 + CaO \rightarrow CaSO_4$$

The method has the advantage of low investment costs but problems are created in the buildup of sulfate slag.

REFERENCES

1. S. Brunauer, "The Adsorption of Gases and Vapors." Princeton Univ. Press, Princeton, New Jersey, 1945.
2. J. W. Hassler, "Activated Carbon." Chem. Publ. Co., New York, 1963.
3. A. Turk, *Ind. Eng. Chem.* **47**, 966 (1955).
4. H. Sleik and A. Turk, "Air Conservation Engineering," 2nd ed. Connor Engr. Corp., Danbury, Connecticut, 1953.

5. A. Turk and K. A. Bownes, *Chem. Eng.* **57,** 156 (1951).
6. H. L. Barnebey, *Heating, Piping, Air Conditioning* **30,** 153 (1958).
7. N. A. Richardson and W. C. Middleton, *Heating, Piping, Air Conditioning* **30,** 147 (1958).
8. A. K. Doolittle, "The Technology of Solvents and Plasticizers," Chapter 9. Wiley, New York, 1954.
9. H. M. Rowson, *Brit. Chem. Eng.* **8,** 180 (1963).
10. H. L. Barnebey, *J. Air Pollution Control Assoc.* **15,** 422 (1965).
11. H. H. Todd, *Air Eng.* **4,** 26 (1962).
12. T. T. Porembski, *Air Conditioning, Heating, Ventilating* **57,** 97 (1960).
13. R. E. Adams and W. E. Browning, Jr., "Removal of Radioiodine from Air Streams by Activated Carbon," At. Energy Comm. Rept. ORNL-2872, UC-70-Radioactive Waste, TID-4500, 15th ed. U.S. At. Energy Comm., Washington, D.C., 1960.
14. D. Bienstock, J. H. Field, S. Katell, and K. D. Plants, *J. Air Pollution Control Assoc.* **15,** 459 (1965).
15. D. Bienstock, J. H. Field, and J. G. Myers, *J. Eng. Power* **86,** No. 3, 353 (1964).
16. A. M. Squires, "Cyclic Use of Calcined Dolomite to Desulfurize Fuels Undergoing Gasification," *Advan. Chem. Ser.* **69** (1967).

GENERAL REFERENCES

Additional pertinent material is in Chapter 5 of "Air Pollution Engineering Manual, Los Angeles APCD" (J. A. Danielson, ed.); PHS Publ. 999-AP-40, DHEW, Cincinnati (1967); and in Chapter 8 of "Air Pollution Manual, Part II," American Industrial Hygiene Assn., Detroit (1968).

48 Nuisance Abatement by Combustion

Harold J. Paulus

I. Introduction

Thousands of different types of combustible organic compounds are released to the atmosphere from many different manufacturing operations. Typical examples of such operations include industrial dryers, ovens, and furnaces employed for the baking of paints, enamels and printing ink, foundry cores, coatings and impregnants on paper, fabric, and plastic, and processes in the manufacture of paints, varnishes, organic chemicals, synthetic fibers, natural and synthetic rubber, and leather goods. In addition, the refining and industrial application of all oils, whether of mineral, animal, or vegetable origin, results in the loss of some of the products to the atmosphere.

The diversity of manufacturing operations which emit combustible contaminants and the need for corrective action has resulted in the use of three rapid oxidation methods: flares, furnaces, and catalytic combustion. When used in an applicable situation, oxidation by these methods reduces the combustible contaminants to odorless, colorless, and innocuous carbon dioxide and water vapor.

Corrective action achieved at the point of release from the process, whether by the use of a flare, furnace, or catalytic system, offers an effective, convenient, single-step means of disposal. However, the explosion and fire hazards of the vaporized combustibles require a thorough knowledge of combustion and an understanding of each oxidation method to obtain a safe and effective system. Such demands generally require professional analysis by engineers experienced in combustion and related protective equipment.

521

II. Principles of Combustion

Combustion is oxidation achieved through the mechanism of rapid chain reactions. The chain reactions or steps involved in reducing undesirable combustible contaminants to water vapor and carbon dioxide are numerous and vary for each compound present in the waste gas stream. However, the occurrence of numerous chain reactions is not detrimental to controlled combustion as this is influenced more by external factors such as concentration, initial gas temperature, volume or flow-through rate, and turbulence. In fact, time, temperature, and turbulence are so predominant in these reactions that they are often referred to as the "three T's" of combustion (1). The speed and completeness of the combustion reaction is directly related to the "three T's" in that oxygen must come into intimate contact with the combustible molecule at sufficient temperature and for sufficient length of time in order that the reaction be completed. The occurrence of incomplete combustion can result in the formation of aldehydes, organic acids, carbon, carbon monoxide, or other products less desirable than that which existed in the waste gas stream.

A mixture is capable of self-propagated combustion or explosion only when the required constituents are within a limited concentration range. This range is significant in that the heat of combustion possessed by the mixture provides sufficient energy to propagate the oxidation process. The limited concentration range is bound by values known as the lower and upper flammable limits (2). These limits usually refer to mixtures of air and a combustible gas or vapor, and are expressed as percent by volume at room temperature, or in terms of total heat of combustion per cubic foot. The latter expression is a convenient unit for engineering and design purposes since it is not dependent on the specific combustible compounds present, hence is applicable to mixtures of compounds. It may be referred to as "fume energy concentration" and is expressed in Btu's per standard cubic foot (scf).

There exists, within the flammable range, an "ideal" air-fuel combination called the stoichiometric air-fuel ratio. This ratio is established by the criterion that just sufficient oxygen is provided to obtain complete combustion of the fuel. A stoichiometric air-hydrocarbon mixture contains heat of combustion equivalent to 100 Btu/scf whereas the lower limit of flammability of a hydrocarbon mixture is approximately 52 Btu/scf. For reasons of safety, most industrial waste gas streams are limited to 25% of the lower limit of flammability, or 13 Btu/scf. Oxidation of this latter mixture produces a temperature rise of approximately 715 °F and the reduced energy content is insufficient to sustain combustion. Hence, supplementary energy is required to complete the oxidation reaction.

The additional or supplementary energy may be supplied in the form of preheaters, fuel-fired burners, or flares. Preheating the air-gas mixture before release at the burner nozzle causes a flame to be sustained somewhat below a mixture energy content of 52 Btu/scf as the lower flammable limit decreases with increasing temperature. A more recent development applicable to oxidation at reduced temperature and energy content is the catalytic combustion system.

A prime design factor in obtaining sustained combustion is knowledge of the minimum temperature required to combust organic vapors in the presence of adequate oxygen. This temperature is known as the autogenous combustion temperature, or catalytic combustion temperature, when referred to direct incinerators or afterburners, and catalytic systems, respectively. It is influenced by the type of combustible matter, oxygen content, energy concentration, flow-through rate, and other conditions. The type of catalyst used in catalytic systems is an additional factor in the catalytic combustion temperature.

Complete oxidation is possible with various flame characteristics realized through the design of the burner. For instance, a luminous diffusion flame results when air and fuel flowing through separate ports are ignited at the burner nozzle. Combustion occurs over an extended area in the combustion chamber, producing a highly radiant flame. The expansion of the gases as the flame progresses provides the necessary turbulence, while a large combustion chamber assures the necessary time at the available temperature to complete the reaction. On the other hand, a burner utilizing the same fuel, but arranged to premix the air and fuel prior to delivery to the burner nozzle, will produce a short, intense, blue flame, permitting complete oxidation within a confined space. In any fuel-fired burner, whether it is of the luminous or premixed type, the continuity of the oxidation reaction depends upon maintaining the air-gas supply to the burner within the flammable range.

III. Flares

A flare is a system for oxidizing gases which is highly efficient when the gas is released at energy concentrations within or above the limits of flammability. Flares are used by many petrochemical plants to dispose of combustibles present with inert gases, such as nitrogen or carbon dioxide. Also, process plants which handle hydrocarbons, hydrogen, ammonia, hydrogen cyanide, or other toxic or dangerous gases are equipped with flares to be used in the event that emergency conditions require the immediate release of such gases for the protection of the personnel and key facilities.

The design and operation of flare facilities varies considerably, depending on the environmental factors, the complementary equipment, and the gas composition. In general, the flare must be designed to protect the surroundings from heat and light, to obtain sufficient mixing of the air and gas, and to assure that an ignition flame will be sustained at varying rates of fuel emission and wind speed. The design of the flare and the resultant flame is also influenced by the fuel composition such as the hydrogen/carbon (H/C) ratio and the presence of inert components.

The height of the flare discharge is established by the proximity of adjacent structures, and the maximum heat release. Some flares utilize ground-level discharge while for others, sufficient protection from the heat of the flame is obtained by elevating the discharge as high as 300 feet above ground level. In addition, flares may be surrounded by an additional length of stack to shield the light produced by the burning gas.

Steam jets are the more satisfactory means for injecting air into the combustion zone and creating good turbulence at the same time. One design of a steam injection-type flare is illustrated in Fig. 1. Steam jets surrounding the flare tip are arranged so that air is induced into the flame along with the steam. Individual flares of this type have been constructed which operate smokelessly with gas flows as high as one million scf/hour, and as low as 1000 scf/hour. Steam requirements vary from 0.05 to 0.30 pounds per pound of disposal gas, depending on the constituents of the latter. The pilot lights are designed to maintain ignition at wind velocities greater than 100 mph.

Flares using steam jets provide an additional benefit in that the steam or water vapor reacts with hydrocarbons to form oxygenated compounds which burn readily at low temperature. In this manner the partial pressure of the fuel is lowered, causing greater separation of the molecules and inhibiting polymerization which is likely to cause smoke. The ratio of steam to hydrocarbon required to maintain the water-gas reaction increases with increased molecular weight and with the concentration of unsaturates in the waste gas.

Although steam injection can make a flare less objectionable, it is often too costly to use an effective quantity of steam. Presently, some refineries are using multijet flares which do not employ steam and promise to be an economical solution to other flaring applications (3). The assembly of the multijet flare consists of parallel pipes, with each pipe containing a row of small nozzles which vertically discharge the gas. Parallel to and directly above the nozzles are mounted solid rods of refractory material against which the gases released from the nozzles impinge. During the impingement process enough air is mixed with the gas to give smokeless combustion. When the discharge rate and heat value of the gas is reasonably stable and where the air-gas mixture can be maintained near 100 Btu/scf, the multijet flare can be sized to provide smokeless and noiseless burning for at least 95% of the expected occurrence of release. The multijet assembly is usually installed at ground level with a flare stack mounted directly above. The flare stack is a steel shell lined with refractory material. It is open on both ends and induces sufficient air past the multijet to maintain the combustion process.

Regardless of the methods used to bring adequate air to the ignition zone, smoke-free burning is less difficult to achieve when the H/C ratio by weight is high (4). For example, methane with an H/C ratio of 0.33 burns in the open air with very little, if any, smoke. In contrast, acetylene, having an H/C ratio of 0.083, burns in the open air with copious release of carbon in the form of soot. Both fuels produce a yellow, luminous flame when the oxygen in the air surrounding the flame comes in contact with the hydrocarbons by diffusion only. The color is evidence that the hydrocarbon molecule is being cracked and free carbon is present in the flame.

Preheating the waste gas stream is often required when the combustible gases are contaminated with inert gases. This preheating is accomplished by surrounding the discharge point of the disposal gas with a ring burner which would be in addition to the pilot burners in Fig. 1. This arrangement is satisfactory if the dilution by the inert gases does not depress the heat of combustion of the mixture below a minimum of approximately 50 Btu/scf.

When entrained oil mist is present in the flare gases, separators at the base of the flare stack, with automatic, continuous removal of the collected material, are vital to safety. Where oxygen-containing gas must be flared with hydrocarbons, additional precautionary steps are required to avoid a possible flashback of the flame to the base of the stack. Flame flashback is usually prevented by establishing, upstream to the flare, a waste gas velocity greater than the rate of flame propagation. A perforated plate with small openings can also prevent flashback when properly located in the gas stream.

Control of the waste gas flow to the flare is often a desirable design feature achieved by compressing the gases to be combusted (5). The gas is put under pressure by adjustable electrically driven compressors and when the discharge rate becomes too great for the compressors the

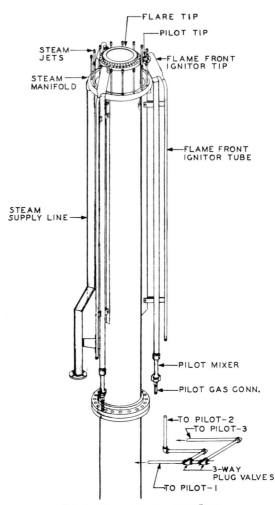

FIG. 1. Steam injection type flare.

exhaust gas is stored to await compression. Aside from flow control, this design helps to reduce the size of the resultant flame and eliminates the variations in quantity of gas to be flared at a particular time.

Flare system safety is a broad subject, and requirements covering such items as ground-level vs. elevated stack discharge, use of purge gas, ignition systems, and many other considerations do not lend themselves to a discussion in terms of standard designs or uniformly applicable procedures (6). The potential hazards of flaring are internal explosions, liquid carry-over from flare stacks, system obstructions, low-temperature failures, and hazards associated with maintenance of the system.

IV. Furnace Disposal

Furnace disposal is basically a method of heating waste gases to the autogenous combustion temperature and maintaining that temperature in the presence of oxygen for sufficient time and with sufficient turbulence to cause the oxidation reaction to occur in an enclosed chamber. A properly designed and operated furnace can destroy gases with an oxidation efficiency greater than 98% even though the gas energy concentration is far below the lower flammable limit. The method is particularly adaptable where: (1) A reliable supply of process waste gas in the flammable range is available for preheat burner fuel. (2) The process exhaust temperature already approaches the autogenous ignition temperature of the contaminants. (3) Low-cost purchased fuel is available. In addition, furnace disposal has preference over catalytic combustion systems when the waste gas stream contains substantial amounts of noncombustible inorganic solids.

Furnace disposal is commonly called "direct flame incineration," since a separately fired burner is conventionally employed to sustain oxidation. The flame, per se, does not change the oxidation process but it does influence the time-temperature-turbulence factors. The flame is characteristically either short and intense, or luminous and diffuse. The luminous, diffuse flame accelerates ignition of entrained particles but the entire fume stream must be heated to the autogenous combustion temperature to oxidize the gaseous contaminants (7). A short, intense flame offers the opportunity of increasing the effective holding time at autogenous combustion temperature, and is believed to result in more economical use of the burner fuel.

Fixed tables of autogenous ignition temperature, or time, for the design of furnace systems do not exist because the limits of flammability, ignition requirements, and burning rates vary for each gaseous composition. Furthermore, available data is not always adequate for a particular gas mixture, but suitable approximations (2) can be used as acceptable design criteria. Generally, furnace construction costs require a practical upper limit on holding time of 0.5 to 0.75 seconds, while the residence temperature requirements may vary from 950 °F for naphtha vapors to 1600 °F for methane. Even higher temperatures may be required for some aromatic hydrocarbons, or when the fume stream contains a high percentage of inerts which tend to act as oxidation depressants.

The determination of residence temperature, and fuel requirement, to oxidize waste gas is best exemplified by a hypothetical process. Assume that 15,000 ft³/min of air at 350 °F ventilates an industrial process which evaporates toluene at the rate of 1 gal/min. Toluene has an ignition temperature of 997 °F and a heat of combustion equal to 901.5 kcal/mole. The mass flow rates of air and toluene are 746 and 7.2 lb/min respectively. The fuel supplied to the burner must release 121,830 Btu of heat every minute to oxidize the toluene vapor. This quantity of heat is obtained by assuming an average specific heat value of 0.25 Btu/pound of air-vapor mixture. During oxidation, the toluene vapor releases 126,744 Btu/min and raises the temperature of the oxidized mixture approximately 615 °F. The gas leaving the furnace at 1615 °F will be essentially free of toluene vapor.

One type of furnace disposal system which embodies desirable design characteristics is a modified form of the scroll-type air heater. This design is illustrated in Fig. 2. The scroll inlet surrounding the burner protects the walls of the combustion chamber from damaging temperatures, and aids in vaporization of organic particles. Mixing is accomplished in the throat, and oxidation is completed in the refractory holding chamber before release to a stack or a waste-heat boiler.

Most furnace assemblies appear simple in design, but it is impossible to overemphasize the potential hazards which exist whenever heat is applied to a mixture of air and combustible vapors. Safety control equipment usually consists of burners equipped with prepurging, ignition, temperature control, and limit protection instrumentation. In addition, process interlocks are almost invariably needed to guard against unanticipated malfunctions. Most control equipment is listed by Underwriter's

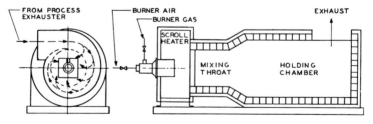

END ELEVATION   SECTIONAL SIDE ELEVATION

FIG. 2. Modified form of the scroll-type air heater.

Laboratories Inc., and Factory Mutual Laboratories, whose listings indicate the appropriateness of the device for varying situations.

It is not possible to obtain a reasonable safety factor in furnace design without diluting high energy fumes. Safety authorities and fire underwriters prefer to limit the concentration to from 1/4 to 1/5 of the lower flammable limit, and this fact should be given full weight in determining the capacity of the system (8). Disregard of this basic requirement with exclusive dependence on duct velocities above the flame propagation rate, or on the flash-arresting property of a water-spray leg, may ultimately lead to disastrous results.

The combustion chamber, stack, and other parts of a furnace disposal system which are subject to high temperatures must be constructed of high temperature alloys or lined with refractory materials. The maximum permissible alloy or refractory temperature for extended operation in a furnace has been established by the Underwriters Laboratories, Inc. (9). In general, refractories are normally used in areas subject to high temperature because they can operate at incandescence, have high thermal insulating properties, and their cost is low compared to high temperature alloys (1).

V. Catalytic Combustion

Catalytic oxidation, a process beneficially used for years by the chemical industry, was first used for air pollution control in 1949 (10). Catalytic combustion systems are capable of eliminating combustible contaminants from waste gas streams at temperatures far below those required by flame combustion. Combustion which normally occurs in disposal furnaces at 1500 °F may be induced at 500 °F in the presence of a suitable catalyst. The catalyst, merely by its presence, evokes the exothermic union of organic vapors and oxygen at temperatures considerably below the natural autogenous temperature and, in the process, does not become a product of the reaction.

Many substances exhibit catalytic properties, but metals in the platinum family are recognized for their ability to produce the lowest catalytic combustion temperatures, and are therefore conventionally used. A survey of 18 single-component oxide catalysts showed that those of cobalt, nickel, manganese, chromium, and iron may be effective when conditions of temperature and concentration are favorable (11). This survey also indicated that, in general, the higher molecular weight hydrocarbons were more easily oxidized than the lower. Hydrocarbons of

Fig. 3. Catalytic fume combustion chamber inside which elements are mounted.

a given carbon number increased in reactivity according to the series: aromatic < branched paraffin alicyclic < normal paraffin < olefinic < acetylenic.

The catalytic oxidation of combustibles proceeds through three steps: (1) adsorption of the gas on the active surface, (2) chemical reaction, or union of the combustible with the oxygen, and (3) the desorption of the reaction products from the surface (12). Hence the catalytic process is a surface reaction and suitable methods of exposing the maximum surface area are prime design criteria. One method of achieving maximum exposed surface consists of electrolytic deposition of platinum alloys on thin nickel-chrome ribbon which is formed into elements similar in appearance to metallic air filter mats. To assure the passage of all gases through the catalyst media, the elements are mounted on an asbestos-gasketed framework inside the fume combustion housing, as illustrated in Fig. 3. Catalyst surfaces are also applied to ceramic rods, beads, pellets, and other shapes. The effect of catalyst support geometry on the performance of platinum catalyst as applied to the oxidation of hydrocarbons has been investigated (13). Regardless of structure, the element must be designed to maintain uniform density under elevated temperature to avoid channeling or bypassing the catalyst. Turbulence is achieved by the passage of the contaminated gases through the elements. Effective catalyst temperatures are generally obtained from the oxidation reaction itself; but, when necessary, burners or electric preheaters are provided. With platinum alloy catalysts, oxidation of hydrogen will be initiated at ambient temperature, naphtha at 450 °F, and methane at 750 °F.

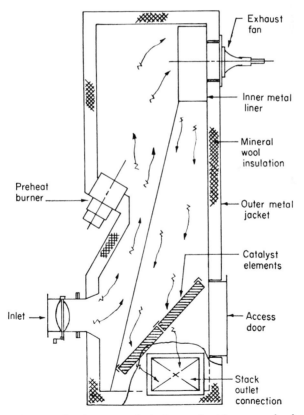

FIG. 4. Catalytic combustion system including preheat burner and exhaust fan.

The catalytic system is not universally applicable because its effectiveness decreases when waste gas characteristics interfere with the surface reaction. Obstruction of the surface reaction is caused by the presence of catalyst poisons (metallic or organometallic vapor), incomplete combustion of carbonaceous material forming deposits on the catalyst surface, or mechanical loss of the catalyst surface by abrasion.

When the entering gaseous mixture is at a temperature above that required to initiate catalytic combustion, the disposal system may consist of no more than an enlargement in the stack to contain the catalyst elements. More frequently, the inlet gas is near room temperature, and the system must include a preheat burner with a component arrangement similar to Fig. 4. Before the oxidized gases are discharged, their heat content is used, by an arrangement of heat exchangers, to superheat steam or preheat the entering fume stream. Process waste gas preheated by this method requires less preheat burner fuel because, after startup, such systems will operate without external fuel if the fumes enter the system at 100 °F, and contain energy concentrations as low as one-tenth the lower flammable limit. By comparison, a conventional furnace disposal system, operating with a stack temperature of 1300 °F would require approximately one million Btu/hour of purchased fuel for each 1000 scf/min of mixture handled. Self-recuperative catalytic fume combustion systems which consume approximately 300,000 Btu/hr of external fuel per 1000 scf/min are in use for the destruction of organic odors in air having essentially zero fume energy concentration.

Precautions relating to the design of disposal furnaces are equally applicable to catalytic combustion systems. The National Fire Protection Association has established a code for catalytic combustion systems (14). Experience has shown that with the codes available and a knowledge of catalysts, their performance, service needs, and limits, such systems have earned an excellent performance record (15).

From an air-correction standpoint, the end results of catalytic combustion are identical to those of furnace disposal. Either system can produce oxidation and odor reduction on hydrocarbon and organic vapors, to the extent of 98% or better, when properly designed, applied, operated, and serviced. Operational differences do exist, however;

1. The problem of generation of nitrogen oxides during disposal is minimized by catalytic combustion. Catalytic systems are, in fact, used for the chemical reduction of those oxides (16–18).

2. The temperature rise due to combustion of contaminants passing through a catalyst element permits reliable monitoring of the energy concentration of the fume stream with limit-protective instrumentation.

3. Catalysts require occasional field cleaning, since no exhaust gas

is completely free of unburnable inorganic dust. Normally, cleaning by a simple washing procedure is required annually or semiannually. However, this problem is minimized by the use of catalytic elements of proper design and composition (*19*).

4. At the present time, the destruction of combustible vapors which may be released from most metal melting operations, from rotating drum-type dryers or other processes which release entrained or vaporized inorganics, can more reliably be accomplished by furnace disposal systems. Continuing research directed toward alleviating this limitation on catalytic systems may prove fruitful.

5. Integration of catalysts into the design of equipment, such as ovens, furnaces, dryers, and pressurized petrochemical units, permits profitable heat recovery, and gives greater opportunity for preventive abatement (*20*).

VI. Summary

Of the three combustion methods described, flares are most suitable to the destruction of off-gases which are constantly released at concentrations above the flammable range, particularly where wide fluctuations in flow rate exist. Process exhaust gases containing combustible contaminants released at concentrations within or below the flammable range can, in most cases, be destroyed effectively by either furnace disposal or catalytic combustion. The choice will usually be based on comparative initial, operating, and service costs, and safety considerations, rather than on abatement efficiency. However, the potential field of application for catalysts to destroy combustibles in process exhaust gases continues to grow with the accumulation of operating records on installations now in daily use.

REFERENCES

1. American Industrial Hygiene Association, "Air Pollution Manual," Part II: Control Equipment. Am. Ind. Hyg. Assoc., Detroit, Michigan, 1968.
2. M. G. Zabetakis, *U.S. Bur. Mines, Bull.* **627** (1965).
3. P. D. Miller, Jr., H. J. Hibshman, and J. R. Connell, *Proc. Am. Petrol. Inst., Sect.* III **38,** 276 (1958).
4. R. J. Reed, *Semi-Ann. Meeting Am. Soc. Mech. Engrs., Los Angeles, 1953* Paper 53-5A-29.
5. P. Brudern, *Erdoel Kohle* **15,** 289 (1962).
6. W. C. Bluhm, *in* "Safe Operations of Refinery Flare Systems" (C. H. Vervalin, ed.), Chapter 39, Gulf Pub. Co., 1964.
7. J. L. Mills and W. F. Hammond, *Proc. 52nd Ann. Meeting Air Pollution Control Assoc., Los Angeles, 1959* Paper No. 59-8.

8. "ASHRAE Guide and Data Book, Fundamentals and Equipment for 1965 and 1966," Chapter 11. Am. Soc. Heating, Refrigerating, and Air Conditioning Engrs., New York, 1966.
9. Underwriters Laboratories, Inc., "Standards for Safety, Commercial-Industrial Gas Heating Equipment," Report UL 795. Underwriters Lab., Chicago, Illinois, 1964.
10. R. J. Ruff, *Ind. Heating* **17,** 10 (1950).
11. K. C. Stein, *et al., U.S. Bur. Mines, Bull.* **608** (1962).
12. H. R. Suter, *J. Air Pollution Control Assoc.* **5,** 173 (1955).
13. M. R. Miller and H. J. Wilhoyte. Paper presented at Air Pollution Control Association Annual Meeting at Cleveland, Ohio, June 11–16, (1967).
14. National Fire Codes, "Occupancy Standards and Process Hazards," Vol. 9, Natl. Fire Protect. Assoc., Boston, Massachusetts, 1965–1966.
15. "The Sentinel," p. 6. Factory Insurance Assoc., Hartford, Connecticut, 1960.
16. C. H. Riesz, F. L. Morritz, and K. D. Franson, *Air Pollution Found. Rept.* **2,** San Marino, California, 1957.
17. H. C. Anderson, W. J. Green, and D. R. Steele, *Ind. Eng. Chem.* **53,** 199 (1961).
18. J. L. Donahue, *J. Air Pollution Control Assoc.* **8,** 209 (1958).
19. J. H. Houdry and C. T. Hayes, *J. Air Pollution Control Assoc.* **7,** 182–186 (1957).
20. R. J. Ruff, *Wire Wire Prod.* **34,** 10 (1959).

GENERAL REFERENCES

Additional pertinent material is in Chapters 5 and 8 of "Air Pollution Engineering Manual, Los Angeles APCD" (J. A. Danielson, ed.), PHS Publ. 999-AP-40, DHEW, Cincinnati (1967); and in Chapters 10 and 11 of "Air Pollution Manual, Part II," American Industrial Hygiene Assn., Detroit (1968); and will be published in the National Air Pollution Control Administration's publication: "Control Technology for Particulate Air Pollutants."

49 Water Pollution Potential of Air Pollution Control Devices

F. E. Gartrell

I. Interrelationships Between Air and Stream Pollution Control Measures

Disposal of waste products from industrial operations is made by any of four general processes. Waste products are discharged for dilution and transport from their source into (1) the atmosphere, (2) a watercourse. They are discharged (3) to open waste lagoons or storage areas, or (4) as in the case of high-level, long-lived radioactive fission products, to permanent storage in closed containers. Air or water pollution problems occur whenever the pollution handling capacity of either the atmosphere, receiving watercourse, or storage area is exceeded. The use of watercourses for disposal of wastes can conflict with other uses of water. Protection of water quality for higher uses than waste disposal places definite limitations upon the quantities of wastes that can be discharged into watercourses.

Devices for air pollution control which reduce the amount of waste material discharged to the atmosphere usually increase the quantities of such materials that must be disposed of by other means. While in many cases the collected materials are returned to process or put to other productive use, a consideration of air pollution control measures must include the ultimate disposal of resulting waste material. This requires integration of air pollution control with overall waste disposal from the operation involved. Wet collectors of many types are used for air cleaning and all types contribute to the total quantity of liquid wastes which may be discharged to watercourses, with or without treatment. Water quality standards are useful in assessing the potential impact on stream pollution control of waste materials to be disposed from air pollution control devices.

II. Water Quality Standards

With industrial development, urban population growth, and rapidly expanding use of water for all purposes, the accompanying need for stream pollution control has led to establishment in most areas of agencies with statutory authority to regulate the discharge of waste materials to surface waters. There are no universally accepted standards for waste disposal from industrial operations. Each situation requires special study of the quantity and type of waste involved, quantity and quality of water available for dilution, and other water uses which might be adversely affected by the discharged wastes.

In most respects water quality requirements for industries are consistent with those for public drinking water supplies. The most widely recognized standards for public water supply are the United States Public Health Service Drinking Water Standards—1962 (1). The portion of these standards related to selected constituents is summarized in Table I. In addition to these requirements the following limits should not be exceeded: turbidity, 5 units; color, 15 units; and threshold odor, 3 units. The water shall have no objectionable taste. It must also meet rigid bacteriological requirements. Where radioactive contaminants are involved, the recommended practice is to keep concentrations in air and water to a minimum.

The following constituents and qualities in water, from either natural or man-made sources, are objectionable in a large number of industrial processes: iron and manganese, hardness, turbidity, color, taste or odor, and high temperature. Quality requirements for specific processes vary widely. Table II summarizes the requirements of selected industrial processes (2).

Modern technology makes it possible to prepare water for almost any use from water of any quality. However, the more nearly a raw water meets process requirements, the less corrective treatment is required. Thus, protecting surface waters from objectionable materials is of definite economic value to water users. In planning air pollution control where discharge of collected waste to streams is contemplated, the potential impact on downstream water users must be considered.

TABLE I

U.S. PUBLIC HEALTH SERVICE DRINKING WATER STANDARDS
REGARDING SELECTED CONSTITUENTS, 1962

	Allowable[a] limit (mg/liter)	Maximum[b] concentration (mg/liter)
Alkyl benzene sulfonate (ABS)	0.5	
Arsenic (As)	0.01	0.05
Chloride (Cl)	250.	
Chromium (hexavalent)(Cr^{+6})		0.05
Copper (Cu)	1.	
Cyanide (CN)	0.01	0.2
Fluoride (F)	0.6–0.8[c]	0.9–1.7[d]
Iron (Fe)	0.3	
Lead (Pb)		0.05
Manganese (Mn)	0.05	
Nitrate (NO$_3$)	45.[e]	
Phenols	0.001	
Sulfate (SO$_4$)	250.	
Total dissolved solids	500.	
Zinc (Zn)	5.	

Radioactivity	Micromicro curies per liter
Radium-226	3
Strontium-90	10
Gross beta (in absence of alpha emitters and strontium-90)	1000

[a] Limit which should not be exceeded where other more suitable supplies can be made available.

[b] Concentration beyond which the supply should be rejected.

[c] For areas where maximum daily air temperature has an annual average between 79.3 and 90.5 °F (averaged over 5-year minimum).

[d] Annual average of maximum daily temperature, 50.0–53.7 °F.

[e] Public should be warned if nitrate content exceeds this limit.

III.   Air Pollution Control Facilities with Stream Pollution Control Features

From a review of water quality standards, it is obvious that many waste materials considered as air pollutants of major concern are likewise objectionable for many water uses, when present in even fairly low concentrations. This is particularly true of wastes involving fluorides, sulfur compounds, and radioactive materials.

TABLE II
SELECTED WATER QUALITY TOLERANCES FOR A FEW INDUSTRIAL APPLICATIONS

Industry	Turbidity (ppm)	Color (ppm)	Hardness (ppm)	pH	Total solids (ppm)	Fe (ppm)	Mn (ppm)	SiO$_2$ (ppm)	CO$_3$ (ppm)	HCO$_3$ (ppm)	General[a]
Air conditioning[b]	—	—	—	—	—	0.5	0.5	—	—	—	A, B
Baking	10	10	[c]	—	—	0.2	0.2	—	—	—	C
Boiler feed:											
0 to 150 psi	20	80	75	8.0+	3000 to 1000	—	—	40	200	50	—
150 to 250 psi	10	40	40	8.5+	2500 to 500	—	—	20	100	30	—
250 psi and over	5	5	8	9.0+	1500 to 100	—	—	5	40	5	—
Canning:											
Legumes	10	—	25 to 75	—	—	0.2	0.2	—	—	—	C
General	10	—	—	—	—	0.2	0.2	—	—	—	C
Carbonated beverages[d]	2	10	250	—	850	0.2	0.2	—	—	—	C
Cooling[e]	50	—	50	—	—	0.5	0.5	—	—	—	C
Food, general	10	—	—	—	—	0.2	0.2	—	—	—	C
Plastics, clear, uncolored	2	2	—	—	200	0.02	0.02	—	—	—	—
Paper and pulp:[f]											
Groundwood	50	20	180	—	—	1.0	0.5	—	—	—	A
Kraft pulp	25	15	100	—	300	0.2	0.1	—	—	—	—

Soda and sulfite	15	10	100	—	200	0.1	0.05	—	—	—	—
Light paper, HL grade	5	5	50	—	200	0.1	0.05	—	—	—	B
Rayon (viscose) pulp:											
Production	5	5	8	—	100	0.05	0.03	25	—	—	—
Manufacture	0.3	—	55	7.8 to 8.3	—	0.0	0.0	—	—	—	—
Tanning[g]	20	10 to 100	50 to 135	8.0	—	0.2	0.2	—	—	—	—
Textiles:											
General	5	20	20	—	—	0.25	0.25	—	—	—	—
Dyeing[h]	5	5 to 20	20	—	—	0.25	0.25	—	—	—	—
Wool scouring[i]	—	70	20	—	—	1.0	1.0	—	—	—	—
Cotton bandage[j]	5	5	20	—	—	0.2	0.2	—	—	—	—

[a] A, No corrosiveness; B, no slime formation; C, conformance to federal drinking water standards necessary.

[b] Waters with algae and hydrogen sulfide odors are most unsuitable for air conditioning.

[c] Some hardness desirable.

[d] Clear, odorless, sterile water for syrup and carbonization. Water consistent in character. Most high quality filtered municipal water not satisfactory for beverages.

[e] Control of corrosiveness is necessary as is also control of organisms, such as sulfur and iron bacteria, which tend to form slimes.

[f] Uniformity of composition and temperature desirable. Iron objectionable since cellulose absorbs iron from dilute solutions. Manganese very objectionable, clogs pipelines and is oxidized to permanganates by chlorine, causing reddish color.

[g] Excessive iron, manganese, or turbidity creates spots and discoloration in tanning of hides and leather goods.

[h] Constant composition; residual alumina 0.5 ppm.

[i] Calcium, magnesium, iron, manganese, suspended matter, and soluble organic matter may be objectionable.

Impact on stream pollution has been experienced in almost every type of industrial situation where extensive air pollution control or abatement has been attempted. Air pollutants involved include fluorine compounds from fertilizer, aluminum, steel, and uranium processing plants; sulfur compounds from smelters, power plants, coke plants, and refineries; particulates from power plants, blast furnaces, ferro-alloy, calcium carbide, and other types of plants; and radioactive wastes from atomic energy installations. Examples follow of stream pollution control features incorporated into air pollution control facilities.

A. CONTROL OF FLUORINE WASTES

1. *Uranium Ore Processing*

The Feed Materials Production Center of the Atomic Energy Commission, located at Fernald, Ohio, produces uranium metal of high purity and fabricates fuel elements for use at the various reactor sites (3). This plant is located on the Miami River. Low flow in the stream, especially during the summer and autumn months, limits the amount of each type of waste that can be disposed of in this manner. Flow in the river varies from 25,000 ft³/sec at flood stage to a low of 100 ft³/sec in dry periods. There are usually periods of several days each year when the average flow does not exceed 300 ft³/sec. The plant water supply is from deep wells on the site. In addition, there are two deep wells on the banks of the Miami River near the outfall of the plant, which serve a public water supply. Therefore, care must be taken to guard against contaminating the ground water.

The problems of waste disposal at this plant are many and varied. The biggest single problem is fluorides. There is excess hydrofluoric acid used in the process, hydrofluoric acid generated by the process, and a metal fluoride product. Off-gases containing HF are scrubbed before discharge to the atmosphere. Both KOH and Ca(OH)₂ scrubber systems have been used. Scrubber solution containing 45% KF is discharged into tank cars and sold. Insoluble fluorides are removed from scrubber systems by filtration and stored on the site in an underground pit especially prepared to prevent ground water contamination. Neutralized soluble fluorides from scrubber systems are discharged with other treated wastes to the river.

All liquid wastes are collected in a central sump from which they are discharged at a controlled rate dependent on concentration of contaminants and the flow in the river. Waste discharges are regulated so that the average level in the river below the outfall does not exceed 1.2 ppm fluoride. Since the stream has a background level of 0.4 ppm fluoride, permissible waste releases are those which will add no more than 0.8 ppm of fluoride to the stream. By careful regulation of waste discharge to stream flow, the fluoride concentration is kept well below the permissible level. An average of 15,000 pounds of fluorides per month has been discharged—from 20 pounds on a low day to more than 4000 pounds on a high day—thereby contributing an average of only 0.1 ppm fluoride to the river.

2. Phosphate Fertilizer Production

A triple superphosphate fertilizer plant at Brewster, Florida, employs a battery of neoprene-lined scrubbers for control of fluoride and sulfur dioxide emissions to the atmosphere (4). The liquid from the scrubber is treated by chemical and physical means to reduce the concentration of fluoride to below 5 ppm before it is discharged to the Alafia River. This conforms to the stream pollution control requirements of the state. The wastes are monitored by continuous water sampling stations located in the plant effluent ditch and in the receiving stream upstream and downstream from the outfall.

At the National Fertilizer Development Center at Muscle Shoals, Alabama, concentrated superphosphate fertilizer containing about 54% available P_2O_5 is produced by reacting concentrated phosphoric acid (containing 73.5% P_2O_5) with pulverized phosphate (5). The reactants are brought together in a rotating drum granulator. The mixture is discharged to a den where it is held for several hours. Fluorine is given off in both the granulator and the den as hydrogen fluoride and silicon fluoride. The total fluorine released is about 20 pounds of fluorine per ton of concentrated superphosphate produced. This release represents about 49% of the total fluorine in the raw materials used in the process.

The concentrated superphosphate plant is equipped with a jet-venturi fume scrubber to remove and scrub the exhaust gases from both the reactor and the den. The scrubber water is recirculated at a rate of 750 gal/min, with about 100 gal/min being discharged and replaced with fresh water. The scrubber removes 98% of the fluorine in the exhaust gas. The water discharged from the scrubber contains up to 5000 ppm of fluorine and may contain as much as 1 ton per day. The production unit is not operated continuously. The fluorine in the water discharged from the scrubber amounts to about 195 tons per year.

Fluorine is removed from the waste water by reacting the water with phosphorus furnace slag. The waste water containing fluorine is pumped to settling ponds on the slag pile. After settling, the water flows to the holding or treatment ponds from which it percolates through the slag pile and discharges as a clear effluent. This treatment removes about

95% of the fluorine from the waste water. The slag consists mainly of calcium silicate and calcium aluminate, and about 93% of the material is smaller than 10 mesh. A large quantity is available as a waste material. The slag combines with the fluorine in a manner similar to the reaction with pulverized limestone, but a great excess of slag over the stoichiometric amount required to form CaF_2 is required. A coating of precipitated CaF_2 forms on the slag particles and prevents the calcium from being fully utilized. Suspended particles of CaF_2 and silica gel occur in the supernatant water above settled slag. For the fluorine removal process the furnace slag is used not only to react with fluorine in the waste water but also to filter out suspended particles resulting from the reaction. The effluent discharges to a creek a short distance above its confluence with the Tennessee River. The treatment ponds have to be remade occasionally because crusts form in the bottom and decrease or stop the flow of water through the slag pile.

A wet-process phosphoric acid plant operated in conjunction with a diammonium phosphate plant at Bartow, Florida, utilizes wet scrubbing for fluorine control (6). Major sources of fluorine fumes are from the digestion, filtration, and sump and vent sections of the plant. The digestion stream, in addition to fluorine, contains particulate matter in the 1- to 5-μ range and with a specific gravity of 2.0 to 2.2. The basic scrubber design is a counter-current, multistage, horizontal spray tower followed by a packed tower tail gas scrubber. Water for the scrubbers is recirculated from the plant's 580-acre gypsum pond, thus eliminating the need for continuous treatment and disposal of contaminated water.

3. Steel Mill

Conventional scrubbing methods were first tried for abatement of a fluoride air pollution problem at a large steel mill near Provo, Utah (7). Discharge to the stream of the large quantities of waste water might have created a contamination hazard more serious than the air pollution problem. The solution finally selected involved reacting the gaseous fluorine with fine particles of calcium and removing the calcium fluoride by cyclones and electrostatic precipitators. The waste material thus collected is buried in a clay pit, where it is covered with the other solid wastes and permanently confined.

B. Control of Radioactive Wastes

The hazardous nature of radioactive wastes associated with nuclear operations places stringent requirements on waste disposal practices. Whether the wastes are concentrated and stored, or diluted and discharged to the atmosphere, soil, or watercourses, the concentrations in the environment must be held to very low levels. Values for maximum permissible concentrations of the various radioisotopes are available to serve as guides in planning treatment and disposal facilities for radio-active wastes (8). However, because of the many uncertainties involved in establishing these values, the recommended practice is to keep the concentrations of radioisotopes in air and water to a minimum.

1. Oak Ridge National Laboratory

Radioactive waste disposal practices at Oak Ridge National Laboratory are illustrative of an integrated program involving air pollution control, land pollution control, and water pollution control (9–12). At this lab-oratory wastes are handled in four ways: by release after treatment of gaseous wastes to the atmosphere through tall stacks, by storage of radio-active solids and high-level liquids for decay, by fixation after treatment of intermediate-level liquid wastes in the soil of the waste disposal area, and by discharge of extremely low-level liquid wastes to the Clinch River. The goal of the laboratory is to hold to a minimum the amount of radioactive material discharged to the environment.

For air pollution control, contaminated air from the various opera-tions is cleaned by various combinations of filtration, precipitation, and scrubbing before it is discharged to the atmosphere through one of several stacks. The gaseous wastes are divided into two separate streams referred to as the cell ventilation system and the off-gas system.

The cell ventilation system draws large volumes of air from laboratory hoods or cells which may contain process equipment. Leaks from this equipment may result in small quantities of radioactive contaminants in the cell ventilation system. This air is passed through roughing and absolute filters and discharged through a 250-foot stack. The filters when changed are disposed of by burying in the laboratory solid waste disposal area.

Off-gas, drawn under vacuum of 45–55 inches of water, from operat-ing equipment constitutes a much smaller volume of air flow but is likely to contain a greater concentration of radioactive contaminants. Depend-ing upon the source of the off-gas, it may be passed through electro-static precipitators and absolute filters or caustic scrubbers, roughing and absolute filters before discharge to the stack. One segment of the system contains charcoal filters for a small proportion of the total gas flow. Here again the particulate filters are disposed of as radioactive solid wastes. The scrubber and precipitator wastes, however, are di-verted into the liquid waste system and treated as described in the follow-ing paragraphs.

Each of the main waste lines of the process waste system is continuously monitored for activity and rate of flow and each is continuously sampled in proportion to flow. To reduce the volume of waste requiring treatment, care is taken to exclude uncontaminated waste water by diverting it around the treatment plant. Low activity level wastes are detained in an equalization basin for radioactive decay of the short-lived constituents before entering the treatment plant. A second and larger emergency basin is available for additional storage if the level of activity is too high for immediate treatment. The horizontal flow plant includes line-soda softening with provision for alternate use of phosphate coagulation for ^{90}Sr removal and clay addition for adsorption of ^{137}Cs. The plant accomplishes 84% removal of strontium, 86% of rare earths and cesium, and 88% of gross beta activity. The effluent is combined with the bypassed uncontaminated wastes and held 2 or 3 days in an open basin for further decay before release into White Oak Creek which flows into the Clinch River.

Intermediate-level wastes from chemical processing and reactor operation are held up and neutralized, if necessary, in stainless steel monitoring tanks and directed to concrete storage tanks from which they are fed to a waste evaporator where a decontamination factor of 10^6 to 10^7 is expected. The condensate combines with the process waste for release to White Oak Creek. The concentrate is jetted to concrete storage tanks and may eventually be injected deep into the earth by hydrofracturing. Liquid wastes having a high level of activity are stored permanently.

Open seepage pits are no longer used for the disposal of even low-level wastes at ORNL. Consequently, the hazard of seepage reaching the surface streams is avoided. The goal of the waste management program is to reduce the concentration of radionuclides in liquid effluents released to the Clinch River to less than one-tenth of the value recommended by the International Commission on Radiological Protection (ICRP) for continuous occupational use. Dilution in the river will reduce the concentration by an additional large factor.

2. Other Atomic Energy Laboratories

Examples may be found at other atomic energy installations where air-cleaning devices contribute materials to the liquid waste disposal systems. At Argonne National Laboratory, caustic batch scrubbers are used to remove chemical fumes and radioactive gases from off-gases of the larger scale process vessels. Dusts from ventilation systems for tools used to machine uranium are removed by an exhaust system incorporating a wet dust collector. Scrubber wastes from these two air-cleaning operations are periodically trucked to the waste treatment building for processing (13).

At Los Alamos Scientific Laboratory, capillary air washers are used at some of the facilities for air cleaning. Liquid wastes from these scrubbers require treatment. From one facility the scrubber effluent is piped to the radioactive liquid waste treatment plant. In another case the water from the capillary air washers is decontaminated in an ion exchange plant before discharge to an adjacent canyon. The ion exchange units are regenerated with acid and treated to form a sludge, which carries all of the radioactivity. This sludge is mixed with cement and buried in the contaminated dump (14).

C. CONTROL OF SULFUROUS WASTES

1. Copper Smelter

Problems associated with sulfur fumes from smelters were among the first air pollution problems for which specific corrective measures were taken. For example, steps to control fumes from copper-smelting activities in the vicinity of Ducktown, Tennessee, were undertaken about 1907. Facilities involving an adaptation of the lead chamber process were installed to recover the sulfur dioxide in the blast furnace gases as sulfuric acid (15).

Before installation of recovery facilities at these smelters, sulfur dioxide fumes and timber overcutting completely destroyed vegetative cover over an area of 7000 acres, partially over a much larger surrounding area. Resulting erosion caused heavy silt loading in streams in the area. The acid-manufacturing operations added acid industrial wastes to the stream pollution problem. In 1940 a stream pollution study of the Ocoee River, which receives wastes from these operations, showed the following: silting up of downstream reservoirs by silt eroded from Ducktown and Copperhill area, unfavorable conditions for fish life, and possible corrosion of hydroelectric installations by acid wastes (16).

Waste treatment facilities have been installed by the industry to control stream pollution. The liquid wastes are neutralized and suspended solids are removed before the wastes are discharged to the river. Control of pH in the receiving stream is difficult owing to fluctuating stream flow from an upstream hydroelectric dam. Acceptable pH control has been achieved, however, by use of automatic recording and chemical feed equipment (17). Parksville Lake, downstream from Ducktown, was stocked with fish in 1950. Fish population studies made through 1953 suggest that recovery of the lake from the effects of prolonged pollution by acid wastes may be a fairly slow process so far as fish are concerned (18).

2. Electric Power Plant

The potential air pollution problem associated with the increasing use of fuels having relatively high sulfur content and the trend to larger capacity plants has led to extensive investigation of possible processes for removal of sulfur dioxide from power plant stack gases (19). However, so far as is known, the only power plants in the world in which full-scale sulfur dioxide removal from stack gases is used are the Battersea and Bankside Stations in London, England. Both plants have used the so-called Battersea process since 1934–1936. Equipment for sulfur dioxide removal was also installed to serve the 150-MW capacity added in 1963 at Bankside.

The gas is washed on grid scrubbers with water from the Thames River, to which a small amount of chalk has been added in order to maintain the alkalinity in the later stages of the washing process. The river water contains most of the alkali that is required to neutralize the sulfur dioxide. Crude manganese is added to the scrubber effluent to activate oxidation of sulfite in the aeration tank. Excess solids are removed in a settler. The effluent containing calcium sulfate in solution is then mixed with water returning to the river from the turbine condensers. Use of this process is applicable only on the seacoast or on a comparatively large river which is so polluted that there can be no risk of interfering with fishing or other riparian rights. The Bankside and Battersea Stations utilize the total dry-weather capacity of the upper and middle tidal reaches of the Thames River to absorb calcium sulfate in solution.

D. CONTROL OF FLY ASH, DUST, AND OTHER PARTICULATE WASTES

1. Calcium Carbide Plant

A separate fluid waste disposal system is an integral part of the air pollution control installations at a large calcium carbide plant at Niagara Falls, New York (20). For fume and dust control at this plant, extensive use is made of wet-collection devices. Pease-Anthony scrubbers remove 95–98% of the dust from the gas from the rotary lime calcining kilns. Fume collected from the calcium carbide electric furnaces is drawn through scrubbers where dust particles are removed by water sprays and centrifugal force. Fine material collected by bag filters used to control dust from the carbide crushing operation is mixed with water and discharged to the fluid-waste disposal system.

Before discharge, the fluid wastes pass through a 130-foot diameter clarifier. Underflow, or sludge, from the clarifier is pumped to a storage lagoon in the refuse area. The overflow from the clarifier is mixed with cooling water to hold solids in the effluent below 50 ppm and maintain a pH of 10.6. It is then discharged to the Niagara River.

2. *Blast Furnace Operations*

Gas washers have been used successfully to clean blast furnace gas at a plant in Donora, Pennsylvania (*21*). The gas from two blast furnaces is handled by two 75,000 ft³/min gas washers. The two washers were installed in an existing stove shell, 24 feet in diameter by 110 feet high. The stove shell was divided vertically into two halves by bulkheading through the center. One washer was installed in each half. Gas enters at the bottom of the washer. It travels upward through a 4-foot bank of ceramic tile equipped with removable inserts. This provides primary cleaning of the gas. A battery of low-pressure spray nozzles is located directly above the tile bank.

From the tile bank the gas ascends through a set of venturi-shaped chambers. Each chamber is equipped with a high-pressure stainless steel nozzle at one end and an adjustable steel deflector cap at the other. The fine spray from the nozzle intimately mixes with the gas and wets the particles of dust. The gas then passes through a moisture eliminator section where it makes a 180° turn. It then passes through a 2-foot bank of ceramic tile, over which is located another battery of low-pressure sprays. The gas contains approximately 3 to 4 grains of dust per cubic foot at the inlet of the washer and is cleaned to 0.025 grain per cubic foot.

Over 9,000,000 gallons of water per day are used in the washing process. The waste water from the washers is treated in a clarifier before being returned to the river. Sludge from the clarifier is recovered and returned to the sintering plant. The water is returned to the river, as clean as when it was removed, and with a slightly higher alkalinity.

3. *Power Plants*

Only a small fraction of the fly ash collected by mechanical and electrostatic precipitators at electric power plants is converted to commercial use. The remainder presents a major waste disposal problem. Where topography is suitable and space is available, use of ash lagoons is standard practice. Ash from the boilers and collectors is carried by a sluice system to the disposal area. The ash settles in the lagoon. The overflow, which is usually alkaline, is discharged into the nearest watercourse. With properly designed lagoons and skimmer devices to prevent discharge of any floating ash, this system of ash disposal from power plants is satisfactory from the standpoint of stream pollution control. For example, over 1,500,000 tons per year of ash are disposed of in this manner at eleven power plants in the Tennessee Valley, without causing adverse effects on streams receiving overflow from the ash lagoons (5).

4. *Chemical Plants*

Spray drying is used in many chemical plants (22). The large volumes of hot air exhausted from spray dryers frequently contain fine particles of the material being dried. At one plant where spray drying is used to dry detergents, the exhaust air from the dryers contains approximately 3 grains per cubic foot. Cyclone collectors are used to recover the particulates dry so they can be returned to process. Effluent from the cyclones contain 0.3 grain per cubic foot. A venturi scrubber is used to further clean the exhaust air to below 0.1 grain per cubic foot before discharge to the atmosphere. Scrubber water is discharged to the plant sewer. Unless there is malfunction of the cyclone separator system, the concentration of detergent in the scrubber effluent is so dilute that no foaming occurs even in the area of high energy collection and separation. Because the gas is hot and humid and the entrained material is sticky, the cyclones or their rotary airlocks can become plugged by the particulates. When this happens, all of the particulates from the cyclones pass into the venturi scrubber. The turbulent mixing in the scrubber and the higher concentration of detergent collected generate foam. Within the plant, this foam boils up out of sewer manholes and visible foam appears on the surface of the body of water receiving effluent from the plant. To control this potential water pollution problem, the cyclones have been equipped with detectors which provide a warning to the operator whenever pressure buildup occurs so that timely corrective action can be taken.

REFERENCES

1. "Public Health Service Drinking Water Standards—1962," Public Health Serv. Publ. No. 956. U.S. Govt. Printing Office, Washington, D.C., 1962.
2. "Manual on Industrial Water and Industrial Waste Water," 2nd ed., ASTM Spec. Tech. Publ. No. 148-F, pp. 24–25. Am. Soc. Testing Mater., Philadelphia, Pennsylvania, 1962.
3. R. C. Heatherton, *Proc. Seminar, Sanit. Eng. Aspects At. Energy Ind., 1955* pp. 275–285. Robert A. Taft Sanit. Eng. Center, Cincinnati, Ohio, 1956.
4. *Chem. Week* **79**, No. 22, 60–61 (1956); personal communication (1958) from W. R. Bradley, Chief Industrial Hygienist, Central Medical Department, American Cyanamid Company, New York.

5. F. E. Gartrell and J. C. Barber, *Chem. Eng. Progr.* **62,** No. 10, 44–47 (1966).

6. H. O. Grant, *Chem. Eng. Progr.* **60,** No. 1, 53–55 (1964).

7. *Intermountain Ind. Mining Rev.* **59,** No. 12, 22–26 (1957).

8. *Natl. Bur. Std. (U.S.), Handbook* **69** (1959) (with addendum 1963); *Health Phys.* **9,** 565–568 (1963).

9. K. Z. Morgan, Testimony before Subcommittee on Radiation—Joint Committee on Atomic Energy, Vol. 3, pp. 2378–2393. Congress of the U.S. 86th Congress, First Session, Jan. 28–30 & Feb. 2–3, 1959.

10. K. E. Cowser, L. C. Lasher, L. Gemmell, and S. G. Pearsall, Operational experience in the treatment of radioactive waste at Oak Ridge National Laboratory and Brookhaven National Laboratory. *Symp. on Practices in the Treatment of Low and Intermediate Level Radioactive Wastes, Vienna, Austria, 1965* Sponsored by IAEA and the European Nuclear Energy Agency of the Organization for Economic Cooperation and Development.

11. J. F. Manneschmidt and E. J. Witkowski, The disposal of radioactive liquid and gaseous waste at Oak Ridge National Laboratory. *Conf. on Light-Water-Moderated Research Reactors, Gatlinburg, Tennessee, 1962* ORNL-TM-282 1962.

12. E. J. Witkowski, Description of ORNL Waste Disposal Systems. Unpublished communication (1966).

13. "Radioactive Waste Disposal at Argonne National Laboratory" (Brochure), Argonne Natl. Lab. Rept. (1958).

14. S. H. Glassmire and J. P. Whalen, *Heating, Piping, Air Conditioning* **28,** 117–121 (1956); personal communication (1958) from C. W. Christensen, Health Div., Los Alamos Sci. Lab. Los Alamos, New Mexico.

15. R. E. Swain, *Ind. Eng. Chem.* **41,** 2384–2388 (1949).

16. G. R. Scott and S. L. Jones, Studies of the Pollution of the Tennessee River System, Tennessee Valley Authority, Knoxville, Tennessee (1945).

17. Public Hearings on Stream Pollution Control Program in Tennessee, Chattanooga, Tennessee, p. 109 (1951).

18. Annual Report, Division of Forestry Relations, Tennessee Valley Authority, Norris, Tennessee, p. 17 (1954).

19. R. L. Rees, *in* "Problems and Control of Air Pollution" (F. S. Mallette, ed.), pp. 143–154. Reinhold, New York, 1955.

20. S. S. Blackmore, *Ind. Wastes* **3,** No. 3, 73–78 (1958); personal communication (1958) with F. E. Gartrell.

21. S. P. Kinney, *Iron Steel Engr.* **30,** No. 5, 2–4 (1953).

22. A. H. Phelps, Jr., *Chem. Eng. Prog.* **62,** No. 10, 37–40 (1966).

Part IX
AIR POLLUTION CONTROL

50 Air Pollution Control Legislation*

Sidney Edelman

* The views expressed herein are those of the author and should not be understood as expressions of any official position.

553

I. Introduction

Air pollution was long considered a matter of obvious pollutants—smoke, odors, and partially burned solids. The first smoke abatement law, adopted by proclamation in 1306, during the reign of Edward I of England, prohibited the use of sea coal as detrimental to health. In 1307, a violator of the prohibition was condemned and executed. Yet even this extreme punishment was not successful in stemming the rising cloud of smoke. In 1661, John Evelyn wrote indignantly that London was wrapped "in Clouds of Smoake and Sulphur, so full of Stink and Darkness." He ingeniously suggested (foreshadowing present zoning proposals) that all industry be moved to the leeward side of the city and that sweet-smelling trees be planted in the city itself.

Early air pollution control legislation, both in the United States and elsewhere, also attempted to deal with the most obvious causes of pollution. Such legislation, while still in force in some states, takes little or no account of the enormous industrial growth which has taken place in recent years. As industrial and scientific processes grew more complex, air pollutants followed suit. Smoke, soot, and odor are still major causes of nuisance and public annoyance in some areas, but new and less obvious contaminants are receiving increased attention from scientists and legislators.

The complexity of the problem and its relationship to the economic base of community life are reflected in the growing complexity of air pollution control statutes and an increasing emphasis on government and industrial cooperation in coping with the problem.

The legal structures established for the control of air pollution, however, usually represent a compromise between the public health and welfare on the one hand, and technical, economic, and political factors on the other. The manner in which this compromise is achieved largely depends on the situation existing in each jurisdiction.

II. Control of Nuisance Conditions

A. Public Nuisance

Public nuisance is a term applied to a miscellaneous group of conditions which cause inconvenience, discomfort, annoyance, damage, or harm to the general public. In most countries such conditions are prohibited and are punishable by criminal sanctions. Generally, the public authorities may also proceed by injunction to prevent the continuation of a nuisance.

Many of the early air pollution laws attempted to deal with the problem by classifying certain discharges into the atmosphere as nuisances and consequently subject to abatement. For example, the emission of "dense smoke," and "thick, black smoke" from a chimney or smokestack was by law declared to be a public nuisance (1). Such laws, while frequently attacked, have in recent years generally been upheld by the courts (2).

This approach has gradually been discarded as cumbersome and uncertain in its results, as well as inadequate to deal with the modern array of pollutants, since it does not overcome the difficulties of proof in identifying sources of less obvious forms of air pollution. Moreover, it makes no provision for the employment of preventive measures or for the use of engineering knowledge and techniques to initiate construction to control emissions which cause or contribute to air pollution.

B. CONTROL BY PRIVATE LITIGATION

Under the law in most countries, a person who suffers injury from air pollution originating from activities conducted on another person's property may sue either to recover for the damages he has sustained or for an injunction to compel the cessation of the activity if it constitutes a continuing nuisance. Despite this abstract protection of the law, private litigation for relief from the effects of air pollution has been unsuccessful as a means of control. The remedy of injunction, which would close down an otherwise lawful business, is so drastic that the courts have been reluctant to grant it (3) and have limited its use to extreme cases. The collection of damages where a plaintiff is successful is often merely a recurrent fee that the defendant is willing to pay.

The failure of individual action as an answer to the problem of air pollution is not at all surprising in the face of the following facts of legal life: (1) the suffering of any given individual has often been neither significant nor irreparable, nor readily enough demonstrable in terms of dollars of damage either to justify his undertaking the expense of litigation or to satisfy the doctrines that limit the granting of effectively deterrent kinds of relief; (2) the difficulty and cost of investigating and of properly proving, from among all possible sources, the source or sources responsible for a given injury have been too far out of proportion to the likely benefits of successful litigation; (3) in an urban setting, pollution may stem from innumerable sources, many of which, although contributing to the harm, constitute no readily identifiable source of injury.

C. Legal Basis for Governmental Control of Air Pollution

An air pollution control statute or ordinance constitutes a legislative determination that certain conditions or circumstances causing or contributing to air pollution, as therein defined, injure or endanger the public health or welfare and are therefore prohibited. Such a prohibition is usually implemented by sanctions such as a fine or imprisonment.

Enactment of legislation of this type is a function of the police power, inherent in the state as a sovereign and conferred on municipalities by statute or charter. It is directed toward the prevention of threatened injury and not merely toward the punishment of threatened harm.

Although the courts have refused to attempt an all-inclusive definition of the police power, on the grounds that such a definition would be undesirable and would tend to give rigidity to the doctrine, an explanation of its basis and function is helpful to an understanding of its application. As stated in McQuillin on Municipal Corporations (3d ed. 1949, Police Power, sec. 24.10), the basis of the police power

. . . is the inherent right of people through organized government to protect their health, life, limb, individual liberty of action, and property, and to provide for public order, peace, safety and welfare. . . . Thus the safeguarding of the public welfare in the most comprehensive sense of the term, is the basis which both creates and requires the exertion of the police power with consequent and unavoidable restrictions on individual actions and the use of property.

Since the police power is based on public necessity, it is not limited to conditions as they exist at any one particular time, and its exercise is capable of modification in accordance with the needs of the public and the growth of knowledge and scientific information.

As the Supreme Court of the United States has said:

While the legislature has no right arbitrarily to declare that to be public nuisance which is clearly not so, a good deal must be left to its discretion in that regard, and if the object to be accomplished is conducive to the public interests it may exercise a large liberty of choice in the means employed. *Lawton v. Steele*, 152 U.S. 133, 14 S.Ct. 499, 502.

The exercise of police powers by municipalities must, of course, be in conformity with statutory authority, either expressly granted or arising by fair implication, or incidental to powers expressly conferred. The burden of proof, however, is upon those who attack the ordinance to show that it is clearly unreasonable.

While the exercise of the police power may result in a restriction of the use of property, such a restriction is not a taking in the constitutional sense so as to require the payment of compensation.

Every citizen holds his property subject to the proper exercise of the police power either by the legislature directly, or by public or municipal corporations to which the legislature may delegate it. It is well settled that laws and regulations of this character, relating to the comfort, health, convenience, good order, and general welfare of the inhabitants, though they may disturb the enjoyment of individual rights, are not unconstitutional, even though no provision be made for compensation for such disturbances. They do not appropriate private property for public use, but simply regulate its use and enjoyment by the owner. If he suffers injury, it is either *damnum absque injuria* (damage without a legal wrong) or, in theory of the law, he is compensated for it by his sharing in the general benefits which the regulations are intended to secure (4).

So far as the Federal Constitution is concerned, we have no doubt that the State may, by itself or through authorized municipalities, declare the emission of dense smoke in cities or populous neighborhoods to be a nuisance subject to restraint as such, and that the harshness of such legislation or its effect upon business interests, short of a merely arbitrary enactment, are not valid constitutional objections. Nor is there any valid Federal Constitutional objection in the fact that the regulation may require the discontinuance of the use of property, or subject the occupant to large expense in complying with the terms of the law or other ordinance (5).

The exercise of the legislative judgment in this regard is not subject to judicial superintendence unless it is plainly beyond the realm of the police power or is palpably unreasonable. Thus, in upholding the validity of a smoke abatement ordinance of the City of Detroit, the United States Supreme Court declared:

The ordinance was enacted for the manifest purpose of promoting the health and welfare of the city's inhabitants. Legislation designed to free from pollution the very air that people breathe clearly falls with the exercise of even the most traditional concept of what is compendiously known as the police power (6).

Furthermore, proof of *actual* injury to health or property is not necessary to support a conviction of violation of the ordinance. Whether persons or property are or may be injured by the prohibited conduct or operation is related to the question of the reasonableness of the ordinance and not to the question of whether the ordinance has been violated.

As the Court said in *Board of Health v. Crew* (7), the "protection of the public health is not required to wait until contamination is shown to exist." It is sufficient, they held, that the statute authorize the administrative agency to act where its observation of conditions, in the light of scientific knowledge of probabilities that might occur in the environment, reasonably lead it to believe that health may be affected. So, it has been held that a statute may properly authorize an administrative agency to prevent water pollution before actual harm results (8). Similarly, under a statute which prohibited a nuisance constituting a "hazard" to the public health and welfare, it was held that the test is not whether the defendant's conduct will "inevitably result in disease, but rather whether the condition constitutes a hazard, danger or peril to the public health from its presence" (9).

In sum, it is clear that the legal machinery for controlling air pollution which injures or endangers the public health and welfare may be established under the police power of the state. The state may delegate the police power to a municipality or other public agency which may, within the scope of the delegation, properly enact an air pollution control ordinance. The legislation or ordinance must establish adequate standards to guide the enforcing agency, and its requirements should not be arbitrary but reasonably related to the purpose sought to be accomplished. Within these restrictions, there is a "large liberty of choice in the means employed" to limit emissions causing or contributing to air pollution.

III.   Legislative Approaches to Air Pollution Control

The control of air pollution necessitates the possession of legal authorities under which control can be effected, of technical means whereby control of pollutants and their emission can be undertaken, of a control organization to see that these things are done and usually of monitoring equipment to ascertain existing conditions and to check the results of action undertaken. The following discussion deals only with the first of these requirements—the nature and scope of the legal authorities which should be provided.

A. SPECIFICATIONS OR PERFORMANCE AS STANDARDS

Apart from consideration of legal criteria, air pollution control legislation raises important questions of public policy. Two opposing trends are apparent in legislation on the subject. The first is to try and control pollution within the limits imposed by the methods available in practice. The second approach is based on the principle that pollution of the atmosphere which is likely to injure the public health or welfare must be controlled and if available techniques are not adequate, to push for the development of necessary new techniques.

Thus, important private and public interests may be in seeming conflict and require consideration of ultimate state public policy in determining the extent and character of air pollution to be permitted in general and in specific cases. Such determinations involve extremely complicated technical and scientific problems, as well as factors of importance to the economic and industrial development of the state. These considerations emphasize the necessity for careful drafting of legislation and call for the exercise of legislative judgment in the light of available scientific knowledge.

The drafting of legislation by a state or local community presents a choice as to whether the statute should be drawn in general terms, furnishing specific guides but leaving its detailed implementation to a qualified administrative body or whether detailed specifications should be enacted, leaving little or no room for the exercise of judgment by the administrative body.

Although the issuance of blanket limitations on emissions by statute or ordinance is understandably appealing, it is an over-simplified approach and may lead to difficulties. Putting aside pollutants which the courts tend to recognize as nuisances per se, e.g., dense smoke, soot, etc., a blanket limitation may be difficult to support as reasonable in the light of scientific knowledge, and may, moreover, impose undesirable rigidity in a field where scientific advances are daily being made. Consideration must be given to the reliability of data relating to many different compounds before a scientific determination fixing the maximum permitted emission in terms of concentration may be made. These and other questions, such as how and where emissions should be measured, call for expertise and scientific judgments which a legislative body, because of other pressures and lack of familiarity, may find it difficult to make.

Some control authorities recommend that standards be established limiting the pollutant load of the atmosphere and that individual sources be controlled as necessary to achieve the desired result.

The consensus of control officials, however, favors the performance approach, specifying only those features which have been established on the basis of experience and scientific criteria relating to the problems under consideration. While standards should not require performance which it is not technically possible to obtain (unless it is intended to prohibit specific pollution, in which case a frank prohibition is preferable) neither should the standards be set so low as to require less than the generally accepted standard of performance.

Important in any consideration of standards is their administration. Mere enactment of legislative standards will not assure that compliance will follow. They must be consistently administered and firmly enforced by qualified and competent staff to obtain community acceptance.

B. COMMUNITY-LEVEL PROGRAMS

Some communities may find their authority to abate public nuisances adequate to cope with the air pollution problem. Most of the larger communities, however, have found the general "public nuisance" approach ineffective and cumbersome and have enacted specific air pollution control ordinances under authority of police power delegated by the state either in the municipal charter or by special legislation. More recently, a number of states have enacted general enabling legislation authorizing cities, counties, and air pollution control districts, whose creation is also authorized by the statute, to adopt comprehensive control programs and to establish the limits of air pollution contaminants which may be emitted from sources within their jurisdiction.

Although the more than 2000 community air pollution control programs authorized by local ordinance constitute 80% of the existing programs in the United States, by far the large majority of communities have no legislation in the field. It is estimated that roughly 7500 communities with local air pollution problems, of which 7000 have populations of less than 25,000, fall into this category.

The larger communities acted early against smoke pollution. By 1912, 23 of 28 cities in the United States with over 200,000 population had smoke abatement programs. The more recently enacted comprehensive air pollution control ordinances, 80% of which were adopted in the past 15 years, evidence the growing concern of smaller communities with the broader aspects of air pollution (10).

Many of these ordinances regulate explicitly the emission of dense smoke and fly ash or dust from the process of combustion and usually deal with emissions of other contaminants by means of a general nuisance clause. The prohibition of smoke above a specified density requires the use of a density standard and a measuring device, which is usually specified in the ordinance as the Ringelmann smoke chart. In a similar manner, the emission of fly ash or dust is regulated in accordance with a recognized procedure based on a weight of particulate matter in relationship to a volume of carrying medium.

Most community air pollution control programs require a permit from the control agency prior to the construction, installation, or alteration of fuel-burning equipment. Upon completion of an installation or repair, an operation permit or certificate is issued. Some local ordinances also provide that certificates of operation be renewed by annual inspection of all fuel-burning equipment.

Such provisions serve to ensure the application of sound engineering principles to combustion equipment, and are not only preventive in nature, but also provide a means of registering potential sources of air pollution. A permit system, however, places increased technical and administrative responsiblities upon the control authority, emphasizing the importance of adequately trained personnel. Small fees are generally charged for installation or repair permits scaled to the size of the unit involved in terms of various parameters. In addition, a number of communities have included detailed requirements regulating the purchase and use of specified fuels, which place limits on ash, sulfur, volatile matter, or olefin content of a fuel.

Penalties are provided for the failure to obtain a permit, for evasion of permit requirements, or the refusal of entry to qualified personnel. Further, many ordinances provide that when three or more violations are cited within a year, the control agency may seal the offending equipment, after an appropriate hearing.

Provision for an appeal by an aggrieved party from administrative action to an impartial hearing board is frequently provided as the final step in agency action before judicial review may be obtained. The appeals procedure furnishes an accepted method of protection against hasty, arbitrary, or unduly oppressive administrative action. It often aids in securing reconciliation of conflicting interests since the appeals board is usually authorized to modify, as well as affirm or reverse, the original control action. It may thus take into account various factors which may not have been considered by the enforcement officer.

Some ordinances provide for variances to be granted by the control officer or the hearing board which, in effect, constitute an exemption from the ordinance for a particular source of air pollution. It is customary to grant variances rather liberally during the initial period of operation of the control program in order to provide a reasonable opportunity for measures which will permit a plant to comply with the limitations on emissions. Such variances are granted for a limited period and are generally subject to renewal for a further period upon a showing of good cause. Apart from allowing for a period of adjustment, variances are justifiable in principle only upon a showing that a strict application of the statute will result in an unnecessary hardship and that if granted, the spirit of the statute will be observed, the public health, safety and general welfare secured, and substantial justice done. It has been suggested, however, that the granting of a variance on an individual basis may be inequitable to other similar plants which have incurred expense in order to operate in compliance with the law.

Where a number of sources cannot, by known available and reasonable methods comply with the standards, and the pollution is not grave enough, in the light of the community interests involved, to justify closing down the plants, exceptions may temporarily be made to the special category of sources involved, pending the development of adequate control devices. The variance, which may be renewed periodically, may exempt the operation entirely or require it to comply with standards consistent with available methods, even though they are lower than the statutory standards. As each variance comes up for renewal, its justification should be reevaluated and reviewed in the light of advances.

C. COUNTY-LEVEL PROGRAMS

As community air pollution control administrators soon discovered, air pollutants do not respect political boundaries. Contaminants from nonregulated areas, beyond the police jurisdiction of the community, may make local control efforts futile.

To meet this problem, some states have enacted legislation enabling all or specified counties to establish air pollution control programs within their political jurisdictions. Recognizing the limitations of such a jurisdictional approach, other states have authorized the establishment of air pollution control districts by two or more adjoining cities or counties, or by combinations of cities and counties.

Such legislation generally requires that before an air pollution control program may be established, or an air pollution control district activated, the governing body must, after a public hearing, determine that there is need for the control of air pollution and that it is impractical to rely on local ordinances. The statute may also require that cities of various classes, which would be included in the proposed district, take similar action. In one state (Massachusetts) the state air pollution control agency may assume jurisdiction at the request of communities adversely affected by air pollution arising in other communities.

Enabling acts of this character which provide for local option are essentially permissive in nature and give no assurance that an effective program will be adopted or, if adopted, will be effectively enforced. In addition to the inherent weakness imposed by a limitation to territorial jurisdiction, the costs of administering an effective control program on a county basis, in terms of personnel and technical services, are sometimes not justified either by the benefits to be derived or the economic resources available to meet these costs.

D. STATE-WIDE PROGRAMS

Within the past few years, a number of states have established air pollution control programs on a state-wide basis. A state air pollution control agency is established either as an independent agency, or as part of the department of health, and is charged with responsibility for the adoption of codes, rules and regulations, and their enforcement. In some cases, enforcement is lodged in the state health department.

Since conditions may vary widely in various parts of the state, depending on the topography, meteorological conditions, sources of pollution, etc., state-wide legislation should provide for varying the emission standards to be applied in any given area, taking into consideration factors such as the population of the area, the degree of industrialization, and other elements which may affect the needs of the particular communities.

These statutes are, in the main, so recent that the accumulated experience is insufficient to permit a sound evaluation of their operation. There has, however, been some criticism of state-wide programs on the grounds, among others, that local sentiment is not given adequate recognition and that nonurban areas are required to help pay for the costs of meeting what is essentially an urban problem.

The validity of these arguments is open to question, since state-wide control does not, as indicated earlier, preclude variances in area standards, and the economic implications of a control program may well affect the well-being of nonurban areas.

E. REGIONAL PROGRAMS

Increasing consideration is being given to a proposal which will combine the strong points of local and state-wide programs and avoid the features which have been the source of criticism. This would be based on the regional approach which recognizes the importance of the physical factors contributing to air pollution. Based on meteorological and topographical studies, the sources and nature of the pollution and its effects, and taking into account other factors such as population concentration, economic resources, land use, etc., regional areas would be established under procedures prescribed by state law. Provision would be made for establishing a regional authority which would establish and enforce an air pollution control program within the region without regard to existing lines of political jurisdiction. Due recognition could be given to local authorities by representation on the regional board and by the use of local enforcement officers under cooperative arrangements. The cost of the program would be met from regional resources.

The state agency would conduct research and provide technical assistance and, under a "march in" provision, assume jurisdiction if, after a reasonable opportunity, the area has been unable to establish a regional control program.

It is an axiom of administration (too often disregarded) that a problem should be handled by the first level of authority capable of dealing with it in its entirety. The characteristics of air pollution are such that, in many cases, the regional agency would constitute the first level of authority (above the city and county) which could handle the problem effectively. An example of the regional approach is the California Bay area air pollution control district act as enacted in 1955 (Chapter 2.5, Health and Safety Code). The act recognizes that the San Francisco Bay area presents a special air pollution control problem and establishes a special Bay Area District to deal with it.

Even a regional authority, however, may stumble on state lines, where the region covers two or more states, and interstate pollution is involved.

F. INTERSTATE PROGRAMS

Interstate air pollution is merely one of the aspects of air pollution which presents a problem because its sources and effects involve more than one political jurisdiction. Since states are involved, however, resolution of the jurisdictional problem is perhaps more difficult.

It has been estimated that one-fourth of the people in the United States live in approximately 23 standard metropolitan areas (as defined by the Census Bureau) that cross state lines and 28 others which extend up to a state line. Problems have arisen in these areas which cannot be dealt with effectively by a single state. As in the case of the regional authority, a level of authority capable of handling the problem in its entirety may have to be established.

Where a state is the complainant, the Supreme Court has jurisdiction (U.S. Constitution Article III, Section 2) to enjoin interstate air pollution. In *Georgia v. Tennessee Copper Co.* (1907) 206 U.S. 230, 26 S. Ct. 618, the court enjoined the defendant from discharging noxious fumes in Tennessee which were alleged to cause a wholesale destruction of forests, crops, and orchards in Georgia. The suit was viewed as one by a state for an injury to it in its capacity as a quasi-sovereign (*11*). Except for such unusual situations, however, recourse to the courts by a state to abate air pollution originating in a sister state holds little promise of success (*12*).

As the Supreme Court said, in a suit by the State of New York to enjoin New Jersey from discharging sewage into New York harbor (*13*):

We cannot withhold the suggestion, inspired by the consideration of this case, that the grave problem of sewage disposal presented by the large and growing populations living on the shores of New York Bay is one more likely to be wisely solved by cooperative study and by conference and mutual concession on the part of representatives of the States so vitally interested in it than by proceedings in any court however constituted.

Uniform laws and voluntary cooperative agreements and action have been suggested as one approach to interstate air pollution. Such arrangements, however, are subject to different levels of enforcement in the interested states, particularly if their strict application would affect the competitive position of local industries. Being subject to unilateral amendment or abrogation, they offer no assurance of continuity of cooperation.

A sounder and more durable legal basis has been suggested in the use of compacts to support interstate action.

A resolution adopted by the Forty-Ninth Governors' Conference on June 26, 1957, recognized "the great importance of air pollution control, particularly in metropolitan areas, and the need for a more intensive attack to be made on this problem." Calling attention to the interstate character of air pollution, the resolution urged that "the states should by interstate action accomplish effective controls with the assistance of the Federal Government." A summary report on air pollution to the Governors' Conference published by the Council of State Governments in May 1958 in response to this resolution suggested state legislation to establish a basis for intrastate and interstate control programs.

National legislation enacted in 1963 gave the consent of Congress to two or more states to negotiate and enter into agreements or compacts for cooperative effort and mutual assistance for the prevention and control of air pollution and the enforcement of their respective laws. Such consent was also extended to the establishment of appropriate agencies by the states for making the compacts effective. However, in the absence of express approval by the Congress, such compacts are not binding on the participating states (14).

Legislation adopted in 1965 by the states of Illinois and Indiana pursuant to such authority established the first interstate air pollution control agency in the United States with jurisdication to control interstate air pollution (15).

In 1966, Ohio and West Virginia also adopted a compact designed to deal with interstate air pollution. A third compact, the Mid-Atlantic States Compact, was adopted in 1967 by the states of New York, New Jersey, and Connecticut and provides for membership by the United States and by the states of Pennsylvania and Delaware. At the time of publication none of these compacts had either become operational or been approved by the Congress (15).

Subsequent to the enactment of this compact legislation, the Clean Air Act was amended by the Air Quality Act of 1967 (Public Law 90-148) which (as discussed in Section IV below) provides for the designation of air quality control regions by the Secretary of Health, Education, and Welfare as the basis for the establishment of air quality standards and emission control requirements. In order to expedite the establishment of air quality standards in an interstate air quality control region (i.e., a region which includes areas in two or more states) federal financial assistance is authorized for the air quality planning program costs of an agency designated by the governors of the affected states for the purpose of recommending air quality standards for the region and plans for their implementation. Such financial assistance may be as much as 100% of the cost of the planning program for two years, and thereafter may not exceed three-fourths of that cost.

An air quality planning commission to develop recommended regulations on air quality standards for an interstate air quality control region may be established by the Secretary to expedite the establishment of such standards. In such case, the members of the commission will be appointed by the Secretary who will also provide the necessary staff and funds for the commission's functions.

The availability of the recommendations of the planning agency established under either of these approaches will undoubtedly facilitate and stimulate consistent approaches to the interstate air pollution problem by the states included in the region, whether or not an interstate compact has been entered into.

Moreover, the review by the Secretary to which the state plans will be subject prior to their becoming effective, under section 108 of the Act (42 U.S.C. 1857d(c)), will assure that the air quality standards and implementing plans are suitable to achieve the desired objectives of both States.

G. ZONING

Planning is the overall consideration of the use to which land in a particular area might be put, having in mind the potential for future growth and desirable changes in land use patterns. Zoning is the legally instrumented guide to private and public land use, preferably in accord with a comprehensive plan, although this is not mandatory in many jurisdictions. The prevailing view in this country is that the two processes may be undertaken separately, while British practice regards them as indivisible (16).

Municipal power to zone stems directly from state enabling acts. Zoning has been upheld by the United States Supreme Court (17) as, in principle, not violative of the due process clause of the Fourteenth Amendment. In each case, however, restrictions imposed by a zoning ordinance must bear a reasonable relationship to the health, morals, safety, or welfare of the community or its inhabitants, in order to sustain their validity as an exercise of the police power.

Planning of the use of land in terms of zoning is receiving greater recognition as a valuable adjunct to the air pollution control activities of a community. While zoning may provide protection for part of an urban area against air pollution, unless provision is made for area-wide control measures, it merely shifts the area affected by air pollution and does not effectively abate it. For specific problems attendant on the growth of a community, it may, however, play an important role in community planning.

Two aspects of air pollution control are involved: (1) site selection for industrial areas so as to preserve the air quality of the community, and (2) physical separation between major pollution sources and residential areas.

Site selection is the process of locating a single industrial plant and is alternatively referred to as plant location. From the standpoint of air pollution control, site selection results in the creation of a single source of pollution as compared with the more complex problem of area or multisource emissions.

The location of the sources of production, the amount to be emitted, and the location of land uses susceptible to air pollution damage lend themselves directly to the principles of planning and zoning.

Traditional zoning effectively groups uses in newly developing areas, has a limited effect on existing uses in old areas, and has the marked disadvantages of divided authority in metropolitan areas where inter-jurisdictional air pollution may be involved (18). The lee side of one city may be the windward side for an adjacent municipality. For effective control, larger air pollution zoning jurisdictions, or even interstate compacts, as mentioned earlier, may be desirable.

To play an effective role in an air pollution control program, zoning must take into account the micrometeorological conditions of the area. Such information together with the use of effective control devices or such other techniques as necessary makes possible more effective planning in regard to a community zoning program.

Three interests are affected by zoning to control air pollution: those of the owner of the plant or the landowner, those of the community and its other inhabitants, and of the nonresidents of the community who will, as a result of the zoning, receive the pollution over their lands. The community in its zoning ordinance may usually be expected to give adequate protection to its own interest and those of its inhabitants, but it should also consider the interests of nonresidents in the area.

Ideally, the community should have at its disposal in making a determination of the reasonableness of the ordinance, a regional plan against which to measure the community plan. The plan would, of necessity, have to take into account more than the local communities' interests and would permit all residents of the region to have some voice in its development. Such a plan would demonstrate that, in the light of the demographic, topographic, meteorological, and physical characteristics of the region, the nature of the pollution problems, and proposed land utilization, the proposed zoning is reasonable and related to the community health and welfare, and is part of the regional program to abate pollution.

The planners of any such ordinance will have to consider carefully the air pollution possibilities, along with the economic and social factors that influence land use and zoning. In making decisions on modification of existing zoning restrictions, the responsible authorities must consider not only pollution arising from the area within their jurisdiction, but also the effect of permitting pollution from the zoned area to add to pollution already reaching the community. In any event, zoning should be accompanied by effective air pollution limitations and controls, if it is to result in the prevention or abatement of air pollution.

IV. General Survey of National Legislation

Throughout the world, legal means for the control of air pollution have recently been newly created or improved. The sheer volume of such material precludes any detailed discussion of the various provisions within the bounds of this chapter. The following pages are mainly concerned, therefore, with the national air pollution control legislation in the United States and Europe, although some information is presented on other countries. Where the text of the national law has not been available, reliance has been placed on the *International Digest of Health Legislation* (19).

A. United States

The Clean Air Act, a federal law enacted in 1963 by the Congress of the United States, and most recently amended by the Air Quality Act of 1967 (20), established a national program for the control of air pollution. Prior to this legislation, the control of air pollution in the United States was left entirely to the states and municipalities. This has resulted in varying levels of air pollution control in different localities, ranging from none at all to extremely strict controls (21–23). Earlier federal legislation on this subject (24) had authorized the U.S. Public Health Service, in the Department of Health, Education, and Welfare to conduct and support research, investigations, surveys, and demonstrations relating to the prevention and control of air pollution, to provide technical assistance, and to support training in air pollution control.

The Clean Air Act, which vested all authorities relating to air pollution in the Secretary of Health, Education, and Welfare (25) expanded the research functions, authorized financial assistance to state and municipal air pollution control programs and, for the first time, provided for a federal program to control air pollution.

In adopting this legislation, the Congress noted that "the growth in the amount and complexity of air pollution brought about by urbanization, industrial development, and the increasing use of motor vehicles, has resulted in mounting dangers to the public health and welfare, including injury to agricultural crops and livestock, damage to and the deterioration of property, and hazards to air and ground transportation" (20a). The Congress recognized that "the prevention and control of air pollution at its source is the primary responsibility of States and local government" (20b). The federal act does not supplant or preempt state and local laws in this field but rather supplements them.

1. Research, Training, and Related Activities

The Secretary of Health, Education, and Welfare is directed to establish a national research and development program, and to conduct and promote research, investigations, experiments, training, demonstrations, surveys, and studies relating to the causes, effects, extent, prevention and control of air pollution. Special emphasis is directed to the problems of preventing and controlling air pollution from the combustion and evaporation of fuels. For these purposes, the Secretary is also authorized to make grants-in-aid to, and contracts with individuals and public or private agencies, institutions, and organizations. Provision is made for cooperative efforts with public and private agencies and institutions, and with industries, as well as for furnishing technical assistance.

2. Potential Air Pollution

The Secretary is also authorized to hold a public conference concerning any potential air pollution problem and if he finds that the discharge or discharges into the atmosphere if permitted to take place or continue are likely to cause or contribute to air pollution which endangers the health or welfare of any persons, he is directed to send such findings together with his advisory recommendations for remedial action to the alleged or potential polluters and to state, interstate, and local air pollution agencies having jurisdiction over the area involved. Although such findings and recommendations are advisory, they and the record of the conference become part of the official record of abatement proceedings held under the Act.

3. *Grants for Support of Air Pollution Control Programs*

The Clean Air Act authorizes the Secretary to make grants-in-aid to assist state, interstate, regional, and municipal air pollution control agencies. Such grants are available in an amount not to exceed two-thirds of the cost of planning, developing, establishing, and improving, and up to one-half the cost of maintaining programs for the prevention and control of air pollution. To provide a financial incentive for programs which serve more than one municipal jurisdiction, whether in the same state or in different states, grants to interstate or intermunicipal agencies may be as much as three-fourths of the cost of planning, developing, establishing, or improving, and up to three-fifths of the cost of maintaining such regional air pollution control programs.

4. *Control of Pollution from Federal Facilities*

Federal agencies are directed to cooperate with the Department of Health, Education, and Welfare in preventing or controlling air pollution resulting from the discharge of pollutants from federal facilities. The Secretary is authorized to issue permits to such agencies for potential pollution sources and is required to make an annual report to the Congress of the status of such permits and compliance therewith.

By Executive Order 11282, May 26, 1966, the President established a national policy and objectives for the prevention, control and abatement of air pollution originating from federal installations. The order directs all federal agencies to establish plans for the prevention and abatement of air pollution from existing and future facilities in order to comply with the more stringent of either state and local requirements or standards established by the Secretary of Health, Education, and Welfare. Regulations of the Secretary (42 CFR Part 76) establish limitations on visible emissions, particulate emissions, and emissions of sulfur oxides as well as restrictions on the open burning of refuse.

5. Air Quality Control Regions, Air Quality Criteria, and Control Technology

Under the Act as amended in 1967, the Secretary is directed to designate air quality control regions, based on urban–industrial concentrations, political boundaries, and other factors necessary to provide adequate implementation of air quality standards. Such regions may be wholly within a single state or may include portions of two or more states. He is also required to develop and issue criteria of air quality requisite for the protection of the public health and welfare and based on best scientific knowledge available. Such criteria will identify the kind and extent of effects on health and welfare produced by air pollutants under varying conditions. Information is also to be published on those recommended pollution control techniques necessary to achieve levels of air quality set forth in the criteria. Such information will include data on control technology, costs of emission controls, and economic feasibility of alternative control methods.

6. Federal Enforcement Authority

The basis for the invocation of federal enforcement authority to abate air pollution is the presence of air "pollution" which "endangers the health or welfare of any persons" (20c). These terms are not limited by definition in the statute, although all language referring to adverse effects on welfare is declared to "include but not be limited to injury to agricultural crops and livestock, damage to and the deterioration of property, and hazards to transportation" (20d).

It should be noted that under the statutory standard, proof of actual injury is not required; if health or welfare is endangered, appropriate action may be taken by the federal authority.

The legal limitations on the territorial jurisdiction of states and local governments in the United States helped shape the jurisdictional basis of federal control action established in the law. Ordinarily, legal authority is exercised by a state or municipality only within its geographical boundaries. Consequently, interstate air pollution, that is, air pollution originating in one state which adversely affects persons in another state, is not subject to abatement by the offended state except in most unusual circumstances (26). While the same rule holds true for municipalities, nevertheless when the municipalities involved are located within the same state, the situation is subject to control by state action.

Accordingly, in recognition of the primary responsibility of states and localities for air pollution control, while the statute provides for essentially the same administrative and judicial procedures for cases involving intrastate as for interstate air pollution, the utilization of the federal control authority against intrastate air pollution is, as pointed out below, subject to action by the state and local governments concerned (27).

In emergency situations, however, where air pollution sources present an imminent and substantial endangerment to the public health and state or local authorities have not acted to abate such sources, the Secretary may request the Attorney General to bring suit in federal court to require the immediate abatement of pollution by those sources.

7. Enforcement Procedures

Under the Clean Air Act, two methods are authorized for federal abatement action; one relies on the conference-hearing technique while the other is based on the regional air quality standards approach.

CONFERENCE HEARING APPROACH

a. Interstate Pollution. In the case of air pollution which is alleged to endanger the health or welfare of persons in a state other than that in which the discharge or discharges (causing or contributing to the air pollution) originate, a conference of the air pollution agencies involved (state, interstate, and local) in both states will be called by the Secretary at the request of the governor of a state, a state air pollution control agency or (with the concurrence of the governor and the state agency of the state in which the municipality is situated), a municipal governing body.

The conference may also be convened at the intitiative of the Secretary, after consultation with state officials of all the affected states, if he has reason to believe that such interstate pollution is occurring.

Although the Secretary and the air pollution control agencies are the only official participants in a conference, the agencies may bring such persons as they desire to the conference. The statute requires that interested persons be given an opportunity to present their views to the conference.

b. Intrastate Pollution. Where only intrastate pollution is involved (i.e., pollution endangering the health or welfare only of persons in the state in which the discharge originates) the conference may be called only upon request, as in the case of interstate air pollution, and such request must also be either made or concurred in by the municipality affected by the pollution or the municipality in which the discharges originate. In such case, however, the Secretary may decline to act if, in his judgment the effect of the pollution is not of such significance as to warrant exercise of federal jurisdiction.

c. International Pollution. A conference will also be called if the Secretary has reason to believe on the basis of reports or studies by a duly constituted international agency that air pollution originating in the United States is endangering the health or welfare of persons in a foreign country or if the Secretary of State so requests. Notification of such conference will be given to the appropriate state, interstate, and local air pollution control agencies and the foreign government will be invited to attend and participate in the conference and in all subsequent proceedings. This provision, however, is applicable to a foreign country only if the Secretary of Health, Education, and Welfare determines that such country has given the United States essentially the same rights respecting the control of air pollution originating in that country.

d. Reports. Prior to the conference, the Secretary may require persons contributing to the pollution to provide reports, based on existing data, concerning discharges and the utilization of control devices. After the conference, such reports may be required only to the extent recommended by such conference.

e. Post-Conference Proceedings. Following the conference discussions, which are to include consideration of (1) occurrence of air pollution subject to abatement; (2) adequacy of abatement measures taken and (3) the nature of the delays in abatement, if the Secretary believes that effective progress is not being made and health or welfare is endangered, he may recommend that necessary remedial action be taken. If appropriate action is not taken within the time prescribed (at least 6 months) the Secretary shall call a public hearing. A hearing board, composed of representatives of the states involved and the federal government, hears the evidence and makes findings on occurrence of air pollution and progress toward its abatement; all interested persons, including the alleged polluter, are to be given an opportunity to present evidence. If the board finds that such pollution is occurring and effective progress is not being made, it is required to recommend "reasonable and suitable remedial measures" to the Secretary.

The findings and recommendations of the board are sent by the Secretary to the individuals, corporations, and public and private agencies causing or contributing to the pollution and to the control agencies concerned, together with a notice specifying a reasonable time to secure abatement.

If appropriate action is not taken within the specified time, and interstate air pollution is involved, the Secretary is authorized to request the Attorney General of the United States to bring a suit on behalf of the United States to abate such pollution. In the case of intrastate pollution, further federal action is dependent on the request of the governor of the state who may ask either for such federal assistance as he considers necessary to assist the state in judicial proceedings to abate the pollution under state and local law or that the Secretary request the Attorney General to bring suit as in the case of interstate pollution.

The court is directed by the law to receive in evidence a transcript of the hearing before the hearing board and a copy of the board's recommendation. It may also receive further evidence in its discretion. Giving due consideration to the practicability of complying with such standards as may be applicable and to the physical and economic feasibility of securing abatement of the pollution proved, the court is authorized to enter such judgment and orders as the public interest and the equities of the case may require.

This abatement authority has to date been invoked in 9 interstate areas, covering parts of 13 different states and the District of Columbia. The problems range from single sources of pollution to the highly complex mix of pollutants in the New York–New Jersey interstate metropolitan area. The total population of the areas involved exceeds 20 million people or more than 10% of the nation's population. Only one of these cases has gone beyond the conference recommendation stage. That case involves a rendering plant in Bishop, Maryland which is charged with emitting vile odors endangering the health and welfare of persons in Selbyville, Delaware, two miles away.

The conference there, which, incidentally, was the first under the Clean Air Act, was called at the request of the Governor of Delaware, and was held on November 10–11, 1965. The hearing took place in May 1967, and suit against the company to secure abatement of the pollution—the first litigation of this kind under the Act—was filed in the Federal District Court in Baltimore on March 7, 1968 but had not been decided at the time of the publication.

REGIONAL AIR QUALITY STANDARDS

In order to invoke federal abatement authority under this approach, the Secretary must first designate air quality control regions and publish air quality criteria and recommended control technology.

Within 90 days after receiving any air quality criteria and recommended control techniques, the governor of a state which wishes to develop and carry out its own program must file a letter of intent that such state will, within 180 days, adopt, after public hearings ambient air quality standards for any designated air quality control region or portions thereof within its jurisdiction, and will, within 180 days thereafter adopt a plan for the implementation, maintenance and enforcement of such air quality standards.

If the Secretary determines that the standards and plan are consistent with the Act, and provide adequate enforcement authority, including authority to deal promptly with emergency air pollution conditions, such standards and plan become the air quality standards applicable to that state and in effect, also become federal air quality standards.

If the state does not take the prescribed action, or if the Secretary finds the standards and plan are not consistent with the Act, he may, after reasonable notice and a conference of representatives of "appropriate federal departments and agencies, interstate agencies, states, municipalities and industries involved" publish standards for air quality regions within that state. Unless, within six months from such publication, the state has adopted its own consistent standards or has asked for a public hearing, the Secretary is directed to promulgate such standards.

Prior to thirty days after the promulgation date of federal standards, the governor of any affected state may ask for a public hearing. The hearing board, on the basis of the evidence presented to it, may approve the standards or modify them and such action is binding on the Secretary.

The statute contemplates that the standards, established by either of the routes outlined above, will be implemented by the state concerned, since further federal action is contingent on findings by the Secretary that: (1) the ambient air quality in the region is below the standards; and (2) that such lowered air quality is due to the failure of a state to take reasonable action to enforce such standards.

If these findings are made, the Secretary is directed to notify the affected state or states, persons contributing to the alleged violation and other interested parties of the violation. Unless reasonable action to enforce the standards is taken within 180 days from such notification, the Secretary may, in the case of pollution "which is endangering the health or welfare of persons in a State other than that in which the discharge or discharges (causing or contributing to such pollution) originate," ask the Attorney General to bring suit on behalf of the United States to abate the pollution.

If only intrastate pollution is involved, the Secretary is not authorized to take action on his own initiative but may, if so requested by the governor, provide technical and other assistance to help the state abate the pollution or ask the Attorney General to bring suit on behalf of the United States to abate the pollution.

If suit is brought, the court will receive in evidence all records of prior proceedings and "such additional evidence, including that relating to the alleged violation of the standards, as it deems necessary to complete review of the standards and to determination of all other issues relating to the alleged violation." After giving due consideration to the practicability and to the technological and economic feasibility of complying with the standards, the court may "enter such judgment and orders enforcing such judgment as the public interest and the equities of the case may require."

It is anticipated that by September 1968 several of the more important regions will have been designated and that several air quality criteria on specific pollutants and the related information on control techniques will have been published.

8. Motor Vehicle Air Pollution Control

The 1965 amendments to the Clean Air Act (*20e*) authorize the Secretary to issue, by regulation, standards applicable to the emission of any substance from new motor vehicles or new motor vehicle engines which in his judgment cause or contribute to, or are likely to cause or contribute to air pollution which endangers the health or welfare of any persons. After the promulgation of such standards, it will be unlawful to introduce into interstate commerce a new motor vehicle or new motor vehicle engine which fails to comply with the applicable standards. A violation of this prohibition is punishable by a fine of not more than $1000, with respect to each vehicle or engine.

The standards, which will also apply to imported new motor vehicles, are to be developed with due consideration given to technological feasibility and economic costs and are subject to amendment from time to time.

Provision is made for the testing of vehicles and the issuance of certificates of conformity, valid for not less than 1 year, with respect to new motor vehicles or new motor vehicle engines which are found to comply with the regulations. Vehicles or engines sold by a manufacturer which are of substantially the same construction as a certified test vehicle or engine are to be deemed to be in conformity with the regulations. Vehicle and engine manufacturers are required to establish and maintain adequate records, available to the Secretary for inspection and copying, as the Secretary may require to enable him to determine whether the manufacturer is complying with the law and regulations (*28*).

The control of emissions from new motor vehicles and new motor vehicle engines is specifically preempted by the federal government, and states and localities are prohibited from imposing any requirements relating to emissions from such vehicles. The statute does not, however, affect their authority to impose requirements on used vehicles and engines, i.e., vehicles for which title has been transferred to an ultimate purchaser.

Provision is also made for the waiver of the prohibition on state action with respect to states which meet the requirements prescribed in the law. Only the state of California, however, is eligible for the waiver. On July 14, 1968, a waiver was given California to have standards for exhaust emission for 1969 and 1970 vehicles, and evaporative emissions for 1970 cars, more stringent than those of the Federal government.

In addition, the Secretary is authorized to require the registration of fuel additives as specified by him together with information identifying the additive, and giving its purpose and chemical composition, together with related information. A failure to comply with registration requirements is punishable by a fine of $1000 for every day the violation continues.

B. AUSTRALIA

Austrialia does not have a national air pollution control law and responsibility for the control of air pollution has been left to the individual states. Thus, under the Clean Air Act of 1957 (29), the state of Victoria prohibited the emission of dark or dense smoke from industrial chimneys, with certain exceptions, and no new industrial fireplace may be installed unless it is, so far as practicable, smokeless when burning the type of fuel for which it is designed. Moreover, the emission of any other air impurities (as defined in the Act) from industrial fireplaces must be minimized, and new industrial fireplaces must be fitted with control devices for such impurities. The Act also provides for the establishment of a clean air committee to carry out studies of air pollution problems, and to make recommendations to the Minister of Public Health for abating such pollution.

In New South Wales, the Clean Air Act of 1961 (30) defines air pollution as the emission into the air of any air impurity. Air impurity is defined to mean smoke, dust, particulate matter, gases, mists, odors, and radioactive substances. The Act establishes a schedule of industrial operations for which a license must be obtained, e.g., cement works, chemical factories, metallurgical works, and works using specified types of combustion equipment. The occupier of scheduled premises must maintain control equipment in efficient condition and must operate it in a proper and efficient manner. Scheduled and unscheduled premises, unless exempted, may not conduct any trade or industry or operate fuel-burning equipment so as to cause or permit emissions in excess of the concentration standard or rate prescribed. The law also provides for an advisory committee to make recommendations to the competent minister for air pollution prevention, abatement, and control. The Clean Air Act of 1963 adopted by Queensland is substantially the same as the New South Wales law.

C. BELGIUM

The law on the Struggle Against Atmospheric Pollution (*31*) adopted on December 28, 1964, allows the authorities to take all appropriate measures to prevent or abate air pollution, and in particular, to prohibit specified air pollution, to regulate or prohibit the use of devices or installations to prevent or abate air pollution.

Section 2 of the Act defines atmospheric pollution as meaning any emission into air, from whatever source, of gaseous, liquid, or solid substances likely to cause harm to human health, to injure animals and plants or to cause damage to property and land. Decrees under the Act are to be proposed jointly by the Minister of Public Health and, depending on the source of the pollution, the Ministers of Mines, Labor, Public Works, and Transport. The Minister of Public Health alone has jurisdiction over air pollution not within the jurisdiction of the named departments. The Minister of Defense, however, alone is competent to act to prevent or abate air pollution from any sources under military authority. The Minister of Public Health is responsible for the coordination of activities such as the sampling and analysis of the substances emitted or of air which is alleged to be polluted, research on the effects of pollution on man and, in collaboration with the laboratories of the Minister of Agriculture, on animals and plants, the development of effective measures for the control of air pollution and the education of the public on the problems of pollution and the methods for its prevention and control. The sampling, analysis, and research is to be carried out in collaboration with public and private laboratories or agencies approved by the Ministry of Public Health, and all information obtained in such collaborative work is sent to the Institute of Hygiene and Epidemiology in the Ministry of Public Health and Family Affairs.

Enforcement officers have the right to enter establishments and dwellings, and to take samples for analysis. Residential premises may be inspected only upon reasonable cause and with authorization by a justice of the peace. Such officers may temporarily prohibit the use of installations and apparatus which because of their design or characteristics are not able to operate in accordance with the implementing decrees and to seal the equipment. Such action shall cease to be in effect after 8 days unless within that period, the users having previously been heard or summoned, the officer in charge of the department to which the officer belongs has confirmed the measures taken. Appeal from such action may be taken to the King. Authority is also given to prescribe occupational requirements for persons engaged in installing devices or installations that may affect air pollution, and criminal sanctions are provided for violations of the Act and decrees thereunder.

D. BULGARIA

In Bulgaria, under the decree of October 24, 1963 (*32*), applicable to industrial undertakings and thermal power stations, air pollution is defined as "any change in the composition of air which renders it dangerous to the health of man or animals and to the growth of vegetation."

The Ministry of Public Health and Social Welfare is responsible for administration of the air pollution provisions of the decree and is directed to establish and enforce sanitary regulations for this purpose.

All agencies and organizations constructing, altering, or expending industrial undertakings and thermal power stations must use production techniques involving a minimum discharge of noxious substances into the air and must not exceed the standards in force applicable to emissions.

All construction plans must include adequate pollution control devices in order to be approved. The operation of industrial plants and thermal electric power facilities before control devices are in service is prohibited except that discharge in excess of the standards may be permitted if there are no known control measures. In such case, necessary measures for the protection of the health of persons and animals and for the preservation of the cleanliness of urban areas must still be taken. Control devices must be checked for efficiency before they are put into operation and must be maintained and operated effectively.

Existing plants must undertake construction programs, supported by economic plans and budgets, approved by the Council of Ministers, on recommendation of the Ministry of Public Health and Social Welfare, for the installation of necessary control devices within time limits established by the Council. Penal sanctions are set out in the decree for violation of its provisions.

E. CANADA

In Canada, the control of air pollution is primarily a provincial responsibility and there is no legislation on the federal level specifically for this purpose except for regulations to control ship smoke issued under the Canada Shipping Act.

Among the provinces, the 1958 Air Pollution Control Act (*33*) of the Province of Ontario authorized municipalities to pass bylaws, subject to limitations specified in the statute, for prohibiting or regulating the emission from any source of any class or type of air contaminant, and to regulate structures and equipment from which air contaminants may be emitted, subject to approval of the Minister of Health. Amendments adopted in 1963 (*34*) authorized the Minister of Health (with the approval of the Lieutenant Governor in Council) to make regulations (1) classifying industrial sources; (2) prohibiting or regulating and controlling emissions of air contaminants from industrial sources; (3) for approval of plans and specifications for such sources. The Act defines an industrial source as including any "action, operation or treatment embracing chemical, industrial or manufacturing processes that may be a source of an air contaminant," but excludes fuel burning equipment used solely for purposes of heating, generating power, or processing steam. Plans and specifications for the construction of industrial sources must have the prior approval of the Minister of Health (35).

The Ontario Air Pollution Control Act of 1967 (15–16 Elizabeth II, 1967) repealed the earlier legislation and provided for provincial control and regulation of air pollution. The Act defines air pollution as the presence of air contaminants (solids, liquids, gases, and odors) in the outdoor atmosphere in quantities that may cause discomfort to or endanger the health or safety of persons, or that may cause injury or damage to property or to plant or animal life, or that may interfere with visibility or the normal conduct of transport or business. A certificate of approval for air pollution control methods and equipment must be obtained from the Minister of Health prior to the construction of a stationary source of air pollution. The Minister may issue orders prohibiting the operation of sources of air pollution or requiring changes in the method of operation or in the control equipment, and, in the case of serious danger to health, may require the immediate discontinuance of operations.

Provision is made for a board of negotiation to negotiate the settlement of claims of persons suffering economic loss from damage to crops or livestock caused by air pollution.

The Act also grants authority for the control of motor vehicle air pollution by the setting of standards for emissions and by requiring motor vehicles to be equipped with control systems or devices.

Regulations issued on January 6, 1968 (O.Reg. 449/67) establish limitations on the emission of smoke, flyash, sulphur dioxide, and other air contaminants.

Alberta introduced provincial regulations for the control of air pollution in 1961. These provide for the control of dust, odors, smoke, and toxic materials on a progressively severe scale depending upon the population of the community to which it is applied. Approval of plans and specifications for all new industries is also required by the Regulations. Administration of the legislation and investigative work on air pollution are functions of the Air and Water Pollution Control Section of the Sanitary Engineering Division of the Department of Public Health.

Saskatchewan introduced an Air Pollution Control Act in 1965 based largely upon the Ontario legislation then existing. Thus controls are divided between the Occupational Health Branch of the Saskatchewan Department of Public Health and municipalities.

In Manitoba, powers were largely delegated to municipalities in amending legislation introduced in 1960. The province also undertakes field studies in air pollution carried out by sections of the health department.

British Columbia amended legislation in 1967 to extend the powers of the Pollution Control Board, which formerly had covered water pollution only, to include air and soil as well.

In the province of Nova Scotia (35a) amendments to section 189 of the Municipal Act were adopted in 1960 and gave municipal councils the power to (1) regulate and control the emission and discharge of smoke, odors and gases and for preventing atmospheric pollution resulting from such emissions; (2) provide standards regulating emissions; (3) require the installation of control equipment, make inspections, and to require owners and operators to file reports. Other provinces, with the exception of Quebec, do not have air pollution problems of sufficient magnitude to necessitate the introduction of legislation nor the maintenance of air pollution staff. In the province of Quebec, air pollution field studies and any necessary control recommendations are made by the Industrial Hygiene Division of the Department of Health.

F. Czechoslovakia

The 1967 Act on Measures to Prevent Air Pollution (36) included an annex setting limitations on the discharge of flyash, sulphur dioxide, and specified harmful substances from any source. Air pollution emissions in excess of these limitations are subject to a fine. In the case of pollution caused by fuel combustion by steam traction facilities, the penalty is computed at a fixed rate per ton of coal consumed. The penalty for pollution resulting from open burning at dumps, quarries, and mines is fixed on the basis of the burning surface or volume. In all other cases, the fine is equivalent to the annual cost of operation of available air pollution control equipment or other measures necessary to comply with the limitations.

The fine so computed is multiplied by a factor corresponding to the classification of the area affected as industrial, residential, recreational, or health resort. An additional penalty is also imposed if the source has not acted to comply with instructions from the State Technical Inspection of Air Protection from Pollution (which is the national control and inspection agency) on measures to mitigate or prevent the air pollution, or if a source fails properly to operate and maintain control equipment or to follow appropriate procedures. In the case of a second similar violation, the penalty is doubled.

The proceeds of all fines and penalties are allocated among the local and municipal committees whose areas of jurisdiction are affected and the National Ministry of Forest Administration and Water Conservation.

G. Denmark

Denmark has no general laws on the prevention of air pollution. Under the Act of January 12, 1858 (37), however, each of the municipalities in the country has passed a public health "bye-law" approved by the Ministry of the Interior. All the bye-laws provide for supervision by the local public health committee of factories and similar commercial establishments in order to avoid health hazards or other serious nuisances to the neighborhood through the emission of noxious fumes, smoke, dust or smells, or in other similar ways. The health committee may issue the necessary injunctions to an enterprise to desist from the nuisances of the above nature. Plants covered by inspection may not be started, constructed, rebuilt or extended before securing permission from the health committee, which is also authorized to approve their location.

H. France

The industrial establishments are classified according to their nuisance under the law of December 19, 1917. In the first class are the establishments which must be constructed outside urban areas and which are subject to authorization only after inquiry and examination. In the second class those which can be erected in urban areas, after inquiry and authorization. In the third class those which need only a declaration and only have to follow general rules of air pollution prevention.

The national law of August 2, 1961 (38) is an enabling act on the prevention of air pollution and noxious odors that is designed to be followed up by decrees regulating air pollution from domestic and industrial sources. The law, in general, requires all buildings and industrial, commercial, handicraft, or agricultural establishments, as well as vehicles or other movable objects to be constructed, operated, or used in such manner as to prevent air pollution and smells, which among other things constitute a public nuisance and menace to the public health. It authorizes the issuance of provisions for the prohibition or restriction of specified contaminants.

Where an establishment not included in the classified list presents serious dangers or inconveniences to the safety, health, or comfort of the surrounding neighborhood, or to public health, the Prefect, after consultation with the mayor and the departmental board of public health, may order remedial action. In case of noncompliance, the operation may be temporarily suspended by the Ministry of Industry. Such suspension may be contested within 2 months before the administrative tribunal whose decision is subject to appeal to the Council of State.

An implementing decree was issued in 1963 (39) which stated, as its purpose, the control of air pollution and odors which inconvenience the population, endanger health or public safety, or harm agricultural production or are prejudicial to the preservation of buildings and monuments or to scenic beauty. Measures under the decree are applicable to the country as a whole but special protection zones as therein provided may be established. The decree deals only with fuel-burning equipment, industrial, and private premises.

The Minister of Industry and the Minister of Public Health and Population are authorized by joint order to establish standards for fuel-burning equipment. Within not more than 2 years after the effective date of such standards, the manufacture, sale, or importation of non-complying equipment is prohibited. Thereafter, all such equipment sold must contain a prescribed notice stating the conditions of installation, adjustment, operation and maintenance, and the fuels for which the plant is designed.

Where an installation causes air pollution threatening public health, the Prefect by order may require remedial measure. In an emergency, if these measures are not complied with, the Prefect, after instituting legal proceedings and upon recommendation of the departmental health council, may take official measures at the expense of the offender to abate the danger, including directions to suspend operations.

Under Title II of the decree, Zones of Special Protection may be established by joint orders of the Minister of Public Health and Population, the Minister of the Interior, the Minister of Industry and the Minister of Construction, on proposal by the Prefect, taking into consideration the population, the concentration by weight and composition of airborne particles, concentration of sulfur dioxide or any other poisonous gas, visibility, and local climatological conditions. Special orders may be issued by the Ministers applicable to heating plants and fuel burning appliances, their use, maintenance, the qualifications of operating personnel, and the use of fuels in any of the zones. In such zones, heating plants exceeding a heat generating rate of 1000 thermes or 1 million kcal/hour are required to have permanent air sampling devices. The Ministers may also require any heating plant more than

10 years old which is unable to meet pollution requirements to suspend operations in not less than 5 years.

I. Federal Republic of Germany

Air pollution is dealt with on the federal level principally under the Industrial and Civil Codes. Under the Federal Act of 1959 (*40*), permits must be obtained for the erection of plants which are likely to incommode, endanger, or cause serious nuisance to the owners or tenants of adjoining property or the public in general. The plants are listed in an order promulgated in 1960. The Technical Directive for Maintaining Purity of the Air promulgated on September 8, 1964, as a "Joint Ministerial Bulletin," prescribes control devices and pollutant emission limits for such plants. These guidelines are to be observed by the licensing authorities in determining the issuance of permits.

Under a 1965 enactment (*41*), the Federal Minister of Health is directed to establish, by decree and with the concurrence of the Bundesrat, districts for the measurement of air pollution without regard to state lines. After measurements have been made, if remedial measures are needed, the Federal Minister of Health will make recommendations for corrective or preventive measures to the appropriate highest state authorities. Each state is required to make annual reports to the Federal Minister of Health concerning its findings and recommendations, and the federal government in turn is to make annual reports to the legislature on air pollution, taking into account the state reports.

Federal legislation has been supplemented in the Confederate States of Baden-Württemberg, Bayern (Bavaria), Neidersachsen (Lower Saxony), and Rheinland-Pfalz through legislation essentially similar to the "Protection from Immissions Act" of April 20, 1962 (*40*) of the *Land* of North Rhine-Westphalia, which is the most industrialized part of the Federal Republic. This Act deals with air pollution and applies to all industrial, workshop, or other plants for which no permit is required under Article 16 of the Industrial Code. It allows the government of the *Land* to require that the installation and operation of a plant shall comply with certain technical requirements; that persons operating such plant shall measure emissions; that emissions from the plant shall not exceed prescribed limits; and that when pollution is serious the use of fuel with certain properties must be restricted in certain districts.

Four sets of regulations have been issued under this Act. They apply to the emission of dark smoke, household-refuse incineration plants, gage measurements and installations for the preparation of bituminous road building material.

J. IRELAND

Section 10 of the Local Government (Sanitary Services) Act (42), adopted in 1962, authorizes regulations for the control of air pollution from any source. Air pollutants include smoke, dust, grit, or gas. Matters which may be covered by the regulations include the testing, measurement, and investigation of air pollution, regulating the establishment and operation of trades and processes having a high pollution potential, and specifying maximum permissible concentrations in the air of specified pollutants.

Specific provisions for the control of alkali, etc., works are contained in Alkali, etc., Works Regulation Act, 1906. This Act also applies to certain cement works and smelting works.

K. ITALY

The Italian Parliament passed a law on July 13, 1966 (No. 615), providing the general framework for control of air pollution. The law covers all fuel burning installations, industrial and residential, including vehicles; and all other means by which the fumes, powders, gases, or odors of whatever kind threaten to change the normal condition of the atmosphere and thereby endanger public health.

A national air pollution commission is established in the Ministry of Health, including representatives of the Ministries of Interior, Public Works, Industry, Transport, Scientific Research, and State Participation. The commission is to examine all aspects of air pollution and promote research in the field.

Each province must also establish an air pollution commission with the same functions.

The law divides the country into zones for air pollution control. Zone A includes communes in northern and central Italy with populations between 70,000 and 300,000 or with lower populations but with exceptional air pollution problems, and communes in southern Italy and the Islands with populations between 300,000 and one million or with special problems. Zone B includes communes in central and northern Italy with populations over 300,000 and communes in southern Italy and the Islands with over a million inhabitants.

The law provides general guidelines on the size of the installations and types of fuels involved, provides penalties for noncompliance with regulations, and establishes responsibility for administering the regulations by provincial fire departments. (In the case of motor vehicles, regulations are to be administered by the Ministry of Transport.) The law provides for regulations to be established by decree within six months, and for local regulations to be put into force by the communes within six months after the nation-wide regulations are decreed. In central and northern Italy, the communes are to conduct a census of all fuel-burning installations covered by the law, within six months of the establishment of communal regulations.

The first regulation issued under the terms of the air pollution law appeared in a Presidential decree dated October 24, 1967 (No. 1788), published in a supplement to the *Official Gazette* of January 9, 1968. These regulations apply only to fuel-burning installations with a capacity greater than 120,000 Btu/hour (30,000 kcal/hour), used for space heating, water heating for civilian use, kitchen dishwashers, sterilizers, medical disinfectors, laundry equipment, waste disposal units, bakeries, and other similar uses. The regulations do not apply to fuel-burning installations included in "a cycle of industrial production" nor to installations where the predominant application is industrial. Regulations for industrial installations and for motor vehicles are currently under study.

L. Japan

The Air Pollution Control Act of 1962 (*43*) is essentially an enabling act to be implemented by cabinet orders. Air pollutants subject to the Act are soot and smoke and "specially designated harmful materials" identified in Article 2 as hydrogen fluoride, hydrogen sulfide, sulfur dioxide and other materials extremely harmful to human health as defined by cabinet orders. Areas specially subject to air pollution by smoke and soot may be designated as air pollution control areas by cabinet order. The Minister of Welfare and the Minister of Trade and Industry will determine the permissible discharge levels of soot and smoke for different types of facilities. After the designation of a control area, no facilities creating smoke and soot may be established unless their emission levels are approved by the provincial governor, and existing facilities may be required, if feasible, to install necessary control equipment. Facilities creating smoke and soot are listed in Cabinet Order 438 of December 1, 1962. The Act also authorizes inspections of plants and provides penalties for its violation.

M. The Netherlands

Under the Public Nuisance Law ("Hinderwet" 1952, as amended in 1958, 1960, and 1964) a permit is required for establishments that may cause danger, damage, or nuisance in its surroundings. The establishments involved are specified in the Public Nuisance Regulation ("Hinderwetbesluit" 1953, as amended until 1967). This regulation contains a rather detailed list of establishments, including any establishment with an installed electric motor capacity of 2 HP or more, covering thus nearly all factories, storages, big heating installations, etc. The permit must be obtained before the beginning of the operation and a new permit is required for any modification. Normally the permit is given by municipal authorities. It may and will mostly contain certain conditions, preferably indicating the means that are required to minimize any nuisance, including air pollution. Small domestic heating apparatus, traffic, and removable installations are not covered by this or any other law. A new law against air pollution was proposed in 1967, but was not enacted at time of publication.

N. NORWAY

The Neighbors Act of June 16, 1961, effective January 1, 1962 (*44*) requires industrial plants and other undertakings to obtain a permit if they spread gas, smoke, radiation, etc., causing harm or inconvenience to many persons or over a wide area. This obligation applies to new plants and increases in the discharges of existing works. Rules have been adopted requiring listed industries, such as iron works, gas and coke works, pulp and paper factories, etc., to apply for a permit in all cases. The application is considered by a Smoke Control Council which decides most cases, with a right of appeal to the Ministry of Industry. Cases of particularly doubtful nature or of great importance may be referred directly to the Cabinet through the Ministry. Permits may be granted subject to a number of conditions, including stack height, control equipment, and monitoring requirements.

O. POLAND

The basic law, adopted on April 21, 1966, covers all sources of air pollution and assigns responsibility to several authorities. Pursuant to this, the following authorities have issued decrees implementing the law as follows:

The Council of Ministers have issued decrees; on September 13, 1966, listing permissible concentrations of air pollutants; on March 23, 1967, authorizing the Chairman of the Central Water Utilization Bureau to establish the width of protective zones around sources of pollution; and on September 26, 1967, covering fines for exceeding permissible dust emission limits, which fines increase as the limit is exceeded.

The Chairman of the Central Water Utilization Bureau has issued decrees: on July 15, 1966, concerning the coordination of responsibility for approving regional, local, site, and construction plans with respect to air pollution between the Central Water Utilization Bureau and the local air pollution control authorities; on July 16, 1966, on the measurement of dispersion of pollutants from sources; on September 15, 1966, requiring the reporting of sources of air pollution and their emissions to the local air pollution control authorities and authorizing these local bodies, acting in agreement with the appropriate state health inspector, to determine the type and amount of substance that these sources may discharge to the air; and on May 30, 1967, establishing protective zone widths.

The Minister of Health and Social Welfare, in concert with the Chairman of the Central Water Utilization Bureau, have issued decrees: on October 17, 1966, on cooperation between the state health inspectorate and local air pollution control authorities; and on January 31, 1967, requiring sources to measure, monitor, and keep records of their emissions and setting forth principles for air quality measurement.

P. PORTUGAL

Although in Portugal there is no specific legislation concerning air pollution, some acts, regulations, and codes permit competent authorities to order measures to abate the effects of pollution, viz: Acts of 17, 8, 1922 and 1, 8, 1923, regulating the installation and functioning of industrial boilers and chimneys. Regulation of 7, 11, 1945, reorganizing the General Health Directorate. Road Code of 20, 5, 1954 and 4, 7, 1966, its regulations and supplements containing orders on air pollution from the automotive vehicles. Regulation of 28, 3, 1966, orders concerning the planning and operation of industrial establishments. Act of 1, 12, 1938, regulating the importation, storage, and treatment of crude oil, its derivatives and residuals. Administrative Code, approved by the regulation of 31, 13, 1940.

Q. SPAIN

On November 30, 1961, the government passed Law 2414 on "Norms to Follow on Disturbing, Unhealthy, Poisonous, and Dangerous Activities." This was published in the government's Official Bulletin No. 292 of December 7, 1962, specifying legislation relative to atmospheric contamination. On March 15, 1963, procedures to be followed in the application of this law were approved. On June 5, 1963, a decree was passed creating the Central Committee of Sanitation. In May 31, 1965, by government order the Central Office of Unhealthy and Dangerous

Activities was created within the Secretariat of the Central Commission of Sanitation for the purpose of advising the Provincial Commissions on Technical Services and to work with Atmospheric Sanitation Services of the Department of Sanitation which is also a government office.

R. SWEDEN

The existing Swedish legislation in the field of air pollution consists of miscellaneous regulations in acts on public health, town and country planning, building and constructions, traffic, etc. The competence of taking action against nuisances is mainly vested in local authorities.

Since 1967, the Swedish Nature Conservancy Office has been the central agency for the prevention of air pollution, water pollution, and noise. In 1969 new legislation is planned concerning these fields. Specified types of works and plants must not be erected without examination in advance.

S. YUGOSLAVIA

The Yugoslav basic law on air pollution, enacted in 1965, and published on pages 1181–1183 of Službeni List SFRJ, No. 30, covers all sources of pollution. It gives authority for organization for air pollution control, research and training to the several constituent republics in the federal union; authority for supervision of execution to the district, republic, and federal sanitary inspectorates; and authority to the Federal Secretary of Health and Social Welfare, with the assistance of the Federal Institute of Public Health, to prepare regulations and set air quality and emission standards. Fines are provided for failure to comply.

T. UNITED KINGDOM

The two principal laws for controlling air pollution are the Clean Air Air Act of 1956 and the Alkali etc. Works Regulation Act of 1906. The former is operated by local authorities and controls the emission of smoke, grit, and dust from domestic and industrial furnaces. The Alkali Act is administered by a small body of qualified inspectors appointed by and responsible to the Minister of Housing and Local Government in England and Wales and the Secretary of State for Scotland. It controls the emission of noxious or offensive gases, smoke, grit and dust from certain specified industries where there are technical difficulties of prevention and control requiring the expertise of chemists, chemical engineers, and fuel technologists. The first Alkali Act was passed in 1863, this being followed by a series of Acts which widened the application to other industries and all were consolidated in the Alkali etc. Works Regulation Act of 1906. Since 1906, additions have been made by Orders and the most recent, the eighth, in 1966 consolidated all the earlier Orders. The Act now covers a large number of special processes, including the bulk of the heavy chemical industry, pharmaceuticals, iron and steel, nonferrous metals, electricity generation, gas making, carbonization, oil refining, petrochemicals, ceramics, lime burning, cement, etc.

Under the Clean Air Act, which is operated by local authorities, it is an offense to emit dark smoke (defined as smoke which is as dark or darker than Ringelmann No. 2) for longer periods than permitted by regulations of the Minister. The Act also provides that no furnace, except small domestic purpose furnaces, shall be installed unless it can be operated, so far as practicable, continuously without emitting smoke when burning fuel of a type for which it was designed. Installation of such furnaces is subject to the approval of the local authority.

A local authority may, by order confirmed by the Minister, declare the whole of a district or any part of it to be a smoke control area in which only approved appliances or approved fuels or both may be used. When such an order applies to dwellings or to churches and buildings used by charities, there is provision for financial contributions from public funds toward the cost of adapting fuel-burning appliances or installing new ones to meet the requirements.

The provisions of the Clean Air Act with respect to dark smoke also apply to railway locomotives and seagoing ships in docks, etc.

The Clean Air Act also empowers local authorities to control emissions of grit and dust from industrial furnaces and there is a system of prior approval for new furnaces burning solid fuel and requiring control equipment to be fitted. The Minister may make regulations for the measurement of grit and dust in furnace emissions. Heights of new chimneys are also controlled under the Clean Air Act.

In addition to the above laws, the nuisance provisions of the Public Health Act 1936 apply to all other aspects of pollution, e.g. offensive odors, miscellaneous grit and dust escapes, acid soot emissions. Finally, an aggrieved citizen or group of citizens can take proceedings under Common Law.

Booklets have been issued by the central government recommending to local authorities standards for chimney heights and grit and dust emissions and methods for the measurement of grit and dust from furnaces.

U. U.S.S.R.

Under an Order issued in 1949 (*47*) no electric power station may be constructed without the simultaneous installation of equipment for dust and ash removal. Corresponding restrictions, relating to gases and particulate matter, apply to factories processing nonferrous metals, coal-tar distilleries, and iron and steel works. Instructions have been issued establishing the maximum permissible concentrations of noxious substances in urban air (see Chapter 51).

V. Model Legislation

To assist local governmental officials who felt a need for specific legal authority for air pollution prevention and abatement programs, various organizations have from time to time prepared model ordinances and legislative guidelines for adoption by communities. The adoption of model laws has, however, generally resulted in a standardized and undesirably rigid approach to air pollution problems as well as a failure to recognize the need for provisions especially designed to deal with problems unique in a given area or arising under a variety of conditions. There is a growing recognition of the desirability of basic criteria for legislation which will permit adjustment to meet particular local situations. The model ordinances would thus constitute but one of the elements which the community could consider in drafting its own legislation.

One of the earliest model ordinances was the "Proposed Standard Smoke Ordinance" prepared in 1924 by a committee of representatives of the American Society of Heating and Ventilating Engineers, The Stoker Manufacturers Association, the American Society of Mechanical Engineers, and members at large. Primarily a smoke control ordinance, the model also contained detailed specifications for boilers, furnaces, etc., and provided for a permit system for new or reconstructed fuel-burning equipment.

This was followed in 1938 by the "Model Smoke-Abatement Ordinance" of the Smoke Prevention Association. This ordinance contained no administrative provisions but was concerned with standards for the construction and performance of fuel-burning equipment and other sources of smoke emission.

An annotated model ordinance "City Smoke Control and Air Pollution Programs" was issued by the National Institute of Municipal Law Officers in 1947. Although it made no specific provision for limiting the emission of dust and other solids, it provided a useful approach and materials for the development of an ordinance in accordance with legal limitations generally applicable to municipalities.

The first model ordinance to include aspects of air pollution other than smoke was "Example Sections for a Smoke-Regulation Ordinance" issued by the American Society of Mechanical Engineers in 1949. In addition to establishing standards for dust in gases, and for smoke emission, it permitted variations for either limited periods or under special circumstances. It also provided in greater detail than previous models for the administration of the air pollution control program.

Reflecting the growing concern over pollutants other than smoke and gases, a subcommittee of the Smoke Prevention Association of America, Inc. in 1950 issued "Standards for Emission of Solids from Chimneys." This was essentially a technical approach to the limitation of the emission of solids.

In 1952, the Manufacturing Chemists Association published "A Rational Approach to Air Pollution Legislation." A second edition, published in 1958, made no substantial change in the basic principles recommended by the association. Essentially, these recommendations placed emphasis on the economic implications of air pollution control, both to the plant owner and the community. They urged that air pollution control be made a matter of local option, with the state furnishing technical assistance to the community. Recognition of the use of air for the disposal of waste products as a reasonable one, to the extent that such use was not harmful to persons or property, was also urged.

A draft "State Air Pollution Control Act" has been developed by the Council of State Governments (Chicago, Ill.) and was published by the Council in its 1967 edition of "Suggested State Legislation."

VI. Guiding Principles for Air Pollution Legislation

The development of air pollution control legislation is largely a problem of the specialized application of accepted principles of administrative law. As in most cases where the administrative law approach has been applied, the efficacy of a particular program depends on many extra-legal elements such as administrative personnel, size of appropriation, and public understanding.

The goal of air pollution legislation should be to maintain a reasonable degree of purity of our air resources consistent with: (1) the public health and welfare; (2) the protection of plant and animal life; (3) the protection of physical property and other resources; (4) the visibility requirements for safe air and ground transportation.

The solution of local problems by local authorities should be encouraged. Municipal and other local agencies should be authorized to establish control programs, and in cases where a need is shown, regional authorities should be authorized. The state agency should, however, be authorized to take action in the absence of a local or regional authority, or its failure to act.

In programs at all levels of government, control can be most effectively brought about only by legislation and regulations which are reasonable and based on technically substantiated criteria. They should provide adequate flexibility, yet be reasonably specific to meet the needs of the area under consideration.

In 1958 a World Health Organization Expert Committee suggested that legislation should be directed toward:

1. The control of sources of pollution by specifying the types of industrial and other processes which should operate under supervision by control authorities, and the types of emission which should be kept to a minimum value.

2. The institution of town-planning practices in which due attention is given to the planning and zoning of industrial sites for the purpose of reducing air pollution, providing always that such action does not make the conduct of industry prohibitively costly or even impossible.

3. The provision of regulations controlling the types of fuel to be burned in installations where combustion emissions are not otherwise controllable (48).

In view of the provisions of the Clean Air Act mentioned earlier, concerning state action in the establishment and enforcement of regional air quality standards, state legislation should also assure that the state air pollution control agency will have adequate authority to meet the requirements of the federal act.

In the light of the above considerations, the following criteria designed to establish and carry out an air pollution control program are suggested for legislation at the state and local level. While these criteria are not all-inclusive, they are intended to provide a convenient check-list of considerations involved in the development of such legislation.

A. GENERAL PRINCIPLES

1. *Statement of Policy*

A declaration of policy in the statute, particularly if a state statute, is desirable. Such a declaration indicates the basic objectives which are to guide the agency in the exercise of authority delegated to it by the legislature and is an aid to the administrative agency and to the courts in the interpretation of the statute.

2. *Definitions*

A definition section is an integral part of a comprehensive air pollution control statute. Such a section is important to the administration and interpretation of the statute, and unduly restrictive or vague definitions should be avoided.

The definition of the term air pollution will control the scope of enforcement activity and should be broad enough to permit comprehensive control measures. The jurisdiction of the agency should be made to extend to those emissions into the atmosphere of the state (or of the police jurisdiction of the agency) causing or contributing to air pollution which may create a nuisance or be actually or potentially harmful, detrimental, or dangerous to human, animal or plant life, or to property, or which adversely affect visibility so as to create an actual or potential hazard to air and surface transportation.

Similarly, the definition of "person" should not be restrictive but should include the state, any municipality, county, sanitary district, public or private corporation, co-partnership, firm or other entity, or individual.

3. Administrative Agency

Administrative authority and responsibility should be vested in a single agency with comprehensive powers. The agency should be so constituted as to take into account the interests and views of affected groups in addition to public health considerations.

The agency might be (1) a single administrator, (2) a board or authority appointed by the chief executive official of the jurisdiction, (3) an ex officio board, composed of heads of departments having related responsibilities such as in a state, health, conservation, agriculture, and in a city, health, building, and public works.

If the agency is placed in an existing department, the health department would seem to be the logical choice, since the health aspects of air pollution constitute a major public interest, and this department usually has trained personnel and facilities needed in the program.

An advisory council, particularly if the agency is a single-administrator type, is generally considered desirable and useful.

4. Comprehensive Planning

The agency should be authorized to undertake comprehensive planning for the control and prevention of air pollution both as regards the maintenance and improvement of air quality and the potential needs of various areas of the jurisdiction.

The agency should also be authorized to engage with another state agency in joint planning, either directly or through a jointly established agency, for the prevention and control of air pollution in an interstate air quality control region designated under the Clean Air Act which lies partly within its own state and partly in the other state or states. Such interstate joint planning activity must include representation of the states and appropriate political subdivisions within the air quality control region and must be capable of recommending to the governors of the states involved standards of air quality and plans for their implementation, as required by the Clean Air Act.

5. *Permits—Registration*

A technique for the control of air pollution is a permit system under which prior agency approval of plans, specifications, and other data for new construction or alterations is required. Approval is given only if the controls to be provided are, in the judgment of the agency, adequate to meet the requirements on the emission of air pollutants.

Such approval does not, of course, necessarily guarantee that the completed installation will be efficiently operated or that it will perform in accordance with its design specifications.

There is, on the other hand, a group of authorities who prefer a procedure which requires registration of all sources of regular or anticipated emissions above some minimum size. It should be recognized that a permit program does involve an administrative responsibility of considerable magnitude. The proponents of a registration program believe that knowledge of location and nature of sources of air pollution with opportunity to inspect will provide as good a foundation for control as a permit program. It is further claimed that the only advantage of permits over registration is that abatement is instituted more simply by withdrawing the permit than by petitioning a court for an injunction, an advantage which to some is offset by the administrative burden of equipment approval. The possible combined use of permit and registration systems might in certain cases prove desirable.

6. *Enforcement*

Discharges into the atmosphere from any source constructed or operated without a permit (if one is required), or in violation of the terms of a permit or of rules, regulations, or orders of the agency should be prohibited. Civil and criminal penalties, abatement authority, and judicial review of agency orders should be provided for.

7. *Administration*

The agency should have sufficient power to carry out its responsibilities. Necessary authority would include power to hold hearings, subpoena witnesses, enforce subpoenas, administer oaths, examine plans and specifications, require maintenance of records and making of reports, and the right to enter on property at reasonable times for purposes of inspection and investigation. The agency should, of course, be empowered to adopt rules and regulations, issue orders, and to take action necessary and appropriate for the administration and enforcement of the statute.

8. Severability

A severability clause may be included to provide that if any part of the statute is declared unconstitutional, the other parts shall continue in force and effect.

B. SPECIFIC CRITERIA

In addition to the general guides set out above, the following checklist is suggested for state-wide control legislation and for regional control legislation.

1. State-wide Legislation

A state air pollution control agency should be authorized to:

1. Conduct a program of research in air pollution, and collect and disseminate information relating to air pollution and its control and prevention.

2. Establish air quality and emission standards, which may be applicable state-wide, or in designated air quality control regions where stricter controls may be necessary, taking into account the purposes of the statute, current scientific knowledge, available control techniques and the need for control after appropriate investigations and a hearing, and to revise such standards from time to time.

3. Issue rules and regulations to implement the statute, and hold public hearings on proposed rules and regulations.

4. Conduct surveys and investigations, either on its own motion or on complaints, into alleged violations, and issue orders, after hearing, to abate discharges or to require remedial measures.

5. Advise, consult, and cooperate with other agencies and local authorities of the state, with other states, interstate or international agencies, the federal government, and with affected groups and industries in the formulation and carrying out of its program; to accept and administer loans and grants from the federal government and from other sources for carrying out any of its functions; and to provide technical assistance and advice to local control organizations, industry, and other affected groups.

6. Employ personnel, including consultants and hearing officers and utilize the personnel and facilities of other state agencies and make reimbursement therefor.

7. Take emergency action to abate air pollution which presents an imminent and substantial endangerment to the public health.

With appropriate modifications to reflect the more limited jurisdiction of local agencies, the above checklist may be helpful in drafting local legislation.

2. Regional Control Legislation

Since some political subdivisions may wish to achieve a higher level of air quality for their jurisdictions than the state air quality standards would provide, the state law should provide this opportunity. Where an air quality control region is involved, however, the statute should assure either that the control agency's jurisdiction is at least the same as the region or provide for effective coordination of progress within the region. Legislation for this purpose should:

1. Specify the procedure by which and conditions under which a local or regional control agency involving one or more cities or counties may be established.

2. Provide for the general and specific powers of the agency, including the authority to issue rules and regulations, orders, and to enforce penalties within the agency's area of jurisdiction.

3. Authorize the local or regional control agency to establish air quality and emission standards no less strict than state standards and to take emergency action to abate air pollution which presents an imminent and substantial endangerment to the public health. Such standards should be subject to approval by the state agency, particularly where local programs within an air quality control region are involved, to assure consistent standards within the region. At the same time, the state standards should continue to be applicable to the region and enforceable directly by the state as may be necessary.

4. Provide for the appointment powers and duties of officers and employees of the agency, and authorize the agency to carry out the purposes of the act.

5. Authorize appropriations to the agencies by counties and cities comprising such agency.

6. Provide for injunctive relief against violations, and for criminal and civil penalties.

7. Provide for appeals from administrative action to appropriate courts on the basis of existing statutes.

REFERENCES

1. Northwestern Laundry v. Des Moines, 239 U.S. 486 (1916); Moses v. United States, 16 App. D.C. 428 (1900).
2. See discussion, 78 American Law Reports, Annotated 1305, 1382–1343.
3. Cf. Hill v. Villarreal, 383 S.W. 2d 463 (Texas, 1964); Waschak v. Moffat, 109 A 2d 310 (Pa. 1954), 54 A.L.R. 2d 748.
4. Munn v. Illinois, 94 U.S. 113 (1876); Welsh v. Morristown, 121 Atl. 697 (N.J., 1923).
5. Northwestern Laundry v. City of Des Moines, 239 U.S. 486, 36 S. Ct. 206 (1916).
6. Huron Portland Cement Company v. City of Detroit, 362 U.S. 440, 80 S. Ct. 813 (1960).
7. (Md., 1957) 129 A. 2d 115.
8. Murphysboro v. Sanitary Water Board of Ill., 134 N.E. 2d 522 (Ill., 1956).
9. Board of Health v. Annet, 62 A. 2d 224 (N.J., 1948); State v. Mundet Cork Co., 86 A. 2d 1 (N.J., 1952).
10. "Digest of Municipal Air Pollution Ordinances." Public Health Serv., U.S. Dept. of Health, Education, and Welfare, Washington, D.C., 1962; "A Compilation of Selected Air Pollution Emission Control Regulations and Ordinances." Public Health Serv., U.S. Dept. of Health, Education, and Welfare, Washington, D.C., 1965.
11. Cf. convention between Canada and the United States of America relating to damage caused in the latter country by emissions from the smelter at Trail, British Columbia. U.S. Treaty Ser. No. 893; 49 Statutes at Large 3245 (1935).
12. See Wisconsin v. Minnesota, 86 S. Ct. 385 (1965), where a suit by Wisconsin to prevent construction of a coal fired electric generating plant in Minnesota, because of its potential air pollution effects in Wisconsin, was dismissed.
13. New York v. New Jersey, 256 U.S. 296, 313 (1921).
14. Section 102 (c), The Clean Air Act, 42 U.S.C. 1857a (c).
15. Bills granting the consent and approval of the Congress to these compacts were introduced in the 90th Congress as follows: Ill.-Ind. Air Pollution Control Compact (H.R. 1150, S. 470); Ohio-W. Va. Interstate Compact on Air Pollution (H.R. 13034, S. 2350); Mid-Atlantic States Air Pollution Control Compact (H.J. Res. 645). None of these bills had been approved at the time of publication.
16. J. R. Taylor, B. S. Hasegawa, and L. A. Chambers, *World Health Organ., Monograph Ser.* **46,** 293 (1961).
17. Euclid v. Ambler Realty Co., 272 U.S. 365, 47 S. Ct. 114 (1925).
18. S. Edelman, *J. Air Pollution Control Assoc.* **13,** No. 7 (1963).
19. Cited hereinafter as IDHL.
20. Public Law 88-206 (Dec. 17, 1963) as amended by Public Law 89-272 (Oct. 20, 1965), and Public Law 90-148 (Nov. 21, 1967) 42 U.S.C. 1857, et seq.; (a) sec. 101 (a) (2); (b) sec 101 (a) 3, 4; (c) sec. 108 (a); (d) sec. 302 (g); (e) sec. 201 et seq.
21. S. M. Rogers and S. Edelman, "A Digest of State Air Pollution Laws." Public Health Serv., U.S. Dept. of Health, Education, and Welfare, Washington, D.C., 1963.
22. "Digest of Municipal Air Pollution Ordinances." U.S. Public Health Serv., Dept. of Health, Education, and Welfare, Washington, D.C., 1962.
23. A discussion of selected State and municipal air pollution control regulations in the United States is contained in "Air Pollution—A Survey of Existing Legislation," pp. 36–42. World Health Organ., Geneva, 1963.
24. Public Law 159, 84th Cong., as amended (Act of July 14, 1955), 69 Stat. 322.
25. Substantially all functions under the Act, are performed by the Surgeon General of the U.S. Public Health Service under a delegation of authority by the Secretary of Health, Education, and Welfare.

26. Georgia v. Tennessee Copper Co., 206 U.S. 230, 27 S. Ct. 618 (1907).
27. See S. Edelman, "Federal Air and Water Control: The Application of the Commerce Power to Abate Interstate and Intrastate Pollution," 33 George Washington Law Review 1067 (June, 1965).
28. For a discussion of these standards, see Chapter 51, p. 601.
29. Act No. 6125 of 1957 (Acts of Parliament, 1957, Part II, pp. 1008–1015) (see 10 IDHL 1959, p. 429).
30. Act No. 69 of 1961 (Statutes of New South Wales 1961, pp. 475–500) (see 15 IDHL IDHL 1957, pp. 7–8).
31. *Moniteur Belge* p. 345 (1965).
32. Decree No. 728 of 24 October 1963 (D'rzhaven Vestnik, 29 October 1963, No. 84, pp. 1–2) (Text reprinted in 16 IDHL Leg. pp. 33–36).
33. Statutes of Ontario, 1958, Chapter 2, p. 8 (see IDHL 489).
34. Act of 26 April 1963, Statutes of Ontario, 1962–1963, Chapter 2, pp. 7–8 (see 15 IDHL 69).
35. Regulations have been issued by the provinces of Manitoba and Alberta which set emission limits for various contaminants, including smoke. (See 14 IDHL pp. 196–197.); (a) id., p. 196.
36. *Law Gazette Czech. Socialist Repbl.*, No. 13, April 18, 1967. Supplemented by Instructions of the Chief Hygienist of the Czechoslovak Socialist Republic; "The Highest Permissible Concentrations of the Most Important Toxic Materials in the Surrounding Atmosphere." Ministry of Health No. HE-325-3.7.67 (July 14, 1967). (*Hygienic Regulations.* **30,** Instruction No. 34, 1967).
37. *European Conf. Air Pollution, 1963* Doc. CPA/RN/14/D/148. Council of Europe.
38. Law No. 61-842 of 2 August 1961 (Journal Official, 3 August 1961).
39. Decree No. 63-963 of 17 September 1963. (Journal Official, 21 September 1963, p. 8539)
40. *European Conf. Air Pollution, 1964* Doc. CPA/RN/14/AL/218. Council of Europe.
41. Act of 17 May 1965, Federal Law Journal, Part I, No. 21, pp. 413–415 (Bonn, 1965).
42. *European Conf. Air Pollution, 1963* Doc. CPA/RN/14/I4/134. Council of Europe.
43. Statute No. 146 of 2 June 1962.
44. *European Conf. Air Pollution, 1963* Doc. CPA/RN/14/141. Council of Europe.
45. Act of 5 July 1956 (Public General Acts and Measures of 1956, Chapter 52, pp. 377–415) (reprinted in full 9 IDHL 181).
46. 15 IDHL 680.
47. Order No. 431 of 14 June 1949 (see 2 IDHL 454).
48. *World Health Organ. Tech. Rept. Ser.* **157** (1958).

51 Air Pollution Standards

Arthur C. Stern

I. Introduction

The preferred sequence of development of air standards is as follows:

1. Prepare air quality criteria, which are analyses of the relationship between pollutant concentrations in the air and the adverse effects associated therewith. World Health Organization calls these "guides."

2. From the air quality criteria, develop air quality goals, which are the concentrations of pollutants with which we believe we can live without adverse effects on health and welfare.

3. From the air quality criteria, develop air quality standards, which are the concentrations of pollutants which we intend to achieve in the immediate future, but which may fall short of our air quality goals

because the standards must give consideration to feasibility of achievement within the immediately foreseeable future.

4. From the air quality goals, develop emission goals, which are the concentration of pollutants in emissions, which by computations based on present assumptions as to the number and nature of sources in the future, will be necessary to achieve air quality goals.

5. From the air quality standards, develop emission standards, which are the concentrations of pollutants in emissions which are necessary now to achieve air quality standards.

6. From the emission standards, develop design standards, which are the limits on choice of site, equipment, and fuel necessary to achieve emission standards.

7. In order to develop any of the above standards, there must also be standards for measurement and testing of the ambient air, effluent gas streams, control and analytical equipment, and air pollution effects.

II.   Air Quality Criteria or Guides*

A. CRITERIA FOR BIOLOGICAL EFFECTS

In developing statements of the relationship between air pollution levels and the effects caused by these levels, many critical decisions must be taken as to the existence or extent of cause-effect relationships. These relationships become quite indistinct in the interpretation of mortality and morbidity data on people, plants, and animals exposed for their lifetime to a multiplicity of stresses, only one of which is air pollution. For many of these stresses, including air pollution, there are inadequate measurements. Doubt exists on how to extrapolate to man data on controlled experiments involving exposure of experimental animals. Doubt also exists on how to extrapolate short-term experiments using relatively pure substances to the exposure of humans, plants, animals, and materials to the aged-irradiated mixture of precursors and reaction products that constitutes our real atmosphere.

In this decision-making process, certain questions continually recur. One is what we mean by injury or damage. As our experimental techniques improve, we are increasingly able to detect subtle physiological and psychological deviations from the norm that can be attributed to pollution. The norm in this case is exposure to unpolluted air and the deviation may be reversible when exposure to the pollutant stops. Some will argue that only irreversible deviations should be considered and that

* See also Volume I, Part III, and Reference (1), p. 717.

any deviation, reversible or irreversible, should be considered benign until proved deleterious. However, the fact that a deviation is reversible upon cessation of exposure to the pollutant is not, of itself, assurance that we are willing to allow such a deviation to occur. Prudence would argue for considering measurable deviations from the norm as deleterious until proved benign.

Within any species there exists a range of resistance and susceptibility to air pollutants. When a representative of a nonhuman species becomes senescent, it means little to us if its demise is hastened by air pollution. We take quite a different view for members of the human species, however. Air pollution levels must be safe for not only the healthy adult but also the ill, the infant, and the aged, who are recognized as being most susceptible to the threatening effects of air pollution.

Even among healthy adults, we can recognize differences in the limitation of physiological performance caused by air pollution. Thus, pollution levels that may so interfere with the oxygen utilization of an athlete as to prevent him from achieving a record-breaking performance may produce no presently measurable diminution in the performance of a sedentary clerical worker.

The question is sometimes raised as to what percentage of the population (i.e., 99.9%; 99.99%; etc.) we should seek to protect by ambient air quality control; and what percentage (i.e., 0.1%; 0.01%) we should take care of by other means such as their relocation to areas or structures having a cleaner air supply, or medical treatment. There are presently no good answers to this question.

There is a difference in resistance and susceptibility to the adverse effects of a pollutant among various species. It is this species difference in response to pollution that offers the best example of the difference between air quality criteria and air quality standards. For any pollutant, one can tabulate the pollutant level that will cause measurable deviation from the norm in each of a number of different species. These are air quality criteria. Among these species will be plants and livestock which normally are grown in a community and those which are not. If the criteria differ between these two groups, the community may elect to set limits to protect only the species of plants and livestock it normally grows. Thus, communities with different ecology could adopt different air quality standards to achieve the same level of protection of their normal plant and animal life. Man, of course, is ubiquitous and requires the same level of protection everywhere. However some of a community's plant or animal life may be more sensitive to some air pollutants than its human population, so that its air quality standards for these pollutants could be based on responses in plants or animals, rather than man.

B. CRITERIA FOR PHYSICAL EFFECTS

Pollution also affects the physical properties of the atmosphere. The determination of what constitutes a physical aberration is as difficult as the similar decision making with respect to biological deviations. The physical properties of the atmosphere affected include its electrical properties; its ability to transmit radiant energy; to convert its water vapor to fog, cloud, rain, and snow; to deteriorate and to soil surfaces. Our concern with atmospheric transmission of radiant energy encompasses the entire radiomagnetic spectrum, but of particular concern is the infrared region, as it affects the terrestrial heat balance; the ultraviolet region, as it affects both biological processes and photochemical reactions in the atmosphere; and the visible spectrum, as it affects both our ability to see things, and our need for artificial illumination.

The physical property most apparent to people is diminution of visibility through the atmosphere. In assessing loss of visibility, we must bear in mind that under certain conditions there will be loss of visibility resulting from fog, wind-blown particles of natural origin, and hazes created by the photochemical reaction in the atmosphere between naturally occurring substances. We therefore cannot use unlimited visibility as the norm for unpolluted air. However, the fact that nature does not provide 100-mile visibility as the norm is no argument for our being willing to accept one-mile visibility in our urban communities.

C. EXAMPLES OF CRITERIA

1. *U.S. Department of Health, Education, and Welfare (DHEW)*

Section 103(c)(2) of the Clean Air Act (Public Law 88-206) called upon the Secretary of Health, Education, and Welfare to publish air quality criteria based on the latest scientific knowledge of the predictable effects of various pollutants in the atmosphere. The first such publication, "Air Quality Criteria for Sulfur Oxides," was released in March, 1967 (*1a*). It included a tabulation of 79 cause-effect statements. The data from these statements were represented graphically on two figures (Figs. 1 and 2)* on which the numbers refer to item numbers in the tabulation. Although these criteria have been published, Sec. 107(b)(1) of the Air Quality Act of 1967 requires that they be reevaluated, and, if necessary,

---

* This form of data presentation, i.e., displaying extent of health and vegetation damage on a pollutant concentration vs. exposure time plot, has been used by Brasser *et al.* (*1b*) and also on p. 326 on Vol. I.

modified and reissued. The revised SO_x criteria, when issued, may not include Figs. 1 and 2.

The next in this publication series are scheduled to be air quality criteria for the photochemical oxidants, carbon monoxide, oxides of nitrogen, hydrocarbons, and particulate matter, each of which will have a similar tabulation.

2. California Department of Public Health

The "Technical Report of California Standards for Ambient Air Quality and Motor Vehicle Exhaust" (1961) (2) contains a 53-item cause-effect tabulation for the sulfur oxides; their January, 1966 publication "The Oxides of Nitrogen in Air Pollution" (3) contains a 94-item cause-effect tabulation for nitrogen dioxide; and their March, 1967 publication "Lead in the Environment and its Effects on Humans" (4) contains a 63-item cause-effect tabulation of quantitated exposures and a 79-item cause-effect tabulation of nonquantitated exposures to lead.

3. Verein Deutscher Ingenieure (VDI)-Kommission Reinhaltung der Luft

Several of the VDI Richtlinien (5) include cause-effect tabulations (Table I).*

4. Union of Soviet Socialist Republics

The author has prepared a cause-effect tabulation based on U.S.S.R. published data (6) on several pollutants, for some of which U.S.S.R. air quality standards have been set (Table II).*

III.   Air Quality Goals†

The obvious goal for urban areas is air the same quality as air from the hinterlands. This can never be lower in any substance than the global background concentration of that substance. Depending upon the substance, global background concentration may be either constant, decreasing, or increasing. A constant or decreasing concentration results when there are sinks to consume the substance at a rate equal to or greater than its rate of introduction to the atmosphere. Otherwise there will be an increasing global background concentration. Among the substances suspected of increasing in background are carbon monoxide

---

* See pp. 660 and 661.
† See also Volume I, Part I.

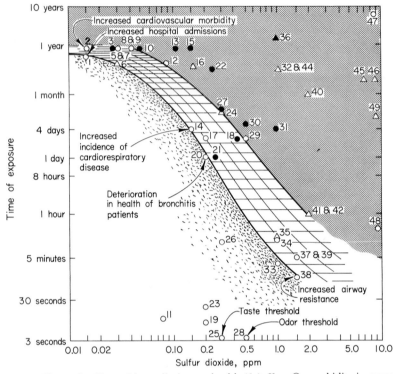

Fig. 1. Effects of sulfur oxides pollution on health (*1a*). Key: ○, morbidity in man; ●, mortality in man; △, morbidity in animals; ▲, mortality in animals; shaded area, range of concentrations and exposure times in which deaths have been reported in excess of normal expectation; grid area, range of concentrations and exposure times in which significant health effects have been reported; speckled area, ranges of concentrations and exposure times in which health effects are suspected.

and carbon dioxide. Some estimates of global background concentration are given in Table III.*

The previously mentioned DHEW "Air Quality Criteria for Sulfur Oxides" (*1a*) includes the following statement: "The concentrations of sulfur dioxide and sulfuric acid and its salts are, therefore, highly correlated, so that sulfur dioxide, which is commonly measured, can be used as an index of total pollution from these compounds," and concludes:

Since the following concentrations are expected in urban communities with diffuse sources having an annual average concentration of 0.015 ppm sulfur dioxide, these sets of ranges of concentrations can be collectively utilized as criteria of acceptable air quality:

* See p. 662.

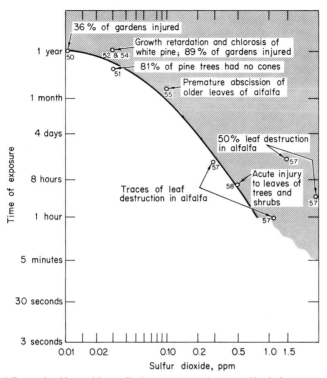

FIG. 2. Effects of sulfur oxides pollution on vegetation (*1a*). Shaded area, range of concentrations and exposure times in which injury to vegetation has been reported; white area, range of concentrations and exposure times of undetermined significance to vegetation.

Time period	Maximum	1 Percentile
24-hour average	0.05–0.08	0.04–0.06
1-hour average	0.12–0.20	0.05–0.11
5-minute average	0.10–0.50	0.05–0.14

Although the quoted sentence speaks of these values as criteria, in the context of this chapter, they are air quality goals. Goals for some other pollutants are listed in Table IV.* They have no official status, and represent the author's evaluation of a variety of published and unpublished data.

IV. Air Quality Standards

At the outset a distinction must be made between air quality standards for the ambient, i.e., outdoor, air and threshold limit values (TLV) for

* See p. 662.

workroom atmospheres, e.g., those published by the American Conference of Governmental Industrial Hygienists (7). These latter are for 8-hours per day, 5-days per week exposure of healthy adult workers. In contrast to this, air quality standards are for 24-hours per day, 7-days per week exposure of all living and nonliving things. The two may not be used interchangeably. The World Health Organization has proposed four air quality levels: Level I—Concentration and exposure time at or below which, according to present knowledge, neither direct nor indirect effects (including alteration of reflexes or of adaptive or protective reactions) have been observed. Level II—Concentrations and exposure times at and above which there is likely to be irritation of the sensory organs, harmful effects on vegetation, visibility reduction, or other adverse effects on the environment. Level III—Concentrations and exposure times at and above which there is likely to be impairment of vital physiological functions or changes that may lead to chronic diseases or shortening of life. Level IV—Concentrations and exposure times at and above which there is likely to be acute illness or death in susceptible groups of the population.

A. Procedures Used in Setting Air Quality Standards

Air quality standards may be set either from air quality criteria and related factors or by several quite different approaches. One such is to use another community's air as the standard. In this approach, community "A" says, "We will be satisfied if our air quality is as good as that which now exists in community 'B'." Knowledge of air quality in community "B" thus provides the standard for community "A."

A second approach is to use as the standard for air quality that air which existed at an earlier time and for which it is believed that adverse effects were either nonexistent or tolerable by the community. In this approach the community says, "We will be satisfied if our air quality is as good as it was here in 1940." If there is objective data on air quality for the earlier date—which is usually not the case—this provides the standard. A variant of this approach is to compute from present-day data what the air quality most likely was at the earlier date.

A third approach is to use as the standard for air quality that air which exists in the community on certain days of good ventilation. In this approach the community says, "We will be satisfied if our air quality every day is as good as it now is on certain days." Knowledge of air quality on these certain days thus provides the standard.

Combinations of several approaches in arriving at an air quality standard are possible by considering not only air quality criteria, but also data from all three of these alternate approaches.

1. *Single or Multiple Standards*

A major decision that must be taken in the adoption of air quality standards is whether there should be one standard for an entire jurisdiction or different standards for different areas within the jurisdiction.

Our present concept for coping with this problem is the "air shed" or air quality region comprising that geographic area which encompasses both the area's air pollution sources and its receptors. All political jurisdictions within an air quality region would have the same air quality standards. In general, air quality regions would not be contiguous but would be separated by nonurban hinterland. If two separated regions were to expand in area in the future until they became contiguous, they would presumably then be merged into one larger air quality region. Since each air quality region would adopt its own air quality standards, they could differ among the several regions. However, there should be a floor below which no region's air quality standards should drop.

Because the residential, commercial, and industrial zones of an urban area are all surmounted by the same air mass, diverse air quality standards within the same jurisdiction or air quality region would seem to be very difficult to administer. One of the banes of air pollution control is the juxtaposition of a community with little or no control to one with stringent control standards. When this happens there is objection on the grounds that air pollution does not recognize jurisdictional boundaries. Yet the use within one jurisdiction of different standards for contiguous land use zones creates the very thing found objectionable when it involves more than one jurisdiction.

The foregoing argument is most valid for relatively small homogeneous jurisdictions such as the city, the county, and the air quality region; but it is less valid when applied to a state or the nation. As has been done in New York (see Section IV,C), a state may wish to preserve the superior air quality presently existing in large areas of the state, e.g., the Adirondack and Catskill Mountain State Park areas, by setting, for these regions, more restrictive standards of air quality than elsewhere in the state. It may also choose, as New York State has, to have less restrictive standards for its major metropolitan areas, on the basis of allowing, as an interim measure, that which is feasible to be done now. Where this is done there should be a procedure to escalate these standards after a predetermined number of years until the standards for such regions approach more closely the state's basic air quality standard.

In American zoning practice, it is relatively easy to keep a lower class use out of a higher class zone. However, it is much more difficult to enforce regulations which keep residences out of lower class zones. Courts are more prone to uphold restraints upon industrial and commercial location than upon the right of an individual to live where he chooses.

2. Economic, Social, and Political Considerations in Setting Air Quality Standards

Setting air quality standards discommodes no one. It is only their implementation, by enforcing emission, fuel, or equipment restrictions to achieve the air quality standard, that does so. Where such restrictions cause economic, social, or political problems, the alternatives include: (1) immediate adoption of air quality goals as standards, but the time phasing of adoption of the restrictions to achieve them; (2) immediate adoption and implementation of restrictions to achieve air quality standards which fall short of air quality goals, but time phasing for later adoption and implementation of air quality standards more closely approaching air quality goals; and (3) immediate adoption of both air quality standards meeting air quality goals and restrictive limitations sufficient to achieve them, but time phasing of the application of these limitations. As a further alternate to time phasing with respect to pollutants, one can time phase with respect to classes of sources, fuels, equipment, etc. The technological feasibility of meeting such standards is a prime consideration in selection of the appropriate alternative.

Economic considerations are sometimes cited as the argument for allowing the air quality standard to be relaxed in cities or industrial areas. The economic consideration of primary concern is the overall economy of the community, region, or nation. However, many things which benefit our overall economy cause hardship to certain individuals, industries, or regions. Thus lowering tariffs on certain imports may benefit our general economy while placing domestic producers of these products at a competitive disadvantage. The same is true of the application of air pollution limitations. Those who have to spend money to achieve a common standard are disadvantaged with respect to those who do not. However, such economic differences may be remedied by means other than the adoption of air pollution standards less stringent than required for the general welfare. These other means include subsidies and tax relief to ease the financial impact on a minority, as well as other means for spreading the cost to all the segments of the economy that are the ultimate beneficiaries. When the British create smokeless zones, they simultaneously provide a subsidy to cover part of the cost of the equipment changeover needed to achieve smokeless operation. The tax laws of several nations and states provide tax relief on expenditures for air pollution control.

There is a widespread delusion that stringent air pollution standards repel new industry whereas relaxed standards attract new industry. This is a fallacy. Los Angeles County, California, the county with the most stringent air pollution regulations in the world, has experienced an unprecedented growth. If anything, the promise of a future of clean air attracts rather than repels both employers and employees.

B. EXPRESSION OF AIR QUALITY STANDARDS

Air quality standards perforce must be expressed in the same terms as are used to categorize air quality data. Air quality data, its measurement, and the manner of its presentation are discussed in detail in Volumes I and II of this edition. At the risk of some repetition of this material, Fig. 3 is included here to show the relationship between atmospheric concentration of a pollutant, the averaging time, and the frequency of occurrence of each concentration-averaging time pair for a specific pollutant at a specific measuring site (8).

If there is only one source of the pollutant being measured, its plume will intercept the measuring site for only one wind direction; whereas if there are many sources of the pollutant uniformly distributed around the site, the measuring site will be subjected to the pollutant for all wind directions. Similarly for two sites with the same source-site relationship, the one with high winds and much vertical mixing will be subject to a different pollutant concentration distribution than the one with low wind velocity and little vertical mixing. These factors, plus variations in source strength, result in differences in slope and ordinate of the lines on charts of the Fig. 3 type for different pollutants and different sites.

If a community wished its present air quality to be its air quality standard, a chart such as Fig. 3 for each pollutant could be its standard for that pollutant since it describes that air quality. Alternatively, it could use one line from the figure, such as the maximum line or the 1% line, as its standard. If the community wished to set its standard at concentrations lower than its present air quality, its new air quality standard could be represented by shifting the ordinate scale of a Fig. 3 type representation of its present air quality. This is not identical to, but has the same effect, as the drawing of a line parallel to and below the ambient air concentration of a pollutant-frequency of occurrence plot on log-probability coordinates of data representing only one averaging time, which has been used in Nashville, Tennessee, St. Louis, Missouri, and other communities as the basis for proposed air quality standards.

Any point on a figure similar to Fig. 3 defined in terms of all three parameters—concentration, averaging time, and frequency of occur-

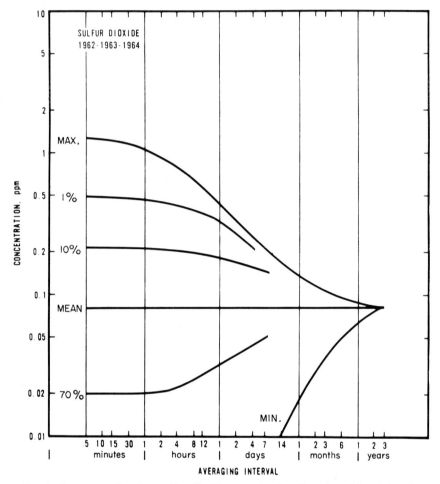

Fig. 3. Frequency of various sulfur dioxide concentrations for selected averaging times in Philadelphia, Pa., January 1, 1962, to December 31, 1964 (8).

rence—may be used to describe the atmosphere and hence may be used as an air quality standard. An air quality standard that does not include frequency of occurrence—in other words, which states a concentration-averaging time pair that shall not be exceeded—defines the point on the "maximum" line for the specified averaging time. An air quality standard which includes neither averaging time nor frequency of occurrence—in other words which states a concentration that shall not be exceeded—defines the point on the "maximum" line for an averaging time corresponding to that of the device or method specified to measure the concentration. If no device or method is specified, it must be assumed to refer to the averaging time of the measuring device or method most likely intended to be employed.

It should be recognized that when a standard states "not to be exceeded more than A times in any period of B hours" and when the averaging time, C, in minutes, is either stated or assumed, it is the same as stating not more than CA minutes in $60 B$ minutes: or less than $[100(60B - CA)]/60B$ percent. For example, a standard of not more than once in 8 hours (30-minute averaging time) computes as 94%. It should be noted that a concentration that is *not* allowed 94% of the time, *is* allowed 6% of the time and would therefore be the point on the 6 percentile line at 30-minute averaging time.

It should be noted that the arithmetic mean concentration of all the data is the same for all averaging times less than the span of the data record. The geometric mean (50% value on Fig. 3) of all the data is essentially the same for all averaging times. Therefore, standards stated in terms of annual mean—either arithmetic or geometric—require no further definition and yet specify an atmosphere with just as much specificity as other forms of definition.

If for the same pollutant and jurisdiction, the several air quality standard values in a sequence such as:

0.02 ppm, annual average

0.10 ppm, 24-hour average, not to be exceeded over 1% of the days in any 3-month period

0.20 ppm, not to be exceeded more than 1 hour in any 4 consecutive days

0.50 ppm, not to be exceeded for more than 5 minutes in any 8-hour period

are derived from different concentration-effect considerations, it may turn out that they are mutually inconsistent, i.e., that the values will not all fall on a figure of the type of Fig. 3 for any one monitoring site in the jurisdiction. However, this does not invalidate the use of such a sequence to set limits on all monitoring sites in the jurisdiction. Consideration should be given to having the values in the sequence as consistent with the concentration-averaging time-frequency of occurrence relationships in the real atmosphere of the jurisdiction as is possible without violating the air quality criteria on which the standards were based.

Brasser *et al.* (*1b*) have proposed that the Netherlands adopt as limits:

Percent occurrence per annum	50	2	0.3
mg/m^3 SO_2 (24 hour average)	0.15	0.3	0.5

In the foregoing, 50% occurrence is an annual average; 2% is essentially any 1 week per year and the 0.3% occurrence any 1 day per year. Intermediate values are determined by two straight lines connecting these three points plotted on log-probability coordinates.

C. TABULATION OF AIR QUALITY STANDARDS

Air quality standards are currently under development all over the world. Section 108 of the United States Air Quality Act of 1967 requires all 50 states to adopt air quality standards as rapidly as air quality control regions involving them are designated, and air quality criteria and recommended control techniques are made available to them by the federal government. Therefore no tabulation prepared in 1968, such as Tables V through VIII,* can hope to be up to date when read in any subsequent year.

In Tables V through VII, where no averaging time was specified in the published standard and one was assumed, this information is included in an appropriate footnote. Where a published standard lists standards for several averaging times, no effort was made to determine whether these several values are mutually consistent, i.e., would both be points on the same figure of a type similar to Fig. 3; or, where an averaging time was assumed, it would be similarly consistent. Although the headings of Table V are "Basic Standard" and "Permissible Standard," because of the foregoing, the distinction between "Basic" and "Permissible" is rather meaningless.

In addition to the standards of Tables V through VIII, which are based on concentrations in the air or on the ground, there is a form of standard that sets a limit on the fluoride level in grasses used or to be used consistently as forage or feed over a substantial period of time. In Florida, this limit is 40 ppm (dry weight basis). The equivalent value in Montana and Ontario is 35 ppm and in New York State is 35 ppm of soluble fluoride (as F) averaged over 4 consecutive months. In Florida, fluoride in the terminal 6 inches of gladiolus foliage may not exceed 35 ppm on a dry weight basis. In essence, these standards use the affected vegetation as the sampling device. Montana also limits gaseous fluorides to 0.0003 $mg/cm^2/28$ days as measured by the calcium formate paper technique. The equivalent limit in Ontario is 0.04 $mg/cm^2/30$ days.

The state of California standard for "adverse" level of particulate matter in the air is "Sufficient to reduce visibility to less than 3 miles when relative humidity is less than 70 percent."

A state of Colorado standard for particulate matter in the air is 0.5

---

* Tables V, VI, VII, and VIII begin on pp. 663, 679, 680, and 681 respectively.

coefficient of haze per 1000 lineal feet of air (CoH) units (3-month average). A CoH unit is a measure of the transmission of light through a filter paper through which a quantity of air has been filtered.

The Missouri Air Conservation Commission Soiling Index standard for the St. Louis Metropolitan area is 0.4 CoH per 1000 lineal feet-annual geometric mean; its standard (and that of the state of Montana) for "reactive" sulfur oxides as measured by the "sulfation" of lead peroxide candles is:

0.25 mg SO_3/100 cm^2/day, maximum annual average
0.5 mg SO_3/100 cm^2/day, maximum month

and its standard for certain settleable acids and alkaline substances is that the difference between downwind and upwind fallout be less than 5 spots on a 15 cm diameter thymol blue and ammonia water-treated yellow gelatine surface.

The Ontario limits for soiling index and sulfation are given in the following tabulation:

| Land use area | COH's/1000 ft of air | | mg SO_3/1000 m^2/day (30 days) |
	Annual geometric mean	90% of 2-hour samplings on a 24-hour basis	
Industrial and commercial	1.1	2.2	1.0
Residential and rural	0.45	1.0	0.4

D. ALERT LEVELS

Alert levels are concentrations of pollutants indicative of approach to danger. There are three such levels promulgated by the Los Angeles County Air Pollution Control District (Table IX).* The first, an initial warning level, the second, a signal for the curtailment of certain significant sources, and the third, the level at which emergency action must be taken. A somewhat similar scheme is in use in New York-New Jersey metropolitan area (Table X).*

The U.S. Air Quality Act of 1967 includes in Section 105(a)(3) a requirement that before any planning grant be awarded any air pollution control agency, the agency must give assurance that it is capable of developing "a system of alerts to avert and reduce the risk of situations in

* See p. 682.

which there may be imminent and serious danger to the public health or welfare from air pollutants." Therefore the number of American communities promulgating alert levels should be expected to increase rapidly.

The Technische Uberwachungs-Verein (TUV) of the Landes (State) Bavaria has developed a system for SO_2 control in the area of Munich in which, starting from a baseline of 24-hour average of 0.4 mg/m³ with not more than five 30-minute periods per 24 hours in excess of 0.75 mg/m³, major industrial emissions of SO_2 (principally from refineries) are to be decreased 20% for each increase of 0.1 mg/m³ in 24-hour average atmospheric SO_2 level or each increase of five 30-minute periods per 24 hours in excess of 0.75 mg/m³.

V.   Emission Standards

A. Procedures Used in Setting Emission Standards

An emission standard is a limit on the amount or concentration of a pollutant emitted from a source. The concentration of pollutant in the effluent may be stated subjectively, in terms of its appearence to the eye or its odor, as determined by the nose; or objectively in terms of its weight or volume. Emission standards may be derived from air quality considerations; process, fuel and equipment considerations; or both. Emission standards sometimes reflect economic, sociological, and political considerations in addition to those which are technological. In some cases, we have the technological ability to control certain pollutants, but are not doing so for economic, sociological, or political reasons. However, despite considerable economic, sociological, and political pressure to more stringently regulate certain emissions, we are not doing so because we lack adequate technological ability.

1. Derivation from Air Quality Standards

Let us assume for the sake of this discussion that (1) a community air quality standard for a pollutant has been set at a level low enough to prevent any injury to vegetation; (2) this level is lower than the human or animal thresholds; (3) in community "A" the ambient air level is considerably below the community air quality standard; and (4) in community "B" the ambient air level is above the community air quality standard but below the human or animal thresholds. Community "A" may elect to maintain its favorable air quality by setting emission standards more stringent than needed to meet air quality standards. This decision imposes an economic burden on new installations greater than needed to meet air quality standards. Conversely, community "B" may elect to maintain the status quo and allow vegetation damage to occur in the community to avoid the economic burden needed to meet an air quality standard based on such damage.

a. Single Sources (see also Chapter 8, Vol. I). If one assumes all possible combinations of wind direction, wind velocity, atmospheric stability, and distance from a single elevated stack, or a group of adjacent elevated stacks which may be considered to act as a single stack, there will be one combination for which (for a specific effluent emission rate and effective stack height) ground level concentration will be greatest. By setting this maximum ground level concentration equal to the air quality standard, the emission limit for the stack or group of stacks may be computed. Although research meteorologists are working to improve the accuracy of this type of computation, the accuracy presently obtainable is good enough to allow use of this methodology for major single sources.

This procedure preempts all the allowable emission for this one stack. If another stack emitting the same pollutant has the proper combination of stack height and distance from the point of maximum ground level concentration of the one stack so that its point of maximum ground level concentration is the same as that for the one stack, these concentrations may be additive. If then the emissions for each stack were computed on the basis of maximum ground level concentration equaling the air quality standard, the resulting ground level concentration could be twice the air quality standard.

When a single source is built there is no way of knowing in advance the number of additional sources that will ultimately share with it the capacity of the atmosphere to dilute pollutants to the air quality standard. There are several possible resolutions to this dilemma. One is the "flexible" emission standard that in the foregoing case allows the single plant an emission limit computed on the basis of its being the only source until the second plant is built, after which *both* plants must meet a revised emission limit half as large as the original limit, and so forth, as a third and fourth, etc. source is built. There is, in this approach, no "grandfather" clause protecting the right of the earlier-built plant or plants to maintain their earlier emissions, but rather they would, as each new source is built, have to decrease their emission. This is an unwieldy approach and difficult to administer but fits certain real situations that need resolution.

Another approach is to make the assumption that there will eventually be X sources; therefore the computation of emission standard should be based initially on the ground level concentration from any source not exceeding one X^{th} of the air quality standard. This penalizes the first few sources but is easier to administer.

A third approach preempts a certain portion (e.g., 90%) of the air quality standard for multiple small sources (see next section), either existing or future, and allows the use of the remainder (e.g., 10%) as the basis for computations by the foregoing procedures for the few large sources.

All of these procedures result in a table or chart to describe the emission standard, rather than a single number. The reason for this is that the computations involved have as variables emission rate, effective stack height, distance, and meteorological values. Dr. John Middleton inserted into the record of the Senate hearings on the Air Quality Act of 1967 (8a) the following example:

> The following is an example of a hypothetical national emission standard for an industrial process:
>
> For this example, we have selected sulfur dioxide emissions from sulfuric acid manufacturing plants using the contact process. On the basis of air quality criteria for sulfur oxides, we selected hypothetical ambient air quality standards for sulfur dioxide of 0.10 p.p.m. (parts of sulfur dioxide per million parts of air) for a 24-hour average; 0.25 p.p.m. for a 1-hour average; and 0.5 p.p.m. for a 5-minute average. It was assumed that the maximum ground concentration of sulfur dioxide attributable to the source to be regulated should not exceed 35 percent of the air quality standard in an area of moderate or low pollution; and 20 percent in an area of relatively high pollution.
>
> Based on the above discussion and considering available technically and economically feasible means for reducing emissions and using meteorological dispersion formulas, the attached table [A] of allowable emissions of sulfur dioxide and minimum stack heights was prepared for plants of various sizes located in each of two types of areas as defined in table [B].

TABLE A

HYPOTHETICAL EMISSION STANDARDS AND STACK HEIGHT REQUIREMENTS
FOR CONTACT PROCESS SULFURIC ACID PLANTS

Plant capacity (tons of 100% sulfuric acid per 24-hr. day)	Maximum allowable emission of SO_2 in tons per day by type of area[a]		Minimum effective stack height in feet[b] by type of area[a]	
	Type A	Type B	Type A	Type B
100	2	1.5	145	150
300	6	4.5	230	270
500	10	7.5	280	320
700	14	10.5	325	370
900	18	13.5	350	400

[a] See table B for definition.

[b] Minimum effective stack heights can be decreased if emissions are less than the maximum allowable. The decrease in effective stack height will be in direct proportion to the extent to which emissions are less than the maximum allowable.

TABLE B

DEFINITION OF AREAS[a]

Type of area	Sulfur dioxide concentration parts per million[b]			Sulfur dioxide emission density tons per square miles per day[c]	Population in 1000's[d]
	24 hour average	1 hour average	5 minute average		
A	0.0–0.05	0.0–0.12	0.0–0.25	0.0–1.3	Less than 200.
B	Greater than 0.05	Greater than 0.12	Greater than 0.25	Greater than 1.3	Greater than 200.

[a] Use sulfur dioxide concentrations if available; if not, use emission density; if neither is available, use population.

[b] Maximum values at any point within 1 mile of the plant after subtracting the calculated concentration attributed to the source to be regulated.

[c] Average for the area within 3 miles of the plant to be regulated on a day of maximum emissions, not including the plant to be regulated.

[d] Population of the standard metropolitan area, or, if not in such an area, of the county in which the source is located.

In some areas it may be necessary to require even more restrictive emission control. It may also be necessary to provide for pollution reduction or maintenance of existing levels by means of land use controls and emission reduction requirements applicable to other sources of pollution. This responsibility would rest with State and local governments.

This hypothetical standard, for the sake of brevity, does not include many of the details that might need to be incorporated in an actual standard.

These same considerations apply to setting emission limits on a large source surrounded by a buffer zone, where the computations are based on the air quality immediately beyond "the fence" surrounding the property, or the equivalent thereof where there is no actual fence. It is not sufficient that the land "within the fence" be owned by the owner of the source at the time of setting the emission limits. There must also be assurance that this buffer zone land cannot later be converted to other than buffer zone use without a concomitant change in applicable emission limits. In the case of emission limits based on ground level air quality in which the land where maximum ground level concentration occurs is in the same ownership as the source, it may be argued that the computation of emission limits should be based upon application of the air quality standard only to the land beyond such common ownership. However, it is use, not ownership, that is the important thing. If the use of the land contemplates the presence of people, the air quality standard should be applied to it for the computation of the emission limit. An exception would be reasonable only if by covenant, deed, zoning restrictions, or stipulation the land in question were converted to a true buffer zone. Since it is unreasonable to expect a control agency to recompute emission limits each time the use of a parcel of property is changed, the practicable procedure for incorporation in regulations is to assume the presence of people and buildings in all land surrounding a source unless such use is legally restricted.

b. Multiple Sources. Very little work has been done on relating emission limits for multiple sources of varied category to air quality standards. Since there is little precedent to follow, innovation will be required. One approach that suggests itself for the general case involving gases or fine particles requires first the preparation of as complete a one-year emission inventory as possible and as complete a multi-year air pollution meteorological analysis of the jurisdiction as possible. A computer program would then be used which, for each pollutant, would compute separately for several ground-level locations, the potential maximum 24-hour and 1-hour pollutant concentration within a year; select the specific day and hour when this maximum concentration would occur; and direct the computer to prepare a table listing the contribution of each source category to the total emission during that day and that hour. The total emission is that from all categories at the same time, not the sum of the maximum emission from each category when these maxima occur at different times. The potential maximum concentration is that which would occur with the concurrence of the worst meteorological conditions and the greatest emissions that can be predicted to occur simultaneously. Tables of this type would be prepared for the latest year for which there are emission data and would be projected ahead 5 and 10 years to assess future levels. The above approach assumes the availability of multi-year air pollution meteorological data and the absence of multi-year air quality measurements. Where air quality measurements exist over a span of years comparable to that for the air pollution meteorological data, measured values, rather than computed ones, should be used to select the day and hour for which emissions should be tabulated.

An alternate to the use of the worst day or hour is to base computed or measured values on the value that will be exceeded by not more than 1% of all days or all hours, which will be called here the 99% values and the 99% day and hour.

The second step is to compare the maximum or 99% concentration values computed or measured, as the case may be, with air quality standards. This comparison will allow, by direct ratio, the computation of total allowable emission beyond which air quality standards would be exceeded during the worst day or hour or the 99% day or hour. The third step is to allocate among the categories the total allowable emission. The final step in the computation of emission limits is the allocation of the emission allowed each category in an equitable manner among all units in the category.

Projections into the future assume the same technology as is used at present. Allocations make the same assumption. Therefore, as technology changes—or can be forced to change by changes in emission standards—projections, allocations, and resulting emission limits will require revision from time to time, and changes in air quality standards will have the same effect.

The steps described above use theoretical or empirical procedures which are currently available, albeit requiring much refinement to achieve the level of accuracy ultimately desired. Up till now these procedures have been developed and used separately. What is needed is to combine them as a systematic method for arriving at emission standards for a community.

Since we have the know-how to compute separately emission limits for the single source and the multiple source situation, it follows that by combining these computations we have the means to treat real situations in real communities in which emissions from major single sources are superimposed on a background of multiple-source emissions.

The above procedure does not take into account chemical or photochemical reaction among pollutants. Several changes in procedure would be needed to set limits on pollutants where air quality standards are based upon the effect of reaction products. First, the computer program would not maximize the time periods of maximum concentrations of the raw pollutant, but rather would tabulate the raw material inventory during time periods which maximize the atmospheric concentration of reaction products. Second, in determining the amount of total raw material permitted in the air, the chemistry of the principal reactions would have to be considered. Last, in allocating this total amount among categories, the ratios of reactants produced by these categories will have to be considered. Although we can specify what the computer must do to account for photochemical reactions, we don't yet have the sophistication to write all the required programs.

2. *Derivation from Rollback and Distance Proportional Considerations*

Rollback procedures to establish emission standards assume three points in time, an earlier time of lower (and presumably acceptable) pollution, the present time, and a future time. A computation estimates the number of source units at the three time periods. Assuming uniform emission per unit source for the several time periods, an estimate based on the present pollutant level is made of the past and future levels.

Finally, the reduction in emission per unit of source necessary to roll back the future pollutant level to that of the past is computed. This was one of the procedures used in setting the California Motor Vehicle Exhaust Emission Standards (2).

The distance proportional approach is used where there is a single dominant source and the fall-off of either pollutant concentration, or its effects, with distance from the source is known. First, it is determined that the concentration or effects at distance D_2 from the source are tolerable, but those at D_1, which are closer to the source, are not.

On this basis, the required decrease in emission and the new emission standard are computed by the known mathematical relationship between pollution concentration and distance from the source.

3. *Derivation from Process and Equipment Considerations*

The direct approach in setting an emission standard is to ask the question: "What are the emissions from the best constructed and best operated plants (or, alternatively, well constructed and operated plants) in this category?" and then rationalize that this performance should set the standard for all such plants. In an analogous approach the first step is to determine for a range of plants from best to worse the pollutant loading of gases leaving the process at a point prior to their passing through any emission control equipment such as dust separator or gas scrubber. The next step is to compute what the emission from each would be if treated by an appropriate unit of emission control equipment. The result will depend upon the collection efficiency assumed for the control equipment. The old adage that "one can have as much control as he is willing to pay for" becomes the test in setting the assumed efficiency high or low. A good combination for such computation is to assume control equipment of better than average efficiency applied to a plant of average control equipment inlet loading.

One commonly used criterion for emission standards is to require the use of the best practicable means to control emissions. The word "practicable" implies not only technological practicability but also economic, sociological, and political practicability. Best practicable means derive not only from the technology within an industry but also from the borrowing of the technology of one industry to improve that of another. Thus, best practicable means utilize either the control actually achieved in the best plants in the industry or that which could be achieved by borrowing the best technology of other industries. Under this concept the emission standard may be made more stringent as the state of the art of control of the process improves over the years. The question as to the extent these more stringent standards should be made retroactive to installations that were in compliance prior to changing the standard but not afterward is provocative. It is more difficult to argue that emission standards be made retroactive when they are based upon process and equipment considerations than when they are based upon air quality considerations. The installation of improved controls in either an existing or a new plant may, by showing an improvement in best practicable means, serve to escalate the emission standard. Should it be shown that an emission standard based upon best practicable means does not result in air which meets an air quality standard, there is no force inherent in the best practicable means approach that is likely to bridge the gap.

B. TABULATION OF EMISSION STANDARDS

The anticipated development of many additional air quality standards noted in Section IV,C, will undoubtedly generate the development of many new emission standards. In the United States, the Air Quality Act of 1967 requires the 50 states, when they adopt air quality standards for air quality control regions, to also adopt a plan for their implementation and enforcement. Such plans will in most cases include emission standards. Therefore tabulations, such as those in this section, are bound to be incomplete almost the day after their publication.

1. *Objective Standards*

Objective standards are expressed as weight or volume of emitted pollutant per unit volume or unit weight of the carrier gas, or per unit of process quantity. Standards on a "per unit volume of carrier gas" basis must be further specified as to the gas temperature and pressure to which volumes are to be reduced. Unless otherwise noted, standards in this chapter are for 760 mm Hg − 15 °C (approx. 30 inches Hg − 60 °F). To account for incidental, accidental, or deliberate dilution with air prior to measurement, it is customary in the case of combustion effluents to specify either the percent excess air or the percent CO_2 to which gas quantity must be reduced.

The objective emission standards listed in Tables XI through XV* are expressed both in their original units and in uniform units to allow comparison. The New York State Air Pollution Control Board has adopted a scheme which specifies the degree of air cleaning required in ranges that are not amenable to incorporation in the above-noted tables or figures. These are shown in Tables XVI and XVII.*

* Tables XI–XVII begin on the following pages: XI, 683; XII, 689; XIII, 690; XIV, 691; XV, 692; XVI, 700; XVII, 701.

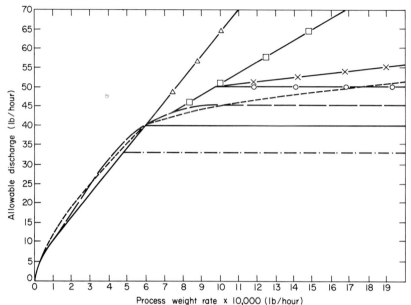

FIG. 4. American emission standards for process dusts. Legend: (—— · —— ·) New York, N.Y., light manufacturing district. (—— O —— O) New York, N.Y., heavy manufacturing district—new installations. (— □ —— □) New York, N.Y., heavy manufacturing district—existing installations. [Use for New York State from 6 to 10 × 10,000 (lb/hour).] (—— △ —— △) Riverside County, Calif. (—— —— ——) San Bernardino County, Calif. (- - - - - - -) Bay Area Air Pollution Control District, San Francisco, Calif.[a] (————) Los Angeles and Orange County Air Pollution Control Districts and City of Riverside, Calif.; Florida; Sarasota, Fla.; Providence, R. I.[b] (—— × —— ×) New York State.

EXTENSION OF VALUES BEYOND FIG. 4

	Allowable discharge (lb/hour)			
Process weight (10,000 lb/hour)	Bay Area A.P.C.A. Calif.[a]	New York, N.Y. heavy mfg. dist. existing installations	Riverside County, Calif.	N.Y.[c] State
25	—	92	154	58.2
50	—	145	304	64.3
75	—	192	454	68.4
100	69	235	604	71.1
200	77.6	—	1204	78.3
500	—	—	—	88.1
600	92.7	—	3604	—

[a] Also Dade County, Florida; St. Louis Metropolitan Area, Missouri; Michigan; Illinois; use for New York State to 6 × 10,000 (lb/hour).

[b] Montgomery and Prince Georges Counties, and Rockville, Maryland; Alexandria, Arlington, Falls Church, and Fairfax County, Virginia—to 60,000 lb/hour:—Beyond—0.066% of process weight in lb/hour, except in Maryland where it is: 55(process weight t/hr)$^{0.11}$-40.

[c] For environmental rating B and C see Table XVI (see also Table XII).

The objective emission standard most widely used in the United States is that for total solid particulate pollutants (fly ash) in effluent gases from the combustion of fuels. It is therefore the one in which trend is most easily observed (Table XIX).* It will be noted that there is a marked downward trend in this emission standard.

In addition to the objective emission standards that are presented here in tabular form, there are those that were issued in graphical form, or which, even though originally issued in tabular form, are preferably presented in graphical form. Several jurisdictions control process emissions by limiting the allowable discharge, in pounds per hour, for various process weight rates, i.e., total hourly weight of all materials introduced into a process operation, including solid fuels, but excluding liquid fuels, gaseous fuels, and combustion air (Fig. 4). A special provision of the Bay Area regulations (which has also been adopted by other jurisdictions) provides that compliance with the process weight regulation noted above need not require the effluent gas to be cleaner than is set forth in Table XIII. It will also be noted from Table XII that Los Angeles County limits emission to 0.3 grains per cubic foot STP; Riverside County to 0.4. The states of Illinois and New York have special process weight tables for jobbing foundries (Table XVIIIA),* and the state of West Virginia has a special process weight table for hot mix asphalt plants (Table XVIIIB).*

The states of New Jersey, Pennsylvania, and Texas limit particulate matter emission depending upon stack height and distance from the stack to the nearest plant property line (Figs. 5–8). Stack height is "effective" stack height, the sum of physical stack height and computed plume rise, provided the latter computation is in form satisfactory to the authorities. The dividing line between coarse and fine particles is 44 μ diameter in New Jersey; and 25 μ diameter (quartz particle) in Pennsylvania and Texas. With specific regard to the New Jersey chart for fine particles, the actual emission permitted is determined by multiplying

FIG. 5. Basic emission for coarse solid particles—Section 2.14, Chapter VII, New Jersey Air Pollution Control Code (p. 626).

FIG. 6. Basic emission for fine solid particles—Section 2.15, Chapter VII, New Jersey Air Pollution Control Code (p. 627).

FIG. 7. Particle fall—Guide for Compliance with Regulation IV, Air Pollution Commission, Pennsylvania Department of Health (p. 628).

FIG. 8A. Suspended Particulate Matter—Guide for Compliance with Regulation IV. Air Pollution Commission, Pennsylvania Department of Health (p. 629).

FIG. 8B. Suspended Particulate Matter—Regulations of the Texas Air Control Board; Type A—residential or recreational; Type B—business or commercial; Type C—industrial; Type D—Areas which do not fall within type A, B, or C land use and which are not normally occupied by people, excluding a rural residence and the area within 100 ft thereof (p. 630).

* Tables XVIIIA and B appear on p. 702; Table XIX, on p. 703.

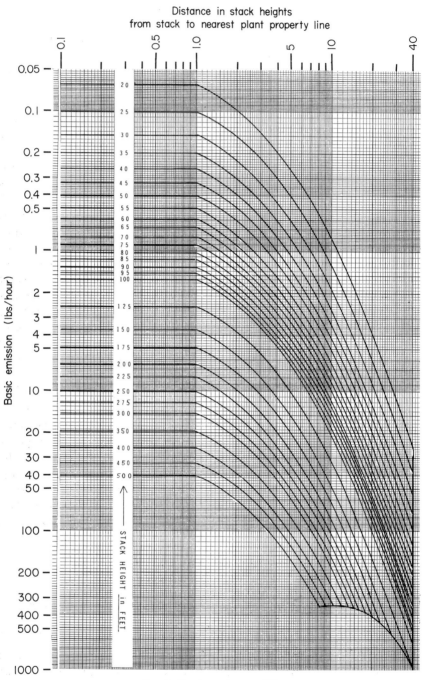

FIG. 5. See legend on p. 625.

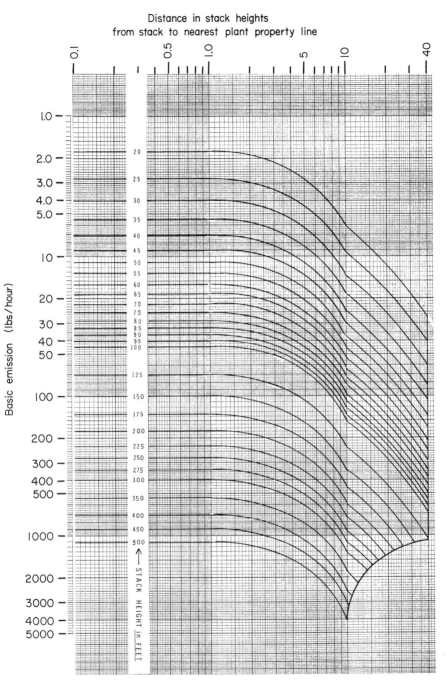

Fig. 6. See legend on p. 625.

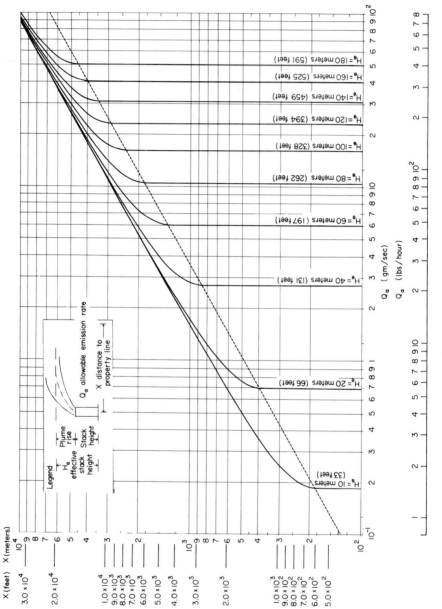

Fig. 7. See legend on p. 625.

628

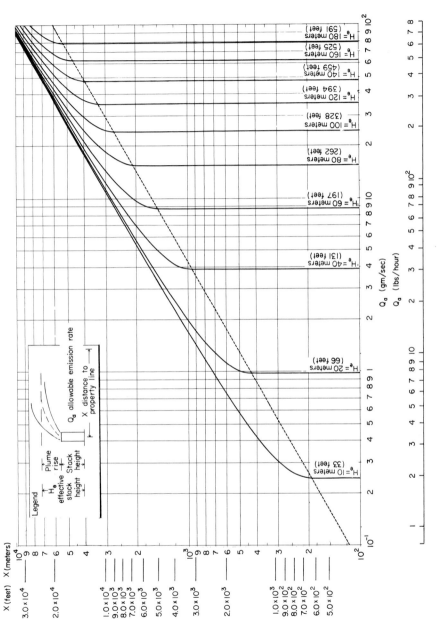

Fig. 8A. See legend on p. 625.

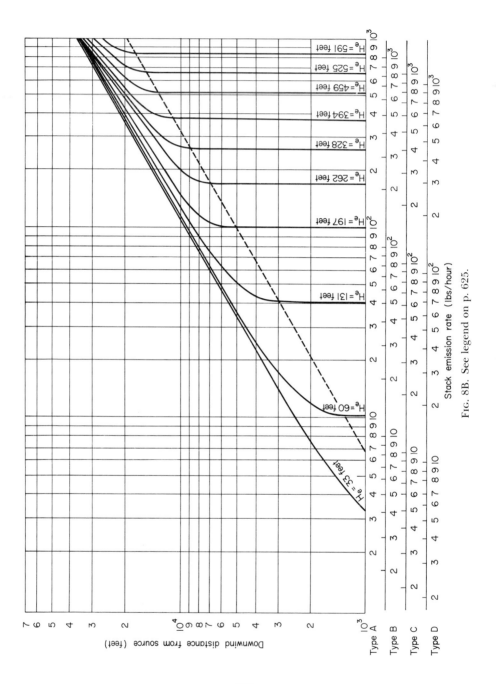

FIG. 8B. See legend on p. 625.

630

the basic emission, read from the chart, by the appropriate effect factor from Table XX.* The New Jersey charts do not apply to emissions from the combustion of solid fuel or refuse, which are differently regulated. The Pennsylvania and Texas charts apply to all classes of sources. There is no Texas chart for coarse particles.

One of the Texas suspended particulate matter emission standards is that the difference between samples taken downwind and upwind of the source shall not (in μg/m^3) exceed, for residential and recreational areas—100; for commercial and business areas—125; for industrial areas—150; and for vacant, range, and agricultural land, except within 100 feet of a residence—175. The number of hours during which samples must be taken to establish the above values depends upon the extent that the 1-hour average values exceed the above values, as follows:

Amount average 1 hour value exceeds above value (μg/m^3)	less than 100	100–300	over 300
Number of hours of sample needed in 24 hours	8	5	3

The other Texas suspended particulate matter emission standard is Fig. 8(b). Also in Texas, particulate matter emissions may not be so great as to impair visibility on urban roads to 1100 feet and, on rural roads, to 2400 feet.

The German Federal Republic has different particulate matter emission limits for total emission, emission of particles larger than 10 μ diameter, existing installations, and new installations (8b). For each of these four conditions there is an allowable emission, in milligrams per cubic meter (STP), which varies with exhaust gas flow, in cubic meters (STP) per hour (Fig. 9). The official fly ash limit in West Germany is set by Fig. 10, which also shows the fly ash standard of the Kommission Reinhaltung der Luft (VDI 2091, 2092, 2093, 2096, 2097, and 2098) (5).

For the regulation of fly ash emission from fuel-burning installations, the form of chart, or tabular sliding scale, most common in the United States varies allowable emission, in pounds per million Btu heat input to the furnace, with total heat input in millions of Btu per hour (Fig. 11). Figure 12 shows a similar chart for Michigan, and Muskegon County, Michigan, in which the abscissa is thousand pounds of steam per hour and the ordinate is pounds of particulate matter per 1000 pounds of flue gas at 50% excess air. Other fly ash emission limits for Michigan communities (Table XXI)* are unique in that they have different "design"

* Table XX appears on p. 703; Table XXI on p. 704.

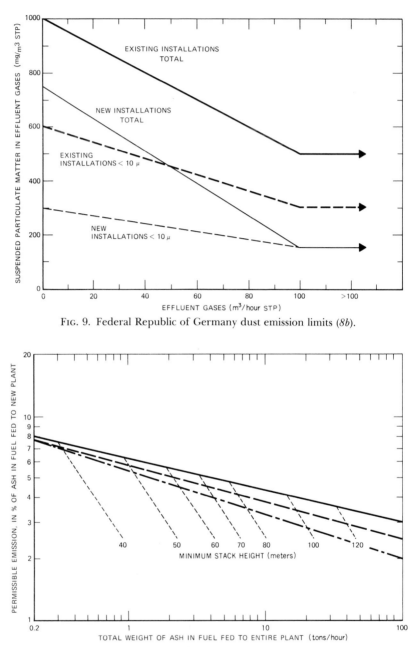

Fig. 9. Federal Republic of Germany dust emission limits (*8b*).

Fig. 10. West Germany fly ash emission standard for new coal-fired boiler furnaces (*8b*). and VDI Richtlinien (VDI 2091, 2092, 2093, 2096, 2097, and 2098). (————) VDI Richtlinien − ≦66% of ash retained in furnace; (— — —) VDI Richtlinien − >66% of ash retained in furnace; (— · — -) Federal Republic of Germany Standard; (- - - - - - -) VDI Richtlinien − Minimum Stack Height—meters.

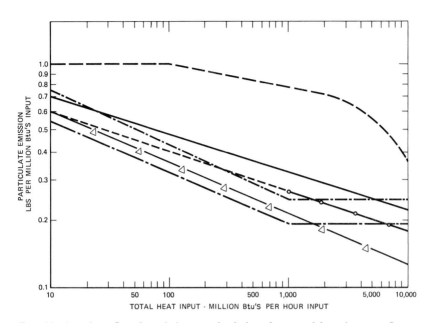

FIG. 11. American fly ash emission standards based on total heat input to furnace. Legend: — — — New Jersey (existing installations). — · — · — · West Virginia (existing installations). ———— New Jersey (new installations). - - - - - - - Federal installations;[a] St. Louis Metropolitan Area, Missouri, Maryland (existing installations), New York, N.Y.[b] — ○ — ○ St. Louis Metropolitan Area, Missouri; Maryland (existing installations), New York, N.Y.[b] —— - —— West Virginia (new installations); —— △ —— △ Maryland (new installations).

[a] Also must comply with local regulations when more stringent.

[b] Montgomery and Prince Georges Counties, and Rockville, Maryland; Alexandria, Arlington, Falls Church, and Fairfax County, Virginia (less than 10 million Btu/hour in fuel = 0.6 lb/million Btu). In Rockville and Montgomery County over 10 million Btu/hour—Emission in (lb/million Btu) = 8.58 $I^{-0.165}$ where I is in Btu/hour.

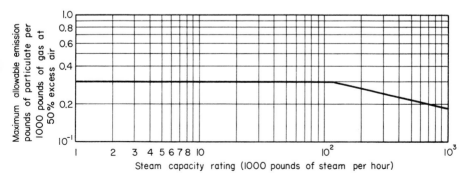
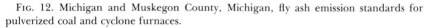

FIG. 12. Michigan and Muskegon County, Michigan, fly ash emission standards for pulverized coal and cyclone furnaces.

633

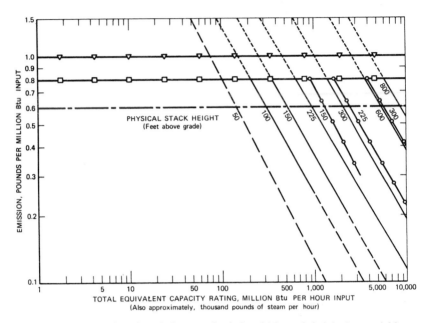

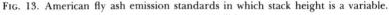

FIG. 13. American fly ash emission standards in which stack height is a variable.

(—— ▽ —— ▽)   South Carolina (existing facilities).

(—— □ —— □)   Illinois (existing facilities outside Standard Metropolitan Statistical Areas, or SMSAS); South Carolina (new facilities).

(– —— – ——)   Illinois (existing facilities in SMSAS and new facilities outside SMSAS); St. Louis Metropolitan Area, Missouri.

(—— —— ——)   St. Louis Metropolitan Area, Missouri.

(- - - - - - -)   St. Louis Metropolitan Area, Missouri.

(——————————)   Illinois (for single stacks); St. Louis Metropolitan Area, Missouri; South Carolina (predominantly residential areas).

(—— ○ —— ○)   South Carolina (predominantly nonresidential and industrial areas).

Conditions: (1) substantially flat terrain; (2) 12% of heat input up stack; (3) no emission greater than 60-μ diameter allowed (for South Carolina this reads "substantially no emission . . ."). In St. Louis Metropolitan Area, Missouri, all installations with a heat input of 5 million Btu per hour or more must have dust collector(s) with a collection efficiency of at least 85%.

For Delaware, the maximum emission for industrial areas is 0.8 lb/million Btu input; for other areas it is 0.6. The 150-ft stack industrial area limit is roughly equivalent to the higher valued 150-ft line; the 100, 150, and 600-ft stack limits for other areas are roughly equivalent to the lower valued lines for these heights. The 100-ft stack industrial area limit is roughly equivalent to the lower valued 225-ft line. The limits for 225 and 300 ft industrial areas, and 225, 300, and 450 other area stacks are jagged lines not on Fig. 13.

and "operating" limits. Figure 13 shows the charts for Illinois, South Carolina and the St. Louis, Missouri, metropolitan area in which stack height is a variable. These are similar to the American Society of Mechanical Engineers Standard APS-1 "Control of Dust Emission—Combustion for Indirect Heat Exchangers" (9) except that the horizontal "cap" line of APS-1 is at 0.8 pound per million Btu input.

The Grit and Dust (i.e., Fly Ash) emission limits recommended by British Ministry of Housing and Local Government, the Scottish Development Department, and the Welsh Office in their 1967 publication "Grit and Dust" (9a) are shown in Figs. 14A and B.

The Italian fly ash emission limit (9b) is: $q = 0.25(1 + A)$ where q is concentration in gm/m^3 and A is a factor derived from Fig. 15.

The German Federal Republic emission standards for new cupolas (Fig. 16) are the same as in Kommission Reinhaltung der Luft (5) specification, VDI 2288.

The New Jersey standards for allowable emission for sulfur compounds from processes other than fuel burning listed in Table XI, incorporate stack height standards that are discussed in Section VI,B.

The standards for Czechoslovakia incorporate both a stack height variable and, for emissions other than fly ash and SO_2 from combustion sources, a unique procedure for computing permissible emission from the air quality standard (Table XXII).*

2. Subjective Standards

The use of the Ringelmann chart and other means for measuring the optical opacity of smoke emissions is discussed in Chapter 29, Vol. II.

The usual regulatory statement applying emission opacity standards prohibits an "emission of a density of A or greater for more than B minutes in any period of C minutes." The principal consideration for establishing period C is the mobility of the source. A stack of a building or factory is stationary and can be observed over a long time, whereas a moving locomotive, marine vessel, or automotive vehicle can be observed from a stationary observation point on the ground for only a short time before it travels out of the observer's view. For stationary sources, the longer the time interval used for C, the stricter the regulation, particularly if the emission time B is cumulative within time period C. The concepts of regulations based upon time B within time C and of time allowances made for smoke released when starting fires had their historical basis in the nature of smoke emission from steam locomotives and hand-fired soft coal industrial boiler furnaces, and represented a compromise to meet the objections of operators of that class of equipment to more stringent regulations. Although the reasons for these compromises have largely disappeared along with the class of equipment they were intended to regulate, their legacy remains embedded in regulatory legislation. When time interval C is long, as it should be for present-day conditions of continuous fuel feed to fuel-burning devices,

* See p. 705.

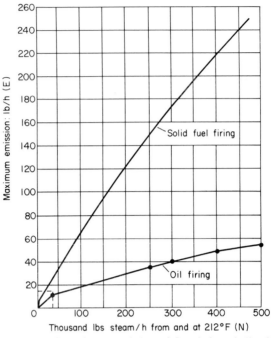

FIG. 14A. Recommended maximum emission of fly ash from boiler furnaces in Great Britain (9a). The following coordinates define those portions of the curves within the dotted box at the origin.

Solid fuel firing:

N	$E =$
0–5	$1.4N$
5–25	$7 + [0.65(N - 5)]$

Oil firing: $E = 0.28N$

allowed emission time B becomes essentially an allowance for operating emergencies. A typical combination of A, B, and C as found in the Cleveland, Ohio, ordinance is:

Source	A Emission- Ringelmann No.	B Time permitted	C Observation time
Stationary plants	2	10 minutes	1 hour
Stationary plants	3	6 minutes	8 hours
Locomotives	3	1/2 minute	4 minutes
Steamships[a]	3	6 minutes	1 hour

[a] This applies principally to steamships at dock, under which circumstances they are essentially stationary plants.

The standard for federal facilities in the United States is No. 1

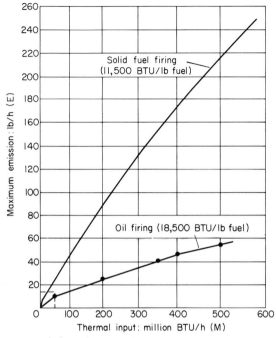

FIG. 14B. Recommended maximum emission of fly ash from indirect or heating furnaces where the material being heated does not contribute to the emission—Great Britain (*9a*). The following coordinates define those portions of the curves within the dotted box at the origin.

Solid fuel firing:

M	E =
0–7.5	0.93M
7.5–40	7 + [0.4(M − 7.5)]

Oil firing: $E = 0.22M$

Ringelmann for new units and No. 2 for existing units, except during startup, cleaning of fires, or soot blowing.

In the early history of smoke regulation, only industrial and locomotive stacks were regulated. Later, when all stacks were regulated, the householder was accorded less stringent limits because it was felt that, with hand-fired coal-burning equipment, he would have more difficulty meeting strict limits than would the industrial plant. The modern approach to varying limits for different categories is to recognize the present availability of smokeless methods for heating homes and hot water, e.g., the following excerpt from the smoke emission regulations of New Haven, Conn.

(*1*) Not darker than No. 1 Ringelmann for domestic installations for heating and hot water in one and two-family dwellings.

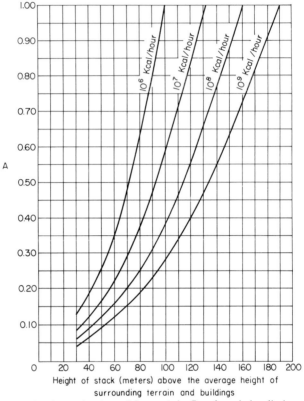

FIG. 15. Figure for determination of factor A in fly ash emission limit computation—(Italy) (*9b*).

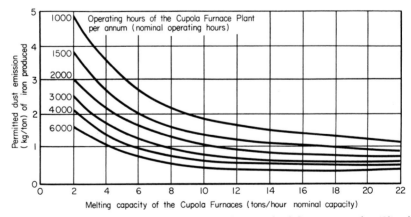

FIG. 16. Federal Republic of Germany emission standard for new cupolas (*8b*); also VDI 2288 (*5*).

(2) Not darker than No. 1 Ringelmann for heating and hot water installations in apartments, office buildings, etc., but densities not greater than No. 3 Ringelmann are permitted for not more than four minutes in any 30 minutes

(3) Not darker than No. 2 Ringelmann for all other stationary installations, but densities not greater than No. 3 are permitted for not more than four minutes in any 30 minutes

The following tabulation shows both the increase in the number of U.S. communities regulating smoke by emission opacity (Ringelmann number) and the tendency, over the past 25 years, toward stricter smoke emission limits:

Emission greater than this Ringelmann number number prohibited[a]	Date of enactment				Status as of end of 1965
	Before 1940	1940– 1949	1950– 1959	1960– 1965	
#3	61	(−1)	(−2)	(−7)	51
#2	14	13	57	20	104
#1	0	0	0	2	2
Total (net)	75	12	55	15	157

[a] Except, in some cases, for special circumstances such as sootblowing, starting cold fires, etc.

The smoke emission regulations applicable to stationary installations in Great Britain are shown in Table XXIII.* Those applying to marine vessels are in a separate regulation (878-1958). The German Federal Republic allows 5 minutes of not greater than No. 3 Ringelmann during firing up; at all other times No. 2 cannot be exceeded. The soot content of flue gas from oil-fired installations is limited to No. 2 on the Bacharach filter paper blackening scale for light oils, and No. 3 for heavy oils.

Several U.S. communities† have adopted "equivalent opacity" regulations, i.e., which apply opacity measurements based on the Ringelmann scale to emissions other than smoke (as customarily defined) and of colors other than black (or gray). While the opacity of a smoke emission is a poor measure of its gravimetric particle loading, the opacity of a smoke-free fly ash emission correlates quite well with its gravimetric loading (Table XXIV).* A special Bay Area (California) provision allows power plant stacks (oil-fired) which exceed the opacity standard of not

* See p. 706.

† California (entire state); Chicago, Illinois; Cleveland, Ohio; Colorado (entire state); Cook County, Illinois; Dade County, Florida; East Chicago, Indiana; East St. Louis, Illinois; Florida (entire state); Gary, Indiana; Hammond, Indiana; Jefferson County, Kentucky; Kentucky (entire state); Muskegon, Michigan; Newark, New Jersey; New York, New York; Orange County, California; Portland, Oregon; Providence, Rhode Island; Riverside, California; St. Louis, Missouri; St. Louis County, Missouri; San Bernardino, California; San Francisco Bay Area, California; Washington, D.C.

more than 3 minutes per hour of No. 2 Ringelmann to alternatively meet a gravimetric emission standard of 0.12 (stack area in square feet)$^{1/2}$ grains/ft^3 at 60 °F.

Some communities apply the same prohibition to motor vehicles as to stationary plants, e.g., Los Angeles County—not more than 3 minutes per hour of No. 2 Ringelmann. New York City limits visible emissions from internal combustion engines to not more than 10 consecutive seconds when stationary and none after the vehicle has moved more than 90 yards from the place where the vehicle was stationary.

Several European countries have adopted standards regulating smoke emission from diesel engine-powered motor vehicles—using either the Bosch or Hartridge smoke meter. The Bosch measures the density of a smoke stain produced by drawing exhaust gas through filter paper and uses a density scale of 0 to 10. The Hartridge uses a scale of 0 to 100 and measures the percentage of light obscured by exhaust gas flowing through the instrument. The limits are as follows:

Country	Hartridge	Bosch
Finland	70	—
Norway	70	5.5
Sweden	—	3.5
Belgium	60	—
France		
Trucks over 19 tons	60	—
Trucks 6–19 tons	50	—
Buses and trucks under 6 tons	45	—
Cars and light trucks	40	—
Fed. Rep. of Germany[a]		
Cars and light trucks	—	6.5
Heavy trucks	—	4.0

[a] Not yet officially adopted.

The approximate correlation between Hartridge (H) and Bosch (B) units is: $H = 13.75B + 4.60$; and the correlation of Hartridge units and visual opacity is approximately:

Hartridge units	Visual density
>75	Dense smoke
55–75	Moderate smoke
30–55	Slight smoke
<30	Hardly visible

In Missouri, odor emission in the St. Louis Metropolitan area is prohibited when it causes an objectionable odor:

1. on or adjacent to residential, recreational, institutional, retail sales, hotel or educational premises,

2. on or adjacent to industrial premises when air containing such odorous matter is diluted with 20 or more volumes of odor-free air,

3. on or adjacent to premises other than those in 1 and 2 when air containing such odorous matter is diluted with four or more volumes of odor-free air.

The above requirements apply only to objectionable odors. An odor is deemed objectionable when 30% or more of a sample of the people exposed to it believe it to be objectionable in usual places of occupancy— if the sample size is at least 20 people; if fewer than 20 people are exposed 75% must believe it to be objectionable.

VI. Design Standards

Design standards are standards relating to site, facility, or process which are intended to help achieve desired air quality. The principal ones are standards for buffer zones, stack height, equipment design, and fuel composition.

A. BUFFER ZONE STANDARDS

The buffer zone concept is incorporated in several of the emission standards (Figs. 5–8). When both a buffer zone and tall stacks are used to protect a community from the emission of a specific plant, and the distance from the plant to the point where its plume comes to ground level at highest concentration is approximately the same as the width of the buffer zone separating the plant from the community, the buffer zone could serve, under certain meteorological situations, to increase, rather than decrease, pollution levels in the community.

Standards promulgated pursuant to U.S.S.R. labor laws require that, using the spring and summer prevailing winds as the criterion, plants expected to discharge objectionable pollutants must be located downwind of nearby residential areas and separated therefrom by what are called "sanitary protection zones." These zones should preferably be planted with species resistant to the pollutants expected, but may not be used as public parks. Under certain conditions, nonpollution-producing industrial, commercial, and public establishments may locate in these zones. There are five categories of such zones, 1000, 500, 300, 100, and 50 meters minimum width, respectively, except that these minima may

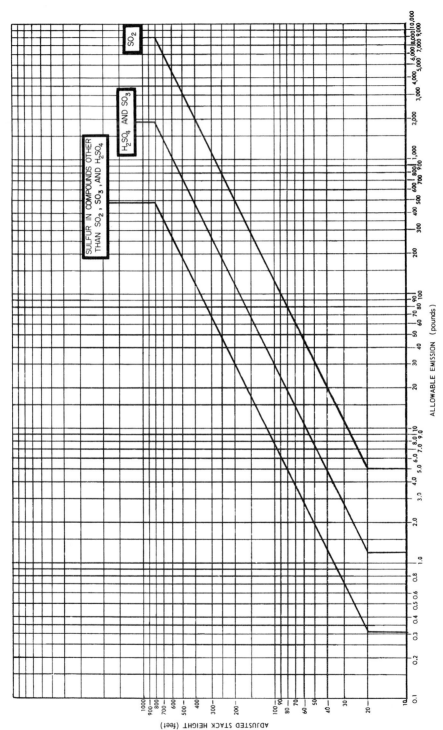

FIG. 17. Allowable emissions for sulfur compounds—New Jersey.

be doubled to protect hospitals, sanitaria, etc. In Poland two hundred and eighty different air polluting industrial, commercial, and public service processes and activities are separately identified in the regulations and assigned to one of these five zone classes. Some processes may be classified into more than one zone category, depending upon production or flow rate, storage quantity, or raw materials composition, e.g., percent sulfur in petroleum. (See Appendix I for Polish buffer zone standards.)

The sanitary protection zones required in the U.S.S.R. for coal-fired boiler plants burning over 3 tons of fuel per hour are based upon four variables: type of fuel, its ash content, rate of fuel consumption, and efficiency of fly ash collection plant (9c) (Table XXV).* Oil-fired plants are treated the same as plants fired with coal of less than 10% ash content and having 90% fly ash collection efficiency. Power plants which consume over 100 tons per hour of high-sulfur-content fuel and which are near residential areas must install SO_2 removal equipment sufficient to meet the air quality standard for SO_2.

In Delaware, open burning is prohibited in: residential, commercial, industrial, and rural areas, within one mile of the corporate limits of any municipality; state boundaries; military, commercial, county, municipal, or private airports or landing strips; primary highways; areas within one-half mile of secondary highways; national reservations; state parks; state forests; wildlife areas; or sites of three or more residences. In addition, such burning is prohibited between one hour after sunset and one hour before sunrise; and during meteorological conditions declared adverse by the commission.

B. STACK HEIGHT STANDARDS

Stack height appears as a parameter in several of the emission standards (Figs. 5–8, 10, 13 and 15, and Table A of the example in Section IV,C,1,a). There are, in addition, stack height standards in which emission standards do not appear as parameters, although undoubtedly utilized in their derivation. Tables XXVI† (9d) through XXIX and Fig. 17 are all intended to decrease sulfur oxide concentration at ground level by discharging it from a high enough stack. In Table XXVI the heights are calculated to give a 3-minute mean ground level SO_2 concentration of 17 parts per hundred million. The adjusted stack height of Fig. 17 is obtained, in the case of stacks less than 200 feet, by multiplying actual stack height by a "stack height adjustment factor" from Table

* See p. 707.
† Tables XXVI and XXVII appear on p. 708; XXVIII and XXIX appear on p. 709.

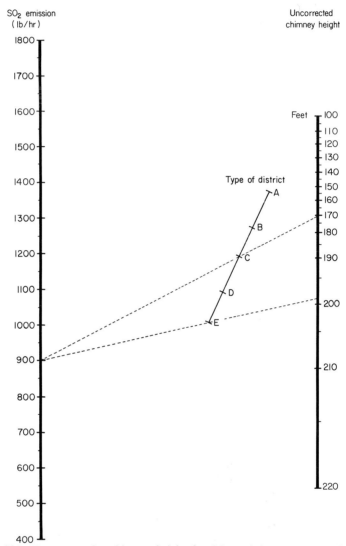

Fig. 18A. Nomogram for chimney height for SO_2 emission—uncorrected chimney heights for large installations—Great Britain (*9d*).

XXX; and, in the case of stacks 200 feet or higher, by adding to or subtracting from the actual stack height the "stack height adjustment," in feet, from Table XXXI.* Table XXXII is intended to protect against both fly ash and sulfur oxides. Tables XXXIII and XXXIV are intended to protect against NO_2 and zinc oxide fume, respectively.

* Table XXX appears on p. 709. Tables XXXI–XXXIV on pp. 710 and 711.

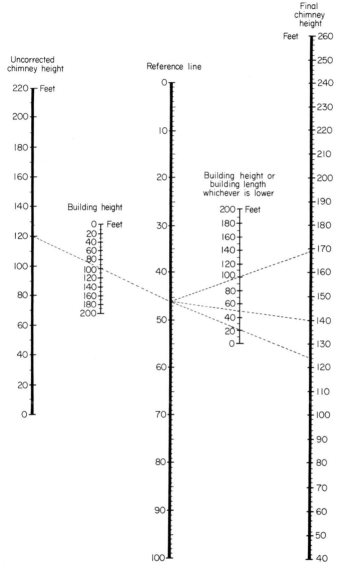

FIG. 18B. Nomogram for chimney height for SO_2 emission—final chimney heights—Great Britain (9d).

In the Netherlands, the limit for total particulate emission from a stack in grains per cubic meter STP is (height of stack (in meters)/50)^2 and the limit for particles larger than 50 μ is 1/40 this total. The increase in allowable particulate matter emission with stack height for Chicago, Illinois, is given in Tables XII and XIV.

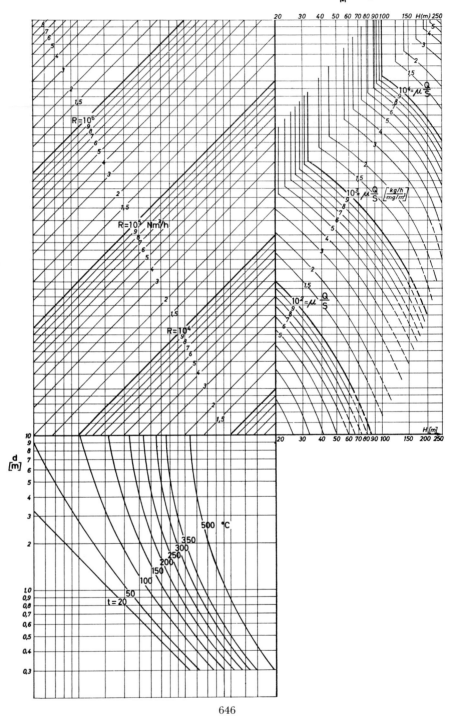

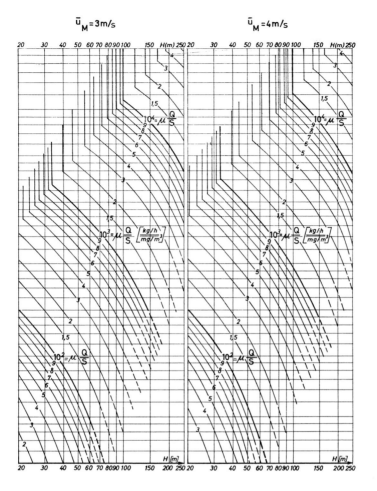

FIG. 19. Federal Republic of Germany Technical Directive for calculating stack height in unimproved terrain (*8b*); also VDI 2289 (*5*).

TABLE OF τ VS. μ

τ	μ	τ	μ	τ	μ
3 minutes	1.48	20 minutes	1.04	4 hours	0.75
4 minutes	1.38	25 minutes	1.02	5 hours	0.72
5 minutes	1.31	30 minutes	1.00	6 hours	0.70
6 minutes	1.26	45 minutes	0.96	12 hours	0.62
8 minutes	1.19	1 hour	0 93	1 day	0.56
10 minutes	1.14	1.5 hours	0.88	2 days	0.51
12 minutes	1.11	2 hours	0.85	3 days	0.50
15 minutes	1.08	3 hours	0.79	4 days	0.49

The Ministry of Housing and Local Government of Great Britain has issued a "Memorandum on Chimney Heights" (*9d*). This memorandum includes nomographs for SO_2 emission covering five types of district, A—undeveloped, B—partially developed, C—built-up residential, D—mixed industrial-residential, and E—mixed heavy industrial-residential. There are four separate nomograms for the determination of uncorrected chimney height for the following ranges of SO_2 emission in pounds per hour: 3–30; 30–100; 100–400; and 400–1800. There are fifth and sixth nomograms for determining final chimney height from uncorrected chimney height, building height, and building length. Only two of these six nomograms are reproduced here (Figs. 18A and 18B). They are for the highest SO_2 emission range.

The regulations of the Federal German Republic incorporate the procedure for determining stack height of Kommission Reinhaltung der Luft (*5*) specification VDI-2289, which utilizes a nomogram (Fig. 19). This nomogram is used as follows:

1. Draw a horizontal line in the lower left diagram at the diameter in meters of the inside exit diameter (*d*) of the stack.

2. From the point of intersection of this line with the curve of appropriate stack exit gas temperature (*t*), in °C, draw a vertical line into the upper left diagram.

3. From the point of intersection of this line with the appropriate diagonal value of total stack effluent gas quantity (*R*), in cubic meters per hour STP, draw a horizontal line through the three remaining diagrams to the right.

4. From each of the three points of intersection of this line with the curves (one in each diagram) of the appropriate value of $(\mu(Q/s))$ draw a vertical line downward to the bottom of the chart. The value of μ is given by the inset table for various values of averaging time (τ). Q is kilograms per hour of emission of the specific pollutant for which s is the maximum increase in ground level concentration over background concentration, in milligrams per cubic meter, which may be contributed by the stack in question.

5. The three points of intersection are at values of stack height (*H*) above ground for three different conditions of average wind velocity, $\bar{u}_M$, in meters per second about 20 meters above ground, namely 2, 3, and 4 m/sec, respectively.

Precautions and limitations on the use of this nomogram are included in the regulation and specification referred to.

The British Alkali Inspectorate has issued "Notes on Best Practicable Means for Cement Works Emissions" (June, 1967) which includes stack height regulations in the form of Table XXXV* for new works with single chimneys, and Fig. 20 for works with multiple chimneys, where

* See p. 712.

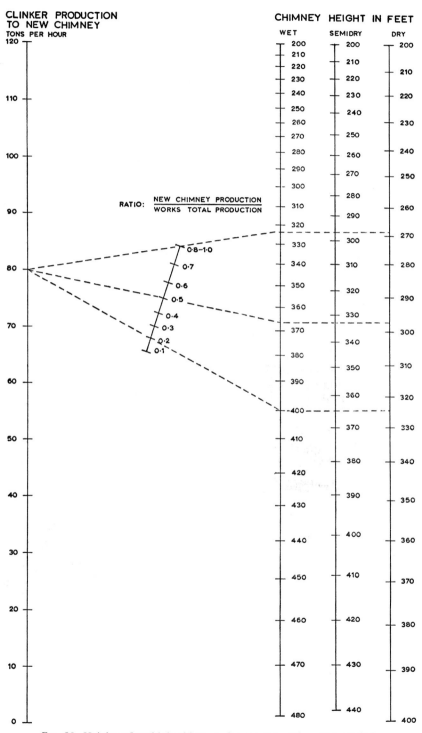

Fig. 20. Heights of multiple chimneys for cement works—Great Britain.

a new chimney is to be installed at a works where existing kilns and chimneys are already in use. [For a completely new works, the ratio: (new chimney production/works total production) is equal to 1.] Chimney exit velocity at maximum production must be not less than 50 feet/sec.

C. Equipment Design Standards

The first standards to be used extensively in air pollution ordinances and regulations were design standards. The incorporation of such standards led to the requirement of the submission of plans and specifications for approval, i.e., for checking for compliance with design standards. Proponents of this approach have argued that it has been the only practicable preventive measure, in the absence of air quality standards and the paucity of emission standards. Opponents raise the hypothetical issue of the plant erected in conformity with design standards but failing to comply with emission or air quality standards. Opponents also have held that design standards stifle engineering ingenuity by preventing designs which contravene the standards but which achieve the desired result in terms of emission or air quality. To avoid these pitfalls, design standards should never be used as a straitjacket on design, but rather as a guide to good design, and appeals procedures should be provided to allow fair consideration for nonstandard designs.

Design standards for stationary fuel-burning equipment relate to such factors as heat release per unit furnace volume, furnace refractory placement and arch design, chimney cross-sectional area and height, stoker setting, fuel oil viscosity, and preheat temperature, etc. Being specific for the characteristics of the fuel used, which differ from region to region, such standards are perforce local and not universal. Design standards tend to become obsolete as technology changes, and therefore should not be incorporated into legislation or regulation that is difficult to amend.

D. Fuel Standards

Fuel standards are a form of design standard in the sense that they limit the kind of fuel that may be burned in equipment of specified design, either all year round or, as in Los Angeles, for certain months of the year. A corollary of the use of fuel standards is fuel dealer licensing, maintenance of lists of approved sources of supply, and policing of fuel deliveries to customers. For details of these procedures, one is referred to the regulations of St. Louis, Missouri, and Pittsburgh, Pennsylvania.

An example of fuel specifications for the purpose of reducing air pollution is the regulation of the olefin content of gasoline by Los Angeles County Air Pollution Control District Rule No. 63, which provides that after December 31, 1961, no gasoline may be used having a degree of unsaturation greater than that indicated by a bromine number of 20 as determined by ASTM Method D1159-57T, modified by omission of the mercuric chloride catalyst.

The sulfur content of fuel is limited by Los Angeles County Air Pollution Control District Rule No. 62 so that between April 15 and November 15, no gaseous fuel may be used containing over 50 grains per 100 ft^3 of sulfur as H_2S, nor any liquid or solid fuel having over 0.5% sulfur by weight. New York City has limited sulfur content of distillate heating oil to 1% and of coal and residual fuel oil to 2.2% in 1967 and 68; 2.0% in 1969 and 1970; 1.0% thereafter.

In the Metropolitan Washington, D.C., area, the State of Maryland; Montgomery County, Prince Georges County, and Rockville, Maryland; and Fairfax County, Virginia, have adopted a 1% fuel sulfur limit—all effective July 1, 1969 for all fuels; in Falls Church, Virginia, it is effective July 1, 1970 but for fuel oil only. The July 1, 1968 value for fuel oil in Maryland and Fairfax County, Virginia, is 1.5%.

The New Jersey limits are as follows:

Grades of commercial fuel oil	% Sulfur by weight		
	Effective 5/1/68	Effective 10/1/70	Effective 10/1/71
No. 2 and lighter	0.3	0.3	0.2
No. 4	0.7	0.4	0.3
No. 5, No. 6, and heavier	1.0	0.5	0.3

These limits do not apply to emissions controlled to the following level:

Grades of commercial fuel oil	Permissible SO_2 emissions (lbs. SO_2 per million BTU gross heat input)		
	Effective 5/1/68	Effective 10/1/70	Effective 10/1/71
No. 4	0.74	0.42	0.30
No. 5, No. 6, and heavier	1.1	0.52	0.30

New York State has adopted a limit for liquid fuels of 0.2 lb of sulfur per million BTU gross heat content, applicable to New York City and three adjoining counties, effective October 1, 1969.

In the St. Louis Metropolitan Area, Missouri, during December–January, 1968–1969; November–February 1969–1970; and October–March, 1970–1971 and thereafter no coal or oil of over 2% sulfur may be burned in any installation of under 2000 million Btu per hour capacity unless the SO_2 emission is less than 2.3 pounds per million BTU.

In the Department of the Seine (France), the use of mineral fuel containing more than 2% sulfur is prohibited in furnaces consuming over 20 kg fuel per hour within 10 km of the perimeter of areas reserved for habitation. The limit on sulfur content of fuel oil generally set by the factory inspectorate in the German Federal Republic is 1.8%. Of 110 United States ordinances studied by Rogers (10), 18 had a limitation of the volatile content of coal (Table XXXVI).*

A fuel standard may reduce a community's economically available sources of supply of fuel. To increase supply, either conforming sources which may have greater production and transportation cost must be tapped, or costly processing must be applied to the product from cheaper nonconforming sources. Since these costs are computable, a community can select the fuel standard for which it is willing to pay. The decrease in sulfur pollution emission associated with a decrease in the sulfur content of a fuel is directly calculable. The resulting decrease in smoke production from hand-fired coal burning can be estimated with considerable accuracy from the decrease in the volatile content of coal.

The British equivalents of fuel standards are the Smokeless Zone provisions of the Clean Air Act, which allow political jurisdictions to elect to limit the type of fuel burned in fireplaces.

VII. Measurement and Test Method Standards

Standards in this category arise from a variety of sources: international, national, and regional; governmental and nongovernmental. They also vary in their degree of authority from designation by the publishing organization as "recommended," "tentative," or "standard" method, to incorporation in official regulations as "the" method which must be used. Most air quality and emission standards include a reference to the measurement method to be used to determine compliance with the standard. There are, however, standards for measurement and

* See p. 712.

test methods which are published separately from air quality and emission standards.

A. AIR QUALITY MEASUREMENT METHOD STANDARDS

The World Health Organization has scheduled for 1968 or 1969 publication a "Guide to the Selection of Methods for Measuring Air Pollutants," prepared with the assistance of Morris Katz, which includes (a) manual analytical methods for particulate arsenic, beryllium, cadmium, chromium, lead, manganese, chlorides, nitrates, sulfates, and sulfuric acid mist; gaseous acrolein, aliphatic aldehydes, ammonia, carbon bisulfide, carbon monoxide, chlorine, fluoride ion, formaldehyde, hydrogen cyanide, hydrogen sulfide, methanol, nitric oxide, oxidant, phenols, and sulfur dioxide; and (b) automatic instrumental methods for carbon monoxide, fluorides (soluble), hydrocarbons, hydrogen cyanide, hydrogen fluoride, hydrogen sulfide, nitric oxide, nitrogen dioxide, oxidant, ozone, and sulfur dioxide.

The Working Party on Methods of Measuring Air Pollution and Survey Techniques of the Organization for Economic Cooperation and Development, Paris, published in 1964 "Methods of Measuring Air Pollution" (11) which contains its recommended methods for measuring smoke, sulfur dioxide, sulfur trioxide, hydrocarbons, and fluorides. This publication contains five proposed international standard calibration curves for the estimation of suspended particulate matter:

(1) Eel reflectometer—Whatman No. 1 filter paper 1-inch diameter
(2) Photovolt reflectometer—Schneider CA 32 filter paper 1-inch diameter
(3) Photovolt reflectometer—Whatman No. 1 filter paper 1-inch diameter
(4) Eel reflectometer—Schneider CA 32 filter paper 1-inch diameter
(5) Eel reflectometer—Fiberglass GF/A filter 1-inch diameter

as well as the British Smoke calibration curves for the Eel reflectometer and Whatman No. 1 filter paper 1-inch diameter for Scotland, Sheffield, Islington, and Greenhithe; and Mean British–Paris–Netherlands curves superimposed on the proposed international standard calibration curve for the above combination of reflectometer and filter paper (Fig. 21).

The U.S. Department of Health, Education, and Welfare in May, 1965 published as Public Health Service Publication No. 999-AP-11 "Selected Methods for the Measurement of Air Pollutants" (12) which includes the following:

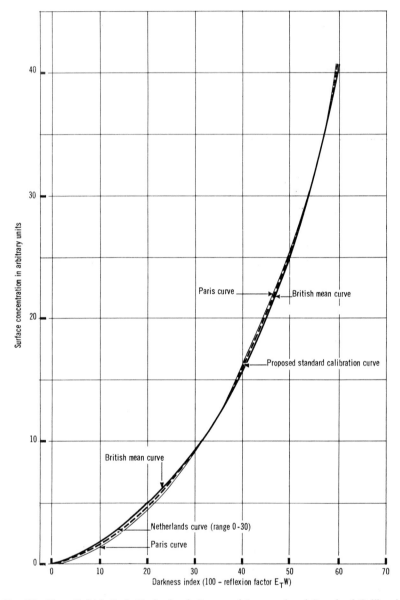

F‌IG. 21. Mean British-Paris-Netherlands Proposed International Standard Calibration Curve for measuring suspended particulate matter (smoke) by reflectance (Eel reflectometer—Whatman No. 1 filter paper 1-inch diameter) (11).

Determination of sulfur dioxide: West and Gaeke method

Determination of sulfur dioxide: hydrogen peroxide method

Determination of nitrogen dioxide and nitric oxide: Saltzman method

Determination of oxidants (including ozone): neutral buffered–potassium iodide method

Determination of oxidants (including ozone): alkaline potassium iodide method

Determination of aliphatic aldehydes: 3-Methyl-2-benzothiazolone hydrazone hydrochloride (MBTH) method

Determination of acrolein: 4-hexylresorcinol method

Determination of formaldehyde: chromotropic acid method

Determination of sulfate in atmospheric suspended particulates: turbidimetric barium sulfate method

Determination of nitrate in atmospheric suspended particulates: 2,4-xylenol method

The analytical procedures of the federally sponsored National Air Sampling Network have been published (13) for: suspended particulates, benzene-soluble organics, beta radioactivity, nitrates, sulfates, ammonium, antimony, arsenic, beryllium, bismuth, cadmium, chromium, cobalt, copper, iron, lead, manganese, molybdenum, nickel, tin, titanium, vanadium, and zinc.

The Los Angeles (California) County Air Pollution Control District (APCD) (14), American Petroleum Institute (API) (15), American Society for Testing and Materials (ASTM) (16), Air Pollution Control Association (APCA) (17), British Standards Institution (BS) (18), California Department of Public Health (SDPH) (19), New Zealand Standards Institute (NZSS) (20), and Verein Deutscher Ingenieure (VDI) (5) all publish numbered standard air quality measurement methods (Table XXXVII).* The last two numbers of the APCD, API, and ASTM standards represent the terminal digits of the year of publication, the terminal "X" of an APCD standard means that it is a revision of an earlier standard, and the terminal "T" of an ASTM standard means that the methods, practices, or definitions are tentative, pending adoption as standards.

The Manufacturing Chemists' Association Air Pollution Abatement Manual includes as Manual Sheets P-7, P-7A, and P-8 [Chapters 6.6 (Suppl. 1), and 7] recommended sampling procedures, measuring equipment, and analytical methods. The original chapters were prepared in 1951 and 1952, the supplement in 1956.

The "Intersociety Committee on Manual for Air Sampling and Analysis," comprising the Air Pollution Control Association, American Industrial Hygiene Association, American Public Health Association,

* Table XXXVII begins on p. 713.

American Society for Testing and Materials, American Conference of Governmental Industrial Hygienists, Association of Official Analytical Chemists, and American Society for Mechanical Engineers, in 1968 approved methods for arsenic, chlorides, ^{210}lead, NO_2 and SO_2; two for fluorides; three for benzo(a)pyrene; and four for ^{222}radon.

The sampling and analytical methods adopted by the U.S.S.R. are listed in "Limits of Allowable Concentrations of Atmospheric Pollutants," edited by Professor V. A. Ryazanov and translated by Dr. B. S. Levine (6). These include in Book 1 (1952) methods for the sampling and analysis of carbon disulfide, carbon monoxide, chlorine, dust, hydrogen sulfide, lead, mercury, oxides of nitrogen, soot, and sulfur dioxide; in Book 2 (1955) new methods for chlorine, lead, mercury, and sulfur dioxide, plus methods for arsenious anhydride, benzene, fluorine, hydrocarbons, manganese, phenol, phosphoric anhydride, and sulfuric acid aerosol; in Book 3 (1957) new methods for mercury and carbon monoxide, plus methods for acrolein and chlorinated hydrocarbons; in Book 4 (1960) methods for formaldehyde and methanol; in Book 6 (1962) methods for acetates, acetone, acetophenone, dimethylformamide, dinyl, ethylene oxide, furfural, isopropyl benzene, isopropyl benzene hydroperoxide, methyl methacrylate, methylstryrol, styrol, and total monobasic carbon-containing acids; in Book 7 (1963) methods for aniline, n-butyl vinyl ester, dimethylterephthalate, phenol with 4-aminoantipyrene, and xylol; and spectrophotometric methods for acetophenene, isopropyl benzene, naphthalene and styrol in the presence of dinyl. A compilation of these methods by M. V. Alekseeva "Determination of Atmospheric Pollutants" (Medgiz, Moskow), originally published in 1958 has since been reissued in a revised edition.

The National Survey of Air Pollution of Great Britain (21) employs British Standard calibration curve, B.S. 1747:Part 2:1964, for measuring suspended particulate matter; and British Standard method, B.S. 1747:Part 3:1963, for measuring sulfur dioxide.

The standard method for assessing ambient air levels of SO_2 in the Federal German Republic (8b) deserves special mention and is best described by citing the applicable sections of the regulation in which it appears as follows:

A. *Density of measuring stations and frequency of measurements to determine the basic load of large areas*
In order to determine the basic load of large areas a measuring density of one measuring station per km² shall be adopted. The position of the measuring stations may be established by the intersections of the grid lines on survey sheets. Four measuring station grids with one measuring point in every 4 km² shall be so overlapped as to provide one measuring station for each km² (Fig. 22). If it is not possible to carry out the measurements at a point corresponding to an intersection of the grid lines (e.g., owing to difficult ground conditions) the measuring station shall be established at the nearest

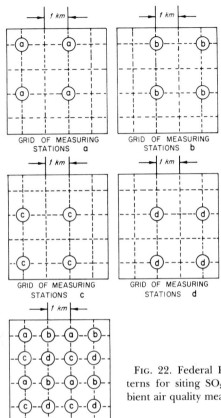

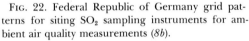

FIG. 22. Federal Republic of Germany grid patterns for siting SO$_2$ sampling instruments for ambient air quality measurements (*8b*).

accessible point. The distance of such points from the intersection points of the grid lines should be below 100 m and must not exceed 200 m.

Each network of measuring stations shall be covered 26 times in one year so that altogether 104 measurements are carried out in every 4 km^2. On the first day of measuring, the measurements are made at the points marked (a) in Fig. 22, on the second day at those marked (b), on the third day at those marked (c), and on the fourth day at those marked (d). The measurement is repeated at each place every two weeks.

As a matter of principle, the measuring days shall be decided upon before the measurements are begun and regardless of the weather. Results recorded during whole days of unfavorable weather shall be disregarded.

In special cases the period of observation may be reduced from a whole year to one-half year including either the months from February to July or the months from August to January. The total number of measurements shall, however, be maintained, so that the measurements shall be repeated at the same place not every second week but every week.

B. *Density of measuring stations and frequency of measurements needed to determine the basic load of small areas and to serve as a basis for calculating the minimum height of chimneys*

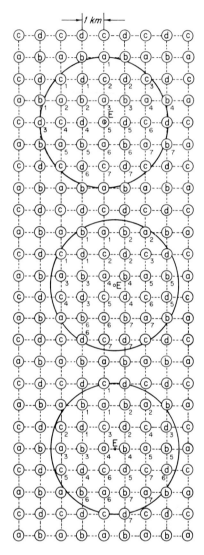

FIG. 23. Federal Republic of Germany grid patterns for siting SO₂ sampling instruments for determining compliance of source "E" with regulations (8b).

In order to determine the basic load in the neighborhood of an existing or projected installation, and also to serve as a basis for determining the minimum height of chimneys, the same procedure as described under [A] shall be followed but it shall be sufficient to arrive at the basic load within a circle of 3 km radius from the plant in question, determined as follows:

Those of the intersections between the vertical and the horizontal lines of the grid on the survey sheets that fall within the circle (at intervals of 1 km) give the positions of the measuring stations. Seven measuring stations are to be established for each of the four measuring grids, thus providing 28 measuring stations in all. If the circle then covers more than 28 measuring stations, the measuring stations in excess are to be omitted, or if it covers fewer the deficiency of measuring stations is to be made up, at those intersection points that fall closest to the arc of the circle.

Figure 23 shows three examples. These serve to explain the selection of measuring points within a measuring point grid in proximity to an emission source (E). All the positions marked "a" are allocated to the measuring grid "a" and the positions b, c, d are allocated to the corresponding measuring grids. Thus in every case grids a, b, c, and d each have seven stations. The points having been so chosen, they are numbered from 1 to 7 continuously within the circle from left to right and from top to bottom. With 28 measuring stations and 26 measuring days for every station each measuring period will, as a rule, yield 728 separate values.

C. *Measurement timing and measuring apparatus*

The measurements shall be carried out between 8 a.m. and 3 p.m.; and in regions where there is a marked evening peak they shall also be carried out 2 hours before and 2 hours after the peak. The measuring apparatus to be used are those described in VDI-Richtlinien (5) 2451 of December 1963.

D. *Evaluation*

The imission (i.e., air quality) limiting the value for sulphur dioxide is not exceeded if evaluation of the measurement results yields the following values:

$$\bar{X} + \Delta\bar{X}_{(P=97.5\%)} \leqq 0.4$$

and

$$\bar{X} + \Delta X_{(P=97.5\%)} \leqq 0.75$$

where

$\bar{X}$ = arithmetic average of all the individual values

$$\Delta\bar{X}_{(P=97.5\%)} = \frac{S_0 \cdot t}{\sqrt{2z}}$$

$$\Delta X_{(P=97.5\%)} = S_0 \cdot t$$

$$S_0 = \pm \sqrt{\frac{2\Sigma(\bar{X} - X_i)^2}{2z - 1}} \text{ for all } X_i > \bar{X}$$

t = the factor for the "student" distribution which, for the 97.5% confidence level, is approximately 2

z = number of all the individual values above the arithmetic average

X_i = individual value

B. EMISSION MEASUREMENT METHOD STANDARDS

Most emission standards include a reference to the measurement method to be used to determine compliance with the standard. Some of the standard methods for ambient air analysis are also applicable to source emission measurement. To the best of the author's knowledge, no international organization has promulgated or published emission measurement standards. Table XXXVIII* lists numbered emission measurement standard methods. The initial and terminal letters and numbers have the same meaning as in Table XXXVII.

* Table XXXVIII begins on p. 715.

TABLE I
DATA ON WHICH SOME VDI AIR QUALITY STANDARDS
ARE BASED (5)

Concentration, in ppm by volume	Effect	Species
Chlorine (VDI 2106—September 1960)		
600	Death	Animals
10–100	Sickness	Animals
1	Irritation	Man
0.3–3.0	Damage	Plants
0.05	Olfactory threshold	Man
Hydrochloric Acid (VDI 2106—Part 2—February 1963)		
100–1000	Leaf Damage	Plants
10–50	No damage	Plants
10	Irritation	Man
5	No organic damage	Man
Hydrogen Sulfide (VDI 2107—April 1960)		
700	Quickly fatal	Man
400–700	Dangerous (30 minutes or less)	Man
170–300	Intense local irritation	Man
100–300	Spontaneous injury	Animals
70–150	Slight symptoms	Man
20–30	Strongly perceptible odor	Man
1.5	Toxic limit	Plants
0.3	Definitely perceptible odor	Man
0.1	Slightly perceptible odor	Man
0.025	Olfactory threshold	Man
Nitric Acid (VDI 2105—Part 2—February 1963)		
25	Damage	Plants
Nitrous Oxides (VDI 2105—May 1960)		
40–80	Pulmonary edema	Animals
10–20	Methemoglobin formation	Man
1–2	Minor irritation	Man
0.1	Olfactory threshold	Man
Sulfur Dioxide (VDI 2108—November 1961)		
100	Strong irritation	Man
10–50	Irritation	Man
1–10	Contradictory findings	Man
1–2	Damage	Plants
0.3–1.0	Perception threshold	Man
0.15	Tolerance limit	Plants

TABLE II
U.S.S.R. Air Quality Criteria (6)

Data measured in mg/m³ Substance	Human odor perception		Human reflex response[a]		Animal chronic exposure[b]	
	Non-perception	Perception	No response	Adverse response	No effect	Adverse effect
Acetone	0.8	1.1	0.35	0.55	0.5	—
Acetephenone	—	0.01	0.003	0.007	—	0.07
Acrolein	—	0.8	—	0.6	—	0.15
Ammonia	0.4	0.5	0.22	0.35	0.2	2.0
Amyl acetate	0.5	0.6	0.12	0.30	—	—
Amylenes and pentenes	—	1.8	—	—	1.9	9.8
Aniline	0.34	0.37	—	0.07	—	0.05
Benzene	—	3.0	—	—	—	3.2
Butyl acetate	0.5	0.6	0.1	0.13	0.1	200.
Carbon disulfide	0.04	0.05	0.03	0.04	—	—
Carbon monoxide	—	—	—	—	1.13	2.65
Chlorine	0.8	1.0	—	1.0	—	—
Chlorobenzol	—	0.4	0.1	0.2	0.1	1.0
Chloroprene	0.25	0.4	—	0.4	0.22	0.48
Chromium (hexavalent)	—	—	—	—	0.0015	0.0025
Cyclohexanol	—	—	0.04	—	0.059	0.61
Cyclohexanone	—	—	0.06	—	0.042	0.46
Dichloroethane	12.2	23.2	—	6.0	—	—
Diketene	0.011	0.019	0.007	0.01	—	—
Dimethyl formamide	0.14	0.88	0.03	0.055	0.03	0.5
Dinitro-o-cresol	—	—	—	—	0.0002	0.036
Dinyl	—	0.08	0.01	0.04	0.01	0.1
Epichlorohydrin	0.2	0.3	0.2	0.3	0.2	2.0
Ethyl acetate	0.5	0.6	0.18	0.3	—	—
Ethylene oxide	—	1.5	—	0.65	—	—
Fluorides	—	—	—	—	—	0.02
Formaldehyde	0.05	0.07	0.07	0.084	—	—
Furfural	—	1.0	—	0.084	—	0.33
Gasoline	6.5	10.0	—	—	20.	100.
Gasoline—shale	0.15	0.3	0.06	0.09	0.06	0.6
Hexamethylenediamine	—	—	—	—	0.001	0.04
Hydrogen chloride	0.05	0.1	—	0.1	—	—
Hydrogen fluoride	—	0.03	—	0.03	0.01	0.1
Hydrogen sulfide	—	0.01	—	—	—	—
Isopropyl benzene	—	0.06	—	0.028	0.014	—
Isopropyl hydroperoxide	—	0.03	—	0.012	0.007	—
Lead	—	—	—	—	—	0.02
Lead sulfide	—	—	—	—	0.0034	0.012
Maleic anhydride	—	1.0	—	—	—	—
Mercury	—	—	—	—	—	0.002
Methanol	—	4.3	1.8	3.3	0.57	5.3
Methyl acetate	0.4	0.5	0.066	0.08	—	—
Nitrobenzene	—	0.0182	0.008	0.0129	0.008	0.08
Nitrogen oxides	—	—	0.3	0.5	—	1.0
Phenol	0.022	0.184	—	0.015	0.01	0.1
Pyridine	0.084	0.21	0.079	0.098	0.1	1.0
Sulfur dioxide	—	0.87	—	0.6	—	1.0
Sulfuric acid	—	0.6	—	0.4	—	—
Styrol	0.02	0.036	0.003	0.005	0.03	0.5
Toluene diisocyanate	0.15	0.2	0.05	0.1	0.02	0.2
Valeric acid vapor	—	—	—	—	0.006	0.14
Vanadium pentoxide	—	—	—	—	0.002	0.006
Vinyl acetate	0.7	1.0	0.21	0.32	—	—
Xylol	—	0.73	0.5	0.6	—	—

[a] The lowest adverse response and the highest no response values of optical chronaxy, dark adaptation and electro-cortical reflex response tests, where data on more than one type of test was available, or of only one of these tests, where data on only one type of test was available. [b] The lowest adverse effect and highest no effect test values reported.

TABLE III
GLOBAL BACKGROUND

Pollutant	Global background concentration
SO_2	0.001–0.002 ppm
NO_2	0.001–0.002 ppm
Oxidant or ozone	0.015–0.03 ppm
Methane	1.2 ± 0.2 ppm
Terpenes (olefins)	0.01 ppm
Carbon monoxide	0.3 ppm
SO_4^{-2}	0.1–1 $\mu g/m^3$
NO_3^-	0.1 $\mu g/m^3$

TABLE IV
AIR QUALITY GOALS

	Annual average (ppm)	Concentration in ppm Averaging time		
		24 hours	8 hours	1 hour
Carbon monoxide	3	—	6[a]	—
Nitrogen dioxide	0.05	—	—	0.15[a]
Oxidant	—	—	—	0.1[b]
Hydrocarbons other than methane[c]	0.3	—	—	1.[a]
Particulate matter	75 $\mu g/m^3$	150 $\mu g/m^{3a}$	—	—

[a] Not to be exceeded more than 1% of the time.
[b] Not to be exceeded more than 1% of the days.
[c] As ppm carbon.

TABLE V
AMBIENT AIR QUALITY STANDARDS

Substance	Political jurisdiction or standard	Basic standard			Permissible standard			Foot-notes[a]
		concentration		Averaging time	concentration		Averaging time	
		mg/m³ STP	ppm		mg/m³ STP	ppm		
Acetaldehyde	VDI 2306	4.	2.	30 min	12.	6.	30 min	1, 2, 3
Acetaldehyde	U.S.S.R.	—	—	—	0.01	0.005	20 min	4, 5
Acetic acid	VDI 2306	5.	2.	30 min	15.	6.	30 min	1, 2, 3
Acetic acid	U.S.S.R.	—	—	—	0.2	0.08	20 min	4, 5, 6
Acetic anhydride	U.S.S.R.	—	—	—	0.1	0.02	20 min	4, 5, 6
Acetone	VDI 2306	120.	50.	30 min	360.	150.	30 min	1, 2, 3
Acetone	U.S.S.R.	0.35	0.15	24 hours	0.35	0.15	20 min	4, 5, 6
Acetophenone	U.S.S.R.	0.003	0.0006	24 hours	0.003	0.0006	20 min	4, 5, 6
Acrolein	U.S.S.R.	0.1	0.04	24 hours	0.3	0.12	20 min	4, 5
Acrolein	VDI 2306	0.01	0.005	30 min	0.025	0.01	30 min	1, 2, 3
Ammonia	Czechoslovakia	0.1	0.14	24 hours	0.3	0.42	30 min	—
Ammonia	Ontario	3.5	5.	30 min	—	—	—	64
Ammonia	U.S.S.R.	0.2	0.28	24 hours	0.2	0.28	20 min	4, 5
Amyl acetate	U.S.S.R.	0.1	0.019	24 hours	0.1	0.019	20 min	4, 5
Amyl acetate	VDI 2306	30.	5.	30 min	90.	15.	30 min	1, 2, 3
Amyl alcohol	VDI 2306	20.	5.	30 min	60.	15.	30 min	1, 2, 3
Amylene	U.S.S.R.	1.5	0.5	24 hours	1.5	0.5	20 min	4, 5, 6
Aniline	VDI 2306	0.8	0.2	30 min	2.4	0.6	30 min	1, 2, 3
Aniline	U.S.S.R.	0.03	0.008	24 hours	0.05	0.013	20 min	4, 5
Arsenic (as As)	Czechoslovakia	0.003	—	24 hours	—	—	—	33
Arsenic (as As)	U.S.S.R.	0.003	—	24 hours	—	—	—	5, 33
Benzene	Czechoslovakia	0.8	0.25	24 hours	2.4	0.75	30 min	—
Benzene	U.S.S.R.	0.8	0.25	24 hours	1.5	0.5	20 min	4, 5, 6

TABLE V (*Continued*)

Substance	Political jurisdiction or standard	Basic standard concentration mg/m³ STP	ppm	Averaging time	Permissible standard concentration mg/m³ STP	ppm	Averaging time	Foot-notes[a]
Benzene	VDI 2306	3.	1.	30 min	10.	3.	30 min	1, 2, 3
Beryllium	New York	0.00001	—	24 hours	—	—	—	—
Beryllium	Montana	0.00001	—	30 days	—	—	—	—
Beryllium	Ontario	0.00001	—	24 hours	0.00001	—	30 min	65
Beryllium	Pennsylvania	0.00001	—	30 days	—	—	—	—
Beryllium	Texas	0.00001	—	24 hours	—	—	—	41
Butane	U.S.S.R.	—	—	—	200.	85.	20 min	4, 5
Butanol	VDI 2306	15.	5.	30 min	45.	15.	30 min	1, 2, 3
Butanol	U.S.S.R.	—	—	—	0.3	0.1	20 min	4, 5
Butyl acetate (-n)	VDI 2306	25.	5.	30 min	75.	15.	30 min	1, 2, 3
Butyl acetate (-n)	U.S.S.R.	0.1	0.021	24 hours	0.1	0.021	20 min	4, 5
Butylene	U.S.S.R.	3.	1.3	24 hours	3.	1.3	20 min	4, 5, 6
Butyric acid	U.S.S.R.	0.01	0.003	24 hours	0.015	0.004	20 min	4, 5
Calcium oxide (lime)	Ontario	0.02	—	30 min	—	—	—	64
Calcium oxide (lime)	Oregon	0.02	—		—	—	—	7, 35
Caprolactum	U.S.S.R.	0.06	0.013	24 hours	0.06	0.013	20 min	4, 5
Caprylic acid	U.S.S.R.	0.005	0.001	24 hours	0.01	0.002	20 min	4, 5
Carbon black (soot)	Czechoslovakia	0.05	—	24 hours	0.15	—	30 min	—
Carbon black (soot)	U.S.S.R.	0.05	—	24 hours	0.15	—	20 min	4, 5
Carbon disulfide	Czechoslovakia	0.01	0.0033	24 hours	0.03	0.01	30 min	—
Carbon disulfide	Ontario	0.45	0.15	30 min	—	—	—	64
Carbon disulfide	Poland	0.015	0.005	30 min	0.045	0.015	30 min	4, 56
Carbon disulfide	U.S.S.R.	0.01	0.0033	24 hours	0.03	0.01	20 min	4, 5, 6
Carbon monoxide	California	33.	30.	8 hours	132.	120.	1 hour	8

Substance	Source							Ref.
Carbon monoxide	Czechoslovakia	1.	0.9	24 hours	6.	5.4	30 min	—
Carbon monoxide	New York	33.	30.	8 hours	—	—	1 hour	—
Carbon monoxide	New York	16.5	15.	8 hours	66.	60.	1 hour	9
Carbon monoxide	Ontario	16.5	15.	8 hours	66.	60.	—	—
Carbon monoxide	Ontario	5.5	5.	30 min	—	—	—	64
Carbon monoxide	Pennsylvania	27.5	25.	24 hours	—	—	—	—
Carbon monoxide	Poland	0.5	0.45	24 hours	3.	2.7	20 min	4, 57
Carbon monoxide	U.S.S.R.	1.	0.9	24 hours	3.	2.7	20 min	4, 5, 6
Carbon tetrachloride	VDI 2306	3.	0.5	30 min	10.	1.5	30 min	1, 2, 3
Carbon tetrachloride	U.S.S.R.	—	—	—	4.	0.7	20 min	4, 5
Chlorine	Czechoslovakia	0.03	0.01	24 hours	0.1	0.033	30 min	—
Chlorine	Ontario	0.3	0.1	30 min	—	—	—	64
Chlorine	U.S.S.R.	0.03	0.01	24 hours	0.1	0.033	20 min	4, 5
Chlorine	Fed. Rep. Germany	0.3	0.1	30 min	0.6	0.2	30 min	2, 11, 12
Chloroaniline (-p)	U.S.S.R.	—	—	—	0.04	0.008	20 min	4, 5
Chlorobenzene	VDI 2306	5.	1.	30 min	15.	3.	30 min	1, 2, 3
Chlorobenzene	U.S.S.R.	0.1	0.02	24 hours	0.1	0.02	20 min	4, 5
Chloroform	VDI 2306	10.	2.	30 min	30.	6.	30 min	1, 2, 3
Chloroprene	U.S.S.R.	0.1	0.028	24 hours	0.1	0.028	20 min	4, 5
Chlorophenyl isocyanate (-m)	U.S.S.R.	0.005	0.001	24 hours	0.005	0.001	20 min	4, 5, 6
Chlorophenyl isocyanate (-p)	U.S.S.R.	0.0015	0.0002	24 hours	0.0015	0.0002	20 min	4, 5, 6
Chromium-hexavalent (as CrO_3)	U.S.S.R.	0.0015	—	24 hours	0.0015	—	20 min	4, 5
Cresol	VDI 2306	0.2	0.05	30 min	0.6	0.15	30 min	1, 2, 3
Cyclohexanol	U.S.S.R.	0.06	0.015	24 hours	0.06	0.015	20 min	4, 5
Cyclohexanone	U.S.S.R.	0.04	0.008	24 hours	0.04	0.008	20 min	4, 5
Cyclohexanone	VDI 2306	10.	2.	30 min	30.	6.	30 min	1, 2, 3
Dichloroethane	VDI 2306	8.	2.	30 min	25.	6.	30 min	1, 2, 3
Dichloroethane	U.S.S.R.	1.	0.25	24 hours	3.	0.75	20 min	4, 5
2-3 Dichloro-1-4 naphthaquinone	U.S.S.R.	0.05	—	24 hours	0.05	—	20 min	4, 5
Diethylamine	U.S.S.R.	0.05	0.02	24 hours	0.05	0.02	20 min	4, 5

TABLE V (Continued)

Substance	Political jurisdiction or standard	Basic standard concentration mg/m³ STP	ppm	Averaging time	Permissible standard concentration mg/m³ STP	ppm	Averaging time	Foot-notes[a]
Diethylamine	VDI 2306	0.03	0.01	30 min	0.09	0.03	30 min	1, 2, 3
Diethyl ether	VDI 2306	65.	20.	30 min	195.	60.	30 min	1, 2, 3
Diketene	U.S.S.R.	—	—	—	0.007	0.002	20 min	4, 5
Dimethylamine	VDI 2306	0.02	0.01	30 min	0.06	0.03	30 min	1, 2, 3
Dimethylaniline	U.S.S.R.	—	—	—	0.0055	0.001	20 min	4, 5
Dimethyl disulfide	U.S.S.R.	—	—	—	0.7	0.18	20 min	4, 5
Dimethylformamide	U.S.S.R.	0.03	0.01	24 hours	0.03	0.01	20 min	4, 5
Dimethyl sulfide	U.S.S.R.	—	—	—	0.08	0.03	20 min	4, 5
Dinitrobenzene	VDI 2306	0.035	0.005	30 min	0.1	0.015	30 min	1, 2, 3
Dinyl (diphenyl + its oxide)	U.S.S.R.	0.01	0.0015	24 hours	0.01	0.0015	20 min	4, 5, 6
Dioxane	VDI 2306	20.	5.	30 min	60.	15.	30 min	1, 2, 3
Divinyl	U.S.S.R.	1.	0.4	24 hours	3.	1.2	20 min	4, 5
Epichlorohydrin	U.S.S.R.	0.2	0.05	24 hours	0.2	0.05	20 min	4, 5
Ethanol	U.S.S.R.	5.	2.5	24 hours	5.	2.5	20 min	4, 5, 6
Ethanol	VDI 2306	100.	50.	30 min	300.	150.	30 min	1, 2, 3
Ethyl acetate	VDI 2306	75.	20.	30 min	225.	60.	30 min	1, 2, 3
Ethyl acetate	U.S.S.R.	0.1	0.029	24 hours	0.1	0.029	20 min	4, 5
Ethylene	U.S.S.R.	3.	2.3	24 hours	3.	2.3	20 min	4, 5, 6
Ethylene	California	0.13	0.1	8 hours	0.62	0.5	1 hour	13
Ethylene oxide	U.S.S.R.	0.03	0.015	24 hours	0.3	0.15	20 min	4, 5
Ethylene oxide	VDI 2306	4.	2.	30 min	12.	6.	30 min	1, 2, 3
Formaldehyde	VDI 2306	0.03	0.02	30 min	0.07	0.06	30 min	1, 2, 3
Formaldehyde	Czechoslovakia	0.015	0.01	24 hours	0.05	0.033	30 min	—
Formaldehyde	U.S.S.R.	0.012	0.01	24 hours	0.035	0.029	20 min	4, 5

Substance	Source			Time			Time	Ref.
Fluorides (as HF)	Montana	0.007	0.001	24 hours	—	—	—	44
Fluorides (as HF)	New York—rural	0.007	0.001	24 hours	—	—	—	15
Fluorides (as HF)	New York—urban	0.0013	0.002	24 hours	—	—	—	15
Fluorides (as HF)	New York—industrial	0.0026	0.004	24 hours	—	—	—	15
Fluorides (as HF)	Ontario	0.0026	0.001	24 hours	—	—	—	53
Fluorides (as HF)	Ontario	0.007	0.01	24 hours	—	—	—	52
Fluorides	Ontario	—	—	30 min	—	—	—	64
Fluorides (as HF) (soluble)	Pennsylvania	0.005	0.0007	24 hours	—	—	—	—
Fluorides (inorganic gaseous)	Czechoslovakia	0.01	—	24 hours	0.03	—	30 min	—
Fluorides (as F)	U.S.S.R.	0.01	—	24 hours	0.03	—	20 min	4, 5
Fluorides (insoluble)	U.S.S.R.	0.03	—	24 hours	0.2	—	20 min	4, 5
Furfural	U.S.S.R.	0.05	0.013	24 hours	0.05	0.013	20 min	4, 5, 6
Furfural	VDI 2306	0.08	0.02	30 min	0.25	0.06	30 min	1, 2, 3
Gasoline	VDI 2306	80.	20.	30 min	240.	60.	30 min	1, 2, 3
Gasoline	Poland	0.75	0.2	24 hours	2.5	0.6	20 min	4, 57
Gasoline (as C) (from crude oil)	U.S.S.R.	1.5	0.38	24 hours	5.	1.25	20 min	4, 5
Gasoline (as C)	U.S.S.R.	0.05	0.01	24 hours	0.05	0.01	20 min	4, 5
Gasoline (as C) (from shale)	U.S.S.R.	0.01	0.002	24 hours	0.01	0.002	20 min	4, 5
Hexamethylene-diamine	U.S.S.R.	0.01	0.002	24 hours	0.01	0.002	20 min	4, 5
Higher alkyl benzols	VDI 2306	—	5.	30 min	—	15.	30 min	1, 2, 3
Hydrochloric acid (as H+)	Czechoslovakia	0.01	—	30 min	—	—	—	—
Hydrochloric acid (as H+)	U.S.S.R.	0.006	—	24 hours	0.006	—	20 min	4, 5, 6
Hydrochloric acid (as HCl)	U.S.S.R.	—	—	—	0.2	0.15	20 min	4, 5, 6
Hydrochloric acid (as HCl)	VDI 2106—Part 2	0.7	0.5	30 min	1.4	1.	30 min	1, 2, 14

TABLE V (*Continued*)

Substance	Political jurisdiction or standard	Basic standard concentration mg/m³ STP	ppm	Averaging time	Permissible standard concentration mg/m³ STP	ppm	Averaging time	Foot-notes[a]
Hydrogen chloride	Ontario	0.05	0.04	30 min	—	—	—	64
Hydrogen fluoride	The Netherlands	0.01	—	24 hours	—	—	—	22
Hydrogen fluoride	U.S.S.R.	0.005	0.008	24 hours	0.02	0.03	20 min	4, 5, 6
Hydrogen fluoride	California	0.15	0.1	1 hour	—	—	—	13
Hydrogen sulfide	Czechoslovakia	0.008	0.005	24 hours	0.008	0.005	30 min	—
Hydrogen sulfide	Missouri	0.045	0.03	30 min	0.075	0.05	30 min	42, 43
Hydrogen sulfide	Montana	0.045	0.03	30 min	0.075	0.05	30 min	43
Hydrogen sulfide	New York	0.15	0.1	1 hour	—	—	—	—
Hydrogen sulfide	Ontario	0.045	0.03	30 min	—	—	—	64
Hydrogen sulfide	Pennsylvania	0.0075	0.005	24 hours	0.15	0.1	1 hour	4, 56
Hydrogen sulfide	Poland	0.02	0.013	24 hours	0.06	0.04	20 min	4, 57
Hydrogen sulfide	Poland	0.008	0.005	24 hours	0.008	0.005	20 min	4, 5, 6
Hydrogen sulfide	U.S.S.R.	0.008	0.005	24 hours	0.008	0.005	20 min	2, 12
Hydrogen sulfide	Fed. Rep. Germany	0.15	0.1	30 min	0.3	0.2	30 min	67
Hydrogen sulfide	Texas	0.12	0.08	30 min	0.18	0.12	30 min	4, 5, 6
Isopropyl benzene	U.S.S.R.	0.014	0.003	24 hours	0.014	0.003	20 min	4, 5, 6
—hydroperoxide	U.S.S.R.	0.007	0.001	24 hours	0.007	0.001	20 min	17
Lead (as Pb)	Czechoslovakia	0.0007	—	24 hours	—	—	—	—
Lead (as Pb)	Montana	0.005	—	30 days	—	—	—	64
Lead (as Pb)	Ontario	0.02	—	30 min	—	—	—	45
Lead (as Pb)	Pennsylvania	0.005	—	30 days	—	—	—	5, 17
Lead (as Pb)	U.S.S.R.	0.0007	—	24 hours	—	—	—	5
Lead sulfide (as Pb)	U.S.S.R.	0.0017	—	24 hours	—	—	—	4, 5
Malathion	U.S.S.R.	—	—	—	0.015	—	20 min	4, 5
Maleic anhydride	U.S.S.R.	0.05	0.01	24 hours	0.2	0.05	20 min	4, 5, 6

668

Substance	Standard							Ref.
Manganese (as Mn)	U.S.S.R.	0.01	—	24 hours	0.03	—	20 min	4, 5, 18
Manganese (as MnO$_2$)	Czechoslovakia	0.01	—	24 hours	—	—	—	—
Mercury (as Hg)	U.S.S.R.	0.0003	—	24 hours	—	—	—	5
Mesidine (2-amino-1,3,5 trimethylbenzene)	U.S.S.R.	—	—	—	0.003	—	20 min	4, 5
Methanol	U.S.S.R.	0.5	0.38	24 hours	1.	0.75	20 min	4, 5, 6
Methanol	VDI 2306	15.	10.	30 min	40.	30.	30 min	1, 2, 3
Methyl acetate	VDI 2306	15.	5.	30 min	45.	15.	30 min	1, 2, 3
Methyl acetate	U.S.S.R.	0.07	0.023	24 hours	0.07	0.023	20 min	4, 5
Methyl acrylate	U.S.S.R.	—	—	—	0.01	0.003	20 min	4, 5
Methyl aniline	U.S.S.R.	—	—	—	0.04	0.01	20 min	4, 5
Methyl ethyl ketone	VDI 2306	30.	10.	30 min	90.	30.	30 min	1, 2, 3
Methyl isobutyl ketone	VDI 2306	20.	5.	30 min	65.	15.	30 min	1, 2, 3
Methyl mercaptan	U.S.S.R.	—	—	—	9×10^{-6}	—	20 min	4, 5
Methyl methacrylate	U.S.S.R.	0.1	0.025	24 hours	0.1	0.025	20 min	4, 5
Methyl parathion	U.S.S.R.	—	—	—	0.008	—	20 min	4, 5
Methylene chloride	VDI 2306	20.	5.	30 min	55.	15.	30 min	1, 2, 3
Methylstyrene (-α)	U.S.S.R.	0.04	0.01	24 hours	0.04	0.01	20 min	4, 5
Monoethyl amine	VDI 2306	0.02	0.01	30 min	0.06	0.03	30 min	1, 2, 3
Monomethyl amine	VDI 2306	0.02	0.01	30 min	0.06	0.03	30 min	1, 2, 3
Naphthalene	VDI 2306	2.5	0.5	30 min	7.5	1.5	30 min	1, 2, 3
Naphthaquinone (-α)	U.S.S.R.	0.005	0.001	24 hours	0.005	0.001	20 min	4, 5, 6
Nitric acid	VDI 2105—Part 2	1.3	0.5	30 min	2.6	1.	30 min	1, 2, 14
Nitric acid (as HNO$_3$)	U.S.S.R.	—	—	—	0.4	0.15	20 min	4, 5, 6
Nitric acid (as H+)	Czechoslovakia	0.01	—	30 min	—	—	—	—
Nitric acid (as H+)	U.S.S.R.	0.006	0.001	24 hours	0.006	0.001	20 min	4, 5, 6
Nitrobenzol	U.S.S.R.	0.008	0.001	24 hours	0.008	0.001	20 min	4, 5
Nitrobenzol	VDI 2306	0.3	0.05	30 min	0.85	0.15	30 min	1, 2, 3
Nitrogen dioxide	California	0.45	0.25	1 hour	—	—	—	13, 19, 20
Nitrogen dioxide	U.S.S.R.	0.085	0.045	24 hours	0.085	0.045	20 min	4, 5, 6
Nitrogen oxides	Colorado	0.18	0.1	1 hour	—	—	—	21
Nitrogen oxides	Czechoslovakia	0.1	0.06	24 hours	0.3	0.16	30 min	19

TABLE V (Continued)

Substance	Political jurisdiction or standard	Basic standard concentration mg/m³ STP	ppm	Averaging time	Permissible standard concentration mg/m³ STP	ppm	Averaging time	Foot-notes[a]
Nitrogen oxides	Ontario	0.18	0.1	24 hours	0.36	0.2	1 hour	—
Nitrogen oxides	Poland	0.2	0.11	24 hours	0.6	0.33	20 min	4, 23, 56
Nitrogen oxides	Poland	0.05	0.03	24 hours	0.15	0.08	20 min	4, 23, 57
Nitrogen oxides	Fed. Rep. Germany	1.	0.5	30 min	2.	1.	30 min	2, 12, 24
Oxidant (by KI)	California	—	0.15	1 hour	—	—	—	13
Oxidant (by KI)	Colorado	—	0.1	1 hour	—	—	—	21
Oxidant (by KI)	Missouri	—	0.15	1 hour	—	—	—	42
Oxidant (by KI)	New York (rural)	—	0.05	24 hours	—	0.1	4 hours	—
Oxidant (by KI)	New York (urban)	—	0.1	24 hours	—	—	—	—
Oxidant (by KI)	New York (all)	—	—	—	—	0.15	1 hour	—
Oxidant (by KI)	Ontario	—	0.1	24 hours	—	0.15	1 hour	—
Oxidant (by KI)	Ontario	—	—	—	—	0.07	—	62
Pentane (-n)	U.S.S.R.	25.	8.	24 hours	100.	33.	20 min	4, 5
Perchlorethylene	VDI 2306	35.	5.	30 min	110.	15.	30 min	1, 2, 3
Phenol	VDI 2306	0.2	0.05	30 min	0.6	0.15	30 min	1, 2, 3
Phenol	Czechoslovakia	0.1	0.026	24 hours	0.3	0.075	30 min	—
Phenol	U.S.S.R.	0.01	0.0026	24 hours	0.01	0.0026	20 min	4, 5
Phosphoric anhydride	U.S.S.R.	0.05	0.0085	24 hours	0.15	0.026	20 min	4, 5
Phthalic anhydride	U.S.S.R.	0.2	0.03	24 hours	0.2	0.03	20 min	4, 5, 6
Propanol	U.S.S.R.	—	—	—	0.3	0.12	20 min	4, 5
Propanol	VDI 2306	50.	20.	30 min	150.	60.	30 min	1, 2, 3
Propylene	U.S.S.R.	3.	1.5	24 hours	3.	1.5	20 min	4, 5
Pyridine	U.S.S.R.	0.08	0.023	24 hours	0.08	0.023	20 min	4, 5
Pyridine	VDI 2306	0.7	0.2	30 min	2.1	0.6	30 min	1, 2, 3

Styrene	U.S.S.R.	0.003	0.0007	24 hours	0.003	0.0007	20 min	4, 5
Sulfates (as H_2SO_4)	Pennsylvania	0.01	—	30 days	0.03	—	24 hours	—
Sulfates (suspended)	Missouri	0.004	—	1 year	0.012	—	—	42, 48
Sulfates (suspended)	Montana	0.004	—	1 year	0.012	—	—	48
Sulfur dioxide	California	0.78	0.3	8 hours	2.6	1.	1 hour	13, 25
Sulfur dioxide	Colorado	0.26	0.1	24 hours	1.3	0.5	1 hour	21
Sulfur dioxide	Czechoslovakia	0.15	0.06	24 hours	0.5	0.19	30 min	—
Sulfur dioxide	Dade County, Florida	0.26	0.1	8 hours	2.6	1.	20 min	—
Sulfur dioxide	Delaware (rural)	0.13	0.05	1 hour	0.55	0.21	1 hour	16
		0.05	0.02	24 hours	0.21	0.08	24 hours	16
Sulfur dioxide	Delaware (residential)	0.18	0.07	1 hour	0.65	0.25	1 hour	16
		0.08	0.03	24 hours	0.26	0.10	24 hours	16
Sulfur dioxide	Delaware (commercial)	0.23	0.09	1 hour	0.73	0.28	1 hour	16
		0.10	0.04	24 hours	0.31	0.12	24 hours	16
Sulfur dioxide	Delaware (industrial)	0.31	0.12	1 hour	0.83	0.32	1 hour	16
		0.16	0.06	24 hours	0.39	0.15	24 hours	16
Sulfur dioxide	Japan	0.52	0.2	3 hours	0.78	0.3	2 hours	26
Sulfur dioxide	Manitoba	0.78	0.3	8 hours	2.6	1.	1 hour	—
Sulfur dioxide	Missouri	0.052	0.02	1 year	0.26	0.1	24 hours	42, 45, 46
Sulfur dioxide	Missouri	0.13	0.05	24 hours	0.26	0.1	1 hour	42, 54
Sulfur dioxide	Missouri	—	—	—	0.65	0.25	5 min	12, 42
Sulfur dioxide	Montana	0.052	0.02	1 year	0.26	0.1	24 hours	21
Sulfur dioxide	Montana	—	—	—	0.65	0.25	1 hour	47
Sulfur dioxide	The Netherlands	0.15	0.05	24 hours	—	—	—	22, 34, 59
Sulfur dioxide	The Netherlands	0.3	0.1	24 hours	—	—	—	22, 34, 60
Sulfur dioxide	The Netherlands	0.5	0.18	24 hours	—	—	—	22, 34, 61
Sulfur dioxide	New York	0.26	0.1	24 hours	0.65	0.25	1 hour	27
Sulfur dioxide	New York	0.39	0.15	24 hours	1.04	0.4	1 hour	28
Sulfur dioxide	Ontario (industrial—commercial)	0.13	0.05	1 year	0.52	0.2	24 hours	—
Sulfur dioxide	Ontario (industrial—commercial)	1.04	0.4	1 hour	0.78	0.3	30 min	65

TABLE V (Continued)

Substance	Political jurisdiction or standard	Basic standard concentration mg/m³ STP	ppm	Averaging time	Permissible standard concentration mg/m³ STP	ppm	Averaging time	Footnotes[a]
Sulfur dioxide	Ontario (residential—rural)	0.05	0.02	1 year	0.26	0.1	24 hours	—
Sulfur dioxide	Ontario (residential—rural)	0.65	0.25	1 hour	0.78	0.3	30 min	65
Sulfur dioxide	Pennsylvania	0.13	0.05	30 days	0.65	0.25	24 hours	—
Sulfur dioxide	Pennsylvania	—	—	—	1.3	0.5	1 hour	—
Sulfur dioxide	Poland	0.35	0.13	24 hours	0.9	0.35	20 min	4, 56
Sulfur dioxide	Poland	0.075	0.03	24 hours	0.25	0.1	20 min	4, 57
Sulfur dioxide	Rumania	0.23	0.09	24 hours	0.68	0.26	20 min	4
Sulfur dioxide	San Francisco, Calif.	—	—	—	—	—	—	29
Sulfur dioxide	South Carolina	0.26	0.1	24 hours	0.78	0.3	1 hour	52
Sulfur dioxide	South Carolina	0.44	0.17	24 hours	1.3	0.5	1 hour	53
Sulfur dioxide	Sweden	0.13	0.05	1 month	0.26	0.1	24 hours	10
Sulfur dioxide	Sweden	—	—	—	0.65	0.25	30 min	10
Sulfur dioxide	Switzerland (March 1–Oct. 31)	0.5	0.2	24 hours	0.75	0.3	30 min	14
Sulfur dioxide	Switzerland (Nov. 1–Feb. 28/29)	0.75	0.3	24 hours	1.3	0.5	30 min	14
Sulfur dioxide	Texas—industrial	0.78	0.3	24 hours	1.3	0.5	30 min	—
Sulfur dioxide	Texas—other	0.52	0.2	24 hours	1.0	0.4	30 min	—
Sulfur dioxide	Trafalgar, Ontario	1.3	0.5	1 hour	—	—	—	—
Sulfur dioxide	U.S.S.R.	0.15	0.058	24 hours	0.5	0.19	20 min	4, 5, 6
Sulfur dioxide	Valois Canton, Sw'd.	0.52	0.2	24 hours	1.3	0.5	1 hour	30
Sulfur dioxide	Fed. Rep. Germany	0.4	0.15	30 min	0.75	0.3	30 min	2, 14

Pollutant	Location									Reference
Sulfuric acid	Missouri	0.004	—	1 year	0.012	—	—	—	—	42, 48
Sulfuric acid	Missouri	—	—	—	0.03	—	—	30 min	—	42, 50
Sulfuric acid	Missouri	—	—	—	0.01	—	—	24 hours	—	42, 51
Sulfuric acid	Montana	0.004	—	1 year	0.012	—	—	—	—	48
Sulfuric acid	Montana	—	—	—	0.03	—	—	1 hour	—	48
Sulfuric acid	New York	0.1	—	24 hours	—	—	—	—	—	4, 56
Sulfuric acid	Poland	0.1	—	24 hours	0.3	—	—	20 min	—	4, 56
Sulfuric acid	Poland	0.05	—	24 hours	0.15	—	—	20 min	—	4, 57
Sulfuric acid (as H+)	Czechoslovakia	0.01	—	30 min	—	—	—	—	—	—
Sulfuric acid (as H+)	U.S.S.R.	0.006	—	24 hours	0.006	—	—	20 min	—	4, 5, 6
Sulfuric acid (as H_2SO_4)	U.S.S.R.	0.1	—	24 hours	0.3	—	—	20 min	—	4, 5, 6
Suspended particulate matter (dust)	Colorado	0.12	—	3 months	—	—	—	—	—	—
Suspended particulate matter (dust)	Czechoslovakia	0.15	—	24 hours	0.5	—	—	30 min	—	—
Suspended particulate matter (dust)	Delaware (rural)	0.06	—	24 hours	0.13	—	—	24 hours	—	16
Suspended particulate matter (dust)	Delaware (residential)	0.075	—	24 hours	0.15	—	—	24 hours	—	16
Suspended particulate matter (dust)	Delaware (commercial)	0.095	—	24 hours	0.17	—	—	24 hours	—	16
Suspended particulate matter (dust)	Delaware (industrial)	0.125	—	24 hours	0.20	—	—	24 hours	—	16
Suspended particulate matter (dust)	Delaware (all)	0.5	—	1 hour	—	—	—	—	—	—
Suspended particulate matter (dust)	Missouri	0.075	—	1 year	0.2	—	—	24 hours	—	42, 48
Suspended particulate matter (dust)	Montana	0.075	—	1 year	0.2	—	—	24 hours	—	49
Suspended particulate matter (dust)	New York	—	—	—	—	—	—	—	—	31

TABLE V (*Continued*)

Substance	Political jurisdiction or standard	Basic standard concentration mg/m³ STP	ppm	Averaging time	Permissible standard concentration mg/m³ STP	ppm	Averaging time	Foot-notes[a]
Suspended particulate matter (dust)	Ontario (industrial—commercial)	0.2	—	30 min	0.175	—	24 hours	63, 66
Suspended particulate matter (dust)	Ontario (industrial—commercial)	0.11	—	1 year	—	—	—	58
Suspended particulate matter (dust)	Ontario (residential—rural)	0.1	—	30 min	0.09	—	24 hours	63, 66
Suspended particulate matter (dust)	Ontario (residential—rural)	0.06	—	1 year	—	—	—	58
Suspended particulate matter (dust)	Oregon (industrial)	0.25	—	—	—	—	—	32, 35
Suspended particulate matter (dust)	Oregon (industrial)	0.3	—	—	—	—	—	35, 36
Suspended particulate matter (dust)	Oregon (other)	0.15	—	—	—	—	—	32, 35
Suspended particulate matter (dust)	Oregon (other)	0.2	—	—	—	—	—	35, 36
Suspended particulate matter (dust)	Pennsylvania	0.15	—	30 days	0.5	—	24 hours	—
Suspended particulate matter (dust)	Pennsylvania	0.15	—	—	—	—	—	41
Suspended particulate matter (dust)	Pennsylvania (air basin)	0.1	—	30 days	—	—	—	37
Suspended particulate matter (dust)	Pennsylvania (fugitive dust)	2.	—	10 min	—	—	—	38, 41

Substance	Location / Standard							Reference
Suspended particulate matter (dust)	Poland	0.2	—	24 hours	0.6	—	20 min	4, 56
Suspended particulate matter (dust)	Poland	0.075	—	24 hours	0.2	—	20 min	4, 57
Suspended particulate matter (dust)	South Carolina	0.025	—	24 hours	0.05	—	1 hour	55
Suspended particulate matter (dust)	South Carolina	—	—	—	0.1	—	15 min	55
Suspended particulate matter (dust)	South Carolina (nonresidential)	0.05	—	24 hours	0.1	—	1 hour	—
Suspended particulate matter (dust)	South Carolina (nonresidential)	—	—	—	0.2	—	15 min	—
Suspended particulate matter (dust)	Texas (residential)	0.125	—	24 hours	—	—	—	39
Suspended particulate matter (dust)	Texas (commercial)	0.15	—	24 hours	—	—	—	39
Suspended particulate matter (dust)	Texas (industrial)	0.175	—	24 hours	—	—	—	39
Suspended particulate matter (dust)	Texas (other)	0.2	—	24 hours	—	—	—	39, 40
Suspended particulate matter (dust)	U.S.S.R.	0.15	—	24 hours	0.5	—	20 min	4, 5
Tetrahydrofuran	VDI 2306	30.	10.	30 min	90.	30.	30 min	1, 2, 3
Thiophene	U.S.S.R.	0.6	—	—	0.6	0.17	20 min	4, 5
Toluene	U.S.S.R.	0.6	0.15	24 hours	0.6	0.15	20 min	4, 5
Toluene	VDI 2306	20.	5.	30 min	60.	15.	30 min	1, 2, 3
Toluene diisocyanate	VDI 2306	0.007	0.001	30 min	0.021	0.003	30 min	1, 2, 3
Toluene diisocyanate	U.S.S.R.	0.02	0.0029	24 hours	0.05	0.0071	20 min	4, 5
Tributyl phosphate	U.S.S.R.	—	—	—	0.01	—	20 min	4, 5
Trichloroethane	VDI 2306	30.	5.	30 min	90.	15.	30 min	1, 2, 3
Trichloroethylene	VDI 2306	30.	5.	30 min	90.	15.	30 min	1, 2, 3

675

TABLE V (Continued)

Substance	Political jurisdiction or standard	Basic standard			Permissible standard			Foot-notes[a]
		concentration		Averaging time	concentration		Averaging time	
		mg/m³ STP	ppm		mg/m³ STP	ppm		
Trichloroethylene	U.S.S.R.	1.	0.17	24 hours	4.	0.67	20 min	4, 5
Triethyl amine	VDI 2306	0.04	0.01	30 min	0.12	0.03	30 min	1, 2, 3
Trimethyl amine	VDI 2306	0.02	0.01	30 min	0.06	0.03	30 min	1, 2, 3
Turpentine	VDI 2306	25.	5.	30 min	75.	15.	30 min	1, 2, 3
Valeric acid (-n)	U.S.S.R.	0.01	0.003	24 hours	0.03	0.008	20 min	4, 5
Vanadium pentoxide	U.S.S.R.	0.002	—	24 hours	—	—	—	5
Vinyl acetate	VDI 2306	20.	5.	30 min	60.	15.	30 min	1, 2, 3
Vinyl acetate	U.S.S.R.	0.2	0.06	24 hours	0.2	0.06	20 min	4, 5
Xylene	U.S.S.R.	0.2	0.05	24 hours	0.2	0.05	20 min	4, 5
Xylene	VDI 2306	20.	5.	30 min	60.	15.	30 min	1, 2, 3

[a] Numbers in this column refer to the following footnotes. *1.* Verein Deutscher Ingenieure—Kommission Reinhaltung der Luft—Richtlinien, VDI—Verlag GmbH. Dusseldorf, Fed. Rep. Germany. *2.* Basic Standard is for long-term exposure. *3.* Permissible standard not to be exceeded more than once in any 4 hours. *4.* Averaging time for permissible standard approximately 20 min. *5.* Also for other countries which adopt identical standards to U.S.S.R. *6A.* If several substances with additive toxic properties are present in the air, the maximum permissible concentration (MPC) of the mixture is calculated from the following formula:

$$X = \frac{A}{M_1} + \frac{B}{M_2} + \frac{C}{M_3} \cdots$$

(1)

where X is the (relative) *MPC*; A, B, C are the concentrations of the substances in the mixture and M_1, M_2, M_3, their respective maximum permissible concentrations.

B. If formula (1) is applied to the following two, three or four component systems, the value X:

should not exceed 1.0 for

(a) acetone and phenol
(b) SO_2 and phenol
(c) SO_2 and NO_2
(d) SO_2 and HF
(e) SO_2 and sulfuric acid aerosol

(f) H_2S and "dinyl"
(g) isopropyl benzene and isopropyl benzene hydroperoxide
(h) furfural, methanol, and ethanol
(i) strong mineral acids (sulfuric, hydrochloric, and nitric, concentrations expressed as H^+)
(j) ethylene, propylene, butylene and amylene

should not exceed 1.3 for

acetic acid and acetic anhydride

should not exceed 1.5 for

(a) acetone and acetophenone   (b) benzene and acetophenone   (c) phenol and acetophenone

C. If (a) H_2S and CS_2, (b) CO and SO_2, (c) phthalic anhydride, maleic anhydride and α-naphthoquinone are present in the mixture, the MPC values of individual substances should not be exceeded.

D. If p-chlorophenyl isocyanate is present together with m-chlorophenyl isocyanate the MPC is determined by the presence of the more toxic substance i.e., of p-chlorophenyl isocyanate. *7.* Above normal background concentration; also deposit standard of 1 ton/sq. mile/month above normal background deposit in residential and commercial areas. *8.* Serious level. *9.* Basic standard—not to be exceeded more than 15% of the time in a year. Permissible standard—not to be exceeded more than 1% of the time in a year. *10.* 24-hour mean not to be exceeded more than once in any 30 days; 30-minute mean not to be exceeded more than 1% of the time in any 30 days. *11.* Same as VDI 2106 (see footnote 1). *12.* Permissible standard not to be exceeded more than once in any 2 hours. *13.* Adverse level. *14.* Permissible standard not to be exceeded more than once in any 2 hours. *15.* Also fluorine and fluorides, as HF. *16.* Annual basis—Basic standard—geometric mean (i.e., fiftieth percentile in log-normal cumulative frequency distribution; permissible standard—95th percentile). *17.* Also its compounds, except tetraethyl lead. *18.* Also its compounds. *19.* As NO_2. *20.* There is also a Serious level Basic Standard of 3 ppm for 1 hour. *21.* Not to be exceeded more than 1% of the time in any 3 months. *22.* Proposed standard, not yet adopted. *23.* As N_2O_5. *24.* Same as VDI 2105 (see footnote 1). *25.* There is also a Serious level Basic Standard of 5 ppm for 1 hour, and an Emergency level Basic Standard of 10 ppm for 1 hour. *26.* "Caution Warning" associated with a meteorological forecast of prolonged duration of levels exceeding standards. There is also an alarm warning at 0.5 ppm $(SO_2 + SO_3)$. *27.* To be exceeded less than 1% of the time in any year in A-1, 2, and 3; B-1, 2, and 3- and C-1, 2, and 3 subregions; less than 2% in D-1, and 2 subregions. A, B, C, and D are geographical regions into which the State is divided—within which subregions are (1) rural, (2) residential, (3) commercial, and (4) industrial. *28.* To be exceeded less than 1% of the time in any year in A-4, B-4, and C-4 subregions; less than 2% in D-3 and 4 subregions, as defined in footnote 27. *29.* Bay Area Air Pollution Control District—(see Table VI). *30.* Outside area of source. *31.* See Table VII. *32.* Above normal background concentra-

677

TABLE V (*Concluded*)

tion. *33.* Also its inorganic compounds, except arsine. *34.* See Section IV, B. *35.* The regulations are intended as a rate, and consequently 24 hour, 1 hour, or 1 minute averaging time can be used. However, it is suggested a 1/2 hour minimum averaging time be used. *36.* Cities of Eugene and Springfield, Oregon. *37.* Based on results from geographically uniformly spaced sampling stations. *38.* From a source near ground level other than a flue. *39.* Not to be exceeded more than 10% of the days in a month. *40.* Vacant, range, or agricultural land, except within 100 feet of a residence. *41.* At any point beyond the property on which the source thereof is located. *42.* St. Louis Metropolitan area. *43.* Basic Standard—not to be exceeded more than twice in any 5 consecutive days; Permissible Standard—not to be exceeded over twice a year. *44.* Averaging time not stated—assumed to be 24 hours. *45.* Tentative. *46.* Basic Standard—24-hour sampling time; Permissible Standard—not to be exceeded over 1 day in any 3-month period. *47.* Not to be exceeded more than 1 hour in any 4 consecutive days. *48.* Permissible Standard—not to be exceeded over 1% of the time. *49.* Permissible Standard—not to be exceeded more than 1% of the days in a year. *50.* Not more than once in any 48 hours; this value appears elsewhere as the hourly average not to be exceeded over 1% of the time. *51.* Not more than once in any 90 days. *52.* Residential or nonindustrial areas. *53.* Industrial areas. *54.* Basic Standard not to be exceeded more than once in any 90 days; Permissible Standard—not more than once in any 4 days. *55.* Predominantly residential areas. *56.* For protected areas. *57.* For specially protected areas. *58.* Geometric mean. *59.* Average value over 1 year. *60.* Not to be exceeded more than 2% of the time. *61.* Not to be exceeded in more than 0.3% of the time, or 1 day/year. *62.* 90% of samplings in any 1 month. *63.* Permissible Standard—90% of 24-hour samplings. *64.* Although this is listed as an ambient air quality standard, it is the maximum ground level concentration from a single point source measured on the center line downwind from the stack and, as such, has the characteristics of an emission standard. *65.* Permissible standard as per 64. *66.* Basic Standard as per 64. *67.* Basic Standard for Residential-commercial areas; Permissible Standard for industrial and all other areas.

TABLE VI

MAXIMUM ALLOWABLE SULFUR DIOXIDE GROUND-LEVEL LIMITS[a,b]
BAY AREA AIR POLLUTION CONTROL DISTRICT, CALIFORNIA (U.S.A.)

Average conc. (c) in ppm (vol.) (1)	Total cumulative daily exposure; duration (t) in hours		Total cumulative monthly exposure; duration (t) in hours	
	Between sunrise and sunset (2)	Between sunrise and next succeeding sunrise (3)	During hours between sunrise and sunset (4)	Any time during month (5)
1.51 or over	0.05	0.10	1.00	2.00
1.5	0.62	1.24	4.40	8.80
1.4	0.67	1.34	5.10	10.20
1.3	0.73	1.46	5.90	11.80
1.2	0.80	1.60	6.90	13.80
1.1	0.89	1.78	8.30	16.60
1.0	1.00	2.00	10.00	20.00
0.9	1.14	2.28	12.40	24.80
0.8	1.33	2.66	15.60	31.20
0.7	1.60	3.20	20.40	40.80
0.6	2.00	4.00	27.80	55.60
0.5	2.67	5.34	40.00	80.00
0.4	4.00	8.00	62.50	125.00
0.3	8.00	16.00	111.00	222.00
0.2 or less	No limit	No limit	No limit	No limit

[a] Interpolation of Columns 2, 3, 4, and 5 shall be based on the formulas $t = 0.8/(c - 0.2)$, $t = 1.6/(c - 0.2)$, $t = 10/c^2$, and $t = 20/c^2$, respectively; where c is the concentration of SO_2 in ppm (vol.) and t is the time of SO_2 exposure in hours and c can vary only between a maximum of 1.5 ppm and a minimum of 0.2 ppm.

[b] Bay Area Pollution Control District Regulation No. 2. San Francisco, California, 1960.

TABLE VII

New York State Ambient Air Quality Objectives for Particulate Matter[a]

Specification of objective	Subregion[b]						
	A-1	A-2 B-1	A-3 B-2 C-1	A-4 B-3 C-2 D-1	B-4 C-3 D-2	C-4 D-3	D-4
Suspended particulate matter—μg/m^3—24-hour sampling period							
50% of values less than	40	45	55	65	80	100	135
84% of values less than	60	70	80	100	120	150	200
Settleable particles—mg/cm^2/month—30-day sampling period							
50% of values less than	0.30	0.30	0.60	0.60	0.90	1.20	1.50
84% of values less than	0.35	0.35	0.80	0.80	1.20	1.70	2.25

[a] Rule 501, pending adoption, would supersede Table VII in areas, after hearings, to classify them into the following new land use areas, I—Rural; II—Sparsely populated; III—Densely populated, light industry; IV—Densely populated, limited heavy industry; V—Extensive heavy industry, for each of which new standards for the 50% and 84% values would be set.

[b] The state will be geographically divided into regions: A, B, C, and D. Within these, the subregions depend on land use: (1) rural, (2) residential, (3) commercial, and (4) industrial.

TABLE VIII
DEPOSITED PARTICULATE MATTER STANDARDS

Jurisdiction	Land use	Standard		Foot-notes[a]
		Original units	Tons/sq. mile/month	
Alberta	Residential	tons/sq. mile/month	15	—
Alberta	Industrial and commercial	tons/sq. mile/month	45	—
Missouri	Nonindustrial	tons/sq. mile/month	10	1
Missouri	Heavy industrial	tons/sq. mile/month	25	1
Montana	Residential	tons/sq. mile/month	15	2
Montana	Heavy industrial	tons/sq. mile/month	30	2
New York	—	tons/sq. mile/month	—	3
Ontario	—	tons/sq. mile/month	15	10
Ontario	Industrial and commercial	tons/sq. mile/month	40	—
Ontario	Industrial and commercial	tons/sq. mile/month	25	8
Ontario	Residential and rural	tons/sq. mile/month	20	—
Ontario	Residential and rural	tons/sq. mile/month	13	8
Oregon	Residential and commercial	tons/sq. mile/month	15	4, 11
Oregon	Industrial	tons/sq. mile/month	30	4, 11
Oregon (Eugene and Springfield)	Residential and commercial	tons/sq. mile/month	20	—
Oregon (Eugene and Springfield)	Industrial	tons/sq. mile/month	50	—
Pennsylvania	Any	1.5 mg/cm²/month	48	5
Pennsylvania	Air basin	1. mg/cm²/month	32	6
Pennsylvania	Emission standard	0.6 mg/cm²/month	19	7
Poland	Protected areas	250 tons/km²/year	48	—
Poland	Specially protected areas	40 tons/km²/year	8	—
Poland	Specially protected areas	6.5 tons/km²/month	15	—
Fed. Rep. Germany	General	0.42 gm/m²/month	36	8, 9
Fed. Rep. Germany	General	0.65 gm/m²/month	55	9
Fed. Rep. Germany	Industrial	0.85 gm/m²/month	72	8, 9
Fed. Rep. Germany	Industrial	1.3 gm/m²/month	110	9

[a] Numbers in this column refer to the following footnotes: *1*. St. Louis Metropolitan Area—3 months average above 5 ton/sq. mile/month background value. *2*. Includes 5 ton/sq. mile/month basic background. *3*. See Table VII. *4*. Above normal background value. *5*. Not to be exceeded as the average of three successive sampling periods. *6*. Based on results from geographically uniformly spaced sampling stations. *7*. At any point outside a person's property. *8*. Average of 12 monthly averages. *9*. Same as VDI 2305 with Bergerhoff measuring method; VDI 2305 also lists standards for Löbner-Leisengang method, which are the Bergerhoff values times 0.77. *10*. Although this is listed as an ambient air quality standard, it is the maximum ground level concentration from a single point source measured on the center line downwind from the stack and, as such, has the characteristics of an emission standard. *11*. Also Virginia.

TABLE IX
Alert Stages for Toxic Air Pollutants
(Rule 156: Los Angeles County Air Pollution Control District)

Gas	In parts per million of air		
	First alert (Still safe but approaching level where preventive action is required)	Second alert (A health menace exists in a preliminary stage)	Third alert (A dangerous health menace exists)
Carbon monoxide	100 for 1 hour 200 for 1/2 hour 300 for 10 min	100 for 2 hours 200 for 1 hour 300 for 20 min	— 200 for 2 hours 300 for 1 hour
Nitrogen oxides	3	5	10
Sulfur oxides	3	5	10
Ozone	0.5	1.0	1.5

TABLE X
Tentative New York-New Jersey Metropolitan Area Standards for Air Pollution Alerts[a]

Alert status	Air Concentrations			Duration sustained levels of air concentrations (hours)	N.Y.-N.J. Metro area meteorology high air pollution potential forecast for next (hours)	Number of pollutants	Action plan
	SO_2 (ppm)	CO (ppm)	Smoke level (COHS)				
Air pollution watch					24		A
First	0.5+	10+	5.0	4 and	18	2	1
	0.7+			2 and	8	1	1
			7.5	2 and	8	1	1
	1.5+			1 and	8	1	1
			9.0	1 and	8	1	1
Second	1.0+	20+	7.5	2 and	8	2	2

[a] See also reference (22), p. 718.

Comments: The standards tabulated above are predicated on the presumption that an air pollution alert should be based on the following criteria:

1. The concentration of the number of pollutants as specified above with sustained levels measured at selected test sites for periods in excess of the duration indicated.

2. A meteorological forecast reporting that high air pollution potential conditions will persist for the tabulated period of time. This would indicate that the levels of concentration will be present for that period of time.

3. The levels of SO_2, CO, and smoke measured and confirmed for the tabulated periods of time together with the forecast of the weather duration of continued high air pollution potential provide the basis for the alert status.

Watch and Alert Status and Action

Plan "A": Upon receipt of a high air pollution potential forecast for the next 24 hours, the Interstate Sanitation Commission will call an air pollution watch and notify cooperating agencies.

Plans 1 and 2: When air pollution measures exceed the standards for an alert and the meteorological forecast indicates profound stable air conditions for the period of time tabulated in the above table, an alert will be recommended by the Interstate Sanitation Commission to the Commissioners of Health of New York and New Jersey or their designee. Detailed actions to implement alerts are specified by the states.

TABLE XI

Emission Standard for Specific Pollutants in Effluent Air or Gases

Substance	Jurisdiction or code	Source of emission	Original units[a]	Standard mg/m³ STP	Standard ppm	Foot-notes[b]
Acrolein	Czechoslovakia	—	3. kg/hour	—	—	26
Ammonia	Czechoslovakia	—	3. kg/hour	—	—	26
Antimony	Great Britain	Less than 5000 cfm	0.05 grains/ft³	115	—	1, 2
Antimony	Great Britain	More than 5000 cfm	0.02 grains/ft³	46	—	1, 2
Antimony	New South Wales	—	0.01 grains/ft³	23	—	1, 3
Antimony	Queensland	—	0.01 grains/ft³	23	—	1, 3
Arsenic	Czechoslovakia	—	0.03 kg/hour	—	—	26, 27
Arsenic	Great Britain	Less than 5000 cfm	0.05 grains/ft³	115	—	1, 2
Arsenic	Great Britain	More than 5000 cfm	0.02 grains/ft³	46	—	1, 2
Arsenic	New South Wales	—	0.01 grains/ft³	23	—	1, 3
Arsenic	Queensland	—	0.01 grains/ft³	23	—	1, 3
Benzene	Czechoslovakia	—	24. kg/hour	—	—	26
Cadmium	Great Britain	Maximum—30 lbs/168 hours	0.017 grains/ft³	39	—	1, 3
Cadmium	New South Wales	—	0.01 grains/ft	23	—	1, 3
Cadmium	Queensland	—	0.01 grains/ft³	23	—	1, 3
Carbon black	Czechoslovakia	(Amorphous carbon)	1.5 kg/hour	—	—	26
Carbon disulfide	Czechoslovakia	—	0.3 kg/hour	—	—	26
Carbon monoxide	Czechoslovakia	—	60. kg/hour	—	—	26
Carbon monoxide	Paris, France	Combustion	1. % by volume	11,000	10,000	—
Carbon monoxide	Japan	Automobile exhaust	3. % by volume	33,000	30,000	4
Carbon monoxide	United States	Automobile exhaust	1.5 % by volume	16,500	15,000	4, 5, 25
Carbon monoxide	United States	Automobile exhaust 100–140 cu. inches	2. % by volume	22,000	20,000	4, 25

TABLE XI (Continued)

Substance	Jurisdiction or code	Source of emission	Standard			Footnotes[b]
			Original units[a]	mg/m³ STP	ppm	
Carbon monoxide	United States	Automobile exhaust 50–100 cu. inches	2.3 % by volume	25,500	23,000	4, 25
Carbonyls	Bay Area A.P.C.D.	Incineration	ppm	—	50	6, 7, 8
Chlorine	Czechoslovakia	—	1. kg/hour	—	—	26
Chlorine	Great Britain	—	0.1 grains/ft³	230	77	3
Chlorine	New South Wales	—	0.1 grains/ft³	230	77	3
Chlorine	Queensland	—	0.1 grains/ft³	230	77	3
Fluorine	Czechoslovakia	Gaseous inorganic compounds	0.3 kg/hour	—	—	26
Fluorine	Florida	—	0.4 lb/ton of P_2O_5	—	—	24
Formaldehyde	Czechoslovakia	—	0.5 kg/hour	—	—	26
Hydrocarbons	Bay Area A.P.C.D.	Incineration	50 ppm	—	50	7, 8
Hydrocarbons	United States	Automobile crankcase	None permitted	—	—	—
Hydrocarbons	United States	Automobile exhaust	275 ppm	—	275	4, 5, 25
Hydrocarbons	United States	Automobile exhaust 100–140 cu. inches	350 ppm	—	350	4, 25
Hydrocarbons	United States	Automobile exhaust 50–100 cu. inches	410 ppm	—	410	4, 25
Hydrochloric acid	Czechoslovakia	(As hydrogen ion)	0.1 kg/hour	—	—	26
Hydrogen chloride	Great Britain	Alkali (saltcake) works	0.2 grains/ft³	460	328	—
Hydrogen chloride	Great Britain	Hydrochloric acid works	0.2 grains/ft³	460	328	—
Hydrogen fluoride	Great Britain	—	0.1 grains/ft³	230	—	9
Hydrogen fluoride	New South Wales	—	0.05 grains/ft³	115	—	—
Hydrogen fluoride	Queensland	—	0.05 grains/ft³	115	—	—
Hydrogen fluoride	VDI 2286	Aluminum reduction	0.005 gm/m³	5	7.5	10
Hydrogen sulfide	Czechoslovakia	—	0.08 kg/hour	—	—	26

Substance	Location	Description		Units			Ref
Hydrogen sulfide	Great Britain	—		ppm	7.5	5	—
Hydrogen sulfide	New South Wales	—		ppm	7.5	5	—
Hydrogen sulfide	Queensland	—		ppm	7.5	5	—
Lead	Czechoslovakia	(Except tetraethyllead)	0.007	kg/hour	—	—	26
Lead	Great Britain	Up to 3,000 cfm of exhaust gas	0.05	grains/ft³	115	—	3, 11
Lead	Great Britain	3,000–10,000 cfm	0.05	grains/ft³	115	—	3, 12
Lead	Great Britain	10,000–140,000 cfm	0.01	grains/ft³	23	—	3, 13
Lead	Great Britain	Over 140,000 cfm	0.005	grains/ft³	12	—	3
Lead	New South Wales	—	0.01	grains/ft³	23	—	3
Lead	Queensland	—	0.01	grains/ft³	23	—	3
Manganese	Czechoslovakia	(as MnO₂)	0.1	kg/hour	—	—	26
Mercury	Czechoslovakia	(Metallic)	0.003	kg/hour	—	—	26
Mercury	New South Wales	—	0.01	grains/ft³	23	—	3
Mercury	Queensland	—	0.01	grains/ft³	23	—	3
Miscellaneous	Great Britain	Superphosphate fertilizer manufacture	0.1	grains/ft³—total acidity as SO_3	230	—	17
Nitric acid	Czechoslovakia	(As hydrogen ion)	0.1	kg/hour	—	—	26
Nitrogen oxides	California	Automobile exhaust		ppm	630	350	4
Nitrogen oxides	Czechoslovakia	(As NO_2)	3.	kg/hour	—	—	26
Nitrogen oxides	Great Britain		1.	grains/ft³	2,300	1,280	9
Nitrogen oxides	Great Britain	Nitric acid plants	2.	grains/ft³	4,600	2,560	9
Nitrogen oxides	New South Wales		1.	grains/ft³	2,300	1,280	—
Nitrogen oxides	New South Wales	Nitric acid plants	2.	grains/ft³	4,600	2,560	—
Nitrogen oxides	Queensland		1.	grains/ft³	2,300	1,280	—
Nitrogen oxides	Queensland	Nitric acid plants	2.	grains/ft³	4,600	2,560	—
Organic compounds	Bay Area A.P.C.D.	As hexane		ppm	—	50	18
Organic compounds	Bay Area A.P.C.D.	As total carbon		ppm	—	300	18
Organic compounds	Bay Area A.P.C.D.		20.	lb/day	—	—	18
Organic solvents	Los Angeles County	Heated or baked	15.	lb/day	—	—	15
Organic solvents	Los Angeles County	Unheated	40.	lb/day	—	—	15
Phenol	Czechoslovakia	—	3.	kg/hour	—	—	26

TABLE XI (Continued)

Substance	Jurisdiction or code	Source of emission	Standard Original units[a]	mg/m³ STP	ppm	Foot-notes[b]
Reactive compounds	Bay Area A.P.C.D.	All olefins, substituted aromatics, and aldehydes	10. lb/day	—	—	18
Reactive solvents	Los Angeles County	Dispose or evaporate	1.5 gallons/day	—	—	16
Sulfur dioxide	Bay Area A.P.C.D.	—	ppm	5,200	2,000	7
Sulfur dioxide	Belgium	Pb and Zn Smelting	1 part/1000 parts	2,600	1,000	28
Sulfur dioxide	Czechoslovakia	—	—	—	—	14
Sulfur dioxide	Dade County, Fla.	—	ppm	5,200	2,000	—
Sulfur dioxide	Eugene, Oregon	Combustion	0.2 % by volume	5,200	2,000	—
Sulfur dioxide	Paris, France	Combustion	1. gm/1000 kcal	—	—	29
Sulfur dioxide	Paris, France	Combustion	4. gm/1000 kcal	—	—	29
Sulfur dioxide	Great Britain	Chamber sulfuric acid plants	4. grains/ft (as SO_3)	9,200	—	—
Sulfur dioxide	Great Britain	Sulfuric acid concentration	1.5 grains/ft³ (as SO_3)	3,450	—	—
Sulfur dioxide	Great Britain	Contact sulfuric acid plants —sulfur burning	2. % of the sulfur burned	—	—	—
Sulfur dioxide	Great Britain	Contact sulfuric acid plants —other than sulfur	4. grains/ft³ (as SO_3)	9,200	—	—
Sulfur dioxide	Japan	—	0.22 % by volume	5,700	2,200	—
Sulfur dioxide	Japan	Petroleum refining and gas manufacturing	0.28 % by volume	7,300	2,800	—
Sulfur dioxide	Los Angeles County	—	0.2 % by volume	5,200	2,000	8
Sulfur dioxide	Manitoba	Combustion	0.2 % by volume	5,200	2,000	—
Sulfur dioxide	Missouri	Existing nonfuel sources	ppm	5,200	2,000	21
Sulfur dioxide	Missouri	New nonfuel sources	ppm	1,300	500	21
Sulfur dioxide	Missouri	Fuel burning sources	2.3 lb/million Btu heat input	—	—	21, 22

Substance	Location	Source / Description	Value	Units			Ref[b]
Sulfur dioxide	Natick, Mass.	Fuel burning sources	0.4	% by volume	10,400	4,000	—
Sulfur dioxide	New Jersey	Other than fuel burning		ppm	7,800	3,000	19, 20
Sulfur dioxide	New Jersey (after 3/1/69)	Other than fuel burning		ppm	5,200	2,000	19, 20
Sulfur dioxide	New Jersey	Sulfur removal from H$_2$S recovery		ppm	39,000	15,000	—
Sulfur dioxide	New South Wales	Metallurgical plant SO$_2$	4.	grains/ft^3	9,200	3,540	—
Sulfur dioxide	New South Wales	Sulfuric acid manufacture	3.	grains/ft^3	6,900	2,650	—
Sulfur dioxide	New York, N.Y.	—		ppm	5,200	2,000	—
Sulfur dioxide	Queensland	Sulfuric acid manufacture	3.	grains/ft^3	6,900	2,650	—
Sulfur dioxide	Riverside County, California	—	0.2	% by volume	5,200	2,000	—
Sulfur dioxide	Sarasota County, Fla.	—	0.2	% by volume	5,200	2,000	—
Sulfur dioxide	South Carolina	—		—			23
Sulfur dioxide	United States	Federal facilities in New York, N.Y.	0.35	lbs/million Btu heat input			—
Sulfur dioxide	United States	Federal facilities in Philadelphia & Chicago	0.65	lbs/million Btu heat input			—
Sulfur in compounds other than SO$_2$, SO$_3$, & H$_2$SO$_4$	New Jersey	—		—			20
Sulfuric acid	Bay Area A.P.C.D.	Acid manufacture from sulfur or pyrites	0.08	grains/ft^3	184		7
Sulfuric acid	Bay Area A.P.C.D.	Acid manufacture from other raw materials	0.3	grains/ft^3	690		7
Sulfuric acid	Czechoslovakia	(As hydrogen ion)	0.1	kg/hour			26
Sulfuric acid	Missouri	Existing nonfuel sources		mg/m^3	70		21
Sulfuric acid	Missouri	New nonfuel sources		mg/m^3	35		21
Sulfuric acid	New Jersey	—	10.	mg/m^3	350		20
Sulfuric acid	New South Wales	—	0.1	grains/ft^3	230		17
Sulfuric acid	Queensland	—	0.1	grains/ft^3	230		17

[a] STP unless otherwise noted.

[b] **Numbers in this column refer to the following footnotes.** *1.* Also compounds of the element. *2.* As the trioxide. *3.* As the element.

TABLE XI (*Concluded*)

4. Average for specified test cycle. 5. Engines of greater than 140 cubic inches displacement. 6. As formaldehyde. 7. Bay Area Air Pollution Control District, San Francisco, California. 8. Corrected to 5% O_2 in the flue gas; 12% CO_2 in the case of Manitoba. 9. As SO_3 equivalent in original units. 10. Verein Deutscher Ingenieure—Kommission Reinhaltung der Luft—Richtlinien, VDI-Verlag GmbH, Dusseldorf, Fed. Rep. Germany. 11. 100 lb/week mass emission limit. 12. 400 lb/week mass emission limit. 13. 1000 lb/week mass emission limit. 14. See Table XXII. 15. Except where there is 85% or more solvent removal from effluent. 16. As defined by Rule 66 of Los Angeles County Air Pollution Control District, Los Angeles, Calif. 17. Or efficiency of condensation of acid gases greater than 99%. 18. Where less than 5% by volume of the organic compounds are "reactive," or "reactive" compound emissions are reduced at least 85%, these limits do not apply. There are other exemptions in Regulation 3. 19. Not applicable with under 3000 cfm of gas, and 50 lb/hour SO_2 emission or 100 lb/hour instantaneous emission rate. 20. See also Fig. 17. 21. St. Louis Metropolitan Area. 22. Different dates of applicability for installations larger and smaller than 2,000,000,000 Btu/hour. 23. The South Carolina Pollution Control Authority has published in its Engineering Guides, seven charts to compute emission limits to meet its air quality standards (see Table V). 24. Primarily emissions from phosphate fertilizer manufacturing. 25. Same as California. 26. Emission rate above which it is necessary to submit a report to the government: Where the discharge is for less than 1 hour, there is a proportionate reduction in emission permissible without such reporting. 27. Inorganic compounds—except arsine. 28. See Table XXVIII. 29. 1. gm/1000 kcal limit applies to installations burning less than 1,000,000 kcal/hour; 4. gm/1000 kcal limit to those burning more than this amount.

TABLE XII

EMISSION STANDARDS FOR TOTAL SOLID PARTICULATE POLLUTANTS IN
EFFLUENT AIR OR GASES FROM SOURCES IN GENERAL

mg/m³ STP	Original units—STP[a]		City, county, or country	Footnotes[b]
1210	1.	lb/1000 lb gas	Detroit, Mich.	*1*
1150	0.5	grains/ft³	Newark, N.J.	—
1030	0.85	lb/1000 lb gas	Cheektowaga, N.Y.	*2*
980	0.425	grains/ft³	Winston-Salem, N.C.	—
920	0.4	grains/ft³	Riverside County, Calif.	*3, 4*
800	0.35	grains/ft³	Chicago, Ill.	*5*
770	0.65	lb/1000 lb gas	Wayne County, Mich.	*1*
690	0.3	grains/ft³	Los Angeles County, Calif.	*10*
480	0.21	grains/ft³	Chicago, Ill.	*6*
460	0.2	grains/ft³	Great Britain, New South Wales, Queensland	*7*
360	0.3	lb/1000 lb gas	New York State	*12, 13*
150		mg/m³	U.S.S.R.	—
150		mg/m³	Fed. Rep. Germany	*8*
120	0.1	lb/1000 lb gas	New York State	*12, 14*
115	0.05	grains/ft³	Great Britain	*9*
—	5.	kg/hour	Czechoslovakia	*11*

[a] Except for New York State, which is for gas at actual conditions.

[b] Numbers in this column refer to the following footnotes: *1*. Less water vapor from wet collector, if employed. *2*. Also Danville, Va.; Jefferson Co., Ky.; Madison, Wis.; Milwaukee Co., Wis.; New Haven, Conn.; New York, N.Y.; Poughkeepsie, N.Y.; St. Paul, Minn.; Tacoma, Wash.; Wheeling, W. Va. *3*. Also Eugene, Springfield; Lane Co., Ore.; Manitoba. *4*. See also Fig. 4. *5*. Stacks under 100 ft high; increase of $0.03(H/100)^2$ grains/scf where H is height of discharge in feet above grade. *6*. Particles larger than 44 μ. *7*. Great Britain—Particles of dust greater than 10 μ. *8*. Exhaust air from screening, crushing, or filling plants or from other similar sources of emission. *9*. Particles of fume less than 10 μ. *10*. Also St. Louis Metropolitan Area, Missouri. *11*. Maximum SiO_2 content: 20%; Emission rate above which it is necessary to submit a report to the government; where the discharge is for less than 1 hour, there is a proportionate reduction in emission permissible without such reporting. *12*. In New York State values are for gas at actual conditions. *13*. Where process weight (Fig. 4) is not applicable, e.g., grinding and woodworking. *14*. For process weights over 100,000 lb/hour, weight discharge may exceed Fig. 4 values if effluent concentration is less than this value.

TABLE XIII

MAXIMUM DUST CONCENTRATION REQUIRED IN
EFFLUENT GASES[a]

Source gas flow scfm	Concentration	
	grains/scf (original units)	mg/m^3 STP
7,000 or less	0.100	228
8,000	0.096	219
9,000	0.092	210
10,000	0.089	203
20,000	0.071	162
30,000	0.062	141
40,000	0.057	130
50,000	0.053	121
60,000	0.050	114
80,000	0.045	103
100,000	0.042	96
120,000	0.040	91
140,000	0.038	87
160,000	0.036	82
180,000	0.035	80
200,000	0.034	78
300,000	0.030	68
400,000	0.027	62
500,000	0.025	57
600,000	0.024	55
800,000	0.021	48
1,000,000 or more	0.020	46

[a] Bay Area Pollution District Regulation, San Francisco, California, 1960; St. Louis metropolitan area Regulations, Missouri Air Conservation Commission, 1967; Dade County, Florida Ordinance, 1963.

TABLE XIV
EMISSION STANDARDS FOR TOTAL SOLID PARTICULATE POLLUTANTS
IN EFFLUENT GASES FROM COMBUSTION OF FUELS (U.S.A.)

mg/m³ STP	Original units	City, county, or country	Foot-notes[a]
Adjusted to either 12% CO_2, 50% excess air, or 6% O_2			
3150	0.75 grains/ft³ at 500 °F	Baltimore, Md; Indianapolis, Ind; Nashville, Tenn.; Tonawanda, N.Y.; Youngstown, Ohio	—
1460	0.35 grains/ft³ at 500 °F	Tampa, Fla.	—
1220	1. lb/1000 lb flue gas	Kingsport, Tenn.; Lorraine, Ohio; Orlando, Fla.	—
1035	1. lb/million Btu heat input	South Carolina	5
1030	0.85 lb/1000 lb flue gas	Akron, Ohio; Alberta, Canada; Asheville, N.C.	2
980	0.425 grains/ft³ STP	Winston Salem, N.C.	—
920	0.4 grains/ft³ STP	Orange and San Bernardino Cos., Calif.; Sarasota Co., Fla.; Lane Co., Ore.; Eugene and Springfield, Ore.	—
840	0.2 grains/ft³ at 500 °F	Dearborn, Mich.	1
800	0.35 grains/ft³ STP	Chicago, Ill.; Cook Co., Ill.	3
790	0.65 lb/1000 lb flue gas	Allegheny Co., Pa.; Cleveland, Ohio; Granite City, Ill.; Wayne Co., Mich.	1
690	0.3 grains/ft³ STP	Bay Area APCD, Los Angeles and Riverside Cos., Calif.	4

[a] Numbers in this column refer to the following footnotes. *1.* Also see Fig. 12. *2.* Also: Battle Creek, Mich.; Birmingham, Mich.; Bridgeport, Conn.; Charlotte, N.C.; Chattanooga, Tenn.; Cheektowaga, N.Y.; Cincinnati, Ohio; Columbia, S.C.; Columbus, Ohio; Danville, Va.; Davenport, Iowa; Dayton, Ohio; East Providence, R.I.; Green Bay, Wis.; Hawaii; Jefferson Co., Ky.; Madison, Wis.; Milwaukee Co., Wis.; Minneapolis, Minn.; Monroe, Mich.; Natick, Mass.; Newark, N.J.; New Haven, Conn.; Niagara Falls, N.Y.; Northhampton, Pa.; Omaha, Neb.; Pawtucket, R.I.; Perth Amboy, N.J.; Philadelphia, Pa.; Poughkeepsie, N.Y.; St. Paul, Minn.; Seattle, Wash.; Syracuse, N.Y.; Tacoma, Wash.; Toledo, Ohio; Wheeling, W. Va.; Zanesville, Ohio. *3.* Chicago, Ill.—Also not over 0.21 grains/scf over 44 μ. for stacks under 100 ft high; for higher stacks = $0.03(H/100)^2$ grains/scf where H is height of discharge in feet above grade. *4.* Bay Area Air Pollution Control District, San Francisco, Calif. *5.* Existing installations; for new installations see Fig. 13.

TABLE XV

Emission Standards for Total Particulate Matter in Effluent Air or Gases from Specific Processes

Source of emission	Jurisdiction or code	Standard original units	mg/m³ STP	Footnotes[a]
INCINERATION OF REFUSE				
	Allegheny County, Pa.	0.2 lb/1000 lb gas	240	—
	Bay Area A.P.C.D.	0.2 grains/ft³	460	1, 2
	Cleveland, Ohio	0.2 lb/1000 lb gas	240	—
	Cincinnati, Ohio	0.4 lb/1000 lb gas	490	3, 42
	Dearborn, Mich.	0.3 grains/ft³ at 500 °F	1280	4
	Florida	0.2 grains/ft³	460	4
	France	mg/m³	400	—
	Japan	0.7 gm/m³	700	—
	New York, N.Y.	0.65 lb/1000 lb gas	790	4, 5
Existing—residential and commercial	Delaware	0.75 lb/million Btu	—	
Existing—industrial and rural	Delaware	1. lb/million Btu	—	
New—industrial and rural	Delaware	0.75 lb/million Btu	—	
New—residential and commercial	Delaware	0.5 lb/million Btu	—	
200 lb/hour and over	Missouri; Maryland	0.2 grains/ft³	460	3, 38
	U.S.A.—Federal Installations	0.2 grains/ft³	460	3, 35
	Falls Church, Va.	0.3 lb/1000 lb gas	370	3, 5
	Montgomery County, Md.	0.3 lb/1000 lb gas	370	3, 5
	Prince Georges County, Md.	0.3 lb/1000 lb gas	370	3, 5
	Rockville, Md.	0.3 lb/1000 lb gas	370	3, 5
Less than 200 lb/hour	Missouri; Maryland	0.3 grains/ft³	690	3, 38
	U.S.A.—Federal Installations	0.3 grains/ft³	690	3
	Falls Church, Va.	0.65 lb/1000 lb gas	790	3, 5
	Montgomery County, Md.	0.65 lb/1000 lb gas	790	3, 5
	Prince Georges County, Md.	0.65 lb/1000 lb gas	790	3, 5
	Rockville, Md.	0.65 lb/1000 lb gas	790	3, 5

Item	Location		Value	Ref.
Less than 20 tons/day	Fed. Rep. Germany		mg/m³	200	6, 7
More than 20 tons/day	Fed. Rep. Germany		mg/m³	150	6, 7
Less than 1000 lb/hour	Illinois	0.35	grains/ft³	805	4
1000 lb/hour and more	Illinois	0.2	grains/ft³	460	4
Up to 10,000 lb/hour	Philadelphia, Pa.	0.2	lb/1000 lb gas	240	3
Over 10,000 lb/hour	Philadelphia, Pa.	0.6	lb/1000 lb gas	740	3
Municipal	Michigan	0.3	lb/1000 lb gas	370	4, 9
Industrial—less than 400 lb/hour	Michigan	0.65	lb/1000 lb gas	790	4, 9
Industrial—more than 400 lb/hour	Michigan	0.3	lb/1000 lb gas	370	4, 9
Residential—less than 200 lb/hour	Michigan	0.65	lb/1000 lb gas	790	4, 9, 10
Residential—more than 200 lb/hour	Michigan	0.3	lb/1000 lb gas	370	4, 9
INDUSTRIAL PROCESSES					
Asphaltic concrete plants	Florida	0.3	grains/ft³	690	40
	Wayne County, Mich.	0.2	lb/1000 lb gas	240	9
	West Virginia		—	—	43
Stationary	Michigan	0.3	lb/1000 lb gas	370	34
Portable— 0–100 tons/hour	Michigan	0.6	lb/1000 lb gas	740	34
—101–150 tons/hour	Michigan	0.5	lb/1000 lb gas	620	34
—151–200 tons/hour	Michigan	0.45	lb/1000lb gas	550	34
—over 200 tons/hour	Michigan	0.35	lb/1000 lb gas	430	34
Cement, grinding, crushing, etc.	Michigan	0.15	lb/1000 lb gas	180	33
New plants	Great Britain	0.1	grains/ft³	230	—
Existing plants	Great Britain	0.2	grains/ft³	460	—
Cement—clinker coolers	Michigan	0.3	lb/1000 lb gas	370	34
Cement grinding, crushing	Fed. Rep. Germany		mg/m³	150	11
Rock crushing—dust handling	Great Britain	0.2	grains/ft³	460	—
Coal briquetting	VDI 2292		mg/m³	300	8, 12
Coal preparation plants	VDI 2293		mg/m³	300	8, 12

TABLE XV (Continued)

Source of emission	Jurisdiction or code	Standard original units		mg/m³ STP	Foot-notes[a]
			mg/m³		
Coke crushing and screening	VDI 2100		150	150	8
Corn Milling (Wet)	Illinois	0.75 grains/ft³		1725	23
Furnaces—calcining					
Electric	Japan	1. gm/m³		1000	—
Gas generating	Japan	0.9 gm/m³		900	—
Glass melting—tank	Japan	1. gm/m³		1000	—
Glass melting—other	Japan	0.7 gm/m³		700	—
Petroleum refinery	Japan	1.2 gm/m³		1200	—
Reactor	Japan	0.7 gm/m³		700	—
	Japan	1.2 gm/m³		1200	—
Kilns—Cement or lime					13
25 tons/hour production	Czechoslovakia	120 kg/hour		—	41
50 tons/hour production	Czechoslovakia	160 kg/hour		—	41
100 tons/hour production	Czechoslovakia	250 kg/hour		—	41
150 tons/hour production	Czechoslovakia	270 kg/hour		—	41
Kilns—cement	Illinois	0.1 grains/ft³		230	36
	Japan	0.6 gm/m³		600	—
	Michigan	0.25 lb/1000 lb gas		310	33
	VDI 2094		mg/m³	150	8
Up to 1500 tons/day clinker	Great Britain	0.2 grains/ft³		460	14
1500 to 3000 tons/day clinker	Great Britain	Sliding scale from 0.2 to 0.1		—	—
3000 and over tons/day clinker	Great Britain	0.1 grains/ft³		230	14
Kilns—ceramic—continuous	Japan	0.7 gm/m³		700	—
Other than continuous	Japan	2. gm/m³		2000	—
Kilns—drying	Japan	1.2 gm/m³		1200	—
Kilns—lime	Japan	1.5 gm/m³		1500	—
	Michigan	0.2 lb/1000 lb gas		240	9, 16
Design	Wayne County, Mich.	0.2 lb/1000 lb gas		240	9, 16
Operation	Wayne County, Mich.	0.3 lb/1000 lb gas		370	9, 17

694

Units—catalytic cracking	Japan	1.	gm/m³	1000	—
	Trafalgar, Ontario	1	ton/day	—	18
METALLURGICAL PROCESSES					
Ferrous or nonferrous					
Furnaces					
Blast	Japan	0.5	gm/m³	500	—
Electric	Japan	0.9	gm/m³	900	—
Metal heating	Japan	0.7	gm/m³	700	—
Metallurgical	New South Wales	0.1	grains/ft³	230	—
	Queensland	0.1	grains/ft³	230	—
Metal refining	Japan	0.7	gm/m³	700	—
Reverberatory	Japan	0.7	gm/m³	700	—
Other	Japan	1.	gm/m³	1000	—
Sintering plants	Great Britain	0.2	grains/ft³	460	—
	Japan	1.	gm/m³	1000	—
Ferrous					
Bessemer converters	Allegheny County, Pa.	0.65	lb/1000 lb gas	790	4, 19
	Cleveland, Ohio	0.2	lb/1000 lb gas	240	20
Blast furnace gas-bled	Allegheny County, Pa.	0.5	lb/1000 lb gas	610	—
	Detroit, Mich.	0.5	lb/1000 lb gas	610	9
	Illinois	0.1	grains/ft³	230	—
	Wayne County, Mich.	0.5	lb/1000 lb gas	610	9
	Fed. Rep. Germany		mg/m³	20	—
Integrated works	Great Britain	0.2	grains/ft³	460	—
Merchant furnaces	Great Britain	0.5	grains/ft³	1150	—
Blast furnace gas-burned	Allegheny County, Pa.	0.35	lb/1000 lb gas	430	—
	Detroit, Mich.	0.2	lb/1000 lb gas	240	9
	Illinois	0.5	grains/ft³	115	—
	Wayne County, Mich.	0.2	lb/1000 lb gas	240	9
	Fed. Rep. Germany		mg/m³	50	9
Cupolas	Chicago, Ill.	0.35	grains/ft³	805	21

TABLE XV (Continued)

Source of emission	Jurisdiction or code	Standard original units	mg/m³ STP	Foot-notes[a]
Cupolas	Cleveland, Ohio	0.5 lb/1000 lb gas	610	—
	Illinois; New York	—	—	37
	Japan	2. gm/m³	2000	—
	Fed. Rep. Germany	—	—	22
New	Allegheny County, Pa.	0.5 lb/1000 lb gas	610	—
Existing	Allegheny County, Pa.	0.65 lb/1000 lb gas	790	—
	Missouri	0.4 grains/ft³	920	38, 39
Hot blast (grit & dust) (fume)	Great Britain	0.2 grains/ft³	460	15
	Great Britain	0.05 grains/ft³	115	15
Jobbing—operation	Detroit and Wayne Counties, Mich.	0.4 lb/1000 lb gas	490	9, 23
	Michigan	0.4 lb/1000 lb gas	490	23
Production—operation	Detroit and Wayne Counties, Mich.	0.25 lb/1000 lb gas	310	9
0–10 tons/hour	Michigan	0.4 lb/1000 lb gas	490	—
11–20 tons	Michigan	0.25 lb/1000 lb gas	310	—
21 and over tons/hour	Michigan	0.1 lb/1000 lb gas	120	—
Production—design	Detroit and Wayne Counties, Mich.	0.1 lb/1000 lb gas	120	9, 23
Furnaces				
Electric	Japan	0.9 gm/m³	900	—
Electric, basic oxygen and open hearth	Allegheny County, Pa.	0.2 lb/1000 lb gas	240	—
	Cleveland, Ohio	0.2 lb/1000 lb gas	240	—
	Illinois	0.1 grains/ft³	230	—
Operation	Detroit and Wayne Counties, Mich.	0.2 lb/1000 lb gas	240	9
	Michigan	0.15 lb/1000 lb gas	180	—

Category	Location		Units		Ref.
Design	Detroit and Wayne Counties, Mich.	0.1	lb/1000 lb gas	120	9
	Michigan	0.1	lb/1000 lb gas	120	—
Heating and reheating	Allegheny County, Pa.	0.3	lb/1000 lb gas	370	—
	Michigan	0.3	lb/1000 lb gas	370	—
	Detroit and Wayne Counties, Mich.	0.3	lb/1000 lb gas	370	9
Open hearth	Japan	0.6	gm/m³	600	—
All oxygen refining processes producing fume	Great Britain	0.05	grains/ft³	115	15
Nonfume problems	Great Britain	0.2	grains/ft³	460	15
Oxygen-using	Japan	1.	gm/m³	1000	24
	Fed. Rep. Germany		mg/m³	150	—
Sintering plants	Allegheny County, Pa.	0.2	lb/1000 lb gas	240	—
	Cleveland, Ohio	0.2	lb/1000 lb gas	240	—
	Illinois	0.1	grains/ft³	230	—
Operation	Detroit and Wayne Counties, Mich.	0.2	lb/1000 lb gas	240	9
	Michigan	0.2	lb/1000 lb gas	240	9
Design	Detroit and Wayne Counties, Mich.	0.15	lb/1000 lb gas	180	9
Continuous operation	Fed. Rep. Germany		mg/m³	150	—
Special cases	Fed. Rep. Germany		mg/m³	300	25, 26
Nonferrous					
Furnace or smelter—general	Cleveland, Ohio	0.2	lb/1000 lb gas	240	—
Aluminum reduction	—			—	—
Alumina grinding	VDI 2286		mg/m³	150	8
Alumina calcining	VDI 2286		mg/m³	100	8
Primary reduction	VDI 2286	0.1	gm/m³	100	8
Secondary recovery	VDI 2441			—	8
Furnaces—rotary	VDI 2441			—	8, 27
Furnaces—other	VDI 2441	0.3	gm/m³	300	8, 27
Copper smelting	Fed. Rep. Germany		mg/m³	500	—
Primary	VDI 2101			—	8
Refining furnaces	VDI 2101	0.3	gm/m³	300	8

TABLE XV (Continued)

Source of emission	Jurisdiction or code	Standard original units	mg/m³ STP	Footnotes[a]
Reverberatory furnaces	VDI 2101	0.3 gm/m³	300	8
Shaft furnaces	VDI 2101	0.3 gm/m³	300	8
Secondary	VDI 2102	—	—	8
Blast furnaces	VDI 2102	0.3 gm/m³	300	8
Converters	VDI 2102	0.3 gm/m³	300	8
Refining furnaces	VDI 2102	0.3 gm/m³	300	8
Hydrometallurgical	VDI 2287	—	—	8, 28
Cobalt calcination	VDI 2287	1. gm/m³	1000	8, 28
Inhibition plant	VDI 2287	0.5 gm/m³	500	8, 28
Roasting plant	VDI 2287	0.1 gm/m³	100	8, 28
Zinc calcination	VDI 2287	—	—	8, 28
Zinc with scrubbing	VDI 2287	3. gm/m³	3000	8, 28
Zinc with hydro-electric dust extraction	VDI 2287	0.5 gm/m³	500	8, 28, 29
Lead smelting	Fed. Rep. Germany	—	—	30
Reducing furnaces	Fed. Rep. Germany	mg/m³	400	30
Refining furnaces	Fed. Rep. Germany	mg/m³	200	30
Slag blowing	Fed. Rep. Germany	mg/m³	100	30
Zinc smelting	Fed. Rep. Germany	—	—	31
Distillation process	Fed. Rep. Germany	mg/m³	200	31
Electrothermic process	Fed. Rep. Germany	mg/m³	100	31
Rotary process	Fed. Rep. Germany	mg/m³	500	31
Stationary retorts	Fed. Rep. Germany	mg/m³	400	31

POWER PLANTS

Electric generating—old plants	Great Britain	0.2	grains/ft³	460	—
New plants	Great Britain	0.05	grains/ft³	115	32
Pulverized coal-burning	Japan	1.2	gm/m³	1200	—
Other	Japan	1.	gm/m³	1000	—

[a] The numbers in this column refer to the following footnotes. 1. Bay Area Air Pollution Control District, San Francisco, Calif. 2. Adjusted to 6% O_2. 3. Adjusted to 12% CO_2. 4. Adjusted to 50% excess air. 5. Maximum emission—250 lb/hour. 6. Adjusted to 7% CO_2. 7. Also VDI 2301 (see footnote 8). 8. Verein Deutscher Ingenieure—Kommission Reinhaltung der Luft—Richtlinien, VDI-Verlag GmbH, Dusseldorf, Fed. Rep. Germany. 9. In Detroit and Wayne Counties, Michigan, less water vapor from wet collectors, if employed. 10. Does not apply to domestic incinerators having less than 5 ft³ storage capacity. 11. Also VDI 2094 (see footnote 8). 12. Limit for industrial exhaust ventilating system effluent—150 mg/m³. 13. Including direct-burning carbon black furnaces. 14. Older kilns—up to 0.5 grains/sfc. 15. Grit and dust—over 10 μ: fume—less than 10 μ. 16. Rotary kilns must have 99% weight collection efficiency, if more restrictive. 17. Rotary kilns must have 98.5% weight collection efficiency, if more restrictive. 18. Or 30 tons per month per 7,000 bbl/day unit. 19. Installations after July 5, 1960 only. 20. Future date of applicability. 21. Also VDI 2099 (see footnote 8). 22. See Fig. 16. 23. Also supplemental regulations. 24. Particles smaller than 10 μ. Also VDI 2112 (see footnote 8). 25. Where, for instance, raw material is to be used in the form of fine dust and the applicant is able to show that, although the present state of technical development does not permit keeping with the 150 mg/m³ limit, no objectionable effects need be feared in the neighborhood. 26. Also VDI 2095 (see footnote 8). 27. Total dust emission not to exceed 1% of aluminum production. 28. Recovery after chloridizing roasting. 29. Output over 30 tons/day of zinc. 30. Also VDI 2285 (see footnote 8). 31. Also VDI 2284 (see footnote 8). 32. New 2000–4000 MW plants must have 99.3% fly ash removal efficiency after 12 months operation. 33. Up to 15,000 barrels per day kiln capacity. Special regulations for over 15,000 barrels per day total plant kiln capacity. 34. In remote location: if no water is available and emission limit of 0.3 lb/1000 lb gas cannot otherwise be satisfied, plant may be located in 1 mile radius uninhabited buffer zone. 35. Shall not normally include particles larger than 60 μ. 36. Or 99.7% collector removal efficiency. 37. See Table XVIIIA. 38. St. Louis and Washington Metropolitan Areas. 39. Or 85% collector removal efficiency. 40. Except for portable plants with less than three inhabited residences within 1 mile. 41. For a chimney height of 70 ± 10 meters. The limits for other chimney heights to be established by the government. 42. Also a discharge, in particles per minute, in residential, business, and industrial districts, of 500,000, 750,000, and 1,000,000, respectively. 43. See Table XVIIIB.

TABLE XVI

ENVIRONMENTAL RATING

Rating	Criteria
A	Includes processes, and exhaust and ventilation systems where the discharge of a contaminant or contaminants results, or would reasonably be expected to result, in serious adverse effects on receptors or the environment. These effects may be of a health, economic, or aesthetic nature or any combination of these.
B	Includes processes, and exhaust and ventilation systems where the discharge of a contaminant or contaminants results, or would reasonably be expected to result, in only moderate and essentially localized effects; or where the multiplicity of sources of the contaminant or contaminants in any given area is such as to require an overall reduction of the atmospheric burden of that contaminant or contaminants.
C	Includes processes, and exhaust and ventilation systems where the discharge of a contaminant or contaminants would reasonably be expected to result in localized adverse effects of an aesthetic or nuisance nature.
D	Includes processes, and exhaust and ventilation systems where, in view of properties and concentrations of the emissions, isolated conditions, stack height, and other factors, it can be clearly demonstrated that discharge of the contaminant or contaminants will not result in measurable or observable effects on receptors, nor add to an existing or predictable atmospheric burden of that contaminant or contaminants which would reasonably be expected to cause adverse effects.

The following items will be considered in making a determination of the environmental rating to be applied to a particular source:
  (a) properties, quantities and rates of the emission
  (b) physical surroundings of emission source
  (c) population density of surrounding area, including anticipated future growth
  (d) dispersion characteristics at or near source
  (e) location of emission source relative to ground level and surrounding buildings, mountains, hills, etc.
  (f) current or anticipated ambient air quality in vicinity of source
  (g) latest findings relating to effects of ground-level concentrations of the emission on receptors
  (h) possible hazardous side effects of contaminant in question mixing with contaminants already in ambient air
  (i) engineering guides which are acceptable to the commissioner

TABLE XVII

USUAL DEGREE OF AIR CLEANING REQUIRED[a] FROM PROCESSES, AND EXHAUST
AND VENTILATION SYSTEMS FOR GASES AND LIQUID PARTICULATE EMISSIONS
(ENVIRONMENTAL RATING A, B, C, AND D) AND SOLID PARTICULATE
EMISSIONS (ENVIRONMENTAL RATING A AND D)

Environ- mental rating	Emission rate potential (lb/hour)								
	Less than 1.0	1 to 10	10 to 20	20 to 100	100 to 500	500 to 1500	1500 to 4000	4,000 to 10,000	10,000 and Greater
A	[b]				99% or greater				
B	See rating D		90– 91%	91– 94%	94– 96%	96– 97%	97– 98%	98– 99%	99% or greater
C	See rating D		70– 75%	75– 85%	85– 90%	90– 93%	93– 95%	95– 98%	98% or greater
D	Degree of air cleaning may be specified by the commissioner providing satisfactory dispersion is achieved.								

[a] Where multiple emission sources are connected to a common air cleaning device, the degree of air cleaning required will be that which would be required if each individual emission source were considered separately.

[b] For an average emission rate potential less than 1.0 lb/hour, the desired air cleaning efficiency shall be determined by the expected concentration of the air contaminant in the emission stream. Where it is uneconomical to employ air cleaning devices, other methods of control should be considered.

TABLE XVIII A
ALLOWABLE EMISSIONS FROM JOBBING FOUNDRY CUPOLAS AND FOUNDRY OPEN HEARTHS (ILLINOIS AND NEW YORK)

Process weight rate 1000 lb/hour	Allowable emission[a] lb/hour	Process weight rate 1000 lb/hour	Allowable emission[a] lb/hour
1	3.05	10	16.65
2	4.70	12	18.70
3	6.35	16	21.60
4	8.00	18	23.40
5	9.58	20	25.10
6	11.30	30[b]	31.30[b]
7	12.90	40[b]	37.00[b]
8	14.30	50[b]	42.40[b]
9	15.50		

[a] Operations exceeding the permissible emission rate acceptable if actual collection efficiency is at least 80% for New York only.   [b] These values for New York only.

TABLE XVIII B
ALLOWABLE EMISSIONS FROM HOT MIX ASPHALT PLANTS (WEST VIRGINIA)

Aggregate process rate lb/hour[a]	Stack emission rate (lb/hour)
10,000	10
20,000	16
30,000	22
40,000	28
50,000	31
100,000	33
200,000	37
300,000	40
400,000	43
500,000	47
600,000	50

[a] For a process weight between any two consecutive process weights stated in this table, the emission limitation shall be determined by interpolation.

TABLE XIX
Number of Communities Adopting Various Emission Standards for Total Solid Particulate Pollutants in Effluent Gases from the Combustion of Fuels (U.S.A.)

mg/m³ STP (equivalent)[a]	Before 1949	1950–1959	1960–1965	Total
Over 1030	4	5	1	10
1030	12	24	4	40
840–1030	0	4	4	8
Under 840	0	3	6	9
Total	16	36	15	67

[a] Adjusted to either 12% CO_2, 50% excess air or 6% O_2.

TABLE XX
Effect Factors for use with Figs. 5 and 6 (New Jersey Air Pollution Control Code)

Material	Effect factor
Coarse solid particles (Fig. 5)	1.0
Fine solid particles (Fig. 6)	
All materials not specifically listed hereunder	1.0
Antimony	0.9
α-naphthylthiourea	0.5
Arsenic	0.9
Barium	0.9
Beryllium	0.003
Cadmium	0.2
Chromium	0.2
Cobalt	0.9
Copper	0.2
Hafnium	0.9
Lead	0.3
Lead arsenate	0.3
Lithium hydride	0.04
Phosphorus	0.2
Selenium	0.2
Silver	0.1
Tellurium	0.2
Thallium	0.2
Uranium (soluble)	0.1
Uranium (insoluble)	0.4
Vanadium	0.2

TABLE XXI

Fly Ash Emission Limits for Michigan and Some Jurisdictions in Michigan

Jurisdiction	Capacity rating (1000/lb steam/hour)	Maximum allowable emission (lb particulate/1000 lb flue gas at 50% excess air)	
		Design	Operating
Pulverized coal firing[a]			
Michigan and Muskegon Co., Mich.	b	—	b
Detroit, Mich.	0–300	0.5 to 0.2[c]	0.6 to 0.3[c]
Detroit and Wayne Co., Mich.	300 and over	0.2	0.3
Wayne Co., Mich.	0–300	0.4 to 0.2[c]	0.5 to 0.3[c]
Other modes of firing			
Michigan and Detroit, Mich.	0–100	—	0.65
Muskegon Co. and Wayne Co., Mich.	100–300	—	0.65 to 0.45[c]
Michigan and Muskegon Co., Mich.	over 300	d	d
Detroit and Wayne Co., Mich.	300–800	—	0.45 to 0.3[c]
Detroit and Wayne Co., Mich.	800 and over	—	0.3

[a] Includes cyclone furnaces in Michigan and Muskegon Co., Mich.

[b] See Fig. 12.

[c] Emission limits for specific ratings determined by linear interpolation between ranges listed.

[d] On application to State Air Pollution Commission or Muskegon County Health Department.

FOOTNOTES TO TABLE XXII (*opposite*)

[a] Where the harmful substances are discharged through two or more chimneys situated within the area of a circle of 1 km in diameter, the chimneys of one and the same establishment are regarded as one chimney. For varying heights of chimneys, the method of calculation shall be established by the Ministry of Forest Administration and Water Conservation in a work instruction manual.

[b] For substances listed for Czechoslovakia in Table V, "K_{max}" is the concentration for 30-minute averaging time; e.g., for ammonia, $K_{max} = 0.3$ mg/m^3. Therefore the permissible emission of ammonia from a 100-m stack is $750 \times 0.3 = 225$ kg/hour.

[c] Where the discharge is for less than 1 hour, there is a proportionate reduction in allowable emission in kilograms.

TABLE XXII
Permissible Emission—Czechoslovakia

Stack height[a] (meters)	Permissible emission in kg/hour		Multiplier for K_{max} for other harmful substances[b,c]
	From combustion of fuel		
	Fly ash	SO$_2$	
7	2.5	2	4
8	3	2.3	4.6
10	4	3.2	6.4
12	5	4.2	8.4
14	7	5.3	10.6
16	9	6.8	13.6
18	11.4	8.4	16.8
20	14	10	20.0
25	21	13.5	27.0
30	31	22.5	45.0
35	42	32.5	65.0
40	55	46	92.0
45	70	60	120.0
50	84	82.5	165.0
55	110	100	200
60	130	122	245.0
65	160	145	290.0
70	192	170	340.0
75	225	195	390.0
80	260	227	455
85	290	257	514
90	325	295	590
95	360	335	670
100	400	375	750
110	490	900	930
120	580	1425	1130
130	675	1950	1340
140	785	2475	1560
150	900	3000	1790
160	1010	3555	2060
170	1130	4110	2320
180	1270	4665	2600
190	1400	5220	2890
200	1550	5779	3200
220	1820	6355	3840
240	2110	6930	4500
260	2400	7510	5160
280	2700	8085	5820
300	3000	8665	6500

NOTE: See footnotes, p. 704.

TABLE XXIII

THE DARK SMOKE (PERMITTED PERIODS) REGULATIONS
—STATUTORY INSTRUMENT 498–1958 MINISTRY OF
HOUSING AND LOCAL GOVERNMENT, GREAT BRITAIN
Not more than 2 minutes of black smoke (i.e., No. 3
Ringelmann) in any 30 minutes and not more aggregate
minutes of dark (i.e., No. 2 Ringelmann) smoke in any
8 hours than:

Number of furnaces per chimney	With soot blowing	Without soot blowing[a]
1	14	10
2	25	18
3	34	24
4	41	29

[a] No continuous emission period to exceed 4 minutes.

TABLE XXIV

RELATIONSHIP BETWEEN FLY ASH LOADING AND EMISSION OPACITY

Fly ash loading			Emission opacity	
Grains/ft^3 of stack gases at 60 °F	mg/m^3 of stack gases at 60 °F	Pounds/1000 lb of stack gases at 50% excess air	Obscuration	Ringelmann No.
0.22	500	0.41	Visible plume	2
0.11	250	0.21	Light haze	1
0.03	68	0.06	Invisible effluent	0

TABLE XXV

Width of Sanitary Protection Zone (in Meters) Required for Coal-Fired Power Plants Burning over 3 Metric Tons of Fuel per Hour (U.S.S.R.)[a]

Fuel ash content %	Fuel consumption[b]	75% Collection efficiency					90% Collection efficiency					
		3–12.5	12.5–25.0	25.0–50.0	50.0–100.0	100.0–200.0	3–12.5	12.5–25.0	25.0–50.0	50.0–100.0	100.0–200.0	200.0–300.0
Up to 10		100	100	300	500	500	100	100	100	300	500	500
10–15		100	300	500	500	500	100	100	300	300	500	500
15–20		100	300	500	1000	1000	100	100	300	300	500	1000
20–25		100	300	500	1000	1000	100	100	300	300	500	1000
25–30		100	300	500	1000	1000	100	300	300	500	1000	1000
30–45		300	500	1000	1000	[c]	100	300	300	500	1000	1000

[a] From Kettner (9c).
[b] Range in metric tons per hour.
[c] Special requirements.

TABLE XXVI
Basic Chimney Heights for Miscellaneous Warm Emissions of Sulfur Dioxide[a]
(For use above range of "Memorandum on Chimney Heights[b])
Alkali Inspectorate—Great Britain

Rate of emission: (tons of SO_2 per day)	3.6	7.5	13	21	30	40
Basic chimney height, feet	100	150	200	250	300	340

[a] To allow for interfering nearby tall buildings the following correction has to be applied.

$$H = 0.625A + 0.935B$$

where H = Final chimney height, feet; A = Basic chimney height, feet; B = Building height, feet.

[b] From (9d).

TABLE XXVII
Basic Chimney Heights for Sulfur-burning
Sulfuric Acid Contact Plants
Alkali Inspectorate-
Great Britain

Production Tons H_2SO_4 per day	Basic Chimney Height, Feet[a]			
	v = 20	v = 30	v = 40	v = 50
100[b]	104	101	99	96
200	142	138	135	132
300	175	167	163	159
400	203	197	192	188
500	226	218	214	210
600	248	241	235	230
700	267	260	253	247
800	286	278	271	266
900	304	294	287	280
1000	319	310	303	296
1100	334	325	317	310
1200	349	340	332	325
1300	363	353	344	337
1400	377	367	358	351
1500	391	381	372	364
1600	405	394	385	376
1700	417	406	397	388
1800	429	418	409	399
1900	441	429	420	409
2000	452	439	430	419

[a] These are based on a calculated 3 minute mean ground level concentration of SO_2 of 20 pphm (parts per 100 million) v = velocity of efflux of gases in feet per second.

[b] Note that the minimum height of chimney for a contact sulfuric acid plant is 120 feet.

TABLE XXVIII
STACK HEIGHT REQUIREMENTS FOR PLANTS EMITTING SO$_2$[a] (BELGIUM)[b]

Degree of dilution of component sulfur gases	Imposed minimum height (meters)	
	For gases or fumes whose temperature is over 150 °C	For gases or fumes whose temperature is under 150 °C
1/12,000	7	10
1/10,000	10	15
1/7,500	14	23
1/5,000	20	35
1/3,000	30	50
1/2,000	40	65
1/1,000	60	100

[a] These requirements apply only to factories roasting or reducing lead or zinc minerals or metals containing lead or zinc.

[b] "Règlement Général pour la Protection du Travail," Chapter II, Mesures spéciales applicables à certaines industries. Sect. I, Ind. des Métaux, A. Art. 364–373.

TABLE XXIX
STACK HEIGHT REQUIREMENT SO$_2$ EMISSION FROM SINTER PLANTS (VDI 2095) (5)

SO$_2$ Emission (kg/hour)	100	500	1000	1500
Minimum stack height (meters)	45	75	90	Special agreement

TABLE XXX
STACK HEIGHT ADJUSTMENT FACTOR—NEW JERSEY[a]

Stack exit velocity (ft/sec)	Temperature at which the gases leave the stack (°F)								
	200 °F or less	300°	400°	500°	600°	700°	800°	900°	1000° or greater
0	0.910	0.910	0.910	0.910	0.910	0.910	0.910	0.910	0.910
5	0.928	0.930	0.932	0.933	0.934	0.935	0.935	0.936	0.936
10	0.946	0.950	0.953	0.956	0.958	0.959	0.961	0.962	0.963
15	0.964	0.970	0.975	0.978	0.981	0.984	0.986	0.988	0.989
20	0.982	0.990	0.996	1.001	1.005	1.008	1.011	1.014	1.016
25	1.000	1.010	1.018	1.024	1.029	1.033	1.037	1.039	1.042
30	1.018	1.030	1.039	1.047	1.053	1.056	1.062	1.065	1.068
35	1.036	1.050	1.061	1.070	1.077	1.082	1.087	1.091	1.095
40	1.054	1.070	1.083	1.092	1.100	1.107	1.112	1.117	1.121
45	1.072	1.090	1.104	1.115	1.124	1.131	1.138	1.143	1.148
50 or greater	1.090	1.110	1.126	1.138	1.148	1.156	1.163	1.169	1.174

[a] Extrapolation below 200 °F or above 1000 °F, or above 50 ft/sec is not permitted.

TABLE XXXI

STACK HEIGHT ADJUSTMENT IN FEET—NEW JERSEY[a]

Stack exit velocity (ft/sec)	Temperature at which the gases leave the stack (°F)								
	200 °F or less	300°	400°	500°	600°	700°	800°	900°	1000° or greater
0	−18.00	−18.00	−18.00	−18.00	−18.00	−18.00	−18.00	−18.00	−18.00
5	−14.40	−13.99	−13.68	−13.44	−13.24	−13.08	−12.94	−12.82	−12.72
10	−10.80	− 9.99	− 9.37	− 8.88	− 8.48	− 8.16	− 7.88	− 7.65	− 7.44
15	− 7.20	− 5.98	− 5.06	− 4.32	− 3.72	− 3.24	− 2.82	− 2.47	− 2.16
20	− 3.60	− 1.97	− 0.74	+ 0.24	+ 1.04	+ 1.68	+ 2.24	+ 2.70	+ 3.12
25	0.00	+ 2.03	+ 3.58	+ 4.80	+ 5.80	+ 6.60	+ 7.30	+ 7.88	+ 8.40
30	+ 3.60	+ 6.04	+ 7.89	+ 9.36	+10.56	+11.52	+12.36	+13.05	+13.68
35	+ 7.20	+10.05	+12.20	+13.92	+15.32	+16.44	+17.42	+18.22	+18.96
40	+10.80	+14.06	+16.52	+18.48	+20.08	+21.36	+22.48	+23.40	+24.24
45	+14.40	+18.06	+20.84	+23.04	+24.84	+26.28	+27.54	+28.58	+29.52
50 or greater	+18.00	+22.07	+25.15	+27.60	+29.60	+31.20	+32.60	+33.75	+34.80

[a] Extrapolation below 200 °F, or above 1000 °F, or above 50 ft/sec is not permitted.

TABLE XXXII

STACK HEIGHT REQUIREMENTS FOR LARGE STEAM POWER PLANTS (U.S.S.R.)[a]

Fuel consumption (metric tons/hour)	Chimney height (meters)[b]	
	High ash coal (over 5%/1000 cal/kg)	Low ash coal (less than 5%/1000 cal/kg)
0–5	30 (45[c])	30 (45[c])
5–15	45	30 (45[c])
15–50	60	45
50–100	80	60
100–200	100	80
200–300	120	100
over 300	150	120

[a] From Kettner (9c).

[b] May use lower stack height when SO_2 removal equipment is used or liquid fuel burned.

[c] When houses 15 meters high are within 200 meters of plant.

TABLE XXXIII

BASIC CHIMNEY HEIGHTS FOR NITRIC ACID PRODUCTION PLANTS—
ALKALI INSPECTORATE—GREAT BRITAIN[a]

Gas volume at STP (ft³/min)	Gas volume at STP (ft³/min)	Effective height (feet)	Plume rise (feet)	Basic chimney height (feet)
175	14,000	205	27	180
350	28,000	287	39	250
530	42,000	353	47	300
700	56,000	412	55	350
1060	84,000	468	68	400

[a] Basis: 1. Efflux velocity 80 ft/sec. 2. Emission has no thermal buoyancy. 3. Maximum g.l.c. for a 3-minute mean is 0.16 ppm NO_2. 4. Concentration of NO_2 is 2.3 grains/ft³ (2.0 grains SO_3). 5. No allowance made for other sources of emission interfering. 6. Wind speed taken as 20 ft/sec.

TABLE XXXIV

BASIC CHIMNEY HEIGHTS FOR COPPER WORKS—ALKALI INSPECTORATE—
GREAT BRITAIN[a]

Rate of melting[b] (tons/24 hours)	25	50	100	150	200	250	300
Basic chimney height (feet)	72	102	144	177	204	228	250

[a] The process to which these are applicable is the recovery of copper and its alloys from scrap fabricated metal, swarf, or residues. It assumes that satisfactory steps have been taken to prevent emissions of dark smoke and that the chimneys are solely to secure satisfactory dispersion of adventitious zinc oxide fume arising during melting and pouring of the copper alloys. Where there is blowing of the molten metal deliberately to remove zinc the standards for general fume emissions are expected to be attempted.

[b] Rate of melting is the aggregate capacity of all furnaces on the works site calculated to a 24-hour day except on a large works where groups of furnaces are so widely separated as to be able to be considered as occupying different sites.

TABLE XXXV

CHIMNEY HEIGHTS FOR CEMENT WORKS—
ALKALI INSPECTORATE—GREAT BRITAIN

Clinker throughput (tons/hour)	Chimney height (feet)[a]		
	Wet process	Semidry process	Dry process
30 and less	200	200	200
60	280	260	240
90	340	310	280
120	390	350	310
240	500	460	415
360	550	500	450

[a] Interpolation between 30 and 360 tons/hour on smooth curves through points in table. Such curves are Fig. 1 of the "notes" referred to in the text.

TABLE XXXVI

REGULATIONS LIMITING THE VOLATILE CONTENT OF COAL:
18 CITIES (U.S.A.)[a]

Maximum percent volatile:	20	21	23	24	26
Number of cities:	5	1	9	1	2

[a] From Rogers (10).

TABLE XXXVII
STANDARD METHODS FOR AIR QUALITY MEASUREMENT[a,b,c]

Standard	Method
A.P.C.A.-APM-1 (Rev. 1)	Recommended Standard Method for Continuing Dust Fall Survey
A.P.C.A.-APM-2	Recommended Standard Methods for Continuing Air Monitoring for Fine Particulate Matter
	APM-2.1—General
	APM-2.2—By Filter Media, Low Volume Samplers
	APM-2.3—By Particle Counting
	APM-2.5—By Filter Media, High Volume Samplers
A.P.C.A.-APM-3	Recommended Standard Methods for Continuous Air Monitoring for Gaseous Contaminants
	APM-3.1—General
	APM-3.3—Hydrogen Sulfide
A.P.C.D. 3-54	K_m Values—Aerosols
A.P.C.D. 4-57X	Metals, Spectrographic
A.P.C.D. 5-46	Aldehydes, Total
A.P.C.D. 6-56	Ammonia and Ammonium Ion
A.P.C.D. 7-53	Dustfall
A.P.C.D. 8-53	Formaldehyde
A.P.C.D. 13-49	Oxides of Sulfur, Barium Sulfate Method
A.P.C.D. 14-56	Ozone
A.P.I. 766-58	Hydrocarbons in the Atmosphere: Mass Spectrometer Freezeout Method
A.P.I. 776-59	Sulfur Dioxide in the Atmosphere (Disulfitomercurate Method)
A.S.T.M.-D 1355-60 (1967)	Continuous Analysis and Automatic Recording of Sulfur Dioxide Content of the Atmosphere
A.S.T.M.-D 1356-67	Terms Relating to Atmospheric Sampling and Analysis
A.S.T.M.-D 1357-57 (1967)	Planning the Sampling of the Atmosphere
A.S.T.M.-D 1391-57 (1967)	Measurement of Odor in Atmospheres
A.S.T.M.-D 1605-60 (1967)	Sampling Atmospheres for Analysis of Gases and Vapors
A.S.T.M.-D 1606-60 (1967)	Inorganic Fluoride in the Atmosphere
A.S.T.M.-D 1607-60	Nitrogen Dioxide with Nitric Oxide Content of the Atmosphere (Modified Griess-Ilosvay Reaction)
A.S.T.M.-D 1609-60	Oxidant (Ozone) Content of the Atmosphere
A.S.T.M.-D 1704-61	Particulate Matter in the Atmosphere (Optical Density of Filtered Deposit)
A.S.T.M.-D 1739-62 (1967)	Collection and Analysis of Dustfall
A.S.T.M.-D 1899-61T	Method of Test for Mass Concentration of Particulate Matter in The Atmosphere (Continuous-Measurement Light Scattering Method)
A.S.T.M.-D 1914-61T	Recommended Practice for Conversion Units and Factors Relating to Atmospheric Analysis
A.S.T.M.-D 2009-65	Collection by Filtration and Determination of Mass, Number, and Optical Sizing of Atmospheric Particulates
A.S.T.M.-D 2010-65 (1967)	Method for Evaluation of Total Sulfation in Atmosphere by the Lead Peroxide Candle
A.S.T.M.-D 2011-65	Method of Test for Continuous Analysis and Automatic Recording of the Oxidant Content of the Atmosphere

TABLE XXXVII (*Continued*)

Standard	Method
A.S.T.M.-D 2012-63T	Method of Test for Continuous Measurement of Nitric Oxide, Nitrogen Dioxide, and Ozone in the Atmosphere
B.S. 1747	Methods for the Measurements of Air Pollution
	Part 1—Deposit gauges (also N.Z.S.S. 1097)
	Part 2—Determination of concentration of suspended matter
	Part 3—Determination of sulfur dioxide
	Part 4—The lead dioxide method
S.D.P.H. 1-A	Sulfur Dioxide in the Atmosphere (Modified West Method) (Manual)
S.D.P.H. 2	Total Oxidant Content of the Atmosphere (Neutral Buffered Potassium Iodide Method) (Manual)
S.D.P.H. 3	Nitrogen Dioxide and Nitric Oxide in the Atmosphere (Saltzman Method) (Manual)
S.D.P.H. 4	Nitrogen Dioxide and Nitric Oxide Content of the Atmosphere (Continuous—Automatic)
S.D.P.H. 5	Total Oxidant Content of the Atmosphere (Continuous—Automatic)
S.D.P.H. 6	Sulfur Dioxide Content of the Atmosphere (Conductivity—Continuous—Automatic)
S.D.P.H. 7	Guide to Operation of Atmospheric Analyzers
S.D.P.H. 8	Sulfur Pollution of Air by Means of Lead Peroxide Candle
S.D.P.H. 9	C_1 through C_5 Atmospheric Hydrocarbons
S.D.P.H. 15	Dustfall Sample Analysis (Draft 6/7/67)
S.D.P.H. 16	Calcium and Magnesium in Dustfall Samples (Draft 6/7/67)
V.D.I. 2119-62	Measurement of Dustfall
V.D.I. 2450-63	Measuring Gaseous Pollutants in the Atmosphere
V.D.I. 2451-63	Measuring Sulfur Dioxide Concentrations in the Atmosphere
V.D.I. 2452-63	Measuring Fluoride-Ion Concentration

[a] A.P.C.A.—Air Pollution Control Association, 4400 Fifth Ave., Pittsburgh, Pa. 15213.

A.P.C.D.—Los Angeles County Air Pollution Control District, 434 S. San Pedro St., Los Angeles, Calif. 90013.

A.P.I.　—American Petroleum Institute, 1271 Ave. of the Americas, New York, N.Y. 10020.

A.S.T.M.—American Society for Testing and Materials, 1916 Race St, Philadelphia, Pa. 19103.

B.S.　—British Standards Institution, British Standards House, 2 Park St., London, W.1, England.

N.Z.S.S.—New Zealand Standards Institute, Departmental Building, Bowen St., Wellington, New Zealand.

S.D.P.H.—California Department of Public Health, 2151 Berkeley Way, Berkeley, Calif. 94704.

V.D.I.　—Verein Deutscher Ingenieure, Kommission Reinhaltung der Luft, Prinz Georg Strasse 77/79, Dusseldorf, Germany.

[b] See also Table XXXVIII.

[c] A.P.C.D. methods which the Los Angeles County Air Pollution Control District considers obsolete have been omitted from this table.

TABLE XXXVIII
Standard Methods for Emission Measurement[a,b]

Standard	Method
A.P.C.D. 1-54	Acetylene
A.P.C.D. 12-56	Oxides of Nitrogen (Phenoldisulfonic Acid Method)
A.P.C.D. 16-57	Organic Acids, Total
A.P.I. 751-54	Collection of Samples
A.P.I. 754-60	Hydrocarbon Evaporation Losses from Oil and Water Separation Processes
A.P.I. 755-54	Measurement of Gas Flow
A.P.I. 756-54	Particulate Matter: Filtration Method
A.P.I. 757-54	Particulate Matter: Impingement Method
A.P.I. 758-54	Particulate Matter: Impaction Method
A.P.I. 762-54	Aldehydes: Bisulfite Absorption Method
A.P.I. 763-54	Ammonia: Kjeldahl and Nessler Reagent Method
A.P.I. 764-54	Carbon Monoxide and Carbon Dioxide: Absorption—Combustion Method
A.P.I. 765-54	Hydrogen Cyanide and Cyanogen: Colorimetric Method
A.P.I. 767-54	Hydrogen Chloride: Turbidimetric Method
A.P.I. 768-54	Inorganic Fluorides: Absorption—Distillation Method
A.P.I. 770-59	Nitrogen Oxides in Gaseous Combustion Products (Phenoldisulfonic Acid Method)
A.P.I. 771-54	Hydrogen Sulfide: Tutweiler Apparatus Method
A.P.I. 772-54	Hydrogen Sulfide: Ammoniacal Cadmium Chloride Method
A.P.I. 773-54	Hydrogen Sulfide and Mercaptans: Electrometric Titration Method
A.P.I. 774-54	Total Sulfur Oxides: Acidimetric Method
A.P.I. 775-54	Sulfur Dioxide and Sulfur Trioxide: Acidimetric Method
A.S.M.E. Power Test Code 21	Test Code for Dust Separating Apparatus
A.S.M.E. Power Test Code 27	Determining Dust Concentration in a Gas Stream
A.S.M.E. Power Test Code 28	Measurement of Small Particulate Matter
A.S.M.E. Power Test Code Supplement on Instruments and Apparatus—Part 20	Smoke Density Determinations
A.S.T.M.-D 1354-60	Concentration of Odorous Vapors
A.S.T.M.-D 1608-60 (1967)	Oxides of Nitrogen in Gaseous Combustion Products (Phenoldisulfonic Acid Procedure)
B.S. 893	Method of Testing Dust Extraction Plant and the Emission of Solids from Chimneys of Electric Power Stations (also N.Z.S.S. 413)
B.S. 1756	Methods for the Sampling and Analysis of Flue Gas Part 1—Methods of Sampling Part 4—Miscellaneous Analyses
B.S. 2740	Simple Smoke Alarms and Alarm Metering Devices
B.S. 2741	Recommendation for the Construction of Simple Smoke Viewers

TABLE XXXVIII (*Continued*)

Standard	Method

B.S. 2742	Notes on the Use of the Ringlemann Chart
	    C: 1957 Ringelmann Chart
	    M: 1960 Miniature Smoke Chart

B.S. 2811	Smoke Density Indicators and Recorders (also N.Z.S.S. 1449)

B.S. 2978	Measurement of Smoke Emission from Industrial Boilers
	    Part 1—Medium capacity coal-fired water tube boilers with traveling grates
	    Part 2—Coal-fired shell boilers with various types of mechanical stoker

B.S. 3405	Simplified Method of Measurement of Grit and Dust Emission from Chimneys
B.S. 3841	Method for the Measurement of Smoke from Manufactured Solid Fuels for Domestic Open Fires
S.D.P.H. 11	n-Butyl Cellosolve in the Air
S.D.P.H. 17	Carbonyl Compounds in Combustion Emissions (Draft 3/15/67)
V.D.I. 2066-66	Measuring Dust Collector Performance

[a] A.P.C.D. —Los Angeles County Air Pollution Control District, 434 S. San Pedro St., Los Angeles, Calif. 90013.

A.P.I.   —American Petroleum Institute, 1271 Ave. of the Americas, New York, N.Y. 10020.

A.S.M.E. —American Society of Mechanical Engineers, 345 East 47th St., New York, N.Y. 10017.

A.S.T.M.—American Society for Testing and Materials, 1916 Race St., Philadelphia, Pa. 19103.

B.S.   —British Standards Institution, British Standards House, 2 Park St., London, W.1., England.

N.Z.S.S. —New Zealand Standards Institute, Departmental Building, Bowen St., Wellington, New Zealand

S.D.P.H. —California Department of Public Health, 2151 Berkeley Way, Berkeley, Calif. 94704.

V.D.I.   —Verein Deutscher Ingenieure, Kommission Reinhaltung der Luft, Prinz Georg Strasse 77/79 Dusseldorf, Germany.

[b] See also Table XXXVII.

REFERENCES

1. The American Industrial Hygiene Association is publishing a series of "Community Air Quality Guides." Those published prior to completion of this chapter were:
   "Rationale," *Amer. Ind. Hyg. Assoc. J.* **29** (1), 1–3.
   "Iron Oxide," *Amer. Ind. Hyg. Assoc. J.* **29** (1), 4–6.
   "Beryllium," *Amer. Ind. Hyg. Assoc. J.* **29** (2), 89–192.
   "Ozone (Photochemical Oxidant)," *Amer. Ind. Hyg. Assoc. J.* **29** (3), 299–303.

The following were announced for future publication (and, with the four above, as a complete set obtainable from the association in Detroit, Michigan): Aldehydes, Carbon Monoxide, Ethylene, Fluorides, Lead, Phenolic compounds, Regional planning, Sulfur compounds, and Total particulate matter.

1a. "Air Quality Criteria for Sulfur Oxides," Public Health Serv. Publ. No. 1619. U.S. Dept. of Health, Education, and Welfare, Washington, D.C., 1967.

1b. L. J. Brasser, P. E. Joosting, and D. van Zuilen, "Sulfur Dioxide—To What Level is it Acceptable?" Rept. G 300 (in English). Research Institute for Public Health Engineering, Instituut voor Gezondheidstechnick TNO, Delft, The Netherlands, 1967.

2. "Technical Report of California Standards for Ambient Air Quality and Motor Vehicle Exhaust." State of California, Dept. of Public Health, Berkeley, California, 1961.

3. "The Oxides of Nitrogen in Air Pollution." State of California, Dept. of Public Health, Berkeley, California, 1966.

4. "Lead in the Environment and Its Effects on Humans." State of California, Dept. of Public Health, Berkeley, California, 1967.

5. Verein Deutscher Ingenieure, Kommission Reinhaltung der Luft, Richtlinien, VDI-Verlag GmbH, Duesseldorf, Federal Republic of Germany.

6. *Gigiena i Sanit.* (1964 et seq.). (Hygiene and Sanitation, Israel Program for Scientific Translations, Clearinghouse for Federal Scientific and Technical Information, Springfield, Virginia); also B. S. Levine, "U.S.S.R. Literature on Air Pollution and Related Occupational Diseases," Vol. 1 (TT-60-21049) 1960; Vol. 2 (TT-60-21188) 1960; Vol. 3 (TT-60-21475) 1960; Vol. 4 (TT-60-21913) 1960; Vol. 5 (TT-61-11149) 1961; Vol. 6 (TT-61-21982) 1961; Vol. 7 (TT-62-11103) 1962; Vol. 8 (TT-63-11570) 1963; Vol. 9 (TT-64-11574) 1964; Vol. 10 (TT-64-11767) 1964; Vol. 11 (TT-65-61965) 1965; Vol. 12 (TT-66-61429) 1966; Vol. 13 (TT-66-62191) 1966; Vol. 14 (TT-67-60046) 1967. Clearinghouse for Federal Scientific and Technical Information, Springfield, Virginia; also V. A. Ryazanov, ed., "Limits of Allowable Concentration of Atmospheric Pollutants" (transl. by B. S. Levine), Book 1 (TT-59-21173) 1952; Book 2 (TT-59-21174) 1955; Book 3 (TT-59-21175) 1957; Book 4 (TT-61-11148) 1960; Book 5 (TT-62-11605) 1960; Books 6 and 7 (TT-64-11574) 1963–1964. Clearinghouse for Federal Scientific and Technical Information, Springfield, Virginia.

7. "Threshold Limit Values for 1967," *Am. Conf. Govtl. Ind. Hygienists, Chicago, Illinois, 1967* pp. 1–26.

8. "Continuous Air Monitoring Program in Philadelphia, 1962–63–64–65." Public Health Serv., U.S. Dept. of Health, Education, and Welfare, Cincinnati, Ohio, 1968 (in press).

8a. Hearings before the Subcommittee on Air and Water Pollution of the Committee on Public Works, U.S. Senate, 90th Congress, 1st Session, S.780—Air Pollution—1967 (Air Quality Act), Part 4. U.S. Govt. Printing Office, Washington, D.C., 1967.

8b. Regulation Z3191A, Joint Ministerial Bulletin No. 26 on Air Pollution Control, Ministry of Health, Published by Ministry of Interior, Federal Republic of Germany, Bad Godesburg, 1964.

9. "Control of Dust Emission—Combustion for Indirect Heat Exchangers," ASME Std., APS-1, p. 30B. Am. Soc. Mech. Engrs., New York, 1966.

9a. Ministry of Housing and Local Government, Scottish Development Department, Welsh Office "Grit and Dust," 10 pp. Her Majesty's Stationery Office, London (1967).

9b. Supplemento ordinario alla GAZZETTA UFFICIALE n.6 del 9 gennaio 1968.

9c. H. Kettner, *Bull. Inst. Wasser-, Boden-, Lufthyg.* **12,** 46 (1957).

9d. Ministry of Housing and Local Government, Scottish Development Department, Welsh Office "Chimney Heights" 2nd ed. 1956 Clean Air Act Memorandum, 10 pp. Her Majesty's Stationery Office, London (1967).

10. S. M. Rogers, *J. Air Pollution Control Assoc.* **7,** No. 4, 308–315, (1958).
11. "Methods of Measuring Air Pollution," Report of the Working Party on Methods of Measuring Air Pollution and Survey Techniques. Organization for Economic Cooperation and Development, Paris, 1964.
12. "Selected Methods for the Measurement of Air Pollutants," Public Health Service Publ. 999-AP-11, pp. 1–54. U.S. Dept. of Health, Education, and Welfare, Cincinnati, Ohio, 1965.
13. "Air Pollution Measurements of the National Air Sampling Network, 1957–1961," Public Health Serv. Publ. No. 978. U.S. Govt. Printing Office, Washington, D.C., 1962.
14. "Laboratory Methods," Air Pollution Control District, County of Los Angeles, Los Angeles, California, 1958.
15. "Sampling and Analysis of Waste Gases and Particulate Matter," Manual on the Disposal of Refinery Wastes, Vol. 5. Am. Petrol. Inst., New York (undated).
16. 1967 Book of ASTM STANDARDS, Part 23, Industrial Water; Atmospheric Analysis, Am. Soc. Testing and Mater., Philadelphia, Pennsylvania, 1967.
17. Air Pollution Control Association, 4400 Fifth Avenue, Pittsburgh, Pennsylvania 15213.
18. British Standards Institution, British Standards House, 2 Park Street, London, W.1.
19. "Recommended Methods in Air Pollution Measurements." California State Dept. of Public Health, Berkeley, California, 1967.
20. New Zealand Standards Institute, Departmental Building, Bowen Street, Wellington, New Zealand.
21. "The Investigation of Air Pollution," National Survey Annual Summary Table 1 for the year ending March 1964. Ministry of Technology, Warren Springs Laboratory, 1964.
22. "Status Criteria for a High Air Pollution Alert and Warning System—A Panel Report." School of Engineering and Architecture, The City College of The City University of New York, New York, 1967, 16 pp.

52 Air Pollution Control Administration

Jean J. Schueneman

I. The Philosophy of Air Pollution Control

A. Objectives of Control Programs

The basic objective of control programs is to preserve the health and welfare of man, both now and in the distant future. Other objectives are protection of plant and animal life, prevention of damage to physical property and interference with its normal use and enjoyment, provision of visibility required for safe air and ground transportation, ensuring continued economic growth and development, and maintenance of an esthetically acceptable and, hopefully, enjoyable environment (*1*).

Those planning or operating air pollution control programs must consider the collective needs and desires of their community and make every effort to translate them into a plan of action. The program should be designed to provide for air resource management in a broad sense and encompass both short and long-range goals.

To accomplish long-range objectives, a series of shorter range objectives must be established if an orderly, planned program is to result. These include collecting fundamental facts, determining conditions existing in the field, analyzing information, developing a plan of action, and putting the plan into effect (2).

As control programs proceed, there is a temptation to move ahead on all fronts simultaneously. This should be avoided in favor of an attack on a manageable part of the problem, preferably engaging first in activities which have the broadest acceptance and the best chance for success. As momentum and support increase, other parts of the problem can be tackled. Unless this is done, the program administrator will find himself and his program in the midst of a confusing, meaningless series of uncoordinated moves and without any complete program segments to show (3).

B. Public Policy in Air Pollution Control

Public policy may be defined as the central ideas and purposes that guide the public actions of individuals and social institutions, both public and private (4). There are four central ideas that should be accepted as axioms of public policy in the air pollution field. First, action should not be postponed until emergency conditions make it compulsory. Drastic action, undertaken on short notice in response to some new Donora-like disaster would be far more costly, and disruptive of normal economic and social patterns, than control measures carefully planned in advance and, perhaps, gradually applied. Second, the air cannot be purified after it is polluted. Prevention rather than cure must be the aim. The control or prevention of air pollutants at their sources, therefore, is of fundamental importance. Third, air pollution control cannot be accomplished without close cooperation among all levels of government, industry, and the public. In the American system of government, the primary source of the police power, on which regulatory programs for air pollution control are based, rests with the states. The need for the states to exercise this power in the air pollution field, either directly or by delegation to appropriate sublevels of government, is therefore obvious, as is participation by the federal government. Preferably, commercial, industrial, municipal, and individual participation should be voluntary, in recognition that their long-term interests are best served by clean air. Finally, the entire structure of any air resource management program rests on enlightened public opinion.

The air resource of any area will be managed—or neglected—to the extent its citizens desire and demand (5).

The establishment of precise statements of public policy in the air resource field is deterred by several factors. The relationships between adverse effects of air pollutant concentrations have not been unequivocally delineated. Policy makers and the public are having difficulty grasping the present and future significance of the population, urbanization, and energy use explosions. The jurisdictional area of policy makers in local government is often too small to encompass the region for which policy needs to be made. Disparity exists between those who pay for the costs of pollution control and those who benefit from it. There are formidable obstacles, but they are not insurmountable (6).

C. THE AIR RESOURCE MANAGEMENT CONCEPT

The basic use of our air resource is to sustain life. All other uses must yield to the maintenance of air quality which will not degrade, either acutely or chronically, the health or well-being of man. There remain but two major areas of possible compromise. These are the esthetics and the economic impact of air pollution and its control. The cost borne by society to achieve a desired quality of air should be in balance with the benefits to be attained (7).

Until recent years, the control of air pollution was based upon the correction of existing problems. Little or no consideration has been given to long-range planning, or how proposed community or regional master plans might influence future ambient air quality. This lack of coordinated planning has tended to maximize the creation of air pollution problems. As long as this situation is allowed to exist, air pollution problems will be created faster than they can be resolved. The use of the air resource management concept should improve this condition materially.

Until recently, local air pollution control programs were oriented along two major lines (1) control of smoke and particulates from combustion sources and (2) control of other discrete emissions into the atmosphere that were deemed a "nuisance," and were capable of technical and economic control. In both cases it was hoped that the "desired" air quality would be achieved. What this "desired" air quality was, remained rather ill-defined (7).

The elements of an air resource management program may be listed as follows (7):

1. Development of a public policy on air conservation.
2. An organizational framework and staff capable of operating along

functional lines (e.g., engineering, technical services, field services) and the funding support.

3. Delineation of realistic short-range goals that can be effectively met in a reasonable time period, say 5 years.

4. Continual assessment of existing air quality and preparation of estimates of the future situation.

5. Assessment in depth, on a continuing basis, of the emissions from all existing pollution sources and those expected to exist in the future.

6. Development of the necessary information about factors that influence the transport of air pollutants.

7. Assessment of the effects of ambient air quality of a community or region on man and his environment.

8. Establishment of ambient air quality goals (referred to, by some, as objectives or standards).

9. Design of remedial measures and programs calculated to bring about the air quality desired.

10. Development of long-range air use plans, fully integrated with other community plans for energy supplies, land use, transportation, recreation, refuse disposal, etc., to cope effectively with changes projected for the community.

11. Development of an understanding of the broad impact of changing science and technology on air resources and the potential effect on the social and economic character of modern society.

12. Development of an effective information and educational program to inform the community of the need to solve air pollution problems promptly and effectively.

The mechanisms and organization for reaching decisions in a community (or state) are of key importance in the success of an air resource management program. They must provide for the assimilation of information into goals and policies, and the subsequent enunciation of a public policy on the management of a community's air resource. Appropriate community involvement in the decision-making process must be encouraged to ensure a base of public support for action.

The degree of success achieved in making decisions and development of policy will depend upon the clear delegation of responsibility to a key individual. It follows that full support by top management (including chief elected executives) is needed to develop and implement a set of program goals.

Long-range planning must be an integral part of an air resource management program. It helps smooth the way for anticipated social and technological changes in the urban environment and makes it possible to consider a much broader scope of alternate programs to achieve or maintain high quality air. For example, in a 25-year plan, consideration could be given to the elimination of certain existing combustion operations and substitution of electrical energy as a heating source, as one means of reducing pollutant emissions—a program too complicated to consider on a short range basis. Planning forces program directors to think ahead about technological changes and predisposes them toward changes which they can agree to and support. Without planning, the director will find himself reacting to changing events rather than influencing them as he should.

The air resource management concept provides a base for organization of tasks so that program directors can perform them systematically, purposefully, with understanding, and with a reasonable probability of accomplishment. It endeavors to develop a point of view, identifies approaches for finding what should be done, and describes how to go about doing it. In this way, it is more likely that the steps required to achieve and maintain desired air quality will be taken expeditiously and in an equitable manner.

II. Governmental Air Pollution Control Programs in the United States

A. LOCAL GOVERNMENT PROGRAMS

1. *Extent of Programs and Budgets*

There were about 130 city, county, and multijurisdictional area air pollution programs in the United States in 1965 which spent more than $5000 per year (Table 1). This included dual coverage in seven geographical areas. It was an increase of 45 agencies over the number reported in 1961 (8). Of the 130 agencies, 39 were not yet, in the usual sense, complete regulatory agencies. Thirty-four were in the process of developing a program and five were conducting surveys. The number of local agencies existing in 1967 was probably about 150.

Total funds expended by local agencies were $14,254,000 in 1965. Of the 1965 total, $10,673,000 were local funds (75%) and $3,581,000 (25%) were federal grants for control programs and surveys. The largest budget was in Los Angeles County ($3,663,000). Of the total budgeted, 38% was in California agencies. The seven largest agencies accounted for 58% of the total. There were 42 agencies with a budget in excess of $50,000. Larger per capita budgets (50 cents or more) existed in smaller communities. Total funds (local plus federal grants) were about $17,400,000 in 1967.

TABLE I
LOCAL AIR POLLUTION PROGRAMS AND BUDGETS
(AGENCIES SPENDING $5000 PER YEAR OR MORE)

City or area	Population 1960 (1000)	Budget, 1965 ($1000)			1965 per capita budget (cents)	1961 budget ($1000) (8)
		Non-federal	Federal[a]	Total		
1. Huntsville, Ala.	72	5	E 10	15	20.8	0
2. Jefferson County (Birmingham) Ala.	635	42	D 121	163	25.7	12
3. Mobile County, Ala.	314	7	D 22	29	9.2	0
4. Maricopa County, Ariz.	664	72	E 57	129	19.5	0
5. Pima County, Ariz.	266	8	D 25	33	12.4	0
6. Humbold County, Calif.	105	7	0	7	6.7	0
7. Los Angeles County, Calif.	6039	3453	I 210	3663	60.8	3402
8. Orange County, Calif. '	704	126	0	126	17.9	117
9. Riverside County, Calif.	306	86	0	86	28.1	67
10. Sacramento County, Calif.	503	28	0	28	5.6	50
11. San Bernardino County, Calif.	504	207	I 77	284	56.3	259
12. San Diego County, Calif.	1000	68	0	68	6.8	79
13. San Francisco Bay Area, Calif.	3291	990	I 58	1048	31.8	560
14. Ventura County, Calif.	199	10	b 20	30	15.1	0
15. Adams and Arapahoe County, Colo.	234	12	E 36	48	20.4	0
16. Boulder City-County, Colo.	74	2	b 7	9	12.2	0
17. Denver City and County, Colo.	494	62	I 89	151	30.5	15
18. Bridgeport, Conn.	157	12	E 22	34	21.6	0
19. Fairfield, Conn.	46	8	D 15	23	50.0	0
20. Middletown, Conn.	33	7	D 12	19	57.6	0
21. New Britain, Conn.	82	7	b 14	21	25.6	0
22. Stratford, Conn.	45	7	D 15	22	48.7	0
23. Washington, D.C.	764	45	I 33	78	10.2	42
24. Metro. Wash. Council of Govts.	1736	7	b 21	28	1.6	0
25. Dade County, Fla.	935	40	I 64	104	11.1	5
26. Hillsborough County, Fla.	398	10	0	10	2.5	0
27. Palm Beach County, Fla.	228	13	E 39	52	22.8	0
28. Pinellas County, Fla.	375	10	0	10	2.7	0
29. Polk-Hillsborough Counties, Fla.[e]	593	142	0	142	23.9	50
30. Atlanta, Ga.	487	13	0	13	2.7	13
31. Fulton County, Ga.	556	6	D 18	24	4.3	0
32. Macon-Bibb County, Ga.	141	5	D 16	21	14.9	0
33. Chicago, Ill.	3550	770	I 393	1163	32.7	364
34. Cook County, Ill.[f]	180	100	I 50	150	83.3	0
35. Peoria, Ill.	103	6	0	6	5.8	8
36. Will County, Ill.	192	6	b 16	22	14.5	0
37. East Chicago, Ind.	58	19	I 15	34	58.7	11
38. Evansville, Ind.	142	14	I 11	25	17.6	10
39. Gary, Ind.	178	43	I 63	106	59.6	0
40. Indianapolis, Ind.	476	40	0	40	8.4	38
41. Terre Haute, Ind.	72	11	0	11	15.3	0
42. Cedar Rapids, Iowa.	92	5	D 11	16	17.4	0
43. Clinton, Iowa.	34	3	b 5	8	23.6	0
44. Kansas City-Wyandotte Co., Kans.	185	8	D 24	32	17.3	0
45. Jefferson Co. (Louisville) Ky.	611	87	I 21	108	17.6	63
46. Anne Arundel County, Md.	207	27	d	27	13.1	0

TABLE I (*continued*)

City or area	Population 1960 (1000)	Budget, 1965 ($1000) Non-federal	Federal[a]	Total	1965 per capita budget (cents)	1961 budget ($1000) (8)
47. Baltimore, Md.	939	77	[d]	77	8.2	70
48. Baltimore County, Md.	492	27	[d]	27	5.5	0
49. Boston Metro. Area, Mass.[e]	1998	99	I 120	219	11.0	52
50. Springfield Metro. Area, Mass.[e]	415	11	D 33	44	10.6	0
51. Worcester, Mass.	187	12	E 23	35	18.6	0
52. Dearborn, Mich.	112	16	0	16	14.3	5
53. Detroit, Mich.	1670	234	c 123	357	21.4	180
54. Grand Rapids, Mich.	177	10	0	10	5.7	6
55. Muskegon County, Mich.	150	5	D 16	21	14.1	0
56. River Rouge, Mich.	18	13	0	13	72.3	0
57. Wayne County, Mich.[g]	996	43	I 90	133	13.3	20
58. Wyandotte, Mich.	44	9	I 18	27	61.5	0
59. Minneapolis, Minn.	483	29	I 38	67	13.8	11
60. St. Paul, Minn.	313	26	I 43	69	22.1	0
61. St. Louis, Mo.	750	134	I 43	177	23.5	118
62. St. Louis County, Mo.[h]	704	69	E 105	174	24.8	0
63. Omaha, Nebr.	302	8	0	8	2.6	20
64. Omaha-Douglas County, Neb.	343	10	b 21	31	9.0	0
65. Clark County, Nev.	127	50	0	50	39.4	0
66. Reno-Sparks-Washoe County, Nev.	85	13	E 28	41	48.2	0
67. Camden, N.J.	117	12	0	12	10.2	7
68. East Orange, N.J.	77	6	D 8	14	18.2	0
69. Elizabeth, N.J.	108	10	0	10	9.3	0
70. Hillside Twp. N.J.	22	8	0	8	36.3	5
71. Newark, N.J.	405	66	0	66	16.3	63
72. Perth Amboy, N.J.	38	30	0	30	78.9	13
73. Albuquerque, N. M.	201	9	I 6	15	7.5	0
74. Albany County, N.Y.	273	2	D 3	5	1.8	0
75. Broome County, N.Y.	213	4	D 8	12	5.5	0
76. Chemung County, N.Y.	99	3	D 5	8	8.1	0
77. Columbia County, N.Y.	47	2	D 4	6	12.7	0
78. Dutchess County, N.Y.	176	2	E 3	5	2.9	0
79. Erie County, N.Y.	1065	38	D 76	114	10.6	0
80. Mt. Vernon, N.Y.	76	3	D 5	8	10.5	0
81. Nassau County, N.Y.	1300	96	D 54	150	11.5	0
82. New Rochelle, N.Y.	77	6	E 6	12	15.5	0
83. New York, N.Y.	7782	1032	I 188	1220	15.7	734
84. Niagara County, N.Y.	242	12	D 35	47	19.4	0
85. Rochester, N.Y.	319	10	0	10	3.3	10
86. Schenectady, N.Y.	82	6	D 3	5	6.1	0
87. Suffolk County, N.Y.	667	8	b 23	31	6	0
88. Syracuse, N.Y.	216	50	0	50	23.2	36
89. Yonkers, N.Y.	191	5	D 9	14	7.3	0
90. Interstate Sanitation Commission-New York and New Jersey	14700	36	b 42	78	0.5	0
91. Asheville, N.C.	59	21	0	21	35.6	16
92. Buncombe, Haywood, Henderson and Transylvania Counties, N.C.	222	8	D 25	33	14.9	0
93. Charlotte, N.C.	202	16	0	16	7.9	19

Continued

TABLE I (continued)

City or area	Population 1960 (1000)	Budget, 1965 ($1000)			1965 per capita budget (cents)	1961 budget ($1000) (8)
		Non-federal	Federal[a]	Total		
94. Durham County, N.C.	112	5	D 13	18	16.1	0
95. Gaston County, N.C.	127	7	D 19	26	20.5	0
96. Guilford County, N.C.	247	6	D 18	24	9.8	0
97. New Hanover County, N.C.	72	4	D 13	17	23.6	0
98. Rowan County, N.C.	83	4	D 13	17	20.3	0
99. Winston-Salem, N.C.	111	17	0	17	15.3	12
100. Akron, Ohio	290	36	D 94	130	44.8	16
101. Cincinnati, Ohio (Area)[i]	542	97	0	97	17.9	165
102. Cleveland, Ohio	876	242	I 35	277	31.6	236
103. Columbus, Ohio	471	74	0	74	15.7	50
104. Dayton, Ohio	262	25	0	25	9.5	55
105. East Cleveland, Ohio	38	5	0	5	13.2	7
106. Lorain, Ohio	69	10	E 19	29	42.1	0
107. Toledo, Ohio	318	39	I 24	63	19.8	12
108. Youngstown, Ohio	167	18	0	18	10.8	17
109. Oklahoma City and County, Okla.	440	3	D 10	13	3.0	0
110. Tulsa City and County, Okla.	346	8	D 25	33	9.6	0
111. Eugene-Springfield, Ore.	71	16	0	16	22.5	10
112. Mid-Willamette Valley, Ore.[j]	278	13	[b] 39	52	18.7	0
113. Portland, Ore.	373	45	I 73	118	31.5	17
114. Allegheny County, Pa.	1629	210	I 160	370	22.7	217
115. Erie, Pa.	138	11	0	11	8.0	15
116. Lehigh Valley Area, Pa.	278	14	E 1	15	5.4	14
117. Philadelphia, Pa.	2003	241	I 125	366	18.2	166
118. Providence, R.I.	207	36	I 7	43	20.8	31
119. Spartanburg, S.C.	44	9	I 10	19	43.0	0
120. Chattanooga, Tenn.	130	23	I 14	37	28.5	16
121. Nashville-Davidson Co., Tenn.	400	16	D 15	31	7.7	13
122. Harris County, Tex.	1243	40	0	40	3.2	42
123. Richmond, Va.	220	29	0	29	13.2	25
124. Roanoke, Va.	97	12	I 2	14	14.4	11
125. Seattle, Wash.	557	35	0	35	6.3	12
126. Seattle-King County Wash.	935	56	D 38	94	10.0	0
127. Tacoma, Wash.	148	12	0	12	8.1	8
128. Wheeling, W. Va.	53	6	0	6	11.3	17
129. Green Bay, Wis.	63	15	0	15	23.8	7
130. Milwaukee County, Wis.	1036	186	0	186	18.0	128
22 agencies existing in 1961 but not in 1965	—	—	—	—	—	308
TOTAL	63362[k]	10673	3581	14254	22.6	8177

[a] Nat'l Air Poll. Control Admin. Program Grant, unless indicated otherwise. E means "Establishment Grant;" D means "Development Grant;" and I means "Improvement Grant."

[b] Funds are Nat'l Air Poll. Control Admin. Survey Grant.

[c] Includes $80,000 Nat'l Air Poll. Control Admin. Survey Grant funds.

[d] Participating in comprehensive survey of Baltimore metropolitan area, supported in part by $225,000 Nat'l Air Poll. Control Admin. Survey Grant made to state of Maryland for all concerned agencies.

[e] Local program operated by the state. Also shown in Table VI.

[f] Serving unincorporated area only. Population is approximate.

[g] Not providing service in Detroit, which is part of Wayne County.

[h] Not providing service in city of St. Louis which is not part of the county government.

[i] Includes $12,000 received from eight communities for services provided by the city.

[j] Benton, Linn, Marion, Polk, and Yamhill Counties.

[k] Not the sum of the numbers in the column because of dual coverage of some areas.

To appraise the nation-wide growth and current status of air pollution programs, a number of analyses of data were made (Tables II and III). Resource data were obtained from past tabulations of local air pollution program expenditures and budgets (8–11) and U.S. Bureau of the Census population data. Table II is a simple tabulation of per capita expenditures of all local agencies. Table III includes only regulatory programs and embodies many adjustments which are explained in footnotes of the table. Budgets of state and local agencies engaged largely or exclusively in conduct of studies and which did not carry out significant regulatory activities were not included in Table III. Also, budgets of the California Air Resources Board and California Highway Patrol were not included since doing so would have warped the long-range picture of "usual" regulatory activities by including a new type of special purpose regulatory activity of major magnitude.

The number of local agencies operating at least minimal regulatory programs increased from 44 in 1952 to 72 in 1961, and 117 in 1965 (Table III). Of particular note is the increase in county agencies since 1961 of from 10 to 46. All but four of the new county programs are in health departments. Six new multijurisdictional agencies came into being or achieved minimal or greater budgets. The number of state programs meeting the assumed criteria for a minimal regulatory program increased from three in 1961 (Delaware, Hawaii, Oregon) to four in 1965 (Oregon, Hawaii, New Jersey, and West Virginia). Total population served by minimal or better state and local regulatory programs in

TABLE II

PER CAPITA EXPENDITURES OF LOCAL AIR POLLUTION CONTROL AGENCIES
(AGENCIES SPENDING $5000 OR MORE PER ANNUM)

Annual expenditures per capita (cents)	1952 (10)		1955 (11)		1961 (8)		1965	
	A[a]	B[b]	A	B	A	B	A	B
1–9	22	49	36	47	36	42	38	29
10–19	16	35	27	36	28	33	46	35
20–29	3	7	7	9	14	17	23	18
30–39	3	7	2	3	3	4	8	6
40–49	0	0	4	5	2	2	5	4
50–59	0	0	0	0	2	2	5	4
60 or more	1	2	0	0	0	0	5	4
Total	45	100	76	100	85	100	130	100
Median (cents per capita)	10.0		10.0		10.8		15.2	

[a] Number of agencies reporting.

[b] Percent of agencies.

TABLE III

BUDGETS AND EXTENT OF LOCAL AND STATE AIR POLLUTION
REGULATORY PROGRAMS; 1952–1965[a]

Descriptive item	Year			
	1952	1955	1961	1965
Number of local programs[b]				
1. City	40	64	58	61
2. County	4	6	10	46
3. Multicounty; multicity; districts	0	0	4	10
4. Total	44	70	72	117
5. Population served by local programs	31,037	36,040	43,456	68,128
6. Number of state programs[c]	0	0	3	4
7. Population served by state programs[c]	0	0	2,495	9,742
8. Total population served by local and state programs	31,037	36,040	45,951	77,870
9. Total U.S. urban population	102,500	111,100	127,100	135,000
10. Ratio of population served to total urban (8 ÷ 9)	0.30	0.33	0.36	0.58
11. Budgets of local agencies[b]	2,525	4,923	7,954	10,518
12. Budgets of state agencies having regulatory programs[c]	0	0	91	492
13. Total state and local budget (lines 12 + 13)	2,525	4,923	8,045	11.010
14. Operating cost index[d]	1.00	1.12	1.44	1.68
15. Total state and local budgets cost adjusted (13 ÷ 14)	2,525	4,400	5,580	6,570
16. Per capita budget for pop. served, cost adjusted 15 ÷ 8)	8.1	12.2	12.2	8.4
17. Per capita budget for total urban pop., cost adjusted (15 ÷ 9)	2.5	4.0	4.4	4.9
18. Federal grants to agencies in lines 4 and 6	0	0	0	3,821
19. Total state, local and Federal funds for programs	2,525	4,923	8,045	14,831
20. Total state, local and Fed. funds, cost adj. (19 ÷ 14)	2,525	4,400	5,580	8,830
21. Total per capita budget for population served (19 ÷ 8)	8.1	13.7	17.5	19.1
22. Total per capita budget for pop. served; cost adjusted (21 ÷ 14)	8.1	12.2	12.2	11.4
23. Total per capita budgets for total U.S. urban population	2.5	4.4	6.3	11.0
24. Total per cap. budget for total U.S. urban pop., cost adj. (23 ÷ 14)	2.5	4.0	4.4	6.5

[a] Population in 1000's; expenditures in 1000's of dollars; per capita expenditures in cents (agencies spending at least $5000 per year).

[b] Agencies spending at least $5000/year (then current dollars) and in 1952, 3.0 cents per capita; in 1955, 3.3 cents per capita; in 1961, 4.3 cents per capita; and in 1965, 5 cents per capita.

[c] States that actually operate regulatory programs and spend at least $5000 per year and spend at a per capita rate as in ([b]) above for the population of the state *not* served by local programs spending as in ([b]) above. Does not include expenditures of California Air Resources Board or Highway Patrol.

[d] Average salary of municipal employees in the U.S. used as an index, with 1952 equal 1.00. Local agencies spend about 70% of their budget on salaries (12).

1965 increased 70% over 1961 and was 2.5 times greater than in 1952. However, the ratio of population served to total United States urban population has not increased as rapidly because of the continuing growth of total urban population, especially since most of the population growth is occurring not in the central cities of urban centers, where many local programs exist, but in urban fringes where there often is no control program.

Budgets of local agencies and states operating at least minimal regulatory programs have increased steadily (Table III). However, operating costs have also increased steadily. To account for this, in several items of Table III, cost was adjusted in accordance with the increase of the average salary of municipal employees (12). This is a reasonably good basis for cost adjustment since agencies spend about 70% of their funds for personal services. Program growth, thus adjusted, is still substantial.

However, on a per capita basis for the population served by at least minimal agencies, the situation is different. Growth in average budget per capita served, after cost adjustment, increased very little since 1952 and actually declined substantially from 1961 to 1965. This decline was brought about partly because of the formation of many new agencies having relatively low per capita budgets and the large growth in population served. When per capita budgets, cost adjusted, are calculated on the basis of the total U.S. urban population, the data indicate only modest growth from 1955 (4.0 cents) to 1965 (4.9 cents).

In 1965, the federal government initiated a program of grants to state and local agencies for air pollution regulatory work. This has had a major impact. Total funds (state, local, federal) available to state and local regulatory programs (in current year dollars) increased from about $2.5 million in 1952 to $8 million in 1961 to $14.8 million in 1965, an increase of 84% in the later 4 years (Table III). On a per capita basis for the population served, this represents an increase from 8.1 cents in 1952 to 17.5 in 1961 to 19.1 in 1965. However, the growth is not as impressive when operating cost and urban population growth adjustments are made.

The major urban centers of the nation are represented by 24 Standard Metropolitan Statistical Areas having a population greater than one million people. These 24 areas contain about 69 million people, about half of the total U.S. urban population. They have increased in population by about 8% since 1961. It is in these areas where air pollution is most likely to be of major concern.

In all but one of these urban centers, there is an air pollution control program. In 18, the program budget was 5 cents per capita or more. The population served by an air pollution regulatory program of at least minimal budget was 33 million in 1961 and 49 million in 1965, an increase of 50%. But, even with this increase, only 72% of the total population of the metropolitan areas is served by at least a minimum program spending 5 cents per capita or more. In some of these urban centers, only a small percentage of the population is covered by a program, e.g., 16% in Kansas City; 32% in Washington, D.C.; 45% in Cleveland, and 64% in Philadelphia. On the other hand, Standard Metropolitan Statistical Areas made up of one county and served by a county-wide agency are completely covered. This situation indicates that increased efforts are needed to provide for air pollution control throughout metropolitan areas.

In the 24 largest metropolitan areas, air pollution budgets (local, certain state programs, and federal grants) total about $11 million, about 75% of the total spent for regulatory programs in the nation. On the basis of total population of these 24 metropolitan areas, total per capita budgets are, however, only about 16 cents.

In 29 Standard Metropolitan Statistical Areas with populations of 0.5 to 1.0 million, containing some 23 million people, only 55% of the population is served by at least a minimum regulatory program. In 8 of the 29 areas, none of the population is served by a minimum regulatory program. A total of $2.1 million is budgeted by local and certain state agencies and provided by federal grants. The average per capita budget is 8.9 cents, based on total metropolitan area population, ranging from nothing to 32.8 cents.

The distribution of funds for various purposes by local air pollution agencies varies widely but the majority of funds in nearly all cases is used for salaries. As an example, in 1964, the City of Chicago budget was as follows (13): personal services, 86%; contractural services, 6%; travel, 2%; commodities and equipment, 2%; capital outlay and contingencies, 3%. In the case of projects supported by federal grants (9), expenditures were 54% for personnel, 28% for equipment, 4% for supplies, 6% for travel, and 8% for other items.

Many agencies recover a part of their operating expenses in fees charged for annual inspection or installations, review of construction plans, and issuance of operating permits. Two tabulations of the percent of annual budget recovered in fees (10, 11) indicate that 18% of the agencies do not collect fees at all; 42% of the agencies recover 1-25% of their budgets in fees; 21% recover 26 to 50% in fees; 14% recover 51–100% in fees; and 5% of the agencies recover more than enough money in fees to cover costs of operating their agencies.

2. Organizational Patterns

Local governmental agencies (cities, counties, etc.) carry on the major portion of the regulatory aspects of air pollution. Until the late 1940's, cities operated nearly all of the air pollution control programs. As recently as 1961, three-fourths of the control agencies were in city governments (Table IV) (8). In the late 1940's, the California law authorizing counties to operate air pollution control districts was adopted. By 1961, seven such districts had been formed, including the six-county San

TABLE IV

ORGANIZATIONAL PATTERNS OF LOCAL AIR POLLUTION PROGRAMS

Type of jurisdictional area	Health dept.		Separate agency[a]		Building dept.		Safety dept.		Other depts.		Total		1961	
	No.	Percent	No.	Percent	No.	Percent	No.	Percent	No.	Percent	No.	Percent	No.	Percent
1956 (14)														
All types	23	28	16	20	19	23	10	12	14	17	82	100	—	—
1965[b]														
Cities	20	33	13	21	8	13	9	15	11	18	61	47	64	75
Counties	34	74	10	22	2	4	0	0	0	0	46	35	15	18
Multi-county	3	50	2	33	0	0	0	0	1	17	6	5	2	2
City-county	8	73	0	0	0	0	0	0	3	27	11	8	1	1
Multi-city	3	50	2	33	0	0	1	17	0	0	6	5	3	4
All types spending $100,000/year or more	14	52	8	30	2	7	2	7	1	4	27	100	—	—
All types newly created since 1961	54	81	6	9	2	3	0	0	5	7	67	100	—	—
All types	68	52	27	21	10	8	10	8	15	11	130	100	85	100

[a] Head of air pollution agency reports to administrative head of government or independent board or commission responsible directly to the head of government or the public.

[b] Derived from Table I and various other sources.

731

Francisco Bay Area district. In 1952, Kentucky also authorized county air pollution control districts. By 1961, two had been formed (Jefferson County—Louisville, and McCracken County—Paducah). County programs were also operated by five county health departments (Allegheny County, Pennsylvania; Philadelphia, Pennsylvania; Harris County, Texas (Houston); Dade County, Florida (Miami) and Wayne County, Michigan (serving all but the city of Detroit). Milwaukee County and the City and County of Denver also operated programs in other than the health department. Other multijurisdictional arrangements existing in 1961 were the Polk and Hillsborough County, Florida district operated by the state; the metropolitan Boston district (28 cities) operated by the state; the Cincinnati intercommunity program (8 cities) operated by Cincinnati; the Lehigh Valley, Pennsylvania, air pollution control agency (5 communities); and the Dayton-Montgomery County, Ohio, contract services arrangement.

By 1965, the situation had changed markedly (Table IV). The number of city programs has decreased by three since 1961. The number of county programs, however, increased from 15 in 1961 to 46. Now county, multicounty and city-county programs make up 48% of the total number of local programs. All but four of the new county, multicounty, and city-county programs were initiated by previously existing health departments.

A number of new interjurisdictional programs have come into being. In North Carolina, four counties (Buncomb, Haywood, Henderson, and Transylvania) with a total population of 228,000 have entered into an agreement to develop an air pollution program to serve their entire area. In Oregon, five counties (Benton, Linn, Marion, Polk, and Yamhill) with a total population of 295,000 have formed the Mid-Willamette Valley Air Pollution Control Authority to develop basic data upon which to establish a regional air pollution control program. The City of Toledo has agreements with surrounding Lucas County to provide air pollution services in the unincorporated parts of the county and similarly with one municipality, both on a contract basis. Akron and Barberton, Ohio are operating a cooperative program as are Springfield and Eugene, Oregon. Cook County, Illinois, is operating a program in the unincorporated parts of the county. Even with this program and the City of Chicago program, however, more than 25% of the total county population is without program services. The state of Massachusetts is in the process of developing a program for 12 communities in the greater Springfield area. The state of Maryland, in cooperation with the city of Baltimore and Anne Arundel and Baltimore Counties is conducting a comprehensive study in the greater Baltimore area. The Interstate

Sanitation Commission (New York and New Jersey, with Connecticut abstaining) in behalf of the New York-New Jersey Cooperative Committee on Interstate Air Pollution (composed of the states of New York and New Jersey and New York City) has developed a management plan and survey protocol for a comprehensive air pollution study in the New York–New Jersey metropolitan area. The Metropolitan Washington Council of Governments, in cooperation with state and local governments, is conducting a study directed toward evaluation of the air pollution problem in metropolitan Washington, with a view toward recommending means of air resource management. In the Denver metropolitan area, a nonprofit corporation known as the Regional Air Pollution Control Agency has been formed by representatives of city and county governments in the five-county area (Adams, Arapahoe, Boulder, Denver, and Jefferson). The agency is to promote cooperative action on the part of governments in the area on the establishment and operation of air pollution prevention and control programs. All of these interlocal arrangements and the trend toward county programs indicate a recognition of the regional nature of air pollution problems and increased efforts to mold governmental organizations and programs to better cope with the problems at hand.

State governmental activity in the regulatory field has expanded. In 1961, only five states (Oregon, Delaware, Hawaii, New Jersey, and Pennsylvania) were engaged in regulatory activities similar in nature to those carried out by local governments. All five programs were very modestly funded and regulatory activity was limited. In addition, Florida and Massachusetts operated one local program each in a limited area. Nine states (Delaware, Hawaii, Illinois, Indiana, New Jersey, New York, Oregon, Pennsylvania, West Virginia) have now entered into regulatory activities in one way or another. In six states (Oregon, Hawaii, New Jersey, Delaware, West Virginia and Pennsylvania) regulatory activities were at a particularly significant level. The regulatory activities of the state of California and, to some extent the state of New York, in the motor vehicle pollution control field were having a marked effect on the role of local programs. A significant development in the states of Arkansas and Louisiana (and possibly South Carolina, pending interpretation of a state law) is enactment of state laws which specifically declare that total responsibility for air pollution control rests with the state government, precluding local governmental programs. How this will work out in practice in these states is yet to be seen.

In 1956, air pollution control activities were widely dispersed in various departments of local government, with health and building departments being most common (Table IV) (14).

There is now still fairly wide distribution but the highest percentage of the local agencies are in health departments (52%). Another 21% of the agencies are independent of other city departments, increasing from 16 such agencies in 1956 to 27 in 1965. The number of agencies in building departments decreased from 19 to 10. The number of agencies in safety and miscellaneous other departments changed by only one (24 in 1956 and 25 in 1965). There is presently little difference in organizational placement of air pollution control agencies between the large agencies (spending $100,000 or more) and the total group of agencies. In both classes, 52% of the agencies are in health departments and 30 or 21% are independent agencies. The agencies created in the period 1961 to 1965 are, however, predominantly in health departments (54 of 67, or 81%).

Depending on the nature of the air pollution problem in a community and the kinds of activities being carried on, the internal organization may take many forms. A fairly common organization is shown in Fig. 1. About 40–60% of the staff will tend to be in the Field Services Division; about 20–30% in Technical Services and the remainder in other activities, varying widely. Technical committees provide advice and consultation to the air pollution control officer on a variety of matters, such as air quality standards, emission control regulations, construction plan approval criteria, air pollution emergency action, public relations, complex scientific questions, etc. Some committees are maintained on a continuing basis, while others may be called together only for a limited time to help with a certain problem. The hearing or appeals board decides on appeals of persons regulated, from actions taken by the air pollution control officer—a means of trying to achieve an equitable settlement of points at issue without time-consuming, costly, and inconvenient court action. Such boards are usually appointed by the mayor or other administrative entity, and consist of three or five people.

3. Activities of Local Agencies

Activities of local programs are principally directed toward bringing about actual control of pollution sources, through enforcement of laws, rules and regulations. The nature and extent of program activities varies tremendously depending on problems existing in the area and money and personnel available for agency operations. Programs having limited staff may only seek abatement of nuisance conditions called to their attention by public complaints (complaint programs). This may require only the part-time services of one person to accept and investigate complaints and to negotiate with responsible parties and secure abate-

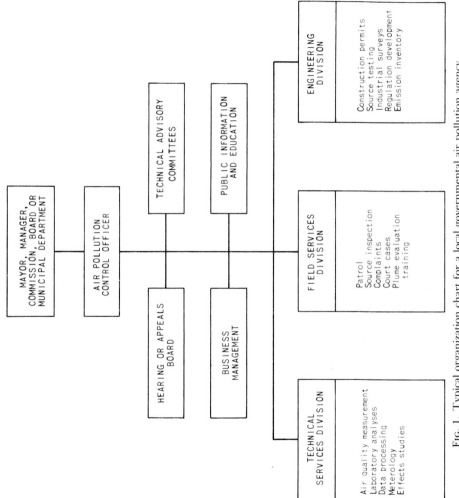

FIG. 1. Typical organization chart for a local governmental air pollution agency.

ment. In complex cases assistance may be secured from consultants, or the state or federal government.

More elaborate programs (nominal programs), in addition to answering complaints, may make regular self-initiated observations and cite violations of visible smoke regulations, seek out violations of nuisance regulations, issue permits for new installations, maintain a registration system for sources of pollution, issue operating permits, and conduct a limited air pollution measurement program.

Large agencies conduct "intensive" programs which include the items already mentioned, and, in addition, enforce a variety of detailed regulations, make extensive measurements of pollution levels, measure effluents from stacks, investigate effects of pollution on health, vegetation and materials, carry on public information programs, maintain a pollutant emission inventory, evaluate and perhaps develop means for emission control, operate a laboratory, and so on.

Ballman and Fitzmorris (15), based on a survey of 216 cities in 24 densely populated states in the eastern part of the country, and using the "complaint," "nominal," and "intensive" classification, demonstrated a relationship between size of community and both the magnitude of the air pollution program operated by the community, and the existence of air pollution legislation (Table V). Only 25% of the cities under 10,000 population had legislation while nearly all cities larger than 200,000 population did. Cities under 200,000 to 500,000 usually had nominal programs; cities of more than a million people usually had intensive programs, with some exceptions in each case.

A large part of most local program efforts is directed toward control of smoke and ash from combustion of refuse, coal, and oil. This is be-

TABLE V

CITIES HAVING AIR POLLUTION LEGISLATION AND GENERAL NATURE OF
AIR POLLUTION CONTROL PROGRAM[a]

Population of city (1000)[b]	Number surveyed	Cities with air pollution ordinance		Cities with complaint program		Cities with nominal program		Cities with intensive program	
		No.	Percent	No.	Percent	No.	Percent	No.	Percent
Under 10	16	4	25	8	50	1	6	0	0
10 to 25	30	12	40	12	40	0	0	0	0
25 to 50	59	36	61	34	58	1	2	0	0
50 to 100	48	32	67	27	56	5	10	0	0
100 to 200	31	25	81	18	58	7	23	0	0
200 to 500	18	17	94	7	39	10	56	1	5
500 to 1000	8	8	100	0	0	6	75	2	25
Over 1000	6	6	100	0	0	2	33	4	67

[a] Adapted from (15).
[b] Central city except for county-wide programs where population is for whole county.

cause these sources are, by far, the most numerous, and because such control activities have been long established in community smoke abatement programs. For example, in Cleveland (1964), of 16,305 devices of concern in an emission compliance program, 10,800 were boilers and other fuel burners, and 4225 were incinerators. Only 8% were industrial process equipment of various kinds (16). In Chicago (1963) 47,082 annual inspections were made of fuel and refuse-burning equipment of various kinds and only 2197 were made of industrial process equipment (17). In Detroit (1963) installation permits were issued for 1164 refuse incinerators, for 114 units of coal and oil-burning equipment, and for two air pollution collectors (18). Many agencies, in fact, have legal authority only to deal with combustion equipment and emissions therefrom.

No comprehensive survey of activities of local air pollution programs has been published since the one reported by Purdom in 1957 (14). No doubt there has been some increase in the number of services provided by agencies and improved adequacy of the services as indicated by the increased budgets of the agencies. Purdom reported that nearly all agencies in all sizes of cities investigate public complaints and seek out violations of smoke emission and other emission regulations. Most agencies, especially those in cities having more than 200,000 population, conduct equipment operation and maintenance surveys, review plans for new installations and issue permits for them, make industrial plant air pollution control surveys and make measurements of particulate matter in the air. Some agencies make area air pollution surveys, measure gases in the air, operate a laboratory, and conduct stack sampling. A few agencies do studies of meteorological conditions and the effects of air pollution on vegetation, and license equipment operators or installers. Purdom noted that only about 10% of the agencies carried on a continuing liason with industry or citizen committees and about one-third of the agencies reported little or no community participation. In the air pollution field, where so much depends on community support and since staffs are limited, it is remarkable that this means of improving effectiveness of operation is not more generally used.

A rough indication of the distribution of manpower in various functions of pollution control agencies can be derived from data from three agencies. In New York City (1962) of 120 staff members, 9 were in executive management, 21 in administration, 56 in field inspection, 19 in engineering (including plan review) and 15 in the laboratory unit (ambient air and stack gas measurements) (19). In Chicago (1964), of 84 staff members, three were in administration, 27 in administrative and technical services (air monitoring, meteorological studies, laboratory), 41 in field services (violation detection, annual inspection and complaint handling), and 13 in engineering services (plan review, certificates of operation, emission inventory, code development and control device work) (13). In Cincinnati (1964) of 24 staff members, 14 were in field activities, 3 in air pollution measurement, and 2 in permit processing (20).

B. STATE GOVERNMENT PROGRAMS

1. Extent of Programs and Budgets

The state of California adopted a law in 1947 permitting the formation of county air pollution control districts. This was the first specific state law concerning air pollution, although previously several states had passed laws enabling cities to control smoke and nearly all states have long had general laws dealing with nuisances. In 1951, Oregon adopted the first statute creating an air pollution control program at the state government level and shortly thereafter began operation with an annual budget of $60,000. By 1956, the states of New Jersey and California had also established identifiable full-time air pollution programs and, for these three states, annual expenditures were about $250,000. In 1961, there were 17 states operating air pollution programs with a budget of $5000 per year or more (Table VI). These programs served a total of 103 million people and had a total budget of a little more than $2 million. However, in only about five of them were the budgets and programs of any consequence when compared with the job to be done (8).

By 1966, 31 states had specific laws which called for some form of air pollution program at the state level. Thirty-four states and Puerto Rico had an air pollution program with a budget of $5000 or more (Table VI). Of these, 13 were newly created within the year, at least in part because of the stimulatory effect of federal program grants which were first made available in 1965. These 35 agencies had budgeted state funds of $4.45 million, an increase of 123% over the amount budgeted by all states in 1961. However, of the $2.45 million increase, 47% was in California alone and $1.6 million (65%) of the increase was in California, New York, New Jersey, and Pennsylvania. Thus, the dollar amount of increase in most states has been modest, although the percent increase in some states has been large. Added to the increase in state budgets was $1.7 million in federal program and survey grant funds, making a total of $6.1 million available to state agencies, more than 3 times the amount in 1961. Even when adjusted for the operating cost index increase and population growth (Table III), the 1965 funds were 2.5 times those in 1961. Incomplete data for 1967 indicate that

TABLE VI

EXTENT OF STATE AIR POLLUTION PROGRAM AND BUDGETS, NOVEMBER, 1965
(THOSE SPENDING $5000 PER YEAR OR MORE)

State	Population, 1960 (1000)	Type of program authorized by law[a]	Budget ($1000) Non-federal	Federal[b]		Total	Per capita budget (cents)	Budget, 1961 ($1000) (8)
1. Alabama	3,300	Technical assistance and studies (Gen. health powers)	5	D	10	15	0.5	0
2. Arkansas	1,800	Comprehensive, including exclusive state-wide control	19	E	39	58	3.2	0
3. California	15,700						15.5	
Dept. of Public Health		Research and technical assistance	1273		0	1273		661
Motor Vehicle Poln. Control Bd.		Regulation of emissions from motor vehicles	561	c	124	685		500
Dept. of Highway Patrol		Regulation of emissions from motor vehicles	479		0	479		0
4. Colorado	1,800	Technical assistance and studies; limited control	52		0	52	2.9	10
5. Connecticut	2,500	Studies; technical assistance; develop legislation	62	D	86	148	5.9	7
6. Delaware	400	Comprehensive	19		0	19	4.8	18
7. Florida								
State in general	5,000	Technical assistance; studies; approve construction plans[d]	25		0	25	0.5	12
Polk-Hillsborough County	(600)	Comprehensive local program operated by state[d]	142		0	142	23.7	51
8. Georgia	3,900	Technical assistance and studies; develop state program	36	D	42	78	2.0	0
9. Hawaii	600	Comprehensive; control by counties authorized	50	I	24	74	12.3	10
10. Idaho	700	Comprehensive; control by local authorities authorized	10		0	10	1.4	0
11. Illinois	10,100	Comprehensive with exemptions for local areas with programs	45	I	79	124	1.2	0
12. Indiana	4,700	Comprehensive; control only in absence of local control	37	I	38	75	1.6	0
13. Kentucky	3,000	Studies; develop legislation and program	21	D	43	64	2.1	0
14. Louisiana	3,300	Comprehensive including exclusive state-wide control	24	E	33	57	1.8	0
15. Maryland	3,100	Technical assistance and studies	55	e	225	280	9.0	38
16. Massachusetts								
State in general	5,100	Comprehensive; control by local authorities authorized	40		0	40	0.8	20
Metro. Boston area	(2000)	Regulatory program operated by state & comprehensive study	99	I	120	219	11.0	52
Metro. Springfield area	(2000)	Comprehensive study conducted by state in local area	11	D	33	44	10.6	0
17. Michigan	7,800	Comprehensive; control by local authorities authorized	62	E	55	117	1.5	20
18. Minnesota	3,400	Develop proposal for state law and program, limited control	5		0	5	0.1	5
19. Missouri	4,300	Comprehensive, with exemptions for local areas with programs	23	E	46	69	1.6	0
20. Montana	700	Studies; develop state program	15	D	10	25	3.6	0

TABLE VI (Continued)

State	Population, 1960 (1000)	Type of program authorized by law[a]	Budget ($1000)			Per capita budget (cents)	Budget, 1961 ($1000) (8)
			Non-federal	Federal[b]	Total		
21. New Hampshire	600	Studies; develop legislation and program	6	D 13	19	3.2	0
22. New Jersey	6,100	Comprehensive; control by local agencies authorized	272	I 251	523	8.7	104
23. New Mexico	1,000	Studies; develop legislation and program	7	D 14	21	2.1	0
24. New York	16,800	Comprehensive; control by local agencies authorized	390	I[c] 139	529	3.1	228
25. North Dakota	600	Studies; develop legislation and program	5	D 10	15	2.5	0
26. Ohio	9,700	Technical assistance and studies	55	0	55	0.6	95
27. Oklahoma	2,300	Technical assistance; develop legislation and program	4	D 8	12	0.5	0
28. Oregon	1,800	Comprehensive; control by local agencies authorized	104	0	104	5.8	63
29. Pennsylvania	11,300	Comprehensive; control by local agencies authorized	191	I 57	248	2.2	60
30. Puerto Rico	2,400	Studies; develop legislation and program	57	D 114	171	7.1	0
31. South Carolina	2,400	Comprehensive; prerogatives of local agencies to be determined	23	E 45	68	2.8	0
32. Tennessee	3,600	Studies; develop state legislation	8	D 17	25	0.7	0
33. Texas	9,600	Comprehensive; control by local agencies authorized	26	D 18	44	0.5	23
34. Washington	2,900	Technical assistance and studies	115	0	115	4.0	24
35. West Virginia	1,900	Comprehensive; local laws existing on 6/1/61 continue in effect	66	I 85	151	8.0	0
TOTAL	154,200		4,449	1,678	6,127	4.0	2,001

[a] Comprehensive includes studies, technical assistance and enforcement authority.

[b] Nat'l Air Pollution Control Admin. Program Grant unless otherwise noted. E means "Establishment Grant;" D means "Development Grant" and I means "Improvement Grant."

[c] Nat'l Air Pollution Control Admin. Survey Grant.

[d] Split of Florida funds estimated by author.

[e] Nat'l Air Pollution Control Admin. Survey Grant for study in metropolitan Baltimore area; City of Baltimore; Anne Arundel County and Baltimore County also participating and contributing funds.

[f] Includes $27,000 Nat'l Air Pollution Control Admin. Survey Grant.

were 35 states and Puerto Rico with total budgets in excess of $5000 per year. Their expenditures, including federal grants, was about $8,900,000 per year.

Air pollution programs are operating in states having a total population of 154 million people or 85% of the national population. This compares to 104 million people served by state programs in 1961—57% of the population. Even now, however, 14 of the programs, serving 47% of the people in these 35 states, had budgets of less than 2 cents per capita. Only 24% of the total people served (19% of the nation's total population) were served by state programs with budgets of 4 cents per capita or more. On an average basis, the per capita budget in the states having programs was 4 cents per capita. The median for the 35 states was 2.2 cents per capita. For the total national population, funds available to states for air pollution programs were 3.3 cents per capita. These data indicate that while substantial progress has been made by state programs, there is still a need for larger budgets.

2. *Organizational Patterns*

Air pollution activities in state governments are generally carried out by the state health department or a separate organization closely associated with the health department. Of the 31 states that have laws specifically authorizing a state air pollution program, 26 have their air pollution programs in the health department. In the other five states, an independent air pollution board or commission is provided to carry out policy-making functions. In these five states, the state health officer is a member of the air pollution control board or commission; and in four of the five, main reliance is placed on the state health department to do the necessary work. In only one state (West Virginia) does the board or commission hire staff separate from other previously existing state departments. In all of the 19 states that do not have laws specifically authorizing state air pollution programs, health departments carry out such air pollution work as may be done, utilizing the broad authority vested in them.

As a general rule (22 of 31 states), state air pollution programs are carried on under the policy guidance of a board, commission, or authority, usually appointed by the governor. In 17 of these 22 states, the board, commission, or authority is tied to the state board of health or state health department. In the other five states (Arkansas, Illinois, Indiana, Texas, and West Virginia) the board or commission is independent of the health department or board of health except that the state health officer is a member and the health department carries on the

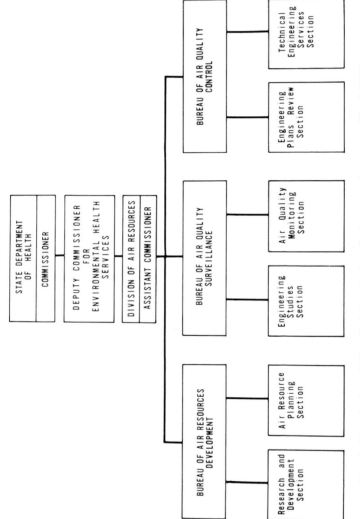

Fig. 2. Organization of New York State's air pollution control program. (April 1967) (21).

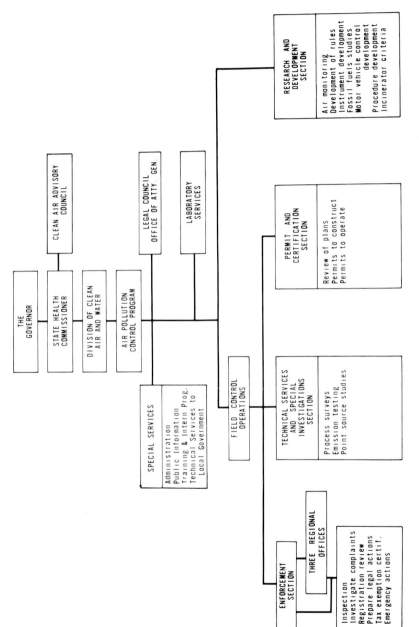

Fig. 3. Organization of New Jersey's air pollution control program. (May 1967) (22).

743

work of the board or commission. In four states (Alaska, Colorado, Hawaii, Minnesota) the state board of health carries out air pollution functions along with its other activities. In three states (Arkansas, Oregon, and South Carolina) the same authority or commission has both air and water pollution control responsibility. Even though the state health officer is nearly always responsible for carrying out the operations of the air pollution program, in only three states, (Louisiana, New York, Washington) is he designated in the law as chairman of the board or commission. Conversely, in two states (Massachusetts, Michigan) the health officer is given authority to promulgate such regulations as he considers necessary to carry out the purpose of the law, rather than vesting this authority in a board or commission.

In those nine states that do not have an air pollution authority, or commission, the state health department has responsibility and authority to implement the law, presumably under the same kind of policy guidance set forth by the state board of health (if there is one) for its other activities.

In 1965, two states (Arkansas and Louisiana) adopted air pollution laws which are unique and which will have a profound effect on the accomplishment of air pollution work in those states. These two laws give sole and exclusive state-wide responsibility for air pollution control to the state agency, thereby precluding cities, counties, or other local governments from such control activity. While this approach avoids conflicting and overlapping jurisdiction, it is difficult to visualize how a state agency will be able to control effectively the thousands of pollution sources in all parts of these large states, especially in view of the transient nature of many pollutant emissions. Only time and experience will reveal the efficacy of this approach. (South Carolina has adopted a law with similar language but its legal interpretation is, as of now, unclear.)

The internal organization of state air pollution programs varies widely, depending on the structure provided in the state air pollution law and the nature of activities conducted by the agency. Examples of the organization of two of the larger agencies are given in Figs. 2 and 3. In New York the Division of Air Resources obtains a small part of its services from the State Labor Department. In New Jersey laboratory services are provided by a general purpose laboratory of the Department of Health.

3. Activities of State Agencies

There are 19 states that have some form of regulatory responsibility at the state level. Included in the 19 were 10 which have active programs actually carrying out some kinds of regulatory program; 8 that have such authority and a budget to run a program, but which have not yet gone into regulatory activities extensively; and one state (California) that has a regulatory program only with respect to motor vehicles. In two of these 19 states (Massachusetts and Florida) most of the regulatory work is done in local districts operated by the state, and there is only limited activity in other parts of the state. In addition to these 19 states, 9 others and Puerto Rico are actively engaged in projects directed toward establishment of a state law and a program expected to include regulatory activities. Currently active regulatory programs serve a total population of about 59 million (not including California), but in only four states (Oregon, Hawaii, New Jersey, West Virginia) is the state budget greater than 5 cents per capita, based on the population living outside of local program jurisdictional areas. Regulatory programs of states may contain all of the elements of local programs, but most do not. The only element included in the regulatory part of most state programs is nuisance and complaint investigation, followed by efforts to secure abatement. Only a very few states review and approve construction plans, seek out violation of emission regulations, issue operating permits, make annual inspections of sources, develop abatement schedules with industry groups, make stack emission measurements, etc. To date, the regulatory activities of all but six state agencies have been at such a modest level as to be almost negligible. Whether state activity will ever be extensive in the regulatory field remains to be seen. However, it is clear that local agencies will continue to carry out a major part of the regulatory activity, as most would agree they should. A possible exception is regulation of motor vehicle emissions, a field already entered extensively by California and to some extent by New York. In at least two states (Arkansas and Louisiana) where the state has exclusive responsibility for regulation of air pollution, the state must do the whole job.

Aside from regulatory work, state programs may embody a wide variety of activities. Most existing programs carry on only a few program elements and even these at a very modest level. The larger agencies, however, carry on extensive activities in a variety of program elements. Perhaps the most important role of the state is to develop a comprehensive plan for air resource management throughout the state. The plan should include evaluation of present and future problems, definition of the roles of the state and various local governments, plans for operation of regulatory programs, mechanisms for establishing air quality goals and emission limitations, time schedules for activities, etc. Such a comprehensive plan might cover a 5–15-year period. While 17 states have conducted state-wide surveys of their air pollution problems, and several others are doing so, only a very few states have developed even the barest outline of a comprehensive plan, had it officially adopted as state policy, and given it wide distribution. This is an activity of high priority to which states should devote substantial attention.

Five states (California, Colorado, Florida, Oregon, New York) have promulgated air quality standards or objectives (see Chapter 51). Many states (about 15) conduct comprehensive community surveys directed toward evaluation of air pollution problems and development of air resource management plans. In New York, for example, the state, in cooperation with local agencies has undertaken surveys in several counties of the state and plans to make such surveys in all parts of the state on a systematic basis. Also, the air pollution situation is monitored in various communities in about 11 states in which continuing state-wide quality monitoring networks of various kinds are operated. Most state programs provide consultation and technical assistance to local governments. A few states have an aggressive program of assistance to local governments in development of air pollution programs. Public information programs of some kind are operated by several states but only three (New York, New Jersey, and California) are known to have professional public information specialists.

A few states conduct comprehensive state-wide studies of specific pollution sources for developing abatement programs. For example, California has done extensive studies of auto exhaust problems; Pennsylvania has studied burning coal mine waste fires (gob or culm pile fires); Oregon has studied wigwam wood waste burners; and Connecticut is studying refuse burning problems.

To provide technical information to local agencies, industry, and others, the state should maintain a good reference library and provide information from it. A few states, notably New York, have made special efforts in this field.

Prevention of new sources of air pollution is an important aspect of air pollution control. Systems for review and approval of construction plans or registration systems directed toward ensuring that new plants do not create unnecessary or excessive air pollution are authorized in many state laws. However, activity in this area has, to date, been limited mostly to five states (Florida, New Jersey, New York, Oregon, Pennsylvania) and even in these states, coverage has been either in a small number of source categories, or sparsely implemented.

Two states operate local air pollution control programs. In Florida, the state operates a program in Polk and Hillsborough Counties, directed largely toward control of pollution from phosphate rock processing plants. In Massachusetts, the state operates a comprehensive program in 28 communities in the greater Boston area. The costs of the program, however, are paid by the local governments. Massachusetts is currently doing a study in the greater Springfield area which may lead to a district similar to the one in the Boston area.

California has in operation a vigorous program directed toward control of motor vehicle emissions. The California Air Resources Board makes extensive studies of emissions and control systems and the state Highway Patrol operates a regulatory program to see that vehicles on the road meet air pollution control requirements. New York has developed criteria for approval of crankcase emission control systems and has approved laboratories that may furnish test data to the state.

Other activities of state programs are research and investigation, including, for example, major studies of effects of pollution on health and vegetation in California; some sociological and health effects studies in New York; conduct of air pollutant emission inventories and listings of potential major pollution sources; conduct of meteorological studies; provision of laboratory services, both for the state program and to some extent as a service to local programs; and conduct of training courses for personnel throughout the state, including training in plume density evaluation.

In two activities, the state will probably retain authority by virtue of governmental powers and duties spelled out in state and national constitutions. These are the matters which involve a neighboring state and the extraordinary police action associated with air pollution emer-

TABLE VII

TOTAL BUDGETS AND POPULATION SERVED BY STATE AND LOCAL AIR POLLUTION PROGRAMS; 1952–1965 (AGENCIES SPENDING AT LEAST $5000 PER YEAR)

Descriptive item	Year			
	1952	1956	1961	1965
1. Budgets of local agencies ($1000)[a]	2,589	5,018	8,075	10,421
2. Budgets of state agencies ($1000)[b]	60	N.A.[c]	2,001	4,449
3. Federal program and survey grants to state and local agencies ($1000)	0	0	0	5,106
4. Total funds (Lines 1 + 2 + 3) ($1000)	2,649	5,018	10,076	19,976
5. Operating cost index[d]	1.00	1.12	1.44	1.68
6. Total funds, cost adjusted (4 ÷ 5) ($1000)	2,649	4,480	7,000	11,900
7. Total U.S. urban population (1000)	102,500	111,100	127,100	135,000
8. Total budget per capita for urban pop. (6 ÷ 7) (cents)	2.6	4.5	7.9	14.8
9. Total budget per capita for urban pop., cost adjusted (8 ÷ 5) (cents)	2.6	4.0	5.5	8.8

[a] Not including state-operated local programs in Boston and Springfield, Mass. and Polk-Hillsborough Counties, Florida.

[b] Including funds for local programs operated by the state given in footnote[a]

[c] Not available. Probably about $250,000 by states of California, Oregon ($60,000) and New Jersey ($28,000).

[d] Average salary of municipal employees in the U.S. used as an index, with 1952 equal 1.00. Agencies spend about 70% of their budgets on salaries (12).

gencies. Such actions are normally beyond the powers available to local governments.

C. Funds Available to State and Local Programs

Total funds available for operation of state and local agencies have increased from $2.6 million in 1952 and $10.1 million in 1961, to $20 million in 1965. On a per capita basis for the total urban population, this is an increase from 2.6 cents to 7.9 cents to 14.8 cents for these years (Table VII). Because of the increase in urban population, which indicates (to a degree) the job to be done, the 7.5-fold increase in funds since 1952 has resulted in only a 5.7-fold increase in per capita expenditures. Furthermore, increased operating costs, as indicated by average salaries of municipal employees, further reduces the apparent gain to a 3.4-fold increase in per capita budgets, adjusted to 1952 indicated operating costs. Considering only the change since 1961, the funds available increased by 71% (adjusted for increased operating costs) and per capita budgets increased 62% (adjusted for increased urban population and operating costs). The federal grants made available in 1966 were a major factor in the growth of expenditures.

D. Interstate Programs

Of the 212 Standard Metropolitan Statistical Areas (1960), there are 24 that include territory in two or more states. These interstate areas have a population of 38.3 million persons, 21.4% of the nation's total, including seven with a population of 1.0 million or more, three with a population of 0.5 to 1.0 million, and seven with a population of 0.25 to 0.5 million. These areas embrace some of the most significant air pollution problems of the nation and yet, interstate action to attack these problems has been very modest.

One interstate compact agency, the Interstate Sanitation Commission, made up of New York, New Jersey, and Connecticut, was originally established in 1936 to deal with water pollution problems. In 1956, the U.S. Congress granted the Commission authority to extend its activities into the air pollution field (23). In 1961, the states of New York and New Jersey adopted laws implementing the authority granted by Congress. Connecticut did not join in this action, making it necessary for the Commission to set up a separate division and financial accounts for its air pollution work. The Commission's principal work involves air pollution measurements, assisting with study of interstate flow of air pollutants, acting as a clearing house for public complaints involving interstate pollution, and participation in design of an area-wide comprehensive study.

Another organization working on interstate problems in the New York City area is the New York-New Jersey Cooperative Committee on Interstate Air Pollution. The committee is made up of representatives of the air pollution control agencies of the states of New York and New Jersey, the City of New York and the Interstate Sanitation Commission. The Committee meets from time to time to discuss mutual problems and to develop action programs which are then implemented individually by the participating agencies. One project of note was development of a regional air pollution warning system and action plan (see Chapter 51). This was developed in cooperation with the air pollution committee of the Metropolitan Regional Council of the New York area.

The states of Illinois and Indiana have adopted companion laws providing for an interstate compact for the prevention and control of air pollution which originates in one state and causes detrimental effects in the other. The state laws were adopted in the early part of 1965. On June 30, 1965, a bill was introduced in the U.S. Congress to grant consent of that body to the two states to proceed to implement the compact, but the bill has not yet been approved by Congress. The compact would create a bi-state commission composed of seven members from each state. The commission would study sources and effects of interstate air pollution and make recommendations for the prevention and control of detrimental conditions. The commission would be empowered to establish standards for enforcement.

In the Lewiston, Idaho-Clarkston, Washington area, the two states, in cooperation with the two cities, the North Central District Health Department (Idaho), and the U.S. Public Health Service conducted a study of interstate air pollution. The report on the study (24) recommended that an air resource management council be established with representation from concerned city and county governments and the two states for the purpose of conducting various air pollution program elements, including development of plans for pollutant emission control. A council representing local governments in the area was formed in early 1966.

A comprehensive study has been made of the air pollution situation in the bi-state St. Louis metropolitan area (25). It was a cooperative venture of the cities of St. Louis, Missouri and East St. Louis, Illinois; St. Louis County; the East Side Health District (Illinois): the states of Missouri and Illinois; the Bi-State Development Agency; the Chamber of Commerce of Metropolitan St. Louis; and the U.S. Public Health Service. The study was directed toward definition of the air pollution problems of the area and development of governmental machinery to provide for air pollution control throughout the metropolitan area.

In the Ohio-Kentucky metropolitan area of Cincinnati, a project has been initiated to develop a comprehensive plan for an air resource management program to control air pollution throughout the bi-state metropolitan area. The agencies participating in the project include the states of Ohio and Kentucky; the City of Cincinnati; Hamilton County Mayors and Township Officials Association; several Ohio and Kentucky cities; Boone, Kenton, and Campbell Counties in Kentucky; the Intercommunity Air Pollution Control Program; and the National Air Pollution Control Administration.

The Metropolitan Washington Council of Governments is conducting a study directed toward augmenting existing knowledge on air pollution in the area and developing comprehensive air pollution control program plans for local agencies. The council is made up of local members of the general Assemblies of Maryland and Virginia, and of the U.S. Congress and members of the governing bodies of three counties in Virginia, two counties in Maryland, six cities in these counties, and the District of Columbia. The National Air Pollution Control Administration is cooperating and assisting in the study.

A New York state statute provides for forfeiture of the charter of a corporation organized under New York law, and revocation of the certificate of authority of a foreign corporation to do business in the state, if, in conduct of its business outside the state, the corporation injures or endangers the health of people within the state by the emission of dust, smoke, odor or fumes (Art. 14, New York General Corporation Law, Section 230-232) (26). In the October, 1964 revision of the New York City Air Pollution Control Code, cognizance of possible use of this corporation law was envisaged in the case of dense smoke emission. The code states (Sec. 9.03 (b)(2)) "In the case of an air contaminant emitted from a source outside of New York, it shall be measured after the plume crosses the jurisdictional boundary of New York City." There has as yet been no application of this provision.

E. Federal Air Pollution Program

1. History

An identifiable federal air pollution program was established in 1955 when the 84th Congress adopted Public Law 159, entitled "An act to provide research and technical assistance relating to air pollution control." The law specifically reserved to the states and communities primary responsibility for the regulatory control of air pollution. Prior to 1955, the U.S. Bureau of Mines had done work in the field of smoke abatement and the U.S. Public Health Service, under authority in Public

Law 78-410 (The Public Health Service Act) had conducted certain limited activities. In 1955, the Public Health Service, U.S. Department of Health, Education, and Welfare established programs to provide technical assistance and training, and to undertake research into the sources, nature, concentration, and control of air pollutants and on the effects of air pollution on health. In September, 1960, a Division of Air Pollution was established in the Public Health Service. In January, 1967 it was renamed the National Center for Air Pollution Control. In June, 1968, a National Air Pollution Control Administration was organized.

Public Law 84-159 authorized a maximum appropriation of $5 million for each of 5 fiscal years. Public Law 86-365 extended this authority for an additional 4 years and Public Law 87-761 further extended the period to 1966. Basic authority and responsibility remained essentially unchanged for the 8 years following 1955 except that in 1960 the Surgeon General of the Public Health Service was directed to study the problem of motor vehicle exhausts and their effects on human health and to report to Congress (27) within 2 years (Public Law 86-493). Also in 1960, Public Law 86-365 declared that all federal agencies should control air pollution from their own facilities. In December, 1963, the "Clean Air Act" was adopted (Public Law 88-206). This act continued provisions of previous laws and added authority for federal abatement action in certain interstate air pollution situations and, on request, in certain intrastate situations. The act also added authority to make grants to state and local governmental air pollution control programs; directed that particular research attention be given to removal of sulfur from fuels; provided for development of air pollution emission control devices; called for formation of a technical committee on motor vehicle pollution (28, 29); strengthened provisions concerning control of air pollution from federal installations; and authorized the promulgation of air quality criteria. In 1965, Public Law 89-272 provided for federal standards for emission of pollutants from motor vehicles; federal action to prevent air pollution from facilities to be built which might cause interstate air pollution; and federal abatement action in certain situations involving international transport of air pollutants. In October, 1966, Public Law 89-675 was adopted which provided authority for federal grants to state, local, and regional governmental agencies for the maintenance of air pollution prevention and control programs and made certain other amendments to the Clean Air Act. In November, 1967, Public Law 90-148 (The Air Quality Act of 1967) was adopted. This act expanded and improved the research and development program, with emphasis on finding better ways to control emissions; provided for a major program for planning and operation of control pro-

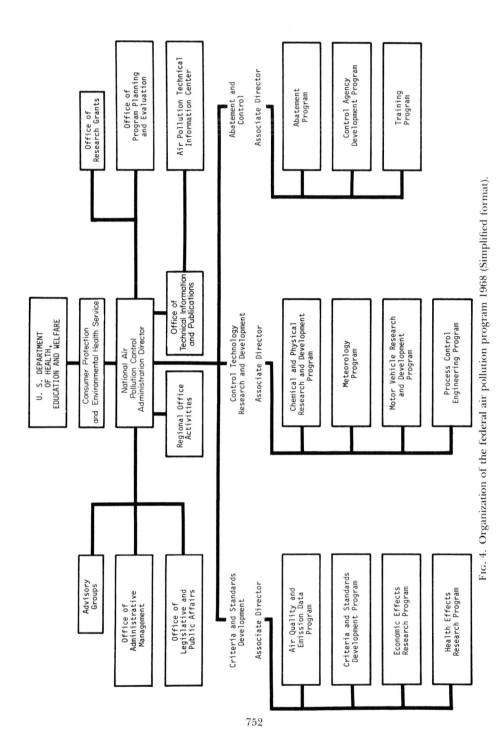

Fig. 4. Organization of the federal air pollution program 1968 (Simplified format).

752

grams on a regional basis; established several advisory groups; provided for registration of fuel additives; and called for comprehensive studies of economic matters and pollution from aircraft (see Chapter 50).

2. *Organization and Budget*

The National Air Pollution Control Administration is made up of three principal operating units, each under the cognizance of an associate director, and a number of staff officers and activities (Fig. 4). As of February, 1968, the Administration employed about 1000 people. The Environmental Sciences Service Administration (ESSA) (U.S. Dept. of Commerce) has staff assigned to the National Air Pollution Control Administration to study the relationships between climate, meteorology, and air pollution. The Department of Agriculture has staff assigned to study effects of air pollution on agriculture. In addition, the Administration funds research by the National Bureau of Standards on atmospheric chemical reactions and chemical analytical procedures; the U.S. Bureau of Mines on motor vehicle pollution, fuel desulfurization, and sulfur compound removal from stack gases; and the Tennessee Valley Authority on dispersion of effluent gases from power plants.

Appropriations for the federal program have grown steadily since 1955, the largest increase coming from fiscal year 1967 to 1968, as a result of the Air Quality Act adopted in midfiscal year 1968 (Table VIII). The "Intramural and contract research" item includes funds transferred to federal agencies other than the Administration.

3. *Activities*

From 1955 to 1963, the federal program focused on research, technical assistance, and training. Since 1963 it has also included financial assistance to state and local air pollution control programs and certain abatement activities. The research encompasses a broad range of investigations of the nature, sources, effects, transport, and control of air pollution. The technical assistance program has centered on defining and characterizing air pollution problems in various cities, states, and interstate areas, and assisting in the development of state and local programs. This has included nine major field investigations, 14 statewide surveys, 16 local surveys intended to provide a basis for control programs, and about 40 short-term technical studies of limited scope. Long-term assistance in the development and improvement of air resource management programs has been a major activity notably in Chicago, St. Louis, northwest Indiana, and North Carolina. Comprehensive reviews have been made of the air pollution aspects of various

TABLE VIII

APPROPRIATIONS FOR THE FEDERAL AIR POLLUTION PROGRAM[a]

Budget category	Fiscal Year													
	1955	1956	1957	1958	1959	1960	1961	1962	1963	1964	1965	1966	1967	1968
Grants														
Research	—	462	530	700	700	1,433	1,553	2,230	2,899	3,851	4,606	5,339	6,218	8,600
Fellowships	—	—	—	—	—	—	—	113	450	{127	252	378	468	468
Training	—	—	105	170	100	100	113}	—	—	{873	998	1,309	2,000	2,691
Control programs	—	—	—	—	—	—	—	—	—	—	4,180	5,000	7,000	20,259
Surveys and demonstrations	—	—	—	—	—	—	—	—	—	—	765	1,850	2,000	2,000
Subtotal	—	462	635	870	800	1,533	1,666	2,343	3,349	4,851	10,801	13,876	17,686	34,018
Intramural and contract														
Research	—	1,054	1,636	2,420	2,436	3,120	4,732	5,617	6,740	6,883	7,885	8,928	16,712	18,300
Technical services	—	166	400	570	488	397	436	582	681	871	1,239	1,441	—	—
Abatement activities	—	—	—	—	—	—	—	—	—	—	566	1,278	—	—
Abatement and control	—	—	—	—	—	—	—	—	—	—	—	—	4,372	9,012
Training	—	40	79	135	136	151	233	258	299	354	429	614	685	1,410
Motor vehicle	—	—	—	—	—	—	—	—	—	—	—	470	1,146	1,445
Subtotal	186	1,260	2,105	3,125	3,060	3,668	5,391	6,457	7,720	8,108	10,119	12,731	22,375	30,167
GRAND TOTAL	186	1,722	2,740	3,995	3,860	5,201	7,057	8,800	11,069	12,959	20,920	26,607	40,061	66,000

[a] Figures in thousands of dollars.

pollution-causing processes or industries. An extensive program in the preparation, acquisition, and distribution of a variety of technical publications is a continuing activity. A major function of the federal program is the training of personnel. In 1967, the training program at the National Air Pollution Control Administration's training facilities in Cincinnati, Ohio, presented 51 courses there and at locations throughout the nation to a total of 1583 trainees. In fiscal year 1967, more than $1 million was provided to 20 universities to provide graduate level training in air pollution. The schools having training grants as of April, 1967 were as follows:

University of California (Riverside)
University of Cincinnati
Drexel Institute of Technology
University of Florida
Harvard University
University of Illinois
University of Michigan
University of Minnesota
New York University
University of North Carolina
Oregon State University
Pennsylvania State University
University of Southern California
Temple University
Texas Agricultural and Mechanical College
Tulane University
University of Utah
Vanderbilt University
University of Washington
West Virginia University
Yale University

The Administration has also made from 10 to 15 fellowships available annually to provide financial support to individuals for advanced studies in air pollution at other institutions. Special training courses designed to train air pollution program administrators and technicians are included in the Pennsylvania State University and University of Southern California programs.

The Clean Air Act directs the Secretary of Health, Education, and Welfare to compile and publish air quality criteria reflecting the latest scientific knowledge useful in indicating the kind and extent of effects which may be expected from various pollutants or combinations of pollutants. The criteria are to be used by the states in establishing air quality standards for air quality control regions designated by the Secretary, as soon as the Secretary also publishes information on emission control technology and costs.

The Administration maintains a Regional Air Pollution Program Director in each of the nine regional offices operated by the U.S. Department of Health, Education, and Welfare. Through these Regional Program Directors, services are made available to state and local programs and others.

The Clean Air Act gives the Secretary of Health, Education, and

Welfare authority to initiate abatement proceedings in interstate areas when he has reason to believe that pollution arising in one state is adversely affecting the health or welfare of persons in another state. The Secretary is also empowered to begin abatement proceedings in interstate or intrastate areas when he is officially requested to do so, in the manner prescribed in the act. The procedures specified in the Clean Air Act include consultation with the states involved, conferences with all affected air pollution control agencies, public hearings, and finally, court actions. Minimum time periods between each step are specified (Fig. 5). Nine actions had been undertaken by 1967.

Research grants are made available by the National Air Pollution Control Administration to universities and other public and private agencies, institutions, and individuals to support their investigations in the field of air pollution. A wide variety of projects in nearly every specialty of the field have been supported. In fiscal year 1967, there were 178 projects under way with grant support totaling $6.2 million. The projects are conceived and conducted by investigators outside the National Air Pollution Control Administration. Special study committes of people from outside the Administration determine the relative merit of project proposals as a means of assisting the allocation of funds.

The control program grants of the National Air Pollution Control Administration made under the provisions of the Clean Air Act are to provide impetus to the establishment and improvement of air pollution prevention and control programs in the states and local communities. Federal funds are made available to match nonfederal funds in excess of the amount expended for air pollution programs by grantee agencies in the year prior to the one in which a supported control project is to begin. To be eligible, the grantee agency must have, or demonstrate intentions to obtain, legal authority for control of air pollution and a "workable program" for reaching specified air pollution control objectives. Federal grant funds in an amount up to two-thirds of the agency "new money" may be awarded to communities and states and up to three-fourths of the agency new money for regional air quality control programs. No more than 10% of the total grant funds available may be expended in any one state. Three types of projects are supported: (1) development projects for determining the need for a program; developing information on legal authority needed; or planning a control program; (2) establishment projects in which an agency is brought into being and starts operating; and (3) improvement projects for upgrading activities of an existing agency (30). In the first year of operations, a total of 100 program grants were made in the amount of $4.6 million. States received 25 grants totaling $1.8 million and 38

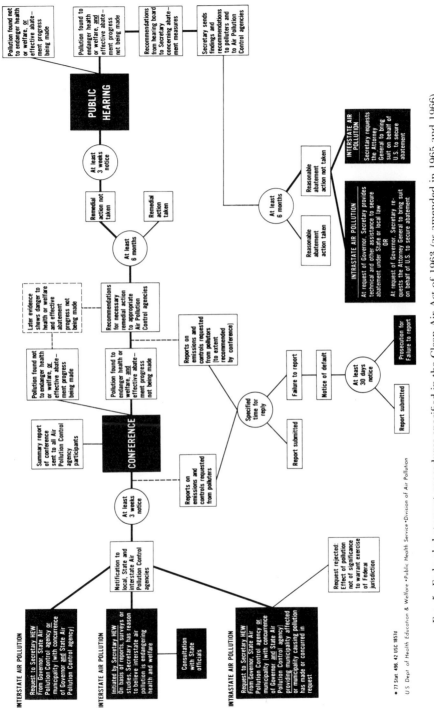

Fig. 5. Federal abatement procedures specified in the Clean Air Act of 1963 (as amended in 1965 and 1966).

local communities received $1.5 million. Of the agencies receiving grants, 10 of the states and Puerto Rico, and 35 local agencies, provided an air pollution budget, having had none in the previous year, indicating the stimulatory effect of the grants (9). In fiscal year 1967, grants were made to 28 state and 109 local agencies in the amount of about $7.0 million.

Federal grants for maintaining air pollution prevention and control programs authorized by the Clean Air Act may be in the amount of up to one-half the cost of state and municipal programs and up to three-fifths of the cost of interstate or intermunicipal programs. The grant funds are intended to supplement and increase nonfederal funds. The grantee agency is required to have an effective control program and adequate legal authority for control of air pollution. Funds in the amount of $10 million were made available for the first time in fiscal year 1968.

The Air Quality Act of 1967 added authority for Federal grants for the planning of state and local air pollution control programs. The proportion of Federal money is the same as for grants for developing, establishing, or improving agencies, except that for an initial two-year period, the Federal grant may be 100% of the cost of operating an agency designated by the governors for planning and establishing air quality standards in an interstate air quality control region designated by the Secretary of Health, Education, and Welfare, with certain conditions.

Survey grant funds are made available to state and local governmental agencies and others to conduct studies, demonstrations, and other work. The agency need not have or intend to obtain legal regulatory powers nor a workable air pollution program outside of the project for which a grant is desired. The relative share of federal and nonfederal funds is not fixed but is generally the same as for program grants. In fiscal year 1965, a total of $765,000 was distributed to 15 survey grant projects. Examples of the projects were: a study of methods for disposal of leaves, testing automotive exhaust control systems, developing a major community study plan, and studying the operation of local air pollution control programs. During fiscal year 1966 and 1967 about $1.5 million was made available for 14 projects to demonstrate methods for preventing and controlling fires in coal mine waste piles in the Appalachia region. Other demonstration projects have included those on means for control of emissions from flue-fed incinerators; development of simplified motor vehicle emission test procedures for use in inspection stations; and systems analyses and pilot studies on control of emissions from municipal incinerators. During fiscal years 1965, 1966, and 1967, a total of about $2.5 million was made available to conduct 24 surveys of the nature and extent of community air pollution problems and to conduct other projects.

III.   Role of Various Levels of Government in Air Pollution Control

A. STATE GOVERNMENT

Since state governmental agencies have not been widely and extensively involved in air pollution activities, their role and program content are still in a phase of development and evolution, and there has been little uniformity of approach. The state's role may be divided into five general categories: (1) leadership, (2) coordination, (3) evaluation, (4) service, and (5) operations (*31, 32*).

Leadership is the primary role of state air pollution agencies. This should take the form of development of a set of comprehensive plans for air resource management throughout the state. The plan should embody both short-and long-range goals and should be updated from time to time. The plan should spell out the duties and responsibilities of various units of government, reasonable in the light of existing or obtainable resources. The plan should be reviewed with local governments and modified as appropriate. Once adopted, it should be given wide distribution and should be used as an operating guide by all concerned. The state should also take the lead in revising existing state laws relating to state-level programs and the powers and duties delegated to local governments. The state air pollution agency should foster establishment of air pollution programs in cities, counties, or regions as may be appropriate and provide substantial assistance in getting such programs started. Similar state action to expand and improve existing programs is another role of importance. The state should also conduct demonstrations, perhaps in cooperation with one or more local agencies or others, of new techniques and equipment, new organizational patterns, better methods or materials for operating control programs, etc. Through such demonstrations, local progress can be accelerated, cost of duplicate or ill-conceived experimentation avoided, and uniformity promoted.

In the field of coordination, the state air pollution agency should first look into activities within the state health department and ensure that these are properly coordinated. Next, the state air pollution agency should examine activities of state offices concerned with industrial

development, land-use planning, agriculture, housing and urban renewal, education, building regulation, public works, motor vehicle
inspection, and others. Efforts should be made to coordinate appropriate
activities of these agencies with that of the state air pollution agency and
also to ensure that policies and programs of these other state agencies
will augment rather than deter activities of local air pollution control
programs. It is often helpful to arrange for periodic meetings of
representatives of the various state agencies and to create a formal
committee to enhance cooperation and coordination. The state air
pollution agency can promote coordination within local government.
A third coordinative role is promotion of uniformity among the local
air pollution control agencies of the state, to the extent appropriate.
Practices, procedures, enforcement policy, codes, and reporting are
among the items where uniformity is possible.

Evaluation of the air quality situation within the state can be done with
a state-wide air quality monitoring program operated by the state with
local agency help. Publication of data obtained is necessary. The state
should also evaluate data on air pollution effects within the state for the
purpose of program design and establishment of priorities for action.
With air quality and effects data and information on sources of pollution,
meteorology, topography, population distribution and trends, governmental structure, staffing of governmental agencies and other data, the
state should prepare and publish an overall evaluation of the air pollution situation from both state-wide and community viewpoints.
Further functions of state air pollution agencies are evaluation of local
air pollution programs, the extent of control being achieved of emissions
from pollution sources, and trends in air quality.

Perhaps the most important role of states in the service category is
training. The training should be designed to supplement the more
basic training available in universities and at federal facilities. It is necessary to provide orientation and training for both new and existing
personnel who will be assuming new responsibilities. Another vital
service is establishment of air quality and emission objectives or standards. Their establishment requires the efforts of a variety of professional
disciplines which may not be available at the local level of government.
States may also provide technical and financial support to local agencies
to foster new programs and improve existing ones. The acquisition,
storage, and retrieval of publications from many sources is a library
function beyond the capability of most local agencies, but the state
should maintain such a library and provide information from it and
other sources to local agencies. Preparation and distribution of technical
publications needed throughout the state can do much to improve

operations. States should provide certain services in connection with review of plans for construction of facilities which may cause air pollution. In the case of industrial process equipment, local agencies often do not receive a sufficient number of plans to maintain competence to review them. In such cases, the state should assume full responsibility or provide consultative services, as may be appropriate. Laboratory services for conducting other than routine analyses should be provided by the state.

In the operations area, the state should assume responsibility for activities connected with air pollution emergencies beyond the capabilities of local agencies. The power to order extraordinary remedial and preventive measures often rests in the hands of the governor. The state air pollution agency should develop necessary plans and procedures for reducing pollution levels, caring for casualties, protective measures, etc. State operations should also include detailed studies of air pollution episodes with a view toward avoiding recurrence and to glean useful information. In the more populous states it is appropriate to conduct a program of research into the effects of pollution as it exists in the state. The work may be done in the state air pollution agency, at the state university, or both. The state should conduct all necessary negotiations and provide leadership in investigating air pollution problems which involve neighboring states and develop solutions to such problems. The state should conduct a broad and continuing public information and education program.

Operations directed toward regulatory control of air pollution may or may not fall within activites of state agencies. If the state has such responsibilities, an additional group of activities, similar to those described in the following discussion of local air pollution programs, will need to be conducted.

B. LOCAL GOVERNMENT

Air pollution programs of cities, counties, and other local agencies are principally directed toward regulatory control of air pollution. The nature of the local program will depend on the nature of the problems, funds and personnel available to operate the program; the nature of state laws setting out the powers and duties of local agencies; and the activities and policies of the state air pollution agency. Local program elements include:

1. Development of a comprehensive air resource managment plan, including short and long range goals.
2. Selection of air quality goals and objectives.

3. Development of a register of air pollution sources, emissions from them, degree of emission control, and related data.
4. Measurement of air quality.
5. Development of rules and regulations concerning pollutant emissions, operating practices, design of equipment, fuel composition, etc.
6. Evaluation of effects of pollution.
7. Investigation of public complaints.
8. Agency-initiated detection of violations of rules and regulations.
9. Negotiating and securing abatement of violations of rules and regulations.
10. Securing abatement of pollution from sources owned by local government.
11. Annual or other periodic inspection of pollution sources.
12. Issuance of operating permits.
13. Development of industry group abatement plans.
14. Measurement of pollutant emissions from stacks.
15. Prevention of new sources of pollution through review of construction plans.
16. Provision of consultative services to industry and equipment purveyors on emission control means.
17. Establishment and operation of a fee system.
18. Conduct of office and formal hearings.
19. Court prosecution of chronic and flagrant violators of the law and regulations.
20. Prevention of air pollution disasters.
21. Providing for cooperation among local governmental agencies such as those concerned with planning, zoning, and inspection.
22. Design and operation of systems for storage and retrieval of data.
23. Preparation of regular activity reports and special topical reports to the public and higher levels in the local government.
24. Conduct of public information program.

C. State-Local Relationships in Regulatory Control of Air Pollution

It is generally accepted that responsibility for regulatory control of air pollution should be at the lowest level of government capable of dealing effectively with the problem in its entirety. With locally controlled action, the program can be better tailored to local needs; economy of operation can be improved; and the program can be more accessible and responsive to local citizens. However, there are problems associated with local control. Cities and counties with small populations are not often in a financial position to hire the needed technical personnel nor to acquire the necessary equipment to run an adequate program. The multiplicity of local governments within metropolitan areas, often in excess of 100, cannot be expected to operate separate programs in an effective and efficient manner. County and multicounty jurisdictional areas are necessary. Industrial and commercial interests sometimes control the actions of local government. If such interests control major pollution sources and, also, do not want to abate pollution from them, the local citizens are unable to have their desires for clean air satisfied. In such cases, the necessity for the state or federal government to provide for needs of the citizens may become evident.

Many states have adopted laws which provide in one form or another, for state enforcement of air pollution control regulations. In many of these states, local control programs are developing concurrently. With the exception of Louisana, Arkansas, and perhaps South Carolina, laws of the states make specific provision that local laws are not superseded by the state law. This dual responsibility can result in lack of clear understanding as to which agency is responsible, which, in turn, can result in overlapping activity, or a lack of any activity—with both the state and local governments hesitating to spend their scarce funds on an air pollution program in hope that the other agency will assume responsibility. In Florida, the state carries out general enforcement only in certain specified districts and reviews plans and seeks abatement of nuisances throughout the state. The Illinois and Missouri laws provide that state enforcement will not proceed in any local area which provides for control of air pollution in a manner not inconsistent with the state law and rules and regulations. Local areas desiring to be exempted from state control activities apply to the state, which may grant the request or, after a hearing, deny it. In the Indiana law, authority of the Air Pollution Control Board to enforce regulations is limited to those areas in which the Board finds, after a hearing, that no local air pollution law or regulation consistent with the state law is in effect; or that the local laws or regulations are not being enforced adequately, and, in the Board's opinion, are not intended to be so enforced. In the New York State Rules to Prevent New Air Pollution, provision is made for the Air Pollution Control Board to accept approval by a municipal agency of plans for new installations in lieu of approval by the state, provided the municipal agency has a qualified technical staff and examines the plans in accordance with standards acceptable to the state board.

Most state laws which provide for enforcement have attempted, in a variety of ways, to provide a voice for local interests in implementation of the law by the state. The most common technique is to require hearings before any state rule or regulation is adopted. Some state laws, e.g., Idaho, Illinois, Indiana, New Jersey, and New York specify that at least one member of the state air pollution control board or commission be a representative of local government. The laws of five states (Hawaii, Idaho, New Jersey, Pennsylvania, and West Virginia) provide for regional air pollution "associations" or "councils" to advise on regional application of proposed rules or regulations. In the Florida law, state-operated control districts may be formed only after a hearing on petition from county commissioners, or free-holders; or on the motion of state authorities. In Michigan, the state health commissioner may take action to regulate air pollution in a local area having an air pollution ordinance if he finds, after consultation with the state air pollution council and local officials, that local laws are not being properly enforced. In Massachusetts, the state may assume joint jurisdiction of an interlocal problem only on request of a local agency. Also, the state may form a state-operated control district only on request of local agencies. When the state of Massachusetts does operate a local-type air pollution control program, the costs are paid by the local areas served. In Minnesota, state regulations have the force of law in cities of the first class only when the state regulations do not conflict with city regulations. In Oregon, the State Sanitary Authority is permitted to delegate its power to grant variances to local governmental bodies. In Pennsylvania, Regional Air Pollution Control Associations are given the opportunity to resolve local complaints before state enforcement action ensues. These several approaches to providing for local participation in the state program have various strong and weak features. No predominant trend to one procedure or another is yet evident, aside from the universal procedure of holding hearings before adopting state regulations.

In general, existing state laws leave much to be desired with respect to providing for orderly, effective, well-defined state-local cooperative effort to abate air pollution. In view of the varying characteristics of the several states, no single approach will be best for all states; however, some general trends are evolving. Experience of the past 20 years indicates that the following general principles have been established:

1. Independent, comprehensive, local control programs should be encouraged in those areas which include a concentrated population great enough to provide adequate financial support for a control program, i.e., about 250,000 or more people. The area should include all of an air quality control region and desirably coincide with the boundaries of existing units of general government, e.g., a county.

2. In metropolitan areas, it is desirable to have a single agency responsible for air pollution control throughout the area. If this cannot be achieved, the best alternative is to have as few responsible agencies as possible within the area.

3. Jurisdictional areas having a population of less than 250,000 can be expected to handle less complex matters such as control of smoke from small combustion operations, open burning, and abatement of nuisances from small industrial and commercial establishments. These smaller jurisdictions can also assist the state by carrying out routine surveillance of sources and air quality monitoring programs.

4. Except as noted above, states should retain and exercise responsibility for control of the larger and more complex air pollution sources. The state cannot be expected to effectively regulate a multiplicity of small sources. In some states, effective county, multicounty, or district programs may largely eliminate the need for a state regulatory program. In California, for example, eight district programs serve 80% of the people of the state.

5. In small, highly urbanized states, a state-operated, state-wide control program may be the best approach. Conduct of certain operations of the state program on a district basis will probably be advisable.

6. States may appropriately retain state-wide responsibility for control of pollution from specified sources, e.g., motor vehicles. The state should also retain the right to assume jurisdiction over major single sources of pollution within areas having comprehensive local programs when pollutants from such sources adversely affect areas outside the area in which the source is located, and the local agency is not effectively dealing with the source.

7. State laws should clearly define those matters which are the responsibility of local jurisdictions and those which are retained by the state.

8. State laws should provide readily usable authority and clear, comprehensive, detailed guidelines, for establishing, operating and financing air pollution control districts—based on location of sources, characteristics of air quality control regions, distribution of population, local desires, and existing governmental structure.

9. States should provide technical assistance and guidelines relative to regulatory programs throughout the state.

10. The state should retain the right to reassume rights and responsibilities it delegates to local jurisdictions when, after a hearing, it is found that the local jurisdiction is not effectively controlling air pollution. To prevent local agencies from abdicating their responsibilities as a means of avoiding the expense of operating an air pollution program, the local

jurisdiction should be obligated to pay for the costs of the state's operating a program for which the local agency is rightfully responsible.

D. INTERJURISDICTIONAL RELATIONSHIPS

The need for changing the geographical jurisdictions and boundaries of local government in many areas, particularly in the major metropolitan areas, arises because of the growing maladjustment between what local governments are called on to do and their ability to perform. The present powers, jurisdictions, and structures of local governments, and the status of intergovernmental relations, especially in metropolitan areas, make it increasingly difficult for local governments to perform independently many functions, including air pollution control, which are area-wide in nature (33). There are four general reasons why local governments as now consituted are unable to perform area-wide functions effectively: (1) fragmentation and overlapping of governmental units; (2) disparities between tax and service boundaries; (3) state constitutional and statutory restrictions; and (4) overlapping of state lines by a metropolitan area. There are a variety of ways for metropolitan areas to adjust their areas and powers to be able to meet the needs of their citizens (33, 34). However, the initiation and operation of air pollution programs cannot wait until major reforms in metropolitan government occur. It becomes necessary, then, to make the best of existing conditions. The preferred organization to handle air pollution control is a unit of general government with a jurisdictional area equal to or larger than the air quality control region. In many cases this will be a county with the county commissioners acting as an air pollution control board or an agency operated by the county such as the health department. In many cases, however, county governments have little authority within incorporated areas, although city-county health departments having jurisdiction throughout the county are becoming more common. If the county health department does not operate in the central city, the situation often will not be too unsatisfactory since the central city and the balance of the county may each have populations large enough to support a good program. The two programs could be operated on a parallel basis by simple, informal coordination. An acceptable, and perhaps politically attainable approach to establishing this type of program organization would be to adopt state enabling legislation permitting county governments, or county boards of health, to operate air pollution programs in all parts of the county or, on local option, in all parts of the county except in incorporated cities larger than some minimum size—say 250,000 population. In metropolitan areas consisting of more than one county (of which there were 79 in 1960) a multicounty air pollution control district is desirable and may be attainable. Failing this, the best choice would be separate county programs, coordinated by informal agreements among the counties.

Intergovernmental agreements under which a governmental unit conducts an activity jointly with one or more other governmental units, or contracts for its performance by another governmental unit are the most widely used means of broadening the geographical base for handling common functions in metropolitan areas (*33*). The greatest weakness of this approach is that a community which has a number of troublesome pollution sources may not agree to enter into such an arrangement.

In spite of all the difficulties which may exist in governmental structure and operation, it is still possible for operating agencies to arrange cooperation and mutual assistance through informal mechanisms. There is rarely any obstacle to prevent agencies in a metropolitan area from sharing certain facilities and equipment; pooling air quality and pollutant emission information; agreeing on air quality and emission standards; and conducting coordinated simultaneous projects of all kinds. This sort of cooperation is the least that should occur in any case.

International situations must be handled at the national level through diplomatic channels or international agencies. Such dealings are, by their very nature, slow and time consuming (*26*). On the Canadian boundary, the International Joint Commission was concerned with air pollution in the Detroit River Area, with special reference to smoke from vessels traversing the Detroit River. The matter was first taken up about 15 years ago (*35*) and was considered closed in late 1966. Also, in 1966 the Commission began consideration of other international air pollution problems referred to it by the governments of the United States and Canada. In the 1965 amendments to the Clean Air Act (Public Law 89-272) provision has been made for the Secretary of Health, Education, and Welfare to seek abatement of air pollution arising in the United States and affecting health or welfare of people in another country, under certain conditions, and provided the other country has established reciprocal arrangements. Even on the international scene, informal cooperation between operating agencies is possible, and is, in fact, practiced by New York and Ontario, and by Detroit and Windsor.

IV. Air Pollution Control Program Elements

A. FINDING AND EVALUATING PROBLEMS

1. *Air Pollutant Emission Inventory*

Knowledge of what pollution is emitted to the atmosphere, where, when, and by whom, is basic to an air pollution control program. Such data, in conjunction with air quality data, indicate the degree of emission control needed to achieve air quality goals, and help establish the priority schedule for abatement action. The most elementary inventory consists of a listing of pollution sources of various kinds such as major coal, oil, and refuse-burning plants, pyrometallurgical plants, chemical factories, cement mills, etc. A more detailed inventory would include the amount and kind of fuel and refuse burned; the amount of various process materials used; the kinds of process and combustion equipment; the nature of emission control equipment or methods and the variation of operations with time. A rough source inventory can be prepared on the basis of published information. Improvements can be made by use of mailed questionnaires. To achieve better accuracy and completeness, field inspection and evaluation are necessary. In some cases, stack emission measurements are needed.

Emission estimates are calculated on the basis of some index of the rate of operation (e.g., amount of fuel used, amount of raw material used), composition of fuels or raw material, nature of process and emission control equipment in use, and an "emission factor" which relates the operating parameters to the rate of emission of various pollutants. Emission factors are based on actual stack emission measurements, process information, materials balances, or theoretical considerations. At least one compilation of such factors has been published (*36*).

Data for keeping a source inventory up to date can be secured in the course of other control program operations including annual inspections, issuance of operating permits, and review of construction plans.

In an emission inventory, data are usually grouped in two ways: (1) by pollutants and (2) by source categories. Pollutants most often included are particulate matter, sulfur dioxide, nitrogen oxides, carbon monoxide, and hydrocarbons. Particulate matter may be subdivided into "fine" (e.g., less than 5 μ in size) and "coarse." They may also be subdivided on the basis of their chemical composition. Other pollutants sometimes inventoried include organic acids, aldehydes, ketones, and ammonia. Source categories include fuel combustion (stationary sources), refuse combustion, transportation, solvent evaporation, gasoline handling, and industrial processes. The later may be subdivided into chemical, metal-lurgical, mineral, and petroleum processing, for example. Several emission inventories may be referred to as examples (*37–40*).

2. *Air Quality Measurements*

Every air pollution control agency should have continuous access to data indicating the quality of its atmosphere in order to determine current and future emission control requirements, evaluate trends in air quality over the years as a measure of control program effectiveness, help in identifying sources of pollution, warn of oncoming problem situations, and use them in establishing standards or goals for air quality. Initially, and at intervals of 5 years or so, relatively intensive studies of air quality are needed to explore variation of concentration of important pollutants with time and geographic location, atmospheric reactions, meteorological relationships, effects of pollution, etc. Between such intensive studies, less intensive continuous monitoring will provide as much information as can be effectively used. The nature of appropriate measurement activities will vary from area to area and from time to time. Local activities should be designed to make maximum use of long-term continuous monitoring being done by state or national agencies. Appropriate arrangements should be made to incorporate data collected by local agencies into data systems operated by state and national agencies, and for publication of data, with interpretation, for the information of all concerned.

Air quality measurements are also needed to appraise the impact of particular sources of pollution on their immediate neighborhoods. While general atmospheric air quality and emission control procedures will take care of the air pollution situation as a whole, localized problems may still develop. In this type of situation, a small area is studied intensively for a few days or weeks, until enough data are available upon which to base a control plan.

3. *Monitoring Air Pollution Effects*

Most of the work on determining relationships between concentrations and effects of pollutants is done by the federal government and universities. However, state and local agencies should conduct special studies to verify the validity of application of general relationships to specific situations in their jurisdictions.

Some monitoring of effects of pollution can be done rather easily. For example, local weather bureau records provide data on change in visibility over the years. Special visibility observations and photographs taken by air pollution control agency personnel at a regular time and place over the years will provide indices of pollution.

Effects on vegetation can be kept under surveillance by horticulturalists in the area, with only brief training and nominal effort. With a bit more work and training, test specimens of selected species of vegetation can be set out in various parts of an area to indicate possible pollutants causing vegetation damage and the day of occurrence of injurious concentrations. Procedures are also available for measuring effects of pollutants on metals, fabrics, and rubber.

Mortality data, analyzed for relationships between pollution levels and time and cause of death, and place of residence, may yield useful information. Studies of morbidity can be made, using data recorded by hospitals, industries, and others. Panels of volunteers can be used to develop information on the prevalence of eye, nose, and throat irritation, odor, and decreased visibility. When repeated from time to time, such studies may yield information on trends toward improved or worsened conditions.

4. *Public Complaints*

Public complaints about air pollution provide a measure of the kinds of air pollution people are able to detect with their senses. Unless matters complained about are corrected, the public will be displeased with the air pollution control program. When analyzed with respect to location, time, and weather, public complaints can help locate troublesome sources, guide pollution control efforts, and contribute toward selection of air quality goals. If the control agency fails to act on complaints, there will be a loss of public support, allegations of favoritism and "politics" in the enforcement effort, and occasionally a time-consuming mandamus suit. However, compared to other control program activities, complaint handling is an inefficient way to obtain a given measure of progress toward control. Efficiency in handling complaints can be enhanced by requiring the complainant to identify himself or by requiring that all complaints be in writing and signed. Every effort should be made to have the complainant identify the source of trouble and to record as much information as possible about the dates, times, and circumstances when the condition complained of exists. Since many of the conditions complained about are transient in nature, the employment of inspectors with radio-equipped automobiles is an advantage, permitting inspection soon after a complaint is made (*41*).

The number of complaints handled by an air pollution control agency varies widely. In general, one to three complaints per year per 1000 population may be expected and 20–40% of them will be about odors. In a recent year, in Detroit, 2257 complaints were received. Open fires were the cause of 38%; odors and "fumes," 21%; smoke and soot, 11%; and other causes (including noise) 30%.

5. Public Interest and Concern

Increasingly in recent years there has been recognition that all problems of the environment must be considered as a whole. At the same time, the definition of "health" has been tending toward the one used by the World Health Organization . . . "a state of complete physical, mental, and social well-being and not merely the absence of disease or infirmity." Thus, increasing attention is being given to sociological and economic matters associated with environmental health problems. Studies directed toward evaluation of public perception of air pollution and the influence such perception has on attitudes and actions (42–45) therefore assume increasing importance. Information obtained from such studies can be used in design of program elements concerned with public information, interjurisdictional relationships, air quality goals, regulations, time schedules, and community organization.

6. Visible Plume Abatement

One of the most important segments of an air pollution regulatory program is the detection and abatement of visible emissions. Regulations which prohibit smoke emissions darker than a specified shade of gray or black as measured using the Ringelmann chart (46) have been applied throughout the world. In addition to reducing visible smoke, emission of certain organic gases and carbon monoxide are reduced since good combustion is necessary to prevent excessive smoke emissions.

In recent years, visible emissions other than smoke (e.g., metallic fumes, dust, ash, mists) have been regulated by a number of jurisdictions, using the equivalent opacity concept (47).

Air pollution programs which limit emission of particulate matter solely on the basis of weight of material discharged are not as effective as those also using visible emission regulation, because of the difficulty of making complex gravimetric emission measurements. In fact, without visible emission limitation, a control program would probably be unworkable. (See Chapter 29, Vol. II). The equivalent opacity concept has been found to be reasonable and legally acceptable (48, 49). The Ringelmann chart (46) is usually the basic reference used in making determinations of the visual appearance of plumes but pocket-sized charts based on Power's Micro-Ringelmann chart (50) have been developed. The Plibrico Co. and the National Coal Association provide pocket-sized charts. The New York City regulation of visible emissions (51) is based on a "Standard Smoke Chart," a reduced sized Ringelmann chart, which is described in detail in the law. A school for training inspectors to quantitate the visual appearance of plumes has been described by Coons (52) and the National Administration provides construction plans for building plume generators for use in training inspectors (53).

The number of visible emission violations occurring in a community will vary greatly depending on industrialization, fuels used, refuse disposal practices, etc. The number of violations actually detected and brought under abatement action will further vary, depending on the kind of enforcement program operated and its intensity. The number of smoke emission violation notices (not including equivalent opacity) issued by control agencies in industrialized cities where considerable coal and oil are burned has been in the range of 20 to 150 per 100,000 population per year.

7. Routine Periodic Inspection of Pollution Sources

Many air pollution programs provide for periodic agency-initiated inspections of installations which may or do cause air pollution. The frequency of inspection may be the same for all kinds of units (e.g., once per year) or more frequent inspections may be made of important sources which have a tendency to cause excessive emissions. An objective of such periodic inspections is to detect faulty equipment and arrange for its repair, thus preventing excessive emissions due to defective equipment. Such periodic inspections are also useful in continually updating pollutant emission inventory data and source registers, keeping in touch with developments as to means being used to control emissions, maintaining interest of operating personnel in air pollution control matters and motivating them to maintain minimum pollutant emissions, and fostering exchange of information among those having similiar source control problems. Also, new practices or equipment, which may require modifications to existing regulations or enactment of new ones, are discovered at an early date, making it possible to curb undesirable situations before they become too widespread. (See Chapter 30 for detailed information.)

8. Stack Sampling

Actual measurement of emission of pollutants is the most accurate and sometimes the only way of determining exactly the emissions from a particular source. However, the procedure is time consuming and expensive and therefore its use is limited, with various estimating procedures being used much of the time.

The purposes of stack sampling are: (1) to determine emissions from particular sources to detect violations of emission regulations; (2) to develop factors for estimating emissions from classes of sources; (3) to obtain information on efficiency of emission control means for reference use in reviewing plans for new installations; and (4) to maintain and improve accuracy of emission inventory data.

Although tests are usually made by the control agency, some laws provide that those responsible for the pollutant source make or have made such emission tests as are reasonably required by the control agency and that the agency will be permitted to prescribe or approve testing methods and witness the testing. Even so, every agency should be capable of doing its own tests or having them done for it by contract. (See Chapter 28 for details of stack sampling.)

B. CORRECTING PROBLEMS

1. *Adopting Air Quality Objectives or Standards*

Ambient air quality objectives, standards, or goals are the keystone to air resource management. They describe the air quality to be achieved or preserved—the end to which control measures are directed. While it is possible to operate air pollution programs without having air quality goals, it is more desirable and sounder technically, to have them. Their key impact is in long-range planning, as a tool in design of preventive actions. Without air quality standards, the program will be largely directed toward correction of existing problems whose detrimental effect is so great as to be almost overwhelming. With air quality standards, it is much more feasible to provide for a sound control program for all sources of pollution even though they may not be, individually, creating a specific nuisance. As important as standards are, however, only a few jurisdictions have adopted them. (See Chapter 51 for details on air pollution standards.)

2. *Adopting Emission Control Regulations*

Regulations which specifically limit emission of pollutants to the atmosphere are the heart of air pollution programs. The nature and extent of emission control regulations are governed by desired air quality, the kinds of pollution sources in the area, dispersive characteristics of the atmosphere and estimates of the total amount of pollutant emissions which can be tolerated. Emission control requirements can be determined by one of four methods: (1) Establishing an air quality goal, measuring present air quality, inventorying current pollutant emissions, and calculating emission reduction needed to meet the air quality goal (54). (2) The "roll-back" approach, based on an assumption that at some time in the past, air quality was satisfactory; estimating what emissions were at that time, and calculating the degree of reduction of present emissions needed to reach the level existing at the earlier time (55, 56). (3) Calculating emission reductions which can be achieved by use of available emission control methods and equipment and estimating improvement in air quality which would result. (4) Selecting a "source fence line" air quality standard and, on the basis of stack gas atmospheric dispersion formulas, calculating the amount of pollutant which may be emitted from a single source, with various stack heights, and not exceed the air quality standard (57, 58).

Preparation of regulations involves extensive technical knowledge and exercise of judgment in a field unfamiliar to many legislators. Therefore, air pollution laws and ordinances often do not contain specific emission control requirements but rather contain general policy statements and provide for administrative machinery to carry out the intent of the law. Authority to adopt regulations is usually given to a board or commission, and, nearly always, public hearings are required before a regulation may be adopted. The board or commission, in drafting regulations, is limited by the language of the basic law granting it regulation-making power and must be careful to remain within its delegated powers lest the regulation be found invalid by a court. In addition, the board must adopt regulations in the manner required by law and its own rules. For example, the regulations must be formally adopted at a proper meeting. A written record must be kept of the vote and the regulation must be filed with a specified official and, perhaps, published in a designated place. A record should be kept of all these actions and the preamble to the regulations should state that the required steps have been taken (59). The regulation should specify upon whom it is binding, who are excepted, and what actions are required or prohibited, so that those regulated will know what is expected of them. (See Chapter 51 for more information on emission regulations.)

After regulations are adopted, the agency should evaluate to see that desired air quality improvement is achieved and what the effects of compliance are on the community. If the regulation is found to be improper for any reason, it should be revised or repealed.

3. *The Enforcement Process*

Once requirements of various kinds have been established in laws, ordinances, and regulations, it becomes the agency's job to see that the public complies. This is done through a combination of programs of education to advise the public what is expected, follow-through on public complaints, finding illegal conditions, securing abatement of illegal conditions through conference, conciliation and persuasion, and prosecution of those few violators who refuse to cooperate.

A vigorous public education program concerning actions expected and prohibited can do much to secure voluntary compliance, thus saving much agency effort in finding and correcting situations one by one.

The most common actions in securing abatement are to bring about compliance with specific regulations. The first action is to find the violation. This done by field inspectors on patrol, area surveys, and investigation of public complaints. When a violation is found, an investigation is made which includes inspection of the offending source, interrogation of responsible parties, and interview of complainants or other witnesses. From this the necessary abatement action is determined, i.e., a decision is made as to whether corrective or punitive action is required. Punitive action is usually taken if the offender has repeatedly violated requirements or there seems to be no good reason why the violation should occur. Such cases include open burning of refuse, smoke emissions due to negligent operation or maintenance, and excessive smoke from vehicles. In such punitive actions, a citation to appear in court is issued or, in some cases a "ticket" is issued, requiring payment of a fine in the same manner as for tickets for illegal vehicle parking. If corrective action is indicated, the responsible party is given a notice specifying the violation which has occurred and indicating the action to be taken. A time for compliance commensurate with the corrective action needed is specified and follow-up action is instituted as dictated by the enforcement policy of the central agency (*60*).

In matters for which there is no specific law or regulation, particularly nuisance abatement, the procedure is somewhat modified. Usually an agency inspector investigates the situation, which may involve odors, dustfall, soiling, or some other condition. If he is of the opinion that a nuisance exists, he attempts to secure abatement by negotiation with the party responsible for the condition. If this fails to bring about correction, a hearing may be held before the pollution control officer or a hearing board. Based on the views of the hearing body, an order to abate the nuisance may be issued or the case may be dismissed. If the order to

abate is not obeyed, the matter may be referred to a court for adjudication. Hearings may also be held when agency inspectors do not
believe a nuisance exists but some citizens do. This allows the hearing
body to get all the facts and opinions upon which to base a decision and
gives the citizens an opportunity to make their views publicly known.

Other enforcement procedures involve failure to obtain a construction
permit, secure or renew an operating permit, provide a required report,
or make a required test. In such cases, it is common practice to allow the
responsible party an opportunity to correct his failure before filing court
action. However, if the person is a repeated violator or seems to have
violated intentionally, the matter may be referred to court immediately
upon discovery.

When the abatement action required is one which will take a long time
to correct, be very costly, or involve a large segment of a community's
industry or public, it is common practice to arrange a long-term abatement schedule. The schedule will require that certain actions be taken at
various times over a period of years. Periodic progress reports may be
required. Such schedules have been developed for 7 to 10 year periods
for the steel industry in Cleveland, Chicago, and Allegheny County,
Pennsylvania. In Cleveland, the schedule is written into an ordinance;
while in the other two areas, the agreement was formally adopted by the
hearing board or administrative agency and the industry. The East
St. Louis, Illinois, ordinance allows 5 years (from February, 1964) for
elimination of hand-fired coal burning installations, except in one-and
two-family dwellings.

Since it is possible that any action taken by the agency may result in
a court action, it is important that all work be accurately done and
meticulously recorded (*10*). The actions must be in accordance with the
law, regulations, and precedents developed in previous court actions.

The enforcement process involved in adjudication of odor problems
is essentially the same as used in other matters. However, there is no
objective method for measuring odors, making it necessary to use the
human nose and human reaction as a means for determining presence
and objectionableness of odorous pollutants. Methods of detecting presence of odors and locating their origin have been described (*61–64*).
(See Chapter 23.) These may be applied in enforcement proceedings.
The reaction of the public to odors may be determined by house-to-
house surveys, student odor surveys, and public opinion polls (*44, 45, 65*).

4. *Variances, Hearings, and Appeals*

A variance is permission granted by the control agency, board, or
commission to build, maintain, or operate an installation which does not

comply with regulations. When a new law is put into effect, unless a period of grace is written into the law, blanket variances, to expire on a certain date, will be needed to allow time to make corrections. Variances may also be needed to allow time to secure equipment, conduct research and pilot plant studies, or budget expenditures. If no satisfactory way to correct a problem is at hand, a variance to give time to develop one may be better than installing unsatisfactory available controls forthwith. Variances should expire on a set date and be renewable only after reconsideration of the case.

Appeal and hearing boards provide a means for individuals aggrieved by actions of the administrator to have their views heard without the expense of a court case. One board may serve the purposes of both an appeal and a hearing body. Appeal and hearing boards can usually grant variances and reject or modify actions taken by the agency administrator. Hearing boards may also consider cases in which the administrator has not been able to secure abatement, and will try to find some means, short of prosecution, to get needed correction of violations.

A few laws require that before the air pollution program administrator can issue an order to correct a violation, a hearing be held before a board or commission. This procedure is unworkable since boards are usually made up of unpaid people who cannot spend the time necessary to hold the required number of hearings; and is unnecessary, since most cases are clear-cut violations which should be corrected. It is preferable to hold hearings only when requested by a regulated person or the program administrator and to authorize the administrator to issue, as he sees fit, orders and notices authorized by law and regulation. Even when hearings are held only on request, the number of hearings may be substantial. For example, in Los Angeles the hearing board holds more than 100 meetings per year.

In addition to formal hearings conducted before hearing boards, most agencies hold many "office" or "administrative" hearings. For example, in 1964 more than 2100 were held in Chicago and more than 700 in New York. These are held when the field inspector is unable to secure abatement or when the issues involved are beyond the ability of the field man to resolve. The hearings are held before responsible executives of the agency for the purpose of examining the facts in the case, reaching a decision as to corrective action to be taken, and motivating the responsible party to take the necessary actions. These informal hearings reduce the number of formal hearings and court prosecutions.

5. Control of New Installations

A key element in an air pollution control program is the regulation of new installations. Some means should be provided which will ensure that all newly constructed facilities will be built in such a way that they can be operated without causing pollutant emissions in excess of those allowed by law or regulations. The most effective way to do this is to require that approval be obtained from the control agency of construction plans before installation begins. Through this procedure, installations are avoided which are poorly designed, will cause air pollution, and thus require costly modification or reconstruction. This does however, impose on the air pollution control agency a requirement that it have available necessary skilled engineering resources to determine from sets of plans and specifications whether an installation will meet emission limitations.

It is desirable to reduce to writing the procedures used in plan approval systems. Los Angeles County has produced a manual of this kind (66). It is also desirable to publish the criteria which will be used in deciding whether plans will be approved. These can be given to inspectors, plan reviewers, engineers, and companies planning to build. This reduces variations among agency personnel and enhances the possibility of plans being approved on first submission.

If an applicant and the agency disagree on whether a proposed installation will perform satisfactorily, a conditional permit can be issued even though the agency feels the installation will not perform adequately. The applicant should acknowledge in writing the fact that the agency believes the installation will not be satisfactory and agree that changes or replacements will be made if necessary. After a permit to construct a facility has been issued and the installation has been built, it must still meet emission control requirements. To ensure that this is the case, each newly built installation should be inspected and emission measurements made. If emissions are satisfactory, a permit to operate is issued. If not, corrections must be made and additional emission measurements conducted. These tests not only ensure that legal requirements are met but also provide information useful in future plan reviews.

In order to help ensure that all new construction is reviewed, it is desirable to make arrangements with other governmental agencies in the jurisdiction that issue permits to call attention of the pollution control agency to proposed facilities becoming known to them.

To reduce the number of plans that must be reviewed, it is well to exempt from construction permit requirements all installations which are habitually designed so as to cause no problems or are of such nature that plan review and approval is unlikely to bring about any significant reduction in pollution emissions. Such sources include gas-fired units, all but very large units fired with light distillate fuel oil, stationary (internal combustion) engines, and others (66).

If, for some reason, a permit system cannot be established, an alternate is to establish a "Registration System." In a registration system, those planning to build a new facility are required to submit only information on the location where the unit will be built, a general description of what it will do, and information on the nature and location of expected pollutant emissions. The agency does not approve or disapprove the installation but merely issues a registration form or certificate. Reliance is placed on the applicant for meeting emission regulations after the unit goes into operation. The registration procedure does, however, give the agency knowledge of the installation so it can be checked after construction and an opportunity to call attention of the applicant to emission requirements, and to offer him advisory services.

6. Sealing Equipment

Authority to seal equipment and thus prevent its use and continued violation of emission regulations is a powerful enforcement tool. It should be used sparingly and cautiously. Application of this punitive and preventive power is often more damaging to the offender than fines levied by a court. Some agencies use this power to ensure correction of defects in space heating equipment by sealing units at the end of the heating season. Thus the owner is not deprived of its use when needed but he knows he must get it corrected during warm weather or face either prosecution for breaking the seal or getting cold. It is also a useful tool in preventing further construction on a unit being built in a manner different from that prescribed in approved plans.

7. Fireman Training

In the past, when coal burning units were responsible for more smoke than they are now, some agencies conducted schools for janitors, firemen, and operating engineers to teach them proper firing and maintenance procedures. Most authorities now favor the concept of restricting use of fuels to devices which can reasonably be expected to burn them without causing excessive smoke. There is still much done on the instruction of equipment operators by field inspection forces in their visits to installations, but formal schools for fireman have all but disappeared. In addition, many agencies publish illustrated charts and leaflets for display in furnace rooms and for general public distribution. Such materials must be written in plain language and be very brief.

8. Disaster Prevention

Preparations should be made to protect the public should an air pollution disaster occur or appear to be developing. The chances of a

catastrophe occurring are remote but the consequences of being un-
prepared are dreadful to think about. Chass *et al.* (67) identify the
principal aspects of disaster prevention programs as follows:

1. Identify pollutants in the air which can induce health disturbances.
2. Establish the concentration of each which will provide a reasonable
   margin of safety.
3. Select and place in operation means for measuring pollutants.
4. Establish plans for action to be taken in the event that pollution
   levels reach potentially harmful levels.

Los Angeles has made extensive use of committees in establishing its
disaster control plan. Committees are also used to keep the plan up to
date and would be used to advise the air pollution control officer should
an emergency situation develop. A lot of work is required to establish
and operate pollution monitoring equipment; obtain, review, and keep
current industry shutdown plans to be used in time of need; inform
the public of its responsibilities; establish and keep in readiness a massive communications network, and so on. In Los Angeles, three stages
of alert, of increasing severity, have been established along with a three-
step plan for preventing a catastrophe. The air pollution control officer
and the governor assume tremendous powers in event of an emergency.
Therefore, legal safeguards require that the program be based on possible serious effects on public health and safety, not on public discomfort.

In the New York City metropolitan area, an air pollution warning
system has been developed (68). An air pollution watch and three levels
of alert have been based on concentrations of sulfur dioxide, carbon
monoxide, smoke levels (COHS), and forecasts of meteorological dispersion conditions. General plans for reduction of pollutant emissions
during times of high pollution concentration have been made.

9. *Motor Vehicle Emission Control*

The vast majority of work to date by state and local governments on
emissions from motor vehicles has been done in California. The state,
in April, 1960, created the Motor Vehicle Pollution Control Board and
gave it authority to control auto, truck, and bus pollutants. Standards
for vehicle emissions however, were established by the State Department
of Public Health. The Motor Vehicle Pollution Control Board had two
basic functions: (1) to establish performance criteria for emission control systems and devices, and (2) to conduct tests to determine whether
control systems and devices met prescribed criteria and emission control requirements. In addition, the Board made appropriate exemptions for certain classes of vehicles and engines, designated approved

testing laboratories, and carried on a public information program. The Board was made up of the Directors of Public Health, Agriculture, Motor Vehicles, and the Commissioner of the Highway Patrol of the State and nine members appointed by the Governor (69). The Board conducted its work with its own staff and by contract. For the year 1965, the Board had a budget of $685,000 including a grant of $124,000 from the U.S. Public Health Service. In late 1967, the Motor Vehicle Pollution Control Board was replaced by an Air Resources Board which was also assigned some of the functions of other state agencies in air pollution control.

California (1967) motor vehicle requirements are that all 1966 and later model cars be equipped to meet requirements for exhaust pipe and crankcase emissions (except very small cars and larger trucks), and vehicles dating back to 1955 models in 10 "high air pollution counties" are required to have crankcase controls upon registration transfer. Exhaust emission standards applicable to vehicles having engines with less than 140 cubic inch displacement became effective in 1968 and for heavy duty trucks, in 1969. A state-wide network of inspection and installation stations examines and certifies required control systems. These stations are licensed by the California Highway Patrol. Mechanics who wish to make installations and inspections are licensed on the basis of examinations administered by the Patrol. The Highway Patrol spot checks vehicles on the roadside to see that they conform with vehicle code safety regulations and air pollution control device requirements. The records of the Department of Motor Vehicles code its master files with regard to air pollution control devices when a vehicle is registered or reregistered (70). The California Highway Patrol had a budget of $479,000 in 1965 to carry out its work in vehicle pollution control, financed by three $1 increases (over a 3-year period) in vehicle registration fees.

The California Department of Public Health promulgated more restrictive standards for exhaust emissions to become effective in 1970; and standards for evaporative losses of gasoline from carburetors and fuel tanks, and for emission of nitrogen oxides in exhausts, both to become mandatory when devices or systems for meeting the standards become available.

Ideally, periodic evaluation of effectiveness of control systems of cars on the road should be based on actual measurement of pollutants emitted. Equipment and procedures for quick inspection of control performance are as yet not available. Inspections are presently based on determination that emission control devices are in place and apparently operating (29).

The state of New York has a law requiring that, with a few exceptions, all motor vehicles registered in the state which were manufactured after June 30, 1963 be equipped with a crankcase ventilating system of a type approved by Air Pollution Control Board. Criteria for approval of devices and systems for control were developed (*71*). The criteria require that test data be developed by an approved laboratory to support applications to the Board for approval of a control system. The Board has approved at least 15 laboratories and has given its approval to 40 to 50 control systems each year since the 1963 model year of vehicles.

Colorado, in April, 1965, adopted a law requiring that all gasoline-powered vehicles manufactured after July 1, 1965, be equipped with a crankcase ventilating system designed to prevent emission of air contaminants. Enforcement will be through a provision that no certificate of inspection and approval will be issued in connection with a previously existing vehicle safety inspection program unless the required control system is in place. Vehicle manufacturers are also required to certify that vehicles offered for sale in the state are properly equipped.

A number of jurisdictions have special regulations applicable to visible smoke emissions from motor vehicles particularly concerned with diesel-powered buses and trucks. In Detroit in 1963, the police issued over 6000 summons, and the air pollution control agency issued over 300, for violation of the vehicle smoke emission law (*18*). In Cincinnati, vehicles going through the safety inspection lane are checked for "excessive smoke." In 1963, over 700 vehicles (0.3% of those inspected) were rejected because of excessive smoke.

In 1965, the U.S. Congress adopted amendments (Public Law 89-272) to the Clean Air Act (Public Law 88-206) which had a profound influence on state and local government activities in the vehicle pollution control field, as well as on the vehicle pollution problem itself. The law is designed to achieve uniform national control by limiting the emission from all new motor vehicles introduced into interstate commerce, whether manufactured in the United States or imported from abroad. The Secretary of Health, Education, and Welfare is authorized to establish standards for emission from a motor vehicle of any substance which in his judgment is, or may be, injurious to the public health or welfare. The Secretary has promulgated such standards, which make it unlawful to introduce a new motor vehicle or new motor vehicle engine into interstate commerce which fails to comply with the standards, or to render inoperative a control device before delivery to the ultimate purchaser. Vehicle and engine manufacturers are required to make available to the Secretary records sufficient to enable him to determine that the manufacturer is complying with the law. The standards may be revised from time to time. The Secretary is required to test systems to determine whether they comply with standards upon application by a manufacturer. Standards for diesel engines have been deferred until control technology is further developed (72).

In January 1968, new emission standards for motor vehicles were proposed, including a limitation on emission of smoke from diesel-powered vehicles; more restrictive exhaust standards for cars and light trucks; standards for exhaust emissions from heavy duty trucks and buses; and regulations applicable to evaporation losses from vehicle fuel tanks and carburetors.

The Air Quality Act of November 1967 (amending the earlier Clean Air Act) prohibited state and local governments from regulating emissions from new motor vehicles and new motor vehicle engines, thus providing for federal preemption in this field. Provision was made, however, for waiver of this prohibition in any state which had adopted vehicle emission standards (other than crankcase emission standards) prior to March 30, 1966. California is the only state that meets this qualification and may be permitted to have its own standards for new motor vehicles, under certain conditions.

The federal program in the vehicle pollution control field should ensure that vehicles leaving manufacturing plants are constructed in such a way that emissions are minimized to the extent feasible within available technology. The job of seeing that control devices are kept in place and are properly maintained, however, is the role of state and local governments. Depending on the nature, durability, and serviceability of the devices and systems applied, it may become advantageous for state and local governments to operate vehicle inspection systems of one sort or another.

In 1964, a federal law was enacted to provide financial assistance to communities for improvement of their urban mass transit systems. This law requires the Secretary of Health, Education, and Welfare to develop specifications that can be applied to equipment and facilities purchased with these funds. Specifications presently require that engine horsepower of buses be at least that which, calculated according to a specified method, will be adequate for the duty required of the vehicle, plus additional smoke emission requirements (73).

Relatively simple engine adjustments and care in operation can minimize smoke from diesel engines. Thus, some air pollution control agencies have continuing liason with owners of fleets of buses and trucks, working toward full utilization of available techniques. These programs yield a reasonable satisfactory return (i.e., reduced smoke) especially if a selective vehicle smoke enforcement program is conducted simultaneously to mete out punitive action to the few who refuse to cooperate.

10. *Fuel Regulation*

Early fuel regulation limited the volatility of coal used in certain furnaces. This was a key to success in the St. Louis and Pittsburgh, and some other smoke abatement programs. A few agencies, notably New York City; New Jersey; St. Louis and St. Louis County, Missouri (and Missouri for the St. Louis Metropolitan area); the Federal government for Federally owned facilities in New York, Chicago, and Philadelphia; and Los Angeles County, regulate the amount of sulfur in fuels as a means of reducing sulfur dioxide emissions. Los Angeles County regulates the olefin content of automotive fuel. This type of regulation is basic in nature, is very effective, and can be enforced readily. An enforcement program involves checking fuel composition at its source (mine or refinery), in transport vehicles, and at distribution depots. Lists of approved fuels are prepared and made public at frequent intervals. Inspections and fuel analyses at the point of use are necessary to substantiate violations. Complaints that illegal fuel is being sold must be checked out. Standards of measurement and procedures for testing must be developed and made public. In some cases, fuels which do not meet required characteristics are permitted provided it can be shown that they can be used and emit no more pollutant than a fuel that does meet the required characteristics. If this is the case, methods of demonstrating emission performance must be established so that "nonstandard" fuels can be tested.

C. OPERATING THE AGENCY

1. *Initiating an Air Pollution Control Program*

Whatever the reason for concern about air pollution in a community or the persons or groups interested in doing something about air pollution, the basic necessity in getting a control program initiated is to develop enough interest among the people of the jurisdiction to support enactment of an air pollution control law and establishment of a full-time governmental control agency. One way to develop interest is to form a "clean air committee," preferably appointed by the mayor or governor. It is helpful for a staff person from government to be assigned to work with the committee, and to act as its executive secretary, since voluntary committee members seldom have the time to carry out all the needed work. Legislative groups often use the "study committee" approach to develop a basis for formulation of laws. These committees may be made up of members of the legislative body or of others from private walks of life. Another commonly used initial step is the conduct of a preliminary survey by an existing governmental agency. For any of these approaches, the general procedure is as follows:

1. Draw in additional people to serve as technical resource people or advisors.
2. Reach preliminary agreement on what the problems are and form subgroups to study various aspects of the problem (e.g., legislation, governmental organization, sources of pollution, effects of pollution, meteorological and topographical aspects).
3. Secure facts from existing information in the community, library research, public meetings, outside consultants, and special studies.
4. Develop possible approaches to solution of air pollution problems.
5. Place a report of the problem and proposed plan of action before the community through mass media, meetings, and individual contacts.
6. Study reactions to the proposal and revise the proposed plan as warranted.
7. Present the plan to appropriate legislators or legislative bodies and support actions to implement the proposal.

An effective way to bring together interested and knowledgeable people is the "governor's or mayor's conference." The head of the government calls the meeting and arranges a program. The purpose is to present as much information as possible about the problem to as large a group of concerned people as can be conveniently assembled. The conference will attract top-flight speakers and listeners and will usually get much coverage by the mass media. After the conference, the head of government will have a better idea of how and where to go and whom to call upon to assist him, and a foundation for public support will have been laid.

Once the program comes into being, it is better to provide for a few program elements in a more concentrated manner than to move on all program aspects at once. It will take time to hire and train personnel and therefore, the relatively simple things should be done first, gradually building up to more complex activities. It may be wise to omit some controversial aspects from initial plans in order to get a start on more generally accepted aspects and take on the more difficult problems as the staff develops know-how. Initial successes on a smaller segment of the problem will do more to create strong public support for an enlarged program than will a scattering of effort, with no completed successes, on many facets of the program.

2. *Intragovernmental Relationships*

Many governmental agencies engage in activities peripheral to air pollution control program operations, such as issuance of building, zoning, and ventilating system permits, industrial inspection, boiler inspection, nuisance abatement, land use planning, civil defense, and refuse disposal. The air pollution program must be coordinated with these other programs if waste and confusion are to be avoided. An example of such coordination is aggreement with the building department that all construction plans be filed there, but that a building permit will not be issued until the air pollution agency has reviewed and approved the plans. Another example is air pollution program representation in activities of planning and zoning agencies.

3. *Public Relationships*

Community recognition of an air pollution problem and an action program to resolve the problem will come about much more readily when the public is convinced that a problem exists, concerns them, and can be solved. A public information program is needed to provide the public with the information they need to arrive at proper decisions. Some specific elements of a public information program are as follows:

1. Inform the people of the nature, extent, causes and effects of air pollution in their community.
2. Describe the steps that need to be taken to control air pollution. Explain the economics of these measures which, in most cases, will indicate that the costs of control will be less than the costs of tolerating pollution.
3. Instill the idea that clean air is a desirable and attainable goal and that a well-planned program will not disrupt community life or industrial progress.
4. Make known the results of successful control efforts undertaken elsewhere.
5. Explain the transport of pollutants from one jurisdiction to another for the purpose of securing control action throughout an air basin.
6. Inform people about things they should do to minimize pollution (e.g., cease open burning of refuse; have automotive emission control systems serviced; keep home heating plants properly adjusted).

Other aspects of public relations activities of air pollution control agencies include work with civic and professional groups, collaboration with industrial groups, publication of monthly and annual reports and information bulletins, awarding of citations for outstanding control work, and use of advisory boards. These are discussed in detail in Chapter 53. The public information programs of Los Angeles (74), New York City (75) and the Air Pollution Control Association (76, 77), have been described.

4. *Air Pollution Control Boards and Commissions*

Until recent years, it was the predominant practice to put details of a control program in a law or ordinance. An administrative agency would then implement the law. However, as the air pollution problem has grown in complexity, legislative bodies have increasingly chosen to put only broad policies into the law, leaving the details to a board or commission. It is easier to change rules and regulations promulgated by a board or commission than to change a law or ordinance. The legislature can also give authority for implementing its policies to an administrative official instead of a board or commission. The principal objection to this is that the administrator might employ an arbitrary approach in adopting and implementing regulations. Thus, the board or commission is often favored as a means of broadening the base of responsibility in this field where many decisions are based on limited information and much judgment. However, boards and commissions are not always responsive to public desires for clean air, particularly if their membership includes a number of industrial representatives. They also detract from the ability of chief executives (mayors and governors) to meet their responsibilities to the public since the terms of office of board and commission members are usually staggered in such a way that a newly elected executive will not be able to control membership or policies. The existence of a board or commission may also cloud and diffuse responsibility between the board itself and the operating agency, thus making it difficult for the chief executive to fix responsibility for inadequate performance and to take remedial action. It is not uncommon for at least some board members to be uninformed or only marginally concerned about air pollution matters thus reducing their effectiveness. These various defects of boards and commissions have prompted some people to favor placing authority and responsibility for air pollution control squarely on the chief executive and the head of the operating air pollution control agency and to give them all necessary powers, including rule and regulation making to implement general policies set out in a basic law. It is reasoned that adequate protection against arbitrary or ill-advised actions by the chief executive and the air pollution control administrator are provided by hearings, recourse to the courts, and the ballot box.

Rogers, in 1957 reported that only 14% of 110 local ordinances provided for an air pollution control board or commission (78). About 38% did, however, provide for an appeal or advisory board. Local ordinances adopted since 1957 have more often provided for a control board or commission. In about 70% of state laws, provision is made for a control board or commission. This difference in practice between state and local governments is a reflection of the more recent date of adoption of state laws as compared with local ordinances. Another reason for more extensive use of boards by states is the infrequency of meetings of state legislatures. Some meet only once every 2 years, making it difficult to make any changes or additions to the law. City legislatures may meet once a week or so.

Most boards and commissions serve without pay although a few receive a nominal per diem allowance, and nearly all are reimbursed for any travel expenses incurred in attending meetings. Membership on boards varies considerably from one place to another. Those included may be governmental officials whose work is related to air pollution and its control, serving in an ex-officio capacity, industrial representatives, doctors, lawyers, engineers, etc. The appointing official (governor or mayor) may be allowed to appoint any person he desires or the law may specify certain general qualifications the appointees must have, such as occupation or professional qualifications.

The air pollution control board may also serve as the hearing and appeal board. This arrangement is considered inappropriate by some, since the board judges the reasonableness of its own actions. The advantages of this dual role for the control board are that fewer people are needed for boards and the fact that the control board is best informed on its own regulations, and is thus better able to interpret them than would be a separate appeal board. Since the board has basic responsibility to the public for protection of air resources, it may be held that an independent appeal board should not be put in a position of being able to obstruct the control board by granting exceptions to the control board's actions, if the appeal board should be so inclined. Protection against arbitrary actions by the control board, in any case, is available to those regulated, by resort to the courts.

5. *Data Storage and Retrieval*

Air pollution control agencies acquire, record, store, retrieve, analyze, and publish large volumes of data. The data result from many of the agency's operations and involve such things as air quality data, pollutant emissions, pollutant sources, emission control equipment, fuels and materials used, source tests made, abatements effected, permits issued, inspections made, hearings held, court actions undertaken, etc. (79). The data may be used to keep case histories, monitor program operations, schedule activities, and to make various statistical tabulations and analyses (80). While the great majority of existing air pollution control programs use manual systems of written records, there is no doubt that modern systems employing punched cards, magnetic tapes, and data processing machines are needed by many agencies if appropriate use is to be made of data available.

In choosing a data system, consideration must be given to initial and operating costs, the needs and uses of the data involved, and the accessibility of the data for program purposes (81). There is, of course, no point in storing data for which there is no forseeable use. Coding should be as simple as possible to minimize errors and reading and coding time. The system should be designed so that transfers of data from one record to another is minimized. Therefore, it is desirable, for example, to punch data record cards directly from field or laboratory reports. The basic record can be overprinted with card column numbers and coding information to reduce the need to refer to coding manuals or rely on memory.

The total data system should be so designed that information from various decks of data cards can be related in any desired manner. For example, one might want to relate air quality measurements at certain locations to pollutant emissions from sources within one mile of the air sampling station. Geographic location coding is particularly necessary not only to interrelate data within the agency but also to make use of data stored by other agencies such as the land-use planning agency. Thus particular attention should be given to location coding, using the method (grid system, census tracts, city block, etc.) of greatest overall utility.

6. Fee Systems

Most air pollution control agencies collect fees for such functions as periodic inspection of pollutant sources, review and approval of construction plans, and issuance of operating permits. Fees are charged on the premise that those who do (or may) pollute the atmosphere should pay a larger share of the cost of operating the control program than the community as a whole. Fee schedules are usually lists of specific classes and sizes of equipment and the charge for the particular governmental action (66).

Two tabulations of the percent of local air pollution program costs recovered in fees (*10, 11*) indicate that most agencies recover less than 25% of their operating expenses from fees, with the median for all agencies being about 20%. However, about 20% of the agencies recover more than half their operating costs in fees. Chicago, in 1964, collected about $531,000 in fees and had a total city appropriation of $770,000, indicating that the net cost to the city for the air pollution program was $239,000.

V.   Community Planning and Air Resource Management

Community planning is a guide for community development. It is not a detailed design nor a substitute for the democratic process. Planning is less a policy-making function than a professional task. A government may spend good money for this professional advice and, although the government may not follow the planners' suggestions, the influence is felt. Even if the plan is not fully adopted, the planning process is important in both molding and influencing community thought. And often the mere existence of a planning body causes a community to think more seriously about its future (*82*).

Land use regulations seek to locate industrial, commercial, and residential areas in such a way that community values and goals, including those related to air pollution, will be served. Planning on a city basis in areas comprising many cities is not feasible. While broad area planning has evolved, broad area zoning, the action phase which follows planning, has not. Individual political jurisdictions have jealously clung to their traditional concepts of home rule in land use regulation. Thus, in metropolitan areas, well-drawn plans have not been well implemented. However, there are some air pollution-related actions in the planning and zoning fields which are worth attempting, particularly in larger political jurisdictions.

The least that should be done to integrate air pollution control activities with community planning work is to establish a firm liason between agencies engaged in these two kinds of work. The air pollution control officer should give testimony at hearings held by planning and zoning agencies. He should comment on zoning applications, especially those involving changes or exceptions to the general zoning law. The planning and zoning agency should routinely notify the air pollution control officer when such actions are to occur. The air pollution control officer should become familiar with comprehensive community plans, planning studies, and the tools that planners use in their work. He should participate in planning and zoning studies, in preparation of plans and zoning maps and in hearings concerning them, and should help defend community plans and zoning schemes against destructive changes (83).

Some specific activities which may be taken to integrate air pollution matters into community planning are as follows:

1. Study plans in existence or being made for transportation, land use, water supply, sewage disposal, open spaces, etc., for the purpose of coordinating these plans with the air resource management plan. Inform others in the planning field of the work being done on air resources.

2. Make projections of pollutant emissions from present and future sources, considering several possible emission control programs and geographical distributions of pollution sources. Consider population growth, transportation, including substitution of mass transit for private autos, industrialization, technological changes, etc.

3. Develop and apply mathematical models for estimating present and future air pollution levels based on meteorological and pollutant emission data and land use patterns. Study pollution levels which would result on the basis of several possible pollution emission control programs and land use patterns.

4. Prepare a series of estimates of the impact of alternatives for control of pollutant emissions and land use which will result in various levels of air quality. Consider such things as cost of control, influence on transportation and social patterns, need for industrial expansion, availability of fuels, community desires and purpose, effects of various pollution levels on health, materials, vegetation, visibility, etc.

5. Study various alternatives for implementing the air resource management program with respect to jurisdictional area served, needed legislation, agencies which could carry out the program, sources of funds, relationships with other jurisdictions, coordination of the program with the program of zoning, transportation, water supply, sewage disposal, refuse disposal, urban renewal and redevelopment, citizen participation, etc.

6. Design air resource management activities in the light of such community planning matters as allocation of land uses and performance standards for new land uses.

The Northeastern Illinois Metropolitan Area Planning Commission has conducted a pioneering air resource planning study (84). The Metropolitan Toronto Planning Board has a vigorous program which provides for air resource management in connection with urban planning activities. Wronski *et al.* (*85*) have listed the measures being instituted as follows:

a. Control of heating equipment in new buildings and encouragement of central district heating plants.
b. Development of publicly operated means of refuse disposal to eliminate pollution caused by existing domestic and commercial refuse disposal facilities.
c. Control of structures of varying height, particularly apartment buildings, so as to reduce to a minimum the adverse effects on amenities resulting from air pollution caused by height differences.
d. Development of a transportation system designed to reduce traffic congestion and thereby reduce air pollution from vehicle exhausts.
e. Prevention of dust through surfacing of streets and parking lots and elimination of unsodded areas.
f. Establishment of a weed control program on public and private lands to reduce pollen counts.
g. Encouraging location of the larger sources of pollution at the greatest possible distance from residential areas.
h. Control of apartment developments in mixed commercial areas so that pollution from commercial premises will not adversely affect the residential buildings.

Zoning ordinances of years ago regulated location of industrial plants on the basis of "use lists." Certain named industries were permitted in some areas and prohibited in others, regardless of the nature of the equipment and performance associated with a particular plant. In recent years, performance standards have had incresing acceptance as a replacement for use lists (*86, 87*). With performance standards, any industry which will operate in compliance with certain specifications concerning noise, glare, appearance, vibration, air pollutant emissions, etc., is permitted to locate in any industrial zone, without regard to the type of operations conducted. People in the planning and zoning field have indicated a willingness to incorporate air pollution performance standards in their regulations but, in many areas, there has been a regrettable lack of communication and coordination between these people and those responsible for air pollution control. Thus, in some areas, zoning regulations may not be consistent with air pollution control regulations; the air pollution aspects of zoning laws may indicate lack of application of the skills of air pollution specialists; and implementation of the air pollution aspects of the zoning law may not be properly coordinated with activities carried out under air pollution control regulations. The trend, however, has been toward better coordination and the future should bring improvements.

Meteorological research has resulted in an improved capability to design mathematical models of the dispersion of pollutants from the multitude of sources in an area (see Chapter 7, Vol. I). Use of electronic computers has been of great assistance. It is now possible, with a knowledge of the pollution sources and meteorological characteristics of an area, to compute air concentrations of pollutants at any point in the area within a reasonable degree of accuracy. Estimates can be made of pollutant emissions from a proposed land use and then computations can be made to determine the air concentrations of pollutants in various parts of the area. By assuming various possible locations for the proposed land use it is possible to select the location which would provide for the best possible protection of the community air supply. This information, along with other considerations, could then be used in preparing land use zoning regulations. More widespread use of this methodology can be expected as it becomes more generally known, understood, developed, and demonstrated.

The problem of air resource management is intimately related to many other community problems. Solutions to air pollution problems may have far-reaching social and economic impact and may influence other environmental factors. Therefore, there is a need for increased attention to the broader aspects of community life and a departure from the past practice of categorical approaches to problems. Incorporation of air pollution considerations into overall community planning is one step that may be taken in this direction.

REFERENCES

1. American Public Health Assoc., "Health Officials Guide to Air Pollution," p. 75. The Association, New York, 1962.
2. F. M. Stead, *Am. J. Public Health* **50,** 312 (1960).
3. J. J. Hanlon, "Principles of Public Health Administration," 2nd ed., p. 128. Mosby, St. Louis, Missouri, 1955.
4. J. P. Dixon, *J. Air Pollution Control Assoc.* **14,** 149 (1964).
5. V. G. MacKenzie, *Paper at Growth Conf. Air, Land, Water Resources, Univ. Calif. at Riverside 1963.*
6. H. H. Humphrey, Vice President of the United States, remarks at a meeting sponsored by the California Manufacturer's Assoc. and Los Angeles County Air Pollution Control District, Los Angeles, California, Nov. 4, 1965.
7. A. N. Heller, J. J. Schueneman, and J. D. Williams, *Proc. 58th Ann. Meeting Air Pollution Control Assoc., Toronto, 1965* Paper No. 65–78.
8. J. J. Schueneman, *J. Air Pollution Control Assoc.* **13,** 116 (1963).
9. C. D. Yaffe, *J. Air Pollution Control Assoc.* **15,** 403 (1965).
10. Air Pollution Control Assoc., "Statistical Tabulation of Air Pollution Control Bureaus, United States and Canada." Pittsburgh, Pennsylvania, 1952.
11. Air Pollution Control Assoc., "Statistical Tabulation, Part I, Air Pollution Control Governmental Agencies, United States and Canada." Pittsburgh, Pennsylvania, 1956.

12. O. F. Nolting and D. S. Arnold, eds., "The Municipal Year Book, 1964," p. 165. Intern. City Mgrs. Assoc., Chicago, Illinois, 1964.

13. City of Chicago, Dept. of Air Pollution Control, "Annual Report, 1964." Chicago, Illinois, 1965.

14. P. W. Purdom, *Public Health Repts.* (*U.S.*) **72**, 957 (1957).

15. H. C. Ballman and T. J. Fitzmorris, *J. Air Pollution Control Assoc.* **13**, 486 (1963).

16. City of Cleveland, Division of Air and Stream Pollution, "Annual Report, 1964." Cleveland, Ohio, 1965.

17. City of Chicago, Dept. of Air Pollution Control, "Annual Report, 1963." Chicago, Illinois, 1964.

18. City of Detroit, Dept. of Buildings and Safety Engineering, "Annual Report, 1963." Detroit, Michigan, 1964.

19. City of New York, Dept. of Air Pollution Control, "Annual Report, 1962." New York, 1963.

20. C. W. Gruber, "Air Pollution Control in Cincinnati." City of Cincinnati, Dept. of Safety, 1964.

21. Private communication, New York State Air Pollution Control Board, Albany, N.Y., May 1967.

22. Private communication, New Jersey State Dept. of Health, Trenton, N.J., May 1967.

23. Public Law 946, 84th U.S. Congress, 2nd Session, Aug. 3, 1956.

24. U.S. Dept. of Health, Education and Welfare, "A Study of Air Pollution in the Interstate Region of Lewiston, Idaho and Clarkston, Washington," Public Health Serv. Publ. No. 999-AP-8, Cincinnati, Ohio, 1964.

25. J. D. Williams, H. C. Mitchell, and C. M. Copley, *Proc. 57th Ann. Meeting Air Pollution Control Assoc., Houston, Texas, 1964* Paper No. 64-14.

26. S. Edelman, *Proc. 55th Ann. Meeting Air Pollution Control Assoc., Chicago, 1962* Paper No. 62-93.

27. U.S. Dept. of Health, Education and Welfare, "Motor Vehicles, Air Pollution, and Health," A report of the Surgeon General to the U.S. Congress, USGPO, Washington, D.C., 1962.

28. U.S. Dept. of Health, Education and Welfare, "Automotive Air Pollution." A report to the U.S. Congress, Senate Doc. No. 7, 89th Congress, 1st Session, USGPO, Washington, D.C., 1965.

29. U.S. Dept. of Health, Education and Welfare, "Automotive Air Pollution." Second report to the U.S. Congress, Senate Doc. No. 42, 89th Congress, 1st Session, USGPO, Washington, D.C., 1965.

30. U.S. Dept. of Health, Education and Welfare, "Air Pollution Control Program Support Under the Clean Air Act (Public Law 88-206), a Fact Sheet." Washington, D.C., 1964.

31. Air Hygiene Committee, Engineering and Sanitation Section, Am. Public Health Assoc., *J. Am. Public Health Assoc.* **50**, 1591 (1960).

32. M. H. Thompson, *J. Am. Public Health Assoc.* **54**, 627 (1964).

33. Advisory Commission on Intergovernmental Relations, "Alternative Approaches to Governmental Reorganization in Metropolitan Areas," Rept. H-11. Washington, D.C., 1962.

34. U.S. House of Representatives, Committee on Government Operations, "Governmental Structure, Organization and Planning in Metropolitan Areas, Suggested Action by Local, State and National Governments." A report by the Advisory Commission on Intergovernmental Relations, Washington, D.C., 1961.

35. International Joint Commission, "Pollution of the Atmosphere in the Detroit River Area." Washington, D.C. and Ottawa, Canada, 1960.
36. M. Mayer, "A Compilation of Air Pollutant Emission Factors for Combustion Processes, Gasoline Evaporation, and Selected Industrial Processes." U.S. Public Health Serv., Cincinnati, Ohio, 1965.
37. R. L. Chass, R. G. Lunche, P. S. Tow, and N. P. Scheffer, *Proc. 52nd Ann. Meeting Air Pollution Control Assoc., Los Angeles, 1959* Paper No. 59-58.
38. J. D. Williams and N. G. Edmisten, *U.S., Public Health Serv., Publ.* **999-AP-18** (1965).
39. A. R. Dammkoehler, *Proc. 58th Ann. Meeting Air Pollution Control Assoc., Toronto, 1965* Paper No. 65-53.
40. State of New York Air Pollution Control Board, "Air Pollution in Erie County." Albany, New York, 1963.
41. M. I. Weisburd, *U.S., Public Health Serv., Publ.* **937,** 135–139 (1962).
42. California Dept. of Public Health, "Air Pollution Effects Reported by California Residents." Berkeley, California, ca. 1958.
43. W. S. Smith, J. J. Schueneman, and L. D. Zeidberg, *J. Air Pollution Control Assoc.* **14,** 418 (1964).
44. J. Schusky, "Public Awareness and Concern with Air Pollution in St. Louis Metropolitan Area." U.S. Dept. of Health, Education, and Welfare, Public Health Serv., Div. Air Pollution, Washington, D. C., 1965.
45. N. Z. Medalia and A. L. Finkner, *U.S., Public Health Serv., Publ.* **999-AP-10** (1965).
46. R. Kudlich (revised by L. R. Burdick), *U.S., Bur. Mines, Inform. Circ.* **7718** (1955).
47. M. I. Weisburd, *U.S., Public Health Serv., Publ.* **937,** 155–166 (1962).
48. Appellate Dept., Los Angeles Superior Court, *People v. International Steel Corp.* (1951) Calif. App. 2d Supp. 935, 226 P. 2d 587, at 938-9 and 1956; 137 C.A. 2nd (Supp.) 859; 291 Pac. 2nd 587.
49. U.S. Supreme Court (351 U.S. 990, 100 L. Ed. 1503). Appellate Dept., Superior Court, Los Angeles, Calif. *People v. Plywood Mfgrs. of Calif.; People v. Shell Oil Co.; People v. Union Oil Co., People v. Southern Calif. Edison Co.* (137 C.A. 2d Supp. 859; 291 P. 2d 587) (1955).
50. Micro Ringelmann Chart, *Power* **98,** 90 (1954).
51. New York City Air Pollution Control Code adopted Aug. 14, 1964.
52. J. D. Coons, H. A. James, H. C. Johnson, and M. S. Walker, *J. Air Pollution Control Assoc.* **15,** 199 (1965).
53. U.S. Dept. of Health, Education, and Welfare, Public Health Service, National Center for Air Pollution Control, Washington, D.C., 20201.
54. J. J. Schueneman, J. D. Williams, and N. G. Edmisten, *Proc. 58th Ann. Meeting Air Pollution Control Assoc., Toronto, 1965* Paper No. 65-77.
55. R. I. Larsen, *J. Air Pollution Control Assoc.* **11,** 71 (1961).
56. California Dept. of Public Health, "Technical Report on California Standards for Ambient Air Quality and Motor Vehicle Exhaust." Berkeley, California, 1960.
57. L. A. Winkelman, *J. Air Pollution Control Assoc.* **14,** 441 (1964).
58. New Jersey Air Pollution Control Code, Regulation VII, "Control and Prohibition of Air Pollution from Solid Particles." Trenton, New Jersey, 1964.
59. American Public Health Assoc., "Health Officials Guide to Air Pollution," pp. 24–32. The Association, New York, 1962.
60. M. I. Weisburd, *U.S., Public Health Serv., Publ.* **937,** 108–114 (1962).
61. A. N. Heller, H. J. Kandiner, W. M. Reiber, and M. Cohen, *Proc. Mfg. Chemists Assoc. Conf. Air Water Pollution Abatement, March 1959.* The Association, Washington, D.C., 1959.

62. N. A. Huey, L. C. Broering, G. A. Jutze, and C. W. Gruber, *J. Air Pollution Control Assoc.* **10,** 441 (1960).

63. American Society for Testing and Materials, "Measurement of Odor in Atmospheres (Dilution Method)," ASTM Designation D 1391-57. Philadelphia, Pennsylvania, 1962.

64. M. I. Weisburd, *U.S., Public Health Serv., Publ.* **937,** 195–206 (1962).

65. S. W. Horstman, R. F. Wromble, and A. N. Heller, *J. Air Pollution Control Assoc.* **15,** 261 (1965).

66. R. L. Chass, R. G. Lunche, E. E. Lemke, J. A. Verssen, R. G. Talens, R. L. Weimer, J. A. Danielson, J. L. McGinnity, and N. R. Shaffer, *et al.,* eds., "Administration of the Permit System," 3rd ed. Los Angeles County Air Pollution Control District, Los Angeles, California, 1965.

67. R. L. Chass, M. Pratch, and A. A. Atkisson, *J. Air Pollution Control Assoc.* **8,** 72 (1958).

68. T. A. Glenn, *J. Air Pollution Control Assoc.* **16,** 22 (1966).

69. California Motor Vehicle Pollution Control Board, "The Auto Smog Story—1964 Biennial Report." Los Angeles, California, 1965.

70. Calif. Motor Vehicle Pollution Control Board *Bulletin IV,* 11 (1965).

71. New York State Air Pollution Control Board, "Criteria for Approval of Crankcase Ventilation Systems-Vehicle Crankcase Ventilation System Compliance Tests." Albany, New York, 1963.

72. V. G. MacKenzie and K. Flieger, "The Clean Air Act Amendments and Solid Wastes Disposal Act of 1965 (P.L. 89-272)." U.S. Dept. of Health, Education, and Welfare, *Indicators,* USGPO, Washington, D.C., 1965.

73. A. C. Stern, *Air Pollution Congr. Swedish Natl. Clean Air Council, Stockholm, Sweden, 1965.*

74. A. A. Atkisson, C. DeKoven, and R. Barsky, *Proc. 51st Ann. Meeting Air Pollution Control Assoc., Philadelphia, 1958* Paper 58-36.

75. K. Kowald, *J. Air Pollution Control Assoc.* **12,** 272 (1962).

76. Air Pollution Control Assoc., "How to Tell the Air Pollution Control Story." 4400 Fifth Ave., Pittsburg, Pennsylvania (undated).

77. J. Fairweather, *Proc. 58th Ann. Meeting Air Pollution Control Assoc., Toronto, 1965* Paper No. 65–150.

78. S. M. Rogers, *Proc. 50th Ann. Meeting Air Pollution Control Assoc., St. Louis, Missouri, 1957.*

79. H. A. James and H. Curris, *Proc. 56th Ann. Meeting Air Pollution Control Detroit, 1963* Paper No. 63-22.

80. M. I. Weisburd, *U.S., Public Health Serv., Publ.* **937,** 114–120 (1962).

81. R. I. Larsen, *J. Air Pollution Control Assoc.* **12,** 423 (1962).

82. M. C. Hope, *Public Health Rept.* (*U.S.*) **75,** 859 (1960).

83. O. Sutermeister, *Public Health Rept.* (*U.S.*) **77,** 389 (1962).

84. J. Dumelle, K. L. Johnson, and W. J. Pelle, *Proc. 58th Ann. Meeting Air Pollution Control Assoc., Toronto, 1965* Paper No. 65-13.

85. W. Wronski, E. W. Anderson, A. E. Berry, A. P. Bernhart, and H. A. Belyea, *Proc. 58th Ann. Meeting Air Pollution Control Assoc., Toronto, 1965* Paper No. 65-10.

86. W. C. McCrone and M. A. Salzenstein, *Proc. 53rd Ann. Meeting Air Pollution Control Assoc., Cincinnati, 1960* Paper No. 60-40.

87. M. A. Salzenstein, *Proc. 58th Ann. Meeting Air Pollution Control Assoc., Toronoto, 1965* Paper No. 65-12.

53   Public Information and Education

John A. Maga

I.   Purpose and Need for Public Information and Education

A. Introduction

An attack on any problem that affects a large segment of the public, that regulates the activities of large numbers of people, and that requires legislation at the local, state, and federal levels of government must have the support of an informed public if it is to be successful. Community-wide air pollution is a problem in which public information and education are of particular importance because of the widespread adverse effects that air pollution has on the community, the differences of opinion that often exist on its causes and solution, and the need for acceptance of control programs by individuals being regulated as well as those adversely affected.

Often there is apathy to problems which have been present for a long time, but in most instances the majority of the public wants to solve the problems of the community in which they live. Efforts to resolve them, however, will be supported only when the public is sufficiently knowledgeable and sufficiently concerned to desire a solution. Not only must the public be made aware of air pollution, it must know something about what actions the community must take if air of satisfactory quality is to be maintained. In instances where air pollution is experienced for the first time or results from a single source, the public may demand an immediate solution. Here the public may have to be informed why an immediate solution is not possible.

Just as the nature of the air pollution problem varies from community to community so do the needs for, and purposes of, public information and education vary depending on the actions desired of the public. Air pollution is a broad and complex community problem in which the technical solution must be worked out in harmony with the social and economic interests of the community. There must be public understanding of the broad implications of the control of air pollution, or lack of control, as well as of the specific technical difficulties in each community.

It is obvious that the program of information and education in each instance must be tailored to the objectives. Short-range informational objectives would be quite different from long-range ones to bring about a good understanding of the specific problem and to change long-held community behavior patterns. A distinction, therefore, should be made between a program of reporting news to the press as it becomes available and a planned program of using media and community organizations to bring about specific actions or change. Individuals concerned with the control of air pollution should understand how to achieve these objectives, keeping in mind the limitations of both the public information approach and the slower educational approach.

B. Public Awareness of Air Pollution as a Problem

Since the mid-1950's the attention given to air pollution by the information media throughout the country has increased steadily. In the past 5 years many articles have appeared in the nation's leading monthly and weekly magazines as well as in the daily press. Air pollution has frequently been the subject of television and radio programs. This is in sharp contrast to the period prior to 1950 when the nation's news media provided much less coverage, and detailed articles describing air pollution as a matter of concern to the nation were seldom found in the leading magazines. It has been encouraging to see that this increased national attention has been accompanied by a growing improvement in the quality of the material presented to the public. Many of the recent reports have given comprehensive and accurate descriptions of the air pollution problem. This developing interest in providing information on community-wide air pollution is also reflected by the publication of several books which were devoted entirely or in part to this problem.

Parallel with the increased interest on the part of the news media have been the more active roles assumed by citizen organizations, voluntary health organizations, conservation groups, and scientific associations in education on the air pollution problem of the nation. Some of these organizations, such as the National Tuberculosis Association, have assumed a leadership role in respiratory disease aspects of air pollution, others, such as the National Audubon Society, have issued bulletins (1) on the air pollution problem. An Air Conservation Commission of the American Association for the Advancement of Science recently reviewed the subject of air pollution and methods for controlling emissions with emphasis on public policy matters and need for public support in air pollution control. In its report the Commission urged the scientific community to participate in informing the public about air pollution and air conservation (2).

At the same time air pollution has been the subject of hearings and legislation by local, state, and federal levels of government. These hearings and the resulting legislation provide a background for attention by the news media. Speeches and statements by U.S. presidents, governors of states, and other key governmental officials restating the importance of clean air are news, and such statements receive the widest possible coverage by the press, radio, and television.

Federal activities in air pollution control, mainly carried on by the U.S. Public Health Service, have been another reason for the increased attention which is being given to air pollution. The expanding federal program, including reports, studies, and press releases, has been a source of information for those engaged in air pollution control and often a source of news. National conferences on air pollution held in Washington, D.C. by the Public Health Service have helped focus national attention on air pollution (3).

Individual companies, trade associations, and publications directed at industrial activities have also accomplished much in public information and education. Although these groups are usually chiefly concerned with the education of their members and their customers, they play a very useful role in bringing information to a wider segment of the public because the materials produced often include information on the broader air pollution problem in the community. Industrial firms have produced a number of good films and reports which fall into this category.

All these activities help to bring about an appreciation that air pollution is of concern to all metropolitan areas and to many small communities, a recognition that steps can be taken to cope with it, and an understanding of the need for legislation.

C. Public Understanding of the Problem Within the Community

Awareness that community-wide air pollution is a problem of modern-day life is desirable and necessary. But this alone is not sufficient to obtain public support of control programs. Here the public must be informed, not only that there is a problem in the community—they probably know that already—but exactly what the problem is, what causes it, and what steps are being taken or are needed to solve it.

In these cases information and education are not merely publicity. They are the deliberate selection and use of appropriate communication methods and facilities, among the many available, to develop a public awareness and support of necessary action. The education program must, therefore, be based on the situation in each community. In some instances it will be necessary to overcome public apathy and to encourage action; in others, to make an explanation as to why an immediate solution is not possible; in still others, to change prevailing public opinion.

The kind of information that is presented by the control agency will be determined by the newness of the program, changes in emphasis of existing programs, or progress being made that requires reporting. In the case of an industry discharging pollutants, it will be determined by the public attitude, actions that have been taken by the company, and plans for installing control equipment. The control agency or the company may know very little on what the public thinks about air pollution or what information should be provided. Before engaging in an information and education program, it may be desirable to learn what the public knows and how the public feels, to serve as a baseline. In some instances it will be necessary to have a public opinion survey to obtain this information. But to be valuable, such surveys must be carefully organized and conducted. The reports on surveys that have been made in the St. Louis Metropolitan Area (4) and in Clarkston, Washington (5), illustrate the use of this approach and might serve as guides for others.

D. Education of the Public to Accept Controls

Those concerned with the control of air contaminants have come to recognize that a few large sources are usually not the major cause of air pollution in metropolitan regions; rather it is the many small sources associated with the daily activities of a community. Combustion of fuel by individuals, commercial establishments, and industries, and the use of motor vehicles are examples of this. Solution of the air pollution problem in these instances is made more difficult and complex because control programs directed at these sources may involve almost every family in the community, have direct economic implication for almost everyone, and require changes in the manner the public has become accustomed to doing things. A more difficult challenge in public communication would not be easy to find.

If the control program is to be successful in these instances it must extend to almost everyone in the community. Ideally, each person affected should be made aware of his contribution to the problem and what action will be required of him. Obviously, even with the best education and information program it will not be possible to reach every person; or, if he is reached, to convince him that the solution being advanced is the correct one. But it is imperative to make the effort to establish effective communication with as large a segment of the public as possible.

E. Cooperation and Support by the Public

Any air pollution control program would be less effective, and in many cases doomed to failure, without voluntary compliance with the control activities by most members of the community involved. This is true even in places where regulations have been adopted and enforcement programs undertaken, because the experience with laws affecting large numbers of people has shown that enforcement alone is not enough. Since maximum voluntary compliance is the ideal to be achieved, it is necessary that a cooperative attitude be developed on the part of those being regulated.

Cooperation implies collective action for mutual benefit. It, therefore, implies more than compliance with laws. It includes participation by community groups in the development of ordinances and support of the control activities by the individuals and industries being regulated as well as by those affected.

Cooperation is achieved through an understanding of the problem by the public. The chances of achieving it are good when the public knows the situation and even better if they have confidence that the control program is sound. To promote this needed understanding and confidence is one of the basic objectives of a public education program. Another is to create support by the community for the air pollution control agency. This support includes the establishment and continued operation of the control agency, the budget to carry out the control activities, and the adoption and enforcement of rules and regulations to reduce the quantity of contaminants being discharged.

F. Industry's Need for Public Information and Education

Industrial plants whose emissions affect nearby residents or contribute to community-wide air pollution have special need for public information and education activities. The community or the plant neighbors may have developed strong feelings about the conditions and about the seeming lack of action by the industry. In these instances, it is important to obtain a more cooperative attitude on the part of the public by developing an understanding of the problem and of the industry's efforts to control emissions.

When a single plant causes a well-defined air pollution problem the needs for public information and education are quite specific. They are to keep the public informed of the plant's efforts to correct the difficulties and report progress being made. If no efforts are being made by the plant to correct an obvious problem, any information and education program will be unsuccessful in obtaining cooperation from the public.

The atmospheric pollutants from industry are only a part of the air pollution problem in large metropolitan areas. The exact contribution of the industrial sources is not always understood and the public may believe that industry is responsible for more of the problem than actually is the case. Here information and education activities of the industry will have to be more extensive. It will be necessary, in addition to providing information on the steps industry has taken to control its pollutants, to explain the many elements in the air pollution problem and to present data on the emission from the industry as compared to the total for the community.

II.   Methods of Public Information and Education—Reaching the Public

It must be recognized that there really is not such a thing as a public— a single group of people with common interests and objectives. Rather, the people who determine public opinion comprise a great diversity of individuals, groups, and community forces.

There are, then, many "publics" with different roles, different postures in the community. There is no one way to reach them, and no one method to elicit a common response. Public information and education cannot, therefore, be done in a casual manner. The program must be well thought out and designed to fit the different objectives and different groups. More must be done than writing news releases, some of which may not even be used by the press. Instead there must be an analysis of interests and forces in the community with a view to finding available channels for reaching the various groups.

Three methods are usually followed in developing a community understanding: mass media, work with community groups, and person-to-person contact.

A. MASS MEDIA APPROACH

Mass media include newspapers, radio, television, pamphlets, reports, exhibits, newsletters, posters, and films. When large numbers of people must be reached, and speed is essential, mass media are most commonly employed.

1. *Radio, Television, and Newspapers*

Basic information on the air pollution problem and all activities dealing with its solution should be prepared and distributed to the press, radio, and television as source material to which they can refer for stories and features. Press releases can be used to provide news and to make known developments of current interest. Speakers, panels, and films can be made available to radio and television stations as appropriate. Spot and feature news are also of interest to radio and television stations but it must be recognized that news channels will use information when it is newsworthy and not just to please the individual, the industry, or the air pollution agency. Therefore, some thought should be given to preparing material which is of public interest and which is stated in a clear and understandable manner. Because air pollution episodes are news the media will give coverage to these even without effort on the part of the local agency. But one should be prepared to meet the increased interest when episodes occur. News coverage at these times can be used to advantage if the press, radio, and television are furnished material which will educate the public on the cause and nature of air pollution and what is being done to correct the problem.

In many instances local newspapers have prepared a series of articles on the subject. This in-depth reporting, which is becoming more common, provides the readers with a look at the whole problem. This approach can be encouraged by furnishing information for the articles to the newspapers.

The Air Pollution Control Association prepared a Public Relations Handbook (6) which presents information on public relations and suggests methods of working with news channels and preparing news releases. The association also provides educational material as a part of

Cleaner Air Week; this material includes posters, bulletins, suggested news releases, and speeches which can be used in drawing attention to air pollution as a part of a nationwide effort. Air pollution control agencies and industries without public relations and education staff can make good use of the prepared material.

Anyone engaged in public information and education should become acquainted with the editors of the local papers and with program directors of radio and television stations before a need for their help arises. By acquainting these people with the steps being taken to control air pollution, and with the objectives and problems involved, one can expect more intelligent cooperation on a year-round basis and at periods of urgent problems.

2. *Other Mass Media*

Leaflets can be used as envelope "stuffers" with gas, electric, and water bills and payroll envelopes. While this method would not be suitable for getting material into the hands of the public at regular intervals, it is an effective means of quickly distributing a single item to a large number of people. The use of leaflets should be considered when a specific action is required of many individuals by a given date. New York City once used this approach to reach fuel dealers. Leaflets could also be used to transmit information on items such as backyard incinerators and the control of motor vehicle emissions. The material presented must be very clear and confined to a few items. Too much information or complex instructions will only cause confusion and misunderstanding.

Newsletters and bulletins are useful in informing groups of people who may have a special interest in air pollution. While these do not normally reach as many people as do newspapers, radio, and television, they can give more detailed information on the subjects covered and they can be better tailored to a specific level of interest. When suitable, they can also be used to provide source material for the local press, radio, and television.

Some of the larger air pollution agencies have made good use of this approach. Examples include the states of California, New York, and Pennsylvania, New York City, and Los Angeles County. The publications of these organizations attempt to report information of particular interest to readers in their jurisdiction. Perhaps the most comprehensive effort to get information into the hands of the public was that of the Los Angeles County Air Pollution Control District, when several years ago it maintained nearly 200 racks in public buildings, transportation terminals, and other locations in the county for distributing pamphlets (7).

Motion pictures and visual aids are an effective means of presenting information to meetings of organizations, civic and community groups, and schools. Well-prepared films can give these groups a good description of the air pollution problem in a short time and can stimulate questions from the audience. Films have been used by a number of industries to present information on what they have done to control air pollution and to educate the public on the causes of air pollution. For example, the National Coal Association has a film on combustion; the Kaiser Steel Corporation has one on the sources of air pollution and the corporation's program to control the emissions from its plant. Unfortunately the high costs of producing good motion pictures makes them prohibitive for most control agencies and small industries. Control agencies with adequate budgets should consider the production of films of their own; smaller agencies can often borrow motion pictures. Small industries may be able to make use of films produced by trade associations in which they have membership.

Exhibits are well known as a means of disseminating information at public gatherings such as fairs, technical conferences, and meetings of organizations. Exhibits should be eye-catching and present only one or, at most, a few ideas. Their main value is in attracting visitors long enough to stop, ask questions, and take more detailed reports or pamphlets. To be most effective, then, the exhibits must be staffed and must have some materials for distribution to visitors.

B. Organizations and Key Individuals in the Community

While mass media are useful in informing the many individuals and groups in the community, they have great limitations if the objective is obtaining the cooperation and support of civic organizations and community leaders. Working with groups and individuals is a direct and personal matter. It can provide opportunities for involving citizens in the work of the control agency. It can create an environment for changing opinions and actions. The personal contact with organization members permits more than merely reporting information, as is largely the case when mass media are used. Questions can be answered and data explained. These contacts are one of the best ways to develop support and assistance because the "thought-leaders" in the community are often also members of the community's more important clubs, organizations, and civic groups.

Industries which have problems and are trying to do something about them benefit from these contacts. It will be possible to explain the steps that have been taken to control emissions, the difficulties that are faced, and plans for solving problems that still exist. The "thought-leaders" and civic organizations can be invited to visit the plant and observe the air pollution abatement efforts of the company.

1. *Scientific and Professional Groups*

Scientific and professional groups play a key role in the community's air pollution problem. As a result of their education and the nature of their work, members of medical, engineering, chemical, and meteorological societies usually have a special interest in air pollution. They are also better able to understand the technical difficulties in eliminating air pollution and the reasons for rules and regulations. Because air pollution is a technical subject, the other segments of the public and legislative bodies look to the scientists and professional people for advice and guidance. These individuals, therefore, can have an important role in interpreting the problem to the public. Physicians, for example, are the key individuals interpreting possible health effects to their patients and to the public.

One way of reaching professional groups is at their conferences and technical meetings. Speakers for local society meetings can be volunteered. Another effective way to reach these organizations is to appoint their representatives to advisory committees on air pollution. Still another way is to organize meetings specifically directed at one or more of the professional interests. For example, the California State Department of Public Health held a series of annual conferences in which research findings on the health effects of air pollution were presented to the medical profession and other interested individuals. One of the reasons this was done was because of the concern that existed in the state on the possible health effects from air pollution.

The type of information presented to the scientific and technical organizations will be very different from that presented to most other groups in the community. It is possible to give detailed data on the technical portions of the air pollution program to these organizations.

2. *Trade and Industrial Associations*

The control of air pollution almost always will affect industrial and commercial establishments in the community. When this is the case, trade and industrial associations can be used to inform their members of the requirements for control of pollutants. They can also be directly involved in the work of the air pollution control agency in a number of ways. Representatives of these groups can be used on committees to assist in developing the control program and in drafting regulations. The need for the specific controls required of industry can be learned at close hand in this way and the associations can then encourage the cooperation of their members in the control program.

The implementation of some regulations and laws depends upon the activities of dealers and service organizations. Fuel dealers, automobile sales agencies, garages, and service stations are some examples. Public attitudes about cars and about the effect of emission control systems on cars are strongly influenced by what the service station attendants and garage mechanics tell the public. Any public information and education program on motor vehicle emission control devices, therefore, should make special efforts to reach the groups engaged in servicing and repairing automobiles.

3. *Community and Civic Groups and Community Leaders*

Community and civic groups, service clubs, and voluntary organizations play an important role in the government of the community and in the programs that are established to solve the community's problems. Community leaders, therefore, are usually active in these groups.

The air pollution story can be brought to these organizations by means of speakers, films, and reports. Such groups should be placed on the mailing lists for publications and reports. This will help to interest them and will stimulate requests for further information and speakers to discuss air pollution problems and control measures.

Individual face-to-face communication, although the most effective means of education, must by necessity be limited to a relatively small number of people. This direct contact with key individuals will, however, achieve much broader benefits because the judgment of these individuals is respected and influences the attitude of other segments of the public which do not have the opportunity for face-to-face communication.

4. *Schools*

Everyone concerned with public education and information soon thinks about the possibility of working with the schools in some manner. This is a logical conclusion because the purpose of schools is to educate. The atmosphere of the school provides the most effective means of transmitting information to a group that will retain the information. The teachers know how best to present the information. The children usually have not yet formulated strong views that have to be changed, and often take the information home to the rest of the family.

Although schools are one of the best means of education, it is not easy to make effective use of them. School administrators are continuously

being requested by organizations outside the schools to provide information on many, many subjects in addition to the usual courses. The school,
however, is limited in the subject matter it can include in its courses.

If the contact with the school is to be successful, one must be prepared
to give the school educational material of high quality which will be valuable to the students. It is most helpful to furnish the school with
material that the students can use to further their education or which
stimulates them into independent studies or work. With this thought in
mind the California Department of Public Health developed a series of
science experiments for use in high schools and junior high schools (8).
Each experiment was designed to demonstrate some phase of air pollution, but at the same time made use of the knowledge the students
acquired in science courses. The experiments were also selected so that
the equipment required would be available in most of the high schools.
One of the important steps in the preparation of the experiments was
their pre-testing by high school teachers and students. Prior to preparation of the booklet, the department staff worked with a committee of
science teachers on the need for the publication, kinds of experiments,
and their use in schools.

This example is cited to show how school people can be brought into
the planning and preparation of material to be used in the classroom
and that it is important to work closely with the school curriculum
people. The involvement of school people was valuable beyond the publication being prepared because it also developed their interest in the
subject of air pollution.

Large schools are often in a position to prepare their own teaching
materials for use in the classroom. As an example, the Los Angeles
County school system prepared several training films on air pollution
for use in its schools. A person skilled in public education from the State
Department of Public Health was useful in providing needed information to the school system.

The interest of schools in education on air pollution is indicated by a
joint conference of the National Science Teachers Association and the
National Center for Air Pollution Control in 1961. One recommendation of this conference was that "in view of its (air pollution) many new
and challenging aspects, it should be dealt with in the science curriculum
of secondary schools" (9). It was further recommended that air pollution not be a separate unit, but be included in those areas of the secondary science curriculum where it logically fits. Carr (9) in suggestions
for teaching about air pollution has prepared a list of activities designed
to help science teachers begin a study of air pollution in regular science
courses.

III. Information and Education Resources

A. EXTENT OF RESOURCES AND EFFORT

The need for information and education seems to be well recognized. It has been discussed at most of the recent annual meetings of the Air Pollution Control Association as well as at the National Conferences on Air Pollution. Control agencies proposing to adopt new regulations covering the discharge of pollutants and companies with contaminant emission problems know that it will be important to have those affected understand what is being done and why.

In view of the apparent appreciation of the need, it is surprising that so few of the control agencies have staff members who are by education and experience skilled in information and education. Williams (10) reported in 1965 that only four full-time personnel were assigned to information and education activities at the state level of government, and that only five such specialists were to be found in 88 full-time local air pollution control agencies in the United States.

Large companies and industrial associations have staff members who are skilled in public relations; they also have resources for preparing most of the materials that would be used for such activities. The small companies, however, are faced with the same difficulties as are the small air pollution control agencies—lack of skilled staff and the resources to develop educational materials.

Because of budget limitations, the control officer or company president must decide between staff needs to meet pressing technical problems, and information and education needs that often do not appear to be so immediate. It may be that, too frequently, staffing requirements are determined solely by the technical problems to be solved. Perhaps it is unrealistic to expect the small plant or the control agency in the small community to have a full-time specialist on public information and education. Some provision, however, should be made to include such skills in their staffs. These activities could be a part-time assignment for a person who has acquired skills in this area, or the control officer or a company official can be the person. In any event, the importance of public education and information should be recognized and staff time devoted to filling the needs in this area. Advice and assistance on programs to be followed and how to deal with specific problems can be obtained from outside consultants. In some control agencies, particularly those associated with health departments, public information and education resources may be available on a part-time basis although it is not often sufficient to meet the needs. These resources could be used to develop skills in the staff of the control agency.

B. FACILITIES AND MATERIALS

Facilities and materials for a public information program will vary depending on need and resources. All control agencies and major dischargers of contaminants should, however, have informational material describing their control program, its purposes, and accomplishments. These should be available for distribution to the news media and to interested persons in the community. Pamphlets, films, and exhibits will also prove useful. In many cases the agency or company may not be able to prepare its own films and pamphlets. Photographs, color slides, film strips, and informational bulletins are, however, within the capabilities of almost every organization.

IV. Limitations and Expectations of Public Information and Education

The information reaching the people within the community comes from many sources; some of it is provided by the control agency, some is provided by industry, but more will probably come from other sources. The individual reaches his final opinion or conclusion from what he has seen, heard, and read. Public attitude is often passive and unreceptive to information not consistent with existing concepts; so the attitudes of a large group of people are not quickly or easily changed. The public may be vitally concerned about air pollution at the time of a severe attack, and then have very little interest once these episodes have ended. The role and efforts of those attempting to educate the public are limited to making information available in a variety of ways.

In view of these limitations to developing constructive attitudes, what should be reasonable objectives in public education and information? It is clear that one cannot expect immediate and complete support of all aspects of the control effort. One should do everything possible to further the understanding by the many groups, individuals, and community forces of the air pollution problem and what is being done about it. To accomplish this the initiative must be taken to maintain everyday good relationships with the community. It will be well to pinpoint the groups and places where the greatest benefits are to be expected.

The goal of public information and education should be to give the facts to the public so the various groups can reach their own conclusions. It is unreasonable to promote, or seek support for, a poor control program or a policy not to place control equipment on an obvious source, or to divert attention from unpleasant facts. The community will evaluate the information it receives in terms of how it perceives the air pollution problem and the efforts being made to bring about a solution. The information released is far more likely to be favorably received if the public knows that the efforts are directed to solving the problem rather than to making alibis. A sound program to bring about a solution, therefore, is the first and most important need if good public understanding and support is to be achieved.

REFERENCES

1. Y. Lyon, "Our Threatened Air Supply." National Audubon Society, New York, 1962.
2. Air Conservation Commission, *in* "Air Conservation," Publ. No. 80, p. 6. Am. Assoc. Advance. Sci., Washington, D.C., 1965.
3. Public Health Service, "National Conference on Air Pollution Proceedings," Public Health Serv. Publ. U.S. Dept. of Health, Education, and Welfare, Washington, D.C., 1022, 1963 and 1669, 1967.
4. Public Health Service, "Public Awareness and Concern with Air Pollution in the St. Louis Metropolitan Area." U.S. Dept. of Health, Education, and Welfare, Washington, D.C., 1965.
5. N. Z. Medalia and A. L. Finkner, "Community Perception of Air Quality: An Opinion Survey in Clarkston, Washington." *U.S., Public Health Serv., Pub.* 999-AP-10 (1965).
6. "APCA Public Relations Handbook." Air Pollution Control Assoc., Pittsburgh, Pennsylvania, 1959.
7. A. A. Atkisson, C. DeKoven, and R. M. Barsky, *Proc. 51st Ann. Meeting Air Pollution Control Assoc., Philadelphia, 1958* Paper No. PP 36, 1–10.
8. G. J. Taylor, M. W. Miller, and Y. Lyon, "Experiments for the Science Classroom." Calif. State Dept. of Public Health, Berkeley, California, 1962.
9. A. B. Carr, *School Sci. Math.* **64,** 229 (1964).
10. T. F. Williams, "Air Pollution and the Public Conscience." Public Health Serv., U.S. Dept. of Health, Education, and Welfare, Washington, D.C., 1965.

54 Air Pollution Literature Resources

John S. Nader

For the reader who cannot find what he seeks in the preceding chapters or their appended references, the following search procedure is offered.

I. Books

Your first resource is to the more important books published in English within the last decade on the general subject of air pollution (*1–7*). Their chapter contents are specific to individual topics, and literature references to published papers are provided.

Next, resource should be had to the group of published proceedings of the several more important, recent, all-embracing air pollution conferences, symposia, and international meetings (*8–23*). It should be noted that the Air Pollution Control Association and its predecessor, the Smoke Prevention Association, for many years published mimeographed proceedings of the papers presented at their annual meetings. These are difficult to obtain, but where available are an excellent resource. Use should also be made of the manuals (*24–28*) on air pollution abatement, control, sampling, and analytical measurement methods.

Next, there are a group of books devoted in their entirety to limited aspects of air pollution but nevertheless comprehensive in the subject matter covered. This applies to subjects such as aerosols, instrumentation, analytical methods, visibility, photochemistry, control, diffusion, etc. (*29–56*).

Then, there are a number of recent popular books (*57–60*) on air pollution that offer good information in a readable style and include references to the technical literature.

Finally, of particular interest are the growing number of volumes of foreign air pollution literature translated into English (*61–66*).

II.   Periodical Literature

The bulk of the English language air pollution technical papers have been published in the following journals (or their predecessor journals): *American Industrial Hygiene Association Journal; Analytical Chemistry; Annuals of Occupational Hygiene; Archives of Environmental Health; Atmospheric Environment; British Journal of Industrial Medicine; Environmental Science and Technology; International Journal of Air Pollution; Journal of Air Pollution Control Association; Journal of Applied Meteorology; Journal of Applied Physiology; Journal of Atmospheric Sciences; Journal of Institute of Fuel; Journal of Occupational Medicine; Journal of Royal Meteorological Society; Occupational Health Review; Proceedings of Royal Society of Medicine; and Public Health Reports.* Cumulative indices have been published for many of these journals.

Because, in addition to these journals, air pollution papers are published in over eight hundred other English and foreign language periodicals (*67, 68*), it is preferable to search the periodical literature through abstract and bibliographic services having wide periodical coverage rather than to start with indices of any of the above-noted journals.

III.   Specialized Bibliographies and Abstracts

The Technical Information Division of the Library of Congress has compiled a two-volume annotated bibliography of published literature on air pollution from 1952 through 1958. Abstracts present test data and experimental results, describe new procedures and equipment, and review legal, economic, and medical development in this field. Volume I (*69*) carries through 1956 and Volume II (*70*) makes the abstract list current through 1958. In January, 1959, the Library of Congress abstracts were merged with Air Pollution Control Association abstracts (*71*) which had started in 1954. The joint venture retained the name *APCA Abstracts* and continues to publish monthly abstracts on air pollution. Some of its monthly issues present summary subject (*72*), and author (*73*) indices which currently serve to supplement Volumes I and II of the Library of Congress bibliography. Prior to the advent of APCA and Library of Congress abstracts, the principal American specialized abstracting service most completely covering air pollution literature was that of the *Journal of Industrial Hygiene and Toxicology* and its successor journals.

The literature up to 1955 has been summarized by Murk (*74*) in an excellent bibliography of bibliographies on air pollution, which includes an annotated bibliography prepared by the author. Additional bibliographies have appeared in the literature (*75–78*), which review quite well the early and intermediate intervals in the history of air pollution studies. More recent revised bibliographies have also appeared (*79–81*). Wilkins (*82*) has compiled selected bibliographies based on published abstracts. The MCA manual (*24*) included an excellent bibliography, as originally published in 1951, and has subsequently included three supplemental bibliographies, added in 1952, 1953, and 1955, respectively. *Industrial and Engineering Chemistry* has had several reviews of applied analyses in air pollution (*83*). *Analytical Chemistry* (*84*) began its reviews in air pollution in 1957 and continues these every other year (*85, 86*). A number of bibliographies (*87–97*) deal with specific areas of interest such as chemical detectors, motor vehicle emissions, particle size analysis, sulfur compounds, ozone, incineration, etc.

A new aid for research personnel is an air pollution research index (*98*) which provides an author index and a bibliographic section for approximately 500 research projects in the United States and abroad. The Pennsylvania State Center for Air Environment Studies also publishes a bimonthly guide to current air pollution literature (*99*). This is known as "Air Pollution Titles" and uses a method of referencing called the Keyword-in-Context (KWIC).

A public technical information center on air pollution was organized in the six-county Bay Area Air Pollution Control District in San Francisco, California. This technical library was originally compiled under the Uniterm coordinate indexing system by Stanford Research Institute. Published and unpublished articles, symposia, and technical conference material on microfilm, plus some original sources, are included in this library's collection. Duplicate files of the Bay Area's Uniterm system have been maintained in the libraries of the National Center for Urban and Industrial Health, Cincinnati, Ohio, the New York State Air Pollution Control Board, Albany, New York; the Air Pollution Technical Information Center, Washington, D.C.; West Virginia University, Morgantown, W. Virginia; The Pennsylvania State University, University Park, Pennsylvania; Division of Air Pollution, Commonwealth of Pennsylvania, Harrisburg, Pennsylvania; University of Southern California, Los Angeles, California; Northern Illinois University, DeKalb, Illinois; University of Western Ontario, London, Ontario; Edgewood Arsenal, Edgewood, Maryland; Air Pollution Control Division, Ontario

Department of Health, Toronto, Ontario; and Bureau of Air Pollution Control, Detroit, Michigan.

The Air Pollution Technical Information Center (APTIC) has been developed by the Office of Technical Information and Publications of the National Air Pollution Control Administration, U.S.D.H.E.W. and has the responsibility for the bibliographic control and the dissemination of the world's technical literature on air pollution, and the establishment of an evaluation center where such information will be assimilated, digested, and reviewed. Its services are available to the public, the scientific community, industry, and officials of other government agencies.

Its program on literature sources includes: screening of 4300 scientific journals and in-house sources such as abstracts by Defense Documentation Center (DDC), by Clearinghouse for Federal Scientific and Technical Information (CFSTI); and report literature or bulletins from National Aeronautics and Space Administration, Engineering Index, American Petroleum Institute, National Library of Medicine, and Science Information Exchange. APTIC (100) will respond to demand requests for technical information by providing citations, abstracts, or extracts.

Cover-to-cover translations of the Russian journal *Gigiena i Sanitariya* and of the German journal *Staub* are available through CFSTI, Springfield, Virginia.

There is active air pollution documentation in a number of foreign countries including Australia, Belgium, France, Germany, Hungary, Japan, The Netherlands, Philippines, Poland, Rumania, Sweden, Switzerland, South Africa, United Kingdom, and the U.S.S.R. The Organization for Economic Co-Operation and Development (OECD) publishes a Guide to European Sources of Technical Information (101) in which information on air pollution activities and literature sources is given for member countries. The United Nations Educational, Scientific and Cultural Organization (UNESCO) publishes a world guide to science information and documentation services (102). The World Health Organization (WHO) with headquarters in Geneva, Switzerland provides an International Documents Service through Columbia University Press in New York City.

Abstracts of air pollution literature have been published in Great Britain (103) on a routine basis since 1932. Other publications having abstracts and an air pollution section are: *Smokeless Air* (The National Society for Clean Air); *Fuel Abstracts* (The Institute of Fuel); and *CEGB Digest* (Central Electricity Generating Board).

In Germany, the journal *Staub* publishes a "Review of Air Pollution"

(*104*) in which is covered an extensive list of journals published in foreign languages. All the papers listed in the "Review" can be referred to as index cards in the International Library of the Documentation Office of the Society of German Engineers, Dusseldorf, Germany.

In France, the *Technological Digest* is published by the Organization for Economic Cooperation and Development and *Pollution Atmospherique* is a publication devoted exclusively to the air pollution problem and is a journal outlet for the activities of a number of technical organizations dealing with various approaches to the prevention of pollution of the atmosphere. The Centre Interprofessional Technique d'Etudes de la Pollution Atmospherique (CITEPA), Paris, publishes a quarterly bibliography with abstracts.

IV. General Bibliographies and Abstracts

In addition to the literature sources specific to air pollution, there are a number of general bibliographies and abstracting sources (*105–121*) which include air pollution in their list of subtopics.

V. Newsletters

A number of air pollution newsletters are being published as a means of quickly disseminating information on new developments in the field of air pollution (*122–132*). Some of these newsletters have coverage combined with developments in water pollution. These vary as to publication rates from biweekly to bimonthly. Publication sources include state and local air pollution control agencies, universities, and private companies. Some trade associations also publish newsletters (*133–137*).*

REFERENCES

Books: General

1. P. L. Magill, F. R. Holden, and C. Ackley, eds., "Air Pollution Handbook." McGraw-Hill, New York, 1956.
2. M. W. Thring, "Air Pollution." Butterworth, London and Washington, D.C., 1957.
3. W. L. Faith, "Air Pollution Control." Wiley, New York, 1959.
4. "American Industrial Hygiene Association Air Pollution Manual." Am. Ind. Hyg. Assoc., Detroit, Michigan, Vol. I, 1960; Vol. II, 1968.
5. World Health Organization, "Air Pollution." Columbia Univ. Press, New York, 1961.
6. S. M. Farber and R. H. L. Wilson, eds. (in collaboration with J. R. Goldsmith and N.

---

* English language listings only.

Pace), "The Air We Breathe; A Study of Man and His Environment." Thomas, Springfield, Illinois, 1961.

7. A. R. Meetham, "Atmospheric Pollution, Its Origin and Prevention," 3rd rev. ed. Pergamon Press, Oxford, 1964.

Proceedings: Conferences, Symposia, International Meetings

8. *Proc. 1st Natl. Air Pollution Symp., Pasadena, Calif., 1949; 2nd (1952); 3rd (1955)*. Sponsored by Stanford Research Institute in cooperation with California Institute of Technology, University of California, and University of Southern California.

9. *Air Pollution Proc. U.S. Tech. Conf. Air Pollution, 1950* McGraw-Hill, New York, 1952.

10. *Probl. Control Air-Pollution, Proc. 1st Intern. Congr. Air Pollution, New York, 1955* Reinhold, New York, 1955.

11. *Proc. Natl. Conf. Air Pollution, Washington, D.C., 1958* U.S. Public Health Serv., Washington, D.C., Publ. **654** (1959).

12. *Conf. Public Health Aspects Air Pollution Europe, Milan, Italy, 1957* Report, *Chronicle World Health Organ.* **12**, No. 1, 14–16 (1958).

13. *Proc. Intern. Clean Air Conf., London, 1959* Natl. Soc. Clean Air, London, 1960.

14. "Air Monitoring and Sampling Networks; Proceedings of the 1959 Seminar." U.S. Public Health Serv., Cincinnati, Ohio; *Robert A. Taft Sanitary Eng. Center, Tech. Rept.* **A60-3** (1960).

15. "Pollution and Environmental Health," Symp. Ser. 57 (35). Am. Inst. Chem. Engrs., New York, 1961.

16. *Proc. Intern. Symp., England, 1960, Inhaled Particles and Vapors*, Pergamon Press, Oxford, 1961.

17. "Air Pollution Measurement Methods Symposium," Tech. Publ. No. 352. Am. Soc. Testing Mater., Philadelphia, Pennsylvania, 1962.

18. "Symposium—Air Over Cities." U.S. Public Health Serv., Cincinnati, Ohio, 1961; *Robert A. Taft Sanitary Eng. Center, Tech. Rept.* **A62-5** (1962).

19. "Symposium. Analysis of Carcinogenic Air Pollutants, Cincinnati, 1961" (E. Sawicki and K. Cassel, Jr., eds.), Natl. Cancer Inst. Monograph No. 9. U.S. Public Health Serv., Cincinnati, Ohio, 1962.

20. *Proc. Natl. Conf. Air Pollution, Washington, D.C., 1962* U.S. Public Health Serv., Washington, D.C., Publ. **1022** (1963).

21. *Proc. Symp. Environ. Meas., Cincinnati, 1963* U.S. Public Health Serv., Cincinnati, Ohio, 1964; *U.S., Public Health Serv., Publ.* **999-AP-15** (1964).

22. *Proc. 1st Natl. Conf. Aerosols, Liblice near Prague, 1962* Czech. Acad. Sci., Prague, 1965.

23. *Proc. Intern. Clean Air Conf., London, 1966* Natl. Soc. Clean Air, London, 1966.

23a. *Proc. Natl. Conf. Air Pollution, Washington, D.C. 1966* U.S. Public Health Serv. Washington, D.C. Publ. 1669 (1967).

Manuals

24. Manufacturing Chemists' Association, "Air Pollution Abatement Manual" (C. A. Gosline, ed.), Washington, D.C., 1951.

25. "Air Pollution Control Field Operations Manual" (A Guide for Inspection and Enforcement) (compiled and edited by M. I. Weisburd). U.S. Public Health Serv., Washington, D.C., 1962; *U.S., Public Health Serv., Publ.* **937** (1962).

26. "ASTM Standards on Methods of Atmospheric Sampling and Analysis," 2nd ed. Am. Soc. Testing Mater., Philadelphia, Pennsylvania, 1962.

27. Air Pollution Control Assoc., "Technical Manual No. 1." Pittsburgh, Pennsylvania, 1963.

28. "Selected Methods for Measurements of Air Pollutants." U.S. Public Health Serv., Cincinnati, Ohio, 1965; *U.S., Public Health Serv., Publ.* **999-AP-11** (1965).

Books: Limited Aspects

29. U.S. Office of Scientific Research and Development, National Defense Research Committee, "Handbook on Aerosols." U.S. Govt. Printing Office, Washington, D.C., 1950.
30. W. E. K. Middleton, "Vision Through the Atmosphere." Univ. of Toronto Press, Toronto, 1952.
31. C. D. Yaffe, D. H. Byers, and A. D. Hosey, eds., "Encyclopedia of Instrumentation for Industrial Hygiene." Univ. of Michigan Press, Ann Arbor, Michigan, 1956.
32. H. C. Van de Hulst, "Light Scattering by Small Particles." Wiley, New York, 1957.
33. C. Orr, Jr. and J. M. DallaValle, "Fine Particle Measurement. Size, Surface, and Pore Volume." Macmillan, New York, 1959.
34. M. B. Jacobs, "The Chemical Analysis of Air Pollutants." Wiley (Interscience), New York, 1960.
35. American Conference of Governmental Industrial Hygienists, Committee on Air Sampling Instruments, "Air Sampling Instruments for Evaluation of Atmospheric Contaminants." 3rd rev. ed., Cincinnati, Ohio, 1967.
36. "Symposium on Air Pollution Control," Tech. Publ. No. 281. Am. Soc. Testing Mater., Philadelphia, Pennsylvania, 1960.
37. W. D. Bamford, "Control of Airborne Dust." British Cast Iron Res. Assoc., Birmingham, England, 1961.
38. P. A. Leighton, "Photochemistry of Air Pollution." Academic Press, New York, 1961.
39. A. Bell and J. L. Sullivan, "Air Pollution by Metallurgical Industries." N.S.W. Dept. of Public Health, Sydney, Australia, 1962.
40. P. A. Kratzer, F. Vieweg, and S. Braunschweig, "The Climate of Cities," Rept. No. AFCRL-62-837. Air Force Cambridge Res. Lab., Bedford, Massachusetts, 1962.
41. F. Pasquill, "Atmospheric Diffusion." Van Nostrand, Princeton, New Jersey, 1962.
42. A. Gilpin, "Control of Air Pollution." Butterworth, London and Washington, D.C., 1963.
43. R. R. Irani and C. F. Callis, "Particle Size. Measurement, Interpretation, and Application." Wiley, New York, 1963.
44. C. E. Junge, "Air Chemistry and Radioactivity." Academic Press, New York, 1963.
45. H. J. White, "Industrial Electrostatic Precipitation." Addison-Wesley, Reading, Massachusetts, 1963.
46. "The Implications of Air Pollution Control," Vol. I. South African Council for Scientific and Industrial Research, Durban, 1964.
47. C. N. Davies, "Recent Advances in Aerosol Research," A Bibliographical Review. Pergamon Press, Oxford, 1964.
48. H. L. Green and W. R. Lane, "Particulate Clouds. Dusts, Smokes, and Mists," 2nd ed. Van Nostrand, Princeton, New Jersey, 1964.
49. "Air Conservation," Publ. No. 80. Am. Assoc. Advance. Sci., Washington, D.C., 1965.
50. D. F. Adams, ed., "Air Pollution Instrumentation." Instr. Soc. Am., Pittsburgh, Pennsylvania, 1965.
51. R. D. Cadle, "Particle Size." Reinhold, New York, 1965.
52. R. N. Rickles, "Pollution Control." Noyes Develop. Corp., New York, 1965.
53. "Restoring the Quality of Our Environment," Report of the Environmental Pollu-

tion Panel, President's Science Advisory Committee. White House, Washington, D.C., 1965.

54. C. N. Davies, ed., "Aerosol Science." Academic Press, New York, 1966.

55. R. D. Cadle, "Particles in the Atmosphere and Space." Reinhold, New York, 1966.

56. H. Wolozin, ed., "The Economics of Air Pollution." Norton, New York, 1966.

56a. R. G. Ridker, "Economic Costs of Air Pollution." F. A. Praeger, New York, 1967.

56b. M. I. Goldman, ed., "Controlling Pollution—The Economics of a Cleaner America." Prentice-Hall, Inc., Englewood Cliffs, N.J. 1967.

Books: Popular

57. C. A. Mills, "This Air We Breathe." Christopher Publ. House, Boston, Massachusetts, 1962.

58. D. E. Carr, "The Breath of Life." Norton, New York, 1965.

59. H. R. Lewis, "With Every Breath You Take." Crown Publ., New York, 1965.

60. L. J. Battan, "The Unclean Sky." Doubleday, Garden City, New York, 1966.

60a. E. Edelson and F. Warshofsky, "Poisons in the Air." Pocket Books, Inc., New York, 1966.

60b. J. Bregman and S. Lenormand, "The Pollution Paradox." Books, Inc. New York, 1966.

60c. A. Lewis, "Clean the Air!" McGraw-Hill Book Co., New York, 1965.

60d. L. Herber, "Crisis in Our Cities." Prentice-Hall, Inc. Englewood Cliffs, N.J., 1965.

Translations of Foreign Books

61. V. N. Uzhov, "Sanitary Protection of Atmospheric Air. Purification of Industrial Discharge Gases From Suspended Substances," Medgiz (State Publisher of Medical Literature), Moscow, 1959. Translation by B. S. Levine, U.S. Dept. of Commerce, Clearinghouse for Federal Sci. and Tech. Inform. U.S. Dept. of Commerce, Springfield, Virginia. Doc. 59-21092, Washington, D.C., 1959.

62. V. A. Ryazanov, ed., "Limits of Allowable Concentrations of Atmospheric Pollutants" (transl. by B. S. Levine), Book 1, Clearinghouse for Federal Sci. and Tech. Inform. U.S. Dept. of Commerce, Springfield, Virginia. Doc. 59-21173. U.S. Dept. of Commerce, Washington, D.C., 1952; Book 2, Doc. 59-21174 (1955); Book 3, Doc. 59-21175 (1957); Book 4, Doc. 61-11148 (1960); Book 5, Doc. 62-11605 (1962).

63. "U.S.S.R. Literature on Air Pollution and Related Occupational Diseases" (transl. by B. S. Levine), Vols. 1–12. Clearinghouse for Federal Sci. and Tech. Inform., U.S. Dept. of Commerce, Springfield, Virginia. [Vol. 1, TT-60-21049 (1960); Vol. 2, TT-60-21188 (1960); Vol. 3, TT-60-21475 (1960); Vol. 4, TT-60-21913 (1960); Vol. 5, TT-61-11149 (1961); Vol. 6, TT-61-21982 (1961); Vol. 7, TT-62-11103 (1962); Vol. 8, TT-63-11570 (1963); Vol. 9, TT-64-11574 (1964); Vol. 10, TT-64-11767 (1964); Vol. 11, TT-65-61965 (1965); Vol. 12, TT-66-61429 (1966); Vol. 13, TT-66-62191 (1966); Vol. 14, TT-67-60046 (1967).

64. J. Juda and K. Budzinski, "Atmospheric Pollution." Warsaw, Poland, 1961. (Translation available from U.S. Dept. of Commerce, Clearinghouse for Federal Sci. and Tech. Inform. U.S. Dept. of Commerce, Springfield, Virginia. Doc. 63-21460. Washington, D.C., 1963.

65. N. A. Fuchs, *in* "The Mechanics of Aerosols" (C. N. Davies, ed.) (transl. by R. E. Daisley and M. Fuchs). Pergamon Press, New York, 1964.

66. E. P. Mednikov, "Acoustic Coagulation and Precipitation of Aerosols" (transl. by C. V. Larrick). Consultants Bureau, New York, 1965.

Specialized Bibliographies and Abstracts

67. *Air Pollution Control Assoc. Abstr.* **13** (4), 17–22 (1967) (Journal Index Issue).
68. *Staub* **24**(12), 1–22 (1964).
69. J. R. Gibson, W. E. Culver, and M. E. Kurz, "The Air Pollution Bibliography," Vol. I. Library of Congress, Washington, D.C., 1957.
70. A. J. Jacobius, J. R. Gibson, V. S. Wright, W. E. Culver, and L. Kassianoff, "The Air Pollution Bibliography," Vol. II. Library of Congress, Washington, D.C., 1959.
71. *Air Pollution Control Assoc. Abstr.* Air Pollution Control Association, Pittsburgh, Pennsylvania.
72. *Air Pollution Control Assoc. Abstr.* **14** (2), 15–46 (1968). (Subject Index Issue).
73. *Air Pollution Control Assoc. Abstr.* **13** (3), 11–15 (1967). (Author Index Issue).
74. J. B. Murk, *Ind. Eng. Chem.* **47**, 976 (1955).
75. S. J. Davenport and G. G. Morgis, "Air Pollution, A Bibliography." U.S. Govt. Printing Office, Washington, D.C., 1954; *U.S., Bur. Mines, Bull.* **537** (1954).
76. "Effects of Atmospheric Pollution on Health of Man," Kettering Lab. of Appl. Physiol., Univ. of Cincinnati, Cincinnati, Ohio, 1957.
77. U.S. Public Health Service, Industrial Hygiene Division, "Biological Aspects of Air Pollution; An Annotated Bibliography." Washington, D.C. (printed by United Steel Workers of America, CIO), 1950.
78. "Air Pollution—Bibliography." Am. Petrol. Inst., New York, 1960.
79. "Air Pollution and Purification-an OTS Selective Bibliography," SB-448 Rev. U.S. Dept. of Commerce, Office Tech. Serv., Washington, D.C., 1963.
80. A. G. Cooper, "Air Pollution Publications," A selected bibliography, 1955–63. U.S. Public Health Serv., Washington, D.C., 1964; *U.S., Public Health Serv., Publ.* **979** (rev. 1964).
81. A. G. Cooper, "Air Pollution Publications," A selected bibliography, 1963–66. U.S. Public Health Serv., Washington, D.C., 1966; *U.S., Public Health Serv., Publ.* **979** (1966).
82. E. T. Wilkins, *Intern. J. Air Water Pollution* **8,** 665–675 (1964); **9,** 135–142 (1965); **10,** 641–645 (1966).
83. K. Kingsley, *Ind. Eng. Chem.* **44**, 1383–1388 (1952); **50,** 1175–1180 (1958).
84. K. Kingsley, *Anal. Chem.* **29**, 589–604 (1957); **31**, 633–645 (1959).
85. J. P. Lodge, Jr., *Anal. Chem.* **33**, 3R-13R (1961).
86. A. P. Altshuller, *Anal. Chem.* **35**, 3R-10R (1963); **37**, 11R-20R (1965); **39,** 10R-21R (1967).
87. E. E. Campbell and H. M. Miller, "Chemical Detectors. A Bibliography for the Industrial Hygienist with Abstracts and Annotations," Vol. I, LAMS-2378. U.S. Dept. of Commerce, Clearinghouse for Federal Sci. and Tech. Inform. U.S. Dept. of Commerce, Springfield, Virginia. 1961; Vol. II, LAMS-2378 (1964).
88. "Motor Vehicle Emissions and Their Control" (annotated bibliography). Air Pollution Found., San Marino, California, 1960.
89. "Micrometeorology, Aerosols, and Air Pollution. Bibliography," AID Rept. B-63-50. Aerospace Inform. Div., Washington, D.C., 1963.
90. A. G. Cooper, "Sulfur Oxides and Other Sulfur Compounds. A Bibliography." U.S. Public Health Serv., Washington, D.C., 1965; *U.S., Public Health Serv., Publ.* **1093** (1965); "Carbon Monoxide," A bibliography with abstracts. U.S. Public Health Serv., Washington, D.C., 1966; *U.S., Public Health Serv., Publ.* **1503** (1966).
91. K. T. Whitby and A. R. McFarland, "Particle Size Analysis. Selected Bibliography, November, 1959." U.S. Public Health Serv., Washington, D.C., 1960.

92. APCA Incinerator Committee, TA-3, *J. Air Pollution Control Assoc.* **12,** 334–339 (1962).

93. P. A. Kenline and J. M. Hales, "Air Pollution and the Kraft Pulping Industry. An Annotated Bibliography." U.S. Public Health Serv., Cincinnati, Ohio, 1963; *U.S., Public Health Serv., Publ.* **999-AP-4** (1963).

94. A. A. Beltran, "Atmospheric Ozone. Its Detection, Measurement and Effects. 1940 to 1959." An annotated bibliography available as Clearinghouse for Federal Sci. and Tech. Inform. U.S. Dept. of Commerce, Springfield, Virginia. Publ. No. 153437. Lockheed Aircraft Corp., Sunnyvale, California, 1960.

95. "Ozone, OTS Selective Bibliography," SB-509 U.S. Dept. of Commerce, Clearinghouse for Federal Sci. and Tech. Inform. U.S. Dept. of Commerce, Springfield, Virginia. Washington, D.C., 1962.

96. W. Ruch, ed., "Chemical Detection of Gaseous Pollutants." Ann Arbor Sci. Publ., Ann Arbor, Michigan, 1966.

97. J. Forman, *Rev. Allergy Appl. Immunol.* **17,** 76–115 (1963).

98. "Index to Air Pollution Research." Center for Air Environment Studies, Pennsylvania State University, University Park, Pennsylvania, 1967.

99. "Air Pollution Titles." Center for Air Environment Studies, Pennsylvania State University, University Park, Pennsylvania, 1968.

100. Air Pollution Technical Information Center, Ballston Center Tower No. 2, 801 North Randolf Street, Arlington, Virginia, 22203.

101. "Guide to European Sources of Technical Information." Organization for Economic Co-Operation and Development, Paris, 1964.

102. "World Guide to Science Information and Documentation Services." United Nations Educational, Scientific and Cultural Organization, Place de Fontenoy, Paris, 1965.

103. Atmospheric Pollution Bulletin, Ministry of Technology, Warren Springs Laboratory, Gunnels Wood Rd., Stevenage, Hertfordshire, England.

104. *Staub,* VDI-Fachgruppe Staubtechnik; Kommission Reinhaltung der Luft, Dusseldorf, Germany.

General Bibliographies and Abstracts

105. "Abstracting and Indexing Services in Science and Technology." National Federation of Science Abstracting and Indexing Services, Washington, D.C., 1963.

106. "Applied Science and Technology Index." Wilson, New York.

107. *Battelle Technical Review,* Battelle Memorial Institute, Columbus, Ohio.

108. *Bibliography of Agriculture,* National Library of Agriculture, Washington, D.C.

109. *Chemical Abstracts,* American Chemical Society, Easton, Pennsylvania.

110. *Engineering Index,* Engineering Index, Inc., New York.

111. *Index Medicus,* National Library of Medicine, Bethesda, Maryland.

112. *Industrial Hygiene Digest,* Industrial Hygiene Foundation, Pittsburgh, Pennsylvania.

113. *International Aerospace Abstracts,* National Aeronautics and Space Administration, Washington, D.C.

114. *Journal of the Iron and Steel Institute,* Iron and Steel Institute, London, England.

115. *Meteorological and Geoastrophysical Abstracts,* American Meteorology Society, Washington, D.C.

116. *Nuclear Science Abstracts,* Division of Technical Information, Atomic Energy Commission, Oak Ridge, Tennessee.

117. *Public Health Engineering Abstracts,* National Center for Urban and Industrial Health, U.S., Public Health Service, Cincinnati, Ohio.

118. Science Information Exchange, Washington, D.C.

119. *Scientific and Technical Aerospace Reports,* National Aeronautics and Space Administration, Washington, D.C.
120. *Technical Abstract Bulletin,* Defense Documentation Center, Defense Supply Agency, Cameron Station, Alexandria, Virginia.
121. *U.S. Government Research and Development Reports,* Clearinghouse for Federal Scientific and Technical Information, Washington, D.C.

Newsletters

122. "Air Currents." Bay Area Air Pollution Control District, San Francisco, California.
123. "Air Pollution." Hofstra University, Hempstead, New York.
124. "Air San." New Jersey State Department of Health, Trenton, New Jersey.
125. "Air and Water News." McGraw-Hill, New York.
126. "Air/Water Pollution Report." Business Publ., Silver Spring, Maryland.
127. "Clean Air News." Commerce Clearing House, Inc., Chicago, Illinois.
128. "Environmental Health Letter." G. W. Fishbein (Publ.), Washington, D.C.
129. "Environmental Technology and Economics." Technomic Publishing Co., Inc., Stamford, Connecticut.
130. "News." City of New York Department of Air Pollution Control, New York.
131. "The Clean Air Quarterly." Bureau of Air Sanitation, Berkeley, California.
132. "Waste Management Report." Patton-Clellan Publ. Co., Washington, D.C.
133. "Air and Water Conservation News." American Petroleum Institute, New York.
134. "Currents." Manufacturing Chemists Assn., Washington, D.C.
135. "Water-Air Legislative Report." American Paper Institute, New York.
136. "Monthly Bulletin." National Council of the Paper Industry for Air and Stream Improvement, New York.
137. "Regulatory Review." National Council of the Paper Industry for Air and Stream Improvement, New York.

List of Potential Air Pollution Producing Industrial Operations

This list is a composite of two lists. Those items which are followed by a roman numeral are from the Polish classification of establishments (May 13, 1967). The roman numeral designates the width of protective zone required in Poland as follows: I = 1000 m; II = 500 m; III = 300 m; IV = 100 m; V = 50 m. The other items are nonduplicating operations from the list prepared by the Los Angeles County Air Pollution Control District to serve as a basis for answering requests from Local Planning Commissions in Los Angeles County as to whether or not certain industrial operations or land uses, likely to be undertaken in the county, should be considered potential sources of air pollution.

Abattoirs (more than 8000 tons/year), II
Abattoirs (less than 8000 tons/year), III
Abattoirs, small animal (less than 1000/day), IV
Abrasive cleaning equipment
Abrasives, manufacture of
Absorption plant
Acetate fiber production, II
Acetic acid production, II
Acetic aldehyde production (using acetylene and mercury), I
Acetic aldehyde production (without mercury), III
Acetylene production (from natural gas or carbohydrates), II
Acrylonitrile fiber production, II
Agar, manufacture of
Albumin production, IV
Alkaloid (galonic preparations) production, IV
Aluminum reduction (electrolytic), I
Aminoenthanthic acid production, I
Ammonia liquor production, III
Ammonia liquor storage, III
Ammonia production (without nitric acid), II
Ammonium carbonate production, I
Ammonium nitrate production, II
Ammonium sulfate production, I
Analine dye intermediates production, ether or benzene series (more than 1000 tons/year), I
Analine dye intermediates production, benzene series (less than 1000 tons/year), II

Animal anatomic and skeleton production, IV
Animal carcass processing or use, I
Animal feed production, from waste food products, III
Animal waste processing or use, I
Animal waste storage, I
Anodizing
Anthracene intermediates production (more than 2000 tons/year), I
Anthracene intermediates production (less than 2000 tons/year), II
Antimony production (metallurgical), II
Apatite mining and preparation, II
Arsenic ore mining and concentrating, I
Arsenic production, I
Asbestos cement products manufacture, IV
Asbestos, manufacture of, III
Asbestos product production, II
Asbestos strip-mining and processing, III
Asphalt, manufacture of
Asphalt strip-mining and processing, III
Asphaltic concrete production (black top plants), III
Automobile assembly
Automobile body and fender works
Automobile painting (spray booths, bake ovens)
Automobile scrapping

Babbitt metal, manufacture of
Bag cleaning
Bake ovens—core, frit, paint, etc.
Bakeries

Barium chloride production (using H_2S), II

Barrel cleaning and reclaiming

Barrels, manufacture of

Basalt, melted, foundries, IV

Bast fiber (linen, flax, etc.) preliminary processing by retting, III

Batching plants, asphaltic and ready-mix concrete

Baths—oil quench, chrome-plating, galvanizing, etc.

Batteries, manufacture of

Bauxite production, I

Biothermic chambers, garbage, II

Blacksmith shops

Blast furnaces, ferrous (1500 m^3 capacity), II

Blasting equipment used in surface cleaning (sand, shot, grit, etc.)

Bleach, manufacture of

Bleaching powder, manufacture of

Blubber melting (fish and sea animals), II

Boiler houses in populated places, IV

Bone distillation

Bone products, manufacture of, V

Booths, spray—lacquer, varnish, paint, enamel, etc.

Bottles, manufacture of

Boxes, manufacture of

Brass and bronze casting

Breweries

Brick, lime-sand, production of, IV

Brick, manufacture of

Bristle processing, IV

Brush, manufacture of, from hair and bristles, V

Building blocks, manufacture of

Burying ground for dead animals, III

Cabinet making

Calcium nitrate production, II

Camphor, synthetic, isomerized, production, II

Can, manufacturing and reconditioning

Canneries, fruit, vegetable, and meat products, V

Caoutchouc reprocessing

Carbide production, I

Carbohydrate (light paraffinic) production (more than 5000 m^3/hr), I

Carbohydrate (light paraffinic) production (1000 to 5000 m^3/hr and less than 25,000 m^3/year of generator gas), III

Carbohydrate (light paraffinic) production (less than 1000 m^3/hr), IV

Carbon black production, I

Carbon dioxide production, V

Carbon disulfide production, I

Cardboard making, V

Carpet production, V

Casein products, manufacture of

Casing (intestine), manufacture of, IV

Catalyst, manufacture of

Caustic soda production (electrolytic), I

Cellophane, manufacture of

Celluloid, manufacture of

Cellulose ester plastics production, II

Cellulose nitrate, manufacture of

Cellulose production (sulfite or bisulfite methods), I

Cement blocks, manufacture of

Cement elevators and reloading stations, IV

Cement, manufacture of

Cement mortar board (reed, straw, chips) manufacture, V

Cement products, manufacture of

Ceramics production, IV

Chalk, manufacture of

Chamois leather production, III

Charcoal production (in other than retort), I

Charcoal production (in retorts), III

China production, IV

Chlorinated hydrocarbon production, I

Chlorine production, I

Chlorine storage tanks, III

Chloroprene rubber production, I

Chromic acid anhydride production, II

Chromium plating

Chromium salt production, II

Cistern purification, washing and evaporation station, IV

Clay processing

Clay product, manufacture of, V

Cleansers, manufacture of

Coal briquette production, III

Coal coking, I

Coal gasification, I

Coal mining, III

Coal tar products, manufacture of

Coal tar residue production, III

Coal yards

Cobalt production (aqueous solution electrolysis), II

Cocoanut oil processing

Coffee roasting, IV

Coke ovens

Composting, garbage, II

Concrete batching plants

Concrete pipes, manufacture of

Concrete products, manufacture of, IV

Confectioneries (more than 20,000 tons/year), V

Construction material from coal waste production, IV

Conveyors—crushed, pulverized, shredded or dusty materials

Cookers—chemical, varnish, animal matter, etc.

Cooperage (ready-made staves), V

Copper—melting and refining

Copper production (aqueous solution electrolysis), II

Cork products, manufacture of

Corundum production, I

Cotton gins

Cotton seed oil, manufacture of, and processing

Crematories

Creosote, manufacture of

Crushers—rock, tile, perlite, etc.

Cryolite production, I

Cyanide compound production, I

Dairies, V

Dehydrators—food, fish meal, citrus waste, garbage, etc.

Delicatessen goods production, V

Detergent, manufacture of

Dextrin production, IV

Diecasting

Dimethyl formamide production, I

Dimethyl tetraphthalene production, I

Dip tanks

Disinfectant, manufacture of

Dolomite production (kiln burning), I

Dolomite strip-mining and processing, III

Down processing, IV

Drop forges

Drugs, manufacture of

Drums, manufacture of, and reclaiming

Dry cleaners

Dry ice (CO_2) production, V

Dumps

Dye, cadmium, production, II

Dye, nitrogen, production, II

Dye, nitrogen-amine, production, II

Dye, organic sulfur, production, I

Dye, sulfuric, production (up to 4000 tons/year), II

Dynamite manufacture

Ebonite production, III

Electric sign manufacture

Electrical equipment manufacture (including small foundries, forges, and heat treating), IV

Electrical equipment manufacture (without foundry), V

Electrical insulating paper and fabric manufacture by continuous varnish or resin impregnation (over 300 tons/year of saturated material), III

Electroplating works

Emery cloth manufacture

Enamel, mixing, manufacture, processing

Engine manufacture

Equipment (containing mercury) production, III

Ester, complex, production, II

Ethyl alcohol production, IV

Ethyl alcohol, synthetic, production (using but not producing H_2SO_4), II

Excelsior (wood wool) manufacture, IV

Excelsior (wood wool) products, manufacture of, V

Explosives, manufacture of

Fabric, cotton, linen and wool, production, including bleaching and dyeing, IV

Fabric, cotton, linen and wool, production—without bleaching, V

Fabric impregnation (involving CS_2 or H_2S), II

Fabric mat plaiting, V

Fabric saturation (chemical solutions other than CS_2), III

Fat rendering

Fatty acid, synthetic, production, II

Fatty oil hydrogenation (nonelectrolytic hydrogen), II

Fatty oil hydrogenation (electrolytic hydrogen), IV

Feather processing, IV

Feed mills, IV

Felt production, IV

Ferroalloy production, I

Fertilizer mixing plants, III

Fertilizer spreading and drying

Fiberboard production, I
Film, photographic, production, V
Fire clay production (kiln burning), I
Fireworks, manufacture of
Fish canning, IV
Fish filleting, IV
Fish processing, IV
Fish smoking, V
Fish, spoiled, processing or use, I
Fish waste processing or use (Fish meal), I
Flour milling, V
Food dehydration
Forging, heavy, II
Foundries, ferrous (over 20,000 tons/year), II
Foundries, ferrous (10,000 to 20,000 tons/year), III
Foundries, ferrous (less than 10,000 tons/year), IV
Foundries, nonferrous (100 to 2000 tons/year), III
Foundries, nonferrous (less than 100 tons/year), IV
Frit, manufacture of
Fruit storage, V
Fur dyeing, III
Fur processing and manufacturing, III
Fur, synthetic, production, V
Furfural production (by hydrolysis of wood pulp or agricultural waste), II
Furnaces, alloying, refining, processing
Furniture, wood, manufacture, V

Galalite (aluminoid base plastics) production, IV
Galvanizing shops
Garbage incineration
Garnetting machines
Gas (generator) production (over 50,000 m³/hr), I
Gas (generator) production (25,000 to 50,000 m³/hr), II*
Gas (generator) production (less than 5000 m³/hr), IV*
Gasoline absorption plants
Gasoline storage and loading
Gelatine production (from animal waste), I

Gelatine production (from fresh, clean or briefly refrigerated material), IV
Glass production, IV
Glass fiber production
Glass wool production, III
Glucose production, IV
Glue production (from waste skin, bones, or other animal waste), I
Glycerine production from glycerine solutions, IV
Grain drying or fermenting
Grain elevators
Graphite production, III
Gravel pits (without explosives), V
Grease, manufacture of
Grinding wheels, manufacture of
Grit milling, V
Guncotton, manufacture of
Gunpowder, manufacture of
Gypsum board (reed, straw, or chips), manufacture of, V
Gypsum products, manufacture of, V

Hair processing, IV
Hair production, III
Hair products, manufacture of
Hard metal alloy production (nonchemical), V
Heat treating of metals, V
Hide curing and tanning
Hide storage, salted or unprocessed (more than 200 hides), III†
Hide storage (less than 20 salted hides), V†
Hoof processing, IV
Horn products manufacture
Horn processing, IV
Hot rolling of metals, I
Hydrazine sulfate production, I
Hydrochloric acid production, I
Hydrocyanic acid production, I
Hydrofluoric acid production, I
Hydrogen, compressed, production, V

Illuminating gas production (more than 50,000 m³/hr), I
Incinerators
Ink, manufacture of
Inorganic derivative production (without Cl), IV

* The hiatus between 5000 and 25,000 m³/hr appears in the original Polish publication
† The hiatus between 200 and 20 hides appears in the original Polish publication

Inorganic salt production—except As, P and Cr, III
Insecticide, manufacture of
Insulated cable, manufacture of, III
Intestine cleaning (outside abattoir), II
Investment casting
Iron smelting (furnaces over 1500m³), I
Iron works

Junk yard
Jute fabrication

Kalsomine, manufacture of
Kettles, varnish, food, plastic, and galvanizing
Kilns, all types
Knitting mills, V

Lace making, V
Lacquer, manufacture of
Lampblack, manufacture of
Land reclamation
Lard, manufacture of
Latex, manufacture of
Latex processing and coating
Lead ore mining and concentrating, I
Lead reduction and melting
Lime, manufacture of
Linoleum, manufacture of
Linseed oil, manufacturing or processing
Lithographing
Livestock railroad car cleaning and washing, II
Liquor distillery
Lumber mill
Lumber yard
Lye, manufacture of

Macaroni production, V
Machine shops, IV
Machinery, manufacture of
Magnesite production (kiln burning), I
Magnesite strip-mining and processing, III
Magnesium production (by chlorination), I
Magnesium production (other than chlorination), II
Magnesium casting
Malt production, V
Manganese ore mining and concentrating, I
Manure or fecal matter spreading (drying), I

Margarine production, IV
Match, manufacture of, IV
Mattress, manufacturing and renovating
Meat packing plants, IV
Mercury production, I
Metal fabricating
Metal pickling
Metallizing (spraying)
Metals, rare, production (by chlorination), II
Mineral processing—earth, perlite, vermiculite
Mining, strip, metallic and nonmetallic ores except Pb, As and Mn, IV
Mining, underground, metallic and nonmetallic ores except Pb, As and Mn, III
Mixers
Morocco leather production, III
Mortar production, IV
Mother-of-pearl, synthetic, production, IV
Mucilage manufacture

Napthalene intermediates production (more than 2000 tons/year), I
Napthalene intermediate production (less than 2000 tons/year), II
Natural gasoline plants
Natural gas treating plants
Newspaper printing
Nickel production (aqueous solution electrolysis), II
Nicotine production, II
Nitrate fertilizer production, I
Nitric acid production, I
Nitric compound derivatives production (without nitric acid), II
Nut processing, including nut oil

Offal reduction
Oil burners
Oil, edible, production, IV
Oil reclaiming
Oil refining
Oil shale mining and preparation, II
Oil shale processing (chemical), I
Oil storage
Oil, vegetable, extraction, IV
Oil wells (crude with more than 5% sulfur content), I
Oil wells (crude with less than 5% sulfur content), III
Oleomargarine manufacture

Open hearth steel furnaces (1 million tons/year), II
Orchard heaters
Ore grinding and reduction
Organic derivative production (without Cl), IV
Organic preparation production, IV
Organic reagent production, II
Ovens
Oxygen, compressed, production, V

Paint, natural mineral, production, IV
Paint spraying and baking
Paint, synthetic mineral, production, III
Paper making, without use of SO_2 as gas, or burning of sulfur containing waste, V
Paper, manufacture from finished cellulose and old paper, III
Paper, sensitive photographic, production, V
Paste, manufacture of
Patent-leather, manufacture of, V
Peat briquette production, III
Peat mining (mechanical cutting), IV
Peat processing (chemical), I
Pencil, manufacture of, IV
Perfume, manufacture of, IV
Pesticide production, I
Petrochemicals, manufacture of
Petroleum refining (over 5% sulfur in crude oil), I
Petroleum refining (less than 5% sulfur in crude oil), II
Petroleum residue (asphalt) production, III
Pharmaceuticals manufacture
Phenol aldehyde resin products manufacture (saturated paper and fabric products), (over 100 tons/year), III
Phenol aldehyde resin products manufacture (saturated paper and fabric products (less than 100 tons/year), IV
Phenolic aldehyde production (more than 300 tons/year), II
Phenol production
Phonograph records, manufacture of
Phosphorite mining and preparation, II
Phosphorus production, I
Photoengraving
Photo finishing
Pickling
Picric acid production, I

Pipe coating
Plasterboard, manufacture of
Plaster, manufacture of
Plaster of paris, manufacture of
Plasticizer production for thermoplastics (PVC, polyurethane, polystyrene, etc.), IV
Plastics extrusion, V
Plastics, moulding, V
Plastics products manufacture—pressing, pressure-casting, vacuum-forming, IV
Plating, metal, including electroplating and finishing
Plywood production, I
Polish, manufacture of
Polyamid compound intermediates production, I
Polyamid fiber production, II
Polyester fiber production, II
Polymer intermediates production, I
Polystyrene, manufacture of
Porcelain enamel, manufacture of, and application
Porcelain production, IV
Pork product curing (more than 3 tons/day), V
Portland cement production (more than 150,000 tons/year), I
Portland cement production (less than 150,000 tons/year), II
Potash production
Potassium carbonate (pharmaceutical) production, IV
Potassium chloride (pharmaceutical) production, IV
Potassium nitrate production, II
Potassium sulfate (pharmaceutical) production, IV
Pottery, manufacture of
Poultry slaughtering (less than 1000 animals/day), IV
Pulp, mechanical, production, V
Pulverized construction material storage elevators, and reloading stations, IV
Pumice, manufacture of
Putty, manufacture of
Pyrite mining and preparation, II

Quarries, gravel, rock, sand, etc.
Quicklime próduction (kiln burning), I

Railroad repair shops
Reactors, chemical
Refractory materials production, IV
Refrigerating plants (more than 600 tons), V
Refuse disposal
Rendering plants
Resin, clay-organic, production, III
Resin, synthetic, production (more than 300 tons/year), II
Rock crushing, III
Rock wool, manufacture of
Rolling mills
Roofing paper or shingles, manufacture of
Rope works, IV
Rotogravure printing
Rubber footwear production, III
Rubber production, III
Rubber products production, III
Rubber reprocessing (reclamation), III
Rubber, synthetic production (other than chloroprene), II
Rubber, synthetic, production, III
Rubber vulcanization (with CS_2), III
Rubber vulcanization (without CS_2), IV
Rugs, manufacture of

Saccharin production, IV
Salt mines (table salt), IV
Salt works and mills, IV
Sand blasting
Sandpaper, manufacture of
Sanitation truck and equipment storage, V
Saturated building felt paper production, III
Sauerkraut, manufacture of
Sausages, manufacture of
Sawmills, IV
Semicellulose production (sulfite or bisulfite methods), I
Sewage treatment fields (more than 5000 m^3 sewage/day) II
Sewage treatment fields (less than 5000 m^3 sewage/day), III
Sewage treatment plants (more than 50,000 m^3/day), II
Sewage treatment plants (100 to 50,000 m^3/day), III
Sewage treatment plants (less than 100 m^3/day), IV

Sewer pipe manufacture
Screens—rotary or vibratory
Shell product, manufacture of
Shellac manufacture of
Shingle, manufacture of
Ship building
Shoe, manufacture of, V
Shoe polish, manufacture of
Shredding
Silk reeling, IV
Sintering, ferrous and nonferrous ores, I
Sintering, pyrite cinder, I
Slag concrete production (more than 150,000 tons/year), I
Slag concrete production (less than 150,000 tons/year), II
Slag grinding, II
Slag wool production, III
Smelters, nonferrous metal, ores and concentrates, I
Smelters, nonferrous metal, secondary—more than 3000 tons/year, I
Smelters, nonferrous metal, secondary—less than 3000 tons/year, III
Smoked meat and fish production
Soap, manufacture of, IV
Soda, calcined (ammoniacal method) (more than 400,000 tons/year), II
Soda, calcined (ammoniacal method) (less than 400,000 tons/year), III
Sodium hydroxide production (nonelectrolytic), III
Sodium nitrate production, II
Sodium nitrite production, I
Solvent extraction and recovery
Spray booths—paint, lacquer, varnish, etc.
Starch production, IV
Steel smelting (more than 1 million tons/year), I
Sterilizing and fumigating
Stills
Stone cutting plants, IV
Stone quarries (without explosives), IV
Stone, synthetic, manufacture, IV
Stoneware (ceramic) production, IV
Storage battery, lead, production, II
Strawboard, manufacture of
Strip mining, brown coal, II
Stucco, manufacture of
Styrene isomer production, III

Styrene production, III
Suet melting (more than 30 tons/year), II
Suet melting (less than 30 tons/year), III
Sugar production, III
Sugar refining, V
Sulfur ore strip mining and concentrating, I
Sulfur recovery
Sulfuric acid production, I
Superphosphate fertilizer production (with sulfuric acid production), I
Superphosphate fertilizer production—with conversion of F to fluorine acids and without sulfuric acid production, II
Synthetic leather production (with volatile organic solvents), II

Talc processing
Tallow processing
Tank farms, petroleum storage
Tank, wooden, construction, IV
Tanks, acid, chrome-plating, oil quench, oil storage or other fume producing materials
Tanning industry extract production, IV
Tanning of hides (large animals), II
Tar processing (chemical), I
Tar production, II
Terra cotta manufacture
Textile printing
Thermoplastic products, manufacture of, III
Thionyl chloride production, I
Tile, manufacture of
Tinning plant
Tire, manufacture of
Tire retreading or recapping
Tin smith shop
Tobacco products, manufacture of, IV
Tool, manufacture of
Top soil storage piles, I
Toys, manufacture of
Trailers, manufacture of
Turpentine, manufacture of
Type founding

Ultramarine production, II

Vanillin production, IV
Varnish, alcohol, production, III

Varnish, clay-organic, production, III
Varnish, fatty, production, III
Varnish, oil, production, III
Varnish, printing, production, III
Varnish, silicone, production, II
Vats, acid, chrome-plating or other fume producing materials
Vegetable cannery
Vegetable drying, salting and pickling, IV
Vegetable oil, manufacture of
Vegetable storage, V
Veneer production, IV
Vinegar, table, production, V
Viscose rayon fiber production, I
Viscose rayon sheet production, I
Volatile oil repackaging

Wagon, farm, works, IV
Wallboard, manufacture of
Water gas production—more than 50,000 m^3/hr, I
White lead, manufacture of
Wineries, V
Wire works, IV
Wood distillation
Wood distillation derivatives production, II
Wood pitch residue production, III
Wood plaiting, V
Wood preservation water solution coating—except with arsenic salts, V
Wood products, manufacture of
Wood treating plants (impregnation and preservation), III
Wool production, III
Wool pulling or scouring plant

Yarn, cotton, linen and wool, production, including bleaching and dyeing, IV
Yarn, cotton, linen and wool, production—without bleaching, V
Yeast, fodder, production (by hydrolysis of wood pulp or agricultural waste), II
Yeast production, V

Zinc alloying, smelting, galvanizing, refining
Zinc production (aqueous solution electrolysis), II

Author Index

Numbers in parentheses are reference numbers and indicate that an author's work is referred to although his name is not cited in the text. Numbers in italics show the page on which the complete reference is listed.

Subject Index

D

F